CONTEMPORARY AUSTRALIAN TORT LAW

SECOND EDITION

Tort law is a dynamic area of Australian law, offering individuals the opportunity to seek legal remedies when their interests are infringed. *Contemporary Australian Tort Law* introduces the fundamentals of tort law in Australia today in an accessible, student-friendly way.

The second edition retains the logical coverage of key aspects of tort law, including negligence, damages and defences, and has been thoroughly updated to cover recent case law and legal developments. In particular, the chapter on defamation has been comprehensively updated to reflect recent amendments to uniform legislation and its application in common law.

Self-assessment tools throughout the text encourage students to continuously test and apply their knowledge of key concepts. These features include case questions and review questions throughout each chapter, as well as longer end-of-chapter hypothetical problems which consolidate and extend students' application of key concepts to realistic contemporary scenarios.

Written by a team of teaching experts, *Contemporary Australian Tort Law* is an engaging and user-friendly resource for students new to studying tort law.

Joanna Kyriakakis is a Senior Lecturer at Monash University Faculty of Law.

Tina Popa is a Senior Lecturer at the Graduate School of Business and Law at RMIT University.

Francine Rochford is an Associate Professor in the Law School at La Trobe University.

Natalia Szablewska is Professor in Law and Society at The Open University (United Kingdom) and an Adjunct Professor at the Royal University of Law and Economics (Cambodia).

Xiaobo Zhao is a Senior Lecturer at the School of Law and Justice, University of Southern Queensland.

Jason Taliadoros is an Associate Professor in the Deakin Law School, Deakin University.

Darren O'Donovan is a Senior Lecturer at La Trobe Law School, Melbourne.

Lowell Bautista is an Associate Professor at the School of Law, University of Wollongong.

Cambridge University Press acknowledges the Australian Aboriginal and Torres Strait Islander peoples of this nation. We acknowledge the traditional custodians of the lands on which our company is located and where we conduct our business. We pay our respects to ancestors and Elders, past and present. Cambridge University Press is committed to honouring Australian Aboriginal and Torres Strait Islander peoples' unique cultural and spiritual relationships to the land, waters and seas and their rich contribution to society.

CONTEMPORARY AUSTRALIAN TORT LAW

SECOND EDITION

Joanna Kyriakakis
Tina Popa
Francine Rochford
Natalia Szablewska
Xiaobo Zhao
Jason Taliadoros
Darren O'Donovan
Lowell Bautista

CAMBRIDGE
UNIVERSITY PRESS

Shaftesbury Road, Cambridge CB2 8EA, United Kingdom

One Liberty Plaza, 20th Floor, New York, NY 10006, USA

477 Williamstown Road, Port Melbourne, VIC 3207, Australia

314–321, 3rd Floor, Plot 3, Splendor Forum, Jasola District Centre, New Delhi – 110025, India

103 Penang Road, #05–06/07, Visioncrest Commercial, Singapore 238467

Cambridge University Press is part of Cambridge University Press & Assessment,
a department of the University of Cambridge.

We share the University's mission to contribute to society through the pursuit of
education, learning and research at the highest international levels of excellence.

www.cambridge.org
Information on this title: www.cambridge.org/highereducation/isbn/9781009348775

First published 2020
Second edition 2024

Cover designed by Simon Rattray, Squirt Creative
Typeset by Integra Software Services Pvt. Ltd.
Printed in China by C & C Offset Printing Co., Ltd, September 2023

A catalogue record for this publication is available from the British Library

A catalogue record for this book is available from the National Library of Australia

ISBN 978-1-009-34877-5 Paperback

Additional resources for this publication at www.cambridge.org/highereducation/isbn/9781009348775/resources

Reproduction and communication for educational purposes
The Australian *Copyright Act 1968* (the Act) allows a maximum of
one chapter or 10% of the pages of this work, whichever is the greater,
to be reproduced and/or communicated by any educational institution
for its educational purposes provided that the educational institution
(or the body that administers it) has given a remuneration notice to
Copyright Agency Limited (CAL) under the Act.

For details of the CAL licence for educational institutions contact:

Copyright Agency Limited
Level 12, 66 Goulburn Street
Sydney NSW 2000
Telephone: (02) 9394 7600
Facsimile: (02) 9394 7601
E-mail: memberservices@copyright.com.au

CONTENTS

ABOUT THE AUTHORS

Joanna Kyriakakis is a Senior Lecturer at Monash University Faculty of Law. Joanna teaches and coordinates the Torts Law subjects for the LLB and JD degrees, as well as teaching elective programs in the areas of International Criminal Law and Animal Law. Her research to date has focused upon corporate accountability for human rights abuses and international criminal law, publishing on a range of related issues in leading books and journals.

Tina Popa is a Senior Lecturer at the Graduate School of Business and Law at RMIT University. Tina has taught tort law for eight years in the JD program, and presently coordinates and teaches tort law in both the undergraduate and postgraduate law programs. Tina's research interests are in tort law, health law and alternative/appropriate dispute resolution, with her doctoral research exploring the challenges in litigation and mediation of medical negligence disputes. Tina's research has been published in leading Australian and international peer-reviewed journals, and she has been a visiting scholar at universities in Canada and Belgium. Tina has extensive experience in the legal industry and has also worked on industry research collaborations, which underpin her approach to research and teaching. Tina is a passionate law teacher committed to implementing innovative and authentic learning design. Between February 2018 and June 2019, Tina held the role of GSBL Online Learning Coordinator, encouraging and supporting law staff to strive for excellence in online teaching and learning. Tina has co-authored journal articles on blended learning design in law teaching, including presenting this work at international law teaching conferences. Tina was invited to present her teaching innovations as Keynote Speaker at the 2019 Teaching & Learning Symposium at the University of Auckland. Tina's work has been recognised through several teaching awards, including the 2018 Vice-Chancellor's Award for Outstanding Contributions to Learning and Teaching (Early Career, Higher Education) and the 2022 Learning & Teaching Enabling Award (awarded jointly with colleagues) from RMIT's College of Business & Law. In 2020, she was recognised as 'Academic of the Year' at the *Lawyers Weekly* Women in Law Awards.

Francine Rochford is an Associate Professor in the Law School at La Trobe University. She currently coordinates and teaches the Torts Law subject in the LLB (Hons) degree as well as teaching into several electives including Education Law, Water Law and Planning Law. Her research has focused on tort law, water law and environmental law, including tortious liability for climate change.

Natalia Szablewska, PhD is Professor in Law and Society at The Open University (United Kingdom) and an Adjunct Professor at the Royal University of Law and Economics (Cambodia). Natalia has over 20 years of professional experience in public policy, research and academia in five countries, during which time she has taught a number of subjects across various jurisdictions, including tort law, constitutional law, public international law and international humanitarian law. She has published extensively for academic and non-academic audiences, and her academic work has appeared in leading journals and with publishers in a number of disciplines. Natalia currently serves on the Modern Slavery Leadership Advisory Group to the New Zealand Government and as a Chair of Business and Human Rights Subcommittee and Executive Management Committee Member at Australian Lawyers for Human Rights. She practised human rights law in a non-governmental organisation in Russia ('Russian Justice Initiative'), litigating before the European Court of Human Rights.

Xiaobo Zhao is a Senior Lecturer at the School of Law and Justice, University of Southern Queensland (UniSQ). He worked as a lecturer in law and legal consultant for several years before taking up his current position at UniSQ. He has taught across a range of law courses for LLB and LLM programs since 2012. He is the course leader of Torts, Water Resource Law and the Sustainable Environmental Governance Research Programme at UniSQ. He is a Senior Research Fellow of the Research Institute of Environmental Law (RIEL), Wuhan University. His research interests focus on comparative environmental law, contaminated land law and torts. He is also the author and co-author of several law books, peer-reviewed journal articles and book chapters.

Jason Taliadoros is an Associate Professor in the Deakin Law School, Deakin University. Jason teaches and coordinates Torts Law units for the LLB and JD degrees and an elective unit in Personal Injuries for the LLB. His research focuses on legal history, torts, and statutory compensation schemes and he has published in these areas in leading books and journals. Jason formerly worked as a legal practitioner in the areas of personal injuries, workers' compensation, and insurance and commercial litigation.

Darren O'Donovan is Senior Lecturer at La Trobe Law School, Melbourne. Darren holds a BCL (Hons), and a PhD from University College Cork, Ireland, where he also lectured from 2009 to 2012. Darren's main specialisation is in administrative law. He has written extensively on rights, oversight and public administration, including the book *Law and Public Administration in Ireland* (co-authored with Dr Fiona Donson). Much of Darren's work has reflected upon the centrality of non-judicial review bodies and first-instance decision-makers to deliver administrative justice. Reflecting these themes, Darren is currently undertaking research projects in relation to the National Disability Insurance Scheme.

Lowell Bautista is Associate Professor at the School of Law and a Staff Member at the Australian National Centre for Ocean Resources and Security (ANCORS), University of Wollongong (UOW). He has taught the Law of Torts at UOW since 2017. Lowell is recognised for his expertise in the Law of the Sea, particularly for his contributions in the area of territorial and maritime disputes in the Asia-Pacific, especially the South China Sea.

He is a lawyer with over two decades of experience in legal and policy research, teaching and consultancy. He holds a BA and LLB degrees from the University of the Philippines, an LLM degree from Dalhousie University, and a PhD from the University of Wollongong. His areas of research expertise primarily involve multi-faceted aspects of international law, law of the sea, ocean governance, maritime security and comparative law, on which topics he has also published.

ACKNOWLEDGEMENTS

The authors and Cambridge University Press acknowledge Liam Webb's research assistance and contribution to Chapter 9.

Tina Popa would like to extend her sincerest thanks to Lucy, Emily and Cambridge University Press. This second edition would not be possible without their support. Her heartfelt thanks to Professor Ian Freckelton, for his mentoring in her tort-related academic endeavours, and Branko, for his unconditional love and support with her tort-related adventures. She also wishes to thank her beautiful tort law students who inspire her to be a better educator every day. Tina dedicates this book to her dear friend Paul Ryan: 'Paul, my deepest thanks for the tort-related conversations, stories and ideas we shared. I will treasure them for years to come'.

Xiaobo Zhao wishes to thank the UniSQ Torts (former Civil Obligations) unit team for the permissions granted to use the teaching and learning materials developed by the team. He especially wishes to thank his colleagues Professor Reid Mortensen, Dr Lingling He and Professor Noeleen McNamara for their endless encouragement and support. His thanks also goes to Emily Baxter for her extraordinary assistance in preparing the second edition.

Jason Taliadoros wishes to acknowledge and thank his colleagues in the Deakin Law School Torts unit teams, whose teaching materials he used in preparing his contribution to this book, in particular Dr Sharon Erbacher. He also thanks Lucy, Emily and the Cambridge University Press editorial team for all their work in preparing this second edition.

Lowell Bautista is grateful to his loving wife, Dr Lyra Reyes, and his little boy, Nathaniel David Bautista, for teaching him what is truly important in life: family. He is thankful for the research assistance of Liam Webb and Aiden Lerch. He appreciates the support and encouragement of Professor Warwick Gullet, who has been a generous and kind mentor.

Extracts from New South Wales Law Reports (NSWLR): reproduced with the permission of the Council of Law Reporting for NSW.

Extracts from Victorian Reports (VR): the publication of extracts from *Myer Stores Ltd v Soo* [1991] 2 VR 597 is made with the consent of the Council of Law Reporting in Victoria.

Extracts from Western Australia Reports (WAR): these extracts are reproduced by permission of the copyright owner, the State of Western Australia.

Extracts from High Court: Queen's Bench Division (EWHC (QB)): reproduced under the Open Government Licence: https://www.nationalarchives.gov.uk/doc/open-government-licence/version/3/.

Extracts from New South Wales legislation: sourced from the New South Wales Legislation website at February 2023. For the latest information on New South Wales Government legislation please go to https://www.legislation.nsw.gov.au. Reproduced under a CC BY 4.0 licence: https://creativecommons.org/licenses/by/4.0/.

Extracts from Victorian legislation: © State of Victoria, Australia. Copyright in all legislation of the Parliament of the State of Victoria, Australia, is owned by the Crown in right of the State of Victoria, Australia. DISCLAIMER: This product or service contains an unofficial version of the legislation of the Parliament of State of Victoria. The State of Victoria accepts no responsibility for the accuracy and completeness of any legislation contained in this product or provided through this service.

Every effort has been made to trace and acknowledge copyright. The publisher apologises for any accidental infringement and welcomes information that would redress this situation.

FIGURES AND TABLES

Figures

TABLE OF CASES

Barilaro v Google LLC [2022] FCA 650, 547, 551
Barisic v Devenport [1978] 2 NSWLR 111, 656
Barker v Adelaide City Corporation [1900] SALR 29, 321
Barker v Furlong [1891] 2 Ch 172, 344
Barker v The Queen (1983) 153 CLR 338, 325–6, 330, 331, 337
Barnett v Chelsea and Kensington Hospital Management Committee [1969] 1 QB 428, 201
Barton v Armstrong [1969] 2 NSWLR 451, 288
Basely v Clarkson (1681) 83 ER 565, 318, 338, 395
Bateman v Shepherd (1997) Aust Torts Reports 81-417, 526
Bathurst City Council v Saban (1985) 2 NSWLR 704, 440
Bathurst City Council v Saban (No 2) (1986) 58 LGRA 201, 440, 441
Battiato v Lagana [1992] 2 Qd R 234, 277
Bauer Media Pty Ltd v Wilson (No 2) (2018) 56 VR 674, 561, 562, 593
Baulkham Hills Shire Council v Domachuk (1988) 66 LGRA 110, 451
Baume v Commonwealth (1906) 4 CLR 97, 590
Baxter v Obacelo Pty Ltd (2001) 205 CLR 635, 655, 657
Bazley v Curry [1999] 2 SCR 534, 491
Bazley v Wesley Monash IVF Pty Ltd [2011] 2 Qd R 207, 341
Bazzi v Dutton (2022) 289 FCR 1, 558
BBMB Finance (Hong Kong) Ltd v Eda Holdings Ltd [1991] 2 All ER 129, 409
Beckingham v Port Jackson & Manly Steamship Co (1957) SR (NSW) 403, 376
Beecham Group Ltd v Bristol Laboratories Pty Ltd (1968) 118 CLR 618, 653
Behrooz v Secretary of the Department of Immigration and Multicultural and Indigenous Affairs (2004) 219 CLR 486, 376
Belbin v Lower Murray Urban and Rural Water Corporation [2012] VSC 535, 548
Belgrave Nominees Pty Ltd v Barlin-Scott Airconditioning (Australia) Pty Ltd [1984] VR 947, 650
Bell v Thompson (1934) SR (NSW) 431, 656
Bendal Pty Ltd v Mirvac Project Pty Ltd (1991) 23 NSWLR 464, 319, 321, 404
Bendigo & Country Districts Trustees & Executors Co Ltd v Sandhurst & Northern District Trustees, Executors & Agency Co Ltd (1909) 9 CLR 474, 652
Beneficial Finance Corporation Ltd v Alzden Pty Ltd (Supreme Court of New South Wales, Equity Division, 10 May 1993), 584
Benic v New South Wales [2010] NSWSC 1039, 152
Bennett v Minister for Community Welfare (1992) 176 CLR 408, 25
Benning v Wong (1969) 122 CLR 249, 444
Bernstein v Skyviews & General Ltd [1978] 1 QB 479, 318, 319–20, 440
Bernstein of Leigh v Skyviews & General Ltd [1978] 1 QB 479, 319
Berry v Humm & Co [1915] 1 KB 627, 646
Beswicke v Alner [1926] VLR 72, 400, 651
Big Top Hereford Pty Ltd v Thomas (2006) 12 BPR 23,843, 352
Bilambil-Terranora Pty Ltd v Tweed Shire Council [1980] 1 NSWLR 465, 340
Bird v Holbrook (1828) 4 Bing 628, 375
Bird v Jones (1845) 7 QB 742, 292, 296–7, 298
BIS Cleanaway v Tatale [2007] NSWSC 378, 411
Bishopsgate Motor Finance Corporation Ltd v Transport Brakes Ltd [1949] 1 KB 322, 356
Bitumen & Oil Refineries (Australia) Ltd v Commissioner for Government Transport (1955) 92 CLR 220, 660
Bjelke-Petersen v Warburton [1987] 2 Qd R 465, 517, 526
Blacker v Waters (1928) 28 SR (NSW) 406, 268, 269
Blackney v Clark [2013] NSWDC 144, 191
Blackwater v Plint [2005] 3 SCR 3, 501
Blades v Higgs (1861) 10 CB (NS) 713, 380, 381, 584
Blake v Burnard (1840) 9 Car & P 626, 290
Blake v JR Perry Nominees Pty Ltd (2012) 38 VR 123, 475–7
Bliss v Hall (1838) 132 ER 758, 425, 435, 447

Bloodworth v Cormack [1949] NZLR 1058, 428
Blundell v Attorney-General (NZ) [1968] NZLR 341, 293
Blundell v Musgrave (1956) 96 CLR 73, 616, 619
Blyth v Birmingham Waterworks Co (1856) 11 Ex 781, 126
Board of Management of Royal Perth Hospital v Frost (Western Australia Court of Appeal, Malcolm CJ, Rowland and Wallwork JJ, 26 February 1997), 180
Bocardo SA v Star Energy UK Onshore Ltd [2011] 1 AC 380, 320, 323
Bodley v Reynolds (1846) 115 ER 1066, 411
Bolam v Friern Hospital Management Committee [1957] 1 WLR 582, 43, 137
Bolton v Stone [1951] AC 850, 154
Bolwell Fibreglass Pty Ltd v Foley [1984] VR 97, 360
Bond v Kelly (1873) 4 AJR 153, 331
Bonnici v Kur-ring-gai Municipal Council (2001) 121 LGERA 1, 420, 421, 447
Bonnington Castings Ltd v Wardlaw [1956] AC 613, 207
Booksan Pty Ltd v Wehbe (2006) Aust Torts Reports 81-830, 677
Bottos v CityLink Melbourne Ltd [2021] VSC 585, 407
Boughey v The Queen (1986) 161 CLR 10, 280
Bourhill v Young [1943] AC 92, 97
Bower v Peate (1876) 1 QBD 321, 437
Bowmakers Ltd v Barnet Instruments Ltd [1945] 1 KB 65, 350
Boyd v Mirror Newspapers Ltd [1980] 2 NSWLR 449, 517, 520–5
Bradley v Schatzel [1911] St R Qd 206, 290, 291
Bradshaw v Griffiths [2016] QCA 20, 322
Brandeis Goldschmidt & Co v Western Transport Ltd [1981] QB 864, 409, 410
Break Fast Investments Pty Ltd v PCH Melbourne Pty Ltd (2007) 20 VR 311, 321, 338, 405, 651
Breen v Williams (1996) 186 CLR 71, 92
Bresatz v Przibilla (1962) 108 CLR 541, 628, 638
Brett Cattle Co Pty Ltd v Minister for Agriculture (2020) 274 FCR 337, 686–8, 689
Bride v Shire of Katanning [2013] WASCA 154, 342
Bridges v Hawkesworth (1851) 21 LJQB 75, 352
Brightwater Care Group v Rossiter (2009) 40 WAR 84, 385
Briginshaw v Briginshaw (1938) 60 CLR 336, 189, 685
Brinsmead v Harrison (1871) LR 6 CP 584, 656
Brisciani v Piscioneri (No 4) [2016] ACTCA 32, 518
British Transport Commission v Gourley [1956] AC 185, 613
Broadway Pty Ltd v Lewis [2012] WASC 373, 406
Brodie v Singleton Shire Council (2001) 206 CLR 512, 141, 417, 444, 453, 455, 667
Brookfield Multiplex Ltd v Owners Corporation Strata Plan 61288 (2014) 254 CLR 185, 87
Broune v Haukyns (1475–83) T 15 Edw 4, 287
Brown v United States, 256 US 335 (1921), 371
Brown v Willington [2001] ACTSC 100, 624
Brunsden v Humphrey (1884) 14 QBD 141, 644
Bryan v Maloney (1995) 182 CLR 609, 62, 85, 89
Bugge v Brown (1919) 26 CLR 110, 473–4
Bulli Coal Mining Co v Osborne [1899] AC 351, 319
Bulsey v Queensland [2015] QCA 187, 304
Bunnings Group Ltd v CHEP Australia Ltd (2011) 82 NSWLR 420, 349, 358, 359, 406, 592
Bunnings Group Ltd v Giudice (2018) Aust Torts Rep 82–402, 152, 153
Bunt v Tilley [2007] 1 WLR 1243, 566
Burford v Allen (1993) 60 SASR 428, 617
Burgess v Florence Nightingale Hospital for Gentlewomen [1955] 1 QB 349, 645
Burke v Butterfield & Lewis Ltd (1926) 38 CLR 354, 677
Burnett v Randwick City Council [2006] NSWCA 196, 346
Burnie Port Authority v General Jones Pty Ltd (1994) 179 CLR 520, 62, 88, 112, 455, 482, 486–7, 501
Burton v Davies [1953] St R Qd 26, 300

Day v Bank of New South Wales (1978) 18 SASR 163, 396
De Freville (1927) 96 LJKB 1056, 296
De Reus v Gray (2003) 9 VR 432, 679–80
De Sales v Ingrilli (2002) 212 CLR 338, 12, 186, 187, 645, 647, 648
Deal v Father Pius Kodakkathanath (2016) 258 CLR 281, 674–5
Dean v Phung [2012] NSWCA 223, 388, 597
Deatons Pty Ltd v Flew (1949) 79 CLR 370, 4, 477, 478
Defteros v Google LLC [2020] VSC 219, 549–50
Delaney v TP Smith Ltd [1946] KB 393, 316
Delta Corporation v Davies [2002] WASCA 125, 594
Denver & Rio Grande Railroad v Lorentzen, 79 F 291 (8th Cir, 1897), 11
Department of Public Prosecutions (Cth) v Hart [2005] 2 Qd R 246, 353
Derrick v Cheung (2001) 181 ALR 301, 78
Dewar v Ollier [2018] WASC 212, 227
Dewey v White (1827) 173 ER 1079, 375
Di Battista v Molton [1971] VR 656, 645
Di Napoli v New Beach Apartments Pty Ltd (2004) 11 BPR 21,493, 323
Diamond v Simpson (No 1) (2003) Aust Torts Reports 81-695, 617
Dickenson v Waters Ltd (1931) 31 SR (NSW) 593, 294
Dingle v Associated Newspapers [1961] 2 QB 162, 659
Dobler v Halverson (2007) 70 NSWLR 151, 140
Dodd Properties (Kent) Ltd v Canterbury City Council [1980] 1 WLR 433, 402
Dodge v Snell [2011] TASSC 19, 246
Dodwell v Burford (1669) 86 ER 703, 277
Doe v Bennett [2004] 1 SCR 436, 491
Dominion Natural Gas Co Ltd v Collins [1909] AC 640, 88
Don Brass Foundry Pty Ltd v Stead (1948) 48 SR (NSW) 482, 424
Donald v Suckling (1866) LR 1 QB 585, 350
Donaldson v Broomby (1982) 60 FLR 124, 292
Donnelly v Joyce [1974] QB 454, 616
Donoghue v Stevenson [1932] AC 562, 22, 23, 57, 58, 59–61, 62, 64, 67, 72, 87, 88, 211
Doodeward v Spence (1908) 6 CLR 406, 341
Dorset Yacht Co Ltd v Home Office [1970] AC 1004, 111, 188
Doubleday v Kelly [2005] NSWCA 151, 231–2
Dovuro Pty Ltd v Wilkins (2003) 215 CLR 317, 162
Dow Jones & Co Inc v Gutnick (2002) 210 CLR 575, 530
Downham v Bellette (1986) Aust Torts Reports 80-038, 395
Drinkwater v Howarth [2006] NSWCA 222, 24
Dryden v Orr (1928) 28 SR (NSW) 216, 407
Duffy v Google Inc (2015) 125 SASR 437, 530–1
Duke of Buccleuch v Cowan (1866) 5 Macpherson 214, 207
Dulieu v White & Sons [1901] 2 KB 669, 97, 213
Duma v Mader International Pty Ltd (2013) 42 VR 351, 677
Dumont v Miller (1873) 4 AJR 152, 313
Dunnage v Randall [2016] QB 639, 130
Dunwich Corporation v Sterry (1831) 109 ER 995, 344
Dutton v Bazzi [2021] FCA 1474, 558
Dymocks Book Arcade Ltd v McCarthy [1966] 2 NSWR 411, 340
Dynamic Flooring Pty Ltd v Carter [2000] NSWSC 992, 424–5
Dynamic Flooring Pty Ltd v Carter [2001] NSWCA 396, 424, 425

E v Australian Red Cross Society (1991) 31 FCR 299, 160
E Hulton & Co v Jones [1910] AC 20, 526–7
Earnshaw v Loy (No 2) [1959] VR 252, 591
Easther v Amaca Pty Ltd [2001] WASC 328, 624

Hunter BNZ Finance Ltd v Australia and New Zealand Banking Group Ltd [1990] VR 41, 350–1, 408
Hunter BNZ Finance Ltd v CG Maloney Pty Ltd (1989) 18 NSWLR 420, 341
Husher v Husher (1999) 197 CLR 138, 613
Hussain v Lancaster County Council [2000] QB 1, 437
Hutchins v Maughan [1947] VLR 131, 271–2, 317
Hyder Consulting (Australia) Pty Ltd v Wilh Wilhelmsen Agency Pty Ltd [2001] NSWCA 313, 603

IBL Ltd v Coussens [1991] 2 All ER 133, 409
ICI Ltd v Trade Practices Commission (1992) 38 FCR 248, 651
Illert v Northern Adelaide Local Health Network Inc [2016] SASC 186, 371
Imbree v McNeilly (2008) 236 CLR 510, 79, 134, 135–7, 233, 246, 256
Indermaur v Dames (1866) LR 1 CP 274, 72, 74
Innes v Wylie (1844) 174 ER 800, 277
Insurance Commissioner v Joyce (1948) 77 CLR 39, 254
Inverugie Investments Ltd v Hackett [1995] 1 WLR 713, 406
Irving v Penguin Books Ltd [2000] EWHC QB 115, 544–5
Isenberg v East India House Estate Co Ltd (1863) 3 De GJ & S 263, 653
Isparta v Richter [2013] 6 SA 529, 559, 570

J & E Hall Ltd v Barclay [1937] 3 All ER 620, 408, 409
Jacobi v Griffiths [1999] 2 SCR 570, 491
Jaensch v Coffey (1984) 155 CLR 549, 62, 98, 586, 593
James v Harrison (1977) 18 ACTR 36, 269
James v Oxley (1939) 61 CLR 433, 357
Jane Doe v Australian Broadcasting Corporation [2007] VCC 281, 572–3
Jane Doe v Fairfax Media Publications Pty Ltd [2018] NSWSC 1996, 669–70
Janney v Steller Works Pty Ltd (2017) 53 VR 677, 5
Jarvis v Williams [1955] 1 WLR 71, 350
JCS v The Queen (2006) 164 A Crim R 1, 306
Jenkins v Jackson (1888) 40 Ch D 71, 437
Jobling v Associated Dairies Ltd [1982] AC 794, 219–20
Joel v Morison (1834) 6 Car & P 501, 472
John F Goulding Pty Ltd v Victorian Railways Commissioners (1932) 48 CLR 157, 359, 361, 362
John Gallagher Panel Beating Co Pty Ltd v Palmer [2007] NSWSC 627, 411
John Lewis & Co Ltd v Tims [1952] AC 676, 292
John Pfeiffer Pty Ltd v Rogerson (2003) 203 CLR 503, 15
John XXIII College v SMA [2022] ACTCA 32, 594
Johns v Delaney (1890) 16 VLR 729, 437
Johnson v Buchanan (2012) 223 A Crim R 132, 313, 321
Johnson v Department of Community Services (2000) Aust Tort Reports 81–540, 32
Johnson v Diprose [1893] 1 QB 512, 344
Johnson Matthey (Australia) Ltd v Dascorp Pty Ltd (2003) 9 VR 171, 408
Jolley v Sutton London Borough Council [2000] 1 WLR 1082, 212
Jones v de Marchant (1916) 28 DLR 561, 355
Jones v Harvey (1983) 1 MVR 111, 292
Jones v Livox Quarries Ltd [1952] 2 QB 608, 227
Jones v Shire of Perth [1970] WAR 56, 600
Jones v Stroud District Council [1988] 1 All ER 5, 603
Joslyn v Berryman (2003) 214 CLR 552, 235, 237

K & S Corporation Ltd v KPMG [2009] SASC 24, 352
Kallouf v Middis [2008] NSWCA 61, 613
Kamasaee v Commonwealth (Ruling on the Settlement Distribution) [2018] VSC 138, 292
Kars v Kars (1996) 187 CLR 345, 620
Kavanagh v Akhtar (1998) 45 NSWLR 588, 213–14
Kay v Barnett [1909] QWN 39, 341

Kaye v Robertson [1991] FSR 62, 277
Kebewar Pty Ltd v Harkin (1987) 9 NSWLR 738, 439–40, 676
Kelsen v Imperial Tobacco Co (of Great Britain and Ireland) Ltd [1957] 2 QB 334, 316, 318, 321
Kennedy v Queensland Alumina Ltd [2016] QCA 159, 227
Kent v Cavanagh (1973) 1 ACTR 43, 440
Kent v Johnson (1972) 21 FLR 177, 452
Kerle v BM Alliance Coal Operations Pty Ltd (2016) 262 IR 381, 93
Khan v Keown [2001] VSCA 137, 371
Khashoggi v IPC Magazines Ltd [1986] 1 WLR 1412, 539
Kiddle v City Business Properties Ltd [1942] 1 KB 269, 446
Kidman v Farmers' Centre Pty Ltd [1959] Qd R 8, 409
King v Crowe [1942] St R Qd 288, 285
King v Philcox (2015) 255 CLR 304, 79, 99–100
Kiobel v Royal Dutch Petroleum Co, 569 US 108 (2013), 15
Kirk v Gregory (1876) 1 Ex D 55, 347–8, 375
Knapp v Railway Executive [1949] 2 All ER 508, 673
Knight v The Queen (1988) 35 A Crim R 314, 288
Knightley v John [1982] 1 WLR 349, 215
Knupffer v London Express Newspaper Ltd [1944] AC 116, 526
Koehler v Cerebos (Australia) Ltd (2005) 222 CLR 44, 68, 69, 70
Kondis v State Transport Authority (1984) 154 CLR 672, 68, 112, 113, 482, 487
Konskier v Goodman Ltd [1928] 1 KB 421, 337, 393
Koremans v Sweeney [1966] QWN 46, 634
Kostik v Giannakopoulos (1989) Aust Torts Reports 80-274, 617
Kostov v Nationwide News Pty Ltd (2018) 97 NSWLR 1073, 560
Kozarov v Victoria (2020) 294 IR 1, 71
Kozarov v Victoria (2022) 273 CLR 115, 68, 69, 70–2
Kraemers v Attorney-General (Tas) [1966] Tas SR 113, 423
Kriz v King [2007] 1 Qd R 327, 623
Kruber v Grzesiak [1963] VR 621, 269
Kruger v Commonwealth (1997) 190 CLR 1, 30
Kuchenmeister v Home Office [1958] 1 QB 496, 296
Kuddus v Chief Constable of Leicestershire [2002] 2 AC 122, 689
Kuhl v Zurich Financial Services Australia Ltd (2011) 243 CLR 361, 65
Kur-ring-gai Municipal Council v Bonnici [2002] NSWCA 313, 420, 432
Kuru v New South Wales (2008) 236 CLR 1, 332, 334–6, 392
Kuwait Airways Corporation v Iraqi Airways Co (Nos 4 and 5) [2002] 2 AC 883, 349, 354–5, 409
KY Enterprises Pty Ltd v Darby [2013] VSC 484, 314

Lachaux v Independent Print Ltd [2020] AC 612, 508, 534, 535
Lagan Navigation Co v Lambeg Bleaching Co [1927] AC 226, 585
Lahoud v Lahoud [2009] NSWSC 623, 340
Lamb v Cotogno (1987) 164 CLR 1, 369, 398, 400, 408, 412, 593, 594, 595–6
Laming v Jennings [2017] VCC 1223, 314
Lamru Pty Ltd v Kation Pty Ltd (1998) 44 NSWLR 432, 406
Lancashire Waggon Co v Fitzhugh (1861) 6 H & N 502, 357
Lang Parade Pty Ltd v Peluso [2006] 1 Qd R 42, 322
Lange v Australian Broadcasting Corporation (1997) 189 CLR 520, 508, 551
Laris v Lin (2017) 18 BPR 36,913, 401
Laut & Loughlin v White Feather Main Reefs (1905) 7 WALR 203, 617
Law v Visser [1961] Qd R 46, 282
Law v Wright (1935) SASR 20, 397
Lawlor v Johnston [1905] VLR 714, 321
Lawrence v Fen Tigers Ltd [2014] AC 822, 426, 427, 442
Le Lievre v Gould [1893] 1 QB 491, 62, 67, 78
League Against Cruel Sports Ltd v Scott [1986] QB 240, 338

Manderson v Wright (No 2) [2018] VSC 162, 427
Mann v O'Neill (1997) 191 CLR 204, 546–7
Manser v Spry (1994) 181 CLR 428, 633
March v E & MH Stramare Pty Ltd (1991) 171 CLR 506, 25, 200–1, 203–5, 206, 210
March v E & MM Stramare Pty Ltd (1989) 50 SASR 588, 204
Marien v Gardiner (2013) 66 MVR 1, 79
Marsh v Baxter (2015) 49 WAR 1, 420, 427, 429, 433
Marshall v Gotham Co Ltd [1954] AC 300, 674
Marshall v Megna [2013] NSWCA 30, 551
Mason v Clarke [1955] AC 778, 317
Masters v Brent London Borough Council [1978] QB 841, 435
Matinca v Coalroc (No 5) [2022] NSWSC 844, 68–9, 93, 194–5
Matsebula v Vandeklashorst [2000] WASCA 141, 291
Matthews v SPI Electricity Pty Ltd (Ruling No 2) (2011) 34 VR 584, 667–9
Matusik v Maher Farms Pty Ltd [2022] VCC 393, 314
Mayfair Ltd v Pears [1987] 1 NZLR 459, 401
Mayfair Trading Co Pty Ltd v Dreyer (1958) 101 CLR 428, 400
McAlpine v Bercow [2013] EWHC 1342, 507
McCarty v North Sydney Municipal Council (1918) 18 SR (NSW) 210, 435
McClelland v Symons [1951] VLR 157, 290, 371, 372
McCracken v Melbourne Storm Rugby Football Club Ltd (2007) Aust Torts Reports 81-925, 613
McCullagh v Lawrence [1989] 1 Qd R 163, 648
McDonald v Ludwig [2007] QSC 028, 393
McDonald v Public Trustee [2010] NSWSC 684, 597
McDowall v Reynolds [2004] QCA 245, 316
McFadzean v Construction, Forestry, Mining and Energy Union (2007) 20 VR 250, 293, 300–2, 305, 593
McFarland v Gertos (2018) 98 NSWLR 954, 407
McGilvray v Amaca Pty Ltd [2001] WASC 345, 639
McGrane v Lot D Preservation Group Inc [2021] VCC 509, 407
McGrath v Marshall (1898) 14 WN (NSW) 106, 336, 388
McHale v Watson (1964) 111 CLR 384, 20, 268, 269, 274–5
McHale v Watson (1966) 115 CLR 199, 129–30, 231, 232–3, 394
McInnes v Ahluwalia [1999] NSWSC 818, 180
McInnes v Wardle (1931) 45 CLR 548, 437
McKay v Essex Area Health Authority [1982] QB 1166, 178, 183
McKenna & Armistead Pty Ltd v Excavations Pty Ltd (1956) 57 SR (NSW) 515, 361
McKeown v Cavalier Yachts Pty Ltd (1988) 13 NSWLR 303, 411
McKew v Holland & Hannen & Cubitts (Scotland) Ltd [1969] 3 All ER 1621, 218
McKiernan v Manhire (1977) 17 SASR 571, 202
McLean v Tedman (1984) 155 CLR 306, 72, 239–40
McMahon v Catanzaro [1961] QWN 22, 432
McMillan Properties Pty Ltd v WC Penfold Ltd (2001) 40 ACSR 319, 342
McNamara v Duncan (1971) 45 FLR 152, 18, 280, 383, 386
McPherson v Breath (1975) 12 SASR 174, 290
McQuire v Western Morning News [1903] 2 KB 100, 11
McWilliam v Hunter [2022] NSWSC 342, 420
Meadows v Ferguson [1961] VR 594, 177–8
Meandarra Aerial Spraying Pty Ltd v GEJ & MA Geldard Pty Ltd [2013] 1 Qd R 319, 152
Medlin v State Government Insurance Commission (1995) 182 CLR 1, 612
Meering v Grahame White Aviation Co Ltd (1919) 122 LT 44, 304–5
Melaleuca Estate Pty Ltd v Port Stephens Council (2006) 143 LGERA 319, 444–5
Mercy Hospitals Victoria v D1 (2018) 56 VR 394, 386, 390–1
Merryweather v Nixan (1799) 101 ER 1337, 659
Merver v Commissioner for Road Transport and Tramways (NSW) (1937) 56 CLR 580, 162
Metals & Ropes Co Ltd v Tattersall [1966] 3 All ER 401, 360

Rigby v Chief Constable of Northamptonshire [1985] 1 WLR 1242, 324, 374, 378–9
RinRim Pty Ltd v Deutsche Bank AG [2017] NSWCA 169, 85
Rinsale Pty Ltd v Australian Broadcasting Corporation [1993] Aust Torts Reports 81-231, 313, 324
Riverman Orchards Pty Ltd v Hayden [2017] VSC 379, 428
Rixon v Star City Pty Ltd (2001) 53 NSWLR 98, 280–2, 292
Roads and Traffic Authority (NSW) v Dederer (2007) 234 CLR 330, 149, 154–6
Roads and Traffic Authority (NSW) v Refrigerated Roadways Pty Ltd (2009) 77 NSWLR 360, 125
Robert v Bass (2002) 212 CLR 1, 551
Roberts v Ramsbottom [1980] 1 WLR 823, 131, 396
Roberts v Roberts (1864) 122 ER 874, 178
Robertson v Balmain New Ferry Co Ltd [1910] AC 295, 297, 298, 299, 394
Robertson v Butler [1915] VLR 31, 383
Robertson v Robin [1967] SASR 151, 646
Robin v Public Trustee (ACT) (2015) 10 ACTLR 300, 341
Robinson v Kilvert (1889) 41 Ch D 88, 428, 429
Robson v Hallett [1967] 2 QB 939, 330
Robson v Leischke [2008] NSWLEC 152, 317, 422, 423
Roche v Douglas (2000) 22 WAR 331, 341
Rodrigues v Ufton (1894) 20 VLR 539, 314
Roe v Ministry of Health [1954] 2 QB 66, 145–6, 149, 484
Rogers v Whitaker (1992) 175 CLR 479, 4, 134, 137, 164–5, 202, 210, 250, 385
Roggenkamp v Bennett (1950) 80 CLR 292, 245, 247
Rolls Royce Industrial Power (Pacific) Ltd v James Hardie & Co Pty Ltd (2001) 53 NSWLR 626, 660
Roman Catholic Church Trustees for the Diocese of Canberra and Goulburn v Hadba (2005) 221 CLR 161, 76
Romeo v Conservation Commission (NT) (1998) 192 CLR 431, 107, 157
Rookes v Barnard [1964] AC 1129, 595
Rootes v Shelton (1967) 116 CLR 383, 246
Rosecell Pty Ltd v JP Haines Plumbing Pty Ltd [2015] NSWSC 1238, 356
Rosecrance v Rosecrance (1995) 105 NTR 1, 617
Rosecrance v Rosecrance (1998) 8 NTLR 1, 617
Rosenberg v Percival (2001) 205 CLR 434, 137
Ross v Warrick Howard (Australia) Pty Ltd (1986) 4 SR (WA) 1, 269
Rowe v Herman [1997] 1 WLR 1390, 482
Roy v O'Neill (2020) 272 CLR 291, 328–30, 332
Ruddock v Taylor (2003) 58 NSWLR 269, 292, 307
Ruddock v Taylor (2005) 222 CLR 612, 292, 294–6, 306
Rufo v Hosking (2004) 61 NSWLR 678, 179–80
Ruhani v Director of Police (No 2) (2005) 222 CLR 580, 292
Rush v Nationwide News Pty Ltd (2018) 359 ALR 473, 541
Rush v Nationwide News Pty Limited (No 7) [2019] FCA 496, 541
Russell v Rail Infrastructure Corporation [2007] NSWSC 402, 233, 234
Russell v Wilson (1923) 33 CLR 538, 350
Rust v Victoria Graving Dock Co (1997) 36 Ch D 113, 402
Ryan v Ann St Holdings [2006] 2 Qd R 486, 474, 478
Rylands v Fletcher (1866) LR 1 Ex 265, 482, 486, 487
Rylands v Fletcher (1868) LR 3 HL 330, 88, 482, 486

S v Department of Immigration and Multicultural and Indigenous Affairs (2005) 143 FCR 217, 488–9
S v G [1995] 3 NZLR 681, 384
S (An Infant) v S [1972] AC 24, 388
Sadcas Pty Ltd v Business & Professional Finance Pty Ltd [2011] NSWCA 267, 408, 409, 410
Sadler v Henlock (1855) 119 ER 209, 473
Safari 4 x 4 Engineering Pty Ltd v Doncaster Motors Pty Ltd [2006] VSC 460, 356
Sahade v Bischoff [2015] NSWCA 418, 292
Samahar Miski v Penrith Whitewater Stadium Ltd [2018] NSWDC 21, 27

TABLE OF STATUTES

Using your VitalSource enhanced eBook

Once you have redeemed your VitalSource access code (see the inside front cover for instructions), the enhanced eBook will be available through your VitalSource account, accessible through the VitalSource Bookshelf website or the VitalSource Bookshelf app, available on all major platforms. The navigation instructions below provide a general overview of the main features available in the enhanced eBook.

VitalSource features

Navigation and search
Move between pages and sections in multiple ways, including via the linked table of contents and the search tool.

Highlight
Highlight text in your choice of colours with one click. Add notes to highlighted passages.

Read aloud
VitalSource Bookshelf includes a read-aloud feature. Controls can be used to increase or decrease the reading speed, or to alter the voice. The feature will remember where you left off and will not be disrupted by navigation to other sections of the book.

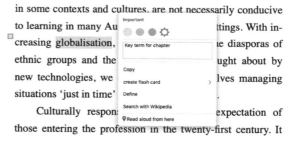

Book features

The VitalSource eBook houses a number of interactive features, outlined below. Note that all solution pop-ups can be moved about the page.

Icons

 This icon is used throughout the textbook to indicate the presence of an interactive component in the eBook. The accompanying descriptor indicates the type of content available.

Jurisdictional tables
Where available, the various state Acts, or specific sections, listed within the textbook's tables are linked to full versions of these texts.

Case links

Where available, a link to the full case under discussion in the case boxes is provided at
the start of the box.

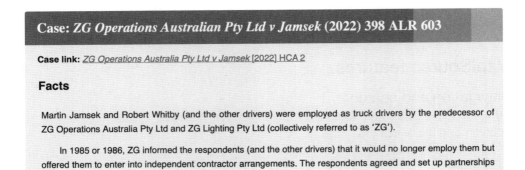

Case: *ZG Operations Australian Pty Ltd v Jamsek* (2022) 398 ALR 603

Case link: *ZG Operations Australia Pty Ltd v Jamsek* [2022] HCA 2

Facts

Martin Jamsek and Robert Whitby (and the other drivers) were employed as truck drivers by the predecessor of
ZG Operations Australia Pty Ltd and ZG Lighting Pty Ltd (collectively referred to as 'ZG').

In 1985 or 1986, ZG informed the respondents (and the other drivers) that it would no longer employ them but
offered them to enter into independent contractor arrangements. The respondents agreed and set up partnerships

Case questions

Respond to the questions and use the guided solutions to assess your responses.

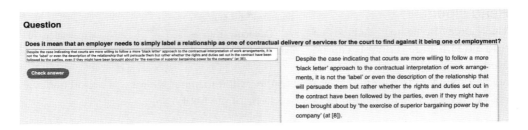

Question

Does it mean that an employer needs to simply label a relationship as one of contractual delivery of services for the court to find against it being one of employment?

Despite the case indicating that courts are more willing to follow a more
'black letter' approach to the contractual interpretation of work arrangements, it is not the 'label' or even the description of the relationship that
will persuade them but rather whether the rights and duties set out in
the contract have been followed by the parties, even if they might have
been brought about by 'the exercise of superior bargaining power by the
company' (at [8]).

Review questions

Respond to the review questions at the end of each major section and use the guided
solutions to assess your responses.

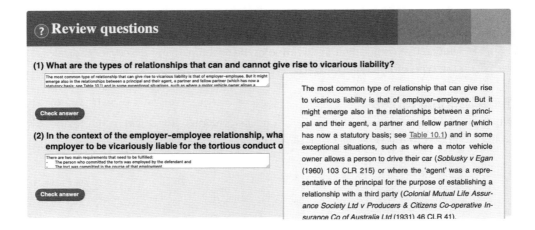

(?) Review questions

(1) What are the types of relationships that can and cannot give rise to vicarious liability?

The most common type of relationship that can give rise
to vicarious liability is that of employer–employee. But it
might emerge also in the relationships between a principal and their agent, a partner and fellow partner (which
has now a statutory basis; see Table 10.1) and in some
exceptional situations, such as where a motor vehicle
owner allows a person to drive their car (*Soblusky v Egan*
(1960) 103 CLR 215) or where the 'agent' was a representative of the principal for the purpose of establishing a
relationship with a third party (*Colonial Mutual Life Assurance Society Ltd v Producers & Citizens Co-operative Insurance Co of Australia Ltd* (1931) 46 CLR 41).

**(2) In the context of the employer–employee relationship, what
employer to be vicariously liable for the tortious conduct o**

There are two main requirements that need to be fulfilled:
- The person who committed the torts was employed by the defendant and
- The tort was committed in the course of that employment.

Multiple-choice questions

Open the multiple-choice questions pop-up box, select your choice of correct answer and click 'Check answer' to assess your results. Note that this box can be moved about the page for you to read text while choosing your responses.

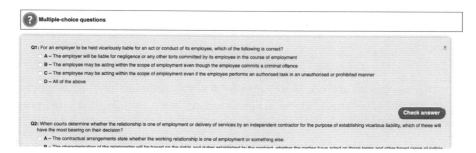

Problem-solving exercises

Respond to the problem-solving exercise at the end of each chapter and use the guided solutions to assess your response.

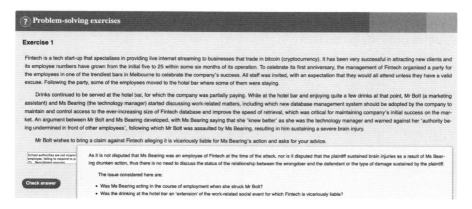

Challenge yourself exercises

Respond to the challenge yourself exercise at the end of each chapter and use the guided solutions to assess your response.

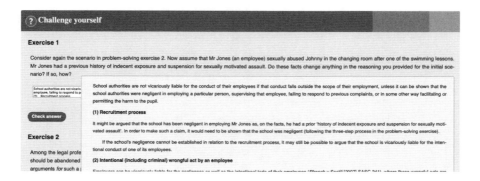

GUIDE TO INSTRUCTOR RESOURCES

A variety of resources for instructors are provided at www.cambridge.org/highereducation/ isbn/9781009348775/resources. These materials are designed to help instructors prepare lectures and tutorials.

- **Tutorial questions:** six questions with guided responses for each chapter for use in tutorials or as homework.

- **Exercises:** four problem-solving or essay-style questions with guided responses for each chapter for use in tutorials or as homework.

- **PowerPoint slides:** a set of slides for each chapter provides an overview of the chapter, featuring key concepts, major headings and all flowcharts and jurisdictional tables from the printed text.

1

INTRODUCTION TO THE LAW OF TORTS

1.1   Introduction and purpose of tort law

Tort law is a compelling and dynamic area of law, affecting many aspects of individuals' lives. A strong understanding of tort principles is important for legal practice, as lawyers may be required to represent clients in a range of tort disputes, from a physical altercation in a bar, to a fall in a supermarket or possibly the lowering of a client's reputation through defamatory material posted on the internet.

1.1.1   What is tort law?

At its core, a tort is a civil wrong. Deriving from the Latin word *tortum* ('wrong'), a tort is an act or omission that infringes upon the rights of individuals in society, allowing the aggrieved individual to seek a legal remedy. It is difficult to provide a comprehensive definition of a tort or the types of actions that lie beneath the 'tort umbrella' as definitions vary between jurisdictions and new torts continue to emerge. Liability in tort is based on protections afforded by the law, such as protection of the right to bodily integrity, protection of the right to possession of land and protection of one's reputation. A cause of action in tort can be pursued separately to an action for breach of contract or for breach of equitable obligations.

The person who occasions a wrong by infringing on the legal rights of another is known as a 'tortfeasor'. The accused tortfeasor is the defendant in legal proceedings usually initiated by an aggrieved individual known as the 'plaintiff'. The two main sources of tort law are common law and statute. Common law refers to the legal principles developed by judges in cases, which carry precedential weight in later, similar cases brought before the courts. Until the late 20th century, Australian tort law was based largely on common law principles. Each state and territory has its own civil liability legislation (although the legislation in the Northern Territory is very limited and the common law largely prevails).[1] Accordingly, cases interpreting the wording of the legislation are only of persuasive value in the courts of another jurisdiction – and only to the extent that the same or similar wording is used in the other jurisdiction's legislation. However, decisions of superior courts, such as the High Court of Australia, are binding across the country so as to create a unified common law.[2]

Historically, Australian tort law was heavily influenced by English jurisprudence, as case law from the United Kingdom was binding, rather than merely persuasive. Appeals to the Privy Council ceased with the passing of the *Australia Act 1986* (Cth). While all foreign cases are now regarded as persuasive only, Australian courts continue to consider and refer to decisions in common law jurisdictions such as England and Wales, Canada and New Zealand. The role of legislation in extending, amending or completely abrogating common law principles has become particularly prominent in the past two decades, with significant reform of personal injury law occurring in all Australian jurisdictions in 2002–3 (discussed in Section 1.2).[3] Defamation laws have also undergone legislative reform with a view to achieving national uniformity,[4] with recent amendments brought in to the most states (save for the Northern Territory and Western Australia) to modernise defamation laws in light of technological advances.[5] The increase in legislative intervention in the law of torts has not diminished the importance of the courts; however, their role has shifted from 'discovering' the law of tort to 'interpreting' and applying the legislation of tort.

Regardless of whether a tort principle derives from common law or legislation, the plaintiff must satisfy the court of all elements of a particular cause of action before initiating proceedings. Generally, the civil liability legislation seeks to lay down the principles previously embodied in the common law, with some variations or limitations on their application. In some instances, the legislation creates new principles and significantly modifies other principles. Yet, many legal terms used in the civil liability legislation depend on a prior understanding of the common law regarding their cause and effect.

---

1 *Civil Law (Wrongs) Act 2002* (ACT); *Civil Liability Act 2002* (NSW); *Civil Liability Act 2003* (Qld); *Civil Liability Act 1936* (SA); *Civil Liability Act 2002* (Tas); *Wrongs Act 1958* (Vic); *Civil Liability Act 2002* (WA). The Northern Territory has the *Personal Injuries (Liabilities and Damages) Act 2003* (NT).

2 *Lipohar v The Queen* (1999) 200 CLR 485, [44]) per Gaudron, Gummow and Hayne JJ.

3 See, eg, *Review of the Law of Negligence* (Final Report, September 2002).

4 *Civil Law (Wrongs) Amendment Act 2006* (ACT) amending the *Civil Law (Wrongs) Act 2002* (ACT); *Defamation Act 2005* (NSW); *Defamation Act 2006* (NT); *Defamation Act 2005* (Qld); *Defamation Act 2005* (SA); *Defamation Act 2005* (Tas); *Defamation Act 2005* (Vic); *Defamation Act 2005* (WA).

5 On 1 July 2021, stage 1 of the *Model Defamation Amendment Provisions 2020* commenced in South Australia, Victoria and New South Wales. The second stage of the reform processes commenced in March 2021 with the release of the *Attorneys-General Review of Model Defamation Provisions: Stage 2* (Discussion Paper, 31 March 2021).

Causes of action in tort can be grouped into three broad categories: intentional torts, negligence and torts of strict liability. As the name of the first category suggests, *intentional torts* are intentional infringements by a tortfeasor of an individual's legal rights. For instance, hitting somebody intentionally is a violation of their bodily integrity and constitutes the tort of battery. In some cases, intention can be established by proving the failure to take care, such as where negligent driving causes injury to another, amounting to battery.[6] Some individual torts can be categorised as intentional torts: trespass to the person (encompassing assault, battery and false imprisonment); trespass to chattels (encompassing trespass to goods, conversion and detinue); and trespass to land. Other torts, such as public and private nuisance, are a hybrid of intentional torts and negligence. Intentional torts are actionable 'per se', meaning that the plaintiff does not have to prove loss to initiate action against the alleged wrongdoer.

In contrast, *negligence* does not require an intentional act by a tortfeasor. Rather, a cause of action arises out of the defendant's failure to take reasonable care regarding an act or omission and the plaintiff has suffered a legally recognised loss. The tort of negligence allows a person who has suffered a legally recognised loss, as a consequence of the tortfeasor's failure to take reasonable care, to sue for compensation. To establish a cause of action in negligence, a plaintiff must prove that the defendant owed a duty of care, that the defendant breached their duty and that the breach caused the harm. As an example of a duty of care, the law recognises that medical practitioners owe patients a duty to take care when providing medical treatment or when warning of the risks associated with a medical procedure.[7] Sometimes two causes of action, such as battery and negligence, can arise out of the same set of facts.[8]

Where liability in tort is *strict*, the law imposes legal responsibility regardless of the tortfeasor's intention or negligence. A common example of strict liability is the vicarious liability of an employer for the actions of an employee.[9] Another example is liability for defamation. Defamation involves publishing a statement that lowers the reputation of a person in the eyes of reasonable members of society. Where a defamatory statement is published, the maker of the statement is liable, regardless of their intention or carelessness.

1.1.1.1   Purpose of tort law

The main purpose of tort law is to provide a remedy to individuals and legal entities whose legal rights have been infringed. The remedy usually comprises *damages*, consisting of sums of money intended to compensate for the harm suffered, for example, personal injury, property damage or economic loss. Damages have a compensatory purpose to correct wrongs. They are designed to restore the plaintiff to their original position (as far as possible), before the wrong was committed. Damages awarded to a plaintiff for a defendant's trespass to the person can also have a deterrent purpose, as courts are permitted to award *aggravated damages* and *exemplary damages*, requiring the tortfeasor to pay additional compensation to the aggrieved individual, including in the absence of damage or injury. The

---

6 *Williams v Milotin* (1957) 97 CLR 465; *Venning v Chin* (1974) 10 SASR 299.
7 *Rogers v Whitaker* (1992) 175 CLR 479.
8 *Ljubic v Armellin* [2009] ACTSC 21. In this case, Dr Armellin's removal of Mrs Ljubic's ovaries without her consent constituted a medical battery and medical negligence.
9 *Hollis v Vabu Pty Ltd* (2001) 207 CLR 21; *Deatons Pty Ltd v Flew* (1949) 79 CLR 370.

rationale for allowing exemplary damages in this context is centred on protecting bodily integrity, punishing the defendant for disregarding the plaintiff's rights and serving as moral retribution or deterrence. For instance, in *Schmidt v Argent*, the Queensland Court of Appeal upheld an award of aggravated and exemplary damages against police officers who showed a blatant disregard for the plaintiff's rights in arresting her without a valid warrant.[10] The award of aggravated and exemplary damages for negligence is prohibited in some states.[11] Tort law can also offer non-monetary remedies, such as an injunction requiring an individual to cease conduct amounting to a trespass or to remove the cause of a nuisance. For example, in *Janney v Steller Works Pty Ltd*,[12] the court awarded an injunction to plaintiffs affected by a tower crane next to residential premises. For a contemporary illustration of damages awards, see the following case example.

Case: *Cruse v Victoria* (2019) VR 241

Facts

On 18 April 2015, police officers raided the plaintiff's home as part of terror raids at six locations. The police arrested the plaintiff (Eathan Cruse) but subsequently released him the following day without charge. No subsequent charges were laid.

During the raid, the plaintiff sustained serious injuries to his head and upper body. He alleged the police partook in several acts of violence including: that he was struck to the left side of his head; that he was lifted and moved from the hallway to the kitchen; that he was slammed against the fridge and pushed to the floor. His wrist was also twisted while the police used profanities and told him: 'Don't say a ******* word'. The plaintiff was diagnosed with post-traumatic stress disorder and major depression, in addition to sustaining physical injuries. The plaintiff sued for battery and assault.

Issue

Was the plaintiff entitled to aggravated and exemplary damages for the excessive nature of the police officers' conduct?

Decision

Richards J awarded the plaintiff $400 000 in damages consisting of:

- $200 000 in general damages
- $20 000 in damages for future economic loss
- $80 000 for aggravated damages
- $100 000 in exemplary damages.

---

10   [2003] QCA 507, [50] (Dutney J). ('Exemplary damages differ from aggravated damages in that they are intended to punish the defendant for conduct showing contumelious disregard for the plaintiff's rights and to deter the defendant from similar conduct in future.')

11   See, eg, *Civil Liability Act 2002* (NSW) s 21. ('In an action for the award of personal injury damages where the act or omission that caused the injury or death was negligence, a court cannot award exemplary or punitive damages or damages in the nature of aggravated damages.')

12   (2017) 53 VR 677.

Significance

The case illustrates the compensatory purpose of tort law and demonstrates that tortfeasors may be liable for additional damages for the brazen disregard of others' rights.

Question

What parts of the police officers' conduct satisfied the judge that aggravated and exemplary damages ought to be awarded?

 Guided response in the eBook

The right to commence tort action is embedded in civil law and these principles can be contrasted with principles of criminal law. A tort is a civil action taken by an individual or legal entity against another individual or legal entity and is initiated in a private context. By contrast, a criminal action is prosecuted on behalf of the State. Also, the purpose of remedies in tort law is mainly to compensate for the harm caused to the plaintiff, whereas the purpose of criminal penalties is mainly to punish the defendant. The same incident can give rise to both civil and criminal actions. For example, if A strikes B, that act can constitute a civil battery and/or assault, as well as a criminal assault. While an injured plaintiff may report an incident (such as a physical altercation) to the police, ultimately it is the plaintiff who elects whether to pursue a civil remedy. In contrast, where a criminal act is committed, the police are almost certain to press charges or impose a penalty to preserve the safety of the general community and deter future misconduct. Table 1.1 illustrates the main differences between a tort and a crime.

Table 1.1   Main differences between a tort and crime

Characteristic	Tort	Crime
Parties	Plaintiff v defendant (the 'v' is said as 'and')	Prosecution v defendant (the 'v' is said as 'against')
Party taking action	Individual or entity	Police/Director of Public Prosecutions (DPP)
Type of wrong	Private wrong against individual or entity	Public wrong against the State or society
Purpose	To restore or compensate	To protect, deter, punish and rehabilitate
Outcome	Damages or injunction	Criminal punishment (fines, imprisonment)
Burden of proof	On the plaintiff	On the police
Standard of proof	On the balance of probabilities	Beyond reasonable doubt

A tort can also be contrasted with a breach of contract. Both originate in civil law. However, pursuing damages for a breach of contract requires an enforceable agreement to exist between the parties, either expressly or through implied conduct. In tort law, no such requirement for a contract exists: plaintiffs may pursue damages for a breach of standards imposed by law. Another fundamental difference between contract and tort is in the operation of damages. In both tort law and contract law, the purpose of damages is to return the plaintiff to the position they would have been in, had it not been for the defendant's wrongdoing. However, in contract, an award of damages for non-performance 'looks forward' to the position the plaintiff would be in were the contract performed; in tort, an award of damages 'looks back' to the position the plaintiff would be in had the wrongful act not occurred. Theoretically, damages in tort can protect a wider range of interests than 'merely' contractual rights, such as the right to bodily integrity, possession of goods or land, or personal reputation. Yet in practice, one can acquire contractual rights over the same matters. For example, a surgeon who performs an operation carelessly can be sued for breach of contract as well as in negligence.

Actions for a breach of contract and a tort can arise out of the same circumstances, as in the example of a surgeon who performs an operation carelessly. In *Chappel v Hart*, a doctor negligently performed an operation on the plaintiff's throat, leaving her with paralysis of the right vocal cord.[13] Gummow J acknowledged that the plaintiff could have recovered nominal damages for breach of contract, but that an action in tort allowed her to pursue a wider range of damages or interests.[14] Table 1.2 illustrates the main differences between a tort and a contract.

Table 1.2   Main differences between a tort and contract

Characteristic	Tort	Contract
Obligations	Obligations imposed by the law based on reasonable standards of conduct	Promises made by parties either expressly or implicitly
Remedies	Damages	Damages and equitable remedies such as an injunction and specific performance
Purpose of damages	To restore the plaintiff to the position they would have been in if the wrong had not occurred	To place the plaintiff in a position they would have been in if the contract had been performed

1.1.2   Theories of tort law

A variety of conceptual frameworks and theories have been applied to tort law, including corrective justice and economic efficiency theory and feminist theory. Understanding the theoretical framework of an area of law is important because it can assist in explaining the basis for the law, understanding reasons behind a judicial decision or justifying certain policy stances. Theories can also justify policy decisions.[15] While theories emerge from the work of eminent scholars, they find contemporary relevance when principles are applied by judges in case law and when legislation is drafted by Parliament. The purpose of this section is to introduce the most prominent theories, which are essential to understanding tort law, and to provide a catalyst for further consideration of these paradigms. It is difficult

---

13 (1998) 195 CLR 232.
14 Ibid 254.
15 Illustrations of policy considerations may also be found in tort law decisions involving wrongful births and wrongful life cases: see *Cattanach v Melchior* (2003) 215 CLR 1; *Harriton v Stephens* (2006) 226 CLR 52.

to claim that a single theory offers a complete account of tort law; therefore it is important to consider the breadth of scholarly literature as it applies to various aspects of that law.

1.1.2.1   Corrective and distributive justice and economic efficiency

Tort law plays an important role in balancing the rights and interests of all members of society. We have noted that where one individual infringes upon the legal rights of another, an aim of tort law is to require the tortfeasor to repair the harm they have caused. This corrective purpose gives aggrieved individuals the right to seek compensation through the courts or non-litigious avenues. However, this right must be balanced with other public interests such as interests in affordable compensation and the ongoing availability of indemnity insurance. Such aims may at times seem to be at odds with one another. This friction is reflected in the principles of corrective justice, distributive justice and economic efficiency theory, which aid in understanding the development of current tort principles. Many tort scholars contend that tort law has a *corrective justice* purpose, since it imposes an obligation on the tortfeasor to correct or remedy wrongdoing to the aggrieved individual.[16] In the tort of negligence, awards of damages arguably have a corrective purpose as they are designed to remediate the harm or damage caused by the tortfeasor. Theorist Ernest Weinrib defines corrective justice as a bilateral relationship in which each party adopts either an active or passive pole of the same injustice.[17] Allan Beever describes this relationship as 'interpersonal justice': if one person wrongs the other by infringing on their legal rights, there is an obligation to restore the equality of the parties.[18] In this way, Beever posits that the law of negligence is best understood in terms of principles of morality.[19]

Corrective justice theory originated with Aristotle, who distinguished between 'corrective justice' and 'distributive justice'.[20] Aristotle envisaged two parties starting in a position of equality. If one party disrupts that equality, corrective justice demands the restoration of equality by deducting something from the party who disturbed the equality and giving it to the disrupted party.[21] Corrective justice requires the negligent person to repair the injured person's loss, which is achieved through compensation. An example of corrective justice theory in operation is a fault-based tort system which requires the plaintiff to prove the element of causation (ie, to demonstrate that the wrongdoer's negligence *caused* the plaintiff's harm).

Corrective justice can be contrasted with *distributive justice*, which is concerned with the equal distribution of goods and wealth in society.[22] Distributive justice addresses justice

---

16   EJ Weinrib, 'Corrective Justice' (1992) 77(2) *Iowa Law Review* 403; EJ Weinrib, 'Toward a Moral Theory of Negligence Law' (1983) 2(1) *Law and Philosophy* 37; EJ Weinrib, 'The Special Morality of Tort Law' (1989) 34(3) *McGill Law Journal* 403; JL Coleman, 'Tort Law and the Demands of Corrective Justice' (1992) 67(2) *Indiana Law Journal* 349; S Erbacher, *Negligence and Illegality* (Hart Publishing, 2017); G Turton, *Evidential Uncertainty in Causation* (Hart Publishing, 2016).

17   EJ Weinrib, *Corrective Justice* (Oxford University Press, 2012) 2. See also EJ Weinrib, 'Corrective Justice in a Nutshell' (2002) 52 *University of Toronto Law Journal* 349; EJ Weinrib, 'The Special Morality of Tort Law' (1989) 34(3) *McGill Law Journal* 403.

18   A Beever, *Forgotten Justice: The Forms of Justice in the History of Legal and Political Theory* (Oxford University Press, 2013) 80.

19   A Beever, *Rediscovering the Law of Negligence* (Hart Publishing, 2007).

20   MDA Freeman, *Lloyd's Introduction to Jurisprudence* (Thomson Reuters, 9th ed, 2014) 481.

21   S Hershovitz, 'Tort as a Substitute for Revenge' in J Oberdiek (ed), *Philosophical Foundations of the Law of Torts* (Oxford University Press, 2014) 89.

22   J Rawls, *A Theory of Justice* (Oxford University Press, rev ed, 1999).

across a community based on a criterion of merit, requiring a broad institution to implement appropriate distribution across the community.[23] An example of distributive justice is a compensation scheme that distributes resources from a pool of funds to members of society who may need them. For instance, a compulsory third party insurance scheme requires all drivers to register their motor vehicles and pay an annual registration fee. Those fees are pooled together to fund state compensation schemes for individuals involved in vehicle collisions.

HINTS AND TIPS

A traditional torts system that requires a plaintiff to establish a causal link between a breach of duty and damage is an example of corrective justice. Statutory schemes, such as a victims of crime compensation scheme or the National Disability Insurance Scheme (NDIS), are examples of distributive justice.

These theoretical frameworks can be illustrated by an example. Imagine that D fails to take reasonable care while driving by using his mobile phone and that this failure causes a car crash with P, who suffers a broken leg. The balance between D and P has been distorted. Corrective justice theory requires D to correct the balance by providing P with a remedy (such as compensation to cover P's medical bills). Yet if D cannot afford the compensation, P's needs will not be met and the wrong will not be rectified. In such circumstances, state compensation schemes (discussed in Section 1.3) can provide much-needed remedies. Given that the injury arose out of a car collision, P's medical expenses will be covered by a state compensation scheme for motor vehicle accidents. Corrective justice theorists assert that the law should facilitate the reparation of harm between the tortfeasor and the injured plaintiff. Yet in practice, it is often difficult to strike the right balance between all members of society.

Economic efficiency theorists are concerned with the distribution of wealth in society.[24] The focus for them is not on how to restore equality between a wrongdoer and a victim, but on how resources can be optimally allocated to serve society's economic wellbeing. Richard Posner contended: 'the common law is best explained as if the judges were trying to maximize economic welfare'.[25] According to the tenets of economic theory, judges should decide cases with the aim of maximising society's total wealth.[26] In other words, justice can be equated to wealth maximisation and the role of tort law is simply to allocate costs with the aims of minimising the cost of accidents and reducing the cost of avoiding them.[27] Hence, if the cost of taking care to avoid injury is less than the cost of compensating for an injury sustained, people should be encouraged to take action to avoid the risk of injury.

23 G Turton, *Evidential Uncertainty in Causation* (Hart Publishing, 2016) 10.

24 R Posner, *The Economics of Justice* (Harvard University Press, 2nd ed, 1983); D Partlett, 'Economic Analysis and Some Problems in the Law of Torts' (1982) 13(3) *Melbourne University Law Review* 398.

25 R Posner, *The Economics of Justice* (Harvard University Press, 2nd ed, 1983) 4.

26 MDA Freeman, *Lloyd's Introduction to Jurisprudence* (Thomson Reuters, 9th ed, 2014) 520.

27 G Calabresi, *The Cost of Accidents* (Yale University Press, 1970).

Economic efficiency theory may best explain the rationale for the 2002–3 statutory civil liability reforms (discussed in Section 1.2), which were argued to be necessary in response to a perceived insurance crisis because the 'efficiency' of resource allocation trumped the notion of a just outcome. In the lead-up to the reforms, certain groups lobbied for restrictions on compensation payments, arguing that the increasing cost of insurance meant that many professionals (such as doctors) could no longer afford indemnity cover. The statutory reforms made drastic changes to negligence principles nationally, curtailing the rights of plaintiffs to access compensation, even in meritorious claims.

One of the criticisms of the pursuit of economic efficiency is that it leads to inequality. Jules Coleman contended that it causes the wealthy to gain more rights and increase their wealth while the poor become worse off.[28] Using the example of the tort reforms, economic efficiency allows professionals (such as doctors) to continue running their practices while claimants injured as a result of medical negligence may struggle to obtain adequate compensation due to the restrictions.

1.1.2.2 Feminist critiques

As with any branch of law, modern tort law needs to be contextualised within its historical setting and social context. The law of torts, as you have already learnt by now, has developed categories of torts to protect certain interests, such as personal interests, property interests and business interests. Thus, it needs to be comprehended within the wider context of changing social norms and how these affect the development of tortious liability vis-à-vis those interests. In that sense, law is never really 'neutral' as it reflects society and its values at a particular time.[29] Thus, it often presents a particular 'point of view', which in consequence means that not all interests of all groups in society are necessarily equally represented. Inevitably, it poses a challenge but, at the same time, it represents an opportunity for a lawyer to contest some of these standards if they do not operate fairly towards all in the society. Feminist critique of tort law is one such attempt.

Feminist theory varies and constantly evolves to adapt to the changing social and cultural environment. In fact, there is more than one feminist theory. But in its basic form, a feminist approach calls for recognition that women and men are equal, and that gender inequality stems from unequal participation in spheres such as family, education and paid labour. But unequal participation does not need to be the case. Hence, feminist scholars critically question the status quo of certain values and perspectives, and consequently how law – including the law of torts – privileges certain groups and their interests, to the detriment of others. This approach challenges 'patriarchy' in society,[30] understood as a male-dominated

---

28 J Coleman, 'Economics and the Law: A Critical Review of the Foundations of the Economic Approach to Law' (1984) 94(4) *Ethics* 649, 662 cited in MDA Freeman, *Lloyd's Introduction to Jurisprudence* (Thomson Reuters, 9th ed, 2014) 521.

29 This explains, for example, the differences between modern Australian and English tort laws, despite their common historical roots and mutual jurisprudential and adjudicative influences.

30 For an excellent overview of the historical development of the patriarchy, see the seminal work by historian G Lerner, *The Creation of Patriarchy* (Oxford University Press, 1987). Lerner's main argument is that patriarchy is neither natural nor biological; rather, it developed as a particular system of organising society, beginning around the second millennium BCE in the ancient Middle East, and thus can be ended by cultural and societal processes.

power structure and hierarchy which produces a systemic bias against women. Although a feminist approach is women centred, it is not women exclusive. As Leslie Bender pointed out, it is not only women but also men who lose out, as 'patriarchy distorts all of our lives' and harm comes from exclusion.[31]

Since the late 1980s, there has been a growing literature on how women's interests are (mis)represented or undervalued in the formation, legal reasoning and application of tort law. For example, consider one of the key concepts in the tort of negligence: the 'reasonable person' test (discussed in Section 3.2). The standard for this test has been developed and applied based on representing a 'reasonable man' or a 'man of reasonable prudence' or, as defined by an English common law maxim, 'the man on the Clapham omnibus'.[32]

The 'reasonable person' principle sets a standard for what is considered reasonable conduct in the circumstances. Thus, it is instrumental in assessing whether the defendant met the legally required standard of care towards the plaintiff. But what might at first glance look like a universal measure for conduct is, in fact, a hypothetical construct that reflects the norms of the society in which it was formulated. Viewed in its historical context, the test was developed in the United Kingdom during the Victorian era (1837–1901), when men and women's roles in society were sharply defined and women were not able to vote, sue or own property.

These days, legal language is more gender neutral, thus 'man' has been replaced with 'person' in the wording of the test. However, changing a noun to a more gender-neutral option might not be sufficient to alter the content of the test, as it continues to rely on a particular conceptualisation of 'rational' and 'reasonable'.[33] This raises a number of questions: What does this conceptualisation mean for legal reasoning? 'Reasonable' according to whose standards? Can it still be said that 'there is less diligence to be exacted or expected from a woman than would be expected from a man'?[34] Some scholars have postulated a 'reasonable woman' criterion.[35] Although such a criterion has not been developed, courts have often taken 'female' characteristics into account when determining tortious liability; a key disagreement is whether there has been too 'much' or too 'little' of this.[36]

The idea of a 'reasonable woman' criterion might not necessarily be unreasonable, given that statistical data indicate differences between the type and extent of personal injuries suffered by women and men, which have further social and economic implications. Statistical data also indicate that men are more likely than women to be injured or killed,[37] including

---

31 L Bender, 'A Lawyer's Primer on Feminist Theory and Tort' (1988) 38(1) *Journal of Legal Education* 3, 8.

32 The phrase is believed to have been used for the first time by Collins MR in *McQuire v Western Morning News* [1903] 2 KB 100, [109].

33 For a critique of the perceived masculine orientation of Western standards of rationality and morality, see G Lloyd, *The Man of Reason: 'Male' and 'Female' in Western Philosophy* (Methuen, 1984).

34 This was a point raised for the consideration of the jury by the judge in a case concerning contributory negligence: *Denver & Rio Grande Railroad v Lorentzen*, 79 F 291, 293 (8th Cir, 1897).

35 See, in relation to US legal history, BY Welke, 'Unreasonable Women: Gender and the Law of Accidental Injury, 1870–1920' (1994) 19(2) *Law and Social Inquiry* 369; M Schlanger, 'Injured Women Before Common Law Courts, 1860–1930' (1998) 21 *Harvard Women's Law Journal* 79.

36 See, eg, A Jacob, 'Feminist Approaches to Tort Law Revisited: A Reply to Professor Schwartz' (2001) 2(1) *Theoretical Inquiries in Law* 211.

37 Australian Bureau of Statistics, *Gender Indicators, Australia, December 2020* (Catalogue No 4125.0, 15 December 2020).

in work-related accidents[38] and motor vehicle accidents,[39] which has led to further studies of the differences in risk-taking (or risk-avoidance) behaviours between genders.[40] This may shed a different light on the level of 'cautiousness' expected or the amount of 'precaution-taking' required when assessing liability in negligence, depending on whether the defendant is female or male. This has implications for insurance claims, and consequently insurance premiums, which in turn can affect legal developments.[41]

A feminist analytical lens can also be useful at the compensation stage when assessing damages for personal injury. For example, as women's life expectancy is usually longer than that of men,[42] it is not uncommon for women and men to be awarded different levels of compensation. As another example, when predicting loss of earning capacity, courts would often assume and take into account that a female plaintiff (but not a male) would take career breaks for child-bearing or child rearing due to 'gender assumptions about women's lack of attachment to the paid labour market and the assumption that women's paid work is secondary to their role as mothers and carers'.[43] However, courts do not automatically give effect to these (actual or perceived) differences. In *De Sales v Ingrilli*, a wrongful death case, the High Court had to consider the prospect of remarriage by the plaintiff and thus whether the discount should apply in assessing damages.[44] Gleeson CJ asserted that 'changing social conditions may … have made it less safe to assume that remarriage will be to the financial benefit of a widow'.[45] Kirby J concurred, highlighting the changing social context and economic position of women in Australia.[46]

We might also consider the differences between genders in relation to the recognised type of harm. Statistical data is again relevant here. The most recent statistics in Australia show that the majority of family and domestic violence is directed against women,[47] and that women suffer more often than men from mental disorders, including anxiety and depression.[48] Thus, from the perspective of a plaintiff, who is probably female, suffering from torts arising within a domestic context, a remedy might not always be available, and the monetary compensation might not be as high as that awarded for torts committed within the public sphere[49] or for 'physical' (bodily) injury.

---

38 This needs to be considered in the context of the type of work performed predominantly by male as opposed to female workers: Safe Work Australia, *Work-related Traumatic Injury Fatalities, Australia* (2020).

39 For the most up-to-date statistics, see Department of Infrastructure, Regional Development and Cities (Cth), *Road Trauma Australia: Annual Summaries*.

40 One such study, which examined the impact of gender and race on risk perception, showed that white men fear various risks less than women and minorities do: DM Kahan et al, 'Culture and Identity-Protective Cognition: Explaining the White-Male Effect in Risk Perception' (2007) 4(3) *Journal of Empirical Legal Studies* 465.

41 As seen in Australia in the early 2000s (see Section 1.2).

42 For the most recent statistics, see Australian Institute of Health and Welfare, *Life Expectancy and Death*.

43 R Graycar, 'Damaging Stereotypes: The Return of "Hoovering as a Hobby"' in J Richardson and E Rackley (eds), *Feminist Perspectives on Tort Law* (Routledge, 2012) 205, 205–6.

44 (2002) 212 CLR 338; [2002] HCA 52.

45 Ibid [26] (Gleeson CJ).

46 Ibid [153] (Kirby J).

47 Australian Bureau of Statistics, *Recorded Crime – Victims, Australia, 2021* (Catalogue No 4510.0, 28 June 2022).

48 Australian Bureau of Statistics, *National Study of Mental Health and Wellbeing, 2020–21, July 2022* (Catalogue No 4326.0, 22 July 2022).

49 On the importance of the public–private divide *in* and *for* law see, eg, K O'Donovan, *Sexual Divisions in Law* (Weidenfeld and Nicolson, 1985).

Unsurprisingly then, the area of psychiatric (mental) harm, or 'nervous shock',[50] has been a focus of feminist debate.[51] A study by Prue Vines, Mehera San Roque and Emily Rumble provided a quantitative and qualitative analysis of Australian case law between 1885 and 2008 in relation to the recognition of psychiatric harm as a compensable type of harm.[52] Their analysis indicates that psychiatric harm is specifically required to be reasonably foreseeable (assessed by the test of 'normal fortitude') and that many statutory provisions continue to put additional limitations on damages recoverable for pure mental harm, requiring the plaintiff to either have witnessed, at the scene, the victim being killed, injured or put in peril, or been in a close relationship with the victim,[53] thereby maintaining the separate status of psychiatric harm (see Section 2.5.1). These findings, confirming earlier studies and literature in this area, indicate that psychiatric injury remains a marginalised form of harm in Australia, an issue which was not adequately addressed by the civil liability reforms (see Section 1.2). Therefore, adopting a feminist approach allows us to refocus on issues that otherwise might be sidelined or perceived as being of less importance – whether predominantly affecting female or male plaintiffs.

Feminist theory, including a feminist challenge to tort law, is a broad and mixed field that deserves further acknowledgement and examination, not only in scholarly debates but also, if not predominantly, in its practical application for achieving justice in civil legal matters.[54] It remains contested whether feminist theory's contribution to tort law has been 'thin' in comparison to its contribution to criminal law.[55] The contribution may also be considered somewhat instrumental in challenging the norms and standards that are often taken for granted. Nonetheless, considering a feminist legal method in tort law is an enlightening way to 'complement traditional legal method by incorporation of alternative views, experiences, perceptions and values which traditional method, in its insistence on logic and deductive thought, may exclude'.[56]

1.1.3   Tort law and human rights

You could ponder the question: how are tort law and human rights law related? Are human rights important for the understanding and development of tort law and tortious liability? Or can we perhaps, through torts claims, strengthen the protection of human rights? The

50 The first use of this term in law was in *Victorian Railways Commissioner v Coultas* (1888) 13 App Cas 222.

51 See, eg, LM Finley, 'A Break in the Silence: Including Women's Issues in a Torts Course' (1989) 1 *Yale Journal of Law and Feminism* 41; E Handsley, 'Mental Injury Occasioned by Harm to Another: A Feminist Critique' (1996) 14(2) *Law & Inequality* 391.

52 P Vines, M San Roque and E Rumble, 'Is "Nervous Shock" Still a Feminist Issue? The Duty of Care and Psychiatric Injury in Australia' (2010) 18(1) *Tort Law Review* 9.

53 See, eg, *Civil Liability Act 2002* (NSW) s 30, requiring the plaintiff to be a 'close member of the family' of the victim (s 30(2)(b)).

54 If you would like to learn more how judgments could be rewritten from a feminist perspective, see H Douglas, F Bartlett, T Luker and R Hunter (eds), *Australian Feminist Judgments: Righting and Rewriting Law* (Hart, 2014), in particular Part II Private Law, Torts.

55 GT Schwartz recognises feminist writings on tort law as important in 'opening up valuable lines of inquiry' but regards it as nevertheless 'thin' in comparison to the substantive contribution made by feminist theory to criminal law (in particular, for example, in relation to the reformulation of the law of rape): 'Feminist Approaches to Tort Law' (2001) 2(1) *Theoretical Inquiries in Law* 175, 209.

56 H Barnett, *Introduction to Feminist Jurisprudence* (Routledge-Cavendish, 1998) 25.

initial response to these questions is that these two branches of law have mutual influence. In a similar fashion, there is a nexus between tort law and contract and criminal laws. The intersection of tort law and human rights law is also an area of increasing jurisprudential interest in relation to the public–private law dichotomy.

As a starting point, these two branches of law have relatively similar aims, that is, to protect and safeguard personal safety and integrity, with implications when these rights are infringed. There are also differences. Most importantly, as noted earlier, tort law is predominantly about facilitating the righting of legal wrongs *between* individuals and other legal entities (inter se), although public authorities can also be defendants in negligence claims, or in torts such as misfeasance in public office and the intentional torts of false imprisonment, assault and battery. Human rights law, on the other hand, has been developed to protect individuals from harm and unwarranted intrusions by the State and its agents (ie, public authorities and public officials) or – when the State fails to investigate human rights violations – to protect the victims of these violations and prosecute the perpetrators. Thus, human rights law has a so-called vertical, as opposed to horizontal, effect: it impacts on the relationship between the State and the individual citizen (or those under the jurisdiction of the State).

In recent years, increasing concern about human rights violations by non-state actors has led to a reconceptualisation of the traditional scope of application of human rights law.[57] However, since holding private or non-state actors accountable for human rights abuses is complicated, the tort framework has been used. For example the *Alien Tort Claims Act 1789* (US) has been used in the United States to hold multinational corporations responsible for their human rights violations in developing countries.[58] The Act grants US courts jurisdiction over 'any civil action by an alien for a tort only, committed in violation of the law of nations or a treaty of the United States'.[59] With varied success,[60] partly due to inconsistent interpretation of the Act among lower courts, non-US nationals have been able to bring claims against corporations for violations of international law (including human rights law) and seek redress in US courts.

One of the more prominent cases where the plaintiffs relied on the *Alien Tort Claims Act* is *Sarei v Rio Tinto plc*.[61] This case involved one of the world's largest mining companies which is publicly listed in Australia. The actions of Rio Tinto on the Papua New Guinea island of Bougainville were challenged by a number of residents of Bougainville seeking compensation from the company and its local subsidiary for their alleged complicity in war crimes, crimes against humanity, genocide and other gross human rights violations.[62] The class action was lodged in 2000. The United States District Court (CD California) dismissed the action in 2002. That decision was overturned by the United States Court of Appeals in 2007, and the case was returned to the District Court in 2008 to determine whether the

---

57 Broadly, the responsibility to ensure and protect human rights rests with states and extending it to non-state actors remains a contentious matter: see, eg, A Clapham, *Human Rights Obligations of Non-State Actors* (Oxford University Press, 2006).
58 28 USC § 1350 (2006).
59 Ibid.
60 See MD Goldhaber, 'Corporate Human Rights Litigation in Non-US Courts: A Comparative Scorecard' (2013) 3(1) *UC Irvine Law Review* 127.
61 221 F Supp 2d 1116 (CD Cal, 2002).
62 See, eg, J Braithwaite and R Nickson 'Timing Truth, Reconciliation and Justice After War' (2012) 27(3) *Ohio State Journal on Dispute Resolution* 443.

applicants needed to exhaust the remedies in their home country before making a claim in the United States. In 2011, reversing the lower court's dismissal of the case, the Court of Appeals upheld the claims regarding genocide and war crimes. However, in 2013 the Court of Appeals vacated the by-now 13-year-old action in light of the United States Supreme Court's decision in *Kiobel v Royal Dutch Petroleum Co*,[63] a class action suit filed on behalf of Nigerian residents who engaged in the 1990s in peaceful protests against environmental degradation in the Ogoni region and were targeted by the Nigerian military allegedly aided by the multinational. The Supreme Court in that case ruled that the *Alien Tort Claims Act* is limited by the 'presumption against extraterritoriality' thus requiring the circumstances of the case to sufficiently 'touch and concern' the territorial jurisdiction of the United States. This decision has significantly curtailed the use of the Act by victims of human rights abuses committed outside the United States to seek compensation from the alleged perpetrators in US courts.

This does not, however, mean that there is no future for common law tort claims when pursuing human rights violations by non-state actors, including for conduct occurring abroad. Although the decision in *Kiobel v Royal Dutch Petroleum Co* seems to limit the scope of application of the *Alien Tort Claims Act* in US courts,[64] this outcome might lead to a revival of the use of human rights-based common law tort action in national courts elsewhere.[65] Yet in Australia and many other countries in relation to interstate and international torts, courts apply – often strictly – the *lex loci delicti* ('the law of the place of the tort').[66] This rule also governs the assessment of damages.[67] Nonetheless, the approach of the common law of tort to human rights litigation has significant prospects of being used and further developed – especially to obtain redress for victims of human rights violations committed abroad by private or non-state actors.

The intersection of tort law and human rights law is of growing importance, and thus of interest to litigation lawyers as well as human rights groups and civil rights advocates. From a practical point of view, human rights law is still a relatively 'young' area of law. The adoption by the United Nations General Assembly of the *Universal Declaration of Human Rights* in 1948 marked the beginning of the modern international human rights law.[68] It is not that human rights law lacks mechanisms for (legal) enforcement, and thus requires the remedial framework of tort law to give effect to these rights; rather, the human rights law enforcement system varies between countries and regions, resulting in myriad complexities and potential limitations.

---

63 569 US 108 (2013).
64 Ibid.
65 See O Webb, '"Kiobel", the Alien Tort Statute and the Common Law: Human Rights Litigation in this "Present, Imperfect World"' (2013) 20 *Australian International Law Journal* 131; L Francisca and H Enneking, *Foreign Direct Liability and Beyond: Exploring the Role of Tort Law in Promoting Corporate Social Responsibility and Accountability* (Eleven International, 2012); PJ Borchers, 'Conflict-of-Laws Considerations in State Court Human Rights Actions' (2013) 3(1) *UC Irvine Law Review* 45, 57.
66 See, eg, *John Pfeiffer Pty Ltd v Rogerson* (2003) 203 CLR 503, 544; *Regie Nationale des Usines Renault SA v Zhang* (2002) 210 CLR 491.
67 *John Pfeiffer Pty Ltd v Rogerson* (2003) 203 CLR 503, 544 (Gleeson CJ, Gaudron, McHugh, Gummow, Hayne JJ) ('*all* questions about the kinds of damage, or amount of damages that may be recovered, would likewise be treated as substantive issues governed by the *lex loci delicti*').
68 GA Res 217 A (III).

Even though the *Universal Declaration of Human Rights* is not legally binding on states, it has led to a range of international instruments, including core human rights treaties, customary international law provisions, regional agreements, domestic human rights bills and constitutional provisions. These have created a comprehensive, albeit complex, system for the protection and promotion of human rights. International treaties need to be ratified by state parties to be legally binding on these states. In addition, they generally must be translated into the domestic legal system of the ratifying state to have national effect.[69] This is the case with Australia. Even though it is a party to most of the core human rights treaties, including the *International Covenant on Civil and Political Rights*,[70] it still lacks a national Bill of Rights. The Australian Capital Territory, Queensland and Victoria have enacted human rights legislation.[71] But so far, the federal Parliament has passed only a handful of laws to give effect to Australia's international human right obligations and to protect individual citizens against violations of their rights by public officials.[72] This makes Australia the only Western country lacking comprehensive national legislation protecting human rights and freedoms.[73]

This means that, unless a claim pertains to matters directly protected by existing domestic legislation, the only avenue for judges in Australia to implement international human rights law domestically is to interpret relevant legal principles *in light of* human rights standards. This was confirmed by the High Court in *Minister of State for Immigration and Ethnic Affairs v Teoh*:

> Where a statute or subordinate legislation is ambiguous, the courts should favour that construction which accords with Australia's obligations under a treaty or international convention to which Australia is a party, at least in those cases in which the legislation is enacted after, or in contemplation of, entry into, or ratification of, the relevant international instrument. That is because Parliament, prima facie, intends to give effect to Australia's obligations under international law.[74]

Thus, even in the absence of a Bill of Rights, the common law can protect human rights through a 'common law bill of rights'.[75] Chief Justice Spigelman, writing extra-curially, argued that a number of rebuttable presumptions of statutory interpretation can serve to protect fundamental rights and freedoms which Parliament is presumed not to have intended to limit or overrule (unless such an intention is made clear) before such a right can be abrogated.[76]

---

69 This follows the 'dualist' approach to the application of international law in states' national systems. The 'monist' approach considers that international law does not need to be translated into national law to have domestic application.

70 (1966) 999 UNTS 171; [1980] ATS 23.

71 *Human Rights Act 2004* (ACT); *Human Rights Act 2019* (Qld); *Charter of Rights and Responsibilities 2006* (Vic).

72 *Age Discrimination Act 2004* (Cth); *Disability Discrimination Act 1992* (Cth); *Racial Discrimination Act 1975* (Cth); *Sex Discrimination Act 1984* (Cth); *Australian Human Rights Commission Act 1986* (Cth).

73 See *Bill of Rights 1960* (Can); *Bill of Rights Act 1990* (NZ); *Human Rights Act 1998* (UK) giving effect to the *European Convention on Human Rights* (1950); *Bill of Rights 1791* (US).

74 (1995) 183 CLR 273; [1995] HCA 20, [26] (Mason CJ and Deane J).

75 Chief Justice James Spigelman, 'The Common Law Bill of Rights' in *Statutory Interpretation and Human Rights* (University of Queensland Press, 2008).

76 Ibid.

The High Court has also articulated the well-established principle of the law of statutory interpretation in Australia:

> The courts should not impute to the legislature an intention to interfere with fundamental rights. Such an intention must be clearly manifested by unmistakable and unambiguous language.[77]

Therefore, a similar presumption might be applied in relation to Australia's international obligations, including those arising under human rights treaties. Even if a 'common law bill of rights' is not identical to the human rights listed in international human rights instruments, there will be a significant overlap between them allowing for the 'articulation of new presumptions'[78] including those relating to non-interference with personal liberty, freedom of movement or freedom of association.[79] Nevertheless, the legislator occasionally steps in to override common law rights, and the law of torts in Australia is a good example of this, with the wide-ranging civil liability reforms of 2002–3 (discussed in Section 1.2). Thus, relying exclusively on the common law might not always be straightforward (or even available), which further limits the possibility of Australian courts awarding a remedy for such violations. It is not surprising then that in 1997 Sir Anthony Mason, a former Chief Justice of the High Court, urged reform of human rights protection in Australia:

> Australia's adoption of a Bill of Rights would bring Australia in from the cold, so to speak, and make directly applicable the human rights jurisprudence which has developed internationally and elsewhere.[80]

Another constraint on the mechanisms of protection and enforcement of human rights in Australia is the lack of a regional human rights system akin to those in Europe, the Americas and Africa.[81] In the United Kingdom, the *Human Rights Act 1998* (UK) and the European Court of Human Rights (ECHR) have enabled the protection of rights in relation to tortious actions that otherwise might have gone unprotected. An example is public authority liability in negligence, which was addressed in the controversial case of *Osman v United Kingdom*.[82] The ECHR challenged the blanket immunity from actions given to police in the United Kingdom by the House of Lords[83] as incompatible with art 6 of the *European Convention on Human Rights* covering the right of access to court.[84] The ECHR eventually overruled its

---

77 *Coco v The Queen* (1994) 179 CLR 427, 437 (Mason CJ, Brennan, Gaudron and McHugh JJ).
78 Chief Justice James Spigelman, 'The Common Law Bill of Rights' in *Statutory Interpretation and Human Rights* (University of Queensland Press, 2008) 24.
79 See also Chief Justice Robert French, 'The Common Law and the Protection of Human Rights' (Speech, Anglo Australasian Lawyers Association, 4 September 2009); Chief Justice Robert French, 'Protecting Human Rights Without the Bill of Rights' (Speech, John Marshall Law School, 26 January 2010).
80 Sir Anthony Mason, 'Rights Values and Legal Institutions: Reshaping Australian Institutions' (1997) *Australian International Law Journal* 1, 13.
81 These are based on the respective regional human rights treaties, the *Convention for the Protection of Human Rights and Fundamental Freedoms* (1950), the *American Convention on Human Rights* (1969) and the *African Charter on Human and Peoples' Rights* (1981).
82 (1998) 29 EHRR 245.
83 See *Hill v Chief Constable of West Yorkshire Police* [1988] 2 WLR 1049.
84 *Convention for the Protection of Human Rights and Fundamental Freedoms* (1950).

decision.[85] However, the case had a profound influence on the subsequent development of the English and Welsh law of public authority negligence.[86]

Human rights standards are, therefore, relevant to the interpretation and development of tort law. For instance, intentional torts are rights-based torts. The torts of battery and assault protect the right to bodily integrity, and the torts of false imprisonment and wrongful detention safeguard the right to liberty. Therefore, it is feasible to indirectly protect at least some human rights through tort law. For example, acts of torture or cruel, inhuman or degrading treatment or punishment[87] would, in most cases, constitute tortious battery. Acts of slavery and slavery-like practices could be litigated as false imprisonment. A tort of invasion of privacy could be used to protect a right to privacy.[88] And actions in negligence could be used to redress harm done to detainees by public officials.[89]

EMERGING ISSUE

The mutual influence of tort law and human rights law will remain strong. Should Australia pass a Constitutional Charter or national bill of rights, this area will continue to attract considerable judicial and scholarly attention.

1.1.4   Overview of intentional torts

The term 'intentional torts' refers to a group of torts that are premised on the need for a tortfeasor to be at 'fault', meaning that the defendant's act was undertaken intentionally, recklessly or negligently.

HINTS AND TIPS

- *Intentional* involves acting intentionally in the sense of 'wanting to' make an interference, such as wanting to strike an opponent in a game of football to get them out of the way.[90]

---

85   See *Z v United Kingdom* [2001] 2 FLR 612. For a critique of that decision, see J Wright, 'The Retreat from Osman: Z v United Kingdom in the ECtHR and Beyond' in D Fairgrieve, M Andenas and J Bell (eds), *Tort Liability of Public Authorities in Comparative Perspective* (British Institute of International and Comparative Law, 2002).

86   'It is difficult to imagine the law of public authority negligence developing as it did in the UK at the end of the 1990s, and in the following years, had it not been for the decision of the ECtHR in the case of *Osman v United Kingdom*': C Booth and D Squires, *The Negligence Liability of Public Authorities* (Oxford University Press, 2006) [3.65].

87   As covered by the *International Covenant on Civil and Political Rights* (1966) 999 UNTS 171; [1980] ATS 23, arts 7, 10.

88   As is the case in New Zealand. There, the right to privacy is not conferred by the *Bill of Rights Act 1990* (NZ). This led the Court of Appeal in *Hosking v Runting* [2003] 3 NZLR 385, after taking into account human rights legislation and New Zealand's international obligations, to conclude that the duty of confidentiality differs from a tort of privacy, which has scope to be further developed.

89   See, eg, *Badraie v Commonwealth* (2005) 195 FLR 119.

90   *McNamara v Duncan* (1971) 45 FLR 152.

- *Recklessness* involves a person foreseeing the likelihood of causing injury but ignoring the risk and acting anyway.[91]
- *Negligent* trespass can occur by acting 'carelessly' through the failure to exercise reasonable care and skill.[92]

Fault in the context of intentional torts is quite different to bringing a general action in negligence, since negligence does not require the defendant to have acted 'intentionally' as such. Put simply, if the failure to adhere to a standard of reasonable care imposed by the law causes harm to the plaintiff, the defendant may be liable in negligence – regardless of their intent.

The historical development of intentional torts can be traced to the English writ system. A *writ* is a formal document issued under a sovereign authority; it enabled a plaintiff to commence either an action in trespass or an action on the case. The plaintiff had to ensure that the facts of the case fitted within the writ. An *action in trespass* was brought for direct acts by the defendant and was actionable per se (without proof of damage). An *action on the case* was brought for indirect acts by the defendant and required the plaintiff to show that they had sustained damage. For example, if D threw a log onto a highway and the log hit P, the action would be taken in trespass because of the directness of the act. However, if D left the log on a highway and P rode over it and was injured, the action would be taken on the case.[93] The system of writs has since been abolished, but the separate causes of action in trespass and negligence remain today. To help you distinguish between an *action on the case* and an *action in trespass*, Table 1.3 provides an overview of the key distinguishing features between the two actions, such as whether damage is required, who bears the onus of proof and the nature of the act.

Table 1.3   Differences between case and trespass

Characteristic	Case	Trespass
Damage	The plaintiff is required to show legally recognised loss, harm or damage	Actionable per se
Onus of proof	The plaintiff must satisfy all elements of a cause of action (eg, duty, breach and causation in negligence)	The plaintiff must show the interference occurred (eg, battery) and the defendant must show they were not at fault
Nature of act (direct or consequential)	Allows for indirect and consequential acts	Requires directness

Intentional torts involve an act of trespass which is an unauthorised interference with the plaintiff's person or property. Broadly, intentional torts can be categorised into trespass to the person, trespass to chattels and trespass to land. The tort of *trespass to the person* encompasses the torts of battery, assault and false imprisonment. These torts have been

---

91 *New South Wales v McMaster* (2015) 91 NSWLR 666, [191] (Beazley P).
92 See *New South Wales v Oubammi* (2019) 101 NSWLR 160 concerning negligent battery.
93 *Reynolds v Clarke* (1725) 1 Str 634.

developed to protect an individual's bodily integrity. For example, the tort of battery involves direct and intentional harmful or offensive contact with a person; therefore, grabbing a person's arm can infringe this legal right and constitute battery.[94] *Trespass to chattels* encompasses the torts of detinue, conversion and trespass to goods. These torts protect possession or ownership of goods and can assist when items are left for repair (such as a car at a mechanic's garage),[95] or lent to another individual[96] or in 'finders-keepers' cases.[97] *Trespass to land* protects against unauthorised interference with the plaintiff's land and all items that are permanently attached to the land. For example, a police officer's entry into the plaintiff's garage in the middle of the night while attempting to arrest the plaintiff's son constituted trespass to land as it was executed without a valid arrest warrant.[98]

HINTS AND TIPS

Intentional torts have four features in common:

(1) the defendant must be at fault
(2) the defendant's act must be direct
(3) the defendant's act must be positive and voluntary
(4) the cause of action is actionable per se (without proof of damage).

The plaintiff must show the defendant's act was direct, positive and voluntary. The burden is then placed on the defendant to show they are not at fault.[99] The requirement of *fault* refers to the defendant's mental state in undertaking the tortious act and can consist of an intentional, reckless or negligent mental state. The defendant must intend the relevant interference with the plaintiff's person or property; however, their motive is irrelevant. For example, in *Carter v Walker*,[100] the Victorian Court of Appeal stated: 'If the act is voluntary, and the defendant "meant to do it" in the sense of meaning to contact the plaintiff, it will be relevantly intentional.'

The requirement for directness refers to the *immediacy* of the act, to ensure that the interference was direct rather than consequential. For example, in *Scott v Shepherd*, the defendant threw a lighted squib (firework) in a market.[101] To avoid injury to themselves, people threw the squib towards one another until it eventually exploded in the plaintiff's face. The Court held that the injury was a result of the defendant's direct act in first throwing the squib, as the intermediaries were simply acting in response to a sudden need to avoid harm.

94 See *Collins v Wilcock* (1984) 3 All ER 374 where a police officer did not validly exercise the power of arrest (eg, caution, charges, reading rights) and was therefore not legally justified in grabbing a woman by the arm.
95 *Wilson v Lombank Ltd* [1963] 1 WLR 1294.
96 *Perpetual Trustees & National Executors of Tasmania Ltd v Perkins* [1989] Aust Torts Reports 80-295.
97 *Chairman, National Crime Authority v Flack* (1998) 86 FCR 16; *Amory v Delamirie* (1722) 93 ER 664; *Parker v British Airways Board* [1982] QB 1004.
98 *New South Wales v Ibbett* (2006) 229 CLR 638; [2006] HCA 57.
99 *McHale v Watson* (1964) 111 CLR 384; *Majindi v Northern Territory* (2012) 31 NTLR 150.
100 (2010) 32 VR 1, [215].
101 (1773) 96 ER 525.

The defendant's act must be *positive* and not passive, which means their conduct needs to be active. The need for a *voluntary* act means that the conduct must have been undertaken with the defendant's free will, as opposed to being coerced by a third party. For example, if A is carried against their will onto another's land by B, A's conduct will not truly be voluntary.[102] Further, where the plaintiff lacks control of their body, such as during an epileptic fit, their conduct will be deemed not to be voluntary.[103]

Finally, intentional torts are *actionable per se*, meaning that the plaintiff need not demonstrate loss or damage to be able to commence action against the defendant. This reflects the rights-based nature of the tort that protects bodily integrity, private property and private land. So, as in the earlier example of grabbing another's arm forcefully, the plaintiff can commence legal action for battery even if they did not sustain any physical injury, though naturally the compensation awarded may be minimal in such circumstances. Table 1.4 succinctly summarises the key features of intentional torts (or actions in trespass) and uses case examples to illustrate how courts interpret and apply principles pertaining to such actions.

Table 1.4 Features of intentional torts

Feature	Definition	Example
Fault	The defendant's mental state must be intentional, reckless or negligent. The defendant does not have to intend the *consequence*, just the *physical interference*.	In *McNamara v Duncan* (1971) 45 FLR 152, the plaintiff was injured during a game of Australian Rules Football. While the defendant might not have intended to cause injury to the plaintiff, he did intend the act of striking the plaintiff in the head with an elbow to get him out of the way.
Directness	The interference must be direct, not consequential. This means that the interference must be immediate upon the act.	In *Scott v Shepherd* (1773) 96 ER 525, the defendant threw a lighted squib (firework) in a market, but to avoid injury the squib was thrown from one person to another until it eventually exploded in the plaintiff's face. The Court held the injury was a result of the defendant's direct act in throwing the squib initially, as the intermediaries were simply acting in response to a sudden need to avoid harm.
Positive act	The defendant's conduct must be active, rather than passive.	In *Innes v Wylie* (1844) 174 ER 800, a police officer's act of merely standing in the doorway was held to be passive.
Voluntary act	The defendant's act must be voluntary, as opposed to being caused by the act of a third party.	In *Smith v Stone* (1647) 82 ER 533, trespass against land was committed by the defendant who carried the plaintiff onto another's land. The plaintiff was not held liable as his act was not voluntary.
Actionable per se	The plaintiff is not required to prove injury or damage, simply a wrongful interference.	In *Dumont v Miller* (1873) 4 AJR 152, the defendant's beagles trespassed onto the plaintiff's property. The cause of action could still be brought by the plaintiff despite no physical damage to the property.

102 *Smith v Stone* (1647) 82 ER 533.
103 *Public Transport Commission (NSW) v Perry* (1977) 137 CLR 107.

1.1.5   Overview of negligence

The tort of negligence refers to a cause of action that arises where the failure by the defendant to take reasonable care causes harm to the plaintiff. The harm can consist of personal injury, damage to property or land or even pure economic loss. Negligence is increasingly used in practice and you may face clients with a variety of legal dilemmas. For instance, cases before the Australian courts have involved a shopper slipping on a greasy potato chip,[104] a patron falling off a chair in a restaurant,[105] consumers eating contaminated oysters[106] and potatoes infected with bacteria causing multimillion-dollar lawsuits.[107]

In 1932, the famous case involving the snail in the ginger-beer bottle laid the foundations of the modern law of negligence and gave rise to Lord Atkin's 'neighbour principle'. The Court in *Donoghue v Stevenson*[108] attempted to provide a formula for the principles of duty of care articulated by Brett MR (writing as part of the minority) in *Heaven v Pender*.[109] In *Heaven* the plaintiff was injured while painting a ship in the defendant's dry dock and was successful in establishing that the defendant had breached his duty of care by inviting the plaintiff onto the unsafe premises.

In 1928, May Donoghue and a friend sat down in a Scottish café for beverages. Donoghue drank ginger beer from an opaque glass bottle which had been bought by her friend. When she poured the ginger beer onto her ice-cream float, a decomposed snail emerged from the bottle. Donoghue suffered vomiting, gastroenteritis and nervous shock. A key feature of this case was Donoghue's inability to sue in contract as she had not purchased the bottle of ginger beer. This presented the Court with a novel duty of care situation. Ultimately the Court held Stevenson, the manufacturer of the ginger beer, liable in negligence. The Court held that a manufacturer is under a legal duty to the ultimate consumer of foods (especially where the item cannot be inspected) to take reasonable care to ensure that the item is free from defects likely to cause harm. In reaching this decision, Lord Atkin developed the 'neighbour principle' (which constituted an extension of the minority view in *Heaven*):

> The rule that you are to love your neighbour becomes in law, you must not injure your neighbour; and the lawyer's question, Who is my neighbour? receives a restricted reply. You must take reasonable care to avoid acts or omissions which you can reasonably foresee would be likely to injure your neighbour. Who, then, in law is my neighbour? The answer seems to be – persons who are so closely and directly affected by my act that I ought reasonably to have them in contemplation as being so affected when I am directing my mind to the acts or omissions which are called in question.[110]

This famous quote illustrates that the concept of duty of care in law is based on whether a defendant should have reasonably foreseen that unless the defendant took reasonable

---

104   *Strong v Woolworths Ltd* (2012) 246 CLR 182; [2012] HCA 5.
105   *Schuller v SJ Webb Nominees Pty Ltd* (2015) 124 SASR 152.
106   *Graham Barclay Oysters Pty Ltd v Ryan* (2002) 211 CLR 540; [2002] HCA 54.
107   *Perre v Apand Pty Ltd* (1999) 198 CLR 180.
108   [1932] AC 562.
109   (1883) 11 QBD 503.
110   *Donoghue v Stevenson* [1932] AC 562, 580–1.

care, a reasonably foreseeable category of people (or an individual) might be at risk of foreseeable injury as a result of any careless conduct.

HINTS AND TIPS

Proof of negligence does not require the defendant to have acted intentionally, but rather, that they failed to adhere to a reasonable standard of care expected in the circumstances.

The tort of negligence consists of three key elements which the plaintiff must prove in order to establish a cause of action:

(1) duty of care

(2) breach of the standard of care

(3) causation and remoteness.

The elements are comprehensively discussed in later chapters and so are only summarised in this section.

The first element – duty of care – requires a plaintiff to demonstrate that the defendant is under a legal obligation to take reasonable care towards a reasonably foreseeable category of people (or an individual) who could sustain reasonably foreseeable harm if reasonable care were not taken.[111] This is a question of law to be decided by judges through reference to existing legal principles. To assist with answering the question of whether a duty of care is owed, the law has developed categories of circumstances where a duty is owed. For example, occupiers owe a duty of care to a person who enters premises controlled by them,[112] road users owe a duty of care to other road users and pedestrians[113] and, as illustrated, manufacturers owe a duty of care to consumers.[114] Categories of duty of care have been developed on a case-by-case basis by judges, and novel cases continue to appear before the courts. Where the law does not automatically impose a duty of care, Australian judges have used various methods to determine whether a duty of care should be imposed. The current approach favoured by the Australian judiciary is based on the 'salient features' derived from numerous decisions of the High Court of Australia.[115] The salient features were usefully summarised by Allsop CJ in *Caltex Refineries (Qld) Pty Ltd v Stavar*.[116] This test requires a plaintiff to demonstrate that the salient features of the case (eg, the defendant's control and assumption of responsibility, the plaintiff's vulnerability, the knowledge and experience of the parties or the degree of harm sustained by the plaintiff) are consistent with the existence of the duty.

---

111 *Chapman v Hearse* (1961) 106 CLR 112, 120.

112 *Australian Safeway Stores Pty Ltd v Zaluzna* (1987) 162 CLR 479.

113 *Chapman v Hearse* (1961) 106 CLR 112.

114 *Donoghue v Stevenson* [1932] AC 562.

115 *Perre v Apand Pty Ltd* (1999) 198 CLR 180; *Sullivan v Moody* (2001) 207 CLR 562.

116 (2009) 75 NSWLR 649.

EMERGING ISSUE

As indicated, duty of care categories do not remain rigidly closed because the courts continue to adapt to contemporary needs in society. For example, Australian courts have recently had to consider the role of torts in climate change litigation. The Federal Court of Australia was required to determine whether a government minister could be held liable in the tort of negligence to Australian children for adverse effects of climate change. At first instance, Bromberg J used the salient features approach to determine that such a novel duty could be imposed.[117] However, on appeal, the Full Court of the Federal Court of Australia ruled that imposition of such a duty was not supported.[118] Nevertheless, the decisions provide a timely example of the remarkable flexibility of the tort of negligence responding to society's needs and changing values.

The second element of negligence involves ascertaining the standard of care applicable in the circumstances, and then determining whether the defendant has breached the requisite standard of care in the particular circumstances. Ascertaining whether a standard has been breached is a question of fact and each case must be assessed individually. The first step in deciding whether there has been a breach of duty of care is to determine the existence of a reasonably foreseeable risk. In *Wyong Shire Council v Shirt*, Mason J stated:

> A risk of injury which is quite unlikely to occur … may nevertheless be plainly foreseeable … when we speak of a risk of injury as being 'foreseeable' … we are implicitly asserting that the risk is not one that is far-fetched or fanciful … A risk which is not far-fetched or fanciful is real and therefore foreseeable.[119]

The defendant need not foresee the precise chain of events or injury, but merely a reasonably foreseeable risk of injury of some kind. Mason J's explanation is important as his Honour's judgment was highly influential in the 2002–3 negligence reforms of the breach principle, subsequently adopted in most Australian jurisdictions.[120] However, the reference to a risk which is not 'farfetched or fanciful' was reframed by the legislature as 'not insignificant' in order to confine liability. In practice, courts have not truly found a substantial difference between the common law and statutory test, as elucidated in *Drinkwater v Howarth*[121] (per Hodgson JA at [25]):

---

117 *Sharma by her litigation representative Sister Marie Brigid Arthur v Minister for the Environment* (2021) 391 ALR 1.

118 *Minister for the Environment v Sharma* (2022) 291 FCR 311; [2022] FCAFC 35. For a discussion of this case and extension of principles to a corporate context see: T Popa, A Kallies, V Johnston and G Belfrage-Maher, 'Do Emerging Trends in Climate Litigation Signal a Potential Cause of Action in Negligence against Corporations by the Australian Public?' (2022) 12(3–4) *Climate Law* 185.

119 (1980) 146 CLR 40, 47.

120 All Australian jurisdictions have adopted this except the Northern Territory where the common law prevails: *Civil Law (Wrongs) Act 2002* (ACT) s 43; *Civil Liability Act 2002* (NSW) s 5B; *Civil Liability Act 2003* (Qld) s 9; *Civil Liability Act 1936* (SA) s 32; *Civil Liability Act 2002* (Tas) s 11; *Wrongs Act 1958* (Vic) s 48; *Civil Liability Act 2002* (WA) s 5B.

121 [2006] NSWCA 222.

... in this case there is no possibility of a different result of applying a test that the risk in question be not insignificant, from applying the test as formulated in *Shirt*, namely that the risk be not far-fetched or fanciful.

The legislative provisions require the plaintiff to establish three matters:

(1)   the risk was foreseeable

(2)   the risk was not insignificant

(3)   a reasonable person in the defendant's position would have taken precautions against the risk of harm.[122]

If the reasonable foreseeability component is satisfied, the court is then required to assess four factors known as the 'calculus of negligence' to determine whether a reasonable person ought to have taken precautions. These factors are:

(1)   the probability of the risk materialising

(2)   the likely seriousness of the harm

(3)   the practicality or burden of taking precautions to avoid the harm

(4)   the social utility of the defendant's conduct.[123]

Case law continues to be used to interpret and provide meaning to the factors in the calculus of negligence.

Causation, the third criterion of negligence, requires a plaintiff to prove a relationship between the damage sustained and the defendant's negligent conduct. In *March v E & MH Stramare Pty Ltd*, Mason CJ explained: 'Generally speaking ... causal connection is established if it appears that the plaintiff would not have sustained his or her injuries had the defendant not been negligent'.[124] Causation is a complex legal principle. It has been described by scholars as 'esoteric' and 'poorly defined'.[125] Chief Justice Spigelman observed, writing extra-curially: 'Nothing is more calculated to excite a common lawyer, or exasperate the uninitiated, than a discussion on the subject of causation'.[126] Causation can be a high hurdle to attainment of compensation, as plaintiffs may be unable to establish a clear causal link between breach of the duty of due care and the injury sustained.

At common law, judges used the 'but for' test to assist them in determining whether there was a causal connection.[127] This test essentially required the court to ask: would the plaintiff have sustained harm or damage but for the defendant's negligence? The 'but for' test has

122   *Civil Law (Wrongs) Act 2002* (ACT) s 43(1); *Civil Liability Act 2002* (NSW) s 5B(1); *Civil Liability Act 2003* (Qld) s 9(1); *Civil Liability Act 1936* (SA) s 32(1); *Civil Liability Act 2002* (Tas) s 11(1); *Wrongs Act 1958* (Vic) s 48(1); *Civil Liability Act 2002* (WA) s 5B(1).

123   *Civil Law (Wrongs) Act 2002* (ACT) s 43(2); *Civil Liability Act 2002* (NSW) s 5B(2); *Civil Liability Act 2003* (Qld) s 9(2); *Civil Liability Act 1936* (SA) s 32(2); *Civil Liability Act 2002* (Tas) s 11(2); *Wrongs Act 1958* (Vic) s 48(2); *Civil Liability Act 2002* (WA) s 5B(2).

124   (1991) 171 CLR 506, 514.

125   M Bagaric and S Erbacher, 'Causation in Negligence: From Anti-Jurisprudence to Principle' (2011) 18(4) *Journal of Law and Medicine* 759.

126   JJ Spigelman, 'Negligence and Insurance Premiums: Recent Changes in Australian Law' (2003) 11(3) *Torts Law Journal* 291, 298.

127   See *March v E & MH Stramare Pty Ltd* (1991) 171 CLR 506 (endorsed in *Bennett v Minister for Community Welfare* (1992) 176 CLR 408).

been criticised for its 'seductive simplicity',[128] with potential to lead to a limited application. This is because the test essentially requires a court to ask whether the plaintiff's injuries would have been sustained but for the defendant's negligence, the response requiring only a 'yes' or 'no' answer. This simplicity led the High Court of Australia to reject the 'but for' test as the sole determining factor proving causation in *March v E & MH Stramare Pty Ltd*.[129]

Some of these difficulties were recognised in the negligence reforms (see Section 1.2), and recommendations were made for a statutory test of causation. Most Australian jurisdictions subsequently adopted a two-part test consisting of factual causation and scope of liability.[130] The first part of the test, the *factual causation* element, requires the plaintiff to prove that negligence was a necessary condition of the occurrence of the harm. Where the plaintiff cannot easily satisfy this test, such as where multiple causes of harm exist, the legislation provides an alternative 'material contribution' test.[131]

Once the first part of the test has been satisfied, through the factual causation (or in the event of an exceptional case via the material contribution test), the plaintiff must also satisfy the second part: the *scope of liability*. The scope of liability element requires the court to assess whether it is appropriate for the scope of the negligent person's liability to extend to the harm so caused. The court must have regard to specific policy considerations that might bear significantly on the outcome. Several High Court cases have interpreted the statutory causation test since the reform and offer insight into how the principles ought to be applied.[132] Yet many scholars ponder whether the statutory reform has made this confusing principle even more complex, due to a lack of clarity and precision in the legislative wording.[133]

Once the three elements of negligence are satisfied, the defendant may still escape liability if they are able to successfully establish a defence. The defence of *contributory negligence* provides that if the plaintiff somehow contributed to their own injury by failing to take reasonable care, their entitlement to damages will be reduced in proportion to their contributory negligence. While a 100 per cent reduction in contributory negligence claims is theoretically possible, it is uncommon, meaning the defendant is likely to remain partially liable. In contrast, the defence of *voluntary assumption of risk* (or *volenti*) is a complete defence if the defendant can establish that the plaintiff had full knowledge of the risks of an activity, and voluntarily accepted those risks in proceeding with the activity. However, the defence may not apply in many circumstances as it exists within narrow limits, as Jerrard

---

128   M Davies and I Malkin, *Torts* (LexisNexis, 7th ed, 2015) 176.
129   (1991) 171 CLR 506.
130   All Australian jurisdictions except the Northern Territory have adopted the statutory test: *Civil Law (Wrongs) Act 2002* (ACT) s 45(1); *Civil Liability Act 2002* (NSW) s 5D(1); *Civil Liability Act 2003* (Qld) s 11(1); *Civil Liability Act 1936* (SA) s 34(1); *Civil Liability Act 2002* (Tas) s 13(1); *Wrongs Act 1958* (Vic) s 51(1); *Civil Liability Act 2002* (WA) s 5C(1).
131   See *Amaca Pty Ltd v Ellis* (2010) 240 CLR 111; *Amaca Pty Ltd v Booth* (2011) 246 CLR 36.
132   See *Adeels Palace Pty Ltd v Moubarak* (2009) 239 CLR 420; *CAL No 14 Pty Ltd v Motor Accidents Insurance Board* (2009) 239 CLR 390; *Amaca Pty Ltd v Ellis* (2010) 240 CLR 111; *Amaca Pty Ltd v Booth* (2011) 246 CLR 36; *Strong v Woolworths Ltd* (2012) 246 CLR 182; *Wallace v Kam* (2013) 250 CLR 375.
133   S Bartie, 'Ambition versus Judicial Reality: Causation and Remoteness Under Civil Liability Legislation' (2007) 33(2) *University of Western Australia Law Review* 415; J Manning, 'Factual Causation in Medical Negligence' (2007) 15(3) *Journal of Law and Medicine* 337; B McDonald, 'Legislative Intervention in the Law of Negligence: The Common Law, Statutory Interpretation and Tort Reform in Australia' (2005) 27(3) *Sydney Law Review* 443.

JA noted in *Leyden v Caboolture Shire Council*: 'Recent authority ... suggests that while the defence of *volenti* may be a highly endangered species, it is not yet extinct. Its boundaries are undoubtedly nowadays confined narrowly.'[134] Apart from contributory negligence and voluntary assumption of risk, the defendant may also rely on defences of *intoxication* or *illegality* by the plaintiff to reduce damages. Additionally, in certain jurisdictions, the defendant may escape liability if the plaintiff suffered harm from an obvious risk associated with dangerous recreational activities.[135]

1.1.6   Tort law and the Stolen Generations litigation

The cases brought by members of the Stolen Generations demonstrate the application of the law in context, since an understanding of social, cultural and historical contexts is necessary for the 'contextualisation' of the legal system. It also shows the potential for tort law to address complex social justice issues. The Stolen Generations litigation is of significance not only to the individual litigants, but also to the Indigenous and non-Indigenous populations of Australia. It shows the intricate relationship between different areas of law, both domestic and international, as well as the impact of policy and policy considerations on the application of the law in Australia. In addition, as a case study for aspiring lawyers, it requires us to comprehend often-complex historical facts, their impact on the present, and their implications for social justice in Australia.

The Stolen Generations litigation cannot be understood without grasping the seminal moments in this part of Australia's history. This history cannot be told better than through the voices of those who endured the consequences of that period.[136] Margaret Tucker wrote:

> As we hung on to our mother she said fiercely: 'They are my children and they are not going away with you.' The police man who no doubt was doing his duty, patted his handcuffs, which were in a leather case on his belt, and which May [my sister] and I thought was a revolver ... 'I'll have to use this if you do not let us take these children now' ... The horror on my mother's face and her heartbroken cry![137]

Another survivor gave this evidence:

> Every morning our people would crush charcoal and mix that with animal fat and smother that all over us, so that when the police came they could only see black children in the distance. We were told always to be on the alert and, if white people came, to run into the bush or run and stand behind trees as stiff as a poker, or else hide behind logs or run into culverts and hide ...

---

134   [2007] QCA 134, [41].

135   See, eg, *Civil Liability Act 2002* (NSW) s 5L. Similar provisions operate in Queensland, Tasmania and Western Australia. For case examples see: *Samahar Miski v Penrith Whitewater Stadium Ltd* [2018] NSWDC 21; *Vreman v Albury City Council* [2011] NSWSC 39; *Castle v Perisher Blue Pty Ltd* [2020] NSWSC 1652.

136   An excellent source of first-hand testimonies is the Stolen Generations' Testimonies Foundation, which collects and curates the personal stories of Australia's Stolen Generations Survivors and shares them online: <www.stolengenerationstestimonies.com>.

137   M Tucker, *If Everyone Cared: Autobiography of Margaret Tucker* (Ure Smith, 1977).

> There was a disruption of our cycle of life because we were continually scared to
> be ourselves. During raids on the camps it was not unusual for people to be shot –
> shot in the arm or the leg. You can understand the terror that we lived in, the
> fright – not knowing when someone will come unawares and do whatever they were
> doing – either disrupting our family life, camp life, or shooting at us.[138]

The term 'Stolen Generations' refers to Australian Indigenous children – Aboriginal and Torres Strait Islanders – who were forcibly removed from their families during the early colonial period in Australia until the late 20th century. Formal government policies developed from the mid-1800s onwards resulted in Indigenous people being placed on reserved land. Indigenous peoples' lives on the reserves was closely controlled. Children were separated from their parents and housed in dormitories with the intention of eventually 'merging' them with the non-Indigenous population and breaking their links with Aboriginal culture.[139]

Each Australian state had its own policy and legislation to effect the removal of Indigenous children from their families. In the late 1930s, merging of Indigenous children of 'mixed descent'[140] into the broader community gave way to the policy of assimilation in Australia. Under this policy, Indigenous children were removed from their families and educated according to 'white' standards after which they were intended to live in the community as white people.[141]

During the assimilation period, Indigenous children were forcibly removed under general child welfare protection legislation which required a child to be 'neglected', 'destitute' or 'uncontrollable' according to Western ideals of family life.[142] When the institutions where the children were placed could no longer cope with the increasing numbers, Indigenous children were adopted, often at birth, or fostered into white families.[143] The policy of assimilation expanded to include removing Indigenous children for the purpose of education.[144]

From 1972, with a change of federal government in Australia, a major shift in policy from assimilation to self-management and self-determination was implemented.[145] However, Aboriginal resistance to the forced removal of Indigenous children became a political force as early as the late 1920s.

Stolen Generations claimants have brought a variety of claims, including for breach of constitutional law, wrongful imprisonment, negligence, breach of statutory and fiduciary duties, vicarious liability, misfeasance in public office and the international crime of genocide (discussed in Section 1.1.6.1). These cases are complex. Claimants face hurdles when suing government defendants and further difficulties if they have suffered high levels of trauma,

---

138 Human Rights and Equal Opportunity Commission, *Bringing Them Home: National Inquiry into the Separation of Aboriginal and Torres Strait Islander Children from Their Families* (1997), pt 2, ch 2, 21 (Confidential evidence 681).
139 Ibid 24.
140 This is preferred to the term used at the time, 'half-caste' (defined in s 2 of the *Northern Territory Aboriginals Act 1910* (SA) to mean 'any person who is the offspring of an aboriginal mother and other than an aboriginal father'), which 'was and is offensive to Indigenous people': ibid 22.
141 Human Rights and Equal Opportunity Commission, *Bringing Them Home: National Inquiry into the Separation of Aboriginal and Torres Strait Islander Children from Their Families* (1997), pt 2, ch 2, 26.
142 Ibid 27.
143 Ibid 28.
144 Ibid.
145 Ibid 29.

abuse and neglect as children. Given this, there have been few claims and even fewer successful litigations.

Chris Cunneen and Julia Grix identified six major limitations of the litigation process for the Stolen Generations claimants:[146]

(1) *Statutory limitation periods:* Statutory limitation periods apply to claims for damages arising from negligence, false imprisonment, breaches of statutory and, by analogy, fiduciary duties. This is relevant not only to the Stolen Generations claims, but it proved to be particularly problematic in these cases because of the lapse of time between the removal of the applicants as children, the accumulative nature of the injury, recognising that an injury has occurred and bringing an action in court.

(2) *Evidentiary difficulties:* It can be and often is difficult to collate evidence and make findings of facts in different contexts, but it is especially difficult when dealing with events that occurred many decades ago. This places a particularly heavy onus of proof on the Stolen Generations claimants in the absence of key witnesses and the loss of records.[147]

(3) *Trauma and (re)victimisation in the adversarial setting:* Expecting claimants to re-live the trauma of abuse, neglect and (often) sexual violence and 'tell their stories' frequently leads to re-victimisation or secondary victimisation (triggered by the impact of negative and insensitive reactions by the community and the wider society to the original victimisation experience). This causes further psychological consequences and compounds the trauma of the initial event.[148] Thus, it is not uncommon for victims of such abuses to choose not to litigate rather than to put themselves through the traumatic events again.

(4) *Financial cost and time involved in litigation:* The costs of litigation are usually high,[149] and the time length and delays add to the barriers faced by the Stolen Generations litigants.

(5) *Establishing specific liability for harms caused:* As we will see, claimants have faced considerable obstacles in not only proving but also establishing liability in their cases.

(6) *The 'standards of the time' justification:* It has been maintained by some, and contested by many,[150] that past action must be judged by the 'standards of the time' rather than present standards, and thus the legislation and policies should be assessed by what would be seen as rational and relevant at the time. Consequently,

146 C Cunneen and J Grix, 'The Limitations of Litigation in Stolen Generations Cases' (Research Discussion Paper No 15, *Australian Institute of Aboriginal and Torres Strait Islander Studies*, 2004).

147 See also A Durbach, 'Repairing the Damage: Achieving Reparations for the Stolen Generation' (2002) 27(6) *Alternative Law Journal* 262, 263.

148 See, eg, U Orth, 'Secondary Victimization of Crime Victims by Criminal Proceedings' (2002) 15(4) *Social Justice Research* 313, 321; J Herman, 'The Mental Health of Crime Victims: Impact of Legal Intervention' (2003) 16(2) *Journal of Traumatic Stress* 159.

149 For example, the direct and indirect costs incurred by the Commonwealth in *Cubillo v Commonwealth (No 2)* (2000) 103 FCR 1; [2000] FCA 1084 amounted to over $11 million; for a breakdown see Commonwealth, *Parliamentary Debates*, Senate, 26 March 2011, 23016 (Robert Hill).

150 This justification can be placed within the context of the theory of reparative justice, when examining how people acquire intergenerational responsibilities and entitlements: see J Thompson, *Taking Responsibility for the Past: Reparation and Historical Injustice* (Polity Press, 2002).

they justified the removal of children as this was done for the children's 'benefit' to integrate and protect them.

To this list, we could also add:

(7) *The 'floodgate' argument:* The policy concern that litigation would 'open the floodgates' to an overwhelming number of Stolen Generations lawsuits has been raised on a number of occasions.

1.1.6.1 Litigation

KRUGER v COMMONWEALTH

The removal of Indigenous children from their families itself has been the subject of litigation. The first case to reach the High Court was *Kruger v Commonwealth*, decided in 1997.[151] It concerned nine applicants who had been removed from their families between 1925 and 1944 and taken to Aboriginal institutions or reserves. The applicants argued that the relevant legislation, the *Aboriginals Ordinance 1918* (NT), was unconstitutional, and thus invalid, as it authorised an act of genocide. Section 6(1) of the Ordinance empowered a Director of Native Affairs to remove Indigenous children of mixed descent from their families 'if in his opinion it [was] necessary or desirable in the interests of the aboriginal or half-caste for him to do so'. Section 16(1) authorised the Director to place the children in Aboriginal institutions or on Aboriginal reserves. This aspect of the plaintiffs' claim relied upon the definition of 'genocide' in the *Genocide Convention*[152] as

> forcibly transferring children of the group to another[153] [and] imposing measures intended to prevent births within a group[154] [with] intent to destroy, in whole or in part, a national, ethnical, racial or religious group.[155]

The High Court concluded that the *Genocide Convention* did not form part of Australian domestic law at the time;[156] but even if it did, the words of the Ordinance, referring to removal 'in the best interests of the child', displayed no intention as required by the Convention and thus did not amount to destroying in whole or in part the Aboriginal Australian people or their culture.[157]

---

151 (1997) 190 CLR 1.
152 *Convention on the Prevention and Punishment of the Crime of Genocide* (1948) 78 UNTS 277; [1951] ATS 2 (*'Genocide Convention'*).
153 *Genocide Convention* art 2(e).
154 Ibid art 2(d).
155 Ibid art 2.
156 *Kruger v Commonwealth* (1997) 190 CLR 1 (Dawson J). Even though Australia ratified the *Genocide Convention* in 1949, the Convention did not become part of Australian law until the passing of the *International Criminal Court (Consequential Amendments) Act 2002* (Cth). The claim of genocide of the Australian Indigenous population was also made in cases relating to land rights and the environment: see, eg, *Nulyarimma v Thompson* (1999) 96 FCR 153; *Thorpe v Commonwealth (No 3)* (1997) 144 ALR 677.
157 *Kruger v Commonwealth* (1997) 190 CLR 1 (Dawson, Toohey, Gaudron, McHugh and Gummow JJ). The National Inquiry into the Separation of Aboriginal and Torres Strait Islander Children from Their Families supports the contention that the forced removal of Indigenous children in Australia was genocide: Human Rights and Equal Opportunity Commission, *Bringing Them Home: National Inquiry into the Separation of Aboriginal and Torres Strait Islander Children from Their Families* (1997), pt 4, ch 13, 266.

CUBILLO v COMMONWEALTH

The *Aboriginals Ordinance 1918* (NT) was placed under judicial scrutiny again in *Cubillo v Commonwealth*.[158] The applicants in this case sued the Commonwealth for wrongful imprisonment, breach of statutory duty, negligence and breach of fiduciary duty. As in *Kruger*, the plaintiffs in *Cubillo* had been removed from their families under ss 6 and 16 of the Ordinance. The decision of O'Loughlin J in the Federal Court was based on the judgment of McHugh J in *Crimmins v Stevedoring Industry Finance Committee*,[159] where various criteria were created to determine 'whether a duty of care should be imposed on a statutory body'.[160] These criteria included: whether it was reasonably foreseeable that the defendant's failure to exercise a statutory power would result in an injury to the plaintiff; the vulnerability of the plaintiff; and whether finding such a duty would impose liability with respect to 'core-policy-making' or 'quasi-legislative' functions.[161]

In *Cubillo v Commonwealth (No 2)*, the foreseeability criterion was not established against the Commonwealth.[162] O'Loughlin J reasoned that guardianship, removal and detention were statutory powers vested in the NT Director of Native Affairs only.[163] Because no act or omission could be charged against the Commonwealth (as the Commonwealth did not have any vicarious liability for the actions of the Director), there could be no foreseeability of injury.[164] To satisfy the Court that a duty of care was owed under the circumstances, the plaintiffs would have had to provide evidence showing that their interests were not taken into account when they were removed from their families and detained in Aboriginal institutions. O'Loughlin J was, however, prepared to consider that once the children had been taken into care, the Director of Native Affairs owed a duty of care to the plaintiffs.

WILLIAMS v MINISTER, ABORIGINAL LAND RIGHTS ACT 1983

While in *Cubillo* a duty of care was found to exist once the children had been taken into care, Abadee J in *Williams v Minister, Aboriginal Land Rights Act 1983* was not prepared to accept a duty of care in similar circumstances.[165] In this case, it was the New South Wales Government that was the defendant.

In the early 1940s, the plaintiff Joy Williams became a ward of the Aborigines Welfare Board as a newborn, with the consent of her mother. She was placed at Bomaderry Children's Home, and at the age of four-and-a-half moved to another institution, Lutanda. Upon leaving Lutanda at the age of 18, she suffered a range of mental disorders, and in 1991 was given a retrospective diagnosis of borderline personality disorder.[166]

---

158 [2000] FCA 1084.
159 (1999) 200 CLR 1, 38–9.
160 J Clarke, 'Cubillo v Commonwealth' (2001) 25(1) *Melbourne University Law Review* 218, 273.
161 *Cubillo v Commonwealth (No 2)* (2000) 103 FCR 1; [2000] FCA 1084, [1230]; ibid.
162 (2000) 103 FCR 1; [2000] FCA 1084.
163 Under *Aboriginals Ordinance 1918* (NT) ss 6, 7, 16.
164 *Cubillo v Commonwealth (No 2)* (2000) 103 FCR 1; [2000] FCA 1084, [1122].
165 [1999] Aust Torts Reports 81-526.
166 Editors, 'Williams v The Minister, Aboriginal Land Rights Act 1983 & Anor (26 August 1999) – Case Summary' (2000) 5(4) *Australian Indigenous Law Reporter* 61. See also Antoni Buti, 'Removal of Indigenous Children from their Families: The National Inquiry and What Came Before' (1998) 3(1) *Australian Indigenous Law Reporter* 1.

Ms Williams instigated legal proceedings against the Board in 1993 for, among other things, trespass (by taking and keeping her at Bomaderry) and breach of duty of care. This required her to seek an extension of time under the *Limitation Act 1969* (NSW). Her request initially failed as the New South Wales Supreme Court held it to be 'neither just not reasonable' to grant an extension.[167] On appeal, the Court of Appeal granted the extension with the judge asserting that her case needed to be heard in full.[168]

The substantive case came before Abadee J in the New South Wales Supreme Court. His Honour reasoned that, as a parent cannot be sued by their child except in specific situations, a failure of parental care towards the child does not breach the civil law (even if it might amount to a criminal offence). By analogy, it would be wrong to impose a higher duty on a third party (including a government care provider) than on the natural parent.[169]

The Court of Appeal upheld the decision of the lower Court that Ms Williams had failed to prove her allegations of breach of duty of care by the Aborigines Welfare Board, as the *Aborigines Protection Act 1909* (NSW) did not transfer guardianship from the mother to the Aboriginal Welfare Board, and remarked that this case suffered from an 'insuperable causation problem'.[170]

JOHNSON v DEPARTMENT OF COMMUNITY SERVICES

In the case of *Johnson v Department of Community Services*, the plaintiff was removed from his family in 1973 at the age of four.[171] He was placed in a foster family and institutions, where he suffered a significant level of abuse, including sexual abuse. Christopher Johnson sought to bring proceedings against the respondents, alleging common law negligence and breach of statutory and fiduciary duties. Here, also, the issue of the limitation period needed to be overcome. Rolfe J in the New South Wales Supreme Court held that the limitation period started to run only after the plaintiff learnt of the facts that constituted a cause of action. His Honour found that the Department of Community Services owed a fiduciary duty to the plaintiff:

> It may also be argued, and in my respectful opinion there would be much force in this argument, that as a matter of policy children, who are basically unable to protect themselves and, therefore, find themselves subject to the control of the respondents, are entitled to expect that they will not be placed in foster care in circumstances where they are likely to be mistreated and, if they are, once again as a matter of policy, that the person with the ultimate control over the foster caring situation should be held to be negligent in failing to act in the child's interest, if it comes to that person's knowledge that the child is being mistreated and that person fails to act.[172]

The case was settled out of court in favour of the plaintiff,[173] with the exact terms not being made public.

---

167 *Williams v Minister, Aboriginal Land Rights Act 1983* (New South Wales Supreme Court, 25 August 1993) 36.
168 *Williams v Minister, Aboriginal Land Rights Act 1983 (No 1)* (1997) 35 NSWLR 497, 514–15.
169 *Williams v Minister, Aboriginal Land Rights Act 1983* [1999] Aust Torts Reports 81-526.
170 *Williams v Minister, Aboriginal Land Rights Act 1983* [2000] Aust Torts Reports 81-578.
171 (2000) Aust Torts Reports 81-540.
172 *Johnson v Department of Community Services* [1999] NSWSC 1156, [100].
173 There were similar outcomes in *Boreham v New South Wales* (2001) and *Jones v New South Wales* (2004).

TREVORROW v SOUTH AUSTRALIA

The only case so far to go to a full hearing and result in a successful outcome for the plaintiff is *Trevorrow v South Australia (No 5)* in the Supreme Court of South Australia.[174] In August 2007, Gray J found in favour of Bruce Trevorrow in his action against the State arising from his forced removal from his parents in 1958 at the age of 13 months. The action had been framed broadly alleging false imprisonment, misfeasance in public office, breach of duty of care and breach of fiduciary and statutory duties. This was the first time that misfeasance in public office had been raised as a cause of action by a Stolen Generations litigant.[175]

In contrast to O'Loughlin J's reasoning in *Cubillo v Commonwealth* against imposing a duty of care on the Commonwealth or the Director of Native Affairs in relation to the plaintiffs' removal,[176] Gray J found that there was 'nothing in the provisions of the Aborigines Act 1934–1939 or the Maintenance Act 1926–1937 or any other relevant statute that exclude[d] the imposition of a duty of care in the present case'.[177] In relation to foreseeability of the type of harm suffered by the plaintiffs, his Honour held that it was 'readily and reasonably foreseeable' that 'the removal and long-term separation of an Aboriginal child from that child's natural parents would give rise to the risk of harm'.[178] Thus, given the existing knowledge in the 1950s and 1960s on the importance of the attachment between mother and child, his Honour concluded that 'the State knew or ought to have known at relevant times that separating a child from its parents and in particular its mother was likely to cause damage to the child'.[179]

As a result, in addition to damages of $450000 the Court also allowed exemplary damages of $75000 in relation to the unlawful removal and detention, that is, in respect of misfeasance in public office and false imprisonment. The defendant appealed the Court's decision in *South Australia v Lampard-Trevorrow*.[180] In 2010, the Full Court of the Supreme Court upheld the finding that the South Australian Government had been negligent in its treatment of Mr Trevorrow. However, it reversed Gray J's findings that the Aborigines Protection Board had breached its fiduciary duty and that there was wrongful detention, stating:

> We do not think it is realistic to describe the care and protection given by the carer of a child as a restraint on the child, in the relevant sense of the term. Bruce Trevorrow was separated from, and denied, the care of his mother, but that does not establish the fact of a restraint. It seems to us that if the notion of restraint for the purposes of the tort of wrongful detention were taken this far, the potential would arise for the tort to expand into previously untouched areas and situations, with unpredictable consequences.[181]

---

174 (2007) 98 SASR 136.
175 A Buti, 'The Stolen Generations and Litigation Revisited' (2008) 32(2) *Melbourne University Law Review* 382.
176 *Cubillo v Commonwealth (No 2)* (2000) 103 FCR 1; [2000] FCA 1084.
177 *Trevorrow v South Australia (No 5)* (2007) 98 SASR 136, [1015]; A Buti, 'The Stolen Generations and Litigation Revisited' (2008) 32(2) *Melbourne University Law Review* 382.
178 *Trevorrow v South Australia (No 5)* (2007) 98 SASR 136, [1046].
179 Ibid [1112] (Gray J).
180 (2010) 106 SASR 331.
181 *South Australia v Lampard-Trevorrow* (2010) 106 SASR 331, [307]. The decision was followed in *Darcy v New South Wales* [2011] NSWCA 413 in relation to the possible false imprisonment of a person with intellectual disabilities who resided in a residential home.

Mr Trevorrow passed away on 20 June 2008 after a long illness, aged 51, before the appeal had been determined. The success of this case rested predominantly on the availability of sufficient evidence, often lacking in the other cases, to substantiate the plaintiff's claims. This case has also reinvigorated the concern about opening 'the floodgates' – which the judiciary remains sensitive to – in terms of the public financial consequences that may flow from a decision attaching state liability for wrongs committed against the Stolen Generations.[182]

COLLARD v WESTERN AUSTRALIA (NO 4)

More recently, in 2013, the Supreme Court of Western Australia handed down a decision in the Collard family case.[183] Eight members of the family were removed without consent and placed in state care between 1958 and 1961. Prichard J dismissed the case, holding that the plaintiffs had failed to establish that the State of Western Australia was subject to the alleged fiduciary duties, and even if it was subject to those duties, the plaintiffs had not established that the State had breached those duties. This case demonstrates the difficulty that Stolen Generations litigants have experienced in bringing their claims, which is not necessarily reflective of their veracity. The main obstacles relate to the matter of evidence, the past standards of the time and policies in place, and the doctrinal arguments. It is arguable that the traditional courtroom setting is not an appropriate forum to address the suffering and loss experienced by the members of the Stolen Generations. Thus, further pressure is placed on non-judicial reparation schemes.[184]

1.1.6.2   Compensation and reparation

The first member of the Stolen Generations to be awarded monetary compensation (on appeal) was Valerie Wenberg Linow, who made a claim against the New South Wales Victims Compensation Tribunal under the *Victims Support and Rehabilitation Act 1996* (NSW).[185] Ms Linow was awarded compensation of $35 000[186] for harm resulting from ill-treatment while in state care.[187]

Mediation has also been used. Even where there is a positive outcome for the applicant, however, this does not set any legal precedent as it is not a court decision.

In June 2011, Neville Austin was the first member of the Stolen Generations in Victoria to be granted compensation for pain and suffering caused by the State of Victoria in its breach of duty of care. The case settled out of court with the quantum of the compensation being covered by a confidentiality agreement (thus not publicly disclosed).

---

182 A Buti, 'The Stolen Generations and Litigation Revisited' (2008) 32(2) *Melbourne University Law Review* 382.

183 *Collard v Western Australia (No 4)* [2013] WASC 455.

184 An example of such a scheme is Canada's Aboriginal Healing Foundation, which operated between 1998 and 2014 to address the legacy of residential schools in Canada and the impact on community health.

185 Notice of Determination, *Claim of Valerie Linow* (Victims of Crime Compensation Tribunal, New South Wales, File Reference 73123, 15 February 2002). This was an unreported case, reasons for which remain confidential. See also C Cunneen and J Grix, 'The Limitations of Litigation in Stolen Generations Cases' (Research Discussion Paper No 15, *Australian Institute of Aboriginal and Torres Strait Islander Studies*, 2004) 10–11, 22.

186 The maximum that could be awarded under the scheme was $50 000: *Victims Support and Rehabilitation Act 1996* (NSW) s 19(1)–(2).

187 A Buti, 'The Stolen Generations and Litigation Revisited' (2008) 32(2) *Melbourne University Law Review* 382.

Although they are important at an individual level, such successes have had only a limited impact on providing redress more widely to the members of Stolen Generations.[188] As Chris Cunneen and Julia Grix noted in relation to Ms Linow's claim:

> While victim compensation is one avenue for dealing with the aftermath of forced removal, it will not provide widespread satisfaction for those who survived Government policies of breeding out and later 'assimilating' Aboriginality.[189]

A more systemic approach is required. Unsurprisingly, already in 1997, the National Inquiry into the Separation of Aboriginal and Torres Strait Islander Children from Their Families recommended that a financial compensation scheme be set up for members of the Stolen Generations.[190] A number of schemes have been launched in different jurisdictions in Australia to address some of the legacies of the past injustices relating to the Stolen Generations, or the Indigenous population in Australia more widely.

The Tasmanian Government was the first in Australia to set up a Stolen Generations reparation scheme. This was established under the *Stolen Generations of Aboriginal Children Act 2006* (Tas), with a total allocation amounting to $5 million. Under ss 4 and 5 of the Act, ex gratia individual payments of up to $5000 per individual and $20 000 per family have been made available to the Stolen Generations survivors.

In 2007, the Western Australian Government opened the Redress WA scheme for the so-called 'forgotten Australians': children and young people abused in the care of the State, including the Stolen Generations. The scheme, which was open between 1 May 2008 and 30 April 2009, had a total budget of $114 million, with just over $90 million being set aside for ex gratia payments. Over 10 000 people had registered with Redress WA by the time the scheme closed; half of those proceeded to the assessment stage and, out of those, just 51 per cent of claims were launched by the members of Stolen Generations.[191]

Eight years after the *Trevorrow* decision,[192] in November 2015, the South Australian Government announced the establishment of an $11 million reparation fund with an estimated 300 members of the Stolen Generations being eligible for payments of up to $50 000, which was then determined to be a flat payment of $20 000.[193] Out of the total sum, $5 million is being used for indirect reparations including memorials, counselling and support programs and other proposals assisting in the healing and reconciliation process.

---

188 On other members of the Stolen Generations successfully making claims of $4000 each under the Criminal Injuries Compensation Scheme in Victoria see, eg, Public Interest Advocacy Centre, *Restoring Identity* (Final Report of the Moving Forward Project, 2nd ed, June 2009) 48.

189 C Cunneen and J Grix, 'The Stolen Generations and Individual Criminal Victimisation: Valerie Linow and the New South Wales Victims Compensation Tribunal' (2003) 14(3) *Current Issues in Criminal Justice* 306, 308.

190 *Bringing Them Home* (Report of the National Inquiry into the Separation of Aboriginal and Torres Strait Islander Children from Their Families, 1997).

191 WA Department for Communities, *Redress WA* (Final Report) 2–3.

192 *Trevorrow v South Australia (No 5)* (2007) 98 SASR 136.

193 For details, see Department of Premier and Cabinet (SA), *Stolen Generations Reparations Scheme*, <www.dpc.sa.gov.au>.

In New South Wales, the Government announced the establishment of a Stolen Generations reparations scheme,[194] operating from 1 July 2017 until 30 June 2023. This provides eligible members of the Stolen Generations with compensation payments of up to $75 000 from the $73 million package. It also provides a collective healing fund of $5 million towards healing centres for the survivors as well as their families, descendants and communities.[195]

On 31 March 2022, the Victorian Government opened the Stolen Generations Reparations Package, which remains open until 31 March 2027. This offers support to address the harm and trauma caused by the forced removal of Indigenous children from 'their families, community, culture and language' and is open to Aboriginal and/or Torres Strait Islander persons who had been removed by a government or non-government agency before 31 December 1976. The Victorian scheme provides for personalised apologies, compensation of $100 000 and access to healing programs.[196]

The Queensland Government established a reparation scheme of $21 million in 2015 to provide compensation to Aboriginal and Torres Strait Islander Queenslanders to address the legacy of stolen wages or savings by previous successive governments under the 'Protection Acts'. The scheme, which closed on 29 September 2017, was the first of a kind in Australia, offering individual reparation payments in relation to past legislative provisions controlling the wages and savings of Indigenous peoples.[197]

On 12 September 2016, a class action was filed in the Federal Court of Australia against the Queensland Government on behalf of 300 Indigenous Australians whose wages were withheld in government-controlled trust accounts for work undertaken in Queensland between 1939 and 1972.[198] The so-called Stolen Wages Class Action found its finale on 9 July 2019 with parties agreeing to a $190 million in-principle settlement that makes an important step forward in the national reconciliation process.[199]

On 23 May 2017, to commemorate the 1997 report, *Bringing Them Home*, the Healing Foundation launched a review, *Bringing Them Home: 20 Years On*.[200] This new study has been instigated by the concern that many of the 54 recommendations of the 1997 report have not yet been fully implemented, leading to further trauma and distress to members of the Stolen Generations and causing a ripple effect on the current generations. The most recent report sets out an action plan to overhaul Australia's Indigenous policy landscape. It sets out a number of recommendations urging the federal government to establish a national

194 Created in response to New South Wales, Parliament, Legislative Council, General Purpose Standing Committee No 3, *Reparations for the Stolen Generations in New South Wales: Unfinished Business* (Report No 34, 23 June 2016).
195 For details, see New South Wales, Aboriginal Affairs, *Stolen Generations Reparations*, <www .aboriginalaffairs.nsw.gov.au>.
196 For details, see Victorian Government, Stolen Generations Reparations Package, <www.vic.gov.au/ stolen-generations-reparations>.
197 This scheme was one of a series of policies introduced in Queensland since 1999, as part of reparations processes. The previous ones included the Compensation for Non-Payment of Award Wages (1975–86) Scheme and the Indigenous Wages and Savings Reparation Process launched in 2002.
198 See *Hans Pearson v Queensland* (Statement of Claim, File No QUD714/201).
199 For more details on the settlement, including the court documents and the Settlement Distribution Scheme, see <www.stolenwages.com.au>.
200 See Aboriginal and Torres Strait Islander Healing Foundation, *Bringing Them Home: 20 Years On* (Report, 2017) <www.healingfoundation.org.au>.

scheme for reparations and initiate a comprehensive study of intergenerational trauma and how to deal with it.[201]

In 2022 the *Territories Stolen Generations Redress Scheme (Facilitation) Act 2021* (Cth) came into force, establishing the Territories Stolen Generations Redress Scheme, seeking to address the harm and trauma suffered by the survivors of Stolen Generations. The $378.6 million Commonwealth Redress Scheme is administered by the National Indigenous Australian Agency and opened for applications on 1 March 2022 and will close on 28 February 2026. It is limited to Stolen Generations survivors removed from their families or communities in the Northern Territory, before 1 July 1978; or Australian Capital Territory, before 11 May 1989; or Jervis Bay Territory. This offers both a financial and well-being package by assisting with healing the trauma, accessing free support services as well as creating an opportunity for the survivors to tell their stories.[202]

Prior to the Redress Scheme being implemented by the Commonwealth Government, a class action had been filed in the New South Wales Supreme Court by Stolen Generations survivors from the Northern Territory. At the time of writing, registration for the class action continues to be open to those who are not eligible to participate in the Redress Scheme.[203] The class action lawsuit has wider eligibility criteria than the Redress Scheme, including that it covers not only survivors but also relatives of those who had passed away before the Scheme was introduced.

EMERGING ISSUE

In June 2021, the Northern Territory Stolen Wages Class Action was filed in the Federal Court of Australia on behalf of Aboriginal and Torres Strait Islander peoples who worked in the Northern Territory between 1933 and 1971 and were affected by wage control legislation.[204] This has become an emerging area of legal interest.

1.1.7   Litigating a tort claim

Earlier in this chapter, we emphasised the importance of a plaintiff satisfying the elements of a cause of action. In practice, there may be instances where a plaintiff is able to fulfil the elements but is nevertheless deterred from pursuing a claim in court. In this section, we explore some of the practical considerations a potential plaintiff faces when pursuing legal action in tort, as well as the procedures a plaintiff must follow to ensure their claim is viable. Consider the example of an individual who has sustained physical injury in a fall due to a slippery floor and wishes to sue in negligence. In addition to the need to establish the legal elements of negligence (duty of care owed by the occupier of premises, breach of that duty,

---

201 Ibid.
202 For more details on the Scheme, see <https://territoriesredress.gov.au>.
203 For more details on the Northern Territory Class Action, see <www.shine.com.au/service/class-actions/northern-territory-stolen-generations-class-action>.
204 See *Minnie Mcdonald v Commonwealth of Australia* (Statement of Claim, File No VID312/2021). For an update on the case, see <www.comcourts.gov.au/file/Federal/P/VID312/2021/actions>.

legal causation), the potential plaintiff faces numerous considerations. Can the plaintiff find witnesses who are willing to testify that the plaintiff fell on a slippery floor? Is there video footage of the incident? Can the plaintiff afford the legal fees and disbursements involved (such as medical report fees)? Does the defendant have sufficient funds or assets to satisfy judgment? Alternatively, does the defendant have insurance that will enable them to pay compensation if the plaintiff succeeds in their claim? These are all important considerations that must be considered before pursuing legal action in court.

1.1.7.1   Procedure

To commence an action, the plaintiff's lawyers will write a letter of demand to the defendant outlining the basis for a claim, setting out the alleged loss and seeking a response from the defendant within a given time frame. The defendant may deny the claim and express their intention to vigorously defend it if the plaintiff proceeds. Alternatively, the defendant may negotiate, either through correspondence or at a formal conference. If the plaintiff is claiming compensation for physical or psychological injury, they will need to obtain medical reports evidencing the type and degree of harm sustained. In defamation cases and professional negligence claims, the plaintiff will need to obtain documentary material evidencing loss. A matter is unlikely to proceed to a court hearing immediately, even in circumstances where a plaintiff appears to have a solid cause of action. Instead, most states have legislation requiring the parties to attempt to resolve the dispute using alternative or appropriate dispute resolution (ADR).[205] Parties and their lawyers will most commonly attend mediation as a form of ADR, where they will negotiate their dispute and aim to reach settlement with the assistance of a neutral third party. If ADR is unsuccessful, the plaintiff will usually initiate court proceedings by filing a writ and statement of claim together with supporting documents such as sworn affidavits. Most personal injury cases are litigated in county or district courts in each state, and many courts have lists specialising in certain types of claims.[206]

When instituting proceedings, plaintiffs should be mindful that litigation is often a lengthy and expensive process. When a plaintiff lodges court documents to initiate a claim, they can expect the defendant to file a defence. Each party will have to disclose relevant documents and attend numerous interim hearings. The parties can expect to wait between 6 and 24 months for the matter to come to trial, and even when a trial date is scheduled, many cases settle immediately before trial.[207] Many law firms now provide legal services on a 'no-win, no-fee' basis, offering to represent clients who have suffered personal injuries without charge unless the claim is successful. While this service can be beneficial in allowing injured individuals to pursue claims, plaintiffs will nevertheless face many out-of-pocket

---

205 Some jurisdictions have mandatory pre-action protocols which are procedural prerequisites that must be satisfied before commencing litigation. For example, the *Civil Dispute Resolution Act 2011* (Cth) introduced pre-litigation procedures into federal civil litigation. Legislation in Victoria imposes an overarching purpose to 'facilitate the just, efficient, timely and cost-effective resolution of the real issues in dispute', which can be realised by an ADR process either agreed to by the parties or ordered by the court: *Civil Procedure Act 2010* (Vic) s 7.

206 For instance, the County Court of Victoria has eight lists with its Common Law Division including a defamation list, medical list, serious injury list, WorkCover list and general list.

207 In some instances, the plaintiff is required to wait 18 months to allow their injury to stabilise before they can institute proceedings. This is the case for 'serious injury' applications in Victoria relating to transport accident or workplace injury matters.

expenses known as 'disbursements'. Further, litigants face the risk of paying the opposing party's costs if the court awards judgment in the opposing party's favour. Finally, even when judgment is rendered, the losing party may initiate an appeal to a higher court if they contend that an error of law has been made.

1.1.7.2 Proof

The plaintiff carries the burden of proof to convince a court that they have sufficient evidence that substantiates their claim. In civil trials, the standard of proof is *on the balance of probabilities*; this requires a plaintiff to show that it is more probable than not that their version of events is true. This is a lower degree of certainty than is required in criminal trials where the prosecution must satisfy the court of the defendant's guilt *beyond reasonable doubt*. This difference between the standard of proof in civil and criminal trials reflects the more serious consequences faced by defendants if they are found guilty of a crime, such as imprisonment. Criminal penalties are severe when compared to the consequences of civil trials, such as an order to pay damages.

A hearing will usually be held before a judge sitting alone rather than in the presence of a jury, though the use of juries in civil trials varies among Australian states and territories. In South Australia and the Australian Capital Territory, civil trials are held before a judge alone.[208] In all other Australian jurisdictions, jury use is at the discretion of the court or the parties, although in Victoria and New South Wales jury trials remain common in civil proceedings.[209] Juries are responsible for deciding *questions of fact* in civil trials (such as whether the defendant was negligent). When a judge hears a case without a jury, they have the sole responsibility for deciding both *matters of law* (such as whether a duty of care was owed) and questions of fact. Where a jury is appointed, they may be permitted to decide on the amount of compensation awarded, though in some areas (such as defamation), legislation has shifted this requirement onto the judge.

1.1.7.3 Time limitations

Once a cause of action arises, a plaintiff has only a limited period in which to commence proceedings. If the time stipulated in legislation has passed, the plaintiff may be prevented from bringing their action. The purpose of time limitations is to ensure that plaintiffs act relatively quickly, as complexities in defending claims increase with the passage of time. Usually the date of action begins when the facts giving rise to the cause of action occur. In the case of an intentional tort, the time commences when the defendant commits the tort, while in negligence cases the date of action occurs when the plaintiff sustains damage.

Legislation provides for a general six-year limitation on tort actions (except personal injury) in all states and territories, except the Northern Territory where the time limitation is three years, and Western Australia where the time limit for claims for trespass to the person is also three years. In personal injury disputes, the time limitation in all states and territories is three years. In defamation claims, plaintiffs have only one year to bring a claim.

---

208 *Supreme Court Act 1933* (ACT) s 22; *Juries Act 1927* (SA) s 5.
209 *Juries Act 1963* (NT) s 7; *Supreme Court Act 1970* (NSW) s 85; *Civil Liability Act 2003* (Qld) s 73; *Supreme Court Civil Procedure Act 1932* (Tas) ss 27–9; *Supreme Court (General Civil Procedure) Rules 2015* (Vic) r 47.02; *Supreme Court Act 1935* (WA) s 42.

In some circumstances the plaintiff may not become aware that they have a cause of action until some time has passed. Legislation now also provides for a 'date of discoverability', which means that the plaintiff has the prescribed amount of time to pursue a claim from the date they *discover* the cause of action.[210] The discoverability provisions are limited by a 'long-stop' provision of 12 years; this is the maximum amount of time the plaintiff has, regardless of when they discover the injury. Table 1.5 outlines time limitations in each Australian state and territory.

Table 1.5 Overview of statutory time limitations

Action and time limits	Section(s)
Tort: 6 years (exception: 3 years in NT and WA (trespass to person))	
Limitation Act 1985 (ACT)	11
Limitation Act 1969 (NSW)	14
Limitation Act 1981 (NT)	12(1)(b)
Limitation of Actions Act 1974 (Qld)	10
Limitation of Actions Act 1936 (SA)	35
Limitation Act 1974 (Tas)	4
Limitation of Actions Act 1958 (Vic)	5(1)
Limitation Act 2005 (WA)	16
Personal injury: 3 years	
Limitation Act 1985 (ACT)	16B
Limitation Act 1969 (NSW)	18A(2), 50C
Limitation Act 1981 (NT)	12(1)(b)
Limitation of Actions Act 1974 (Qld)	11
Limitation of Actions Act 1936 (SA)	36
Limitation Act 1974 (Tas)	5A
Limitation of Actions Act 1958 (Vic)	5(1A), 27D, 27F
Limitation Act 2005 (WA)	6, 55
Defamation: 1 year	
Limitation Act 1985 (ACT)	21B
Limitation Act 1969 (NSW)	14B
Limitation Act 1981 (NT)	12(2)(b)
Limitation of Actions Act 1974 (Qld)	10AA
Limitation of Actions Act 1936 (SA)	37
Defamation Act 2005 (Tas)	20A
Limitation of Actions Act 1958 (Vic)	5(1AAA)
Limitation Act 2005 (WA)	15

In some instances, the statutory time limitation bar may be waived or suspended, either through legislation or leave of the court. For example, all states and territories have introduced no limitation periods for institutional child abuse (see Section 10.4.1, in particular Table 10.6).[211]

---

210 *Limitation Act 1969* (NSW) s 50C; *Limitation Act 1974* (Tas) s 5A; *Limitation of Actions Act 1958* (Vic) s 27F.
211 See, eg, *Limitation Act 1985* (ACT) s 21C; *Limitation Act 1969* (NSW) s 6A; *Limitation Act 1981* (NT) s 5A; *Limitation of Actions Act 1974* (Qld) s 11A; *Limitation of Actions Act 1936* (SA) s 3A; *Limitation Act 1974* (Tas) s 5B; *Limitation of Actions Act 1958* (Vic) s 27P (see pt IIA div 5 more generally); *Limitation Act 2005* (WA) s 6A.

1.1.7.4   Uninsured defendant

In Australia's fault-based tort system, insurance companies play a critical role in compensating injured individuals. In many types of negligence claims, successful plaintiffs are compensated by insurance companies whose role is to indemnify the defendant. This reflects the loss-shifting paradigm within which tort law operates. Indemnity insurance is commonly held by professionals (such as lawyers, doctors and financial advisers) and by occupiers. The cost of the insurance is borne by the policyholder who pays an annual premium to the insurer with the purpose of being indemnified if a claim is made against them. Once a claim has been commenced, the insurer (or their legal representative) manages the claim and finances compensation if damages are awarded. Note, however, that the plaintiff must commence action against the individual tortfeasor(s) rather than the insurer, as ultimately it is not the insurer who has occasioned the wrong. Recovering compensation can prove difficult where the defendant is uninsured and has insufficient income or assets to satisfy a court judgment. In such circumstances, compensation schemes operated by state and territory governments (such as statutory schemes for transport accidents, workplace accidents or victims of crime: see Section 1.3) can provide much-needed avenues of recovery. In many instances, individuals who have sustained harm and are unable to earn an income may need to rely on government benefits or the healthcare system as their primary form of financial assistance.

REVIEW QUESTIONS

(1) What are the differences between an action in trespass and an action in negligence?

(2) How do theories such as corrective justice, distributive justice and economic efficiency assist us to understand the tort of negligence?

(3) Should courts consider amending the standard of care to take into account the relevant gender differentials (eg, that women are believed to be more risk-averse and more concerned with safety than are men)? What consequences would that have for the application of the relevant standard of care?

(4) Summarise the Stolen Generations claims and why the actions failed. How can the outcome of these cases be reconciled with the wrongs committed against the Stolen Generations and thus what should be the 'way forward'?

 Guided responses in the eBook

1.2   Civil liability reforms

In recent years, legislative intervention has encroached upon common law tort principles by amending, eliminating or restricting certain rights. The most significant legislative reforms to tort law occurred in 2002–3 as a result of the recommendations of the *Review of the Law of Negligence* ('Ipp Report'), released in September 2002.[212] In this section, the reforms which were implemented by the states and territories stemming from the report are referred to as the 'civil liability reforms'. This section discusses the background to the reforms, outlines the amendments, discusses the legal community's response to the reforms and explains the general effects of the reforms on the public. This section is intentionally concise as the impact of the civil liability legislation will be discussed in more depth in later chapters of this book.

1.2.1   Background to the reforms

By 2002, myriad factors were contributing to the high cost and low availability of medical indemnity insurance. Australia found itself in an insurance 'crisis' due to a legal compensation system perceived as being 'out of control'.[213] Australia's second-largest insurance company, HIH Group, collapsed; Australia's largest medical defence organisation, United Medical Protection, fell into liquidation;[214] substantial compensation payouts were highly publicised; and litigation surged due to the rise of 'no-win, no-fee' firms.[215]

In response, the Commonwealth, state and territory governments commissioned a review of the law of negligence, to be led by the Honourable David Ipp. The Review Panel was charged with reformulating the common law in order to limit liability and limit the quantum of damages in personal injury cases.[216] The recommendations of the Ipp Report led to the introduction of, or in some instances amendment of, civil liability legislation in each jurisdiction which severely restricted the amounts of compensation payable in personal injury claims in many states. The recommendations adopted by the state and territory governments varied, with some jurisdictions introducing new legislation, some making amendments to existing legislation and others retaining common law principles. The reforms affect all personal injury claims arising out of negligence by imposing statutory provisions for principles which were previously governed by the common law.[217] These reforms created additional barriers for claims with a lower level of impairment, and they adversely impacted plaintiffs with severe injuries through the limited calculation of damages.

---

212 *Review of the Law of Negligence* (Final Report, September 2002) ('Ipp Report').
213 SS Clark and C Harris, 'Tort Law Reform in Australia: Fundamental and Potentially Far-Reaching Change' (2005) 72(1) *Defense Counsel Journal* 16, 16–17.
214 J Burdon, 'Medical Indemnity Insurance in Australia' in RG Beran (ed), *Legal and Forensic Medicine* (SpringerVerlag, 2013) 629.
215 SS Clark and Christina Harris, 'Tort Law Reform in Australia: Fundamental and Potentially Far-Reaching Change' (2005) 72(1) *Defense Counsel Journal* 16, 16–17. See also SS Clark and R McInnes, 'Unprecedented Reform: The New Tort Law' (2004) 15(2) *Insurance Law Journal* 1; L Skene and H Luntz, 'Effects of Tort Law Reform on Medical Liability' (2005) 79(6) *Australian Law Journal* 345, 346; P Underwood, 'Is Ms Donoghue's Snail in Mortal Peril?' (2004) 12(1) *Torts Law Journal* 39, 39–42.
216 Ipp Report 26 [1.7].
217 For example, the test of foreseeability of a risk as neither 'far-fetched' nor 'fanciful' was outlined in *Wyong Shire Council v Shirt* (1980) 146 CLR 40, 47–8 (Mason J). The equivalent test is now contained in *Wrongs Act 1958* (Vic) s 48.

1.2.2   Overview of the key amendments

The recommendations of the Ipp Report spanned a wide range of tort issues. A key recommendation was that a national response to tort reform be enacted in a single statute in each jurisdiction.[218] Others were the adoption of a modified *Bolam* standard of care for medical practitioners;[219] a legislative statement that medical practitioners have a duty to inform patients;[220] and statutory provisions about recreational services[221] warning of obvious risks,[222] emergency services[223] and time limitations for bringing claims.[224] With regard to negligence, the Review Panel recommended that principles regarding foreseeability, standard of care, causation and remoteness should be legislatively stated.[225] The panel also recommended the defences of contributory negligence and voluntary assumption of risk be extended,[226] the common law principles relating to recovery for mental harm altered[227] and liability of public authorities limited.[228] Various recommendations were made regarding entitlements to claim for damages, including the introduction of permanent impairment thresholds and caps on damages.[229]

1.2.3   Response to the reforms

The implementation of the civil liability legislation prompted prominent academics and legal practitioners to question the coherency of the current tort regulatory framework.[230] Advocates of the reforms argued that the changes alleviated the 'insurance crisis',[231] whereas opponents of the reforms questioned whether legislative intervention had been genuinely required or if the response was an 'instantaneous, unreasoned political reaction to popular outcry'.[232] Both the driver of the reforms (the alleged insurance crisis) and the manner in which the review was undertaken were comprehensively criticised by distinguished commentators who declared that the two-month evaluation time frame had been too short, and that allegations of an 'insurance crisis' was public policy hype, utterly unsubstantiated

---

218 Ipp Report 35 Recommendation 1.
219 Ibid 41–2 Recommendation 3. The *Bolam* test stems from the English case *Bolam v Friern Hospital Management Committee* [1957] 1 WLR 582 which provided that a medical practitioner is not negligent if they acted in accordance with opinion widely held by the medical profession.
220 Ipp Report 45–53 Recommendations 5–7.
221 Ibid 62–4 Recommendation 11.
222 Ibid 67–8 Recommendation 14.
223 Ibid 69–70 Recommendation 16.
224 Ibid 85–99 Recommendations 23–6.
225 Ibid 101–19 Recommendations 28–9.
226 Ibid 121–30 Recommendations 30–2.
227 Ibid 135–49 Recommendations 33–8.
228 Ibid 151–63 Recommendations 39–42.
229 Ibid 181–227 Recommendations 45–61.
230 L Skene and H Luntz, 'Effects of Tort Law Reform on Medical Liability' (2005) 79(6) *Australian Law Journal* 345; P Underwood, 'Is Ms Donoghue's Snail in Mortal Peril?' (2004) 12(1) *Torts Law Journal* 39; D Mendelson, 'Australian Tort Law Reform: Statutory Principles of Causation and the Common Law' (2004) 11(4) *Journal of Law and Medicine* 492.
231 H Coonan, 'Insurance Premiums and Law Reform: Affordable Cover and the Role of Government' (2002) 25(3) *University of New South Wales Law Journal* 819.
232 P Underwood, 'Is Ms Donoghue's Snail in Mortal Peril?' (2004) 12(1) *Torts Law Journal* 39, 39.

by empirical evidence.[233] Academic and legal experts highlighted the unreasonableness to the plaintiff in the post-Ipp framework.[234] In the Victorian context, John Chu asserted that the overall effect of the existing regime is 'unfair' for individuals because of the 'significant injury' thresholds and the caps on damages.[235]

1.2.4   Effects of the reforms

The ongoing effects of the civil liability reforms continue to be felt by injured individuals throughout Australia, particularly in states that adopted restrictions for non-economic loss damages.[236] These restrictions require the plaintiff to satisfy minimum injury levels and limit the quantum of compensation through caps on non-economic loss damages. In 2013 the Victorian Government commissioned the Victorian Competition and Efficiency Commission (VCEC) to undertake an inquiry responding to concerns that the law had imposed 'unreasonable barriers' and 'limitations' to legitimate personal injury claims.[237] The scope of the inquiry was to make recommendations to address any anomalies, inequities or inconsistencies in the *Wrongs Act 1958* (Vic) relating to personal injury damages, without undermining the objectives of the 2002–3 tort reforms.[238] The VCEC recommended that the Government lower the injury threshold for psychiatric and spinal injuries, and increase the compensation cap for damages for non-economic loss. On 18 November 2015, the *Wrongs Act* was amended to enact many of the VCEC's recommendations.[239] A thorough evaluation of the amendments is necessary to ascertain their long-term effects on the rights of injured individuals.

1.2.5   Additional reforms around institutional child abuse

Contemporary developments in society have placed the spotlight on societal issues that have warranted legislative intervention. The Royal Commission into Institutional Responses to Child Sexual Abuse released its final report in December 2017. Further reforms have taken

---

233 H Luntz, 'Reform of the Law of Negligence: Wrong Questions – Wrong Answers' (2002) 25(3) *University of New South Wales Law Journal* 836; Peter Cashman, 'Tort Reform and the Medical Indemnity "Crisis"' (2002) 25(3) *University of New South Wales Law Journal* 888; JJ Spigelman, 'Negligence and Insurance Premiums: Recent Changes in Australian Law' (2003) 11(3) *Torts Law Journal* 291; P Cane, 'Reforming Tort Law in Australia: A Personal Perspective' (2003) 27(3) *Melbourne University Law Review* 649; P Underwood, 'Is Ms Donoghue's Snail in Mortal Peril?' (2004) 12(1) *Torts Law Journal* 39.

234 J Chu, 'Analysis and Evaluation of Victorian Reform in General Damages for Personal Injury under the Tort of Negligence' (2007) 10(2) *Deakin Law Review* 125; J King, 'When Justice is Significantly Injured' (2012) 86(3) *Law Institute Journal* 26; J North, 'Tort Reforms: Futile or Necessary?' (Speech, Insurance Law Conference, 28 July 2005) 4.

235 J Chu, 'Analysis and Evaluation of Victorian Reform in General Damages for Personal Injury under the Tort of Negligence' (2007) 10(2) *Deakin Law Review* 125, 168.

236 For recent studies on the effects of the reforms, see T Popa, 'Practitioner Perspectives on Continuing Legal Challenges in Mental Harm and Medical Negligence: Time for a No-Fault Approach?' (2017) 25(1) *Tort Law Review* 19; T Popa, 'Righting *Wrongs*: Lawyers' Reflections on the Amendments to the *Wrongs Act 1958* (Vic) on Medical Negligence and Mental Harm Claims' (2017) 24(1) *Torts Law Journal* 64; T Popa, 'Criticising Current Causation Principles: Views from Victorian Lawyers on Medical Negligence Legislation' (2017) 25(1) *Journal of Law and Medicine* 150.

237 Victorian Competition and Efficiency Commission, *Adjusting the Balance: Inquiry into Aspects of the Wrongs Act 1958* (Final Report, 26 February 2014) vii–viii.

238 Ibid 1.

239 *Wrongs Amendment Act 2015* (Vic).

place in response to the need to impose a clear legal duty to prevent child abuse within organisations. For example, in Victoria a statutory duty of care was created to impose a clear legal duty to take responsibility to prevent child abuse.[240] A plaintiff who can show child abuse occurred will have a cause of action, and the responsibility shifts to the defendant to show they took reasonable precautions to prevent the abuse from occurring. This effectively reverses the onus of proving breach. Similar provisions are contained in most state jurisdictions.[241] (See further Section 10.4.1.)

REVIEW QUESTIONS

(1) Outline the arguments for and against restricting compensation in personal injury claims. Support the arguments by referring to theories of tort law where possible.

(2) Do you think some of the restrictions emanating from the civil liability reforms are consistent with the aims of tort law?

 Guided responses in the eBook

1.3 Australian statutory compensation schemes

In most cases, tort law can assist individuals whose rights have been infringed to obtain a remedy, but as we have seen, tort law has limitations. Litigating a claim is a lengthy and expensive process which can be emotionally stressful for the parties; satisfying the standard of proof in court can be a challenging exercise; and in circumstances where the defendant is uninsured, difficulties can arise in obtaining compensation. The following box summarises some of the main challenges with Australia's fault-based system of tort law.

HINTS AND TIPS

- Litigation can be costly, due to the lengthy and adversarial nature of proceedings.
- It may be difficult to issue tort proceedings if: the tortfeasor cannot be identified; they have insufficient funds; and/or they are not insured.

240 See *Wrongs Amendment (Organisational Child Abuse) Act 2017* (Vic). The amendments are contained within *Wrongs Act 1958* (Vic) ss 88–93.

241 *Civil Liability Act 2002* (NSW) ss 6D–6F; *Civil Liability Act 2003* (Qld) s 33D; *Civil Liability Act 1936* (SA) s 50E; *Civil Liability Act 2002* (Tas) s 49F; *Civil Liability Act 2002* (WA) ss 15A–15M; *Civil Law (Wrongs) Act 2002* (ACT) ss 114A–114M; *Personal Injuries (Liabilities and Damages) Act 2003* (NT) s 17D.

- Delays in litigation can increase stress, prevent injury rehabilitation and re-traumatise individuals, thus having an adverse impact on wellbeing.[242]
- Lump sums can be problematic because it is difficult to foresee and calculate the plaintiff's precise loss.[243]
- Litigation is stressful and emotional for the parties.[244]
- Litigation takes place in a public courtroom which can attract unwanted media coverage.

State statutory schemes have been implemented to overcome some of these deficiencies. Statutory schemes are not codes; therefore, claimants can pursue compensation through a scheme and/or pursue a claim under general tort law. The main schemes relevant to tort law are outlined in the following sections.

1.3.1   Transport accident compensation

In some states and territories, individuals involved in a motor vehicle collision are entitled to access compensation under a statutory scheme. Individuals pay a yearly motor vehicle registration fee and receive some benefits under these schemes if involved in a collision.

Victoria, Tasmania and the Northern Territory operate a 'no-fault' motor accident compensation system, meaning that individuals involved in a motor vehicle collision can obtain limited compensation regardless of whether they were at fault in causing an accident.[245] In these jurisdictions, individuals are entitled to claim for income support, medical expenses (including hospital and rehabilitation expenses), home services and lump sum compensation. The right to take common law action has been abolished in the Northern Territory but remains available in Tasmania. Victoria operates a complex system which allows individuals to access a variety of payments depending on whether they are at fault and whether they meet the minimum whole person impairment. If a claimant is at fault, they are entitled to make a no-fault claim if their impairment level is 10 per cent or less. If the claimant's impairment level is more than 10 per cent, they are permitted to make a no-fault claim *and* pursue impairment lump sum benefits. If the claimant is not at fault, they are entitled to seek common law damages if they have sustained a minimum 30 per cent whole person impairment.

Recent amendments in New South Wales have introduced a no-fault statutory compensation scheme, entitling claimants to receive compensation covering medical

---

242 MK Miller and BH Bornstein, 'Stress, Trauma, and Wellbeing in the Legal System: An Overview' in MK Miller and BH Bornstein (eds), *Stress, Trauma, and Wellbeing in the Legal System* (Oxford University Press, 2012).

243 P Vines and A Akkermans (eds), *Unexpected Consequences of Compensation Law* (Hart Publishing, 2020).

244 A Akkermans, 'Achieving Justice in Personal Injury Compensation: The Need to Address the Emotional Dimensions of Suffering a Wrong' in P Vines and A Akkermans (eds), *Unexpected Consequences of Compensation Law* (Hart Publishing, 2020).

245 *Motor Accidents Compensation Act 1979* (NT); *Transport Accident Act 1986* (Vic); *Motor Accidents (Liabilities and Compensation) Act 1973* (Tas).

treatment expenses and lost wages for a period of six months.[246] If the other driver was at fault, the injured claimant may be entitled to receive medical treatment and lost wages for longer than six months. The legislation commenced on 1 December 2017 and represents a shift from the previous system where compensation to drivers was restricted to a maximum of $5000 on a no-fault basis.

The Australian Capital Territory and South Australia have limited statutory schemes and entitlements vary depending on whether the claimant was at fault.[247] In the Australian Capital Territory, individuals who are not at fault can claim a maximum of $5000 in medical expenses and separately for compensation for personal injury. In South Australia, individuals who are not at fault have access to compensation for medical expenses, loss of earnings and non-economic loss (such as pain and suffering).

In Queensland and Western Australia, individuals who are deemed to be at fault are not entitled to receive compensation under a statutory scheme. Individuals who are not at fault are, nevertheless, entitled to claim for economic loss, pain and suffering and medical expenses.[248]

1.3.2   Workers compensation

All the states and territories have a statutory system of workers compensation to compensate people who are injured as a result of their employment.[249] Compensation is payable without the worker needing to prove that the employer was at fault. Under these schemes, employers have an obligation to take out insurance. Injured individuals can claim compensation if they are an employee and the injury occurred in the course of employment.[250] Workers will be entitled to compensation if their employment was a significant contributing factor to the injury. Compensation can also be provided to workers injured during a recess break or while travelling as part of their duties.

Workers are entitled to a range of benefits including loss of income, medical and rehabilitation expenses and superannuation entitlements. Claims are administered by a statutory body, usually the WorkSafe body in each jurisdiction.[251] In the Australian Capital Territory, Victoria and Tasmania, claimants are entitled to pursue a common law claim for damages, although they must satisfy certain requirements.[252] For a common law action, the

---

246 *Motor Accidents Injuries Act 2017* (NSW).
247 *Road Transport (Third Party Insurance) Act 2008* (ACT); *Motor Vehicles Act 1959* (SA).
248 *Motor Accident Insurance Act 1994* (Qld); *Motor Vehicle (Third Party Insurance) Act 1943* (WA).
249 *Safety, Rehabilitation and Compensation Act 1988* (Cth); *Workers Compensation Act 1951* (ACT); *Workplace Injury Management and Workers Compensation Act 1998* (NSW); *Workers Rehabilitation and Compensation Act 1986* (NT); *Workers' Compensation and Rehabilitation Act 2003* (Qld); *Return to Work Act 2014* (SA); *Workers Rehabilitation and Compensation Act 1988* (Tas); *Accident Compensation Act 1985* (Vic); *Workers' Compensation and Injury Management Act 1981* (WA).
250 The common law relies on a test of vicarious liability while the statutory tests, in some cases, can be far broader.
251 In the Australian Capital Territory, the Northern Territory, Victoria, Tasmania and Western Australia the statutory body is WorkSafe within that particular jurisdiction. The relevant body in New South Wales is the State Insurance Regulatory Authority, in Queensland it is the Office of Industrial Relations and in South Australia it is Return To Work SA.
252 In Victoria, for instance, a claimant must demonstrate that they have sustained a 'serious injury': *Accident Compensation Act 1985* (Vic) s 134AB.

worker has to demonstrate that the employer was liable in the tort of negligence. South Australia and the Northern Territory have abolished the right to claim common law damages, while the remaining states have severely restricted such entitlement.

1.3.3   National Disability Insurance Scheme

A recent example of the adoption of an Australia-wide no-fault scheme is the National Disability Insurance Scheme (NDIS). The NDIS was introduced in response to a 2011 Productivity Commission inquiry which recommended a no-fault national scheme for 'catastrophic' injury.[253] The scheme was established under the *National Disability Insurance Scheme Act 2013* (Cth) and is administered by the National Disability Insurance Agency. The NDIS provides a level of compensation to disabled individuals for support services deemed reasonable and necessary, but it does not compensate for lost income.[254] The NDIS is funded through government revenue (including a diversion of all usual disability services funding to the NDIS) and an increase to the Medicare levy.[255] The scheme replaces the previous system under which the Australian Government was responsible for providing employment services to people living with a disability, and providing funding to individual states to allow them to facilitate support services. In order to access support under the NDIS, the scheme requires individuals to be under the age of 65, be an Australian citizen or permanent resident, and have a permanent disability or one that is likely to be permanent.[256]

The NDIS is similar to the no-fault scheme operating in New Zealand, although its coverage is broader as it applies to individuals born with a disability as well as those who have sustained an injury. Unlike the New Zealand scheme, the NDIS does not provide income support. While the implementation of a national scheme seems promising, expert scholars have criticised the absence of a single source of funds that caters to all needs of individuals with disabilities.[257]

1.3.4   Victims of crime compensation schemes

Each of the states and territories has a scheme created to compensate victims of crime.[258] The purpose of such schemes is to provide compensation in circumstances where an offender may not have sufficient financial means to satisfy a civil judgment in tort. Further,

---

253 Productivity Commission, *Disability Care and Support* (Inquiry Report No 54, July 2011) 2 vols. The Productivity Commission also recommended the introduction of a National Injury Insurance Scheme (NIIS); however, the recommendation was not adopted by the Australian Government or the states or territories, except for Queensland.

254 For a comprehensive overview of the scheme, including background, implementation, eligibility and coverage, see B Madden, JF McIlwraith and R Brell, *The National Disability Insurance Scheme Handbook* (LexisNexis, 2014).

255 Australia, Parliament, *The National Disability Insurance Scheme: A Quick Guide* (Web Page) <www.aph.gov.au>.

256 *National Disability Insurance Scheme Act 2013* (Cth) ss 21–5.

257 H Luntz, 'Compensation Recovery and the National Disability Insurance Scheme' (2013) 20(3) *Torts Law Journal* 153, 207.

258 *Victims of Crime (Financial Assistance) Act 1983* (ACT); *Victims Support and Rehabilitation Act 1996* (NSW); *Crimes (Victims Assistance) Rules 2002* (NT); *Criminal Offence Victims Act 1995* (Qld); *Victims of Crime Act 2001* (SA); *Victims of Crime Assistance Act 1976* (Tas); *Victims of Crime Assistance Act 1996* (Vic); *Criminal Injuries Compensation Act 2003* (WA).

in instances where the criminal perpetrator cannot be identified, it is almost impossible for the victim to instigate civil proceedings. The amount of financial assistance available under these schemes is limited, and certainly far lower than can be expected through a civil judgment. Compensation provided can cover medical and counselling expenses, safety-related expenses, loss of income and replacement of clothing. An individual who has received benefits from the victims of crime scheme is not prevented from bringing an action in tort against the offender.

1.3.5   Emerging and ad hoc schemes

Parliament can implement ad hoc statutory schemes in response to emerging issues or society's needs. These schemes may be implemented relatively quickly, for example, to compensate individuals with a vaccine reaction during a pandemic, or they may be implemented to address historic wrongs, such as compensating victims of child sexual abuse. The following is a brief outline of a selection of examples of ad hoc schemes:

- **Stolen Generation schemes:** These schemes have been created to address the trauma sustained by Indigenous children due to forced removal from their families, community and land. For example, in 2022, Victoria commenced the Stolen Generations Reparations Package aimed at Aboriginal and/or Torres Strait Islander persons who were removed by government and non-governmental agencies before 1976 while they were under 18 years of age.[259] Other Australian states introduced similar schemes in preceding years.[260]

- **National Redress Scheme:** This scheme is a response to recommendations to the Australian Royal Commission into Institutional Responses to Child Sexual Abuse. It aims to acknowledge that many children were subjected to sexual abuse in Australian institutions, recognises suffering sustained as a result of these abuses, holds child institutions accountable and assists affected people with access to counselling and a redress payment.[261]

- **COVID-19 Vaccination Scheme:** In response to the COVID-19 pandemic, the Australian Government developed a vaccine claims scheme to allow individuals who have experienced an adverse side effect of the vaccine access to limited compensation through a claims scheme.[262] The scheme follows in the steps of international jurisdictions which already had vaccine compensation systems in place at the time of the pandemic or were swift in implementing one.[263]

---

259 *Stolen Generations Reparations Package,* <www.vic.gov.au/stolen-generations-reparations-package>.
260 Tasmania in 2006; Western Australia in 2007; Queensland in 2012; South Australia in 2015; New South Wales in 2017 and Commonwealth Territories in 2021.
261 National Redress Scheme, *About the National Redress Scheme,* <www.nationalredress.gov.au/about/about-scheme>.
262 Services Australia, *COVID-19 vaccine claims scheme,* <www.servicesaustralia.gov.au/covid-19-vaccine-claims-scheme>.
263 See K Watts and T Popa, 'Injecting Fairness into COVID-19 Vaccine Injury Compensation: No-Fault Solutions' (2021) 12(1) *Journal of European Tort Law* 1.

REVIEW QUESTIONS

(1) How do statutory schemes complement deficiencies in the common law tort system?

(2) Do you believe that a single source of funds within one scheme should be implemented to cater to the needs of individuals with permanent disabilities?

Guided responses in the eBook

1.4   International compensation schemes

1.4.1   No-fault schemes

Australia's fault-based tort system has been criticised by scholars as 'slow, costly, inefficient, stressful and often inequitable and unpredictable'.[264] Resolving disputes can be protracted and complex as litigation is known to be a key stressor for disputants.[265] Inequities can arise if a claimant has sustained an injury but is unable to satisfy the legal requirements for compensation.[266] This can be particularly devastating for victims of medical negligence, as presently Australian jurisdictions do not facilitate statutory schemes to compensate for medical injuries.[267] An alternative to the existing fault-based tort system is the introduction of a no-fault compensation system similar to those currently operating in countries such as New Zealand, Sweden, Finland and Denmark.[268] As New Zealand has a common law legal system, it offers a valuable model for Australia.

1.4.1.1   New Zealand

In New Zealand, individuals who sustain an injury as a result of an accident are entitled to claim no-fault benefits. The injured person is not required to prove fault or negligence on the part of the person who caused the accident. The scheme provides financial support for a range of physical injuries, medical treatment injuries, work-related injuries, serious injuries and disabilities, mental injuries, injuries caused by sexual violence as well as death. Injuries that do not arise as a result of an accident (such as conditions that worsen over time) are not compensable. Claimants are not required to prove fault in court to receive

264   D Weisbrot and KJ Breen, 'A No-Fault Compensation System for Medical Injury is Long Overdue' (2012) 197(5) *Medical Journal of Australia* 296.

265   M King and R Guthrie, 'Using Alternative Therapeutic Intervention Strategies to Reduce the Costs and AntiTherapeutic Effects of Work Stress and Litigation' (2007) 17(1) *Journal of Judicial Administration* 30.

266   D Weisbrot and KJ Breen, 'A No-Fault Compensation System for Medical Injury is Long Overdue' (2012) 197(5) *Medical Journal of Australia* 296.

267   T Popa, 'Don't Look for Fault, Find a Remedy! Exploring Alternative Forms of Compensating Medical Injuries in Australia, New Zealand and Belgium' (2019) 27(2) *Tort Law Review* 120.

268   T Vansweevelt and B Weyts (eds), *Compensation Funds in Comparative Perspective* (Intersentia, 2020); K Watts, *A Comparative Law Analysis of No-Fault Comprehensive Compensation Funds* (Intersentia, 2023).

compensation. Instead, an injured person is required to complete a claim form, consult with a healthcare provider to verify their injury, and lodge the claim with the NZ Accident Compensation Corporation.[269] Funding for the no-fault scheme is sourced from employment taxes, government revenue and taxes on petrol and vehicle registrations.[270]

During the period of the civil liability reforms (discussed in Section 1.2), former Australian Government Minister, the Honourable Joe Hockey, intended to introduce a no-fault scheme similar to the New Zealand scheme, but faced vehement opposition due to fears of the exorbitant cost and liability such a system could attract.[271] However, Andrew Field observed that most of these arguments were untethered to any justification and lacked evaluation of the true cost of such a model.[272] In his view, the arguments against a no-fault scheme carried significant political weight before the introduction of thresholds, and before the removal of common law protections. In light of the current legislative tort restrictions, it might be worthwhile considering the alternatives again.[273] David Weisbrot and Kerry J Breen supported the introduction of a no-fault scheme.[274] They conceded that elements of opponents' arguments are legitimate, regarding the social costs of the no-fault scheme, but emphasised that funding can be sought from the community through taxpayer funds, rather than being limited to compulsory medical indemnity cover.[275]

The no-fault system has been widely accepted in Australia through its operation in transport accident and workplace injury compensation schemes, and thus is not a foreign process. It may be timely to seriously contemplate whether it can be implemented as a better system to manage injuries.

REVIEW QUESTIONS

(1) Describe the theoretical framework that best explains the operation of a no-fault scheme.

(2) Outline the arguments in favour of and against the adoption of a no-fault scheme for injuries in Australia.

  Guided responses in the eBook

---

269 Accident Compensation Corporation, *What To Do If You're Injured* (Web Page) <www.acc.co.nz/im-injured/what-to-do>.

270 C Hodges and S Macleod, 'New Zealand: The Accident Compensation Scheme' in S Macleod and C Hodges (eds), *Redress Schemes for Personal Injuries* (Hart Publishing, 2017) 35–7.

271 A Field, '"There Must Be a Better Way": Personal Injuries Compensation since the "Crisis in Insurance"' (2008) 13(1) *Deakin Law Review* 67, 92.

272 Ibid 93.

273 Ibid 95–7.

274 D Weisbrot and KJ Breen, 'A No-Fault Compensation System for Medical Injury is Long Overdue' (2012) 197(5) *Medical Journal of Australia* 296.

275 Ibid 297.

KEY CONCEPTS

- **principles of tort law:** in Australia derived from common law, but in the past 20 years were impacted substantially by civil liability legislation. Apart from common law tort principles, various Australian statutory compensation schemes can assist injured individuals.

- **tort:** can be distinguished from a breach of contract because the right to seek a remedy does not depend on the existence of an enforceable agreement between two individuals. It can be distinguished from a crime because its primary focus is not protection of society but, rather, enabling an aggrieved individual to seek a remedy from the wrongdoer.

- **tort law:** facilitates 'the righting of legal wrongs' between members of society, corporations and other entities with separate legal personality. Tort law is also a distinct body of law that is different to equity.

- **tort law theories:** such as corrective justice, distributive justice, loss spreading, economic efficiency, human rights and feminist critiques can assist us to understand tort law.

 Complete the multiple-choice questions in the eBook to test your knowledge

PROBLEM-SOLVING EXERCISES

Exercise 1

Paul Bryan is an IT specialist employed by Computer Sparks Pty Ltd. One afternoon, after a birthday lunch with colleagues where he drank a standard glass of wine, Paul returns to his work office before the end of his lunch break. He becomes involved in an animated conversation about a new learning management system his team has created for university students and thus fails to notice an electric cord on the floor. Paul trips over the cord and breaks his arm. Too stubborn to accept a ride in an ambulance, Paul takes some codeine tablets to ease the pain of his broken arm and decides to drive himself to the nearest hospital. On the way to the hospital, Paul becomes disorientated and crashes his car into a van driven by Angelo Saint. As a result of the accident, Angelo's van is substantially damaged and Paul sustains a leg injury. As Paul tries to get out of the car to apologise for causing the accident, Angelo menacingly paces over to Paul and immediately starts yelling at him. The two men get into a heated argument and an enraged Angelo punches Paul in the face.

A distraught Paul has now come to your legal office seeking advice on compensation for his injuries. Advise Paul about the various avenues of compensation available to him. You are not required to advise Paul on the substantive elements of a cause of action.

Note: The legal issues in this scenario are limited to the avenues of compensation available to Paul for his injuries. The problem intentionally does not stipulate an Australian jurisdiction, so you can give advice based on the law in your state or territory.

Guided response in the eBook

Exercise 2

Millie Max is out at a restaurant with friends one evening. During a festive evening, she accidentally spills her glass of red wine on a fellow restaurant patron, Hanna Hope. Millie apologises profusely and says it was an accident, but Hanna does not accept the apology. She claims her expensive dress has been ruined. The two women get into an argument. Hanna, who has had too much to drink, shouts menacingly, 'You'll pay for this!' She lunges at Millie, grabs a champagne bottle and hits Millie over the head. The act causes Millie to sustain head lacerations and severe injuries which require emergency hospital treatment. Millie has since sought legal advice from your office about possible claims against Hanna.

Adopt the role of Millie's solicitor and advise her on: (a) the various torts arising from the scenario and (b) avenues of compensation available to her. You are not required to advise Millie on the substantive elements of a cause of action.

 Guided response in the eBook

CHALLENGE YOURSELF

Exercise 1

Consider again the Paul and Angelo scenario in problem-solving exercise 1.

(1) Could Angelo initiate an action in the tort of negligence against Paul? If so, what are the elements that would need to be satisfied? For this problem, you are required to disregard any statutory schemes and structure your advice using your preliminary understanding of the principles of negligence from this chapter.

(2) Adopting the role of Angelo's solicitor, write a letter of demand to Paul seeking compensation for damage caused to Angelo's van as a result of Paul's alleged negligent driving.

 Guided responses in the eBook

Exercise 2

Consider again the Millie and Hanna scenario outlined in problem-solving exercise 2. In your answer, you were required to discuss possible causes of action in tort law that Millie can instigate against Hanna. Challenge yourself by applying the elements of intentional torts to extend your answer and determine whether Hanna's act in throwing a bottle at Millie amounts to a tort.

 Guided response in the eBook

DUTY OF CARE

2.1   Introduction

As we have seen, to establish that a defendant is liable in negligence, the plaintiff must establish: (1) that a duty of care is owed; (2) that the duty has been breached; and (3) that the breach has caused damage within the scope of liability. The concept of duty of care can be the most challenging to establish because it is difficult to define it in a meaningful way. In reality the duty question does not arise often, as there will often be a precedent establishing that the plaintiff and defendant are in an established relationship of duty. At present, where a set of facts requires us to consider whether a duty of care is owed, the following general approach (illustrated in Figure 2.1) is used:[1]

(1)   Determine whether there is a relevant precedent establishing that a duty of care is owed to a **person in the plaintiff's position** by a **person in the defendant's position** for **this type of harm**. This may require some reasoning by analogy, a process considered in more detail later in the chapter.

---

1   There may be other statutory 'hurdles' in legislation in some states. For instance, in Victoria there are special requirements where the damage claimed is pure mental harm. See Table 2.4.

Figure 2.1   Duty of care

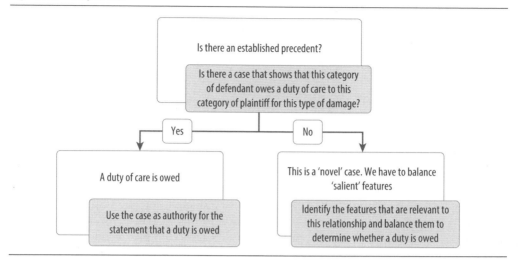

(2)   If there is no established precedent (in other words it is a 'novel' case), balance the 'salient' features of the relationship (the multi-factorial approach). Courts have enumerated a number of salient features which may apply to different types of case, but others may arise.

The journey to the current approach has not been smooth, and many relatively recent cases retain the marks of the history of the judicial approach. In this chapter we consider the development of the concept of duty of care from the seminal case of *Donoghue v Stevenson* to the modern approach.[2] *Donoghue v Stevenson* widened the concept of duty from a series of particular relationships and established a general tort of 'negligence'. The House of Lords based the relationship of duty of care on the 'reasonable foreseeability' of the plaintiff. However, 'reasonable foreseeability' is an unexacting test: if used as the *only* criterion of duty, it would expand the potential liability of a class of defendant too widely. Accordingly, both common law courts and the legislature have sought a description of the relationship in a way that places appropriate limits on the duty owed by one person to another. Some of those approaches have not been helpful, and in Australia the 'salient features' approach is now used (discussed in Section 2.4.2).

'Salient features' are the factual circumstances relevant to a particular case. This means that the legal question of whether a duty is owed will often be answered by considering *factual* circumstances. However, even though the question of duty should not be considered to be determined by a 'test' or algorithm, there are useful approaches to a problem-solving question (or, indeed, a case) which aid in the resolution of the issue.

The question of duty is asked in retrospect – that is, after the injury has occurred and the plaintiff is looking for redress knowing how the injury occurred. In retrospect, the relationship between the plaintiff and the defendant seems clear – obviously the defendant's conduct *can* affect the plaintiff, because it *has*. It is a mistake, however, to consider that

2 [1932] AC 562.

the plaintiff is within the range of foreseeable harm just because harm has occurred – 'foreseeability' is all about whether a reasonable person should have anticipated that their actions could affect the plaintiff. This is one of the things that makes the duty concept difficult. The existence and content of any duty of care must be determined *prospectively in retrospect* and without focusing on the specific circumstances of breach.[3]

2.2   Duty of care: general principles

A duty of care is imposed by law (not as a matter of fact). Often there will be a binding precedent that establishes that this category of defendant (eg, manufacturers) owes a duty to this category of plaintiff (eg, consumers of the manufacturer's product) to guard against this type of harm (eg, physical injury).

Where there is no precedent that establishes that a duty of care is owed to this category of plaintiff by this category of defendant in relation to this type of harm, it is a novel, or 'new', type of case. Where this happens, the courts have adopted a range of strategies over time to determine whether a duty exists or not. The test of reasonable foreseeability, derived from *Donoghue v Stevenson*,[4] has contributed to a trend of expansionism in the law of negligence, creating the need for additional 'gatekeepers.' At present the Australian approach to the question of whether there is a duty of care in a novel case requires first, foreseeability of harm and second, a 'salient features' test.[5] This is the broad structure of the approach – legislation in each state may have an impact in certain situations.[6]

Table 2.1 sets out an approach to address a question dealing with duty of care. Each step of this process is dealt with in this chapter, so you may like to refer back to this table as you work through the chapter.

2.2.1   The 'neighbour' principle

The starting point for the analysis of duty of care is the initial premise that a duty is not owed to everyone. A duty is owed only to those within the scope of potential risk from the defendant's actions. We thus need to determine how to define that group. Historically, a duty was owed only to specific categories based on pre-existing relationships (eg, occupier and entrant or common carrier and consignor) or in relation to certain types of products (eg, inherently dangerous goods). Over time the categories of pre-existing relationships expanded.[7] However, there was no single general statement governing liability for damage due to the negligent actions of another.

Donoghue v Stevenson did attempt a statement of general application[8] and thereby widened the potential of the negligence action beyond defined categories. In that case Lord

---

3   *CAL No 14 Pty Ltd v Motor Accidents Insurance Board* (2009) 239 CLR 390, 418 (Hayne J).
4   [1932] AC 562.
5   Addressed in detail under Section 2.4.2.
6   See, for instance, Section 2.5.4.
7   For instance, in *Coggs v Bernard* (1703) 92 ER 999 the liability of a 'common carrier' (an established relationship) was extended to a gratuitous (ie, unpaid) arrangement.
8   [1932] AC 562.

Table 2.1   Decision table

Umbrella issue	More specific issue	Principles – selection criteria	Principles
Is D liable in negligence to P for the property loss, personal injury or economic loss?			
	Does D owe a duty of care to P to take reasonable care to prevent property loss, personal injury or economic loss?		
		Is there an established precedent? (To determine if there is a relevant precedent you would, in practice, have to do some research and may have to reason by analogy).	For instance: **Manufacturer–consumer** for physical injury **Employer–employee** for physical injury including recognised psychiatric harm **Occupier–entrant** for physical injury **Doctor–patient** for physical harm **Teacher–pupil** for physical and psychological harm **Users of the highway–other users** for injury to persons and damage of property of other users
		If there is no established precedent, which salient features apply to this case?	Of the salient features (see Section 2.4.2), give more weight to the vulnerability of the plaintiff and the degree and nature of control of the defendant

Atkin said 'in English law there must be, and is, some general conception of relations giving rise to a duty of care, of which the particular cases found in the books are but instances'.[9] Thus, you owe a duty only to your 'neighbour' – Lord Atkin's 'neighbour principle' stated:

> [A]cts or omissions which any moral code would censure cannot in a practical world be treated so as to give a right to every person injured by them to demand relief. In this way rules of law arise which limit the range of complainants and the extent of their remedy.

9 Ibid 580.

The rule that you are to love your neighbour becomes in law, you must not injure your neighbour; and the lawyer's question, Who is my neighbour? receives a restricted reply. You must take reasonable care to avoid acts or omissions which you can reasonably foresee would be likely to injure your neighbour. Who, then, in law is my neighbour? The answer seems to be – *persons who are so closely and directly affected by my act that I ought reasonably to have them in contemplation as being so affected when I am directing my mind to the acts or omissions which are called in question.*[10]

In Lord Atkin's reference to 'the lawyer's question' you will see the influence of the Christian view of the world. This is an allusion to the Gospel of St Luke (10:25), which states:

And, behold, a certain lawyer stood up, and tempted him, saying, Master, what shall I do to inherit eternal life?

He said unto him, What is written in the law? how readest thou?

And he answering said, Thou shalt love the Lord thy God with all thy heart, and with all thy soul, and with all thy strength, and with all thy mind; and thy neighbour as thyself.

And he said unto him, Thou hast answered right: this do, and thou shalt live. But he, willing to justify himself, said unto Jesus, And *who is my neighbour?*[11]

What follows is the parable of the good Samaritan. In that parable, the duty to rescue and care for the injured person is described in terms of morality. Lord Atkin's passage notes that the *law* does *not* impose that duty. The lawyer's question 'who is my neighbour?' receives a *restricted reply*. Much of the decided law about the 'duty of care' is intended to place limits on the duty owed. While the decision was moving away from the old, confined categories of relationship, it was not intended to open an unrestricted responsibility for harm caused to others.

Case: *Donoghue (M'Alister) v Stevenson* [1932] AC 562

Facts

May Donoghue (née M'Alister) went into a retail store, Minchella's, famous in Paisley, Scotland, for its ice cream. Her companion purchased for her a bottle of ginger beer to pour over the ice cream. The ginger beer was in an opaque bottle so the contents could not be seen while they were in the bottle. After Donoghue had consumed most of the bottle, she upended the rest into her glass, along with the remains of a mostly decomposed snail. She suffered shock at the sight of the snail and gastroenteritis from having consumed the ginger beer.

Issue

At the time the law allowed recovery if there was a contract or in certain specific relationships. Recovery in 'negligence' of a manufacturer to an end consumer was, for instance, available in the

---

10 Ibid (emphasis added).
11 Emphasis added.

case of a dangerous article or an article which was dangerous because of a defect known to the manufacturer. There was no 'general' duty of care.

Decision

The House of Lords held that the manufacturer of the soft drink was liable in negligence to the consumer for an injury due to the goods.

Significance

The decision broadened the availability of a remedy in negligence beyond the previous restricted categories and stated a generalised approach to determine whether a duty of care is owed. The approach was immediately applicable to the manufacturer–consumer relationship where the consumer suffered physical injury due to negligence in the production process. However, the test was generalisable to apply the duty concept to other relationships and, eventually, other types of harm.

Question

What is the 'neighbour principle' from *Donoghue v Stevenson*?

 Guided response in the eBook

Donoghue v Stevenson was a decision of the English House of Lords and therefore not binding in Australia. In *Grant v Australian Knitting Mills Ltd*[12] a South Australian doctor developed dermatitis as a result of wearing long woollen underwear produced by the defendant. The cuffs and ankle ends of the garment had contained a chemical which acted as an irritant. The Privy Council found that Grant could recover damages for the injury he had suffered, and in doing so applied *Donoghue v Stevenson*. The Privy Council was at the time part of the hierarchy of courts in Australia, so this had the effect of bringing *Donoghue v Stevenson* to Australia.

2.2.2   The rise and fall of 'proximity'

Courts in Australia used the 'neighbour' principle to derive the 'test' to determine whether or not a duty was owed in a particular case. Iterations of the test usually commenced with the requirement of 'reasonable foreseeability' of harm. 'Foreseeability' means 'able to be foreseen'. For instance, if I eat food purchased from a vendor, it is foreseeable that I may become affected by the state of the food. If a vendor sells me food contaminated with salmonella, I am in the range of people (purchasers) who may be harmed by the vendor's actions. Injury to purchasers is foreseeable. Similarly, injury to others to whom I serve the contaminated food is also foreseeable; even though they are not purchasers, it could be foreseen that I may serve the food to others. These eventual consumers are, however, less foreseeable than the immediate class of purchasers, so we are extending the potential liability of the vendor to this new class of non-purchasing consumers. Lord Atkin's test tried to manage this extension of potential liability by using the term 'reasonable': we owe a duty only to those who are *reasonably* foreseeable.

However, the test of 'reasonable' foreseeability was still too indiscriminate. Once new categories of harm, such as pure economic loss and mental harm, were accepted by the courts, it became too difficult to determine the limits of 'reasonable' foreseeability. Mere foreseeability was no longer a sufficient 'gatekeeper' of liability.

In *Jaensch v Coffey*,[13] the High Court of Australia redefined the test of foreseeability to include consideration of the degree of proximity between the parties. In its simplest form 'proximity' could just mean 'nearness' or 'closeness' in physical terms. The term 'proximity' was used in *Donoghue v Stevenson*[14] itself as deriving from previous cases[15] but extended beyond physical proximity 'to such close and direct relations that the act complained of directly affects a person whom the person alleged to be bound to take care would know would be directly affected by his careless act'.[16] It was later described as taking in physical, circumstantial or causal proximity.

The concept of proximity came to be used to introduce value judgments on 'matters of policy and degree'.[17] The breadth of the concept left the way clear for the development or recognition of other factors determining the presence of proximity, such as reliance,[18] assumption of responsibility,[19] and (possibly) expectation.[20] The requirement of proximity was said to be a limitation on the extent to which the test of foreseeability will leave the defendant open to liability[21] and would draw considerations of public policy into the question, along with assessments of community standards and demands.

The champion of this 'conceptual taxonomy' was Deane J, whose view was endorsed by a majority of the High Court.[22] However, it was also criticised as being 'nebulous and devoid of legal content'.[23] Justice Brennan decried it as 'a juristic black hole into which particular criteria and rules would collapse and from which no illumination of principle would emerge'.[24]

---

13 (1984) 155 CLR 549.
14 [1932] AC 562.
15 See, eg, *Le Lievre v Gould* [1893] 1 QB 491, 497.
16 [1932] AC 562, 581 (Lord Atkin).
17 Ibid.
18 *Sutherland Shire Council v Heyman* (1985) 157 CLR 424, 498; *San Sebastian Pty Ltd v Minister Administering the Environmental Planning and Assessment Act 1979 (NSW)* (1986) 162 CLR 340, 355.
19 *Sutherland Shire Council v Heyman* (1985) 157 CLR 424, 498.
20 *Hawkins v Clayton* (1988) 164 CLR 539, 596–7 (Gaudron J).
21 Douglas Brodie expresses proximity as a 'control device' frequently employed by British courts in recent years in cases involving public bodies: D Brodie, 'Public Authorities and the Duty of Care' (1996) 2 *Juridical Review* 127, 137.
22 The requirement of proximity was given weight in a series of cases: *Sutherland Shire Council v Heyman* (1985) 157 CLR 424, 461–2, 506–7; *Stevens v Brodribb Sawmilling Co Pty Ltd* (1986) 160 CLR 16, 30, 50–2; *San Sebastian Pty Ltd v Minister Administering the Environmental Planning and Assessment Act 1979 (NSW)* (1986) 162 CLR 340, 354–5; *Cook v Cook* (1986) 162 CLR 376, 381–2; *Gala v Preston* (1991) 172 CLR 243. *Gala* is of particular significance, because in it a majority of the High Court (Mason CJ, Deane, Gaudron and McHugh JJ) joined in an explicit adoption of the proximity criterion (at 252–3). *Burnie Port Authority v General Jones Pty Ltd* (1994) 179 CLR 520 was the high-water mark of the concept of proximity. Since that point, however, there has been a retreat: *Perre v Apand Pty Ltd* (1999) 198 CLR 180.
23 M McHugh, 'Neighbourhood, Proximity and Reliance' in PD Finn (ed), *Essays on Torts* (Law Book, 1989) 5.
24 *Bryan v Maloney* (1995) 182 CLR 609, 655.

In *Hill v Van Erp* the High Court found that proximity was not a useful guide to the determination of a duty of care in any particular case.[25] The correct approach in Australia is first to focus 'on established categories in which a duty of care has been held to exist; analogies are then drawn and policy considerations examined in order to determine whether the law should recognise a further category, whether that be seen as a new one or an extension of an old one.'[26] The end of proximity as a determinant of duty was reinforced in *Perre v Apand Pty Ltd.*[27] Chief Justice Gleeson said that 'the concepts of proximity and fairness are not susceptible of any such precise definition as would be necessary to give them utility as practical tests'.[28] Justice McHugh described proximity as 'neither a necessary nor a sufficient criterion for the existence of a duty of care.'[29] Justice Hayne said that 'to search … for a single unifying principle lying behind … a relationship of proximity is … to search for something that is not to be found'.[30]

2.2.3   The current law

The current position in Australia has been stated by the High Court in *Sullivan v Moody*[31] and subsequent cases, as modified by legislation in each jurisdiction. In summary it requires the following steps (see Table 2.1):

(a)   Is there an established category (ie, a binding precedent) which has found that a duty of care is owed by this category of defendant to this category of plaintiff for this type of harm?

(b)   If there is no established category – so it is a 'novel' case – the matter is to be considered by reference to 'salient features' of the relationship.

REVIEW QUESTIONS

(1)   What was significant about *Donoghue v Stevenson* (ie, how did it change the previous law)?

(2)   In law, 'who is my neighbour'?

(3)   What is the role of 'proximity' in establishing the duty of care in negligence?

(4)   A doctor treated X for a sexually transmitted disease. X continued to have unprotected sex with his wife Y. Y now wishes to sue the doctor in negligence. State the 'issue' which, if answered, will determine most effectively whether the doctor owed a duty in negligence to Y.

   Guided responses in the eBook

25   (1997) 188 CLR 159, 175–9 (Dawson J), 188–90 (Toohey J), 210–11 (McHugh J), 237–9 (Gummow J).
26   (1997) 188 CLR 159, 189 (Toohey J).
27   (1999) 198 CLR 180.
28   Ibid 194 (Gleeson CJ).
29   *Perre v Apand Pty Ltd* (1999) 198 CLR 180, 211, citing Dawson J in *Hill v Van Erp* (1997) 188 CLR 159, 176–7.
30   Ibid 301.
31   (2001) 207 CLR 562.

2.3   Duty of care: established categories

In most cases a duty will have been established in a previous case. As Kirby J noted in *Harriton v Stephens*: '[i]n practice, the absence of an agreed legal formula has not caused difficulty for the overwhelming majority of tort actions. Most tort actions fall within a recognized duty of care category.'[32]

Where there is a recognised category, it is sufficient to show that the case at issue falls into that category. So, for instance, in *Donoghue v Stevenson* the issue could be stated as follows: Does the manufacturer (Stevenson) owe a duty to take reasonable care to avoid physical injury to a consumer (Donoghue)?[33] That case established that *yes*, a manufacturer *does* owe a duty of care to a consumer, so this means that we have an *established category of duty* for this particular harm. Similarly, a doctor owes a duty of care to a patient to take reasonable steps to avoid physical injury, and a driver owes a duty of care to a passenger to avoid physical injury. Normally, in those simple cases, it is enough to find an authority to establish that this is the case; it is likely that the issue of duty will not arise at trial or will be conceded by the defendant.

The real difficulty of establishing whether a duty exists will only arise in a 'novel' case. A case may be novel because it involves a new category of plaintiff (eg, does a doctor owe a duty of care to the *spouse* of a patient?) or a new category of harm (eg, does a doctor owe a duty of care to a patient to avoid pure economic loss?). So even where the plaintiff and the defendant do fall within the relationship category, it is possible that the authority may be *distinguished* on the basis that the type of harm arising in the case differs from that in the case authority. For instance, there are precedents that establish a school owes a duty of care to school pupils to take reasonable care for their physical protection during school hours.[34] That duty may extend beyond school hours and outside school premises in some cases. It may also extend to psychological harm, for instance due to bullying at school. At this stage, however, no Australian case has held that a school owes a student a duty of care to prevent 'failure to learn'. This, therefore, would be considered a 'novel case' and would have to be determined by reference to the salient features considered later in this chapter.

In determining whether a case is 'novel' in terms of the duty of care, therefore, the articulation of the *issue* is important. The 'issue' in a case is the question that has to be answered in order to resolve the case – something like: *Is the defendant liable in negligence to the plaintiff?* However, that question is too broad, because it might be clear from the question that a duty is owed, or that the duty has been breached. The real question might be whether damage was caused by the breach.

If we confine ourselves to an issue related to the question of duty, we could state the issue as: *Does the defendant owe the plaintiff a duty of care?* But again, that issue is stated too broadly. There may be a case which shows that the defendant owes the plaintiff a duty in relation to physical injury *but not in relation to economic loss*, for instance. If an issue is stated too broadly it may fail to identify that it is a novel relationship.

---

32   (2006) 226 CLR 52, 73 (Kirby J).
33   [1932] AC 562.
34   *Commonwealth v Introvigne* (1982) 150 CLR 258.

It is also important to note that this question sometimes strays into the *breach* question. The distinction between the *existence* and the *scope* or *content* of the duty of care (ie, what obligations arise out of the duty) can be difficult to draw, as we will see in relation to the legislative reforms (see Table 2.1).

In problem-solving terms, there are several mental steps in the search for the appropriate rule or principle:

(1) Identify the scope of the duty of care. This is often done in terms of the obligation to prevent a certain type of damage to a certain category or group of people by taking reasonable care in carrying out certain acts to prevent a certain type of damage. The High Court has said that, when formulating a duty of care, its scope and its content 'must neither be so broad as to be devoid of meaningful content, nor so narrow as to obscure the issues required for consideration'.[35]

(2) Check for established cases where a duty has been held to exist to guard against the type of harm. In these situations, the case is an authority which establishes that a duty is owed by the defendant to guard against the plaintiff suffering that type of harm. You will, of course, need to consider the weight of that authority (eg, its recency – whether the authority has been affected by legislation or other changes in the law – jurisdiction and whether there are any distinguishing features).

(3) If there is no established case (in other words it is a 'novel case'), it is necessary to use some version of the test for determining the duty of care. In those cases Australian courts will use a salient features or multi-factorial approach.

(4) Check the legislation in the relevant jurisdiction to see if it supplements the duty principle. For instance, legislation has introduced restrictions in the case of pure mental harm and the duty owed by public authorities.

When articulating the issue, the 'scope' of the duty of care at step (1) will frame, or limit, your research in steps (2) to (4). This can have quite radical effects on the way the case is argued. Thus, if we look at the example of *Badenach v Calvert*, we could have a number of possible alternative articulations of an issue relating to duty of care in one case (if only one correct one):[36]

• Does a solicitor owe a duty of care to the testator to advise the testator that he could avoid exposing his estate to a claim under the testator's family maintenance legislation by taking certain steps? This was the articulation of the duty urged by the plaintiff, and was framed 'retrospectively', in light of the knowledge of the particular breach, and too narrowly. In other words, the scope of the duty was incorrectly framed.

• Does a solicitor owe a duty of care to the testator to give advice as to the client's property interests and future estate? This is more general than the previous articulation, but probably equivalent.

• Does a solicitor owe a duty of care to the beneficiary to advise the testator that he could avoid exposing his estate to a claim under the testator's family maintenance legislation by taking certain steps? This articulation was not urged by the parties,

---

35   *Kuhl v Zurich Financial Services Australia Ltd* (2011) 243 CLR 361, 371.
36   (2016) 257 CLR 440; [2016] HCA 18.

but you can see in this statement that the person to whom the duty is owed is correct, but the scope is still incorrect.

- Does a solicitor owe a duty of care to the client to use reasonable care in the preparation of the client's will? This is a well-established tortious and contractual duty and was not relevant to the claims of the plaintiff, who was not the client.

- Does a solicitor owe a duty of care to the beneficiary of the testator to use reasonable care in the preparation of the will? This was the issue as articulated by the High Court. As stated, this was a novel issue because the facts of the previous case did not cover it.[37] This meant that the duty issue had to be determined as a novel case.

- Does a solicitor owe a duty of care to the client to use reasonable care in the preparation of the will so as to prevent loss of a chance?[38]

- Does a solicitor owe a duty of care to the beneficiary to use reasonable care in the preparation of the will so as to prevent loss of opportunity to avoid a detriment?[39]

Note the importance, in stating the issue, of identifying the person to whom the duty is owed and the scope of the duty, which in this case was (as determined by the solicitor's retainer) 'the preparation of the will'. Gageler J noted that 'the Testator did not retain … the Solicitor to give general estate planning advice. The Testator retained the Solicitor specifically to prepare a will giving the whole of his estate to [the plaintiff]'.[40] This determined the scope of the duty in this case and distinguished the case from the established precedent in *Hill v Van Erp*.[41]

Note, in the last two articulations, the reference to the damage claimed. This is not always noted in an issue statement relating to duty of care; but as we saw in Table 2.1, it can be relevant because, as in this case, if the damage is not the same as the damage claimed in the relevant precedent, it could be a distinguishing feature – it could make it a novel case.

So, whenever the issue of 'duty of care' arises, the first step will be to determine whether there is an existing precedent which is *analogous* with the situation in terms of the relationship between the plaintiff and the defendant and the type of harm suffered. The next section considers some very common 'established relationships.'

HINTS AND TIPS

To work out whether there is an 'existing category' of duty it can be worthwhile to:

(1) Identify the group or category of the plaintiff and the defendant (eg, consumer–manufacturer, school–student). This is important because, sometimes, altering the category (from 'road user' to 'passenger' for instance) might make it easier to find a precedent, or might give you grounds to distinguish a precedent.

---

37 The High Court held that *Hill v Van Erp* (1997) 188 CLR 159 (which was the authority relied upon by the plaintiff) did not support the case. The facts of *Hill* 'were particular, and the duty of care to the intended beneficiary found to exist was limited. In that case, a will was properly drawn but, in executing the will, the relevant formalities were not complied with. The negligence arose on the execution of the will': *Badenach v Calvert* (2016) 257 CLR 440; [2016] HCA 18, [84] (Gordon J).

38 This was the articulation of Estcourt J in the Full Court: *Calvert v Badenach* [2015] TASFC 8, [134], [141].

39 This was the articulation of Porter J in the Full Court: *Calvert v Badenach* [2015] TASFC 8, [93].

40 *Badenach v Calvert* (2016) 257 CLR 440; [2016] HCA 18, [52] (Gageler J).

41 (1997) 188 CLR 159.

(2) Identify the category of harm (eg, physical harm, psychological harm, economic loss).
(3) Review your textbook to establish whether there is an existing category of relationship for this particular type of harm.
(4) If the textbook does not give you a clear answer, use a full text searchable database (eg, AustLII, BarNet Jade, Lexis Advance or WestLaw) and use key words to see if you can find a precedent in your jurisdiction for the plaintiff and defendant for this category of harm.
(5) Make sure that you check the status of the case – is it still current? It is worthwhile checking the online legal databases in your library that provide access to the *authorised* reports. You should become familiar with the icons that indicate how a case has been treated in later cases. The databases will show, for instance, whether 'positive', 'cautionary', 'negative' or neutral treatment has been indicated in later cases. It thus indicates whether it is a strong authority for the case you are citing.

2.3.1   Manufacturer–consumer

Donoghue v Stevenson itself is authority for the established category of manufacturer–consumer, obliging the manufacturer to take reasonable care to prevent physical injury.[42] The principle was derived from statements made in *Heaven v Pender*[43] and *Le Lievre v Gould*:[44]

> That this is the sense in which nearness or 'proximity' was intended by Lord Esher [in *Heaven v Pender*] is obvious …
>
> This (ie, the rule he has just formulated) *includes the case of goods, etc., supplied to be used immediately by a particular person or persons,* or one of a class of persons, where … the goods would in all probability be used at once by such persons before a reasonable opportunity for discovering any defect which might exist, and where the thing supplied would be of such a nature that a neglect of ordinary care or skill as to its condition or the manner of supplying it *would probably cause danger to the person or property of the person for whose use it was supplied, and who was about to use it* …
>
> Lord Esher emphasizes the necessity of goods having to be 'used immediately' and 'used at once before a reasonable opportunity of inspection' … to exclude the possibility of goods having their condition altered by lapse of time, and to call attention to the proximate relationship, which may be too remote where inspection even of the person using, certainly of an intermediate person, may reasonably be interposed.[45]

The proviso that the plaintiff had not been able to inspect the contents of the bottle (because it was opaque) has led to some 'cautionary' treatment of the case itself. In *Voli v Inglewood Shire*

---

42 [1932] AC 562.
43 (1883) 11 QBD 503.
44 [1893] 1 QB 491.
45 [1932] AC 562, 581–2 (Lord Atkin) (emphasis added).

Council,[46] Windeyer J noted Lord Atkin's reference to products sold 'in such a form as to show that [the manufacturer] intended them to reach the ultimate consumer in the form in which they left him with no reasonable possibility of intermediate examination'. He noted that the appropriate question is 'whether it was contemplated that, in the ordinary course, the article would be examined, or tested, or in some way treated before it was taken into consumption or use'[47], but this in itself was not intended as a 'complete criterion'.[48] You can see by this process of interpreting, applying and reinterpreting the precedents in their factual context that it may be possible to refine, or even to distinguish, an apparently applicable authority.

It is worth noting that most simple cases of manufacturer liability to a single consumer would not reach litigation stage, so a case resembling *Donoghue v Stevenson* would be unlikely today. Strong legislative provisions protecting consumers also provide a simpler way of seeking a remedy in the case of a manufacturer defect.[49] However, more complex manufacturer–consumer litigation may feature a tortious claim.

2.3.2   Employer–employee/master–servant

The employer–employee relationship is a longstanding, established duty relationship for certain categories of harm such as physical injury, and a more modern relationship in terms of other categories of harm such as the duty to take reasonable care to avoid causing employees a recognisable psychiatric injury.[50] The scope of the common law general duty of care includes the provision of a safe workplace, a safe system of work, and safe tools and equipment.[51]

While it may be the case that the employer's duty to the employee is confined to the place of work and within working hours, the duty may extend outside working hours and outside work premises – so there are circumstances in which 'the temporal or spatial scope of the duty'[52] might be expanded. Traditionally this is tied to whether the injury occurs 'in the course of employment',[53] where the 'course of employment is not a narrow conception'. This is a question of law, but it is 'fact-sensitive depending upon all of the circumstances of the case and the totality of the particular employment relationship between the employer and employee in question.'[54] In *Matinca v Coalroc (No 5)*,[55] the New South Wales Supreme Court found that the duty of care of an employer coal-mining company extended to the employee's journey home. The plaintiff employee, Matinca, was seriously injured in a single-vehicle collision 259 kilometres from the mine and 2 hours and 20 minutes after Matinca had left

---

46 [1963] Qd R 256.
47 Ibid.
48 *Haseldine v CA Daw & Son Ltd* [1941] 2 KB 343, 362 (Scott J).
49 See, for instance, consumer guarantees of acceptable quality contained in the *Australian Consumer Law*. See as an example *Capic v Ford Motor Co of Australia Pty Ltd* (2021) ACSR 235.
50 *Koehler v Cerebos (Australia) Ltd* (2005) 222 CLR 44; *Kozarov v Victoria* (2022) 273 CLR 115; [2022] HCA 12.
51 *Kondis v State Transport Authority* (1984) 154 CLR 672, 687–8 (Mason J); *Govic v Boral Australian Gypsum Pty Ltd* (2015) 47 VR 430, 436; *Hingst v Construction Engineering (Australia) Pty Ltd (No 3)* (2018) 281 IR 70.
52 *Matinca v Coalroc (No 5)* [2022] NSWSC 844, [101].
53 *ACI Metal Stamping and Spinning Pty Ltd v Boczulik* (1964) 110 CLR 372, 378–9 (Kitto J).
54 *Matinca v Coalroc (No 5)* [2022] NSWSC 844, [103].
55 [2022] NSWSC 844.

the mine site to drive home. The employer argued that the spatial and temporal scope of the duty did not extend to the site and time of the accident, but the Court concluded that the duty of care 'extends beyond [the] hours and place of work to his journey to and from work at least so far as the risk of work induced fatigue injury is concerned. The duty is, of course, in accordance with the formulation of an employer's duty generally to see that reasonable care is taken to obviate that risk.'[56]

Employer–employee cases also involve a contractual relationship governing the relationship, and federal and state legislation also governs the relationship. *Koehler v Cerebos (Australia) Ltd*[57] addressed the implications if the law of negligence developed in a way that would inhibit the capacity of contracting parties to make agreements, although the majority did not find it significant in that instance as 'insistence upon performance of a contract cannot be in breach of a duty of care.'[58] The majority considered the relevance of external standards by which the work requirements of a contract could be assessed, but noted that this would 'invite attention to fundamental questions of legal coherence.'[59] In *Kozarov v Victoria*[60] the High Court reconsidered the effect of *Koehler* on the duty of care owed by an employer and the interaction of that duty with contractual obligations. Chief Justice Kiefel and Keane J noted that 'the fundamental proposition for which *Koehler* stands is that the content of the obligation of an employer to take reasonable care for the safety of employees at work cannot be determined in isolation from the obligations which the parties owe each other under their contract of employment'. In *Kozarov*, unlike *Koehler*, the employment contract was on the footing that employees would be protected by policies to protect their mental health.

In addition, legislation in all jurisdictions provides no-fault compensation for physical injury occurring in the workplace.[61] Typically, common law (tortious) compensation is only available according to the terms of the legislation in each state, which provides that compensation will only be awarded where the injury exceeds a statutory threshold for seriousness.

Case: *Hamilton v Nuroof (WA) Pty Ltd* (1956) 96 CLR 18

Facts

The defendants were using bitumen to repair the roof of a six-storey building. They engaged the plaintiff as a labourer on the day the work began to move hot bitumen up to roof level. The method deployed involved lifting 18-kilogram vessels of molten bitumen in front of the body high enough for a man to seize it by its handle from above. While he was passing a bucket of molten bitumen to the leading hand, the plaintiff spilt it on himself and sustained severe injuries.

Issue

Was the employer liable for failing to avoid exposing its employee to a risk of injury?

---

56 [2022] NSWSC 844, [121].
57 (2005) 222 CLR 44; [2005] HCA 15.
58 Ibid [29] (McHugh, Gummow, Hayne and Hayden JJ).
59 Ibid [31] (McHugh, Gummow, Hayne and Hayden JJ). For a discussion of coherence see Section 2.4.2.17.
60 (2022) 273 CLR 115; [2022] HCA 12.
61 See, eg, *Workers' Compensation and Rehabilitation Act 2003* (Qld).

Decision

The accident arose out of the method adopted to handle the hot bitumen. The High Court noted that the dangers of such a manner of work were very apparent and there were alternative methods of raising the bitumen, for instance, by using a rope.

Significance

This decision clarified the duty of the employer to create a safe *system* of work – not merely to identify and remedy particular dangers.

Notes

The scope of the duty of the employer was expressed as a duty 'to take reasonable care to avoid exposing the employee to unnecessary risk of injury'.[62] In *Koehler v Cerebos (Australia) Ltd*[63] this issue was revisited in the context of the duty of the employer to take reasonable care to avoid *psychiatric* injury. The plurality[64] in *Koehler* held that 'a reasonable person in the position of the employer would not have foreseen the risk of psychiatric injury' to the employee.[65] However, that determination had to be made by reference to the employment contract – what the employee agreed to do. To determine whether there is a duty to take reasonable steps to avoid psychological harm it must be determined whether 'psychiatric injury to the *particular* employee is reasonably foreseeable.'[66] This question was revisited in *Kozarov v Victoria*[67]

Question

What was the *scope* of the employer's duty of care in *Hamilton v Nuroof (WA) Pty Ltd*?

 Guided response in the eBook

Case: *Kozarov v Victoria* (2022) 273 CLR 405

Facts

Kozarov was a solicitor working for the Victorian Office of Public Prosecutions in the Specialist Sexual Offences Unit (SSOU). She suffered psychiatric injury which she claimed was due to vicarious trauma from the nature of the work she was required to do (causation was at issue in the case). The SSOU had a Vicarious Trauma Policy in effect at the commencement of Kozarov's employment, but no measures were taken under that policy to protect her mental health.

---

62   *Hamilton v Nuroof (WA) Pty Ltd* (1956) 96 CLR 18, 25.
63   (2005) 222 CLR 44; [2005] HCA 15.
64   McHugh, Gummow, Hayne and Heydon JJ.
65   (2005) 222 CLR 44; [2005] HCA 15, [26].
66   Ibid [35] (italics in original).
67   (2022) 273 CLR 115; [2022] HCA 12.

Issue

A key issue was whether the duty would engage only after Kozarov began to display signs of adverse effects on her mental health, or whether that duty existed from the point of employment.

Decision

At first instance Kozarov was successful. It was held that the employer had been put on notice of the risk to mental health, requiring that steps be taken including a rotation out of the SSOU, that Kozarov would have accepted a rotation out of the SSOU, and that a rotation would have avoided an exacerbation of the mental harm.[68] On appeal the Court of Appeal held that Kozarov had not established that the State's actions caused the injury.[69] The High Court allowed Kozarov's appeal.

Significance

Kozarov occurs in the context of an increasing number of claims against employers by employees for psychological harm. It particularly engages the issue of harm caused by vicarious trauma. From the perspective of the duty of care of the employer for the employee's psychological harm the significance of *Kozarov* is the way in which it builds upon *Koehler v Cerebos (Australia) Ltd*[70] to clarify the circumstances in which a duty of care arises. In *Koehler* the plurality in the High Court had noted that an employer engaging an employee to perform stated duties 'is entitled to assume, in the absence of evident signs warning of the possibility of psychiatric injury, that the employee considers that he or she is able to do the job.' However, in this case, the employer had in place a policy relating to psychological harm resulting from exposure to vicarious trauma, as did the employer in *Kozarov*, and the trial judge had found as a matter of fact that 'the nature and intensity of the work carried an obvious risk of psychiatric injury from exposure to vicarious trauma.'[71] In other words, the assumption from *Koehler* that an employee is able to do the job does not remove the obligation to maintain a safe system of work, and the requirement to prove that psychiatric injury to a particular employee was reasonably foreseeable was satisfied in this case by the existence of a Vicarious Trauma Policy.

Notes

The unchallenged findings of the trial judge were that a safe system of work should have included:

> an active OH&S framework; more intensive training for management and staff regarding the risks to staff posed by vicarious trauma and PTSD; welfare checks and the offer of referral for a work-related or occupational screening, in response to staff showing heightened risk; and, a flexible approach to work allocation, especially where required in response to screening, including the option of temporary or permanent rotation from the SSOU where appropriate.[72]

---

68 *Kozarov v State of Victoria* [2020] VSC 78; 294 IR 1.
69 *State of Victoria v Kozarov* [2020] VSCA 301; 301 IR 446.
70 [2005] HCA 15.
71 *Kozarov v Victoria* (2020) 294 IR 1, 126 [564]; *Kozarov v Victoria* (2022) 273 CLR 115; [2022] HCA 12, [27] (Gageler and Gleeson JJ).
72 *Kozarov v Victoria* (2022) 273 CLR 115; [2022] HCA 12, [82] (Gordon and Steward JJ).

That duty extended to establishing, maintaining and enforcing a safe system of work, given that the employer could 'prescribe, warn, command and enforce obedience to [its] commands'.[73]

Question

How does the decision in *Kozarov v Victoria* affect the principle arising from *Koehler v Cerebos (Australia) Ltd*[74] in relation to the duty of care owed by an employer for psychological injuries?

 Guided response in the eBook

HINTS AND TIPS

It can be difficult to distinguish the *scope* of the duty of care from the question of *breach*. The distinction can be unclear, even in judgments. When thinking about duty, it can help to think in terms of category (eg, the category of the relationship between the plaintiff and the defendant, and the category of harm). Don't think about the specifics of the plaintiff's situation, because the question is set in the abstract and prospectively.

2.3.3   Occupier–entrant

The occupier–entrant tortious relationship predated the generalised duty of care in negligence. However, the common law had developed differentiated standards of care depending on the category of entrant (see Table 2.2). *Indermaur v Dames* required a 'fine gradation of standards corresponding to the degree of benefit which [an occupier] derives from [an entrant's] visit'.[75] *Indermaur* predated the definition of the duty relationship in *Donoghue v Stevenson*[76] but the categories continued to have influence for a long time.

Table 2.2   Categories of entrant under common law

Lawful entrants	Unlawful entrants
Invitees	Trespassers
Licensees	
Persons entering under contract	
Persons exercising a legal power of entry	
Persons entering as of public right	

---

73 *McLean v Tedman* (1984) 155 CLR 306, 313.
74 (2005) 222 CLR 44.
75 (1866) LR 1 CP 274.
76 [1932] AC 562.

In the case of the trespasser, the duty initially was minimal: not to cause the trespasser injury intentionally or recklessly. However, over time the High Court found a way around this rule by holding that in suitable circumstances an occupier could be concurrently subject to an ordinary duty of care towards a trespasser that would override the narrower duty. The last case in which this approach was used is *Hackshaw v Shaw*,[77] in which a farmer shot at a car whose driver was stealing petrol from his bowser, injuring a girl crouching in the front seat.

In the case of lawful entrants, the duty owed by the occupier to invitees was more stringent than that owed to licensees. This is because licensees were persons who entered with the consent or permission of the occupier, whereas invitees were persons who entered at the occupier's invitation or request and for the occupier's benefit. Persons who entered as of public right (eg, entrants to public parks) were unlike invitees in that their presence did not usually confer any material benefit on the occupier but were also unlike licensees in that they did not need the permission of the occupier to enter. The duty owed to these people was the same as that owed to invitees, as was the duty owed to persons who entered in exercise of a legal (ie, common law or statutory) power of entry. Visitors entering under the terms of a contract were the final subcategory. If the contract made reference to the duty owed by the occupier to the contractual entrant – which was not common – then this governed the situation. Otherwise, the law implied into the contract a duty of reasonable care. This made the occupier liable not only for negligence on its part or that of its employees, but also for the negligence of its independent contractors. Thus, the high level of duty owed to the contractual entrant was justified by the fact that the occupier had received payment for allowing entry.

In *Australian Safeway Stores Pty Ltd v Zaluzna*,[78] the High Court held that there was no need to determine the existence of the special duty qua (in the capacity of) occupier: 'the fact that the respondent was a lawful entrant upon the land of the appellant establishes a relationship between them which of itself suffices to give rise to a duty on the part of the appellant to take reasonable care to avoid a foreseeable risk of injury to the respondent.'[79] Some states, such as Victoria, had made statutory provision for occupiers' liability prior to *Zaluzna*: see, for example, *Occupiers' Liability Act 1983* (Vic) (now pt IIA of the *Wrongs Act 1958* (Vic)). In other states there had been proposals to modify the legislation,[80] but these were abandoned in the light of *Zaluzna*. The interaction between statutory provisions and the common law can cause difficulties.[81] Table 2.3 shows some of the relevant statutory provisions.

---

77 (1984) 155 CLR 614.

78 (1987) 162 CLR 479.

79 Ibid 488 (Mason, Wilson, Deane and Dawson JJ).

80 In New South Wales, the New South Wales Law Reform Commission, *Working Paper on Occupiers' Liability* (Working Paper No 3, July 1969); in Tasmania, the Law Reform Commission of Tasmania, *Occupiers' Liability* (Report No 53, 1988).

81 For further information see P Handford and B McGivern, 'Two Problems of Occupiers' Liability: Part One – The Occupiers' Liability Acts and the Common Law' (2015) 39(1) *Melbourne University Law Review* 128.

Table 2.3   Occupier liability – statutory provisions

Legislation	Section
Civil Law (Wrongs) Act 2002 (ACT)	168
Personal Injuries (Liabilities and Damages) Act 2003 (NT)	9
Civil Liability Act 1936 (SA)	20
Wrongs Act 1958 (Vic)	14B
Civil Liability Act 2002 (WA)	5

Case: *Australian Safeway Stores Pty Ltd v Zaluzna* (1987) 162 CLR 479

Facts

A customer in a Safeway store was injured after she fell heavily on a wet floor. It was raining, and other customers had tracked water inside.

Issue

Did the supermarket owe a general duty of care in negligence, or the inviter's duty to their invitee 'to take reasonable care to prevent damage from unusual danger of which it knew or ought to have known', as articulated by Willis J in the occupier's liability case *Indermaur v Dames*?[82]

Decision

A majority of the High Court noted that the 'plain tenor' of the articulation of the duty of an occupier to an invitee in *Indermaur v Dames* was 'that an invitor's obligation with respect to dangers on his premises should be measured by the flexible standard of reasonable care, as part of the general law of negligence. Unfortunately it has been treated more as a statutory definition of exclusive application to the occupier of dangerous premises in their relationship to invitees.'[83]

Significance

This case is significant mainly for the High Court's rejection of the previous common law approach to occupier's liability, by which the duty owed to the entrant varied according to whether the entrant was an invitee, a licensee, a person entering under contract, a person entering in exercise of a legal power of entry, a person entering as of public right, or an unlawful entrant. The High Court held that the general duty of care applied to all entrants, and the circumstances of entry were relevant in applying the calculus of negligence (the standard of care to be applied).

---

82 (1866) LR 1 CP 274, 288.
83 *Australian Safeway Stores Pty Ltd v Zaluzna* (1987) 162 CLR 479, 487.

Notes

The majority in *Zaluzna* concluded:

> there remains neither warrant nor reason for continuing to search for fine distinctions between the so-called special duty enunciated by Willes J [in *Indermaur v Danes*] and the general duty established by *Donoghue v Stevenson*. The same is true of the so-called special duties resting on an occupier of land with respect to persons entering as licensees or trespassers.[84]

Question

What is the effect of the circumstances of the plaintiff's entry on the liability of the occupier?

   Guided response in the eBook

2.3.4   Doctor–patient

The relationship between medical practitioner and patient is one of the earliest recognised duties. Usually a patient visits a general practitioner or specialist's rooms, or at a hospital, where the doctor attends them. The duty relates to diagnosis, professional advice and treatment. There have been a number of extensions to the duty. For instance, it has been 'established that health care providers owe a duty to an unborn child to take reasonable care to avoid conduct which might foreseeably cause prenatal injury. Such a duty has been held to exist even before conception'.[85]

HINTS AND TIPS

Remember that a case can be distinguished in a number of ways. If you are trying to work out whether an 'existing category' such as doctor–patient is applicable to your case (or whether it can be distinguished), you might have to consider: (1) whether the legislation in your jurisdiction has affected the precedent; (2) whether your case involves a different type of harm (eg, economic loss instead of physical harm); and (3) whether your case involves a different category of plaintiff (eg, cases have distinguished pregnant women and foetuses).

---

84 *Australian Safeway Stores Pty Ltd v Zaluzna* (1987) 162 CLR 479, 487.
85 *Harriton v Stephens* (2006) 226 CLR 52, 74 (Kirby J) citing *Watt v Rama* [1972] VR 353.

2.3.5   Teacher–pupil and school authority–pupil

A school owes a duty to take reasonable care for the protection of students against reasonable risk of physical harm. The rationale for this duty is the:

> need of a child of immature age for protection against the conduct of others, or indeed of himself, which may cause him injury coupled with the fact that, during school hours the child is beyond the control and protection of his parent and is placed under the control of the schoolmaster who is in a position to exercise authority over him and afford him, in the exercise of reasonable care, protection from injury.[86]

Roman Catholic Church Trustees for the Diocese of Canberra and Goulburn v Hadba is a more recent articulation of this duty.[87]

The liability of the school may extend to before and after-school hours. In *Geyer v Downs* the High Court held that the duty covered the period before school commenced.[88] The duty might also extend beyond school grounds. In *Trustees of the Roman Catholic Church for the Diocese of Bathurst v Koffman* the physical bullying of a 12-year-old student took place at a bus stop 400 metres from the school grounds, but the Court held that, since the school knew that students used the bus stop as a matter of routine, and it ought to have known that problems could occur by the mixing of students, the school authority owed a duty of care.[89] In *Horne v Queensland* students had been told to make their own way to a tennis centre outside the school as part of school-organised activities, and were permitted to cycle.[90] The 13-year-old plaintiff suffered serious injuries after she fell off her bicycle and landed on the road in front of the rear wheels of a semi-trailer which ran over the lower part of her body. It was clear that a duty was owed to the student, and that the duty had been breached when the school allowed students to ride along the road unsupervised.

Case: *Geyer v Downs* (1977) 138 CLR 91

Facts

The plaintiff was an eight-year-old girl who was accidentally struck by a softball bat in the school grounds before the commencement of classes. There was no teacher supervision at the time. The school knew that students would congregate in the playground before classes and Departmental Instructions indicated the need to supervise children in the playground.

Issue

Did the school owe a duty of care to the student before school hours?

---

86   *Richards v Victoria* [1969] VR 136, 138–9 (Winneke CJ).
87   (2005) 221 CLR 161.
88   (1977) 138 CLR 91.
89   (1996) Aust Torts Reports 81-399.
90   (1995) 22 MVR 111.

Decision

It was acknowledged that a duty was owed by the school to students. In this case the 'temporal ambit' of that duty was at issue. This was to be determined by the circumstances of the relationship, and not by the capacity of the school to provide supervision. The headmaster had permitted (although not encouraged) students to enter the school from 8:15 am, and the school knew that many students were on school grounds between 8:15 and 9:00 am.

Significance

This case established that a duty may arise to supervise students outside school hours. Prior to this there was no case clearly establishing that there was *no* duty. The headmaster knew that students were accessing the school well before school commenced and that risks of injury arose in the absence of supervision.

Notes

The gates were not opened for the students specifically; they were opened for the teachers, delivery of milk and food, toilet pan delivery and so on. However, it was well-known that students started entering through the gates well before 'school hours'. The headmaster conceded that there were a lot of working mothers in the area and that it would be dangerous to lock the children out of the school on a busy road. The headmaster discouraged them from coming early through 'frequent admonitions.' No precautions were taken to supervise them before the commencement of school. There were rules against playing games, but no method of enforcement except asking passing teachers to admonish students who were playing games.

Question

The defendant argued that there could be no duty arising before school hours because, according to Department Instructions, the headmaster had no authority to require teachers to supervise before school. Are Departmental Instructions such as this irrelevant to the question of duty of care?

 Guided response in the eBook

2.3.6   Duty owed to a rescuer

The foreseeability of injury to a plaintiff attempting to assist the victim of a defendant's negligence has long been recognised. The duty does not rely on whether there had been a request for assistance:

> Danger invites rescue. The cry of distress is the summons to relief … The wrong that imperils life is a wrong to the imperilled victim; it is a wrong also to his rescuer … The wrongdoer may not have foreseen the coming of a deliverer. He is accountable as if he had.[91]

91   *Wagner v International Railway Co*, 232 NY 176, 180 (1921) (Cardozo J).

It is not necessary that the precise sequence of events leading to the need for rescue be foreseeable. In *Haynes v Harwood*, a boy threw a stone at a horse which was tethered to the defendant's unattended van.[92] The horse bolted, endangering passers-by. A considerable distance away a policeman saw that people were in danger and intervened. The horse fell on him and he was seriously injured. The Court said: 'It is not necessary to show that this particular accident and this particular damage were probable, but it is sufficient if it is of a class that might well be anticipated as one of the reasonable and probable results of the wrongful act.'[93]

Where the damage suffered by a rescuer includes psychological harm there will be additional considerations in determining whether a duty of care exists. This has been considered by a number of recent cases. *Wicks v State Rail Authority of New South Wales*[94] and *Watson v New South Wales*[95] both involved psychological harm of those, including rescuers, responding to a train derailment near the Waterfall railway station in New South Wales, at which 7 people were killed and 42 injured. The derailment was caused by the negligence of the State Rail Authority. Whether or not a duty of care for psychological harm was owed to rescuers had to be resolved by reference to the legislative provisions limiting liability for psychological harm.[96] *Watson* related to a triggering of the trauma associated with the rescue, which did not occur until 2018 – delayed onset post-traumatic stress disorder.

2.3.7   Users of the highway

It is axiomatic that the driver of a motor vehicle owes a duty of care to the person and property of other users of the road. It is foreseeable that the actions of a user of a motor vehicle may physically injure another road user. In *Le Lievre v Gould*, Lord Esher said:

> if a man is driving along a road, it is his duty not to do that which may injure another person whom he meets on the road, or to his horse or his carriage. In the same way it is the duty of a man not to do that which will injure the house of another to which he is near. If a man is driving on Salisbury Plain, and no other person is near him, he is at liberty to drive as fast and as recklessly as he pleases … So, too, if a man is driving along a street in a town, a similar duty not to drive carelessly arises out of contiguity or neighbourhood.[97]

Where a duty is of such long standing you may find it difficult to find relevant authorities. It could be called 'trite' or obvious law in the sense that the precedent is of long standing and buried by time.[98] In *Derrick v Cheung*[99] the duty of a driver to a pedestrian (a 21-month-old child who darted in front of the car the defendant was driving) was assumed, and only

---

92   [1935] 1 KB 146.
93   Ibid 156 (Greer J).
94   (2010) 241 CLR 60; [2010] HCA 22.
95   (2021) 96 MVR 413.
96   See Section 2.5.1.
97   [1893] 1 QB 491, 497.
98   See the analysis of trite law in Australia in R Haigh, '"It is Trite and Ancient Law": The High Court and the Use of the Obvious' (2000) 28(1) *Federal Law Review* 87.
99   (2001) 181 ALR 301; [2001] HCA 48.

the question of breach was at issue. In *Marien v Gardiner*[100] the New South Wales Court of Appeal notes that '[t]he duty of the driver of a motor vehicle to users of the roadway, including pedestrians, is to take reasonable care for their safety having regard to all the circumstances of the case'.[101] In *Girmay v Green*[102] the Tasmanian Supreme Court made the same point without citing authority.[103]

Thus, we owe a duty of care to take reasonable steps to prevent another road user from suffering physical injury. Clear instances of duty include drivers of other vehicles and passengers.[104] There may be instances where a defendant will argue that a plaintiff does not fall within the established boundaries of that duty, so it will be necessary to provide an explicit authority. So, for instance, in *Collins v Insurance Australia Ltd*[105] the issue was whether a driver owes a duty of care to other drivers not involved in the original collision. The plaintiff was injured when she took evasive action to avoid colliding with a queue of vehicles stopped on a rural highway as a result of an accident caused by another driver's negligence. In an appeal against the decision to refuse payment under the negligent driver's compulsory third-party insurance, the New South Wales Court of Appeal had to determine whether a duty of care was owed to the plaintiff, despite the physical distance and the period of time between the original accident and the plaintiff's accident. Finding that a duty of care was owed, Basten AJA, with whom Meagher JA agreed, noted in a case involving physical injury there is a 'simple proposition that the duty of the insured to other road users [is] to exercise proper care in driving so as not to cause a collision.'[106] He said 'constraints as to space and time which have arisen in developing a duty of care not to cause mental harm should not be imported into this discussion. Nor is assistance obtained from introducing in this context concepts such as vulnerability, used to control the potentially indeterminate scope of a duty to avoid economic loss.'[107]

In *King v Philcox*[108] the issue was whether the duty of a driver extended to mental harm suffered by those who had observed the outcome of a motor vehicle accident.[109] The novel aspect of this case was whether a duty of care to guard against mental harm was owed to a person who saw the aftermath of an accident, but later discovered that they were related to one of the victims. The common law rules relating to mental harm have been affected by the Civil Liability Acts in most jurisdictions.[110] This case is considered in more detail below.[111]

In *Watt v Rama*[112] the issue was whether the established duty extended to an unborn child injured due to a negligent driver but later born alive. Chief Justice Winneke and Justice

---

100 (2013) 66 MVR 1.
101 Ibid [33].
102 (2021) 34 Tas R 64.
103 Ibid [27].
104 *Imbree v McNeilly* (2008) 236 CLR 510.
105 (2022) 109 NSWLR 240; [2022] NSWCA 135.
106 Ibid [127] (Basten AJA).
107 Ibid [128] (Basten AJA).
108 (2015) 255 CLR 304; [2015] HCA 19.
109 The question of duty of care for mental harm is considered later under Section 2.5.1.
110 See Table 2.4.
111 See Section 2.5.1.
112 [1972] VR 353.

Pape in the Full Court of the Victorian Supreme Court (now the Court of Appeal) described the issue of duty as 'an interesting and important point in the law of torts upon which there is no authority which binds this Court.'

Case: *Watt v Rama* [1972] VR 353

Facts

On 15 May 1967, a car driven by Rama (the defendant) collided with a car driven by the plaintiff's mother, Watt, as a result of Rama's negligence. Watt was rendered a quadriplegic. At the time of the collision she was pregnant, and she later gave birth to the plaintiff who was born with brain damage and epilepsy as a result of the accident. She sued the defendant in negligence. The defendant argued that at the time of the accident the plaintiff was not 'a person or a human being ... and ... had no separate existence apart from her mother. Accordingly, she was not a legal person to whom a duty of care could be owed'.[113]

Issue

This case raised the interesting, and at the time novel, question of whether a driver owed a duty of care not to cause injury to an unborn infant whose mother was driving a car at the time, or whether the defendant driver owed a duty to the unborn infant not to injure the mother.

Decision

It was reasonably foreseeable that a driver may, upon failure to take reasonable care, cause injury to a pregnant woman, and that the child, when born, may be injured. The duty 'crystallised' when the baby was born.

Significance

This case was significant insofar as a duty could not be owed directly to the unborn child, but was nevertheless held to be a contingent duty capable of ripening into a duty when the child was born injured.

Notes

While the defendant clearly owed a duty of care to the mother, the unborn child was not a legally defined person at the time of the collision. The problem was considered by analogy to the situation, in law, where a person is a member of a class but is not, themselves, defined.

Question

Does *Watt v Rama* establish that an unborn child is owed a duty of care?

 Guided response in the eBook

REVIEW QUESTIONS

(1) What categories of persons are, as a matter of precedent, owed a duty by other persons?

(2) Explain the circumstances in which a case involving an established category of duty (eg, driver–passenger, doctor–patient) might be distinguished?

 Guided responses in the eBook

2.4   Duty of care in the novel case

2.4.1   Identifying risk: what is foreseeable?

Foreseeability is a well-established component of the duty of care. However, foreseeability is an undemanding requirement:

> In almost every case in which a plaintiff suffers damage it is foreseeable that, if reasonable care is not taken, harm may follow. The conclusion that harm was foreseeable is well-nigh inevitable. As Dixon CJ said in argument in *Chapman v Hearse*, 'I cannot understand why any event which does happen is not foreseeable by a person of sufficient imagination and intelligence'. Foresight of harm is not sufficient to show that a duty of care exists.[114]

The test of foreseeability is unable to control the range of potential plaintiffs, so courts have developed a range of additional gatekeeper mechanisms. These are commonly called 'salient features', or the 'multi-factorial approach'.

2.4.2   'Salient features' or the 'multi-factorial' approach

'Salient features' are factors to be considered when determining whether a duty of care is owed when there is *no existing precedent*. A list of the salient features was helpfully compiled by Allsop P in *Caltex Refineries (Qld) Pty Ltd v Stavar*,[115] and has been extensively utilised in later novel cases.

HINTS AND TIPS

The 17 features identified by Allsop P are not exhaustive, and they are not to be treated as a 'shopping list'[116] to be applied indiscriminately. They do not appear to be in any particular order and there is no indication of the relative weight to be given to each feature. It is not necessary to satisfy each feature – identify the ones relevant to the relationship at issue.

---

114 *Modbury Triangle Shopping Centre Pty Ltd v Anzil* (2000) 205 CLR 254, 288 (Hayne J).
115 (2009) 75 NSWLR 649.
116 *Strategic Formwork Pty Ltd v Hitchen* (2018) 277 IR 220.

The multi-factorial or salient features approach tends to involve a mix of policy, fact and law. According to Allsop P, it is an 'oversimplification' to regard the question of duty as a question of law, because '[t]he existence of a duty depends in part on findings of fact and part on value judgments and legal policy'.[117] His Honour continued:

> the 'multi-factorial' approach … requires consideration of a congeries of disparate elements, some of which are entirely factual in nature, others of which require value judgment and others an infusion of legal policy. There was always a degree of irony in maintaining that the existence of a duty involved a question of law (and thus not for determination by a jury) when the concept of reasonableness itself invoked consideration of community standards.[118]

The weighting to be applied to these factors has not been fully articulated, but in recent cases two factors have received greater attention than others:

(1)   the degree and nature of control able to be exercised by the defendant to avoid harm

(2)   the degree of vulnerability of the plaintiff to harm from the defendant's conduct, including the capacity and reasonable expectation of a plaintiff to take steps to protect itself (the plaintiff's autonomy).[119]

HINTS AND TIPS

It may be useful to arrange the salient features in any particular case into 'affirmative' and 'negative' features – affirmative salient features indicate that a duty would be owed, but they must be balanced against negative features, which speak against the imposition of a duty in that context. There are some features that are neither positive nor negative, but are preliminary enquiries: for instance, 'the nature of harm alleged,' 'the nature of the activity' and the 'existence of a category of relationship'. Whether these factors indicate that a duty is owed or not depends on the analysis of the feature.

For the sake of simplicity, each of the factors will be considered in the order listed in *Caltex Refineries (Qld) Pty Ltd v Stavar*.[120] This discussion also uses some of the same wording, as it is consistent with the cases from which the salient features were drawn.

---

117   *Caltex Refineries (Qld) Pty Ltd v Stavar* (2009) 75 NSWLR 649, [159].
118   Ibid [160].
119   *Precision Products (NSW) Pty Ltd v Hawkesbury City Council* (2008) 74 NSWLR 102 (Allsop P, Beazley and McColl JJA).
120   (2009) 75 NSWLR 649.

2.4.2.1   Foreseeability

In *Caltex Refineries (Qld) Pty Ltd v Stavar*, Allsop P noted:

> I have described 'foreseeability' as a salient feature; it is perhaps better expressed that
> the use of salient features operates as a control measure on foreseeability ... In a novel
> area, reasonable foreseeability of harm is inadequate alone to found a conclusion of
> duty.[121]

If it is reasonably foreseeable that the defendant's actions, if carried out without reasonable care, will cause damage to a person in the 'category' of the plaintiff, this is a necessary but not a sufficient determinant of duty. In straightforward cases of physical injury it is likely that a duty relationship will ordinarily have been established in previous cases. However, other types of harm will normally give rise to the necessity for other control mechanisms.

2.4.2.2   Plaintiff's harm

It follows that the nature of the harm alleged will be relevant to the expansion of a duty to a new category of plaintiff (see the earlier discussion of 'special duty relationships' especially Sections 2.4.1 and 2.4.2). As already indicated, where the plaintiff suffers physical injury only, it is likely that the duty of care has been established by precedent (although there may, of course, be exceptions). However, where a plaintiff has suffered physical injury but is seeking redress from a new class of defendant (say, a regulatory authority which failed to oversee the activities of the *primary* wrongdoer), it is possible that a case involving physical injury will be a novel case.

Other types of damage, like pure economic loss and mental harm, give rise to policy issues and therefore attract further control mechanisms. Many of the relevant policy issues are included as salient features, but note that these are not exhaustive of the potential issues. Potential indeterminacy of liability is of particular relevance as it is in the interests of justice that a defendant can determine with reasonable certainty the degree to which they are exposed to liability, and a category of duty that does not enable this certainty is inconsistent with other aims of the law of negligence – such as the capacity of the defendant to manage or respond to risk or the coherence of the common law and the expansion of the tort of negligence into other areas of law.

2.4.2.3   Control

The degree and nature of control able to be exercised by the defendant to avoid harm can be relevant, particularly where a duty is asserted in relation to a new category of defendant. The obligation to control may arise out of statute, as in the case of a public authority exercising oversight of building, safety or quality. It could also be alleged that there is an obligation to control arising out of contract, but not necessarily a contract with the plaintiff. In *Perre v Apand Pty Ltd*, the defendant company, Apand, controlled the activity on the Sparnons' farm because it had introduced bacterial wilt to the farm.[122] This triggered the quarantine of nearby farms, including that of the plaintiff, Frank Perre, and the loss of the market for potato

---

121 Ibid [106].
122 (1999) 198 CLR 180.

growers. Of course, the defendant's control over the circumstances leading to the plaintiff's damage will often also signal the plaintiff's *lack* of control – and therefore contribute to their vulnerability, which is also a salient feature. McHugh J in *Perre v Apand Pty Ltd* noted:

> Although each category will have to formulate a particular standard, the ultimate question will be one of fact. The defendant's control of the plaintiff's right, interest or expectation will be an important test for vulnerability.[123]

The same point was made in *Hill v Van Erp*, in which the solicitor's control over the finalisation of a will also meant that the plaintiff – the intended beneficiary – was vulnerable because of their 'unavoidable [dependence] upon the proper performance of a function within the sole province of the solicitor'.[124]

The idea of 'control' has been an issue in relation to cases alleging a responsibility to control third parties. In these cases, the plaintiff may be seeking damages from the actual wrongdoer, but there may be reasons, such as the impecuniosity of the primary wrongdoer, or an inability to identify them, which will make the defendant a more attractive option. These issues are considered in more detail in Section 2.5.5.

2.4.2.4 Vulnerability

The vulnerability of the plaintiff to harm from the defendant's conduct has been given particular emphasis. In *Woolcock Street Investments Pty Ltd v CDG Pty Ltd*[125] the High Court noted:

> 'Vulnerability', in this context, is not to be understood as meaning only that the plaintiff was likely to suffer damage if reasonable care was not taken. Rather, 'vulnerability' is to be understood as a reference to the plaintiff's inability to protect itself from the consequences of a defendant's want of reasonable care, either entirely or at least in a way which would cast the consequences of loss on the defendant.[126]

The idea of vulnerability includes consideration of the plaintiff's capacity to look after themselves, and the reasonable expectation that they will do so.

The following facts have been argued to give rise to vulnerability:

- the plaintiff being a foetus in utero[127]
- the defendant being the only potential source of the information on which the plaintiff relied[128]
- the plaintiff's inability to do anything to protect themselves from a quarantine resulting in economic loss[129]

---

123 Ibid 229 (McHugh J).
124 (1997) 188 CLR 159, 175 (Dawson J; Toohey J agreeing).
125 (2004) 216 CLR 515.
126 (2004) 216 CLR 515, 530 (Gleeson CJ, Gummow, Hayne and Heydon JJ).
127 *Harriton v Stephens* (2006) 226 CLR 52, 76 (Kirby J).
128 *Central Highlands Regional Council v Geju Pty Ltd* [2018] 3 Qd R 550.
129 *Perre v Apand Pty Ltd* (1999) 198 CLR 180; [1999] HCA 36, [351]: 'the appellants were vulnerable for the reasons detailed above. In particular, by reason of the physical proximity of the [genetically modified or "GM"] canola on Sevenoaks, Eagle Rest was uniquely vulnerable to an incursion of GM swaths. The appellants were also uniquely vulnerable to the consequence of that incursion, being loss of the certification of the land as organic. The respondent had actual knowledge of these vulnerabilities.'

- the inability of an intended beneficiary to ensure that the client's solicitor properly performed the client's retainer[130]
- the inability of the plaintiff to check the quality of the builder's work themselves – and hence, reliance on the builder[131]
- reliance itself, which has been regarded as 'an indicator of vulnerability'.[132]

Conversely, the plaintiff could protect themselves in a range of ways (and therefore not be vulnerable), including by:

- 'negotiating with the vendor for a warranty of freedom from defect or an assignment in lieu of the vendors' rights against third parties in relation to defects'[133]
- seeking a warranty that land was zoned 'industrial'[134]
- where there are other sources of information available – making their own inquiries about the financial position of the company instead of relying on another[135]
- retaining a solicitor before contracting[136]
- being a 'sophisticated investor which had all the information it needed to determine whether it should seek to participate' in a share offer.[137]

2.4.2.5 Reliance

The degree of reliance by the plaintiff upon the defendant has been a significant factor in a series of cases including *Bryan v Maloney*,[138] the negligent misrepresentation cases and the 'duty to control' cases. Many of these cases precede the full articulation of the 'salient features' test, but it seems clear that courts are utilising arguments from these cases. In many cases reliance, assumption of responsibility and vulnerability (in the sense of having no other option than to rely on the defendant) are factors that are present in the same fact situations. Reliance on the defendant is one of the indicators of vulnerability.

In the negligent misrepresentation cases reliance has sometimes been coupled with the requirement that the reliance was 'reasonable'. This requirement was articulated, for instance, in *Mutual Life & Citizens' Assurance Co Ltd v Evatt*,[139] in *Shaddock & Associates Pty Ltd v Parramatta City Council (No 1)*[140] and in *Esanda Finance Corporation Ltd v Peat Marwick Hungerfords ('Esanda')*.[141]

---

130 *Hill v Van Erp* (1997) 188 CLR 159 (Brennan CJ, Dawson, Toohey, Gaudron, McHugh and Gummow JJ).
131 *Woolcock Street Investments Pty Ltd v CDG Pty Ltd* (2004) 216 CLR 515.
132 *Perre v Apand Pty Ltd* (1999) 198 CLR 180, 228 (McHugh J). But 'the High Court has so far not held that a duty of care arises in negligent misstatements cases merely because it is foreseeable that a plaintiff unknown to the defendant falls within a broadly defined class of persons who might suffer economic loss by reasonably relying upon a statement made by the defendant': *Central Highlands Regional Council v Geju Pty Ltd* [2018] 3 Qd R 550.
133 *Woolcock Street Investments Pty Ltd v CDG Pty Ltd* (2004) 216 CLR 515.
134 *Central Highlands Regional Council v Geju Pty Ltd* [2018] 3 Qd R 550.
135 *Esanda Finance Corporation Ltd v Peat Marwick Hungerfords* (1997) 188 CLR 241.
136 *Central Highlands Regional Council v Geju Pty Ltd* [2018] 3 Qd R 550.
137 *RinRim Pty Ltd v Deutsche Bank AG* [2017] NSWCA 169.
138 (1995) 182 CLR 609.
139 (1968) 122 CLR 556, 571 (Barwick CJ), 584 (Kitto J).
140 (1981) 150 CLR 225, 230–1 (Gibbs CJ).
141 (1997) 188 CLR 241.

In *Esanda* the issue was whether the auditor (Peat Marwick Hungerfords) of a company which had failed (Excel) owed a duty of care to a finance provider (Esanda) which had lent money to Excel and subsequently suffered pure economic loss.[142] Toohey and Gaudron JJ noted that the authorities did not provide a clear articulation of the requirements to establish duty in the case of voluntary provision of information or advice, but that reliance or assumption of responsibility and special knowledge or expertise seemed necessary as a matter of common sense. In addition, 'ordinary principles require that the relationship does not arise unless it is reasonable for the recipient to act on that information or advice without further inquiry. Similarly, ordinary principles require that it be reasonable for the recipient to act upon it for the purpose for which it is used.'[143]

In *Central Highlands Regional Council v Geju Pty Ltd*, the Supreme Court of Queensland articulated this requirement in the modern duty framework.[144] As in *Shaddock*[145] the defendant in *Geju* was a local council. It issued a planning and development certificate to the new owner of a block of land which incorrectly noted the land as zoned 'industrial', whereas it was zoned 'rural'. The certificate was a 'limited' certificate, and one of the issues was whether it was reasonable for the plaintiff to act on the information without further inquiry. The Supreme Court held that the reliance by the plaintiff on the certificate was not reasonable. Some time had elapsed between the issue of the certificate and the purchase of the land and the certificate was a limited one.

On the current state of the law, the reasonableness of the plaintiff's reliance on the defendant is still considered.

2.4.2.6 Assumption of responsibility

As an indicator of duty, an assumption of responsibility by the defendant also predates the current duty framework. As a criterion it was typically associated with cases involving public authorities or negligent misstatement giving rise to pure economic harm. In *Esanda* Toohey and Gaudron JJ noted:

> The decided cases do not identify precisely what it is that results in liability for economic loss suffered in consequence of the voluntary provision of information or advice. However, commonsense requires the conclusion that a special relationship of proximity *marked either by reliance or by the assumption of responsibility* does not arise unless the person providing the information or advice has *some special expertise or knowledge, or some special means of acquiring information which is not available to the recipient.*[146]

2.4.2.7 Proximity

While proximity no longer plays a dominant part in the articulation of the duty of care, it remains relevant. In *Central Highlands Regional Council v Geju Pty Ltd*, Fraser JA reiterated: 'that the … rejection of proximity as a touchstone for a duty of care … did not render

---

142 Ibid.
143 (1997) 188 CLR 241, 265 (Toohey and Gaudron JJ).
144 [2018] 3 Qd R 550.
145 *Shaddock & Associates Pty Ltd v Parramatta City Council (No 1)* (1981) 150 CLR 225.
146 (1997) 188 CLR 241, 265 (emphasis added).

irrelevant to the duty question the underlying factors which had been held to give rise to such a relationship.'[147] In essence, proximity retains its original meaning of 'nearness' of the plaintiff to the defendant but is not limited to physical proximity. It 'extend[s] to such *close and direct* relations that the act complained of directly affects a person whom the person alleged to be bound to take care would know would be directly affected by his careless act'.[148]

In many cases physical closeness will not be a necessary consideration because cases involving physical closeness have already resulted in an established precedent. For instance, a plaintiff suffering physical injury as a result of physical closeness to a motor vehicle accident will ordinarily be within an established category of duty (motor vehicle driver–road user). Furthermore, 'proximity in the sense of nearness or closeness is hardly a useful concept in most cases of pure economic loss'.[149] The usefulness of proximity as a separate category for consideration is likely to be most apparent in new categories of loss where the 'causal', 'relational' or 'circumstantial' closeness of the defendant's act to the plaintiff's consequence must be measured.

2.4.2.8 Category of relationship

The existence or otherwise of a category of relationship between the defendant and the plaintiff or a person closely connected with the plaintiff is naturally one of the matters that should be considered, not least because it will help to identify whether it is a novel case. However, in this context 'category' is interpreted more broadly. In *Caltex Refineries (Qld) Pty Ltd v Stavar*, Allsop P noted:

> The employment relationship brings with it the well-known duty to exercise care in the provision of a safe system of work. The use of an independent contractor by a principal, rather than the direct engagement of employees, is a significant factor in the existence or not of responsibility of the principal arising from the conduct or activity of the subcontractor and its employees or agents … Circumstances will arise, however, where the principal remains subject to a duty of care in respect of damage or harm that may arise from, or in connection with, the conduct of the independent contractor.[150]

2.4.2.9 Nature of the activity

It is difficult to imagine commencing a discussion determining whether a duty of care is owed without first considering the nature of the defendant's activities. A driver's liability is considered in the context of their activities as a driver, for instance; or a surgeon's activities arising from their work as a surgeon. The nature of the activity undertaken by the defendant will provide the scope of the duty of care, particularly in cases in which the defendant's activities are defined by agreement or by other duties. There are some cases in which the nature of the activity will raise particular concerns – if it is dangerous or involves significant responsibilities.

---

147 [2018] 3 Qd R 550, [23] referring to *Owners Strata Plan No 61288 v Brookfield Australia Investments Ltd* (2013) 85 NSWLR 479, 486, quoted by French CJ in *Brookfield Multiplex Ltd v Owners Corporation Strata Plan 61288* (2014) 254 CLR 185, 199–200.

148 *Donoghue v Stevenson* [1932] AC 562, 581 (Lord Atkin).

149 *Perre v Apand Pty Ltd* (1999) 198 CLR 180, 211.

150 *Caltex Refineries (Qld) Pty Ltd v Stavar* (2009) 75 NSWLR 649, [108].

2.4.2.10   Nature or degree of danger or hazard

The nature or the degree of the hazard or danger liable to be caused by the defendant's conduct or the activity or substance controlled by the defendant was relevant to the 'action on the case', predating the law of negligence.[151] It was a consideration articulated in *Rylands v Fletcher*, which involved the escape of water which had been stored on the defendant's land into the mines of the plaintiff.[152] The rule in *Rylands v Fletcher* is now absorbed into the principles of the law of negligence in Australia[153] but the relevance of the nature or degree of the hazard is clearly enunciated in *Burnie Port Authority v General Jones Pty Ltd*[154]:

> a person who takes advantage of his or her control of premises to introduce a dangerous substance, to carry on a dangerous activity, or to allow another to do one of those things, *owes a duty of reasonable care to avoid a reasonably foreseeable risk of injury or damage to the person or property of another* … that duty of care both varies in degree according to the magnitude of the risk involved and extends to ensuring that such care is taken.[155]

Similarly, the old rules relating to 'inherently dangerous goods' such as firearms and explosives[156] will have an effect at the duty stage (as well as the 'breach' stage – more dangerous activities will heighten the standard of care). In *Donoghue v Stephenson* Lord Atkin noted that 'the person dealing with [an inherently dangerous article] may well contemplate persons as being within the sphere of his duty to take care who would not be sufficiently proximate with less dangerous goods; so that not only the degree of care but the range of persons to whom the duty is owed may be extended.'[157]

2.4.2.11   Knowledge that the conduct will cause harm

The 'knowledge' (either actual or constructive) by the defendant that the conduct will cause harm to the plaintiff can generate a sufficiently close relationship to give rise to a duty of care.[158] This was noted by Stephen J in *Caltex Oil (Australia) Pty Ltd v The Dredge Willemstad* as part of an extension of the duty of care to cases involving purely economic loss.[159] Originally knowledge of potential to cause harm was one of the concepts which enabled incremental development of the duty of care where the plaintiff has not suffered any physical injury or damage, but has suffered economic loss. To meet the criterion in *Willemstad*, the knowledge had to be that the plaintiff as a particular person, not merely as a member of an unascertained class, would be likely to suffer economic loss as a consequence of his negligence.[160] Where the knowledge is of the plaintiff specifically, the case does not

---

151 For instance, liability for escape of dangerous animals or fire.
152 (1868) LR 3 HL 330.
153 *Burnie Port Authority v General Jones Pty Ltd* (1994) 179 CLR 520.
154 (1994) 179 CLR 520.
155 Ibid 556–7 (Mason CJ, Deane, Dawson, Toohey and Gaudron JJ) (emphasis added). See also Section 2.5.6.
156 Those who 'sent forth' inherently dangerous articles were subject to a common law duty to take precautions: *Dominion Natural Gas Co Ltd v Collins* [1909] AC 640, 646 (Lord Dunedin).
157 [1932] AC 562, 596.
158 *Caltex Refineries (Qld) Pty Ltd v Stavar* (2009) 75 NSWLR 649, [103].
159 (1976) 136 CLR 529.
160 *Caltex Oil (Australia) Pty Ltd v The Dredge Willemstad* (1976) 136 CLR 529.

give rise to the concern that the imposition of a duty would 'involve the creation of a liability which is indeterminate as to quantum, identity of plaintiff, or time'.[161]

2.4.2.12   Potential indeterminacy of liability

Indeterminacy of liability may indicate that a duty of care should not be recognised, or that a duty should not extend to a particular type of harm.[162] In *Caltex Refineries (Qld) Pty Ltd v Stavar*, Allsop P noted that indeterminacy, the risk of harm and the reasonable methods of risk interact.[163] In the context of that case (which considered liability for injury caused by asbestos exposure), he noted that with the state of knowledge at the time, the nature of the risk and how to alleviate it, there was no impermissible indeterminacy.[164]

In cases in which the damage is purely economic loss, particularly where it is the result of negligent misstatement, the potential to create a class of plaintiffs whose limits could not be determined was an important consideration to the question of duty. This was noted in *Bryan v Maloney*: '[o]ne policy consideration which may militate against recognition of a relationship of proximity in a category of case involving mere economic loss is the law's concern to avoid the imposition of liability "in an indeterminate amount for an indeterminate time to an indeterminate class".'[165] Indeterminacy in this sense is as to quantum (of potential damage), identity of the plaintiff, or the time period over which damage may occur due to the defendant's negligence. In *Gunns Ltd v Tasmania*[166] the issue was whether the Minister owed a duty of care to those applying for a water licence to make a decision within a reasonable time. In terms of indeterminacy of liability the Court noted the link between the indeterminacy of the class and the capacity to manage the risk of litigation:

> If the suggested duty of care exists, the Minister may well owe anyone whose interests might be affected by such an application a duty to make a decision within a reasonable time. And a breach of that duty could result in the State being exposed to claims for damages for all sorts of economic loss by many and various actual and potential water users.[167]

Indeterminacy of liability is an indicator that a duty of care should not be imposed – at least without other control mechanisms (thus it is typically a 'negative' salient feature); however, it is important to distinguish between the *size* of the potential class of plaintiffs and its indeterminacy.

2.4.2.13   Avoidance of harm

The nature and consequences of any action that can be taken to avoid the harm to the plaintiff will be relevant to the vulnerability of the plaintiff to the actions of the defendant. In the context

---

161 *Hill v Van Erp* (1997) 188 CLR 159, 233–4.
162 *Perre v Apand Pty Ltd* (1999) 198 CLR 180; [1999] HCA 36, [15], [32], [101]–[111], [202], [243], [329], [336]–[338] and [390]–[395]; see also *Collins v Insurance Australia Ltd* (2022) 109 NSWLR 240; [2022] NSWCA 135.
163 (2009) 75 NSWLR 649, [113].
164 *Caltex Refineries (Qld) Pty Ltd v Stavar* (2009) 75 NSWLR 649, [112].
165 (1995) 182 CLR 609, 618 (Mason CJ, Deane and Gaudron JJ), citing *Ultramares Corporation v Touche*, 174 NE 441, 444 (1931) (Cardozo CJ).
166 (2016) 25 Tas R 276.
167 Ibid [21] (Blow CJ).

of *Caltex Refineries (Qld) Pty Ltd v Stavar*, this was relevant to the means to alleviate harm from the risk of asbestos exposure.[168] So, from the perspective of that risk, the avoidance of harm was a matter for consideration to determine the indeterminacy of harm. Avoidance required steps to prevent the domestic exposure (of the kind identified by the medical literature to be a ready category of potential vulnerability) by taking reasonable and appropriate steps to prevent workers returning home in a contaminated state. These steps would involve, but not be limited to, warnings of the risk of wearing contaminated clothes home.[169]

2.4.2.14   Effect on autonomy or freedom

The extent of imposition on the autonomy or freedom of individuals, including the right to pursue one's own interests, was highlighted in the *Review of the Law of Negligence* and subsequent reforms[170] and if it is relevant it favours the argument that no duty is owed. It will often be relevant when it is argued that the defendant should have protected or controlled the plaintiff.

In *Stuart v Kirkland-Veenstra*, the High Court was required to consider whether police officers were negligent in not preventing a person from committing suicide.[171] It was held that, as the circumstances did not trigger the application of the *Mental Health Act 1986* (Vic), no duty in common law was owed to Mr Veenstra or his wife. Gummow, Hayne and Heydon JJ in a joint judgment noted:

> The duty which the plaintiff alleged the police officers owed her late husband was a duty to control *his* actions, not … to prevent harm to a stranger, but to prevent him harming himself. On its face, the proposed duty would mark a significant departure from an underlying value of the common law … Personal autonomy is a value that informs much of the common law. It is a value that is reflected in the law of negligence. The co-existence of a knowledge of a risk of harm and power to avert or minimise that harm does not, without more, give rise to a duty of care at common law … the value described as personal autonomy leaves it to the individual to decide whether to engage in conduct that may cause that individual harm.[172]

2.4.2.15   Conflicting duties

Conflicting duties arising from other principles of law or statute are of particular relevance in cases involving a public authority. The question will often be whether a public authority or an authority with statutory duties or obligations has a separate common law duty of care. In *Hunter and New England Local Health District v McKenna*[173] a mentally ill patient was discharged into the care of Stephen Rose, a friend he subsequently killed. The issue was whether a hospital and/or its doctors owed a duty of care to Mr Rose or his relatives. The High Court noted that the doctors and the hospital, when making the decision to discharge the patient, had other statutory duties. One of these duties was:

---

168   (2009) 75 NSWLR 649.
169   Ibid [112] (Allsop P).
170   *Review of the Law of Negligence* (Final Report, September 2002).
171   (2009) 237 CLR 215; [2009] HCA 15.
172   Ibid, [87]–[89] (emphasis in original).
173   (2014) 253 CLR 270; [2014] HCA 44.

not to detain or continue to detain a person unless the medical superintendent was of the opinion that no other care of a less restrictive kind was appropriate and reasonably available to the person [a duty not] consistent with a common law duty of care [to those] with whom the mentally ill person may come in contact when not detained.[174]

The High Court noted that 'if a suggested duty of care would give rise to inconsistent obligations, that would ordinarily be a reason for denying that the duty exists'.[175]

2.4.2.16   Consistency with statute

In relevant cases the existence or scope of a common law duty of care will be affected – or governed – by legislation that governs the defendant's actions. Again, this criterion will overlap with other salient features, such as conflicting duties, so the discussion in Section 2.4.2.15 about *Hunter and New England Local Health District v McKenna* is also relevant here.[176] The statute may also create an immunity from civil suit or specify a particular forum to determine the matter.

Case: *Electricity Networks Corporation v Herridge Parties* (2022) 406 ALR 1

Facts

A statutory corporation maintained an electricity distribution network (including poles and wires) to deliver electricity to premises. A rotten pole caused a live wire to fall to the ground and cause a bushfire, which damaged a number of properties in Parkerville, Western Australia.

Issue

Did the corporation owe a duty of care to persons in the vicinity of the property to take reasonable steps to avoid harm due to fire to person or property?

Decision

A common law duty of care was owed to landowners. It:

> had a duty to take reasonable care in the exercise of its powers, and the content of that duty relevantly required it to avoid or minimise the risk of injury ... and loss or damage to their property, from the ignition and spread of fire in connection with the delivery of electricity through its electricity distribution system ... The common law imposed that duty in tort ... alongside the rights, duties and liabilities created by statute (at [52]).

Significance

The High Court considered the question of the proposed duty in the context of the statutory framework governing the establishment and functions of the electricity corporation. It noted that

---

174   *Hunter and New England Local Health District v McKenna* (2014) 253 CLR 270; [2014] HCA 44, [29].
175   Ibid, citing *Sullivan v Moody* (2001) 207 CLR 562, 582.
176   (2014) 253 CLR 270; [2014] HCA 44.

the corporation was created as a commercial body and had a profit-making function. The High Court made a detailed review of the provisions of the legislation in order to make its decision.

Notes

The rotted pole which, in falling, caused the fire, was on private land. The public authority, in defence, focused on ownership of the pole. However, the powers and functions of the authority were authorised on both private and public land.

Question

What salient factors might apply to the relationship between a power authority and a landowner?

 Guided response in the eBook

2.4.2.17   Conformance and coherence of structure and fabric of common law

Alongside the need for consistency with statute, the coherence of the common law is relevant where an argument is made for extending the duty of care. This has been described as 'the desirability of, and in some circumstances, need for conformance and coherence in the structure and fabric of the common law'.[177] In early cases, the existence of alternative causes of action more consistent with the interests being preserved was a countervailing policy argument – the courts were reluctant to allow the extension of a duty of care in negligence when an established cause of action was more appropriate to the interests being protected. In *Breen v Williams*, Gaudron and McHugh JJ noted that 'any changes in legal doctrine, brought about by judicial creativity, must "fit" within the body of accepted rules and principles'.[178] This point was reiterated in *Perera v Genworth Financial Mortgage Insurance Pty Ltd* by Leeming JA who noted 'that the law of negligence is but one part of the Australian legal system, and is not to be extended so as to obliterate or undercut other principles, which may serve other important values'.[179] The Court described various forms of incoherence:[180]

- It would be incoherent for a duty of care in tort to be owed by a mortgagee exercising a power of sale to the mortgagor because that would be a misconstruction of the nature of legal and equitable property.
- A duty of care is unlikely to exist if it would cut across areas of law which serve other interests. Indeed, for a long time a duty of care in tort could not coexist with a duty of care in contract. This is no longer the case.[181]

---

177 *Caltex Refineries (Qld) Pty Ltd v Stavar* (2009) 75 NSWLR 649, [103] (Allsop P).
178 (1996) 186 CLR 71, 115.
179 (2017) 94 NSWLR 83, [42].
180 (2017) 94 NSWLR 83.
181 *Astley v Austrust Ltd* (1999) 197 CLR 1; [1999] HCA 6, [44]–[48].

- Courts are resistant to finding a duty of care in tort where it 'subverts' or 'cuts across' well-established defences or immunities.[182] For instance, extending the duty of care in tort into situations which are covered by the law of defamation would undercut existing defences in defamation law.

Case: *Matinca v Coalroc (No 5)* [2022] NSWSC 844

Facts

The plaintiff was injured in a single-car collision over two hours after he had finished work at a remote mine site. He sued his employer.

Issue

Did the employer owe a duty of care to protect against physical injury to the employee which extended to his commute from the site of employment?

Decision

The New South Wales Supreme Court held that the employer's duty of care extended to the commute home.

Significance

While it is well-established that an employer owes a duty of care to an employee, the scope or extent of that duty will vary. In this case the extension of the temporal and spatial scope of the duty, while a question of law, was 'also fact-sensitive depending upon all of the circumstances of the case and the totality of the particular employment relationship between the employer and employee in question' [103]. The Court considered the employer's own policies, including the fatigue management procedures, to find that there was a duty owed to the employee during the commute.

Notes

This case demonstrates a balancing of salient factors. The employer argued that after that point the right to exercise control over the employee ended, and that to extend the duty would be 'inimical to [the employee's] right of personal autonomy including his right of freedom of movement, which would be contrary to fundamental values the common law tended to support.'[183] Conversely, salient factors which would extend the duty to the employee's journey home might include the fact that the employer created the risk by requiring certain patterns of work, the vulnerability of the employee to the impact of the fatigue of the employer's required work patterns (for instance, 12-hour shifts and/or consecutive night shifts), the fact that the employee is responding to the demands of the employment (remote mine sites), and the fact that the employer alone could reduce or manage the risk by altering work systems.[184]

---

182 *CAL No 14 Pty Ltd v Motor Accidents Insurance Board* (2009) 239 CLR 390, 406–7, 410.
183 *Matinca v Coalroc (No 5)* [2022] NSWSC 844, [105].
184 *Kerle v BM Alliance Coal Operations Pty Ltd* (2016) 262 IR 381, [109]–[112] (McMeekin J), a case also involving a single-car collision during a long commute after shiftwork in a mine.

Question

Which are 'affirmative' and which are 'negative' salient features?

 Guided response in the eBook

EMERGING ISSUE

Recent cases have considered whether a duty of care is owed to take measures to prevent harm caused by climate change. In *Sharma by her litigation representative Sister Marie Brigid Arthur v Minister for the Environment*[185] ('Sharma 1') Justice Bromberg in the Federal Court held that the Minister for the Environment owed a duty of care to the plaintiff children when making decisions about whether to approve an extension of a coal extraction project. The decision was successfully appealed in *Minister for the Environment v Sharma*[186] ('Sharma Appeal').

Affirmative salient features supporting a duty were that it was foreseeable to a reasonable person in the position of the Minister that approval of the project would expose the children to a risk of personal injury,[187] that the Minister had complete control over the risk[188] and knowledge of the risk of harm, that the children were vulnerable[189] and reliant[190] and that there was relational proximity between the Minister and the children.[191] The negative salient features included incoherence of the suggested duty with a statutory scheme and with administrative law, although at length no incoherence was found. Indeterminacy of liability was also argued but rejected – the number of potentially affected children was wide, but not indeterminate. The Full Court of the Federal Court allowed the appeal – there was held to be no duty of care in the circumstances.

 ## REVIEW QUESTIONS

(1) What is the current test for determining whether a duty of care is owed to a person?

(2) Explain the 'salient features' test. How is it applied? When is it applied?

---

185 (2021) 391 ALR 1.
186 (2022) 291 FCR 311; [2022] FCAFC 35.
187 (2021) 391 ALR 1, [186].
188 Ibid [271].
189 Ibid [296].
190 Ibid [299].
191 Ibid [313].

(3) What 'gatekeeper' concepts are imposed by the civil liability statute in your jurisdiction before the common law test for establishing duty of care is applied? How has this affected the law (if at all)?

(4) A prisoner who had served the majority of his sentence for aggravated rape of a particular woman (his wife) is released on parole. He subsequently reoffends, targeting another woman on a random basis. Assuming that this is a 'novel' case (ie, there is no existing precedent covering this particular situation)[192] which salient features would you argue to be relevant in this case?

 Guided responses in the eBook

2.5   Special duty relationships

As the common law develops incrementally, plaintiffs seeking damages for negligent acts leading to new types of damage challenge traditional rules. For instance, cases claiming purely economic loss and mental harm necessitated a wider range of considerations to manage potential liability. The courts' approach to different types of damage reflects an unease with the advance of negligence, and various 'control mechanisms'[193] have been adopted and discarded in an attempt to find some coherent principle. At the moment, the courts use the 'salient features' or 'multi-factorial' approach. In some types of case, legislation has also been deployed to manage the growth of liability in negligence or to address particular policy issues.

2.5.1   Duty to prevent psychological injury ('mental harm')
2.5.1.1   What is mental harm?

Mental harm may arise as a result of other injury (in which case it is 'consequential') or it may be pure mental harm. In relation to duty, issues arise in the context of pure mental harm.

The common law has described psychological harm in various ways. The descriptor for this type of harm has changed as the criteria for recovery has changed. Early cases used the term 'nervous shock' and the criteria for recovery included being in the 'zone of danger' and experiencing a sudden shock.[194] Modern cases and legislation use the term 'mental harm' (see Table 2.4).

---

192 This is a thought exercise: the matter has been litigated. See M Cuerden, 'He Should Have Been in Prison' (2006) 72 *Precedent* 28.

193 D Butler, 'Proximity as a Determinant of Duty: The Nervous Shock Litmus Test' (1995) 21(2) *Monash University Law Review* 159, 160.

194 See, eg, *Dulieu v White & Sons* [1901] 2 KB 669.

Table 2.4   Duty of care: mental harm*

Legislation	Section
Civil Law (Wrongs) Act 2002 (ACT)	34
Civil Liability Act 2002 (NSW)	32
Law Reform (Miscellaneous Provisions) Act 1956 (NT)	25
Civil Liability Act 1936 (SA)	33
Civil Liability Act 2002 (Tas)	34
Wrongs Act 1958 (Vic)	72
Civil Liability Act 2002 (WA)	5S

* Additional limitations apply to the damages available for claims involving mental harm: *Civil Liability Act 2002* (NSW) s 30, *Civil Liability Act 1936* (SA) s 53, *Civil Liability Act 2002* (Tas) s 32, *Wrongs Act 1958* (Vic) s 73.

2.5.1.2   Policy factors in mental harm cases

Cases in which compensation has been sought for mental harm have developed incrementally, with courts considering a number of policy factors contributing to their reluctance to widen compensation. Those policy factors have included the following.

THE POTENTIAL RANGE OF LIABILITY

There are competing policy considerations when expanding the range of potential plaintiffs. An expansive precedent must balance two positive but contradictory goals: 'either to provide a remedy to everyone who suffers mental damage as a result of a wrong or extending exposure to tort liability almost without limit.'[195] When liability for psychiatric harm is extended beyond the immediate victim to secondary victims, who suffer mental damage as a result of seeing another injured, there is a risk of extending liability further than would be just.

POTENTIAL DISPROPORTIONALITY OF LIABILITY

Extending liability for pure psychiatric harm could impose a burden on defendants which is disproportionate to the wrongfulness of their actions. Extending the range of potential plaintiffs beyond those immediately involved in the incident without further controls risks an uncontrolled widening of the class, particularly when incidents may be televised or spread by social media.

PROOF OR EVIDENCE

Early cases demonstrated concern that mental harm was not physically discernible, and there remains a greater level of diagnostic uncertainty in cases involving mental harm. These concerns have largely been alleviated.

2.5.1.3   Early decisions

It has long been established that a plaintiff can recover for 'direct nervous shock' resulting from bodily injury suffered by a plaintiff due to the defendant's negligence. This follows

---

195   NN Chin, 'A Remedy for Nervous Shock or Psychiatric Harm – Who Pays?' [2002] *Murdoch University Electronic Journal of Law* 46, 47.

from the wider principle that if a person suffers an actionable loss, such as personal injury or property damage, they can also recover damages for other losses consequential upon the initial loss. The simplest case involves nervous shock due to a negligent act against oneself. In *Dulieu v White & Sons* Dulieu, who was pregnant, was a bartender working behind the bar when White's carriage crashed through the wall of the pub.[196] Dulieu was in shock, and she gave birth to her baby prematurely. The case was the first English authority to permit recovery for negligently inflicted psychiatric damage and is the source of the 'zone of danger' rule which limited the range of plaintiffs who would or could recover this type of loss. Kennedy J stated: '[t]he shock where it operates through the mind, must be a shock which arises from a reasonable risk of immediate personal injury to oneself.'

Conversely *Bourhill v Young* held that a duty was not owed to a bystander by a negligent road user.[197] In that case Bourhill heard, but did not see, a collision between a motorcyclist and a motor car which was due to the negligence of the motorcyclist, Young (who dies as a result of the crash). Bourhill was pregnant at the time, and subsequently miscarried and suffered nervous shock. In an action against the executor of the motorcyclist's estate, it was held that no duty was owed to Bourhill. Lord Wright said:

> My Lords, that damage by mental shock may give a cause of action is now well established and it is not disputed … If, however, the appellant has a cause of action it is because of a wrong to herself. She cannot build on a wrong to someone else … I cannot accept that John Young could reasonably have foreseen, or, more correctly, the reasonable hypothetical observer could reasonably have foreseen, the likelihood that anyone placed as the appellant was, could be affected in the manner in which she was.[198]

Early cases maintained the zone of danger analysis. In *Chester v Municipality of Waverley*, the Court refused to extend the duty of care to the mother of a child killed due to the negligence of the Council.[199] The defendant Council excavated a trench which filled with water. The plaintiff's son, aged seven-and-a-half years, fell into the trench and drowned. The plaintiff was present when his dead body was recovered and received a severe nervous shock. Latham J noted the difficulty of stating the limits of the duty proposed:

> If a duty of the character suggested exists at all, it is not really said that it should be confined to mothers of children who are injured. It must extend to some wider class – but to what class? There appears to be no reason why it should not extend to other relatives or to all other persons, whether they are relatives or not. If this is the true principle of law, then a person who is guilty of negligence with the result that A is injured will be liable in damages to B, C, D and any other persons who receive a nervous shock (as distinguished from passing fright or distress) at any time upon perceiving the results of the negligence, whether in disfigurement of person, physical injury, or death.[200]

---

196 [1901] 2 KB 669.
197 [1943] AC 92.
198 Ibid 111 (Lord Wright).
199 (1939) 62 CLR 1.
200 Ibid 7.

In dissent, Evatt J noted the special vulnerability of parents, picturing the plight of the mother, and this dissent prompted the NSW Parliament, and subsequently two Australian territories, to legislate to allow recovery for nervous shock where it was suffered by certain categories of family members.

In states that did not enact the legislation, the common law continued to develop until *Jaensch v Coffey*, when the High Court extended recovery to the wife of a victim who had attended the 'aftermath' of the accident.[201] The plaintiff, the injured man's wife, was not physically injured in the accident, did not see or hear it or its consequences, and was at no time in the area of potential danger. She did, however, hear and see enough at the hospital to become afraid that her husband might die, and developed a psychiatric illness because of this. The High Court held that the plaintiff was owed a duty to take reasonable care to prevent mental harm.

2.5.1.4 Development of liability

The development of precedent in relation to nervous shock has been incremental, based upon the category of relationship between the person suffering the nervous shock and the person whose injury gave rise to the nervous shock. Over the course of the decisions, courts have imposed a number of limitations on the range of duty, for instance:

*   whether the plaintiff was personally in danger
*   whether the plaintiff witnessed the incident giving rise to the injury
*   whether the plaintiff was related to the injured person
*   the closeness of the relationship[202]
*   whether the incident would have caused psychological harm to a person of ordinary fortitude.

However, in *Tame v New South Wales; Annetts v Australian Stations Pty Ltd* the High Court held that the relevant criteria for the existence of a duty were the same as in all negligence cases.[203] The High Court dealt together with two quite different fact situations in which the plaintiffs suffered mental harm. *Annetts v Australian Stations Pty Ltd* involved a case of mental harm to parents as a result of the death of their son, James. James had been employed by Australian Stations at 16 years of age. He was sent to work alone 100 kilometres away and was subsequently found to be missing. His parents were informed by telephone and Mr Annetts collapsed. James's parents made several trips to search for him, but his body was not found for five months. Mr and Mrs Annetts suffered psychiatric illness upon hearing that James had disappeared and later when told of his death.

In *Tame v New South Wales*, there was a motor vehicle accident between the plaintiff and a drunk driver. A police officer accidentally noted a high blood-alcohol reading against both drivers in the Police Accident Report. This mistake was identified and corrected quickly; however, the plaintiff alleged that she had suffered psychiatric injury after learning of the error. In judgment Gaudron J noted:

201 (1984) 155 CLR 549.
202 *Tame v New South Wales; Annetts v Australian Stations Pty Ltd* (2002) 211 CLR 317, 405 (Hayne J) ('requirements of nearness, hearness and dearness, or, as they have also been called, physical proximity, temporal proximity and relational proximity').
203 (2002) 211 CLR 317.

> The three 'rules' in issue may conveniently be described as the 'sudden shock rule', the 'normal fortitude rule' and the 'direct perception rule'. Whatever purpose those 'rules' might hitherto have served in the development of the law relating to pure psychiatric injury, they now serve to emphasise that … something more than foreseeability of the likelihood of harm of the kind in issue is necessary before a defendant will be held to owe a duty of care to take reasonable steps to avoid a risk of that kind.[204]

The additional factors, alongside foreseeability, that would point to the existence of a duty to take reasonable care to prevent psychological harm included the knowledge of the employers in *Annetts*, relied upon by the plaintiff to ensure the safety of their son; the limited class of potential plaintiffs (reducing the potential for indeterminate liability); the defendant's control over the conditions of employment; and the vulnerability of the employee (and the parents). Negative features included the potential inconsistency with statutory and other duties in *Tame*.[205]

Civil liability statutes in most jurisdictions provide additional constraints. Section 32 of the *Civil Liability Act 2002* (NSW) is representative, requiring that a duty of care is not to be found unless 'the defendant ought to have foreseen that a person of normal fortitude might, in the circumstances of the case, suffer a recognised psychiatric illness' (see Table 2.4). In the case of pure mental harm, the legislation in most jurisdictions reinstates some of the previous common law requirements, requiring the court to consider:

- whether or not the mental harm was suffered as the result of a sudden shock
- whether the plaintiff witnessed, at the scene, a person being killed, injured or put in peril
- the nature of the relationship between the plaintiff and any person killed, injured or put in peril
- whether or not there was a pre-existing relationship between the plaintiff and the defendant.[206]

Some legislation applies additional restrictions which apply at the point of damage, rather than duty of care. Section 53 of the *Civil Liability Act 1936* (SA) restricts the award of damages for mental harm to cases in which the injured person was physically injured or at the scene of the accident, or was a parent, spouse, domestic partner or child of a person killed, injured or endangered in the accident.[207] The South Australian legislation was applied in *King v Philcox*.[208] Philcox developed a major depressive disorder after the death of his brother in a motor vehicle accident caused by the negligence of George King. Philcox heard of the accident a few hours after it had occurred. At that point he realised that he had driven past the location of the accident earlier that day while the vehicle in

---

204   Ibid 339.
205   *Tame v New South Wales* (2002) 211 CLR 317.
206   *Civil Liability Act 2002* (Tas) s 34 has different wording, enumerating only the requirements that 'the circumstances of the case include the following: (a) whether or not the mental harm was suffered as the result of a sudden shock; (b) whether or not there was a pre-existing relationship between the plaintiff and the defendant.'
207   Equivalent limitations are specified in *Civil Liability Act 2002* (NSW) s 30 and *Civil Liability Act 2002* (Tas) s 32.
208   (2015) 255 CLR 304; [2015] HCA 19.

which his brother was trapped and dying was still there. The Court held that under s 33 of the *Civil Liability Act 1936* (SA):

> the foreseeability of risk must relate to 'a person of normal fortitude in the plaintiff's position'. The circumstances set out in s 33(2) are not necessary conditions of the existence of a duty of care. Rather they are to be treated as relevant to the assessment of that foreseeability of harm that is a necessary condition.[209]

French CJ and Kiefel and Gageler JJ noted that it was 'not strictly necessary to decide whether the Full Court erred in holding that King owed a duty of care not to cause pure mental harm to Ryan Philcox', because of the disentitling provision in s 53. However, their Honours did go on to interpret the wording of s 33, the primary 'duty' provision in this case, and noted:

> At common law, as under s 33, the existence of a duty of care not to cause another person pure mental harm is dependent upon a number of variables which inform the foreseeability of risk. Section 33 does not prescribe any particular pre-existing relationship. It does not require the plaintiff to have witnessed at the scene a person being killed, injured or put in peril. It does not require a sudden shock. It does require that the defendant has in contemplation a person of normal fortitude in the plaintiff's position … To say that a duty of care is owed to a parent, spouse, child, fellow employee or rescuer of a victim is not to say that it cannot be owed to the sibling of a victim. The terms of s 33 are consistent with that approach for they include, as one of the circumstances relevant to the foreseeability that is a necessary condition of the duty of care, 'the nature of the relationship between the plaintiff and any person killed, injured or put in peril'. A sibling relationship is a circumstance of that character.[210]

2.5.2   Duty to prevent pure economic loss

Economic loss may arise as a result of other loss (in which case it is 'consequential' economic loss) or it may be pure economic loss. The latter may be due to a number of circumstances, for instance:

- negligent misrepresentation
- economic loss as a result of regulatory activity
- negligent performance of a service
- negligent supply of shoddy goods or structures.

2.5.2.1   The difference between pure and consequential economic loss

Economic loss sustained in conjunction with physical injury routinely attracts compensation. For instance, if the negligent actions of a defendant caused physical injury, as a result of which the plaintiff was unable to work, the economic loss suffered as a result of that injury

---

209   Ibid [13] (French CJ, Kiefel and Gageler JJ).
210   Ibid [29].

would routinely be compensated. However, economic loss which is not accompanied by other loss was not always compensated.

The early position is represented by *Cattle v Stockton Waterworks Co.*[211] This case established the rule that a plaintiff was not entitled to recover for economic or financial loss not consequential upon damage to his person or property. In that case, the plaintiff entered into an agreement with Knights to construct a tunnel under a road for a fixed sum. The job became more expensive because of a leak from the defendant's pipes which they failed to fix. The plaintiff sought compensation for the extra cost of completing the tunnel but could not sue in his own name for the loss he had sustained.

The Court was particularly concerned about the potential of indeterminate liability; it said that to allow an action to a contractor whose activity had become less profitable because of damage to the land on which he was working would be to

> establish an authority for saying that [in a case such as where a landowner was liable for flooding of a neighbouring mine], the defendant would be liable, not only to an action by the owner of the drowned mine, and by such of his workmen as had their tools or clothes destroyed, but also to an action by every workman and person employed in the mine, who in consequence of its stoppage made less wages than he would otherwise have done.[212]

2.5.2.2   Pure economic loss due to negligent misstatement

The reluctance of courts to provide compensation for pure economic loss was demonstrated over a series of cases. Typically, policy considerations were dominant in precluding recovery – particularly the potential for indeterminate liability. This situation changed, theoretically at least, with *Hedley Byrne & Co Ltd v Heller & Partners Ltd.*[213] In this UK case the plaintiff was an advertising firm. The defendant was a merchant bank. The plaintiff placed, on behalf of its client, Easipower Ltd, substantial orders for advertising time on television programs and for advertising space in certain newspapers. The advertisements were placed on credit terms, so the plaintiff would be financially exposed if Easipower did not pay. To protect itself the plaintiff made enquiries through its own bank to determine the creditworthiness of Easipower, who was a customer of the defendant. The defendant bank gave the company satisfactory references. These references turned out to be unjustified. On the basis of the bank's references, the plaintiff did not cancel the orders for advertising. Easipower subsequently failed, and the plaintiff had to pay the bill of some £17 000.

The House of Lords clearly established that recovery for negligent misstatement was possible, even when the misstatement resulted in purely economic loss. Several members of the House of Lords said the requirement of physical injury was illogical. Lord Devlin said:

> If, irrespective of contract, a doctor negligently advises a patient that he can safely pursue his occupation and he cannot and the patient's health suffers and he loses his livelihood, the patient has a remedy. But if the doctor negligently advises him that he cannot safely pursue his occupation when in fact he can and he loses his livelihood,

---

211 (1875) LR 10 QB 453.
212 Ibid 457 (Blackburn J).
213 [1964] AC 465.

there is said to be no remedy. Unless, of course, the patient was a private patient, and the doctor accepted half a guinea for his trouble: then the patient can recover all.[214]

In principle, the plaintiff could recover damages. However, in *Hedley Byrne* there was a disclaimer clause which was an effective defence.

In the Australian case of *Mutual Life & Citizens' Assurance Co Ltd v Evatt*, the High Court ruled on the negligent provision of advice causing economic loss.[215] The respondent sought advice from MLC on the investment performance of HG Palmer, which was a subsidiary of one of the MLC companies. He was advised that HG Palmer would continue to be financially stable and that it would be safe to invest further in it. On the strength of this advice, Mr Evatt did invest further in it and suffered when the company subsequently went into liquidation. The High Court gave judgment in favour of the plaintiff in a 3:2 majority. Barwick CJ said that 'a cause of action for breach of a duty of care in the gratuitous giving of information and advice by a person who does not profess a calling or particular capacity can be maintained'.[216] On appeal, the Privy Council disagreed on the basis that MLC's business did not include giving advice on investments and that it did not claim to have the necessary skill or competence to give such advice. However, the approach of the High Court was subsequently adopted in *Shaddock & Associates Pty Ltd v Parramatta City Council (No 1)*.[217] Shaddock & Associates were purchasing a piece of land in Parramatta. Solicitors for the plaintiff rang the City Council and asked an unidentified Council employee if the land was going to be affected by road-widening proposals. The employee replied 'no'. The solicitor then gave the Council a standard printed enquiry form on which was the same question: Is the land in question affected by any road-widening proposals? No reply was given to the enquiry and the plaintiff gave evidence that the practice of the Council was to give an answer if road-widening works were proposed and to leave it blank if they were not. In fact, there were road-widening proposals. As a result of these proposals the plaintiff suffered financial loss of $174 000.

The defendants relied on the Privy Council decision in *Mutual Life & Citizens' Assurance Co Ltd v Evatt*[218] and argued that a duty of care would only arise where the defendant providing the information in the course of business professed to have skill or competence in the giving of that information. The High Court adopted its own approach in *Mutual Life & Citizens' Assurance Co Ltd v Evatt*[219] (not the subsequent Privy Council decision) and found in favour of the plaintiff, Shaddock. The Court held that a person has a duty to take reasonable care in the provision of information or advice if he or she carries on a business or profession in the course of which advice or information is provided. The Court also said that it is not necessary that the person providing the information knew the precise purpose to which the information was being put; it was sufficient that the defendant knew that the plaintiff was asking for the information for a serious purpose.

The case of *Shaddock* involved information given in response to a request.[220] However, there are cases in which information was transmitted to a third party, or was not given in

---

214   *Hedley Byrne & Co Ltd v Heller & Partners Ltd* [1964] AC 465.
215   (1968) 122 CLR 556; on appeal to the Privy Council (1970) 122 CLR 628.
216   (1968) 122 CLR 556, 577–8.
217   *Shaddock & Associates Pty Ltd v Parramatta City Council (No 1)* (1981) 150 CLR 225 ('Shaddock').
218   (1970) 122 CLR 628.
219   (1968) 122 CLR 556.
220   (1981) 150 CLR 225.

response to a particular request. The Court in *San Sebastian Pty Ltd v Minister Administering the Environmental Planning and Assessment Act 1979 (NSW)* noted that there is no need for a request by the plaintiff for information or advice.[221] The existence of an antecedent request may be helpful in demonstrating reliance, but it is not crucial.

In *Hill v Van Erp*,[222] when the High Court finally revised the role of proximity in novel cases, the approach to the determination of duty of care in a case involving negligent misstatement causing purely economic loss was again in question (see Section 2.4.2.7).

Esanda was an opportunity for the High Court to give guidance on the new approach,[223] but the decision did not give a fully developed approach to the question of duty. It was a striking-out application, and the case was not fully argued. What was clear in all the judgments was that something more than foreseeability was required; whether that was called proximity or not was not to the point.

Case: *Esanda Finance Corporation Ltd v Peat Marwick Hungerfords* (1997) 188 CLR 241

Facts

Esanda Finance Corporation ('Esanda'), a finance provider, lent money to Excel and associated companies. Esanda accepted a guarantee from Excel and purchased debts from Excel on terms which included an indemnity by Excel against any shortfall. Excel subsequently went into liquidation and Esanda suffered financial loss. It sought to recover the loss from Peat Marwick Hungerfords, who were Esanda's auditors. Esanda claimed negligence, arguing that Peat Marwick Hungerfords were negligent in their conduct of Excel's accounts. The action before the High Court was a strikeout application – that is, an application to have the proceedings struck out as disclosing no cause of action. Because of this the Court only considered whether the statement of claim lodged by Esanda was capable of giving rise to a duty of care. Figure 2.2 represents the facts in *Esanda*.

Figure 2.2   The facts in *Esanda Finance Corporation Ltd v Peat Marwick Hungerfords* (1997) 188 CLR 241

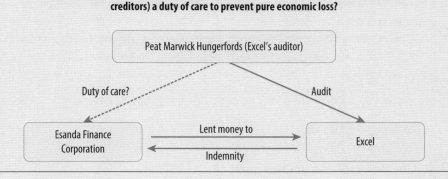

Does Peat Marwick Hungerfords (Excel's auditor) owe Esanda Finance Corporation (Excel's creditors) a duty of care to prevent pure economic loss?

221 (1986) 162 CLR 340.
222 (1997) 188 CLR 159.
223 Ibid 241.

Issue

Was a duty of care owed by the auditors of a company to the creditors (finance providers) of a company?

Decision

The Court found that the auditors did not owe a duty of care to the creditors.

Significance

At the time this case was heard (the late 1990s), there was significant uncertainty as to the extent of an auditor's liability. There were a number of actions and potential actions against auditors as a result of a financial downturn which had caused financial loss to creditors, shareholders and others. Many hoped that the High Court would provide a 'bright line' rule clarifying the test for duty of care, but because there were a number of separate judgments, the case did not provide real certainty. Nonetheless, this case is an early example of the application of salient features.

Notes

The High Court dismissed Esanda's claim that Peat Marwick Hungerford owed it a duty of care. The policy reasons for expanding the liability of auditors, and those for restricting liability, were considered. Some of these factors were detailed by McHugh J, who said they might include the following:

- If a duty was owed to third parties, the supply of auditing services would fall because of an inability to obtain insurance or the costs of insurance, and the consequent increase in fees.
- The administration of the court system would be adversely affected by a large number of lengthy claims involving auditors.
- The interests of justice in allowing a claim must be balanced against the type of plaintiff involved. Investors, creditors and others who read and rely on audit reports and financial statements are not the equivalent of ordinary consumers. They are sophisticated and financially literate. The demands of corrective justice do not require that these people should be able to pass the loss on to auditors.
- If the risk passed to the auditors, they would not be able to guard against that risk and the risk would be difficult to determine.
- The Court had insufficient information on who is the most efficient absorber of the loss.

Question

Why was the effect on auditors one of the potential policy implications of extending liability in this case?

 Guided response in the eBook

2.5.2.3   Pure economic loss due to other factors

Pure economic loss can arise due to a number of other events: regulatory action, physical damage to property from which another would obtain a benefit, negligent performance of a service, or the acquisition of shoddy goods or structures, for instance. Reluctance to impose liability for purely economic loss characterised early cases. Even after *Hedley Byrne* (in 1964) theoretically allowed recovery for purely economic loss as a result of negligent misstatement, there was still a marked reluctance to allow recovery in the United Kingdom.[224]

Earlier English cases concerning the negligent infliction of purely economic loss denied recovery on the basis that pure economic loss was not recoverable except in cases of negligent misstatement.[225] This position changed in *Caltex Oil (Australia) Pty Ltd v The Dredge Willemstad*.[226] In that case the defendant's knowledge of the potential for economic loss as a result of the defendant's actions was significant to the successful claim. There was also no danger, in this case, that liability would be indeterminate.

The next analogous case to come before the High Court was *Perre v Apand Pty Ltd*.[227] In this case, Apand introduced onto the Sparnons' farm seed potatoes that were infected with bacterial wilt. This caused that farm, and a number of neighbouring farms, to be put into quarantine. Perre owned a neighbouring farm that did not suffer bacterial wilt but was put into quarantine, so suffered pure economic loss. The High Court found that a duty of care was owed to the neighbouring farms. No general principle allowing easy application emerges from the case as all seven Justices delivered separate judgments. A number of relevant factors were identified and many of these are now included in the modern list of salient features.

2.5.3   Special defendants: occupiers

Occupiers' liability is liability of the person in control of 'premises' to those injured due to the state of those premises. At common law 'premises' means more than land; it includes fixtures on land such as bridges, wharves and diving towers. Some movable structures such as cars, scaffolding and ships are also 'premises'. The basis of the duty owed by an occupier in relation to the physical state or condition of the premises is control over, and knowledge of, the state of the premises.[228]

2.5.3.1   Meaning of occupier

The test to determine whether a person is an occupier is the degree of control a person has over the premises. In *Wheat v Lacon & Co* the House of Lords considered the definition.[229] The premises were a public house with a flat above, both of which were owned by the defendant. The licensees of the public house were permitted by the defendant to have

224 *Hedley Byrne & Co Ltd v Heller & Partners Ltd* [1964] AC 465.
225 See, eg, *Weller & Co v Foot and Mouth Disease Research Institute* (1966) 1 QB 569; *SCM (United Kingdom) Ltd v WJ Whittall & Son Ltd* [1971] 1 QB 337; *Spartan Steel & Alloys Ltd v Martin & Co (Contractors) Ltd* [1973] 1 QB 27.
226 (1976) 136 CLR 529.
227 (1999) 198 CLR 180.
228 *Commissioner for Railways v McDermott* [1967] 1 AC 169, 186.
229 [1966] AC 552.

paying guests. A guest was killed while descending a poorly lit staircase, which only had a partial handrail. The defendant was held to be the occupier of the premises on the basis of their control over the premises, such that they should have realised that any failure of care on their part may result in injury to a person coming there.[230] The licensee, however, was not an occupier because, as a servant of the brewery, they were not responsible for the condition of the premises. The test is, therefore, a factual one: does the person have some control, any control, over the premises such that they can prevent injury to visitors?

2.5.3.2   Early law: categories of entrant

The common law approach to an occupier's standard of care was a 'highly complex pattern of legal rules' which fitted the plaintiff into one of a number of categories, before assigning the standard to be applied to each (see Table 2.2).

2.5.3.3   Modern law

The technical rules for distinguishing between categories of entrant survived in most jurisdictions in Australia[231] until *Australian Safeway Stores Pty Ltd v Zaluzna*.[232] The current law relating to duty is expressed in *Zaluzna* and represented in cases such as *Libra Collaroy Pty Ltd v Bhide*.[233] In *Bhide* it was clear that the landlord of residential premises owed a duty to tenants, and household members and the tenant owed a duty to occupants and to entrants.[234] The landlord's duties were not non-delegable and could be delegated to a managing agent.[235]

The events considered in *Australian Safeway Stores Pty Ltd v Zaluzna* occurred in a supermarket in Melbourne.[236] A customer slipped and fell heavily because the supermarket foyer was wet due to rain. A majority of the High Court concluded that there was

> neither warrant nor reason for continuing to search for fine distinctions between the so-called special duty enunciated by Willes J [in *Indermaur v Danes*] and the general duty established by *Donoghue v Stevenson*. The same is true of the so-called special duties resting on an occupier of land with respect to persons entering as licensees or trespassers.[237]

The demise of the technical distinctions between invitees, licensees and trespassers did not render the circumstances of entry entirely irrelevant. It may, for instance, be of great

---

230 Ibid 577 (Denning LJ).
231 In England the distinctions between lawful entrants were abolished by the *Occupiers' Liability Act 1957* (UK). Australian legislatures were slow to follow suit, and those that did were swiftly overtaken by the common law. Prior to *Australian Safeway Stores Pty Ltd v Zaluzna* (1987) 162 CLR 479, Victoria had passed the *Occupiers' Liability Act 1983* (Vic) (now pt IIA of the *Wrongs Act 1958* (Vic)), which abolished the old technical distinctions.
232 (1987) 162 CLR 479.
233 [2017] NSWCA 196.
234 Ibid [176]–[177].
235 See Section 2.5.6.
236 (1987) 162 CLR 479.
237 *Australian Safeway Stores Pty Ltd v Zaluzna* (1987) 162 CLR 479, 487 (Mason, Wilson, Deane and Dawson JJ).

importance in determining whether there has been a breach.[238] The circumstances of the entry onto premises will affect the calculus of negligence in the sense that entry by one class of persons, say, a trespasser, is usually less probable than entry by a licensee. The precautions taken by a reasonable landowner to guard against injury to a trespasser would be correspondingly less onerous.[239]

2.5.4   Special defendants: public authorities

Public authorities, sometimes called statutory authorities, are bodies set up by statute for a public service. That means that they have to exercise their powers in the public interest, not just as they choose, and they may be liable as a matter of public law if they exercise their powers outside the public interest. Thus, the first and most obvious remedy if a public authority is doing something wrong is recourse to administrative law. There is also a tort called 'breach of statutory duty' which is a separate tort (discussed in Section 13.2). However, it is also possible to sue public authorities in negligence in certain circumstances.

At common law the Crown could not be sued because it would be a contradiction for the King to be subject to his own courts. The position now is that public authorities are to be treated, so far as possible, just like other defendants. However, there is a need for special principles in the case of negligence actions against public bodies. Liability has been excluded where 'the purposes or functions peculiar to government'[240] gave rise to the potential liability, or where the Crown's prerogative or traditional immunities are involved. Accordingly, government bodies have frequently enjoyed some level of immunity in relation to matters of 'policy' – as opposed to the implementation of policy (called the 'policy/operational' distinction).

In many cases liability arises from the authority's occupation of premises or land.[241] These cases are to be determined more or less in the same way as other occupiers' liability cases, subject to statutory provisions and resource allocation concerns. Other cases involve negligent misstatement,[242] or a public authority being held liable for causing physical injury.[243]

However, there are some cases where the facts do not fall within a common law category. The relationship between these matters and the 'salient features' approach may not be readily apparent; in *Fuller-Wilson v New South Wales*[244] Basten JA in the New South Wales Court of Appeal noted that features compiled by Allsop P in *Stavar* 'were expressed in terms equally applicable to private parties and to public authorities' but that 'a different focus is required with respect to public authorities'.[245] In particular, the court has to take account of:

238 *Wyong Shire Council v Shirt* (1980) 146 CLR 40, 47–8 (Mason J).
239 Prior to *Australian Safeway Stores Pty Ltd v Zaluzna* (1987) 162 CLR 479, Victoria had passed the *Occupiers' Liability Act 1983* (Vic) (now pt IIA of the *Wrongs Act 1958* (Vic)), which abolished the old technical distinctions. However, the effect of the legislation was quickly overtaken by the common law.
240 *Maguire v Simpson* (1977) 139 CLR 362, 393–5 (Stephen J), 408 (Murphy J); *Commonwealth v Evans Deakin Industries Ltd* (1986) 161 CLR 254.
241 *Nagle v Rottnest Island Authority* (1993) 177 CLR 423; *Romeo v Conservation Commission (NT)* (1998) 192 CLR 431.
242 *Shaddock & Associates Pty Ltd v Parramatta City Council (No 1)* (1981) 150 CLR 225.
243 *Nader v Urban Transit Authority (NSW)* (1985) 2 NSWLR 501.
244 [2018] NSWCA 218.
245 Ibid [15].

- the legislation creating the statutory authority
- the need to maintain coherence in the law
- the need to 'avoid the imposition of a duty which may be inconsistent with, or incompatible with the public duties imposed by statute or the common law'[246]
- any special factors applicable to the statutory authority which may negative a duty of care.

The Civil Liability Acts also supplement the common law requirements, requiring consideration of the functions, activities and resources of the authority. The main relevant sections are listed in Table 2.5.

Table 2.5   Duty of care: public authorities

Legislation	Section(s)
Civil Law (Wrongs) Act 2002 (ACT)	110, 114
Civil Liability Act 2002 (NSW)	42, 44, 45, 46
Civil Liability Act 2003 (Qld)	35, 37
Civil Liability Act 1936 (SA)	42
Civil Liability Act 2002 (Tas)	38, 41, 42, 43
Wrongs Act 1958 (Vic)	82, 83, 85
Civil Liability Act 2002 (WA)	Part 1C (ss 5U–5AA)

The provisions can differ in detail between jurisdictions so care should be taken when considering cases from different jurisdictions. They require analysis of the legislation establishing and governing the public authority in question. As a fairly typical example, s 42 of the *Civil Liability Act 2002* (NSW) requires consideration of whether the authority's functions are limited by resource limitations that are reasonably available to the authority, and the general allocation of resources by the authority is not open to challenge. The functions are to be determined by reference to the broad range of its activities, not just the matter at issue. Compliance with general procedures and standards for the exercise of functions is evidence of proper exercise of functions.

The duty of care of a public authority was considered in *Graham Barclay Oysters Pty Ltd v Ryan*[247] which involved a failure to regulate for the contamination of water in the context of the supply and consumption of contaminated oysters. The oysters were grown in and harvested from Wallis Lake in New South Wales. Ryan consumed a number of oysters contaminated with the hepatitis A virus caused by rainfall run-off contaminated with faecal matter. Ryan was diagnosed with hepatitis A and sued the Council and the State (as well as other parties) in negligence. The main issues were whether the Council and the State owed a duty to carry out the functions which would have prevented the injury.

The High Court revisited the question of the liability of public authorities in *Electricity Networks Corporation v Herridge Parties*.[248] Western Power, a statutory corporation, operated an electricity distribution system to supply electricity to consumers. It contracted

---

246 Ibid [75] (Basten JA).
247 (2002) 211 CLR 540; [2002] HCA 54.
248 (2022) 406 ALR 1 (Kiefel CJ, Gageler, Gordon, Edelman and Steward JJ).

with another company (Thiess) to carry out inspections and repairs of poles and cables. A deteriorated electricity pole and the electrical cable connected to it fell to the ground and caused a bushfire, which damaged a large area in Western Australia. So this case concerned the exercise of statutory power (rather than the wrongful failure to exercise power – an omission to act). The High Court noted that the 'focus of the analysis is upon the relevant legislation – the powers that have been exercised in the performance of the authority's statutory functions – and the positions occupied by the parties.'[249] If this analysis gives rise to a common law duty of care, that duty is in addition to rights and obligations created by the statute.

2.5.4.1   Interpretation of the relevant statute/s

The decision as to whether a duty of care is owed by the public authority must be made in the context of the statutes empowering the authority to carry out the actions or make the decision being considered. The statute which creates and empowers the statutory authority operates 'in the milieu of the common law'; unless the legislation excludes liability, the common law will apply.[250] Aside from this possibility, the statute will have an impact on the existence or otherwise of a common law duty of care. As Gummow and Hayne JJ stated in *Graham Barclay Oysters Pty Ltd v Ryan*:

> The existence or otherwise of a common law duty of care allegedly owed by a statutory authority turns on a close examination of the terms, scope and purpose of the relevant statutory regime. The question is whether that regime erects or facilitates a relationship between the authority and a class of persons that, in all the circumstances, displays sufficient characteristics answering the criteria for intervention by the tort of negligence.[251]

If the reading of the statute *does* indicate that a common law duty of care is owed, the duty in tort exists *alongside* the rights, duties and liabilities created by statute. If there is no statutory duty of care, the common law will not usually impose one, except in certain limited circumstances.

In many circumstances there will be more than one statute relevant to the functions of the public authority in the context of the case. In *Fuller-Wilson v New South Wales*[252] for instance it was argued that the functions of the police in the context of the case were to be determined by reference to the *State Emergency and Rescue Management Act 1989* (NSW), the *Essential Services Act 1988* (NSW), the *Coroners Act 2009* (NSW), the *Law Enforcement (Powers and Responsibilities) Act 2002* (NSW) and the *Police Act 1990* (NSW). In that case police attended at the scene of a motor vehicle accident at which a person had been killed. Police and other state officers had to remove the body and clothing from the scene, but some bodily remains were left at the scene. These were recognised by members of the victim's family who visited the scene, who claimed compensation for psychological harm. At first instance the primary judge had summarily dismissed the claim on the basis that no

249 *Electricity Networks Corporation v Herridge Parties* (2022) 406 ALR 1, [27].
250 *Crimmins v Stevedoring Industry Finance Committee* (1999) 200 CLR 1.
251 (2002) 211 CLR 540; [2002] HCA 54, [146].
252 [2018] NSWCA 218.

duty of care was owed. An appeal was allowed, the Court of Appeal finding that although the weight of authority supported the view that no duty was owed, 'there is a reasonable argument that the common law in Australia should recognise a wider scope of liability'[253] and thus the proceedings should not have been summarily dismissed.

2.5.4.2   Common law duty of care

As well as an interpretation of the relevant statute, the Court in *Graham Barclay Oysters Pty Ltd v Ryan* noted that where a novel duty was being urged salient features should be consulted, focusing on the relevant legislation and the positions of the parties:

> It ordinarily will be necessary to consider the degree and nature of control exercised by the authority over the risk of harm that eventuated; the degree of vulnerability of those who depend on the proper exercise by the authority of its powers; and the consistency or otherwise of the asserted duty of care with the terms, scope and purpose of the relevant statute. In particular categories of case, some features will be of increased significance.[254]

Civil liability legislation in state jurisdictions has inserted additional requirements: see Table 2.5.

2.5.5   Special defendants: a duty to control others

To what extent must a person who has control of another person take steps to prevent that other person causing injury or damage to some third person? Jane Stapleton has called this an issue of 'peripheral liability' – liability of a defendant for the actions of a more blameworthy person. Stapleton noted in 1995 that 'the most noteworthy and troublesome form of this phenomenon [of peripheral liability] is the increase in the past 20 years in the number of novel claims alleging that the defendant had negligently failed to control or deter the active injuring party or warn the plaintiff about the latter'.[255] This species is considered to be most problematic because 'there can very often be a mismatch between who is being sued and the perceived relative unimportance of that party's role in producing the damage: in other words, very often, the party who is alleged to have failed to control the third party is peripheral in a causal sense'.[256] She notes:

> To impose liability in such a case carries two dangers. First, it is often true that a plaintiff could plausibly implicate the omissions of very many parties to control the third party who in fact injured him or her. Hence to hold liable all those whose omissions were so implicated would signal a vast inhibition on freedom. Secondly, imposing liability on a peripheral party who had merely failed to control a third party deflects attention away from the party or parties directly and principally responsible for the damage.[257]

---

253   Ibid [80] (Bastin JA).
254   (2002) 211 CLR 540; [2002] HCA 54, [149] (Gummow and Hayne JJ).
255   J Stapleton, 'Duty of Care: Peripheral Parties and Alternative Opportunities for Deterrence' (1995) 111(2) *Law Quarterly Review* 301, 311.
256   Ibid.
257   Ibid.

An early analysis of the relevant relationship was made in *Smith v Leurs*,[258] quoted with approval in *Dorset Yacht Co Ltd v Home Office*[259] and subsequently by Lord Mackay in the leading judgment in *Smith v Littlewoods Organisation Ltd*.[260] In *Smith v Leurs* Dixon J said:

> one man may be responsible to another for the harm done to the latter ... on the ground that the act of the third person could not have taken place but for his own fault or breach of duty ... It is, however, exceptional to find in the law a duty to control another's actions to prevent harm to strangers. The general rule is that one man is under no duty of controlling another man to prevent his doing damage to a third.[261]

There are some well-established situations in which a person owes a duty to control another. Examples are schools and parents owing a duty to control young children,[262] and prison authorities to control inmates.[263] In the absence of such a relationship of control, courts are reluctant to hold one person liable for the actions of a third party. For instance, in *Hill v Chief Constable of West Yorkshire Police*, police were held not to owe a duty of care to a plaintiff injured by third parties.[264]

In *Modbury Triangle Shopping Centre Pty Ltd v Anzil*[265] the Court had to consider the position of the defendant, who was the owner of a shopping centre, when an employee of a tenant of the centre was injured in an attack by a third party in the car park as the employee was leaving work.[266] The lights of the car park were not turned on, and the employee was set upon and injured by assailants. He sued the owners of the shopping centre as occupiers. The High Court held that a duty to take reasonable care to prevent harm from the criminal behaviour of third parties was not owed:

> [The] appellant had no control over the behaviour of the men who attacked the first respondent, and no knowledge or forewarning of what they planned to do ... The inference that they would have been deterred by lighting in the car park is at least debatable. The men were not enticed to the car park by the appellant. They were strangers to the parties.[267]

Accordingly, there was no duty to take reasonable care to protect the plaintiff from this risk.

2.5.6   Non-delegable duties

Non-delegable duties are 'duties not just to take care, but to see or ensure that care is taken'.[268] Although a non-delegable duty normally arises where one person has engaged another to perform a task or obligation, it may also arise in other defined situations. For example, it is possible that

---

258   (1945) 70 CLR 256.
259   [1970] AC 1004.
260   [1987] 1 AC 241.
261   (1945) 70 CLR 256, 262.
262   *Smith v Leurs* (1945) 70 CLR 256; *Allen v Kerr* [1995] Aust Torts Reports 81-354; *Carmarthenshire City Council v Lewis* [1955] AC 549; *Hogan v Gill* [1992] Aust Torts Reports 81-182; *Curmi v McLennan* [1994] 1 VR 513.
263   *Dorset Yacht Co Ltd v Home Office* [1970] AC 1004.
264   [1988] 2 WLR 1049.
265   (2000) 205 CLR 254; [2000] HCA 61.
266   Ibid.
267   Ibid 263 (Gleeson CJ).
268   JP Swanton, 'Non-delegable Duties: Liability for the Negligence of Independent Contractors' (1991) 4(3) *Journal of Contract Law* 183, 183.

the potential plaintiff stands in a special relationship with the defendant which would give rise to a non-delegable duty. The scope of the 'special relationship' sufficient to give rise to this non-delegable duty is a little unclear. Mason J said in *Kondis v State Transport Authority*:

> In these situations the special duty arises because the person on whom it is imposed has undertaken the care, supervision or control of the person or property of another as to assume a particular responsibility for his or its safety, in circumstances where the person affected might reasonably expect that due care will be exercised.[269]

There are several categories in which this relationship is established: employer and employee,[270] school and pupil,[271] occupier and contractual entrant,[272] and hospital and patient.[273] These relationships tend towards some 'undertaking of care supervision or control' or an 'assumption of a particular responsibility for the safety' of another.[274] See also the detailed discussion of non-delegable duties in Section 10.3.

2.5.6.1 Occupier and entrant

In *Burnie Port Authority v General Jones Pty Ltd*, the Court considered the position of an occupier in regard to a lawful entrant.[275] Although the Court did not find it necessary to conclude on the question of whether the occupier owed a non-delegable duty to the lawful visitor, the majority said that 'the ordinary processes of legal reasoning by analogy, induction and deduction would prima facie indicate that it is'.[276] This case is discussed in detail in Section 10.3.1.3.

2.5.6.2 Independent contractors

Glanville Williams defined an independent contractor as 'any person, other than a servant, who is employed to do work'.[277] As a result of trends in law and management, the use of independent contractors in place of employees became common, and it has become more difficult to legally distinguish the categories.

The general position in relation to independent contractors is fairly settled:

> [W]here a person who is under a duty of care entrusts the performance of the duty to an apparently competent contractor, he is not generally (so far as his own duty of care goes) under a duty to check the contractor's work, being entitled to rely on its proper performance. This is particularly obvious where the property of the work can only be ascertained by an expert, for otherwise the duty to employ experts would be one of infinite regress. Thus, where a person employs an apparently competent contractor, his liability is vicarious or nothing.[278]

However, some duties will not be delegable. The problem is to define their extent.

---

269 (1984) 154 CLR 672, 687.
270 *Kondis v State Transport Authority* (1984) 154 CLR 672.
271 *Commonwealth v Introvigne* (1982) 150 CLR 258.
272 *Calin v Greater Union Organisation Pty Ltd* (1991) 13 CLR 33.
273 *Ellis v Wallsend District Hospital* (1989) 17 NSWLR 553.
274 B McDonald and J Swanton, 'Non-delegable Duties in the Law of Negligence' (1995) 69(5) *Australian Law Journal* 323, 326.
275 (1994) 179 CLR 520.
276 Ibid 557.
277 G Williams, 'Liability for Independent Contractors' (1956) 14(2) *Cambridge Law Journal* 180.
278 Ibid 183.

2.5.6.3   Employer and employee

The obligation of an employer to provide proper staff, premises, plant and system of work, whether to an independent contractor or to another employee, is non-delegable.[279] This anomaly has been described as a 'typical piece of judicial legislation, designed to mitigate the mischief of the doctrine of common employment [using] devious reasoning and the fictitious use of language.'[280] Originally restricted to default by the employee in the course of their employment,[281] it was later extended to the acts of independent contractors.[282] Despite the demise of common employment, the non-delegable duty of the employer to the employee remains in addition to the vicarious liability of the employer for acts of the employee in the course of employment.[283]

The effect of the doctrine, however, has been tempered substantially in most jurisdictions by the introduction of compulsory insurance, which limits the extent to which the employee can pursue a common law claim against the employer.

2.5.6.4   School authorities

In *Commonwealth v Introvigne* a pupil sued the Commonwealth Government for injury sustained in the school playground.[284] The school was situated in the Australian Capital Territory; however, the Commonwealth had given the State of New South Wales responsibility for running the public school system. As a consequence, the teachers were employees of the Education Department of New South Wales, and the selection and control of the teachers were not responsibilities undertaken by the Commonwealth. In this situation, the State of New South Wales was not a subcontractor. However, the High Court held that the position of a school authority was a special one:

> The liability of a school authority in negligence for injury suffered by a pupil attending the school is not a purely vicarious liability. A school authority owes to its pupil a duty to ensure that reasonable care is taken of them whilst they are on the school premises during hours when the school is open for attendance … the duty is not discharged by merely appointing competent teaching staff and leaving it to the staff to take appropriate steps for the care of the children. It is a duty to ensure that reasonable steps are taken for the safety of the children, a duty the performance of which cannot be delegated.[285]

Parents were obliged to have their children enrol at a school in the Territory maintained by or on behalf of the Commonwealth[286] and to cause their children to attend that school; the

---

279 Ibid 190; H Luntz and D Hambly, *Torts: Cases and Commentary* (Butterworths, 4th ed, 1995) [7.8.4], [17.5.13C] ff.
280 G Williams, 'Liability for Independent Contractors' (1956) 14(2) *Cambridge Law Journal* 180, 190.
281 *Wilsons & Clyde Coal Co v English* [1938] AC 57, 78.
282 *Paine v Colne Valley Electricity Supply Co Ltd* [1938] 4 All ER 803, 807 (Goddard LJ); see G Williams, 'Liability for Independent Contractors' (1956) 14(2) *Cambridge Law Journal* 180, 191.
283 *Kondis v State Transport Authority* (1984) 154 CLR 672. See also Section 10.3.1.4.
284 (1982) 150 CLR 258. See also Section 2.3.5.
285 *Commonwealth v Introvigne* (1982) 150 CLR 258, 269–70 (Mason J).
286 *Education Ordinance 1937* (ACT) ss 8, 9.

Commonwealth had had the school established and maintained on its behalf, and thus the duty was owed directly by the Commonwealth to the pupil. The Commonwealth did not cease to owe the duty because it arranged the State to operate the school on its behalf. Thus, although the State of New South Wales was not a subcontractor and it was not appropriate for the principles relating to subcontractors to be applied to this case, the Commonwealth was held to be personally liable. Mason J said:

> it is appropriate that a school authority comes under a duty to ensure that reasonable care is taken of pupils attending a school ... The immaturity and inexperience of the pupils and their propensity for mischief suggest that there should be a special responsibility on a school authority to care for their safety, one that goes beyond a mere vicarious liability for the acts and omissions of its servants.[287]

The duty of the school authority was likened to that owed by a hospital to its patient; both give rise to a personal duty on the part of the hospital or school authority. Neither the duty, nor its performance, is capable of delegation.

Case: *Commonwealth v Introvigne* (1982) 150 CLR 258

Facts

Introvigne was a student at Woden Valley High School in the Australian Capital Territory (ACT). ACT schools were established by the Commonwealth, but the teachers were employees of the State of New South Wales. Introvigne and his friends were gathered in the school grounds at 8:30 am. From 8:20 to 8:25 am, almost all the teachers were at a meeting called by the acting school principal to announce the death of the school principal. A single staff member was patrolling the school. There were 900 students.

Introvigne and his friends were launching themselves off the steps near the flagpole, using the halyard attached to the pole to make themselves airborne. When Introvigne did this, the 'truck' at the top of the flagpole became detached and fell on his head. He was seriously and permanently injured.

Issue

Did the Commonwealth owe a duty of care to the student in these circumstances, separate from the duty owed by the teaching staff (who were employed by New South Wales)?

Decision

The Commonwealth had a duty of care which could not be delegated to the State (a non-delegable duty). This is separate from the vicarious liability of an employer for the tortious actions of the employee.

Significance

This case followed *Ramsay v Larsen*[288] and *Geyer v Downs*[289] in finding that the school authority and teaching staff owe a duty to the pupils to take reasonable care to prevent reasonably foreseeable

---

287 *Commonwealth v Introvigne* (1982) 150 CLR 258, 271.
288 (1964) 111 CLR 16.
289 (1977) 138 CLR 91.

risks (ie, risks that are not far-fetched or fanciful). The case also discussed non-delegable duties, standard of care and vicarious liability. The duty of care of the teaching staff was conceded by the Commonwealth; but it was argued that the Commonwealth also owed a duty of care similar in material respects to that owed by the teaching staff. The Court held that the Commonwealth had a duty of care which was non-delegable, and required the Commonwealth to ensure that care was taken:

> The liability of a school authority in negligence for injury suffered by a pupil attending the school is not a purely vicarious liability. A school authority owes to its pupil a duty to ensure that reasonable care is taken of them whilst they are on the school premises during hours when the school is open for attendance. [26] (Mason J).

Notes

The school, the State of New South Wales and the Commonwealth Government were sued in negligence. The High Court found that the school owed a duty of care to students at the school and that the duty extended to the period before the commencement of classes. The case was argued on the basis of the State's vicarious liability as employers for the tortious actions of the teacher/employees. However, the Commonwealth was also liable quite separately from the vicarious liability. The Court held that a duty of care was owed by the Commonwealth and that it was a non-delegable duty.

Question

What is a 'non-delegable duty'?

 Guided response in the eBook

REVIEW QUESTIONS

(1) What is the role of policy in the determination of a duty of care? How useful is the duty of care concept in achieving the goals of the law of negligence?

(2) What is the importance of vulnerability in determining whether a duty of care is owed? Is vulnerability more important in some situations than others? Which situations?

(3) What policy reasons originally prevented the common law from recognising pure mental harm, and what motivated acceptance of this form of harm?

 Guided responses in the eBook

KEY CONCEPTS

- **duty of care:** not owed to everyone in the world. It has a 'gatekeeper' role – it keeps the law of negligence within reasonable bounds.

- **established duty:** currently, Australian courts first determine whether there is an 'established duty' in relation to the category of relationship between the plaintiff and the defendant for that type of harm. If there is no established duty (ie, it is a novel case), courts refer to salient features.

- **foreseeability of harm:** the original basis for a duty of care, but this concept was found to be too broad, so later courts introduced additional controls.

 Complete the multiple-choice questions in the eBook to test your knowledge

PROBLEM-SOLVING EXERCISES

Exercise 1

Hemi was driving to pick up his girlfriend Ruiha during rush hour. The traffic was worse than usual, and Hemi realised that there had been an accident. Two cars had collided at the intersection. On his way back home he drove past the accident again. By that time police and emergency vehicles were there. Later he drove past the intersection again and noticed that one of the cars had severe damage and had been cut open to retrieve someone inside. He wondered, then, if someone had been badly hurt.

At 10:30 pm that night, his parents arrived and told him that his brother Mikaere had been killed in a car accident caused by a driver, Piripi, travelling through a stop sign. Hemi then realised that he had passed the accident several times that evening, without knowing that his brother was in the car, possibly dying. Hemi was distraught. He thought that when he had passed the accident site earlier in the day, he should have known that Mikaere was there. He should have stopped and done something to help. Over the next few months, Hemi finds that he is not getting over the tragedy. He is diagnosed with a major depressive disorder with significant anxiety-related components of a post-traumatic stress reaction.

Assume that there was a breach and that Hemi's illness was caused by the breach. Did the driver Piripi owe Hemi a duty of care to guard against this damage?

 Guided response in the eBook

Exercise 2

Harriet is a graduate teacher at a state school in Melbourne. Her high-achieving nature has resulted in perfectionism and a tendency to become depressed when things go wrong. The headmaster, Barry, has counselled her on this.

Bridie is a student in Harriet's Year 9 science class. She has been diagnosed with a disorder on the autism spectrum but despite the school's efforts to obtain a full-time aide she only has an aide in some classes. Harriet finds teaching the Year 9 class to be very stressful. The class is very disruptive and Harriet feels inadequately prepared to teach science, since her primary degree was in English literature. Bridie has become very critical of Harriet and often loudly interrupts the class to say that Harriet 'doesn't know what she's talking about'. This upsets Harriet, as it seems to reflect her own insecurities and she feels that it must be obvious that this is the first time she has taught science. Over the course of the school term Bridie's behaviour becomes more and more disruptive. She often walks around the room, upsetting experiments and playing with equipment. Harriet feels too ashamed to mention it to other teachers, as she thinks it might make it seem that she is not doing a good job. However, the aide mentions several times to other teachers in the staff room that 'Bridie is giving Harriet a pretty hard time. I'm a bit worried about Harriet – she's a bit high-strung.' Other teachers notice that Harriet is becoming more and more quiet, and that she looks unhappy. Harriet has to leave classrooms twice because a student's comment has brought her to tears.

Harriet has not returned to teaching. She has been diagnosed with a long-term severe depressive condition as a result of her experience in the classroom. Does the State of Victoria (who runs the school) owe a duty of care to Harriet in relation to mental harm?

 Guided response in the eBook

CHALLENGE YOURSELF

Exercise 1

The Council was carrying out repairs to some rural roads in the Shire. It had deployed plastic road barriers to protect workers and control traffic while the repairs were going on. These plastic barriers were designed to be filled with water onsite so that they could not be readily moved, whereas the concrete barriers needed to be put into position with a crane. When empty, the plastic barriers weighed 65 kilograms; when full, they weighed 610 kilograms. In arranging the barriers around the worksite, the Council had deployed filled barriers to protect workers, but had used empty barriers at the end of the work site to warn traffic. These were left empty so that, if a car did collide with them, they would not cause too much damage. Sometime during the night, somebody moved the two end (empty) barriers so that they obstructed traffic. Pierre, riding his motorcycle, collided with one of the barriers and was injured.

Does the Council owe a duty of care to Pierre to take reasonable steps to avoid his physical injury?

 Guided response in the eBook

Exercise 2

The Abingdon Council decided to organise a musical event, a 'Day of Pop' which would run in the local showgrounds. The event marketing targeted teenagers but the event was not limited to a particular age group. Barry, who was seven years old, was handed a Day of Pop flyer when he attended an after-school activities session. It said:

> *Fun for all the family*
> Come to the showgrounds for a family-friendly day of music.
> Bring a picnic rug and a fun attitude!

Cassie was a single mother and often struggled to cope with Barry, who was extremely energetic and often 'acted out'. Cassie felt that the Day of Pop would be an opportunity for her to get some shopping done and go to a hair appointment. Cassie rang the Council office and asked Evelyn, who answered the phone, whether the event was suitable for younger children. Evelyn replied, 'Parents are welcome to bring their younger children'.

On the day of the event Cassie drove to the showgrounds at 10:00 am and dropped Barry at the gates. Barry wandered around the showgrounds for about 30 minutes, but then he became bored. He wandered away from the band area to a different part of the showgrounds. Temporary fencing around two metres high had been erected, and signs on the fence said 'No Entrance! Warning – Construction'. Barry couldn't read the signs, although he could tell that he wasn't supposed to go past the fence. With some difficulty he climbed over the fence panels and crawled into an abandoned shed. Inside it was very dark, and Barry fell over and twisted his ankle and it was too sore for him to move.

Cassie came at 4:00 pm to pick Barry up, and for half an hour she looked for him in vain among the crowd, becoming increasingly anxious. At 4:30 pm, she came up to one of the security guards at the gate and explained that her son was missing. A search of the showgrounds began immediately, and he was found at 6:00 pm when his cries alerted the search team. By that time Cassie was extremely upset. She herself had got lost for two days when she was young, and she was now convinced that Barry was lying dead somewhere. She was later diagnosed with serious post-traumatic stress disorder (PTSD) and became unable to continue with her employment as a retail assistant.

Cassie intends to sue Abingdon Council, saying that it is liable for her PTSD. Advise Abingdon indicating, with reasons, the likelihood that she would be owed a duty of care.

 Guided response in the eBook

3

BREACH OF DUTY OF CARE

3.1   Introduction

Once the plaintiff has established that the defendant owed him or her a duty of care, the next question is whether the defendant breached that duty of care. In its broadest terms, breach is about whether the defendant has engaged in negligent conduct, which can be understood as failing to take the precautions against certain risks of harm that a reasonable person, in the circumstances, would have taken.

So how do we work out which precautions the reasonable person would have taken in the circumstances? As illustrated by Figure 3.1, this analysis has two main parts:

(1)   A court determines the qualities of the reasonable person against whom the behaviour of the defendant will be compared. For example, the comparison might be with a person who possesses a particular set of skills or some other attribute. This is sometimes referred to as *setting* the standard of care.

(2)   The court then decides what that reasonable person would have done if placed in the same circumstances the defendant was in. It does so by addressing a series of questions. This is sometimes referred to as *applying* the standard of care to the facts of the case.

What the defendant actually did or did not do is then compared to that standard of expected carefulness. If the defendant's conduct was less careful than what the court decides the hypothetical reasonable person would or would not have done, the defendant is said to have fallen below the standard of care expected of them and will have breached their duty of care.

Figure 3.1   Second element of a negligence claim

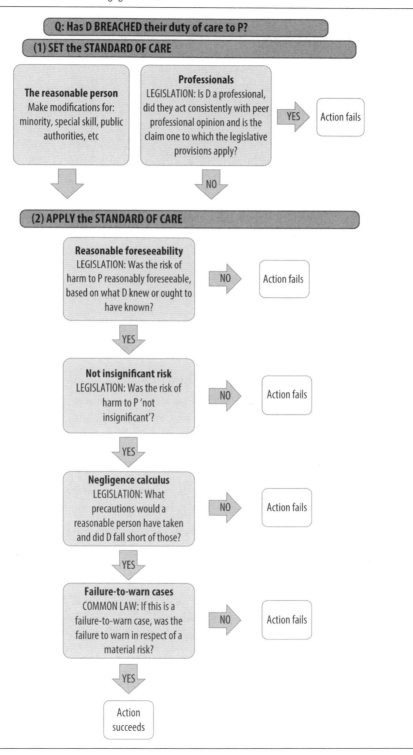

3.1.1   What is negligent conduct?

Negligent conduct is a failure to take reasonable care against certain risks of harm to the plaintiff (or class of plaintiff). Negligent conduct might occur either in the form of positive acts (eg, throwing a dart in the direction of other people) or in the form of omissions (eg, a doctor failing to warn their patient about risks of surgery). Precisely what the standard of care requires of the defendant is dependent upon the exact circumstances of each case, but a few broad principles are relevant:

(1)   As noted earlier, the defendant's behaviour is compared to that of a hypothetical person who is reasonable and prudent. This hypothetical person may also have certain specific qualities, but it is always an objective standard.

(2)   A person is only expected to take precautions against foreseeable and 'not insignificant' risks.

(3)   A range of considerations determine what precautions the reasonable person would have taken in response to foreseeable and 'not insignificant' risks. This is sometimes referred to as the negligence calculus and involves weighing up various factors such as: the probability and likely seriousness of harm created by the risk, the burden of taking precautions against the risk, and the social utility of the defendant's risk-producing activity.

(4)   Some special rules apply where the defendant is a professional or in cases where the alleged carelessness by the defendant is a failure to warn of risks.

Each of these principles is elaborated upon more fully in dedicated sections of this chapter. First, however, we will discuss a few preliminary matters.

of people and institutions, and the nature of the world and society'.[1] As Burns argues, this is probably unavoidable given the nature of the tort of negligence and its purpose in our community. However, it does raise risks that judges should be alert to, such as the possibility that the social facts they claim are common sense are outdated or fail to take account of the lived experiences of marginalised groups, such as members of the LGBTIQA+ community or people with disabilities.[2]

3.1.2   No degrees of breach

It is important to note that there are no degrees of breach. What this means is that it is irrelevant, for the purposes of breach, whether the defendant has only just failed to meet the standard of care expected of them or whether they have fallen short of that standard to a significant degree. In other words, both minor and major examples of carelessness are effectively equivalent at the breach stage. In either case, the defendant will have breached their duty.

The reasons that the law does not concern itself with degrees of breach include:

- There is no necessary connection between the degree of negligence on the part of the defendant and the seriousness of harm that befalls a plaintiff. A person may be only slightly careless but still cause an enormous amount of damage.
- Accordingly, people should not think it is acceptable to take even apparently small risks on the presumption that the law will treat them more favourably than those acting in obviously dangerous ways.
- Moreover, depending upon the theory one adopts as to the purposes of tort law, the degree of carelessness which brought about harm to the plaintiff may be irrelevant. Tort law is not about defendant culpability but rather about ensuring compensatory outcomes for plaintiffs or ensuring defendants meet their duties of repair. Minor or major breaches do not impact differentially upon those purposes (see Section 1.1.2).

Having said this, the question of the degree of the defendant's carelessness may become relevant when apportioning liability between the plaintiff and the defendant in cases where the plaintiff is found to have been contributorily negligent (discussed in Section 5.2).

3.1.3   Relevance of past findings of breach

As we will see in Section 3.2.1, the qualities of the reasonable person against whom the defendant is compared are a question of law. What this means is that this part of the breach inquiry is determined by the application of existing legal precedents that dictate the qualities that are (and are not) held by the reasonable person. For example (and as discussed in Section 3.2), the reasonable person may be deemed to have certain skills (say, the skills of a doctor) but will not be deemed to be of a certain gender (say, uniquely female) and this is based entirely on precedent.

---

1   K Burns, 'It's Not Just Policy: The Role of Social Facts in Judicial Reasoning in Negligence Cases' (2013) 21(2) *Torts Law Journal* 73, 73.
2   Ibid 85–6.

By contrast, the determination of whether and what specific precautions that reasonable person would then have taken if placed in the same circumstances as the defendant is a question of fact.[3] While the divide between questions of fact and questions of law at the breach stage is not quite as simple as this would suggest,[4] in broad terms this means that the question of what a reasonable person would have done as appropriately careful behaviour in the circumstances is deeply fact driven. In other words, this question can only be decided by close attention to the facts of the given case.

The relevance of this distinction is that courts may be bound by other courts' findings of law, but not their findings of fact. And so the mere finding by one court in one case that conduct engaged in by a defendant was a breach of a duty of care will not bind another court deciding another case, even where the facts appear similar. This is because the circumstances of each case will differ in slight but potentially significant ways.

To give an example, we can consider *Qualcast (Wolverhampton) Ltd v Haynes*.[5] In that case, the plaintiff was an experienced moulder working in the defendant's foundry. While the plaintiff had only recently commenced working for the defendant, he had been in the same line of work for many years. When the plaintiff was working one day, a ladle of molten metal he was holding slipped and some of the metal splashed on his foot, causing an injury. The question was whether a reasonable employer would have instructed the plaintiff to wear protective clothing that could have kept them safe from injury, and by failing to do so this defendant was in breach.

The judge at first instance found negligence on the part of the defendant, but reluctantly. He did so because he considered himself bound by earlier cases that had found that employers must not merely provide protective equipment to their workers but must urge them to wear it, in order to satisfy their duty of care. In this case, however, the plaintiff needed no apparent urging as his own experience meant he was well aware both of the risks he took when working and of the availability of specialist protective clothes.[6] The House of Lords subsequently corrected the trial judge and held that there was no negligence in this case. It held that the earlier cases were not binding and that this particular employer had behaved sufficiently carefully given his particular employee's experience and appreciation of the risk.

3.1.4   Importance of the civil liability legislation

A final preliminary matter is the importance of the civil liability legislation in shaping determinations of breach by Australian courts today. As noted in Section 1.2, substantial legislative reforms of the various state and territory civil liability regimes followed the conclusion of a review headed by the Honourable David Ipp into personal injury claims ('Ipp Review').[7] A number of those amendments bear in important ways upon the breach element of a negligence claim.

Some provisions simply codify what was already the norm under the common law. What this means is that they reiterate in legislation the principles that were already operating

---

3   *Teubner v Humble* (1963) 108 CLR 491, 503–4 (Windeyer J).
4   K Barker et al, *The Law of Torts in Australia* (Oxford University Press, 5th ed, 2012) 442–4.
5   [1959] AC 743.
6   *Qualcast (Wolverhampton) Ltd v Haynes* [1959] AC 743, 754 (Lord Keith quoting Judge Norris at trial).
7   *Review of the Law of Negligence* (Final Report, September 2002) ('Ipp Report').

under the common law. For example, many of the civil liability statutes now confirm that 'negligence means failure to exercise reasonable care and skill'.[8]

However, some of the amendments to civil liability regimes in the wake of the Ipp Review introduced new principles relevant to breach. One such example is the addition of a requirement that risks must be 'not insignificant' in order to warrant precautions.[9] Importantly, however, the legislation introduced around Australia operates against the backdrop of pre-existing common law principles of negligence.[10]

Table 3.1 lists the core provisions[11] of the various civil liability statutes in Australia that set out the basic framework for determining breach. This chapter is broadly structured according to this (largely common) framework, within which the relevant common law principles are also considered.

Table 3.1   Breach of duty: general principles

Legislation	Section(s)
Civil Law (Wrongs) Act 2002 (ACT)	42, 43, 44
Civil Liability Act 2002 (NSW)	5B, 5C
Civil Liability Act 2003 (Qld)	9, 10
Civil Liability Act 1936 (SA)	31, 32
Civil Liability Act 2002 (Tas)	11, 12
Wrongs Act 1958 (Vic)	48, 49, 50
Civil Liability Act 2002 (WA)	5B

HINTS AND TIPS

Because the civil liability statutes do not 'cover the field' on the element of breach, it is important to remember that the common law continues to be relevant. This means you need to work with the legislation in your state or territory together with the common law rules that apply. Remember that legislation overrules common law if there is any inconsistency of principles between those sources of law.

It is also important to be aware that in many jurisdictions injuries arising in certain contexts are excluded from aspects of the civil liability legislation, including those related to breach. While they vary, the kinds of claims that might be excluded from the civil liability statutes include:

---

8   *Civil Law (Wrongs) Act 2002* (ACT) s 40; *Civil Liability Act 2002* (NSW) s 5; *Civil Liability Act 2003* (Qld) sch 2 (definition of 'duty of care'); *Civil Liability Act 1936* (SA) s 3; *Wrongs Act 1958* (Vic) s 43.
9   *Civil Law (Wrongs) Act 2002* (ACT) s 43(1)(b); *Civil Liability Act 2002* (NSW) s 5B(1)(b); *Civil Liability Act 2003* (Qld) s 9(1)(b); *Civil Liability Act 1936* (SA) s 32(1)(b); *Civil Liability Act 2002* (Tas) s 11(1)(b); *Wrongs Act 1958* (Vic) s 48(1)(b); *Civil Liability Act 2002* (WA) s 5B(1)(b).
10 See, eg, *Roads and Traffic Authority (NSW) v Refrigerated Roadways Pty Ltd* (2009) 77 NSWLR 360, 397.
11 Note that in some instances these provisions are misleadingly included under the heading 'duty of care' but nonetheless relate to breach considerations: see, eg, *Adeels Palace Pty Ltd v Moubarak* (2009) 239 CLR 420, 432–3 (commenting on the relevant New South Wales provisions).

- claims related to acts that are intended to cause injury or death or involve sexual assault
- claims related to injuries at work or in the context of a motor vehicle accident
- certain dust disease and smoking related claims.[12]

Where excluded, such personal injury claims are instead determined according to common law principles and any specialised legislation governing the area, as well as any provisions of the civil liability statutes that are explicitly preserved.

REVIEW QUESTIONS

(1) What is negligent conduct and what does it mean to say that assessing a defendant's breach of duty is a comparative exercise?

(2) Does the degree to which a defendant has fallen short of the requisite standard of care play a role in determinations of breach?

(3) If a court found in Case A that a defendant driver of a motor vehicle was expected to slow to a near stop when approaching a T-intersection, would a court in Case B be bound to find the same if its case also involved a motor vehicle collision at a T-intersection?

 Guided responses in the eBook

3.2   Setting the standard of care: the reasonable person

3.2.1   An objective standard

Baron Alderson, in an oft-quoted statement from *Blyth v Birmingham Waterworks Co*, described negligence as 'the omission to do something which a reasonable man, guided upon those considerations which ordinarily regulate the conduct of human affairs, would do, or doing something which a prudent and reasonable man would not do'.[13] This reference to what a prudent and reasonable person would do reflects the objective and impersonal legal standard that is applied when a court assesses whether a defendant has acted with sufficient care in a particular circumstance.

What does it mean that the court uses an objective standard as the measure of carefulness? It means that typically a court will not take into account the particular idiosyncrasies of the defendant in determining whether they behaved reasonably. Instead, the defendant's behaviour is measured against the likely conduct of the reasonable person.[14] For example,

---

12 See, eg, *Civil Law (Wrongs) Act 2002* (ACT) s 41(2); *Civil Liability Act 2002* (NSW) ss 3B, 5A; *Personal Injuries (Liabilities and Damages) Act 2003* (NT) s 4; *Civil Liability Act 2003* (Qld) s 5; *Civil Liability Act 2002* (Tas) ss 3B, 10; *Wrongs Act 1958* (Vic) s 45; *Civil Liability Act 2002* (WA) s 3A.

13 (1856) 11 Ex 781, 784.

14 *Vaughan v Menlove* (1837) 3 Bing NC 468.

whether or not the defendant has a lower-than-average level of intelligence is not relevant when determining the standard of carefulness expected of them. As described by Lord Macmillan in *Glasgow Corporation v Muir*, 'the standard of foresight of the reasonable man is in one sense an impersonal test. It eliminates the personal equation and is independent of the idiosyncrasies of the particular person whose conduct is in question'.[15] Moreover, the reasonable person is prudent, meaning that the rule 'requires in all cases a regard to caution such as a man of ordinary prudence would observe'.[16] They are a person free of both over-apprehension and overconfidence.[17]

The imposition of an objective reasonable-person standard can sometimes lead to what appear to be unjust results with respect to certain categories of defendants who, due to personal characteristics, resources or ill luck, would be inherently unable to meet that standard. To some extent, this risk is protected against by the fact that the reasonable person is 'situated' in the position of the defendant, meaning that what could be expected depends on the circumstances in which the defendant in fact found themselves.[18] For example, in *Allen v Chadwick*, the High Court considered a female plaintiff's age, gender and condition of pregnancy as being relevant factors that any reasonable person would take into account if they were weighing up risks related to available avenues for action.[19] To illustrate, that case involved a car accident which occurred in the early hours of the morning just outside of a small country town in regional South Australia.[20] At the time of the accident, the plaintiff, Danielle Chadwick, was a young woman of 21 years of age who had known she was pregnant for about 9 or 10 weeks. Shortly prior to the car accident, which resulted in serious spinal injuries to the plaintiff, Chadwick had been driving her then intimate partner, the defendant, Alex Allen, and another friend, both of whom were very intoxicated, around the area for about 10-15 minutes to look for cigarettes. During this time, the trial judge accepted that the plaintiff had become disoriented as to their proximity to the town in which they were staying.[21] After the plaintiff stopped the car and exited it briefly, the defendant took the wheel and demanded the plaintiff re-enter as a passenger. The High Court accepted that the plaintiff's assessment of the alternative avenues available to her (to accept the lift with a clearly intoxicated driver or try to find her own way back to the town) reasonably took account of the objective facts of her circumstances, which included the risks associated with walking an uncertain distance back to the town in the dark while young, female and pregnant (which the court considered rendered her more vulnerable to serious consequences of an assault, should one occur).[22] While this case addressed the question of the plaintiff's contributory negligence, the High Court made it clear that this determination involved the application of the same general principles that apply to a determination of the reasonable care and skill expected of a defendant.[23]

---

15 [1943] AC 448, 48.
16 *Vaughan v Menlove* (1837) 3 Bing NC 468, 475 (Tindal CJ).
17 *Glasgow Corporation v Muir* [1943] 2 All ER 44, 48.
18 For an excellent discussion of how characteristics that are personal to the defendant and their external circumstances can factor into the 'application' of the standard of care, versus modifying the reasonable person standard, see J Dietrich and I Field, '"The Reasonable Tort Victim": Contributory Negligence, Standard of Care and the "Equivalence Theory"' (2017) 41(2) *Melbourne University Law Review* 602, 612–20.
19 *Allen v Chadwick* (2015) 256 CLR 148.
20 Ibid 154–5 (recounting the circumstances of the accident).
21 Ibid 158.
22 Ibid 167.
23 Ibid 156, 164–5.

In addition to accounting for a person's 'situatedness' when determining what reasonable care would involve, there are certain (limited) characteristics peculiar to the defendant's circumstances that the courts have decided are relevant when setting the standard of care. These characteristics are set out below. Finally, there are signs of a recent judicial tendency towards aligning legal expectations more closely with what people could genuinely do in real life.[24]

Nonetheless, there remain potential situations where the rule may operate harshly on a defendant, though this might be justified on a few bases:

(1)   Negligence is an ethical concept concerned with a person's responsibility for their behaviour. It is thus about how they ought to have behaved, not how they were capable of behaving. Indeed, if a person was not in a position to undertake all the precautions demanded, they ought not to have engaged in the risk-creating activity at all.[25]

(2)   The current rule serves to recognise and reinforce the full human agency of a defendant, by refusing to treat matters beyond our control as part of an equation as to our responsibility.[26]

(3)   If torts are concerned not with moral culpability but responsibilities of repair and of compensation (distributive justice considerations), a stricter, more demanding, standard is warranted. This argument carries even more weight in situations where insurance operates to effectively indemnify the defendant and to provide a robust compensatory remedy to the plaintiff.[27]

(4)   To fix standards of care according to the idiosyncrasies of defendants – such as according to the levels of intelligence or experience or judgment of the individual defendant – would be an overly cumbersome task for courts and would result in infinite varieties of due care, rather than a standard measure, contrary to the general function of negligence law.[28]

Whatever the justification, the objective standard of the reasonable person is now reflected in the various civil liability statutes,[29] although the Australian Capital Territory and South Australian statutes provide the most complete restatement of the common law principle, providing:

Standard of care

For deciding whether a person (the defendant) was negligent, the standard of care required of the defendant is that of a reasonable person in the defendant's position who was in possession of all the information that the defendant either had, or ought reasonably to have had, at the time of the incident out of which the harm arose.[30]

---

24 See, eg, *Tame v New South Wales* (2002) 211 CLR 317, 354 (McHugh J). See also H Luntz et al, *Torts: Cases and Commentary* (LexisNexis Butterworths, 8th ed, 2017) 221–4.

25 K Barker et al, *The Law of Torts in Australia* (Oxford University Press, 5th ed, 2012) 430.

26 Ibid 430–1.

27 On the relevance of insurance see, eg, *White v White* [1949] 2 All ER 339, 351 (Lord Denning).

28 See, eg, *Vaughan v Menlove* (1837) 3 Bing NC 468, 474–5 (Tindal CJ).

29 References to the 'reasonable person' appear throughout the negligence provisions of the various civil liability statutes. A particularly relevant provision states that the precautions expected of a defendant will be according to those which 'a reasonable person in the person's [defendant's] position would have taken': *Civil Law (Wrongs) Act 2002* (ACT) s 43(1)(c); *Civil Liability Act 2002* (NSW) s 5B(1)(c); *Civil Liability Act 2003* (Qld) s 9(1)(c); *Civil Liability Act 1936* (SA) s 32(1)(c); *Civil Liability Act 2002* (Tas) s 11(1)(c); *Wrongs Act 1958* (Vic) s 48(1)(c); *Civil Liability Act 2002* (WA) s 5B(1)(c).

30 *Civil Law (Wrongs) Act 2002* (ACT) s 42; *Civil Liability Act 1936* (SA) s 31(1).

3.2.2   Relevant characteristics of the defendant

There are some qualities or characteristics associated with a defendant that courts have decided should modify the reasonable person standard that is used when determining breach. While these do not convert the standard from an objective to a subjective one, they do affect what a court might objectively expect of the defendant as reasonable care in the circumstances, by either raising expectations or lowering them. The established categories are briefly explored here.

3.2.2.1   Age

Where the defendant is a child, it is appropriate to take into account that child's age when considering reasonably prudent behaviour in the circumstances. This means comparing the behaviour of the child defendant in question to that of an ordinary child of the same age. This principle was established in *McHale v Watson*, a case involving a 12-year-old defendant.

Case: *McHale v Watson* (1966) 115 CLR 199

Facts

Barry Watson (the defendant) was a 12-year-old boy who, after playing a game of tag with some other children, threw a sharpened steel rod he had with him at a nearby post being used to set the parameters of the game. Unfortunately, the rod either missed or glanced off the post, and instead landed in the eye of Susan McHale (the plaintiff), a 9-year-old girl standing nearby. As a result, the plaintiff lost sight in her injured eye.

Issue

The issue in this case was whether the standard of care expected of the defendant differed from the ordinary standard due to his young age.

Decision

The majority of the High Court held that, on account of his age, the defendant should be held to a lower standard than that of the reasonable (adult) person. Their Honours were of the view that a child could not be expected to have the degree of foresight, prudence or experience of an adult in assessing risk. For that reason, the standard of reasonable prudence and foresight against which the conduct of a child defendant should be measured is that of an ordinary child of comparable age.

This does not mean that a child cannot be negligent. Nor did the Court consider that this modification of the standard offends the established principle of negligence that idiosyncrasies of the individual are irrelevant when setting the standard of care. This is because, in relation to foresight and prudence, 'normality is, for children, something different from what normality is for adults' (at 213).

Significance

This case is authority for the principle that the standard of care is modified where the defendant is a child, to reflect the degree of care we can reasonably expect of a child at that age.

Notes

One point of difference between two of the majority Justices was whether, in addition to considering the ordinary prudence and foresight of a child of comparable age when determining the standard of care for children, a court is also entitled to take into account the intelligence and experience of the child defendant. Kitto J was opposed to this proposition, considering it a difference from the general rule that could not be justified (at 213). By contrast, Owen J felt the test was to compare the child defendant to a child of 'the same age, intelligence and experience' (at 234). The better view is likely to be that intelligence and experience will not be taken into account, as this is more consistent with the general principles of negligence law.

Question

What is the justification for setting a different (lower) standard of care for children?

 Guided response in the eBook

There is no rule in the civil law as to when a child ceases to be a child; in other words, there is no set age of majority. What is clear is that as a child increases in age, the standard of care rises to eventually reach the point at which a distinction from the reasonable (adult) person standard cannot be justified.

So far as adults are concerned, the general rule is that everyone is subject to the same standard of reasonable care. Unlike the law related to children, it is less clear whether any modification can be made to the standard to reflect infirmities associated with old age, something which may become a greater issue in the future given our ageing population.[31] However, the better view seems to be that there is no equivalent modification of the standard of care applicable to the elderly, other than any modification relevant to physical or mental impairment, in so much as those would operate (see Section 3.2.2.2). Indeed, the elderly (as distinct from children) can be expected to modify their behaviours as necessary to avoid risk-generating activities that they are no longer competent to adequately protect against.

3.2.2.2 Physical and mental impairment

There is some uncertainty about the precise implications of a defendant's physical impairment on the proper standard of care for breach; however, it is likely that such impairment (short of involving unexpected automatism) will not modify the reasonable person standard.[32] The reasons include that the nature of a defendant's impairment can often be incorporated into the characterisation of the defendant's negligence and thus any modification of the reasonable person standard becomes irrelevant. To explain: a person's

---

31 N Bromberger, 'Negligence and Inherent Unreasonableness' (2010) 32(3) *Sydney Law Review* 411, 411.
32 See, eg, *Corr v IBC Vehicles Ltd* [2008] 1 AC 884; *Dunnage v Randall* [2016] QB 639.

knowledge that they have, or may have, a physical impairment that would pose risks to others and failure to protect against such risks could be described as their negligent conduct.[33] By contrast, sudden and unexpected physical incapacity which renders the defendant's resulting action reflexive or automatic is such that even a reasonable person could not protect against it.

For example, compare the situation of a driver who is feeling dizzy as a precursor to experiencing a stroke shortly after, with the situation of a driver who is unexpectedly stung by a bee and causes an accident almost immediately. Both cases involve a subjective physical incapacity that affects the defendant's inherent ability to act to the standard of a reasonable, fully able-bodied driver. However, in the first instance advance notice exists which allows the driver acting as a reasonable person to pull over and thus nullify the risk they now pose. By contrast, in the second instance even a reasonable driver would be unable to avoid the loss of control that might ensue.[34] Indeed, the difference between such cases can also be explained as turning on the presence or absence of voluntariness on the part of the defendant, with voluntariness a necessary, though often implicit, requirement of any fault-based tort, including negligence.[35]

For the purposes of contributory negligence, under an older common law approach, courts were willing to consider a person's physical and mental incapacities or infirmities when determining the degree of carefulness expected in respect of oneself. However, new lines of authority, following the introduction of the uniform civil liability regime, have tended to maintain an objective standard, notwithstanding a particular plaintiff's physical or mental conditions which may undermine or remove their ability to act according to that reasonable person standard. Doing so is intended to bring the treatment of plaintiffs (for the purpose of contributory negligence) into alignment with the strict approach adopted for defendants at the breach stage (see Section 5.2.2).[36]

By contrast to the somewhat piecemeal case law on physical impairment, there is clear authority with regard to the position where a defendant is suffering from a mental health condition that reduces their inherent capacity to act to the standard of a reasonable person. The most recent Australian authority is *Carrier v Bonham*, which confirms that no modification is made to account for a defendant's mental impairment when setting the standard of the reasonable person against whom their conduct will be compared.[37] It is interesting to note that, on this particular question, the law as it is sits in marked contrast with the view taken by tort academics of what it should be.[38]

---

33 H Luntz et al, *Torts: Cases and Commentary* (LexisNexis Butterworths, 8th ed, 2017) 230–1; R Balkin and J Davis, *Law of Torts* (LexisNexis Butterworths, 5th ed, 2013) 278–80.

34 See, eg, *Roberts v Ramsbottom* [1980] 1 WLR 823 (liability despite a stroke while driving, with an alternative basis for the finding of liability being the notice the defendant had, by way of dizziness, of some disabling symptoms). Compare *Scholz v Standish* [1961] SASR 123 (no liability given bee sting immediately prior to collision). See also *Leahy v Beaumont* (1981) 27 SASR 290 (driver liable as he had the opportunity to cease driving when a coughing fit pre-empted a full loss of consciousness).

35 J Dietrich and I Field, '"The Reasonable Tort Victim": Contributory Negligence, Standard of Care and the "Equivalence Theory"' (2017) 41(2) *Melbourne University Law Review* 602, 625–7.

36 For a critique of the 'equivalency' approach to the standard of care of defendants and plaintiffs, see ibid.

37 [2002] 1 Qld R 474. See also *Adamson v Motor Vehicle Insurance Trust* (1957) 58 WALR 56.

38 Nikki Bromberger, 'Negligence and Inherent Unreasonableness' (2010) 32(3) *Sydney Law Review* 411, 417 n 38.

Case: *Carrier v Bonham* [2002] 1 Qd R 474

Facts

Keith Carrier (the plaintiff) was injured after the bus he was driving collided with John Bonham (the defendant). The defendant was attempting suicide by stepping in front of the bus. The plaintiff tried, but was unable, to avoid the collision. While the defendant suffered some minor injuries, it was the plaintiff who was most seriously injured, developing an adjustment disorder which caused him to give up bus driving. The defendant had a long history of chronic schizophrenia and was a patient at the Royal Brisbane Hospital. On the evening in question, he had escaped from the hospital with the intention of killing himself.

Issue

The question was whether the defendant's conduct that night was to be assessed against that of a reasonable person, notwithstanding his mental health condition which rendered him unable to rationalise about risk in the way that standard would demand.

Decision

The Queensland Court of Appeal held that both precedent and policy supported the finding that the standard of the reasonable and ordinary person is not modified by virtue of a defendant's unsoundness of mind.

Significance

This case is authority for the principle that the standard of care expected of a person is *not* modified where they have a mental impairment that might otherwise affect their personal capacity to exercise due care.

Notes

The Court in *Carrier v Bonham* explained its decision using the following arguments:

*   The purpose of negligence is not to punish and blame but to provide redress. To this extent it is less a question of culpability than on whom the risk should fall.
*   It would be practically impossible to apply a standard of care modified by mental impairment, because the nature of psychiatric illness is such that it makes little sense to speak of the reasonably psychiatrically ill person.
*   Mental impairment is unlike childhood, in that it is not a stage of development common to, and broadly uniform across, all human beings. Instead, it impacts only some people, and not others, and occurs in such a vast variety of degrees and shades that no objective standard could be predicated upon it.
*   Setting a different (lower) standard would have adverse policy implications for the mentally ill, as it may push policy towards the reintroduction of institutionalisation on the basis that they are incapable of being held accountable by ordinary mechanisms of distributive justice and thus should be removed from the general community.

Each of these rationales has been critiqued by tort academics.[39]

Question

How did the Court in *Carrier v Bonham* justify its view that the decision not to modify the standard of care of the reasonable person to account for mental impairment is consistent with the willingness of courts to modify the standard in the case of children?

     Guided response in the eBook

3.2.2.3   Intoxication

A related but distinct issue is the implication of the defendant or plaintiff's intoxication on the setting of the standard of care for the purpose of determining breach. In general, a defendant's state of intoxication will not modify the standard of reasonable care expected of them, for the reasons discussed in Section 3.2.2.2. In South Australia, however, some leeway is given to an involuntarily intoxicated defendant of a certain kind. Section 31(2) of the *Civil Liability Act 1936* (SA) provides that the reasonable person is taken to be sober, notwithstanding any intoxication on the part of the defendant, unless the intoxication is attributed wholly to the correct use of drugs as prescribed by a medical practitioner. In such a case, the reasonable person standard will be lowered to reflect the level of care expected of a person intoxicated to the same extent as the defendant.

In addition, New South Wales, Queensland and Victoria have legislative provisions that relate to the standard of care owed by the defendant where it is the *plaintiff* who is intoxicated. In New South Wales and Queensland, the legislation confirms that the fact of a plaintiff's intoxication 'does not of itself increase or otherwise affect the standard of care owed to the person'.[40] This serves to clarify that a court should not readily increase expectations of what will constitute due care on the part of a defendant because they are dealing with a plaintiff who is less capable of taking due care of themselves. In Victoria, the language of the relevant statutory provision is somewhat more ambiguous, stating simply that a court must consider a plaintiff's voluntary intoxication or engagement in illegal activity as part of its determination of breach.[41] Nonetheless, this too is presumably intended to warn courts not to increase expectations of defendants on that basis alone. Having said this, it is worth noting that there are circumstances where it might be reasonably foreseeable by a reasonable person that they will be dealing with intoxicated persons (eg, in running a licenced venue) which will demand consideration of the special risks of harm such intoxication might pose.[42]

---

39 See, eg, N Bromberger, 'Negligence and Inherent Unreasonableness' (2010) 32(3) *Sydney Law Review* 411.
40 *Civil Liability Act 2002* (NSW) s 49; *Civil Liability Act 2003* (Qld) s 46.
41 *Wrongs Act 1958* (Vic) s 14G.
42 This goes more to the question of breach (discussed in Section 3.3) than to the legal standard of care of the reasonable person. It should be noted that the question of whether a duty of care is owed by a publican to an intoxicated patron, and the scope of that duty, is in itself a significant prior question to be determined: see, eg, *CAL No 14 Pty Ltd v Motor Accidents Insurance Board* (2009) 239 CLR 390.

3.2.2.4   Possession of special skills

Where a person engages in an activity that demands the application of special skills in order to do so carefully and appropriately, the reasonable person standard is modified to reflect the attribution of those skills. Hence, a doctor will be assessed according to the standard of care and skill expected of a reasonable and ordinary doctor, a driver of a motor vehicle will be assessed according to the standard of care and skill expected of a reasonable and ordinary driver, and so on. This rule therefore increases the degree of care and skill that the reasonable defendant would be expected to exercise.

This modification of the standard of care to account for special skill is well established under the common law. In *Phillips v William Whiteley Ltd*, the plaintiff went to a jeweller (the defendant) to have her ears pierced.[43] The jeweller did so, sterilising the piercing needle by exposing it to a naked flame and dipping it in Lysol. The plaintiff subsequently developed an abscess she attributed to an infection acquired through the hole of the piercing. All parties admitted that the defendant had not taken all the precautions that a doctor or surgeon would take in preparing the piercing instrument. However, the jeweller was not expected to act to that standard, since he was not holding himself out to be anything other than a jeweller. For this reason, he was required to exercise that degree of care and skill expected of an ordinary and reasonable jeweller, a standard higher than that of the ordinary and reasonable person but not so high as that applicable had the plaintiff sought the procedure from a doctor or surgeon. It is also worth noting that specialisations within particular skill sets (eg, the distinction between a general practitioner and a specialist in some areas of medical practice) will be reflected in their expected standards of care[44] (see further Section 3.2.2.6).

It is important to note that this principle holds not simply when a person *in fact* possesses the relevant skills in question (though they often will) but whenever they *hold themselves out* as possessing them. The mere fact of doing an activity which presupposes special skills may constitute such 'holding out'. Moreover, the 'special skills' principle may 'trump' other factors such as age, meaning that even a young person holding themselves as having special skills by engaging in a particular activity (say, driving a car) is held to the same adult standard of skill irrespective of their youth.[45]

The 'special skills' principle has now been codified in the South Australian and Victorian civil liability statutes, as listed in Table 3.2.

Table 3.2   Breach of duty: special skills

Legislation	Section
Civil Liability Act 1936 (SA)	40(a)
Wrongs Act 1958 (Vic)	58(a)

It is important to note that, in addition to the 'special skills' principle, most of the civil liability statutes have introduced special rules regarding the standard of care for professionals (discussed in Section 3.3.3.6).

---

43   [1938] 1 All ER 566.
44   See, eg, *Rogers v Whitaker* (1992) 175 CLR 479, 483 (describing the 'reasonable person' standard of care in that case as demanding 'the skill of an ophthalmic surgeon specializing in corneal and anterior segment surgery').
45   *Imbree v McNeilly* (2008) 236 CLR 510.

3.2.2.5   Experience

Where the purported exercise of special skills (see Section 3.2.2.4) and professional skills (see Section 3.2.2.6) imports a higher expectation of care, the particular experience level of the defendant in the doing of that activity is not relevant to the standard of care. In other words, if you are working as a solicitor in a law firm, the standard of care expected of you is the same regardless of whether you have been acting as a lawyer for many years or whether you are in your first year of practice. This principle has been affirmed by the High Court in the case of learner drivers, where experience level is not taken into account in setting the standard of the reasonable driver.[46] It is likely to be the case for other categories of defendants also.

Some cases suggested that there are situations where a lower standard of care may be set for defendants who are particularly inexperienced in the risk-creating activity they are undertaking, and where a special relationship exists between them and the plaintiff such that the plaintiff is *aware* of their inexperience but relies upon their care in undertaking that activity regardless.[47] However, the High Court in *Imbree v McNeilly* rejected this line of argument, at least as it pertains to learner and unlicensed drivers and their passengers.[48] Moreover there may be good reasons not to vary the standard of care in other activity categories, given that the issue of plaintiff knowledge can be taken into account when considering applicable defences, such as contributory negligence and voluntary assumption of risk.[49]

Case: *Imbree v McNeilly* (2008) 236 CLR 510

Facts

Paul Imbree (the plaintiff) was on a four-wheel drive trip through the Northern Territory with two of his sons and one of their friends, Jesse McNeilly (the defendant). The plaintiff knew that the defendant (then 16 years old) did not yet have his learner's permit to drive. The plaintiff nonetheless allowed the defendant (as well as the other boys) to drive his vehicle for about 30–40 minutes at a time during the journey when he assessed the off-road terrain to be less demanding. The defendant, while driving on one such occasion, misjudged how to handle a piece of tyre debris on the road and, as a result, caused the car to roll over. The plaintiff suffered severe spinal injuries as a result of the accident, rendering him tetraplegic.

Issue

The question was whether it was appropriate to expect a lesser standard of care from the defendant in light of his inexperience as a driver and the plaintiff's knowledge of that inexperience.

---

46 *Imbree v McNeilly* (2008) 236 CLR 510.
47 For example, in *Cook v Cook* (1986) 162 CLR 376, the High Court allowed a modified standard of care as between a husband and wife for an accident she caused when learning to drive under his instruction. For a discussion of other examples, see K Barker et al, *The Law of Torts in Australia* (Oxford University Press, 5th ed, 2012) 434–6.
48 (2008) 236 CLR 510; [2008] HCA 40.
49 See, eg, *Imbree v McNeilly* (2008) 236 CLR 510; [2008] HCA 40, 514–15 (Gleeson CJ), 532 (Gummow, Hayne and Kiefel JJ).

Decision

The High Court held that, notwithstanding the plaintiff's knowledge of the defendant's inexperience in driving a motor vehicle, the standard of care the defendant owed to the plaintiff was precisely the same as the standard owed to all other road users: that of the reasonable driver.

Significance

This case overturned earlier High Court authority that set a lower standard of care for an inexperienced driver in relation to passengers aware of their inexperience.

Notes

The High Court in *Imbree v McNeilly* explained its decision by relying on the following arguments (at 561–3):

- Setting a different standard of care owed by a defendant to one particular plaintiff (their passenger), as opposed to all other potential plaintiff groups (other road users), is anomalous in negligence law and is not justifiable.
- In practice, inexperience is difficult to apply as a modified standard as it involves so many variants and is thus closely related to the idiosyncrasies of the defendant. In that sense, to modify the standard on that basis would be inconsistent with the objective standard of care which is applied in other cases.
- The issue of the plaintiff's knowledge of the defendant's inexperience and of the defendant's supervisory role can be better and properly addressed as a matter of potential defences. Moreover, it was inconsistent in early cases to adopt a modified standard owed by a learner driver to their supervisor and not to extend this to all other road users aware of the learner driver's status.
- Kirby J also took the view that the existence today of compulsory insurance in cases involving motor vehicle accidents further justifies not modifying the standard of care for inexperienced drivers, given the implications for distributive justice.

Question

How might the existence of compulsory insurance bear on the question of whether the standard of care for inexperienced and learner drivers should remain that of the 'reasonable driver' in all circumstances?

 Guided response in the eBook

3.2.2.6   Status of professionals

Imagine that you go to a doctor to receive medical advice and treatment and suffer some harm. You attribute it to carelessness by the doctor. However, the doctor is able to demonstrate that the course of action they took in treating you would be endorsed by other doctors working in the same field. Should the view of the other medical professionals prevail? Or should a court be entitled, notwithstanding such a view, to find that a reasonable doctor would have acted more prudently in some way?

In the United Kingdom, this kind of situation is covered by the so-called *Bolam* principle, named after the case in which it was first articulated.[50] In essence, this principle provides that a doctor will not be liable if they acted in accordance with a practice accepted as proper by a responsible body of their peers and notwithstanding the existence of a contrary view among some of the profession.[51] In other words, the standard of care for medical professionals in their treatment of patients in the United Kingdom is set (under this principle) not by the courts but as a 'matter of medical judgment'.[52]

The High Court of Australia, however, rejected the *Bolam* principle for the purposes of Australian negligence law.[53] While it did not object to the importance of considering the opinion of medical experts when determining what reasonable care demands of medical professionals, it did object to such opinion being determinative.[54] This means that the position on the standard of care for medical professionals under the common law in Australia is consistent with the position taken for all other categories of defendants when assessing their liability. That is, a defendant's adherence to a common or accepted practice within their field is a relevant consideration as to what constitutes reasonable care in the circumstances of the case, but it does not determine the standard. (See further Section 3.3.3.6.)

The same issue was the subject of specific consideration by the Ipp Review, which was asked to 'develop and evaluate options for a requirement that the standard of care in professional negligence matters (including medical negligence) accords with the generally accepted practice of the relevant profession at the time of the negligent act or omission'.[55] That review led to the introduction by all states of provisions related to the standard of care for professionals. Unfortunately, these provisions are not uniform. Nor do they entirely correspond with the recommendations of the 2002 *Review of the Law of Negligence* ('Ipp Report'). Moreover, the Australian Capital Territory and Northern Territory have not introduced any such provisions and remain governed by the common law approach. There are thus concerns regarding the potential for significant variations on the question of

---

50 *Bolam v Friern Hospital Management Committee* [1957] 1 WLR 582.
51 Ibid 587 (McNair J).
52 *Sidaway v Bethlem Royal Hospital Governors* [1985] AC 871, 881 (Lord Scarman).
53 *Rogers v Whitaker* (1992) 175 CLR 479 (addressing a doctor's failure to provide information to a patient about certain risks associated with her eye surgery). This case is taken to have rejected the *Bolam* principle not only in cases involving a doctor's failure to provide adequate information, but also in relation to the provision of treatment by medical professionals: *Naxakis v Western General Hospital* (1999) 197 CLR 269.
54 *Rosenberg v Percival* (2001) 205 CLR 434, 439 (Gleeson CJ).
55 Ipp Report x. The recommendations on that issue are set out at 37–57.

professional negligence liability across Australian jurisdictions, notwithstanding that a goal of the Ipp Review was to encourage uniformity.[56]

Despite differences, there are some common features across the various civil liability statutes.[57] In essence, they provide that certain professionals *will not be liable* for negligence if they acted in a manner that was widely accepted by peer professional opinion as competent professional practice. Such peer professional opinion thus operates, unlike the common law in Australia but similarly to the *Bolam* principle, as determinative of the standard of care for the relevant professionals. To operate as determinative, the peer professional opinion being relied upon by the defendant to justify their actions does not need to have been universally accepted. Nor does the existence of a conflict between widely accepted peer opinions negate any one of those opinions being relied upon for the purpose of using this principle. Courts do, however, have some leeway to overrule professional opinion where it is deemed irrational or unreasonable. Moreover, in most states these principles do not apply to cases where the defendant's alleged breach constitutes a failure to provide sufficient information regarding a risk of harm (see further Section 3.3.4). The provisions setting out these principles in each of the relevant civil liability statutes are listed in Table 3.3.

Table 3.3 Breach of duty: professionals

Legislation	Section(s)	Application
Civil Liability Act 2002 (NSW)	50, 5P	• Applies to professionals • Peer opinion must be widely accepted in Australia to be relied upon • Peer opinion cannot be relied upon if court considers it irrational • Does not apply to cases involving failure to warn as to risk of injury or death to a person associated with any professional service
Civil Liability Act 2003 (Qld)	20, 22	• Applies to professionals • Peer opinion must be widely accepted by a significant number of respected practitioners to be relied upon • Peer opinion cannot be relied upon if court considers it irrational or contrary to a written law • Does not apply to cases involving failure to warn about risk to a person associated with any professional service
Civil Liability Act 1936 (SA)	41	• Applies to persons who provide a professional service • Peer opinion must be widely accepted in Australia to be relied upon • Peer opinion cannot be relied upon if court considers it irrational • Does not apply to cases involving failure to warn about risk of injury or death to a person associated with a healthcare service
Civil Liability Act 2002 (Tas)	22	• Applies to professionals • Peer opinion must be widely accepted in Australia to be relied upon • Peer opinion cannot be relied upon if court considers it irrational • Does not apply to cases involving failure to warn about risk of harm associated with any professional service

---

56 C Mah, 'A Critical Evaluation of the Professional Practice Defence in the Civil Liability Acts' (2014) 37(2) *University of Western Australia Law Review* 74.

57 The formulation adopted here is taken from ibid 77–8.

Table 3.3   *(cont.)*

Legislation	Section(s)	Application
Wrongs Act 1958 (Vic)	57, 59, 60	• Applies to professionals • Peer opinion must be widely accepted in Australia by a significant number of respected practitioners to be relied upon • Peer opinion cannot be relied upon if court considers it unreasonable, though court must provide reasons for that finding in writing • Does not apply to cases involving failure to warn about risk or other matter associated with any professional service
Civil Liability Act 2002 (WA)	5PA, 5PB	• Applies to health professionals • Peer opinion must be widely accepted by peers to be relied upon • Does not preclude liability if conduct of health profession so unreasonable that no reasonable health professional would have behaved in that way • Does not apply to cases involving failure to warn about risk of injury or death associated with: (a) treatment proposed for a patient or foetus; or (b) a diagnostic procedure for a patient or foetus

With that common framework in mind, it is worth noting several points of difference among the state civil liability statutes:

- *Professionals covered:* In most states, the relevant statutory provisions operate to the benefit of all 'professionals' (meaning a person 'practising a profession'); in South Australia they relate to 'persons providing a professional service' (presumably a wider category of defendants); in Western Australia they apply only to medical professionals.

- *Widely accepted:* In some states, a particular opinion must be 'widely accepted in Australia' to be relied upon, whereas in other states the drafting refers to wide acceptance in general and makes no reference that confines the opinion geographically to Australian expert opinion. Moreover, only Queensland and Victoria particularise the need for a 'significant number of respected practitioners' to agree, in order to meet the threshold of a widely held view.

- *Irrational or unreasonable as grounds to disregard peer opinion:* In most states, the legislation disallows reliance on peer professional opinion as the standard of care where the opinion is deemed by a court to be 'irrational'. The language of irrationality suggests a very high bar before this preclusion would operate. By contrast, Victoria requires an opinion to be deemed unreasonable by a court before it can be disregarded, which provides significantly more leeway to courts to do so. This is tempered somewhat by the obligation that courts provide reasons in writing when they exercise this power. It has, nonetheless, been suggested that the language of 'unreasonableness' ostensibly places the Victorian courts in the same position they were in under the common law in terms of regard to peer professional opinion.[58] Queensland also provides, in addition to irrationality, that an opinion that is contrary to a written law is a further ground for a court to disregard it. Finally, Western Australia adopts a test familiar in public law, namely that peer opinion

---

58 Ibid 91–2.

cannot be relied upon by a defendant where their behaviour is so unreasonable that no reasonable practitioner would have done the same, which seems unlikely to have much purchase where an opinion is widely held.

- *Failure to warn:* Each state precludes the application of the statutory standard of care for professionals in cases where the defendant's breach relates to a failure to give adequate information (discussed in Section 3.3.4). Differences lie, however, in respect of which professional service settings and what kinds of information the alleged breach must relate to, in order for the preclusion to operate.

The relevant provisions in each state on the standard of care for professionals are listed in Table 3.3, together with a summary of their requirements on each of these points of difference.

HINTS AND TIPS

It is debatable precisely where in the framework of a negligence claim the statutory provisions on the standard of care of professionals ought to be addressed: whether as a matter of defence or as a question of establishing the standard of care. The better view is that the provisions form part of the process of establishing the relevant standard of care, albeit that the onus falls on the defendant to lead evidence establishing that standard.[59] To treat the principle at the defence stage of the inquiry would lead to inconsistent findings in the context of the same action. Specifically, it would involve a finding first that the defendant did not act reasonably (breach), and subsequently that the defendant did act reasonably (defence).[60]

In so much as the provisions interplay with the breach inquiry, they overlap with both the setting of the standard of care of the reasonable person comparator (the subject of our discussions in this section) and with its application to the case at hand (the subject of discussions in Section 3.3). The practical reason why it may be worthwhile addressing this issue in your own answers on breach right at the outset when you are setting the standard of care is that, where they operate and are satisfied, the statutory provisions on the standard of care for professionals ostensibly 'trump' all other issues in breach. In other words, if it is determinative, peer professional opinion renders the other factors you would ordinarily have to address to determine breach irrelevant.

For this reason, it is worthwhile doing the following when you are reviewing a problem scenario involving a potential professional defendant with a view to providing some legal advice on breach:

(1) Identify (and explain) whether your defendant is the kind of professional to which your state's statutory peer professional opinion provisions apply. Moreover, identify (and explain) whether the kind of claim being made

59   See, eg, *Dobler v Halverson* (2007) 70 NSWLR 151, 166–8 (Giles JA, Ipp and Basten JJA agreeing) (commenting on *Civil Liability Act 2002* (NSW) s 50).

60   Richard Cheney SC, 'Competent Professional Practice: Section 50 of the *Civil Liability Act 2002* (NSW)' (Paper presented to Greenway Chambers CPD Program, Sydney, 8 March 2018) 9–10.

against the defendant is such as to allow or preclude the operation of those provisions. (For example, if you have a failure to warn case, are these provisions inapplicable?) If you are working within the jurisdiction of either of the territories, you bypass this issue and address common practice later, as part of your negligence calculus.

(2) If the statutory provisions on professional standards of care apply, consider whether the formal requirements might be satisfied based on the information provided in the problem, explaining why in your answer. For example, was the defendant's behaviour consistent with an opinion widely held by their peers?

(3) If those provisions are satisfied, you can conclude that there was no breach.

(4) If those provisions are not satisfied, continue with the other considerations demanded when determining whether a defendant has breached their duty of care (as discussed in Section 3.3).

3.2.2.7 Public authorities

As noted in Section 2.5.4, public authorities form a special category of defendant that raises peculiar issues when questions of their alleged negligence arise. A public authority is an entity empowered by statute to perform public functions. The social role of such entities, to engage in decision-making around policy and public interest concerns, differentiates them from private actors, whose behaviours are driven primarily by private interests. For that reason, the common law has carved out special considerations that are relevant when determining whether public authorities owe a duty of care should their activities injure private interests and in determining whether they have breached any such duty.

At the breach stage of a negligence inquiry, at least two variations under the common law provide a degree of leniency as to the standard of care expected of public authorities. First, a court is entitled to take into account the limited resources of a public authority and their need to distribute those across various responsibilities when assessing breach. Second, a court is entitled to allow for the legitimate expectation that individuals will protect themselves against obvious dangers.[61] There are also some decisions by public authorities that will raise such 'core' policy questions that they are not amenable to a reasonableness assessment by a court in a negligence claim, though the precise scope of this principle is uncertain.[62]

There are now also statutory provisions in most states and territories that bear on the standard of care expected of public authorities.[63] The exceptions are South Australia and the Northern Territory, where the common law alone continues to apply. The new provisions

---

61 J Bell-James and K Barker, 'Public Authority Liability for Negligence in the Post-Ipp Era: Sceptical Reflections on the "Policy Defence"' (2016) 40(1) *Melbourne University Law Review* 1, 14. Strictly speaking, these factors overlap with the *application* of the 'standard of care' rather than the *setting* of the standard. All issues related to public authorities are, however, dealt with here for simplicity.

62 See, in particular, *Crimmins v Stevedoring Industry Finance Committee* (1999) 200 CLR 1; *Brodie v Singleton Shire Council* (2001) 206 CLR 512; [2001] HCA 29; *Graham Barclay Oysters Pty Ltd v Ryan* (2002) 211 CLR 540; [2002] HCA 54.

63 These were introduced based on recommendations by the Ipp Review Panel. See Ipp Report ix [3(a)]. The recommendations on that issue are set out at 151–61.

introduced across Australian jurisdictions raise complexities. They are not uniform; nor do they entirely resemble the recommendations made by the Ipp Report.[64] However, a few general rules regarding the modified standard of care in a negligence claim can be identified.

First, all of those jurisdictions that introduced statutory reforms related to public authorities include a provision that directs the courts to consider the following when determining questions of either duty or breach related to a public authority:

(a)   the functions required to be exercised by the authority are limited by the financial and other resources reasonably available to the authority for exercising the functions

(b)   the general allocation of the resources by the authority is not open to challenge

(c)   the functions required to be exercised by the authority are to be decided by reference to the broad range of its activities (and not only by reference to the matter to which the proceeding relates)

(d)   the authority may rely on evidence of its compliance with the general procedures and applicable standards for the exercise of its functions as evidence of the proper exercise of its functions in the matter to which the proceeding relates.[65]

These considerations are all drafted in broadly the same terms across the various Australian jurisdictions and appear in the statutory provisions listed in Table 3.4. It is unclear how far (if at all) they modify the existing common law, which (as noted earlier) already allowed a modified standard to account for the resources and duties of public authorities.[66]

Table 3.4   Breach of duty: public authorities and resources

Legislation	Section
Civil Law (Wrongs) Act 2002 (ACT)	110
Civil Liability Act 2002 (NSW)	42
Civil Liability Act 2003 (Qld)	35
Civil Liability Act 2002 (Tas)	38
Wrongs Act 1958 (Vic)	83 (excludes category (b))
Civil Liability Act 2002 (WA)	5W

Second, some jurisdictions have introduced what has been described as a statutory 'policy defence',[67] although it may be more accurate to describe such provisions as lowering the

---

64 J Bell-James and K Barker, 'Public Authority Liability for Negligence in the Post-Ipp Era: Sceptical Reflections on the "Policy Defence"' (2016) 40(1) *Melbourne University Law Review* 1, 3.

65 It is worth noting that the precise definition, and thus scope, of the concept of a 'public authority' differs slightly in each jurisdiction: *Civil Law (Wrongs) Act 2002* (ACT) s 109; *Civil Liability Act 2002* (NSW) s 41; *Civil Liability Act 2003* (Qld) s 34; *Civil Liability Act 2002* (Tas) s 37; *Wrongs Act 1958* (Vic) s 79; *Civil Liability Act 2002* (WA) s 5U.

66 J Bell-James and K Barker, 'Public Authority Liability for Negligence in the Post-Ipp Era: Sceptical Reflections on the "Policy Defence"' (2016) 40(1) *Melbourne University Law Review* 1, 23.

67 For a discussion of the provisions that create such so-called 'policy defences' and the complexities of their implications see ibid 24–37.

standard of care expected of public authorities when exercising certain statutory functions.[68] Variants of this modified standard of care appear in the provisions listed in Table 3.5. While the drafting within each of the relevant civil liability Acts differs, the core notion is that the exercise of certain statutory functions or powers by public authorities cannot give rise to liability unless they are so unreasonable that no reasonable authority could have done the same. It is not clear precisely how far these provisions reduce the standard of care applicable to public authorities when they apply, though lower the standard they certainly do. It may be at least equivalent to the standard of care of professionals acting in compliance with peer professional opinion (see Section 3.2.2.6), if not potentially more accommodating to the defendant given the full range of 'reasonable' decisions it would allow.[69] It is certainly an attenuated standard that has parallels with the *Wednesbury* standard of unreasonableness under public law and that operates to 'significantly alter the otherwise applicable standard of care at common law.'[70] Because some of the provisions listed in Table 3.5 refer to proceedings 'based on breach of statutory duty', there is some uncertainty as to whether those provisions are limited to claims brought under the distinct tort of breach of statutory duty. However, there is authority that suggests they apply more broadly, including to claims brought in negligence.[71]

Table 3.5   Breach of duty: public authorities and the exercise of a statutory duty or function

Legislation	Section(s)
Civil Law (Wrongs) Act 2002 (ACT)	111
Civil Liability Act 2002 (NSW)	43, 43A
Civil Liability Act 2003 (Qld)	36
Civil Liability Act 2002 (Tas)	40
Wrongs Act 1958 (Vic)	84
Civil Liability Act 2002 (WA)	5X, 5Y

Finally, some jurisdictions have introduced provisions that specifically limit the liability of road authorities[72] or that introduce an added hurdle to public authority liability in cases involving a claim that the authority should have exercised a power, but did not do so.[73]

---

68 *Queensland Bulk Water Supply Authority v Rodriguez & Sons Pty Ltd* (2021) 393 ALR 162, 199.
69 J Bell-James and K Barker, 'Public Authority Liability for Negligence in the Post-Ipp Era: Sceptical Reflections on the "Policy Defence"' (2016) 40(1) *Melbourne University Law Review* 1, 29–37.
70 *Southern Properties (WA) Pty Ltd v Executive Director, Department of Conservation and Land Management* (2012) 42 WAR 287, 310 (McLure P, Buss JA agreeing). See also *Queensland Bulk Water Supply Authority v Rodriguez & Sons Pty Ltd* (2021) 393 ALR 162, 199–205; *Curtis v Harden Shire Council* (2014) 88 NSWLR 10, 68–72 (Basten JA).
71 See, eg, *Queensland Bulk Water Supply Authority v Rodriguez & Sons Pty Ltd* (2021) 393 ALR 162, 185–7 (interpreting s 36 of the *Civil Liability Act 2003* (Qld)).
72 *Civil Law (Wrongs) Act 2002* (ACT) s 113; *Civil Liability Act 2002* (NSW) s 45; *Civil Liability Act 2003* (Qld) s 37; *Civil Liability Act 1936* (SA) s 42; *Civil Liability Act 2002* (Tas) s 42; *Civil Liability Act 2002* (WA) s 5Z.
73 *Civil Law (Wrongs) Act 2002* (ACT) s 112; *Civil Liability Act 2002* (NSW) s 44; *Civil Liability Act 2002* (Tas) s 41. In addition, Tasmania has a 'recreational activities' limitation on the liability of public authorities, where they provide an appropriate risk warning to users: *Civil Liability Act 2002* (Tas) s 39.

EMERGING ISSUE

Climate change litigation is an increasingly common phenomenon all around the world. Such litigation seeks to influence the behaviour of decision-makers whose choices affect global warming. Australia is no exception. An emerging issue is the use of negligence law as one vehicle for such claims. One significant example of this kind is *Minister for the Environment v Sharma*.[74] At first instance, a Federal Court judge held that the federal Minister for the Environment owes Australian children a duty of care when deciding whether to approve new coalmining in light of the future impacts of climate change on their health and wellbeing.[75] The Full Court of the Federal Court overturned this decision on appeal.[76] Some of the judges did so in part on the basis that the purported duty of care would raise for consideration at the point of breach 'matters that are core policy questions unsuitable in their nature and character for judicial determination' (at 207). According to this line of thinking, a duty of care in this case would demand a court assess the reasonableness of a ministerial decision shaped by Australian governmental policy of the highest order – policy that, among other things, reflects Australia's cooperation with other countries in relation to managing greenhouse gas emissions (at 279–83). Not all of the judges agreed on this point, and it remains open whether similar future claims might proceed, particularly as the actual impacts of climate change on Australian communities start to be experienced.

3.2.2.8   Institutions and child abuse

In 2015, the Royal Commission into Institutional Responses to Child Sexual Abuse made a number of recommendations as to how to reform civil liability laws to address the historical widespread phenomenon of child sexual abuse in institutional settings in Australia. Among other things, this included recommending the introduction of a statutory duty of care on the part of institutions with care, supervision or control over a child to take reasonable steps to prevent the child being subject to abuse by persons associated with the institutions.[77] A number of jurisdictions have now introduced this statutory duty, via the provisions listed in Table 3.6. Those provisions operate not only to construct a presumed duty of care; they also serve to modify the standard of care expected, as well as reversing the onus of proof in relation to breach. While the precise drafting of the scope of the duty in each jurisdiction varies, common to each is that a breach of duty will be presumed if child abuse is proven to have been committed by a relevant associated person, unless the institution can prove it took either 'reasonable steps' or 'all reasonable steps' to prevent the abuse. To varying degrees, each jurisdiction also sets out indicative factors that a court may take into account

---

74 (2022) 291 FCR 411.
75 (2021) 391 ALR 1.
76 *Minister for the Environment v Sharma* (2022) 291 FCR 411.
77 *Royal Commission into Institutional Responses to Child Sexual Abuse: Redress and Civil Litigation Report* (Report, September 2015) 54–7.

in determining breach. To illustrate, some of the factors set out in s 50F of the *Civil Liability Act 1936* (SA) include:

* the nature of the institution
* the resources that were reasonably available to the institution
* the relationship between the institution and the child
* the position in which the institution placed the person (who committed the abuse of the child) in relation to the child, including the extent to which the position gave the person authority, power or control over the child or an ability to achieve intimacy with the child or gain the child's trust.

Table 3.6   Breach of duty: institutional child abuse

Legislation	Section(s)
Civil Liability Act 2002 (NSW)	6F
Personal Injuries (Liabilities and Damages) Act 2003 (NT)	17E (abuse by associated individual) 17F (abuse by another child)
Civil Liability Act 2003 (Qld)	33E
Civil Liability Act 1936 (SA)	50F
Civil Liability Act 2002 (Tas)	49H
Wrongs Act 1958 (Vic)	91

3.2.3   Time of assessment

Often, there can be significant delays between the time when an allegedly negligent act or omission occurred, and the date when the plaintiff's legal claim regarding that incident is adjudicated by a court (or a settlement reached between the parties). The question thus arises: is the reasonableness of what the defendant did or did not do assessed according to: (a) what a reasonable person would (or would not) have done at the time of the events in question, or (b) what a reasonable person would (or would not) do today? The implications for a defendant of the difference can be quite significant, given that our knowledge and understanding of certain risks can alter substantially over time. Indeed, the very events which are the subject of a plaintiff's legal action may themselves generate new knowledge and understanding about risks of the kind the plaintiff was exposed to.

The answer is that the court must assess the defendant's conduct against the reasonable person imbued with the kind of knowledge and appreciation of risk that could be expected *at the time of the events in question*. This is as a matter of fairness and to ensure judgment free from the bias of hindsight. Given that fault is a part of the tort of negligence, it would be unfair to the defendant if they were expected to behave to a standard that not even the most prudent among us at the time would have appreciated was necessary.

The potential importance of this principle was demonstrated in the 1954 case of *Roe v Ministry of Health*.[78] In that case, two patients (the plaintiffs) had been in hospital in 1947 for minor surgery. In each instance, their surgery required the administration of a spinal anaesthetic. The way this was done by the hospital at the time was by using an

---

78   [1954] 2 QB 66.

anaesthetic contained in small glass ampoules that were, in turn, stored in larger containers containing phenol (carbolic acid). This system of storage had been recently introduced to sterilise the ampoules and reduce the risk of their transferring infection to the patient. What was not appreciated, however, was the potential for microscopic cracks in the ampoules, undetectable by a simple visual inspection, to allow the carbolic acid to seep into the anaesthetic. This seepage had occurred to the anaesthetic used on the two plaintiffs and as a result they were rendered paraplegic by the injections.

It was suggested that the use of dark dyes in the carbolic acid solution could have alerted the anaesthetist to this risk eventuating and provided a means of averting a potentially dire outcome. Indeed, by 1951, it was a risk that had become known and was warned about in UK medical journals. Nonetheless, the Court held that the standard of care was that of a reasonable anaesthetist and hospital according to what was reasonably known and knowable in 1947. Based on that knowledge, this case could not be described as negligence but as misadventure. The risk of reasoning with the benefit of hindsight can also arise in facts situations that involve a much shorter period.[79]

Most jurisdictions have now codified the principle as to the time of an assessment of breach, in general terms[80] or in relation specifically to the conduct of professionals or persons with special skills.[81] Some civil liability statutes now explicitly provide that the subsequent taking of action that would have avoided the risk of harm if taken earlier does not of itself constitute an admission of liability.[82]

REVIEW QUESTIONS

(1) What does it mean to say that the reasonable person is an objective standard?

(2) Identify at least two characteristics of the defendant that we know, by law, will serve to modify the standard of care of the reasonable person where relevant to the case at hand, either by potentially raising or reducing expectations. For each category, think of a reason why a modification to the standard might be justified.

(3) Identify two characteristics of the defendant that we know, by law, will *not* serve to modify the standard of care of the reasonable person, even if present in the case at hand. For each category, think of a reason why a modification to the standard is considered not to be justified.

    Guided responses in the eBook

---

79 See, eg, *Tapp v Australian Bushmen's Campdraft & Rodeo Association Ltd* (2022) 273 CLR 454 (on whether reliance on evidence that the defendant ploughed the grounds of a campdrafting competition a day after a horse's fall tended to demonstrate the foreseeability the day before as to the deteriorated condition of the grounds).

80 *Civil Law (Wrongs) Act 2002* (ACT) s 42; *Civil Liability Act 1936* (SA) s 31(1).

81 *Civil Liability Act 2002* (NSW) s 50; *Civil Liability Act 2003* (Qld) s 23(1); *Civil Liability Act 1936* (SA) ss 40(b), 41(1); *Civil Liability Act 2002* (Tas) s 22(1); *Wrongs Act 1958* (Vic) ss 58(b), 59(1); *Civil Liability Act 2002* (WA) s 5PB(1).

82 See further Section 3.4.2.

3.3   Applying the standard of care: demonstrating breach

In order to determine what a reasonable person would have done if placed in the same circumstances as the defendant, most of the civil liability statutes now set out a framework of issues that courts must address. These statutory frameworks are substantively uniform across the jurisdictions that have adopted them and in a large part reflect the process for determining breach as it already existed under the common law, albeit with some variations. Only the Northern Territory does not provide an overarching statutory framework for determining breach and thus remains subject solely to the common law.

Section 5B of the *Civil Liability Act 2002* (NSW) is an example of the breach framework the other states and territories have also adopted. It provides:

> (1)   A person is not negligent in failing to take precautions against a risk of harm unless:
> > (a)   the risk was foreseeable (that is, it is a risk of which the person knew or ought to have known), and
> > (b)   the risk was not insignificant, and
> > (c)   in the circumstances, a reasonable person in the person's position would have taken those precautions.
>
> (2)   In determining whether a reasonable person would have taken precautions against a risk of harm, the court is to consider the following (amongst other relevant things):
> > (a)   the probability that the harm would occur if care were not taken,
> > (b)   the likely seriousness of the harm,
> > (c)   the burden of taking precautions to avoid the risk of harm,
> > (d)   the social utility of the activity that creates the risk of harm.

The comparable provisions in each of the other jurisdictions are listed in Table 3.7.

Table 3.7   Breach of duty: general framework

Legislation	Section
Civil Law (Wrongs) Act 2002 (ACT)	43
Civil Liability Act 2002 (NSW)	5B
Civil Liability Act 2003 (Qld)	9
Civil Liability Act 1936 (SA)	32
Civil Liability Act 2002 (Tas)	11
Wrongs Act 1958 (Vic)	48
Civil Liability Act 2002 (WA)	5B

What is very important today is that each step in the breach inquiry framework must be assessed as an independent consideration. This was a crucial aspect of the recommendations of the Ipp Report and flowed from concerns that some courts were treating step 1 (foreseeability) as sufficient, where it alone does not satisfy the requirements of liability.[83] We will work through each step of the breach inquiry in turn.

---

83 Ipp Report 105 [7.14].

HINTS AND TIPS

When working on the breach element of a negligence problem, this statutory framework provides you with a fairly straightforward structure you can adopt in your own answer. Once you have established the reasonable person standard that is applicable to your scenario (as per the discussion in Section 3.2), you can structure your answer according to the steps set out in the relevant 'framework' provision of the civil liability statute that applies in your jurisdiction.

   This part of your analysis also involves thinking very clearly about precisely which precautions a reasonable person would have taken in the circumstances. Remember to address each item independently as required by the civil liability legislation and that there may be additional provisions and issues that become relevant, depending upon the nature of your scenario. Demonstrations of how these various issues can be argued is provided in the practice problems at the end of this chapter.

3.3.1   Reasonable foreseeability

According to both the common law and the statutory frameworks listed in Table 3.7, a person is only required to take precautions in relation to foreseeable risks. This means that, if a court determines that the risk of harm to the plaintiff was not foreseeable to a reasonable person in the defendant's position at the time (which includes any special knowledge the defendant in fact has), there can be no question of a breach of duty of care. It might thus be described as a hurdle requirement that must be satisfied before the other aspects of the breach inquiry become relevant.

   As explained by Glass CJ in *Minister Administering the Environmental Planning and Assessment Act 1979 v San Sebastian Pty Ltd*, the concept of foreseeability arises at various stages of a negligence claim (duty, breach and remoteness) but each raises different issues that 'progressively decline from the general to the particular'.[84] At the breach stage, the inquiry relates to the precise risk the plaintiff complains they were exposed to; in other words, it relates to the kind of carelessness complained of by the plaintiff. However, this only requires the potential for foresight of a risk of an injury of the same general kind and not the specific injury the plaintiff has suffered:

> The breach question requires proof that it was reasonably foreseeable as a possibility that *the kind* of carelessness charged against the defendant might cause damage of *some kind* to the plaintiff's [or class of plaintiffs'] person or property.[85]

The application of this test therefore relies crucially upon the plaintiff making clear precisely the risks they allege the defendant should have protected against, though this need only go to the class of injury suffered by the plaintiff, not their precise injury or the precise way in

84 [1983] 2 NSWLR 268, 295.
85 *Minister Administering the Environmental Planning and Assessment Act 1979 v San Sebastian Pty Ltd* [1983] 2 NSWLR 268, 296 (Glass JA) (emphasis in original).

which it came about.[86] In fact, identifying the precise risk of harm to the plaintiff, in terms of the 'true source of potential injury', is crucial to all steps in the breach inquiry.[87]

Moreover, the way in which the plaintiff characterises the risk of harm to them at the breach stage (including the level of specificity and generality of the risk) is also important to how a court assesses other related elements of the claim in negligence. The same characterisation of risk as is applied at the breach stage is also the correct way in which to approach the question of causation (whether the risk in question caused the injury to the plaintiff) and when determining whether or not the risk was an obvious one.[88] It is also important to appreciate that the foreseeability of a risk is not equivalent to the probability that the risk may (or may not) eventuate.[89] Probability refers to the statistical likelihood of something occurring whereas foreseeability refers to one's capacity to know about and thus anticipate something occurring. While these things may overlap, they also may not. What the defendant actually knows or ought to know are crucial to the foreseeability inquiry, but not to the question of probability. Having said this, these concepts are apt to become confused in light of the way in which probability of a causal outcome informs our foresight of what might or might not occur.[90] The probability of a risk eventuating is a scientific notion that may or may not be known at a particular time in history.[91] This point was demonstrated in the case of *Roe v Ministry of Health* (discussed in Section 3.2.3).[92] Moreover, something may have a low chance of occurring but be self-evident as a potential risk (albeit a small one).

The leading case on the reasonable foreseeability test at the breach stage is *Wyong Shire Council v Shirt*.

Case: *Wyong Shire Council v Shirt* (1980) 146 CLR 40

Facts

Brian Shirt (the plaintiff) was an inexperienced water-skier who was skiing in a circuit of lakes habitually used by water-skiers. The southernmost of those lakes was quite shallow. The Council of the Shire of Wyong (the defendant) had recently undertaken dredging work in that southernmost lake to create a channel. It had erected signs in the bed of the lake adjacent to the channel on which the words 'Deep Water' were written. The plaintiff mistakenly understood the signs as indicating water depth in a part of the lake which, in fact, remained quite shallow. He therefore chose to ski, he argued, somewhere he thought was safe (deep water) rather than dangerous to a learner like himself (shallow water). While water-skiing, he fell and struck his head and as a result was rendered quadriplegic.

---

86 On the latter, see *Chapman v Hearse* (1961) 106 CLR 112, 120; *Tapp v Australian Bushmen's Campdraft & Rodeo Association Ltd* (2022) 273 CLR 454, 491–2 (Gordon, Edelman and Gleeson JJ).

87 *Roads and Traffic Authority (NSW) v Dederer* (2007) 234 CLR 330; [2007] HCA 42, 351 (Gummow J).

88 *Tapp v Australian Bushmen's Campdraft & Rodeo Association Ltd* (2022) 273 CLR 454, 489–94 (Gordon, Edelman and Gleeson JJ). For more on obvious risks see Section 5.3.2.1.

89 *Wyong Shire Council v Shirt* (1980) 146 CLR 40, 47 (Mason J).

90 For an example of the complex relationship between foresight and the question of causality of harm, see *Minister for the Environment v Sharma* (2022) 291 FCR 311.

91 See, eg, Ipp Report 103–4 [7.10].

92 [1954] 2 QB 66.

Issue

The appeal to the High Court turned on the correct test of reasonable foreseeability at the breach stage of a negligence claim.

Decision

The High Court held that the test was whether the precise risk to the plaintiff was such as would be foreseeable to a reasonable person in the defendant's position as a real risk, meaning it was not far-fetched or fanciful. The majority of the Court held that in this case the question was thus whether a reasonable person could foresee that a water-skier might be induced to believe a certain area of the lake was deeper than in fact it was because of the position of the sign. They held that this specific risk was not far-fetched and was thus foreseeable.

Significance

This case is routinely referred to both as correctly articulating the reasonable foreseeability test under the common law as it relates to determining breach, and as demonstrating how the negligence calculus is to be applied when determining what a reasonable person would do in response to a foreseeable risk.

Notes

Mason J, while finding the risk in the case to be foreseeable, acknowledged that it 'is a question on which minds may well differ, as indeed they have done. It [the foreseeability test] is not a question which a judge is necessarily better equipped to answer than a layman'.[93] Indeed, in this case, Wilson J dissented on the outcome of the reasonable foreseeability test. He found instead that the risk to the plaintiff was unforeseeable given the visibility (in his view) of the shallowness of the water and the fact that the signs were directed (properly, he thought) not to water-skiers who could adjudge the issue, but to swimmers who might be at risk in deeper water.

Question

If you read the judgment of Wilson J, do you think he agrees or disagrees with the test of foreseeability at the breach stage as articulated by Mason J?

 Guided response in the eBook

Given the threshold of 'not far-fetched or fanciful', the reasonable foreseeability inquiry at the breach stage can be described as a relatively undemanding hurdle. This might be justified on the basis that to fix a higher standard (eg, that a risk must be 'not unlikely to occur') would strip negligence of much of its importance and function, as it would become tantamount to liability for deliberate harm.[94] Importantly, however, the foreseeability test alone is not determinative of breach. As discussed in *Wyong Shire Council v Shirt*, once

---

93   *Wyong Shire Council v Shirt* (1980) 146 CLR 40, 48–9 (Mason J).
94   Ibid 49–50 (Murphy J).

foreseeability was satisfied under the common law, the next inquiry was what (if anything) a reasonable person would do in response to the foreseeable risk, which involves weighing up various practical factors (discussed in Section 3.3.3).[95] However, a further preliminary hurdle must now be satisfied under the civil liability statutory schemes, which is an inquiry into whether the relevant risk was not insignificant.

HINTS AND TIPS

In order to apply the reasonable foreseeability test as it arises at the breach stage, you must identify the precise risk or risks of injury underpinning the plaintiff's claim. This can be described as 'characterising the risk'. It is worth doing this at the outset of your discussion of breach, as we have seen (in Section 3.2) that if your case is best characterised as a failure-to-warn claim, this may also have some bearing on setting the correct standard of the reasonable person. Moreover, as demonstrated in the discussion in Section 3.3.1, how you characterise the risk for the purposes of demonstrating breach has implications for other aspects of the claim in negligence, such as causation and obvious risk. It is thus a very critical part of a plaintiff's claim. It is also worth noting that there may be more than one risk that the plaintiff argues that the defendant should have foreseen and protected against which might be argued concurrently or alternatively in presenting their case.

3.3.2 'Not insignificant' risk

In response to concern regarding the apparent ease with which a plaintiff might satisfy the common law reasonable foreseeability test, the Ipp Review recommended the addition of a further hurdle requirement for breach, in the form of the 'not insignificant risk' test.[96] This test has now been adopted uniformly across all jurisdictions except the Northern Territory.[97] In essence, it provides that a person is only expected to take precautions against foreseeable risks that are not insignificant. In other words, a risk may be foreseeable but be sufficiently insignificant as to warrant a reasonable person doing nothing further in respect of it.

Like foreseeability, the 'not insignificant risk' test is a matter of layperson judgment assessed prospectively from the perspective of a reasonable person in the defendant's position, in light of what the defendant knew or ought to have known. There are a couple of questions the test raises. The first question goes to how 'significance' should be measured. As the legislation does not specify, a range of logical measures might arguably be used (eg, a risk involving severe consequences, even if relatively improbable, might nonetheless be described as significant). However, the comments of the Ipp Review Panel suggest that the insignificance of risk is to be assessed by reference to the *probability* of the risk occurring, as

---

95 Ibid 44–7 (Mason J).
96 Ipp Report 105–7.
97 *Civil Law (Wrongs) Act 2002* (ACT) s 43(1)(b); *Civil Liability Act 2002* (NSW) s 5B(1)(b); *Civil Liability Act 2003* (Qld) s 9(1)(b); *Civil Liability Act 1936* (SA) s 32(1)(b); *Civil Liability Act 2002* (Tas) s 11(1)(b); *Wrongs Act 1958* (Vic) s 48(1)(b); *Civil Liability Act 2002* (WA) s 5B(1)(b).

opposed to the likely seriousness of harm if it materialises.[98] To date, the case law seems to confirm this approach,[99] though there is also judicial scepticism as to whether this is correct, on the basis that if 'the purpose of the assessment is to determine whether a reasonable person would have taken precautions which the defendant did not take, arguably the seriousness of the possible consequences should not be excluded.'[100]

A second question goes to the precise threshold implied by the language of the test. On this question, the Ipp Report again provides guidance in the following manner:

> The phrase 'not insignificant' is intended to indicate a risk that is of a higher probability than is indicated by the phrase 'not far-fetched or fanciful', but not so high as might be indicated by a phrase such as 'a substantial risk'. The choice of a double negative is deliberate. We do not intend the phrase to be a synonym for 'significant'. 'Significant' is apt to indicate a higher degree of probability than we intend.[101]

In case law, the threshold has been interpreted as imposing a more demanding standard than the 'reasonable foreseeability' test, but 'not by very much'.[102] It has alternatively been described as 'not particularly high' and 'not particularly demanding'[103] and as 'a slightly more demanding standard than one that is far-fetched or fanciful'.[104] In *Collins v Insurance Australia Ltd,* Basten AJA noted:

> Levels of risk may need to be assigned a place on an ascending scale along the following path: no risk → foreseeable risk → insignificant risk → not insignificant risk → significant risk → ... [certainty].[105]

In that case, the NSW Court of Appeal held that the consequential risks of injury to a driver attempting to avoid a traffic jam following an accident on a highway was 'not insignificant' notwithstanding that other drivers had successfully navigated the hazard. In explaining this decision, Kirk JA stated that 'taking account of the not particularly demanding nature of the requirement, a risk may have a low likelihood of occurrence but still be characterised as not insignificant.'[106] Victoria alone has codified the threshold for its 'not insignificant risk' test in s 48(3) of the *Wrongs Act 1958*, which states:

> (3) For the purposes of subsection (1)(b) –
>> (a) *insignificant risks* include, but are not limited to, risks that are far-fetched or fanciful; and
>> (b) risks that are *not insignificant* are all risks other than insignificant risks and include, but are not limited to, significant risks.

---

98 Ipp Report 105.

99 *Benic v New South Wales* [2010] NSWSC 1039, [101] (Garling J).

100 *Collins v Insurance Australia Ltd* (2022) 109 NSWLR 240; [2022] NSWCA 135, [135] (Basten AJA, Meagher JA agreeing).

101 Ipp Report 105 [7.15].

102 *Shaw v Thomas* (2010) Aust Torts Reports 82-065, [44] (Macfarlan JA, Beazley and Tobias JJA agreeing). See also *Meandarra Aerial Spraying Pty Ltd v GEJ & MA Geldard Pty Ltd* [2013] 1 Qd R 319, 333 (Fraser JA, White JA and Mullins J agreeing).

103 *Bunnings Group Ltd v Giudice* (2018) Aust Torts Rep 82–402, [54] (per Leeming and White JJA and Emmett AJA, summarising prior case law).

104 *Prouten v Chapman* [2021] NSWCA 207, [24] (Meagher and Leeming JJA).

105 (2022) 109 NSWLR 240; [2022] NSWCA 135, [132] (Meagher AJA agreeing).

106 Ibid [40].

An example of where the application of this test defeated the plaintiff's claim despite the risk being foreseeable is the case of *Vincent v Woolworths Ltd.*[107] In that case, the plaintiff was working for Woolworths (the defendant) which had provided her with a small step to reach higher shelves without having to strain. While using the step, the plaintiff stepped backward onto a passing customer's shopping trolley and was injured. The NSW Court of Appeal agreed with the lower courts that the risk of injury to the plaintiff, while 'plainly reasonably foreseeable', did not meet the 'not insignificant risk' threshold.[108] This was because the 'commonplace character of the activity' that led to her harm was such that the defendant could expect workers to guard against it.[109]

3.3.3   The negligence calculus

Even when a plaintiff has demonstrated that a particular risk was foreseeable and was not insignificant, this tells us only that a reasonable person would thus contemplate some possible precautions against the risk. It does not determine precisely what precautions (if any) such a person would have taken. Indeed, as noted earlier, this is a matter on which the plaintiff is generally expected to direct the court. To resolve the inquiry requires the court to balance a variety of considerations, identified by Mason J in *Wyong Shire Council v Shirt* as:

- the magnitude of the risk
- the degree of probability of its occurrence
- the expense, difficulty and inconvenience of taking alleviating action
- any other conflicting responsibilities the defendant may have.[110]

The weighing up of these factors is commonly referred to as the 'negligence calculus',[111] though the High Court has warned that this process does not denote a mathematical calculation but rather a matter of judgment.[112] Crucially, no single factor is alone determinative and indeed the relative weight that each consideration should be given depends upon the circumstances of the case.

The negligence calculus has been codified within the various Australian statutory breach frameworks, using the following terms: the *probability* of harm if precautions were not taken, the likely *seriousness* of the harm, the *burden of taking precautions* to avoid the risk of harm, and the *social utility* of the risk-creating activity.[113] Other factors may also be relevant. We consider each briefly now.

3.3.3.1   Probability

The basic position is that the greater the probability of a harm occurring, the greater the degree of care that a reasonable person would take in respect of that risk. The probability

---

107   [2016] NSWCA 40. For another example, see *Bunnings Group Ltd v Giudice* (2018) Aust Torts Rep 82-402.
108   *Vincent v Woolworths Ltd* [2016] NSWCA 40, [20] (Macfarlan JA quoting trial Judge Campbell).
109   Ibid [35] (Macfarlan JA).
110   (1980) 146 CLR 40, 47–8.
111   For a brief discussion of the source of, and judicial responses to, this terminology, see H Luntz et al, *Torts: Cases and Commentary* (LexisNexis Butterworths, 8th ed, 2017) 188–9.
112   *Mulligan v Coffs Harbour City Council* (2005) 233 CLR 486, 490 (Gleeson CJ and Kirby J).
113   *Civil Law (Wrongs) Act 2002* (ACT) s 43(2); *Civil Liability Act 2002* (NSW) s 5B(2); *Civil Liability Act 2003* (Qld) s 9(2); *Civil Liability Act 1936* (SA) s 32(2); *Civil Liability Act 2002* (Tas) s 11(2); *Wrongs Act 1958* (Vic) s 48(2); *Civil Liability Act 2002* (WA) s 5B(2).

that a particular harm may occur, even where it raises the risk of serious physical injury to a person, might be so small as to warrant no further precautions.

For example, in *Bolton v Stone*, the defendant/appellant was a cricket club that occupied and regularly organised cricket matches at a local cricket ground.[114] A two-metre-high fence surrounded the ground but, by virtue of the natural slope of the grounds, the top of the fence was in fact five metres above the cricket pitch. Adjacent to the cricket grounds were some residential properties, including that of Ms Stone (the plaintiff). One day during a match, the plaintiff was standing on the road outside her house, about 90 metres from the pitch, and was struck on the head by a cricket ball that had been batted beyond the boundary of the grounds.

One factor principally led the House of Lords to find no breach. This was the very low risk of this type of harm occurring. In that respect, it is worth noting that the risk was understood in a specific way: as the risk of the ball exiting the grounds *and causing injury*. Evidence was presented that the occurrence of a ball exiting the grounds was quite rare (perhaps only six times in 30 years).[115] While the risk of this occurring and thus causing injury was hence foreseeable, it was so small as to demand no further precautions. Lord Normand observed: 'It is not the law that precautions must be taken against every peril that can be foreseen by the timorous'.[116] Lord Reid described the relevant question as 'whether the risk of damage to a person on the road was so small that a reasonable man in the position of the appellants, considering the matter from the point of view of safety, would have thought it right to refrain from taking steps to prevent the danger'.[117] Lord Radcliffe held that 'a reasonable man, taking account of the chances against an accident happening, would not have felt himself called on' to take further preventative measures.[118]

As *Bolton v Stone* demonstrates, in ascertaining the probability of harm occurring it is important to properly characterise the risk of harm according to the real source of the plaintiff's injury. Moreover, a defendant's obligation is to take reasonable care, not to prevent injury. These two principles are also illustrated by *Roads and Traffic Authority (NSW) v Dederer*.

Case: *Roads and Traffic Authority (NSW) v Dederer* (2007) 234 CLR 330

Facts

Philip Dederer (the plaintiff) was a 14-year-old boy who dived off a bridge into the waters of an estuary below. On the occasion in question, the water level below the bridge was particularly low (only about two metres deep) and as a result the plaintiff struck his head on the bottom of the estuary and was rendered partially paraplegic. The bridge was part of a road under the care of the Roads and Traffic Authority (NSW) (the defendant) and the tide below the bridge was known by

---

114   [1951] 1 All ER 1078.
115   *Bolton v Stone* [1951] AC 850, 864 (Lord Reid).
116   Ibid 1082.
117   Ibid 1086.
118   Ibid 1087.

it to be variable. (The plaintiff later added the Great Lakes Shire Council as a co-defendant to the case.) The plaintiff's dive at that spot on the bridge was not unusual: for many years young people had jumped and dived from that location. For its part, the Council co-defendant had erected a pictogram sign prohibiting diving. Before the plaintiff's case, there had been no injuries arising from this prohibited practice.

Issue

The issue was whether the Council had done enough, in response to the risk posed by young people diving from its bridge, by erecting pictogram signs prohibiting such diving.

Decision

Both the trial judge and the Court of Appeal held that the defendant had breached its duty of care by failing to take further precautions against this known and grave risk, either by improving signage (which was apparently ineffective given the continuation of the practice) or by modifying the design of the bridge to make access for diving more difficult. However, Gummow J (with Heydon and Callinan JJ agreeing) held that the lower courts had misapplied certain basic principles of negligence. First, the lower courts had misconstrued the real probability of harm in this case by mischaracterising the risk of injury as the risk of people diving or jumping from the bridge, whereas it was the risk of making impact with shallow water. Characterised in this way, the risk was not one of high probability; rather it was very low, as demonstrated by the lack of injuries over many years. Second, Gummow J clarified that the exercise of reasonable care will discharge a defendant's duty of care. Such an obligation is not equivalent to the more stringent requirement of preventing harm, which was in his view the (incorrect) standard the lower courts had applied.

Significance

The case clarified the principle that a defendant is not obliged to eliminate risks in order to be acting with due care. The case is also important as it demonstrates how the courts today take a measured and not overly demanding approach to what constitutes reasonable care.

Notes

Kirby J, with whom Gleeson CJ agreed, dissented in this case on the basis that concerns had been communicated to the defendant about the risk (particularly to children) of the ineffectiveness of its signs. His Honour held (at 373–4) that the defendant needed to take measures beyond mere reliance on signs known to be ineffective, which otherwise would operate as a kind of 'automatic, absolute and permanent panacea' for the purpose of its duty of care.

Question

Were negligence calculus factors other than probability of risk considered by Gummow J in his judgment in *Roads and Traffic Authority (NSW) v Dederer*?

 Guided response in the eBook

3.3.3.2 Seriousness

The basic position is that the more serious or grave the nature of a harm that is likely to occur (if such harm does indeed eventuate), the greater the degree of care that a reasonable person would take in respect of that risk. Moreover, a defendant's awareness of the potential for uniquely 'grave' impacts of a risk of harm upon some specific person or persons should be factored into the assessment of due care.

For example, in *Paris v Stepney Borough Council*, the plaintiff was working as a fitter in a garage run by the Council (the defendant).[119] His employer knew that the plaintiff was blind in one eye due to an injury he had sustained during World War I. One day, while the plaintiff was doing maintenance work on a car, he struck a rusty bolt with a steel hammer, to loosen the bolt. A chip flew from the bolt into his good eye, blinding him in that eye and thus blinding him totally. The question was whether his employer had breached its duty of care to him by not providing him with protective goggles.

A key issue for the House of Lords was whether the defendant's awareness of the plaintiff's disability, and thus of the special risk of an increase in the *severity* of a particular kind of injury should it befall him, had a bearing upon the precautions that the employer was obliged to take. On this question, the Court unanimously found in the affirmative, with Lord Morton of Henryton describing the principle in the following terms:

> I think that the more serious the damage which will happen if an accident occurs, the more thorough are the precautions which an employer must take. If I am right as to this general principle, I think it follows logically that if A and B, who are engaged on the same work, run precisely the same risk of an accident happening, but if the results of an accident will be more serious to A than to B, precautions which are adequate in the case of B may not be adequate in the case of A, and it is a duty of the employer to take such additional precautions for the safety of A as may be reasonable. The duty to take reasonable precautions against injury is one which is owed by the employer to every individual workman.[120]

Lord Normand posed the argument in terms of common sense applied to the precise circumstances in question, noting that the amount of care expected of a prudent person would vary infinitely depending on the circumstances, including the known existence of a peculiar vulnerability to grave injury. To demonstrate, he observed: 'No prudent man in carrying a lighted candle through a powder magazine would fail to take more care than if he was going through a damp cellar.'[121]

3.3.3.3 Burden of taking precautions

The basic position is that the greater the burden on the defendant involved in taking precautions against a risk, the less likely that a reasonable person in their position would take such precautions. This is also sometimes referred to as the *practicality* of adopting a

---

119 [1951] 1 All ER 42.
120 *Paris v Stepney Borough Council* [1951] AC 367, 385.
121 Ibid 381.

particular precaution. Burden may exist in the form of expense, inconvenience or difficulty. At its most extreme, burden may involve the cessation of a risk-producing activity in its entirety. By contrast, a relatively simple precaution will point towards an expectation that a reasonable person would adopt it, short of other compelling considerations.

It should be recalled that, with few exceptions such as occupiers and public authorities (whose obligations are thrust upon them), the inquiry regarding the practicality of precautions is not to be directed at the precise resources available to the specific defendant in question. This is a result of the objectiveness of the reasonable person standard (discussed in Section 3.2). However, even an objective standard must consider the implications upon an ordinary, albeit prudent, person's pool of likely resources. Indeed, an extremely grave risk of harm (in terms of the nature of the injury it would produce if it eventuated) might not demand additional precautions should other factors, such as the probability of its occurrence and the highly burdensome nature of protecting against it, weigh against further action.

This idea has been demonstrated in numerous cases. For example, in *Romeo v Conservation Commission (NT)*, the plaintiff fell from a sheer cliff in a reserve managed by the defendant and onto a beach many metres below.[122] The reserve was an area of natural beauty that extended across 8 kilometres of coastline in the Northern Territory. The plaintiff, who was aged 16 at the time and had been drinking before the fall, was severely injured due to the fall. The majority of the High Court recognised the gravity of harm that could eventuate from a fall of this kind and accepted that it was a foreseeable risk. However, the obviousness of the risk posed by the sheer cliff face rendered the probability of falls by people taking due care low. Moreover, the proposed precaution (fencing the relevant section of the cliff face) was considered impracticable in part because it implicitly demanded that the defendant protect against similarly placed risks, thus implying a duty to fence other lengths of the reserve's cliff face. This would not only be costly but also have implications for the preservation of the aesthetics of the natural environment.[123] Most jurisdictions have now introduced provisions in the relevant civil liability Acts that provide that a court must consider the burden of taking precautions to avoid similar risks of harm for which the defendant is responsible when determining their burden to take precautions against the risk of harm specifically to the plaintiff.[124]

Another example of where the impracticality of taking precautions was ultimately determinative of breach is *Graham Barclay Oysters Pty Ltd v Ryan*.

---

122 (1998) 192 CLR 431.

123 In their separate dissenting judgments, Gaudron and McHugh JJ disputed the majority's view of the practical implications of the plaintiff's claims, arguing that the presence of a car park and common usages of the area in the vicinity where the plaintiff fell differentiated it sufficiently such that fencing that area alone, rather than the cliff face more broadly, was implied by the duty to take reasonable precautions in this instance: *Romeo v Conservation Commission (NT)* (1998) 192 CLR 431, 453 (Gaudron J), 462–3 (McHugh J). See also *Caledonia Collieries Ltd v Speirs* (1957) 97 CLR 202 (where the majority of the High Court found that the defendant's obligation to install catchpoints on its railway line to prevent risks at a particular level crossing did not imply the need to do so at every other level crossing in the state).

124 See further Section 3.4.2.

Case: *Graham Barclay Oysters Pty Ltd v Ryan* (2002) 211 CLR 540

Facts

Grant Ryan, together with a number of other consumers (the plaintiffs), contracted the hepatitis A virus after consuming oysters that had been harvested from the waters of Wallis Lake in New South Wales. The waters had been polluted by faecal matter following particularly heavy rainfall. The pollutant had flushed into the lake from nearby private septic tanks and stormwater drains that had not been maintained. This had, in turn, caused the virus to be present in the oysters.

The Barclay group (the defendant) was the grower and supplier of the oysters. The plaintiffs argued that the defendant should have taken precautions (beyond those in fact taken by it) to protect against this eventuality. The defendant had, in fact, temporarily ceased oyster production for a few days following the heavy rains and had subjected the oysters to a usual cleaning process. However, it knew that the oyster-cleaning technology was not capable of ensuring the oysters were entirely free from contamination. Importantly, at the time of the events, there were no further scientific tests that the defendant could have practically accessed to detect the virus in the water or in its oysters.

Issue

The issue was whether (and what) precautions could be reasonably expected of the oyster company in light of the grave, but improbable, risk that its operations posed.

Decision

In determining breach, the High Court considered the negligence calculus. All of the Justices recognised the gravity of harm that might befall consumers if something of this nature occurred, and recognised that harm was foreseeable. They also considered that the probability of this harm occurring was extremely low. This was the first occasion involving an outbreak of an oyster-related disease in almost 100 years of production in Lake Wallis. Taking this into account, together with the extremely burdensome nature of any further precautions, the majority held there was no breach. It is worth noting the precautions available to the defendant, and their implications. On the various precautions proposed, the majority of the Court held the following:

(1) The defendant could have suspended production and sale of oysters until a survey of the conditions of septic tanks and stormwater drains was performed by the relevant public authorities. This, however, was an uncertain period of delay to production, given that the defendant had no capacity to either oblige this to happen or to carry it out itself.

(2) The defendant could have warned customers of the risk of contracting a virus by consuming its oysters. This would be tantamount to ceasing sales entirely, given the unlikelihood that anyone would purchase and consume such oysters.

(3) The defendant could have moved its operations to a different lake beyond the proximity of human settlement. This was not feasible, given the lack of evidence that any such location was available.

For each of these precautions, the burden was so onerous as to be equivalent to the defendant ceasing its commercial operations, which no reasonable company would do on the basis of an admittedly grave, but extremely unlikely, risk of harm.

Significance

This case illustrates how we analyse the burdens that proposed precautions might involve for the defendant and weigh those against the other calculus factors when determining breach.

Notes

Kirby J and Callinan J separately dissented on the question of the reasonableness of precautions taken by the defendants. They held that some further (though unstated) period of cessation of production and sale was demanded given how serious the risk to consumers was. It is worth noting that this case also involved claims against the local and state authorities responsible for the management of Lake Wallis; however, those claims failed on the basis of a lack of duty of care on the part of those public authorities.

Question

What do you think is demonstrated by the majority decision in this case in relation to the liability of the defendant?

 Guided response in the eBook

Some cases have emphasised the importance of the *plaintiff* identifying and proving to the requisite standard the practical precautions that they claim the defendant ought to have taken if that defendant were acting with due care.[125]

There are also certain statutory provisions today related to evidentiary considerations that overlap with how a court should approach its assessment of the burden upon a defendant of taking certain precautions (discussed in Section 3.4.2).

HINTS AND TIPS

In order to weigh up the burden of taking precautions in an answer, it is critical that you identify what precaution or precautions you think a plaintiff could argue were available to the defendant as a means of protecting against the harm that occurred. This allows you to evaluate the burden that such precautions would involve.

---

125 See, eg, *Swain v Waverley Municipal Council* (2005) 220 CLR 517, 534–9 (McHugh J).

3.3.3.4   Social utility

In some instances, a defendant may undertake an activity that creates risks of harm but that also has a particular social value to another person or to the community at large. For example, when emergency services vehicles are being driven to an accident, the drivers may take certain risks that we would ordinarily condemn but that we consider justified in their case in order to render emergency assistance.

This idea is encapsulated in the *social utility* principle. It allows a court to consider conflicting (and sometimes statutory) responsibilities that a defendant may have towards another person or the general community that will justify their not taking precautions against risks of harm that might otherwise be expected. The basic position is that the greater the benefit a defendant's overall activity will bring to others, the less likely it is that a reasonable person would take precautions that undermine the achievement of that social benefit.

An example of this principle applied in an emergency services context is *Watt v Hertfordshire County Council*.[126] In that case, a fire department was called to the location of an accident. It was possible that a particular, heavy piece of equipment (a jack) might be needed to free a trapped accident victim. The only fire department vehicle that was equipped to properly secure the jack was at the time being used in another service. For this reason, the jack was transported to the accident site unfixed (along with fire officers) via a lorry. During that journey, the jack fell on one fire officer when the lorry driver had to brake suddenly. The House of Lords found no breach by the Council fire department, with Denning LJ stating the relevant principle as follows:

> It is well settled that in measuring due care one must balance the risk against the measures necessary to eliminate the risk. To that proposition there ought to be added this. One must balance the risk against the end to be achieved. If this accident had occurred in a commercial enterprise without any emergency, there could be no doubt that the servant would succeed. But the commercial end to make profit is very different from the human end to save life or limb. The saving of life or limb justifies taking considerable risk, and I am glad to say there have never been wanting in this country men of courage ready to take those risks, notably in the fire service.
>
> In this case the risk involved in sending out the lorry was not so great as to prohibit the attempt to save life. I quite agree that fire engines, ambulances and doctors' cars should not shoot past the traffic lights when they show a red light. That is because the risk is too great to warrant the incurring of the danger. It is always a question of balancing the risk against the end.[127]

The concept of social utility is not limited to emergency services. It has also been applied, for example, to the public health benefit of an availability of blood stocks,[128] the value of sport and physical activity,[129] the importance of education services in general and to special

---

126   [1954] 2 All ER 368.

127   *Watt v Hertfordshire County Council* [1954] 2 All ER 368, 371.

128   *E v Australian Red Cross Society* (1991) 31 FCR 299.

129   See, eg, *Wilson v Nilepac Pty Ltd* [2011] NSWCA 63. See also B Richards, M De Zwart and K Ludlow, *Tort Law Principles* (Lawbook Co, 6th ed, 2013) 351–2.

needs children in particular,[130] and the value of risk-taking as a part of children learning independence.[131] As with other areas of breach, a challenge that can arise with arguing social utility is how to best characterise the risk-creating activity. The more broadly it is characterised (for example, the provision by the defendant of personal training facilities), the more it may tend to elevate a social utility argument. By contrast, characterising a risk-creating activity narrowly (say, the use by the defendant of a hard exercise ball as part of their personal training service) may tend to make it harder to prove the social utility of that activity.

3.3.3.5   Legislative standards

How does the fact that a defendant has complied with, or deviated from, legislative standards interplay with the question of whether they have breached their duty of care? For example, if a plaintiff claims that the defendant failed to exercise reasonable care while undertaking a particular risk-creating activity (say, driving), but the defendant can show they were behaving consistently with the relevant legislation governing that activity (road traffic statutes and regulations), does that fact determine that there was no breach? Likewise, does the fact of non-compliance with such laws determine that there was a breach of duty of care?

The answer to that question is: evidence that the defendant was either complying with or breaching relevant legislation is *not* determinative of breach; rather, it is a consideration that weighs into the court's calculation of due care.[132] There are a few justifications for this position, which include:

- Legislation may have little or no bearing on the precise carelessness alleged against the defendant and what the circumstances demanded by way of due care.
- Legislation may set minimum, rather than exhaustive, standards of care.
- Committing a technical breach may, in some circumstances, be the most prudent thing for a person to do – for example where breaching a road rule avoids significant physical harm to a person.[133]
- The purposes of legislation (eg, deterring particular kinds of conduct) may be quite distinct from the purposes of negligence law (eg, compensation and distributive justice) and thus inappropriate for fixing the standard of care.[134]

3.3.3.6   Common practice

In Section 3.2.2.6, we saw that certain professionals are deemed by statute to have demonstrated due care if their conduct is shown to have been consistent with the professional opinion of their peers as reasonable in the circumstances. As discussed, the civil liability legislation has therefore introduced a statutory defence for certain professionals which is similar to the *Bolam* principle under English common law.

---

130 *Gem v New South Wales* [2017] NSWDC 108.
131 See, eg, *Sanchez-Sidiropoulos v Canavan* [2015] NSWSC 1139.
132 *Sibley v Kais* (1967) 118 CLR 424. See also *Tucker v McCann* [1948] VLR 222.
133 These arguments were canvassed by Herring CJ in *Tucker v McCann* [1948] VLR 222, 223–8.
134 K Barker et al, *The Law of Torts in Australia* (Oxford University Press, 5th ed, 2012) 440.

However, there remain circumstances where the way in which a defendant's behaviour conforms to, or deviates from, common practice is determined according to the principles under the common law. These include:

- in the Australian Capital Territory and the Northern Territory, where no statutory provisions related to professionals have been introduced
- in all other states, where the defendant is not considered a 'professional' for the purpose of the standard of care for professionals provisions
- in relevant failure-to-warn cases.

It is thus important to remain familiar with the common law position. As a reminder, the principle under the common law is that a defendant's adherence to a common or accepted practice within their field is a consideration in – but does not determine – the standard of due care demanded by the circumstances.[135] In this sense, the operative principle is ostensibly the same as that which operates in respect of a defendant's compliance with legislation (see Section 3.3.3.5).

In *Mercer v Commissioner for Road Transport and Tramways (NSW)*, the plaintiff was a tram passenger injured as a result of a collision with another tram on the same line.[136] The collision was a result of the driver collapsing at the controls but not due to any negligence on his part. The plaintiff argued that the defendant (which controlled the tramway system in Sydney) should have installed a device known as a 'dead man's handle', which would stop a tram if the driver removed pressure from it. The defendant, however, presented expert evidence that this device was not used in any tramway system for trams of the kind on which the plaintiff was travelling, due to risks that came along with it. In other words, the defendant argued that not using such a device was considered common practice in the field.

By a 3:2 majority, the High Court confirmed the jury's finding of breach by the defendant on the basis that common practice, while prima facie a good measure of the care and skill required, is not determinative of due care. This is in part because the common practice itself may be negligent. Moreover, practices in the field may not have kept pace with new developments, or may have originally been designed to serve the interest of the industry rather than those subject to the risk.[137] Hence, the full range of evidence must be evaluated by the court to determine what due care demands in the circumstances. Having said this, courts must be careful when departing from common practice, to ensure they are not applying a type of hindsight bias.[138]

3.3.4 Failure to warn

As noted in Section 3.2.2.6, there are some cases where a plaintiff's allegation of negligence is that the defendant failed to give full and adequate information allowing the plaintiff to make informed decisions in respect of matters affecting them. This issue, sometimes (perhaps misleadingly) referred to as 'failure to warn', most commonly arises in cases

---

135 *Mercer v Commissioner for Road Transport and Tramways (NSW)* (1937) 56 CLR 580.
136 (1937) 56 CLR 580.
137 *Mercer v Commissioner for Road Transport and Tramways (NSW)* (1937) 56 CLR 580, 589 (Latham CJ);
     F v R (1983) 33 SASR 189, 194 (King CJ).
138 *Dovuro Pty Ltd v Wilkins* (2003) 215 CLR 317, 329 (McHugh J).

involving alleged medical negligence. This is because it is possible for a risk that is inherent in a medical treatment to eventuate and cause harm to a patient, notwithstanding that the treatment was undertaken with all due care by the medical professional. The complaint of the patient in such cases will be that this particular risk ought to have been made known to them, so they could decide if they wished to go ahead with the treatment despite the possibility of harm. While failure-to-warn cases most often arise in medical contexts, a failure in the provision of information could also form the basis of a negligence claim in other contexts, such as claims of pure economic loss by misstatement.

In the medical context, it is important to differentiate between a claim involving an allegation of a failure to provide full and adequate information to a patient versus one which relates to actual errors of treatment. The reason for this is that unique principles have been developed both under the common law and under the various civil liability schemes that address the particular nature of a failure-to-warn case.

We look first at the common law. In *F v R,* the plaintiff went to the defendant (an obstetrician and gynaecologist) to inquire about the best option for sterilisation available to her.[139] The defendant recommended a tubal ligation as the most effective option, without advising that the failure rate of such procedures was between 0.5 and 1 per cent. The tubal ligation was undertaken with all due care; however, the inherent risk of the procedure failing in its objective eventuated, and the plaintiff subsequently became pregnant. She sued the doctor for failing to tell her about the risk, arguing that if she had known about it, she would have demanded a more extensive intervention. Two factors were ultimately important in the finding by the South Australian Supreme Court that the defendant had not been negligent in failing to warn of that risk. The first was the fact that the plaintiff had not made any specific request about the failure rate for this procedure, which remained (as she had requested) the most effective option for sterilisation. The second was that no more effective surgical intervention was medically available as an alternative at the time.

Importantly, King CJ set out the relevant circumstances that a court must consider in determining what information should be disclosed by a doctor as a matter of due care:

(1) *Nature of the matter to be disclosed:* Adequate notice means giving information liable to influence the decision-making of a reasonable person in the position of the plaintiff. The significance of the information relative to the consequences of having or not having the particular treatment bears on this.

(2) *Nature of the treatment:* The more drastic the intervention, as well as the question of the availability of alternatives, the more the obligation of disclosure tends to increase.

(3) *The patient's desire for information:* The more a patient demonstrates the desire to know information related to their treatment, the more notice a doctor has been given of their desire to be fully informed in order to exercise their right of control over matters affecting them. This increases the obligation of disclosure.

(4) *The patient:* The temperament and health of a patient, together with the doctor's judgment that disclosure may be harmful to the patient, or be such that the patient is unable to use the information in a rational way, provide a basis for the doctor not to disclose certain information.

---

139 (1983) 33 SASR 189.

(5) *General circumstances:* The existence of an emergency situation or other surrounding circumstances may reduce expectations of disclosure.

(6) *Common practice:* Whether and when particular information is commonly provided should be kept in mind, though this remains only a factor in the assessment of the degree of disclosure demanded and is not determinative.[140]

These considerations, set out by King CJ in *F v R*, were approved by the High Court in *Rogers v Whitaker*, which described the doctor's duty in terms of a duty to warn of material risks.

Case: *Rogers v Whitaker* (1992) 175 CLR 479

Facts

Maree Whitaker (the plaintiff) consulted Dr Christopher Rogers (the defendant), an ophthalmic surgeon, regarding the possibility of surgery to improve the vision and appearance of her right eye which had been blinded by an injury in her youth. The defendant advised on, and subsequently carried out, a surgery that was hoped would improve both the aesthetics and vision of the plaintiff's right eye. While the surgery was undertaken with due care, the defendant had failed to advise the plaintiff of an inherent risk of a slightly higher than 1-in-14 000 chance that the surgery may result in 'sympathetic ophthalmia'. This condition involves a sympathetic loss of vision in the patient's other eye, rather than improvement in the damaged eye. This is what happened, rendering the plaintiff blind.

Issue

The Court had to determine the question whether the risk of sympathetic ophthalmia was one the doctor had a duty to disclose.

Decision

To determine that question, the High Court developed the notion of 'material risk'. It stated (at 490):

> The law should recognize that a doctor has a duty to warn a patient of a material risk inherent in the proposed treatment; a risk is material if, in the circumstances of the particular case, a reasonable person in the patient's position, if warned of the risk, would be likely to attach significance to it or if the medical practitioner is or should reasonably be aware that the particular patient, if warned of the risk, would be likely to attach significance to it.

The High Court found unanimously that the risk in this case was material. First, any reasonable person in the position of the plaintiff would attach significance to information regarding this risk. Second, in light of the degree of interest and concern the plaintiff had expressed regarding the risks of surgery to her good eye, she would personally have attached great significance to it.

---

140 Ibid 192–4.

Significance

The High Court articulated the principle of material risk. This principle is crucial when deciding whether and what a doctor is obliged to disclose by way of risks to their patients. The case also contains a valuable discussion of the concept of therapeutic privilege.

Notes

The High Court allowed that there are exceptions to the obligation of a doctor to disclose material risks to a patient. These include emergency situations or circumstances otherwise special to the patient that the doctor judges as rendering disclosure contrary to the patient's best interests. The latter is sometimes referred to as a doctor's 'therapeutic privilege' to exercise their informed judgment regarding ways in which disclosure may harm a patient.

Question

The High Court in *Rogers v Whitaker* dealt at length with the question of whether it was bound to follow the *Bolam* principle, namely that under Australian law, the question of medical negligence should be determined by the opinion of the medical profession itself as to what constituted due care. What did it decide in that regard?

 Guided response in the eBook

As noted earlier, each of the states has introduced provisions specific to the question of duties to warn a person of a risk of harm. While these vary from state to state, they do fall into some broad forms:

- *Duty discharged through due care:* In Victoria, s 50 of the *Wrongs Act 1958* clarifies that a person discharges their duty of care in respect of warning or giving information to another person if they take reasonable care in the giving of that information.

- *Obvious risks:* Most states provide that a defendant's duties do not extend to having to warn of obvious risks. Precisely how such risks are defined, and the exceptions to that principle, vary slightly from state to state. An illustrative example is the definition of obvious risk set out in s 5F of the *Civil Liability Act 2002* (NSW) which provides that an obvious risk is 'a risk that, in the circumstances, would have been obvious to a reasonable person in the position of that person.'[141] Generally, the rule that a defendant is not required to warn a plaintiff about obvious risks is limited to the defendant's proactive duty, meaning it does not apply to cases where a plaintiff has explicitly requested the information. Another important exception is where the defendant is a professional and the risk relates to a risk of death or personal injury or harm to the plaintiff from the provision of a professional service. In Victoria, the equivalent provision on obvious risk operates somewhat differently; rather than

---

141 See also *Civil Liability Act 2003* (Qld) s 13; *Civil Liability Act 1936* (SA) s 36; *Civil Liability Act 2002* (Tas) s 15; *Wrongs Act 1958* (Vic) s 53; *Civil Liability Act 2002* (WA) s 5F.

preclude a duty it shifts the onus to the plaintiff to prove that they did not have an awareness of a particular risk or information if their claim is a failure to warn.

- *Proactive and reactive duties of doctor to warn:* Queensland and Tasmania have introduced specific provisions that broadly codify the two variants for identifying a material risk set out in *Rogers v Whitaker*, describing these as the 'proactive' and 'reactive' duties of disclosure respectively.

The relevant provisions of each state's civil liability statute are listed in Table 3.8.

Table 3.8   Breach of duty: failure to warn

Legislation	Sections
Civil Liability Act 2002 (NSW)	5H: No proactive duty to warn of obvious risk except where the plaintiff has requested the information; it is required by written law; or the defendant is a professional and the risk is a risk of death or personal injury to the plaintiff from the provision of a professional service
	5P: Statutory standard of care for professionals does not apply to cases involving failure to warn of the risk of injury or death to a person associated with any professional service
Civil Liability Act 2003 (Qld)	15: No proactive duty to warn of obvious risk except where the plaintiff has requested the information; it is required by written law; or the defendant is a professional (other than a doctor) and the risk is a risk of death or personal injury to the plaintiff from the provision of a professional service
	21: Proactive and reactive duty of doctor to warn of risk
	22(5): Statutory standard of care for professionals does not apply to cases involving failure to warn as to risk to a person associated with any professional service
Civil Liability Act 1936 (SA)	38: No duty to warn of obvious risk except where the plaintiff has requested the information; it is required by written law; or the defendant is a professional and the risk is a risk of death or personal injury to the plaintiff from the provision of a professional service
	41(5): Statutory standard of care for professionals does not apply to cases involving failure to warn as to risk of injury or death to a person associated with a healthcare service
Civil Liability Act 2002 (Tas)	17: No proactive duty to warn of obvious risk except where the plaintiff has requested the information; it is required by written law; or the defendant is a professional (other than a medical practitioner) and the risk is a risk of death or personal injury to the plaintiff from the provision of a professional service
	21: Proactive and reactive duty of registered medical practitioner to warn of risk
	22(5): Statutory standard of care for professionals does not apply to cases involving failure to warn as to risk of harm associated with any professional service
Wrongs Act 1958 (Vic)	50: A duty to warn of risk is satisfied by the exercise of reasonable care
	56: In a failure-to-warn case, the plaintiff bears the onus of proving that the plaintiff was not aware of risk or information
	60: Statutory standard of care for professionals does not apply to cases involving failure to warn as to risk or other matter associated with any professional service
Civil Liability Act 2002 (WA)	50: No duty to warn of obvious risk except where the plaintiff has requested the information; it is required by written law; or the defendant is a professional and the risk is a risk of harm to the plaintiff from the provision of a professional service
	5PB(2): Statutory standard of care for professionals does not apply to cases involving failure to warn as to risk of injury or death associated with a treatment proposed for a patient or foetus or a diagnostic procedure for a patient or foetus

Review questions

(1) What are the four main considerations that must be weighed up when determining what precautions (if any) a reasonable person would have taken in respect of a foreseeable and 'not insignificant' risk? What term is commonly used to refer to the evaluative process for weighing up these factors?

(2) To what extent does the fact that a defendant has acted in conformity with the opinion and common practice of their peers influence a determination on the question of breach of duty of care?

(3) How is the scope of the 'social utility' consideration malleable?

(4) What is meant by the concept of a 'material risk'?

(5) What are some examples of how social fact assumptions form a part of determinations of breach? Why should this be of some concern to jurists?

 Guided responses in the eBook

3.4   Proving breach

Under our adversarial model of law, one of the two parties, either the defendant or the plaintiff, always has the burden of proving any fact or issue that is crucial to their legal claim (alternatively referred to as the *burden* or *onus of proof*). The party bearing the burden of proof is responsible for demonstrating a relevant matter to the requisite standard required for the court to accept it as proven. In a negligence action, the burden of proof falls on the plaintiff in terms of satisfying the court that the elements of duty, breach, causation and remoteness have all been made out. Put in the negative, if the plaintiff fails to prove any issue necessary to make out any of those elements, their claim will fail.

The *standard of proof* refers to the objective threshold that has to be met to satisfy the court that a given matter is proven. The normal standard for all issues in a negligence action is proof on the balance of probabilities. This means that a court must be satisfied that facts, and their relevant implications, are 'more probable than not'.[142] The burden and standard of proof as it applies to the plaintiff in a negligence action have been codified in some of the civil liability statutes, particularly in relation to the element of causation.[143] This codification was undertaken in respect of causation in particular, as there were concerns that the courts, through the introduction of various principles, may have inadvertently reversed the onus of proof or lowered the standard of proof in certain cases involving evidentiary gaps.[144]

---

142 *Holloway v McFeeters* (1956) 94 CLR 470, 480–1 (Williams, Webb and Taylor JJ).

143 *Civil Law (Wrongs) Act 2002* (ACT) s 46; *Civil Liability Act 2002* (NSW) s 5E; *Civil Liability Act 2003* (Qld) s 12; *Civil Liability Act 1936* (SA) s 35; *Civil Liability Act 2002* (Tas) s 14; *Wrongs Act 1958* (Vic) s 52; *Civil Liability Act 2002* (WA) s 5D.

144 Ipp Report 109–11.

3.4.1   The use of inference in negligence law

In order to satisfy the burden and standard of proof, a party will present evidence to support their contentions. In many negligence cases, there may only (or primarily) be *circumstantial evidence* upon which a party depends to demonstrate a matter at issue. This is evidence of a fact, or series of facts, from which a judge or jury is asked to infer the existence (or otherwise) of negligence. These are pieces of information that do not, of themselves, show that something occurred in a particular way, but which collectively paint a picture of what most likely happened. By contrast, *direct evidence* is evidence that (if accepted) alone resolves an issue in the claim. For example, if a person goes missing, leaving behind all their clothes and other property, and their bank account is no longer being accessed, this may be circumstantial evidence to conclude they have been the subject of foul play, even if their body is never recovered. However, if that person's body is found, that would be direct evidence that the victim has died. If an eyewitness saw another person hit the victim with their vehicle, that would be direct evidence of *how* that victim was killed.

The use of inferences drawn from circumstantial evidence is allowed in a civil action. However, when some element of a negligence claim depends in whole (or part) upon inferences drawn from circumstantial evidence, a question that arises is the test that should be applied by a court to determine whether a fact can be accepted as proven based on the drawing of such inferences.

This issue was discussed in *Holloway v McFeeters*.[145] In that case, the plaintiff's husband was killed in a hit-and-run accident. There were no witnesses to the accident but only various pieces of evidence about how the accident might have occurred. These included a witness who spoke to the victim shortly before the accident and could attest to his condition; and tyre marks, vehicle debris and the position of the victim's body suggesting a point of impact and the probable movement of the offending vehicle. The vehicle and its driver were, however, never identified so as to provide evidence of what happened. Nor did anyone see the actual collision leading to the victim's death. The sole legal question for the High Court was whether there was sufficient evidence upon which the jury could infer and conclude that the accident was caused by the (unknown) driver's negligence.

The majority of the High Court held that there was sufficient evidence for a jury to draw the inference of negligence on the part of the driver of the vehicle, notwithstanding a range of possibilities that might be compatible with a finding of no breach (eg, the driver having no reasonable time to avoid collision). Their Honours described the relevant test for drawing such an inference from the available evidence as follows:

> It is clear that it is a mistake to think that because an event is unseen its cause cannot be reasonably inferred ... Inferences from actual facts that are proved are just as much part of the evidence as those facts themselves. In a civil cause 'you need only circumstances raising a more probable inference in favour of what is alleged ... where direct proof is not available it is enough if the circumstances appearing in the evidence give rise to a reasonable and definite inference; they must do more than give rise to conflicting

---

145 (1956) 94 CLR 470.

inferences of equal degree of probability so that the choice between them is mere matter of conjecture … All that is necessary is that according to the course of common experience the more probable inference from the circumstances that sufficiently appear by evidence or admission, left unexplained, should be that the injury arose from the defendant's negligence. By more probable is meant no more than that upon a balance of probabilities such an inference might reasonably be considered to have some greater degree of likelihood'.[146]

Another important concept to be aware of in the context of proving breach is the notion of *res ipsa loquitur* ('the thing speaks for itself'). This principle is discussed in Section 4.2.1.1.

3.4.2   Evidential considerations

Finally, it is worth noting that most of the civil liability statutes now include some provisions that direct the courts as to appropriate factors that may or may not be taken into account when determining breach.

Section 5C of the *Civil Liability Act 2002* (NSW) illustrates the kinds of principles that are replicated in other civil liability legislation. It provides:

> **In** proceedings related to liability for negligence:
>
> (a)   the burden of taking precautions to avoid a risk of harm includes the burden of taking precautions to avoid similar risks of harm for which the person may be responsible, and
>
> (b)   the fact that a risk of harm could have been avoided by doing something in a different way does not of itself give rise to or affect liability for the way in which the thing was done, and
>
> (c)   the subsequent taking of action that would (had the action been taken earlier) have avoided a risk of harm does not of itself give rise to or affect liability in respect of the risk and does not of itself constitute an admission of liability in connection with the risk.

The comparable provisions in other civil liability statutes are listed in Table 3.9.

Table 3.9   Breach of duty: evidential considerations

Legislation	Section(s)
Civil Law (Wrongs) Act 2002 (ACT)	44
Civil Liability Act 2002 (NSW)	5C
Civil Liability Act 2003 (Qld)	10
Civil Liability Act 2002 (Tas)	11(3), 12
Wrongs Act 1958 (Vic)	49

---

146   *Holloway v McFeeters* (1956) 94 CLR 470, 480–1 (Williams, Webb and Taylor JJ) (original sources omitted).

REVIEW QUESTIONS

(1) Who has the burden of proving breach in a negligence claim and what is the requisite standard of proof to discharge that burden?

(2) If a defendant subsequently takes action that would have, had it been taken earlier, avoided a risk that was the cause of harm to the plaintiff, does this prove the defendant breached their duty of care to the plaintiff?

 Guided responses in the eBook

KEY CONCEPTS

- **breach of duty:** involves an inquiry into whether the defendant has engaged in negligent conduct, meaning whether they have failed to take the appropriate precautions demanded against certain risks of harm that the reasonable person, in the circumstances, would have taken.

- **civil liability Acts:** the main statutes in each state or territory that set out the statutory rules that apply to the determination of negligence in that jurisdiction. These operate in conjunction with common law rules on negligence.

- **negligence calculus:** a term used to describe the series of factors that a court weighs up when assessing what kinds of precautions a reasonable person would have taken in response to a foreseeable risk.

- **reasonable foreseeability:** the degree of foresight of risk that must exist for a reasonable person to be expected to take precautions against it. A risk is reasonably foreseeable if the defendant knew or ought to have known about it.

- **reasonable person:** the hypothetical person whose actions are the basis for comparison in determining what is due care. The reasonable person is a person acting with ordinary care and skill when doing something that involves risks to others.

- **standard of care:** the standard of carefulness demanded by the circumstances in which the defendant found themselves. The defendant is compared to this standard; if they fall short of it, they have breached their duty of care.

 Complete the multiple-choice questions in the eBook to test your knowledge.

PROBLEM-SOLVING EXERCISES

Exercise 1

For the last three years, Samara has coached a swimming team, the Dockland Sharks, who compete in ocean swim meets around Australia. Samara has a degree in sports management from the well-regarded Meyer Sports Institute, a US tertiary institution concerned with the training of Olympic-grade athletes. She is also on the board of the Australian Swim Instructors Society.

Ramone, who is 16-years-old, is one of the best swimmers in the Dockland Sharks. Samara believes he may have a real chance of winning the upcoming Australian Ocean Swims Championship, which is the most prestigious event on the Australian ocean swimming calendar. In order to train him for the event, Samara directs Ramone to add to his schedule two swims each week in the Olympic-length pool located at her home, to which he agrees. To replicate the conditions of ocean swimming in Ramone's training regime, Samara adds a type of artificial salt to the water of her pool to simulate the buoyancy of ocean water.

The method employed by Samara to treat her pool for this purpose is not generally known or used in Australia, but it is widely accepted by trainers in the United States as a preferred method for Samara's purposes. Samara has used it as a technique for training her best swimmers for more than 15 years, without it causing any injury. However, recently a small handful of US sports journals have reported on medical cases where the particular artificial salt used by Samara was found to have caused some people (with particular allergies) serious skin irritations and sometimes permanent skin scarring.

After 10 weeks of regular swims in Samara's pool, Ramone develops serious and painful skin lesions all over his body. It turns out he is one of a very small number of people with an allergy to the artificial salt she has been using in her pool. Ramone attends his GP, Sangeeta, who advises that the salt in the pool has triggered a very serious skin condition that will require laser treatment administered over the course of a few months. Samara, upon learning of what happened to Ramone, has ceased using the artificial salt in her pool when training her swimmers.

Advise Ramone as to whether Samara has breached her duty of care to him. Assume that Samara owes a duty of care to Ramone and that the events outlined in the scenario took place in your jurisdiction.

 Guided response in the eBook

Exercise 2

Phuong is a childcare worker at Brunsburg Childcare Centre, a service offered to local residents by the Brunsburg Council in northern Melbourne. Phuong and one other childcare worker are the available staff for managing the children on any given day. Phuong has complained a few times about feeling overwhelmed by how much she has to manage on her own as a result of the low staff numbers.

On a Friday morning in September, Phuong is alone at the centre supervising about 10 children in the outside play area. The other childcare worker, Samuel, is away at the time depositing the centre's income for the week at the local bank, as is expected by the centre. During that morning's outdoor play, one child complains of nausea and begins to vomit. Phuong knows that this child has food allergies that must be responded to urgently, and so is particularly concerned to arrange care for her quickly. Phuong takes the child inside to check her medications and to call her parents and/or for medical assistance. She is away from the outside play area for about five minutes.

While she is away, four-year-old Timmy tugs at the legs of three-year-old Sally while Sally is using the flying fox, causing her to fall and strike her head. All the children have been taught that they are not to interfere with other children when they are using the flying fox. That rule is regularly repeated by the childcare workers, but Timmy is a known 'troublemaker'.

Sally suffers a serious injury to her head. Her parents, upset and outraged, wish to sue for damages. Advise Sally's parents as to whether Phuong has breached her duty of care to their daughter.

Assume that Phoung has a duty of care to Sally and that the events outlined in the scenario took place in your relevant jurisdiction.

 Guided response in the eBook

Exercise 3

Rosalina is a 19-year-old horse rider who regularly competes in campdraft competitions. Campdrafting is a sport that involves a rider on horseback working cattle by rounding the cattle up into an enclosed space. Over one weekend, Rosalina attends and competes in a campdraft competition organised and managed by Cattle Corrallers Pty Ltd (CC). Over the course of the two-day event, hundreds of competitive rides are held on the grounds of the event organised into different divisions for different age categories. (On the afternoon of the second day, Rosalina is preparing to ride in an Open Division competition. Open Division means the best riders of all age groups will compete.)

The first day and the morning of the second day of the competition run smoothly. However, in the two hours just prior to Rosalina's Open Division ride, there are four falls (where the rider falls from the horse in some way) in various places around the competition grounds. CC volunteers who are patrolling the event designate these falls as 'bad falls'. This designation means they involved a risk of injury.

After witnessing the last of these falls, an experienced competitor, Mason, approaches the CC director, Allende, to advise that the condition of the ground seems dangerous and that the organisers should stop the event. In response, Allende suspends the start of the Open Division ride for five minutes and walks across the competition grounds to confer with the event organising committee. The committee decide that competitors must 'ride to the conditions of the terrain' and that it would be unfair to stop the competition in order to plough the grounds, as this would give subsequent riders a competitive advantage. (Ploughing turns over the topsoil of the ground and makes it more compact, and thus safer for riding.) The committee decide instead to announce over the loudspeaker that any competitor who wishes to withdraw from the competition will be reimbursed their competitor fee. The competition is then resumed.

Rosalina, who is concentrating on preparing for her ride and is some distance from the loudspeaker, does not hear the announcement. Soon after she starts to compete, she feels the feet of her horse slip. The horse falls heavily, throwing Rosalina to the ground. As a result, she suffers a serious spinal injury.

The following day, CC plough the competition grounds. Upon doing so, it becomes clear that the condition of the grounds had deteriorated significantly over the course of the two-day competition.

Advise Rosalina as to whether CC has breached its duty of care to her. Assume that the conduct of Allende and the organising committee can be attributed to CC, that CC owes Rosalina a duty of care and that the events outlined in the scenario took place in your jurisdiction.

Guided response in the eBook

CHALLENGE YOURSELF

Exercise 1

Consider again the scenario in the first problem-solving exercise. Now assume that when Ramone visits his GP, Sangeeta, she fails to tell him that the laser treatment she is recommending for his skin lesions carries a 1-in-14 000 chance of triggering an ongoing overall pain condition (fibromyalgia), even if the treatment is carried out with all due care. This is precisely what happens to Ramone as a result of the laser treatment he undertakes with Sangeeta. As an alternative treatment, patients with the kind of skin lesions Ramone has presented with can use a topical ointment; however, this treatment is far less effective at eradicating the problem. Sangeeta has also failed to tell Ramone about this alternative treatment option. Most GPs, like Sangeeta, do not advise, or recommend, this alternative treatment to patients or tell them about the risks of the laser treatment causing fibromyalgia, unless they are explicitly asked. Ramone is 16 years old and did not make many enquiries of Sangeeta regarding risks and alternatives to the laser treatment she suggested.

Indicate how your previous answer would now vary if Ramone were to argue a breach of duty of care by Sangeeta.

 Guided response in the eBook

Exercise 2

Consider again the scenario in the second problem-solving exercise. Now assume that Sally's parents decide to sue Brunsburg Council for the harm to Sally.

Brainstorm how your previous answer would now vary if Sally's parents were to argue a breach of duty of care by the Council. Consider the direct liability of the Council here (and not its vicarious liability for any negligence on the part of Phuong).

 Guided response in the eBook

Exercise 3

Consider again the scenario in the third problem-solving exercise. Now assume that Rosalina heard the loudspeaker announcement. Brainstorm how your previous answer would vary in light of this change in the facts, if at all.

 Guided response in the eBook

4

DAMAGE:
FACTUAL
CAUSATION
AND SCOPE
OF LIABILITY

4.1   Introduction

As we have already seen, there are three basic elements to a successful action in negligence:

(1)   a duty to take reasonable care owed by the defendant to the plaintiff

(2)   a breach of that duty of care by the defendant

(3)   damage resulting to the plaintiff from that breach.

HINTS AND TIPS

Even though the exercise looks relatively simple, drawing a clear distinction between these three elements is often complicated in practice. Often the parties themselves do not choose to argue their case in a way that allows each element to be easily separated out.[1] That said, following the proposed three-step approach will make comprehending a negligence claim more accessible, especially at the early stages of your learning.

In an action for negligence the plaintiff must prove all three elements. In addition to proving that the defendant owed the plaintiff a duty of care and breached that duty, the plaintiff must show that the damage they sustained resulted from the defendant's breach. To prove this, the plaintiff must show that the defendant's negligence *caused* his or her damage (causation in fact) and that the damage the plaintiff suffered was within the appropriate scope of liability (legislative requirement) or not too *remote* (at common law). In practice, the evidence for the plaintiff must satisfy the court that, on the balance of probabilities, the defendant's conduct caused the damage suffered by the plaintiff.

1 See *Cole v South Tweed Heads Rugby League Football Club Ltd* (2004) 217 CLR 469.

This chapter deals with the third element. As illustrated by Figure 4.1, this stage involves taking (yet again) three steps:

(1)   Identify the damage having an adverse effect on the plaintiff to be recognised by law as damage for which compensation can be sought.

(2)   Link the defendant's conduct (act or omission) to the damage suffered by the plaintiff.

(3)   Establish the scope of the defendant's liability or, putting it differently, establish the extent to which the defendant should be found liable for the harm suffered by the plaintiff *or* the type of harm suffered was within the scope of foreseeability.

Figure 4.1   Third element of a negligence claim

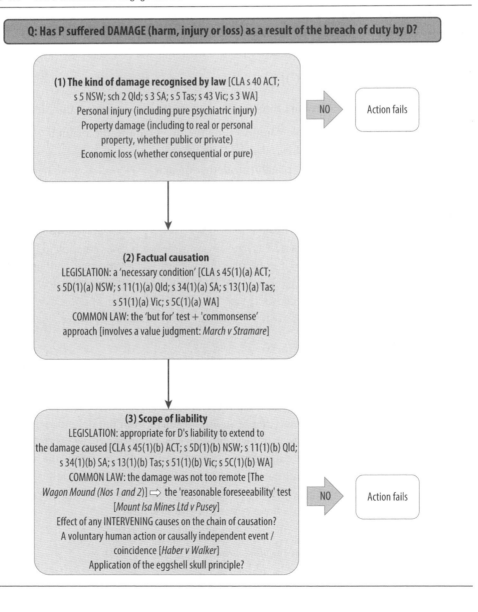

HINTS AND TIPS

Unless each of these steps is satisfied – that is, proven on the balance of probabilities, by the plaintiff – an action in negligence will fail.

Steps (2) and (3) have been given statutory form in all Australian states and territories except the Northern Territory. Thus, even though they need to be considered in light of common law principles, reference must be made to the relevant civil liability legislation.

4.1.1   The kind of damage recognised by law

Before arguing the causation element in a negligence claim, it is necessary to assess whether the kind of damage claimed to be suffered by the plaintiff is actionable; if it is not, the claim will fail. This is because damage is at the heart of an action in negligence. Without actual damage or loss, there cannot be liability in negligence. This is unlike trespass which is actionable per se (not requiring proof that damage was suffered). The third element of a successful action in negligence is, therefore, often referred to as the 'gist' of a negligence action.[2]

The first step is to establish whether the damage suffered by the plaintiff is of a kind that is recoverable in a negligence action, as not all 'loss' or 'harm' suffered by a plaintiff is compensable. As Crennan J (with whom Gleeson CJ, Gummow and Heydon JJ agreed) explained in *Harriton v Stephens*:

> Because damage constitutes the gist of an action in negligence, a plaintiff needs to prove actual damage or loss and a court must be able to apprehend and evaluate the damage, that is the loss, deprivation or detriment caused by the alleged breach of duty. Inherent in that principle is the requirement that a plaintiff is left worse off as a result of the negligence complained about, which can be established by the comparison of a plaintiff's damage or loss caused by the negligent conduct, with the plaintiff's circumstances absent the negligent conduct.[3]

Thus, the plaintiff must prove that the damage they suffered was caused through another's negligence[4] and was of a type that is recognised by the law. This includes (see Table 4.1):

- personal injury (including pure psychiatric injury; see Section 2.5.1)
- property damage (including to real or personal property, whether public or private)
- economic loss (whether consequential or pure; see Section 2.4.2).

On policy grounds, there are further limitations on what will be recognised as compensable, such as when the loss or damage results from illegal or fraudulent activities. This was confirmed in *Meadows v Ferguson* where Hudson J delivered the concluding judgment, stating:

---

2 See *Williams v Milotin* (1957) 97 CLR 465, 474.
3 (2006) 226 CLR 52, 126.

Table 4.1   Overview of statutory provisions on the definition of 'harm'

Legislation	Provision
Civil Law (Wrongs) Act 2002 (ACT)	s 40
Civil Liability Act 2002 (NSW)	s 5
Civil Liability Act 2003 (Qld)	sch 2
Civil Liability Act 1936 (SA)	s 3
Civil Liability Act 2002 (Tas)	s 9
Wrongs Act 1958 (Vic)	s 43
Civil Liability Act 2002 (WA)	s 3

> if the conclusion is reached that the earnings of which the plaintiff has been deprived are earnings derived from an illegal employment or activity, I am of opinion that on grounds of public policy the Court should not recognize those earnings as affording a proper basis for the award of damages.[5]

Similarly, if the form of loss cannot be calculated or quantified (such as grief, general anxiety or emotional disturbance), it will not be recoverable.[6] In such circumstances, the question is whether it is possible to satisfy the principle of *restitutio in integrum* (restoration of the injured party to the state they would have been in, if not for the injury or harm sustained). An example of where this has proven difficult is in the so-called wrongful life claims. As we will see in Section 4.1.2.2, wrongful life claims are brought by the plaintiff (child) against the defendant (usually the medical practitioner or medical service provider) for allowing the plaintiff to be born at all and, consequently, requiring them to live with a (severe) disability. In the leading English case, *McKay v Essex Area Health Authority*, the Court of Appeal had to consider whether the plaintiff's 'life' (however disabled) could constitute compensable damage.[7] The Court held that such a finding would lead to an 'intolerable and insoluble problem',[8] in that it would require the Court to compare the relative value of 'existence' with 'non-existence'. As Ackner LJ observed:

> how can a court begin to evaluate non-existence, 'the undiscovered country from whose bourn no traveller returns'? No comparison is possible and therefore no damage can be established which a court could recognise. This goes to the root of the whole cause of action.[9]

Likewise, if damage is deemed to be too 'vague', the plaintiff will not be compensated for it. In *Roberts v Roberts* an expulsion from a social club was perceived too vague to be recognised as damage at law.[10] Also, an action in negligence might not be available when

---

4   See *Cattanach v Melchior* (2003) 215 CLR 1; [2003] HCA 38, [197] (Hayne J).
5   [1961] VR 594, 598.
6   See *Calveley v Chief Constable of Merseyside Police* [1989] AC 1228; *Tame v New South Wales* (2002) 211 CLR 317; [2002] HCA 35; *Leonard v Pollock* [2012] WASCA 108.
7   [1982] QB 1166.
8   *McKay v Essex Area Health Authority* [1982] QB 1166, 1192 (Griffiths LJ).
9   Ibid 1189 (Ackner LJ).
10   (1864) 122 ER 874.

a more appropriate action is available (eg, if dealing with harm to one's reputation, in defamation; see Chapter 11).

Traditionally, the term 'damage' has been used interchangeably with 'harm' or 'loss' or 'injury'.[11] More recently, following the introduction of the civil liability legislation, preference has been given to the use of the term 'harm', which is defined as meaning 'any kind of harm' that includes personal injury or death, damage to property or economic loss.

HINTS AND TIPS

The application of the civil liability legislation might be subject to specific exclusions. For example, under s 5 of the *Civil Liability Act 2003* (Qld) that Act does not apply to claims for damages for personal injury if the harm involves:

- an injury defined under the *WorkCover Queensland Act 1996 (Qld)* or the *Workers' Compensation and Rehabilitation Act 2003* (Qld), except as expressly stated
- an injury that is a 'dust-related condition' or
- an injury resulting from smoking or other use of or exposure to tobacco products and smoke.

See also *Civil Law (Wrongs) Act 2002* (ACT) s 41(2); *Civil Liability Act 2002* (NSW) s 3B; *Civil Liability Act 1936* (SA) s 4; *Civil Liability Act 2002* (Tas) s 3B; *Wrongs Act 1958* (Vic) s 19C(2); *Civil Liability Act 2002* (WA) s 3A.

4.1.2   The 'loss of a chance' in medical negligence

As discussed in more detail in Section 4.3.1, the plaintiff needs to show on the balance of probabilities that they sustained harm or injury because of the defendant's conduct (act or omission). In the context of medical negligence, the plaintiff might want to claim 'loss of a chance' of a more favourable outcome, in that the lack of appropriate diagnosis or treatment either caused them to lose an opportunity to recover or led to deterioration of their condition.

In *Rufo v Hosking*, the New South Wales Court of Appeal had to grapple with whether a claim of loss or diminution of a more favourable medical outcome could, in fact, be considered an actionable 'damage'.[12] The Court argued that, should the plaintiff be able to prove on the balance of probabilities that (1) there was a chance of a better outcome *and* (2) the plaintiff would have acted upon that chance by undertaking a particular course of treatment or operation, loss of a chance can afford a proper basis for compensation.[13]

There were a number of cases in Australia before the introduction of the civil liability legislation that dealt with the loss of a chance in medical negligence.[14] The change of approach came with the *Tabet* litigation. The judge at first instance felt bound to follow the

---

11 See *Harriton v Stephens* (2004) 59 NSWLR 694, [42] (Spigelman CJ).
12 (2004) 61 NSWLR 678.
13 *Rufo v Hosking* (2004) 61 NSWLR 678, [40] (Santow JA).

decision in *Rufo v Hosking*,[15] and awarded the plaintiff (a six-year-old girl) damages for her loss of a chance of a better outcome because 25 per cent of her brain damage might have been avoided had the defendant not delayed a CT scan (which, when eventually performed, revealed a medulloblastoma).[16] The defendant appealed. The New South Wales Court of Appeal overruled the trial decision, stating a number of reasons for (and practical difficulties with) applying the doctrine of loss of a chance.[17] The plaintiff appealed, and the case made its way to the High Court.[18] By a unanimous decision (6:0), the High Court dismissed the appeal on the grounds that the plaintiff had not been able to prove the loss of a chance, and that the third element of a negligence action (damage) should not be redefined in terms of 'chance'. Despite the rejection of the doctrine in the case, some justices left open the possibility for a claim to succeed should the circumstances differ. Gummow ACJ observed:

> this outcome will not require acceptance in absolute terms of a general proposition that destruction of the chance of obtaining a benefit or avoiding a harm can never be regarded as supplying that damage which is the gist of an action in negligence.[19]

The current position in Australia is that courts are unlikely to recognise that loss of chance in itself will constitute 'damage' for the purpose of the tort of negligence. Courts are also unlikely to recognise that the burden of proof shifts away from the plaintiff who is still required to show that, on the balance of probabilities, the defendant's negligence caused or materially contributed to the harm suffered by the plaintiff (and proving an 'increased risk' is not sufficient).

HINTS AND TIPS

Note, as a matter of caution, that the approach to the doctrine of the 'loss of a chance' has developed differently across different jurisdictions.[20] In Australia, the High Court rejected the doctrine in *Tabet v Gett* (2010) 240 CLR 537, but the matter may be far from settled.

Keeping in mind the difficulties of proving loss of a chance by a plaintiff in medical malpractice cases, the following sections look more closely at claims of so-called 'wrongful birth', 'wrongful life' and 'wrongful death'.

---

14 See, eg, *Board of Management of Royal Perth Hospital v Frost* (Western Australia Court of Appeal, Malcolm CJ, Rowland and Wallwork JJ, 26 February 1997); *McInnes v Ahluwalia* [1999] NSWSC 818; *Gavalas v Singh* (2001) 3 VR 404; *Rufo v Hosking* (2004) 61 NSWLR 678.

15 (2004) 61 NSWLR 678.

16 *Tabet v Mansour* [2007] NSWSC 36.

17 *Gett v Tabet* (2009) 109 NSWLR 1.

18 *Tabet v Gett* (2010) 240 CLR 537.

19 Ibid [27].

20 For a recent overview of the loss of chance doctrine comparing legal approaches in China, Europe and Australia, see RG Beran, VL Raposo and Y Manman, 'Loss of Chance across Different Jurisdictions (the Why and Wherefore)' (2020) 8(2) *Peking University Law Journal* 143.

4.1.2.1   The wrongful birth cases

The term 'wrongful birth' is used to describe claims by parents for compensation for the costs of raising a child who would not have been born if not for the negligence of the defendant (usually a practitioner or hospital). These types of cases typically arise in relation to negligently performed sterilisation, negligently performed abortion that results in continued pregnancy, supply of defective contraceptives, or a failure to warn of the risk associated with sterilisation procedures of them failing to prevent conception.

In *Cattanach v Melchior*, the High Court found in favour of the respondents who sued the appellants for their negligence in performing a tubal ligation (sterilisation) that allowed Mrs Cattanach to conceive and give birth to a healthy but unintended child.[21] Mrs Melchior claimed compensation from Dr Cattanach (among others) for the costs of rearing the child. The majority of the High Court (4:3) found in favour of the parents, allowing them to recover the costs of raising the child as those costs were causally related to the doctor's negligence. The majority of Justices rejected the argument that the birth of a child should not be construed in terms of a legal 'harm', thus recognising it as capable of protection by law and something for which compensation might be sought. The Court pointed out that the harm or loss for which the damages were awarded were not for the 'birth' of the child, but for the negligence of the defendant.

Following the decision in *Cattanach*, legislation was passed in New South Wales, Queensland and South Australia to limit the availability of damages for economic loss from rearing and maintaining a healthy child. The legislation did not affect claims for additional costs associated with caring for a disabled child born due to medical negligence.

Case: *O'Loughlin v McCallum* [2021] WADC 77

Facts

The plaintiff (Ms O'Loughlin), a mother of six children at the time, underwent a sterilisation procedure (tubal ligation) by her gynaecologist (Dr McCallum; first defendant) which subsequently led to a surprise pregnancy five years later and the birth of a healthy son. The plaintiff spent most of her adult life caring for her children, and both her husband's and her sole income came from Commonwealth social security payments.

Dr McCallum admitted to performing the procedure negligently and Western Australia Country Health Service (second defendant) admitted vicarious liability for the first defendant's negligence. The plaintiff made a claim for damages.

Issue

Was the plaintiff entitled to damages for loss of earning capacity, general damages for pain and suffering and loss of amenities, and the costs of raising the child?

---

21 (2003) 215 CLR 1; [2003] HCA 38.

Decision

The District Court of Western Australia assessed the quantum of damages, and the plaintiff was successful in claiming:

- loss of earning capacity in the sum of $20 000
- general damages of $22 000 (which was subject to the restriction pursuant to s 9 of the *Civil Liability Act 2002* (WA))
- the costs of raising the child (in accordance with *Cattanach v Melchior*[22]) of $83 347, consisting of $25 116 for the past costs and $52 957 for the future costs up to age 18.

Significance

The case is an example of a compensation claim for 'wrongful birth' if there is no legislation to the contrary, whereby a child's birth was unplanned or unexpected and came about by virtue of negligence in advice or treatment by a medical practitioner. In Western Australia, there are no legislative restrictions on damages for 'wrongful birth' claims which are assessed by reference to the common law and general principles.

Question

What factors satisfied the judge that the 'costs of raising a child' damages should not be offset against social security benefits?

 Guided response in the eBook

EMERGING ISSUE

The decision in *Cattanach v Melchior* (2003) 215 CLR 1 remains the leading common law authority on claims for compensation in 'wrongful birth' cases, except in New South Wales, Queensland and South Australia (see Table 4.2). The assessment of damages, and the underpinning considerations, will continue to require further judicial and legislative clarification to ensure appropriate compensation for medical negligence in similar cases.

Establishing the type of harm suffered or causation in relation to wrongful birth cases is usually a straightforward exercise: the negligence of the defendant (eg, failing to perform a sterilisation or abortion correctly) resulted in the plaintiff's loss requiring compensation (for the costs of birth services or/and bringing up an unwanted child, who might or might not be unhealthy). However, the issues of causation and what would constitute 'damage' become more complicated in relation to the so-called 'wrongful life' claims.

---

22 (2003) 215 CLR 1; [2003] HCA 38.

Table 4.2   Overview of statutory provisions relating to 'wrongful birth' claims

Legislation	Section(s)	Application
Civil Liability Act 2002 (NSW)	71	• If the child is born healthy, an award of damages for economic loss is not available for costs relating to rearing or maintaining the child. • If the child is born with a disability, the claim can include compensation for rearing or maintaining the child that arise because of the disability.
Civil Liability Act 2003 (Qld)	49A, 49B	• An award of damages cannot be made for economic loss arising out of the costs ordinarily associated with rearing or maintaining a child as a result of failed sterilisation procedures and failed contraceptive procedures or contraceptive advice. • Costs associated with the birth, such as antenatal, obstetric and labour care, or pain and suffering, can be claimed. • The legislation does not address a right to claim costs for rearing a disabled child or a child born with a serious condition.*
Civil Liability Act 1936 (SA)	67	• When negligent action or innocent misrepresentation by words or conduct has resulted in the unintended conception of a child, or the failure of attempted abortion or the birth of a child that would have been aborted, no compensation can be awarded to cover the 'ordinary costs' of raising a child; 'ordinary costs' include all costs associated with the child's care, upbringing, education and advancement in life. • Other costs relating to the birth, including antenatal, obstetric and labour care, or pain and suffering, can be claimed. • If a child is born mentally or physically disabled, any amount that exceeds the 'ordinary costs' if the child were not disabled may also be claimed.

*   In *Veivers v Connolly* [1995] 2 Qd R 326, recovery of such costs was allowed. It can be presumed that this case will be followed by the courts as there is a lack of statutory provision to the contrary.

4.1.2.2   The wrongful life cases

These types of cases usually involve considering a claim where a child has been born with a (severe) disability and, if not for the medical negligence (eg, failure to diagnose a condition in the foetus), the parents would have had a choice of lawfully terminating the pregnancy. These cases raise a number of legal and policy arguments in relation to: (1) proving causation (the lost opportunity for the mother to regulate her fertility);[23] (2) whether 'life' or 'existence' can constitute the type of 'harm' recognised as actionable in the law of torts; (3) establishing the scope of the duty of care (ie, the obligation not to injure the plaintiff prior to or after birth);[24] and (4) linking the breach of that duty with the damage element.

In *Harriton v Stephens*, the majority of the High Court (6:1) believed that this type of 'harm' should not be recognised at law, even though the defendant (Dr Stephens) had been

---

23 As noted by Stephenson LJ in *McKay v Essex Area Health Authority* [1982] QB 1166, 1177–8. This is based on the argument of protecting the right to the bodily integrity of the mother, whereby pregnancy and childbirth, if unwanted, constitute a violation of this right.

24 *Edwards v Blomeley* [2002] NSWSC 460, [63] (Studdert J).

found to be negligent in diagnosing rubella in Ms Harriton's mother while she was pregnant leading to the plaintiff being born with severe congenital disabilities.[25] Had the parents known of the presence of the rubella virus, they would have terminated the pregnancy. The majority did not find it appropriate (on moral and ethical grounds) to extend the doctor's duty of care to a child who, if the doctor had performed that duty correctly, would not have been born, as it is one thing to 'su[e] the doctor for causing physical damage, being the disability' and another to 'su[e] the doctor for causing a "life with disabilities"'.[26] On policy grounds, it was argued that should liability for 'wrongful life' be recognised, it could lead to devaluing the worth of the lives, and could constitute differential (ie, discriminatory) treatment, of the disabled.[27]

Kirby J, in his dissenting judgment, did not consider some of the views of his fellow Justices to warrant a rejection of wrongful life actions. He argued that some of these views were 'premised on a misunderstanding of the tort of negligence [or] a distorted characterisation of wrongful life claims'.[28] In relation to the hold by the majority 'impossible comparison' argument, he argued that awarding damages would in fact offer the plaintiff 'a degree of practical empowerment' and enable the child to 'lead a more dignified existence'.[29] His Honour perceived that such actions could succeed on 'ordinary principles of negligence law' and would further strengthen the requirement that 'health care providers such as the respondent exercise reasonable care to detect and warn of risks' that a foetus could face.[30]

In *Waller v James*, a case of negligent genetic screening, the High Court also refused to recognise a medical negligence claim, finding that this was impossible under the law of torts.[31] The Court noted that it requires an assessment of the situation of the child had the wrongful act not been committed (the child not having been born) and an assessment of the situation after the wrongful act was committed (the child living with the disability). The Court found it impossible to compare 'existence' of the plaintiff with 'non-existence' for the purpose of establishing tortious liability.[32]

4.1.2.3   The wrongful death cases

These types of cases are brought by close relatives of the deceased when the death is caused by a wrongful act of another. They are often referred to as *Lord Campbell's Act* actions. They can arise in relation to medical negligence (damages claims based on loss of a chance of recovery or survival), but not exclusively. This area of law requires an understanding of the historical context within which it has emerged and an appreciation of the cross-jurisdictional differences.

---

25 (2006) 226 CLR 52.
26 *Harriton v Stephens* (2006) 226 CLR 52; [2006] HCA 15, [245] (Crennan J).
27 Ibid [262]–[263] (Crennan J).
28 Ibid [110] (Kirby J).
29 Ibid [122] (Kirby J).
30 Ibid [120] (Kirby J).
31 (2006) 226 CLR 136.
32 On the critique of the denial of wrongful life claims in *Harriton v Stephens* (2006) 226 CLR 52 and *Waller v James* (2006) 226 CLR 136 as an 'unjust decision ... that, probably unlike the plaintiffs themselves, would have been better off not existing', see D Stretton, 'Harriton v Stephens; Waller v James: Wrongful Life and the Logic of Non-Existence' (2006) 30(3) *Melbourne University Law Review* 972, 1001.

Until the mid-19th century, under the common law rule in England and Wales,[33] it was not possible to make a tortfeasor liable for paying damages for causing a wrongful death. Two principles guided such a rule. First, a personal action (with some exceptions) was only available to a party who was alive and would not survive to a deceased's estate.[34] Second, as laid down in *Baker v Bolton*,[35] even if the wrongful death caused financial loss to a living plaintiff, it was not possible to make a living defendant liable for it, as damages were available only if the wrongful act caused physical damage to the plaintiff or their property.[36] The expansion of the railways in the 1830s brought an increase in railway-related accidents and this mobilised the legislature to reconsider the law. In 1846, Parliament reformed the *Baker v Bolton* rule by enacting a statute allowing for the compensation of the families of persons wrongfully killed. This was the *Fatal Accidents Act 1846*, commonly known as *Lord Campbell's Act*.[37] The purpose of the Act was to open a way to developing principles at common law allowing an award of damages for wrongful death. However, no action was available for wrongful death, apart from that arising under *Lord Campbell's Act*, until the introduction of the *Law Reform (Miscellaneous Provisions) Act 1934*, on which the Australian legislation was largely modelled.[38] Today, in Australia, all jurisdictions have a statutory cause of action for wrongful death (see Table 4.3).

Table 4.3   Overview of legislation on the *Lord Campbell's Act* type of action

Legislation	Provision
Civil Law (Wrongs) Act 2002 (ACT)	pt 3.1
Compensation to Relatives Act 1897 (NSW)	s 3(1)
Compensation (Fatal Injuries) Act 1974 (NT)	s 7
Civil Proceedings Act 2011 (Qld)	pt 10
Civil Liability Act 1936 (SA)	pt 5
Fatal Accidents Act 1934 (Tas)	s 4
Wrongs Act 1958 (Vic)	pt III
Fatal Accidents Act 1959 (WA)	s 4

In all Australian jurisdictions, an action can be brought by either the legal dependants of the deceased[39] or the executor/executrix or administrator/administratix of the estate of the deceased.[40] Thus, the principle underlying liability for a wrongful death action is loss to the eligible relatives and loss to the estate. In both cases, even though there is an overlap between the claims, there is a different purpose for the damages that can be claimed. Should an action be successful, the eligible relatives are awarded damages under the dependants' action legislation (eg, the *Compensation to Relatives Act 1897* (NSW)), whereas the estate

33 At the time, the rule in Scotland differed.
34 Not reformed until the passing of the *Law Reform (Miscellaneous Provisions) Act 1934*, 24 & 25 Geo 5.
35 (1808) 170 ER 1033.
36 See WS Malone, 'The Genesis of Wrongful Death' (1965) 17(6) *Stanford Law Review* 1043.
37 *Fatal Accidents Act 1846*, 9 & 10 Vict, c 93.
38 *Law Reform (Miscellaneous Provisions) Act 1934*, 24 & 25 Geo 5, c 41. Currently, in England and Wales, the applicable provisions can be found in the *Fatal Accidents Act 1976* (UK).
39 Under the *Supreme Court Act 1995* (Qld) these include the child, spouse (including certain de facto partners) or parent of the deceased.
40 See, eg, *Supreme Court Act 1995* (Qld) s 18(1).

can be awarded damages under, for example, the *Law Reform (Miscellaneous Provisions) Act 1944* (NSW).

As a general rule, the estate is able to claim for pecuniary losses from the time of injury or death (eg, funeral or medical expenses),[41] whereas the dependants can claim damages for future financial losses resulting from the wrongful death (eg, loss of income, domestic services[42] or superannuation).[43] The family members who are entitled to make a claim can apply only for damages for pecuniary (financial) loss,[44] with the most common being loss of income; damages for non-pecuniary losses (eg, grief or sorrow) are not usually available.

HINTS AND TIPS

Despite the general rule being that only pecuniary loss can be claimed by the eligible relatives, provision is made for solatium (a non-pecuniary loss) in the Northern Territory and South Australia, under the *Compensation (Fatal Injuries) Act 1974* (NT) s 10(3)(f) and *Civil Liability Act 1936* (SA) s 30.

An example of a successful action for wrongful death is *Haber v Walker*.[45] This case concerned a plaintiff's husband who sustained brain injury following a car accident, and subsequently became depressed and committed suicide. (On the relevant issue of breaking the chain of causation, see Section 4.3.2.1.) Mr Haber left behind eight dependent children and a wife. The Court had to consider the application of s 16 of the *Wrongs Act 1958* (Vic) which provides:

> Whensoever the death of a person is caused by a wrongful act neglect or default and the act neglect or default is such as would (if death had not ensued) have entitled the party injured to maintain an action and recover damages in respect thereof, then and in every such case the person who would have been liable if death had not ensued shall be liable to an action for damages notwithstanding the death of the person.

The majority (2:1) found in favour of the plaintiff's claim that Mr Haber's suicide was a consequence of the car accident caused by the defendant's negligence. Following this, the Court awarded the surviving members of the family £11700 (reduced by 10 per cent by the finding of contributory negligence on the part of Mr Haber). The damages awarded would have differed had the case been decided after the amendment to s 26(4) of the Victorian statute, following which contributory negligence of the deceased is no longer taken into account when accessing damages for the beneficiary of an action under *Lord Campbell's Act*.[46]

---

41 See, eg, *Law Reform (Miscellaneous Provisions) Act 1944* (NSW) s 2.
42 See *Nguyen v Nguyen* (1990) 169 CLR 245.
43 See, eg, *Compensation to Relatives Act 1897* (NSW) s 3(1).
44 *Woolworths Ltd v Crotty* (1942) 66 CLR 603, 618 (Latham CJ); *De Sales v Ingrilli* (2002) 212 CLR 338.
45 [1963] VR 339.
46 A similar approach has been adopted in the Australian Capital Territory under *Civil Law (Wrongs) Act 2002* (ACT) s 27.

You might recall the discussion in Section 1.1.2.2 of the High Court decision in *De Sales v Ingrilli*.[47] In that case the appellant contended that applying the 'remarriage discount' to the assessment of damages was not in line with the 'modern day realities'. The wrongful death claim was brought by the widow of the deceased under the *Fatal Accidents Act 1959* (WA) on behalf of herself and two children. The compensation sought was for an 'injury' defined as 'the loss of a benefit the claimant would otherwise have reasonably expected to receive from the deceased, had the accident not occurred'.[48]

Since the introduction of the apportionment legislation (see Section 5.2.4), there are differences across jurisdictions as to what can be claimed and by whom, which requires the relevant statutes to be consulted. But, as a general rule, for the plaintiff to succeed in an action for wrongful death, they must show that the defendant's wrongful conduct (act or omission) caused the death of the deceased, as well as that the deceased would have been entitled to bring an action against the defendant had they still been alive. For example, if the limitation period would have expired for the deceased to bring civil proceedings, the entitled family members will be barred from making a claim for wrongful death as well.[49] However, in the Northern Territory a 'settlement, release or judgment in respect of the wrongful act … given or obtained by the deceased' will not prevent action by the dependants.[50] In South Australia, should the deceased have received damages for loss of earning capacity before their death, the dependants' damages will be discounted accordingly.[51]

Since Lord Ellenborough's assertion in *Baker v Bolton* that 'in a civil court, the death of a human being could not be complained of as an injury',[52] this common law rule has been subject to statutory refinement in Australia and other common law countries, allowing liability for death caused wrongfully to arise.

REVIEW QUESTIONS

(1)   Can any kind or type of 'damage' give rise to compensable claims in negligence?

(2)   What is the difference between the terms 'damage' and 'damages' in the law of torts?

(3)   Is the 'loss of a chance of a better outcome' in medical negligence claims an actionable damage in Australia?

(4)   Why are courts willing to accept 'wrongful birth' claims but remain reluctant to do so for 'wrongful life' claims?

 Guided responses in the eBook

---

47   (2002) 212 CLR 338.

48   *De Sales v Ingrilli* (2002) 212 CLR 338; [2002] HCA 52, [11] (Gleeson CJ).

49   See, eg, *Emmett v Eastern Dispensary and Casualty Hospital*, 396 F 2d 931 (DC Cir, 1967). The wrongful death claim by the deceased's son was dismissed at first instance as it had been commenced after the expiry of the limitation period under the local limitations statute.

50   *Compensation (Fatal Injuries) Act 1974* (NT) s 7(2).

51   *Civil Liability Act 1936* (SA) s 54(3).

52   (1808) 170 ER 1033, 1033.

4.2   Factual causation

When considering the question of causation, note the comments of Gaudron J in *Chappel v Hart*: 'Questions of causation are not answered in a legal vacuum. Rather, they are answered in the legal framework in which they arise.'[53] Thus, the matter of causation in the law of torts is a much narrower and more purposeful exercise than it is in the sciences, but equally crucial. In the sciences, understanding causal relations (that A leads to B) is essential for explaining what has gone before, and thus allowing us to predict what will come in the future, in order to effect any necessary changes to influence the desired outcome. Answering such a question in the sciences is influenced by the theory of probability which attempts to measure the likelihood of a particular event occurring on a scale of '0' (denoting impossibility) to '1' (signifying certainty). In the law of negligence, on the other hand, the question is not so much 'how' probable something is, but rather whether 'it is more probable than not' that the negligence of the defendant caused the plaintiff the harm.

Consequently, courts have approached the matter of causation as a limiting element in establishing the defendant's liability. But the basis for that liability has been referred to in different and not always consistent ways, including describing the wrongful act as 'the real effective' cause,[54] the 'direct' cause,[55] the 'natural and probable' cause[56] or the 'proximate cause'.[57] On its surface, this might sound like a relatively simple exercise but, in practice, causation is a complex legal principle that has significant implications for the ability of the plaintiff to be awarded compensation. Therefore, it is often criticised as being overly 'esoteric' and 'poorly defined',[58] and even 'metaphysical'.[59] It was no surprise that the matter of causation was one of the areas to be reformed by the civil liability legislation introduced in the early 2000s (see Section 1.2).

4.2.1   Onus and standard of proof

The 'onus of proof' refers to the burden of proving what has occurred. In an action for negligence, the plaintiff bears the onus of establishing each of the three elements of negligence (duty, breach and damage). It is only if the defendant raises a defence, such as contributory negligence (see Section 5.2), that the onus of proof shifts to the defendant to establish that defence.

The onus of proof will be discharged if the proof meets a certain standard. The standard of proof requires a determination of whether, in the words of Lord Denning, it is 'more probable than not' that something has occurred.[60] The court does not require certainty, but it must be satisfied that it is more likely than not that what is alleged took place,

---

53   (1998) 195 CLR 232, 238.
54   *Leyland Shipping Co v Norwich Union Fire Insurance Society* [1918] AC 350, 370.
55   *Re Polemis* [1921] 3 KB 560.
56   *Haynes v Harwood* [1935] 1 KB 146, 156; *Dorset Yacht Co Ltd v Home Office* [1970] AC 1004, 1028–30.
57   *Yorkshire Dale Steamship Co v Minister of War Transport* [1942] AC 691.
58   M Bagaric and S Erbacher, 'Causation in Negligence: From Anti-jurisprudence to Principle – Individual Responsibility as the Cornerstone for the Attribution of Liability' (2011) 18(4) *Journal of Law and Medicine* 759.
59   J Edelman, 'Unnecessary Causation' (2015) 89(1) *Australian Law Journal* 1.
60   *Miller v Minister of Pensions* [1947] 2 All ER 372, 374.

after considering all the available evidence and witness statements. This process is often considered to involve a calculation of odds: is there a greater than 50 per cent chance that one version of events is more probable than the other?

The High Court in *Briginshaw v Briginshaw* cautioned against engaging in a purely 'mathematical' calculation, clarifying that courts are instead required to:

> feel an actual persuasion of its occurrence or existence before it can be found. It cannot
> be found as a result of a mere mechanical comparison of probabilities independently
> of any belief in its reality ... [A]t common law ... it is enough that the affirmative of an
> allegation is made out to the reasonable satisfaction of the tribunal.[61]

You might view this as a balancing act where tilting the scale one way or another establishes proof of a fact. But it is possible for there to be an element of doubt involved, as certainty is not a requirement. The *standard of proof* in an action for negligence is 'on the balance of probabilities',[62] which is a lesser standard from that applied in criminal matters requiring proving 'beyond reasonable doubt'. For an overview of statutory provisions on the 'onus of proof', see Table 4.4.

Table 4.4   Overview of statutory provisions on 'onus of proof'

Legislation	Section
Civil Law (Wrongs) Act 2002 (ACT)	46
Civil Liability Act 2002 (NSW)	5E
Civil Liability Act 2003 (Qld)	12
Civil Liability Act 1936 (SA)	35
Civil Liability Act 2002 (Tas)	14
Wrongs Act 1958 (Vic)	52
Civil Liability Act 2002 (WA)	5D

Keeping in mind that the onus of proof remains on the plaintiff, there might be circumstances where it is simply not possible to explain the events in any other way than by the defendant's negligence; this is when the maxim *res ipsa loquitur* might apply.

4.2.1.1   The maxim *res ipsa loquitur*

The maxim *res ipsa loquitur*, meaning 'the thing (or fact) speaks for itself', applies to situations where the plaintiff cannot establish the cause of the accident, but *the very fact that the accident occurred* and that an injury was sustained establishes a prima facie case of negligence against the defendant. A prima facie (at first sight) case is sometimes referred to as 'a case to answer'. Thus, it allows the plaintiff to treat the very fact of the injury as evidence of the defendant's negligence.

---

61 (1938) 60 CLR 336, 361–2 (Starke J).
62 In New South Wales, this standard of proof is prescribed by *Evidence Act 1995* (NSW) s 140 which
    provides that the standard of proof is 'on the balance of probabilities' (which applies in all civil
    proceedings).

This common law maxim (sometimes referred to as a principle, rule or doctrine) plays a role in situations when it would be very difficult, if not impossible, for the plaintiff to provide direct evidence of the defendant's negligence. It is then for the defendant to disprove the allegation of negligence: that is, to rebut it by explaining that they took all reasonable care or that the injury was caused by something other than the defendant's negligence.

HINTS AND TIPS

Even when *res ipsa loquitur* is found to apply, the plaintiff still bears the onus of proving factual causation on the balance of probabilities.

The first case in which the doctrine appeared was the English case of *Byrne v Boadle*.[63] As the plaintiff was walking along a street, a barrel of flour fell on him causing him to lose consciousness. Neither the plaintiff nor any witnesses could see *how* the accident happened. As the defendant's shop was adjacent to the road on which the plaintiff was walking, that was found to be sufficient to presume negligence on the part of the defendant. As this case shows, applying the doctrine of *res ipsa loquitur* requires the use of inferential reasoning to prove negligence: that is, the court infers a causal connection between the action (or inaction) of the defendant (eg, lack of inspection or a poor maintenance system) and the incident (eg, the barrel falling out of a window).

Following the doctrine's development, it is for the plaintiff to present sufficient evidence to show that it is more probable than not that the defendant was the responsible party, and the incident leading to the injury (eg, the fact of the barrel falling) becomes prima facie evidence of negligence. Since the introduction of the maxim, there have been numerous attempts to prescribe the boundaries of its application; nevertheless, its application continues to be confused.

In *Schellenberg v Tunnel Holdings Pty Ltd*, the High Court rejected the application of this rule in the particular circumstances, but confirmed its applicability and refrained from abandoning it altogether,[64] as has been done elsewhere (eg, in Canada).[65] The decision in *Schellenberg* affirmed the following:

(1) The principle of *res ipsa loquitur* does *not* reverse the onus of proof (even though there might be an inference of negligence, it is still up to the plaintiff to prove negligence on the balance of probabilities).[66]

(2) The occurrence must be such that it could not ordinarily happen *without* the defendant's negligence.

---

63 (1863) 159 ER 299.
64 (2000) 200 CLR 121.
65 See *Fontaine v British Columbia (Official Administrator)* [1998] 1 SCR 424, where the Supreme Court of Canada noted at 435 that this doctrine was not more than 'an attempt to deal with circumstantial evidence'. See also M McInnes, 'The Death of Res Ipsa Loquitur in Canada' (1998) 114(4) *Law Quarterly Review* 547.
66 *Schellenberg v Tunnel Holdings Pty Ltd* (2000) 200 CLR 121; [2000] HCA 18, [24] (Gleeson CJ and McHugh J). As Kirby J noted at [108]: 'The defendant can remain silent and still succeed'.

(3)   The *res* (thing), whether the instrument or agent causing or contributing to the injury, was within the exclusive *control* or *management* of the defendant.[67]

(4)   Once there was an *explanation* for the occurrence, the principle had no further application, as the doctrine relies on the *absence* of explanation.[68]

Thus, the maxim continues to be applicable in Australia, but the commentary by Kirby J in this case gives clear direction as to the doctrine's assumed 'separate' nature, and points to it being no more than an 'inferential reasoning' to the facts in a negligence claim:

> Perhaps *res ipsa loquitur* will continue to linger for a time as yet another indication of the attraction of lawyers to exotic labels. This case may have the merit of acting as a reminder of its limitations, the danger of treating it as a rule of law and the necessity to limit its use to that of an aid to logical reasoning by inference when considering whether the plaintiff has, or has not, established a cause of action in negligence.[69]

Despite the doctrine being not often successfully invoked, the application of the maxim occasionally leads to a favourable outcome for the plaintiff. In *Blackney v Clark*, the doctrine was successfully applied.[70] The plaintiff, Mr Blackney, was successful in bringing a claim for damages against the defendant, Mr Clark, for injuries sustained while coming to the rescue of Mr Clark and his boat. The presiding judge confirmed that those who voluntarily place themselves in a position of danger owe a duty of care to their rescuers, since rescue is reasonably foreseeable when, as in this case, a mariner puts himself in a position of danger. His Honour found that a prima facie case of negligence was found on the facts:

> the defendant allowed his vessel to get so close to the breakers that his vessel was dragged into shore by the breakers. Without more, that bespeaks negligence. It is a position where the principle of *res ipsa loquitur* applies. The defendant, if his navigation was blameless, could have entered the witness box and told me so. He did not. This is not a case of reversing the onus of proof, but relying on such proof as the plaintiff can adduce to determine whether there is evidence to suggest negligence on the part of the defendant and then throwing the evidentiary onus back to the defendant where the defendant is the only person who can elucidate the position.[71]

In order for the doctrine to succeed, it must be shown that there is more than a mere possibility that a certain event is the explanation of the plaintiff's damage that the court should accept. Even if the defendant raises some other explanation, it is still up to the court to assess the range of evidence available and decide which of the explanations proposed by each party is more probable in the circumstances.

---

67   Ibid [49] (Gleeson CJ and McHugh J).
68   Ibid [32], [35]–[36] (Gleeson CJ and McHugh J).
69   Ibid [124] (Kirby J).
70   [2013] NSWDC 144.
71   Ibid [28] (Neilson DCJ).

4.2.2   Civil liability legislation

You learnt in Chapter 1 about the reforms that followed the 2002 *Review of the Law of Negligence* ('Ipp Report'), which made 61 recommendations in total.[72] The law reforms relevant for our discussion are those that introduced a statutory test of causation (Recommendation 29):

Recommendation 29

The Proposed Act should embody the following principles:

Onus of proof

(a)   The plaintiff always bears the onus of proving, on the balance of probabilities, any fact relevant to the issue of causation.

The two elements of causation

(b)   The question of whether negligence caused harm in the form of personal injury or death ('the harm') has two elements:

   (i)   'factual causation', which concerns the factual issue of whether the negligence played a part in bringing about the harm; and

   (ii)   'scope of liability' which concerns the normative issue of the appropriate scope of the negligent person's liability for the harm, once it has been established that the negligence was a factual cause of the harm. 'Scope of liability' covers issues, other than factual causation, referred to in terms such as 'legal cause', 'real and effective cause', 'commonsense causation', 'foreseeability' and 'remoteness of damage'.

Factual causation

(c)   The basic test of 'factual causation' (the 'but for' test) is whether the negligence was a necessary condition of the harm.

(d)   In appropriate cases, proof that the negligence materially contributed to the harm or the risk of the harm may be treated as sufficient to establish factual causation even though the but for test is not satisfied.

(e)   Although it is relevant to proof of factual causation, the issue of whether the case is an appropriate one for the purposes of (d) is normative.

(f)   For the purposes of deciding whether the case is an appropriate one (as required in (d)), amongst the factors that it is relevant to consider are:

   (i)   whether (and why) responsibility for the harm should be imposed on the negligent party, and

   (ii)   whether (and why) the harm should be left to lie where it fell.

(g)   (i)   For the purposes of sub-paragraph (ii) of this paragraph, the plaintiff's own testimony, about what he or she would have done if the defendant had not been negligent, is inadmissible.

   (ii)   Subject to sub-paragraph (i) of this paragraph, when, for the purposes of deciding whether allegedly negligent conduct was a factual cause of the harm, it is relevant to ask what the plaintiff would have done if the defendant had not been negligent, this question should be answered subjectively in the light of all relevant circumstances.

---

72 *Review of the Law of Negligence* (Final Report, September 2002).

Scope of liability

(h) For the purposes of determining the normative issue of the appropriate scope of liability for the harm, amongst the factors that it is relevant to consider are:

(i)   whether (and why) responsibility for the harm should be imposed on the negligent party; and

(ii) whether (and why) the harm should be left to lie where it fell.

The statutory provisions appear to be relatively similar to the common law approach to causation (as we will discuss in more detail later) but the main aim of the legislative reforms in this area was to simplify the tests used by courts in relation to causation. Thus, in all jurisdictions except the Northern Territory, the approach is to draw a distinction between 'factual causation' (ie, whether the damage was caused or materially contributed to by the defendant's breach, which is a question of fact) and 'scope of liability' (ie, whether the damage was a foreseeable consequence of that breach, which is a question of law for the judge to determine).

Even though the clear separation of the process into two stages has helped with some of the confusion surrounding the issue of causation, it continues to attract scholarly and judicial criticism. As the legislative changes relied on the recommendations of the Ipp Report, it is worth considering how some of the issues relating to causation were assessed by the Ipp Review Panel.

The Ipp Report made a number of references to common law terms such as 'real cause', 'effective cause', 'remoteness of damage' and 'foreseeability' but the interpretations of some of these terms are at odds with their common law application.[73] For example, at common law, the 'reasonable foreseeability' test is used to assess duty of care, breach of duty and remoteness of damage, rather than the first element of causation (factual causation), leading to confusion. It should be remembered that the 'reasonable foreseeability' test in this context is not identical to that used at the other stages of a negligence action. Further, the Ipp Report associated the 'scope of liability' element with the notion of common sense. However, at common law, the commonsense approach is more closely affiliated with the first element (ie, factual causation). Another point of contention is that the scope of liability stage lacks precision and clarity by offering a 'broad judicial discretion to determine causation in individual cases by reference to idiosyncratic notions of "policy" and "justice"',[74] and thus does not necessarily offer more clarity than the common law 'commonsense' approach.

As a matter of caution, make sure that you are clear about whether the issue of causation in a particular case was decided under common law principles, or following the introduction of the civil liability legislation and under the relevant statutory provisions.

---

73 On this point, see B McDonald, 'Legislative Intervention in the Law of Negligence: The Common Law, Statutory Interpretation and Tort Reform in Australia' (2005) 27(3) *Sydney Law Review* 443.

74 M Bagaric and S Erbacher, 'Causation in Negligence: From Anti-jurisprudence to Principle – Individual Responsibility as the Cornerstone for the Attribution of Liability' (2011) 18(4) *Journal of Law and Medicine* 759, 765.

Case: *Matinca v Coalroc (No 5)* [2022] NSWSC 844

Facts

The plaintiff (Mr Matinca) was employed by the defendant (Coalroc) as an underground coal miner on a weekend roster with three shifts of 12 hours each Friday, Saturday and Sunday. At the time of the plaintiff's employment, the company had a personal travel management plan in place for its employees.

Approximately two hours and 20 minutes after Mr Matinca left the mine precinct heading home, he was involved in a motor vehicle accident that caused him serious personal injury (at [2]), including:

- a traumatic brain injury involving retrograde and post-traumatic amnesia (the latter for a period of about 18 days)
- multiple facial fractures
- a degloving injury of the right arm.

The plaintiff sued the defendant for damages for breach of the duty of care owed to him by Coalroc as his employer.

Issue

Did the work-related fatigue cause the relevant incident resulting in the plaintiff's injury?

Decision

The New South Wales Supreme Court had to decide whether the incident 'was caused or materially contributed to by work-induced fatigue occasioned by the nature and conditions of his employment with Coalroc and that the temporal or spatial scope of the duty Coalroc owed him in the circumstances extended to that occurrence' (at [6]).

Campbell J was satisfied that the fatigue-induced inattention was a necessary cause of Mr Matinca's loss of control and the subsequent collision and was not satisfied with the defendant's argument that the speed of the driver or the condition of the road was *the* causal factor. He further reasoned that, due to the nature of the defendant's business, the employer's duty of care extended beyond the employee's work hours and place of work.

The workplace fatigue management procedure in place was indicative of the recognition of the dangers of work-related fatigue on Coalroc's employees and thus it was a failure on part of the defendant not to ensure that Mr Matinca submitted his personal travel management plan.

The employer was found to be negligent and ordered to pay the employee $1 130 782.28.

Significance

This case shows that the employer's scope of liability will be extended to situations outside the employee's working hours or workplace if it can be shown on the balance of probabilities that the work-induced fatigue caused or materially contributed to the injuries sustained by the employee.

Notes

In this case, the matter of evidence and expert opinions were considered, with Campbell J stating that 'I am of the view that the experts have approached what might be categorised as the question of factual causation in a restricted manner by which they have looked to see whether the objective evidence identifies a salient factor which can be described as the primary or sole cause' (at [85]). Instead, he argued, the legal standard of causation applied in the law of negligence should not be seen to be the same as the one applied by engineers looking for 'a single factor which yields greater than a 50 per cent contribution to the occurrence of the accident' (at ibid.)

The question for establishing the legal standard is, somewhat, 'easier' in that it requires showing on the balance of probabilities that the defendant's negligence merely *caused* or *materially contributed* to the plaintiff's injury, which led the judge to conclude that 'Mr Matinca's single vehicle collision was caused by a combination of factors including speed, the prevailing driving conditions and momentary inattention caused by fatigue. Of these I think fatigue the most significant' (at [91]). Thus, even though fatigue was not strictly speaking 'a necessary condition', Campbell J was satisfied it 'constituted a very substantial, material contribution to the occurrence of the accident' (at [99]).

Question

Notwithstanding the relevant workers compensation legislation, does it mean that the employer is always going to be liable for incidents occurring while their employees are travelling home from work?

 Guided response in the eBook

HINTS AND TIPS

Be aware that the 'remoteness of damage' aspect of causation (which under common law would determine whether the plaintiff's loss should be attributed to the defendant's negligence) is now part of the second stage of the causation inquiry, namely the 'scope of liability' test.

4.2.2.1   The 'necessary condition' test

The first step in establishing whether a breach of duty on the part of the defendant caused the particular harm to the plaintiff involves establishing whether there is a link between the defendant's act (or failure to act) and the damage suffered by the plaintiff. To satisfy this step, the plaintiff must show that the defendant's negligence was a 'necessary condition' of the occurrence of the harm (see Table 4.5).

This first requirement of the damage element closely resembles the common law 'but for' test (see Section 4.2.3.1), but they are not identical. It is not uncommon for courts to approach the 'necessary condition' test as though it were simply a 'statutory statement of the "but for"' test for causation.[75] However, the statutory test uses a different formulation of words making it a *positive* test, in that it must be shown that the defendant's negligence

Table 4.5   Overview of statutory provisions on the 'necessary condition'

Legislation	Section
Civil Law (Wrongs) Act 2002 (ACT)	45(1)(a)
Civil Liability Act 2002 (NSW)	5D(1)(a)
Civil Liability Act 2003 (Qld)	11(1)(a)
Civil Liability Act 1936 (SA)	34(1)(a)
Civil Liability Act 2002 (Tas)	13(1)(a)
Wrongs Act 1958 (Vic)	51(1)(a)
Civil Liability Act 2002 (WA)	5C(1)(a)

led to the plaintiff's harm. By contrast, the 'but for' test is a *negative* test under which the plaintiff's harm is conditional on the defendant's negligence.

Section 5D(1)–(3) of the *Civil Liability Act 2002* (NSW) provides:

(1)   A determination that negligence caused particular harm comprises the following elements:

    (a)   that the negligence was a necessary condition of the occurrence of the harm ('factual causation'), and

    (b)   that it is appropriate for the scope of the negligent person's liability to extend to the harm so caused ('scope of liability').

(2)   In determining in an exceptional case, in accordance with established principles, whether negligence that cannot be established as a necessary condition of the occurrence of harm should be accepted as establishing factual causation, the court is to consider (amongst other relevant things) whether or not and why responsibility for the harm should be imposed on the negligent party.

(3)   If it is relevant to the determination of factual causation to determine what the person who suffered harm would have done if the negligent person had not been negligent:

    (a)   the matter is to be determined subjectively in the light of all relevant circumstances, subject to paragraph (b), and

    (b)   any statement made by the person after suffering the harm about what he or she would have done is inadmissible except to the extent (if any) that the statement is against his or her interest.

This new statutory formula for causation was applied in the case of *Finch v Roberts*, which concerned a plaintiff with testicular cancer who had to undergo a number of chemotherapy courses.[76] Mr Finch underwent four, rather than three, courses of chemotherapy due to the defendant's failure to advise him to see an oncologist to discuss the possibility of the existence of other tumours. It was determined that it was the fourth course of chemotherapy that caused his ongoing disabilities and gave rise to the action. Kirby J in his judgment concluded:

---

75   *Strong v Woolworths Ltd* (2012) 246 CLR 182; [2012] HCA 5, [18]; *Adeels Palace Pty Ltd v Moubarak* (2009) 239 CLR 420; [2009] HCA 48, [55].

76   [2004] NSWSC 39.

> I consider the defendant's negligence was a necessary condition of the harm that ensued (s 5D(1)(a)). I further believe that it is appropriate that the scope of the defendant's liability extend to the harm so caused (s 5D(1)(b)). The consequences were in each case a foreseeable result of the breach. [The defendant] himself recognised … that a failure to detect any early change in the tumour may have created the need for more chemotherapy than may otherwise have been necessary.[77]

This test involves considering whether the plaintiff would have been injured even if the defendant had not been negligent, and how likely it was that the plaintiff would have been injured if not for the defendant's negligence. First, it requires considering whether that injury would arise to start with. Second, it looks at assessing the likelihood of the injury arising, that is: *Is it more likely than not that the plaintiff would have sustained this type of injury or loss anyway?* Being a positive test, it requires the court to look into the effective cause of the damage, notwithstanding that there might be other causes. A case where this question needed to be answered was *Cox v New South Wales*, which concerned profound and ongoing bullying at school.[78] The student was persistently bullied by a fellow pupil in a primary school run by the defendant, the State of New South Wales. The Supreme Court held that the defendant owed a duty of care and breached that duty by failing to restrain the bullying child. The Court had to consider whether the psychological harm that the plaintiff had suffered was causally connected to the defendant's failure to restrain the bully. The complication in this case was that the plaintiff's mother and father had psychological problems, including severe depression, and that the mother had, as was claimed, a malign influence on him. It was alleged that these were the operative causes of the psychological damage that the plaintiff was attempting to recover damages for from the defendant.

The Court had to consider the question of causation. Had the plaintiff suffered the psychological illness anyway, irrespective of the negligence on the part of the defendant, there would be no link between the lack of action by the defendant and the plaintiff's psychological condition. It was held that the question of causation is not whether the plaintiff would, in some other circumstances and at some other time, suffer some kind of psychological disorder, but whether the defendant's negligence was the 'necessary condition' of the occurrence of that particular harm. It does not need to be the sole cause, but it is enough that it is the substantial cause of that harm.

In *Adeels Palace Pty Ltd v Moubarak*, the High Court emphasised that the 'first point to make about the question of causation is that … it is [now] governed by the Civil Liability Act'.[79] Thus, it is not necessary to consider whether, or even to what extent, the statutory provision is similar (or not) to the causation determination, but simply that the statutory provisions must be observed. As to the point of ensuring the division between the first and the second element in determining causation in a negligence action, their Honours held:

> Dividing the issue of causation in this way expresses the relevant questions in a way that may differ from what was said by Mason CJ, in *March v E & M H Stramare* Pty Ltd to be the common law's approach to causation. The references in *March* to causation

---

77   *Finch v Roberts* [2004] NSWSC 39 [148].
78   (2007) 71 NSWLR 225.
79   (2009) 239 CLR 420; [2009] HCA 48, [41].

being 'ultimately a matter of common sense' were evidently intended to disapprove the proposition 'that value judgment has, or should have, no part to play in resolving causation as an issue of fact'. By contrast, s 5D(1) [of the *Civil Liability Act 2002* (NSW)] treats factual causation and scope of liability as separate and distinct issues.[80]

The decision by the High Court in *Strong v Woolworths Ltd* provides another example of the consideration of causation under s 5D of the *Civil Liability Act 2002* (NSW).[81] This is one of the so-called 'slip and fall' cases, where the plaintiff claims that the occupier of premises or property owner (or their employee) failed to recognise a dangerous condition (a pothole or slippery substance on the floor) and did not remove or repair the potential hazard.

Case: *Strong v Woolworths Ltd* (2012) 246 CLR 182

Facts

The plaintiff (appellant), who walked with the aid of crutches due to her leg being amputated above the knee, slipped on a greasy chip on the sidewalk sales area in a shopping centre. The incident took place at around 12:30 pm, and the last time the area had been inspected on that day was at 8 am. As a result of the fall, the plaintiff suffered a serious spinal injury. The plaintiff sued Woolworths and CPT Manager Limited, the owner of the centre, in negligence.

Issue

Was the defendant's negligent failure in ensuring a periodic system of inspection and cleaning of the sidewalk a necessary condition for the occurrence of the plaintiff's injury?

Decision

The plaintiff brought an action in negligence in the New South Wales District Court and was successful against Woolworths. (The claim against CPT Manager was dismissed.) Woolworths appealed the decision.

The New South Wales Court of Appeal was satisfied that the defendant owed the plaintiff a duty to take reasonable care for the safety of the persons on its premises. However, it was not satisfied that the appellant had successfully proven that her fall was caused by Woolworths' negligence. The Court found that the plaintiff had failed to prove, on the balance of probabilities, the time when the chip was dropped – whether earlier in the day or just before the plaintiff slipped on it. If the latter was the case, then even if the defendant had had an 'appropriate' cleaning regime in place, that might not have prevented the plaintiff from being injured.

The appellant was granted special leave to appeal to the High Court. The majority of the High Court (French CJ, Gummow, Crennan and Bell JJ) did not agree with the Court of Appeal's ruling that it was not due to Woolworths' negligence that the appellant had slipped on the chip. On the balance of probabilities, had there been an 'appropriate' cleaning system in operation, that chip

---

80 Ibid [43].
81 (2012) 246 CLR 182; [2012] HCA 5.

would have been detected and removed sometime between 8 am (the last inspection) and when the incident took place (at around 12:30 pm):

> Proof of the causal link between an omission and an occurrence requires consideration of the probable course of events had the omission not occurred ... [The plaintiff] was required to prove that, had a system of periodic inspection and cleaning of the sidewalk sales area been employed on the day of her fall, it is likely that the chip would have been detected and removed before she approached the entrance to Big W.[82]

Significance

The onus of proof rests on the plaintiff, but they are not required to show the definite sequence of events. All the plaintiff is required to prove on the balance of probabilities is that the defendant's conduct (in this case, an omission in ensuring that an 'appropriate' cleaning regimen was in place) was a necessary condition for the occurrence of their harm. In assessing the causal link between the defendant's omission and the occurrence, the court will consider the probable course of events had that omission not taken place.

Notes

This case is an example of where, even though the burden is on the plaintiff, the defendant might be required to explain how and why something might have happened. As discussed in Section 4.2.1.1 on *res ipsa loquitur*, once the plaintiff can prove that there was a substance on the floor, the court will find it as prima facie evidence of negligence unless the defendant can show that they had taken all reasonable steps, notwithstanding that there was a spillage on the floor.

In such cases, it is not that the owner or occupier is responsible for the spillage but that they should have taken reasonable steps to clean it up. In keeping with the requirement under s 5E of the *Civil Liability Act 2002* (NSW) that the plaintiff bears the onus of proof (see Section 4.2.1), it would be near impossible for the plaintiff to show a causal relationship (between the spillage and their fall) unless they were able to prove how long that spillage was on the floor. Thus, courts are more prepared to accept a plaintiff's claim that there is no other or better explanation but that the cause of the incident was the lack of a system of periodic inspection and cleaning in place.

As you know by now, in the law of torts the standard of proof is on the balance of probabilities. Thus, in situations like this, it is often an exercise in drawing odds. The majority of the High Court, overturning the Court of Appeal's decision, found at [38]:

> The probabilities favoured the conclusion that the chip was deposited in the longer period between 8 am and 12.10 pm and not the shorter period between 12.10 pm and the time of the fall.

However, not all the Justices agreed. In his dissenting judgment, Heydon J took a hardline approach and remained sceptical that the plaintiff was able to provide sufficient evidence from 'which to draw a circumstantial inference on the balance of probabilities' (at [66]) that the chip fell

---

82 *Strong v Woolworths Ltd* (2012) 246 CLR 182; [2012] HCA 5, [32] (French CJ, Gummow, Crennan and Bell JJ).

sometime between 8 am and 12:10 pm, rather than later. Thus, he found the 'appellant's recourse to what she called "probability theory" unconvincing' (at [75]).

Question

In similar cases, which do you think should prevail, 'probability theory' or the 'common knowledge and experience approach', when assessing what might have happened?

 Guided response in the eBook

4.2.3   Common law (historical overview and interpretive framework)

In order to fully grasp the current requirements for satisfying the causation element, it is necessary to understand how it operates under common law (which is still the case in the Northern Territory). Traditionally, two things had to be shown. First, the damage suffered by the plaintiff must have been caused by the defendant; this was referred to as 'causation'. Second, the damage suffered by the plaintiff had to be of the type that the defendant should be required to compensate the plaintiff for; this was known as 'remoteness'.

HINTS AND TIPS

In all jurisdictions except the Northern Territory, where the common law approach continues to apply, an inquiry into the 'damage' element should be based on the relevant civil liability legislation, even if these provisions largely follow and are based on the common law approach.

This two-stage approach was clearly followed in the High Court's judgment in *March v E & MH Stramare Pty Ltd ('Stramare')*.[83] The approach taken by McHugh J drew on the work of Jane Stapleton, whose research had also been considered by the Ipp Panel.[84] Professor Stapleton had argued that the use of the term 'causation' is confusing and that it should be reserved for a description of fact (ie, whether the defendant's negligence led to the plaintiff's damage).[85] All other issues, including the application of the 'but for' test, should be considered as resting on the principle of responsibility (a matter of policy) rather than being disguised in the language of causation.[86]

---

83 (1991) 171 CLR 506.
84 'The Panel's consideration of and recommendations about causation have been greatly assisted by the work of Jane Stapleton': Ipp Report 109 [7.27] n 6.
85 J Stapleton, 'Causation-in-fact and the Scope of Liability for Consequences' (2003) 119(3) *Law Quarterly Review* 388.
86 Ibid.

The test used to assess remoteness of damage before the 1991 decision in *Stramare* proved to be too broad. This necessitated the High Court to consider the policy arguments. A major concern was that policy factors were being hidden in the determination of causation. This concern led McHugh J to advocate that policy considerations should be articulated clearly and considered only at the 'remoteness of damage' stage of causation, which he aptly called the 'scope of the risk' test.[87] This concern also explains the legislative reforms recommended by the Ipp Report and subsequently built into the civil liability legislation in most jurisdictions. If you look again at ss 5D and 5E of the *Civil Liability Act 2002* (NSW), which are largely to the same effect in other jurisdictions, you can see the influence of the views of McHugh J in *Stramare* and Professor Stapleton.

4.2.3.1   The 'but for' test

The 'but for' test is a *negative* test which asks this question: *If not for the negligent conduct by the defendant, would the plaintiff have suffered this damage?* If the answer is 'yes' (ie, the plaintiff's injury or loss would have occurred anyway), causation is not established (and so the action fails).

This was the outcome of the English case of *Barnett v Chelsea and Kensington Hospital Management Committee*.[88] A hospital doctor was alleged to have failed in his duty of care by refusing to examine a patient (Mr Barnett) who complained of vomiting after drinking tea. The doctor advised the patient to go home and to contact his doctor should he continue to feel unwell in the morning. Mr Barnett died five hours later of arsenic poisoning. The Court had to decide whether there was some causal connection between the failure of the doctor to act and the death of Mr Barnett. The Court held that the causation element was not satisfied, as the patient would have died of poisoning even if he had been admitted and offered medical treatment at the time he arrived at the hospital. Thus, the Court had to compare what actually had happened with what might have happened if the person who owed the duty satisfied their obligations under that duty. The 'but for' test is a *hypothetical* test as the court is essentially trying to compare what happened with what hypothetically (ie, probably) would have happened if not for the negligent conduct of the defendant. Assume that you are driving a car that you know has faulty brakes when you run into another car stopped at traffic lights. Initially, the accident does not look too major. However, it causes the driver of the stationary car, an elderly woman, to sustain serious injury that requires her to be hospitalised. While convalescing at the hospital, she trips and falls on the stairs, sustaining further and even more serious injuries to her back. If we were to apply the 'but for' test, the question asked of you would be: *Would the injury to the woman's back have been occasioned, if not for your act of driving a car with faulty brakes?* On a strict application of the test, the answer would be 'no': if you had not driven the car with faulty brakes, the other driver would not have been injured and thus taken to the hospital where she sustained further injuries. In cases like these, courts need to consider how strictly to apply the 'but for' test.

This can be illustrated by comparing two cases (see Table 4.6) that looked similar on the facts, but where the application of the 'but for' test yielded different results.

---

87 (1991) CLR 506, [25].
88 [1969] 1 QB 428.

Table 4.6 Comparison of cases involving application of the 'but for' test

Case	*McKiernan v Manhire* (1977) 17 SASR 571	*Pyne v Wilkenfeld* (1981) 26 SASR 441
Facts	P tripped in the hospital while recovering from her primary injury caused by D's negligence.	P tripped as a result of wearing a neck brace due to her initial injury and caused herself further injury as a result of falling.
Decision	The tripping could have happened anywhere; the fact that it happened in the hospital was irrelevant.	The tripping was caused by the neck brace worn by P; as wearing the neck brace was the result of D's negligent act, P was able to recover damages from D.
Relevance	Did the initial injury merely secure P's presence in a particular location where the subsequent injury was sustained?	Did the initial injury or its ongoing treatment impair P's capacity to respond to the surrounding environment as they otherwise would have?
The 'but for' test	The test was applied unsuccessfully for P.	The test was applied successfully for P.

Can the different outcomes in these cases be explained by the inconsistency in the application of the 'but for' test, or something else? It is arguable that if the person's initial injury simply secured their presence in a particular location where the plaintiff suffered a further injury (eg, a hospital, as in *McKiernan v Manhire*[89]), the courts are unlikely to find in favour of the plaintiff. On the other hand, if the person's capacity to respond to the surrounding environment is impaired by the injury itself or its ongoing treatment (eg, wearing a neck brace, as in *Pyne v Wilkenfeld*[90]), the application of the 'but for' test might yield a positive outcome for the plaintiff by apportioning the liability for that injury to the initial tortfeasor.

Such considerations are relatively frequent in medical negligence and 'failure to warn' cases. In *Rogers v Whitaker* the question was whether the plaintiff, who had sight in only one eye, would have consented to the eye operation if she had been properly informed of its risks.[91] The Court found that the surgeon had failed to explain to the plaintiff the risk of sympathetic ophthalmia to her good eye. The plaintiff was able to establish to the satisfaction of the Court that if she had known the odds were a 1-in-14 000 chance of losing the sight in both eyes, she would not have proceeded with the operation, and would have retained the sight in her good eye.

Similarly, in *Chappel v Hart* the High Court found a causal connection between a surgeon omitting to warn the patient of risk inherent in an operation, and the risk materialising.[92] The plaintiff alleged that she would have not proceeded with the operation had she known the danger. The High Court (3:2) held that the factual cause of harm was the defendant's failure to warn of the risk, even though the operation itself was performed without negligence.

In such cases, what a person would have done had they know of the risk is assessed subjectively, which is a process distinct from assessing the conduct of a reasonable

---

89 (1977) 17 SASR 571.
90 (1981) 26 SASR 441.
91 (1992) 175 CLR 479.
92 (1998) 195 CLR 232.

person (ie, whether a reasonable person in the plaintiff's position would want to know the information).[93] This has now been clarified by the civil liability legislation in most jurisdictions (see Table 4.7).

Table 4.7   Overview of statutory provisions on the test determining what the person who suffered harm would have done if the negligent person had not been negligent

Legislation	Section
Civil Liability Act 2002 (NSW)	5D(3)
Civil Liability Act 2003 (Qld)	11(3)(a)
Civil Liability Act 2002 (Tas)	13(3)(a)
Wrongs Act 1958 (Vic)	51(3)
Civil Liability Act 2002 (WA)	5C(3)(a)

It is also worth keeping in mind that in four jurisdictions (see Table 4.8), statements made by the injured person about what they would have done are inadmissible except when the statement is against the person's interest.

Table 4.8   Overview of statutory provisions on admissibility of statement made by the injured person

Legislation	Section
Civil Liability Act 2002 (NSW)	5D(3)(b)
Civil Liability Act 2003 (Qld)	11(3)(b)
Civil Liability Act 2002 (Tas)	13(3)(b)
Civil Liability Act 2002 (WA)	5C(3)(b)

The main advantage of the 'but for' test is that it is simple to apply. However, it is not difficult to see that in certain circumstances it can be too easily satisfied, leading to absurd or arguably unjust outcomes. On the other hand, if the plaintiff's injuries are an outcome of multiple causes operating concurrently, the plaintiff's loss can be established only by bringing an action against all the defendants; however, in doing so, the position of each defendant must be considered individually and the reasons stated for bringing the defendant within the scope of liability.[94] Not only might it often be impossible to demonstrate that there is a more than 50 per cent likelihood that the cause led to the breach of the duty (the burden for which is on the plaintiff), but also in certain circumstances the test can be too narrowly applied, to the detriment of the plaintiff who is left uncompensated despite an obvious breach of a duty of care.

Unsurprisingly, in *Stramare* the High Court rejected the 'but for' test as the sole determining factor proving causation, particularly where there is more than one act sufficient to cause injury to the plaintiff.[95]

---

93 See also T Cockburn and B Madden, 'Proof of Causation in Informed Consent Cases: Establishing What the Plaintiff Would Have Done' (2010) 18(2) *Journal of Law and Medicine* 320.

94 This relates to assigning responsibility under existing common law principles, but the Australian Capital Territory [*Civil Law (Wrongs) Act 2002* s 45(2)] and South Australia [*Civil Liability Act 1936* s 34(2)] have also introduced statutory conditions.

95 (1991) 171 CLR 506.

Case: *March v E & MH Stramare Pty Ltd* (1991) 171 CLR 506

Facts

The defendant parked his fruit and vegetable truck in the middle of the road with the rear and hazard lights on, as it was early in the morning. The plaintiff, who was drunk at the time, drove his car into the back of the defendant's truck and as a result sustained injury. The plaintiff sued the defendant, arguing that his injuries were caused by the defendant's negligence in parking his truck in the middle of the road.

Issue

Is the application of the 'but for' test satisfactory in circumstances where there is more than one act sufficient to cause injury to the plaintiff?

Decision

At the first instance, the trial judge held that both the truck driver and the plaintiff were negligent. Thus, it was an issue of contributory negligence, and he apportioned liability on the basis of 70 per cent to the car driver and 30 per cent to the truck driver. The defendant appealed on the basis that his action was not the cause of the subsequent collision, and the plaintiff cross-appealed claiming that attributing 70 per cent of the fault to him was too high.

The majority of the Supreme Court of South Australia (Bollen and Prior JJ, with White J dissenting) did not find that the act of the truck driver 'wholly or partly' caused the collision, and that it was possible to establish 'causal proximity' between that act and the injuries sustained by the car driver.[96] The case reached the High Court.

The High Court unanimously affirmed the trial judge's decision and overturned the Supreme Court's decision on finding the drunkenness of the driver to be sufficient to displace the liability of the defendant.[97] Mason CJ held:

> [T]he 'but for' test, applied as a negative criterion of causation, has an important role to play in the resolution of the question ... Generally speaking ... causal connection is established if it appears that the plaintiff would not have sustained his or her injuries had the defendant not been negligent.[98]

Significance

The application of the 'but for' test must be subject to a number of qualifications. The application of the 'but for' test can be difficult or even troublesome in some situations where there are multiple acts or events leading to the plaintiff's injury. The test is not to be used as the exclusive test of causation in negligence cases.

---

96   *March v E & MM Stramare Pty Ltd* (1989) 50 SASR 588.
97   *March v E & MH Stramare Pty Ltd* (1991) 171 CLR 506.
98   Ibid 514 (Mason CJ).

Notes

The limitations of the 'but for' test were considered in this case. The case indicates that the test is not as helpful in identifying the cause of harm if more than one factor has contributed to the harm sustained by the plaintiff. There were two independent causes of the plaintiff's harm – the defendant's negligent parking in the street, and the plaintiff's negligent driving under the influence of alcohol – but neither was sufficient on its own to cause the accident. The defendant was found to be liable as his tortious conduct created the risk of injury, but the damages were reduced by 70 per cent due to the plaintiff's contributory negligence.

Dean J argued that the 'but for' test should not be used as the exclusive test for causation as it:

> would lead to the absurd and unjust position that there was no 'cause' of an injury in any case where there were present two or more independent and sufficient causes of the accident in which injury was sustained ... the mere fact that something constitutes an essential condition (in the 'but for' sense) of an occurrence does not mean that, for the purpose of ascribing responsibility or fault, it is properly to be seen as a 'cause' of that occurrence as a matter of either ordinary language or common sense. Thus, it could not, as a matter of ordinary language, be said that the fact that a person had a head was a 'cause' of his being decapitated by a negligently wielded sword notwithstanding that possession of a head is an essential precondition of decapitation.[99]

Question

Does the 'but for' test identify all the factors that may be treated as the cause of the harm or loss suffered by the plaintiff?

 Guided response in the eBook

The 'but for' test remains important. However, even before the legal reforms, judges would apply the commonsense approach and use it to account for public policy considerations in more 'complex' cases.

4.2.3.2   The 'commonsense' test

The commonsense approach[100] does not necessarily provide an ultimate answer to problems of causation. The major criticism of the commonsense approach is that '[it] does not clearly indicate what a court should do in any particular case'.[101] Dixon J observed in *Gunnersen v Henwood* that the commonsense approach is not a legal test at all, and equated it with

---

99   Ibid 523 (Dean J).

100   The commonsense approach also applies in criminal law, which largely asks the same question (ie, whether the accused made a significant contribution to the death of the victim) and hence causation is a matter of common sense for the jury to determine: *Campbell v The Queen* (1981) WAR 286, 290 (Burton CJ).

101   *State Rail Authority (NSW) v Wiegold* (1991) 25 NSWLR 500.

'personal views' and 'speculations'.[102] Thus, this approach also has its limitations, as what is common sense to one person might not be so for someone else. It begs a question: how *common* is the common sense?

In *Stramare*, McHugh J in his dissenting judgment opined that the commonsense approach should only be used in 'unusual cases' where there were two or more separate and independent events or acts 'each of which was sufficient to cause the damage'.[103] McHugh J suggested that the 'normative considerations' (the commonsense inquiry) should occur at the 'remoteness of damage' stage, noting that he favoured the 'scope of the risk' test:

> Once it is recognised that foreseeability is not the exclusive test of remoteness and that policy-based rules, disguised as causation principles, are also being used to limit responsibility for occasioning damage, the rationalisation of the rules concerning remoteness of damage requires an approach which incorporates the issue of foreseeability but also enables other policy factors to be articulated and examined.
>
> ... [T]he 'scope of the risk' test enables relevant policy factors to be articulated and justified in a way which is not possible when responsibility is limited by reference to commonsense notions of causation or to be more specific criteria such as '*novus actus interveniens*', 'sole cause' or 'real cause', all of which conceal unexpressed value judgments.[104]

The legal reforms did not end the use of the commonsense approach, and the courts are still directed by the civil liability legislation to incorporate this test in the process of determining whether to impose responsibility for the harm on the party in breach in exceptional cases. Thus, in an exceptional (some jurisdictions use 'appropriate') case, where the breach of duty is established but the requirement of 'factual causation' is not satisfied, the court is required to consider (among other relevant things) whether or not and why responsibility should be imposed on the defendant. This provision (see Table 4.9) is not very specific and thus, presumably, leaves it to the judge's discretion whether or not and why the defendant should be liable in such circumstances.

Table 4.9   Overview of statutory provisions on 'exceptional cases'

Legislation	Section
Civil Liability Act 2002 (NSW)	5D(2)
Civil Liability Act 2003 (Qld)	11(2)
Civil Liability Act 2002 (Tas)	13(2)
Wrongs Act 1958 (Vic)	51(2)
Civil Liability Act 2002 (WA)	5C(2)

4.2.3.3   The 'material contribution' test (cases of cumulatively caused injury)

Let us now consider circumstances where there are multiple causes of the plaintiff's harm or loss. In such cases, the plaintiff needs to demonstrate not that the defendant's actions

---

102 [2011] VSC 440, [379].
103 (1991) 171 CLR 506, 516.
104 *Stramare* (1991) 171 CLR 506, 535 (McHugh J).

were the 'but for' cause of the damage, but instead that the defendant's actions *materially contributed* to the damage suffered. In this sense, material contribution is a contribution that is more than *de minimis* (trivial or minor).

The expression 'material contribution' can been traced back to the 19th-century Scottish case *Duke of Buccleuch v Cowan* and the development of the law of nuisance.[105] The Court held that each of the polluters 'made a material contribution' to the river pollution, and thus it was not necessary to prove that it was the pollutants discharged by the defendant's factory that were the sole reason giving rise to a nuisance.[106] However, it must be noted that the phrase 'material contribution' has been used inconsistently in the context of causation in torts.

In the English case of *Bonnington Castings Ltd v Wardlaw*, the House of Lords held that it was not necessary for the plaintiff to demonstrate that the breach of duty of care by the defendant had been the sole or principal cause of the damage, but it must have materially contributed to it (what is known now as the *Bonnington* test).[107] In this case, a factory worker contracted pneumoconiosis by inhaling air with silica dust. The plaintiff claimed that it was the employer's negligence in not installing an extractor fan that had contributed to a larger exposure to silica dust than would have been the case had the employer taken the necessary precautions. Thus, even though some silica dust (the non-guilty or 'non-tortious' dust) would have been present irrespective of the defendant's action, it was the additional (guilty or 'tortious' dust) that the plaintiff had to demonstrate to have made a material contribution to the disease.

The High Court of Australia considered the *Bonnington Castings* decision in *Amaca Pty Ltd v Ellis*, a case which concerned an injury caused by uncertain pathogenesis.[108] The High Court had to determine whether the lung cancer and subsequent death of Mr Cotton was due to him working in unsafe conditions that exposed him to respirable asbestos fibres (due to the negligence of multiple defendants), or due to him smoking 15–20 cigarettes each day for more than 26 years. Assessing which of these was the more probable cause of Mr Cotton's lung cancer was a difficult undertaking for the Court which faced a lack of definite expert evidence on the cause of Mr Cotton's cancer. It found that the relative risk of smoking was the more probable cause of lung cancer than exposure to asbestos. Thus, the plaintiff (the executor of Mr Cotton's estate) was not able to establish that asbestos was a 'necessary condition' of cancer. Their Honours distinguished *Bonnington Castings*, noting that the matter of 'material contribution' did not in fact arise in the circumstances as, on the balance of probabilities, the plaintiff did not show a causal link between the asbestos exposure and Mr Cotton's cancer.[109] The High Court clarified the relevance of the 'material contribution' test, which it said is to be considered only *after* proving causation. That is, in cases relating to epidemiological risks, it is necessary to show that the risk caused by (in this case) asbestos fibres needs to be established first before determining whether the specific exposures to asbestos (brought about by successive tortfeasors) made a material contribution to the asbestos-related injury.

---

105 (1866) 5 Macpherson 214.
106 See also S Steel and D Ibbetson, 'More Grief on Uncertain Causation in Tort' (2011) 70(2) *Cambridge Law Journal* 451, 453.
107 [1956] AC 613.
108 (2010) 240 CLR 111.
109 *Amaca Pty Ltd v Ellis* (2010) 240 CLR 111, 135–6.

Where there are multiple causes of the damage, the plaintiff is not required to prove that the defendant's negligence was the sole or only cause of harm to satisfy the 'but for' or 'necessary condition' requirement. Notwithstanding this, as the majority in *Amaca Pty Ltd v Booth* noted, applying the 'but for' test is 'troublesome in various situations in which multiple acts or events led to the plaintiff's injury'.[110]

In cases where there is an evidentiary gap that makes it impossible for the plaintiff to prove causation (eg, where there exist multiple potential causes of the harm), relevant statutory provisions have been introduced in South Australia and the Australian Capital Territory to deal with such a situation (see Table 4.10).

Table 4.10   Comparison of South Australian and Australian Capital Territory legislation

Civil Liability Act 1936 (SA) s 34(2)	*Civil Law (Wrongs) Act 2002* (ACT) s 45(2)
Where, however, a person (the plaintiff) has been negligently exposed to a similar risk of harm by a number of different persons (the defendants) and it is not possible to assign responsibility for causing the harm to any one or more of them –	However, if a person (the plaintiff) has been negligently exposed to a similar risk of harm by a number of different persons (the defendants) and it is not possible to assign responsibility for causing the harm to one or more of them –
(a) the court may continue to apply the principle under which responsibility may be assigned to the defendants for causing the harm; but	(a) the court may continue to apply the established common law* principle under which responsibility may be assigned to the defendants for causing the harm; but
(b) the court should consider the position of each defendant individually and state the reasons for bringing the defendant within the scope of liability.	(b) the court must consider the position of each defendant individually and state the reasons for bringing the defendant within the scope of liability.

* *The differing text.*

REVIEW QUESTIONS

(1) What is the difference, if any, between the 'but for' test and the 'necessary condition' test?

(2) Can the plaintiff argue that the very fact that particular harm occurred is sufficient proof to infer that the defendant was negligent?

    Guided responses in the eBook

4.3   Scope of liability

The second step in proving a causal link between the defendant's negligent conduct and the damage sustained by the plaintiff involves considering the issue of remoteness of damage. What must be established is not just that the damage was factually caused by the defendant, but also whether that damage should be within the scope of the defendant's liability.

110 (2011) 246 CLR 36, 62 (Gummow, Hayne and Crennan JJ).

In its simplest form, this involves establishing whether the damage suffered by the plaintiff *should be* attributed to the defendant's negligence: *Would it be reasonable to hold the defendant liable for the plaintiff's injuries?* This requires taking into account a number of normative considerations (eg, is it 'fair' or 'right' that the defendant should bear the loss?). It also reintroduces the concept of 'reasonable foreseeability'.

This assessment involves making a value judgment about the just allocation of responsibility for the harm suffered by the plaintiff, once it is established that the harm or loss is a consequence of negligence by the defendant.

Table 4.11 provides an overview of statutory provisions on the 'scope of liability'.

Table 4.11   Overview of statutory provisions on the 'scope of liability'

Legislation	Section
Civil Law (Wrongs) Act 2002 (ACT)	45(1)(b) and (3)
Civil Liability Act 2002 (NSW)	5D(1)(b) and (4)
Civil Liability Act 2003 (Qld)	11(1)(b) and (4)
Civil Liability Act 1936 (SA)	34(1)(b) and (3)
Civil Liability Act 2002 (Tas)	13(1)(b) and (4)
Wrongs Act 1958 (Vic)	51(1)(b) and (4)
Civil Liability Act 2002 (WA)	5C(1)(b) and (4)

As noted in Section 4.2.3.2, the 'commonsense' test was used to determine causation when the 'but for' inquiry yielded unsatisfactory results. Notions of common sense and policy considerations determined whether the cause of the accident should be attributed to the defendant's negligence. Following the introduction of the civil liability legislation, the notions of common sense and policy became relevant at the 'remoteness of damage' stage and are now referred to as the 'scope of liability'.

HINTS AND TIPS

As with the 'necessary condition' statutory test for establishing the first element (factual causation), common law instructed the development of the second element (scope of liability).

The case of *Wallace v Kam* illustrates this well.[111] It is also an example of how the courts have tightened causation in medical negligence cases. The decision in *Wallace v Kam* establishes that in order to show factual causation, the plaintiff must prove on the balance of probabilities that they have 'sustained, as a consequence of having chosen to undergo the medical treatment, physical injury which [they] would not have sustained if warned of all material risks' by the doctor.[112] In this case, Dr Kam operated on Mr Wallace to improve the condition of his lumbar spine. Dr Kam failed to advise Mr Wallace that there was a risk

---

111 (2013) 250 CLR 375.
112 *Wallace v Kam* (2013) 250 CLR 375; [2013] HCA 19, [17].

that the operation could injure nerves (causing neurapraxia) in his thighs and another risk (assessed at 5 per cent) that he could suffer paralysis. Mr Wallace developed neurapraxia, and the risk of paralysis did not materialise. The trial judge found that, even if the plaintiff had been warned of the risks, he would have still consented to the operation, thus the 'failure to warn' of the risk of paralysis could not have been the legal cause of the neurapraxia. The Court of Appeal (in a split decision) found that Dr Kim was not liable for the neurapraxia. Mr Wallace appealed the decision by special leave to the High Court. The High Court followed the majority decision of the Court of Appeal and dismissed Mr Wallace's appeal. The High Court accepted that, had he been warned of all material risks, Mr Wallace would not have chosen to undergo the surgical procedure (the 'factual causation' element), but Dr Kim's liability should not extend to the personal injury sustained in circumstances where the patient was prepared to accept the risk that in fact materialised (ie, the neurapraxia [the 'scope of liability' element]). This case highlights that the plaintiff needs to satisfy *both* elements of the two-limbed test for causation to succeed in a negligence claim.

HINTS AND TIPS

Compare this case with *Rogers v Whitaker* (discussed in Section 4.2.3.1) in which the High Court declared that the law should recognise that 'a doctor has a duty to warn a patient of a material risk inherent in the proposed treatment', explaining that 'risk is material if, in the circumstances of the particular case, a reasonable person in the patient's position, if warned of the risk, would be likely to attach significance to it or if the medical practitioner is or should reasonably be aware that the particular patient, if warned of the risk, would be likely to attach significance to it'.[113]

The 'scope of liability' includes considerations of policy on issues such as the application of the eggshell skull rule and whether an intervening cause breaks the chain of causation.

4.3.1   Remoteness of damage

The element of remoteness of damage in the tort of negligence is concerned with the *limits* of the defendant's liability for damage caused by the defendant's negligence. As mentioned earlier, in *Stramare* the element of causation was treated as a fusion of factual (evidence-based) assessment and normative (or value-based) considerations.[114] Following the introduction of the civil liability legislation, the policy considerations are now to be kept separate from the first element of factual causation and dealt with under the second element of the appropriate scope of liability.

The scope of liability inquiry, therefore, overlaps the remoteness of damage inquiry, as both are legal (rather than factual) tests that are mainly concerned with whether the damage suffered by the plaintiff ought to be treated as a consequence of negligent conduct by the defendant. The question of causation (first element) focuses on negligent conduct, whereas remoteness of damage focuses on the consequences of that conduct.

---

113 (1992) 175 CLR 479, 483 (Mason CJ, Brennan, Dawson, Toohey and McHugh JJ).
114 (1991) 171 CLR 506.

The inquiry into remoteness of damage asks the question: *Was the damage suffered by the plaintiff not too remote to impose liability on the defendant?* This can be broken down to two questions that assist in the inquiry:

(1)   Was the *kind* of harm reasonably foreseeable?

(2)   Was the *way* the harm occurred reasonably foreseeable?

The aim of this exercise is to determine whether it is reasonable to hold the defendant liable for the damage that occurred as a result of their negligence.

Historically, defendants were liable for *all the direct consequences* of their negligence, as laid down in *Re Polemis* in 1921.[115] However, after the decision in *Donoghue v Stevenson* expanded the categories of duties of care beyond the restricted class, the potential liability for damages in an action for negligence was greatly increased.[116] At the time, there was no concept of limitation of liability, and hence the defendant would be responsible for all losses caused directly by the defendant's breach of duty.

The 'direct consequence' test, as applied in *Re Polemis*, would allow a consequence to be considered as 'too remote' only if it was 'due to the operation of independent causes having no connection with the negligent act, except that they could not avoid its results'.[117] Unsurprisingly, this was considered unfair as the defendant could be made liable for damage that was not foreseeable and hence could not have taken the necessary steps to prevent it. Some 40 years later, the decision in *Re Polemis* was replaced by the Privy Council in *Overseas Tankship (UK) Ltd v Mort's Dock & Engineering Co Ltd ('The Wagon Mound (No 1)')* with a new test for determining whether damage was not too remote from the defendant's breach was introduced: the 'reasonable foreseeability' test.[118]

4.3.1.1   The 'reasonable foreseeability' test

In 1961 the 'direct consequences' test was replaced by the 'reasonable foreseeability' test in *The Wagon Mound (No 1)*.[119] In this case, the defendant's ship, *The Wagon Mound*, leaked furnace oil in Sydney Harbour. The oil was eventually ignited by sparks from welding operations at the wharf, causing damage to other ships and the wharf itself. The Privy Council introduced a new test limiting the liability of the defendant to damage that was reasonably foreseeable as a consequence of the defendant's negligence.

Six years later, the Privy Council considered what would constitute 'reasonably foreseeable damage' in *Overseas Tankship (UK) Ltd v Miller Steamship Co ('The Wagon Mound (No 2)')*.[120] The Law Lords found that even though the risk of damage was small, the chief engineer of *The Wagon Mound* should have realised that that risk was not too remote, as it would occur to a reasonable person in the defendant's position. The test was that the risk of damage would occur to the mind of a reasonable person and they would not consider it to be far-fetched.

---

115   *Re Polemis* [1921] 3 KB 560.
116   *Donoghue v Stevenson* [1932] AC 562.
117   [1921] 3 KB 560, 577 (Scrutton LJ).
118   [1961] AC 388 ('*The Wagon Mound (No 1)*').
119   Ibid.
120   [1967] 1 AC 617 ('*The Wagon Mound (No 2)*'). This case arose out of the same accident as *The Wagon Mound (No 1)* and the defendants were the same. However, the plaintiffs this time were owners of some ships that were also damaged in the fire.

Although we are again inquiring as to reasonable foreseeability (see Figure 4.2), the remoteness of damage inquiry as to reasonable foreseeability is different to that used in the duty of care and standard of care inquiries.

Figure 4.2   'Reasonable foreseeability' test for elements of a negligence claim

(1) Duty of care	(2) Standard of care	(3) Remoteness of damage
Was P in a reasonably foreseeable class of persons likely to be affected by D's act or omission?	Was the risk of injury reasonably foreseeable as a result of D's conduct?	Was P's damage reasonably foreseeable as a consequence of D's negligence?

What needs to be reasonably foreseeable is the *kind, type or class* of damage suffered by the plaintiff, *not the extent* of that damage. In *Hughes v Lord Advocate*, the House of Lords held that the *kind* of injury suffered by the plaintiff was reasonably foreseeable.[121] In this case, two boys aged eight and ten were exploring a manhole that was left unattended by workmen taking a break. As they ventured into the manhole, they took with them a paraffin lamp left by the workmen. One of the boys dropped the lamp which exploded resulting in extensive burns to the boys. It was held that it was foreseeable that the boys may suffer a burn from the lamp (even if the explosion itself was unforeseeable), and it was immaterial that the *extent* of the burns was greater than was reasonably foreseeable. It was also considered not necessary to show that the manner in which the damage was occasioned was foreseeable (see supporting question (2) in Section 4.3.1).

In *Jolley v Sutton London Borough Council*, the House of Lords affirmed the approach taken in *Hughes*, namely that damage was not too remote if it was foreseeable.[122] However, in relation to whether the manner in which the harm occasioned or its extent should also be foreseeable, Lord Steyn stated:

> The scope of the two modifiers – the precise manner in which the injury came about and its extent – is not definitively answered by either *The Wagon Mound [No 1]* or *Hughes v Lord Advocate*. It requires determination in the context of an intense focus on the circumstances of each case.[123]

In Australia, the High Court applied the same approach in *Mount Isa Mines Ltd v Pusey* finding that the plaintiff's schizophrenia was not too remote a consequence of the defendant's negligence.[124] Windeyer J stated:

> Foreseeability does not mean foresight of the particular course of events causing the harm. Nor does it suppose foresight of the particular harm which occurred, but only of some harm of a like kind.[125]

---

121 [1963] AC 837.
122 [2000] 1 WLR 1082.
123 *Jolley v Sutton London Borough Council* [2000] 1 WLR 1082, 1090.
124 (1970) 125 CLR 383.
125 *Mount Isa Mines Ltd v Pusey* (1970) 125 CLR 383, 402.

However, Windeyer J went on to identify a difficulty with the 'some harm of a like kind' approach:

> This comfortable latitudinarian doctrine has ... the obvious difficulty that it leaves the criterion for classification of kinds or types of harm undefined and at large.[126]

HINTS AND TIPS

The leading case on the basic test of remoteness of damage is *The Wagon Mound (No 1)*. The High Court discussed the 'reasonable foreseeability' test (for remoteness of damage) in *Mount Isa Mines Ltd v Pusey*.

4.3.1.2   The eggshell skull principle

The final aspect of the remoteness of damage inquiry is the concept of the eggshell skull. The eggshell skull principle (or thin skull rule or *talem qualem* rule) is often expressed as 'taking your victim as you find them'.

The application of this principle enables the plaintiff to recover damages for the full extent of their injuries despite the injuries being more severe because of some characteristic of the plaintiff such as a pre-existing medical or psychological condition as 'there is no difference in principle between an eggshell skull and an eggshell personality'.[127] This follows from the English case of *Dulieu v White & Sons* where Kennedy J stated:

> If a man is negligently run over or otherwise negligently injured in his body, it is no answer to the sufferer's claim for damages that he would have suffered less injury, or no injury at all, if he had not had an unusually thin skull or an unusually weak heart.[128]

In the New South Wales Court of Appeal case *Commonwealth v McLean*, Handley and Beazley JJ noted:

> Under this principle a defendant is liable for additional damage of a foreseeable kind suffered by a plaintiff who has some special vulnerability.[129]

HINTS AND TIPS

The rule applies only to damage of the same kind or type as that which was foreseeable. This legal doctrine applies in all areas of torts, with a similarly constructed doctrine in criminal law.

At common law, the eggshell skull principle has been successfully applied, including in cultural or religious settings. In the case of *Kavanagh v Akhtar*, Mrs Akhtar, a Muslim

---

126   Ibid.
127   *Malcolm v Broadhurst* [1970] 3 All ER 508, 511 (Lane J).
128   [1901] 2 KB 669, 679.
129   (1996) 41 NSWLR 389, 406.

woman, had her long hair cut as a result of an injury, without her husband's permission.[130] This led to her husband leaving her. As a consequence, she suffered from depression and suicidal tendencies. The Court had to consider whether the kind of damage was reasonably foreseeable (ie, not too remote). Mason J held:

> In any event, the possibility that a person will desert a partner who has been disfigured
> in the eyes of the deserter is sufficiently commonplace to be foreseeable.[131]

It was not necessary for the defendant to have foreseen the exact nature of their act. The psychological impact and the psychiatric illness that followed was foreseeable, as it is not too far-fetched to see a psychiatric injury as a foreseeable consequence of a physical injury, and the family setting, cultural predisposition and context should be taken into account in such circumstances.

EMERGING ISSUE

With the exception of the Northern Territory and Queensland, the civil liability statutes across Australia have somewhat limited the application of the eggshell skull principle to mental harm requiring that the defendant foresaw, or ought to have foreseen, that a person of 'normal fortitude' might, in the circumstances, suffer recognised psychological illness if reasonable care were not taken. See, for example, s 74(1)(a) of the *Wrongs Act 1958* (Vic) and s 32(1) of the *Civil Liability Act 2002* (NSW).

4.3.2   The chain of causation and intervening causes

Earlier we noted that when applying the 'but for' test, almost anything following the negligent conduct could be said to have been *caused* by that negligent conduct. However, when there is a new act or event that occurs after the original tortious act, causing further injury or exacerbating the original harm to the plaintiff, it might be perceived as a *novus actus interveniens* (Latin for a 'new intervening act') which breaks the chain of causation (see Figure 4.3).

The test that is applied to determine whether the chain of causation may be broken by an intervening act, relieving the original tortfeasor of liability, differs depending on whether that intervening event is attributed to a third party or the plaintiff.

4.3.2.1   Breaking the chain of causation

When dealing with a new act by a third party, the test applied is whether that act was foreseeable. That needs to be put into the context of the current statutory requirements (in all jurisdictions except the Northern Territory). Thus, even if the consequences of the act are seen as highly probable, the court still needs to assess where the liability for its consequences should be placed under the second limb of causation (ie, scope of liability).

---

130 (1998) 45 NSWLR 588.
131 Ibid 601 (Mason J).

Figure 4.3   Effect of an intervening event or act on the chain of causation

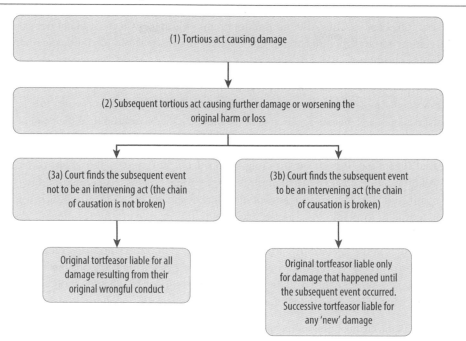

In *Chapman v Hearse*, the High Court defined 'reasonable foreseeability' in such circumstances as 'mark[ing] the limits beyond which a wrongdoer will not be held responsible for damage resulting from his wrongful act',[132] thus leaving space for normative reasoning and policy considerations to be applied.

Where the act of that third party is tortious, it is more likely to break the chain of causation.[133] However, it still depends on how foreseeable that act was (and hence whether the original defendant's liability should extend to the subsequent harm), even if that new act was tortious. For example, imagine a situation when negligent medical treatment follows a tortious act that created the very situation that led to that medical treatment. In this case, the question that follows is: *Should the original tortfeasor be liable for the consequences of the tortious medical treatment as well?*

The case of *Mahony v J Kruschich (Demolitions) Pty Ltd* concerned Mr Glogovic who was injured by the negligence of his employer, Kruschich Demolitions.[134] Mr Glogovic alleged that as a consequence of his injuries he required extensive medical treatment. Dr Mahony was one of the medical practitioners who treated Mr Glogovic. Kruschich Demolitions brought a cross-claim against Dr Mahony alleging he was negligent in some of the medical treatment of the plaintiff, 'caus[ing] or contribut[ing] to the plaintiff's continuing injuries and incapacities'.[135] The High Court found that the subsequent medical treatment was not an intervening act and the initial tortfeasor could not avoid liability for a plaintiff's

---

132   (1961) 106 CLR 112, 122.
133   See *Knightley v John* [1982] 1 WLR 349.
134   (1985) 156 CLR 522.
135   *Mahony v J Kruschich (Demolitions) Pty Ltd* (1985) 156 CLR 522.

subsequent injury, even if that subsequent injury was tortiously inflicted.[136] Some risk of medical negligence in the treatment of an injury resulting from the initial tortious act is reasonably foreseeable. Thus, the medical treatment or advice will most likely not constitute an intervening act and thus not make the original tortfeasor liable for the 'exacerbation' of the plaintiff's condition, unless the treatment is:

> 'inexcusably bad' … or 'completely outside the bounds of what any reputable medical practitioner might prescribe' … or 'so obviously unnecessary or improper that it is in the nature of a gratuitous aggravation of the injury' … or 'extravagant from the point of view of medical practice or hospital routine'.[137]

A case that illustrates how the courts might approach the issue of the chain of causation being broken by a new act of the plaintiff is *The Oropesa*.[138] This case concerned two ships, *The Oropesa* and *The Manchester Regiment*, which were involved in a collision for which each was partially to blame. As the sea was rough, the master of *The Manchester Regiment* did not think that his ship would stay afloat, so he started to ferry his 50-member crew across to *The Oropesa*. On the second trip, the lifeboat capsized and the ship master and nine crew members who were on board drowned. The Court of Appeal had to consider whether the act of leaving the sinking ship and setting off in the lifeboat broke the chain of causation. Lord Wright, who delivered the leading judgment, reached the following conclusion:

> To break the chain of causation it must be shown that there is something … ultroneous, something unwarrantable, a new cause which disturbs the sequence of events, something that can be described as either unreasonable or extraneous or extrinsic. I doubt whether the law can be stated more precisely than that.[139]

In essence, the Court had to assess whether the act by the master could be perceived as naturally resulting from the heavy damage to *The Manchester Regiment*. Given the circumstances, it could have been considered an act of 'self-preservation' (wholly reasonable in the circumstances) and thus it was not found to be a *novus* act.

Further guidance on when a subsequent act or event will be classified as a new intervening act can be found in *Haber v Walker*.[140]

Case: *Haber v Walker* [1963] VR 339

Facts

The plaintiff's husband (Mr Haber) was injured in a car accident caused by the defendant (Mr Walker). Mr Haber sustained severe (physical and mental) injuries and ultimately committed suicide.

Issue

Was the suicide a *novus actus interveniens* that severed the chain of causation?

136 Ibid 726.
137 Ibid 726–7.
138 [1943] P 32.
139 *The Oropesa* [1943] P 32, 39.
140 [1963] VR 339.

Decision

At the first instance, it was held that suicide could not be reasonably foreseeable, but on appeal the Court found for the plaintiff. Lowe J reasoned (at [352]) that whether the chain of causation is broken is 'very much a matter of circumstance and degree, and … a question of fact'. If the act is not the deliberate act of a 'sane person' then it does not break the chain of causation, and an act is not a 'voluntary' act when the person's choice is taken away.

Significance

For the intervening act or event to sever the chain of causation it must be voluntary or causally independent and not a coincidence.

Notes

If the defendant makes a successful plea on the basis of a *novus actus interveniens* breaking the chain of causation, they can avoid liability for the harm ultimately suffered by the plaintiff. In *Haber v Walker* the Court had to consider whether the defendant's liability should extend to Mr Haber's depression and subsequent suicide. The action was brought by the plaintiff under s 16 of the *Wrongs Act 1958* (Vic) as administratrix of the deceased's estate, on behalf of herself as the widow and the eight young children of the deceased.

The Court offered a lengthy consideration of the relevant authorities, including whether the issue of 'legal' insanity should be considered in such circumstances, and whether it was insanity produced as a direct consequence of injuries inflicted by the defendant that led to the suicide. If it was found, it would not sever the causal connection between the injury and death of Mr Haber. Smith J explained what is considered to be the crux of such an assessment (at [359]):

> for an act to be regarded as voluntary it is necessary that the actor should have exercised a free choice. [This involves a] question of degree [and] if his choice has been made under substantial pressure created by the wrongful act, his conduct should not ordinarily be regarded as voluntary.

The majority of the Court (Lowe and Smith JJ, with Hudson J dissenting) held that Mr Haber's suicide did not break the chain of causation, and thus Mrs Haber and the children of the deceased were able to recover damages resulting to them from his death.

Question

Does the case of *Haber v Walker* mean that 'suicide' will never be considered a new intervening act?

 Guided response in the eBook

In *Haber v Walker* the majority of the Victorian Supreme Court held that the death of the plaintiff's husband by suicide 18 months after the motor vehicle accident was caused by the accident. The act of suicide, not being a 'voluntary human action', did *not* break the chain of causation. Even though his act could have been considered to be deliberate, it was not regarded as fully voluntary as it was performed under severe mental stress. It was not a voluntary act but one that could be attributed to Mr Haber's depression, which was itself caused by the defendant's breach of duty of care. In order for the subsequent act to break the chain of causation (to be a *novus actus interveniens*) it must be either:

(1) a voluntary human action, or

(2) a causally independent event which by ordinary human standards is so unlikely to occur as to be termed a coincidence.[141]

In circumstances where subsequent events supersede or follow upon the original event, it might be held that the defendant's negligent conduct did not cause the damage; that is, the scope of liability should not be extended to include harm or harms that occurred after the initial wrongful act. However, if the defendant's conduct generated the very risk of injury that subsequently followed, the defendant's liability will be extended to include the damage.

HINTS AND TIPS

For a new act by a third party to break the chain of causation, that act must be *foreseeable* (and subject to statutory requirements under the 'scope of liability'). When the act of a third party is negligent, it is more likely to break the chain of causation. (But see *Mahony v J Kruschich (Demolitions) Pty Ltd*.)

When the new act is by the plaintiff, the court will assess whether that act was *reasonable* in the circumstances (*The Oropesa*), as well as whether it can be regarded as a voluntary human action or mere *coincidence* (*Haber v Walker*).

4.3.2.2 Voluntary human action

In order for the plaintiff's action to break the chain of causation, it is necessary that the plaintiff is considered to be of sound mind and that the act is independent and voluntary. In order for the courts to consider the plaintiff's action to break the chain of causation, that action needs to be reasonable, which is assessed according to an objective test.[142] If that condition is not satisfied (ie, it was 'unreasonable' conduct), it will constitute a *novus actus interveniens*.

HINTS AND TIPS

Keep in mind that there often is a fine line between arguing 'unreasonable conduct' and 'contributory negligence' (see Chapter 5 for more details). The distinction is a value judgment for the court to make on the facts of each case.

---

141 Ibid 358 (Smith J).

142 See *McKew v Holland & Hannan & Cubitts (Scotland) Ltd* [1969] 3 All ER 1621, 1623 (Lord Reid): 'if the injured man acts unreasonably he cannot hold the defender liable for injury caused by his own unreasonable conduct'.

In the case of *Yates v Jones*, the plaintiff was injured in a car accident caused by the defendant's negligence.[143] A drug dealer suggested she try heroin as pain relief, which she did and she subsequently developed an addiction. It was held that the introduction of the plaintiff to heroin was a separate and independent cause of her addiction. Samuels JA held that the addiction was not a reasonably foreseeable consequence of the defendant's negligence. The outcome of this case can also be explained on policy grounds: if taking drugs was perceived to be a 'nonvoluntary' act, this could lead to unacceptable applications of the law in relation to personal responsibility.

The courts will distinguish between cases where the plaintiff has full capacity, enabling them to make a choice, and cases where the plaintiff has no capacity, being deprived of reasonable options to act. In the former case, the plaintiff's deliberate voluntary act may break the chain of causation; in the latter, the chain of causation will not be considered to be broken. The voluntary nature of the intervention will negate a causal connection between the defendant's conduct and the damage, irrespective of how foreseeable the harm was.

4.3.2.3 Causally independent events

In situations when an independent event is so unforeseeable and unrelated to the original tortfeasor's wrongful act that it can be called a coincidence, the chain of causation will be severed.

This may be the case where there is a natural event that might cause further injury or loss to the defendant. For example, imagine your car is damaged by the negligent driving of another driver. While you are awaiting breakdown towing services, your car is hit by lightning and catches fire. The question that follows is: *Should the initial tortfeasor be held responsible for the initial (in this case, minimal) damage only, or for the full damage?* The test applied here is whether the conjunction of these two events causing damage to your car can be considered to be reasonably foreseeable. If, in our scenario, the lightning can be considered a 'supervening event' and not a consequence of the earlier car crash, the defendant will not be responsible for the loss that followed from their wrongful act, as that would be considered unfair.

A case where the plaintiff's injury was attributed to natural causes or regarded as a 'vicissitude of life' is *Jobling v Associated Dairies Ltd*.[144] Mr Jobling was employed as a butcher at Associated Dairies. He had slipped on the floor, due to his employer's negligence, and sustained an injury (a slipped disc). As a result of this injury, he was unable to work to his full capacity, which led to his earnings being reduced by 50 per cent. Four years later, and before the trial, Mr Jobling was diagnosed with a pre-existing spinal condition, which was not a result of the original accident and which would make him unable to work at all. The issue considered by the Court was whether Mr Jobling should be compensated by his employer for the partial incapacity and the loss of future earnings, or for the four years only. The trial judge followed *Baker v Willoughby* (see Section 4.3.2.4),[145] but on appeal the House of Lords distinguished (but did not overrule) that case and stated that the employer was liable for damages and loss of earnings for the four years only. Mr Jobling's

---

143 [1990] Aust Torts Reports 81-009.
144 [1982] AC 794.
145 [1970] AC 467.

pre-existing medical condition was considered to be wholly unconnected to the original accident and thus it had to be considered in the final assessment in order not to award Mr Jobling excessive damages.

4.3.2.4   Successive causes leading to a similar damage

In circumstances of successive events where a successive event is also tortious, the original tortfeasor will be found liable for the entire damage as if the successive event did not occur. The House of Lords held in *Baker v Willoughby* that when two accidents happen concurrently and contribute to the same injury, the original tortfeasor is liable for the harm resulting from the overall injury.[146] In this case, Mr Baker's leg was severely injured by Mr Willoughby's negligent driving, which resulted in Mr Baker needing to look for new employment. Mr Baker sued Mr Willoughby for loss of income. In the meantime, as Mr Baker took up his new position, his new employer was raided by robbers and he was shot in his already injured leg. Mr Baker's leg had to be amputated as a result of the complications following the initial injury combined with the new wound.

It needed to be considered whether the shooting was a new intervening act breaking the chain of causation, or whether Mr Willoughby was liable also for the loss of income following the robbery. The House of Lords took the view that if the initial tortfeasor had not been negligent in the first place, the plaintiff would not have lost his leg. Mr Willoughby was found liable to pay compensation to Mr Baker for losses including after the amputation.[147]

REVIEW QUESTIONS

(1) Given the substantial hurdle that plaintiffs must overcome in satisfying the second element (the scope of liability), which is particularly evident in medical negligence cases, what reforms would you suggest to address some of these difficulties?

(2) The 'reasonable foreseeability' test is used in determining the duty of care, breach of the duty and remoteness of damage. Can you explain how the test differs for each of these three elements?

(3) Go back to the discussion about the theories of corrective justice and distributive justice in Section 1.1.2.1 and then answer the following question: Which of these two theories provides a stronger basis for the element of causation in a negligence claim?

    Guided responses in the eBook

---

146   Ibid.
147   Ibid.

KEY CONCEPTS

- **causation:** the 'gist' of a negligence action, linking the behaviour with the harm caused. In most jurisdictions in Australia it involves a two-stage test to establish: (1) factual causation; and (2) the scope of liability.

- **chain of causation:** determines whether the defendant's liability should extend to the subsequent damage suffered by the plaintiff following a supervening cause (described as a *novus actus interveniens*).

- **damage:** at the heart of an action in negligence, as without proof of compensable damage there cannot be liability in negligence (unlike in trespass which is actionable per se). The term 'damage' is used interchangeably with 'harm', 'loss' and 'injury'.

- **eggshell skull principle:** provides that the defendant must take the plaintiff as found, meaning that the defendant will be liable for the full extent of the plaintiff's injury, even if the injury is significantly greater than it would be had it not for the plaintiff's pre-existing condition.

- **factual causation:** links the defendant's conduct with the plaintiff's harm. It requires the application of the 'necessary condition' statutory test in all jurisdictions except the Northern Territory where the 'but for' common law test is followed.

- ***novus actus interveniens:*** means a 'new intervening act or event' that breaks the chain of causation resulting from an earlier wrongful act.

- **'reasonable foreseeability' test:** limits the defendant's liability for negligence by assessing whether the damage was reasonably foreseeable as a consequence of the defendant's negligence.

- ***res ipsa loquitur:*** a law maxim meaning 'the facts speak for themselves', which provides an inference of negligence, even if it might not dictate such a finding.

- **scope of liability:** denotes asking normative questions and raising policy considerations as to whether it would be appropriate to extend the defendant's liability to the harm or loss caused to the plaintiff (at common law, the question posed is whether the damage was not too remote.)

 Complete the multiple-choice questions in the eBook to test your knowledge

PROBLEM-SOLVING EXERCISES

Exercise 1

Ms Smith is a well-established fashion model with prospects of an international career. Recently her modelling agency secured for her a very lucrative contract in Paris. She is married with two young children. Mr Jones (her husband) is a 'stay-at-home' dad who gave up his career as a lawyer a few years ago to support his wife's career and take care of their children.

On her way to a photo shoot, Ms Smith is involved in a car accident which is mainly due to the negligence of the other driver. As a result of that accident, she sustains serious injuries to her face. Ms Smith is admitted to a local hospital where she is provided with reasonable treatment. When her bandages are taken off and she sees her face, she starts crying uncontrollably. She realises that she will no longer be able to pursue her career as a model and her dream of moving to Paris falls into pieces. She develops anxiety.

A few months after she leaves the hospital, her anxiety continues to worsen and she decides that she cannot go on like this. She decides to consult a plastic surgeon (Dr Snip) to 'give her the face she used to have'. Unfortunately, Dr Snip fails to advise her of any risks associated with such an operation. The plastic surgery does not go as planned, aggravating her facial disfiguration.

Ms Smith is left with no income from modelling. Her children are scared by her looks and afraid to come near her. As a result, she becomes deeply depressed and attempts suicide. She is now on life support with the doctors holding little hope for her recovery.

Who should be liable for the harm suffered by Ms Smith: the initial negligent car driver and/or the plastic surgeon? For the purpose of this exercise, you are only required to comment on the third element (damage) of a negligence claim.

 Guided response in the eBook

Exercise 2

Due to his negligent driving, Tom causes his lorry to overturn near an exit of a one-way tunnel. Two police officers arrive at the scene. The officer in charge (Jerry) forgets to close off the entry to the tunnel and negligently orders his colleague (Sophie) to ride her motorcycle back to the entry of the tunnel to seal it off. As Sophie is riding against the flow of oncoming traffic, she is hit by an oncoming car and is severely injured.

Should Tom bear the liability for Sophie's injuries?

 Guided response in the eBook

CHALLENGE YOURSELF

Exercise 1

Consider again the scenario in problem-solving exercise 1.

(1)   Would it make any difference if Ms Smith had prior suicidal tendencies? Would that change the way the court would view the voluntariness of her act?

(2)   Imagine that the events recently occurred in Victoria, under the *Wrongs Act 1958* (Vic). Would this make any difference to the application of the eggshell skull principle?

Guided responses in the eBook

Exercise 2

Consider again the scenario in problem-solving exercise 2 with the following change of facts:

> Due to his negligent driving, Tom causes his lorry to overturn near the exit of a tunnel. Two police officers arrive at the scene. As the police officers leave their patrol car to assist Tom, one of them is struck by another lorry driver who negligently collided with her.

What is the difference between the scenario in problem-solving exercise 2 and this one? Would the first defendant (Tom) still be liable for the officer's injury, and if so, why?

Guided response in the eBook

5

DEFENCES TO NEGLIGENCE

5.1   Introduction

Once a plaintiff has established that a duty of care is owed and has been breached and that the breach has resulted in damage the burden of proof then shifts to the defendant. In an action for negligence, the plaintiff's claims can be defeated (or, in the case of contributory negligence, damages may be reduced) if the defendant can prove a relevant defence. The key defences to an action in negligence are the following (see Figure 5.1):

- The plaintiff's failure to take reasonable care of their own safety, or 'contributory negligence', can result in the damages awarded being reduced, or 'apportioned'.
- The plaintiff's previous acceptance of the risk – their voluntary assumption of the risk created by the defendant's conduct – is a complete defence. The plaintiff will receive no damages, because they chose to bear the risk.
- The plaintiff's intoxication or willing undertaking of dangerous recreational or unlawful activities may operate as a defence in some jurisdictions. In others, it may be relevant to establishing that a breach has occurred.
- Statutory defences, including the plaintiff's delay in initiating proceedings, may bar the plaintiff's claim.

Figure 5.1   Negligence

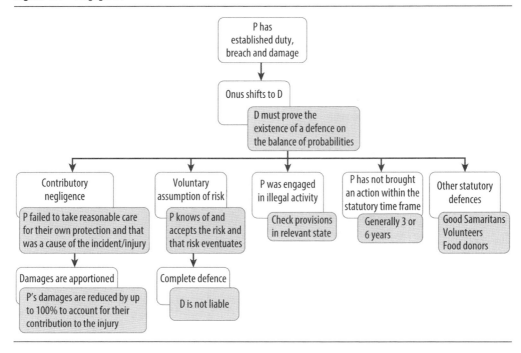

A defendant who wishes to rely on one of these defences must: (1) plead these matters by filing a defence that raises the matters; and (2) produce evidence to prove them on the balance of probabilities. The defendant bears the onus of proving the defence.

HINTS AND TIPS

A defence may be arguable but not pressed for various reasons. Think about strategic issues related to:

- Burden of proof (check the legislation – in some cases the burden of proof will shift by the creation of a presumption
- Outcome of defence (for instance, is it a complete defence or will it result in apportionment of damages?)
- The difficulty in establishing the different elements of the defence.

Very often, matters which are relevant may not be fully argued. Where you are asked to outline an argument, it is worth indicating whether there are other potential arguments but they are not being pressed (and give reasons).

5.2   Contributory negligence

Contributory negligence is a *plaintiff's* failure to meet the standard of care necessary for *their own* protection where that failure is a *contributing cause* to the incident or injury. For example, a defendant may claim that a plaintiff contributed to their own injury by:

- getting into a car with an intoxicated driver[1]
- failing to wear a seatbelt while riding in a car[2]
- looking at a mobile phone while walking (and falling in a wet carpark)[3]
- failing to comply with safety instructions in a workplace[4]
- an employee entering a pen to separate two fighting dogs despite being told not to do so[5]
- entering into a loan knowing that the repayments were unaffordable[6]
- a property developer's failure to understand and act upon important provisions in a contract, resulting in failure to apply for an extension of time[7]
- holding onto the back of a car to 'hitch a ride' while riding a skateboard[8]
- walking on a bitumen road in the dark with one's back to oncoming traffic[9]
- jumping out of a moving vehicle[10]
- climbing onto the back of a vehicle to hitch a ride[11]
- riding a skateboard on a busy road[12]
- riding a bicycle on an elevated railway line without barriers or guards.[13]

To find contributory negligence at common law it is necessary to show:

(1) The plaintiff failed to take reasonable care for their own safety or for the protection of their interests.

(2) This negligence was a cause of the plaintiff's harm.

(3) The harm that eventuated was within the risk created by the plaintiff's conduct.

If a defendant successfully establishes that the plaintiff was contributorily negligent, the damages are apportioned between the plaintiff and the defendant – the plaintiff's award of damages is reduced in proportion to their contribution to the accident or damage. Figure 5.2 sets out a simplified process to assist your problem-solving.

1 *Allen v Chadwick* (2015) 256 CLR 148; [2015] HCA 47; *Solomons v Pallier* (2015) 72 MVR 365.
2 *Froom v Butcher* [1976] 1 QB 296.
3 *Coles Supermarkets Australia Pty Ltd v Bridge* [2018] NSWCA 183.
4 *Kennedy v Queensland Alumina Ltd* [2016] QCA 159.
5 *Futter v Williams* [2021] VCC 1198.
6 *Dewar v Ollier* [2018] WASC 212.
7 *Shoal Bay Beach Constructions No. 1 Pty Ltd v Mark Hickey (No 5)* [2021] NSWSC 1499.
8 *Verryt v Schoupp* (2015) 70 MVR 484.
9 *Walker v Smith* (2022) 99 MVR 280.
10 *Lim v Cho* (2018) 84 MVR 514. The trial judge held that the contributory negligence of the plaintiff was sufficient to reduce liability by 100 per cent. On appeal, the Court of Appeal held that there was no negligence by the defendant, so found it unnecessary to interfere with the findings in relation to contributory negligence.
11 *Jones v Livox Quarries Ltd* [1952] 2 QB 608.
12 *Cruickshank v Radojicic* [2015] NSWDC 312.
13 *Consolidated Broken Hill Ltd v Edwards* (2005) Aust Torts Reports 81-815.

Figure 5.2   Contributory negligence – summary process

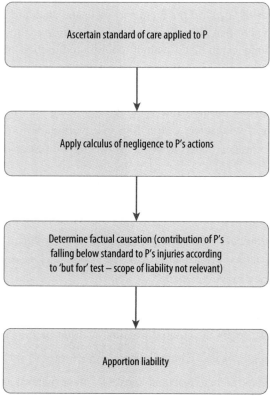

5.2.1   Definitions and rationale

Contributory negligence as a defence reflects the aspect of fault or culpability underlying the law of negligence. Apportioning damages to take account of the respective faults of the plaintiff and defendant is a natural concomitant of the apportionment of responsibility and this is reflected in the wording of the various apportionment statutes. The obligation of plaintiffs to take proper precautions for their own protection is also a reflection of the agency and autonomy of the individual. This was noted in the *Review of the Law of Negligence* ('Ipp Report'):

> there is in the Australian community today a widely held expectation that, in general, people will take as much care for themselves as they expect others to take for them. This is an application of the fundamental idea that people should take responsibility for their own lives and safety, and it provides powerful support for the principle that the standard of care for negligence and contributory negligence should be the same.[14]

---

14 *Review of the Law of Negligence* (Final Report, September 2002) ('Ipp Report') 123 [8.10].

In *Vairy v Wyong Shire Council* Callinan and Heydon JJ also emphasised the individual's responsibility to society to take care for their own protection:

> The 'duty' to take reasonable care for [their] own safety that a plaintiff has is not simply a nakedly self-interested one, but one of enlightened self-interest which should not disregard the burden, by way of social security and other obligations that a civilized and democratic society will assume towards him if he is injured. In short, the duty that he owes is not just to look out for himself, but not to act in a way which may put him at risk, in the knowledge that society may come under obligations of various kinds to him if the risk is realized.[15]

5.2.2   The standard of care for contributory negligence

5.2.2.1   General rule

At common law the plaintiff was not held to the same standard of care as the defendant. As a result of implementation of the Ipp Report recommendations, legislation has affected the common law rules for the standard of care to be applied to the plaintiff. The general rule is now that the principles that apply to the defendant in working out whether they have fallen below the standard of care also apply to the plaintiff in working out whether they have been contributorily negligent. The standard of care of the plaintiff is generally the standard of a reasonable person in the position of the plaintiff, determined on the basis of what that person knew or ought to have known at the time.

The application of the same standard of care would imply that the calculus of negligence would be used to determine whether the plaintiff has fallen below the standard required for their own protection. The Ipp Report recommended this,[16] although it is not explicitly included in the legislation. The provisions in the relevant statutes are included in Table 5.1.

Table 5.1   Contributory negligence: standard of care

Legislation	Section
Civil Liability Act 2002 (NSW)	5R
Civil Liability Act 2003 (Qld)	23
Civil Liability Act 1936 (SA)	44
Civil Liability Act 2002 (Tas)	23
Wrongs Act 1958 (Vic)	62
Civil Liability Act 2002 (WA)	5K

The text of most of these statutes follows a similar formula – applying the same standard of care to the plaintiff as applies to the defendant, determined on the basis of what the plaintiff knew or ought to have known at the time. An exception is s 44 of the *Civil Liability Act 1936* (SA), which has no equivalent to sub-s (2).

---

15 (2005) 223 CLR 422, 483; [2005] HCA 62, [220].
16 Ipp Report 13 Recommendation 30(c).

Accordingly, the *plaintiff's standard of care* would be determined by reference to:

(1)   the probability that the harm would occur if care were not taken
(2)   the likely seriousness of the harm
(3)   the burden of taking precautions to avoid the risk of harm
(4)   the social utility of the activity that creates the risk of harm.

These considerations are the same as the 'calculus of negligence' applied in relation to the defendant.

The issue that arises from the wording of these provisions is what is meant by 'a reasonable person in the position of that person'. The provision presents the *objective 'reasonable person'* test articulated in *Wyong Shire Council v Shirt*.[17] In the case of plaintiffs with particular skills or experience this may manifest as a heightened standard. In *Shoal Bay Beach Constructions No. 1 Pty Ltd v Mark Hickey (No 5)*[18] for instance, the plaintiff company, acting through an agent, failed to fully appreciate the significance of a contractual requirement. The defendants claimed that the plaintiff's failure was so significant that it should result in reduction of the defendant's liability by 100 per cent. The Court disagreed, noting that 'the contractual provisions were, for non-lawyers, relatively complex' and that the plaintiff 'were entitled to rely on the defendant's expertise … and could not reasonably be expected … to bear the full responsibility'.[19] Nevertheless a reasonable person in the plaintiff's position would have appreciated the importance of the provisions. The Court assessed the reduction for the plaintiff's contributory negligence at 30 per cent.

As with the common law test, however, particular issues arise in regard to the standard of care to be applied to children, to mentally incapacitated persons, to intoxicated persons and to employees injured in the course of their employment.

HINTS AND TIPS

It may be difficult to find cases in your jurisdiction which consider the provisions of the relevant statute. Many cases are still relevant, even though they may precede amendments to the statutes or may apply statutes in other state jurisdictions. When reading a case it is worth noting whether legislation from another state is being applied, and whether that legislation has the same wording as in your own state.

5.2.2.2   Children

In relation to children, the civil liability legislation has been interpreted consistently with the common law. A child defendant is held to the standard of care of an ordinary child of the same age, and that is also the standard applied to the child plaintiff when determining whether there has been contributory negligence.

This is consistent with Recommendation 30 of the Ipp Report, which noted that 'applying the same standard of care to contributory negligence as to negligence does not entail

---

17   (1980) 146 CLR 40, although that case was applying the standard to the defendant.
18   [2021] NSWSC 1499.
19   Ibid [193].

ignoring the identity of the plaintiff or the nature of the relationship between the plaintiff and the defendant'.[20]

The common law position was stated in *McHale v Watson*.[21] Watson, a boy of 12, injured McHale, a young girl playing nearby, when he threw a sharpened welding rod which hit her in the eye. A majority of the High Court held that a child was not to be held to the standard of an adult but to that of a child of the same age and experience.[22] In obiter, McTiernan ACJ noted that 'in cases dealing with alleged contributory negligence on the part of young children they are expected to exercise the degree of care one would expect, not of the average reasonable man, but of a child of the same age and experience'.[23] Kitto J considered this to be consistent with the objective standard:

> The standard of care being objective, it is no answer for [a child], any more than it is for an adult, to say that the harm he caused was due to his being abnormally slow-witted, quick-tempered, absent-minded or inexperienced. But it does not follow that he cannot rely in his defence upon a limitation upon the capacity for foresight or prudence, not as being personal to himself, but as being characteristic of humanity at his stage of development and in that sense normal. By doing so he appeals to a standard of ordinariness, to an objective and not a subjective standard.[24]

As a result of the application of the statutes listed in Table 5.1, this standard of care will also be applied to the plaintiff where contributory negligence is claimed. In *Doubleday v Kelly* the NSW Court of Appeal had occasion to consider the interpretation of s 5R of the *Civil Liability Act 2002* (NSW).[25] The plaintiff in that case was a seven-year-old girl who was injured at the house of a friend when she climbed onto a trampoline while wearing roller skates. It was contended on behalf of the defendant that the provision should be interpreted to exclude the age of the plaintiff. The Court noted that this 'radical departure from the Common Law' was not intended.[26] The legislation is to be interpreted consistently with *McHale v Watson*.[27]

Case: *Doubleday v Kelly* [2005] NSWCA 151

Facts
The plaintiff was, at the time of the incident, seven years old. She was attending her first 'sleepover' at a friend's house. She woke early in the morning and she and her friend put roller skates on and, without supervision, went to play outside. Thinking the trampoline was a hard surface on which to roller skate, the plaintiff got onto the trampoline, rolled backwards and fell off. She suffered injury to her arm and permanent loss of sensation in her dominant hand. She sued, alleging negligence of the occupier for failure to supervise.

20 Ipp Report 123–4 [8.12].
21 (1966) 115 CLR 199.
22 McTiernan ACJ, Kitto and Owen JJ.
23 *McHale v Watson* (1966) 115 CLR 199, 205.
24 Ibid 213.
25 [2005] NSWCA 151.
26 Ibid [26] (Bryson JA, Young CJ in Eq and Hunt AJA agreeing).
27 (1966) 115 CLR 199.

Issue

In getting onto a trampoline while wearing roller skates, was the seven-year-old plaintiff contributorily negligent?

Decision

The argument for contributory negligence failed in the Court of Appeal. The Court considered the position of children at common law and under ss 5R and 5S of the NSW Act. Section 5R, which sets out that the standard required of the plaintiff was the same as the standard required of the defendant, did not change the common law position on the relevance of the age of the plaintiff – that 'the characteristics of a reasonable person in the position of the person who suffered harm include the characteristics of being a child of seven years' (at [26]).

Significance

The case clarifies the standard of care required of a child plaintiff under the legislation.

Notes

The Court also considered the application of the obvious risk provisions (ss 5F, 5K and 5L of the NSW Act and agreed that 'subs. 5F(1), which requires consideration of the position of the person who suffers harm and whatever else is relevant to establishing that position. The characteristics of being a child of seven with no previous experience in the use of trampolines or roller skates, who chose to get up early in the morning and play unsupervised, is part of that position' [28].

The Court of Appeal also affirmed the decision of the trial judge in relation to liability (although the assessment of damages was varied).

Question

What is the standard of care required of a plaintiff?

 Guided response in the eBook

5.2.2.3   Plaintiffs with disabilities

Disabilities, including the mental incapacity of the plaintiff, have raised more difficult issues. In *McHale v Watson* the Court rejected the proposition that the mental deficits of a plaintiff should be taken into account in determining a question of contributory negligence:

> when men [sic] live in society, a certain average of conduct, a sacrifice of individual peculiarities going beyond a certain point, is necessary to the general welfare. If, for instance, a man is born hasty and awkward, is always having accidents and hurting himself or his neighbours, no doubt his congenital defects will be allowed for in the courts of Heaven, but his slips are no less troublesome to his neighbours than if they sprang from guilty neglect. His neighbours accordingly require him, at his proper peril,

to come up to their standard, and the courts which they establish decline to take his personal equation into account.[28]

More recent cases supported the application of a different standard of care in cases of inexperience.[29] These would have provided strong grounds for varying the standard of care in cases involving plaintiffs with disabilities. The aberrant course of authority, since overruled, commenced with *Cook v Cook*.[30] The plaintiff was an experienced driver who had invited the defendant, an inexperienced and unlicensed driver, to drive her car while she was a passenger. The plaintiff knew the defendant could not drive. During the journey the defendant crashed the car and the plaintiff was injured. The High Court held that the defendant's conduct should be measured against the standard of the reasonable learner driver rather than the standard of the ordinary driver. Even when measured against the standards of the inexperienced driver, the defendant had fallen below the standard of care.

This course of authority was overruled by the High Court in *Imbree v McNeilly*.[31] The plaintiff was an experienced driver travelling with the defendant (and others) in the Northern Territory. The plaintiff, knowing that the 16-year-old defendant did not have a learner's permit, allowed him to drive. An accident occurred while the defendant was driving, and the plaintiff was awarded damages for the defendant's negligence. Damages were reduced for contributory negligence and the plaintiff was given leave to appeal to the High Court. He contended that the apportionment of damages against him had been influenced by the application to the defendant of the standard of care for learner drivers previously laid down in *Cook v Cook*.[32]

Gummow, Hayne and Kiefel JJ in a joint judgment held:

> There is no warrant for the distinction that was drawn in *Cook v Cook*. *Cook v Cook* should no longer be followed in this respect … *Cook v Cook* departed from fundamental principle and achieved no useful result … The plaintiff who was supervising the learner driver, the plaintiff who was another passenger in the vehicle, the plaintiff who was another road user are all entitled to expect that the learner driver will take reasonable care in operating the vehicle. The care that the learner should take is that of the reasonable driver.[33]

Consistent with the affirmation of the objective standard in *Imbree*, the current rule is that the plaintiff's disabilities will *not* be taken into account when determining the standard of care required for their own protection. Disabled plaintiffs will be measured against the objective standard of the reasonable person in the position of the plaintiff. The rationale for this principle, which on its face may appear to be unfair, was stated in *Allen v Chadwick*:

> the purpose of the law of negligence is to adjust losses between members of the community in a way which balances the value of personal autonomy with the need to

---

28 Ibid 232 (Owen J).
29 *Cook v Cook* (1986) 162 CLR 376 and *Gala v Preston* (1991) 172 CLR 243, which were significant to the reasoning that resulted in the decision in *Russell v Rail Infrastructure Corporation* [2007] NSWSC 402.
30 (1986) 162 CLR 376.
31 (2008) 236 CLR 510; [2008] HCA 40. See also Chapter 3.
32 (1986) 162 CLR 376.
33 (2008) 236 CLR 510; [2008] HCA 40, [71]–[72].

moderate excessive risk taking and to compensate its victims. The reasonable person is the standard by which the responsibility of the tortfeasor and the victim are measured in order to meet that balance. The effect of striking the balance in that way is that some victims of negligence will be expected to do more than they can subjectively do to protect their safety.[34]

An example of the *old course of authority* (which had some influence at common law prior to *Imbree v McNeilly*[35]) can be seen in *Russell v Rail Infrastructure Corporation*.[36] The plaintiff was a 21-year-old woman who was mildly intellectually handicapped. She walked through a missing panel in a fence to gain access to the Port Botany freight line and climbed onto the side of a goods train. When it gathered speed, she was dragged across the rocks alongside the track, suffering severe injuries to her right leg which was later amputated below the knee. Applying the old course of authority (ie, prior to *Imbree*), the Court held that the standard required of the plaintiff is that of a reasonable adult having a mild degree of intellectual handicap.

The new course of authority is demonstrated in *Town of Port Hedland v Hodder (No 2)*.[37] The plaintiff, Reece Hodder, had multiple physical and intellectual disabilities. He mounted a diving block at the shallow end of the South Hedland swimming pool and entered the water head first, striking his head on the bottom of the pool and fracturing his cervical spine, rendering him quadriplegic. The Town of Port Hedland owned the pool, but engaged the YMCA to manage it. The trial judge found that the Town had breached its duty of care by failing to remove the diving blocks and that the breach had caused the injuries. The YMCA was held at first instance to have breached its duty of care, but the breach was not causative of the plaintiff's injury.

The standard of care required of a plaintiff with a disability was considered on appeal. The trial judge had concluded that the standard was to be determined on an entirely objective basis – without reference to any disability. He apportioned damages 90 per cent to the Town and 10 per cent to the plaintiff, so Hodder's award of damages was reduced by 10 per cent. The trial judge concluded that s 5K of the *Civil Liability Act 2002* (WA) required him to assess the issue of contributory negligence on an objective basis – by reference to the position of a reasonable adult without disabilities. A reasonable adult would have recognised that diving from a block into shallow water, without training or experience, was imprudent.

On appeal, the 10 per cent apportionment was overturned, but each judge provided different reasons. A majority decision held that Hodder was entitled to 100 per cent of the damages.[38] A different majority concluded that the standard of care to be applied was the objective standard of the ordinary person without regard to the physical or intellectual disabilities of the plaintiff.[39]

---

34 (2014) 120 SASR 350 (Kourakis CJ, Gray and Nicholson JJ).
35 (2008) 236 CLR 510; [2008] HCA 40.
36 [2007] NSWSC 402.
37 (2012) 43 WAR 383.
38 Martin CJ and McLure P.
39 McLure P and Murphy JA.

Martin CJ considered that to assess the plaintiff's standard of care on the basis that he was 'a normal able-bodied 23-year-old man, with normal hearing and vision, and of normal intellectual ability' was problematic:

> The harshness, injustice and unfairness in this approach is manifest. It assumes a miracle of biblical proportions and requires the court to assess the question of contributory negligence in some parallel universe in which the blind can see, the deaf can hear, the lame can walk or even run, and the cognitively impaired are somehow restored to full functionality.[40]

His Honour 'instinctively recoil[ed]' against assessing the plaintiff's contributory negligence without regard to his disabilities and would not do so unless compelled by authority or the 'unequivocal language of s 5K'.[41] After a review of the authorities and of the recommendations of the Ipp Review, his Honour concluded that in relation to s 4K:

> the word 'reasonable' is properly construed as connoting a norm of behaviour which the person in the position of the plaintiff must achieve, or be found contributorily negligent. But there is nothing in the language of the section, or in logic or in practice, which prevents such a norm of behaviour being imposed by reference to the physical defects and incapacities of the plaintiff.[42]

In relation to physical disabilities, then, His Honour considered that the physical defects or incapacities of the plaintiff should be taken into consideration when assessing the standard of care for the purposes of contributory negligence. However:

> Difficult questions could arise if it is decided there are some conditions of mind such as insanity or fundamental cognitive or intellectual impairment which can be taken into account. As I have observed, plainly, qualities of temperament such as carelessness or impetuosity must be excluded.[43]

Martin CJ did not consider it necessary to resolve this issue, since the impairment critical to the plaintiff's contributory negligence was a physical disability – his visual impairment. Failing to take this disability into consideration would be inconsistent with the second limb of s 5K(2), which refers to both the subjective and objective knowledge of the plaintiff.

McLure J agreed that the 10 per cent apportionment should be set aside, but did not agree that the standard for assessing contributory negligence should be subjective. Applying the decision of the High Court in *Joslyn v Berryman* (which dealt with intoxicated plaintiffs),[44] her Honour considered that 'generally, the standard of care in negligence is both objective and impersonal' and the attenuation of the standard made for children 'has not been widened to include other classes of people with impaired capacity for foresight or prudence'.[45] However, in McLure J's view the trial judge had erred in finding that Mr Hodder had been contributorily negligent because the diving blocks were placed so as to be an invitation to use them.

---

40 *Town of Port Hedland v Hodder (No 2)* (2012) 43 WAR 383, 49 (Martin CJ).
41 Ibid 53 (Martin CJ).
42 Ibid 73 (Martin CJ).
43 Ibid.
44 (2003) 214 CLR 552; [2003] HCA 34.
45 *Town of Port Hedland v Hodder (No 2)* (2012) 43 WAR 383, 87 (McLure P).

Murphy J considered that the standard of care of the physically or mentally impaired plaintiff should be the same as the standard of care of the physically or mentally impaired defendant. His Honour concluded:

> Where a person has a physical disability which impairs their capacity to undertake an activity involving risk, the application of the standard of care is not so crude as to impute to them the ability to do that which they are physically unable to do. However, it does require them to take other steps in order to exercise reasonable care for their safety and the safety of others. That may include ... deferring the activity or not undertaking it at all. The objective standard also precludes exculpation on the basis that the person failed, through intellectual impairment or otherwise, subjectively to comprehend the risk which they were posing to themselves or others in undertaking the activity in question.[46]

On that reasoning, the majority held that a plaintiff's physical disabilities should not be taken into account when determining if the plaintiff was contributorily negligent.

However, applying normal principles, where the *defendant knew* of the plaintiff's disability, the plaintiff's contributory negligence is not measured in the same way; where the fact of the disability is causative of the injury, it is part of the negligence of the defendant. It is not then attributed to the lack of reasonable care of the plaintiff. In other words, as Martin CJ noted, 'the standard of care required [of the defendant] may be influenced by the vulnerabilities of the person or class of persons to whom the duty is owed, if known, actually or constructively by the putative tortfeasor'.[47]

This reasoning, which reinforces the common law view of the objective standard but suggests a capacity to take account of the objectively ascertainable facts, was also applied in *Anwar v Mondello Farms Pty Ltd*[48] in the context of s 33 of the *Civil Liability Act 1936* (SA). The point at issue was the plaintiff's capacity to recover for psychological harm, which was subject to the control mechanisms in the legislation. The Court considered that 'the phrase "in the plaintiff's position" does not allow the Court to have regard to subjective personality traits which would undermine the normal fortitude standard'.[49] However, objective factors could be relevant:

> A person of normal fortitude in the position of the plaintiff is an unskilled migrant worker with a poor grasp of the English language and minimal training who was carrying out his duties in a lawful manner. That person would respond to adversity and injury in the manner expected of a person with those characteristics and without peculiar vulnerability or susceptibility to psychiatric illness.[50]

On this course of authority it appears that the plaintiff's disabilities, where they are objectively ascertainable, can be considered to be part of the defendant's negligence in suitable cases – where the defendant is aware of the disability by reason of its obviousness to an external viewer. Otherwise, the plaintiff is judged against an objective standard, so that a disability which is not objectively ascertainable cannot be taken into account for the benefit of the plaintiff in the defence of contributory negligence.

---

46 Ibid 465.
47 Ibid 50.
48 (2015) 123 SASR 321.
49 Ibid [2].
50 Ibid [17].

EMERGING ISSUE

The course of authority thus continues to apply an objective standard to the plaintiff's level of care in the determination of contributory negligence. However, the developing case law relating to the wording of the statutes in each jurisdiction may give rise to a nuanced approach to the standard of care required of a plaintiff for their own protection.

5.2.2.4   Intoxication

In *Joslyn v Berryman* the High Court considered the relevance of intoxication to the standard of care of the injured plaintiff.[51] Sally Joslyn was a passenger in a car driven by Allan Berryman. Both were intoxicated, having been drinking at a party until 4:00 am. She noticed that Mr Berryman was falling asleep at the wheel, so she insisted on driving. While she was driving the vehicle overturned, causing injury to Mr Berryman who sued in negligence. His contributory negligence was at issue. It was held that Mr Berryman had contributed to his own injury; the standard of care was that of a reasonable person in his position. McHugh J noted that the tradition of leniency in assessing the plaintiff's conduct in comparison to the defendant's arose from the historical position that contributory negligence was a complete defence. Apportionment of damages means that lenience is no longer justified, yet:

> some modern cases concerned with passengers accepting a lift from intoxicated drivers have also taken a lenient view of the passengers' conduct. But in principle, any fact or circumstance which a reasonable person would know or ought to know and which tends to suggest a foreseeable risk of injury in accepting a lift from an intoxicated driver, is relevant in determining whether the passenger was guilty of contributory negligence in accepting the lift.[52]

Some of the modern Acts contain a presumption of contributory negligence when a person is intoxicated or relies upon a person known to be intoxicated. There are significant differences in the wording of the provisions (see Table 5.2).

Table 5.2   Presumptions in contributory negligence

Legislation	Section(s)
Civil Law (Wrongs) Act 2002 (ACT)	94, 95, 96, 97
Civil Liability Act 2002 (NSW)	50
Personal Injuries (Liabilities and Damages) Act 2003 (NT)	14, 15
Civil Liability Act 2003 (Qld)	47, 48, 49
Civil Liability Act 1936 (SA)	46, 47, 48
Civil Liability Act 2002 (Tas)	5
Wrongs Act 1958 (Vic)	14G
Civil Liability Act 2002 (WA)	5L

---

51 (2003) 214 CLR 552; [2003] HCA 34.
52 Ibid [19].

In *Allen v Chadwick* the High Court revisited the matter of contributory negligence in cases involving the intoxication of the plaintiff, applying s 47(2) of the *Civil Liability Act 1936* (SA).[53] The two issues were whether the injured plaintiff, Chadwick, was contributorily negligent when she was injured after she got into the car driven by Allen, who she ought to have known was intoxicated;[54] and when she failed to engage her seatbelt.[55] Sections 47 and 49 of the Act create a presumption of contributory negligence in those two cases. The presumption of contributory negligence in the case of intoxication is irrebuttable unless the plaintiff can establish, on the balance of probabilities, 'that the intoxication did not contribute to the accident; or the injured person could not reasonably be expected to have avoided the risk'. There is a fixed statutory reduction of 25 per cent if the presumption cannot be rebutted. In *Allen v Chadwick* the plaintiff argued that the circumstances in which she got into the car meant that the second exception applied. The defendant had insisted on driving, and although the plaintiff felt 'helpless, anxious and confused' this was a subjective circumstance that had 'nothing to do with a reasonable evaluation of relative risk … [She] could reasonably be expected to have walked back into the township in order to avoid the risk of riding with Mr Allen if walking back to town and the hotel could reasonably have been assessed as a less unsafe course of conduct'.[56] The High Court noted:

> a defendant who inflicts harm on another by unreasonable conduct is not excused from liability in negligence because of a reduced personal capacity for reasonable decision-making. Section 44 of the Act operates to apply the same rule to determining whether a plaintiff has been contributorily negligent. In either case, confusion or panic on the part of the actor does not reduce what reasonableness requires. To take into account a mental or emotional state which subjectively reduces the capacity for reasonable decision-making would be inconsistent with the objectively reasonable assessment of risk which s 47(2)(b) postulates.[57]

The effect of the statutes is that, where the plaintiff is intoxicated there is a presumption that the plaintiff is contributorily negligent. The onus then shifts to the plaintiff to show that the intoxication was not, in fact, a cause of the incident or injury.

5.2.2.5   Obvious recreational risks

The Civil Liability Acts have introduced provisions dealing with cases in which recreational activities have obvious risks and those risks materialise. While in some states these provisions interact with the defence of voluntary assumption of risk,[58] the interaction between these provisions and the defences of contributory negligence was considered in *Cox v Mid-Coast Council*.[59] The plaintiff was a recreational pilot who, when approaching an airstrip, collided

---

53 (2015) 256 CLR 148; [2015] HCA 47.
54 *Civil Liability Act 1936* (SA) s 47.
55 Ibid s 49.
56 *Allen v Chadwick* (2015) 256 CLR 148; [2015] HCA 47, [56] (French CJ, Kiefel, Bell, Keane and Gordon JJ).
57 Ibid.
58 See Section 5.3.2.1.
59 [2021] NSWCA 190.

with a Ferris wheel. The plaintiff pilot brought an action in negligence against the Council claiming that it was negligent in allowing the erection of the Ferris wheel, which effectively obstructed the safe landing of aircraft in the Council-controlled airport. The question of appeal related to the statutory defence under s 5L. It was contended that the Ferris wheel was an obstruction that amounted to an obvious risk, thus activating the statutory provisions in the NSW legislation. The NSW Court of Appeal noted that s 5L of the *Civil Liability Act 2002* (NSW) excludes liability in negligence where the harm is suffered as a result of the materialisation of an obvious risk of a dangerous recreational activity. If that provision is successfully established, then contributory negligence will not be necessary – the defendant will have a complete defence. If the defence under s 5L had failed, then the contributory negligence of the pilot would have reduced liability by 35 per cent. In this case the Court of Appeal agreed with the primary judge that the pilot was engaged in a dangerous recreational activity and that the obstacle (the Ferris wheel) was an obvious risk. The collision was the materialisation of an obvious risk.

5.2.2.6   Employees

Where an employee suffers injury in the course of their employment, it is most likely that the injury will be covered by compulsory statutory no-fault workers compensation schemes (see Table 5.3). The legislation generally excludes common law claims, so most injuries arising from negligence in the workplace will not be litigated in negligence.

Table 5.3   Workers compensation legislation

Jurisdiction	Legislation
Australian Capital Territory	*Workers Compensation Act 1951*
New South Wales	*Workers Compensation Act 1987; Workplace Injury Management and Workers Compensation Act 1998*
Northern Territory	*Return to Work Act 1986*
Queensland	*Workers Compensation and Rehabilitation Act 2003*
South Australia	*Workers Rehabilitation and Compensation Act 1986*
Tasmania	*Workers Rehabilitation and Compensation Act 1988*
Victoria	*Accident Compensation Act 1985; Accident Compensation (WorkCover Insurance) Act 1993*
Western Australia	*Workers' Compensation and Injury Management Act 1981*

Where the injury is permanent and sufficiently severe, the plaintiff may be able to claim in common law negligence. Legislation defines whether the injury is severe enough (and this varies from state to state). Where employees have been injured in the course of their employment, the court will start with the assumption that the employer had failed to discharge its obligations to take reasonable care for the worker. This might mean, for instance, that the employer had failed to institute a safe system of work. In *McLean v Tedman* a garbage collector was injured when he was struck by a motor vehicle.[60] He

60 (1984) 155 CLR 306.

had run across the road from behind the garbage truck to collect a bin and did not see an oncoming car, even though it was being driven on the correct side of the road and would have been visible to a person in the plaintiff's position from approximately 200 metres away. A majority of the High Court concluded that the plaintiff had not been contributorily negligent but that his conduct amounted to mere inadvertence, inattention or misjudgment.[61]

On the same basis the court may consider the longstanding practice of the plaintiff which had the apparent or actual authority of the defendant. In *Davies v Adelaide Chemical & Fertiliser Co Ltd* the High Court had to determine whether an employee contributed to his own injury when he reached under a moving conveyor belt to grease a roller.[62] It had been the employee's longstanding practice to carry out his duty in this way. It did not involve a great deal of risk and he had never been instructed to stop the machine to carry out the operation. The High Court (Latham CJ, Dixon and McTiernan JJ) held that the defence of contributory negligence had not been made out. Dixon J said:

> in following such a practice at the time of the accident the plaintiff was ... not acting contrary to any rule, instruction, advice or practice made, given or established by the defendant as his employer or in his own interest or for his own convenience ... [he] was performing his duties according to his habitual and longstanding practice for which he had the ... approval of the factory management who treated it as part of his ordinary work.[63]

Otherwise, courts had long had regard 'to the long hours and the fatigue, to the slackening of attention which naturally comes from constant repetition of the same operation, to the noise and confusion in which the man works, to his pre-occupation in what he is actually doing at the cost perhaps of some inattention to his own safety'.[64] The 'inattention borne of familiarity and repetition' causing a 'temporary inadvertence to danger' was considered not to amount to contributory negligence in *Commissioner of Railways v Ruprecht*.[65]

5.2.3 Causation

To amount to *contributory* negligence, the failure of the plaintiff to comply with the standard of care must have contributed to the plaintiff's injury. This requires that the plaintiff's failure was one cause of the injury to the plaintiff. It is only necessary to show factual causation; this is different from the *plaintiff's* obligation to show that the defendant's breach caused their injury (factual causation) *and* was within the scope of liability (legal causation). The requirement that the defendant prove that the plaintiff's own conduct caused the incident or injury is also implicit in the outcome of the application of the doctrine of contributory

---

61 Mason, Wilson, Brennan and Dawson JJ, Gibbs CJ dissenting.
62 (1946) 74 CLR 541.
63 Ibid 551.
64 *Caswell v Powell Duffryn Associated Collieries Ltd* [1940] AC 152, 178–9.
65 (1979) 142 CLR 563.

negligence – apportionment of damages by reference to relative responsibility for the injury. The onus of proving causation is on the defendant.[66] The principles for determining causation are those applicable to a determination that negligence has caused harm. Causation is determined by asking whether the wrong was a necessary condition of the harm (see Section 4.2.2.1). The statutory requirement of 'scope of liability' is not to be applied.[67] In other words, it is a question of factual causation only.

The requirement that the plaintiff's contributory negligence is a cause (not necessarily the only cause) of the injury appears inconsistent with the statutory provisions that allow the plaintiff's damages to be reduced by 100 per cent (see Section 5.2.4); it remains to be seen how courts will deal with this. In *Lim v Cho* it was argued that the plaintiff's contributory negligence was jumping from a vehicle which was travelling at 50 km/h.[68] The trial judge held that it was just and equitable to reduce damages by 100 per cent. On appeal the Court of Appeal held that the plaintiff had not fallen below the standard of care but found it unnecessary to interfere with the decision on apportionment.

5.2.4   Apportionment

If the defendant establishes that the plaintiff failed to take reasonable care for their own safety, the damages will be apportioned (see Table 5.4). This means that the damages suffered by the plaintiff will be reduced by the proportion due to the plaintiff's failure to take care.

Table 5.4   Contributory negligence: apportionment

Legislation	Section(s)
Civil Law (Wrongs) Act 2002 (ACT)	102
Law Reform (Miscellaneous Provisions) Act 1965 (NSW)	9
Personal Injuries (Liabilities and Damages) Act 2003 (NT)	17
Law Reform (Miscellaneous Provisions) Act 1956 (NT)	16
Civil Liability Act 2003 (Qld)	24
Law Reform (Contributory Negligence and Apportionment of Liability) Act 2001 (SA)	7
Wrongs Act 1954 (Tas)	4
Wrongs Act 1958 (Vic)	26, 62, 63
Law Reform (Contributory Negligence and Tortfeasors' Contribution) Act 1974 (WA)	4

Courts usually work out the apportionment by examining the conduct of both plaintiff and defendant in all the circumstances of the incident, comparing the plaintiff's and the defendant's relative share of responsibility for the damage.

---

66 This was the rule at common law. In *Nicholson v Nicholson* (1994) 35 NSWLR 308, the Court held that this had not been altered by *Motor Accidents Act 1988* (NSW), s 74. In *Verryt v Schoupp* (2015) 70 MVR 484, the NSW Court of Appeal approved this reasoning.
67 *Verryt v Schoupp* (2015) 70 MVR 484.
68 (2018) 84 MVR 514.

Case: *Podrebersek v Australian Iron & Steel Pty Ltd* (1985) 59 ALJR 492

Facts

This case was an appeal by the plaintiff from a decision of the NSW Court of Appeal. At first instance, the jury in the NSW Supreme Court had determined that the defendant employer, Australian Iron & Steel, was liable in negligence and that the plaintiff was contributorily negligent.

The plaintiff was cleaning gas pipes for the defendant when an explosion of gas injured him. The explosion was caused when a pin which was meant to seal off a hole in the gas pipe fell out, allowing gas to escape. The pin was meant to be screwed into the hole but it had only been screwed in for half a turn instead of the necessary three to four turns. The plaintiff was said to have contributed to the incident by failing to use a spanner to secure the pin as he had been instructed to do when he was trained.

Issue

The High Court (Gibbs CJ, Mason, Wilson, Brennan and Deane JJ) noted (at [10]):

> The making of an apportionment as between a plaintiff and a defendant of their respective shares in the responsibility for the damage involves a comparison both of culpability, i.e. of the degree of departure from the standard of care of the reasonable man ... and of the relative importance of the acts of the parties in causing the damage ... It is the whole conduct of each negligent party in relation to the circumstances of the accident which must be subjected to comparative examination. The significance of the various elements involved in such an examination will vary from case to case; for example, the circumstances of some cases may be such that a comparison of the relative importance of the acts of the parties in causing the damage will be of little, if any, importance.

Decision

The High Court considered that on the evidence the jury was entitled to find contributory negligence. On the question of apportionment the High Court refused, on several grounds, to allow the appeal despite the deficient direction to the jury.

Significance

The High Court in this case provided a definitive statement about the approach to be adopted in making an apportionment of damages where the plaintiff has fallen below the standard required for their own protection.

Question

What is meant by the plaintiff's 'culpability' in the context of contributory negligence? How does the plaintiff's 'culpability' affect the apportionment of damages?

 Guided response in the eBook

Apportionment is generally a straightforward process. If it is established that a plaintiff was 25 per cent responsible for damage in an accident, and the defendant was 75 per cent responsible, the plaintiff's damages will be reduced by the amount of 25 per cent of the loss. The defendant will have to pay to the plaintiff an amount representing 75 per cent of the plaintiff's loss. In *Pennington v Norris* the High Court noted that the court's task is to arrive at a 'just and equitable' apportionment as between the plaintiff and the defendant of 'responsibility' for the damage.[69]

In *Pennington v Norris* the plaintiff was struck by a car but was partly at fault having failed to keep a proper lookout while crossing the road.[70] The trial judge found the defendant liable, but reduced damages by 50 per cent based on a finding that the plaintiff was 50 per cent contributorily negligent. On appeal the High Court had to take account of s 4(1) of the *Tortfeasors and Contributory Negligence Act 1954* (Tas) which stated that regard had to be had to 'the claimant's share in the responsibility for the damage'. The Court said that this involves a 'comparison of culpability':

> By 'culpability' we do not mean moral blameworthiness but degree of departure from the standard of care of the reasonable man ... the plaintiff's 'contributory' negligence is not a breach of any duty at all, and it is difficult to impute 'moral' blame to one who is careless merely of his own safety ... The negligence of the defendant was in a high degree more culpable, more gross, than that of the plaintiff.[71]

The Court held that a 'fair and reasonable allocation' of responsibility was 80 per cent to the defendant and 20 per cent to the plaintiff.

Is it possible for the damage to be attributed entirely to the plaintiff – that is, for the award of damages to be reduced by 100 per cent? The traditional answer was 'no', but under legislation the answer can now be 'yes'. In *Wynbergen v Hoyts Corporation Pty Ltd* the High Court held that it is not possible to reduce damages by 100 per cent because that would mean that the plaintiff was entirely responsible for their injury.[72] This is logically inconsistent with the plaintiff's harm being caused by the defendant. Wynbergen, the plaintiff, worked for Hoyts Corporation, the defendant. His first job, each day, was to check the toilets for damage. The toilets were cleaned by Hoyts' staff who mopped the tiled floors, leaving them wet. Mr Wynbergen slipped on the wet floor and fell, injuring his right knee. He said there were no signs at the entrance to the toilet warning of the wet floor and he had no reason to believe that the floor was wet. He sued Hoyts and, although Hoyts was found to be negligent, the plaintiff was found to be 100 per cent contributorily negligent. He appealed to the Court of Appeal. That Court dismissed the appeal. It held that the apportionment of 100 per cent for the appellant's contributory negligence was open to the jury and was not inconsistent with the facts or the finding that Hoyts was negligent. He appealed to the High Court on the issue of whether the court can award contributory negligence of 100 per cent. The Court[73] held that apportionment legislation is predicated upon a finding that damage is

---

69 (1956) 96 CLR 10, 16 (Dixon CJ, Webb, Fullagar and Kitto JJ).
70 (1956) 96 CLR 10.
71 Ibid 16–17 (Dixon CJ, Webb, Fullagar and Kitto JJ).
72 (1997) 72 ALJR 65.
73 Considering the effect of *Law Reform (Miscellaneous Provisions) Act 1965* (NSW) s 10.

partly a result of the fault of others and partly a result of the person's own fault. That means that 'no matter how culpable the claimant may be, if the damage results from the fault of the person who suffers the damage and the fault of another, it is not possible to say that the damages recoverable in respect of that damage are to be not simply reduced but are to be entirely eliminated'.[74]

Despite this apparent illogicality, the Ipp Report recommended that a court should be entitled to reduce a contributorily negligent plaintiff's damages by 100 per cent. This recommendation has been implemented by statute in most states (see Table 5.5). In *Axiak v Ingram* this issue arose in relation to a 'blameless motor accident' as defined by s 7A of the *Motor Accidents Compensation Act 1999* (NSW).[75] The plaintiff had alighted from a school bus and then run behind the bus into the path of an oncoming car. The proceedings required the Court to consider whether there was 'fault' for the purposes of the *Motor Accidents Compensation Act 1999* (NSW) because if the accident was a 'blameless motor accident' the plaintiff's injuries would be deemed to have been caused by the fault of the driver. The driver argued that the accident was not blameless but had been caused by the child. The Court of Appeal held that the words 'fault of any other person' in the Act did not refer to the plaintiff's contributory negligence. More relevantly, the Court of Appeal held that the principles on apportionment derived from *Podrebersek v Australian Iron & Steel Pty Ltd* did not apply to 'blameless motor accidents' and the concept of contributory negligence under the Act was to be applied in a different manner than the usual comparison of responsibility.[76]

Table 5.5   Legislative provisions: apportionment of 100 per cent

Legislation	Section
Civil Law (Wrongs) Act 2002 (ACT)	47
Civil Liability Act 2002 (NSW)	5S
Civil Liability Act 2003 (Qld)	24
Civil Liability Act 1936 (SA)	50
Wrongs Act 1954 (Tas)	4
Wrongs Act 1958 (Vic)	63
Law Reform (Contributory Negligence and Tortfeasors' Contribution) Act 1974 (WA)	4

Note: Section 50 of the *Civil Liability Act 1936* (SA) does not specifically provide that damages may be reduced by 100 per cent.

In addition to the common law's role in apportionment, many of the statutes apply fixed statutory reductions in specified cases: notably, intoxication and failure to wear a seatbelt, as indicated earlier. The overall thrust of the provisions is to require the plaintiff to apply the same standard of care for their own protection as is required of the defendant. To ensure the appropriate level of responsibility, statutory provisions reverse the onus of proof where the plaintiff is intoxicated or engaged in illegal activity at the time of the incident causing the harm.

---

74   *Wynbergen v Hoyts Corporation Pty Ltd* (1997) 72 ALJR 65, [68].
75   (2012) 82 NSWLR 36.
76   (1985) 59 ALJR 492.

HINTS AND TIPS

Try isolating each of the plaintiff's injuries and working out, in relation to each injury, how much of it was due to the plaintiff's own lack of care.

REVIEW QUESTIONS

(1) Against which standard of care is the adult plaintiff's conduct measured when determining whether the defence of contributory negligence will apply?

(2) Against which standard of care is the child plaintiff's conduct measured when determining whether the defence of contributory negligence will apply?

(3) What principles apply to the question whether the plaintiff's failure to comply with the relevant standard of care contributed to the loss suffered?

(4) How do courts arrive at an 'apportionment' of damages?

 Guided responses in the eBook

5.3   Voluntary assumption of risk

If a plaintiff, prior to the activity which caused the injury, freely and voluntarily agreed to accept the risk of injury or loss due to participation in that activity, and that particular risk eventuated, this is a *complete defence* to a future claim in negligence. This is called 'voluntary assumption of risk'.

5.3.1   Definitions and rationale

In judicial terms, '[o]ne who has invited or assented to an act being done towards him cannot, when he suffers from it, complain of it as a wrong'.[77] In Latin, this defence is *volenti non fit injuria* which, roughly translated, means 'there can be no injury to the willing'. According to McClellan CJ at LC: 'The Latin maxim "*volenti non fit injuria*" originated in the civil law and literally refers to the situation where a free citizen of Rome would, in concert with another, permit himself to be sold as a slave in order to share in the purchase price.'[78] For example, a defendant may claim that a plaintiff voluntarily assumed the risk of injury by:

- getting into a car knowing that it is driven by an intoxicated driver[79]
- instructing a learner driver knowing they are inexperienced[80]

---

77 *Smith v Baker & Sons* [1891] AC 325, 360 (Lord Herschell).
78 *Carey v Lake Macquarie City Council* (2007) Aust Torts Reports 81-874, [70].
79 *Roggenkamp v Bennett* (1950) 80 CLR 292. Note that this fact situation may also give rise to the defence of contributory negligence.
80 *Nettleship v Weston* [1971] 2 QB 691.

- playing a sport where certain risks are well known to be part of the game[81]
- undertaking dangerous recreational activities.[82]

The rationale for this rule is the principle of human autonomy – the idea that a person is capable of making choices as an expression of their human agency. This idea is expressed in the dissenting judgment of Lord Hobhouse in *Reeves v Commissioner of Police*:

> Where a natural person is not under any disability, that person has a right to choose his own fate. He is constrained in so far as his choice may affect others, society or the body politic. But, so far as he himself alone is concerned, he is entitled to choose ... A corollary of this principle is ... the principle that a person may not complain of the consequences of his own choices ... The autonomy of the individual human confers the right and the responsibility. To qualify as an autonomous choice, the choice made must be free and unconstrained – ie, voluntary, deliberate and informed.[83]

It has been said that the defence of voluntary assumption of risk rarely succeeds,[84] and many illustrative cases predate compulsory workers compensation legislation. In some jurisdictions the defence does not apply in cases involving motor vehicle accidents.[85] Workers compensation legislation has also abolished the defence in employer–employee cases. However, changes to legislation in all states have modified the common law to make it easier for the defendant to prove that the plaintiff knew of an 'obvious risk'. Figure 5.3 sets out the simplified process for analysing a case involving voluntary assumption of risk.

To successfully argue this defence the defendant must prove on the balance of probabilities the following three elements:

(1) The plaintiff knew of the danger.
(2) The plaintiff fully appreciated the risk of injury created by the danger.
(3) The plaintiff voluntarily agreed to accept the risk and its consequences.

---

81 *Rootes v Shelton* (1967) 116 CLR 383. But compare *Dodge v Snell* [2011] TASSC 19. In *Rootes v Shelton*, Barwick CJ at 385 stated: 'By engaging in a sport or pastime the participants may be held to have *accepted risks* which are inherent in that sport or pastime ... but this does not eliminate all duty of care of the one participant to the other ... the rules of the sport or game may constitute one of those circumstances: but ... they are neither definitive of the existence nor of the extent of the duty; nor does their breach or non-observance necessarily constitute a breach of any duty found to exist' (emphasis added). It has been argued that, in the United Kingdom, as a result of *Caldwell v Maguire* [2002] PIQR 6, 'it is inherently impossible to plead *volenti* in sports cases and that a variable standard of care has been introduced through the need to examine a sport's "playing culture"': D McArdle and M James, 'Are you Experienced? "Playing Cultures", Sporting Rules and Personal Injury Litigation after *Caldwell v Maguire*' (2005) 13(3) *Tort Law Review* 193, 194.
82 *Goode v Angland* (2017) 96 NSWLR 503; *Stewart v Ackland* (2015) 10 ACTLR 207.
83 [2000] 1 AC 360, 394.
84 *Imbree v McNeilly* (2008) 236 CLR 510; [2008] HCA 40, [79] (Gummow, Hayne and Kiefell JJ, Gleeson CJ and Crennan J agreeing), quoting JG Fleming, *The Law of Torts* (LBC Information Services, 9th ed, 1998) 334.
85 *Motor Accidents Act 1988* (NSW) s 76; *Motor Accidents Compensation Act 1999* (NSW) s 140; *Civil Liability Act 1936* (SA) s 47(6).

Figure 5.3   Voluntary assumption of risk – summary process

| Knowledge of risk – actual knowledge, subjective test (*Scanlon v American Cigarette Company (Overseas) Pty Ltd (No 3)* [1987] VR 289 **unless** | **Voluntary** assumption of risk – **the plaintiff must have acted voluntarily and with full appreciation of the risks involved.** | If the defendant can prove that the plaintiff agreed to undertake the risk, the defendant has a complete defence – the plaintiff cannot recover for the injury at all. |

- Obvious risk (check legislation) which reverses the onus of proof. Legislation defines 'obvious risk' objectively, but see *Doubleday v Kelly* [2005] NSWCA 151 in relation to children.
- Alleged failure of duty to warn, in which case check legislation – may need to prove unawareness of risk

P may need:
- Absence from constraint: *Bowater v Rowley Regis Corp* [1944] KB 476 (c.f. *Imperial Chemical Industries Ltd v Shatwell* [1965] AC 656)
- Freedom from intimidation, reasonable time make assessment of risk: *Avram v Gusakoski* [2006] WASCA 16
- Sufficient capacity (argued but not often accepted in cases of intoxication of P)

5.3.2 Knowledge of risk

To establish the defence, the defendant generally has to show that the plaintiff had knowledge of the risk. In *Roggenkamp v Bennett* McTiernan and Williams JJ noted that the question of acceptance of risk was one of fact and it may be inferred from conduct:

> The inference may more readily be drawn in cases where it is proved that the plaintiff knew of the danger and comprehended it, as, for example, where the danger was apparent, or proper warning was given of it, and there was nothing to show that he was obliged to incur it, than in cases where he had knowledge that there was danger but not full comprehension of its extent, or where, while taking an ordinary and reasonable course, he had not an adequate opportunity of electing whether he would accept the risk or not.[86]

The test at common law was subjective.[87] As explained by McColl JA in *Carey v Lake Macquarie City Council*:

> The plaintiff must have actually perceived and fully appreciated a risk before he or she could be said to have voluntarily accepted it. Actual knowledge will be more readily inferred where a risk is obvious … but a risk does not have to be obvious in order to satisfy the test.[88]

In terms of constructive knowledge the common law position was set out in *Scanlon v American Cigarette Co (Overseas) Pty Ltd (No 3).*[89] The Court held that it is insufficient for a cigarette manufacturer to allege that a user ought to have known of the harmful character of the product as a basis for raising the defence.

---

86 (1950) 80 CLR 292, 300.
87 *Scanlon v American Cigarette Co (Overseas) Pty Ltd (No 3)* [1987] VR 289.
88 (2007) Aust Torts Reports 81-874, [75].
89 [1987] VR 289.
90 Ibid 289.

Case: *Scanlon v American Cigarette Co (Overseas) Pty Ltd (No 3)* [1987] VR 289

Facts

The plaintiff, Ruth Scanlon, smoked the defendant's cigarettes for about 20 years. She developed cancer and sued the defendant. The defendant pleaded voluntary assumption of risk. In this case Scanlon was seeking to have parts of the defendant's defence struck out.

Issue

Paragraphs 5 and 14 of the defence claimed:

> if it proved to be the case, that the smoking of the said cigarettes involved risk of injury as alleged (which is not admitted), the plaintiff knew or ought to have known that the smoking of the said cigarettes involved such risk and the plaintiff accepted, consented to and voluntarily assumed the same.[90]

The plaintiff argued that the inclusion of the words 'ought to have known' should be struck out, because this is not part of the defence of voluntary assumption of risk.

Decision

Nicholson J accepted the plaintiff's argument and struck out the relevant portions of the defences. He said:

> the pleading clearly asserts that it is sufficient to establish a volens defence for a defendant to establish that a plaintiff ought to have known as distinct from having actual knowledge of the relevant matters in question.
>
> Either this proposition is correct or it is not, and I have found that it is not, and the relevant words will accordingly be struck out of both defences.[91]

Significance

This case reflects the common law position in relation to the requirement of knowledge in cases involving the defence of voluntary assumption of risk. The defence, at common law, required actual knowledge.

Notes

The case is interesting for the general test in relation to constructive knowledge, but it is particularly important in the wake of the legislative reforms because of the special position in relation to tobacco litigation. This case remains relevant to tobacco litigation since the provisions relating to obvious risks do not apply to cases involving smoking or the use of tobacco products.[92]

---

91 Ibid 294.
92 See, eg, *Civil Liability Act 2002* (NSW) s 3B; *Civil Liability Act 2003* (Qld) s 5; *Civil Liability Act 2002* (Tas) s 3B; *Wrongs Act 1958* (Vic) s 45; *Civil Liability Act 2002* (WA) s 3A.

Question

What is the difference between what is 'known' and what 'ought to be known'?

 Guided response in the eBook

5.3.2.1   Obvious risks

As discussed in earlier chapters, the Ipp Review had as one of its concerns the recalibration of responsibility between the plaintiff and the defendant in negligence cases. In response to the recommendations of the Ipp Report, the civil liability legislation changed the requirement of actual knowledge in the case of obvious risks and manifestation of inherent risks.[93] In the view of the Ipp Review Panel, the defence had become 'more or less defunct since the introduction of apportionment for contributory negligence',[94] because courts were unwilling to hold that the plaintiff knew of the risk or that the plaintiff had freely and voluntarily accepted the risk, and they tended to define the risks 'narrowly and at a relatively high level of detail. The more narrowly a risk is defined, the less likely it is that a person will have been aware of it.'[95]

Accordingly, the civil liability legislation (see Table 5.6) generally focused on reversing the onus of proof in relation to awareness of risks where those risks are obvious and, in relation to awareness of risk, to establish that all that is required is awareness of a risk of the general type, rather than the precise risk.[96]

Table 5.6   Comparative provisions: obvious risks

Legislation	Section(s)
Civil Liability Act 2002 (NSW)	5F, 5G
Civil Liability Act 2003 (Qld)	13
Civil Liability Act 1936 (SA)	36, 37
Civil Liability Act 2002 (Tas)	15, 16
Wrongs Act 1958 (Vic)	53, 54
Civil Liability Act 2002 (WA)	5F, 5M, 5N

Where the risk is an obvious risk, the plaintiff is taken to have been aware of the risk unless the plaintiff proves, on the balance of probabilities, that they were not actually aware of the risk. This is the effect of legislation in all Australian jurisdictions.

---

93 Ipp Report 129–30.
94 Ipp Report 129.
95 Ibid.
96 Ipp Report 130.

5.3.2.2   Unavoidable risks

Inherent risks are generally defined in the statute as 'risks of something occurring that cannot be avoided by the exercise of reasonable care and skill'.[97] Legislation in most states reiterates that the defendant is not liable for 'inherent risks' (other than in cases involving failure to warn) (see Table 5.7). There can be no liability for an 'inherent risk' because, by definition, if something cannot be avoided then its occurrence cannot be due to negligence.[98] Conversely, to show that something is an inherent risk 'it must be proven that the risk cannot be avoided by the exercise of reasonable care and skill'.[99] For example, in *Paul v Cooke* the plaintiff underwent an operation which involved an unavoidable risk of intra-operative rupture followed by stroke.[100] The risk was unavoidable, so there could be no negligence if it eventuated; it was an inherent risk. This situation must be distinguished from cases where the plaintiff is suing because of a *failure to warn* of an unavoidable risk. For instance, in *Rogers v Whitaker* the patient underwent an operation which had an unavoidable risk, but she was not warned of that risk.[101] The legislation generally excludes 'failure to warn' from the 'inherent risk' exclusion.

Table 5.7   Comparative provisions: inherent risks

Legislation	Section
Civil Liability Act 2002 (NSW)	5I
Civil Liability Act 2003 (Qld)	16
Civil Liability Act 1936 (SA)	39
Wrongs Act 1958 (Vic)	55
Civil Liability Act 2002 (WA)	5P

5.3.3   Appreciation of the risk of injury

The defendant must next establish that the plaintiff fully appreciated the danger. There is some difficulty in distinguishing 'knowledge' of the risk and full comprehension of the nature and extent of the risk.

The civil liability legislation has altered the common law, and the legislative provisions differ between jurisdictions. In *Carey v Lake Macquarie City Council* the Court considered ss 5F and 5G of the *Civil Liability Act 2002* (NSW) in relation to the knowledge requirement that triggers the 'obvious risks' rebuttable presumption.[102] It was held that the plaintiff cannot rebut the presumption that a risk is 'obvious' by claiming that, despite knowing of the general risk of harm, they were not aware of all of its possible manifestations.

The South Australian legislation differs from the NSW provisions considered in *Carey*. In *Schuller v SJ Webb Nominees Pty Ltd* the plaintiff was dancing on a chair while inebriated

---

97   See, eg, *Civil Liability Act 2002* (NSW) s 5I(2).
98   B McDonald, 'Legislative Intervention in the Law of Negligence: The Common Law, Statutory Interpretation and Tort Reform in Australia' (2005) 27(3) *Sydney Law Review* 443, 461.
99   *Nominal Defendant v Cooper* (2017) 82 MVR 254, [110].
100   (2013) 85 NSWLR 167.
101   (1992) 175 CLR 479.
102   (2007) Aust Torts Reports 81-874, [90].

and fell, injuring her leg.[103] She sued the defendant owner of the premises in negligence. The trial judge found that the defendant had successfully made out the defence of voluntary assumption of risk. In the context of ss 36 and 37 of the *Civil Liability Act 1936* (SA) it was held that dancing on a chair while inebriated was an obvious risk.[104] The issue before the Full Court of the Supreme Court of South Australia was 'whether sections 36 and 37 abrogate the need to prove that the appellant voluntarily assumed the risk'[105] – in other words, whether it is necessary under the statute to prove both knowledge of the risk and acceptance of it.

The Court considered these provisions to be intended to make it easier for the defendant to establish the defence of voluntary assumption of risk in two ways. The first was by reversing the onus of proof in cases of obvious risk, as indicated earlier. Second, Stanley J stated that 's 37(2) provides that it is not necessary to show that the plaintiff knew of the exact nature or manner of occurrence of the risk. It is enough to show that he or she knew of the type or kind of risk or, alternatively, that a risk of this type or kind was obvious.'[106] The Court considered that the provisions were intended to overcome the tendency of the common law to put obstacles in the way of successful pleading of the defence:

> One obstacle was that courts were unwilling to find that a plaintiff actually knew about the risk so as to assume it. Another was that courts tended to define risks narrowly and at a high level of detail, and so required the defendant to prove that the plaintiff knew not only of the risk of bodily injury from the activity, but also of the risk of suffering injury in a particular way.[107]

The different wording of the civil liability legislation will have to be tested, but it does not appear likely that, in the case of obvious risks, the courts would reintroduce a requirement that the plaintiff knew of all the potential manifestations of that risk.

Case: *Tapp v Australian Bushmen's Campdraft and Rodeo Association Limited* [2022] HCA 11

Facts

Tapp was a participant in a campdraft competition. This competition involves the participant, on horseback, riding into groups of cattle and separating one from the group. While she was competing, her horse slipped and she fell, suffering a serious spinal injury. She sued the Association, arguing that the surface of the arena caused her horse to fall and that the Association, by allowing the event to continue, breached its duty to take reasonable care for her safety. The Association, she said, should have ploughed the arena when it became unsafe. The stages of *Tapp* are shown in Table 5.8.

---

103 (2015) 124 SASR 152.
104 The NSW legislation has no provision equivalent to *Civil Liability Act 1936* (SA) s 37(3).
105 (2015) 124 SASR 152, [40] (Stanley J).
106 Ibid [49].
107 Ibid [50] (Stanley J).

Table 5.8   Stages of *Tapp v Australian Bushmen's Campdraft and Rodeo Association Limited*

Hearing	Parties	Outcome
First instance [2019] NSWSC 1506 Lonergan J	Emily Tapp (Plaintiff) Australian Bushmen's Campdraft & Rodeo Association Limited (Defendant)	Tapp's claim dismissed
Appeal [2019] NSWSC 1506 Basten, Payne and McCallum JJA	Emily Tapp (Appellant) Australian Bushmen's Campdraft & Rodeo Association Ltd (Respondent)	Tapp's appeal dismissed
Appeal [2022] HCA 11 Kiefel CJ, Keane, Gordon, Edelman and Gleeson JJ	Emily Tapp (Appellant) Australian Bushmen's Campdraft & Rodeo Association Ltd (Respondent)	Tapp's appeal **allowed**

Issue

The issue, for the purposes of the question of 'obvious risk', is whether the Association was liable for harm suffered from 'obvious risks of dangerous recreational activities' under the terms of the *Civil Liability Act 2002* (NSW) s 5L.

Here there were two sets of risk – the risk inherent in campdrafting competitions (falling from the horse, for instance) and the risk arising from the deterioration of the ground over the course of the competition.

Decision

Tapp was successful, and s 5L of the *Civil Liability Act 2002* (NSW) did not operate to remove liability. The application of the section by the plurality occurs from paragraph [150]ff. Once the relevant risk – the risk of the deterioration in the ground – was identified, it was held that the risk of injury would not have been obvious to a reasonable person in Tapp's position because (a) she had no opportunity to examine the ground so had no means of assessing the condition of the ground; (b) from the information available (her own rides and the observations of other contestants) a reasonable person would not have had concerns about the ground; (c) in the circumstances a reasonable person would have relied on the Committee to make an appropriate decision about the surface of the ground, given that they were maintaining it and they were more experienced than the teenaged competitor.

While there was a delay in her event, there was no warning given about the state of the ground, and although there was an announcement allowing competitors to withdraw with a refund of the entry fee:

> there was no suggestion that the announcement was loud enough that a reasonable person in her position, while warming up her horse in the separate arena, would have heard it. In any event, a reasonable person in Ms Tapp's position would have known, as she knew, that events were held up for other reasons such as 'an injured beast … coming out of the yard'.[108]

---

108   *Tapp v Australian Bushmen's Campdraft and Rodeo Association Ltd* (2022) 273 CLR 454; [2022] HCA 11, [156].

Significance

The High Court decision clarified the point at which the 'obvious risk' provisions operated: in New South Wales, s 5L operates as a defence, requiring the defendant to prove that the plaintiff was engaged in a 'recreational activity' that was dangerous in the sense that it involved a 'serious risk of harm', that risk was obvious, and the harm that the plaintiff suffered was a result of the materialisation of that obvious risk. The 'obvious risk' defence applied to the risks inherent in the campdraft competition, but the plaintiff's injury was attributable to the condition of the ground, which is a risk at a different level of generality.

The case clarified that the risk, for the purposes of s 5L of the NSW Act, should be at the same level of generality as the risk considered for the purposes of the breach of duty. Under these provisions the breach must be determined first, and then s 5L applied.

Notes

The 'obvious risk' provisions in the legislation are not uniform across the states; see for instance the difference in wording of the Victorian and the NSW legislation.

Question

Did the High Court in *Tapp v Australian Bushmen's Campdraft and Rodeo Association Limited* hold that there was no obvious risk in riding in a campdraft competition?

 Guided response in the eBook

5.3.4   Voluntary acceptance of risk

It is not enough that the plaintiff knew of the risk: they must have fully accepted the risk. This is a factual question that can be difficult to establish because the acceptance may not be express – it may have to be inferred from conduct. Aside from the abolition of the *volenti* defence in relation to some industrial and transport accidents (see Section 5.2.2.5), the common law position in relation to this has generally not been affected by legislative reform. The Ipp Review Panel expressly did not recommend any provision dealing with the issue of voluntariness: 'Whether or not a risk was taken voluntarily is ultimately an evaluative question about which it would be difficult to make general provision.'[109] However, the removal of provisions relating to workplaces does render inapplicable a significant number of cases involving a degree of pressure on the plaintiff.

Problematically, 'there will rarely, if ever, be direct evidence that a plaintiff voluntarily agreed to accept a risk. Their agreement will usually have to be implied or inferred from their conduct.'[110] Clearly this may be a difficult factual question. Often the courts will infer that the plaintiff voluntarily accepted a risk where it has been proved that they actually

---

109   Ipp Report 130 [8.32].
110   *Carey v Lake Macquarie City Council* (2007) Aust Torts Reports 81-874, [76] (McClellan CJ).

perceived and appreciated the risk but nevertheless engaged in the action.[111] In *Carey v Lake Macquarie City Council* McClellan CJ made a number of useful points in this determination:

- Courts are less likely to infer that agreement is voluntary where the alternative to agreement is 'onerous or repugnant'.[112] In *Insurance Commissioner v Joyce* Dixon J noted: 'consent or voluntary assumption of risk is not to be implied where, notwithstanding knowledge, the person concerned has exposed himself to the danger only because of the exigency of the situation in which he stands. If he has no real or practical choice he does not voluntarily consent.'[113] Conversely, participation in recreational activity is voluntary: 'places of recreation are not places to which people are compelled to resort, and nor are they obliged, if they do, to participate in physical activities there.'[114]

- Voluntary consent is easier to infer when the plaintiff has engaged in a positive act (rather than an omission). It seems that a 'conscious choice' is more readily inferred in the case of a positive act.[115]

- 'Even if a plaintiff perceived and fully appreciated a risk, the inference of free and voluntary agreement cannot be made if the plaintiff had a genuine belief that the risk would not materialise.'[116] There have been several cases in which the plaintiff was a passenger in a car driven by a defendant who was under the influence of alcohol, but the defence of *volenti* failed because the plaintiff believed that the driver was capable of driving safely.[117]

Thus, to establish the defence of voluntary assumption of risk, the defendant must prove on the balance of probabilities that the plaintiff knew of the danger of engaging in the activity, fully appreciated the risk of injury created by the danger and voluntarily agreed to the consequences.

Case: *Avram v Gusakoski* (2006) 31 WAR 400

Facts

The plaintiff and the defendant had both been drinking in Joondanna, Western Australia, and were drunk. Another person, Reid, was not drinking and was to drive. The defendant insisted on driving and demanded the keys aggressively. His attitude was described as being intimidating. He was a big man who had in the past assaulted the plaintiff. The plaintiff objected but Reid allowed the defendant to drive. There was an accident due to the defendant's negligent driving.

Issue

Had the plaintiff fully appreciated the risk of improper driving caused by the driver's intoxicated condition *and voluntarily accepted it?*

---

111 Ibid [77] (McClellan CJ).
112 Ibid [79].
113 (1948) 77 CLR 39, 57 quoted in *Carey v Lake Macquarie City Council* (2007) Aust Torts Reports 81-874, [78].
114 *Vairy v Wyong Shire Council* (2005) 223 CLR 422; [2005] HCA 62, [217] (Callinan and Heydon JJ).
115 *Carey v Lake Macquarie City Council* (2007) Aust Torts Reports 81-874, [81] (McClellan CJ).
116 Ibid [82] (McClellan CJ).
117 See, eg, *O'Shea v Permanent Trustee Co of NSW Ltd* [1971] Qd R 1; *Suncorp Insurance & Finance v Blakeney* [1993] Aust Torts Reports 81-253.

Decision

Pullin JA (with whom Malcolm CJ and Murray AJA agreed) noted that 'the [defendant's] conduct imposed on the [plaintiff] the obligation to make a decision about whether he would assume the risk of staying in the vehicle and the appellant did not allow a reasonable time for the respondent to make that assessment. Murray AJA noted (at [80]–[81]):

> there was nothing to indicate that the [plaintiff] should be taken to have assumed the legal risk of injury; that he should be taken to have agreed, if he was injured, to bear the liability entirely himself.
>
> [The plaintiff] might be taken to have appreciated that the appellant had had a lot to drink over the day and that he was intoxicated … But that is not to say that by remaining in the vehicle, he was impliedly accepting that the risk of any collision, as a result of alcohol caused misjudgement of driving conditions, would be borne by him.

Significance

Consent is not voluntary if procured by some sort of pressure. In this case there was held to be no voluntary consent where a drunken, aggressive, intimidating driver left the passenger with little time to consider alternatives.

Notes

The accident occurred before amendments to the *Civil Liability Act 2002* (WA) in 2003. Relevant provisions include ss 5F (definition) and 5N (presumption of knowledge in the case of obvious risks).

Question

Would the conclusion in this case be different under the provisions of the *Civil Liability Act 2002* (WA)?

 Guided response in the eBook

REVIEW QUESTIONS

(1) What is the difference between contributory negligence and the defence of voluntary assumption of risk (*volenti non fit injuria*)?

(2) What is the effect on the pleading of a case if the defendant, in a *volenti* defence, claims that the risk was obvious?

 Guided responses in the eBook

5.4   Illegality

5.4.1   Is illegality a defence?

The illegality of the conduct of the plaintiff has been a matter for consideration in a number of cases in negligence. It is clear that illegality in and of itself will not absolve the defendant from liability.[118] However, there are some circumstances in which the plaintiff's illegal conduct will be relevant to the resolution of a case in negligence. This was the position at common law. The civil liability legislation also, to a degree, addresses the question (see Table 5.9). It is not clear, however, that illegality per se should be considered a defence.

Table 5.9   Comparative provisions: illegal activity

Legislation	Section
Civil Law (Wrongs) Act 2002 (ACT)	94
Civil Liability Act 2002 (NSW)	54
Personal Injuries (Liabilities and Damages) Act 2003 (NT)	10
Civil Liability Act 2003 (Qld)	45
Civil Liability Act 1936 (SA)	43
Civil Liability Act 2002 (Tas)	6
Wrongs Act 1958 (Vic)	14G

5.4.2   The common law position

In *Gala v Preston* the High Court considered the 'defence' of illegality – particularly in the context of 'joint illegal enterprises'.[119] However, in the analysis the illegality of the plaintiff's conduct was treated as a factor to consider in determining whether a duty of care was owed or whether the joint illegality would prevent the construction of a standard of care. The Court reached a decision on the basis of the proximity of the relationship between the parties and by reference to *Cook v Cook*.[120] After the demise of proximity as a consideration in determining the duty of care, *Cook* was no longer considered good law.[121]

In *Miller v Miller* the High Court revisited the issue in the context of a motor vehicle accident where the plaintiff was a passenger in a stolen vehicle illegally driven by the defendant.[122] After reviewing the relevant authorities, the Court identified the following propositions:

> First, the fact that a plaintiff was acting illegally when injured as a result of the defendant's negligence is not determinative of whether a duty of care is owed. Second, the fact that plaintiff and defendant were both acting illegally when the plaintiff suffered injuries of which the defendant's negligence was a cause and which would not have been suffered but for the plaintiff's participation in the illegal act is not determinative. Third, there are

118   *Miller v Miller* (2011) 242 CLR 446; [2011] HCA 9, [13] (French CJ, Gummow, Hayne, Crennan, Kiefel and Bell JJ).
119   (1991) 172 CLR 243.
120   (1986) 162 CLR 376.
121   Ibid. This case was overruled in *Imbree v McNeilly* (2008) 236 CLR 510; [2008] HCA 40.
122   (2011) 242 CLR 446; [2011] HCA 9.

cases where the parties' joint participation in illegal conduct should preclude a plaintiff recovering damages for negligence from the defendant. Fourth, different bases have been said to found the denial of recovery in some, but not all, cases of joint illegal enterprise: no duty of care should be found to exist; a standard of care cannot or should not be fixed; the plaintiff assumed the risk of negligence. Fifth, the different bases for denial of liability all rest on a policy judgment. That policy judgment has sometimes been expressed in terms that the courts *cannot* regulate the activities of wrongdoers and sometimes in terms that the courts *should not* do so.[123]

Whether or not the illegality of the plaintiff's conduct is relevant to the liability of the defendant depended, first, on the statutory purpose of the legislation creating the offence; and second on the nature of the conduct. If the conduct in which the defendant and plaintiff were jointly engaged was one which created a risk of injury (eg, driving dangerously), it would be difficult to determine a standard of care. In *Miller* the evidence showed that the plaintiff had attempted to remove herself from the vehicle before the accident, thus removing her complicity in the conduct.

5.4.3   State legislative variations

State legislation varies in its treatment of the illegal activities of the plaintiff. Section 54 of the *Civil Liability Act 2002* (NSW) provides that a court is not to award damages where the plaintiff's injury or death:

(a)   ... occurred at the time of, or following, conduct of that person that, on the balance of probabilities, constitutes a serious offence, and

(b)   that conduct contributed materially to the death, injury or damage or to the risk of death, injury or damage.

The section does not apply where the defendant's own conduct was an offence and that conduct caused the death, injury or damage of the plaintiff.

Section 14G of the *Wrongs Act 1958* (Vic) operates differently; it requires the court to consider whether or not the plaintiff was engaged in illegal activity as part of the question of establishing the breach of the duty of care.

REVIEW QUESTIONS

(1)   Is the illegality of the plaintiff's conduct a defence to an action in negligence?

(2)   How has the civil liability legislation affected the common law position in relation to the plaintiff's illegal activity?

 Guided responses in the eBook

---

123   Ibid [70] (emphasis in original).

5.5 Other defences

5.5.1 Limitation of actions

Legislation in all jurisdictions sets a limitation period beyond which a plaintiff is barred from bringing an action in negligence against the defendant (see Table 5.10). This period is generally six years for an action in tort, or three years in the case of negligence giving rise to personal injury. The periods have been extended in relation to child abuse actions.[124]

Table 5.10 Limitation of actions

Legislation	Section
Limitation Act 1985 (ACT)	11
Limitation Act 1969 (NSW)	14
Limitation Act 1981 (NT)	12
Limitation of Actions Act 1974 (Qld)	10
Limitation of Actions Act 1936 (SA)	35
Limitation Act 1974 (Tas)	4
Limitation of Actions Act 1958 (Vic)	5
Limitation Act 2005 (WA)	13

The relevant limitation period runs from the time the cause of action 'accrues' (ie, is complete). In the tort of negligence, damage is the gist of the action so the cause of action is not complete until the plaintiff suffers the required damage.

To prevent these limitation of action Acts barring plaintiffs from suing in circumstances of gradual onset injury, the definition of harm must take account of injuries which may be latent but of which the plaintiff may not be aware until the symptoms become manifest. The test is basically whether the damage is discoverable (an objective test) or discovered by the plaintiff (a subjective test). This was considered in *Alcan Gove Pty Ltd v Zabic*.[125]

The respondent, Zorko Zabic, was employed by Alcan Gove at its refinery from 1974 to 1977. He regularly carried out repairs and maintenance of pipelines, during which time he was exposed to and inhaled materials containing asbestos dust and fibre. He experienced chest pain and shortness of breath in November 2013 and was diagnosed with malignant mesothelioma in January 2014. He subsequently commenced proceedings at common law, arguing that Alcan Gove knew of the dangers of asbestos and failed to take any precautions for his safety.

Mr Zabic argued that the cause of action arose with the inhalation of asbestos dust and fibre which caused mesothelial cell changes before 1 January 1987. Alternatively, Alcan Gove argued that the cause of action accrued when Mr Zabic developed symptoms of mesothelioma after 1 January 1987. The issue, therefore, was whether Mr Zabic was statute barred. The Northern Territory Court of Appeal overturned the decision of the trial judge. The High Court agreed with the Court of Appeal and unanimously dismissed an appeal:

---

124 *Limitation Act 1985* (ACT) s 21C; *Limitation Act 1969* (NSW) s 6A; *Limitation Act 1981* (NT) s 5A; *Limitation of Actions Act 1974* (Qld) s 11A; *Limitation of Actions Act 1958* (Vic) s 27P; *Limitation Act 2005* (WA) s 6A.

125 (2015) 257 CLR 1; [2015] HCA 33.

> [T]he respondent's mesothelial cells were so damaged shortly after inhalation of asbestos
> fibres between 1974 and 1977 as 'inevitably and inexorably' to lead to the eventual
> onset of the malignant mesothelioma … the damage done to the mesothelial cells
> shortly after inhalation was non-negligible compensable damage sufficient to found a
> cause of action and that the subsequently developed malignant mesothelioma was part
> of the damage arising in that accrued cause of action.[126]

The Court also stated:

> [W]ithout more, a risk of developing a compensable personal injury cannot sustain a
> cause of action in negligence for damages for personal injury. It is only when and if the
> risk eventuates that compensable damage is suffered and, therefore, it is only then that
> the cause of action in negligence accrues.[127]

5.5.2   Good Samaritans and volunteers

Good Samaritans are protected from civil suits in all jurisdictions provided the assistance is
provided in good faith and without payment or expectation of payment. It includes advice
provided over the telephone. Immunity will not apply if the act or omission that causes
harm was given before the advice, assistance or care was provided by the good Samaritan.

Volunteers are protected by a limited immunity in some jurisdictions if they are providing
service for a community group or charity in good faith. The civil liability statutes also
introduce protection for food donors from liability for the consumption of the food where
the food 'was donated in good faith for a charitable or benevolent purpose, and with the
intention that the consumer of the food would not have to pay for the food'.[128]

Good Samaritan provisions are intended to allay the concerns of people, particularly
health professionals, about the possibility of liability in negligence arising from giving
assistance in emergencies. Despite the Ipp Panel having no evidence before it of litigation in
these circumstances, many state legislatures opted to include protections for good Samaritans.
Relatively indicative is the *Civil Liability Act 2002* (NSW) which defines a good Samaritan in
s 56 as 'a person who, in good faith and without expectation of payment or other reward,
comes to the assistance of a person who is apparently injured or at risk of being injured'.

The main provisions are set out in Table 5.11.

Table 5.11   Comparative provisions: Good Samaritans and volunteers

Legislation	Good Samaritan section	Volunteer section(s)	Food donor section(s)
Civil Law (Wrongs) Act 2002 (ACT)	5	6–11	11A–11B
Civil Liability Act 2002 (NSW)	57	61	58C
Personal Injuries (Liabilities and Damages) Act 2003 (NT)	8	7	7A
Civil Liability Act 2003 (Qld)	–	39	38A

---

126   Ibid [3] (French CJ, Kiefel, Bell, Keane, Nettle JJ).
127   Ibid [37] (French CJ, Kiefel, Bell, Keane, Nettle JJ).
128   *Civil Liability Act 2002* (NSW) s 58C.

Table 5.11 *(cont.)*

Legislation	Good Samaritan section	Volunteer section(s)	Food donor section(s)
Civil Liability Act 1936 (SA)	74	–	74A
Civil Liability Act 2002 (Tas)	35B	47	35F
Wrongs Act 1958 (Vic)	31B	37	31F
Civil Liability Act 2002 (WA)	5AD	–	–

REVIEW QUESTIONS

(1) The plaintiff has a limited time within which to bring an action in negligence. When does this time start to 'run'?

(2) What is the effect of 'good Samaritan' provisions?

 Guided responses in the eBook

KEY CONCEPTS

• **contributory negligence:** the plaintiff's failure to take care for their own protection, where that failure is a cause of the damage. A successful claim of contributory negligence will result in apportionment of damages.

• **defences to negligence:** once the plaintiff has established the requirements of a case in negligence by establishing that a duty is owed, that it has been breached and that the breach has resulted in damage, the defendant must prove the existence of a relevant defence. Defences to negligence existed at common law, but have been heavily modified by statute.

• **illegality, intoxication or willing engagement:** operate as a defence in dangerous recreational activities in some jurisdictions; in other jurisdictions they may affect the standard of care.

• **statute barred:** a plaintiff's failure to bring proceedings within the time period stipulated by legislation can result in an action being 'statute barred'.

• **voluntary assumption of risk:** occurs where the plaintiff, with knowledge of the risk, voluntarily accepts the risk. This is a complete defence but is not often successfully invoked.

 Complete the multiple-choice questions in the eBook to test your knowledge.

PROBLEM-SOLVING EXERCISES

Exercise 1

Davo, aged 15, and his two mates, Eccs (aged 14) and Baz (aged 11), were skateboarding on the street outside their homes. They had just got to the bottom of a hill and were facing the long climb back up when a car driven by Wokka drew alongside. Wokka's son, BJ, was a good friend of Davo. Davo, Eccs and Baz asked Wokka if they could skitch a ride back up the hill – meaning that they would hang on to the back of the car while Wokka drove. Wokka agreed to do this, as he had done before. While the boys held on, he drove slowly (at 10–20 km/h) up the hill. Halfway up the hill, BJ saw Baz start to wobble, and then he saw him let go of the back of the car and fall on the road. Baz was not wearing a helmet and when he fell, he hit the back of his head, causing a fracture to the occipital region of his skull. Contrecoup injury was caused to his frontal lobe by the 'transmitted forces' in the skull. This damage to his frontal lobe caused injuries affecting his cognition and behaviour, whereas the damage to the occipital region did not cause many problems at all.

What defences are available to Wokka? Disregard any transport accident legislation.

 Guided response in the eBook

Exercise 2

Ahna was turning 10 and her father, Aayush, decided to take her and two of her friends to visit 'Outback Adventures', a two-hectare farmlet just outside of Sydney with activities including a dirt-bike riding track. Ahna told Aayush that she wanted to ride on the dirt bikes. Aayush filled out the paperwork while Ahna and her friends were at the petting zoo. The form stated 'Quad bike riding involves a significant risk of physical harm or personal injury including permanent disability and/or death. Any such injury may result not only from your actions including physical exertion but also from the action, omission or negligence of others.'

As Ahna and her friends approached the quad bike track, there was a sign which said:

> Please be advised that quad biking is an inherently dangerous activity. You are required at all times to ride at a speed which is within your ability and that is suitable for the ground conditions you may experience.
>
> If you decide to go quad bike riding, you are advised that you do so entirely at your own risk.
>
> All riders need to pass our training assessments to qualify to go out on our rides. All instructions given by our guides and staff must be obeyed for the safety and enjoyment of everyone.

Ahna and her friends spent half an hour with an instructor, Jed. He told them that they must follow him at all times, and reiterated that they had to follow his instructions for their own safety. They all 'passed' the training assessment.

After that, they followed the instructor along the quad bike track to the back of the property. They spent an hour travelling around the track. At the end of that period they were told by the instructor to follow him back to the main buildings. The instructor was travelling quite fast. Mindful of Jed's instructions to follow him at all times, Ahna and her friends tried to keep up, but Ahna lost control of her quad bike. She overturned it and was seriously injured.

Assuming that a duty of care existed and has been breached, what defences may be available to Outback Adventures? What further facts do you need to assess this?

 Guided response in the eBook

CHALLENGE YOURSELF

Exercise 1

Sixteen-year-old Cian heard about a 'big party' to be held on Friday night in the neighbouring suburb. He took a bus and arrived at the party at 9 pm. By midnight he realised that none of his friends were coming. He was so embarrassed and unhappy, he had his first alcoholic drink. By 1 am he was mildly drunk. By 2 am he had a new best friend, Aoife, who was 17 and had a P-plate licence. Aoife offered to drive him home. Aoife was also a little drunk and was showing off a bit. She swerved along the road, aiming for the wheelie bins. The first time she did it, she found Cian's obvious fear was so funny that she did it again. She oversteered and ran into a parked car. Cian was seriously injured.

What defences are available to Aoife? Disregard any transport accident legislation and refer only to the tort of negligence.

 Guided response in the eBook

Exercise 2

Janet and Bruce were both 18, but had not yet attained their driver's licences. On Saturday night they were bored and decided to go 'on the town'. Janet's elder brother Harry said that they could use his car if they took something over to a mate in another suburb. Janet, always curious, asked what that 'something' was, and Harry told them it was just a 'bit of meth' (in other words, the drug methamphetamine). Janet said they'd do it 'only if we have some too'. Harry agreed to this. Janet and Bruce, after both of them had used the drug, got into the car and started to drive around Newcastle. Before they got to the 'mate's' house, Janet told Bruce she was feeling a bit woozy, and she thought she might be having a bad reaction to the drug. She wanted Bruce to take over the driving, but he said that he wasn't in the right state. He told Janet to keep on driving and 'she'd be fine'. Janet began to drive erratically, then lost control. The car left the road and overturned, and Bruce suffered serious and permanent injuries. Janet claims that since both she and Bruce were engaged in an 'illegal activity', she should not be liable for Bruce's injuries.

Ignoring the effects of the statutory compensation schemes in each state, assess the relevance of the illegality of the actions in which Janet and Bruce were involved.

 Guided response in the eBook

6

TRESPASS TO THE PERSON

6.1   Introduction

'Trespass' is a generic term encompassing a set of wrongs involving direct, and usually intentional, interference with either the person or property affected. There are three different forms of trespass actions:

- trespass to the person
- trespass to land
- trespass to goods (chattels).

These trespass actions create a number of fundamental common law rights protecting a plaintiff's personal dignity, desire for autonomy, interests in the physical integrity of people's body and the exclusive possession of land and goods. While the common aim of these forms of action is to protect the fundamental common law rights of a person, the ingredients of each tort are quite disparate. In order to fully understand each form of trespass action, we must first briefly consider their origins and their features.

6.2   Historical origins of trespass and relationship with negligence

The law of torts began with the trespass action which evolved from the criminal action for trespass in the early days of common law (ie, the Middle Ages). Torts were developed in England from about the 13th century onwards in the King's common law courts. In the early years of the common law, every action had to be commenced by the issue of a royal writ. A writ was a command on behalf of the King that a case be heard by the Royal Courts. The writ set out the cause of action available to a plaintiff in a set form, known as a 'form of action'.

In order to succeed in an action, medieval plaintiffs had to ensure that the substance of their claim was covered by a standard writ. That means, if the facts of the plaintiff's claim did not fall within one of the recognised writs, the plaintiff had no remedy. The types of actions for which a writ could be issued were limited. *Trespass* and *action on the case* were two principal forms of writ in the early common law.

6.2.1   Trespass

The writ of trespass was applied to deal with forcible, direct and immediate injury to the plaintiff's:

- person
- land – *quare clausum fregit* ('wherefore he broke the close')
- goods – *trespass de bonis asportatis* ('trespass of goods carried').

The various forms of writs of trespass were the predecessors of what are now the actions of battery, assault and false imprisonment. Trespass in the early period was both a crime and a tort and both aspects could be disposed of by the court in one proceeding. This explains the tie between trespass and criminal law. The primary purpose of the writ of trespass was peacekeeping. It was based on the principle that in a trespass action, the defendant was at fault for having acted *vi et armis et contra pacem Domini Regis* ('with force and arms and contrary to the King's peace'). The idea was that if a person could bring an action in relation to a direct interference with their person or property, it would discourage people from taking the law into their own hands and retaliating in a manner that might constitute a breach of the peace.

Trespass actions are actionable per se ('as is'). Consequently, a trespass action can be brought for the trespass itself, without requiring proof that the trespass caused damage. The reason was that the direct interference (eg, use of force or direct invasion of property) involved a breach of the King's peace and was in itself wrongful; thus, it is not necessary that the defendant's conduct resulted in any kind of injury to the plaintiff. For the same reason, and because of the importance the law attaches to the interests protected, rules on the onus of proof require the plaintiff in trespass actions to prove the existence of direct interference, then shift the onus to the defendant to disprove fault or otherwise justify their conduct. In addition, since the rationale behind the writ of trespass was to prevent conduct that would lead to immediate retaliation, the law was interested in the *causal sequence* of events rather than the *intentions* of the defendant in a trespass action. A plaintiff who successfully pleaded and proved the alleged trespass was entitled to recover damages from the defendant.

6.2.2   Action on the case

The writ of *action on the case*, originally referred to as the writ of 'trespass on the case' or simply the 'case', evolved later. It was developed to complement the trespass action in the 14th century, as a remedy for a wide range of wrongs originally not covered by trespass. The writ for action on the case was available for the miscellaneous collection of injuries that were *indirect* and *consequential*. For example, it was invoked by owners of goods against carriers for losing or destroying the goods in the course of transit, by homeowners against neighbours for maintaining a nuisance in the neighbourhood, and by animal owners against veterinarians for incompetent medical treatment.

Unlike trespass, the plaintiff had to prove all the elements, including injury or damage as a result of the interference, as part of the cause of action.

In the 14th century, there was a distinct separation between trespass and actions on the case, and differences between these two forms of action were both procedural and substantive. It was vital for the plaintiffs and their lawyers to differentiate and choose the right form of action in the early days. Choosing an incorrect writ led to the plaintiff's case being 'nonsuited' (ie, abandoned before verdict), and the action would have to be started again with the correct pleading.

6.2.3   Choosing between trespass and case

Against such a background, some guidelines were needed to decide the circumstances in which trespass or case should be brought. By the early 17th century, the prevailing formulation suggested that the existence of directness (ie, a direct causal connection between the defendant's conduct and the interference with the plaintiff's rights) was adopted in practice to mark a line between trespass and the action on the case. A classic explanation in relation to the directness of the interference was given in *Reynolds v Clarke* where Fortescue J stated:

> if a man throws a log into the highway, and in that act it hits me, I may maintain trespass, because it is an immediate wrong; but if as it lies there I tumble over it, and receive an injury I must bring an action upon the case; because it is only prejudicial in consequence, for which originally I could have no action at all.[1]

The difficulties with this broad approach were obvious, especially for cases whose factual situations made it difficult to decide whether the interference was direct or indirect. For example, in *Scott v Shepherd*, the Court held that the defendant's act was direct and not consequential, which meant that the plaintiff's action in trespass was correctly brought.[2] Blackstone J dissented on the ground that the injury was indirect (because the two intervening persons were free agents) and case should have been brought instead.

Case: *Scott v Shepherd* (1773) 96 ER 525

Facts

In October 1770, Shepherd (the defendant) threw a lighted gunpowder squib (firework) onto a market stall owned by Yates. It was picked up and thrown on by two other people, acting in self-preservation, and then exploded in the face of Scott (the plaintiff) putting out one of his eyes. Scott sued Shepherd for trespass and assault for throwing, casting and tossing the lighted squib. The jury returned a verdict in favour of the plaintiff. The defendant appealed.

---

1 (1725) 1 Str 634, 636.
2 (1773) 2 W Bl 892.

Issue

Was the injury to the plaintiff directly caused by the defendant's actions, or by a new force of a third person?

Decision

The Court dismissed the appeal. It held that the injury to the plaintiff was the direct and unlawful act of the defendant who originally threw and intended to throw the squib, and so the defendant was liable in trespass.

Blackstone J stated that he 'took the settled distinction to be that where the injury is immediate, an action of trespass will lie; where it is only consequential, it must be an action on the case' (at 894).

Significance

This is one of the most famous tort cases in history, elucidating the arcane distinction between trespass and action on the case.

Notes

The majority of the King's Bench held that the defendant directly inflicted the plaintiff's injury. The two intermediaries did not act as free agents but, according to De Grey CJ, acted 'under a compulsive necessity for their own safety and self-preservation … the true question is whether the injury is the direct and immediate act of the defendant; and I am of opinion that in this case it is' (at 899). Nares J agreed and stated: 'Being, therefore, unlawful, the defendant was liable to answer for the consequences, be the injury mediate or immediate' (at 893). Blackstone J dissented, arguing that the defendant had committed a trespass only to the stall owner. The intermediate actors had acted on their own judgment and there was no immediate injury passing from the defendant to the plaintiff, without which no action of trespass can be maintained. At the time, the law forbade the plaintiff from suing in both trespass and case (joinder of forms of action), otherwise there would be no remedy for him. The rule against the joinder of forms of action was abolished by the English legislature in 1852.[3]

Question

Why was the appeal in the case of *Scott v Shepherd* eventually dismissed by the Court? What solution would you suggest to the scenario of *Scott v Shepherd*?

    Guided response in the eBook

---

3   *Common Law Procedure Act 1852*, 15 & 16 Vict, c 76 (UK).

With the passage of time, the rigidity of the law in differentiating the forms of action and difficulties in deciding which was correct form of action created hurdles for the plaintiffs and their lawyers. Lawyers challenged the distinction between trespass and case in so-called running down cases on the highway,[4] which were the historical equivalent of today's traffic accident cases. A lawyer in a running down case was confronted with a dilemma because the procedural rules required him to choose from one of the two writs at the outset of litigation; this often meant that the choice had to be made in the absence of critical information that would help identify the proper writ to use.

Developments then occurred in response to this and other potential litigation traps. English common law courts in the 1830s decided to allow any claim of negligently caused injury or damage to be brought under the case writ, regardless of whether the injury involved the direct or indirect application of force.[5] This removed the difficulty over choosing the correct pleading. The old forms of action, including trespass and case, were abolished by the English legislature in the *Supreme Court of Judicature Act 1873*, 36 & 37 Vict, c 66 (UK). As a result the plaintiff only needed to set out the relevant facts in their statement of claim. This is still the position in England and all Australian jurisdictions.[6]

After the removal of the differences in pleading between trespass and actions on the case, the English case law experienced a period of uncertainty in differentiating the types of action during the 19th century. The distinction between direct and consequential injury remains fundamental to the choice of action. Case law developed that trespass can be established only if the injury was direct – either intentional or unintentional. Action on the case would be available where the injury was consequential, even if intentional or where it was direct and unintentional.[7] Furthermore, as highway trespass emerged in England, fault (in the form of either intention or negligence) became a necessary element in all forms of trespass.[8]

A new trend developed in 1959 in England. In *Fowler v Lanning* Diplock J stated that 'trespass to the person does not lie if the injury to the claimant, although the direct consequence of the act of the defendant, was caused unintentionally and without negligence on the defendant's part'.[9] This suggested the existence of the form of 'negligent trespass'. The English Court of Appeal in *Letang v Cooper* judicially abolished negligent trespass.[10]

---

4 For example, cases in which someone was run over by a horse or a horse-drawn cart, or injured in a collision of vehicles: *Leame v Bray* (1803) 102 ER 724; *Hopper v Reeve* (1817) 129 ER 278; *Williams v Holland* (1833) 131 ER 848.

5 *Williams v Holland* (1833) 131 ER 848. For a detailed introduction to the historical development of running down cases see K Barker et al, *The Law of Torts in Australia* (Oxford University Press, 5th ed, 2012) 31.

6 See *Federal Court Rules 1979* (Cth) r 11.2; *Court Procedures Rules 2006* (ACT) r 406; *Uniform Civil Procedure Rules 2005* (NSW) r 14.7; *Supreme Court Rules 1987* (NT) r 13.02; *Uniform Civil Procedure Rules 1999* (Qld) r 149(1); *Supreme Court Civil Rules 2006* (SA) r 98(2); *Supreme Court Rules 2000* (Tas) r 227(1); *Supreme Court (General Civil Procedure) Rules 1996* (Vic) r 13.02; *Rules of the Supreme Court 1971* (WA) O 20 r 8(1).

7 *Holmes v Mather* (1875) LR 10 Ex 261.

8 See, eg, *Stanley v Powell* [1891] 1 QB 86; *Blacker v Waters* (1928) 28 SR (NSW) 406; *McHale v Watson* (1964) 111 CLR 384.

9 [1959] 1 QB 426.

As Denning MR pointed out in *Letang*, the key distinction between trespass and case is the issue of *intention* rather than *directness*. That means, unintentional interferences can no longer give rise to a cause of action in trespass, as the tort of negligence would be the only cause of action; intentional, direct interference to the plaintiff's person may only be brought in trespass.[11] The ruling in this case remains the present position in England. These developments have not been followed in Australia, where it is the *directness* of the interference, rather than *intention*, that determines the form of cause of action.[12] The basic position regarding choice of action or actions to seek a remedy is that *direct* and *intentional* interferences are still dealt with by trespass, while *indirect* and *unintentional* interferences are dealt with by a separate tort: negligence. Nonetheless, there is still room for overlap of the two types of action.

Negligent trespass, as suggested by the High Court's joint judgment in *Williams v Milotin*,[13] continues to exist in Australia,[14] case law suggesting that where direct unintentional injury to the person is complained of, the plaintiff is entitled to sue in trespass or negligence or both.[15]

Case: *Williams v Milotin* (1957) 97 CLR 465

Facts

On 7 May 1952, the plaintiff was riding a bicycle along a public road when he was struck from behind by a motor truck which was being driven by the defendant in a negligent manner. The plaintiff received serious bodily injuries. Relying on s 36 of the *Limitation of Actions Act 1936* (SA), he sued the defendant for damages, alleging that the collision was due to the defendant's negligence, and consequently the action fell within the statutory time period. The defendant pleaded that the collision was trespassory and had occurred more than three years before the

---

10 [1965] 1 QB 232. The case involved a car accident. The defendant, while driving his car negligently, ran over the female plaintiff's leg while she was sunbathing in the grass car park of a hotel. She sought damages on the basis of trespass to the person, as a claim in negligence was time-barred. The English Court of Appeal held that the plaintiff could not recover damages based on trespass to the person, as the defendant's actions were accidental and not intentional.

11 *Letang v Cooper* (1965) 1 QB 232, 239 (Lord Denning MR), 242 (Danckwerts LJ) and endorsed in *Stubbings v Webb* [1993] AC 498, 507 (Lord Griffiths).

12 *Williams v Milotin* (1957) 97 CLR 465; *Blacker v Waters* (1928) 28 SR (NSW) 406; *Exchange Hotel Ltd v Murphy* [1947] SASR 112.

13 (1957) 97 CLR 465, 473.

14 See, eg, *Ross v Warrick Howard (Australia) Pty Ltd* (1986) 4 SR (WA) 1; *Parsons v Partridge* (1992) 111 ALR 257, 259–60 (Morling CJ); *New South Wales v Knight* [2002] NSWCA 392; *Cooper v Neubert* [2017] TASSC 33.

15 See *Venning v Chin* (1974) 10 SASR 299, 308, where the Supreme Court of South Australia considered the English position and declared itself bound by the High Court's decision. Note, however, the obiter comments of the High Court in *Hackshaw v Shaw* (1984) 155 CLR 614, 667–8. Cases involving the countenancing of negligent trespass include: *West v Peters* (1976) 18 SASR 338; *Elliot v Barnes* (1951) 51 SR (NSW) 179; *Kruber v Grzesiak* [1963] VR 621; *McHale v Watson* (1964) 111 CLR 384; *Tsouvalla v Bini* [1966] SASR 157; *James v Harrison* (1977) 18 ACTR 36, 38; *Horkin v North Melbourne Football Club Social Club* [1983] 1 VR 153, 157; *Ross v Warrick Howard (Australia) Pty Ltd* (1986) 4 SR (WA) 1; *Platt v Nutt* (1988) 12 NSWLR 231; *Wilson v Horne* [1999] Aust Torts Reports 81-504, 65790–1 (Cox CJ); *New South Wales v Knight* [2002] NSWCA 392.

institution of the action; the action was therefore barred by the same Act. Sections 35 and 36 of the Act provided as follows:

> 35. The following actions namely: ... (c) actions which formerly might have been brought in the form of actions called actions on the case and ... (k) actions for libel malicious prosecution arrest or seduction and any other actions which would formerly have been brought in the form of actions called trespass on the case: shall, save as otherwise provided in this Act, be commenced within six years next after the cause of such action accrued but not after.
>
> 36. All actions for assault, trespass to the person, menace, battery, wounding or imprisonment shall be commenced within three years next after the cause of such accrued but not after.

Issue

Could the plaintiff bring an action in negligence when the limitation period for trespass had expired?

Decision

The Full Court of the Supreme Court of South Australia declared that the plaintiff's action was not barred by s 36. The defendant then appealed to the High Court. The High Court decided that the plaintiff could frame his cause of action not only as a negligent trespass to the person, but also in the tort of negligence. The Court stressed:

> The two causes of action are not the same now and they never were. When you speak of a cause of action you mean the essential ingredients in the title to the right which it is proposed to enforce. The essential ingredients in an action of negligence for personal injuries include the special or particular damage – it is the gist of the action – and the want of due care. Trespass to the person includes neither, but it does include direct violation of the protection which the law throws round the person ... It happens in this case that the actual facts will or may fulfil the requirements of each cause of action. But that does not mean that within the provisions of the *Limitation of Actions Act 1936* ss 35 and 36, only one 'cause of action' is vested in the plaintiff. If he had chosen to discard negligence and special or particular damage as ingredients in his cause of action and rely instead on the elements amounting to trespass or assault, something might be said for the defendant's reliance on s 36. But not otherwise [at 474].

Significance

This case is the leading authority confirming that negligent trespass remains in Australia. It confirms that in the absence of intention, a violation may be actionable as either trespass or in the tort of negligence.

Question

What is the main implication of the High Court decision in *Williams v Milotin*?

    Guided response in the eBook

REVIEW QUESTIONS

(1) Can a plaintiff bring an action in negligence after the limitation period for trespass has expired? Explain why or why not.

(2) If a case with a similar scenario to *Scott v Shepherd* arose today, how could the plaintiff frame the statement of claim against the defendant?

 Guided responses in the eBook

6.3   The trespass action

As we noted earlier, trespass is a generic term which covers trespass to the person, trespass to land and trespass to goods. It was the remedy for all direct injury whether intentional or unintentional, while action on the case covered the situation where the injury was consequential or indirect. All forms of trespass torts share a number of distinctive features:

(1) They involve a direct interference with the plaintiff's person, land or goods.

(2) The defendant is at fault.

(3) They are actionable per se.

(4) The onus of proof differs upon the trespass being classified as 'highway' or 'non-highway'.[16] We shall deal with each feature in turn.

6.3.1   Direct interference

The trespass action is only available in circumstances where the plaintiff can show that the interference with the plaintiff's person, land or goods is a direct consequence of the defendant's voluntary act. Directness has long been required by the trespass action. We touched on this feature while discussing the historical methods of choosing between trespass and case (see Section 6.2.3). The requirement of directness is less controversial in some of the most obvious instances of trespass actions (eg, slapping someone's face or stepping onto someone's land without authorisation). However, in some marginal cases, it would be difficult to determine the directness of the interference. For example, in *Hutchins v Maughan* the defendant laid poisoned baits on his unfenced land and warned the plaintiff not to cross the land because of this.[17] The plaintiff thought the defendant was bluffing and brought his sheep and sheep dogs onto the land. The plaintiff's dogs picked up the baits and died as a result. The police magistrate gave judgment for the plaintiff for this trespass claim

---

16 Highway trespass can be broadly understood as trespass on or to land adjoining a highway. The importance of differentiating highway trespass and non-highway trespass is attached to the onus of proof. After 1959, trespass to the person on the highway no longer differs from trespass committed anywhere else and the plaintiff bears the burden of proof. Australian law, through *Venning v Chin* (1974) 10 SASR 299, held that in the case of a highway trespass the burden of proof of fault, whether in the form of intentional or negligent conduct, lay on the plaintiff, while in non-highway trespass the defendant had the burden of proof.

17 [1947] VLR 131.

and awarded him damages for the loss of the dogs. The defendant appealed. The Supreme Court of Victoria held that trespass did not lie, as the injury was consequential upon the defendant's act and not immediately or directly occasioned by it. Citing *Scott v Shepherd*[18] and *Leame v Bray*,[19] Herring CJ explained that 'it should rather be regarded merely as consequential upon it (the defendant's act) and not as directly or immediately occasioned by it. And so trespass does not lie in respect of defendant's act in laying the baits'.[20]

Immediacy has been thought to be one possible means to establish directness. The most frequently cited case on this point is *Reynolds v Clarke* in which the log on the highway example was used to explain the concept.[21] Nevertheless, it is worth noting that cases concerning trespass to land (see Chapter 7) show that immediacy is not always necessary where there are no intervening causes between the act and its consequences. The feature of *direct interference* will be revisited when the elements of the respective forms of trespass action are examined.

6.3.2 Fault of the defendant

In trespass, the act complained of must have been done with intention or with a lack of reasonable care, generally referred to as 'fault'. Both intention and negligence are sufficient to satisfy fault for the purposes of trespass.

6.3.2.1 Intention

With respect to intention, the defendant only has to intend the interference. This means that the defendant must have intended to bring about the alleged interference with the plaintiff's person or property, or must have been aware that such a consequence would occur. The motive of the defendant is irrelevant.[22] It is sufficient if the defendant should have known that the consequences of the act were certain to happen and persisted in acting.

However, the defendant's act must be voluntary for it to be regarded as intentional. That means it must be directed by the will or conscious mind of the defendant. Therefore, automatic conduct that occurs while sleepwalking, or involuntary bodily actions during an epileptic fit, are not seen as blameworthy. For example, in *Smith v Stone* it was held that a defendant did not commit an actionable trespass by going onto the plaintiff's land involuntarily.[23] The rule was applied in the High Court case of *Public Transport Commission (NSW) v Perry*.[24] In that case, while awaiting the arrival of a train, a passenger involuntarily fell onto the rail tracks after suffering an epileptic fit. The majority of the High Court held that there was no trespass to land as the passenger's presence on the premises came about involuntarily.[25] Older cases often described this as an inevitable accident which would not be actionable in trespass.[26]

---

18 (1773) 96 ER 525 (Blackstone J).
19 (1803) 102 ER 724 (Le Blane J).
20 [1947] VLR 131, 134.
21 (1725) 1 Str 634.
22 *Murray v McMurchy* [1949] 2 DLR 442.
23 (1647) 82 ER 533.
24 (1977) 137 CLR 107.
25 See also *Morris v Marsden* [1952] 1 All ER 925, 928.
26 *Stanley v Powell* [1891] 1 QB 86.

Case: *Stanley v Powell* [1891] 1 QB 86

Facts

The defendant (Powell), who was a member of a shooting party, fired at a pheasant, but one of the pellets from his gun glanced off the bough of a tree and accidentally wounded the plaintiff (Stanley), another member of the shooting party.

Issue

Could the defendant be held liable in trespass?

Decision

The jury held that the defendant was not liable. If the defendant's act had been wilful or negligent, the defendant would have been liable. Denman J held that the defendant could not be liable in trespass, stating:

> no decision was quoted, nor do I think that any can be found which goes so far as to hold, that if A is injured by a shot from a gun fired at a bird by B, an action of trespass will necessarily lie, even though B is proved to have fired the gun without negligence and without intending to injure the plaintiff or to shoot in his direction.[27]

Significance

This case reflects the principle that there is no liability in trespass where the trespassory act was committed without fault by the defendant.

Question

How has the case *Stanley v Powell* impacted subsequent court decisions in Australia?

 Guided response in the eBook

6.3.2.2   Lack of care

With respect to 'lack of care' or 'recklessness', a person who acts recklessly and thereby commits a direct interference may be liable in trespass. Recklessness exists where the consequences of a defendant's act were so likely that the defendant should have foreseen them, but the defendant consciously disregarded any substantial risks flowing from the act. As Spigelman CJ stated in *Nationwide News Pty Ltd v Naidu*, 'a test of reckless indifference to a result will, in [the context of the tort of wilful infliction of harm], satisfy the requirement of intention'.[28] Intention and recklessness are subjective states of mind. In this aspect they are distinguishable from negligence, which is determined objectively.

As negligent trespass exists in Australia, negligence is therefore a sufficient state of mind to satisfy the fault requirement for trespass.[29] This means that if the defendant acted with less

---

27   Ibid 88.
28   (2007) 71 NSWLR 471, [80].
29   *Williams v Milotin* (1957) 97 CLR 465; *New South Wales v Ouhammi* (2019) 101 NSWLR 160.

care than a reasonable person would in the same situation, the defendant was at fault and the trespassory action was blameworthy.

6.3.3   Actionable per se

All trespass actions are actionable per se. This means that for the tort to be actionable, the plaintiff does not have to show that they suffered any loss or damage as a result of the interference. The main reason is that trespass actions protect people's fundamental common law rights of bodily integrity or property interests, and the law presumes damage on the direct interference with these rights.[30] Such loss or damage will, however, be taken into account in awarding damages to the plaintiff.

6.3.4   Onus of proof

When the onus of proof in a trespass action is considered, the general rule is that the plaintiff is only required to prove that the trespassory act occurred (eg, the fact of contact, or the threat or deprivation of liberty). Then, the onus shifts to the defendant to disprove fault.[31] This shift in the onus derives from the deterrence function of the tort and reflects the right-based nature of the tort.

An exception to this rule has developed with respect to the highway cases (ie, cases involving trespasses on or to land adjoining a highway). In such cases, the plaintiff bears the onus of proving fault on the part of the defendant.[32] The rationale for this exception is that, again, there have been developments in the English law which have not been followed in Australia. The English law has abolished the distinction between highway and non-highway cases. In the English case of *Fowler v Lanning*, the Court of Appeal held that the plaintiff must show either intention or negligence in all trespass cases.[33] This was confirmed in *Letang v Cooper* and continues to be the current position in English law.[34] However, it appears that in Australian law the plaintiff will only bear the onus of proving fault in a highway case.[35]

Case: *McHale v Watson* (1964) 111 CLR 384

Facts

The defendant, a 12-year-old boy, threw a sharpened piece of steel which hit the eye of a 9-year-old girl, with whom the boy was playing. The girl's parents sued the defendant in trespass and negligence, and the boy's parents in negligence.

---

30   *Nicholls v Ely Beet Sugar Factory Ltd* [1936] Ch 343, 349–50 (Lord Wright MR).
31   See the High Court's decision in *McHale v Watson* (1964) 111 CLR 384, which confirms that the onus in a non-highway case lies on the defendant to prove the fault (intention or negligence) in respect of a trespass. See also *Hackshaw v Shaw* (1984) 155 CLR 614; *Anton v White* [2001] NSWCA 66.
32   *Holmes v Mather* (1875) LR 10 Ex 261.
33   [1959] 1 QB 426.
34   [1965] 1 QB 232.
35   *Venning v Chin* (1974) 10 SASR 299; *New South Wales v Ouhammi* (2019) 101 NSWLR 160 (in which the Appellate Court of New South Wales had to decide which party carries the burden of proof where the tort of battery has been alleged).

Issue

Did the plaintiff bear the burden of proof in showing fault?

Decision

Windeyer J in the High Court (sitting alone) held that in the action in trespass, the onus of proof is on the defendant. On this view, if the defendant could not prove on the balance of probabilities that he did not intend to hit the girl and that he was not negligent in throwing the steel, he would be liable for the trespassory actions. The Court held that the defendant was not negligent. When explaining the onus of proof, Windeyer J stated (at 388):

> But the question remains, is it for the plaintiff to establish that the missile with which she was hit was thrown with intent to hit her or so negligently that it did so – or is it for the defendant who threw it to prove an absence of intent and negligence on his part? I think the latter view is correct.

The plaintiff appealed, but the High Court in the appellate case, *McHale v Watson* (1966) 115 CLR 199, mainly dealt with the standard of care to be expected of a junior (see Sections 3.2.2.1 and 5.2.2.2).

Significance

This case reflected the Australian position regarding the onus of proof in a trespass action. In a non-highway case, the onus of proof lies on the defendant (to disprove fault).

Question

Why did the High Court in *McHale v Watson* hold that in the action in trespass, the onus of proof is on the defendant?

 Guided response in the eBook

REVIEW QUESTIONS

(1) Explain the onus of proof in a trespass action.

(2) How do you understand 'fault' as an element of the trespass action?

 Guided responses in the eBook

6.4   Trespass to the person

It has long been recognised that, in most societies, the law places the highest value on the individual's bodily integrity. Therefore, it is understandable that one of the earliest remedies provided by tort law was for forcible wrongs against the person, by the writ of trespass. Interference, no matter how slight, with a person's civil right to 'security of the person, and self-determination in relation to his own body, constitutes trespass to the person'.[36] This section deals with the tort of trespass to the person as well as three nominate torts under this *form* of action (see Figure 6.1):

- battery (unlawful physical touching)
- assault (an apprehension or threat of unlawful touching)
- false imprisonment (unlawful confinement or restraint).[37]

Figure 6.1   Trespass to the person

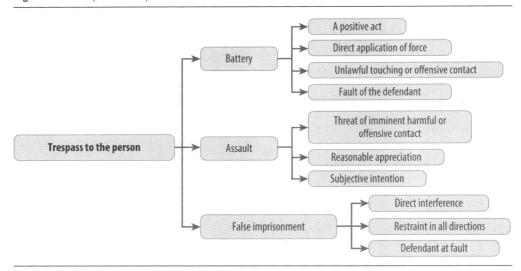

These torts are all descended from the ancient writ of trespass and each has its own distinctive focal point. A straightforward example of a battery is a deliberate punch to someone's nose. The idea of an assault is captured by a situation in which one person points a gun at another who is standing nearby and threatens to shoot him. Deliberately locking someone in a room against their will is a typical instance of false imprisonment.

36 JF Clerk, MA Jones and WHB Lindsell, *Clerk & Lindsell on Torts* (Sweet & Maxwell, 21st ed, 2015) ch 15, s 1.

37 As a preliminary matter of terminology, trespass to the person is a *form* of action, but assault, battery and false imprisonment are *causes* of action. 'Cause of action' can be defined as a factual situation that entitles one person to obtain a legal remedy in court from another person: see BA Garner and HC Black, *Black's Law Dictionary* (West, 9th ed, 2009) 215 ('cause of action').

6.4.1   Battery

The tort of battery occurs when the defendant commits an intentional or negligent act which directly causes physical contact with the person of the plaintiff without their consent. The interests protected by battery include 'physical integrity as well as personal dignity'.[38] Often the tort of battery is committed along with the tort of assault, which as we will see involves the apprehension by the plaintiff of an imminent battery. However, it is possible for the defendant to commit the tort of battery only. The following are some recognised examples of battery:

- striking a horse so it throws its rider[39]
- throwing a firework that is passed on by several parties until it hits and injures a person[40]
- cutting someone's hair against their will, or without their consent[41]
- shining the flashlight of a camera in the eyes of a hospital patient, thereby causing him injury[42]
- hitting someone on the head without causing any injury[43]
- spitting in someone's face[44]
- pulling a chair from a person so that they are thrown to the floor and injured.[45]

The elements of battery include:

- a positive act
- direct application of force
- unlawful touching or offensive contact
- fault of the defendant.

6.4.1.1   A positive act

The interference complained of in a battery must be a positive and affirmative act, not a passive act or omission. For example, in *Innes v Wylie* the plaintiff alleged that the defendant, a policeman, prevented him from entering a room by standing in the doorway, and that this constituted battery.[46] However, the Court held that the defendant had stood 'entirely passive like a door or a wall put to prevent the plaintiff from entering the room' and that this could not amount to battery.[47]

This will not be disputed in most cases as it will be clear that the interference caused was either positive or passive. However, a failure to act in some cases may be nevertheless regarded by the law as a positive act. For example, in *Fagan v Commissioner of Metropolitan Police*, the defendant (Fagan) was instructed by a police officer to park his car to answer questions.[48] The defendant accidentally drove the vehicle onto the police officer's foot.

---

38 *Stingel v Clark* (2006) 226 CLR 442; [2006] HCA 37, [57] (Gummow J). See also *Williams v Milotin* (1957) 97 CLR 465, 474; *Collins v Wilcock* (1984) 3 All ER 374; *Cooper v Neubert* [2017] TASSC 33.
39 *Dodwell v Burford* (1669) 86 ER 703.
40 *Scott v Shepherd* (1773) 96 ER 525.
41 *Forde v Skinner* (1830) 4 C & P 239; *Coffey v Queensland* [2012] QSC 186.
42 *Kaye v Robertson* [1991] FSR 62.
43 See *Battiato v Lagana* [1992] 2 Qd R 234.
44 *R v Cotesworth* (1704) 87 ER 928; *Majindi v Northern Territory* (2012) 31 NTLR 150.
45 *Hopper v Reeve* (1817) 129 ER 278. See also *Garratt v Dailey*, 279 P 2d 1091 (Wash, 1955).
46 (1844) 174 ER 800.
47 Ibid [263].
48 [1969] 1 QB 439.

Only after being asked several times to remove it did the defendant move the wheel off the plaintiff's foot. The defendant appealed his assault conviction on the ground that his failure to move the car was an omission. The Court held that the action of the appellant may have been initially unintentional, but from the moment he became aware of his wheel resting on the policeman's foot, the action could not be regarded as mere omission or inactivity.[49] In this case, both the driving of the car onto the policeman's foot and the failure to remove the car were thought to be part of one continuous positive act.

In addition, the positive act must be voluntary in the sense that it must be 'directed by the defendant's conscious mind'.[50]

6.4.1.2   Direct application of force

As a trespass action, battery requires that the interference with the plaintiff's person is direct. In other words, the contact with the plaintiff's person should be the immediate result of the defendant's action. All the general rules concerning directness in trespass claims apply in battery. In *Carter v Walker*, the third plaintiff arrived in the immediate aftermath of a physical altercation between two police officers, his elderly mother (second plaintiff) and his brother (first plaintiff), but he did not directly witness that altercation.[51] The third plaintiff claimed in battery for his nervous shock. The Victorian Court of Appeal held that the third plaintiff did not have a cause of action in battery as he had not been directly harmed by the actions of the defendants; nor did he have any physical contact with the defendants. Buchanan, Ashley and Weinberg JJA noted that 'directness has been a requirement of [battery] in English, and then Australian, law. The requirement of directness, and its role in the development of the action on the case, has often been explained'.[52]

Although the contact must be the direct result of the defendant's act, the defendant need not actually touch the plaintiff, or even be present at the time of the contact, to commit a battery. For example, the defendant may not touch the plaintiff at all, but poke the plaintiff with a long pole or stretch a wire across the sidewalk as the plaintiff approaches, causing the plaintiff to fall. And, as in *R v Cotesworth*[53] and *Majindi v Northern Territory*,[54] spitting at someone may constitute a battery. Although no part of the defendant's body touched the plaintiffs in these examples, the defendants imposed an unauthorised *contact* on the plaintiffs.

Battery may be committed by using instruments (eg, a gun or gardening shears)[55] or animals. In *Haystead v Chief Constable of Derbyshire*, the defendant hit a mother in the face as she held her child.[56] As a result of the punches, the child fell from his mother's arms and hit his head on the floor. The Court held that a battery could be inflicted even though the force was applied indirectly. In *Darby v Director of Public Prosecutions (NSW)*, the Court held that a police dog handler's action in allowing his police dog repeated bunting and

49   Ibid 442 (Lord Parker CJ, Bridge and James JJ).
50   *Morris v Marsden* [1952] 1 All ER 925, 927.
51   (2010) 32 VR 1.
52   Ibid [216].
53   (1704) 87 ER 928.
54   (2012) 31 NTLR 150.
55   See, eg, *Croucher v Cachia* (2016) 95 NSWLR 117 where an altercation between two neighbours led to one being seriously injured by the gardening shears wielded by the other.
56   (2000) 3 All ER 890.

nudging of a person's genital area could amount to battery.[57] Giles JA pointed out that the dog in the case was an instrument through which battery could be committed.[58]

6.4.1.3   Unlawful touching or offensive contact

Unlawful touching (or offensive contact) is the element that distinguishes battery from other trespass actions. For a battery to occur, the defendant's act must be offensive – at least unwelcome or unwanted – contact with the plaintiff's person. In earlier times it was said that the application of force had to be hostile: 'the least touching of another in anger is a battery'.[59] That means, no matter how slight or trivial the contact is, it may give rise to a battery if the contact was of a hostile nature. Malice, ill will, anger, threatening conduct or touching the plaintiff while speaking unfriendly words are all indicators of 'hostility'.

HINTS AND TIPS

When is a touching to be called hostile? In the English Court of Appeal case *Wilson v Pringle* [1987] QB 237 Croom-Johnson LJ said (at 252–3):

> In our view, the authorities lead one to the conclusion that in a battery there must be an intentional touching or contact in one form or another of the plaintiff by the defendant. That touching must be proved to be a hostile touching. That still leaves unanswered the question 'when is a touching to be called hostile?' Hostility cannot be equated with ill will or malevolence. It cannot be governed by the obvious intention shown in acts like punching, stabbing or shooting. It cannot be solely governed by an expressed intention, although that may be strong evidence. But the element of hostility, in the sense in which it is now to be considered, must be a question of fact for the tribunal of fact ... Where the immediate act of touching does not itself demonstrate hostility, the plaintiff should plead the facts which are said to do so.

Indeed, many batteries, such as domestic violence, physical abuse and rape, will be hostile in this sense. However, touching that is not hostile can also give rise to battery on an equal basis. A typical example is a doctor performing medical treatment without the patient's consent, even if the treatment was performed to save the patient's life.[60] In *Re F (Mental Patient: Sterilisation)*, Lord Goff referred to various potential batteries which entail no hostility:

> [A] 'prank that gets out of hand', 'an over-friendly slap on the back', or 'surgical treatment by a surgeon who mistakenly thinks that the patient has consented to it', all these things may transcend the bounds of lawfulness, without being characterised as hostile.[61]

---

57   (2014) 61 NSWLR 558.
58   Ibid [73].
59   *Cole v Turner* (1704) 90 ER 958.
60   *Collins v Wilcock* (1984) 3 All ER 374 (Lord Goff).
61   [1990] 2 AC 1, 73.

Case law has suggested that 'hostility' is not essential in the modern parlance of battery.[62] Instead, battery should be broadly understood as touching with a lack of the plaintiff's consent (whether express or implied). This means that if the contact is lawful and consented to, there is no battery.[63]

The absence of consent to the application of force is not clearly stated as an element of common law battery.[64] In English law, the absence of consent is an element of the tort itself, so that the plaintiff must prove that they did not consent to the contact.[65] However, the position is not the same in Australia. Australian courts take the view that consent is a defence (see Chapter 8); thus, the defendant bears the onus to prove that the plaintiff did consent to the offensive contact.[66] The High Court endorsed the principle of personal inviolability in *Secretary, Department of Health and Community Services v JWB* ('*Marion's Case*'), where McHugh J said:

> In England, the onus is on the plaintiff to prove lack of consent. That view has the support of some academic writers in Australia, but it is opposed by other academic writers in Australia. It is opposed by Canadian authority. It is also opposed by Australian authority. Notwithstanding the English view, I think that the onus is on the defendant to prove consent ... The contrary view is inconsistent with a person's right of bodily integrity. Other persons do not have the right to interfere with an individual's body unless he or she proves lack of consent to the interference.[67]

However, as an exception to the tort of battery, bodily contact that arises from the exigencies of everyday life is not legally actionable. For example, if a person gets into a crowded lift or is brushed against by another person in a crowd, the touching is part of ordinary life and will not be deemed an action of battery.[68] Quoting *Collins v Wilcock*,[69] the High Court Justices in *Marion's Case* accepted that in modern society there needs to be 'a general exception [to liability in battery] embracing all physical contact which is generally acceptable in the ordinary conduct of daily life'.[70] *Rixon v Star City Pty Ltd* further explains the circumstances when touching another's person is or is not a lawful touching.[71] In the case, touching the plaintiff's shoulder to gain his attention was found not to be an unlawful touching.

---

62 See, eg, *Rixon v Star City Pty Ltd* (2001) 53 NSWLR 98. There is some doubt about whether it is still true that the touching must be 'in anger' for it to constitute a battery in England: see *Wilson v Pringle* [1987] QB 237, 252–3 (Croom-Johnson LJ). While the case law suggests that hostility is not an essential ingredient of battery, the point has been made that 'hostility or hostile intent may convert what would otherwise be an ordinary incident of social intercourse into a battery': *Boughey v The Queen* (1986) 161 CLR 10, 24–5 (Mason, Wilson and Deane JJ).

63 *McNamara v Duncan* (1971) 45 FLR 152; *Pallante v Stadiums Pty Ltd* [1976] VR 331; *Murphy v Culhane* [1977] QB 94.

64 See, eg, *Christopherson v Bare* (1848) 11 QB 473; *Carter v Walker* (2010) 32 VR 1, [215]; *Secretary, Department of Health and Community Services v JWB* (1992) 175 CLR 218, 311 (McHugh J) ('*Marion's Case*').

65 *Freeman v Home Office (No 2)* [1984] QB 524.

66 See, eg, *McNamara v Duncan* (1971) 45 FLR 152, further discussed in Chapter 8.

67 (1992) 175 CLR 218, 310.

68 *Campbell v Samuels* (1980) 23 SASR 389.

69 (1984) 3 All ER 374, 378.

70 (1992) 175 CLR 218, 233 (Mason CJ, Dawson, Toohey and Gaudron JJ).

71 (2001) 53 NSWLR 98.

Case: *Rixon v Star City Pty Ltd* (2001) 53 NSWLR 98

Facts

The plaintiff, Brian Rixon, was identified playing roulette in the defendant's casino. At the time, the plaintiff was the subject of an exclusion order issued by the defendant under the *Casino Control Act 1992* (NSW). One of the defendant's employees approached the plaintiff and placed his hand on the plaintiff's shoulder, asking him to accompany the employee to an interview room. The plaintiff was detained for approximately 1.5 hours in the room while waiting for the police to arrive. The plaintiff sued the defendant for unlawful arrest, assault and false imprisonment.

Issue

Did the touching without anger or hostile attitude constitute battery?

Decision

The trial judge rejected the plaintiff's claims of assault and battery because the defendant's employee who touched the plaintiff 'lacked the requisite intention in relation to assault and the requisite anger or hostile attitude in relation to battery' (at 107). The actions for false imprisonment and unlawful arrest also failed as the defendant (Star City) acted within the scope of its legislatively conferred power in detaining the plaintiff (Rixon).

The Court of Appeal affirmed these findings, but offered different reasons. Sheller JA (with whom Priestley and Heydon JJA agreed) followed Lord Goff's judgments in *Collins v Wilcock* (1984) 3 All ER 374 and *Re F (Mental Patient: Sterilisation)* [1990] 2 AC 1, reiterating the fundamental principle that 'every person's body is inviolate, and that any touching of another person, however slight [,] may amount to a battery' (at [112], [114]). In the meantime he emphasised some important exceptions, including those special instances where the control or constraint is lawful and a broader exception has been created to allow for the exigencies of everyday life. Thus the conduct of the defendant's employee in the circumstances was generally acceptable in the ordinary conduct of daily life. The appeal was dismissed.

Significance

This case refers to 'the fundamental principle, plain and incontestable, that every person's body is inviolate, and any touching of another person, however slight, may amount to battery' (at 112–13). It also confirmed an important exception that implied consent is a defence to battery (eg, hand shaking at a party, a friendly slap on the back) and that 'physical contact [is] generally acceptable in the ordinary conduct of daily life' (at 113).

Question

To what extent is the element of hostility relevant in an action for battery?

 Guided response in the eBook

It is worth noting that knowledge of the contact is not an essential element of battery. The plaintiff need not be aware of the interference at the time it is committed. It may, therefore, be battery to move or kiss a sleeping girl without consent. The rule has also been confirmed by some sport-related battery cases, where the plaintiff knew that the offensive acts or the injuries may occur during the game.[72] To establish the tort of battery, the plaintiff must show evidence of the contact, or evidence of those who saw the contact take place. If witnesses can testify that the act took place, a battery against the defendant is established. A defendant who does not know the contact has actually taken place may still be liable for battery. For example, a defendant in a car who ran down the plaintiff believing the object was not a person might incur liability in battery.[73]

6.4.1.4   Fault of the defendant

The element of fault is common to all trespass actions, as discussed in Section 6.3.2. As already seen, in battery the defendant's act must have been intentional or negligent.[74] While intention is considered, any of three types of intent on the defendant's part can suffice for a battery:

(1)   a wilful intent to apply force to the plaintiff

(2)   a reckless indifference as to the plaintiff suffering the application of force

(3)   the negligent application of force.

Wilful intent is the most common type of fault in battery. For example, in *Collins v Wilcock*,[75] the police constable deliberately touched the plaintiff's arm and the wilful intent of that sort was obvious. In battery, intention is judged solely by looking at the consequences of the act. Therefore, if the defendant intended to batter someone, it does not matter if they accidentally hit the plaintiff, rather than the person they intended to hit. What does matter is whether the consequences suffered by the plaintiff were intended by the defendant.[76] If the answer to this question is 'yes', the defendant's behaviour will constitute battery. Finally, it should be borne in mind that the requisite intent on the defendant's part is to deliberately apply force to the plaintiff, rather than an intent to cause harm or injury to the plaintiff.

Recklessness may suffice in certain, less usual instances. That is, if the contact was the result of the defendant's reckless disregard or lack of care, fault could be established.[77] So, the defendant should be liable for battery if he kicks out at random and happens to connect with the plaintiff.[78]

---

72   See, eg, *Sibley v Milutinovic* (1990) Aust Torts Reports 81-013;ʻ*Canterbury Bankstown Rugby League Football Club Ltd v Rogers* [1993] Aust Torts Reports 81-246.

73   *Law v Visser* [1961] Qd R 46; D Mendelson, *The New Law of Torts* (Oxford University Press, 3rd ed, 2014) 134.

74   *Cole v Turner* (1704) 90 ER 958; *Exchange Hotel Ltd v Murphy* [1947] SASR 112.

75   (1984) 3 All ER 374, 378.

76   See, eg, *Giumelli v Johnston* (1991) Aust Torts Reports 81-085 where the Court held that the defendant's failure to keep his elbow down and his jumping motion in contravention of the rules suggested that his actions were intended to cause bodily harm to the plaintiff, or that he knew or ought to have known, that such harm was likely to follow from his actions.

77   *Carter v Walker* (2010) 32 VR 1, [215].

78   *R v Venna* [1976] QB 421.

As noted in Section 6.2.3, negligent trespass is recognised in Australia. Negligent battery could therefore be established where the act of the defendant was not proved to have been either intentional, reckless or negligent.[79] Negligent battery is a tort only, whereas intentional battery is both a tort and a crime. A feature of negligent battery, pointed out by the Court in *Carter v Walker*, is that it 'maintained the requirement of directness, but that it accommodated negligent rather than intentional acts in the sense that the defendant's act, though intended, was careless with respect to contact with the plaintiff'.[80] In negligent battery, while the burden of proof is still based on the civil standard of the balance of probabilities, it must reflect the seriousness of the allegation. It has been generally accepted that, in negligent battery (except in highway cases), it is for the defendant to prove that there was no fault on their part to avoid liability.[81]

Case: *New South Wales v Ouhammi* (2019) 101 NSWLR 160

Facts

Mr Ouhammi (the respondent) was arrested and held in a holding cell by police while he was heavily intoxicated. When a senior constable opened the holding cell door, the respondent approached the door. The senior constable rushed to close the door, which caught and severed the respondent's thumb, resulting in a partial amputation. The respondent sued the constable's employer, the State of New South Wales (the appellant), alleging assault, battery and negligence. The trail judge held that the State was vicariously liable and awarded damages of $82 000 on the basis that 'the closing of the door on Mr Ouhammi's thumb was a battery, and that the defendant had failed to negative fault' (at [51] per Brereton JA). The State appealed. The NSW Court of Appeal had to determine which party bears the onus of proof with respect to fault in the case of non-intentional battery (where intention to cause injury could not be established).

Issue

Which party should bear the onus of proof in an allegation of non-intentional battery?

Decision

When the fault element in the tort of negligent battery is considered, Brereton JA agreed with Simpson AJA, holding that the onus of negativing fault is borne by the defendant (at [54]). The appellant judges unanimously accepted that, except in highway cases, a defendant will be excused from liability of battery if the violation was 'utterly without fault' (at [15]), and the onus of establishing this lies on the defendant. It is not the case that the plaintiff needs to prove negligence for the purposes of establishing a cause of action in the tort of battery. Brereton JA stated:

---

79 See C Sappideen and P Vines (eds), *Fleming's The Law of Torts* (Lawbook Co, 10th ed, 2011) [2.20].
80 (2010) 32 VR 1, [215] (9).
81 See, eg, Gummow J in *Stingel v Clark* (2006) 226 CLR 442; [2006] HCA 37, [47]; *New South Wales v Ouhammi* (2019) 101 NSWLR 160.

Thus – leaving aside highway accident case ... at least before the CLA, the position in New South Wales was that:

(1) neither intention nor negligence was part of the cause of action in battery;

(2) however, a defendant would be excused from liability if it could show that the violation was utterly without fault on its part; and

(3) this required more than negativing negligence in the sense of a failure to use reasonable care and skill, and involved (at the least) proof that the defendant's act was involuntary, and/or that the exercise of ordinary care and caution on the defendant's part could not possibly have prevented the physical contact [at [102]–[103]].

Significance

It reiterated the general law principle that, except in highway cases, it is the defendant who bears the onus of negativing fault where the tort of battery is alleged.

Question

Who bears the onus of proof in a negligent battery or non-intentional battery allegation?

 Guided response in the eBook

HINTS AND TIPS

Originally, trespass simply required that the act of the defendant be voluntary, and it is for the defendant to argue that it was not in order to jump out of liability. However, as the tort of negligence evolved, trespass actions recognised a defence that the alleged contact or threat was neither intended nor negligent. Therefore, the modern form of trespass actions, such as assault, battery and trespass to land and goods (see Chapter 7), effectively requires not only that the defendant's act be voluntary, but also that the fiscal contact or threat be either intentional or negligent (ie, the defendant was at fault).

6.4.2   Assault

The tort of assault occurs when the defendant, by an intentional (or negligent) act, directly places the plaintiff in reasonable apprehension of imminent harmful or offensive contact with the plaintiff's person. Like battery, assault protects physical integrity and personal dignity. It should be noted that in ordinary usage, and in criminal law, the word 'assault' is often used compendiously by lawyers and non-lawyers to refer to conduct that tort law defines as 'battery'.[82] This is partly because the torts of assault and battery are often, although

---

82 Thus it is important to be precise about the use of the word 'assault' in the law of torts.

not always, committed in close succession. However, as already noted, an assault may occur without a battery (eg, where the assailant points a gun at the victim who fears being shot), and vice versa (eg, where the assailant delivers a blow from behind, or offensively touches a sleeping person). A person can be the victim of an assault that is not a battery. Likewise, it is not necessary for the battery to include an assault, if we consider batteries committed on unconscious plaintiffs, or surreptitious batteries (eg, poisonings). Moreover, an assault might arise from an attempt at battery, but it need not. For example, the defendant's purpose may have been all along to scare rather than touch the plaintiff.

Assault differs from battery because it gives effect to the right to physical integrity and personal dignity by protecting against certain apprehensions of contact, rather than contact itself. In this sense, it is misleading to describe assault as an action for unrealised or incomplete battery. Rather, an assault is a suit for a fully realised wrong; it is completed when the requisite apprehension is generated in the victim.

HINTS AND TIPS

In practice, the term 'assault' is sometimes used by judges, lawyers and non-lawyers to refer to what is strictly battery, rather than what is strictly assault. For example, as noted by James J in *Fagan v Commissioner of Metropolitan Police*, 'although *assault* is an independent crime and is to be treated as such, for practical purposes today *assault* is generally synonymous with the term *battery* and is a term used to mean the actual intended use of unlawful force to another person without his consent'.[83]

Since the early days of the common law, assault has been recognised not only as a tort, but as a crime as well. In Queensland, the courts have directly applied the definition of assault in s 245 of the *Criminal Code Act 1899* (Qld) to civil actions for trespass to person.[84] Nonetheless, the onus of proof for such cases in Queensland remains the civil standard (ie, on the balance of probabilities).[85]

As a trespass action, assault shares some common elements of trespass such as directness, being actionable per se and fault. The element of fault in assault is common to all trespass actions and has been discussed in Section 6.3.2. To amount to an assault, it is not sufficient that it was reasonably foreseeable that the plaintiff would be put in fear of imminent harmful contact from the defendant's act.

To establish a cause of action for the tort of assault, the plaintiff must prove the following elements:

- a threat of imminent harmful contact upon the plaintiff
- a reasonable apprehension on the part of the plaintiff that the threat is to be carried out by the defendant
- a subjective intention on the part of the defendant.

---

83   [1969] 1 QB 439, 444.
84   *Origliasso v Vitale* [1952] St R Qd 211; *Greban v Kann* [1948] QWN 40; *King v Crowe* [1942] St R Qd 288.
85   *Greban v Kann* [1948] QWN 40.

To be an assault, the defendant must commit a positive act indicating infliction of an imminent harmful threat upon the plaintiff. The threat may be conveyed by a threatening conduct (gesture or act) or be coupled with a verbal threat. Nonetheless, not every threat will suffice to give rise to liability.

Section 245 of the *Criminal Code Act 1899* (Qld) (*'Criminal Code'*) provides:

> (1)   A person who strikes, touches, or moves, or otherwise applies force of any kind to, the person of another, either directly or indirectly without his consent, or with his consent if the consent is obtained by fraud, or who by any bodily act or gesture attempts or threatens to apply force of any kind to the person of another without his consent, under such circumstances that the person making the attempt or threat has actually or apparently a present ability to effect his purpose, is said to assault that other person, and the act is called an *assault*.
>
> (2)   In this section – *applies force* includes the case of applying heat, light, electrical force, gas, odour, or any other substance or thing whatever if applied in such a degree as to cause injury or personal discomfort.

As some writers have observed, the application of the s 245 definition of assault in civil cases does not change the law of trespass. As in Queensland, there are very few civil actions for trespass to person because 'magistrates in criminal proceedings are empowered, upon conviction, to order payment of compensation to the injured person'.[86] All the same, the crime of assault has not always been equated with the tort of assault. There are three distinctions between the common law definitions of assault and battery and the definition of assault in s 245 of the *Criminal Code*. First, s 245 includes the application of *indirect* force, which would not amount to a trespass to the person under the common law. Second, lack of consent of the plaintiff is expressly included in the *Criminal Code* definition as an element; thus, the onus is on the plaintiff to prove their lack of consent (express or implied). That point is, as we mentioned in Section 6.4.1.3, debatable under the common law. Third, the *Criminal Code* recognises provocation as a valid defence (in s 269) whereas the common law does not. Evidence of provocation affects the assessment of damages.[87]

In some other common law jurisdictions (eg, the United States) in recent years, criminal statutes have been amended to make conduct that constitutes assault in the tort sense punishable as a criminal assault as well. A majority of US states now make either act – attempted battery or placing in fear of a battery – a criminal offence.[88]

6.4.2.1   Threat of imminent harmful or offensive contact

HARMFUL NATURE OF THE THREAT

The threat must be of a harmful nature. A threat might be itself legally 'neutral' as it is merely an expression of a proposed action. According to Lord Dunedin in *Sorrell v Smith*, whether the threat is actionable will depend upon whether the proposed action is legal or illegal (ie,

---

86   See A Stickley, *Australian Torts Law* (LexisNexis Butterworths, 4th ed, 2016) 42. See also *Victims of Crime Assistance Act 2009* (Qld), ch 3, pt 16.

87   *Fontin v Katapodis* (1962) 108 CLR 177; *Farah Constructions Pty Ltd v Say-Dee Pty Ltd* (2007) 230 CLR 89; [2007] HCA 22, [135].

88   See WR LaFave, *Criminal Law* (West, 5th ed, 2011) [16.3(b)].

tortious).[89] Only if the threat involves an intimation of a tortious act will a person have the right to sue.[90]

IMMINENT HARMFUL CONTACT

The apprehended threat must be *imminent*, as distinguished from any contact in the future. The question of whether a fear of imminent or immediate physical interference has been created depends on the circumstances of the case. The oft-quoted example is *Tuberville v Savage*, in which the question arose whether it was an assault for the plaintiff to lay his hand upon the handle of his sword and say 'If it were not assize-time, I would not take such language from you'.[91] The Court agreed that there was no assault as the immanency of the threat was negated by the defendant's words.

Another example is *Zanker v Vartzokas*.[92] In this case, the plaintiff accepted a lift in a van being driven by the defendant. After it started moving, the defendant offered to give the plaintiff money in exchange for sexual favours. The plaintiff rejected this request and demanded to be let out. The defendant refused this and threatened the plaintiff, saying, 'I am going to take you to my mate's house. He will really fix you up.' Frightened for her safety, the plaintiff leapt out of the moving vehicle suffering some actual injury. The trial judge held that there was no fear of 'immediate violence' and dismissed the charge of assault. The plaintiff succeeded on appeal. White J noted in the decision that the threat was of violence that included its perpetration very shortly. He pointed out that the threat was a continuing one, presumably up to the moment the victim leapt from the moving vehicle:

> The threat was, it is true, to be carried out in the future but there was no indication by the defendant whether the 'mate's house' was around the next corner or several or more streets away in the suburban area. A present fear of relatively imminent violence was instilled in her mind from the moment the words were uttered and that fear was kept alive in her mind, in the continuing present, by continuing progress, with her as prisoner, towards the house where the feared sexual violence was to occur.[93]

Higgins CJ referred to *Zanker* in *R v Gabriel*, where he said that the word 'imminent' does not necessarily mean that the violence will commence 'without any delay'; it is sufficient if it be 'soon' which means in the immediate future.[94] Therefore, imminent contact does not mean instantaneous contact, as where the defendant's fist is about to strike the plaintiff's nose. A better understanding might be that there will be no significant delay.[95]

---

89 [1925] AC 700.
90 See, eg, *Broune v Haukyns* (1475–83) T 15 Edw 4, described in J Baker, *The Oxford History of the Laws of England: 1483–1558* (Oxford University Press, 2003) vol 6, 782, cited in D Mendelson, *The New Law of Torts* (Oxford University Press, 3rd ed, 2014) 139.
91 (1669) 86 ER 684.
92 (1988) 34 A Crim R 11.
93 Ibid 114.
94 (2004) 182 FLR 102, 112.
95 In the United States, the notion of 'imminent' in civil assault is suggested by the *Restatement (Second) of Torts* as follows: 'It is not necessary that one shall be within striking distance of the other, or that a weapon pointed at the other shall be in a condition for instant discharge. It is enough that one (the defendant) is so close to striking distance that he can reach the plaintiff almost at once, or that he or she can make the weapon ready for discharge in a very short interval of time': American Law Institute, *Restatement (Second) of Torts* (1979) § 29 cmt (b).

Likewise, text messages, email or other electronic messages containing threats must refer to an imminent harmful contact in order to constitute assault.[96] In *Slaveski v Victoria*,[97] the judge reviewed *Zanker*[98] and *R v Gabriel*[99] and concluded:

> there is no rule preventing a threat of physical harm which is not accompanied by any physical contact, such as a threat made over the telephone or by email or other electronic means, from constituting an assault. Such a threat can constitute an assault provided that all the elements of the tort are established, including that the threat is to inflict immediate physical harm.[100]

MERE WORDS

At one time it was thought that mere words without accompanying action could not amount to an assault. For example, in *R v Meade and Belt* Holroyd J pointed out that 'no words or singing are equivalent to an assault'.[101] However, this proposition was challenged by courts in later decisions. For example, in *Barton v Armstrong*[102] and *Knight v The Queen*[103] the courts held that threats made over the phone could amount to assault.

In contrast to this, mere silence may constitute assault in certain circumstances. In *R v Ireland*, the defendant made multiple telephone calls to three different women during which he remained silent, and the House of Lords held that a 'silent caller' should be liable for assault.[104] Therefore, words alone or mere silence are just as potent as acts as a means of instilling a reasonable fear and arousing necessary apprehension in the recipient although there is no threat of immediate physical contact.

CONDITIONAL THREAT

Assault can be carried out through conditional threats. In *Police v Greaves*, the Court considered the issue of conditional threats and whether or not a threat made to a police officer – that if they came closer, they would be stabbed – amounted to a conditional threat.[105] The defendant said: 'Don't you bloody move. You come a step closer and you will get this straight through your guts.' The Court held that the defendant's words constituted assault because they threatened imminent and direct violence unless the plaintiff desisted from lawful acts in the course of his police duties.

Accordingly, such actions may constitute an assault even though the defendant's threat of violence is conditional on the plaintiff doing or refraining from doing an act. Most often,

---

96 *Balven v Thurston* [2013] NSWSC 210.
97 [2010] VSC 441.
98 Ibid [232]–[235].
99 Ibid [238].
100 Ibid [240] (Kyrou J).
101 (1823) 1 Lew CC 184, 185. See also *Read v Coker* (1853) 13 CB 850 where the plaintiff was a tenant of the defendant. When the defendant told the plaintiff to leave the premises, the plaintiff refused. The defendant then called some of his employers to see the defendant off the premises. These men pulled up their sleeves and showed their fists and told the plaintiff that if he did not leave, they would break his neck. The Court accepted in principle that words spoken between parties in each other's presence may constitute assault.
102 [1969] 2 NSWLR 451.
103 (1988) 35 A Crim R 314.
104 [1998] AC 147.
105 [1964] NZLR 295.

a conditional threat implies an application of force unless something is done; this may constitute assault.

For example, if a mugger said to their victim 'your wallet or you get knifed' and the threat is sufficiently immediate, this might be actionable. Sometimes a conditional threat will constitute assault even where the defendant makes it clear that no bodily contact will ensue if the plaintiff obeys the unlawful instructions (eg, 'I won't stab you if you hand over your wallet'). In both scenarios, the imminent harmful bodily contact is conditional upon non-compliance with the stated request, and the main issue is whether the offered alternative is an acceptable command.

Whether a conditional threat is calculated to cause apprehension of imminent harmful contact will depend on the surrounding circumstances. For example, if the defendant, who was engaged in beating up A, turned to the plaintiff and said 'Piss off, or you're next', this too could amount to an assault. Contrary to this, a threat to use lawful force (eg, where an entitled occupier threatens a trespasser by saying, 'Stop, or I'll shoot') may not be assault if the force to be applied is proportionate.

6.4.2.2   Reasonable apprehension

APPREHENSION

As noted in Section 6.4.2.1, the central issue in assault is whether the plaintiff has been placed in apprehension of imminent physical violence against them or someone under their control. In the context of assault, the word 'apprehension' simply means the perception or anticipation of an imminent harmful or offensive contact.[106] In other words, the plaintiff knows and expects that the physical interference is about to take place. Thus, where the plaintiff has no knowledge of the threat, there can be no assault. In *R v Phillips*, the defendant pushed a girl to the ground, causing her to strike her head and become unconscious.[107] He dragged her body to the edge of a river and left her there. When the tide came in, she drowned. The Court considered whether there had been assault by moving the victim to the edge of the river. Barwick CJ stated:

> The deceased at all times relevant in this connection was unconscious. There was thus no question of assault in the common law sense of the word. Such an assault necessarily involves the apprehension of injury or the instillation of fear or fright.[108]

REASONABLENESS OF THE APPREHENSION

In addition, for there to be an assault, the plaintiff's apprehension must be *reasonable*. The general rule is that it will be deemed to be reasonable if the defendant has, from the plaintiff's perspective, the means and capacity to carry the threat of force into immediate effect.[109] The rule was stated by Tindal CJ in *Stephens v Myers*: 'It is not every threat, when there is no actual personal violence, that constitutes an assault, there must, in all cases, be the means of carrying the threat into effect'.[110] In this case, the plaintiff chaired a turbulent parish meeting,

---

106   K Barker et al, *The Law of Torts in Australia* (Oxford University Press, 5th ed, 2012) 47.
107   (1971) 45 ALJR 467.
108   Ibid 472.
109   *Zanker v Vartzokas* (1988) 34 A Crim R 11; *R v Gabriel* (2004) 182 FLR 102.
110   (1830) 172 ER 735, 350.

in which the defendant was voted to be ejected from the parish hall. The defendant refused and advanced towards the plaintiff, waving his clenched fist and saying that he would rather pull the plaintiff out of the chair than be ejected from the hall. The defendant was stopped by the churchwarden before he got within striking distance. The plaintiff sued for assault and his claim succeeded. Another example is *Cobbett v Grey*, in which Pollok CB remarked that if the defendant stands some distance away from the plaintiff, saying 'I'm going to hit you', there will be no assault as the defendant lacks capacity to put the words or acts into effect.[111]

When assessing the reasonableness of the plaintiff's apprehension, the important thing is not whether the plaintiff actually apprehended an immediate violence but whether, in the circumstances of the case, a reasonable person would have done so. In *MacPherson v Beath* Bray CJ stated:

> The reasonableness of the [plaintiff's] apprehension may or may not be necessary. I do not pause to canvass that, though it seems to me … that if the defendant intentionally puts in fear of immediate violence an exceptionally timid person known to him to be so then the unreasonableness of the fear may not prevent conviction.[112]

Nevertheless, a defendant does not need to have the necessary means to carry out their intention with immediate effect; it is sufficient if the plaintiff in the circumstances believes on reasonable grounds that the defendant will act imminently. Suppose, for example, the defendant points an unloaded or a realistic toy gun at the plaintiff; the plaintiff does not know that it is unloaded or is an imitation gun but believes that the weapon is loaded or real; in this case, there is an assault. In *Bradey v Schatzel*, the appellant pretended to load the rifle she was holding and then aimed it at the respondent police officer.[113] This was held to be sufficient to constitute assault, even though it was later discovered that the rifle had never been loaded.[114] As Higgins CJ said in *R v Gabriel*:

> It is also important to note that for the presented fist to constitute an assault, it does not matter that the accused does not strike the blow or that he or she has no intention to do so. The issue is the identification of the threat, next what the victim concludes from the threat, and, finally, what he or she was intended by the accused to conclude.[115]

Similar views were expressed in *R v St George*,[116] *Blake v Burnard*,[117] *R v Hamilton*[118] and *McClelland v Symons*.[119]

---

111 (1849) 4 Ex 729 (CA) 744. However, it should be noted that striking distance is only one factor that may negate the capacity of the defendant. Case law suggests that a threat to strike a person, even made at such a distance as to make contact impossible, may constitute an assault if it instils a fear of immediate violence in the mind of the plaintiff: see *R v Mostyn* (2004) 145 A Crim R 304, [71].

112 (1975) 12 SASR 174, 177. Bray CJ's reasoning was applied by Anderson J in *White v South Australia* (2010) 106 SASR 521, [364]. (Protesters at the Beverley Uranium Mine were detained by police for seven hours in an old ship container. The Court held that there was false imprisonment as the arrests were unlawful since the protestors had not been asked to leave before they were arrested.)

113 [1911] St R Qd 206.

114 See also *McClelland v Symons* [1951] VLR 157, 163–4.

115 (2004) 182 FLR 102, 129.

116 (1840) 9 Car & P 483.

117 Ibid 626.

118 (1891) 12 LR (NSW) 111, 114.

119 [1951] VLR 157, 163–4.

APPREHENSION NOT FEAR

It should also be noted that the plaintiff's fear is not necessary to constitute an assault although its existence may help clarify the apprehension.[120] In *Bradey v Schatzel* the fact that the police officer was not scared was thought irrelevant to establishing the assault, given that a reasonable person in such circumstances would have been.[121] So, in *ACN 087 528 774 Pty Ltd v Chetcuti* Hargrave AJA said:

> The threat must in fact create in the mind of the plaintiff an apprehension that the threat will be carried out forthwith. It is not necessary for the plaintiff to fear the threat, in the sense of being frightened by it. It is enough if the plaintiff apprehends that the threat will be carried out without his or her consent. The apprehension in the mind of the plaintiff must be objectively reasonable.[122]

6.4.2.3   Subjective intention

To be an assault, the requisite intent must be present. That is, the defendant must intend to inflict immediate force or violence on the plaintiff. According to *Tuberville v Savage*, 'the intention as well as the act makes an assault. Therefore, if one strikes another upon the hand, or arm, or breast in discourse, it is no assault, there being no intention to assault'.[123]

In *ACN 087 528 774 Pty Ltd v Chetcuti* the requisite intention to constitute an assault was described by Hargrave AJA as:

> [a] subjective intention on the part of the defendant that the threat will create in the mind of the plaintiff an apprehension that the threat will be carried out forthwith. It is not necessary to prove that the defendant in fact intends to carry out the threat.[124]

The relevant intent can be either intention or recklessness, as stated by Lord Hope in the English Court of Appeal decision of *R v Ireland*: 'any act by which [the defendant], intentionally or recklessly, cause[s] [the plaintiff] to apprehend immediate and unlawful personal violence'.[125]

In an assault, particularly an intentional assault, the defendant must either have intended to harm the plaintiff or intended to create an apprehension of imminent harm in the plaintiff. According to Smith and Kennedy JJ in *Hall v Fonceca*, for a defendant to be liable for assault, they must actually intend to apply force.[126] In other words, they must turn their mind to using force against the plaintiff or creating the apprehension of force in the mind of the plaintiff. This explained why, in *Rixon v Star City Pty Ltd*, the NSW Court of Appeal held that an employee putting his hand on the plaintiff's shoulder to attract the plaintiff's

---

120 B Richards et al, *Tort Law Principles* (Thomson Reuters (Professional) Australia, 2nd ed, 2017) 60.
121 [1911] St R Qd 206.
122 (2008) 21 VR 559, [16] (citations omitted).
123 (1669) 86 ER 684.
124 (2008) 21 VR 559, [16] (citations omitted).
125 [1997] QB 114, 117.
126 [1983] WAR 309. In *Hall v Fonceca*, the Court accepted that 'an intention on the part of the assailant either to use force or to create apprehension in the victim is an element in an assault.' See also *Hayman v Cartwright* (2018) 53 WAR 137; *Matsebula v Vandeklashorst* [2000] WASCA 141, [11]–[12].

attention was not assault – there was not 'the necessary intention to create in Mr Rixon an apprehension of imminent harmful or offensive contact'.[127]

An exception to this rule is the negligent assault. It has been suggested that mere negligence as to the commission of an assault may suffice in an appropriate case.[128] Negligent assault cases are rare in practice.[129]

6.4.3 False imprisonment

The tort of false imprisonment involves an intentional or negligent act of the defendant which directly causes the total deprivation of the liberty of the plaintiff without lawful justification. The tort protects the interest in freedom from confinement and protects against the loss of personal liberty, which has long been identified as one of the most important common law rights. As Fullagar J observed in *Trobridge v Hardy*, the right to be free from interference with one's person and liberty is one of the 'the most elementary and important of all common law rights'.[130]

In Australia, there is no constitutional bill of rights, thus interference with personal liberty is mainly regulated by common law. As such, the tort of false imprisonment plays a significant role in the protection of human rights in Australia, particularly freedom from arbitrary detention and freedom of movement.[131] Accordingly, false imprisonment most commonly arises in the context of the following situations: arrests by police officers;[132] restraint by prison authorities;[133] confinement by a retailer of a suspected shoplifter;[134] and immigration detention matters.[135]

Conduct amounting to false imprisonment in these circumstances is often accompanied by an assault or battery or other trespass. However, it is not necessary that the plaintiff should be assaulted or battered to be subject to false imprisonment.[136] When the nature or scope of the restraint is considered, false imprisonment cases fall into two major classes. The first class involves deprivation of liberty by means of close physical restraint such as

---

127 (2001) 53 NSWLR 98, [59]. See also *Hall v Fonceca* [1983] WAR 309.
128 *R v Savage* [1992] 1 AC 699.
129 For further examples, see *New South Wales v McMaster* (2015) 91 NSWLR 666 and *Sabade v Bischoff* [2015] NSWCA 418, [71]–[73].
130 (1955) 94 CLR 147, 152. See also *Ruhani v Director of Police (No 2)* (2005) 222 CLR 580; [2005] HCA 43, [63]–[65].
131 See FA Trindade, 'The Modern Tort of False Imprisonment' in N Mullany (ed), *Torts in the Nineties* (LBC Information Services, 1997) 231. See also C Sappideen, P Vines and P Watson, *Torts: Commentary and Materials* (Lawbook, 13th ed, 2021) 55.
132 See, eg, *Symes v Mahon* [1922] SASR 447; *Little v Commonwealth* (1947) 75 CLR 94; *Watson v Marshall* (1971) 124 CLR 621; *John Lewis & Co Ltd v Tims* [1952] AC 676; *Donaldson v Broomby* (1982) 60 FLR 124; *Jones v Harvey* (1983) 1 MVR 111; *Re Bolton; Ex parte Beane* (1987) 162 CLR 514; *Slaveski v Victoria* [2010] VSC 441.
133 See, eg, *Cowell v Corrective Services Commission (NSW)* (1988) 13 NSWLR 714 (miscalculation of prisoner's sentence); *R v Deputy Governor of Parkhurst Prison; Ex parte Hague* [1992] 1 AC 58 (lawful prisoner cannot be falsely imprisoned by prison authority); *R v Governor of Brockhill Prison; Ex parte Evans (No 2)* [2001] 2 AC 19.
134 See, eg, *Myer Stores Ltd v Soo* [1991] 2 VR 597; *Coles Myer Ltd v Webster* [2009] NSWCA 299.
135 See, eg, *Goldie v Commonwealth* (2002) 117 FCR 566; *Ruddock v Taylor* (2003) 58 NSWLR 269; *Ruddock v Taylor* (2005) 222 CLR 612; [2005] HCA 48; *Fernando v Commonwealth* (2014) 231 FCR 251; *Kamasaee v Commonwealth (Ruling on the Settlement Distribution)* [2018] VSC 138; *Lewis v Australian Capital Territory* [2019] ACTCA 16.
136 *Bird v Jones* (1845) 7 QB 742, 749 (Patteson J).

in a prison or in similar physical confinement. The second class of cases are 'psychological' types of false imprisonments, which means restraint does not arise from actual physical confinement but extends beyond the use of force to restraint by threats[137] or submission to an assertion of authority – provided it has an effect of depriving the liberty of the plaintiff. As noted by the Court in *McFadzean v Construction, Forestry, Mining and Energy Union*: 'the essence of the action of false imprisonment is the compelling of a person to stay at a particular place against his or her will'.[138]

Therefore, no matter which form it may take, and however short, complete deprivation of liberty without lawful cause will amount to false imprisonment.

Like other forms of trespass to the person, false imprisonment is actionable per se. Thus, it is not necessary for the plaintiff to prove that actual damage has been suffered as a result of the wrongful imprisonment. To establish the tort of false imprisonment there must be:

- direct interference
- restraint of the plaintiff in all directions (or total restraint)
- fault on the part of the defendant.

6.4.3.1   Direct interference

In common with other trespass actions, directness of the defendant's act is required to establish false imprisonment. That is, the deprivation of the plaintiff's liberty must be a direct result of the defendant's conduct. A false imprisonment will normally result from some positive act, but *Herd v Weardale Steel, Coal & Coke Co* confirmed that a false imprisonment can be committed by mere omission to act.[139] Although the defendant must directly cause the imprisonment, it can come about either through the defendant's own actions or in a situation where the defendant instructs others to restrain the plaintiff.

A defendant may also effect the plaintiff's imprisonment through the agency of a third party. For example, in *Flewster v Royle*, the defendant, a jilted fiancée, stated positively to the commander of a press-gang that the plaintiff was liable to be impressed.[140] The plaintiff was in fact exempted from the impress law. In consequence of the defendant's information, the plaintiff was seized and held on board a ship. The Court held that the defendant (the ex-fiancée) was liable for false imprisonment. Likewise, in *Aitken v Bedwell*, it was held that the person who was 'active in promoting and causing' the confinement should be liable for false imprisonment.[141]

Where the defendant upon the information of another restrains a plaintiff, it is usually difficult to decide who should be sued for the false imprisonment. This is particularly true for the so-called 'police informant' cases.[142]

---

137 Case law shows that a person's liberty may be restrained in various ways, including by physical restraint, by threats or by other intimidating conduct or coercion. The threat may be against the plaintiff or some other person, or even valuable personal property: see, eg, *Homsi v The Queen* [2011] NSWCCA 164; *Myer Stores Ltd v Soo* [1991] 2 VR 597; *McFadzean v Construction, Forestry, Mining and Energy Union* (2007) 20 VR 250; *R v Garrett* (1988) 50 SASR 392.
138 (2007) 20 VR 250, [41].
139 [1913] 3 KB 771 (CA), affd [1915] AC 67 (HL).
140 (1808) 170 ER 924.
141 (1827) 173 ER 1084.
142 See, eg, *Dickenson v Waters Ltd* (1931) 31 SR (NSW) 593; *Blundell v A-G (NZ)* [1968] NZLR 341; *Bahner v Marwest Hotel Co Ltd* (1969) 6 DLR (3d) 322; *Myer Stores Ltd v Soo* [1991] 2 VR 597; *Davidson v Chief Constable of North Wales* [1994] 2 All ER 597.

As a general principle, who should be sued (the police officer or the police informant) will be determined according to whether the police officer exercised their own judgment and made a decision to effect an arrest.[143] For example, in *Dickenson v Waters Ltd*, the plaintiff was shopping at the defendant store; she was accused of shoplifting by the shop inspector and taken to the manager's office.[144] When the attending police officer asked the manager, 'Do you wish to proceed?', the manager replied 'yes'. The plaintiff was subsequently charged with larceny and later acquitted. The defendant store, not the police officer, was found to be liable for the false imprisonment. In this case, the arrest would not have been effected by the police officer in the circumstances if there had been no affirmative request from the manager. Although this case demonstrates that a defendant will be liable if they 'are active in promoting and causing the imprisonment',[145] it is unusual in the sense that arresting police are normally considered to be exercising their own judgment and discretion. In such a case, it may be found that both the retail employee who initially detains the plaintiff and the arresting police officer have committed separate torts of false imprisonment.[146]

This principle was reasserted by the High Court in *Ruddock v Taylor*:

> So the question in such cases is whether a complainant has issued a direction to arrest the plaintiff or has merely complained of the plaintiff's behaviour. If the arrest of the plaintiff is the result of the officer's independent assessment of the evidence of the complainant, the defendant is not liable. But if the officer acts on a direction of the defendant, the defendant will be liable.[147]

Case: *Ruddock v Taylor* (2005) 222 CLR 612

Facts

The respondent (Taylor), a British citizen, lived in Australia holding a permanent transitional visa. In 1996, the respondent pleaded guilty to eight sexual offences against children. He was sentenced to a term of imprisonment. After he was released from prison, the Commonwealth twice cancelled his visa under s 501 of the *Migration Act 1958* (Cth). Following each cancellation decision (which was later found to be unlawful), the appellant was detained in immigration detention for two lengthy periods. After his release he sued the Ministers who had made the two decisions to cancel his visa

---

143 See, eg, *Dickenson v Waters Ltd* (1931) 31 SR (NSW) 593, 595–6; *Pike v Waldrum* [1952] 1 Lloyd's Rep 431, 454–5; *Davidson v Chief Constable of North Wales* [1994] 2 All ER 59.

144 (1931) 31 SR (NSW) 593.

145 See also *Hopkins v Crowe* (1836) 111 ER 974; *Myer Stores Ltd v Soo* [1991] 2 VR 597, 617. Compare the cases concerning the removal of Aboriginal children from their families (the 'Stolen Generations'), where the action for false imprisonment has been used, not always successfully. In *Cubillo v Commonwealth (No 3)* (2001) 112 FCR 455, 457 the Federal Court stated: 'A person who is active in promoting and causing the imprisonment is jointly and severally liable with the person who effects the imprisonment, ordinarily because their acts are done in furtherance of a common design'. The appellants' claims for false imprisonment (as well as three other causes of action) were dismissed.

146 See *Bahner v Marwest Hotel Co Ltd* (1969) 6 DLR (3d) 322; *Myer Stores Ltd v Soo* [1991] 2 VR 597.

147 (2005) 222 CLR 612; [2005] HCA 48, [115] (Gleeson, Gummow, Hayne and Heydon JJ).

and the Commonwealth. In the NSW District Court, he claimed damages for false imprisonment, and succeeded. The Ministers and the Commonwealth appealed to the NSW Court of Appeal. The Court found that the cancellation was unlawful and the Ministers who cancelled the visas should be liable for false imprisonment. Philip Ruddock, the then Minister for Immigration and Multicultural Affairs, Senator Kay Patterson and the Commonwealth appealed to the High Court.

Issue

Did the circumstances of the detentions give rise to liability in tort for false imprisonment?

Decision

On appeal, the High Court held that s 189 of the *Migration Act 1958* (Cth) allowed an officer to detain a person whom the officer knew or reasonably suspected to be an unlawful non-citizen, as long as the officer had the subjective state of mind when detaining the respondent that the detention was lawful. The Court held:

> it follows from the considerations just mentioned that s 189 may apply in cases where the person detained proves, on later examination, not to have been an unlawful non-citizen. So long always as the officer had the requisite state of mind, knowledge or reasonable suspicion that the person was an unlawful non-citizen, the detention of the person concerned is required by s 189. And if the Minister brought about a state of affairs where an officer knew or reasonably suspected that a person was an unlawful non-citizen by steps which were beyond the lawful exercise of power by the Minister, it does not automatically follow that the resulting detention is unlawful. Rather, separate consideration must be given to the application of s 189 – separate, that is, from consideration of the lawfulness of the Minister's exercise of power. If it were suggested that the Minister had exercised power where the Minister knew or ought to have known that what was done was beyond their power, an action may lie for the tort of misfeasance in public office. But that has never been the respondent's case in this matter.[148]

Significance

False imprisonment requires the intention to detain. Under s 189 of the *Migration Act 1958* (Cth), the immigration officers were required by law to detain the respondent. The inevitable consequence of cancelling the visa was detention – thus, there was no opportunity for them to exercise independent discretion.

Question

The case of *Ruddock v Taylor* raises important issues about the basis of the immigration officers' liability for false imprisonment in the context of immigration detention. In this case, on what basis did the High Court hold that the Minister is not liable for false imprisonment?

 Guided response in the eBook

---

148 Ibid [28] (Gleeson, Gummow, Hayne and Heydon JJ) (citations omitted).

Where the imprisonment follows indirectly upon the defendant's conduct, the imprisonment must cause actual damage in order to support an action for negligence or an action on the case for intentional, indirect injury to the person.[149] In *Sayers v Harlow Urban District Council*, the plaintiff became locked inside a public cubicle of the defendant's lavatory due to the defective and negligent maintenance of the lock of the cubicle.[150] The plaintiff climbed to the top of the cubicle wall trying to escape but then slipped and injured herself. The plaintiff was successful in recovering damages in negligence from the defendant. The case was brought in negligence, not false imprisonment. However, had there been no injury to the plaintiff, there would have been no cause of action, because the imprisonment of the plaintiff arose indirectly here and false imprisonment would not have been available. This rests on the assumption that the imprisonment itself would not have amounted to actual damage for the purpose of suing in negligence. The case also demonstrates that merely providing the occasion for the imprisonment is insufficient for false imprisonment: a direct cause of the imprisonment is required.

As negligent trespass remains in Australian law, it may well be possible to bring an action for negligent false imprisonment. As many writers observe, the majority of cases concerning negligent trespass are battery cases. It is not clear whether negligent false imprisonment can be recognised.[151]

6.4.3.2   Restraint in all directions

To be a false imprisonment, the restraint of the plaintiff's free movement must be total or whole. Whether there is a total deprivation of the plaintiff's liberty depends on whether there is any reasonable means of escape. In *Bird v Jones* Patteson J emphasised that, for the first time, false imprisonment must be 'the total restraint of the liberty of the person' and 'not a partial obstruction of his will, whatever inconvenience it may bring him'.[152] Thus, a mere obstruction of movement in one direction only is insufficient.[153]

Case: *Bird v Jones* (1845) 7 QB 742

Facts

The plaintiff was prevented by two police officers from using part of a bridge because a number of seats had been placed there for spectators who had paid to view a boat race. The plaintiff was told he could pass in another direction, but he refused and stood in the same place. He was later taken into custody by the police.

---

149 See B Richards et al, *Tort Law Principles* (Thomson Reuters (Professional) Australia, 2nd ed, 2017) 68.
150 [1958] 1 WLR 623.
151 See C Sappideen et al, *Torts Commentary and Materials* (Thomson Reuters, 12th ed, 2016) 61. Compare *De Freville* (1927) 96 LJKB 1056. See also the comments on *De Freville* in B Richards et al, *Tort Law Principles* (Thomson Reuters (Professional) Australia, 2nd ed, 2017).
152 (1845) 7 QB 742, 744.
153 See also *Kuchenmeister v Home Office* [1958] 1 QB 496.

Issue

Had the defendant totally deprived the plaintiff of his liberty and thus committed a false imprisonment?

Decision

The Court found that there was no false imprisonment because his restraint had not been total. Although the plaintiff had been blocked in one direction, he was at liberty to move off in another direction and no restraint or actual force was used against him. He could have turned around and been free to go in any other direction he pleased. Coleridge J stated:

> a prison may have its boundary large or narrow, visible and tangible, or, though real, still in the conception only; it may itself be moveable or fixed: but a boundary it must have; and that boundary the party imprisoned must be prevented from passing; he must be prevented from leaving that place, within the ambit of which the party imprisoning would confine him, except by prison-breach.[154]

Significance

The case reflects the principle that partial obstruction and disturbance does not constitute imprisonment.

Question

Why is *Bird v Jones* still an important consideration today when defining false imprisonment?

 Guided response in the eBook

Similarly, the Court in *Balmain New Ferry Co Ltd v Robertson* explained that partial restraint could not amount to false imprisonment. It found that the plaintiff had reasonable, alternative means of escape, although the means of escape would have involved leaving the wharf via the ocean.[155] In *Louis v Commonwealth* the plaintiffs were deported from Hong Kong to Melbourne in the defendant's aircraft. An argument that the imprisonment continued after they were released in Australia was rejected by Kelly J in the Supreme Court of the Australian Capital Territory: 'it seems to me to be impossible to say that persons who are at perfect liberty to move around Australia, as I am satisfied the plaintiffs were, are suffering a state of imprisonment'. The restraint was not total as the plaintiffs were not constrained financially from leaving Australia.[156]

---

154 (1845) 7 QB 742, 744.
155 (1906) 4 CLR 379, affd [1910] AC 295 (PC).
156 (1987) 87 FLR 277, 282.

Case: *Balmain New Ferry Co Ltd v Robertson* (1906) 4 CLR 379

Facts

Balmain New Ferry Company ran a steam ferry from Sydney to Balmain. Mr Robertson paid a penny to enter a wharf to board a ferry. When he realised that the next ferry was not due for 20 minutes, he decided to leave the wharf by means of another turnstile. As he refused to pay another penny to exit through the turnstile, he was restrained on the wharf. Mr Robertson brought an action against the company in the Supreme Court of New South Wales for assault and false imprisonment. The Court held that Mr Robertson had been assaulted and falsely imprisoned. The company then appealed.

Issue

Was requiring the payment of another penny to enable Mr Robertson to leave the wharf a false imprisonment?

Decision

The case of the respondent (Mr Robertson) failed in both the High Court of Australia and the Privy Council. The High Court took the view that he had contracted to depart the wharf by ferry and that if he decided to leave the wharf by means of the turnstile, the condition of paying a penny was not unreasonable. O'Connor J stated (at 388):

> The abridgement of a man's liberty is not under all circumstances actionable. He may enter into a contract which necessarily involves the surrender of a portion of his liberty for a certain period, and if the act complained of is nothing more than a restraint in accordance with that surrender he cannot complain. Nor can he, without the assent of the other party, by electing to put an end to the contract, become entitled at once, unconditionally and irrespective of the other party's rights, to regain his liberty as if he had never surrendered it.

The High Court's decision was upheld on appeal to the Privy Council in *Robertson v Balmain New Ferry Co Ltd* [1910] AC 295, where Loreburn LC stated (at 299):

> The defendants were entitled to impose a reasonable condition before allowing him to pass through their turnstile from a place to which he had gone of his own free will. The payment of a penny was a quite fair condition, and if he did not choose to comply with it the defendants were not bound to let him through. He could proceed on the journey he had contracted for.

Significance

This case establishes that even where a person is totally obstructed, this will not constitute false imprisonment if there is a reasonable condition to passing, and that entry into a contract is sufficient to make lawful an imprisonment. The case narrows the law on false imprisonment set out in *Bird v Jones* (1845) 7 QB 742.

Notes

For a full explanation of this case (including a thorough exploration of the facts), see Mark Lunney, 'False Imprisonment, Fare Dodging and Federation: Mr Robertson's Evening Out' (2009) 31(4) *Sydney Law Review* 537.

In *Herd v Weardale Steel, Coal & Coke Co* [1913] 3 KB 771 the plaintiff was a miner employed by the defendant. He descended into the coal mine to begin work at 9:30 am, and in the ordinary course of work he would be entitled to be raised to the surface at the end of his shift at 4 pm. The plaintiff and his workmates refused to work, arguing that the work was dangerous. At 11 am he requested that the defendants raise him to the surface. The defendant employer refused on the basis that there was no contractual obligation to return the worker to the surface until the shift ended. The plaintiff was finally drawn up at about 1:30 pm. He sued the defendants for false imprisonment. Following the decision in *Robertson v Balmain New Ferry Co Ltd* [1910] AC 295, the House of Lords held that the plaintiff was only entitled to the use of the exit on the terms on which he had entered. The plaintiff miner who refused to work was held to have no right to be brought to the surface until completion of his shift. This breach of contract justified his detention in the mine at the end of his shift.

Balmain New Ferry and *Herd* are authorities for the proposition that entry into a contract is sufficient to make lawful an imprisonment. However, this proposition has been criticised by different writers, who argue that the decision does not rest on a firm basis.[157] One of the problems associated with it is that restraint of another is not a legitimate means of enforcing a contractual obligation.[158] Cases such as *Vignoli v Sydney Harbour Casino*[159] and the Canadian case *Bahner v Marwest Hotel Co Ltd*[160] are authority for the proposition that a person cannot be detained if they fail to pay a bill or debt.

Additionally, it has been said that the question of whether the contractual condition of exit is reasonable is not relevant to the issue of whether the restraint amounts to a false imprisonment. According to the critics, a better way to view this type of situation is in terms of consent. If a person withdraws their consent to a restriction of liberty (eg, when on a train or bus), they should be released unless it is not possible or would cause inconvenience to others (eg, other passengers).[161] The *Herd* case was also criticised on these grounds and it has been argued that the defendant company should not have treated the plaintiff miner's consent to remain in the mine as irrevocable.[162]

---

157 See G Williams, 'Two Cases for False Imprisonment' in GW Keeton, RHC Holland and G Schwarzenberger (eds), *Law, Justice and Equity: Essays in Tribute to GW Keeton* (Pitman, 1967) 47–55. See also C Sappideen et al, *Torts: Commentary and Materials* (Thomson Reuters, 12th ed, 2016) 57; B Richards et al, *Tort Law Principles* (Thomson Reuters (Professional) Australia, 2nd ed, 2017) 69; RP Balkin, *Law of Torts* (LexisNexis, 5th ed, 2013) 53–4.
158 See B Richards et al, *Tort Law Principles* (Thomson Reuters (Professional) Australia, 2nd ed, 2017) 69.
159 [1999] Aust Torts Reports 81-541.
160 (1969) 6 DLR (3d) 322 (BCSC), affd (1970) 12 DLR (3d) 646 (BCCA).
161 See KF Tan, 'A Misconceived Issue in the Tort of False Imprisonment' (1981) 44(2) *Modern Law Review* 166.
162 See, eg, C Sappideen et al, *Torts: Commentary and Materials* (Thomson Reuters, 12th ed, 2016) 57; B Richards et al, *Tort Law Principles* (Thomson Reuters (Professional) Australia, 2nd ed, 2017) 69; RP Balkin, *Law of Torts* (LexisNexis, 5th ed, 2013) 54.

Question

If a case with a scenario similar to *Herd v Weardale Steel, Coal & Coke Co* arose today, do you think the court's decision would still favour the employer?

 Guided response in the eBook

NO REASONABLE MEANS TO ESCAPE

If the plaintiff has a means of escape from the place of imprisonment but that means is not a reasonable one, the imprisonment will be deemed to be total. For example, in *Zanker v Vartzokas*[163] and *Burton v Davies*[164] it was held that the defendant's conduct in driving at speed to prevent the plaintiff from reasonably alighting amounted to false imprisonment.[165] As Townley J stated in *Burton v Davies*:

> If I lock a person in a room with a window from which he may jump to the ground at the risk of life or limb, I cannot be heard to say that he was not imprisoned because he was free to leap from the window.[166]

Whether there was a reasonable means to escape is a question of fact. What is regarded as *reasonable* very much depends on the case facts and thus should be considered case by case. Generally, the means of escape will not be considered as reasonable in following circumstances:

- The only way of escape is dangerous to the plaintiff's life or limbs (eg, jumping from a fifth-floor window or an aircraft at its cruising altitude).[167]
- The plaintiff is justified in believing that any attempt to escape would involve a risk of public embarrassment or application of physical force by the defendant.[168]
- The possible means of escape is unknown to the plaintiff (eg, a concealed trapdoor leading to the outside).
- The plaintiff is afraid for their own or another's safety.[169]

Case law also suggests that factors such as threat or danger to property (including property of others),[170] distance, the time it will take to escape and the legality of escape should also be taken into account in deciding the reasonableness of the possible means of escape.[171]

---

163 (1988) 34 A Crim R 11.
164 [1953] St R Qd 26.
165 See also *R v Macquarie* (1875) 13 SCR (NSW) 264, which involved the plaintiff being cast adrift in a boat.
166 [1953] St R Qd 26, 30.
167 See, eg, *Burton v Davies* [1953] St R Qd 26; *Sayers v Harlow Urban District Council* [1958] 1 WLR 623.
168 See, eg, *Bahner v Marwest Hotel Co Ltd* (1969) 6 DLR (3d) 322 (BSCS), affd (1970) 12 DLR (3d) 646 (BCCA); *Myer Stores Ltd v Soo* [1991] 2 VR 597.
169 See, eg, *R v Garrett* (1988) 50 SASR 392, 405 (the will of a person may be overborne by threats of immediate physical force to the safety of another person).
170 For example, in *Ashland Dry Good Co v Wages*, 195 W 2d 312 (1946), the defendant retained the plaintiff's purse and caused the plaintiff's nervous condition to become worse, resulting in additional treatment. The plaintiff sued for false arrest and compensatory damages were awarded.
171 *McFadzean v Construction, Forestry, Mining and Energy Union* (2007) 20 VR 250.

Case: *McFadzean v Construction, Forestry, Mining and Energy Union* (2007) 20 VR 250

Facts

The plaintiffs were anti-logging protestors who had engaged in an anti-logging demonstration in the Otway Ranges in Victoria. They applied various protest techniques to prevent the defendants, forestry workers, from logging native forests. In response, the defendants set up a picket line outside the camp the plaintiffs had made in the forest. The picketers constituted of loggers and their families who had serious concern for the future of the logging industry in the Otways. The picketers' leaders offered to escort the plaintiffs safely through the picket line if they agreed never again to be involved in any form of protest at a logging coupe. The plaintiffs refused to enter into any such agreement. The defendants also used chainsaws, beat makeshift drums, ran generators close to the protestors' camp, threw stones against their tents and cars and engaged in other like conduct in order to harass and annoy them. Among many other claims, the plaintiffs sued the defendants for false imprisonment from the time the picket line was established until the time it came to an end, as the plaintiffs had feared violence if they had attempted to cross the picket line.

Issue

Had the defendants totally deprived the plaintiffs of their liberty by setting up a picket line? If so, was it a reasonable means of escape to seek assistance from police in leaving the protest site?

Decision

The Supreme Court of Victoria held unanimously that there had been no false imprisonment because there was a reasonable means of escape – leaving the protest site on foot through the bush. In analysing the reasonableness of the means of escape, the Court held:

> For some people perhaps, it might not be reasonable to expect that they make use of the bush gate. The evidence of those who walked through the bush as to the necessity to hold on, the difficulty of the terrain and its condition, the lack of visibility of holes and the fear of bone breakages, together with the need to look out for snakes and leeches, suggest that the experience may have been for some both difficult and unpleasant. But the judge was not concerned with just some people. His task was to assess the reasonableness of egress through the bush gate for this group of plaintiffs who it appeared were not unfamiliar with a bush environment and who had chosen to remain in this area of bush as their stamping ground for a protest about logging. We are not persuaded, in the circumstances of this case, that the evidence called for the conclusion that the bush gate for such people should be regarded as an unreasonable means of egress.[172]

---

172 Ibid [83].

Significance

This case illustrates the principle that, to be a false imprisonment, the deprivation of the plaintiff's liberty must be total.

Question

How was the reasonableness of the means of escape defined by the Supreme Court of Victoria in *McFadzean v Construction, Forestry, Mining and Energy Union*?

    Guided response in the eBook

PHYSICAL RESTRAINT NOT NECESSARY

Although the trespass refers to imprisonment, it is not necessary that the plaintiff be confined in some defined physical place (eg, a prison). Older cases showed that false imprisonment required the actual detention of the plaintiff in some physical place.[173] However, the modern approach is to ask whether the plaintiff submitted himself or herself to the defendant's power, reasonably thinking that there was no way of escape that could reasonably be taken. Therefore, if the plaintiff was not actually restrained in a specific place, and even if it would not be apparent to others that the plaintiff was being restrained, the restraint to a plaintiff may still be deemed to be total. For example, *Symes v Mahon* shows that a plaintiff may be falsely imprisoned by non-physical boundaries if they are deprived of liberty by a submission to the defendant's power.[174] The Appeal Court in *McFadzean v Construction, Forestry, Mining and Energy Union* confirmed this proposition in stating that 'restraint must be total, although it need not imply the use of physical force – it is sufficient if there be submission to the control of another after being given to understand that without submission there will be compulsion'.[175] Similarly, in *Myer Stores Ltd v Soo* the plaintiff submitted to the control of the defendant's representatives and at no point was he physically restrained, but the restraint was deemed to be total and to amount to false imprisonment.[176] Likewise, in *Ferguson v Queensland*, the Supreme Court of Queensland reasserted that, to establish false imprisonment, the fact that the plaintiff has submitted to the defendant's power is sufficient.[177] It is not necessary 'for the defendant to have used force and acts or words are sufficient where a plaintiff believes that force would be used if he does not submit'.[178]

---

173   *R v Macquarie* (1875) 13 SCR (NSW) 264.
174   [1922] SASR 447.
175   (2007) 20 VR 250, [23].
176   [1991] 2 VR 597, 615.
177   [2007] QSC 322.
178   Ibid [13].

Case: *Myer Stores Ltd v Soo* [1991] 2 VR 597

Facts

The respondent (Soo) was shopping at the store of the first appellant (Myer). Two police officers were called by a security officer of Myer and informed that the respondent, a person of interest due to shoplifting, was present at the store. The police officers and the security officer requested the respondent to accompany them to Myer's security office to sort out the matter. The respondent was then escorted by the three to the security office, where he was interviewed for an hour before being allowed to leave. Subsequently, a search warrant to search the respondent's home was granted and commenced. The respondent also agreed to attend at the police station for further interview and he did so voluntarily. After the interview, the investigating officer concluded that the respondent had been exonerated. The respondent brought an action for false imprisonment against both Myer and the police.

Issues

(1) Was the escorting of the respondent to the security office by the police officers and store security officer total deprivation of liberty amounting to false imprisonment?

(2) Was the questioning of the respondent for an hour a false imprisonment?

(3) Was the respondent's attendance at the police station for further interview a false imprisonment?

Decision

The trial judge found that the respondent had been falsely imprisoned and awarded him $5000 in damages. The appellants appealed, and the respondent cross-appealed on the question of damages. The respondent successfully established that the security officer had falsely imprisoned him when the officer escorted him to the store security office for interrogation, but failed to establish that his voluntary journey to a police station constituted false imprisonment. With regards to the first and the second issue, O'Bryan J stated:

> In my opinion, the evidence accepted by the learned judge inevitably required him to find that shortly after the third appellant spoke to the respondent in the hi-fi department his freedom of movement was totally restrained. The respondent knew, and the second and third appellants intended, that he had to accompany them to a place at which they could ask him questions about shoplifting. The conduct and words spoken to the respondent in the hi-fi department constituted imprisonment, in my opinion … The conduct which constituted imprisonment taken up by Evans, Mann and Sterling whereby the respondent proceeded from the department to the security room on the ground floor behind Evans, who led the way, followed by Mann and Sterling a few paces behind. A bystander would readily appreciate that the respondent was being escorted on a journey. The respondent was not invited to proceed at his own pace and by his own route to the security room; it was intended that he should proceed there under escort.
>
> … I am very clearly of the opinion that the respondent not a truly voluntary attendant in the security room and that the second third appellants intended, at all material times, to detain the respondent the room. That is not to say that they would necessarily have

used physical force but their conduct was enough to show the respondent that he was under restraint and had no choice but to remain in the room.[179]

Significance

This is one of the most frequently cited cases confirming that, to amount to false imprisonment, the deprivation of the plaintiff's liberty must be total, even though the deprivation is actuated by non-physical boundaries.

Question

Did the plaintiff need to be confined in some defined physical place for there to be a false imprisonment?

 Guided response in the eBook

It is clear that words or an assertion of authority may also constitute false imprisonment, provided the total restraint is procured by the threat of imminent and direct force to get the plaintiff to submit himself or herself to the defendant's power.[180]

KNOWLEDGE OF THE RESTRAINT

Knowledge of the restraint is not an essential element of false imprisonment. Although there is some early authority to the contrary,[181] false imprisonment can arise even if the plaintiff is not aware of the detention until it is over.[182] In *Meering v Grahame-White Aviation Co Ltd*, the plaintiff agreed to attend the defendant's office to give evidence in relation to some stolen items.[183] Unknown to the plaintiff at the time, three detectives had been stationed outside the room with instructions to stop the plaintiff from leaving if he attempted to do so. The House of Lords held by a majority that the plaintiff was falsely imprisoned. Atkin LJ said:

> It appears to me that a person could be imprisoned without his knowing it. I think a person can be imprisoned while he is asleep, while he is in a state of drunkenness, while he is unconscious, and while he is a lunatic. Those are cases where ... the person might

---

179 *Myer Stores Ltd v Soo* [1991] 2 VR 597, 614–15.
180 See, eg, *Symes v Mahon* [1922] SASR 447; *Harnett v Bond* [1925] AC 669; *Warner v Riddiford* (1858) 4 CB (NS) 180; *Bulsey v Queensland* [2015] QCA 187.
181 See, eg, *Herring v Boyle* (1834) 149 ER 1126 where an action was brought on behalf of a schoolboy detained at school by his headmaster during the holidays because of his parents' failure to pay the fees. The judge was influenced by the fact that the boy was unaware of his detention. Since the decision of *Meering v Grahame-White Aviation Co Ltd* (1919) 122 LT 44, knowledge of confinement is no longer required for a plaintiff to have an action for false imprisonment.
182 See, eg, *Meering v Graham-White Aviation* (1919) 122 LT 44; *Murray v Ministry of Defence* [1988] 1 WLR 692; *Myer Stores Ltd v Soo* [1991] 2 VR 597, 615; *Hart v Herron* [1984] Aust Torts Reports 80-201, where the jury found that the plaintiff was falsely imprisoned after being detained and given deep-sleep therapy without his consent, even though the plaintiff had no recollection of the imprisonment.
183 (1919) 122 LT 44.

properly complain if he were imprisoned, though the imprisonment began and ceased while he was in that state. Of course, the damages might be diminished and would be affected by the question whether he was conscious of it or not. So a man might in fact … be imprisoned by having the key of a door turned against him so that he is imprisoned in a room in fact although he does not know that the key has been turned.[184]

The House of Lords in *Murray v Ministry of Defence*[185] disapproved *Herring v Boyle*[186] and endorsed *Meering*, stating that actual knowledge of detention is not a necessary element of false imprisonment. Thereafter, in *Myer Stores Ltd v Soo*,[187] O'Brien J followed the House of Lords' ruling in *Murray*, holding that the victim need not be aware of the fact of the denial of liberty; knowledge of unlawful restraint may be relevant to the issue of damage.

However, if the plaintiff is aware of the potential for total restraint by the defendant but voluntarily chooses not to exercise their right to freedom of movement for their own reasons, there is no false imprisonment.[188]

To sum up, the plaintiff need not have been aware that they were being imprisoned at the time they were physically restrained; but where no force is used, the plaintiff must have reasonably believed that force would be used to restrain them if they had not submitted. If the plaintiff has knowledge of the imprisonment but gives up the right to leave, there is no false imprisonment.

6.4.3.3   The defendant at fault

As with the torts of battery and assault, the tort of false imprisonment requires proof of fault on the defendant's part. That is, the defendant must have intended the imprisonment or have been negligent in bringing it about. In relation to the issue of intention, the defendant must intend to commit the act which is substantially certain to cause the confinement *and* deprive the plaintiff of their liberty. In other words, in false imprisonment all that must be intended is the confinement or detention. The requisite intent may be proven by either *wilful intent* or *recklessness* as to whether an imprisonment would be likely to flow from the act. This is not problematic for cases where the intention to deprive the plaintiff's liberty is obvious. In such cases, as long as the defendant's action is voluntary, the requisite intention to imprison can be present.

False imprisonment can also arise where the defendant brings about the imprisonment negligently. An example is where a security guard locks the door of a library, believing that everybody, including the plaintiff, has gone home for the night, not realising that the plaintiff is in fact in the building, using the toilet. If the security guard has performed all the routine checks as required, the guard cannot be liable for false imprisonment – because the act of locking was deliberate, it was done without any intention to deprive the plaintiff of their liberty.

Suppose, however, that the security guard failed to perform this due diligence and negligently locked the plaintiff in the building. Should the guard be liable for false imprisonment? As

---

184   Ibid 53–4.
185   [1988] 1 WLR 692.
186   (1834) 149 ER 1126.
187   [1991] 2 VR 597, 615.
188   *McFadzean v Construction, Forestry, Mining and Energy Union* (2007) 20 VR 250, [41].

observed by Professor John Fleming in *The Law of Torts*, there are two different views. One is that the plaintiff should prove all the elements of actionable negligence – including actual injury – to justify the claim. This issue would be less important if loss of liberty qualified as recognised harm for the tort of negligence. The other view is that, if there can still be negligent trespass, then it is likely that the plaintiff can sue for negligent false imprisonment, without proof of loss.[189] As noted in Section 6.2.3, negligent trespass is recognised in Australia. Thus, technically, at least in Australia, there is no reason why a false imprisonment could not arise in the situation where the defendant negligently but directly causes the plaintiff's imprisonment.[190] In our example, the security guard is highly likely to be liable for negligent false imprisonment if the other elements of false imprisonment can be fulfilled.

As with the other torts of trespass to the person, intention in false imprisonment does not require the defendant to have intended to act unlawfully or injure the plaintiff in any way.[191] In this sense, liability in false imprisonment can be seen as strict.[192] Mistaken belief on the defendant's part is not relevant; a false imprisonment can be committed even though the defendant had a reasonable but mistaken belief in their right to imprison the plaintiff.[193] For example, if a prisoner is held past the term for which they are lawfully imprisoned, due to an honest and reasonable mistake of the prison authority, the defendant will nevertheless be liable for false imprisonment.[194] However, there are some rare exceptions mainly based on policy concerns such as maintaining a 'disciplined and effective defence force'.[195] In this case, the High Court held that the plaintiff, a member of the defence forces, could not succeed in false imprisonment against another member, although the command to detain the plaintiff had been made under invalid legislation:[196]

> Obedience to lawful command is at the heart of a disciplined and effective defence force. To allow an action for false imprisonment to be brought by one member of the services against another where that other was acting in obedience to orders of superior officers implementing disciplinary decisions that, on their face, were lawful orders would be deeply disruptive of what is a necessary and defining characteristic of the defence force. It would be destructive of discipline because to hold that an action lies would necessarily entail that a subordinate to whom an apparently lawful order was directed must either question and disobey the order, or take the risk of incurring a personal liability in tort.[197]

---

189 See C Sappideen and P Vines (eds), *Fleming's The Law of Torts* (Lawbook Co, 10th ed, 2011) 40.
190 The English law and Australian law hold different views on the question of whether an action can lie for a negligent false imprisonment. In England, it is likely that there is no negligent false imprisonment; instead, the action is brought in negligence and the plaintiff needs to prove that their negligent detention resulted in actual damage: *Sayers v Harlow Urban District Council* [1958] 1 WLR 623.
191 *R v Vollmer* [1996] 1 VR 95; *JCS v The Queen* (2006) 164 A Crim R 1.
192 *Ruddock v Taylor* (2005) 222 CLR 612; [2005] HCA 48, [140] (Kirby J).
193 See also *R v Governor of Brockhill Prison; Ex parte Evans (No 2)* [2001] 2 AC 19.
194 See *Cowell v Corrective Services Commission (NSW)* (1988) 13 NSWLR 714; *R v Governor of Brockhill Prison; Ex parte Evans (No 2)* [2001] 2 AC 19. It was concluded in both cases that false imprisonment is a tort of strict liability and the defendant should be liable for false imprisonment even though they have acted upon a good faith interpretation of the law, which was proved incorrect and unlawful. See also *Kable v New South Wales* (2012) 293 A Crim R 719.
195 *Haskins v Commonwealth* (2011) 244 CLR 22; [2011] HCA 28.
196 *Defence Force Discipline Act 1982* (Cth) pt VII div 3.
197 *Haskins v Commonwealth* (2011) 244 CLR 22; [2011] HCA 28, [67].

Furthermore, motive or malice for the intention to detain the plaintiff is not an element of false imprisonment. As Meagher JA stated in *Ruddock v Taylor*, if a defendant without statutory provision wrongfully imprisons a plaintiff, he is guilty of the tort – 'no matter how innocent, ignorant or even idealistic he may be'.[198] However, evidence of malice, both in the sense of ill will or spite, does affect the assessment of damages in the context of false imprisonment actions.[199] In *Myer Stores Ltd v Soo*, the actions of Myer's security officer were not premeditated and were not malicious per se, but his persistence in the accusation (suspecting that Mr Soo was a shoplifter) evidenced 'unreasoning prejudice' of which the law does not approve.[200] Similarly, in *R v Governor of Brockhill Prison; Ex parte Evans (No 2)*, a prisoner was successful in suing the governor of the prison for false imprisonment.[201] Although the defendant argued that he had acted honestly, it did not reduce the protection afforded by the tort of false imprisonment which is one of strict liability; the plaintiff was entitled to damages.

REVIEW QUESTIONS

(1) How does one differentiate the torts of battery and assault?

(2) If A sent an email to B threatening to shoot B dead, could B's apprehension of imminent threat ever be considered reasonable?

 Guided responses in the eBook

6.5 Remedies for trespass to the person

Although the torts of battery, assault and false imprisonment are all actionable per se, damages may be awarded to the plaintiff by way of remedy. As Murphy J emphasised in *Myer Stores Ltd v Soo*:

> The damages in an action for false imprisonment are generally awarded not for a pecuniary loss but for a loss of dignity, mental suffering, disgrace and humiliation. Any deleterious effect on the plaintiff's health will also be compensated.[202]

Note that the civil liability legislation would apply to limit an award of damages for personal injury caused by an intentional tort. An injunction may also be awarded to restrain future apprehended interferences with the plaintiff's person.[203] This remedy and the civil liability legislation are further discussed in Chapter 8.

---

198 (2003) 58 NSWLR 269, [73].
199 D Mendelson, *The New Law of Torts* (Oxford University Press, 3rd ed, 2014) 150.
200 [1991] 2 VR 597, 625.
201 [2001] 2 AC 19.
202 [1991] 2 VR 597, 633.
203 See, eg, in the case of domestic violence: *Daley v Martin (No 1)* [1982] Qd R 23; *Zimitat v Douglas* [1979] Qd R 454; *Corvisy v Corvisy* [1982] 2 NSWLR 557. See also, eg, *Domestic Violence and Family Protection Act 1989* (Qld).

REVIEW QUESTION

What are the usual remedies sought for trespass to the person?

 Guided response in the eBook

KEY CONCEPTS

- **action on the case:** originally referred to as the 'writ of trespass on the case' or simply 'case', this action was developed to complement the trespass action as a remedy for injuries originally not covered by trespass. It was available for the miscellaneous collection of injuries that were *indirect* and *consequential* and is the ancestor of negligence.

- **trespass:** a generic term encompassing a set of wrongs involving direct, and usually intentional, interference with either the person or property affected. There are three forms of trespass action: trespass to the person, trespass to land and trespass to goods (chattels).

- **trespass to the person:** refers to interference with a person's civil right to security of the person, and self-determination in relation to a person's own body. The tort of 'trespass to the person' includes three nominate torts (ie, torts that have specific names): battery (unlawful physical touching); assault (an apprehension or threat of unlawful touching); and false imprisonment (unlawful confinement or restraint).

 Complete the multiple-choice questions in the eBook to test your knowledge

PROBLEM-SOLVING EXERCISES

Exercise 1

One evening, when Stephen is watering his garden, he hears a noise outside his yard. Looking over the fence, he sees a boy lying on the ground and two teenagers kicking him. Frightened for the boy's safety, Stephen calls the police. A few moments later, the police arrive on the scene and arrest the two attackers. When John, one of the attackers, is being put into the police car, he sees Stephen looking over the fence. John realises that it must have been Stephen who called the police. He points at Stephen and shouts: 'I'm coming back for you later! Be afraid, be very afraid!'

Does Stephen have a claim for assault?

Guided response in the eBook

Exercise 2

Sally drives into the Brisbane CBD in mid-December to do some Christmas shopping. She enters a multistorey car park, taking a ticket from a booth at the entrance. When she takes the ticket from the booth, the entry boom gate is activated to allow her car to enter the car park. She drives around all five levels of the car park but is unable to find a space available. She decides to try another parking station, so she proceeds to the exit gate. At the exit gate, there is a booth manned by an attendant and another boom gate. Sally hands the attendant her ticket and asks to be let out through the boom gate because she could not find a space to park. The attendant refuses to let her through unless she pays the minimum $5 fee. Sally refuses to pay. After a five-minute stand-off between Sally and the attendant, the car park manager emerges from her office and instructs the attendant to raise the boom gate and let Sally proceed.

Can Sally sue the car park for false imprisonment?

 Guided response in the eBook

CHALLENGE YOURSELF

Exercise 1

Consider again the scenario in problem-solving exercise 2. Sally continues her Christmas shopping. She is stopped at the checkout of a supermarket and asked to show the operator the contents of her handbag. Sally happily complies as she knows it is a condition of her entry into the store. However, the operator finds an item in Sally's bag which he says he needs to check to see if it is from the supermarket's stock. Sally tells him it is not, but he replies that she must wait at the service desk while he gets his manager to check. Sally waits by the service desk for 10 minutes until the manager appears and tells her she is free to go.

Could this be considered false imprisonment?

 Guided response in the eBook

Exercise 2

(This case scenario was inspired by the US case of *Davis v Giles* 769 F 2d 813 (DC Cir 1985).)

Peter was a parking lot attendant. One evening, John parked his car in the parking lot where Peter worked. Next morning, after consuming beers all night at a pub nearby, John returned to the parking lot to retrieve his car. When John was paying the parking fee, Peter told John that his car battery might be dead because the car lights had been left on all night. John blamed Peter – why didn't he force his way into the car and turn off the lights? Peter explained that the policy of the parking lot prohibited him from entering locked cars. John was upset. He approached Peter with his fists clenched, and said: 'Okay mate, let me teach you a lesson!' Frightened for his own safety, Peter shut the door of the booth. John pinned the door from the outside using a stick, and said: 'You coward, now you can stay there!' John walked away, leaving Peter locked inside the booth. After about five minutes, Peter managed to escape the booth, but he broke his arm.

Advise potential trespass actions available to Peter.

 Guided response in the eBook

7

TRESPASS TO LAND AND TRESPASS TO PERSONAL PROPERTY

7.1   Introduction

Having discussed how the law of torts protects a person's physical integrity and freedom of movement in the previous chapter, we will now consider how the law protects a person's interests in property against certain types of interference, including trespass to land and trespass to personal property. Figure 7.1 indicates the relationship of different forms of trespass actions. In this chapter, we will explore the definitions and features of these trespass actions.

Figure 7.1   Different forms of trespass actions

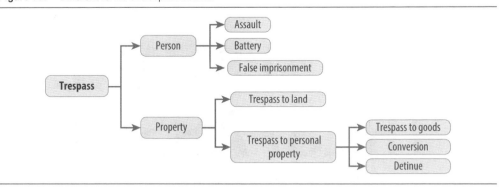

7.2   Trespass to land

Trespass to land is one of the earliest common law actions. It occurs when there is a direct interference, either intentional or negligent, with land in the possession of the plaintiff, and the interference is without lawful justification. In early times, the trespass *quare clausum fregit* ('wherefore he broke the close' or a breaking of the plaintiff's boundaries) was used in the trespass writ to indicate that the wrong complained of was a direct, forcible interference with the property rights of a plaintiff. In modern terminology this is 'trespass to land'. It should be noted that trespass to land is not a criminal offence at common law, but it has been criminalised by numerous statutory provisions in relation to enclosed lands.[1]

Trespass to land has evolved to serve a variety of purposes. Originally, this tort was a remedy for forcible breach of the King's peace, protecting people's real property from physical intrusion.[2] Later it was used as a means of resolving boundary disputes, determining title to land and preventing the acquisition of property rights by trespassers.[3] It also protects against interference with the plaintiff's privacy and security where the violation involves unlawful intrusion onto the plaintiff's land or premises.[4] Injunctions and aggravated and exemplary damages have been awarded by courts in appropriate cases where the defendant intruded onto the plaintiff's property for the purpose of televising film and sound recordings.[5] However, the action in trespass to land cannot be used as a general remedy for violations of privacy.[6] The primary function of this tort is to protect rights in property, rather than simply to provide compensation or protect ownership.

As with other forms of trespass, trespass to land is actionable per se. It is actionable even if the interference causes no damage or diminution of value to the plaintiff's land.[7] All that needs to be proven is that the alleged act was committed. This point is made in this oft-quoted passage from *Entick v Carrington*:

> Our law holds the property of every man so sacred that no man can set foot upon his neighbour's close without his leave. If he does, he is a trespasser, though he does no damage at all; if he will tread upon his neighbour's ground he must justify it by law.[8]

Subject to the highway exception (discussed in Section 6.3.4), the defendant bears the onus of disproving fault. Examples of trespass to land include situations where a defendant:

- enters upon the plaintiff's land without permission – no matter how slight that entry may be
- throws an object onto or removes an object from the plaintiff's land

---

1   *Crimes Act 1914* (Cth) s 89(1); *Public Order (Protection of Persons and Property) Act 1971* (Cth) ss 11–12, 20; *Enclosed Lands Protection Act 1943* (ACT) s 4; *Trespass on Territory Land Act 1932* (ACT) s 4; *Inclosed Lands Protection Act 1901* (NSW) s 4; *Trespass Act 1987* (NT) ss 5–8, 11; *Summary Offences Act 2005* (Qld) s 11; *Summary Offences Act 1953* (SA) ss 17, 17A; *Police Offences Act 1935* (Tas) ss 14A–14D, 19A; *Summary Offences Act 1966* (Vic) s 9(1)(d); *Criminal Code* (WA) s 70A.

2   See C Sappideen and P Vines (eds), *Fleming's The Law of Torts* (Lawbook, 10th ed, 2011) 49.

3   See, eg, *Lemmon v Webb* [1894] 3 Ch 1, 24.

4   *Plenty v Dillon* (1991) 171 CLR 635, 647, upheld in *New South Wales v Ibbett* (2006) 229 CLR 638; [2006] HCA 57, [30]; *Armidale Local Aboriginal Lands Council v Moran* [2018] NSWSC 1133, [13] (the defendant had no right to enter, occupy or remain on the Council's land as a squatter).

5   See, eg, *Emcorp Pty Ltd v Australian Broadcasting Corporation* [1988] 2 Qd R 169; *Rinsale Pty Ltd v Australian Broadcasting Corporation* [1993] Aust Torts Reports 81-231; *Lincoln Hunt Australia Pty Ltd v Willesee* (1986) 4 NSWLR 457; *Australian Broadcasting Corporation v Lenah Game Meats Pty Ltd* (2001) 208 CLR 199; [2001] HCA 63.

6   It should be noted that there is no separate tort of privacy in Australia, although law reform commissions in some jurisdictions have recommended the introduction of a statutory cause of action for intruding on privacy.

7   For example, in *Dumont v Miller* (1873) 4 AJR 152, entering upon the plaintiff's land with his dogs for the purpose of hunting was trespass, even though no physical damage to the plaintiff's property had occurred. See also *Johnson v Buchanan* (2012) 223 A Crim R 132, where hanging an arm 'partially to protrude over the fence' was held to be trespass on a neighbour's property, even though no harm had been caused.

8   (1765) 2 Wils KB 275, 291; 95 ER 807, 817. See also the judgment of Brennan J in *Halliday v Nevill* (1984) 155 CLR 1, 10.

- refuses to leave the plaintiff's land when permission to be there has been withdrawn
- builds a fence or a shed on someone else's property
- affixes brackets to the plaintiff's wall without authorisation
- dumps rubbish on the plaintiff's property
- sprays graffiti on buildings or structures
- parks a car on an 'employees only' car port or enters a 'staff only' area without authorisation.

Remedies for trespass to land are discussed in Chapter 8.

7.2.1   Defining trespass to land

As already mentioned, the tort of trespass to land covers the situation where the defendant, by an intentional or negligent act, causes a direct and unauthorised interference with the plaintiff's possession of land. The definition can be broken down in several ways. However, the following elements must be established in order for an action in trespass to land to succeed:

- The plaintiff must have the requisite title to sue.
- There must be direct interference with the plaintiff's land.
- The defendant must be at fault.

7.2.2   Title to sue: possession

7.2.2.1   Plaintiff's interest

As stated earlier, the tort of trespass to land protects against interference with the possession of land. Only the person who is in possession of the land at the time of the interference has the right to sue. Because of its emphasis on interference with the plaintiff's possession, it is not the function of the tort to protect ownership. Thus, an owner whose land has been leased to another may not have the requisite title to sue for trespass to land, even though the action of ejectment may enable the owner to regain possession.[9] Contrary to this, a lessee or tenant who acquires exclusive possession may bring an action for trespass to land against third parties or even the landowner whose land is the subject of the lease.[10]

What is 'possession' is a question of fact. At common law, it involves both factual possession (actual control) and *animus possidendi* ('intention to possess, and exclude others').[11] To decide whether the plaintiff has exclusive possession of particular land at the time of the trespass, the appropriate degree of factual possession and *animus possidendi* must be proved.[12]

---

9 *Rodrigues v Ufton* (1894) 20 VLR 539.

10 *Moore v Devanjul Pty Ltd (No 5)* [2013] QSC 323.

11 According to Slade J in *Powell v McFarlane* (1977) 38 P & CR 452, 471, *animus possidendi* refers to 'the intention, in one's own name and on one's own behalf, to exclude the world at large, including the owner with the paper title if he be not himself the possessor, so far as is reasonably practicable and so far as the processes of the law will allow'. Cited with approval in *Whittlesea City Council v Abbatangelo* (2009) 259 ALR 56; *KY Enterprises Pty Ltd v Darby* [2013] VSC 484; *Gibson v Allard* [2017] VSC 788; *Spiteri v Fibreglass Industrial Products Pty Ltd* [2017] VSC 768; *Laming v Jennings* [2017] VCC 1223; *Matusik v Maher Farms Pty Ltd* [2022] VCC 393.

12 It also includes the situation of constructive possession, which is a legal fiction to describe a situation where an individual has actual control over chattels or real property without having physical control of them.

On the one hand, preference is given to the plaintiff with legal title. That is, if there is no evidence to the contrary, the law will ascribe possession either to the owner of the land with the paper title or to persons who can establish a title through the paper owner.[13] A landowner as possessor needs only to establish actual control over the land to prove their exclusive possession. In such circumstances, any active step in relation to the land (such as enclosing the land,[14] cultivating it or living on it) is not required. As the Privy Council pointed out in *Ocean Estates Ltd v Pinder*, the 'slightest acts by the person who has title to the land, indicating his intention to take possession, are sufficient to enable him to bring an action for trespass against a defendant entering upon the land without any title', unless his intention to abandon the exclusive possession can be shown.[15] Moreover, exclusive possession remains even if the land in question is out of physical occupation for a period (eg, due to the occupier leaving for a holiday or letting the land lie fallow for a few years). On the other hand, if the prospective plaintiff is not the landowner, or a person has no paper title, both factual possession and *animus possidendi* should be proved in order for the courts to attribute possession of the land to the plaintiff.[16] It should be noted that the *animus possidendi* or the intention to exclude the world at large is a crucial element of possession, the absence of which explains why there is trespass when social activists occupy sites to draw attention to environmental damage or to pursue other socially desirable goals,[17] or when squatters intrude onto a property asserting they have no place to go.[18]

We have stated that possession rather than ownership is the key for title to sue in trespass to land. Thus, for the purpose of a trespass action, a plaintiff need not establish a legal or equitable title (indicating any proprietary or contractual right) to the land. A possessor, even an unlawful possessor (eg, a squatter), can sue for trespass – the mere fact of their exclusive possession will justify their title to sue.[19] The possessor of the land without a legal title may still maintain a trespass action against any person who lacks a better title when the interference occurs.[20] Therefore, a squatter with earlier possession can sue a subsequent

---

13 *Powell v McFarlane* (1977) 38 P & CR 452, 470 (Slade J); quoted with approval in *Whittlesea City Council v Abbatangelo* (2009) 259 ALR 56, 58 [5] (Ashley and Redlich JJA, and Kyrou AJA).

14 *Seddon v Smith* (1877) 36 LT 168, 169.

15 [1969] 2 AC 19, 25.

16 *Powell v McFarlane* (1977) 38 P & CR 452, 470 (use of the adjacent land by grazing a cow and a goat there were not sufficient to amount to factual possession); *Techild Ltd v Chamberlain* (1969) 20 P & CR 633, 642 (which confirms that factual possession cannot be based on trivial acts of possession such as occasionally allowing someone's horse to graze on another's property).

17 For example, animal rights organisations: *Australian Broadcasting Corporation v Lenah Game Meats Pty Ltd* (2001) 208 CLR 199; [2001] HCA 63; *Windridge Farm Pty Ltd v Grassi* (2011) 254 FLR 87; and anti-fracking protesters: *Wensley v Persons Unknown* [2014] EWHC 3086 (interim injunction against protesters). See C Sappideen, P Vines and P Watson, *Torts: Commentary and Materials* (Lawbook, 13th ed, 2021) 91.

18 *Secretary of State for the Environment v Meier* [2009] 1 WLR 2780 (exclusion of homeless travellers from government land).

19 As stated by Bowen CJ in *Mulcahy v Curramore Pty Ltd* [1974] 2 NSWLR 464, 475, a long period of continuous possession that is 'open, not secret; peaceful, not by force; and adverse, not by consent of the true owner' can give legal title to the squatter.

20 *Newington v Windeyer* (1985) 3 NSWLR 555, 563 (McHugh JA, Kirby P and Hope JA agreeing). As some writers have observed, the law of trespass to land is not concerned with who has the *best* claim to exclusive possession of the land but with who has the *better* claim to exclusive possession. Thus if the possession of land is disputed, the person who has a superior or better title wins. Generally, a person with factual possession has a better relative claim to possession than a passer-by, but a lesser relative claim to possession than someone who has the legal right to possession. See D Fox, 'Relativity of Title at Law and Equity' (2006) 65 *Cambridge Law Journal* 330. See also K Barker et al, *The Law of Torts* (Oxford University Press, 5th ed, 2012) 162.

intruder, but not the true owner or someone acting on behalf of the true owner.[21] In *Delaney v TP Smith Ltd* the plaintiff possessed a house under a lease that was legally ineffective.[22] The owners reclaimed possession of the house by forcibly ejecting the plaintiff. The plaintiff brought an action against the owners for trespass to land. The English Court of Appeal held that there was no trespass because the defendant's right to excusive possession overrode the plaintiff's actual possession.

7.2.2.2   Tenants and lessors

It is well accepted that a tenant who is in lawful possession of demised premises while the lease continues has a title to sue in trespass. In fact, a tenant in possession of land is entitled to sue the landlord for trespass if the landlord or the landlord's belongings enter without authority.[23] The landlord in such circumstances is 'tantamount to a stranger'.[24]

However, this common law position has been modified by legislation which provides the lessor with certain rights of entry or re-entry onto rented premises. For example, in Queensland, ss 129–204 of the *Residential Tenancies and Rooming Accommodation Act 2008* (Qld) govern entry onto rented premises by lessors. In case a lease is broken by the tenant, the lessor will regain immediate possession of the land. This deprives the tenant of title to sue in trespass to land.[25]

7.2.2.3   Licensees

Whether a licensee can sue in trespass to land is unclear. Old case authority suggested that a mere licence to use the land does amount to exclusive possession of the land, even if the acts done interfere with the licensee's use and enjoyment of the licence.[26] Thus, a licensee, like a hotel guest, does not necessarily have exclusive possession of the land even he or she has permission to enter. The position of Australian courts today remains that a mere licensee lacks sufficient title.[27] However, in certain circumstances, if a licensee has sufficient exclusive occupation of the land and exercises actual control over such premises, he or she can maintain an action of trespass against third parties who interfere with the possession.[28]

---

21   For example, *NRMA Insurance Ltd v B & B Shipping & Marine Salvage Co Pty Ltd* (1947) 47 SR (NSW) 273 (which summarised the position that *jus tertii* ['third party rights'] is no defence to an action for recovery of land); *Nicholls v Ely Beet Sugar Factory Ltd* [1931] 2 Ch 84; *Corporation of Hastings v Ivall* (1874) LR 19 Eq Cas 558, 585. The defendant in an action of trespass to land should only be able to plead the better right of the third party, not the true owner. See M Wonnacott, *Possession of Land* (Cambridge University Press, 2006) 32–4.

22   [1946] KB 393.

23   *Kelsen v Imperial Tobacco Co (of Great Britain and Ireland) Ltd* [1957] 2 QB 334 (the defendant landlord's advertising sign projected into the airspace above the plaintiff's single-storey shop constituted a trespass).

24   *Moore v Devanjul Pty Ltd (No 5)* [2013] QSC 323, [20] (McMeekin J).

25   *Baker's Creek Consolidated Gold Mining Co v Hack* (1894) 15 LR (NSW) Eq 207.

26   *Hill v Tupper* (1864) 3 H & C 121; *Vaughan v Shire of Benalla* (1891) 17 VLR 129, 135, affd *Western Australia v Ward* (2002) 213 CLR 1, 226 (McHugh J). *Simpson v Knowles* [1974] VR 190, 195–6 (Norris J); *McDowall v Reynolds* [2004] QCA 245, [7] (McPherson JA).

27   *Georgeski v Owners Corporation SP 49833* (2004) 62 NSWLR 534, [105]–[106] (Barrett J).

28   See, eg, *Moreton Bay Regional Council v Mekpine Pty Ltd* (2016) 256 CLR 437; [2016] HCA 7; *Sorrento Medical Service Pty Ltd v Chief Executive, Department of Main Roads* (2007) 2 Qd R 373; *Hinkley v Star City Pty Ltd* (2011) 284 ALR 154; *Shannon v New South Wales* [2015] NSWDC 69 (a plaintiff who was in possession of the land, 'as a matter of fact and practicality, the only person who could be approached

7.2.2.4   Easements and *profit à prendre*

A *profit à prendre* ('right of taking') is the right to enter the land of another, to take something which is part of the land and to carry it away as the property of the grantee. Rights to take minerals, timbers or wild animals from the land of another are classic forms of *profits à prendre*. An easement is a set of rights to enable one person to cross or otherwise use someone else's land for a specified purpose, including access, drainage, sewerage or supply of water or gas. A *profit à prendre* is clearly distinguishable from an easement as it involves a right to profit. A person with a right in the form of an easement or *profit à prendre* may be entitled to sue in trespass.[29]

7.2.2.5   Co-owners

If the land is owned by more than one person in the form of either a joint tenancy or a tenancy in common, each co-owner is entitled to exclusive possession to all of the land and is able to sue the trespasser. As a general rule, however, a co-owner (A) cannot sue another co-owner (B) unless A is wrongfully excluded from the land.[30] In addition, if the land is co-owned but not all owners occupy the land, only the co-owner in possession of the land at the time of the interference has title to sue in trespass.[31]

7.2.3   Actionable interferences

7.2.3.1   Direct interference

As in all trespass actions, the act of the defendant must directly cause the interference or intervention. The directness of the interference means that the interference (or injury) follows so immediately upon the act of the defendant that it may be termed part of that act.[32] An obvious example of a direct interference is where a person walks on or throws an object onto land in the possession of another. Indirect interference, such as a mere interference with the possessor's amenity or use and enjoyment of the land, is not an interference which gives rise to an action for trespass to land. The possible action will be nuisance (see Chapter 9) or negligence (see Chapters 2–4).[33]

Sometimes it is difficult to draw a distinction between direct and indirect interferences. For example, in *Southport Corporation v Esso Petroleum Co Ltd*, a trespass action was brought by the plaintiff against Esso Petroleum Co for discharging a considerable amount of oil from

---

for permission to enter the land', has title to sue for trespass to land); *Burwood Land Co Ltd v Knox* (1895) 21 VLR 381 (FC) (the mortgagor and a grazing licensee jointly in possession could maintain a trespass action for injury to their possessory rights); *Vaughan v Shire of Benalla* (1891) 17 VLR 129 (FC) (the plaintiff could sue in trespass for interference with his rights under a grazing licence).

29 *Fitzgerald v Firbank* [1897] 2 Ch 96; *Mason v Clarke* [1955] AC 778, followed in Australia in *Unimin Pty Ltd v Commonwealth* (1977) 45 LGRA 338 (rights to work a quarry).

30 *Luke v Luke* (1936) 36 SR (NSW) 310.

31 See the New Zealand High Court case *Baker v Police* [1997] 2 NZLR 467.

32 *Hutchins v Maughan* [1947] VLR 131, 133 (Herring CJ).

33 For example, water flowing from a defendant's land onto a plaintiff's is a consequential interference: *Reynolds v Clarke* (1725) 1 Str 634; damage caused by tree boughs from neighbouring land encroaching onto the plaintiff's land due to a storm was not trespass: see *Lemmon v Webb* [1894] 3 Ch 1 (CA), affd [1895] AC 1. See also *Young v Wheeler* [1987] Aust Torts Reports 80-126; *Robson v Leischke* [2008] NSWLEC 152; *Clambake Pty Ltd v Tipperary Projects Pty Ltd (No 3)* (2009) 77 ATR 242.

its tanker into the Ribble Estuary, oil which was then carried onto the plaintiff's foreshore by the tide.[34] Denning LJ observed that the plaintiff could not maintain an action for trespass because the interference with the foreshore was not a physical act done directly on the plaintiff's land.[35] Denning LJ further explained that the oil being carried onto the land by the tide was a consequential rather than a direct act, and the proper cause of action would be an action on the case for public nuisance (see Chapter 9). Morris LJ disagreed with Denning LJ and found that 'if something is thrown upon land or if the force of the wind or of moving water is employed to cause a thing to go on to land', the interference would be sufficiently direct to give rise to an action in trespass.[36]

In two similar cases, *Gregory v Piper*[37] and *Watson v Cowen*,[38] instead of assuming the directness of the interference, the courts looked to whether the interference was a 'natural' and 'probable' consequence of the defendant's act.[39] In *Gregory v Piper*, the defendant employer ordered his employee to pile up rubbish outside the plaintiff's land; the rubbish dried out and rolled against the plaintiff's wall and gate. In *Watson v Cowen*, the defendant ordered his independent contractor to bulldoze some land at the top of a slope. The earth shifted down the slope and eventually settled on the land of the plaintiff. In both cases, the issue of directness was either ignored or assumed and the defendants were held liable for trespass. Therefore, principles upon which the court will determine whether the interference is direct or consequential should be developed on a case-by-case basis.

7.2.3.2   Interference with land

As the subject matter of the tort, the term 'land' is used in a technical sense. Traditionally in common law, land has broadly covered the actual land or soil, the airspace above it and the area below the surface.[40] The actual land includes soil and earth to a certain depth[41] and buildings, plants, grass, unsevered crops and any other fixtures attached to the land.[42] This notion was reflected by the Latin maxim *cuius est solum, eius est usque ad coelum et ad inferos* ('for who owns the soil, his it is up to heaven and down to the centre of the earth'). As Sir William Blackstone explained:

> no man may erect any building, or the like, to overhang another's land: and downwards, whatever is in a direct line between the surface of any land, and the center of the earth, belongs to the owner of the surface; as is every day's experience in the mining

---

34   [1954] 2 QB 182, revd [1956] AC 218 (HL).

35   [1954] 2 QB 182, 196. Lord Denning's observation was supported on appeal by Redcliffe and Tucker LL in the House of Lords.

36   [1954] 2 QB 182, 204.

37   (1829) 109 ER 220.

38   [1959] Tas SR 194.

39   *Gregory v Piper* (1829) 109 ER 220, 593 (Bayley J), 595 (Parke J) (B & C).

40   See, eg, *Kelsen v Imperial Tobacco Co (of Great Britain and Ireland) Ltd* [1957] 2 QB 334, cited by *HS South Brisbane Pty Ltd v United Voice* (2019) 2 QR 556; *Bernstein v Skyviews & General Ltd* [1978] 1 QB 479.

41   See, eg, *Stoneman v Lyons* (1975) 133 CLR 550.

42   See, eg, *Basely v Clarkson* (1681) 83 ER 565; *Lincoln Hunt Australia Pty Ltd v Willesee* (1986) 4 NSWLR 457; *Port Stephens Shire Council v Tellamist Pty Ltd* (2004) 135 LGERA 98 (where destruction of trees on land owned by the respondent was trespass, the respondent was entitled to nominal damages for the wrongful acts of the Council); *Paridaen & Anor v Mahaside Pty Ltd* [2022] QSC 109.

countries. So that the word 'land' includes not only the face of the earth, but every thing under it, or over it.[43]

Compared with its traditional notion, the scope of the land in a trespass action is more limited in the modern era. As a general rule, the owner's right to the airspace above the surface is limited to 'such height as is necessary for the ordinary use and enjoyment of [the] land and the structures upon it' (the *Bernstein* test).[44] Case authorities involving subterranean caves, minerals or treasure have also tested the limits below the surface of land in trespass actions.[45] The rationale behind the change is that the rights of the public to the beneficial use of airspace (eg, for passing aeroplanes or satellites) and subsoil (eg, for extraction of mineral and petroleum resources) must be balanced against the rights of a person in possession of land.

AIRSPACE

As airspace is land that can be interfered with, intrusions into the airspace above the plaintiff's land may be actionable. Earlier cases showed that shooting the plaintiff's cat, which was on the roof of a shed on the plaintiff's land, constituted trespass by invasion of the plaintiff's airspace.[46] It has also been held that encroachments into airspace from neighbouring properties are trespass.[47]

However, not every interference with the airspace will amount to a trespass. For example, in *Bernstein v Skyviews & General Ltd*, the English High Court held that flying an aeroplane over the plaintiff's land for the purpose of photographing it was not a trespass.[48] The *Bernstein* test was further illustrated by the Northern Territory Supreme Court in *Schleter v Brazakka Pty Ltd*.[49] In this case the Court stated that Griffiths J in *Bernstein* 'did not deny the existence of rights with respect to airspace nor did he decide that interference with the upper airspace is never actionable'.[50] The Court held that the defendant's flights at a height of some 600 feet were not a trespass.

Case: *Bernstein v Skyviews & General Ltd* [1978] 1 QB 479

Facts

The defendant company flew over the plaintiff's property and took aerial photographs of it. The defendant later offered to sell the plaintiff a copy of the photographs. The plaintiff complained that the photographs had been taken without his consent, and that taking them was an invasion of his privacy and trespass into his airspace. The plaintiff sued the defendant for trespass to land, and demanded the negatives to be handed over or destroyed.

---

43 W Blackstone, *Commentaries on the Laws of England* (The Legal Classics Library, 1765) vol II, bk II, ch 2, 18.
44 *Bernstein of Leigh v Skyviews & General Ltd* [1978] 1 QB 479.
45 See, eg, *Elwes v Brigg Gas Co* (1886) 33 Ch D 562; *Bulli Coal Mining Co v Osborne* [1899] AC 351; *Edwards v Sims*, 24 SW 2d 619 (1929).
46 *Davies v Bennison* (1927) 22 Tas LR 52.
47 See, eg, *Bendal Pty Ltd v Mirvac Project Pty Ltd* (1991) 23 NSWLR 464; *Piazza v Strata Corporation 10147 Inc* (2020) 136 SASR 483.
48 [1978] 1 QB 479.
49 (2002) 12 NTLR 76.
50 Ibid [29].

Issue

Did the defendant's single flight over the plaintiff's airspace at a considerable height from the ground constitute a trespass?

Decision

The Court found that there was no trespass. Griffiths J observed (at [484]):

> The problem is to balance the rights of an owner to enjoy the use of his land against the rights of the general public to take advantage of all that science now offers in the use of air space. This balance is in my judgment best struck in our present society by restricting the rights of an owner in the air space above his land to such height as is necessary for the ordinary use and enjoyment of his land and the structures upon it, and declaring that above that height he has no greater rights in the air space than any other member of the public.

Significance

This case confirmed the rule that not every interference with airspace will amount to trespass. Griffiths J in this case highlighted the importance of balancing the rights of an owner to enjoy the use of their land with the rights of the general public in the use of airspace.

Notes

Griffiths J held the view that to apply the *cuius est solum* maxim literally would lead to 'the absurdity of a trespass at common law being committed by a satellite every time it passed over a suburban garden': at [484]. Therefore, the operation of the maxim was restricted in the modern law – this is the main basis of the decision in *Bernstein*: see *Finlay Stonemasonry Pty Ltd v JD & Sons Nominees Pty Ltd* (2011) 28 NTLR, [39].

The right of an owner to the subsoil has also been restricted and for the same reason. In the British case *Bocardo SA v Star Energy UK Onshore Ltd* [2011] 1 AC 380, the defendant petroleum company had been drilling for petroleum under the plaintiff landowner's land. Although the defendant was holding a licence to extract petroleum, it did not have the plaintiff's permission. The plaintiff sued the defendant in trespass. The English Court of Appeal held that the *cuius est solum* maxim was not part of English law because literal application (ownership to the centre of the earth) would lead to absurdities. Citing the decision in *Bernstein*, Lord Hope explained the current status of the maxim:

> In my opinion the brocard [ie, maxim] still has value in English law as encapsulating, in simple language, a proposition of law which has commanded general acceptance. It is an imperfect guide, as it has ceased to apply to the use of airspace above a height which may interfere with the ordinary user of land (at [26]–[28]).

Question

What limitations are imposed on rights to airspace in the context of an action for trespass to land?

 Guided response in the eBook

Thus, whether an intrusion into the airspace over another's land amounts to trespass depends on the height and nature of the interference. It is trespass if that portion of airspace is needed for the 'ordinary use' of the land which the possessor may see fit to undertake. Whether the incursion in fact affects or interferes with the possessor's use at the time of the interference is irrelevant.[51]

The *Bernstein* test, or 'ordinary user' principle, has been liberally interpreted by the courts in cases where the intrusion has taken place in the course of building operations, even if it does not interfere with general use and enjoyment. In particular, where airspace is commercially exploitable, the courts have favoured the landowner's right and awarded substantial damages and/or injunctions to stop a continuing trespass. For example, in *LJP Investments Pty Ltd v Howard Chia Investments Pty Ltd*,[52] the defendant (a commercial developer) sought the consent of the plaintiff (its neighbour) to allow it to erect scaffolding which would extend over the plaintiff's land. The plaintiff asked for a fee for this but the request was rejected by the defendant. The defendant erected the scaffolding anyway. The scaffolding was about 4.5 metres above ground level, and protruded 1.5 metres into the plaintiff's airspace. The plaintiff sued the defendant, alleging that the incursion of the scaffolding into the airspace above its land constituted a trespass. The Supreme Court of New South Wales held that there was a trespass to the plaintiff's land. Hodson J, in applying the *Bernstein* test and endorsing *Graham v KD Morris & Sons Pty Ltd*[53] and *Kelsen v Imperial Tobacco Co (of Great Britain and Ireland) Ltd*[54] stated:

> I think the relevant test is not whether the incursion actually interferes with the occupier's actual use of land at the time, but rather whether it is of a nature and at a height which may interfere with any ordinary uses of the land which the occupier may see fit to undertake.[55]

The Court granted a mandatory injunction against the defendant, required it to remove the scaffolding in question and awarded damages to the plaintiff.[56]

In some jurisdictions, statutory regimes have been created to allow temporary access to a neighbouring property without attracting penalties for trespass. For example, s 88K

---

51 *LJP Investments Pty Ltd v Howard Chia Investments Pty Ltd* (1989) 24 NSWLR 490, 495 (Hodgson J). See also *Bendal Pty Ltd v Mirvac Project Pty Ltd* (1991) 23 NSWLR 464, 470 (Bryson J).
52 (1989) 24 NSWLR 490.
53 [1974] Qd R 1.
54 [1957] 2 QB 334.
55 *LJP Investments Pty Ltd v Howard Chia Investments Pty Ltd* (1989) 24 NSWLR 490, 494.
56 Cases of similar causes of action: *Johnson v Buchanan* (2012) 223 A Crim R 132 (plaintiff trespassed by inadvertently allowing his arm to intrude over and down into his neighbour's property when he leant on the fence dividing their properties); *Break Fast Investments Pty Ltd v PCH Melbourne Pty Ltd* (2007) 20 VR 311 (defendant trespassed by attaching metal cladding to parts of the western face of its 12-storey building which encroached between 3 and 6 centimetres into the airspace over the plaintiff's adjoining land); *Graham v KD Morris & Sons Pty Ltd* [1974] Qd R 1 (a crane jib occasionally suspended directly above the plaintiff's roof was trespass); *Woollerton & Wilson Ltd v Richard Costain Ltd* [1970] 1 WLR 411 (incursion of a crane into the plaintiff's airspace was trespass and an injunction was awarded); *Kelsen v Imperial Tobacco Co (of Great Britain and Ireland) Ltd* [1957] 2 QB 334 (defendant's advertising sign projecting a few inches into airspace above plaintiff's shop was trespass); *Barker v Adelaide City Corporation* [1900] SALR 29 (an electric cable suspended across a public street at a certain distance from the ground was trespass); *Lawlor v Johnston* [1905] VLR 714 (ventilating pipes overhanging neighbouring premises was trespass).

of the *Conveyancing Act 1919* (NSW) provides that the Supreme Court of New South Wales may make an order 'imposing an easement over land if the easement is reasonably necessary for the effective use or development of other land that will have the benefit of the easement'.[57]

It should be noted that the capacity of an aircraft flight to give rise to a trespass has been directly addressed by legislation in all Australian states except Queensland. This legislation should be consulted instead of common law doctrine to deal with the exemptions from trespass. These statutes exclude actions being brought in trespass for the mere transient invasion of airspace.[58] For example, s 72 of the *Civil Liability Act 2002* (NSW) provides:

> No action shall lie in respect of trespass or nuisance, by reason only of the flight of an aircraft over any property at a height above the ground which, having regard to wind, weather, and all the circumstances of the case is reasonable, or the ordinary incidents of such flight, so long as the provisions of the Air Navigation Regulations are duly complied with.

However, to counterbalance this exemption, the legislation imposes strict liability on the owners of aircraft for all material loss or damage to persons or property caused by that aircraft. If damage is caused to the land below by an aircraft (or an object falling from it) while in flight, taking off or landing, the owner of the aircraft will be strictly liable (without proof of negligence or intention or other cause of action) for the loss or damage suffered as a result.[59]

SUBSOIL

It has been accepted that a person who possesses the surface of land generally also possesses the subsoil below the land,[60] even if the existence of the object below the surface is not known[61] or the owner is unable to use the subsoil.[62] For example, in the US case of *Edwards v Sims*, the defendant made money by conducting tours into a network of caves under the plaintiff's property.[63] The entrance to those caves was, however, located on the

---

57 Similar provisions can be found in *Access to Neighbouring Land Act 2000* (NSW) ss 7–8; *Property Law Act 1974* (Qld) s 180; *Law of Property Act 2000* (NT) ss 163–4; *Conveyancing and Law of Property Act 1884* (Tas) s 84; *Land Titles Act 1980* (Tas) s 110(4)–(12). More recent examples reflecting the exercise of the flexible statutory regime include *Bradshaw v Griffiths* [2016] QCA 20; *Lang Parade Pty Ltd v Peluso* (2005) 1 Qd R 42; *2040 Logan Road Pty Ltd v Body Corporate for Paddington Mews CTS 39149* [2016] QSC 40; *Clarence City Council v Howlin* (2016) 219 LGERA 226.

58 *Civil Liability Act 2002* (NSW) s 72; *Civil Liability Act 1936* (SA) s 62; *Damage by Aircraft Act 1963* (Tas) s 3; *Wrongs Act 1958* (Vic) ss 30, 31; *Damage by Aircraft Act 1964* (WA) s 4.

59 Actual damage to a person or property on the surface caused by an aircraft is covered by international conventions and legislation. Provisions concerning strict liability for damage raised from trespass include *Civil Liability Act 2002* (NSW) s 73; *Civil Liability Act 1936* (SA) s 63; *Damage by Aircraft Act 1963* (Tas) s 4; *Wrongs Act 1958* (Vic) s 31; *Damage by Aircraft Act 1964* (WA) s 4.

60 *Elwes v Brigg Gas Co* (1886) 33 Ch D 562.

61 *Re Cohen; National Provincial Bank Ltd v Katz* [1953] Ch 88; *Corporation of London v Appleyard* [1963] 2 All ER 834.

62 *Edwards v Sims*, 24 SW 2d 619 (1929).

63 Ibid.

defendant's property. The Court of Appeals of Kentucky held by majority that the plaintiff was entitled to bring a trespass action despite the fact that he himself could not utilise the caves, as the only access to them was located on the defendant's property. In *Stoneman v Lyons*, the appellant's workers dug a trench along the boundary of his property and undermined the adjoining landowner's garage wall, causing it to collapse after rain.[64] The High Court of Australia held that there was a trespass. Therefore, unless consented to or authorised by statutory provisions, extracting minerals, laying sewer or drainage pipes, digging a tunnel or pouring water or other fluids under a plaintiff's property constitutes trespass.

However, whether any limits apply to the depth of soil for the purpose of a trespass action is not clear. This issue was considered by the Supreme Court of the United Kingdom in *Bocardo SA v Star Energy UK Onshore Ltd*.[65] The Court held that the running of pipelines below a property constituted an actionable trespass at depths of between 250 and 850 metres. The Australian position is that, in general, a similar principle to *Bernstein* can apply. For example, in *Di Napoli v New Beach Apartments Pty Ltd*, the Supreme Court of New South Wales held that trespass to land may be committed beneath the surface of the plaintiff's land.[66] In that case, the plaintiff and the defendant were occupiers of adjoining lands. In the course of constructing a large building on the defendant's land, the defendant's builder placed rock anchors which projected beneath the plaintiff's land. Young CJ stated that, with respect to subterranean rights, 'a person has substantial control over land underneath his or her soil for considerable depth'.[67]

It should be noted that although at common law there is a presumption that the landowner owns everything on or below the land, mineral rights in Australia are normally vested in the Crown pursuant to statute (see Table 7.1). Unless mineral rights have been granted, the landowner will not be able to sue for trespass on the ground of interference with these mineral rights.

Table 7.1   Statutory provisions in relation to mineral rights in Australia

Legislation	Provision(s)
Mining Act 1992 (NSW)	s 62
Mineral Resources Act 1989 (Qld)	ss 50, 125
Mining Act 1971 (SA)	s 9
Mineral Resources Development Act 1995 (Tas)	s 79
Mineral Resources (Sustainable Development) Act 1990 (Vic)	ss 45, 46
Mining Act 1978 (WA)	s 8A, div 3, s 46

64 (1975) 133 CLR 550.
65 [2011] 1 AC 380.
66 (2004) 11 BPR 21,493.
67 Ibid [18]. See also, eg, *Burton v Spragg* [2007] WASC 247; *Piazza v Strata Corporation 10147 Inc* [2019] SADC 38.

7.2.4   Interference without lawful justification

To be an actionable trespass to land, the interference with the plaintiff's possession of land must be unauthorised or without consent.[68] If a person who enters the plaintiff's land has the plaintiff's consent or licence to do so, there will be no trespass.[69]

Unlawful entry is the most common form of trespass to land. Trespass to land will occur if the defendant unlawfully entered the plaintiff's land personally, or directly introduced animate or inanimate objects onto the land.[70] Interferences mentioned in Section 7.2.3.2 (eg, shooting the plaintiff's cat sitting on the plaintiff's roof, and allowing an advertising sign to project into airspace above the plaintiff's shop) were held to be trespassory. In these types of cases, the illegitimacy of the plaintiff's act seems obvious and consent or licence does not exist from the very beginning of entry. Entry with the plaintiff's consent, called a 'licence to enter', does not constitute a trespass.[71] The entrant with the consent of the plaintiff is called a 'licensee'. A licence to enter may arise from the plaintiff's express or implied consent, or by the authority of law. The onus of proving the existence of a licence rests on the licensee (ie, the entrant).

7.2.4.1   Express licence

The person in possession expressly consenting to another's visiting is the most straightforward example of an express licence to enter. Generally, contracts (eg, concert tickets or contracts to build on property) will give rise to a licence to enter property for particular purposes.[72] Once the purpose of the licence has been fulfilled, the licence expires and the licensee should leave within a reasonable time. If the licensee refuses to depart within a reasonable time, he or she becomes a trespasser. For example, a plumber called by the plaintiff to undertake repair work enters the plaintiff's property under an express licence; once the job has been done, the plumber should leave within a reasonable time to avoid liability.

If a defendant entered the plaintiff's property for a lawful purpose under an implied licence, but then acted beyond the scope of the licence, that licence will be void and the person will become a trespasser from the outset. For example, in *TCN Channel Nine Pty Ltd v Anning*, the New South Wales Court of Appeal recognised that a reporter has a limited licence to enter premises and seek permission to interview and film.[73] The scope of an implied licence in this case was for the purpose of entering to interact with the defendant's tyre business situated on their race track; to interview and film footage for a television program was beyond the scope of the implied licence.[74]

----

68 Although consent is normally regarded as a defence to the trespass actions, recent cases suggest that for an actionable trespass to land, it is necessary for the plaintiff to negate consent: *Lord v McMahon* [2015] NSWSC 1619, [148].

69 *Woodley v Woodley* [2018] WASC 333.

70 See, eg, *Rigby v Chief Constable of Northamptonshire* [1985] 1 WLR 1242 (QBD).

71 *Amess v Hanlon* (1873) 4 AJR 90 (VSCFC). See also *TCN Channel Nine Pty Ltd v Anning* (2002) 54 NSWLR 333; *Farrington v Thomson* [1959] VR 286; *Amstad v Brisbane City Council (No 1)* [1968] Qd R 334; *Singh v Smithenbecker* (1923) 23 SR (NSW) 207; *Semple v Mant* (1985) 39 SASR 282.

72 *Cowell v Rosehill Racecourse Co Ltd* (1937) 56 CLR 605, 621; *TCN Channel Nine Pty Ltd v Anning* (2002) 54 NSWLR 333.

73 (2002) 54 NSWLR 333.

74 Ibid [349]. See also *Rinsale Pty Ltd v Australian Broadcasting Corporation* [1993] Aust Torts Reports 81-231, where journalists entered premises with cameras rolling even though an interview proposal had been refused. It was held that there was a trespass from the moment of entry and no implied licence.

Case: *TCN Channel Nine Pty Ltd v Anning* (2002) 54 NSWLR 333

Facts

The respondent (Henry Anning) leased a large block of fenced rural land and built a motorcycle race track on it. He also purchased and stored a large quantity of used tyres on that property. The appellant (TCN Channel Nine) produced a television program known as *A Current Affair*. On the day in question, a television crew employed by the appellant, accompanying inspectors from the Environmental Protection Agency, members of the local council and the police, entered the respondent's property through a gate that was unlocked. The respondent asked them to leave the property.

Issue

Did the appellant's employees have a licence, either implied or express, to enter the respondent's property?

Decision

The New South Wales Court of Appeal upheld the trial judge's finding that the appellant had committed the tort of trespass to land. The Court adopted the reasoning of the High Court in *Halliday v Nevill* (1984) 155 CLR 1, *Plenty v Dillon* (1991) 171 CLR 635 and *Coco v The Queen* (1994) 179 CLR 427, and pointed out that although there might be an implied licence to allow the entry, the scope of the licence was not unlimited. The mere fact that the respondent had not relocked the gate after a delivery did not, of itself, establish an implied licence to enter. The scope of an implied licence would be for the purposes of the conduct of the used tyre business or for the conduct of a race track:

> Whatever may have been the scope of a permission for entry with respect to the conduct of the used tyre business or the conduct of a race track, nothing the appellant did was referable to any such purpose. If there was an implied licence to enter for any such purpose, the appellant did not avail itself of such a licence [at [43]].
>
> [The appellant] entered the land for the purposes of filming the raid, recording the Respondent's use of the land, conducting such interviews as it could with a view to broadcasting a programme. It was wholly outside any implied licence [at [78]].

Significance

This case is an important authority confirming that if a defendant entered the plaintiff's land with an implied licence, but then acted beyond the scope of the licence, the licence will be void and the person became a trespasser from the outset.

Notes

For a defendant who enters with an implied licence, the defendant's true purpose for entry must come within the scope of the implied licence. The importance of ascertaining the scope of a licence was explained by Brennan and Deane JJ in *Barker v The Queen* (1983) 153 CLR 338:

> It is possible that the question whether a particular entry is within the scope of a limited permission can involve difficulty in the identification of the limits of the permission and

the definition of the actual entry. An obvious example is the case where the permission is confined by reference to a particular purpose and an entry is made for that purpose and some other illegitimate purpose … the identification of the limits of the authority, like the definition of the actual entry for the purposes of ascertaining whether it comes within those limits, is essentially a question of fact to be determined by reference to the circumstances of the particular case [at 364–5].

Question

Was there any licence, either implied or express, enjoyed by the defendant in *TCN Channel Nine Pty Ltd v Anning*?

 Guided response in the eBook

7.2.4.2   Implied licence

A licence to enter may also arise from implied consent. In general, temporary and harmless entries in daily life may fall within the scope of implied licence. For example, there is an implied licence for pedestrians to use a pathway or driveway to the front door of a building, unless it is indicated that such entry is prohibited; to step upon an occupier's open driveway to avoid a vehicle parked on the footpath; or to enter the driveway for insignificant entries, such as to retrieve some item or an errant child.[75] An implied licence may also exist where the person enters the land on lawful business, communicating with the owner or making a delivery to a person in the premises.[76] That is why a sales person does not usually commit trespass by stepping onto a person's land and knocking on the front door, unless the person has already declared that the sales person is unwelcome.[77]

Case: *Halliday v Nevill* (1984) 155 CLR 1

Facts

Two police officers on a motorised patrol noticed the appellant, who was known to one of the police officers as a disqualified driver, reversing a car out of the driveway of a house. Having reversed onto the street, the appellant saw the police car approaching and immediately drove back into the driveway. The police officers walked down the driveway, entered the premises and arrested the driver. The magistrate held that the arrest was unlawful because the police officer conducting the arrest was a trespasser on the premises at the time of the arrest.

---

75 *Plenty v Dillon* (1991) 171 CLR 635, 647 (Gaudron and McHugh JJ).
76 *Halliday v Nevill* (1984) 155 CLR 1, 7 (Gibbs CJ, Mason, Wilson and Deane JJ).
77 This licence will typically be confined to the means of access (such as path, driveway or both) leading to the entry to the dwelling: see *Halliday v Nevill* (1984) 155 CLR 1, 7 (Gibbs CJ, Mason, Wilson and Deane JJ).

Issue

Did the police officers have an implied licence to enter the driveway?

Decision

The High Court held, by a majority of 4:1 (Brennan J dissenting), that the police officers had an implied licence to enter the driveway of the premises; thus they were not trespassers. The licence was implied as there was no suggestion that the driveway was closed off by a locked gate or any other obstruction, or that any notice or other indication prohibited the entry of visitors, including members of the police force. Gibbs CJ, Mason, Wilson and Deane JJ stated (at [6]–[7]):

> While the question whether an occupier of land has granted a licence to another to enter upon it is essentially a question of fact, there are circumstances in which such a licence will, as a matter of law, be implied unless there is something additional in the objective facts which is capable of founding a conclusion that any such implied or tacit licence was negated or was revoked. The most common instance of such an implied licence relates to the means of access, whether path, driveway or both, leading to the entrance of the ordinary suburban dwelling-house. If the path or driveway leading to the entrance of such a dwelling is left unobstructed and with entrance gate unlocked and there is no notice or other indication that entry by visitors generally or particularly designated visitors is forbidden or unauthorized, the law will imply a licence in favour of any member of the public to go upon the path or driveway to the entrance of the dwelling for the purpose of lawful communication with, or delivery to, any person in the house. Such an implied or tacit licence can be precluded or at any time revoked by express or implied refusal or withdrawal of it. The occupier will not however be heard to say that while he or she had neither done nor said anything to negate or revoke any such licence, it should not be implied because subjectively he or she had not intended to give it.
>
> ... The question which arises is whether, in those circumstances, the proper inference as a matter of law is that a member of the police force had an implied or tacit licence from the occupier to set foot on the open driveway for the purpose of questioning or arresting a person whom he had observed committing an offence on a public street in the immediate vicinity of that driveway. The conclusion which we have reached is that common sense, reinforced by considerations of public policy, requires that that question be answered in the affirmative [citations omitted].

Significance

The majority of the High Court in this case stated that whether an occupier of land has granted a licence to another to enter land is a question of fact. Such a licence may be implied unless there is obstruction or some indication that entry is forbidden or the implied permission has been revoked.

Notes

In this case Brennan J delivered an influential dissenting judgment. Quoting from the judgment cf Lord Camden LCJ in *Entick v Carrington* (1765) 95 ER 807, 817, Brennan J pointed out that the rule stating 'every invasion of private property … is a trespass' remains true. According to Brennan J (at [4]):

> This case is about privacy in the home, the garden and the yard. It is about the lawfulness of police entering on private premises without asking for permission. It is a contest between public authority and the security of private dwellings … The principle applies alike to officers of government and to private persons. A police officer who enters or remains on private property without the leave and licence of the person in possession or entitled to possession commits a trespass and acts outside the course of his duty unless his entering or remaining on the premises is authorized or excused by law.

In considering the relationship between the common law privileges that secure the privacy of the individual and the statutory powers in aid of the law enforcement, Brennan J observed (at [6]): 'although the common law has long protected the privacy of the home, it has never treated that privacy as inviolate against the exercise of a power to arrest.'

Questions

(1) What was the factual situation that give rise to the claim in *Halliday v Nevill*?
(2) In the view of the majority in *Halliday v Nevill*, what is the scope of the implied licence to enter private premises?

  Guided responses in the eBook

Case: *Roy v O'Neill* (2020) 272 CLR 291

Facts

The appellant was subject to a domestic violence order (DVO) for the protection of her partner. On 6 April 2018, three Northern Territory police officers attended the appellant's unit to conduct 'proactive domestic violence duties', including proactively checking DVO compliance by going to people's premises. While on the appellant's premises, the officers administered a breath test to the appellant which returned a positive result for alcohol, suggesting a violation of a condition of the DVO. The appellant was arrested and charged.

The trial judge held that the police did not have the power to attend at the unit to check the appellant's compliance with the DVO, and the appellant was found not guilty. On appeal, the Supreme Court of the Northern Territory agreed with the trial judge, holding that the police did not have an implied licence for the purpose of investigating whether a breach of the law had occurred. The prosecution further appealed to the Northern Territory Court of Appeal and succeeded. The appellant then appealed to the High Court.

Issue

(1) Did the police officers commit a trespass when they entered the premises occupied by the appellant, or did they have an implied licence to enter and to approach the front door to communicate with the appellant or her partner?

(2) Did the implied licence terminate and the police officers become trespassers when they asked the appellant to provide a sample of her breath?

Decision

The appeal was dismissed. A majority (3:2) of the High Court found that the police officers entered onto the premises with an implied licence. The Court held that at common law there will be no implied licence for police where entry is for the sole purpose of exercising coercive powers.

Kiefel CJ found that the implied licence described in *Halliday v Nevill* (1984) 155 CLR 1 would readily admit the police officers' entrance on the appellant's property. She held (at [18]):

> It is implied by the law so that police might undertake such enquiries and observations of the appellant as were necessary if she was present at the dwelling unit, to ascertain whether the DVO had been breached and an offence committed, as Constable Elliott expected might be the case. Whether this be called a 'check' or an investigation does not matter. It is a non-coercive aspect of police business which involves no adverse effect upon any person … It involves no interference with the occupants' possession. It is difficult to imagine how police could go about their business and more particularly how they could be expected to prevent domestic violence in the public interest unless they were able to make such enquiries and observations of the subject of a DVO and the person it is intended to protect.

However, the majority found that police do not lose implied licence to communicate where the motive for communication is to investigate the occupier for an offence. Checking on the welfare of the appellant's partner constituted a sufficient ground for an implied licence. Once the officers found the appellant was intoxicated, they had the requisite belief for the purposes of s 126(2A) of the *Police Administration Act 1978* and were authorised to remain on the premises and to require a sample of the appellant's breath.

Significance

The decision has implications for proactive policing Australia-wide as it gives the police confidence that they can, in certain circumstances, lawfully enter land and speak with occupants in the absence of express statutory authority. The authority does remain subject to limitations. The licence will not extend to authorise the entrance onto property if the sole purpose is to subject the occupant to a coercive process. The High Court's proposition is important for government agencies and their officers, including police, health, housing and welfare workers. It not only allows them to conduct their duties proactively, but also protects them from liability at the agency level.

Notes

The High Court in this case discussed the situation where the entrant has a dual purpose, including lawful communication, that entrance will usually be authorised. Citing *Barker v The Queen*, their Honours held at [72]:

> This implication in law of a licence in instances of mixed purposes reflects the realities and incidents of social life. The realities and incidents of social life do not require the drawing of imperceptible, jurisprudential distinctions based upon whether a purpose within a licence is or is not accompanied by other subjective motivations or purposes that might lie outside the licence, especially where the other subjective motivations or purposes might be conditional, subservient, or uncertain, or might never be acted upon. If such distinctions were drawn the operation of an implied licence would be practically unworkable.

Turning to entrance by police, the Court held that police do not lose implied licence to communicate where the motive for communication is to investigate the occupier for an offence, as found in *Robson v Hallett* [1967] 2 QB 939.

Question

In *Roy v O'Neill*, Bell and Gageler JJ took a different view of the legality of entry with a 'dual purpose': both to communicate, but also to coerce if cooperation was not forthcoming. In their view, entrance with such a mixed purpose was unlawful.

Do you agree with the reasoning of Bell and Gageler JJ in dissent which held that the implied licence to 'knock and talk' does not extend to compel the occupant to do anything – such as to take a sample of the appellant's breath for alcohol analysis?

 Guided response in the eBook

7.2.4.3   Exceeding the licence

The defendant will be a trespasser if he or she enters for a purpose outside the scope of the licence (whether express or implied). That is because one basic effect of a licence to enter is that it makes the entrant's lawful presence on the land conditional on the entrant continuing to observe the conditions. Once an entrant breaches one of the conditions of entry, the plaintiff's consent is withdrawn and the entrant becomes a trespasser. For example, in *Singh v Smithenbecker*, the defendant lawfully entered the plaintiff's land to take some sheep he had purchased from the plaintiff.[78] He then wrongfully removed the plaintiff's gate, rounded up certain sheep and drove away without the plaintiff's

---

78 (1923) 23 SR (NSW) 207.

permission. The defendant's acts were held to be trespassory from the outset as they exceeded the scope of the licence.[79]

Similarly, in *Barker v The Queen*, the defendant had the authority of the house owner to keep an eye on the property while the owner was away.[80] However, the defendant entered the house and committed theft. The High Court held that the defendant was a trespasser as he had obtained authority to enter the house for the purpose of security, but instead he had entered for the purpose of committing theft. Mason J pointed out that 'a person who enters premises for a purpose alien to the terms of a licence given to him to enter the premises enters as a trespasser', and if that is the case, the person 'stands in no better position than a person who enters with no authority at all'.[81]

The question of the scope of the implied right to enter has arisen in cases dealing with entry onto business premises by reporters and crews from television current affairs programs. One general principle is that an implied licence only covers the situation where the defendant enters the property with a bona fide, legitimate purpose. For example, in *Lincoln Hunt Australia Pty Ltd v Willesee* the crew entered the plaintiff's premises with one of the plaintiff's customers and took a video camera to record the interior of the premises.[82] The New South Wales Court of Appeal held that the defendant's implied right to enter the plaintiff's business premises was limited to those members of the public who were bona fide seeking information and business. It did not extend to unwanted visitors, such as people wishing to enter to rob the premises, or intrusive media crew members harassing the inhabitants by asking questions which would later be televised.

Similar views were held by the Queensland Court of Appeal in *Gallagher v McClintock*.[83] The appellant had attended a church for many years, but had been forbidden from entering the church property after a dispute arose between him and the church leaders about the manner of worship. To regain access to the premises of the church, the appellant sought an interlocutory injunction against the pastor and church board. The Court refused the application, holding that the church leadership had absolute 'discretion to allow or refuse any person a licence to enter their property' without prior notice or reason.[84] To comply with statutory requirements in relation to religious worship[85] and to behave in reasonable conformity with the requirements of the religion in which he was participating, were held to be implied conditions of the licence to enter.[86]

However, a difficult question will arise if the defendant entered the plaintiff's premises with mixed purposes. For example, in *Byrne v Kinematograph Renters Society Ltd*, cinema

79 See also *Bond v Kelly* (1873) 4 AJR 153 (after lawfully entering plaintiff's land, defendant acted outside his work order and cut down more trees than permitted, thereby committing trespass to land); *Horkin v North Melbourne Football Club Social Club* [1983] 1 VR 153; *Plenty v Dillon* (1991) 171 CLR 635; *TCN Channel Nine Pty Ltd v Anning* (2002) 54 NSWLR 333.

80 (1983) 153 CLR 338.

81 *Barker v The Queen* (1983) 153 CLR 338, 346–7 (Mason J).

82 (1986) 4 NSWLR 457.

83 [2014] QCA 224.

84 *Gallagher v McClintock* [2013] QSC 292, [2], [44]. See also *Kuru v New South Wales* (2008) 236 CLR 1, 14–15; [2008] HCA 26, [43]; *Lambert v Roberts* [1981] 2 All ER 15, 19; *Halliday v Nevill* (1984) 155 CLR 1; *Mackay v Abrahams* [1916] VLR 681, 684.

85 Set out in *Criminal Code* (Qld) s 207.

86 *Gallagher v McClintock* [2014] QCA 224, [24]–[25].

inspectors visited the plaintiff's cinema to investigate suspected fraud.[87] They bought tickets and watched a performance, but in fact the purpose of their entry was to check the numbers on the tickets and the number of audience members. Harman J held that the inspectors were not trespassers since the invitation to persons to enter the cinema was in general terms and the motives of the inspectors in entering were irrelevant. This can be compared with the decision in *Healing (Sales) Pty Ltd v Inglis Electrix Pty Ltd*.[88] In that case, the defendant had a contractual right to enter the plaintiff's premises to retake possession of certain goods, but in exercising this right also took other goods belonging to the plaintiff. Barwick CJ and Menzies J held that there was no trespass to land despite the fact that the defendant exceeded the licence to enter, as in respect of the original entry, there could not be a partial trespass to land which was for both a lawful and an unlawful purpose.[89] While agreeing with this proposition, Kitto J also held that the original entry was non-trespassory but the subsequent step taken by the defendant for the purpose of removing goods not subject to the contract 'was an unlicensed step and therefore a trespass'.[90] This proposition has been further reiterated by Keane and Edelman JJ in *Roy v O'Neill*,[91] where their Honours referred to established authority to the effect that police do not lose implied licence to communicate where the motive for communication is to investigate the occupier for an offence and do something coercive, such as administering a breath test.

7.2.4.4   Revocation or withdrawal of licence

A licence to enter (whether express or implied) can be revoked or withdrawn by the possessor. If the licensee does not leave within a reasonable time after the licence is withdrawn or revoked, the licensee becomes a trespasser unless the person has some independent legal authority to be present on the land. In *Cowell v Rosehill Racecourse Co Ltd*, the plaintiff had bought a ticket to enter the racecourse and watch the races.[92] He was asked to leave as it was alleged that he had misbehaved and breached the contract of entry. The plaintiff sued the racecourse operator on the ground that, as a licensee, he had a right or permission to stay on the premises. The High Court held that the plaintiff was a trespasser as he refused to leave within a reasonable time after the licence was revoked. The defendant racecourse operator had the right to evict the plaintiff. If the revocation amounts to a breach of contract, as in *Cowell*, the proper remedy for the licensee is an action for breach of contract – not trespass. What is a reasonable time depends on the facts, but generally a reasonable time allows the licensee to withdraw from the land and take away any belongings he or she has brought onto the land.[93]

To effectively revoke a licence, notice must be given to the licensee informing him or her that the licence is revoked. This requires a communication to the licensee which 'the licensee understands as a revocation of the licence' or which 'a reasonable person in the position of

---

87   [1958] 1 WLR 762.
88   (1968) 121 CLR 584.
89   Ibid 598–9.
90   Ibid 606.
91   (2020) 272 CLR 291; [2020] HCA 45, [72].
92   (1937) 56 CLR 605.
93   *Wilson v New South Wales* (2010) 278 ALR 74, [50] (Hodgson JA, McColl and Young JJA agreeing); *Cowell v Rosehill Racecourse Co Ltd* (1937) 56 CLR 605 (Dixon J); *Kuru v New South Wales* (2008) 236 CLR 1; [2008] HCA 26.

the licensee would understand as a revocation of the licence'.[94] Whether there has been a communication of revocation is a question of fact. Although a sign such as 'Private property' has been held to be insufficient to negate an implied licence,[95] taking other steps such as locking gates and displaying written notices like 'No Entry' or 'No Trespass' to warn off strangers would likely be sufficient.[96] In addition, prior communication with the possessor may be sufficient to negate an implied licence. In *Plenty v Dillon*, although the owner of the property had declared he would not accept service of summons to his daughter, two police officers entered anyway to serve a summons.[97] The High Court held that the police trespassed onto the property as the implied licence to enter had been revoked clearly by the plaintiff in prior communication.

If a property is co-owned by tenants in common, a tenant in common may permit an invitee to use the common property. However, if the permission given to the invitee is not reasonable and incidental to the tenant's proper use and enjoyment of the common property, the licence may be revoked by another tenant in common.[98]

7.2.4.5 Authorised by law

Apart from an express or implied licence, an entry may also be authorised by law. A number of statutes confer power to enter land or premises without the consent of the plaintiff. For example, s 122 of the *Animal Care and Protection Act 2001* (Qld) allows inspectors to enter places and vehicles for the purpose of investigating and enforcing compliance with the Act. Sections 9 and 10 of the *Law Enforcement (Powers and Responsibilities) Act 2002* (NSW) allow police officers to enter in emergencies and to arrest or detain someone in specific situations.[99] Occupiers who prevent a public official's statutory right of entry may attract a penalty or termination of the relevant service.[100] Statutory powers authorising certain persons to enter without committing trespass also extend to officers of local government and inspectors of some private organisations.[101] As a precondition, the statutory authority to engage in what otherwise would be tortious conduct must be 'clearly expressed in unmistakable and unambiguous language'.[102]

Under the common law, a police officer or citizen can enter private premises for the purpose of making an arrest, preventing a murder or following an offender who is running

---

94 Similarly, in the foregoing case *Gallagher v McClintock* [2014] QCA 224, the appellant's licence to be on Church land was revoked by the Church Board by its letter to the appellant in 2013.

95 *Thompson v Vincent* (2005) Aust Torts Reports 81-799, [123] (Mason P).

96 See, eg, *TCN Channel Nine Pty Ltd v Anning* (2002) 54 NSWLR 333; *Maynes v Casey* [2010] NSWDC 285; *Wilson v New South Wales* (2010) 278 ALR 74.

97 (1991) 171 CLR 635.

98 *New South Wales v Koumdjiev* [2005] NSWCA 247, which considered *Robson-Paul v Farrugia* (1969) 20 CLR 820, *Annen v Rattee* [1985] 1 EGLR 136 and *Hong v Choo* [2004] HKEC 64.

99 Section 10(1) of the Act provides that a police officer may 'enter and stay for a reasonable time on premises to arrest a person, or detain a person under an Act, or arrest a person named in a warrant'. Sections 9 and 10 of the Act were successfully applied by the Court in *New South Wales v McCarthy* (2015) 251 A Crim R 445.

100 For example, *Electricity Act 1994* (Qld) s 138 provides that supply may be disconnected if entry to read the meter is refused or obstructed.

101 See, eg, *Local Government Act 1993* (NSW) s 191; *Prevention of Cruelty to Animals Act 1979* (NSW) s 24E.

102 *Coco v The Queen* (1994) 179 CLR 427, 436 (Mason CJ, Brennan, Gaudron and McHugh JJ).

away from an affray. In such circumstances there is power not only to enter premises but to break into the premises where necessary. A condition of any lawful breaking of premises in such circumstances is that the person seeking entry has demanded and been refused entry by the occupier.[103] Restrictions on the power of police to enter premises were further addressed by the High Court in *Kuru v New South Wales*,[104] where a majority (Gleeson CJ, Gummow, Kirby and Hayne JJ with Heydon J dissenting) allowed the appeal, finding that police had neither a statutory[105] nor a common law justification to remain on the defendant's property after investigating a domestic disturbance. The High Court pointed out that the police's common law power to prevent a breach of the peace did not extend to entering and remaining on the premises to investigate whether a breach of the peace had occurred or was likely to occur.[106]

Case: *Kuru v New South Wales* (2008) 236 CLR 1

Facts

Six police officers went to the appellant's flat following a report of domestic violence in progress at the premises. When police arrived, the front door of the flat was open. The police entered the premises and found the appellant. The appellant's then fiancée (now wife) had had a noisy argument with him and left the flat with the appellant's sister. At first, the appellant invited the police to conduct a cursory check of the premises, but later withdrew his permission and repeatedly asked the police to leave. The police officers refused and a physical altercation ensued. The appellant was arrested and detained at the police station until the next morning. The trial judge dismissed the charges against the appellant, held that the police were trespassers and awarded the appellant damages. The State of New South Wales appealed. The New South Wales Court of Appeal in *New South Wales v Kuru* (2007) Aust Torts Reports 81-893 concluded that the police were not trespassers when the appellant first made physical contact with one of the officers. The appellant appealed.

Issue

Was there lawful justification for the police to remain on the appellant's property after the appellant revoked his consent?

Decision

A majority of the High Court (Gleeson CJ, Gummow, Kirby and Hayne JJ with Heydon J dissenting) allowed the appeal, finding that the police had neither a statutory nor a common law justification for remaining on the appellant's property after his permission had been withdrawn. The majority found that although police officers have a common law power to enter private premises to prevent a breach of the peace, they have no power to enter or remain on premises

103 *Plenty v Dillon* (1991) 171 CLR 635, [5].
104 (2008) 236 CLR 1.
105 Under *Crimes Act 1900* (NSW) ss 357F, 357H.
106 (2008) 236 CLR 1; [2008] HCA 26, [40]–[54].

to investigate whether a breach of the peace has occurred or is imminent. Their Honours stated (at [32]):

> The express provisions of s 357G reinforce the view that s 357F dealt only with entry to a dwelling house by invitation, and then for only so long as the relevant invitation remained unrevoked. In all but the case for which s 357F(4) provided, revocation by an occupier of an invitation to enter or remain sufficed to terminate then and there the permission for a police officer to remain on the premises. Only an invitation to enter or remain issued by the person reasonably believed to be the victim of a domestic violence offence trumped the occupier's revocation of permission.

The majority also held (at [53]):

> However broadly understood may be the notion of a duty or right to take reasonable steps to make a person who is breaching or threatening to breach the peace refrain from doing so, that duty or right was not engaged in this case. It was not engaged because, by the time police arrived at the appellant's flat there was no continuing or threatened breach of the peace. And no breach of the peace was later committed or threatened before the eruption of the violent struggle that culminated in the appellant's arrest.

Accordingly, the 'continued presence of police officers in the appellant's flat' after the appellant had asked them to leave 'and a reasonable time for them to leave had elapsed, could not be justified as directed to preventing a breach of the peace'.

Significance

This is a very important case about the authority to enter a plaintiff's land. The majority of the High Court, referring to the decision in *Plenty v Dillon* (1991) 171 CLR 635, summarised three significant rules concerning the police powers to enter private premises. Gleeson CJ, Gummow, Kirby and Hayne JJ stated (at [43]):

> First, a person who enters the land of another must justify that entry by showing either that the entry was with the consent of the occupier or that the entrant had lawful authority to enter. Secondly, except in cases provided for by the common law and by statute, police officers have no special rights to enter land. And in the circumstances of this case it is also important to recognise a third proposition: that an authority to enter land may be revoked and that, if the authority is revoked, the entrant no longer has authority to remain on the land but must leave as soon as is reasonably practicable.

Notes

The power which the police have at common law to prevent breaches of the peace does not extend to a power to enter and remain on the premises to investigate breaches of the peace. Neither s 357F nor s 357H of the *Crimes Act 1900* (NSW) authorised the police to remain on the premises.

Question

The High Court confirmed that generally implied licence – to 'knock and talk' – applies as much to an officer of the state as it does to your neighbour or to a door-to-door salesman. Do you think this proposition will change if the police's purpose to entry is both to talk and to coerce?

 Guided response in the eBook

To overcome the limits on police powers to enter property, legislation in various Australian jurisdictions gives the police lawful authority to interfere with possession. For example, s 9 of the *Police Powers and Responsibilities Act 2000* (Qld) provides that a police officer may enter and stay on premises for a reasonable time in circumstances that may otherwise be trespass.[107]

7.2.4.6   Trespass ab initio

Where a person enters the plaintiff's land with lawful authority (ie, under statute or common law) but then commits a wrongful act beyond that authority, the person becomes a trespasser *ab initio* ('from the beginning'). Trespass ab initio is based upon abusive behaviour of the defendant that negates the processor's original permission to be on the land. The rule was first defined in *Six Carpenters' Case*.[108] The rule does not apply where the defendant entered with the consent of the plaintiff rather than lawful authority. Conditions constituting trespass ab initio include:

(1)   The act is one of positive misfeasance (eg, refusal to pay for food and wine consumed in a restaurant or hotel), not mere nonfeasance or neglect of duty.[109] In *Six Carpenters' Case*, six carpenters went into an inn, consumed some bread and wine and paid for it. Later, they requested more wine but refused to pay. The Court held that the entrants abused the authority to enter, which could retrospectively render their entry unlawful.

(2)   The right to enter was conferred by law, not by licence or consent of the plaintiff.[110] As already mentioned, if the plaintiff gave consent but later revoked the consent, trespass can be committed if the entrant failed to leave within a reasonable time. However, trespass ab initio occurred only when a person has abused the authority to enter granted by law: either under common law rules (eg, a police officer in pursuit of a felon) or statutory provisions (eg, a gas meter reader).

---

107   There are similar provisions in *Crimes Act 1914* (Cth) s 3T; *Law Enforcement (Powers and Responsibilities) Act 2002* (NSW) ss 9, 10; *Police Administration Act 1978* (NT) s 119; *Summary Offences Act 1953* (SA) s 72B; *Crimes Act 1958* (Vic) s 459A; *Criminal Investigation Act* (WA) s 33.
108   (1610) 77 ER 695 (QB).
109   *Six Carpenters' Case* (1610) 77 ER 695 (QB).
110   *Windeyer v Riddell* (1847) 1 Legge 295; *McGrath v Marshall* (1898) 14 WN (NSW) 106.

(3)   There is no ground justifying the original entry, even though trespassory acts were also committed later on the land.[111] In *Elias v Pasmore*, police officers had legally entered the plaintiff's land to arrest a man. While there, they seized a number of items – some of them unlawfully. It was held that trespass had only been committed in respect of the documents unlawfully removed; there was no trespass ab initio since some of the documents were lawfully taken.

The role of the doctrine of trespass ab initio in the modern law is unclear. The very existence of the doctrine was doubted by Denning LJ in the Court of Appeal case *Chic Fashions (West Wales) Ltd v Jones*.[112] In that case, the police searched the plaintiff's premises and seized some goods they wrongly thought to be stolen. The seizure was held to be lawful because the police had entered the premises with a warrant authorising them to remove anything they believed to be stolen. Denning LJ said trespass ab initio was no longer law as it contradicted the principle that if an act was lawful while it was conducted, subsequent events cannot make it unlawful; the rest of the Court of Appeal treated it as obsolete.[113] However, Denning LJ took a different view in *Cinnamond v British Airports Authority*, where the Court applied the ab initio principle to prohibit some mini-cab drivers unlawfully entering the airport and touting for business.[114]

A more substantive function of the doctrine, suggested by Professor John Fleming, is that it is 'justifiable at best as a constitutional safeguard against abuse of governmental authority' (eg, the exercise of police powers) in modern times.[115] Australian courts have not ruled definitively on the issue, although in *Barker v The Queen* Deane JJ stated:

> If the doctrine of trespass *ab initio* survives, it is, in a modern context, perhaps best seen as an anomalous rule of evidence which is applicable in a case of an alleged civil trespass by a person who relies upon an authority under the general law and which precludes the alleged trespasser from denying that he entered the land for the purpose of doing thereon the precise things which he subsequently did.[116]

Therefore, when determining whether one's behaviour was abusive it is necessary to consider whether it was consistent with an express or implied permission to enter.

7.2.4.7   Continuing trespass

Trespass is said to be 'continuing' if, after an initial trespassory entry or failure to leave, the person or object remains on the land. Continuing trespass gives rise to new causes of action arising from day to day; it can justify a series of legal actions until they are removed.[117] The

---

111   *Elias v Pasmore* [1934] 2 KB 164.
112   (1968) 2 QB 299.
113   *Chic Fashions (West Wales) Ltd v Jones* (1968) 2 QB 299, 313 (Denning LJ), 317 (Diplock LJ).
114   (1980) 1 WLR 582, 588–9.
115   See C Sappideen and P Vines (eds), *Fleming's The Law of Torts* (Lawbook, 10th ed, 2011) 52.
116   (1983) 153 CLR 338, 363–4.
117   See, eg, *Konskier v Goodman Ltd* [1928] 1 KB 421 where rubbish left behind after the completion of building work was held to be a trespass. *Konskier* itself cites an earlier authority to the same effect: *Hudson v Nicholson* (1839) 151 ER 185. Both cases were cited with approval by the Supreme Court of New South Wales in *Lord v McMahon* [2015] NSWSC 1619 (building table drains near the boundary of two subdivided rural properties causing erosion of the plaintiff's property was a trespass).

limitation period for the trespass runs from the last day of the presence. For example, in *Holmes v Wilson*, the highway authorities had built buttresses for a road on the plaintiff's land.[118] Building these supports was held to be a trespass, and the defendant had to pay damages. The defendant was found liable in a subsequent action for trespass for failing to take the buttresses away.[119]

This doctrine is of particular importance for both a subsequent transferee of land and purchaser of the offending objects.[120] It should be noted that the doctrine applies only to continuing trespassory invasion (ie, failure to leave or remove items from the land); it does not apply to unrepaired damages to the land following from the trespass.[121]

7.2.5 Fault

To be actionable in trespass to land, the interference with the plaintiff's possession of the land must be either intentional or negligent. That is, the defendant must be at fault. There will be no liability for trespass if the defendant can show that there was no intention or negligence on their part. An example of a case where the trespass action failed because there was no fault on the part of the defendant is *Public Transport Commission (NSW) v Perry*.[122] In this case, a railway passenger at a train station who suffered an epileptic fit fell on the railway tracks and sustained injury. In defending an action for negligence, the Commission argued that the passenger was trespassing by her presence on the railway tracks. A majority of the High Court held that the involuntary movement of the passenger onto the tracks did not constitute a trespass. Similarly, if a defendant was pushed or involuntarily propelled onto someone's land without permission, there will be no trespass due to lack of intention.[123]

It should be noted that in trespass to land, liability arises even where the defendant was not aware that he or she had intruded on another's property. In this sense, liability for trespass to land is strict in substance. For the same reason, if the defendant was mistaken about the ownership or boundaries of land, or about the availability of permission, the intention for the purpose of trespass to land can still be established.[124]

Trespass to land may also be committed negligently. In *League Against Cruel Sports Ltd v Scott* the Court held that a master of hounds was liable for an entry by the hounds onto the plaintiff's land.[125] It was said that the master was liable if he intended the hounds' entry or if by negligence he failed to prevent them from entering.[126]

---

118 (1839) 113 ER 190.

119 *Holmes v Wilson*, ibid, was applied with approval by McKechnie J in *SSYBA Pty Ltd v Lane* [2013] WASC 445, [60].

120 *Hudson v Nicholson* (1839) 151 ER 185; *Break Fast Investments Pty Ltd v PCH Melbourne Pty Ltd* (2007) 20 VR 311.

121 See *Clegg v Dearden* (1848) 12 QB 576 (where the defendant failed to fill up a pit he dug in his neighbour's land, only the initial entry was treated as trespass).

122 (1977) 137 CLR 107.

123 *Smith v Stone* (1647) 82 ER 533.

124 *Basely v Clarkson* (1681) 83 ER 565.

125 [1986] QB 240.

126 *League Against Cruel Sports Ltd v Scott* [1986] QB 240, 247–52 (Park J).

REVIEW QUESTIONS

(1) Who can sue for trespass to land?

(2) What may constitute the subject matter of the tort of trespass to land?

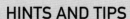

Guided responses in the eBook

HINTS AND TIPS

Before dealing with problem questions in relation to trespass to land, it is important to be familiar with the following issues:

- the scope of land for the purpose of trespass to land
- who has title to sue for trespass to land
- the circumstance where an implied licence exists
- the effect of revoking or withdrawing a licence for entry to a property
- the types of interference that may give rise to trespass to land.

7.3   Trespass to personal property

Trespass to personal property is an act by the defendant that directly interferes with the plaintiff's possession of the property. There are three intentional torts relating to personal property: trespass to goods, conversion and detinue. These torts are separate torts and the elements of each are quite distinct. However, they overlap to some extent and there are situations where the plaintiff can maintain an action in more than one of these torts (see Table 7.2).

Table 7.2   Comparison of trespass to goods, conversion and detinue

	Trespass to goods	Conversion	Detinue
Definitions	• An intentional or negligent act directly causes an unauthorised interference with goods or chattels in the possession of the plaintiff.	• An intentional act seriously interferes with the possession of the plaintiff in a manner repugnant to the right of the plaintiff.	• A wrongful refusal to deliver up goods to a person having the immediate right to the possession of those goods causes deprivation of possession of the goods.
Elements	• The plaintiff has the requisite title to sue. • There is a direct interference with goods. • The defendant is at fault.	• The plaintiff has the requisite title to sue. • There is to be a direct interference with the plaintiff's goods that amounts to a repugnant dealing. • The defendant is at fault.	• The plaintiff has the requisite title to sue. • There is a demand and refusal. • The defendant is at fault.

Table 7.2 (cont.)

	Trespass to goods	Conversion	Detinue
Types of interference	• Mere taking or asportation of goods. • Handling of goods without authority. • Unauthorised use of goods. • Causing material damage to the goods.	• Wrongful use. • Wrongful taking or dispossessing. • Wrongful destruction or alteration. • Wrongful disposition (sale and delivery or wrongful delivery).	• Detaining the plaintiff's goods while the goods are in the defendant's possession. • An inability to return goods due to wrongful loss or destruction of the goods by the defendant.

Who can sue	• Person who has actual or constructive possession at the time of the interference.
	• In limited circumstances, the person who has immediate right to possession (eg, bailor) may sue for trespass to goods.
	• A special or temporary right to present possession would be sufficient to support an action for trespass. Thus, a lienee, a carrier or a bailee who has had actual possession of goods may sue.
		• A person with actual physical or constructive possession of the goods at the time of the conversion, or an immediate right to possession, may sue for conversion:
		(1) bailment at will:
		  • bailee
		  • bailor
		(2) bailment for a term:
		  • bailee
		  • owner
		  • bailees and bailors
		  • co-owners
		  • finders.
			• A person with actual physical or constructive possession of the goods at the time of the interference, or an immediate right to possession:
			(1) bailment at will
			  • bailee
			  • bailor
			(2) bailment for a term
			  • bailee
			  • bailor (but only when goods were lost or destroyed by the bailee).

The subject matter of the actions for trespass to goods, conversion and detinue is 'personal property'. This term refers to movable property and can be used interchangeably with both 'goods' and 'chattels'. Real property, like land or buildings permanently attached to land (fixtures), cannot be the subject of trespass to personal property actions; the proper action will be trespass to land. However, if the item was detached from the land (eg, trees or a shed), it becomes a movable property and can therefore become the subject of an action in trespass.[127]

Generally, pure intangibles such as intellectual property rights, an internet domain name, an internet protocol (IP) address, an autonomous system number (ASN) or a telephone number cannot be the subject of such actions.[128] Money in a bank account is not personal property for the purposes of an action in conversion, detinue or trespass to goods.[129] However, documentary intangibles such as cheques and shares have been recognised as a

---

127 *Dymocks Book Arcade Ltd v McCarthy* [1966] 2 NSWR 411; *Bilambil-Terranora Pty Ltd v Tweed Shire Council* [1980] 1 NSWLR 465; *Laboud v Laboud* [2009] NSWSC 623.
128 *Hoath v Connect Internet Services Pty Ltd* (2006) 229 ALR 566; *Telecom Vanuatu Ltd v Optus Networks Pty Ltd* [2008] NSWSC 1209.
129 See *Ferguson v Eakin* [1997] NSWCA 106.

proper subject of the torts under consideration, due to the fact that the document establishing or evidencing the right is itself a chattel which may be tortiously interfered with.[130] In such a case, the value of the document is not in the paper itself but in the right it represents. In addition, instruments that are not negotiable interests (eg, life insurance policy, guarantee) can potentially be converted.[131]

There was a debate as to whether human body parts or corpses could form the basis of an action in trespass. In *Doodeward v Spence*, the High Court held that a corpse is not property and could not be the subject matter of an action for trespass to personal property.[132] However, Griffith CJ pointed out that a body part which has been the subject of 'work or skill' such that it 'has acquired some attributes differentiating it from a mere corpse awaiting burial' might be property and subject to possessory rights.[133] Subsequent decisions have recognised that parts of a corpse which have been dissected or preserved for scientific or exhibition purposes could constitute property.[134]

EMERGING ISSUE

More recent cases have confirmed rights in human body parts, tissues and fluids. For example, in *Roblin v Public Trustee (ACT)*, the Supreme Court of the Australian Capital Territory held that stored sperm taken with consent was property.[135] In that case, the sperm was deposited after the deceased was diagnosed with cancer, as he was advised that treatment for the cancer might affect his fertility.[136] Mossop M stated:

> The mere fact that the semen was formerly part of a human body is not sufficient to deny that it is property. The fact that the sperm constitutes human gametes is not sufficient at common law to take it out of the conception of property. There has been no legislative intervention that requires it to be treated differently to other material that might constitute property because it was formerly part of a human body, or because of its particular status as being human gametes.[137]

130   See, eg, *Wilton v Commonwealth Trading Bank of Australia* [1973] 2 NSWLR 644; *Hunter BNZ Finance Ltd v CG Maloney Pty Ltd* (1989) 18 NSWLR 420 (cheques); *NIML Ltd v Man Financial Australia Ltd* (2006) 15 VR 156 (cheques); *Haddow v Duke Co NL* (1892) 18 VLR 155 (shares); *Hardy v Cotter* (1881) 7 VLR (E) 151 (shares); *Kay v Barnett* [1909] QWN 39 (title deeds).

131   *Watson v McClean* (1858) 120 ER 435 (life insurance policy); *M'Leod v M'Ghie* (1841) 133 ER 771 (life insurance policy or a guarantee).

132   (1908) 6 CLR 406.

133   Ibid [414].

134   See, eg, *R v Kelly* [1999] QB 621.

135   (2015) 10 ACTLR 300. The similar issues have been considered by different courts across Australian jurisdictions in recent years, especially by the Supreme Court of NSW. See, for example, *Hosseini v Genea Ltd* [2021] NSWSC 1568; *Re Application by Adams (a pseudonym) (No 2)* [2021] NSWSC 794; *Chapman v South Eastern Sydney Local Health District* (2018) 98 NSWLR 208.

136   Similar examples include *Roche v Douglas* (2000) 22 WAR 331, *Yearworth v North Bristol NHS Trust* [2010] QB 1 and *Bazley v Wesley Monash IVF Pty Ltd* [2011] 2 Qd R 207, which were considered by the Court in *Roblin v Public Trustee (ACT)* (2015) 10 ACTLR 300.

137   (2015) 10 ACTLR 300, [28].

A similar position was held by the Supreme Court of Queensland in *Re Cresswell*.[138] The applicant alleged that she was entitled to possession of the sperm of her late partner, extracted shortly after his death under a court order, to be used in assisted reproductive treatment. The Court held that the applicant is entitled to possession and use of the sperm on certain conditions.

Even so, whether human bodies (including some early forms of life such as embryos and gametes) and tissues can be the subject of property rights remains a complex and developing area of the law. There are a number of unresolved matters. The Australian Law Reform Commission considered whether genetic samples are capable of being regarded as property ownership and concluded by recommending that 'proprietary rights in preserved samples should continue' but that 'there should be no legislation to confer property rights on human genetic samples'.[139] Due to the complex and developing nature of this area of law, the Supreme Court of Queensland pointed out that it would be appropriate to leave the issue to be considered by the Law Reform Commission, even though it is likely that some issues will need to be resolved by Parliament.[140] This attitude might extend to the protection of intangible assets such as computer files, digital information, e-tickets and so forth in the new cyber environment.

All actions involving trespass to personal property protect the plaintiff's possession rather than ownership. Therefore, the plaintiff need not prove a title or ownership to the goods but need only to show possession, either actual or constructive, to the goods.[141] There are three forms of legal possession of personal property: (1) actual possession, which refers to the situation where goods are under the physical control of the plaintiff; (2) constructive possession, which refers to the situation where the plaintiff has actual control over the goods without physically controlling them; and (3) right to possession, which means the plaintiff, as the temporary keeper or the long-term owner, has a legally enforceable right to gain possession of the goods.

The rules concerning the plaintiff's title to sue vary depending on which of the three torts – trespass to goods, conversion or detinue – is being pursued.

---

138 [2019] 1 Qd R 403.
139 Australian Law Reform Commission, *Essentially Yours: The Protection of Human Genetic Information in Australia* (Report No 96, 30 May 2003) Recommendation 20–1. See also C Sappideen, P Vines and P Watson, *Torts: Commentary and Materials* (Lawbook, 13th ed, 2021) 120.
140 See *Re Cresswell* [2019] 1 Qd R 403, [235].
141 Even so, the person who is in possession of, but does not own, the property cannot prevent a non-owner in possession from bringing an action in trespass to goods. Even a person who obtained a property unlawfully (eg, a thief) can obtain a property right to exclude all others except those with a better right, if the person has physical control of the chattel and the intent to exercise that control on their own behalf to exclude others. See *Costello v Chief Constable of Derbyshire Constabulary* [2001] 1 WLR 1437, [31] (Lightman J, Keene and Robert Walker LLJ agreeing); *McMillan Properties Pty Ltd v WC Penfold Ltd* (2001) 40 ACSR 319, 325–6 [44]; *Bride v Shire of Katanning* [2013] WASCA 154, [72]; cited by *Hocking v Director-General of the National Archives of Australia* (2020) 271 CLR 1; [2020] HCA 19, [204].

7.3.1   Trespass to goods

As 'goods' and 'chattels' can be used interchangeably with 'personal property', so trespass to goods can be used as an umbrella concept encompassing all three nominate torts. However, 'trespass to goods' also refers to a particular nominate tort. As a nominate tort, it involves an intentional or negligent act on the part of the defendant which directly causes an unauthorised interference with goods or chattels in the possession of the plaintiff.

Trespass to goods assumes various forms. Taking a motor car, a mobile phone, documents or jewellery out of the possession of another; vandalising a chattel; injuring pets or animals of others could all be actionable as a trespass to goods. To establish trespass to goods, the following elements must be established:

- the plaintiff has the requisite title to sue
- there is a direct interference with goods
- the defendant is at fault.

As this action is a form of trespass action, the general rules for trespass claims apply, requiring the plaintiff to establish direct interference, proof of damage and fault (see Section 6.3). The interference with the plaintiff's goods must be a direct result of the defendant's act; if the interference is intentional but indirect, this gives rise to an action on the case, but not an action in trespass. In the meantime, possession for the purpose of trespass to goods is established in the same way as trespass to land and both intention and physical control are required (see Section 7.2.3.1).

Trespass to goods is actionable without proof of actual damage. Lord Blanesburgh's dictum in *Leitch v Leydon*[142] is often cited to support the view that trespass to goods is always actionable per se.[143] However, there is some doubt about whether a mere touching of goods causing no damage is actionable. For example, in *Everitt v Martin*, the High Court of New Zealand held that a mere negligent touching of goods resulting in no damage was not trespass.[144] In *Wilson v Marshall*, the Supreme Court of Tasmania held that a police officer unlocking a car door using a piece of wire did not commit trespass to goods.[145] There is limited Australian authority on this point, but it would seem that trespass should, in theory, be available in such circumstances, if the law does not take the touching as trifling.[146]

Remedies for trespass to goods include an award of damages and grant of an injunction. These are discussed in Chapter 8.

---

142   [1931] AC 90, 106.
143   Even so, the person in possession but does not own the property cannot prevent a non-owner in possession from bringing an action in trespass to goods. See *Costello v Chief Constable of Derbyshire Constabulary* [2001] 1 WLR 1437, [31] (Lightman J, Keene and Robert Walker LLJ agreeing); *Hocking v Director-General of the National Archives of Australia* (2020) 271 CLR 1; [2020] HCA 19.
144   [1953] NZLR 298.
145   [1982] Tas R 287.
146   Based on similar observations, some academic writers also conclude that there has been a consensus among them that an intentional touching of goods is trespass, even if there is no damage or dispossession. See, eg, RP Balkin and JLR Davis, *Law of Torts* (LexisNexis Butterworths, 4th ed, 2009) 95, cited by M Davies and I Malkin, *Focus: Torts* (LexisNexis Butterworths, 9th ed, 2021) 908.

7.3.1.1 Title to sue

The action of trespass to goods is concerned with protection of the plaintiff's possession. Therefore, the general rule is that only the person who has actual or constructive possession at the time of the interference may sue for trespass to goods. A special or temporary right to present possession would be sufficient to support an action for trespass. Thus, a lienee, a carrier or a bailee who has had actual possession of goods is entitled to sue for trespass to goods.[147] There are, however, some apparent exceptions to the rule that possession is essential. In the following exceptions, the plaintiff could sue for trespass to goods even though the plaintiff was not in actual possession of the goods at the time of the defendant's act:

- A trustee may sue for direct interference with goods, even though the goods are possessed by a beneficiary.[148]
- The executor or administrator of an estate may sue for trespass to the goods of a deceased person, even though the trespassory act occurred prior to the executor or administrator taking actual possession.[149]
- The owner of a franchise in a wreck may sue for an interference with franchise goods which took place prior to actual possession being taken by the franchisee.[150]
- A person with an immediate right of possession can sue where there is interference by a third party (other than the bailee) with the actual possession of the plaintiff's servant, agent or bailee under a revocable bailment (see Section 7.3.1.2). This important exception was addressed by the High Court in *Penfolds Wines Pty Ltd v Elliott*.[151]

7.3.1.2 Bailment exception

Of the exceptions to the rule that possession is essential outlined in Section 7.3.1.1, the bailment exception has the most practical importance. A bailment is an arrangement, often made by contract, where one person (the bailee) takes possession of a chattel from another person (the bailor) on the understanding that the chattel will be returned to the bailor, or otherwise disposed of pursuant to the bailor's directions, once the purpose of the agreement has been fulfilled. During the period a bailment exists, the bailor parts with possession of the goods rather than the ownership.

As already mentioned, a bailee who is in actual possession may sue in trespass and that is not disputed. However, the bailor's title to sue in trespass to goods is less clear. If the bailment is terminable by the bailor at any time (normally called a 'revocable bailment' or 'bailment at will'), the bailor will have a right to immediate possession and be entitled to sue for trespass to goods.[152] But if the bailment is for a term, a bailor out of possession may

---

147   *Standard Electronic Apparatus Laboratories Pty Ltd v Stenner* [1960] NSWR 447, 451 (Walsh J), citing E Bullen, S Leake and J Jacob, *Bullen & Leake & Jacob's Canadian Precedents of Pleadings* (Thomson Reuters, 3rd ed, 2017) 414. See also *Johnson v Diprose* [1893] 1 QB 512, 515; *Penfolds Wines Pty Ltd v Elliott* (1946) 74 CLR 204 (Dixon J).
148   *Barker v Furlong* [1891] 2 Ch 172.
149   *Tharpe v Stallwood* (1843) 5 Man & G 760.
150   *Dunwich Corporation v Sterry* (1831) 109 ER 995.
151   (1946) 74 CLR 204, 227 (Dixon J).
152   *Penfolds Wines Pty Ltd v Elliott* (1946) 74 CLR 204. See also *Lotan v Cross* (1810) 170 ER 1219; *Wilson v Lombank Ltd* [1963] 1 WLR 1294 (a bailor can sue for trespasses to the bailee at will's possession based on the constructive possession in the bailor).

not sue for trespass to goods during the term. This is because during the term the bailor has no right to demand return of the goods from the bailee and therefore has no entitlement to immediate possession; what the bailor has is a mere reversionary interest.[153]

This exception has only limited application because it will not arise where the bailment is for a term which has not expired or been terminated; nor will it apply where the tortious act complained of was committed by or with the consent of the bailee.[154]

HINTS AND TIPS

Bailment exception has the most practical importance. The usual requirement that a plaintiff must have possession of the chattel at the time of the trespass in order to sue will be problematic if this rule is strictly adhered to in practice. Bailment exception enables a plaintiff with only an immediate right to possession to sue in trespass. It is therefore important to differentiate various forms of possession (actual possession, constructive possession and an immediate right to possession) in establishing title to sue in actions of trespass to goods.

Case: *Penfolds Wines Pty Ltd v Elliott* (1946) 74 CLR 204

Facts

The plaintiff (Penfolds Wines Pty Ltd) made wine and sold it in bottles. The bottles were embossed with the plaintiff's name and an information informing purchasers that the bottles were the property of the plaintiff at all times. Notations on their invoices accompanying the bottles also informed possessors that Penfolds retained ownership of the bottle. Once the contents had been consumed, the empty bottles were supposed to be returned to Penfolds on demand; they were not to be damaged, destroyed, parted with or used for purposes other than retail or consumption. The defendant (Elliott) was a licensed hotelier carrying on business at a hotel in New South Wales. He sold bulk wine to customers by filling whatever bottles they brought to his hotel. Among these bottles were some belonging to the plaintiff. The plaintiff asserted that the defendant, without its consent, had been receiving, collecting and handling its embossed bottles, using them in his business and filling them with liquids not produced or marketed by Penfolds. The plaintiff sought an injunction to restrain the defendant's practice, alleging trespass to goods and conversion by Elliott.

Issue

Had the defendant committed trespass to the plaintiff's goods (wine bottles) by filling them with liquids made by other producers?

Decision

The trial judge found that the plaintiff did not have title to sue and therefore could not succeed in trespass to goods. The plaintiff appealed. By a majority of 3:2 (Latham CJ and Williams J

---

153 *Gordon v Harper* (1796) 101 ER 828; *Ward v Macauley* (1791) 100 ER 135.
154 *Penfolds Wines Pty Ltd v Elliott* (1946) 74 CLR 204.

dissenting), the High Court held that no injunction should be granted on the ground that the evidence showed only a rare and casual act. As Dixon J pointed out (at [224]–[225]):

> Trespass is a wrong to possession. But, on the part of the respondent, there was never any invasion of possession. At the time he filled the two bottles his brother left with him, he himself was in possession of them. If the bottles had been out of his own possession and in the possession of some other person, then to lift the bottles up against the will of that person and to fill them with wine would have amounted to trespasses. The reason is that the movement of the bottles and the use of them as receptacles are invasions of the possession of the second person. But they are things which the man possessed of the bottles may do without committing trespass. The respondent came into possession of the bottles without trespass. For his brother delivered possession to him of the two bottles specifically in question. In the same way, if any other customer ever left bottles of the appellant with him for wine to be poured into them, those customers must have similarly delivered possession of the bottles to the respondent. His possession of the appellants' bottles was, therefore, never trespassory. That his brother was in possession of the two bottles specifically in question there can be no doubt.

Significance

In this frequently cited case in relation to trespass to personal property, the High Court elucidated the essence and elements of conversion. Dixon J pointed out that 'the gist of the action of trespass must be the wrong to the right of possession'. His Honour also explained (at 229) that 'the essence of conversion is a dealing with a chattel in a manner repugnant to the immediate right of possession of the person who has the property or special property in the chattel'. In addition, when deciding the plaintiff's title to sue in trespass to goods, Dixon J considered the 'bailment exception' (see Section 7.3.1.2).

Notes

The action for trespass to goods protects possession rather than ownership. Therefore, a person with possession (either physical or constructive) of goods at the time of the interference is entitled to sue in trespass to goods. This rule was stated by Dixon J in *Penfolds Wines Pty Ltd v Elliott*:

> It is submitted that the correct view is that right to possession, as a title for maintaining trespass, is merely a right in one person to sue for a trespass done to another's possession; that this right exists whenever the person whose actual possession was violated held as servant, agent, or bailee under a revocable bailment for or under or on behalf of the person having the right to possession.[155]

Therefore, where a company's goods were unduly interfered with, a company officer or an employee (or agent on the plaintiff's behalf, according to Dixon J) may have the title to sue for trespass to goods, even though such a person does not have possession or a right to immediate possession personally: *Burnett v Randwick City Council* [2006] NSWCA 196.

---

155 Quoting F Pollock and R Wright, *An Essay on Possession in the Common Law* (Clarendon Press, 1888) 3–4.

The majority (Dixon, McTiernan and Williams JJ) in *Penfolds Wines Pty Ltd v Elliott* held that there was no trespass to goods. Dixon J said there was no trespass as there was 'no infringement upon the possession of any one' (at [224]). Even so, Dixon J suggested, as an exception, that the bailor could sue the bailee for trespass if the goods were destroyed or the nature of the goods was completely changed (at [228]). Latham CJ (dissenting) held that there was trespass to goods. His Honour concluded that the bailment had expired once the bailee acted 'in a manner absolutely repugnant to the terms of the bailment' (at [217]). That meant, when the bottles were handed to the defendant by the bailee, the bailment was terminated and the person with the immediate right to possession (Penfolds) was entitled to sue in trespass to goods.

Dixon also pointed out that the defendant's action could not be an innominate injury to the plaintiff's right to possession because the defendant did no damage to the plaintiff's goods (the bottles). Therefore, although the plaintiff could not sue in trespass to goods or detinue in such circumstances, the remedy for an innominate injury 'would have been a special action on the case' (at [224]).

Question

According to the majority, why was there no trespass to goods in *Penfolds Wines Pty Ltd v Elliott*?

 Guided response in the eBook

Thus, as a general rule, a bailee cannot commit trespass with respect to the goods he or she is holding for the bailor. However, there may be an exception to this general rule. In *Penfolds* Dixon J suggested that the complete destruction of the chattel by the bailee may amount to trespass.[156]

The case also involved a claim in conversion, which we will look at in Section 7.3.2.

7.3.1.3   Direct interference

Any direct interference with the plaintiff's possession (or that of the plaintiff's bailee at will) may give rise to a cause of action.[157] The distinction between a direct and consequential act was discussed in Section 6.2.3. Therefore, to lock goods in a room is not an actionable trespass to goods as the interference with possession is indirect.[158]

Latham CJ in *Penfolds Wines Pty Ltd v Elliott* outlined the types of interference that will constitute a trespass to a good.[159] Examples include mere taking or asportation of goods without the infliction of any material damage, handling of goods without authority, unauthorised use of goods and causing material damage to the goods.

The mere taking or asportation of a good can amount to trespass. For example, in *Kirk v Gregory*, the defendant removed jewellery from the bedroom of a recently deceased person into another room for safekeeping, but it could not later be found, probably due to theft.[160]

---

156   *Penfolds Wines Pty Ltd v Elliott* (1946) 74 CLR 204, 227–8.
157   *Covell v Laming* (1808) 170 ER 1034.
158   *Hartley v Moxham* (1842) 114 ER 675.
159   (1946) 74 CLR 204, 214.
160   (1876) 1 Ex D 55.

The executor of the estate sued the defendant for trespass. The defendant was held liable for removing the goods even though the Court accepted that the defendant was not liable for the theft (or conversion) of the goods.

Similarly, simply handling someone else's goods without their authority or consent can constitute trespass.[161] Trespass can also arise where there has been an unauthorised use of goods. Therefore 'unauthorised acts of riding a horse, driving a motor car, using a bottle, are all equally trespasses'.[162]

Causing material damage to the goods is the typical form of trespass to goods.[163] However, as we will see, trespass is actionable per se so there is no need to show actual, material damage.

7.3.1.4   Fault

As in all trespass actions, fault is an element of trespass to personal property. Liability will not arise if the court finds that the interference was not intentional and the defendant was not negligent. For example, in *National Coal Board v JE Evans & Co (Cardiff) Ltd*, the defendant escaped liability after cutting the plaintiff's underground electricity cable, the presence of which the defendant neither knew or ought to have known about.[164] As with other forms of trespass, intention in the context of trespass to goods refers to the intention to do the act which gave rise to the actionable interference, rather than any intention to commit a trespass.[165] In this sense, if the defendant interferes with goods due to the mistaken belief that they are entitled to the goods, this is not sufficient to avoid liability. It is the plaintiff who bears the onus of proving that the defendant intended to, or negligently did, commit the act.

7.3.2   Conversion

Conversion consists of an intentional act on the part of the defendant which seriously interferes with the possession of the plaintiff in a manner 'repugnant' to the right of the plaintiff. The tort of conversion is the successor of the action of *trover* (from the Old French *trouver*, meaning 'to find'), which was developed out of the earlier writ of trespass *de bonis asportatis* ('trespass of goods carried'). It was based on the fiction that the plaintiff possessed a certain chattel and casually lost it, the defendant found it and refused to return it to the plaintiff on request, then the defendant converted the chattel to his or her own use.[166] As the torts continued to develop up to the modern day, the elements of conversion changed to cope with the development of society. As Dixon J explained in *Penfolds Wines Pty Ltd v Elliott*:

> The essence of conversion is a dealing with a chattel in a manner repugnant to the immediate right of possession of the person who has the property or special property

161 *Slaveski v Victoria* [2010] VSC 441 (handling of documents and removing them within the premises was an actionable trespass).
162 *Penfolds Wines Pty Ltd v Elliott* (1946) 74 CLR 204, 214–15 (Latham CJ).
163 *Fouldes v Willoughby* (1841) 151 ER 1153, 1157 (Alderson B).
164 [1951] 2 KB 861.
165 *Clissold v Cratchley* [1910] 2 KB 244.
166 For a detailed history of trover and conversion, see JB Ames, 'History of Trover' (1897) 11(5) *Harvard Law Review* 277, 374; JW Salmond, 'Observations on Trover and Conversion' (1905) 21(1) *Law Quarterly Review* 43, 47; D Mendelson, *The New Law of Torts* (Oxford University Press, 3rd ed, 2014) 244.

in the chattel. It may take the form of a disposal of the goods by way of sale, or pledge or other intended transfer of an interest followed by delivery, of the destruction or change of the nature or character of the thing, as for example, pouring water into wine or cutting the seals from a deed, or of an appropriation evidenced by refusal to deliver or other denial of title. But damage to the chattel is not conversion, nor is use, nor is a transfer of possession otherwise than for the purpose of affecting the immediate right of possession, nor is it always conversion to lose the goods beyond hope of recovery. An intent to do that which would deprive 'the true owner' of his immediate right to possession or impair it may be said to form the essential ground of the tort.[167]

Allsop P in *Bunnings Group Ltd v CHEP Australia Ltd*,[168] referring to *Penfolds Wines* and *Kuwait Airways Corporation v Iraqi Airways Co (Nos 4 and 5)*,[169] pointed out that the basic features of conversion involve 'an intentional act or dealing with goods inconsistent with or repugnant to the rights of the owner, including possession and any right to possession. Such an act or dealing will amount to such an infringement of the possessory or proprietary rights of the owner if it is an intended act of dominion or assertion of rights over the goods'.[170]

The action will only arise where the defendant commits an intentional act. Mere negligence will not suffice with this tort.[171] A defendant does not, however, have to intend to convert the article. What is necessary is that the defendant intended to deal or interfere with the article and that dealing or interference amounts to a conversion. A conversion does not depend on actual or constructive knowledge on the part of the defendant. In other words, a conversion can be committed even though the defendant did not know, or had no reason to suspect, that the plaintiff had rights in the good.[172]

To establish an action in conversion, the following elements must be established:

- the plaintiff has the requisite title to sue
- there was a direct interference with the plaintiff's goods that amounted to a repugnant dealing
- the defendant is at fault.

7.3.2.1   Title to sue

A person who has an actual or immediate right to possession at the time of the alleged interference can sue.[173] As with most property-related torts (eg, trespass to goods), title to sue for conversion is not based upon the ownership of the goods. Thus, although the normal plaintiff in conversion is the owner or one who derives title from the owner (eg, a bailee or hirer holding a special property), a party with mere possession of a chattel, even without

---

167   (1946) 74 CLR 204, 229.
168   (2011) 82 NSWLR 420.
169   [2002] 2 AC 883.
170   (2011) 82 NSWLR 420, [124] (Giles and Macfarlan JJA agreeing).
171   See, eg, *Payne v Dwyer* (2013) 46 WAR 128, [113] (Pritchard J) (the Court was not convinced that it could infer that the defendant intended to interfere with any minerals which may have been contained in the gravel).
172   See, eg, the liability of the auctioneer in *Union Transport Finance Ltd v British Car Auctions Ltd* [1978] 2 All ER 385 (auctioneer mistakenly believed the sale had been authorised by the true owner).
173   *Penfolds Wines Pty Ltd v Elliott* (1946) 74 CLR 204, 229 (Dixon J).

title, can sue. The joint judgment of Isaacs and Rich JJ in *Russell v Wilson* confirmed that a person with a possessory title is entitled to sue in conversion:

> Possession … is not merely evidence of absolute title: it confers a title of its own, which is sometimes called a 'possessory title'. This possessory title is as good as the absolute title as against, it is usually said, every person except the absolute owner.[174]

The phrase 'immediate right to possession' suggests that to be entitled to bring conversion, immediacy of possession is required. It distinguishes the case where the right is to future, rather than present, possession. Thus a plaintiff with a right to future possession only does not have a title to sue.

As a general rule, the right to immediate possession must be established on the basis of a proprietary or possessory interest in the good. Case law has suggested that finders;[175] persons having commercial interests in goods, such as lienees[176] and pledgees;[177] licensees;[178] and, in certain circumstances, possessors who have acquired their possessions illegally,[179] are entitled to sue in conversion. Therefore, it is possible that a 'true owner' of goods may be held liable to a person with an immediate right to possession of the goods in an action. For example, a bailee is entitled to sue a bailor for conversion during a bailment for a term.[180] However, mere contractual right to possession will be insufficient to maintain a claim for conversion.[181]

OWNER

An owner of goods who has not transferred his or her right to immediate possession could sue, as the owner would have an immediate right to possession at the time of the conversion. And in fact, actual ownership is the most obvious basis on which to establish a right to maintain conversion. However, there are some restrictions on the ability to establish a title to sue in conversion through a plaintiff's ownership of the goods.

Ownership without some form of possession at the time of interference is not sufficient; the owner of the goods must also prove the right to immediate possession of them.[182] If the owner has surrendered that right through bailment for a period of time, then during the bailment term the bailor (or 'true owner') does not have an immediate right to possession; in such circumstances, only the bailee has the title to sue a third party.[183] In *Hunter BNZ Finance Ltd v Australia and New Zealand Banking Group Ltd*, it was held that the drawer of

---

174 (1923) 33 CLR 538.
175 See, eg, *Armory v Delamirie* (1722) 93 ER 664; *South Staffordshire Water Co v Sharman* [1896] 2 QB 44; *Parker v British Airways Board* [1982] QB 1004.
176 See, eg, *Standard Electronic Apparatus Laboratories Pty Ltd v Stenner* [1960] NSWR 447.
177 See, eg, *Donald v Suckling* (1866) LR 1 QB 585; *Halliday v Holgate* (1868) LR 3 Exch 299.
178 See, eg, *Northam v Bowden* (1855) 156 ER 749, 750 (Martin B) (in limited circumstances a licensee may have sufficient title to sue for conversion).
179 If possession of goods is obtained illegally by the parties through illegal transactions (eg, an illegal contract), the parties are entitled to sue a third party in conversion based on the parties' property right to the goods: *Russell v Wilson* (1923) 33 CLR 538; *Bowmakers Ltd v Barnet Instruments Ltd* [1945] 1 KB 65 (CA); *Singh v Ali* [1960] AC 167. Such title to sue cannot be negated based on the plaintiff's mere intention to engage in criminal conduct with the goods: *Gollan v Nugent* (1988) 166 CLR 18.
180 *City Motors (1933) Pty Ltd v Southern Aerial Super Service Pty Ltd* (1961) 106 CLR 477.
181 *Jarvis v Williams* [1955] 1 WLR 71.
182 *Wertheim v Cheel* (1885) 11 VLR 107.
183 Ibid; *Short v City Bank of Sydney* (1912) 15 CLR 148 (Isaacs J).

a cheque in favour of a third party remains the true owner and has the right to immediate possession of the cheque before it reaches the hands of the payee.[184] However, once the cheque has actually reached the person who is the payee authorised to receive it, the action for conversion is available only to the payee.[185]

BAILEES AND BAILORS

Where goods are the subject of a bailment at will, it is of course the bailee who has the immediate right to possession and who can sue if the goods are converted by a third party.[186] Meanwhile, a bailor may sue a bailee if the bailment is revocable at will, even though the bailor is not in physical possession of goods.[187] In *Perpetual Trustees & National Executors of Tasmania Ltd v Perkins*, three sisters inherited certain family paintings and passed them to another family member under a bailment at will. When that family member died, the executor of the deceased sold the paintings to the Art Gallery of South Australia. One of the sisters, as the previous custodian of the paintings, demanded the return of the items from the Art Gallery, but it refused to do so. The plaintiffs, as bailors of the paintings, sued the Art Gallery for conversion. It was held that the plaintiffs were entitled to succeed in conversion, as the bailors' title was superior to that of the current possessor. For a more recent example concerning the bailor's title to sue in conversion under a bailment at will, refer to *Toll Holdings Ltd v Stewart*, where the seller bailor was entitled to sue the logistics company bailee in conversion.[188]

By contrast, a bailor for a term cannot sue a third party in conversion because the bailor has no right to immediate possession of the good during the term.[189] If, however, it is the bailee who converts the bailor's goods, then the bailor can bring an action, as the act of conversion being repugnant to the bailment gives the bailor the immediate right to possession and therefore title to sue.[190]

CO-OWNERS

If the converted goods are co-owned by different parties, one co-owner can only sue another co-owner in conversion if the defendant co-owner's act 'amounts to the destruction of the property', or a complete extinction of possessory rights.[191] In *Hill v Reglon Pty Ltd*, the New South Wales Court of Appeal held that one co-owner may convert the joint property (scaffolding under a bailment by contract) by asserting exclusive possession as against the

---

184 [1990] VR 41. See also *Australia and New Zealand Banking Group Ltd v Hunter BNZ Finance Ltd* [1991] 2 VR 407 (FC); *Citibank Ltd v Papandony* [2002] NSWCA 375.

185 *Perpetual Trustees Australia Ltd v Heperu Pty Ltd* (2009) 76 NSWLR 195.

186 *The Winkfield* [1902] P 42 (CA).

187 *Perpetual Trustees & National Executors of Tasmania Ltd v Perkins* [1989] Aust Torts Reports 80-295, 69203 (Green CJ).

188 (2016) 338 ALR 602.

189 *Gordon v Harper* (1796) 101 ER 828; *Wertheim v Cheel* (1885) 11 VLR 107; *Short v City Bank of Sydney* (1912) 15 CLR 148 (Isaacs J).

190 See *Penfolds Wines Pty Ltd v Elliott* (1946) 74 CLR 204, where a majority of members of the High Court took the view that the plaintiff's immediate possession of goods gave title to sue in conversion. See also *Myer Stores Ltd v Jovanovic* [2004] VSC 478; *Nominal Defendant v Andrews* (1969) 121 CLR 562; *Nominal Defendant v Morgan Cars Pty Ltd* (1974) 131 CLR 22; *Citicorp Australia Ltd v BS Stillwell Ford Pty Ltd* (1979) 21 SASR 142.

191 *Gwinnett v Day* [2012] SASC 43, [40] (Stanley J).

other co-owner.[192] In *Payne v Dwyer*, the defendant extracted gravel from his land and sold it to a third party. The gravel contained minerals that were co-owned by the defendant and plaintiffs. The Supreme Court of Western Australia held that the plaintiffs could not sue that defendant co-owner in conversion.[193]

FINDERS

It is clear that actual possession of a finder is sufficient to enable the finder to bring conversion against a third party except the true owner, or a person with an earlier subsisting right to possession.[194] Finders' possessory title was originally recognised in *Armory v Delamirie*, where the plaintiff, a chimney-sweep's boy, found a jewel in the chimney and brought it to the defendant jeweller for valuation.[195] The jeweller offered to buy the jewel, but the boy refused. The Court held that the plaintiff was entitled to succeed in conversion against the defendant jeweller.

However, title of the finder will be subject to any prior possessory title. Therefore, if the good is found attached to, or under, land occupied by another, the landowner or occupier will have a better title than that of the finder.[196] That possessory title of a landowner or occupier is based on the legal principle that the occupier had actual possession of the good before it was found, and the occupier is presumed to have an intent to control the good, even without knowing of its existence. For example, in *National Crime Authority v Flack*, the Federal Court held that the appellant should return to the respondent the briefcase, and the money in it, seized from the respondent's premises.[197] This was because the respondent, as occupier and tenant, manifested sufficient intention to exercise control over the premises and all goods within them – even without knowing of the existence of the seized goods within the premises.

If the good is found on the surface of another's land (eg, the floor of a building), the general rule is that the finder will have possession; the occupier only obtains possessory title if he or she has somehow manifested an intention to exercise an exclusive control over the area where the good is found. For example, in *Parker v British Airways Board*, the English Court of Appeal upheld the verdict of conversion in favour of the plaintiff who found a bracelet on the floor of the executive lounge of the defendant's airway.[198] There was insufficient manifestation by the defendant of an intention to exercise control on the area where the bracelet was found. The same rule applies to both private land and land which enables public access.[199]

---

192 [2007] NSWCA 295, [93] (Beazley JA). Compare *Flynn v Flynn* [2011] WADC 141 (one co-owner of a racehorse was liable in conversion to another for refusing to share winnings with the plaintiff co-owner). See also *ACN 116 746 859 v Lunapas Pty Ltd* [2017] NSWSC 1583.
193 (2013) 46 WAR 128.
194 *Parker v British Airways Board* [1982] QB 1004, 1017 (Donaldson LJ).
195 (1722) 93 ER 664.
196 See, eg, *Elwes v Brigg Gas Co* (1886) 33 Ch D 562; *Ranger v Giffin* (1968) 87 WN (Pt 1) (NSW) 531 (items found underneath the land surface); *South Staffordshire Water Co v Sharman* [1896] 2 QB 44; *City of London Corporation v Appleyard* [1963] 1 WLR 982 (QB) (items found attached to land).
197 (1998) 86 FCR 16.
198 [1982] QB 1004. See also *Hannah v Peel* [1945] 1 KB 50; *Byrne v Hoare* [1965] Qd R 135; *Big Top Hereford Pty Ltd v Thomas* (2006) 12 BPR 23,843.
199 *Bridges v Hawkesworth* (1851) 21 LJQB 75 (customer who found a roll of banknotes on the floor of a shop open to the public had a better right than the shop owner), cited in *K & S Corporation Ltd v KPMG* [2009] SASC 24, [26]; *Waverley Borough Council v Fletcher* [1996] QB 334 (owner rather than finder using metal detector on council property had possession of goods).

If the finder is an employee or agent who finds in the course of employment, the general rule is that the possessory rights of the finder vests in the employer or principal.[200] However, if the finder did not find the good due to the scope or nature of his or her work (ie, the employment only provided the occasion of the finding), the finder will acquire a sufficient interest in the good.[201] In *Byrne v Hoare*, the Queensland Supreme Court held that an on-duty police officer who found a gold ingot near the public exit of a drive-in cinema had possession of the gold as the finding was not made by reason of his employment.

7.3.2.2   Repugnant dealing

From our definition of conversion in Section 7.3.2, the most important feature of the tort of conversion is that the defendant has dealt with the good in a manner 'repugnant' to the possession, or right to immediate possession, of the plaintiff. That is, the interference is so seriously inconsistent with the plaintiff's right to possession of the good that it amounts to a denial of that right.[202] Apart from wrongful use of a good, which *Penfolds Wines Pty Ltd v Elliott* shows can constitute a conversion,[203] there are various types of defendant's conduct which have been held sufficient for conversion. They include wrongful taking of goods, destruction of goods (eg, crashing a car),[204] alteration of goods (eg, converting them into something else),[205] delivery of goods to the wrong person, and wrongful disposition of goods by a bailee. Below are some typical forms of interference through which conversion may be committed. The list is not exhaustive and there are overlaps between some forms of interference. Other interferences that are unable to be readily classified may also give rise to conversion.[206]

WRONGFUL USE

Any unjustified use of goods is conversion if the use is 'for the purpose of affecting the immediate right to possession'.[207] That is, to amount to conversion, the use must occur in a particular way that encroached on the plaintiff's immediate right to possession. For example, in *Milk Bottles Recovery Ltd v Camillo*, the Supreme Court of Victoria held that the defendant's use of the plaintiff's milk bottles, without the plaintiff's permission, to sell his own milk was conversion.[208] Moreover, if the defendant uses the plaintiff's good for unlawful purposes and exposes the good intentionally to a serious risk of loss, the defendant's use amounts to conversion. For example, in *Moorgate Mercantile Co Ltd v Finch* [1962] 1 QB 701, the defendant who used the plaintiff's car to smuggle Swiss watches across the border

---

200 *Willey v Synan* (1937) 57 CLR 200, 216 (Dixon J); *DPP (Cth) v Hart* [2005] 2 Qd R 246; QCA 51, [22] (McPherson JA).

201 *Byrne v Hoare* [1965] Qd R 135.

202 *Penfolds Wines Pty Ltd v Elliott* (1946) 74 CLR 204, 229 (Dixon J, Williams J dissenting at 242–3). See also *Perpetual Trustees Australia Ltd v Heperu Pty Ltd* (2009) 76 NSWLR 195, [58] (Allsop P and Handley AJA, Campbell JA agreeing); *CHEP Australia Ltd v Bunnings Group Ltd* [2010] NSWSC 301, [181]–[182] (McDougall J).

203 (1946) 74 CLR 204.

204 *Schemmell v Pomeroy* (1989) 50 SASR 450.

205 *Hollins v Fowler* (1875) LR 7 HL 757.

206 *England v Cowley* (1873) LR 8 Exch 126 (Bramwell B).

207 *Penfolds Wines Pty Ltd v Elliott* (1946) 74 CLR 204, 229 (Dixon J).

208 [1948] VLR 344.

was caught by customs officials, and the car in question was confiscated. The defendant was held to be liable for conversion.[209]

WRONGFUL TAKING OR DISPOSSESSING

To take goods out of the possession of, or to dispossess, another can constitute conversion. What must be shown is that the taking or dispossession was committed with the intention of exercising dominion over the goods – either temporarily or permanently. Therefore, committing a theft or seizing goods under legal process without justification is certainly conversion.[210] However, mere taking or moving of goods without intention to exercise dominion over the goods may give rise to an action in trespass to goods, but not conversion. For example, in *Fouldes v Willoughby*, the defendant put the plaintiff's horses ashore with no intention to exercise dominion over them.[211] The Court held that no conversion was committed. Contrary to this, if the defendant intends to exercise dominion over the plaintiff's goods and the plaintiff is accordingly excluded from possession, the defendant's interference may amount to conversion.[212] *Kuwait Airways Corporation v Iraqi Airways Co (Nos 4 and 5)* concerned the Iraqi military occupation of Kuwait in 1990 in which Iraqi forces seized 10 commercial aircraft belonging to the plaintiff (Kuwait Airways). The aircraft were later removed to Iraq on Iraqi Government orders. Thereafter the defendant (Iraqi Airways) treated the aircraft as its own, repainting the planes with the Iraqi Airways colours and incorporating them into its own fleet. The planes were used for an occasional flight within Iraq. Subsequently four of the aircraft were destroyed by coalition bombs and the remaining ones were sent to Iran, where they were impounded before being returned to the plaintiff in August 1992. The plaintiff sued the defendant in conversion, seeking the return of the planes or payment of their value, and damages resulting from the defendant's wrongful interference (including the sum the plaintiff had paid Iran for keeping, sheltering and maintaining the planes). The House of Lords held that the defendant's acts could constitute conversion under English law. Lord Nicholls said:

> The flaw in [the defendant's] argument lies in its failure to appreciate what is meant in this context by 'depriving' the owner of possession. This is not to be understood as meaning that the wrongdoer must himself actually take the goods from the possession of the owner. This will often be the case, but not always. It is not so in a case of successive conversions. For the purposes of this tort an owner is equally deprived of possession when he is excluded from possession, or possession is withheld from him by the wrongdoer … Similarly, mere unauthorised retention of another's goods is not conversion of them. Mere possession of another's goods without title is not necessarily

209 See also *Grant v YYH Holdings Pty Ltd* [2012] NSWCA 360 (defendant converted the plaintiff's sheep by breeding them to produce lambs); *Anderson Formrite Pty Ltd v Baulderstone Pty Ltd (No 7)* [2010] FCA 921 (defendant contractor converted the plaintiff's formwork by locking the plaintiff's employees out of the building site). In both examples, the defendants abused the plaintiffs' possession by unlawful use of the plaintiffs' goods.

210 For example, *Rick Cobby Haulage Pty Ltd v Simsmetal Pty Ltd* (1986) 43 SASR 533; *Tinkler v Poole* (1770) 5 Burr 2657; *Burton v Hughes* (1824) 2 Bing 173; *Chubb Cash Ltd v John Crilley & Son* [1983] 2 All ER 294.

211 (1841) 151 ER 1153.

212 See *Kuwait Airways Corporation v Iraqi Airways Co (Nos 4 and 5)* [2002] 2 AC 883.

inconsistent with the rights of the owner. To constitute conversion detention must be adverse to the owner, excluding him from the goods. It must be accompanied by an intention to keep the goods. Whether the existence of this intention can properly be inferred depends on the circumstances of the case. A demand and refusal to deliver up the goods are the usual way of proving an intention to keep goods adverse to the owner, but this is not the only way.[213]

Temporary taking (eg, taking a car for a joyride), even though there is an intention to return the car, was held to be conversion in the New Zealand case *Aitken Agencies Ltd v Richardson* (where the defendant took the plaintiff's van for a joyride before abandoning it).[214] There is contrasting Australian authority. In *Schemmell v Pomeroy*, the Supreme Court of South Australia pointed out that not all wrongful use of a vehicle was conversion, unless the defendant joyrider had a wrongful intent to drive the car recklessly or destructively at the time of taking the car, or the car was actually destroyed.[215] Although there is debate about whether the taking must result in a major or serious interference with the plaintiff's possession to constitute conversion,[216] it would be acceptable to conclude that a taking of goods that results in a minor interference of short duration might be too trifling to amount to conversion.

WRONGFUL DESTRUCTION OR ALTERATION

In addition, there is conversion if the defendant intentionally destroys the plaintiff's good or changes its form.[217] Destruction is crucial: mere damage to goods does not amount to conversion.[218] For the purpose of conversion, the degree of damage must amount to the good being regarded as destroyed or its utility eliminated as a good in its original form.[219] Where there is only partial damage to the goods, plaintiffs may sue in trespass or negligence, but not in conversion.

This can create difficulty because it is sometimes difficult to draw a clear line between damaged goods and destroyed goods. Generally, a change of identity amounting to destruction may constitute conversion. For example, crushing grapes in order to produce wine, grinding another's corn to make flour, spinning cotton into yarn – if done without the authority of the owner, are conversion.[220] Equally, to draw some wine out of the plaintiff's

---

213 Ibid [40]–[41].
214 [1967] NZLR 65.
215 (1989) 50 SASR 450, 451–2 (White J).
216 For example, in *Model Dairy Pty Ltd v White* (1935) 41 Arg LR 432, it was held that 'a slight deprivation of possession is not in itself sufficient for conversion': at 433 (Gavan Duffy J). Similarly, Professor Fleming has suggested that to amount to conversion, the taking must have resulted in a 'substantial interference with the owner's rights as to warrant a forced sale': see C Sappideen and P Vines (eds), *Fleming's The Law of Torts* (Lawbook, 10th ed, 2011) 70. But this view was not accepted by the Supreme Court of Tasmania in *Triffit v Dare* (Cox, Wright and Crawford JJ, 18 August 1993) [14]. For responses to these arguments, see K Barker et al, *The Law of Torts* (Oxford University Press, 5th ed, 2012) 118.
217 *Penfolds Wines Pty Ltd v Elliott* (1946) 74 CLR 204, 229 (Dixon J). It has been held that purely accidental destruction is not conversion: *Simmons v Lillystone* (1853) 8 Exch 431.
218 *Fouldes v Willoughby* (1841) 151 ER 1153, 1156 (Alderson B).
219 *Jones v de Marchant* (1916) 28 DLR 561 (making a fur coat from animal skins).
220 *Hollins v Fowler* (1875) LR 7 HL 757.

cask and then fill up it with water to make good the deficiency is conversion.[221] Nevertheless, it is not conversion to bottle another's wine in order to preserve it.[222]

WRONGFUL DISPOSITION (SALE AND DELIVERY)

It is conversion if the defendant purported to sell and deliver the plaintiff's goods to a third party without the permission of the plaintiff who has an immediate right to possession. In such circumstances, both the seller and the purchaser of the goods may be liable for conversion. For example, in *Perpetual Trustees & National Executors of Tasmania Ltd v Perkins* (see Section 7.3.2.1), both the seller (executors of the deceased) and the purchaser (Art Gallery of South Australia) committed conversion.[223]

To amount to conversion, the act of the defendant under this head must be purported to affect the title to the plaintiff's goods. Therefore, if the defendant receives the goods in good faith, merely keeping them or restoring them to the person who deposited the goods with him, no conversion is committed,[224] because the purpose of the dealing was not to affect the plaintiff's title to the goods. Conversely, in *Citicorp Australia Ltd v BS Stillwell Ford Pty Ltd*, the defendant purchased a car from a car yard, without knowing of the plaintiff's existence or having any notice of the plaintiff's right to the car.[225] The Court held that there was a conversion because the purchase was intentional interference with the plaintiff's title and inconsistent with the plaintiff's right to immediate possession.[226]

It is clear that where a wrongful sale gives good title to the purchaser, the sale will itself amount to a conversion, because the purchase and taking possession of the goods constitute a denial of the plaintiff's immediate right to possession.[227] However, where a purchaser buys a stolen item from a seller without notice of the rights of the original owner, or a seller has no right to sell the goods but nevertheless sells them to the purchaser, the purchaser can rarely acquire good title from the seller due to the common law rule *nemo dat quod non habet* ('a person who does not have good title may not pass good title to another').[228] This raises the question whether a purported but ineffective sale, which does not pass title to the goods to the purchaser, is a conversion. The usual rule is that, if the sale is purported but

221 *Richardson v Atkinson* (1723) 93 ER 710.

222 *Philpott v Kelley* (1835) 111 ER 353.

223 [1989] Aust Torts Reports 80-295. See also *Moorgate Mercantile Co Ltd v Twitchings* [1977] AC 890. The basis of both parties' liability in conversion was addressed in *Rosecell Pty Ltd v JP Haines Plumbing Pty Ltd* [2015] NSWSC 1238, [40] (White J): 'Where a person acquires goods by purchase from a person not authorised to sell them, it is the purchase and acquisition of the goods that are the acts inconsistent with the true owner's right to possession'.

224 *Hollins v Fowler* (1875) LR 7 HL 757, 767 (Blackburn J): the defendant's conduct was of a 'mere ministerial nature'. See *Hollins v Fowler* (1875) LR 7 HL 757, 757, 766-7.

225 (1979) 21 SASR 142.

226 See also *Safari 4 x 4 Engineering Pty Ltd v Doncaster Motors Pty Ltd* [2006] VSC 460, where a bona fide purchaser for value without notice buying a car that belonged to someone else was a conversion. The defendant purchaser intended to deny the 'owner's right and did assert a right which was inconsistent with the owner's right by purchasing the vehicle': Gillard J at [97].

227 For more detail, see C Sappideen, P Vines and P Watson, *Torts: Commentary and Materials* (Lawbook, 13th ed, 2021) 145, 149.

228 See *Bishopsgate Motor Finance Corporation Ltd v Transport Brakes Ltd* [1949] 1 KB 322, 336 (Denning LJ). There are some statutory exceptions to the *nemo dat* rule. For example, a purchaser may gain good title to uncollected goods: see *Disposal of Uncollected Goods Act 1967* (Qld) s 15; *Uncollected Goods Act 1995* (NSW) s 34.

ineffective, it is not a conversion unless there is delivery to effect the transfer of possession to the purchaser.[229] Therefore, a purchaser should be liable for conversion due to the purchase and taking possession of the goods, even if the purchaser acts in good faith without notice of the rights of the original owner and pays full value for the converted goods.

Because of the apparent harshness of the *nemo dat* rule, parliaments have developed several statutory exceptions to protect an innocent purchaser in certain circumstances. These exceptions apply only in favour of a purchaser who acquires the goods in good faith and without notice of any lien or other rights of the original owner.[230]

WRONGFUL DELIVERY

There will also be a conversion where the defendant delivers the goods to the wrong person.[231] This clearly covers the situation where a courier or carrier delivers goods, which are the subject matter of the contract of carriage or bailment, to the wrong address.[232] However, if failure to deliver was due to the fact that the goods have been lost or destroyed by accident or carelessness, there will be no conversion.[233] Nor is it conversion if a delivery is made in accordance with the sender's instructions which resulted in delivery to the wrong person.[234] Equally, there is no conversion if a bailee or pledgee redelivers goods to the person from whom they were obtained without notice of the claim of the true owner.[235] But that would not be the case if a claim has been made by the plaintiff.[236]

There is another exception to the general rule in cases where the bailment is involuntary[237] (eg, when goods are incorrectly left at a person's address) stating that a person or involuntary bailee will not be liable for any further misdelivery if he or she has acted with reasonable care.[238]

As noted earlier, conversion is a tort of strict liability; it is not a defence that the defendant acted under a reasonable, though mistaken, belief that it was entitled to deliver the chattel

---

229 See *Lancashire Waggon Co v Fitzhugh* (1861) 6 H & N 502 (a person who intends to sell goods to which he has no title but does not transfer possession of the goods commits no conversion, although in such circumstance the seller may be liable for malicious falsehood); *Short v City Bank of Sydney* (1912) 15 CLR 148 (a mere assertion of title to a good did not amount to conversion); *Motor Dealers Credit Corporation Ltd v Overland (Sydney) Ltd* (1931) 31 SR (NSW) 516 (a seller who had no possession but dealt with the plaintiff's title to goods was held liable for conversion).

230 See, eg, *Sale of Goods Act 1954* (ACT) s 29(2); *Sale of Goods Act 1923* (NSW) s 28(2); *Sale of Goods Act 1972* (NT) s 28(2); *Sale of Goods Act 1895* (SA) s 25(2); *Sale of Goods Act 1896* (Tas) s 30(2); *Goods Act 1958* (Vic) s 31; *Sale of Goods Act 1895* (WA) s 25(2).

231 *Youl v Harbottle* (1791) 170 ER 81.

232 See, eg, *Tozer Kemsley & Millbourn (Australasia) Pty Ltd v Collier's Interstate Transport Service Ltd* (1956) 94 CLR 384; *Sydney Corporation v West* (1965) 114 CLR 481; *Helson v McKenzies (Cuba Street) Ltd* [1950] NZLR 878.

233 *Owen v Lewyn* (1672) 1 Vent 223; *The Arpad* [1934] P 189, 232.

234 *M'Kean v M'Ivor* (1870) LR 6 Ex 36.

235 *Hollins v Fowler* (1875) LR 7 HL 757, 767; *Union Credit Bank Ltd v Mersey Docks and Harbour Board* [1899] 2 QB 205.

236 *Penfolds Wines Pty Ltd v Elliott* (1946) 74 CLR 204.

237 Involuntary bailment refers to a bailment that arises where a person accidentally, but without any negligence, comes into possession of goods against that person's wishes. It occurs where goods are found by someone or taken into possession through a process of inertia selling; or a departing tenant leaves goods on the landlord's premises; or mail is delivered to a wrong address: see NE Palmer, *Bailment* (Law Book, 1979) 379.

238 *James v Oxley* (1939) 61 CLR 433, 477.

to the third party. For example, in *Union Transport Finance Ltd v British Car Auctions Ltd*, an auctioneer who sold and delivered a car on hire purchase, in the mistaken belief that the vendor was entitled to sell the vehicle, was nevertheless liable for conversion.[239] Indeed, the liability of intermediaries (eg, eBay or Amazon) who facilitate delivery depends on the nature of the defendant's conduct. As Blackburn J said in *Hollins v Fowler*, a defendant would not be liable in conversion if his or her conduct was of a 'mere ministerial nature'.[240] Any of the defendant's actions purporting to affect the title to the goods could not be seen as 'ministerial':

> One who deals with goods at the request of the person who has the actual custody of them, in the bona fide belief that the [custodian] is the true owner, or has the authority of the true owner, should be excused for what he does if the act is of such a nature as would be excused if done by the authority of the person in possession ...
>
> Thus a warehouseman with whom goods have been deposited is guilty of no conversion by keeping them, or restoring them to the person who deposited them with him, though that person turns out to have had no authority from the true owner ...
>
> And the same principle would apply to ... persons acting in a subsidiary character, like that of a person who has the goods of a person employing him to carry them, or a caretaker, such as a wharfinger.[241]

WRONGFUL DETENTION

A wrongful detention of goods can also amount to conversion. It overlaps with and covers much of the same ground as the tort of detinue. In such a case, liability will arise only if the defendant intended to retain the good in defiance of a plaintiff with an immediate right to possession.[242] This is usually evidenced by the plaintiff's unconditional demand for the goods and the defendant's wrongful refusal to return them.[243]

The demand made by the plaintiff must be lawful and reasonable. In addition, a person in possession of a good may not be liable for conversion if the refusal was to enable reasonable time to investigate the validity of a demand (eg, to clarify the plaintiff's title to the goods)[244] or if the goods were not sufficiently identified.[245] Meanwhile, if the demand is made by the plaintiff's agent, it would be reasonable for the defendant to require evidence of the agent's authority to make the demand.[246] But the reason for the refusal may not include, for example, concern about the risk of strike action by employees.[247]

---

239 [1978] 2 All ER 385.
240 (1875) LR 7 HL 757.
241 Ibid 757, 766–7.
242 *Oakley v Lyster* [1931] 1 KB 148; *Glass v Hollander* (1935) 35 SR (NSW) 304.
243 *Bunnings Group Ltd v CHEP Australia Ltd* (2011) 82 NSWLR 420.
244 See, eg, *Flowfill Packaging Machines Pty Ltd v Fytore Pty Ltd* [1993] Aust Torts Reports 81-244, 62520 (Young J): the 'reasonable time to investigate' rule will not apply if there is no doubt of the plaintiff's title to the goods. See also *Hollins v Fowler* (1875) LR 7 HL 757 (Blackburn J: if the refusal is by a person who does not know the plaintiff's title and has a bona fide doubt as to the title to the goods, and who detains the goods for a reasonable time to clear up that doubt, this is not a conversion).
245 *Bunnings Group Ltd v CHEP Australia Ltd* (2011) 82 NSWLR 420, [22] (Allsop P).
246 *Clayton v Le Roy* [1911] 2 KB 1031; *Pratten v Pratten* [2005] QCA 213.
247 *Howard E Perry & Co Ltd v British Railways Board* [1980] 2 All ER 579.

7.3.2.3   Fault

The fault element in conversion is narrower than that in trespass, because negligence is not sufficient to create liability in conversion. Conversion can only be committed by the defendant's international and voluntary conduct. As Allsop P stated in *Bunnings Group Ltd v CHEP Australia Ltd*:

> The tort is one of strict liability and thus a mental element in knowing that a wrong is being committed is not required. Nevertheless, intention is not irrelevant. The act or dealing in question must be intentional; further, the intention must be the exercise of such dominion as is repugnant to the rights of the owner.[248]

It is sufficient if the defendant intended to deal with the plaintiff's goods in a manner which was an assertion of dominion contrary to the rights of the plaintiff. There is no requirement of wrongful motive or any dishonest intent; nor is there a requirement that the defendant intended to effect a conversion. This was shown in *Ashby v Tolhurst*.[249] The plaintiff left his car at the defendant's car park, and the defendant's car park attendant negligently allowed a stranger to get in and drive the plaintiff's car away. The House of Lords held that the defendant was not liable in conversion as the attendant had no intention to deal with the car in a manner that was inconsistent with the plaintiff's right to immediate possession.

As mentioned earlier, conversion is usually described as a tort of strict liability. The tort can, therefore, be committed by a defendant who does not even know of the existence of the plaintiff, or who mistakenly believes that he or she has a right to deal with the goods. That is why an auctioneer who sells and delivers a stolen item in good faith to a purchaser is liable for conversion, a purchaser who unknowingly buys a stolen item is liable for conversion (see 'Wrongful disposition (sale and delivery)' in Section 7.3.2.2). The purchaser's good faith is not a defence;[250] nor can ignorance or mistake be used as a defence, no matter how reasonable the mistake is.

7.3.3   Detinue

The tort of detinue deals with a wrongful detention of the plaintiff's goods. The action arises where the plaintiff demands the return of the goods in question and the defendant fails to deliver them in response to that demand. The essence of detinue, as stated by McDougall J in *CHEP Australia Ltd v Bunnings Group Ltd*, 'lies in the wrongful refusal to deliver up goods to a person having the immediate right to the possession of those goods'.[251] This is normally evidenced by a request for their return and a refusal to comply.[252]

Clearly, there is an overlap between this action and conversion, because many interferences with goods involve the detaining of goods from the person with immediate right to possession. There are, however, some important differences between the two torts.

---

248   (2011) 82 NSWLR 420, [125].
249   [1937] 2 KB 242.
250   *Hollins v Fowler* (1875) LR 7 HL 757.
251   [2010] NSWSC 301, [183], cited and applied by McColl JA in *Grant v YYH Holdings Pty Ltd* [2012] NSWCA 360, [43]; *Re NL Mercantile Group Pty Ltd* [2018] NSWSC 1337, [165] (Gleeson J) (the defendant is liable for damages in detinue for failure to return a sport motor vehicle).
252   *John F Goulding Pty Ltd v Victorian Railways Commissioners* (1932) 48 CLR 157, 167.

One of these differences stems from the fact that a detinue action can arise from a negligent interference, but conversion relies solely on an intentional act of misfeasance by the defendant. In addition, while demand and refusal constitute the gist of the action of detinue, demand and refusal constitute just one of many forms of conversion.[253] Other differences relate to remedies and will be considered in Chapter 8.

7.3.3.1 Title to sue

With respect to the issue of title to sue, the actions of conversion and detinue are the same. The plaintiff must have been in actual possession[254] or have had an immediate right to possession at the time of the defendant's refusal to return the goods.[255] Therefore, bailors in a bailment at will may sue in detinue, but bailors in a bailment for a term cannot sue in detinue before the expiry of that term. Bailees and sub-bailees are entitled to sue in detinue where withholding of the goods gives rise to interference to a right to immediate possession.[256] It includes the situation that a bailee can sue a bailor wrongfully in possession during the term of a bailment in detinue.[257]

To sue in detinue, the plaintiff's interest in the property must be lawful. In *Carolan v New South Wales*, the plaintiff was found in possession of a suitcase containing $702000 in cash which was later seized by police officers prior to criminal action.[258] The plaintiff sought a declaration that detention of the money by police constituted trespass to goods, conversion or detinue. The Supreme Court of New South Wales held that there was no conversion as the Court was not satisfied on the balance of probabilities that the plaintiff was lawfully entitled to the cash.[259]

Finally, as with conversion, the plaintiff in detinue need not establish that he or she has the best right to possession; instead, a better right to possession than the person being requested to return the goods is sought.[260]

7.3.3.2 Demand and refusal

As discussed, this action is based on wrongful detention as shown by a demand for the return of goods followed by a refusal to do so. The demand can be either an oral request or a demand in writing. It must, however, be fairly specific and set out a time and a place for the delivery of the demanded goods to the plaintiff. For an example of insufficient demand, see *Lloyd v Osborne* where the plaintiff sent the defendant a letter demanding the return of some sheep without indicating where the sheep should be delivered or who the agent

---

253 For further discussion concerning the differences between conversion and detinue, see B Richards and M de Zwart, *Tort Law Principles* (Thomson Reuters Australia, 2nd ed, 2016) 117.

254 See, eg, *Metals & Ropes Co Ltd v Tattersall* [1966] 3 All ER 401 (plaintiff who sued in detinue was said to be in actual (or constructive) possession of the subject matter (boilers)).

255 Like in conversion, the entitlement to sue in detinue is not based on ownership: *Bolwell Fibreglass Pty Ltd v Foley* [1984] VR 97, 99 (Young CJ); *Penfolds Wines Pty Ltd v Elliott* (1946) 74 CLR 204, 241 (Williams J).

256 *Premier Group Pty Ltd v Followmont Transport Pty Ltd* (2000) 2 Qd R 338, [6]–[7] (Pincus JA).

257 *City Motors (1933) Pty Ltd v Southern Aerial Super Service Pty Ltd* (1961) 106 CLR 477.

258 [2014] NSWSC 1566.

259 Ibid. See also *Gollan v Nugent* (1988) 166 CLR 18.

260 *Premier Group Pty Ltd v Followmont Transport Pty Ltd* (2000) 2 Qd R 338, [7]–[8] (Pincus JA, Moynihan and Atkinson JJ).

was.[261] However, a demand may not be effective if the plaintiff required the defendant to return the goods to a particular place, unless the defendant was obligated to do so due to pre-existing contractual obligations. For example, in *Capital Finance Co Ltd v Bray*, the plaintiff (a hire purchase company) requested the defendant (a hirer) to deliver up the car he was hiring to one of three named places at his own expense.[262] The Court held that the demand was not a proper one as the defendant was never under an obligation to return the car to one of these addresses.

On the other hand, there may be some cases where there is no need for the plaintiff to show a demand and refusal. This is the case where it is clear that if the demand had been made, the defendant would have refused to accede to it.[263]

In many cases, the demand is obviously made to the defendant if he or she is still in possession. However, there may be cases where the defendant is no longer in possession of the good; this occurs in the majority of cases where a bailment exists between plaintiff and defendant.[264]

First, the defendant can still be liable for detinue in such circumstances if their lack of possession is due to an intentional act (eg, converting the goods by selling to another person). The only difference between the causes of action in such a case relates to the limitation period. In the case of conversion, the cause of action dates from the act of conversion; in detinue, it dates from the time of demand and refusal.[265]

Second, the defendant will still be liable if their lack of possession of the goods (eg, goods having been lost or destroyed) arose from their negligence.[266]

Third, if the defendant was a bailee and the goods are no longer in his or her possession due to a failure to comply with the terms of the bailment, the defendant will be liable for detinue even though there was no intentional or negligent loss or destruction of the good on the part of the defendant. For example, in *Lilley v Doubleday*,[267] the defendant bailee stored goods in a warehouse other than the one required by the bailment terms; the goods were destroyed by fire; and the defendant was held liable for detinue.[268]

As for the refusal, there is some debate as to whether an express refusal is necessary. The question has been raised as to whether failing to take notice of a specific demand constitutes a refusal. The better view is probably that failure to respond is equivalent to a refusal.[269]

---

261 (1899) 20 LR (NSW) 190. See also *Flowfill Packaging Machines Pty Ltd v Fytore Pty Ltd* [1993] Aust Torts Reports 81-244. The Court held that the plaintiff's claim in detinue failed, because the plaintiff's demand did not state the place and to whom the machines were to be delivered, and because the plaintiff knew where the machines were and would have been able to repossess them without interference from the defendant.
262 [1964] 1 All ER 603.
263 See, eg, *Crowther v Australian Guarantee Corporation Ltd* [1995] Aust Torts Reports 80-709 (defendant had clearly shown an intention to retain the goods).
264 See, eg, *John F Goulding Pty Ltd v Victorian Railways Commissioners* (1932) 48 CLR 157, 167 (Stark, Dixon and McTiernan JJ); *Slaveski v Victoria* [2010] VSC 441, [326]–[327] (Kyrou J).
265 *John F Goulding Pty Ltd v Victorian Railways Commissioners* (1932) 48 CLR 157.
266 *Houghland v RR Low (Luxury Coaches) Ltd* [1962] 1 QB 694; *Westpac Banking Corporation v Royal Tongan Airlines* [1996] Aust Torts Reports 81-403.
267 (1881) 7 QBD 510.
268 See also *McKenna & Armistead Pty Ltd v Excavations Pty Ltd* (1956) 57 SR (NSW) 515.
269 *Lloyd v Osborne* (1899) 20 LR (NSW) 190, 194 (Darley C); *Ming Kuei Property Investments Pty Ltd v Hampson* [1995] 2 Qd R 251.

7.3.3.3   Fault

The fault requirement for conversion works like that for trespass to goods. For the purpose of showing that a defendant has committed the tort of detinue, there must be evidence that the defendant's conduct was either intentional or lacking in care.[270] An unintentional loss of goods by a bailee has been suggested to be the only situation that can give rise to detinue but not conversion. In *John F Goulding Pty Ltd v Victorian Railways Commissioners*, the High Court held that by delivering the plaintiff's goods to an unauthorised third party, the defendant had been negligent and was liable in detinue.[271] The rule also applies to a gratuitous bailee who negligently fails to return goods within a reasonable time of the demand for their return.[272]

HINTS AND TIPS

When dealing with a problem question concerning a trespass to personal properties, it is important to be familiar with the following issues:

- The elements of each of the available actions (trespass to goods, conversion and detinue)
- The nature of the interferences which may give rise to the available actions
- The similarities and differences between these causes of action
- The plaintiff's title to sue in each of the causes of action
- Potential defences to and remedies for the plaintiff.

REVIEW QUESTIONS

(1)   What is trespass to goods? What elements might be sufficient for the tort of trespass to goods?

(2)   What is conversion? What title to sue is required for conversion?

   Guided responses in the eBook

---

270   *Houghland v RR Low (Luxury Coaches) Ltd* [1962] 1 QB 694 (the normal standard of reasonable care in the circumstances will apply). See also *Trans-Motors v Robertson Buckley & Co* [1970] 2 Lloyd's Rep 224; *Fairbairn v Miller* (1918) VLR 615.

271   (1932) 48 CLR 157.

272   *Mitchell v Ealing London Borough Council* [1979] QB 1; *Waldron v Baz* [2005] WADC 187, [116] (Deane DCJ).

KEY CONCEPTS

- **conversion:** consists of an intentional act on the part of the defendant which seriously interferes with the possession of the plaintiff in a manner repugnant to the right of the plaintiff.

- **detinue:** deals with the wrongful detention of the plaintiff's goods. The action arises where the plaintiff demands the return of the goods in question and the defendant fails to deliver them in response to that demand.

- **trespass to goods:** involves an intentional or negligent act on the part of the defendant which directly causes an unauthorised interference with goods or chattels in the possession of the plaintiff.

- **trespass to land:** occurs when there is a direct interference, either intentional or negligent, with land in the possession of the plaintiff without lawful justification.

 Complete the multiple-choice questions in the eBook to test your knowledge.

PROBLEM-SOLVING EXERCISES

Exercise 1

Smith owns a two-storey split level in southern Queensland. Joe, who is a local builder, owns a vacant lot next to Smith's house. Two months ago, Joe decided to develop and construct a multi-storey building on that lot. In the course of construction, it was necessary to anchor a deep excavation as part of the development. This was done by drilling a series of bore holes under the land on which Smith's house stood. Joe tried to contact Smith to get his permission but failed, because at the time Smith was travelling in South Africa with his partner. Due to the tight schedule, Joe decided to drill the bore holes without Smith's permission. He inserted rock anchors, grouted them and tensioned them into place. After that, the tension was released and the anchor cables were left on site. Joe also used a construction crane to lift items from the street to the building site. The horizontal arm of the crane projected into the airspace of Smith's house for about two metres.

On returning from South Africa, Smith found the anchor cables and realised what had happened to his land. He became very uneasy when he saw the crane suspended directly above his roof. Smith asked Joe to remove the crane immediately and to pay $5000 in compensation. Joe rejected his proposal.

Does Smith have any cause of action in trespass against Joe?

 Guided response in the eBook

Exercise 2

Nick is a sales representative for a technology firm. Before he joined his current employer in March 2022, Nick worked as an engineer at Hibot Pty Ltd ('Hibot'), a local manufacturer of artificial intelligence (AI) equipment in Brisbane. In April 2022, Nick had to visit Hibot's factory in the course of this new job. When Nick arrived, he found that the visitors' parking was full. It was raining and Nick was reluctant to park on the street some distance away. Therefore, he parked in a parking space that was reserved for Hibot's staff. When he finished his work in the main office, Nick decided to go to Hibot's workshop to speak with some of his old friends. He entered the workshop building, waved to the receptionist and went through the door behind her that led into the workshop. There was a large sign on the door that stated: 'Workshop staff only. No admittance to visitors'.

Near the entrance of the workshop was a display area. Nick was attracted by some robots on display. Ignoring the 'No photos' sign, Nick took a few photos of the robots with his mobile phone, with the intention of showing them to his new work colleagues.

Advise Hibot as to the potential claims in trespass it may have.

 Guided response in the eBook

CHALLENGE YOURSELF

Exercise 1

Peter Burns is the captain of a well-known Australian cricket team. Shortly after he won a medal in the Champions Trophy, he purchased a second-hand Ferrari sports car priced at $190000. Two weeks ago, Peter found that his car bounced up and down when he stopped short. He sent the car to a local garage owned by Sam. After conducting a preliminary diagnosis, Sam told Peter the brake was not working properly. Peter left the car with Sam for a complete diagnosis and repair. In the meantime, he told Sam not to wash or polish the car because he had recently applied some special coating material to protect the vehicle's paint and had been advised not to wash or polish the exterior until the materials fully dried out. Sam assured Peter that his instructions would be followed and the car would be ready for collection two weeks later. Sam delegated the work to his chief mechanic, Celia, telling her to check and fix the brake problems. However, their conversation was interrupted by a phone call and Sam forgot to tell Celia of Peter's particular instruction about cleaning the car. Celia replaced the brake system, then thoroughly cleaned the car and polished the exterior (which were standard operations of the garage's service package).

Comprehensively advise Peter of any trespass actions available to him. Ensure that your advice includes references to relevant case authority.

 Guided response in the eBook

Exercise 2

In the above case, Celia finished working on Peter's car before the deadline. She called her boyfriend, Martin, asking him to collect her from work so they could eat out to celebrate. When Martin arrived, Celia told him she would take a shower first and that Martin could wait in the workshop. Martin was attracted to the Ferrari. He decided to take the car for a quick drive and return it before Celia finished her shower. Because it was rush-hour and Martin was not familiar with the car, he rear-ended a city bus, resulting in extensive damage to the Ferrari.

Apart from the possible actions against Celia as you have suggested in exercise 1, advise Peter of any other appropriate action(s) against Martin in trespass.

 Guided response in the eBook

8

DEFENCES TO AND REMEDIES FOR TRESPASS

8.1   Introduction

This chapter deals with defences to the trespass actions discussed in Chapters 6 and 7. As a general rule, the defendant bears the burden of proving the facts necessary to constitute a defence.[1] Where the defence is established, the defendant will be relieved of liability.

It should be noted that some statutory defences, which are similar to common law defences, are provided by the civil liability legislation and/or Criminal Code in most Australian states and territories.[2] Therefore, when considering such defences, the relevant legislation in a particular jurisdiction must be consulted. This chapter will discuss some of the most important defences available for trespass to the person, trespass to land and trespass to personal property.

The defences fall within three roughly divided categories:[3]

---

1 See C Sappideen, P Vines and P Watson, *Torts: Commentary and Materials* (Lawbook, 13th ed, 2021) 167.

2 For example, the statutory defence of self-help can be found in: *Civil Liability Act 2002* (NSW) s 52; *Criminal Code* (NT) s 43BD (contained in *Criminal Code Act 1983* (NT) sch 1); *Criminal Code* (Qld) ss 270–8 (contained in *Criminal Code Act 1899* (Qld) sch 1); *Criminal Code* (Tas) s 46 (contained in *Criminal Code Act 1924* (Tas) sch 1); *Criminal Code* (WA) ss 247–55 (contained in *Criminal Code Act Compilation Act 1913* (WA) app B).

3 There are different ways to organise the defences to trespass. For example, Professor John Murphy et al place defences to trespass within a threefold system: (1) 'absent element defences' (defences in this category are denials of one or more of the elements of a particular tort); (2) 'justification defences' (once defences in this category are accepted, the defendant's act can be justified on the ground that he or she acted reasonably in committing a tort); (3) 'public policy defences' (the defendant will not be liable even though he or she committed a tort for no good reason): J Murphy et al, *Street on Torts* (Oxford University Press, 13th ed, 2012) 324. The classification used in this chapter is borrowed from SW Howe et al, *Torts* (LexisNexis Butterworths, 2nd ed, 2012) 218.

(1)   *Self-help based defences:* These defences cover situations where the defendant's trespassory act was 'the result of an attempt to help or defend themselves or a third party'.[4]

(2)   *Justification-based defences:* But for the availability of these defences, the defendant's act would be tortious and the defendant liable for its consequences.

(3)   *Fault-based defences:* A lack of fault on the defendant's part is the feature that the fault-based defences have in common.

We also consider a number of factors that are not defences to trespass at the end of this chapter (in Section 8.2.9). The defences to be discussed in this chapter are shown in Figure 8.1.

Figure 8.1   Defences to trespass

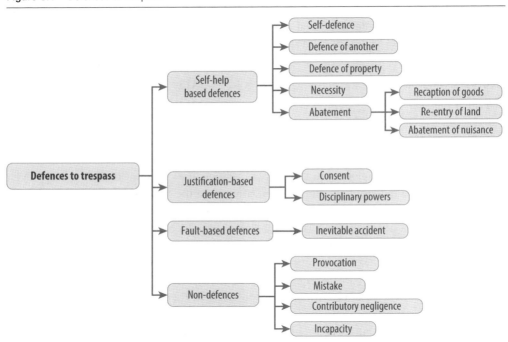

The remedies generally sought for trespass actions include damages and injunctions. Damages are a monetary sum awarded to the plaintiff.[5] An injunction is a court order that compels the defendant to do or refrain from doing specific actions.[6] These remedies are not mutually exclusive, and the plaintiff may be entitled to more than one remedy should the cause of action be established.

The most common remedy for trespass actions is an award of damages. As the torts of battery, assault and false imprisonment are all actionable per se, damages may be awarded

---

4   SW Howe et al, *Torts* (LexisNexis Butterworths, 2nd ed, 2012) 218.

5   The term 'damages' as a monetary remedy for civil wrong should be differentiated from 'damage' as a synonym of 'harm or injury'. See C Sappideen, P Vines and P Watson, *Torts: Commentary and Materials* (Lawbook, 13th ed, 2021) 554.

6   *Black's Law Dictionary* (West, 9th ed, 2009) 855 ('injunction').

to the plaintiff irrespective of whether loss (arising from personal injury, damage to property or financial loss) has been suffered. There are four types of damages:

(1) *Nominal damages:* These are awarded where the plaintiff's rights have been infringed but the plaintiff has not suffered any actual loss or harm. The purpose of nominal damages is not to compensate the plaintiff. Instead, they have a declaratory function to record the fact that the plaintiff's rights have been interfered with.[7] Therefore, typical nominal damages will be a token amount.

(2) *Compensatory damages:* The plaintiff is entitled to recover compensatory damages for his or her loss arising from the tortious act committed by the defendant. An award of compensatory damages means 'that sum of money which will put the party who has been injured … in the same position as he would have been in if he had not sustained the wrong for which he is now getting his compensation or reparation'.[8] This means that the idea of compensatory damages is to restore the plaintiff to the position he or she would have been in if the tort had not happened.

(3) *Aggravated damages:* These damages may be awarded to compensate for injured feelings caused by tortious conduct that was particularly officious, abusive, insulting or humiliating.[9]

(4) *Exemplary damages:* These damages may be awarded where tortious conduct was so outrageous as to deserve the inclusion of a punitive element in the assessment of damages. The purpose of these awards is to punish the defendant for gross disregard of the plaintiff's rights and to deter the defendant from repeating the conduct.

The remedies to be discussed in this chapter are shown in Figure 8.2.

8.2   Defences to trespass

8.2.1   Self-defence

Trespass actions may be justified on the ground of self-defence if the act of the defendant was to avert the threat of imminent harm to their person (as opposed to their property). The defence of self-defence will be available to a defendant who uses reasonable force to repel a battery by the plaintiff, or to prevent or terminate a false imprisonment of the defendant herself or himself. It is worth noting that in the case of self-defence, the threat of imminent harm arises from the plaintiff's own actions, and is faced by the defendant herself or himself. If the application of the force is a response to trespass to the person or property of a third party, then 'defence of another' (see Section 8.2.2) or 'defence of property' (see Section 8.2.3) will apply, respectively. Furthermore, if the threat of imminent harm arises from the defendant's own actions, the proper defence will be 'necessity' (see Section 8.2.4).

---

7   See, eg, *New South Wales v Stevens* (2012) 82 NSWLR 106, [26] where McColl JA (Ward JA agreeing) said that nominal damages are 'vindicatory, not compensatory'.

8   *Livingstone v Rawyards Coal Co* (1880) 5 App Cas 25, 39. A similar discussion was had by Mason CJ, Dawson, Toohey and Gaudron JJ in *Haines v Bendall* (1991) 172 CLR 60, 63.

9   As defined by the High Court in *Lamb v Cotogno* (1987) 164 CLR 1, 8–9.

Figure 8.2   Remedies for trespass

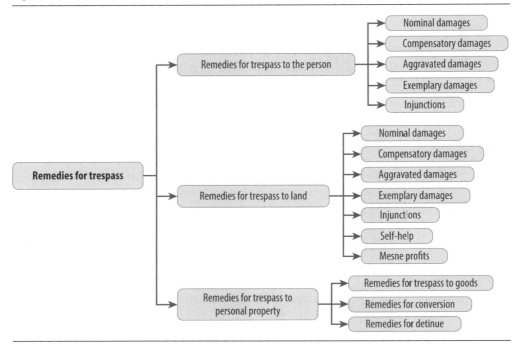

In the High Court case of *Zecevic v Director of Public Prosecutions (Vic)*, the appellant (accused) killed a neighbour after an altercation between them.[10] The appellant believed that the neighbour had a knife at hand and might have had a shotgun in his car; thus, the act of killing was necessary to defend himself. Wilson, Deane and Dawson JJ stated that the test to make out self-defence relies on:

> whether the [defendant] believed upon reasonable grounds that it was necessary in self-defence to do what he did. If he had that belief and there were reasonable grounds for it, or if the jury is left in reasonable doubt about the matter, then he is entitled to an acquittal.[11]

Although *Zecevic* dealt with self-defence in relation to criminal acts, this test has been frequently cited with approval by courts in civil cases.[12]

In order to establish this defence in civil cases, the defendant will need to prove:

(1)   there was a threat of imminent harm to their person[13]

(2)   there were reasonable grounds to believe that it was necessary to use force to protect herself or himself.[14]

10   (1987) 162 CLR 645.
11   Ibid 661.
12   See, eg, *Illert v Northern Adelaide Local Health Network Inc* [2016] SASC 186; *Watkins v Victoria* (2010) 27 VR 543; *Carter v Walker* (2010) 32 VR 1.
13   See, eg, *Watkins v Victoria* (2010) 27 VR 543.
14   See, eg, *Zecevic v DPP (Vic)* (1987) 162 CLR 645; *Fontin v Katapodis* (1962) 108 CLR 177; *Pearce v Hallett* [1969] SASR 423; *Bennett v Dopke* [1973] VR 239; *Howard v Wing* [2000] TASSC 147.

Imminent danger turns on how immediate and serious the threat posed to the defendant was, and the subjective reasonableness of the defendant's perception of that immediacy.[15] Imminent danger generally means that there is little opportunity or possibility for the defendant to rationally consider all the possible means to neutralise the threats. In referring to the High Court decision in *Zecevic*, Hinton J in *Illert v Northern Adelaide Local Health Network Inc* stressed the importance of this element, stating:

> the imminence and seriousness of the threat to which the [defendant] was supposedly responding are important, and often critical, factual considerations going to the [defendant's] supposed belief, and the reasonableness of his belief.[16]

Therefore, an imminent danger should be assessed based on the defendant's subjective belief, rather than an actual need for defensive force or what a hypothetical reasonable person in the defendant's position might have believed in the circumstances.[17]

The reasonableness or proportionality element requires that the amount of force used by the defendant was reasonable or proportionate to the threat posed.[18] On the one hand, to be a successful self-defence, the force used by the defendant must have been reasonable.[19] What constitutes reasonable force is a question of fact to be determined in view of the circumstances on a case-by-case basis. It will be relevant to consider, for example, the way that the defendant resisted the plaintiff, whether a weapon or object was used, and the number of times the plaintiff was struck. However, it should also be noted that the defendant's acts must not be judged too harshly, because self-defence normally takes place under extreme circumstances. In those circumstances, a defendant 'cannot be expected to weigh precisely the exact measure of self-defensive action which is required'.[20]

On the other hand, proportionality of defensive force is, as observed in *Zecevic*, relevant but not determinative of whether the defence of self-defence was made out.[21] For example, spitting on the defendant's face does not require the defendant to respond by shooting the plaintiff. Such a response would be neither necessary nor proportionate. Shooting at the plaintiff would be considered more appropriate where the defendant was threatened with a gun or knife. In *Miller v Sotiropoulos*, Meagher JA observed that a minor push could not possibly justify a lethal punch in return.[22] In contrast, in *McClelland v Symons*, the plaintiff pointed a loaded rifle at the defendant saying, 'I've brought the gun to shoot you and here it is'.[23] The defendant then picked up a metal bar and struck the plaintiff on the head. The

---

15 See, eg, in *New South Wales v McMaster* (2015) 91 NSWLR 666, NSW Court of Appeal considered the situation that constitutes an imminent peril.

16 [2016] SASC 186, [58].

17 *Zecevic v DPP (Vic)* (1987) 162 CLR 645; *Watkins v Victoria* (2010) 27 VR 543.

18 *Fontin v Katapodis* (1962) 108 CLR 177.

19 Ibid.

20 *Watkins v Victoria* (2010) 27 VR 543, [72]. Holmes J famously observed in *Brown v United States*, 256 US 335 (1921) that 'detached reflection cannot be demanded in the presence of an uplifted knife' (at 343). This observation has been cited by a number of Australian courts when considering the claim of self-defence: see, eg, *Queensland Police Service v Skennar* [2017] QMC 11; *R v Forsyth* [2013] ACTSC 174; *Khan v Keown* [2001] VSCA 137.

21 *Zecevic v DPP (Vic)* (1987) 162 CLR 645.

22 [1997] NSWCA 204, [14].

23 [1951] VLR 157.

plaintiff suffered considerable injuries and sued the defendant for battery. The Court held that the defendant's act was proportionate to the threat confronting him. The defendant was acting in reasonable self-defence; thus, no battery had been committed. Once the imminent danger or threat is neutralised (eg, the plaintiff has been disabled) and the defendant's safety is secure, further acts by the defendant will not be covered by self-defence. The onus of proving the existence of the elements outlined earlier in this section lies on the defendant.[24] When the allegation is one of excessive force, it is the plaintiff who has the burden of proving further acts beyond self-defence.[25] The burden then passes to the defendant to justify necessity and reasonableness of the force in the circumstances.[26]

Case: *Fontin v Katapodis* (1962) 108 CLR 177

Facts

The plaintiff (Katapodis) was a customer at a hardware store. The defendant was employed in the glass department to cut glass with various tools. The defendant told the manager that the plaintiff had not paid for goods but in fact the plaintiff had done so. The defendant refused to apologise to the plaintiff and the two began to argue. At one point, the plaintiff picked up a wooden T-square from the bench and hit the defendant on the shoulder twice. When the plaintiff raised the T-square to hit the defendant for a third time, the defendant picked up a piece of offcut glass and threw it at the plaintiff's face. The plaintiff raised his hand attempting to protect his face and sustained permanent injury to his hand. The plaintiff sued the defendant for battery and the defendant argued self-defence.

Issue

Was throwing a piece of glass at the plaintiff by the defendant a self-defence in the circumstances?

Decision

The High Court held that the defendant's acts did not amount to self-defence because they were not reasonably necessary to avert the plaintiff's attack. The plaintiff's action in battery succeeded. McTiernan J said (at 181–2):

> It is clear that Fontin had a right to defend himself against being beaten by Katapodis. The question is whether, in the circumstances, it was reasonably necessary for him to throw the piece of glass at Katapodis ... Perhaps Katapodis may have struck more severe blows if Fontin had not prevented him. But to throw the piece of glass at Katapodis as a means of self-defence was out of all reasonable proportion to the emergency confronting Fontin. No other weapon was available to Fontin but instead of throwing the piece of glass at Katapodis he could easily have moved away from him and thus have avoided further blows from the T-square. Fontin had no need to stand his ground and it was not reasonably necessary for him to throw at Katapodis the cruel and cutting missile which he did throw. It was somewhat of the nature of a deadly weapon.

---

24 *Croucher v Cachia* (2016) 95 NSWLR 117; *McClelland v Symons* [1951] VLR 157, 161–3 (Sholl J).
25 *Pearce v Hallett* [1969] SASR 423, 428 (Bray CJ).
26 Ibid.

Significance

In this case the High Court considered what may constitute an excessive force in self-defence.

Question

How do you understand 'reasonableness' or 'proportionality' as an element of the defence of self-defence?

 Guided response in the eBook.

In addition to this common law defence to intentional torts, statutory self-defence exists in most Australian jurisdictions. In the Northern Territory, Queensland, Tasmania and Western Australia, self-defence under the Criminal Codes also applies to civil cases.

HINTS AND TIPS

Although the common law and criminal defences may result in the same outcome, important differences exist between them. Thus, attention should be given to the specific requirements and conditions for the application of common law self-defence and statutory self-defence, as well as the differences between jurisdictions.

EMERGING ISSUE

We know that, on the one hand, the reasonableness or proportionality element of self-defence requires that the amount of force used by the defendant was reasonable or proportionate to the threat posed; on the other hand, we cannot expect a person, usually the defendant, to precisely weigh the exact measure of self-defensive action which is required. What happens if a burglar who intruded into your house, hit by a heavy object you threw towards him, sues you for trespass to the person? While the common law rules concerning self-defence can be applied to justify the force you have used, it does not automatically resolve the issue of whether the convicted burglar can sue you for trespass to the person.

In the United Kingdom, this issue was addressed in s 329 of the *Criminal Justice Act 2003*, which provides that a person who is convicted of an 'imprisonable offence' (eg, murder, manslaughter, rape, theft and burglary, and many more minor offences) can only sue for trespass relating to the same incident with the permission of a court. If permission is given, the defendant will only be liable if the force was 'grossly disproportionate'. This is a weaker test than the normal one for self-defence, providing some extra protection to victims of serious crime. There is no comparable provision in Australia. The issue is open for discussion and to be assisted by further judicial input.

8.2.2　Defence of another

The early common law permitted a family member to use reasonable defensive force to protect another family member such as a spouse, parent or child, as well as a servant.[27] This defence has gained a wider basis for application in modern conditions. As Bray CJ observed in *Pearce v Hallett*, 'every man has the right of defending any man by reasonable force against unlawful force'.[28] This means that the defence is no longer limited to protection of a person of 'some defined relationship' to the defendant; it extends to the defending of 'any person, whether relative, friend or stranger'.[29] The test for self-defence has been held to apply to cases involving defence of another.[30] That is, the defendant must believe on reasonable grounds that it was necessary for him or her to use force to protect another person from an imminent danger. In the meantime, the force used must be reasonable or proportionate, and the onus of establishing that is upon the defendant.[31] In Queensland, s 273 of the *Criminal Code* (Qld) addresses the defence of another, which also applies to civil actions. In New South Wales, s 52 of the *Civil Liability Act 2002* (NSW) is a similar provision.

HINTS AND TIPS

From the above, we know that self-defence can be broadly applied to justify trespass actions against the person if the defendants were using reasonable force which they honestly and reasonably believed was necessary to protect themselves, or someone else, or property or to prevent a crime. How much force is 'reasonable' for self-defence to apply? This is a question of fact to be determined in view of the circumstances on a case-by-case basis, but the basic principle is that the type and strength of force used must be balanced against the danger the defendant was protecting against. The way that the defendant resisted the plaintiff, whether a weapon or object was used, and the number of times the plaintiff was struck are factors which may be relevant. It should be noted that the defendant's acts must not be judged too harshly, because self-defence normally takes place under extreme circumstances.

8.2.3　Defence of property

At common law, defence of one's own property based upon an immediate necessity to act is a good defence.[32] However, examples in this regard are limited to situations where the person in possession of land or premises is entitled to use reasonable force to eject

---

27　See, eg, *Seaman v Cuppledick* (1614) 74 ER 966; *Tickell v Read* (1773) 98 ER 617; *Barfoot v Reynolds* (1733) 93 ER 963. Compare *Leward v Basely* (1695) 91 ER 937; *A-G's Reference (No 2 of 1983)* [1984] QB 456.

28　[1969] SASR 423.

29　*R v Portelli* (2004) 10 VR 259, [13] (Ormiston JA).

30　*Watkins v Victoria* (2010) 27 VR 543, [75]; *R v Portelli* (2004) 10 VR 259, [23]. In *R v Portelli*, Ormiston JA stated (at [19]) that the defence is not limited to defence of a person of 'some defined relationship' to the defendant; it also extends to 'any person, whether relative, friend or stranger' should the force used be reasonably necessary.

31　*Goss v Nicholas* [1960] Tas SR 133.

32　See, eg, *Greyvensteyn v Hattingh* [1911] AC 355; *Cope v Sharpe (No 2)* [1912] 1 KB 496; *Proudman v Allen* [1954] SASR 336; *Rigby v Chief Constable of Northamptonshire* [1985] 1 WLR 1242 (QB).

a trespasser on the property, or deter a trespasser from entering that property.[33] The test for defence of property is similar to that applied in self-defence cases: specifically, for the defence to be established, there must be immediate danger to property.[34] In addition, the force used by the defendant must be reasonably proportionate to the danger to the property.[35] For the same reason, protection of property does not necessarily justify shooting a trespasser. For example, in *Bird v Holbrook*, the Court held that the erection of a spring-gun to deter trespassers from entering went beyond what was reasonably necessary to protect the defendant's land and goods.[36] Contrary to this, the defendant has a right to shoot trespassing dogs if the property in the form of livestock is in real and imminent danger and there is no other feasible method to protect the property.[37]

There is little authority clearly stating that defence of property can extend to defence of another's property.[38] A better view is probably that using reasonable force to defend another's property (both real property and personal property) can be justified by the defence of necessity (discussed in Section 8.2.4).[39] A good example is where a defendant entered onto the plaintiff's land to start a firebreak to protect the neighbour's property.[40]

8.2.4 Necessity

The defence of necessity can sometimes protect a defendant against liability in circumstances where consent could not be obtained. Even so, necessity has a broader application. It may justify intervention for the preservation of oneself, another person, one's own property or the property of another.

Typical situations where the defence of necessity can apply include entering another's land to fight fires,[41] towing someone's vessel away in order to prevent destruction of the

---

33 See, eg, *Holmes v Bagge* (1853) 118 ER 629; *Stroud v Bradbury* [1952] 2 All ER 76; *Horkin v North Melbourne Football Club Social Club* [1983] 1 VR 153 (a drunken patron injured while being ejected from a club successfully sued in assault and battery).

34 See, eg, *Kirk v Gregory* (1876) 1 Ex D 55; *Carter v Thomas* [1893] 1 QB 673; *Southwark London Borough Council v Williams* [1971] Ch 734.

35 *Norton v Hoare (No 1)* (1913) 17 CLR 310, 321–2 (Isaacs, Gavan, Duffy and Rich JJ).

36 (1828) 4 Bing 628. See also *Hackshaw v Shaw* (1984) 155 CLR 614 (a farm owner who shot a trespasser in the night owed a duty of care to a trespasser).

37 *Cresswell v Sirl* [1948] 1 KB 241; *Ramage v Evans* [1948] VLR 391 (shooting marauding dogs to protect sheep in both cases). It should be noted that the liability for the act of dogs is now subject to statutory regulations in Australia. A statutory right of self-defence also applies to this area. For example, in Queensland, the 'defence of premises against trespassers: removal of disorderly persons' is contained in *Criminal Code* (Qld) s 277. A similar provision can be found in *Civil Liability Act 2002* (NSW) s 52(2)(d).

38 See, eg, *Workman v Cowper* [1961] 2 QB 143.

39 Compare *Workman v Cowper* [1961] 2 QB 143 (shooting a dog which posed a danger to another's livestock) with *Cresswell v Sirl* [1948] 1 KB 241; *Ramage v Evans* [1948] VLR 391.

40 *Cope v Sharpe (No 2)* [1912] 1 KB 496. Statutory provisions in all Australian jurisdictions provide that fire officers are entitled to destroy property for the purpose of protecting life or property in controlling or extinguishing fire. See *Emergencies Act 2004* (ACT) s 34; *Fire Brigades Act 1989* (NSW) ss 13, 16; *Fire and Emergency Act 1996* (NT) s 23(3); *Fire and Emergency Services Act 1990* (Qld) s 53(2); *Fire and Emergency Services Act 2005* (SA) s 59; *Fire Service Act 1979* (Tas) s 29; *Country Fire Authority Act 1958* (Vic) s 30; *Fire Brigades Act 1942* (WA) s 34.

41 *Cope v Sharpe (No 2)* [1912] 1 KB 496 (entering onto the plaintiff's land to start a firebreak to prevent the existing fire spreading to neighbour's property); *Dewey v White* (1827) Mood & M 56; 173 ER 1079 (firefighters justified in throwing down the plaintiff's chimney to avoid its falling onto highway).

wharf,[42] throwing someone's cargo overboard to prevent a ship from sinking,[43] destroying clothing infected with a virulent disease,[44] and performing surgery to separate conjoined twins in order to avoid the death of both of them.[45] Again, the medical treatment context provides a good example. For instance, a heart-attack victim who arrives at a hospital in an unconscious state cannot consent to lifesaving medical treatment. However, the doctor who performs such treatment will not have committed a trespass due to the operation of the defence of necessity. What the doctor must show is that the treatment is reasonably necessary to prevent imminent harm to the plaintiff's person or reduce the likelihood of such harm, and that the interference is a reasonably proportionate response to that harm.[46] The defence also applies in a similar manner to justify an interference with property (land or goods) where such interference is necessary to protect or preserve that property.[47]

In order to make out this defence, the following elements must be established by the defendant:

(1)   There was an *imminent danger* to person or property.

(2)   There was a *reasonable necessity* for the defendant to act for the preservation of person or property.

(3)   The imminent danger was *not due to the defendant's fault*.

(4)   The steps taken were *reasonable and proportionate* to the danger to be avoided.

8.2.4.1   Imminent danger

For the defence of necessity to apply, the circumstances must amount to a real and imminent danger. For example, a conflagration approaching a house can be an imminent danger.[48] In *Proudman v Allen*, the Supreme Court of South Australia illustrated the circumstances which may amount to threat of imminent danger.[49] When establishing this element, the actual effect of the defendant's act (eg, damaged or even destroyed property) was irrelevant.[50]

---

42   *Beckingham v Port Jackson & Manly Steamship Co* (1957) SR (NSW) 403.

43   *Mouse's Case* (1608) 77 ER 1341 (one passenger threw the cargo belonging to another passenger overboard to save the ship and the lives of passengers threatened by a storm).

44   *Seavey v Preble*, 64 Me 120 (1874) (the government was not liable for the costs of destroying wallpaper in the homes of smallpox victims).

45   *Re A (Children) (Conjoined Twins: Surgical Separation)* [2000] 4 All ER 961.

46   A discussion of the circumstances in which the defence of necessity will protect a medical practitioner who does not have a patient's consent was considered in *Re F (Mental Patient: Sterilisation)* [1990] 2 AC 1.

47   See, eg, *Proudman v Allen* [1954] SASR 336.

48   *Cope v Sharpe (No 2)* [1912] 1 KB 496. See also *Cosenza v Origin Energy Ltd* [2017] SASC 145, [36] (Blue J). The defence of necessity has also been applied in criminal cases and, similarly, the notion of danger or peril is required to justify its application. For example, in the High Court case *Behrooz v Secretary of the Department of Immigration and Multicultural and Indigenous Affairs* (2004) 219 CLR 486; [2004] HCA 36, Gray J pointed out that there was no suggestion that the appellant was compelled to escape (from the prison) to avoid some peril, thus a defence of necessity would not apply (at [15]).

49   [1954] SASR 336.

50   Ibid.

Case: *Proudman v Allen* [1954] SASR 336

Facts

The defendant saw that a car was rolling driverless down a slope. He ran to the car, opened the door and tried to stop it but failed. The defendant then turned the steering wheel to avoid the car crashing into other parked vehicles. The collision was avoided but the car ran into the sea.

Issues

Was the defendant's act reasonably necessary to protect a third party's property from a threat of an imminent danger? Could the defence of necessity apply to the defendant?

Decisions

The Court held that there was an imminent danger and the defendant's action was a reasonably apparent necessity to protect a third party's property. Hannan AJ stated:

> It would seem that in principle the present respondent should not be absolutely liable for damage caused by his interference with the property of another when he acted in the reasonable belief that his interference was justified by the necessity of the situation and was intended to benefit the owner ... These works of charity and necessity must be lawful as well as right. The test of justification seems to be the actual presence of imminent danger and a reasonably apparent necessity of taking such action as was taken.
>
> ... the immunity for the consequences of such acts of interference is not limited to persons having an interest in the chattels concerned or a duty to preserve them, but extends to everyone who acts reasonably in a real emergency for the purpose of saving the goods of another from damage or destruction, whether he or she derives or is likely to derive any pecuniary advantage from the action or not, or is fulfilling any legal obligation [at 338–41].

Significance

This case illustrates circumstances that may amount to an imminent danger for the defence of necessity to apply.

Question

The defence of necessity can sometimes protect a defendant against liability in circumstances where consent could not be obtained. Can the defence of necessity justify intervention for the preservation of the property of another?

 Guided response in the eBook

In contrast, in *Southwark London Borough Council v Williams*, the Court held that there was no imminent danger to the defendants and the defence of necessity could not apply.[51] In that case, the defendants were a homeless family squatting in the plaintiff Council's empty property. The Council wished for immediate possession and applied to the Court for an order for this purpose. One of the arguments used by the defendants was that they acted out of necessity. The Court had to decide the question of whether necessity justifies the encroachment on private property. Lord Denning MR said:

> The reason is because, if hunger were once allowed to be an excuse for stealing, it would open a way through which all kinds of disorder and lawlessness would pass. So here, if homelessness were once admitted as a defence to trespass, no one's house could be safe. Necessity would open a door which no man could shut. It would not only be those in extreme need who would enter. There would be others who would imagine that they were in need, or would invent a need, so as to gain entry. Each man would say his need was greater than the next man's. The plea would be an excuse for all sorts of wrongdoing.[52]

8.2.4.2   Reasonable necessity

The defendant's act must be reasonably necessary in all the circumstances.[53] As with the defence of self-defence, whether the steps taken by the defendant are necessary and reasonable depends on the individual facts of each case. For example, in *Cope v Sharpe (No 2)*, the defendant entered the plaintiff's land and burnt heather there in order to prevent an existing fire from spreading to his master's property.[54] Setting fire to the heather was held to be reasonable in the circumstances and the defendant was exempted from liability.

However, although the steps taken by the defendant must be reasonably necessary, the defendant needs to show that if the steps had not been taken the property would have been destroyed or injured.[55]

8.2.4.3   Imminent danger not due to the defendant's fault

Necessity is very similar to the self-help based defences such as self-defence, defence of property and defence of another (see Section 8.2.2). However, necessity differs from self-defence because it is not used as a response to danger or threats caused by the defendant's own fault, either via negligence, tortious behaviour or breach of statutory duty. In *Rigby v Chief Constable of Northamptonshire*, Taylor J pointed out that the defence of necessity is only available 'in the absence of negligence on the part of the defendant creating or contributing to the necessity'.[56] In that case, the police used gas canisters to flush out a dangerous psychopath hiding in the plaintiff's gun shop, despite knowing that the psychopath had spread gunpowder on the floor. At the time there was no fire-fighting equipment available

---

51 [1971] Ch 734.
52 Ibid 744.
53 *Murray v McMurchy* [1949] 2 DLR 442 (performing sterilisation by tubal ligation for medical reasons, although there was no imminent threat to life, was held not to be reasonably necessary).
54 [1912] 1 KB 496.
55 *Proudman v Allen* [1954] SASR 336.
56 [1985] 1 WLR 1242, 1254.

to hand. The gas combined with the gunpowder caused a fire and burnt out the plaintiff's shop. The Court held that the defence of necessity was not allowed in this case due to negligence of the police.

Likewise, in *Simon v Condran* the plaintiff and the defendant were next-door neighbours and both of them owned dogs.[57] On the day in question the dogs got into a fight. The plaintiff followed her dog and entered the defendant's house where she was bitten on the hand by the defendant's dog. The plaintiff claimed damages, arguing that the trespass to land was necessary to handle the emergency. The Court held that the defence of necessity did not apply because the plaintiff's own negligence gave rise to the occasion for the necessary intervention.

8.2.4.4   Proportionate to the danger to be avoided

In addition, the steps taken by the defendant must be reasonable and proportionate to the imminent danger to be avoided. In *Re A (Children) (Conjoined Twins: Surgical Separation)* the English Court of Appeal invoked necessity to justify an order to authorise the separation of conjoined twins.[58] Medical evidence showed that an operation would hasten the imminent death of one twin who was the weaker and most dependent. However, if the twins were left as they were without the operation, both of them would die. The Court held that the evil inflicted (the death of one child) was not disproportionate to the evil to be avoided (the death of both children). This position was adopted by the Supreme Court of Queensland in *Queensland v Nolan*, which dealt with a similar situation (separation of conjoined twin girls) and the defence of necessity was relied upon.[59] The Supreme Court of Queensland authorised the operation by reference to the decision in *Re A* as well as the medical practitioners' statutory obligation imposed by s 286 of the *Criminal Code* (Qld). The Court held that the operation would be in the best interests of each of the twins and the operation was not unlawful.[60]

8.2.5   Abatement

Abatement arises where a person takes reasonable steps to ameliorate or terminate a tortious interference with their goods (or chattels) or land. Abatement is a generic term, the forms of which generally include recaption of goods, re-entry of land and abatement of nuisance.

8.2.5.1   Recaption of goods

Recaption of goods is a common law remedy exercised by a person who has been wrongfully deprived of the possession of goods. Through recaption, a person in actual possession of goods who loses his or her possession of the goods as a result of unlawful interference is entitled to use reasonable force to retake the goods. However, if the plaintiff's initial taking of the goods was consensual, and the defendant's recaption of the goods is based on a right to immediate possession (eg, where there is a bailment), the application of reasonable force to regain those goods should be subject to certain restrictions. In *Toyota Finance Australia*

57 (2013) 85 NSWLR 768.
58 [2000] 4 All ER 961.
59 [2002] 1 Qd R 454.
60 Ibid 522.

Ltd v Dennis, a majority of the New South Wales Court of Appeal held that the defence of recaption of goods only operates in cases where the plaintiff wrongfully came into possession.[61] Sheller JA (Meagher JA agreeing), citing Professor Fleming, stated:

> According to the better opinion, force is not justified unless the plaintiff's adverse possession was wrongful from its inception. Against a bailee, for example, the owner must resort to law, at any rate if repossession cannot be accomplished peacefully.[62]

Case: *Toyota Finance Australia Ltd v Dennis* (2002) 58 NSWLR 101

Facts

The respondent lessee's husband (Dennis) hired a vehicle from the appellant lessor Toyota Finance Australia (Toyota). The respondent was in arrears with his payments and the appellant was entitled to repossess the vehicle pursuant to the hire purchase agreement. When the appellant was attempting to take possession of the vehicle, the respondent resisted and a struggle for the car keys followed, in the course of which the appellant grabbed and pulled on the arm of the respondent's wife. The respondent sued the appellant, claiming damages for assault and battery.

Issue

Was the appellant's act justified by its right of recaption of the car?

Decision

The New South Wales Court of Appeal held that the appellant was not entitled to use force to regain possession of the vehicle and his conduct constituted assault. By a majority (Meagher and Sheller JJA, with Handley JA dissenting), the Court declined to follow the principle stated in *Blades v Higgs* (1861) 10 CB (NS) 713 and concluded that an owner's right of forcible recaption of a good unlawfully detained from another was limited to situations where that other's adverse possession was wrongful from its inception. In this case, the respondent had originally come into possession of the car lawfully under the lease. Thus, the appellant was not entitled to use force to regain possession and his conduct amounted to assault. Quoting Professor Fleming's text (*The Law of Torts* (9th ed, 1998) 100), Sheller JA (Meagher JA agreeing) stated (at [134]):

> The scope of the privilege widened steadily since medieval times with increasing confidence in the ability of law to regulate extra judicial redress; but this trend, which

---

61 (2002) 58 NSWLR 101. In *StockCo Agricapital Pty Ltd v Tucki Hills Pty Ltd* (2022) 405 ALR 453, Stewart J discussed the uncertainty of the law with regard to recaption that is demonstrated by the divergent judgments in *Toyota Finance Australia Ltd v Dennis* (2002) 58 NSWLR 101. While there are few Australian cases on recaption, in *StockCo Agricapital Pty Ltd* Stewart J referred to some valuable scholarship, which includes: L Aitken, 'The Abandonment and Reception of Chattels' (1994) 68(4) *Australian Law Journal* 263; PW Young, 'Recaption of Chattels' (2003) 74(4) *Australian Law Journal* 223; L Aitken, 'Recovery of Chattels in the Common and Civil Law: Possession, Bailment and Spoliation Suits' (2008) 82(6) *Australian Law Journal* 379; J O'Hara, 'The Nature of Recaption' (2019) 93(10) *Australian Law Journal* 866.

62 (2002) 58 NSWLR 101, [134].

reached its zenith during the last century, is likely to be reversed rather than followed today. Still, owing to the dearth of modern authority and some conflict among the older decisions, the present position cannot be stated in all respects with a high degree of confidence ... According to the better opinion, force is not justified unless the plaintiff's adverse possession was wrongful from its inception. Against a bailee, for example, the owner must resort to law, at any rate if repossession cannot be accomplished peacefully.

Sheller JA further explained (at [141], [144]):

I do not think we should follow *Blades v Higgs* ... With due respect, *Blades v Higgs* is not a convincing decision. It is not based on precedent and for no satisfactory reason encourages forcible, perhaps violent, redress where none is required ... In my opinion, [the appellant] had no right to seek forcibly to seize the vehicle and in the course of doing so, to assault.

Significance

In *Toyota Finance Australia Ltd v Dennis* the principle stated in *Blades v Higgs* was rejected. This means that, in Australia, the defence of recaption of goods does not apply to cases where the initial possession was not unlawful.

Notes

In *Toyota Finance Australia Ltd v Dennis*, one difficult question to be answered by the Court was whether the right to use force to repossess goods should be limited to cases where the wrongdoer's possession was wrongful from its inception. The English position on this question was originally reflected by the frequently cited case *Blades v Higgs* (1861) 10 CB (NS) 713. In *Blades v Higgs*, the plaintiff obtained some dead rabbits which had been poached from the Marquis of Exeter. The defendant servants of the Marquis used force to prevent the plaintiff from taking the rabbits away. The Court held that the defendant did not commit battery by using reasonable force to retake the rabbits from the plaintiff. Erle CJ observed that it had been a rule that a person entitled to possession of a good could use force to retake the good he or she had been unlawfully dispossessed of, and that the principle also extended to circumstances where the good was wrongfully taken by a plaintiff who was not the original taker. That means, no matter how the plaintiff originally came into possession of the good, adverse possession is itself sufficient to justify recaption of goods.

When *Toyota Finance Australia Ltd v Dennis* was decided, there was no legislation in New South Wales addressing how self-defence is to operate in civil proceedings. The *Civil Liability Act 2002* (NSW) s 52(2) provides that:

(2) A person carries out conduct in self-defence if and only if the person believes the conduct is necessary:
   (a) to defend himself or herself or another person, or
   (b) to prevent or terminate the unlawful deprivation of his or her liberty or the liberty of another person, or

(c) to protect property from unlawful taking, destruction, damage or interference, or

(d) to prevent criminal trespass to any land or premises or to remove a person committing any such criminal trespass, and the conduct is a reasonable response in the circumstances as he or she perceives them.

Therefore, if a case of the same factual scenario occurred today in New South Wales, the defendant might be able to rely on the statutory defence of self-defence under s 52 to justify his or her tortious activities.

Question

A majority of the New South Wales Court of Appeal (Meagher and Sheller JJA, with Handley JA dissenting) declined to follow *Blades v Higgs* (1861) 10 CB (NS) 713 and concluded that an owner's right of forcible recaption of a good unlawfully detained from another was limited to situations where that other's adverse possession was wrongful from its inception. If the situation in *Toyota Finance Australia Ltd v Dennis* occurred today in New South Wales, do you think the court decision would be different?

   Guided response in the eBook

The defence of recaption of goods may also justify trespass to land, where a defendant with a right to immediate possession of a good entered the plaintiff's land for the purpose of retaking the good.[63] In *Haniotis v Dimitriou*, the plaintiff (tenant) rented a factory from the defendant (landowner) but then breached the lease by refusing to pay rent. The defendant entered the property, removed the plaintiff's goods and changed the locks to eject the plaintiff. The Court held that the defendant had not committed trespass to land or trespass to goods. However, if there was no breach of the lease, the tenant may sue the landowner in trespass to land.[64] The Criminal Codes of most Australian jurisdictions give rights to retake possession of goods using reasonable force from any person who is in possession of them but does not hold them under a claim of right.[65] Therefore, original wrongful taking by that person is not required in such jurisdictions.

---

63 *Haniotis v Dimitriou* [1983] 1 VR 498.

64 *Moore v Devanjul Pty Ltd (No 5)* [2013] QSC 323. For residential properties, in all jurisdictions except Victoria and Tasmania legislation prohibits the landlord from entering or retaking possession of premises without an order for possession from a court or the relevant residential tenancy tribunal. See *Residential Tenancies Act 1997* (ACT) s 37; *Residential Tenancies Act 2010* (NSW) s 120; *Residential Tenancies Act 1999* (NT) pt 9; *Residential Tenancies and Rooming Accommodation Act 2008* (Qld) s 353; *Residential Tenancies Act 1995* (SA) s 95; *Residential Tenancies Act 1987* (WA) s 80. In Victoria and Tasmania, statutory law provides that without the tenant's permission, a landlord has no right to enter the premises.

65 *Criminal Code* (ACT) s 38; *Criminal Code Act 1983* (NT) s 27(k); *Criminal Code* (Qld) s 276; *Criminal Code* (Tas) s 45; *Criminal Code* (WA) s 253.

8.2.5.2   Re-entry of land

A person who has a right to immediate possession of land may use reasonable force to eject the person in possession of the land. The defence justifying the use of reasonable force is referred to as 're-entry of land'. The right to re-entry of land overlaps with defence of property and necessity, where actual possession or the right to exclusive possession is required to justify the reasonable force used to eject a trespasser. In *Cowell v Rosehill Racecourse Co Ltd*, the plaintiff (Cowell) refused to leave the defendant's racecourse after his licence was revoked.[66] The plaintiff thereby became a trespasser and the defendant used reasonable force to physically eject the plaintiff from the land. The plaintiff alleged that the physical ejectment amounted to a battery. The defendant argued that the ejectment was justified as a way to abate the plaintiff's trespass to land. The Court agreed and held the defendant not liable for the battery committed to the plaintiff. Whether possession has been retaken is a question of fact. Acts that would be sufficient upon a small parcel of land may be insufficient over a large parcel of land, and vice versa.[67]

8.2.5.3   Abatement of nuisance

The defence of abatement of nuisance bears a resemblance to the defences of recaption of goods and re-entry, and can operate to justify an action for trespass to land. This defence involves the defendant entering the land of another or taking other self-help measures to abate a nuisance which substantially interferes with the enjoyment of his or her own land. For example, in *Lemmon v Webb*, cutting off branches of overhanging trees was not trespass.[68] It should be noted that statutory provisions in many jurisdictions address the lopping of overhanging or encroaching tree branches.[69] Therefore, statutory provisions should be consulted before action is taken by a person to abate a nuisance.

8.2.6   Consent

Consent is a defence to trespass to the person (assault, battery and false imprisonment), trespass to land and interferences with personal property (trespass to goods, conversion and detinue). There can be no trespass if the interference occurs with the plaintiff's consent.[70] As already seen when discussing trespass to the person, it seems that in Australia, the onus is on the defendant to establish the existence of consent.[71] This means that consent is more properly regarded as a defence to the trespass rather than an element of the action. A similar position

---

66 (1937) 56 CLR 605.
67 See, eg, *Robertson v Butler* [1915] VLR 31, entry upon disputed land, walking, hunting, and picnicking upon the land a few times a year was deemed not to be a retaking of possession by the document owner. See also *Hodgson v Thompson* (1906) 6 SR (NSW) 436, 440, quoted by Justice O'Neill in *Alford v Evans and Registrar of Titles* [2010] VCC 475.
68 [1895] AC 1. Self-help measures to abate a nuisance also include, for example, unblocking drains (*Nicol v Nicol* (1887) 13 VLR 322) and removing encroaching roots and branches (*Young v Wheeler* [1987] Aust Torts Reports 80-126).
69 See, eg, *Trees (Disputes Between Neighbours) Act 2006* (NSW) s 5; *Neighbourhood Disputes Resolution Act 2011* (Qld) s 54.
70 See, eg, *McNamara v Duncan* (1971) 45 FLR 152.
71 *Secretary, Department of Health and Community Services v JWB* (1992) 175 CLR 218, 310–11 (McHugh J) ('*Marion's Case*').

was held by the Supreme Court of Canada in *Non-Marine Underwriters, Lloyd's of London v Scalera*, where the Court held that the defendant must prove that the bodily contact was made with volitional consent.[72] 'Lack of consent' is not an element of battery because 'when a person interferes with the body of another, a prima facie case of violation of the plaintiff's autonomy is made out'.[73] The position in Australia and Canada is opposite to the English and New Zealand position.[74] For example, in *Freeman v Home Office (No 2)*, McCowan J ruled that the burden is on the plaintiff to establish his or her own lack of consent.[75]

Some changes in the Australian position have been observed in recent years. In *White v Johnston*,[76] the New South Wales Court of Appeal departed from the approach of McHugh J in *Marion's Case*[77] and held that the better view is to treat 'lack of consent' as part of the definitions (element) of assault and battery. In *White v Johnston*, Leeming JA concluded that a plaintiff 'who sues in assault and battery in all cases bears the legal burden of establishing an absence of consent on his or her part'.[78]

Therefore, the current Australian position on whether lack of consent is an element of trespass and accordingly for the plaintiff to prove, or whether the issue of consent in trespass is a defence and the defendant bears the onus, remains unsettled. However, in Queensland, 'lack of consent' is an element of battery due to the fact that the criminal definition of assault in s 245 of the *Criminal Code* (Qld) also applies to civil cases.

Outlined here are a number of factors affecting the validity of consent which must be considered in practice. Each of these factors will be examined in turn:

(1)   Consent can be given either expressly or impliedly.

(2)   Consent must be real and be given voluntarily.

(3)   The plaintiff must have the legal capacity to consent.

(4)   Consent may come to an end through revocation or expiration.

(5)   The scope of the consent cannot be exceeded.

8.2.6.1   Express or implied consent

EXPRESS CONSENT

Consent can be either express or implied. A common example of express consent being sought and obtained is found in the context of medical procedures.[79] A medical procedure or treatment that involves physical interference or touching of the patient will, if performed without consent, constitute battery.[80] Obviously, there will be no real consent if the plaintiff

---

72   (2000) 185 DLR (4th) 1.

73   Ibid 565–7.

74   See also *S v G* [1995] 3 NZLR 681, 687 (CA); *H v R* [1996] 1 NZLR 299, 305 (HC).

75   [1984] QB 524, 537.

76   (2015) 87 NSWLR 779.

77   *Marion's Case* (1992) 175 CLR 218, 310–11 (McHugh J).

78   (2015) 87 NSWLR 779, [130].

79   For example, the *Consent to Medical Treatment and Palliative Care Act 1995* (SA) explains the nature, consequences and risks of proposed medical treatment and the likely consequences of not undertaking the treatment. This Act provides one exception to the rule that broad knowledge of the treatment is sufficient to establish valid consent.

80   See, eg, *Marion's Case* (1992) 175 CLR 218, 310 (McHugh J): 'every surgical procedure is an assault unless it is authorized, justified or excused by law'.

patient has no understanding of the interference to which they are consenting. In Australia, it has been held that for the purpose of trespass, the patient need only be told the broad nature of the interference.[81] If the treatment performed is different to what the plaintiff consented to, there will be a trespass.[82] Notably, a signed consent form is not conclusive evidence of consent by the plaintiff.[83]

The courts value very highly the individual's right to refuse consent to medical treatment even if such treatment would be lifesaving, or the refusal may result in deterioration of the patient's condition or may lead to premature death. In *Re T*, the Court held that an adult patient who suffers from no mental incapacity has an absolute right to choose whether to consent to medical treatment, to refuse treatment or to choose any other alternatives being offered.[84] Whether the reasons for making the choice are rational, irrational, unknown or non-existent is irrelevant.[85] In *X v Sydney Children's Hospital Network*,[86] Basten JA quoted the Ontario Court of Appeal in *Malette v Shulman*,[87] stating:

> The state's interest in preserving the life or health of a competent patient must generally give way to the patient's stronger interest in directing the course of her own life … Recognition of the right to reject medical treatment cannot, in my opinion, be said to depreciate the interest of the state in life or in the sanctity of life. Individual free choice and self-determination are themselves fundamental constituents of life. To deny individuals freedom of choice with respect to their healthcare can only lessen, and not enhance, the value of life.[88]

A question arises in relation to these rules: if the patient's refusal of treatment not only endangers her own life but also endangers the life of an unborn foetus, can the right to refuse treatment gain its common law foundations? The English and Canadian courts have confirmed that the interests of an unborn foetus will not be elevated above the common law rights of pregnant women, whose autonomy is protected by the common law doctrine of consent.[89] In *St George Healthcare NHS Trust v S*, Butler-Sloss LJ stated:

> while pregnancy increases the personal responsibilities of a woman it does not diminish her entitlement to decide whether or not to undergo medical treatment … She is

---

81 *Rogers v Whitaker* (1992) 175 CLR 479, 490 (Mason CJ, Brennan, Dawson, Toohey and McHugh JJ) (a doctor's failure to warn the patient of risks inherent in an eye operation constituted a breach of duty), affd in *Reeves v The Queen* (2013) 304 ALR 251 (gynaecologist who removed the entire vulva and clitoris of a patient without 'informed consent' was found guilty).

82 *Chatterton v Gerson* [1981] QB 432, 443; *Murray v McMurchy* [1949] 2 DLR 442.

83 See *Chatterton v Gerson* [1981] QB 432.

84 (1992) 3 Med LR 306.

85 See also *Airedale NHS Trust v Bland* [1993] AC 789, 891 ('a doctor has no right to proceed in the face of objection, even if it is plain to all, including the patient that adverse consequences and even death will or may ensue'); *Re B (Adult: Refusal of Medical Treatment)* [2002] 2 All ER 449; *Brightwater Care Group v Rossiter* (2009) 40 WAR 84; *Hunter and New England Area Health Service v A* (2009) 74 NSWLR 88.

86 (2013) 85 NSWLR 294.

87 (1990) 67 DLR (4th) 321.

88 *X v Sydney Children's Hospital Network* (2013) 85 NSWLR 294, [58].

89 See, eg, *St George's Healthcare NHS Trust v S* [1999] Fam 26; *R (Pretty) v DPP* [2002] 1 AC 800 (both cases reiterate the principle that a competent patient cannot be compelled to accept lifesaving treatment); *Winnipeg Child and Family Services (Northwest Area) v G* (1997) 152 DLR (4th) 193; *Re Baby R* (1988) 53 DLR (4th) 69 (BCSC); *Re A* (1990) 72 DLR (4th) 722 (ONUFC).

entitled not to be forced to submit to an invasion of her body against her will, whether her own life or that of her unborn child depends on it.[90]

The Supreme Court of Victoria had the opportunity to rule upon the same matter in *Mercy Hospitals Victoria v D1*.[91] However, the question whether the Court should be concerned with 'the interests and wellbeing of [the pregnant teen's] unborn baby, or of the baby when born',[92] in the context of exercising its *parens patriae* jurisdiction,[93] was not clearly stated. Therefore, this issue remains open in Australia and decisions in other common law jurisdictions can be referred to.

In all Australian jurisdictions, consent by both adults and minors for the removal of human tissue (including blood) for transplantation is governed by statutory provisions.[94]

IMPLIED CONSENT

An example of implied consent is when a person who engages in a sport consents to bodily contact in the course of the game.[95] Implied consent is given to those incidental contacts within the rules of the game. The implied consent may even extend to certain rule infringements such as stripping or pushing.[96] However, battery may be committed if the contact is outside the rules of the game to a serious extent and the application of force aims 'to cause bodily harm', or the defendant 'knows, or ought to have known, that such harm is the likely result of his actions'.[97]

Implied consent is also referred to as 'implied licence' in trespass to land cases. If the defendant entered the plaintiff's land with consent or implied licence, there will be no trespass. In *Halliday v Nevill* the High Court observed an implied or tacit licence to enter the plaintiff's premises 'can be precluded or at any time revoked by express or implied refusal or withdrawal of it'.[98]

Therefore, unless there is a fence or notice indicating that entry of land is forbidden, implied licence exists for a person entering property unintentionally (or intentionally for the purposes of legitimate communication), to avoid an obstruction on the footpaths, to retrieve an item that has fallen or blown upon the land or to recover a straying child or animal.[99]

---

90 [1999] Fam 26, 50.
91 (2018) 56 VR 394. This case is more relevant to the issue of a minor's capacity to refuse medical treatment, which will be further discussed in Section 8.2.6.3 (capacity to consent).
92 Ibid [6](c) (Macaulay J).
93 The Latin term *parens patriae* means 'parent of the country'. It is a doctrine that grants the state inherent power and authority to act as guardian for persons (both adults and children) who are legally unable to act on their own behalf. For instance, under this doctrine the courts may change custody, or authorise the performance of certain medical treatments for a child's wellbeing.
94 *Transplantation and Anatomy Act 1978* (ACT); *Human Tissue Act 1983* (NSW); *Transplantation and Anatomy Act 1979* (NT); *Transplantation and Anatomy Act 1979* (Qld); *Transplantation and Anatomy Act 1983* (SA); *Human Tissue Act 1985* (Tas); *Human Tissue Act 1982* (Vic); *Human Tissue and Transplant Act 1982* (WA).
95 *McNamara v Duncan* (1971) 45 FLR 152. See also *Giumelli v Johnston* [1991] Aust Torts Reports 81-085; *Canterbury Bankstown Rugby League Football Club Ltd v Rogers* [1993] Aust Torts Reports 81-246 (a head-high tackle, which was a foul play in a rugby league game, constituted a battery, and the player's club was held to be vicariously liable).
96 [1991] Aust Torts Reports 81-085.
97 *Giumelli v Johnston* [1991] Aust Torts Reports 81-085; *Sibley v Milutinovic* (1990) Aust Torts Reports 81-013.
98 (1984) 155 CLR 1, 7 (Gibbs CJ, Mason, Wilson and Deane JJ).
99 *Plenty v Dillon* (1991) 171 CLR 635.

Case: *Giumelli v Johnston* (1991) Aust Torts Reports 81-085

Facts

The plaintiff and the defendant were players on opposing teams in an Australian Rules Football match. While the plaintiff had the ball, the defendant collided with him in a 'hip and shoulder' bump, which is permitted by the rules of the game.

Issue

Had the plaintiff consented to contact that would otherwise amount to a battery simply by participating in the game, given that the rules permitted physical contact?

Decision

King CJ (Mohr and Prior JJ agreeing) said (at [68709]–[68710]):

> The rules of Australian Rules Football permit bodily contact, including strong bodily contact, in the course of the game. Those who participate in a football match are taken to consent to the infliction on them of such physical force as is permitted by the rules of the game. It was accepted by the [plaintiff], moreover, that some bodily contact outside the rules of the game is to be expected as an ordinary incident of a football match …
>
> Although a player's consent to the application of force to him in the course of the game extends not only to the application of force within the rules of the game but also to certain commonly encountered infringements of the rules … such consent cannot be taken to include physical violence applied in contravention of the rules of the game by an opposing player who intends to cause bodily harm or knows, or ought to know, that such harm is the likely result of his actions.

Significance

This is a frequently cited case concerning the circumstances where implied consent exists.

Question

In which circumstances will a plaintiff player not be regarded as having consented to the physical contact?

 Guided response in the eBook

Although the implied consent by the plaintiff may preclude an action for battery, it is still possible for the plaintiff to sue in negligence.

8.2.6.2   Real and voluntarily given

Consent will only be valid if it is real, in the sense of 'genuine', and given freely by the plaintiff. For consent to be effective, the plaintiff must have sufficient knowledge to understand the nature and character of the act to be performed. For example, in *S (An Infant) v S*, the Court held that there is no genuine consent to medical procedures when consent is procured under sedation.[100]

On the one hand, consent will not be valid if it is procured by fraud. As a general rule, fraud may nullify consent if the act consented to is not identical to the act actually performed. For example, in *R v Williams*, the defendant singing coach gained the consent of the plaintiff (a female pupil) to perform a surgical operation to improve her singing; instead he had sexual intercourse with the plaintiff.[101] It was held that the plaintiff's consent was vitiated by fraud as to the nature and quality of the act. However, not every fraudulent misrepresentation will vitiate consent. For example, fraudulent misrepresentations about marital status[102] or non-disclosure of sexual disease as an inducement to consent to sexual relations do not vitiate the plaintiff's consent so as to convert permitted acts into trespasses.[103] In such circumstances, the act performed is not materially different from what has been consented to, and the plaintiff understands the nature and character of the interference. In the fraudulent misrepresentation cases, such as *Hegarty v Shine*,[104] although the plaintiff cannot sue in battery, the fraud itself may be actionable and the plaintiff may succeed in the tort of negligence or intentional, non-trespassory infliction of sexual diseases. In cases where consent is obtained by fraud, it is the plaintiff who bears the burden of proving that fraud.[105]

Consent will not be valid if it is obtained by physical force,[106] threats or mental duress, such as a coercive relationship of employment or even imprisonment. In *Symes v Mahon*,

---

100 [1972] AC 24.
101 [1923] 1 KB 340.
102 See, eg, *McGrath v Marshall* (1898) 14 WN (NSW) 106; *Papadimitropoulos v The Queen* (1957) 98 CLR 249 (where a woman consented to sexual intercourse in the belief that she was married to a bigamist, the fraudulent misrepresentation by the bigamist did not turn that sexual intercourse into rape). The decision in *Papadimitropoulos* has been reversed by statutory provisions in some jurisdictions: see, eg, *Crimes Act 1900* (NSW) s 61HE(6).
103 See, eg, *Hegarty v Shine* (1878) 4 LR Ir 288 (QBCA), where the defendant had sexual intercourse with the plaintiff without revealing his syphilitic condition and thereby infected the plaintiff. See also *R v Clarence* (1888) 22 QBD 23, where the defendant had sexual intercourse with his wife without revealing that he was infected with gonorrhoea. In both cases, the Court held that there was no battery. The plaintiff understood the nature of the act to be performed, and the defendant's silence did not vitiate her consent. However, like *Papadimitropoulos v The Queen* (1957) 98 CLR 249, the decision in *R v Clarence* is outdated and no longer authoritative: see *R v Dica* [2004] 3 WLR 213; *R v Brady* [2006] EWCA Crim 2413.
104 *Hegarty v Shine* (1878) 4 LR Ir 288 (QBCA). See also *McGrath v Marshall* (1898) 14 WN (NSW) 106; *Papadimitropoulos v The Queen* (1957) 98 CLR 249.
105 *Dean v Phung* [2012] NSWCA 223.
106 See, eg, *Michael v Western Australia* (2008) 183 A Crim R 348 (where the plaintiff consented after being physically threatened).

the Court held that consent procured by duress was ineffective and false imprisonment was therefore established.[107]

8.2.6.3 Capacity to consent

Only a person who has legal capacity to consent can give valid consent.[108] In *Neal v The Queen*, Nettle and Redlich JJA and Kyrou AJA stated that a person is deemed not to be capable of giving consent to trespass (in that case sexual penetration) if 'the person is asleep, unconscious or so affected by alcohol or another drug as to be incapable of freely agreeing'.[109] Even so, whether a particular person has the capacity to consent is to be assessed on a case-by-case basis.

In the medical procedure context, it is well established by case law that an adult with legal capacity has the right to consent or refuse consent to medical treatment. For example, in the Canadian case *Malette v Shulman* (discussed in Section 8.2.6.1), an adult's refusal of a blood transfusion for religious reasons was held to be valid.[110] This common law right has been reinforced by legislation in relation to advance health directives in several Australian jurisdictions.[111] A medical practitioner who failed to follow a valid and applicable advance health directive may be liable in trespass.[112]

However, the courts have had to deal with the question of whether a person under the age of 18, technically a minor, can provide valid consent. The leading High Court authority on the issue is *Marion's Case*.[113] The High Court rejected a fixed-age approach and accepted the view adopted in the earlier House of Lords decision in *Gillick v West Norfolk and Wisbech Area Health Authority*.[114] That is, a minor is capable of giving consent when he or she 'achieves a sufficient understanding of and intelligence to enable him or her to understand fully what is proposed'.[115] The test is known as '*Gillick* competence' and has become an integral aspect of medical and family law. If the child lacks *Gillick* competence, consent must be sought from the child's parents or guardian. Even so, the informed decision

107 [1922] SASR 447.
108 See, eg, *Marion's Case* (1992) 175 CLR 218; *Gillick v West Norfolk and Wisbech Area Health Authority* [1986] AC 112.
109 (2011) 32 VR 454, [77].
110 (1990) 67 DLR (4th) 321 (Can) [19], cited with approval in *X v Sydney Children's Hospital Network* (2013) 85 NSWLR 294.
111 Statutory provisions enable adults (by themselves, agents or alternative agents) to express their wishes about specific healthcare decisions through an advance health directive. See *Medical Treatment (Health Directions) Act 2006* (ACT) pt 2; *Powers of Attorney Act 2006* (ACT); *Advance Personal Planning Act 2013* (NT) pt 2; *Powers of Attorney Act 1998* (Qld) ch 3; *Consent to Medical Treatment and Palliative Care Act 1995* (SA) s 8; *Advance Directive Act 2013* (SA); *Medical Treatment Act 1988* (Vic) ss 5A, 5B(2); *Guardianship and Administration Act 1990* (WA) s 110P. There are no statutory advance directives in New South Wales or Tasmania; the common law applies in both jurisdictions.
112 *Hunter and New England Area Health Service v A* (2009) 74 NSWLR 88 (a 'worksheet' prepared by the patient refusing dialysis for religious reason should be followed by the hospital).
113 (1992) 175 CLR 218, 237–8.
114 [1986] AC 112. See also *Re LG* [2017] FCWA 179, [37] (Duncanson J), where the Family Court of Western Australia held that the child (LG) was *Gillick* competent to consent to Stage 3 treatment, in order to facilitate the child's future gender reassignment.
115 [1986] AC 112, 187.

of a *Gillick*-competent minor or his or her parent or guardian can be overruled by a court exercising *parens patriae* jurisdiction.[116]

Case: *Mercy Hospitals Victoria v D1* (2018) 56 VR 394

Facts

The defendant (D1) was a 17-year-old woman who had been pregnant for 38 weeks. She consented to a caesarean section being performed to deliver her baby if necessary. The Mercy Hospitals Victoria sought her consent to a blood transfusion during or after delivery, if necessary, to save her life or prevent serious injury during or after the delivery. Because such administration is contrary to her faith as a Jehovah's Witness, the defendant refused consent. The defendant's mother, for the same reason, also informed the hospital that she would refuse to give such consent if asked. The hospital therefore brought an urgent application to the Supreme Court of Victoria, seeking a court declaration to authorise doctors to administer a blood transfusion to the defendant, where necessary, without the defendant's consent.

Issue

Should the hospital be allowed to administer a blood transfusion, which is necessary to save the minor's life or prevent serious injury to the minor's health, without consent of the minor or the minor's parent?

Decision

The Court held that the hospital was authorised to administer a blood transfusion during or after the delivery.

The Court considered whether allowing the minor's choice to refuse a blood transfusion based on religious conviction was in accord with the 'welfare and best interests' standard. While agreeing with White J's thoughts in *Children, Youth & Women's Health Service Inc v YJL* (2010) 107 SASR 343 (at 350 [41]) that a child's spiritual welfare should be of equal concern, Macaulay J pointed out that the 'particular attributes of the child must remain in clear focus' in the exercise of the Court's *parens patriae* jurisdiction.

Macaulay J thought Basten JA's view in *X v Sydney Children's Hospital Network* (2013) 85 NSWLR 294, [60], was helpful when assessing a choice made by a minor, even a *Gillick*-competent minor. Quoting Basten JA's statement, Macaulay J pointed out:

---

116 See, eg, *Mercy Hospitals Victoria v D1* (2018) 56 VR 394; *Minister for Health v AS* (2004) 29 WAR 517; *X v Sydney Children's Hospital Network* (2013) 85 NSWLR 294. Guardianship legislation in many jurisdictions empowers emergency treatment, including blood transfusion, without consent of the minor or his or her parent or guardian. For example, *Children and Young Persons (Care and Protection) Act 1998* (NSW) s 174 permits a medical practitioner to carry out medical treatment on a child without the consent of the child or the parents 'if the medical practitioner is of the opinion that it is necessary, as a matter of urgency, to carry out the treatment on the child or young person in order to save his or her life or to prevent serious damage to his or her health'. Other states and territories have similar provisions: see, eg, *Emergency Medical Operations Act 1973* (NT) s 3; *Consent to Medical Treatment and Palliative Care Act 1995* (SA) s 13.

The interest of the state in preserving life is at its highest with respect to children and young persons who are inherently vulnerable, in varying degrees. Physical vulnerability diminishes (usually) with age and is at its height with respect to babies. Intellectual and emotional vulnerability also diminish with age but, as the facts of this case illustrate, may be a function of experience (including but by no means limited to education) as well as age. Vulnerability lies at the heart of the disability identified by legal incapacity.

The Court also evaluated the impacts of two statutes, the *Human Tissue Act 1982* (Vic) and the *Medical Treatment Planning and Decisions Act 2016* (Vic), which were relevant to the Court's exercise of jurisdiction in this case.

Taking into account the above matters and observations, Macaulay stated:

> I am not satisfied D1 does have a sufficient understanding of the consequences of her choice ... I do not consider that allowing her, in effect, to choose to die or only survive with serious injury is in her best interests taking into account a holistic view of her welfare (physical, spiritual and otherwise) [at [76]].

Significance

This case confirmed that the informed decision of a *Gillick*-competent minor or his or her parent or guardian can be overruled by a court, and that 'particular attributes' such as the intellectual and emotional vulnerability of a minor should be the focus when assessing a minor's capacity to consent or refuse medical treatment.

Question

At common law, a minor is capable of giving consent to medical treatment when he or she 'achieves a sufficient understanding of and intelligence to enable him or her to understand fully what is proposed'. The test is known as '*Gillick* competence'. Can and should the decision of a '*Gillick*-competent' child be overridden by the court?

 Guided response in the eBook

In the case of an intellectually disabled child, the disability may deprive him or her of the capacity to consent to medical treatment. In such circumstances, as a general rule, the parents would retain the power to consent on their child's behalf.[117] However, *Marion's Case* made it clear that there is an important exception in relation to consent to a sterilisation procedure (unless it is an incidental result of surgery performed to cure a disease or correct some malfunction) which the Court concluded 'falls outside the ordinary scope of parental powers'.[118] In that case, it was held that court authorisation was needed. In addition, parental consent to treatment with respect to non-therapeutic procedures, such

---

117 *Marion's Case* (1992) 175 CLR 218.
118 Ibid [53] (Mason CJ, Dawson, Toohey and Gaudron JJ).

as sterilisation of a mentally disabled child in *Marion's Case*, organ donation and gender reassignment, are beyond the capacity of parents.[119] An order or direction from the Family Court or Guardianship Board should be sought in those circumstances.

There is an important exception to the general principles governing consent. The common law allows medical practitioners to provide emergency medical treatment to a person without obtaining consent if the treatment is reasonable and necessary in order to save a person's life or to prevent serious damage to a person's health.[120] However, emergency treatment can only be given to a person who has not refused consent to the treatment.[121] In the context of emergency treatment, if no person authorised to give consent is available, the medical practitioners can apply the defence of necessity to avoid liability (for the general principles governing the defence of necessity, see Section 8.2.4).

In many jurisdictions, the guardianship legislation authorises emergency treatment for an adult patient who does not have the capacity to give consent.[122]

8.2.6.4   Revocation and expiration of consent

Consent, either express or implied, can be revoked or withdrawn by the plaintiff. In *Plenty v Dillon*,[123] the High Court applied the principles in *Halliday v Nevill*,[124] holding that where the implied licence is withdrawn, there is no right at common law for a police officer to enter private premises to serve a summons. The implied licence had been expressly revoked before the police officers' entry onto the premises. Revocation or withdrawal may also take place after the act consented to has taken place. For example, in *Cowell v Rosehill Racecourse Co Ltd*, it was held that by failing to leave the defendant's racecourse after his licence was revoked, the plaintiff became a trespasser.[125]

To be an effective revocation of consent, a defendant must be allowed a reasonable amount of time to cease the interference (eg, leaving the plaintiff's premises, withdrawing treatment, or otherwise ceasing the activity) after the revocation of the consent. In the case of a licence permitting entry onto land, notice must be given to the defendant informing him or her that the licence is revoked.[126] For further discussion about revocation of licence see Section 7.2.4.4.

---

119 See, eg, *Re Inaya (Special Medical Procedure)* (2007) 213 FLR 278; *Re GWW and CMW* (1997) 136 FLR 421 (both cases involving bone marrow donation); *Re A* (1993) FLC 92-402; *Re Jamie* [2015] FamCA 455 (both involving gender reassignment); *Re LG* [2017] FCWA 179.
120 *Marion's Case* (1992) 175 CLR 218, 310; *Gillick v West Norfolk and Wisbech Area Health Authority* [1986] AC 112.
121 *Hunter and New England Area Health Service v A* (2009) 74 NSWLR 88, [31] (the person's directive to refuse dialysis should be followed).
122 *Guardianship Act 1987* (NSW) s 37; *Emergency Medical Operations Act 1973* (NT) ss 2, 3; *Guardianship and Administration Act 2000* (Qld) s 63; *Guardianship and Administration Act 1995* (Tas) s 40; *Guardianship and Administration Act 1986* (Vic) s 42A; *Guardianship and Administration Act 1990* (WA) s 110ZH.
123 (1991) 171 CLR 635.
124 (1984) 155 CLR 1.
125 (1937) 56 CLR 605. See also *Kuru v New South Wales* (2008) 236 CLR 1; [2008] HCA 26 (police officers became trespassers when they failed to leave the appellant's property within a reasonable time after revocation of consent).
126 *Wilson v New South Wales* (2010) 278 ALR 74.

Where the plaintiff's consent has expired and interference with the plaintiff's interest continues, the defence of consent will be ineffective.[127] In *Konskier v Goodman Ltd*, the defendant contractor was given permission to leave building rubble on the plaintiff's land during the demolition of a building. However, the defendant failed to remove the rubble after completion of the work. The Court held that there was a trespass as the consent had expired.

8.2.6.5 Scope of consent

For consent to be effective, the interference cannot exceed the scope of the consent, or the terms and conditions attached to the consent. Therefore, if there is any divergence from the terms or conditions as consented to, the entire conduct may become trespassory.[128] For example, in *Murray v McMurchy*, consent had only been granted for one operation (caesarean section), but a second operation (sterilisation procedure) was performed by the surgeon on the grounds of 'convenience' rather than 'necessity'.[129] The Court held that consent had not been extended and the second operation amounted to trespass. Similarly, in *White v Johnston*, the Court held that if a dentist is solely motivated by an unrevealed non-therapeutic purpose, the patient's consent to dental treatment is not valid and assault and battery will be made out.[130]

Exceeding the scope of consent in trespass to land cases is discussed in detail in Section 7.2.4.3.

In some instances, assault can be committed even where the plaintiff's consent existed.[131] If a plaintiff has consented to a criminal act, the criminal nature of the deed does not automatically invalidate consent. Therefore, in the criminal context, consent will be a valid defence in civil proceedings, although the defendant may still be criminally liable.[132]

8.2.7 Disciplinary powers

Certain persons, including parents, teachers, captains of aeroplanes and masters of ships, may use the defence of disciplinary powers to justify the physical chastisement of children and pupils, or restraint of passengers.

Parents have a right to use moderate and reasonable corporal punishment to correct children in wrong behaviour.[133] However, there are some limits to that right, which include: '(1) the punishment must be moderate and reasonable; (2) it must have a proper relation to

---

127 *Konskier v Goodman Ltd* [1928] 1 KB 421.

128 See, eg, *Murray v McMurchy* [1949] 2 DLR 442; cited by *McDonald v Ludwig* [2007] QSC 028.

129 *Murray v McMurchy* [1949] 2 DLR 442.

130 (2015) 87 NSWLR 779. However, in this case, the Court of Appeal pointed out there was no evidence to show that the work done by the dentist (Ms White) was exclusively for non-therapeutic purposes or without clinical justification. The consent was therefore valid.

131 Examples include: (1) assaults committed in the course of an unlawful prize fight (*R v Coney* (1882) 8 QBD 534); (2) sexual intercourse with a juvenile under the age of 16 (*Madalena v Kuhn* (1989) 61 DLR (4th) 392); (3) sadomasochistic assaults causing actual bodily harm in the course of homosexual activity (*R v Brown* [1993] 2 WLR 556); and (4) death (*R v Stein* (2007) 18 VR 376). See B Richards and M de Zwart, *Tort Law Principles* (Thomson Reuters, 2nd ed, 2017) 155–6.

132 *Bain v Altoft* [1967] Qd R 32, 41.

133 *Ramsay v Larsen* (1964) 111 CLR 16.

the age, physique and mentality of the child; and (3) it must be carried out with a reasonable means or instrument'.[134]

Likewise, teachers have disciplinary powers over pupils. However, the power of a school teacher to administer corporal punishment to a pupil is not based on implied delegation of authority from the parents of the child, but the power vested by the government in state school teachers to maintain order and discipline.[135]

In a majority of Australian jurisdictions, the use of corporal punishment as a means of discipline is prohibited by government education authorities.[136] For example, corporal punishment was abolished in Queensland through that state's government policy.[137]

In addition, masters of ships and aircraft may use reasonable force to restrain passengers and crew in order to preserve 'necessary discipline and the safety' of the vessel or those on board the vessel.[138] Similarly, there are statutory provisions which confirm such discipline powers.[139]

8.2.8 Inevitable accident

Inevitable accident is a defence to trespass actions. As discussed in Chapter 6, for a defendant to be liable for trespass, the act complained of must have been done with intention or with a lack of reasonable care.[140] That is, the defendant must be at fault. This defence is only necessary where the plaintiff is seeking to establish a non-highway trespass and the onus of proving the absence of fault lies on the defendant. This can be achieved if a defendant can prove that the conduct was neither intentional nor negligent.[141] For example, in *Stanley v Powell*, there was no battery to the plaintiff from the accidental ricochet.[142] Likewise, in *Public Transport Commission (NSW) v Perry*, a person with epilepsy involuntarily falling onto railway tracks was not a trespass to land but an inevitable accident.[143] Both cases are discussed in detail in Chapter 6.

8.2.9 Non-defences

Under this heading, we will briefly mention a number of non-defences to liability raised from trespass actions. These include provocation, mistake, contributory negligence and incapacity.

---

134 *R v Terry* [1955] VLR 114, 116 (Scholl J). See also *Police (SA) v G, DM* (2016) 124 SASR 544. *White v Weller; Ex parte White* [1959] Qd R 192 (blows to the head are unreasonable).

135 *R v Terry* [1955] VLR 114.

136 *Education Act 2004* (ACT) s 7(4); *Education Act 1990* (NSW) ss 35(2A), 47(h); *Education Act 1994* (Tas) s 82A; *Education and Training Reform Regulations 2007* (Vic) reg 14 (government schools); *School Education Regulations 2000* (WA) reg 40(2) (government schools).

137 See Queensland, Department of Education, *Annual Report: 1994–1995* (Report, 1995) 6. Employees of the Queensland Department of Education and Training must not impose 'corporal punishment on a student in the course of their professional duties': Queensland, Department of Education and Training, *Standard of Practice* (February 2016) 7, <https://qed.qld.gov.au/aboutus/rti/DisclosureLogs/182806.pdf>.

138 See *Robertson v Balmain New Ferry Co Ltd* [1910] AC 295; *Hook v Cunard Steamship Co Ltd* [1953] 1 WLR 682.

139 *Crimes (Aviation) Act 1991* (Cth) ss 34, 49; *Criminal Code* (Qld) s 281; *Criminal Code* (WA) s 258.

140 See *Stanley v Powell* [1891] 1 QB 86, as summarised in Section 6.3.2.1.

141 *McHale v Watson* (1966) 115 CLR 199.

142 [1891] 1 QB 86.

143 (1977) 137 CLR 107.

8.2.9.1   Provocation

It is generally accepted that mere provocation is not a defence to trespass in civil proceedings. Provocation may, however, be relevant to an award of exemplary or aggravated damages. In *Fontin v Katapodis*, the Court held that the plaintiff's provocative conduct was not a defence to assault and battery, but the conduct could operate to prevent or reduce an award of exemplary damages.[144] Likewise, in *Whitbread v Rail Corporation (NSW)*, the plaintiffs' offensive behaviour could constitute provocation and reduce the award of aggravated damages even though it did not amount to assault or battery.[145]

Note that the provisions of the Criminal Codes also apply to civil cases of battery and assault in Queensland and Western Australia.[146] This means that while provocation is not available at common law to defend a trespass action, statutory provocation under the relevant sections can be raised.[147] The burden of proof of provocation lies with the defendant on the balance of probabilities.[148]

8.2.9.2   Mistake

As observed in previous chapters, mistake is not a defence to intentional torts. A defendant who acts mistakenly, even though reasonably, may be liable for trespass.[149] That is because it is the intention rather than the motive of the defendant that is relevant in determining whether the cause of action of trespass can be made out. Therefore, a man who embraces a woman thinking her to be his wife commits battery; the reasonableness of the mistake is irrelevant. Some examples follow.

- A defendant who entered another's land, cut down grass and took it away in the mistaken belief that the land was his own was held liable in trespass.[150]

- A prison authority which did not release a prisoner in time due to a mistaken belief that the prisoner was not due for release was held liable in false imprisonment.[151]

- A police officer who required a person to accompany him to Adelaide police station mistakenly believed that the defendant was the person the subject of an arrest warrant was held liable in false imprisonment.[152]

- A defendant who seized plant and materials in the mistaken belief that it had the right to do so was held liable in detinue.[153]

- An auctioneer who sold goods under the mistaken belief that the client who delivered the goods for auction had title, was liable in conversion.[154]

---

144 (1962) 108 CLR 177, 184 (McTiernan J).

145 [2011] NSWCA 130. See also *Downham v Bellette* (1986) Aust Torts Reports 80-038 (the plaintiff's provocative conduct was not a defence to compensatory damages but it prevented an award of aggravated damages).

146 *Criminal Code* (Qld) ss 268–70, 272; *Criminal Code* (WA) ss 245–7.

147 *White v Connolly* [1927] St R Qd 75; *Wenn v Evans* (1985) 2 SR (WA) 263.

148 *Grehan v Kann* [1948] QWN 40.

149 See, eg, *Symes v Mahon* [1922] SASR 447; *Cowell v Corrective Services Commission (NSW)* (1988) 13 NSWLR 714; *Consolidated Co v Curtis & Son* [1892] 1 QB 495.

150 *Basely v Clarkson* (1681) 83 ER 565.

151 *Cowell v Corrective Services Commission (NSW)* (1988) 13 NSWLR 714; *R v Brockhill Prison; Ex parte Evans (No 2)* [2000] 2 AC 19.

152 *Symes v Mahon* [1922] SASR 447.

153 *Egan v State Transport Authority* (1982) 31 SASR 481.

154 *Consolidated Co v Curtis & Son* [1892] 1 QB 495.

8.2.9.3   Contributory negligence

The weight of Australian authority is that contributory negligence is not a defence to assault and battery, either at common law or under the apportionment legislation.[155] In *Venning v Chin*, Bray CJ held:

> It is clear that contributory negligence could never be a defence to an intentional tort, or perhaps it would be preferable to say to the intentional consequences of a tort.[156]

In *Horkin v North Melbourne Football Club Social Club*, the drunken plaintiff refused to leave the defendant's club when asked, and the employees of the defendant club used excessive force to throw the plaintiff out of the club premises.[157] The defendant argued that the plaintiff's tortious conducts, such as the tort of trespass (committed by entering the club premises) and the tort of battery (by striking the defendant's employees), constituted 'fault' on the plaintiff's part for the purposes of apportionment legislation in Victoria. The Court held that the plaintiff's trespass and battery would not have constituted 'fault' for the purposes of the apportionment legislation, because the extended definition applied to the defendant's fault only, not the plaintiff's.

In addition, case law shows that contributory negligence is not a defence for conversion and presumably other intentional torts to goods.[158] In *Wilton v Commonwealth Trading Bank of Australia*, it was held that, as contributory negligence had not been a defence to an action in conversion at common law, apportionment under the legislation could not apply.[159]

8.2.9.4   Incapacity

A defence based on incapacity is generally associated with two groups of persons: those who are mentally ill and minors. A person who is mentally ill may be liable for trespass (normally assault and battery) only if that person knows the nature and quality of that act, even if he or she did not know that the act was morally wrong.[160] Thus mental incapacity itself is not a defence to trespass.

However, if the mental state rendered the person's acts involuntary, then involuntariness will be a good defence to the trespassory activities.[161] Even so, the defendant may be in

---

155 See, eg, *Quinn v Leathem* [1901] AC 495, 537; *Fontin v Katapodis* (1962) 108 CLR 177; *Venning v Chin* (1974) 10 SASR 299; *Horkin v North Melbourne Football Club Social Club* [1983] 1 VR 153, 166 (Brooking J); *New South Wales v Riley* (2003) 57 NSWLR 496, [104] (Hodgson JA).

156 (1974) 10 SASR 299, 317. However, it should be noted that for the purposes of applying contributory negligence in the context of trespass, the court would be comparing intentional wrongdoing on the part of the defendant with carelessness on the part of the plaintiff (incommensurate fault states), the operation of which is quite different to that of the defence in the context of negligence. For example, in *Horkin v North Melbourne Football Club Social Club* [1983] 1 VR 153, Hodgson JA pointed out at [107]: 'where there are indirect and unintended consequences of the trespass, I think the better view is that the defence of contributory negligence is available in respect of those unintended consequences'.

157 [1983] 1 VR 153.

158 See, eg, *Wilton v Commonwealth Trading Bank of Australia* [1973] 2 NSWLR 644; *Day v Bank of New South Wales* (1978) 18 SASR 163; *Grantham Homes Pty Ltd v Australia & New Zealand Banking Group Ltd* (1979) 37 FLR 191; *Australian Guarantee Corporation Ltd v Commissioners of the State Bank of Victoria* [1989] VR 617.

159 [1973] 2 NSWLR 644.

160 *Morris v Marsden* [1952] 1 All ER 925.

161 *Roberts v Ramsbottom* [1980] 1 WLR 823.

breach of duty if the onset of his or her mental state was attributed to the defendant's negligence (eg, negligent failure to take necessary medication).[162]

In the case of minors, minority itself is not a defence to trespass.[163] For a successful defence, a minor must be able to establish an inability to understand the nature of the act. Thus a defence based on incapacity would only cover the very young and the question will be one of capacity.[164]

REVIEW QUESTIONS

(1) In order to make out the defence of necessity, what elements should be established by the defendant?

(2) Is provocation a defence to assault and battery?

(3) For the defence of another to be applied, what elements need to be established?

  Guided responses in the eBook

8.3   Remedies for trespass

8.3.1   Remedies for trespass to the person

8.3.1.1   Nominal damages

As already noted, nominal damages are not awarded in actions for personal injury; however, they may be awarded where a plaintiff's legal rights have been infringed but the plaintiff has suffered no actual loss or harm.[165] In *Stephens v Myers*, the Court held that there was an assault but only awarded the plaintiff nominal damages of one shilling as the plaintiff did not suffer any injury.[166] In *Law v Wright*, the plaintiff sued in trespass to the person for an assault where the only damage in the case was hurt feelings.[167] By considering the circumstances, such as 'the rank and motives of the parties' and 'the degree of personal insult',[168] the Court held that nominal damages could be awarded.[169]

8.3.1.2   Compensatory damages

Compensatory damages can be awarded if the plaintiff suffered loss or harm, provided that the damage was the 'natural and probable consequence' of the tortious act (eg, battery,

---

162 Ibid.
163 *Smith v Leurs* (1945) 70 CLR 256.
164 Ibid.
165 See, eg, *New South Wales v Stevens* (2012) 82 NSWLR 106.
166 (1830) 172 ER 735.
167 (1935) SASR 20.
168 *Law v Wright* (1935) SASR 20, 25 (Piper J).
169 See also *Hill v Cooke* [1958] SR (NSW) 49.

assault, false imprisonment).[170] There have been numerous cases of compensatory damages for trespass to the person. The purpose of compensatory damages is, as noted in Section 8.1, to restore the plaintiff to the position he or she would have been in if the tort had not been committed.[171] Under the common law, compensatory damages for personal injury may fall within one of two broad categories:

(1)   *Non-economic loss:* Previously known as general damages, this covers bodily injury, pain and suffering; loss of amenities of life; loss of expectation of life; and disfigurement.

(2)   *Economic loss:* This covers the loss of expected benefits (including earnings) and any out-of-pocket expenses, such as hospital and medical costs.

The civil liability legislation in all Australian jurisdictions imposes some restrictions on compensatory damages. A significant question is whether or not the limitations on recoverable damages in the legislation apply equally to personal injury resulting from intentional torts. The civil liability Acts in New South Wales, Tasmania, Victoria and Western Australia all provide that the limitations on recoverable damages do not apply to intentional torts committed with an intention to cause injury or death, or to commit sexual assault or other sexual misconduct.[172] There are no significant exclusionary provisions in South Australia and the Australian Capital Territory. The Northern Territory and Queensland do not mention intention in their exclusions. However, the *Civil Liability Act 2003* (Qld) would apply to limit an award of damages for personal injury caused by an intentional tort. Section 52 of the Act provides that exemplary, punitive or aggravated damages cannot be awarded in relation to a claim for personal injury damages.

8.3.1.3   Aggravated damages

Aggravated damages can be awarded for injury to the 'plaintiff's feelings caused by insult, humiliation and the like';[173] as such, aggravated damages are compensatory in nature. They are to be assessed from the plaintiff's point of view with reference to the aggravated manner in which the tortious act was done.[174] Therefore, the worse the defendant's behaviour was, the more generous the aggravated damages considered by the court. As Lord Hailsham stated in *Cassell & Co Ltd v Broome*:

> In awarding 'aggravated' damages the natural indignation of the court at the injury inflicted on the plaintiff is a perfectly legitimate motive in making a generous rather than a more moderate award to provide an adequate solatium. But that is because the

---

170   *Palmer Bruyn & Parker Pty Ltd v Parsons* (2001) 208 CLR 388; [2001] HCA 69; *TCN Channel Nine Pty Ltd v Anning* (2002) 54 NSWLR 333, [103] (Spigelman CJ).

171   See, eg, *Winky Pop Pty Ltd v Mobil Refining Australia Pty Ltd* [2016] VSCA 187, [299] (Warren CJ, Ashley and Osborn JJA).

172   *Civil Liability Act 2002* (NSW) s 3B(1)(a); *Civil Liability Act 2002* (Tas) s 3B(1)(a); *Wrongs Act 1958* (Vic) s 28C(2)(a); *Civil Liability Act 2002* (WA) s 3A(1). Note that the wording and expressions in relation to the limitation differ in these Acts.

173   *Lamb v Cotogno* (1987) 164 CLR 1, 11 (Mason CJ, Brennan, Deane, Dawson and Gaudron JJ).

174   *New South Wales v Abed* (2014) 246 A Crim R 529, [230]; *New South Wales v Zreika* [2012] NSWCA 37, [60]–[64].

injury to the plaintiff is actually greater and, as the result of the conduct exciting the indignation, demands a more generous solatium.[175]

There have been numerous cases where aggravated damages were awarded for trespass to the person. For example, in *Henry v Thompson*, the Queensland Supreme Court awarded $10 000 aggravated damages to a plaintiff who was beaten up by police and urinated on by one officer, on the basis that the behaviour of the police had caused 'great emotional hurt, insult and humiliation'.[176] Likewise, aggravated damages (as well as compensatory damages) were awarded in *Vignoli v Sydney Harbour Casino*, where the plaintiff was falsely imprisoned by the defendants even though no injury was suffered.[177]

Provocation of the defendant may result in a reduction or elimination of aggravated damages.[178] In addition, civil liability legislation in some jurisdictions imposes restrictions on the right to claim for aggravated damages for personal injury in certain circumstances. For example, s 21 of the *Civil Liability Act 2002* (NSW) specifies that the awarding of aggravated damages does not apply to claims of personal injury caused by negligence.[179]

Aggravated damages have also been used to compensate the plaintiff in a wide range of trespass actions such as trespass to land, trespass to goods and the tort of defamation.

8.3.1.4   Exemplary damages

Exemplary damages, also referred to as 'punitive damages', are awarded to punish the defendant and deter repetition of the tortious conduct.[180] Therefore, unlike aggravated damages, exemplary damages are punitive in nature, rather than compensatory. Exemplary damages will be available if the defendant committed 'a wrongdoing in contumelious disregard of another's rights'.[181] In *Pratten v New South Wales*, the plaintiff alleged, among other things, wrongful arrest and false imprisonment by police. It was held that exemplary damages should not be allowed as the 'plaintiff [had] not demonstrated conscious wrong-doing in contumelious disregard of another's rights'.[182]

It should be noted that exemplary damages can only be awarded where the defendant's conduct was 'high-handed' or 'outrageous'.[183] Accordingly, the degree of outrageousness of

---

175 [1972] AC 1027, 1073.
176 [1989] 2 Qd R 412.
177 (2000) Aust Torts Reports 81-541. See also *Myer Stores Ltd v Soo* [1991] 2 VR 597 (aggravated damages of $10 000 awarded for distress suffered by the plaintiff as a result of the false imprisonment committed by an employee of the defendant); *New South Wales v Riley* (2003) 57 NSWLR 496 (aggravated damages awarded for assault and false imprisonment by police officers resulting in hurt feelings of the plaintiff); *Varmedja v Varmedja* [2008] NSWCA 177 (aggravated damages awarded for humiliation and insulting behaviour of the defendant); *Eaves v Donelly* [2011] QDC 207 (aggravated damages awarded for embarrassment experienced by the plaintiff); *Attalla v New South Wales* [2018] NSWDC 190 (aggravated damages awarded for wrongful arrest and imprisonment).
178 *Fontin v Katapodis* (1962) 108 CLR 177.
179 See also *Personal Injuries (Liabilities and Damages) Act 2003* (NT) s 19; *Civil Liability Act 2003* (Qld) s 52.
180 See *XL Petroleum (NSW) Pty Ltd v Caltex Oil (Australia) Pty Ltd* (1985) 155 CLR 448 (exemplary damages awarded for the purpose of deterrence).
181 *Uren v John Fairfax & Sons Pty Ltd* (1966) 117 CLR 118, 154 (Windeyer J).
182 [2018] NSWDC 299, [228] (Hatzistergos DCJ).
183 *New South Wales v Riley* (2003) 57 NSWLR 496, [138] (Hodgson JA).

the defendant's tortious conduct and the effect it may have had on the plaintiff are relevant to the assessment of exemplary damages.[184]

As with aggravated damages, the availability of exemplary damages is limited by civil liability legislation in some jurisdictions. For example, in New South Wales, Queensland and the Northern Territory, exemplary damages cannot be awarded in tortious claims seeking damages for personal injury or death.[185] In addition, exemplary damages will not be available for certain types of claims, such as motor accidents and cases involving industrial injuries.[186] Further, it has been accepted that exemplary damages may not be awarded where substantial punishment has already been imposed upon a defendant for the same conduct (ie, where it was the subject of both civil and criminal actions). In such a case the purpose for the awarding of exemplary damages is thought to be wholly fulfilled and a result of 'double punishment' should be avoided.[187] Along with aggravated damages, exemplary damages may be reduced or even prevented if there is provocation.[188]

8.3.1.5   Injunctions

An injunction may be awarded to restrain future apprehended interferences with the plaintiff's person.[189] Generally, an injunction to protect against assault or battery can be awarded where damages would be an insufficient remedy for the plaintiff: in particular, where irreparable damage would be suffered by the plaintiff should there be no intervention from the court.[190] Other factors in favour of an award of an injunction include that the tort is continuing or particularly serious; or the wrong is likely to be repeated should there be no intervention by the court.[191]

8.3.2   Remedies for trespass to land

The most common remedies for trespass to land are damages and/or an injunction. Additionally, in certain circumstances, a limited form of self-help is available to the plaintiff. The type of remedies and amount of damages depend upon whether the plaintiff suffered any loss and the circumstances surrounding the case.

---

184   *Gray v Motor Accident Commission* (1998) 196 CLR 1, 9. The defendant had deliberately struck the plaintiff with his car causing serious injury to the plaintiff. In subsequent negligence proceedings against the defendant's vehicle insurer (who was substituted as defendant), the Court held that exemplary damages should not be awarded because the defendant had already been substantially punished in criminal proceedings.

185   See *Civil Liability Act 2002* (NSW) s 21; *Civil Liability Act 2003* (Qld) s 52; *Personal Injuries (Liabilities and Damages) Act 2003* (NT) s 19.

186   See, eg, *Motor Accidents Act 1988* (NSW) s 81A; *Motor Accidents Compensation Act 1999* (NSW) s 144; *Workers Compensation Act 1987* (NSW) s 151R; *Motor Accident Insurance Act 1994* (Qld) s 55; *Workers' Compensation and Rehabilitation Act 2003* (Qld) s 309; *Motor Vehicles Act 1959* (SA) s 113A; *Transport Accident Act 1986* (Vic) s 93(7); *Accident Compensation Act 1985* (Vic) s 135A(7)(c).

187   *Gray v Motor Accident Commission* (1998) 196 CLR 1, 40 (Gleeson CJ, McHugh, Gummow and Hayne JJ).

188   *Lamb v Cotogno* (1987) 164 CLR 1; *Andary v Burford* [1994] Aust Torts Reports 81-302 (the plaintiff's conduct was so provocative that the amount awarded for exemplary damages was substantially reduced).

189   See, eg, in the case of domestic violence: *Parry v Crooks* (1981) 27 SASR 1; *Daley v Martin (No 1)* [1982] Qd R 23; *Corvisy v Corvisy* [1982] 2 NSWLR 557; *Zimitat v Douglas* [1979] Qd R 454.

190   See the above-cited domestic violence cases.

191   *Beswicke v Alner* [1926] VLR 72, 76 (Cussen J); see also *Mayfair Trading Co Pty Ltd v Dreyer* (1958) 101 CLR 428, 451 (Dixon CJ).

As already seen, trespass to land is actionable per se and no proof of damage is required to establish the cause of action.[192] The purpose of damages is not merely to compensate the plaintiff for damage to the land, but also to vindicate 'the plaintiff's right to the exclusive use and occupation of his or her land'.[193] Therefore, if the plaintiff suffers no actual damage, nominal damages may be awarded to vindicate the plaintiff's right to exclude any trespasser from the property.[194] However, if the plaintiff does suffer actual damage as a result of the trespass, he or she can recover such damage.[195] On occasion, the plaintiff can also recover aggravated damages and exemplary damages.[196] Liability for loss or damage caused by aircraft is regulated by statute.[197]

8.3.2.1   Nominal damages

Where the plaintiff suffers no actual damage but the interference with the plaintiff's possession can be proven, nominal damages can be awarded. For example, in *Windridge Farm Pty Ltd v Grassi*, animal rights activists took photos and video footage by trespassing on the plaintiff's property.[198] The Court confirmed that the plaintiff was entitled to damages to vindicate its right to exclusive possession of its property even though the plaintiff suffered no actual loss. In *Finesky Holdings Pty Ltd v Minister for Transport (WA)*, the Court awarded a nominal sum of $1000 to vindicate the plaintiff's right to the exclusive possession of the subleased mining land which had been trespassed upon by the defendant.[199] Other examples are *Hill v Higgins*,[200] where a sum of $220 nominal damages was awarded even though the trespass to the plaintiff's land had caused no actual loss, and *TCN Channel Nine Pty Ltd v Anning*,[201] where a sum of $25 000 nominal damages was awarded.

8.3.2.2   Compensatory damages

In cases of physical damage to land, the plaintiff is entitled to recover compensatory damages for his or her loss if the damage was a 'natural and probable consequence' of the tortious act.[202] What constitutes a natural and probable consequence of a trespass is a question of fact to be judged from all the circumstances of a case.[203]

---

192 *Halliday v Nevill* (1984) 155 CLR 1, 10 (Brennan J).
193 *Plenty v Dillon* (1991) 171 CLR 635, 645 (Mason CJ, Brennan and Toohey JJ).
194 See, eg, *Mayfair Ltd v Pears* [1987] 1 NZLR 459, 465; *Laris v Lin* (2017) 18 BPR 36,913; *Sydney Local Health District v Macquarie International Health Clinic Pty Ltd* (2020) 105 NSWLR 325.
195 *Finesky Holdings Pty Ltd v Minister for Transport (WA)* (2002) 26 WAR 368, [260].
196 See, eg, *XL Petroleum (NSW) Pty Ltd v Caltex Oil (Australia) Pty Ltd* (1985) 155 CLR 448; *New South Wales v Ibbett* (2006) 229 CLR 638; [2006] HCA 57.
197 *Damage by Aircraft Act 1999* (Cth) ss 10, 11; *Civil Liability Act 2002* (NSW) s 73; *Civil Liability Act 1936* (SA) ss 61–2; *Damage by Aircraft Act 1963* (Tas) s 4; *Wrongs Act 1958* (Vic) ss 29–31; *Damage by Aircraft Act 1964* (WA) s 5.
198 (2011) 254 FLR 87.
199 (2002) 26 WAR 368.
200 [2012] NSWSC 270.
201 (2002) 54 NSWLR 333.
202 *Palmer Bruyn & Parker Pty Ltd v Parsons* (2001) 208 CLR 388; [2001] HCA 69; *TCN Channel Nine Pty Ltd v Anning* (2002) 54 NSWLR 333, [103] (Spigelman CJ).
203 As stated by Spigelman CJ: 'What is a natural and probable consequence arising from a trespass to land must depend on all the circumstances of a case. It is essentially a question of fact.' *TCN Channel Nine Pty Ltd v Anning* (2002) 54 NSWLR 333, [104].

As noted, the purpose of compensatory damages is to restore the plaintiff to the position he or she would have been in if the tort had not been committed.[204] Therefore, the guiding principle in assessing compensatory damages is that the plaintiff should receive full restitution for their loss. Damages required to achieve full restitution are assessed on one of two bases: either the diminution in market value of the property or the cost of restoring the property to its pre-damaged condition.[205] The overriding requirement is that damages should be a 'fair and reasonable compensation to the plaintiff for the injury he has suffered'.[206]

When deciding on which basis the compensatory damages should be made, some factors are relevant. If the defendant's desire to restore the property is unreasonable or the cost of restoration is disproportionate to the diminution in the land's market value, the cost of restoration will not be awarded.[207] Where there is a conflict about which basis the compensatory damages should rely on, whether the basis sought by the plaintiff is reasonable should be assessed.[208] The test for the reasonableness of the plaintiff's desire was illustrated by Samuels J in *Evans v Balog*.[209] Quoting the test proposed by the authors of *McGregor on Damages*,[210] his Honour stated:

> The test which appears to be the appropriate one is the reasonableness of the plaintiff's desire to reinstate the property; this will be judged in part by the advantages to him of reinstatement in relation to the extra cost to the defendant in having to pay damages for reinstatement rather than damages calculated by the diminution in value of the land … Hence, it is sometimes said that a plaintiff may have the cost of restoration provided that it is not disproportionate to the diminution in value.[211]

In addition, if the plaintiff chooses a more expensive replacement when an exact replacement is available, the damages will be limited to the cost of that exact replacement.[212] However, if to reinstate is the only reasonable course of action, the cost of restoration can be awarded, although it is much higher than the diminution in value.[213] Moreover, if the repairs required are performed by the plaintiff and/or volunteers, damages for repair can be awarded if assessment on that basis is considered reasonable.[214] Consequential loss, such as financial loss, loss of rent and loss of use of premises flowing from the damage to land, are recoverable by the plaintiff.[215]

---

204   See, eg, *Winky Pop Pty Ltd v Mobil Refining Australia Pty Ltd* [2016] VSCA 187, [299] (Warren CJ, Ashley and Osborn JJA).
205   See, eg, *Commonwealth v Amann Aviation Pty Ltd* (1991) 174 CLR 64, 116 (per Deane J).
206   *Port Stephens Shire Council v Tellamist Pty Ltd* (2004) 135 LGERA 98, cited with approval in *Rasco Pty Ltd v Lucas* [2017] VSC 703.
207   *Evans v Balog* [1976] 1 NSWLR 36; *Public Trustee v Hermann* (1968) 88 WN (NSW) 442, 447–8 (Isaacs J); *Hansen v Gloucester Developments Pty Ltd* [1992] 1 Qd R 14.
208   *Evans v Balog* [1976] 1 NSWLR 36; *Port Stephens Shire Council v Tellamist Pty Ltd* (2004) 135 LGERA 98.
209   [1976] 1 NSWLR 36.
210   H MacGregor and JD Mayne, *McGregor on Damages* (Sweet & Maxwell, 13th ed, 1972) 713.
211   *Evans v Balog* [1976] 1 NSWLR 36, 39–40.
212   *Gagner Pty Ltd v Canturi Corporation Pty Ltd* (2009) 262 ALR 691, [105], citing *Darbishire v Warran* [1963] 1 WLR 106 with approval.
213   See *Harbutt's Plasticine Ltd v Wayne Tank & Pump Co Ltd* [1970] 1 QB 447.
214   *Powercor Australia Ltd v Thomas* (2012) 43 VR 220.
215   See, eg, *Rust v Victoria Graving Dock Co* (1997) 36 Ch D 113; *Dodd Properties (Kent) Ltd v Canterbury City Council* [1980] 1 WLR 433; *Lollis v Loulatzis* [2007] VSC 547.

8.3.2.3   Aggravated damages

Aggravated damages are potentially available in the case of a trespass to land, where the interference with possession was carried out in a high-handed, insulting or oppressive manner.[216] The general principles governing the award of aggravated damages for personal injury also apply to trespass to land. For example, in *Greig v Greig*, the defendant, who was the plaintiff's brother, secretly entered the plaintiff's property and installed a recording device in the room to record conversations of his brother's housekeeper.[217] A sum of £100 in aggravated damages was awarded by the Court as a solatium for the plaintiff's 'injured feelings'.[218] Aggravated damages have also been awarded in some typical trespass to land cases involving media intrusion. For example, in *TCN Channel Nine Pty Ltd v Anning*, aggravated damages were awarded to compensate the plaintiff's mental trauma as a result of trespass to land;[219] and in *Craftsman Homes Australia Pty Ltd v TCN Channel Nine Pty Ltd*, aggravated damages were awarded for the hurt of feelings, humiliation and affront to dignity experienced by the plaintiff.[220] In a more recent case, *Balven v Thurston*, the Supreme Court of New South Wales upheld the local court's decision and awarded aggravated damages to compensate the plaintiff.[221] The reason is that trespass to land was committed in the context of intimidation and stalking, and Ms Thurston's mental harm was a probable and/or intended consequence.[222]

Additionally, aggravated damages can be extended to cover situations where the trespass actions disturbed family members and other persons involved in a 'bona fide domestic relationship' with the plaintiff.[223]

HINTS AND TIPS

The award of aggravated damages for personal injury is also affected by statutory defences under the civil liability legislation, the application of which differs from defence to defence and from jurisdiction to jurisdiction. For example, in Queensland, aggravated damages in personal injury cases can only be awarded if the act that gives rise to personal injury was 'an unlawful intentional act done with intent to cause personal injury' or 'an unlawful sexual assault or other unlawful sexual misconduct' (s 52 of the *Civil Liability Act 2003* (Qld)). Similarly, aggravated damages for personal injury are not recoverable in the Northern Territory (s 19 of the *Personal Injuries (Liabilities and Damages) Act 2003* (NT)). In New South Wales, aggravated damages for personal injury are not recoverable in cases where the act or omission that caused the 'injury or death was negligence' (s 21 of the *Civil Liability Act 2002* (NSW)). Therefore, in awarding aggravated damages for personal injury, the civil liability legislation of the particular jurisdiction must be consulted.

---

216   *Uren v John Fairfax & Sons Pty Ltd* (1966) 117 CLR 118, 129–30.
217   [1966] VR 376.
218   Ibid 380 (Gillard J).
219   (2002) 54 NSWLR 333, [19].
220   [2006] NSWSC 519.
221   [2015] NSWSC 1103.
222   Ibid [39].
223   *New South Wales v Ibbett* (2006) 229 CLR 638; [2006] HCA 57, [31].

8.3.2.4 Exemplary damages

Exemplary damages may be awarded in cases of trespass to land to punish the conduct which is in contumelious disregard of the plaintiff's rights. For example, in *LJP Investments Pty Ltd v Howard Chia Investments Pty Ltd*, exemplary damages, the amount of which was greater than the market value of the use of the plaintiff's airspace, were awarded to punish the defendant for its deliberate disregard of the plaintiff's rights.[224] Exemplary damages will be considered by courts especially when 'the amount of general and aggravated damages did not adequately serve the purposes of punishment and deterrence'.[225] In *TCN Channel Nine Pty Ltd v Ilvariy Pty Ltd*, the Court awarded $60 000 in exemplary damages to recognise that the defendants 'have engaged in conscious wrong doing in contumelious disregard of the rights' of the plaintiff and to give 'particular weight … to the fact that the award of $110 000 by means of general and aggravated damages, although expressed as compensatory, also has an effect by way of punishment and deterrence'.[226] Another case that is frequently cited in this regard is *XL Petroleum (NSW) Pty Ltd v Caltex Oil (Australia) Pty Ltd*, where the High Court affirmed the amount of exemplary damages awarded by the Court of Appeal.[227]

8.3.2.5 Injunctions

As with trespass to the person, the plaintiff may seek an injunction to prevent continuing or future interference to land,[228] or to require a trespasser to restore the land to its pre-tort state.[229] There are two types of injunctions: prohibitory injunctions and mandatory injunctions. Prohibitory injunctions may order the defendant to cease or refrain from a tortious act (eg, to stop entering the plaintiff's land); mandatory injunctions compel a defendant to do a particular act (eg, to remove an object that constitutes a trespass from the plaintiff's land). In *LJP Investments Pty Ltd v Howard Chia Investments Pty Ltd*, the Court granted a mandatory injunction in vindication of the plaintiff's right to exclusive possession of land.[230] In a number of Australian jurisdictions, courts may make orders to create an easement over land to permit an encroachment to remain or for the effective use or development of another's land that will gain the benefit.[231]

In general, an injunction can be granted to restrain an anticipated trespass (ie, a future wrong), in particular if irreparable harm would be suffered by the plaintiff if an injunction were not granted.[232] In *Lincoln Hunt Australia Pty Ltd v Willesee*, Young J observed:

224 (1989) 24 NSWLR 490.
225 *TCN Channel Nine Pty Ltd v Ilvariy Pty Ltd* (2008) 71 NSWLR 323, [4] (Spigelman CJ, Beazley and Hodgson JJA agreeing).
226 (2008) 71 NSWLR 323, [28], [40] (Spigelman CJ, Beazley JA agreeing).
227 (1985) 155 CLR 448; [1985] HCA 12.
228 Numerous cases involve the granting of an injunction to prevent a continuing trespass to land: see, eg, *Bendal Pty Ltd v Mirvac Project Pty Ltd* (1991) 23 NSWLR 464 (injunction granted to stop a trespass to the plaintiff's airspace); *Graham v KD Morris & Sons Pty Ltd* [1974] Qd R 1 (injunction granted to prevent a crane overhanging the plaintiff's roof).
229 *HB Holmes Pty Ltd v Beers* [1986] 2 Qd R 739.
230 (1989) 24 NSWLR 490.
231 See *Encroachment of Buildings Act 1922* (NSW) s 3(2); *Conveyancing Act 1919* (NSW) s 88K; *Law of Property Act 2000* (NT) ss 163–6; *Property Law Act 1974* (Qld) s 180; *Conveyancing and Law of Property Act 1884* (Tas) s 84J. It has been recommended in Victoria, see Victorian Law Reform Commission, *Review of the Property Law Act 1958* (Final Report, September 2010).
232 See, eg, *Lincoln Hunt Australia Pty Ltd v Willesee* (1986) 4 NSWLR 457.

> If a trespass to land is threatened it can be enjoined if it appears that the defendant is likely to carry out his threat and that the plaintiff will suffer irreparable damage if he does. If a defendant has once trespassed and appears likely to repeat his trespass then an injunction can be granted either at common law or in equity.[233]

In contrast, where trespass is a past and completed occurrence rather than a continuing one, no injunction will be granted.[234] Therefore, to convince the court to grant an injunction, it is important for the plaintiff to prove that the anticipated interference is imminent or highly likely to occur.[235]

In addition, a court may award damages in lieu of, or in addition to, an injunction. These damages are known as equitable damages. Conditions for the award of equitable damages were set out by Smith LJ in the leading case of *Shelfer v City of London Electric Lighting Co.*[236] These conditions include:

(1)   The injury to the plaintiff's legal rights is small.

(2)   The injury is one which is capable of being estimated in money.

(3)   The injury can be adequately compensated by a small money payment.

(4)   It would be oppressive to the defendant to grant an injunction.[237]

Equitable damages are now conferred in the various Australian state and territory Supreme Court Acts.[238]

8.3.2.6   Self-help

In addition to damages and injunction, the remedy of self-help is of particular importance to trespass to land. A plaintiff in possession of the land may use reasonable force to repel or expel a trespasser or to remove objects placed on land that constitute trespass. For example, a plaintiff in possession of land can cut overhanging branches or an encroaching root on his land.[239] Defences based on self-help are normally regarded as both remedies for and defences to intentional torts (see Section 8.2.1 for more information about this remedy).

8.3.2.7   Mesne profits

A plaintiff is entitled to claim damages against a tenant who fails to vacate the leased premises at the end of a lease; these damages are known as *mesne* ('middle') profits. The claim for mesne profits was always brought after re-entry and usually after a successful writ of ejectment.[240] The claim is not available if the plaintiff does not exercise sufficient acts of

---

233   Ibid 462.

234   *Sherman v Condon* [2014] QDC 189.

235   *Barbagallo v J & F Catelan Pty Ltd* [1986] 1 Qd R 245.

236   [1895] 1 Ch 287.

237   See also *Break Fast Investments Pty Ltd v PCH Melbourne Pty Ltd* (2007) 20 VR 311 (a mandatory injunction was appropriate to require the appellant to remove all cladding attached to the respondent's building).

238   *Supreme Court Act 1933* (ACT) s 34; *Supreme Court Act 1970* (NSW) s 68; *Supreme Court Act 1995* (Qld) s 244; *Supreme Court Act 1935* (SA) s 30; *Supreme Court Civil Procedure Act 1932* (Tas) s 11; *Supreme Court Act 1958* (Vic) s 38; *Supreme Court Act 1935* (WA) s 25.

239   *Lemmon v Webb* [1895] AC 1.

240   *Hampton v BHP Billiton Minerals Pty Ltd (No 2)* [2012] WASC 285, 310.

physical possession when the claim is brought.[241] In addition, the common law does not allow a landlord to seek possession of the land and mesne profits in the same action.[242] Mesne profits are claimed from the date when the lease came to an end through to the date when the plaintiff regained possession. The quantification of mesne profits is the value of the 'usual' or 'general' market rent that the trespasser should have paid over the period of alleged trespass.[243] The common law position in this regard has been changed by legislation in most of the Australian jurisdictions.[244] This enables a plaintiff in those jurisdictions to bring a single action seeking ejectment and mesne profits.

EMERGING ISSUE

Squatting has been a contentious issue worldwide for centuries. A squatter refers to a person who occupies land or a building without any legal claim or title.[245] In the context of trespass to land, the terms trespasser and squatter in effect mean the same thing and can be used interchangeably. Squatting can be a criminal offence, but usually, it is viewed by the law as a civil dispute between the owner of the property and a property squatter.

Obviously, the squatter's rights start with a wrongful action – and occupying an empty house belonging to someone else is an obvious example of trespass to land. In general, a property squatter must vacate the premises when requested to do so by the rightful owner, through legal action such as ejectment. However, if the rightful owner failed to defend his rights against the wrongful action for a period of time (eg, 12 years or more), then the question of 'squatter's rights' will arise.

The term 'squatter's rights' refers to the rights 'to acquire title to real property by adverse possession, or by pre-emption of public lands'.[246] When a certain set of criteria is met, that occupier (generally a squatter) can assume the title of the property and gain ownership.[247] Most Australian states have introduced legislation that deals specifically with adverse possession claims over the title of houses, and they vary in their specifics.[248] In *Mulcahy v Curramore Pty Ltd*,[249] the Court held that main elements to establish adverse possession include: (1) the possession must be open, not secret; (2) possession must be peaceful, not by force; (3) the possession must be

---

241   *Minister of State for the Interior v RT Co Pty Ltd* (1963) 107 CLR 1.
242   *Hampton v BHP Billiton Minerals Pty Ltd* [2012] WASC 285; *Broadway Pty Ltd v Lewis* [2012] WASC 373.
243   *Hampton v BHP Billiton Minerals Pty Ltd (No 2)* [2012] WASC 285, [344]. See, eg, *Inverugie Investments Ltd v Hackett* [1995] 1 WLR 713, 717 (Lord Lloyd); *Swordheath Properties Ltd v Tabet* [1979] 1 WLR 285, 288 (Megaw LJ); *Lamru Pty Ltd v Kation Pty Ltd* (1998) 44 NSWLR 432, 439 (Cohen J); *Bunnings Group Ltd v CHEP Australia Ltd* (2011) 82 NSWLR 420, [198] (Giles JA).
244   *Landlord and Tenant Act 1899* (NSW) s 8; *Property Law Act 1974* (Qld) s 147; *Landlord and Tenant Act 1936* (SA) s 6; *Landlord and Tenant Act 1935* (Tas) s 69; *Supreme Court Act 1986* (Vic) s 79.
245   BA Garner, *Black's Law Dictionary* (St. Paul: West Publishing Co., 5th ed, 2009) 1533.
246   Ibid 1534.
247   In New South Wales, Western Australia, Queensland and Tasmania, the period to qualify for adverse possession is 12 years; in Victoria and South Australia it is 15 years.
248   Adverse possession claims can be made in most of the Australian states, except the Northern Territory and the Australian Capital Territory, with various pieces of legislation developed in these states to deal with the issue.
249   [1974] 2 NSWLR 464.

without consent of the owner. More factors and principles in relation to this have been addressed by courts in some recent decisions.[250]

Although unusual, the issue of squatters and adverse possession claims do happen from time to time in Australia and have frequently appeared in the national news media in recent years. These cases are not always about squatters. In fact, most adverse possession claims deal with boundary line disputes between shop owners, or farmers who have been working on the land for decades. Adverse possession itself is not a remedy for trespass to land, but it closely relates to this form of trespass action. The criteria set by law (either by common law rules or statutory provisions) make adverse possession claims exceptionally hard to prove. While adverse possession laws continue to be in contention, this topic needs future discussion in multiple areas of law, such as land law and torts.

8.3.3   Remedies for trespass to personal property

Common remedies for trespass to personal property are self-help, damages and injunctions. We have discussed self-help in Section 8.2.1. Injunctions as an equitable remedy can be granted by a court where an award of damages would be an inadequate remedy. A plaintiff can seek an injunction for an adequate remedy: for example, to restrain or prevent further interference with the goods, or to request return of the goods.

8.3.3.1   Remedies for trespass to goods

The primary remedy for trespass to goods is damages. Nominal damages can be awarded if the defendant committed trespass to goods without damaging them. For example, nominal damages have been awarded where the goods were merely trespassed by 'asportation'. In *Slaveski v Victoria*, the plaintiff claimed damages for trespass to goods.[251] The Court awarded $200 in nominal damages for trespass to goods by asportation and $900 in nominal damages for an unconsented transcription of the contents of the plaintiff's documents.

A plaintiff can claim compensatory damages where his or her goods are damaged as a result of the defendant's trespass. If the goods have been totally destroyed, the prima facie rule is that the plaintiff will be entitled to the value of the goods as assessed at the time of the trespass.[252] If the goods are merely damaged, the plaintiff will recover for the diminution in value of the goods.[253] The diminution in value is generally assessed on two bases. Where repair is reasonable in the circumstances, the plaintiff can claim the reasonable cost of repairing the goods.[254] If the repair and reinstatement were done by the plaintiff or others

---

250 See, eg, *Hungry Jack's Pty Ltd v The Trust Company (Australia) Ltd* [2018] WASC 64; *McFarland v Gertos* (2018) 98 NSWLR 954; *Hardy v Sidoti* (2020) 19 BPR 40,535; *Bottos v CityLink Melbourne Ltd* [2021] VSC 585; *McGrane v Lot D Preservation Group Inc* [2021] VCC 509.
251 [2010] VSC 441.
252 *Dryden v Orr* (1928) 28 SR (NSW) 216.
253 Ibid.
254 *Pargiter v Alexander* (1995) 5 Tas R 158.

on a voluntary basis, the reasonable cost of repairing and reinstating is compensable.[255] However, the plaintiff may sell the damaged goods without repairing and then claim the difference between the value of the goods before and after the damage.[256]

A plaintiff can claim exemplary or aggravated damages in appropriate circumstances. Aggravated damages may be awarded where the trespass to goods was committed in an aggravated manner.[257] For example, in *Private Parking Services (Vic) Pty Ltd v Huggard*, the plaintiff's vehicle was unlawfully towed away, detained and damaged.[258] A sum of $2000 in aggravated damages was awarded for the associated worry, anxiety and mental upset. Likewise, in *Moore v Lambeth County Court Registrar (No 2)*, the plaintiff was wrongfully dispossessed of his goods, and the Court awarded aggravated damages to compensate the plaintiff for the resultant injury to his feelings.[259] Exemplary damages may also be awarded to punish the defendant.[260]

Consequential economic loss flowing from the trespass is recoverable.[261] If the goods are profit earning, the plaintiff may also recover loss of profits. For example, in *William Holyman & Sons Pty Ltd v Marine Board of Launceston*, the plaintiff recovered the cost of repairs to the ship and loss of net profits while the ship was being repaired.[262] If the plaintiff hires a substitute, the cost of that hire may be recovered.[263]

Non-economic loss, such as the loss of use or enjoyment of goods, is also recoverable. To claim such damages, the plaintiff need not prove that the goods in question would in fact have been used during the time of deprivation.[264]

8.3.3.2   Remedies for conversion

Along with trespass to goods, the typical remedy for conversion is a judgment for damages. The compensatory damages for established conversion are generally assessed as the full market value of the converted goods at the time of the conversion, together with any consequential loss that may be proved by the plaintiff.[265] The main reason is that the conversion is complete at the time of the conversion, and satisfaction of judgment for conversion effects a forced sale to the converter. In *Hill v Reglon Pty Ltd*, Beazley JA explained:

255   See, eg, *Powercor Australia Ltd v Thomas* (2012) 43 VR 220 (damages are recoverable where fixtures were reinstated by plaintiff's own labour or by labour of volunteers).
256   See *Davidson v JS Gilbert Fabrications Pty Ltd* [1986] 1 Qd R 1.
257   See, eg, *Lamb v Cotogno* (1987) 164 CLR 1, 8–9.
258   (1996) Aust Tort Reports 81–397.
259   [1970] 1 QB 560.
260   See also *Pargiter v Alexander* (1995) 5 Tas R 158; *Hunter BNZ Finance Ltd v Australia and New Zealand Banking Group Ltd* [1990] VR 41; *Caltex Oil (Australia) Pty Ltd v XL Petroleum (NSW) Pty Ltd* [1982] 2 NSWLR 852; *Healing (Sales) Pty Ltd v Inglis Electrix Pty Ltd* (1968) 121 CLR 584.
261   *Liesbosch (Dredger) v The Edison* [1933] AC 449.
262   (1929) 24 Tas LR 64. See also *Thomson v STX Pan Ocean Co Ltd* [2012] FCAFC 15.
263   *Athabaska Airways v Sask Government Airways* (1957) 12 DLR (2d) 187.
264   *The Mediana* [1900] AC 113, 117–18 (Earl of Halsbury LC).
265   *ACN 116 746 859 v Lunapas Pty Ltd* [2017] NSWSC 1583. See also *Semenov v Pirvu* [2011] VSC 605, [19] (Dixon J); *Anderson Formrite Pty Ltd v Baulderstone Pty Ltd (No 7)* [2010] FCA 921; *Johnson Matthey (Australia) Ltd v Dascorp Pty Ltd* (2003) 9 VR 171; *Sadcas Pty Ltd v Business & Professional Finance Pty Ltd* [2011] NSWCA 267, [75] (Giles JA), [84] (Handley AJA); *Furness v Adrium Industries Pty Ltd* [1996] 1 VR 668, 669 (Fullagar J); *Flowfill Packaging Machines Pty Ltd v Fytore Pty Ltd* [1993] Aust Torts Reports 81-244; *Ley v Lewis* [1952] VLR 119, 121–2 (O'Bryan and Dean JJ); *J & E Hall Ltd v Barclay* [1937] 3 All ER 620, 623 (Greer LJ).

the basis of damages as being that the act of conversion is a sufficiently serious infringement of the plaintiff's right of control over the converted goods to justify 'the drastic sanction of compelling the wrongdoer to buy the plaintiff out'.[266]

Thus, if the market value of the goods can be determined, the measure of damages will likely be the price at which replacement goods can be purchased in that market.[267] In such circumstances, it is the plaintiff who has the onus of proving the market value of the converted goods.[268] However, if there is no such market and the market value of the goods is therefore not available, the damages can be assessed as the replacement cost of the converted goods.[269]

The purpose of compensatory damages for conversion is to place the plaintiff in the position he or she would have been in if the tort or torts had not been committed.[270] Therefore, if the actual loss suffered by the plaintiff is less than the full value of the goods, damages should be assessed upon the actual loss sustained by the plaintiff, rather than the full value of the goods. This rule was confirmed by the High Court in *Butler v Egg & Pulp Marketing Board*.[271] In that case, Butler was obliged, by virtue of a statute, to deliver eggs to the Board. The Board would pay a fixed sum for the eggs and then process the sale of those eggs. The Board therefore had a right to immediate possession of the eggs once they came into existence. Butler converted the eggs by selling them instead of supplying them to the Board. The Board sued for conversion and claimed damages. The High Court held that the measure of damages was not the full value of the eggs at the date of the conversion. Instead, the damages were limited to reflect the amount that the Board would have been bound to pay the egg producer.[272]

If the converted goods are returned to the plaintiff, credit must be given for their then value and the plaintiff is entitled to damages for diminution in value of the goods.[273] Even so, the plaintiff cannot be compelled to accept the return of the converted goods.[274]

Consequential losses resulting from conversion, such as the reasonable costs of any necessary repairs and damages for loss of use, are compensable.[275] However, the consequential losses must be 'of a kind that should have been within the contemplation of the defendant as a likely consequence having regard to the defendant's knowledge (or express notice) of the facts'.[276]

---

266 [2007] NSWCA 295, [154] quoting N Palmer, *Palmer on Bailment* (Law Book, 2nd ed, 1991) 214.
267 *Furness v Adrium Industries Pty Ltd* [1996] 1 VR 668, 669 (Fullagar J); *Sinclair v Haynes* [2000] NSWSC 642, [3] (Hamilton J).
268 *Sinclair v Haynes* [2000] NSWSC 642, [3]; *Longden v Kenalda Nominee* [2003] VSCA 128 ff., [10].
269 See *J & E Hall Ltd v Barclay* [1937] 3 All ER 620, 624 (Greer LJ); *BBMB Finance (Hong Kong) Ltd v Eda Holdings Ltd* [1991] 2 All ER 129, 131 (Lord Templeman).
270 *Butler v Egg and Pulp Marketing Board* (1966) 114 CLR 185.
271 Ibid.
272 See also *IBL Ltd v Coussens* [1991] 2 All ER 133, 139 (Neill LJ); *Brandeis Goldschmidt & Co v Western Transport Ltd* [1981] QB 864, 870 (Brandon LJ).
273 *Sadcas Pty Ltd v Business & Professional Finance Pty Ltd* [2011] NSWCA 267, [75] (Giles JA), [84] (Handley AJA). See also *Hiort v London & North Western Railway Co* (1879) 4 Ex D 188; *Solloway v McLaughlin* [1938] AC 247.
274 *Kidman v Farmers' Centre Pty Ltd* [1959] Qd R 8. See also the discussion in *Craig v Marsh* (1935) 35 SR (NSW) 323, 329.
275 *Kuwait Airways Corporation v Iraqi Airways Co (Nos 4 and 5)* [2002] 2 AC 883, [67] (Lord Nicholls).
276 *National Australia Bank Ltd v Nemur Varity Pty Ltd* (2002) 4 VR 252, [10].

If the converted goods are profit earning, it is appropriate for the plaintiff to claim the hire value of the goods throughout the period that the goods would have been hired out.[277] In addition, damages may include hiring charges of a substitute good until the good was reasonably replaced.[278] If goods that have been let under a hire purchase agreement are converted, the damages will not be assessed as the full market value of the goods. Instead, the usual measure of damages is the balance of the hire purchase price outstanding.[279]

As for trespass to goods, aggravated and exemplary damages can be awarded for conversion. For example, in *Private Parking Services (Vic) Pty Ltd v Huggard,* it was held that aggravated damages were available to compensate for conversion.[280] Likewise, in *Hesketh v Joltham Pty Ltd,* the Court held that it was appropriate to award aggravated damages to compensate for the distress due to loss of converted items of sentimental, but not commercial, value.[281] See also *Healing (Sales) Pty Ltd v Inglis Electrix Pty Ltd,* where exemplary damages were awarded for conversion (as well as trespass to goods) by employees of the defendant.[282]

8.3.3.3   Remedies for detinue

As discussed in Chapter 7, the tort of detinue arises upon the wrongful detention of goods and refusal to return the goods after request. Therefore, the general remedies for detinue include an order for return of the goods and/or damages to compensate the plaintiff for the detention of the goods.

If the detained goods are ordinary items of commerce and by the time of the judgment are still in possession of the defendant, the plaintiff can seek one of the following forms of judgment:

(1)   the value of the goods as assessed and damages for their detention

(2)   return of the goods or recovery of their value as assessed and damages for their detention

(3)   return of the goods and damages for their detention.[283]

However, if the goods are no longer possessed by the defendant (eg, they have been lost or destroyed), the plaintiff can be awarded compensatory damages to the value of the goods at the time of the judgment, plus the damages for the detention or deprivation of the goods.[284]

---

277   *Sadcas Pty Ltd v Business & Professional Finance Pty Ltd* [2011] NSWCA 267, [78] (Giles JA); *Egan v State Transport Authority* (1982) 31 SASR 481.
278   *Flowfill Packaging Machines Pty Ltd v Fytore Pty Ltd* [1993] Aust Torts Reports 81-244, 62523 (Young J).
279   *Western Credits Pty Ltd v Dragan Motors Pty Ltd* (1973) WAR 184, 187 (Jackson CJ).
280   (1996) Aust Tort Reports 81–397, 63535 (Batt J).
281   [2000] QCA 44.
282   (1968) 121 CLR 584.
283   See *General & Finance Facilities Ltd v Cooks Cars (Romford) Ltd* [1963] 2 All ER 314, 319 (Diplock LJ), cited with approval in *Wade Sawmill Pty Ltd v Colenden Pty Ltd* [2007] QCA 455, [18]. Statutory provisions in a number of jurisdictions, including New South Wales, Queensland and Victoria, allow the court to make any of three forms of order if a plaintiff succeeds in an action of detinue. See *Civil Procedure Act 2005* (NSW) s 93; *Civil Proceedings Act 2011* (Qld) ss 80–2; *Supreme Court (General Civil Procedure) Rules 2005* (Vic) r 21.03.
284   *Re NL Mercantile Group Pty Ltd* [2018] NSWSC 1337, [168] (Gleeson J), citing *Gaba Formwork Contractors Pty Ltd v Turner Corporation Ltd* (1991) 32 NSWLR 175, 178. See also *Brandeis Goldschmidt & Co v Western Transport Ltd* [1981] QB 864.

If the good in question is of 'special value or interest' to the plaintiff, the court may order specific restitution as a remedy.[285] That is because damages would not be adequate in certain cases due to the uniqueness, special value and irreplaceable nature of the good. Even so, the character of the good is only one factor to be considered when deciding whether restitution of the good should typically be ordered. If the good itself is replaceable (not unique), but an award of damages would not be an adequate remedy, specific restitution may still be ordered.[286] Specific restitution of goods in a detinue claim may also be justified if obtaining the goods in question on the market was possible only with 'great difficulty'.[287]

General rules in relation to assessment of damages also apply to a claim of detinue. For example, reasonable consequential losses flowing from detention of goods are compensable. In *Hannaford v Stewart (No 2)*, it was held that expenses in respect of the insurance, transportation and storage of the detained goods are 'necessarily incurred in the delivery up of the paintings to the plaintiffs' and accordingly should be compensated.[288] Damages for loss of use during the detention are available to the plaintiff.[289] If the goods detained are used by the plaintiff in businesses, damages may include the cost of hiring substitute goods. Where the plaintiff hires out the goods, damages may be assessed by reference to the profits that would have been earned from hiring the goods out.[290]

Along with trespass to goods and conversion, exemplary damages can be awarded for detinue.[291]

In addition, a plaintiff can seek an injunction in detinue for the return of goods or, in proper circumstances, for recovery of value and damages for detention of the goods.[292]

REVIEW QUESTIONS

(1) What are nominal damages and in which circumstances would a court consider awarding nominal damages?

(2) Is it possible for a court to award damages either in lieu of or in addition to an injunction?

285 *Whitely Ltd v Hilt* [1918] 2 KB 808, 819 (Swinfen Eady MR). Goods that have been identified as sufficiently special that they deserve an order for specific restitution include: a family portrait or original paintings (*Perpetual Trustees & National Executors of Tasmania Ltd v Perkins* [1989] Aust Torts Reports 80-295; *Hannaford v Stewart* [2011] NSWSC 448); a yacht (*McKeown v Cavalier Yachts Pty Ltd* (1988) 13 NSWLR 303); horses (*Fitz-Alan v Felton* [2004] NSWSC 1118; *Circuit Finance Pty Ltd v Goodwood Road Pty Ltd* [2006] VSC 399); and mortgage documents (*Patroni v Conlan* [2004] WASC 1).
286 See *BIS Cleanaway v Tatale* [2007] NSWSC 378, [6] (McDougall J) (packing pallets should be returned to CHEP although they are not uniquely identifiable).
287 *Howard E Perry & Co Ltd v British Railways Board* [1980] 2 All ER 579.
288 [2011] NSWSC 722, [31]–[32] (Hall J). See also *John Gallagher Panel Beating Co Pty Ltd v Palmer* [2007] NSWSC 627, [23] (damages for consequential loss not too remote are recoverable in detinue); *Macrocom Pty Ltd v City West Centre Pty Ltd* [2003] NSWSC 898, [45]; *National Australia Bank Ltd v Nemur Varity Pty Ltd* (2002) 4 VR 252; *Bodley v Reynolds* (1846) 115 ER 1066 (damages were awarded to compensate a carpenter, whose tools of trade were wrongfully detained, for loss of trade).
289 *John Gallagher Panel Beating v Palmer* [2007] NSWSC 627, [27].
290 *Gaba Formwork Contractors Pty Ltd v Turner Corporation Ltd* (1991) 32 NSWLR 175, 178.
291 See *Egan v State Transport Authority* (1982) 31 SASR 481; *Healing (Sales) Pty Ltd v Inglis Electrix Pty Ltd* (1968) 121 CLR 584; [1968] HCA 60.
292 See, eg, *General & Finance Facilities Ltd v Cooks Cars (Romford) Ltd* [1963] 2 All ER 314; *Pratten v Pratten* [2005] QCA 213.

(3) *Marion's Case* concerns the question of whether consent could be given to perform a hysterectomy and ovariectomy on a 14-year-old girl who suffered from mental retardation which prevented her giving consent herself, even if she had been older. How did the High Court determine whether consent was required here?

Guided responses in the eBook

KEY CONCEPTS

- **abatement of nuisance:** a defendant may enter the land of another or take other self-help measures to abate a nuisance which substantially interferes with the person's enjoyment of his or her land.

- **aggravated damages:** may be awarded to compensate for injured feelings caused by tortious conduct that was particularly officious, abusive, insulting or humiliating.[293]

- **compensatory damages:** aim to restore the plaintiff to the position he or she would have been in if the tort had not been committed.

- **consent:** there can be no trespass if the interference occurs with the plaintiff's consent.

- **defence of another:** allows a defendant to use reasonable force to protect another person from an imminent danger based on a reasonable belief that it was necessary to do so.

- **defence of property:** a defendant may take reasonable steps to protect his or her own property based upon an immediate necessity to act.

- **disciplinary powers:** a defence open to certain persons (eg, parents, teachers, captains of aircraft or masters of ships) to justify the physical chastisement of children and pupils, or restraint of passengers.

- **exemplary damages:** may be awarded where tortious conduct was so outrageous as to warrant the inclusion of a punitive element in the assessment of damages.

- **injunction:** a judicial order either: restraining a person from beginning or continuing to interfere with the plaintiff's legal rights to their person, land or personal property; or compelling a person to carry out a certain act.

- **necessity:** a defence that may justify intervention for the preservation of oneself, another person, one's own property or the property of another.

- **nominal damages:** awarded where the plaintiff's rights have been infringed but the plaintiff has not suffered any actual loss or harm; typical nominal damages are merely a token amount.

---

293 *Lamb v Cotogno* (1987) 164 CLR 1, 8–9.

- **recaption of goods:** entitles a person in actual possession of goods who loses possession of those goods as a result of unlawful interference to use reasonable force to retake the goods.

- **re-entry of land:** entitles a person who has a right to immediate possession of land to use reasonable force to eject the person in possession of the land.

- **self-defence:** a defence that enables a defendant to use reasonable force to repel a battery by the plaintiff, or to prevent or terminate a false imprisonment of the defendant.

 Complete the multiple-choice questions in the eBook to test your knowledge.

PROBLEM-SOLVING EXERCISES

Exercise 1

Mackenzie is a 24-year-old single woman who has suffered from aortic valve disease for a couple of years. She ordinarily lives with her mother and sister in a northern suburb of Melbourne. Both Mackenzie and her mother are adherents of the Jehovah's Witness faith.

About half a year ago, Mackenzie's condition deteriorated and she was admitted to a local hospital (Hospital A) with sepsis and progressive renal failure. The hospital sought Mackenzie's consent to a blood transfusion to save her life. Mackenzie refused because she thought such administration was contrary to her religious belief. The local hospital therefore provided Mackenzie with an alternative treatment. Unfortunately, Mackenzie's symptoms could not be effectively alleviated.

Four months later, Mackenzie's condition has worsened and she is transferred to a major hospital (Hospital B) with septic shock and renal failure. The treating doctors are of the view that Mackenzie is at a significantly increased risk of death if the septic shock and renal impairment cannot be effectively controlled. The doctors also recommend an urgent blood transfusion as part of her treatment. Because Mackenzie is unable to communicate, the hospital decides to administer the blood transfusion immediately.

Knowing the hospital's decision, Mackenzie's mother, Doris, informs Hospital B that Mackenzie would not want to receive any blood or blood products in her treatment because she is a Jehovah's Witness. Doris argues that Mackenzie expressly rejected Hospital A's recommendation for a blood transfusion in her previous treatment. However, Mackenzie's sister, Fiona, who has a very good relationship with her, insists that Hospital B is obligated to try all possible means, including the administration of a blood transfusion, to preserve her sister's life.

Due to the divided opinion between Mackenzie's close family members, and a concern about its own tortious liability, Hospital B is seeking your advice.

 Guided response in the eBook

Exercise 2

Stella is a 12-year-old girl in Grade 6. Every day, her mother, Lucy, picks her up from school and drives her home. One day, on their way home, a car ran a red light and collided with Lucy's car. Lucy was not injured, but Stella suffered a severe leg injury. Stella was treated by a first aid officers on the roadside. An officer told Stella he would give her a tetanus shot. Stella has a phobia of pain; she refused and shouted: 'Don't you dare touch me!' Lucy told the officer not to listen to her so the officer gave Stella the tetanus shot anyway. If Stella sued the officer for battery, are there any defences available to them?

 Guided response in the eBook

CHALLENGE YOURSELF

Exercise 1

Assume, in the case discussed in problem-solving exercise 1, that Mackenzie signed an advance care directive when she was 20, refusing a blood transfusion should she require it, and the directive included a statement saying that her wishes were not to be overridden in any circumstances by any person. Would your answer differ due to the existence of such a document?

 Guided response in the eBook

Exercise 2

Rand is a rugby player who had played rugby league for most of his life. Recently, Rand's team, the Night Owls, made it to Grand Final for the first time in over 20 years. Rand is hoping to win the Grand Final for his team and then retire from playing rugby. However, Rand's team are up against some tough competition and are scheduled to play against The Duke in the Grand Final.

On the day of the Grand Final, Rand's team was in the lead when one of the players from The Duke, Dodgy, struck Rand with a head-high tackle, which is against the rules of the game. Rand's head was severely injured. He had to come off the field and could no longer play. Rand then missed out on seeing his team win the Grand Final.

Is the defence of implied consent available to Dodgy in these circumstances?

 Guided response in the eBook

NUISANCE

9.1   Introduction

Nuisance is one of the oldest and most interesting of the law of torts. It developed early in the common law to protect a person's interest in land.[1] The emergence and rise of the modern tort of negligence has posed a challenge to the precise scope and relevance of the tort of nuisance.[2] An action in nuisance covers conduct of the defendant that is excessive, substantial and unreasonable, which interferes with the plaintiff's use and enjoyment of his or her land.[3] Nuisance covers both physical and non-physical damage.

There are two types of nuisance. The first is *private nuisance*, which is engaged when a plaintiff's use and enjoyment of his or her land is interfered with by an act or omission of the defendant. The second is *public nuisance*, which can be used by a plaintiff to sue a defendant who interferes with the plaintiff's public right, which causes the plaintiff to suffer particular or special damage that is greater than, or different to, that suffered by the general public.

Since liability in nuisance is strict, the defendant must establish his or her defence once a prima facie case has been established.[4] A defendant is only liable for a harm that is foreseeable; thus, foreseeability is essential to establish the tort of nuisance.[5] The tort of nuisance protects the pleasure, comfort and enjoyment derived by a plaintiff in the occupancy and use of both public and private rights in land. The elements of each tort will now be considered.

9.1.1   Private nuisance: interference with the use and enjoyment of land

Hargrave v Goldman is the landmark Australian High Court decision on the tort of private nuisance.[6] In that case, Windeyer J defined the tort as 'an unlawful interference with a person's use or enjoyment of land or some right over, or in connection, with it'.[7] The action is related to the tort of trespass to land (discussed in Chapter 7) as both actions protect the plaintiff's interest in his or her land. However, the central distinction lies on whether the harm suffered by the plaintiff is direct or consequential. This was illustrated by the Queen's Bench in *Southport Corporation v Esso Petroleum Co Ltd*.[8] In that case, the defendant discarded 400

---

1   In addition to the tort of private nuisance, trespass to land and negligence also protect a person's interest in land. While there can be potential overlap with nuisance and negligence, nuisance and trespass to land do not overlap. Nuisance covers acts which are indirect, while trespass must be direct.

2   In *Southern Properties (WA) Pty Ltd v Executive Director, Department of Conservation and Land Management* (2012) 42 WAR 287, McLure P observed that private nuisance remains a separate tort apart from negligence (at [117]–[119]); however, public nuisance in 'highway cases' has been absorbed into the general tort of negligence: *Brodie v Singleton Shire Council* (2001) 206 CLR 512; [2001] HCA 29, [55] (Gaudron, McHugh and Gummow JJ; Kirby J agreeing at [226]).

3   *Hargrave v Goldman* (1963) 110 CLR 40, 59.

4   *Southern Properties (WA) Pty Ltd v Executive Director, Department of Conservation and Land Management* (2012) 42 WAR 287, [97].

5   *Butler Market Gardens Pty Ltd v GG & PM Burrell Pty Ltd* [2018] VSC 768, [98].

6   (1963) 110 CLR 40.

7   *Hargrave v Goldman* (1963) 110 CLR 40, 59.

8   [1954] 2 QB 182.

tonnes of oil from its ship, as it was stranded in the estuary of a river. The oil was carried by the tide onto the plaintiff's land, causing considerable damage. The plaintiff sued, inter alia, in private nuisance and trespass to land. When considering whether the tort of nuisance or trespass was committed, Lord Denning ruled:

> I am clearly of opinion that the Southport Corporation cannot here sue in trespass. This discharge of oil was not done directly on to their foreshore, but outside in the estuary. It was carried by the tide on to their land, but that was only consequential, not direct. Trespass, therefore, does not lie.[9]

In other words, as the oil was not directly dumped onto the plaintiff's land, it cannot be a trespass. Rather, because the oil spilt onto the plaintiff's land in consequence of the tide, an action in nuisance lies. The central distinction between the two torts is therefore whether the injury to the plaintiff's interest in land by the defendant is direct or consequential.

The tort of private nuisance was developed to 'protect the right of an occupier of land to enjoy it without substantial and unreasonable interference'.[10] The test to determine whether the interference is unreasonable or wrongful is according to the ordinary usages of mankind living in a particular society.[11] The harms against which protection is afforded by the tort of private nuisance include:

- any physical damage to land, such as damage to buildings by flooding due to a neighbouring defendant blocking a watercourse,[12] or damage to trees due to toxic fumes[13]

- interference with the use and enjoyment of land, such as disturbance of the comfort or convenience of the plaintiff by smell,[14] noise,[15] vibration[16] or fear for one's safety,[17] despite there being no physical damage.

The tort of nuisance, generally speaking, is not intended to protect people, but rather property values.[18] However, as explained by Professor Fleming, even more sophisticated interests that are given very limited protection by law can be protected.[19] An example of such an interest is highlighted in *Thompson-Schwab v Costaki*,[20] where the English Court of Appeal held that a nuisance was established where a business of prostitution affronted the interests of reasonable neighbours in a suburban area. Lord Evershed MR found that

---

9 Ibid 196.
10 *R v Rimmington* [2006] 1 AC 459, [5] (Lord Bingham).
11 *Elston v Dore* (1982) 149 CLR 480, 488, quoting Lord Atkin's judgment in *Sedleigh-Denfield v O'Callaghan* [1940] AC 880.
12 *Thorpes v Grant Pastoral Co Pty Ltd* (1954) 92 CLR 317.
13 *St Helen's Smelting Co v Tipping* (1865) 11 ER 1483.
14 *Bamford v Turnley* (1860) 122 ER 25.
15 *Oldham v Lawson (No 1)* [1976] VR 654; *Uren v Bald Hills Wind Farm Pty Ltd* [2022] VSC 145, [32].
16 *Sturges v Bridgman* (1879) 11 Ch D 852.
17 *Evans v Finn* (1904) 4 SR (NSW) 297.
18 FH Newark, 'The Boundaries of Nuisance', (1949) 65(4) *Law Quarterly Review* 480, 488–9; per Young J in *Gray v New South Wales* (Supreme Court of New South Wales, Young J, 31 July 1997); *Hunter v Canary Wharf Ltd* [1997] AC 655, 696.
19 J Fleming, *The Law of Torts* (Law Book Co, 9th ed, 1998) 465–6.
20 [1956] 1 WLR 335.

the prostitutes and their customers, who frequently wolf-whistled and displayed overly affectionate acts on the public street, constituted more than just an interference to the sensibilities of a reasonable person. In his Lordship's view, such a business interfered with the comfortable and convenient enjoyment of a family lifestyle and neighbourhood.

However, not every slight annoyance will constitute an *unreasonable* interference.[21] For example, the mere presence of a building is not a nuisance,[22] and neither is the obstruction of a pleasing view from one's home.[23] As we will see in Section 9.2, the courts will look to a variety of factors when considering whether the plaintiff's use and enjoyment of land has been interfered with to constitute a nuisance. Ultimately, the tort of private nuisance reflects the common law trying to balance two conflicting interests: the right of an occupier to use and enjoy his or her land, and the right of the occupier's neighbour to undertake activities as he or she sees fit.

HINTS AND TIPS

It is essential for you to understand and identify the difference between the tort of nuisance and the tort of trespass to land. A tip: the best way to do this is to determine whether the interference occurred directly or consequentially as a result of the defendant's actions.

For example, the directors of a coal mine in northern Queensland decide to dump sulphur dioxide waste material onto Farmer A's land and into the Flinders River. Farmer A immediately notices the material. Farmer B, on the other hand, lives 50 kilometres away from Farmer A and the Flinders River runs through her land. Twelve months after the dumping, Farmer B discovers the presence of sulphur dioxide on her property. Will the farmers have an action against the coal mine in tort?

The answer to this question can be found by identifying whether the interference that occurred to each farmer was direct or consequential. Farmer A will have an action in trespass against the mine, as the waste material was *directly* dumped by the mine onto his land.

Farmer B, on the other hand, will not have an action in trespass, as the waste was not directly placed onto her land by the mine. However, Farmer B will have an action in private nuisance, because as a result of the dumping of the waste into the Flinders River, the waste has consequentially dispersed onto Farmer B's land. The coal mine's actions can be said to have *consequentially* interfered with the use and enjoyment of Farmer B's land. Thus, both Farmer A and Farmer B will likely have an action against the mine in tort law.[24]

21 *Fraser v Booth* (1949) 50 SR (NSW) 113, 116.
22 *Hunter v Canary Wharf Ltd* [1997] AC 655.
23 *Aldred's Case* (1611) 77 ER 816.
24 Note that Farmer B may also have an action in public nuisance: see Section 9.9.

9.2   Unreasonable interference

To constitute a nuisance, the interference with the plaintiff's use or enjoyment of his or her land must be unreasonable.[25] The crucial issue when applying the tort is therefore whether the defendant's conduct was objectively[26] reasonable, according to the ordinary usage of those living in that particular society.[27] However, it is important to understand that a court is not concerned about whether the defendant took reasonable care in a negligence sense. Rather, in determining whether or not an interference is reasonable, a court will balance the desire of the plaintiff to use and enjoy property rights without interference against the desire of others to undertake the activity that causes the interference.[28] For example, if D plays a musical instrument at night that disturbs P's sleep, all that P will need to show is that her sleep, a corollary of her enjoyment of her land, has been interfered with. The court will then determine whether P's right to sleep should not be interfered with by D's right to play music in his home. The fact that D may have acted reasonably (in the negligence sense) by using the best soundproof material that he could find is irrelevant if the bare minimum sound still interferes with P's sleep. It follows that if a court considers an interference to be unreasonable, then the fact that the defendant has taken all reasonable care provides no defence: the smallest interference possible is itself a nuisance.[29] Such a principle was acknowledged by Sperling J in *Bonnici v Kur-ring-gai Municipal Council*[30] and subsequently affirmed by the New South Wales Court of Appeal.[31]

Reasonableness is determined by a number of factors, such as the type and extent of the damage, the locality, the intensity, time and duration of the interference, the plaintiff's sensitivity, the nature of the defendant's activity, whether the defendant could have avoided causing the interference and whether there was malice on the part of the defendant. The critical problem for the courts when considering these factors is the need to balance the conflicting interests of the plaintiff and the defendant. This is known as the 'live and let live' principle.[32]

A modern-day example of the rule is found in the case of *Southwark London Borough Council v Tanner*.[33] The tenants of an apartment block complained that their right to enjoy their land had been interfered with as they could hear all the sounds made by their neighbours, including arguments, crying babies, cleaning, cooking and sexual intercourse. The House of Lords had to balance the interest of the plaintiffs in living in a quiet apartment, with the interest of the defendants in making the usual noises of habitation. The House ultimately held that the plaintiffs could not establish 'unreasonable' interference. On balance, the House ruled that such noises were necessary for the common and ordinary use and occupation of

---

25   *Hargrave v Goldman* (1963) 110 CLR 40, 60 (Windeyer J); *McWilliam v Hunter* [2022] NSWSC 342, [35], applying the earlier NSWSC authority of *Trewin v Felton* [2007] NSWSC 851, [73].
26   The Western Australian Court of Appeal has confirmed that the test is an objective one: *Marsh v Baxter* (2015) 49 WAR 1, [247]. See Section 9.2.5 for a discussion of the facts and reasoning of the decision.
27   *Sedleigh-Denfield v O'Callaghan* [1940] AC 880, 903 (Lord Wright).
28   *St Helen's Smelting Co v Tipping* (1865) 11 ER 1483, 1485.
29   See J Goudkamp and E Peel, *Winfield & Jolowicz on Tort* (Sweet & Maxwell, 19th ed, 2014) [15.010].
30   (2001) 121 LGERA 1, [187].
31   See *Kur-ring-gai Municipal Council v Bonnici* [2002] NSWCA 313.
32   *Bamford v Turnley* (1860) 122 ER 25, 33.
33   [2001] 1 AC 1.

land and houses and the activities were done with proper consideration for the interest of neighbouring occupiers.[34] This principle reflects the common law's recognition that living in any society requires some level of reasonable interference with others.

The 'live and let live' principle must be thought of as an overarching framework when considering whether the defendant's interference is reasonable. Within this framework are various factors that courts use to balance the conflicting interests of the parties. Such factors will now be considered.

Case: *Bonnici v Kur-ring-gai Municipal Council* (2001) 121 LGERA 1

Facts

Mr and Mrs Bonnici (the plaintiffs) purchased a block of land in 1977 in Gordon on Sydney's North Shore. In 1979, they built their family home on the land. However, when the plaintiffs purchased the land there was no street drainage system in place. In 1980, the local council (the defendant) commenced works which implemented a stormwater drain system in the area. However, in 1982, following heavy rain, water poured from this drainage system onto the plaintiffs' land and flooded the entire backyard. By December 1983, the property had been flooded more than 17 times, with water depths of up to 500 millimetres against the walls of the house. It resulted in damage to the house, its foundations and the natural state of the land. As a result, the defendant completed various works to prevent the stormwater flowing onto the plaintiffs' land. Despite the Council's efforts, water still unnaturally flowed onto the plaintiffs' land. The plaintiffs sued the Council, inter alia, in private nuisance.

Issue

The primary issue in the case was whether the defendant's interference was unreasonable, despite the fact that it took all reasonable steps available to mitigate it.

Decision

Sperling J in the New South Wales Supreme Court upheld the plaintiffs' claim in private nuisance. His Honour held that the defendant had been guilty of a nuisance in causing or allowing stormwater to flow directly and indirectly onto the plaintiffs' land; thus, the plaintiffs were to be awarded damages for the resulting damage. Importantly, however, an injunction was also granted to restrain the defendant from causing any stormwater to flow onto the plaintiffs' land. His Honour held that while the Council had taken all reasonable steps to mitigate the nuisance, the remaining interference due to the indirect stormwater that entered the plaintiffs' property still constituted an unreasonable interference and thus a nuisance.

Significance

This case is significant because it demonstrates that interference can still be said to be unreasonable, even though the defendant who created that interference has taken all reasonable steps available to mitigate it.

---

34   Ibid 21 (Lord Millett).

Question

Explain why Sperling J still awarded an injunction (and acknowledged that the nuisance was continuing) in this case, despite the fact that the defendant had taken all reasonable steps available to it to mitigate the nuisance.

    Guided response in the eBook

9.2.1   Type of damage

The first step when considering whether a defendant's interference is unreasonable is to determine what type of harm the plaintiff has suffered. It was established in *Hunter v Canary Wharf Ltd* that courts recognise three types of harm relevant to the tort of private nuisance.[35] This was neatly summarised by Preston CJ in *Robson v Leischke*:

> Three kinds of interference are recognised by the law as constituting a nuisance:
> (a) causing encroachment on the neighbour's land, short of trespass;
> (b) causing physical damage to the neighbour's land or any building, works or vegetation on it;
> (c) unduly interfering with a neighbour in the comfortable and convenient enjoyment of his or her land.[36]

These categories of harm will be explained further. Of central importance is that the plaintiff's onus of proof will differ depending on what type of harm the defendant's interference has allegedly caused.

The reason why the courts have treated the types of harm differently can be traced back to the House of Lords' decision in *St Helen's Smelting Co v Tipping*.[37] Their Lordships distinguished physical damage from harm in the form of an interference with a plaintiff's enjoyment. Lord Westbury established that where the harm is non-physical, the question of whether the interference is unreasonable will centre upon what is reasonable in that specific locality where the plaintiff lives. In contrast, where physical damage occurs, the locality of the plaintiff's land is less of a material factor. Thus, the common law of both England and Australia has long reasoned that a distinction must be made between these two types of harm when determining if a private nuisance has occurred.

9.2.1.1   Physical: material damage

The tort of private nuisance protects plaintiffs from consequential physical damage done to their land. This includes the first two categories of harm outlined in Section 9.2.1. Category (a) is often caused by tree roots from a neighbouring property growing onto the defendant's

35 [1997] AC 655, 695 (Lord Lloyd of Berwick).
36 [2008] NSWLEC 152, [54] (citations omitted).
37 (1865) 11 ER 1483.

land. Category (b), on the other hand, is any physical damage done to any part of the land, including any buildings, trees, fixtures or attachments to fixtures.[38] It often arises from fire, toxic chemicals, flooding and the like.

Once the plaintiff has established that the defendant's interference caused consequential physical damage, regardless of whether such damage could have been reasonably anticipated, this renders the interference prima facie unlawful. The plaintiff, having satisfied onus of proof, is entitled to succeed unless the defendant can prove lawful justification or show that its activity was reasonable.[39] Such a principle was originally established by Windeyer J's leading High Court judgment in *Gartner v Kidman*.[40] It has since been applied by the New South Wales Court of Appeal in *Corbett v Pallas*,[41] where the Court held that if the nuisance is one where substantial (see Section 9.2.2) material damage has been caused, the onus of proof will lie with the defendant to show that its activity was reasonable.

9.2.1.2   Non-physical: interference with use and enjoyment of land

The tort of private nuisance also protects plaintiffs from consequential interference with the use and enjoyment of their land. Nuisances of this kind will likely arise from something emanating from the defendant's land.[42] Preston CJ in *Robson v Leischke* gave a useful summary:

    (a)   noise (egs, *Halsey v Esso Petroleum Co Ltd, Vincent v Peacock* and *Cohen v City of Perth*);

    (b)   vibrations (egs, *Shelfer v City of London Electric Lighting Co* and *Hoare & Co v McAlpine*);

    (c)   dust (egs, *Pwllbach Colliery Company Ltd v Woodman, Thompson v Sydney Municipal Council* and *Kidman v Page*);

    (d)   sediment from soil erosion (eg, *Van Son v Forestry Commission of New South Wales*);

    (e)   noxious smuts and pollution (egs, *St Helen's Smelting Company v Tipping* and *Halsey v Esso Petroleum Co Ltd*);

    (f)   smoke (egs, *Crump v Lambert* and *Manchester Corp v Farnworth*); and

    (g)   offensive odours and stenches (eg, *Walter v Selfe*).[43]

The interference can also be a concern for one's health and safety (eg, the constant fear of being shot at)[44] or the annoyance of a particular neighbouring business or trade.[45] If the harm caused is this kind of non-physical interference, then the onus of proof is on the plaintiff to prove that the interference is unreasonable according to the locality in which the plaintiff lives and the various other factors we will consider.[46] Table 9.1 provides examples

---

38 See *Halsey v Esso Petroleum Co Ltd* [1961] 1 WLR 683 (damage to clothes on the plaintiff's clothes line due to the defendant's acid smuts was recognised as physical damage for the purposes of a private nuisance).

39 *Kraemers v A-G (Tas)* [1966] Tas SR 113, [123].

40 (1962) 108 CLR 12, 48.

41 (1995) 86 LGERA 312, 317.

42 *Hunter v Canary Wharf Ltd* [1997] AC 655, 685.

43 *Robson v Leischke* [2008] NSWLEC 152, [85] (citations omitted).

44 *Evans v Finn* (1904) 4 SR (NSW) 297.

45 *Thompson-Schwab v Costaki* [1956] 1 WLR 335.

46 *St Helen's Smelting Co v Tipping* (1865) 11 ER 1483, 1486.

and states who bears the burden of proof for private nuisance that causes either physical or non-physical damage.

Table 9.1   Physical damage and non-physical damage

	Physical damage	Non-physical damage
Examples	Any property damage: • Flooding • Fire • Damage to trees or plants • Damage to soil due to neighbouring tree roots.	Likely to be something emanating from the defendant: • Toxic smells or dust or pollution • Loud noise or vibrations • Smoke • Offensive business (eg, prostitution).
Burden of proof	• Once the plaintiff has established material damage caused by the defendant's interference, then the plaintiff has satisfied its onus. • The onus now reverses and the defendant must prove that its activity was reasonable.	• The onus of proof is on the plaintiff to prove that the interference is unreasonable according to the locality and various other factors that go to prove reasonableness.

9.2.2   The principle of triviality

Irrespective of whether the consequential harm caused is physical or non-physical, the interference must be substantial.[47] Therefore, once the type of harm has been identified, consideration must be given to whether it is 'substantial' in order to constitute a private nuisance. This test was established by Knight-Bruce V-C when he held in *Walter v Selfe* that the interference must be:

> an inconvenience materially interfering with the ordinary comfort physically of human existence, not merely according to elegant or dainty modes and habits of living but according to plain and sober and simple notions among the English people.[48]

This test has been adopted by Australian courts on numerous occasions.[49] It is important to note, however, that the substantiality of the plaintiff's harm does not necessarily need to be quantified. It should be seen more like an impermissible 'range' of harm, which differs depending upon the circumstances of each case. This is evident in the reasoning of Hodgson CJ in *Dynamic Flooring Pty Ltd v Carter*.[50] In that case, Mr Carter was the neighbour of Mr Lambert. Mr Lambert made alterations to his property, such that the general stormwater which flowed onto his land also flowed onto Mr Carter's land. Mr Carter alleged that this action constituted a nuisance, as in 1995 and 1997, floods occurred which led to 600 millimetres of water being dispersed around the plaintiff's land and

---

47   *Walter v Selfe* (1851) 64 ER 849.
48   Ibid 852.
49   See *Don Brass Foundry Pty Ltd v Stead* (1948) 48 SR (NSW) 482; *Cohen v City of Perth* (2000) 112 LGERA 234; *Dynamic Flooring Pty Ltd v Carter* [2001] NSWCA 396.
50   [2000] NSWSC 992.

taking some days to disperse. When considering whether the harm caused to Mr Carter was substantial, Hodgson CJ held:

> it was in my opinion unreasonable, and to some extent irresponsible, to bring such a large amount of soil on to number 20 without any attempt to consult the neighbour and no real precautions being taken to prevent damage being caused. Having regard to this, and my views on the affectation of number 18, I find that a nuisance was created … I think some damage in the sense of loss of amenity is proved. As I have said, *it is only proved in the most general sense and it is extremely difficult to quantify.*[51]

On appeal, the New South Wales Court of Appeal affirmed Hodgson CJ's finding and held that the substantial harm requirement is not necessarily an objective quantification that is similar in every case, but rather a range of minimum harms that can vary depending upon the circumstances of the individual facts at hand.[52] It is therefore important to consider all of the relevant factors of the case before making a judgment on whether the harm is in fact substantial.

9.2.3 Locality

Central to whether a defendant's interference is unreasonable – particularly for non-physical interferences – is the question of what level of interference is to be expected given the locality in which it occurs. It must be determined what type and level of interference a normal person should reasonably put up with given the locality in which the defendant's activity was carried out.[53]

The first step when considering the effect of locality is to determine its character. Different areas in our society are used for various enterprises. A suburb or region can be used for residential purposes, agriculture or industry and the like. Therefore, what might be a nuisance in one location might not be a nuisance in another. For example, a plaintiff who lives in an industrial area cannot expect the same standard of air quality as someone who lives in a residential suburb.[54] Thus, the type and level of interference to be expected in the area in which the plaintiff lives is pivotal in determining whether the interference is unreasonable. Take a busy inner-city suburb – for example, Newtown, Sydney. An ordinary person living there should reasonably expect to put up with a certain level of music and the sounds of partygoers during the night. But residents of this area should not reasonably expect to be awoken from a midday nap by the sounds of a sheep shearer who has moved in next door.

Even though a locality is industrial or residential in character, interferences that are inherent within such localities may be so substantial that they can still be held to be unreasonable. In *Feiner v Domachuk* the plaintiff sued in private nuisance due to an offensive smell from the defendant's neighbouring mushroom farm.[55] Brownie J in the New South Wales Supreme Court held that the offensive smells due to keeping compost made from straw mixed with urine and horse manure still constituted a nuisance. Despite the fact

---

51 Ibid [70], [75] (emphasis added).
52 *Dynamic Flooring Pty Ltd v Carter* [2001] NSWCA 396, [44].
53 *Bliss v Hall* (1838) 132 ER 758.
54 Ibid.
55 (1994) 35 NSWLR 485.

that the plaintiff lived in a rural area and the defendant had an agricultural zoning permit, the interference they caused went over and beyond the smells expected in an ordinary rural zone.[56]

Other than assessing the character of the locality generally, two factors are further relevant to identifying it. The first is local government planning and zoning law. There will be certain cases where such laws are of assistance, but generally they are irrelevant. It has been held that planning permission given by a local authority to a defendant will be a relevant factor that can be taken into account where the project undertaken by the defendant is of a large scale and is the result of a policy decision by the authority leading to a fundamental change in the use of that locality.[57] However, the fact that land is being used in accordance with permission of a planning authority adhering to zoning and licensing law[58] does not of itself prevent it being a nuisance[59] and should therefore play a minimal role in determining whether the interference is unreasonable. Trial courts must be wary of the extent to which they rely upon relevant zoning law when assessing the reasonableness of the defendant's interference, as the United Kingdom Supreme Court in *Lawrence v Fen Tigers Ltd* criticised the lower courts for overstating the significance of planning permission.[60]

The second issue relevant to an assessment of the character of a particular locality is the extent to which the defendant's own activities can be taken into account. In *Coventry v Lawrence*, the plaintiff moved into a cottage approximately 600 metres from a car racing stadium and a motorcycle track. The United Kingdom Supreme Court had to consider whether a nuisance was committed as a result of the noise created by speedway racing and other activities that took place inside and outside the stadium about eight times per year. Central to this issue was the locality in which the plaintiff lived: her cottage was half a mile away from the nearest residential property and a small village was located about a mile from the stadium. In assessing the locality, Lord Neuberger held:

> I accept that one starts, as it were, with the proposition that *the defendant's activities are to be taken into account when assessing the character of the locality* ... Where I part company with the Court of Appeal is on the issue of whether one ignores the fact that those activities may constitute a nuisance to the claimant. In my view, *to the extent that those activities are a nuisance to the claimant, they should be left out of account when assessing the character of the locality*, or, to put it another way, they should be notionally stripped out of the locality when assessing its character. Thus, in the present case, where the judge concluded that the activities at the stadium and the track were actually carried on in such a way as to constitute a nuisance, although they could be carried on so as not to cause a nuisance, the character of the locality should be assessed on the basis that (i) it includes the stadium and the track, and (ii) they could be used for speedway, stockcar and banger racing and for motocross respectively, but (iii) only to an extent which would not cause a nuisance.[61]

---

56 Ibid 492–3.
57 *Gillingham Borough Council v Medway (Chatham) Dock Co Ltd* [1993] QB 343.
58 See, eg, *Liquor Act 2007* (NSW); *Liquor Control Reform Act 1988* (Vic); *Liquor Licensing Act 1997* (SA).
59 *Wheeler v Saunders* [1996] Ch 19, 30 (Staughton LJ).
60 [2014] AC 822 (Lord Neuberger of Abbotsbury PSC).
61 Ibid [63]–[65] (emphasis added).

This reasoning holds that the defendant's noise and any other activity that occurs in the neighbourhood can properly be taken into account when assessing the character of the locality, to the extent that it does not give rise to an actionable nuisance or is otherwise unlawful. This principle has not yet been adopted by the Australian High Court, but it has been cited with approval[62] and considered[63] on numerous occasions in Australia.

Finally, it is important to appreciate that the nature of localities can change. For example, one location may change from a predominantly rural area to a predominantly suburban one. Thus, courts are required to decide which of the two conflicting uses of land the law of nuisance should facilitate.[64]

HINTS AND TIPS

In order to illustrate the principles in *Lawrence v Fen Tigers Ltd* [2014] AC 822, they are applied in the following example:

> In December 2013, Aqua Adventures was given local council permission to open in a quiet, residential neighbourhood of Ballarat, a city in Victoria. Jane, an Australian bush poet, lived in the closest house to the water park. She usually writes in the silence of her lounge room, but due to the sounds of screaming children and loud music emanating from the water park, she can no longer write her poetry. You are a solicitor working on Jane's case and have been asked to assess the locality of the neighbourhood for a possible claim in nuisance.

In assessing whether a defendant's interference is unreasonable, it must be determined whether the defendant's conduct was objectively reasonable according to the ordinary usage of people living in that particular society: *Sedleigh-Denfield v O'Callaghan* [1940] AC 880, affirmed in *Marsh v Baxter* (2014) 49 WAR 1. Thus, it must be determined what level of noise a person should reasonably expect in a quiet suburb of Ballarat.

The water park is situated next to a 'quiet, residential neighbourhood of Ballarat'. Given this suburban character, there will likely be substantial noise from activity during the day, but these sounds would be unlikely to pierce the walls of a house with closed doors. The general sounds of Aqua Adventures can be taken into account in considering the objective noise of the locality, but not to the extent that it constitutes a nuisance (*Lawrence v Fen Tigers Ltd*). The fact that Aqua Adventures was given local council permission to open the water park, however, is irrelevant as this mere fact, without certain details of whether noise is permitted, is of no assistance to the defendant (*Lawrence v Fen Tigers Ltd*). Thus, it is likely that the noise created by Aqua Adventures will be unreasonable when it goes beyond the sounds made by day-to-day activities such that it is so loud that it can be heard by a reasonable person inside their house with all of the doors closed.

---

62 See *Sino Iron Pty Ltd v Mineralogy Pty Ltd (No 2)* [2017] WASCA 76; *Coles Group Property Developments Ltd v Stankovic* [2016] NSWSC 852; *Manderson v Wright (No 2)* [2018] VSC 162.

63 See *Emprja Pty Ltd v Red Engine Group Pty Ltd* [2017] QSC 33; *Mineralogy Pty Ltd v Sino Iron Pty Ltd (No. 6)* (2015) 329 ALR 1.

64 *Sturges v Bridgman* (1879) 11 Ch D 852.

9.2.4   Intensity, time and duration

The intensity, time and duration of the interference will also be relevant to whether it is unreasonable. The type of injury will have a direct bearing on the influence of these factors. If the plaintiff suffers considerable personal injury, the fact that it only occurred once for a short period of time will not make it reasonable.[65] In contrast, if the plaintiff suffers non-physical interference, then the time of day, intensity and length of this interference will have direct bearing on whether it is unreasonable. In *Haddon v Lynch*, the plaintiff alleged that the sounds of the defendant church ringing its bells constituted a nuisance.[66] The Court reasoned that while the sound of the bells was generally not a nuisance, it was in fact an unreasonable interference when the bells were rung before 9 am on Sundays and public holidays. Thus, the time of day and the day on which the interference occurs will affect its reasonableness.[67]

The relevance of the duration and intensity of the interference will depend on all of the circumstances of the case. It has been held that a continuing state of affairs is normally necessary for a nuisance to occur.[68] However, this is arguably an incorrect assumption. Rather, a consideration of all the factors of the case at hand must be undertaken as, in some cases, the interference need not be continuous. For example, in *Andrea v Selfridge & Co Ltd*,[69] it was held that a serious interference for a short period of time may still be unreasonable, especially if it occurs at night or in the early morning in a residential area.[70] Lord Greene MR did, however, qualify this statement when it came to the facts of the individual case and held that when one is dealing with temporary operations such as construction work or demolition, everybody has to put up with a degree of discomfort.[71] In *Uren v Bald Hills Wind Farm Pty Ltd*, the Victorian Supreme Court ruled that while the noise from wind turbines was intermittent, it amounted to a substantial interference with the plaintiff's enjoyment of his property at night, particularly, 'his ability to sleep undisturbed in his own bed in his own house on his own rural property'.[72]

9.2.5   The sensitive plaintiff

The reasonableness of the defendant's conduct is an objective test. Thus, a plaintiff will not succeed in establishing that an interference is unreasonable where he or she has an unusual subjective sensibility or idiosyncrasy in person or property that caused the plaintiff to be easily disturbed or inconvenienced.[73] The law pays no regard to delicacy or sensitivity in a plaintiff's person and therefore the elderly,[74] persons with disabilities[75] and persons sensitive

---

65 *Riverman Orchards Pty Ltd v Hayden* [2017] VSC 379, [179].
66 [1911] VLR 5.
67 See also *Seidler v Luna Park Reserve Trust* (Supreme Court of New South Wales, Hodgson J, 21 September 1995).
68 *SCM (United Kingdom) Ltd v WJ Whittall & Son Ltd* [1971] 1 QB 337.
69 [1938] Ch 1.
70 This principle was explicitly affirmed by the Victorian Supreme Court in *Munro v Southern Dairies Ltd* [1955] VLR 332.
71 *Andrea v Selfridge & Co Ltd* [1938] Ch 1, 5.
72 *Uren v Bald Hills Wind Farm Pty Ltd* [2022] VSC 145, [32].
73 *Robinson v Kilvert* (1889) 41 Ch D 88.
74 *Spencer v Silva* [1942] SASR 213, 219.
75 *Bloodworth v Cormack* [1949] NZLR 1058, 1064.

to noise[76] are given no assistance. Furthermore, the sensitive use to which a plaintiff puts his or her property cannot be taken into account. For example, in *Marsh v Baxter* the appellants were approved growers of organic produce on their property.[77] They lost their organic produce certification in 2010 when it was found that genetically modified seed from the respondent's land had blown onto their property. The appellants suffered pure economic loss and sued, inter alia, in private nuisance. On the question of whether the appellants were unusually sensitive because they grew organic crops, the Western Australian Court of Appeal held:

> the appellants could not, by putting their land to an abnormally sensitive use, thereby 'unilaterally enlarge their own rights' and impose limitations on the operations of their neighbours to an extent greater than would otherwise be the case … The appellants were, of course, entitled to enter into arrangements which had the effect that their land was being put to an abnormally sensitive use, but their neighbours did not then fall under an obligation to limit their farming activities on their own land so as not to interfere with that use of the appellants' land.[78]

Thus, as a general rule, a plaintiff's unusual sensitivity cannot be taken into account when assessing whether the defendant's interfering conduct was reasonable. However, the New South Wales Supreme Court has acknowledged an exception to this principle. In *Onus v Telstra Corporation Ltd* the defendant was granted local council permission to build a 35-metre tower next to the plaintiff's airfield.[79] Thus, in exactly the same way as in *Marsh v Baxter*, the plaintiff's use of his land constituted an abnormal sensitivity and it was because of this that such a tower would pose a danger to aviation safety at the airfield. However, when assessing the reasonableness of the defendant's interference, Price J held:

> I should mention that the present case is very different to the circumstances upon which *Robinson v Kilvert* was decided. In that case, the court was not concerned with issues of public safety or the gravity of the consequences that might arise because of the nuisance. Moreover, the predominant use of the airfield has been for many years pilot training and the strong probability is that the proposed construction of the tower will have a substantial prejudicial impact upon the ordinary enjoyment of the airfield by the plaintiff. The balancing exercise leads me firmly to the conclusion that the public interest in aviation safety must prevail.[80]

Although Price J framed his analysis as a distinction from the principle in *Robinson v Kilvert*,[81] it is arguable that it is an exception. This is because Price J held that the plaintiff's sensitivity in relation to the use of his land can be taken into account when there are serious issues of public safety due to the defendant's interference having the capacity to cause grave harm. It is likely that this exception due to social development in the law can be applied in cases of

---

76 *Spencer v Silva* [1942] SASR 213, 219.
77 (2015) 49 WAR 1.
78 Ibid [785]–[786].
79 [2011] NSWSC 33.
80 Ibid [136].
81 (1889) 41 Ch D 88.

personal sensitivity, such that if a person with asthma were of serious risk of dying due to a defendant's noxious dust, it would be hoped that the law would give that person a remedy. The exception ultimately serves as a reminder that the assessment of reasonableness of the defendant's interference is always a task of balancing all of the individual factors at hand.

9.2.6   The nature of the defendant's activity and the public interest

The nature of the defendant's conduct is another relevant factor in assessing reasonableness, 'for the law, in judging what constitutes a nuisance, does take into consideration both the object and duration of that which is said to constitute the nuisance'.[82] The utility of a defendant's conduct must therefore be taken into account. For example, any plaintiff must put up with the temporary construction work of his or her neighbour provided that all reasonable precautions are being taken to minimise disturbance.[83] Furthermore, certain interferences may have utility because their object is in the interest of the community. Thus, some consideration will be given to the fact that a type of interference is essential and unavoidable in the particular locality due to its social utility.[84] For example, the neighbours of a power plant cannot complain that the plant is operating at night, as its operation is essential to the nation's energy resources.

However, just because the interfering conduct has utility does not mean that the plaintiff's private rights can be infringed. It is no defence for the defendant to assert that, due to the high public interest in his actions, only the plaintiff should suffer the burden of the interference.[85]

In *Cohen v City of Perth*,[86] the defendant local council collected garbage from an apartment block very late at night and at very early hours of the morning, using an old garbage truck which created significant noise. The plaintiff lived in the apartment above the main bin area, and complained that the truck removing the garbage during these hours constituted a nuisance. The defendant argued that it was in the public interest to remove waste from the apartment block and therefore its actions did not constitute unreasonable interference. The Supreme Court of Western Australia disagreed, and held that while the actions did have some level of utility, the plaintiff did not have to suffer the inconvenience of its noise before 7 am on weekends and after 7:30 pm on weekdays.[87] In *Uren v Bald Hills Wind Farm Pty Ltd*, the Supreme Court recognised that while 'the generation of renewable energy by the wind farm is a socially valuable activity';[88] however, 'there is not a binary choice to be made between the generation of clean energy by the wind farm, and a good night's sleep for its neighbours.'[89] It should be possible to achieve both by the defendant taking measures to reduce the noise.[90] Finally, malicious activity will have no utility (see Section 9.2.8).

---

82 *Harrison v Southwark Water Co* [1891] 2 Ch 409, 414 (Vaughan Williams J).
83 *Andrea v Selfridge & Co Ltd* [1938] Ch 1.
84 *Munro v Southern Dairies Ltd* [1955] VLR 332; *Uren v Bald Hills Wind Farm Pty Ltd* [2022] VSC 145, [13].
85 *Munro v Southern Dairies Ltd* [1955] VLR 332, 337.
86 (2000) 112 LGERA 234.
87 Ibid [1], [180] (Roberts-Smith J).
88 *Uren v Bald Hills Wind Farm Pty Ltd* [2022] VSC 145, [13], [243], [334].
89 Ibid [13] [244].
90 Ibid [13], [307]–[333].

Case: *Uren v Bald Hills Wind Farm Pty Ltd* [2022] VSC 145

Facts

Noel Uren and John Zakula (the plaintiffs) owned and resided on neighbouring rural plots of land in Gippsland, Victoria. In 2015, Bald Hills Wind Farm (the defendant) began operating adjacent to their land, consisting of 52 individual wind turbines approximately 110 metres in height. The wind farm was the subject of substantial community opposition when it was first proposed, and the development was allowed to proceed with conditions relating to 'acoustic amenity' (ie, relating to the noise levels generated by the wind farm). In 2020, the plaintiffs commenced this action in private nuisance against the defendant, alleging that noise from the wind farm had caused a substantial interference with both plaintiffs' enjoyment of their land, including their ability to sleep undisturbed.

Issues

The first issue in this case was whether the defendant's interference was unreasonable. As a part of this issue, the sub-issues were to determine the nature and extent of the interference, the relevance of the public interest value in operating the turbines, and the relevance of whether or not the defendant had complied with the noise conditions of its permit.

Decision

Richards J in the Victorian Supreme Court held the plaintiff's claim in private nuisance. Her Honour held that the defendant had been guilty of a nuisance in causing loud noises to be emanated from the wind farm to the plaintiffs' properties. Her Honour found that the emanation of noise was not an unreasonable interference during daylight hours, but that the noise was unreasonable at night when it interfered with the defendants' right to sleep undisturbed on their respective properties. Her Honour was not satisfied that the defendant had demonstrated compliance with the conditions of its operation relating to noise, but also stated that compliance with conditions in itself would not preclude a finding of nuisance given that she had already found the disturbance to be unreasonable. Her Honour acknowledged the public interest value of the wind turbines operating, but found that the public interest benefits were not mutually exclusive with the avoidance of nuisance, and that the wind farm could be operated in a manner which avoided the unreasonable noises. Her Honour gave judgment in the form of an injunction restraining the defendant from causing the noise to occur at night, as well as awards of damages for both plaintiffs.

Significance

This case demonstrates a number of crucial factors which must be weighed up in the determination of whether interference is unreasonable or not. It clarifies that timing is an important factor, as her Honour only held that the night-time noise constituted a nuisance. Furthermore, it demonstrates the weighing-up process that is carried out in relation to nuisances which have a public interest element is significant, because it demonstrates that interference can still be said to be unreasonable even though the defendant who created that interference has taken all reasonable steps available to mitigate it.

Question

Explain why Richards J did not find the interference to be a nuisance when it occurred during the daytime on the plaintiffs' properties.

 Guided response in the eBook

9.2.7   Practicality of avoiding interference

If a plaintiff complains of a defendant's interfering conduct, a material factor will be whether the defendant could have achieved the same purpose without causing the interference or causing it to a lesser extent. If this is so, then the courts will almost conclusively presume that the defendant's interference is unreasonable.[91] In *Painter v Reed*, the defendant was a horse trainer who broke in horses.[92] The defendant decided that the appropriate time to do this was in the early hours of the morning, from 4 am onwards. The plaintiff was the defendant's neighbour and sued in nuisance due to the fact that his sleep was severely disturbed by the sound of the movements and stomping of horses. Richards J, in the South Australian Supreme Court, held that there was clearly a private nuisance because there were practical options for the defendant to take to avoid the interference: he could easily have decided to train his horses at a more convenient hour or even in a stable further away from the plaintiff's premises.

On the other hand, the High Court has established that courts are not to place an intolerable burden on defendants,[93] and that private nuisance cases must be decided on a 'balanced consideration of what could be expected of the particular [defendant] as compared with the consequences of inaction'.[94] Thus, in *Spark v Osborne*, the High Court held that the defendant was not required to spend hours each day weeding his property to keep down a noxious weed which already grew naturally on his land, so as to prevent it from spreading onto neighbouring land.

Factors relevant to whether there was a viable alternative method available to the defendant to mitigate the interference include the cost of the method,[95] the extent to which it would have reduced interference[96] and its reasonableness.[97] It is important to remember, however, that even if the defendant has taken all reasonable steps to mitigate the interference (and is therefore not negligent), the bare minimum interference can still be unreasonable and constitute a nuisance (see Section 9.2).[98]

91   *Painter v Reed* [1930] SASR 295, 304 (Richards J).
92   [1930] SASR 295.
93   *Sparke v Osborne* (1908) 7 CLR 51.
94   *Goldman v Hargrave* [1967] 1 AC 645, 664.
95   *Painter v Reed* [1930] SASR 295.
96   *McMahon v Catanzaro* [1961] QWN 22.
97   *Cohen v City of Perth* (2000) 112 LGERA 234.
98   *Kur-ring-gai Municipal Council v Bonnici* [2002] NSWCA 313.

9.2.8 Malice

If the defendant's interference is malicious, in the sense that its sole purpose is to cause annoyance or harm, then the interference will be treated as unreasonable where harm can be proven, irrespective of any other relevant factors.[99] This principle was established in *Christie v Davey* where the defendant, aggravated by his neighbour's music lessons, started frequently whistling, shrieking and beating on trays and walls to disturb his neighbour.[100] The Court granted the claimant an injunction because the defendant had acted maliciously for the purpose of agitating her.

The principle was later developed in *Hollywood Silver Fox Farm v Emmett*.[101] In that case, the claimant used his land for a sensitive purpose by farming silver foxes, which are extremely nervous during breeding time. The defendant frequently and deliberately fired guns on his own land, neighbouring the claimant's, in order to scare the silver foxes. The claimant thus suffered pure economic loss, as the foxes did not breed properly due to the disturbance. The King's Bench held that even though the plaintiff was using his land for a sensitive purpose, where a defendant acts maliciously to disturb this sensitivity, he will be held liable for an action in private nuisance.[102]

The Australian courts have adopted both of these principles.[103] Furthermore, the Supreme Court of New South Wales has contemplated the effect of a plaintiff's own maliciousness. In *Fraser v Booth*, Roper CJ had to consider the effect of maliciousness where the plaintiff acted intentionally and created her own nuisance, in response to the defendant's nuisance.[104] In that case, Booth was training hundreds of pigeons, which caused substantial noise as well as noxious smells from the faeces they dropped all over Fraser's land. In response, Fraser let off firecrackers to scare the pigeons. Roper CJ held that the plaintiff's actions were justifiable because they were taken under stress from an existing nuisance in the hope of alleviating it.[105] This case is, therefore, authority for the principle that a plaintiff may intentionally respond to a nuisance in order to abate or mitigate its effects.

9.2.9 An ultimate question of fact

Ultimately, all of the considerations in Sections 9.2.1 to 9.2.8 must be taken into account, where applicable, when considering whether a defendant's interfering conduct is unreasonable. As reiterated on numerous occasions, the test is a balanced one that will be applied differently in every case depending on its facts and circumstances. Figure 9.1 exemplifies the multifarious nature of assessing whether a defendant's interference is unreasonable.

---

99 *Christie v Davey* [1893] 1 Ch 316.
100 Ibid.
101 [1936] 2 KB 468.
102 Ibid 471.
103 See, eg, *Michos v Council of the City of Botany Bay* (2012) 189 LGERA 25, [58]; *Marsh v Baxter* (2015) 49 WAR 1, [249].
104 (1949) 50 SR (NSW) 113.
105 Ibid 117.

Figure 9.1 Unreasonable interference

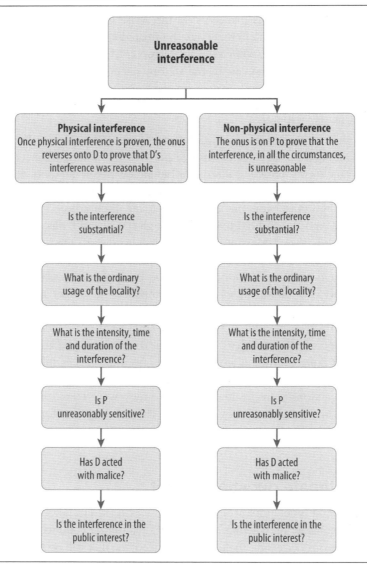

REVIEW QUESTIONS

(1) Which party in an action for private nuisance bears the onus of establishing that a defendant's conduct is unreasonable? Does it differ depending on the type of damage suffered?

(2) What factors are relevant in determining whether a defendant's conduct is unreasonable? Are the factors the same in every case?

 Guided responses in the eBook

9.3   Who can sue?

The law of private nuisance does not protect persons without an interest in land.[106] Thus, in order to have title to sue, a plaintiff must have an interest in the land on which a nuisance was committed.[107] Those who are considered to have proprietary interests sufficient to sue in private nuisance include:

- an owner-occupier[108]
- a tenant-lessee with actual possession[109]
- an owner of an incorporeal hereditament such as a negative covenant or easement.[110]

A reversioner[111] can only sue in private nuisance if the interference permanently harms the land and thus damages his or her reversionary interest.[112] For example, a reversioner can sue for vibrations causing structural damage to a house in which he or she has a reversionary interest, as the injury will continue indefinitely and thus reduce the value of his or her proprietary interest.[113] A licensee, however, has no standing to sue.[114] Licensees can include guests, lodgers and members of the freeholder's or tenant's family who reside on the property.[115] The reason provided by the common law for this principle is that neighbouring occupiers often come to agreements where one or both will allow some temporary nuisance. Thus, if a licensee were given standing to sue, the neighbour who was committing the agreed temporary nuisance could not rely on the agreement to avoid liability to the licensee.[116]

EMERGING ISSUE

The High Court of Australia has never ruled on the issue of standing in private nuisance. Thus, the principles in this section are based on the law of the United Kingdom. This is arguably problematic, given that the United Kingdom's law is influenced by the human rights provisions it is obliged to enforce under the *Human Rights Act 1998* (UK) (see Section 1.1.3), which Australian courts are not bound to follow. Australian intermediate

---

106 *Hunter v Canary Wharf Ltd* [1997] AC 655, 703 (Lord Hoffmann). It is important to note that the Australian High Court has never before ruled on this principle. Thus, the persuasive precedent of the English House of Lords must be relied upon.

107 Note that a plaintiff may sue in respect of a continuing interference which existed prior to taking possession of the land: *Bliss v Hall* (1838) 132 ER 758.

108 *Malone v Laskey* [1907] 2 KB 141.

109 *Masters v Brent London Borough Council* [1978] QB 841.

110 *Nicholls v Ely Beet Sugar Factory Ltd* [1936] Ch 343.

111 An example of a common reversioner is someone who may have the title to the fee simple once a life interest has passed. Another is a lessor who has leased his or her premises.

112 *McCarty v North Sydney Municipal Council* (1918) 18 SR (NSW) 210.

113 *Colwell v St Pancras Borough Council* [1904] 1 Ch 707.

114 *Malone v Laskey* [1907] 2 KB 141; *Oldham v Lawson (No 1)* [1976] VR 654.

115 *Oldham v Lawson (No 1)* [1976] VR 654.

116 *Hunter v Canary Wharf Ltd* [1997] AC 655, 693 (Lord Goff).

courts have diverged on this issue, in some cases allowing mere licensees to bring a claim.[117] It is time the High Court made a ruling on the principles of standing to sue in nuisance, as this would clarify the rules applicable to Australian tort law.

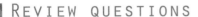

R EVIEW QUESTIONS

(1) Who can bring an action for private nuisance? Do they need to have an interest in the land?

(2) Does Australian tort law have its own unique principles of standing in private nuisance compared to those of the United Kingdom?

  Guided responses in the eBook

9.4   Who can be sued?

It was once thought that a person could only be sued in private nuisance if the unreasonable interference emanated from that person's land. The High Court overruled this principle in *Hargrave v Goldman*, holding that persons can be liable in nuisance even when they have no proprietary interest in the land on which they commit an interference.[118] Australian common law has since developed to create three categories of defendants who can be held liable when a private nuisance occurs: creators of a nuisance, those who authorise a nuisance, and those who adopt or continue a nuisance.

9.4.1   Creators of a nuisance

A person who creates a nuisance will be liable as a defendant. However, we have established that this person does not need to have any proprietary interest in the land on which the interference emanates. Thus, in *Fennell v Robson Excavations Pty Ltd*, a contractor working for the owner of land was held liable in private nuisance where its excavation work damaged the lateral support of the neighbouring plaintiff's land.[119] Essential to liability arising, however, is that the creator of the nuisance has some form of direct control over the activity that creates the unreasonable interference.[120] Where a defendant with a proprietary interest in land creates a nuisance on that land, the defendant will not be absolved of responsibility simply

---

117 *Bald Hills Wind Farm Pty Ltd v South Gippsland Shire Council* [2020] VSC 512, [12]–[14]; *Toll Transport Pty Ltd v National Union of Workers* [2012] VSC 316; cf *Hoxton Park Residents' Action Group Inc v Liverpool City Council* (2010) 178 LGERA 275.
118 (1963) 110 CLR 40, 60 (Windeyer J).
119 (1977) 2 NSWLR 486.
120 *Casley-Smith v FS Evans & Sons Pty Ltd (No 5)* (1988) 67 LGRA 108, 141.

by changing the nature of his or her interest.[121] Such a situation frequently arises where an owner-occupier of land creates a nuisance and then sells or leases the land to another, with the nuisance continuing, in the hope of avoiding responsibility for its consequences.[122]

9.4.2   Authorisation of a nuisance

The second category of persons that can be held liable as defendants are those who authorise a nuisance. Such authorisation commonly arises in a tenancy relationship, as a lessor who lets premises for a specific purpose that will naturally create a nuisance will be held liable if that nuisance occurs.[123] Examples of such liability include an owner-occupier who allowed gypsies to camp on his land,[124] and a landlord council which permitted its tenants to use the land for go-kart racing.[125] This principle is confined to circumstances in which the nuisance either has been *expressly* authorised or is certain to result from the *purposes* for which the property is let.[126] However, if the nuisance arises from the way in which the tenant uses the premises, rather than the purpose for which they have been let, the tenant will be liable and not the landlord.[127] Thus, it was held by the New South Wales Court of Appeal in *Wilkie v Blacktown City Council* that a lessor will not be liable for a lessee's nuisance if the purpose of the tenancy does not entail at least a high degree of probability that the tenants will create such a nuisance.[128] It is important to recognise, however, that in this example the liability is not vicarious.

An employer will be vicariously liable for a nuisance created by an employee in the course of employment.[129] There is also authority suggesting that an occupier will be liable for the acts of independent contractors where such work can be said to cause a foreseeable risk of harm.[130] Such a principle is premised upon the fact that owners and occupiers of premises owe a duty to their neighbours which they cannot delegate to independent contractors.[131] It has been applied to hold an occupier of premises liable when an independent contractor has removed the lateral support of neighbouring land[132] or allowed the escape of a fire.[133] However, the High Court in *Torette House Pty Ltd v Berkman* held that this principle is relatively narrow and an occupier will not be held liable if the independent contractor caused harm which was not a natural consequence of the contract of engagement.[134]

---

121 *Thompson v Gibson* (1841) 151 ER 845.
122 Even if such a fact situation arises, a lessee or purchaser could *also* be held liable: see Section 9.4.3.
123 *Harris v James* (1876) 45 LJ QB 545; *Jenkins v Jackson* (1888) 40 Ch D 71; *Sampson v Hodson-Pressinger* [1981] 3 All ER 710.
124 *Page Motors Ltd v Epsom and Ewell Borough Council* (1981) 80 LGR 337.
125 *Tetley v Chitty* [1986] 1 All ER 663.
126 *Rich v Basterfield* (1847) 4 CB 783; *Ayers v Hanson, Stanley & Prince* (1912) 56 SJ 735; *Smith v Scott* [1973] Ch 314.
127 *Sykes v Connolly* [1895] 11 WN (NSW) 145; *Hussain v Lancaster County Council* [2000] QB 1 (CA).
128 (2002) 121 LGERA 444, [81].
129 *Spicer v Smee* [1946] 1 All ER 489, 493 (Atkinson J).
130 *Bower v Peate* (1876) 1 QBD 321, 326.
131 See *Torette House Pty Ltd v Berkman* (1940) 62 CLR 637, 640–1, 646–7 (Latham CJ).
132 *Johns v Delaney* (1890) 16 VLR 729.
133 *McInnes v Wardle* (1931) 45 CLR 548.
134 *Torette House Pty Ltd v Berkman* (1940) 62 CLR 637, 647–8 (Latham CJ).

9.4.3   Adopting or continuing a nuisance

The final category of defendants that can be held liable are those who adopt or continue a nuisance. The difference between authorising a nuisance and adopting or continuing one is outlined in Table 9.2. A person will be liable for a nuisance he or she did not create where that person knew or ought to have known of the nuisance and did not remedy it.[135] For example, an occupier can be held liable for nuisances created by mere licensees[136] or if an occupier makes use of a nuisance created by the previous owner.[137] It is important to recognise, however, that the defendant in these circumstances will only be liable for the harm caused *after* he or she is said to have the requisite level of knowledge of the nuisance and failed to reasonably abate it.

Table 9.2   The difference between authorising a nuisance and adopting or continuing one

	Authorising a nuisance	Adopting or continuing a nuisance
Explanation	A defendant will be said to have authorised a nuisance where the nuisance has either been expressly authorised or is certain to result from the purposes of an agreement.	A defendant will have adopted or continued a nuisance where they knew or ought to have known of the nuisance but did not remedy it.
Examples	• An employer will have authorised a nuisance where an employee creates a nuisance in the course of his or her employment. • A lessor will have authorised a nuisance where the lessor expressly agrees in the lease agreement that the lessee can use the premises as an auction yard with high volumes of traffic and loud announcements, despite the fact that a local public school is situated next door.	• A lessor will have adopted a nuisance where, upon inspection of the property, it can be determined that the lessee has unjustifiably altered the stormwater drains so that all of the stormwater flows onto the property next door. • A person will have adopted a nuisance where, despite identifying the presence of bed bugs, the person fails to try and remove them thereby allowing them to move into the apartments below and above.

This principle was established by the English House of Lords in the landmark case of *Sedleigh-Denfield v O'Callaghan*[138] and adopted by the Australian High Court in *Goldman v Hargrave*.[139] In *Goldman*, the defendant's tree caught on fire after being struck by lightning and naturally created a nuisance. However, when the defendant saw the burning tree and gained knowledge of the nuisance, instead of dousing the flames with water, he left it to burn itself out and thus adopted the nuisance. He was therefore held liable for the damage that ensued when the fire spread to neighbouring properties.

The High Court identified that liability in this category will ultimately turn on two elements: first, whether (and when) the person has, or should have, knowledge of the

---

135   *Sedleigh-Denfield v O'Callaghan* [1940] AC 880, 897 (Lord Atkin).
136   *Page Motors Ltd v Epsom and Ewell Borough Council* (1981) 80 LGR 337.
137   *Sedleigh-Denfield v O'Callaghan* [1940] AC 880.
138   Ibid.
139   (1963) 110 CLR 40.

nuisance; and second, whether the person has allowed the nuisance to continue without taking reasonably prompt and efficient means for its abatement.[140] When considering this second element, the Privy Council in *Goldman v Hargrave* held that an objective test in the subjective circumstances of the defendant is to be used:

> In such situations the standard ought to be to require of the occupier what it is reasonable to expect of him in his *individual circumstances*. Thus, less must be expected of the infirm than of the able bodied: the owner of a small property where a hazard arises which threatens a neighbour with substantial interests should not have to do so much as one with larger interests of his own at stake and greater resources to protect them: if the small owner does what he can and promptly calls on his neighbour to provide additional resources, he may be held to have done his duty: he should not be liable unless it is clearly proved that he could, and reasonably in his individual circumstance should, have done more.[141]

The particular circumstances of the defendant must therefore be taken into account when assessing the reasonableness of the defendant's actions in abating the nuisance.

REVIEW QUESTIONS

(1) Who can be sued in the tort of private nuisance?

(2) Can a plaintiff sue all three types of defendants, or is the plaintiff limited to suing just one type?

 Guided responses in the eBook

9.5   Unprotected interests

The tort of private nuisance protects the use and enjoyment of land from unreasonable interference. Given the ambiguity in what constitutes the 'use and enjoyment of land', there has been significant debate over what rights the tort protects. As a result, some interests have been left unprotected.

9.5.1   The right of support

Interference with the natural right to support of land is actionable in private nuisance. As such, an owner of land has the right to have their land supported by the land of their neighbour, and any removal of lateral support from land will be actionable.[142] However, this right is restricted to the land being supported while it is in its natural state, meaning that the

---

140 Ibid.
141 (1966) 115 CLR 458, 467 (Lord Wilberforce) (emphasis added).
142 *Pantalone v Alaouie* (1989) 18 NSWLR 119.

right to the support of buildings or any structures on the land is therefore not protected.[143] This means that if the land beneath a building subsides due to some action of the defendant, the defendant will only be liable if the land would have subsided had it been in its natural state (ie, had it not been built upon).[144] As McHugh JA put it in *Kebewar Pty Ltd v Harkin*, if the land subsided because of the additional weight of the buildings, then the plaintiff will not have a right to support and no action in nuisance will lie.[145]

9.5.2   The right to a view and aesthetic appearance

The tort of private nuisance will not give a plaintiff a remedy if the defendant has obstructed a pleasing view from the plaintiff's premises.[146] However, if the construction of the building is unlawful, then a private nuisance will have occurred.[147]

A further development that has caused serious debate[148] across the common law jurisdictions of Australia, the United Kingdom, the United States and Canada is whether the aesthetic values of plaintiffs can be protected. Courts in the United States and Canada have refused to recognise aesthetic nuisances as, in the words of the California Court of Appeal, 'the essence of a private nuisance is interference with the use and enjoyment of land and unpleasant appearance alone does not interfere with such a right'.[149] The Australian common law developed in a different direction when Fox J, in *Kent v Cavanagh*, held in obiter dicta that a building that is aesthetically displeasing could constitute a nuisance.[150] While there is contrasting authority which suggests that an unsightly building alone is not enough to constitute a nuisance,[151] unreasonable interference is a combination of a totality of factors and therefore a displeasing building combined with other factors such as malice or the circumstances of the locality could arguably constitute a private nuisance in Australia.

9.5.3   The right of privacy

Another contentious issue in the law of private nuisance is whether the tort will protect a plaintiff's enjoyment of privacy in his or her own home. It has long been established in Australian law that private nuisance does not give a plaintiff freedom from the view and inspection of neighbouring occupiers or of other persons.[152] This principle was developed to hold that an occupier of property is also not protected from being photographed by someone outside the property.[153] Furthermore, in the English case of *Bernstein v Skyviews & General Ltd*,[154] the English High Court held that there was no actionable nuisance when an

---

143   *Kebewar Pty Ltd v Harkin* (1987) 9 NSWLR 738.
144   *Walker v Adelaide City Corporation* (2004) 88 SASR 225, [256]–[259].
145   (1987) 9 NSWLR 738, 743.
146   *Phipps v Pears* [1965] 1 QB 76.
147   *Campbell v Paddington Corporation* [1911] 1 KB 869.
148   See R Coletta, 'The Case for Aesthetic Nuisance' (1987) 48(1) *Ohio State Law Journal* 141.
149   *Oliver v AT&T Wireless Services*, 76 Cal App 4th, 524 (1999) 534.
150   (1973) 1 ACTR 43 (SC).
151   See *Bathurst City Council v Saban (No 2)* (1986) 58 LGRA 201.
152   *Victoria Park Racing & Recreation Grounds Co Ltd v Taylor* (1937) 58 CLR 479, 507 (Dixon J).
153   *Bathurst City Council v Saban* (1985) 2 NSWLR 704.
154   [1978] 1 QB 479.

aerial photographer photographed the plaintiff's private country estate. There is, however, obiter dicta holding that constant videotaping of a property by cameras using a bright light may constitute a private nuisance.[155] It is likely that the protection of privacy through the tort of nuisance or the development of a common law tort of invasion of personal privacy will only continue to grow as technology develops.[156]

Case: *Raciti v Hughes* (1995) 7 BPR 14,837

Facts

The plaintiffs' and the defendants' properties adjoined one another. The defendants decided to install on their property floodlights and camera surveillance equipment, for the very purpose of illuminating the plaintiffs' adjoining backyard. This was so the defendants could videotape what occurred in the plaintiffs' yard.

The floodlight system would be activated by a sensor, which switched on the lights and recording camera in response to movement or noise, such as activity in the backyard or a dog barking. The plaintiffs became distressed about using their backyard, and due to the constant floodlights, they could not sleep. They sued the defendants in private nuisance.

Issue

The primary issue in the case was whether the invasion of the plaintiffs' privacy amounted to an actionable private nuisance.

Decision

Young J in the New South Wales Supreme Court held that there was an actionable nuisance. He agreed with the plaintiffs' submission that the categories of nuisance are never closed, and held first that the floodlights, in themselves, constituted a nuisance. His Honour then went on to distinguish the case from *Bathurst City Council v Saban (No 2)* (1986) 58 LGRA 201, based on the fact that the defendants' actions were 'a deliberate attempt to snoop on the privacy of a neighbour and to record that on video tape'. Thus, it can be argued that the tort of private nuisance will only protect the privacy of plaintiffs where the actions of a defendant are for the very purpose of disturbing the privacy of the plaintiff. Ultimately, Young J awarded the plaintiffs an injunction preventing the defendants from using the floodlights and surveillance cameras.

Significance

This case is authority for the principle that, in certain circumstances, the tort of private nuisance can be used to protect privacy interests.

---

155 See *Raciti v Hughes* (1995) 7 BPR 14,837, relied on by Kunc J in *Au v Berlach* (2022) 20 BPR 42,231, [117].

156 A Lerch, 'The Judicial Law-Making Function and a Tort of Invasion of Personal Privacy' (2021) 43(2) *Sydney Law Review* 133, 146.

Question

What is the distinguishing factor behind the different outcomes in *Bernstein v Skyviews & General Ltd* and *Raciti v Hughes*?

 Guided response in the eBook

REVIEW QUESTIONS

(1) To what extent is a right to support of land protected by Australian nuisance law?

(2) When will the tort of private nuisance protect a plaintiff's privacy?

 Guided responses in the eBook

9.6 Defences

9.6.1 Prescription

If a defendant can establish that his or her interference amounted to an easement by prescription, the defendant will have a defence to private nuisance.[157] Such a right of prescription can only be established if the defendant has committed the interference *as of right* for more than 20 years and the plaintiff, or a previous title holder, could have taken action to sue for actionable nuisance but failed to do so.[158] For the nuisance to be as of right, it must not be exercised by violence, or secretly or by stealth, or by permission asked from time to time, on each occasion or even on many occasions of using it.[159] However, this does not mean that the plaintiff (or previous occupiers) are required to have actual knowledge of the nuisance. Rather, as was put by Lord Neuberger in *Lawrence v Fen Tigers Ltd*, the essential question will be whether the nature and degree of the activity of the defendant, taken as a whole, should make a reasonable person in the position of the plaintiff aware that a continuous right to enjoyment is being asserted and ought to be challenged if it is intended to be resisted.[160] Thus, the time period will commence once a reasonable person would have become so aware.

---

157 But not public nuisance: see *Hulley v Silver Springs Bleaching & Dyeing Co* [1992] 2 Ch 268.
158 *Sturges v Bridgman* (1879) 11 Ch D 852.
159 *Fernance v Simpson* [2003] NSWSC 121.
160 *Lawrence v Fen Tigers Ltd* [2014] AC 822, [142].

HINTS AND TIPS

For a defendant to establish an easement by prescription is quite difficult, and the defendant making such a claim must show very particular circumstances have arisen in order to rely on this in relation to a claim in nuisance. It is essential for you to understand and verify all of the relevant circumstances when asserting that a prescriptive easement has arisen.

Consider the example of a car-washing business which causes water to run across a neighbouring parcel of land. This may be found to be a nuisance, as the water indirectly interferes with the ability of the neighbouring land to be used and enjoyed. For the car-washing business to defend an action in nuisance by way of establishing an easement by prescription, it is first necessary for the offensive behaviour – namely, the flowing of water onto the neighbouring land – to have occurred for more than 20 years. Second, it is necessary that the car wash owner did not do anything to hide the offensive behaviour, and they also must not have threatened or coerced the neighbour into allowing the behaviour. Additionally, the car wash owner must not have made attempts to obtain permission; they must have continuously acted as if they have the right to use the easement throughout the period. Lastly, it will be fatal to proving this defence if the neighbouring property owner at any time prior to the 20 years elapsing makes efforts to enforce their property rights or to request that the offensive behaviour be stopped.[161] Only if the car wash owner can establish that none of these things have occurred, will they then be able to successfully argue that an easement has arisen by prescription.

9.6.2 Statutory authorisation

Many activities that interfere with the use and enjoyment of land are authorised by statute. In 1912, Isaacs J in the High Court in *Nielsen v Brisbane Tramways Co Ltd* held that if Parliament has authorised something which, after all reasonable care is taken, creates a nuisance, then Parliament must be taken to have authorised a nuisance to that extent.[162] This decision was the inception of the statutory authorisation defence in Australia. It exemplifies the 'live and let live' principle, as it recognises that certain activities are essential for the running of a sophisticated society and cannot be carried out without creating some sort of nuisance.

The defence pivots on the proper construction of the statute and whether the damage that arises from the exercise of the powers is intra vires ('within the powers authorised by') the statute.[163] The defendant bears the burden of proving this on the balance of probabilities.[164] As was propounded by the Western Australian Court of Appeal in *Southern Properties (WA)*

---

161 *Fernance v Simpson* [2003] NSWSC 121.
162 (1912) 14 CLR 354.
163 This includes delegated legislation: *Gillingham Borough Council v Medway (Chatham) Dock Co Ltd* [1993] QB 343.
164 *Manchester Corporation v Farnworth* [1930] AC 171.

Pty Ltd v Executive Director, Department of Conservation and Land Management, there are two steps that must be considered to determine whether the defence should be applied.[165]

First, it must be asked what duty is imposed on the defendant by the statute.[166] This will set up the framework for the following analysis. Most importantly, the distinction between a statute which requires an activity to be carried out, or a statute which merely permits an activity to be carried out, must be identified.

Second, it must be asked whether the creation of the nuisance is authorised by the statutory duty.[167] However, the question of authorisation is determined by whether the statutory provision requires an activity to be carried out or simply permits such activity.[168]

If the activity is *required* to be carried out by the statute, then any nuisance resulting from the activity will be authorised unless it is caused by negligence.[169] Thus, the specified activity must be performed with reasonable care.[170] In assessing whether there has been negligence, the courts consider whether the authorised activity could have been done in a different manner so that the nuisance, or the extent of the nuisance, could have been mitigated.[171] For example, a statute requires the state government to run a train service. Although the government was given such authorisation, it would be an actionable nuisance if the authority in charge of the service decided to save funds by omitting to put noise reducers on the trains, particularly those that ran at night. There is clearly a reasonable alternative to reduce the effect of such a nuisance, meaning that the interference is still actionable.

If, however, the statute only *permits* the activity to be carried out, then the defendant must prove not only that the activity was carried out with reasonable care, but also that *a nuisance* was an *inevitable consequence* of the performance of the statutory duty, in order for the defence to apply.[172] This is a more stringent test that focuses on the decisions relating to whether, when or how to undertake the authorised activity. In *Melaleuca Estate Pty Ltd v Port Stephens Council*, the plaintiff sued the local council defendant after it carried out drainage works that caused the total amount of stormwater from all of the surrounding properties to be discharged onto the plaintiff's land.[173] The Council relied on s 241 of the *Local Government Act 1919* (NSW) as its defence, which stated that 'for the purpose of draining or protecting any public road any Council may ... make, open, cleanse and keep open any ditch, gutter, tunnel, drain or watercourse'.

The New South Wales Court of Appeal found that there was an actionable nuisance.[174] It held that the Council had designed and constructed a piping system that effectively drained the area, and committed no negligence. However, it found that the performance of the statutory power as outlined in s 241 did not have the inevitable consequence of creating a

---

165 (2012) 42 WAR 287.
166 Ibid [121].
167 *Bankstown City Council v Alamdo Holdings Pty Ltd* (2005) 223 CLR 660; [2005] HCA 46.
168 *Southern Properties (WA) Pty Ltd v Executive Director, Department of Conservation and Land Management* (2012) 42 WAR 287, [121].
169 Ibid [122].
170 *Brodie v Singleton Shire Council* (2001) 206 CLR 512, 577.
171 *Benning v Wong* (1969) 122 CLR 249, 325.
172 *Southern Properties (WA) Pty Ltd v Executive Director, Department of Conservation and Land Management* (2012) 42 WAR 287, [123].
173 (2006) 143 LGERA 319.
174 Ibid [59].

discharge of polluted water directly onto the plaintiff's land, thus resulting in a nuisance.[175] Therefore, as the nuisance created by the Council was not an inevitable consequence of the performance of the statutory duty imposed on it, the statutory authorisation defence could not apply.

Case: *Southern Properties (WA) Pty Ltd v Executive Director, Department of Conservation and Land Management* (2012) 42 WAR 287

Facts

The plaintiff owned a winery, in which they grew grapes to make wine. In March and April of 2014, the Western Australian Department of Conservation and Land Management (the defendant) conducted a prescribed burn of the Warren National Park in order to prevent bushfires. Smoke from the burn tainted the plaintiff's grapes, causing a loss of $620 000. The plaintiff sued, inter alia, in private nuisance and negligence.

In the Western Australian Supreme Court, Murphy J found in favour of the defendant. His Honour held that the defendant did not owe a general duty of care in negligence to avoid smoke damage to the plaintiff's grapes. His Honour did not, however, consider whether the defendant was liable in nuisance.

Issue

One of the primary issues in the case was whether the defendant could rely upon the statutory authorisation defence. Section 57 of the *Conservation and Land Management Act 1984* (WA) provided that the defendant must follow the proposed management plan that is published in the Gazette. The approved management plan required the defendant to conduct a fire management plan, which included the annual undertaking of back-burning.

Section 132 then provided:

(1) A person does not incur civil liability for anything done by the person in good faith in, or in connection with, the performance or purported performance of functions under this Act or the *Wildlife Conservation Act 1950*.

(2) The State is also relieved of any civil liability for anything done or omitted to be done in good faith in, or in connection with, the performance or purported performance of a function under this Act or the *Wildlife Conservation Act 1950* in relation to preventing, managing or *controlling fire on land* to which this Act applies, section 8A land or section 8C land.[176]

Decision

The Western Australian Court of Appeal held in favour of the respondent (defendant). Giving the leading judgment, McLure P held that when considering whether the statutory authorisation

---

175 Ibid [60]–[61].
176 Emphasis added.

defence applies, a distinction must be made between statutory provisions that require an activity to be carried out and a provision that permits an activity to be carried out:

- If a statutory provision requires a specified activity to be carried out, the defendant need not prove that the nuisance created was an inevitable consequence of the activity. The nuisance will be authorised so long as the activity was performed with reasonable care.
- If a statutory provision permits an activity to be carried out, the defendant must prove that the nuisance created was an inevitable consequence of the activity and it was performed with reasonable care.

McLure P then reasoned that as the back-burning of the National Park was required by s 57 of the *Conservation and Land Management Act 1984* (WA), all that needed to be proven by the defendant was that it performed such an activity with reasonable care. This was satisfied on the evidence, and thus the statutory authorisation defence applied.

Significance

The case is significant as it is authority for the two following propositions: (1) If a statutory provision requires a specified activity to be carried out, the defendant need not prove that the nuisance created was an inevitable consequence of the activity. The nuisance will be authorised so long as the activity was performed with reasonable care. (2) If a statutory provision permits an activity to be carried out, the defendant must prove that the nuisance created was an inevitable consequence of the activity and it was performed with reasonable care.

Notes

This case demonstrates that the statutory authorisation defence is premised on identifying whether a statutory provision requires a specific activity to be carried out, or simply permits such an activity. It is therefore essential that such a distinction is made when applying the defence.

Question

Would the reasoning in this case have been different if the statute merely permitted the back-burning to be carried out?

    Guided response in the eBook

9.6.3   Non-defences

9.6.3.1   Coming to the nuisance

The consent of the plaintiff, by word or deed, to an action which amounts to a nuisance will operate as a defence.[177] At common law, an action in nuisance can be defeated if the plaintiff consented or acquiesced to the existence of the nuisance. However, 'coming to

---

177 *Kiddle v City Business Properties Ltd* (1942) 1 KB 269; *Leakey v National Trust for Places of Historic Interest or Natural Beauty* [1980] QB 485, 515 (Megaw LJ), followed in *Ozibar Pty Ltd v Laroar Holdings Pty Ltd (No 2)* [2016] QSC 82, especially at [272].

a nuisance' is not capable of providing a defence to a nuisance claim.[178] What this means is that it is no defence to claim that the plaintiff had come to occupy premises which he or she knew may be affected by the defendant's nuisance, and therefore should be required to live with it. For example, in *Champagne View Pty Ltd v Shearwater Resort Management Pty Ltd* the defendant owner of a golf course had operated for many years without there being an issue with golf balls often flying into neighbouring properties. When the plaintiff moved into a unit next door to the golf course in 1997, she found that almost 30 golf balls a day intruded into her property and seriously interfered with her physical health and mental wellbeing. Gillard J in the Victorian Supreme Court held that a nuisance had been committed irrespective of the fact that the nuisance had been committed in the location for many years and no other neighbour had made a claim for private nuisance.[179]

9.6.3.2   Nuisance due to numerous independent acts

It is no defence to a nuisance to assert that it was created by the independent acts of different persons. This principle was established in *Thorpe v Brumfitt*, where the English Court of Appeal held that if more than one person contributes to a nuisance, all are individually liable even if the contribution of any one of them would be insufficient on its own to constitute a nuisance.[180] Australian courts have since adopted the principle.[181] For example, in *Bonnici v Kur-ring-gai Municipal Council*, the plaintiff sued the local council for private nuisance due to the fact that stormwater from various neighbours' properties could only flow onto the plaintiff's property. Sperling J in the Supreme Court of New South Wales applied the principle in *Thorpe* to hold that while the amount of stormwater from the various properties was the usual amount that flowed onto neighbouring lands individually and did not constitute a nuisance, the aggregate stormwater incursion onto the plaintiff's property constituted a nuisance.[182]

R E V I E W   Q U E S T I O N S

(1)   What is, and what is not, a defence to private nuisance?

(2)   Does the statutory authorisation defence apply differently if a statute merely permits an activity to take place, rather than requires that such an activity be undertaken?

   Guided responses in the eBook

---

178   *Bliss v Hall* (1838) 132 ER 758; *Miller v Jackson* [1977] QB 966, 986–7.
179   *Champagne View Pty Ltd v Shearwater Resort Management Pty Ltd* [2000] VSC 214, [60]–[63].
180   *Thorpe v Brumfitt* (1873) 8 Ch App 650, 656.
181   See, eg, *Westfield Management Ltd v Perpetual Trustee Co Ltd* (2007) 233 CLR 528; [2007] HCA 45; *Plumpton Park Developments Pty Ltd v SAS Trustee Corporation* (2018) 19 BPR 38,531.
182   *Bonnici v Kur-ring-gai Municipal Council* (2001) 121 LGERA 1, [197].

9.7   Remoteness of damage

If a plaintiff can show that a defendant has unreasonably interfered with the plaintiff's use and enjoyment of his or her land, the plaintiff is prima facie entitled to an injunction.[183] However, if the plaintiff seeks damages for the harm he or she has suffered, it must also be proven that the harm caused by the interference was reasonably foreseeable. This principle was established by the English House of Lords,[184] and was relatively adopted by the New South Wales Court of Appeal in *Gales Holdings Pty Ltd v Tweed Shire Council*.[185] In that case, the local council had constructed new stormwater drains which consequentially led stormwater to run onto the plaintiff's land and to pool there. In an unusual turn of events, a colony of Wallum froglets, an endangered species, built a habitat on the plaintiff's land. When the plaintiff later sought to develop its land, it was prohibited from doing so due to the *Threatened Species Conservation Act 1995* (NSW).

The plaintiff therefore sued the defendant in private nuisance. The plaintiff claimed for injunctive relief, to prevent further stormwater being released onto its land, and for $600000 in damages due to the fact that the value of the land had now been significantly reduced. The New South Wales Court of Appeal held that a private nuisance had been committed.[186] However, while it granted the injunctive relief, it refused to award damages. The Court first distinguished between nuisance and damage occasioned by the nuisance:

> It is important to draw a distinction between the nuisance, on the one hand, and the damage occasioned by the nuisance, on the other. The nuisance was the channelling of stormwater runoff onto the land. The damage was the wetting up of the land. The channelling was an unreasonable interference from when it began … Whether and when that nuisance occasioned damage to [the plaintiff] is a different question.[187]

After making this distinction, the Court held that damages will only be awarded in private nuisance if the damage suffered by the plaintiff due to the defendant's nuisance is reasonably foreseeable.[188] Thus, the relevant issue was whether the Council could reasonably foresee that the consequence of continuing the nuisance, after the construction of the drains, would be that a habitat for a *protected* species (rather than any species) might be established. The Court ultimately held that the population of such a species due to the nuisance was not reasonably foreseeable.[189]

This case analysis demonstrates that remoteness of damage is not a factor to be taken into account at the unreasonable interference stage. Rather, it must only be considered if the plaintiff intends to seek damages for the defendant's nuisance. Damages will only be awarded if the harm suffered by the plaintiff was a reasonably foreseeable consequence of the defendant's nuisance. Alternatively, injunctive relief will almost always be available.

---

183 See *Gales Holdings Pty Ltd v Tweed Shire Council* (2013) 85 NSWLR 514, [174], [272]; *Lawrence v Fen Tigers Ltd* [2014] AC 822, [121] (Lord Neuberger).
184 See *Cambridge Water Co v Eastern Counties Leather plc* [1994] 2 AC 264.
185 (2013) 85 NSWLR 514.
186 Ibid [165] (Emmett JA).
187 Ibid [213] (Emmett JA).
188 Ibid [142]–[144] (Emmett JA).
189 Ibid [259] (Emmett JA).

REVIEW QUESTIONS

(1) Is remoteness of damage considered when establishing the elements of the tort of private nuisance or when assessing whether the plaintiff should be awarded damages?

(2) What is the remoteness test that must be satisfied for damages to be awarded in the tort of nuisance?

 Guided responses in the eBook

9.8   Relationship with other torts

9.8.1   Private nuisance and public nuisance

A private nuisance protects plaintiffs from interference with the use and enjoyment of their *private* land. It thus requires the plaintiff to have some sort of interest in the land which is interfered with. In contrast, public nuisance (discussed in Section 9.9) occurs when a public right is interfered with. While public nuisance is generally a public crime, if a plaintiff can show that he or she has suffered particular damage, then that plaintiff will be able to sue using the civil tort of public nuisance, even if none of his or her rights or privileges in land were invaded.

The distinction between the two torts was exemplified in *Tate & Lyle Industries v Greater London Council*.[190] In that case, the defendant built ferry terminals on the Thames, which later caused silting and prevented large ships accessing the claimant's jetty. As a result, the claimant had to dredge the channels in the river to make the jetty usable again, costing it £540000. The House of Lords dismissed the action in private nuisance on the ground that as the jetty itself was unaffected, the claimant's private rights in it had not been unreasonably interfered with. However, the House went on to hold that the silting had caused interference with the public right of navigation. The fact that the claimant had suffered particular damage, through having to expend money in order to use this public right, was sufficient to establish the tort of public nuisance.

It is important to recognise, however, that public and private nuisances do not represent mutually exclusive dichotomies.[191] For example, in picketing cases the interference sometimes occurs on a public roadway, preventing entry onto premises.[192] But the picketing also interferes with the plaintiff's right to use its property by entering and leaving it as it pleases. Thus, the interference of the pickets can give rise to a public and private nuisance.

---

190 [1983] 2 AC 509.
191 *Shogunn Investments Pty Ltd v Public Transport Authority of Western Australia* [2016] WASC 42, [106]. See also *Yakult Australia Pty Ltd v National Union of Workers* [2018] VSC 151.
192 *Shogunn Investments Pty Ltd v Public Transport Authority of Western Australia* [2016] WASC 42, [105].

9.8.2   Private nuisance and negligence

The tort of nuisance remains distinct from the tort of negligence.[193] As discussed earlier, a consideration of reasonableness in nuisance examines whether the defendant's interference and its consequences were reasonable, according to the ordinary usage of those living in that society. On the other hand, a consideration of reasonableness in negligence looks at whether the defendant has taken all the proper and reasonable steps to mitigate a risk of harm. Furthermore, the tort of nuisance will protect plaintiffs against substantial interference with enjoyment of their land – for example, from toxic fumes, noise and offensive businesses. In contrast, the tort of negligence will never protect the 'amenity' of an occupier, as the tort does not recognise that type of harm (eg, toxic fumes and smells) as 'damage'.

But this is not to say that liability in nuisance and liability in negligence are completely distinct. Rather, the torts overlap.[194] A common example of this is a lateral support case. In such cases, if a defendant excavator working on land next door to the plaintiff carelessly removes the *natural* lateral support from the plaintiff's land (see Section 9.5.1), the plaintiff can sue in either nuisance or negligence for the damage. This is because the defendant owes both a duty of care in the negligence sense to perform its excavation duties properly and with reasonable care, and also owes a duty not to unreasonably interfere with the use and enjoyment of the plaintiff's land. If, however, the defendant had, with all due care and skill, excavated the land and still removed the lateral support of the plaintiff's land, the plaintiff would continue to have an action in nuisance given that its use of the land was unreasonably interfered with.

A defendant can be found liable in both negligence and nuisance. In *Prestage v Barrett*, the Tasmanian Supreme Court found two defendants liable in negligence and nuisance for losses caused by the 2013 Forcett bushfire, which burnt 25 520 hectares of land and resulted in damage to the properties of 400 plaintiffs.[195] The finding of negligence was based on a campfire lit in a tree stump and not fully extinguished, which reignited and the bushfire spread to surrounding areas.[196] The Supreme Court of Tasmania found that the harm was reasonably foreseeable and that the failure of the defendants to abate the harm amounted to fault.[197] The Court found that occupiers of land have a non-delegable duty of care regarding hazardous actions carried out on their property.[198] As in any fact scenario where multiple torts can arise, it will be up to the discretion of counsel to determine which cause of action should be made out, depending on the reasonable prospects of success. It is likely that where the facts make out a cause of action in nuisance and negligence, the action in nuisance should be preferred given that the tort will avoid most of the restrictions outlined in the civil liability legislation.

---

193 *Prestage v Barrett* [2021] TASSC 27, [713].
194 *Miller v Jackson* [1977] QB 966, 985–6 (Geoffrey Lane LJ).
195 *Prestage v Barrett* [2021] TASSC 27, [5]–[6].
196 Ibid [82], [111], [673]
197 Ibid [743].
198 Ibid [637].

9.8.3   Nuisance and trespass to land

As discussed in Section 9.1, nuisance and trespass are separate torts that do not intertwine. Trespass will be established where an intentional or negligent act *directly* interferes with the plaintiff's land. Nuisance, on the other hand, will only be established where the intentional or negligent act *consequentially* causes an unreasonable interference.

REVIEW QUESTIONS

(1)   What is the difference between private and public nuisance?

(2)   Can a plaintiff sue in both private nuisance and negligence?

 Guided responses in the eBook

9.9   Public nuisance

Nuisances are divided into two categories: public and private. A public nuisance is a common law crime,[199] while a private nuisance is a tort. A public nuisance is one that affects the reasonable comfort and convenience of a class of the public who come within its interference.[200] The effect of a public nuisance being widespread and indiscriminate, action is usually taken by the Attorney-General on behalf of all citizens.[201] However, as we will see later, specific individuals can establish civil liability for the special or particular damage suffered by them due to a public nuisance.

Public nuisances are generally those that interfere with a public space. For example, it is a public nuisance to pollute water to make it unfit for consumption,[202] obstruct a highway[203] or waterway,[204] make false bomb threats in a crowded building,[205] or even for an authority which owns a public park to interfere with it so substantially that it undermines the public's ability to enjoy it as a park.[206] There are two advantages to employing the tort of public nuisance over private nuisance. First, a plaintiff need not establish an interest in the land on which the interference has occurred. And second, as we will see, there is authority suggesting that a plaintiff will be entitled to damages for personal injury in public nuisance.

To make out *civil liability* for the tort of public nuisance, two elements must be satisfied: unreasonable and substantial interference; and special or particular damage.

---

199   *R v Rimmington* [2006] 1 AC 459. Note, however, that there is ambiguity about whether the crime exists in Criminal Code states and territories, given that the Code is said to replace the common law.

200   *A-G v PYA Quarries Ltd* [1957] 2 QB 169, 184.

201   Ibid 190 (Denning LJ); *Baulkham Hills Shire Council v Domachuk* (1988) 66 LGRA 110, 122.

202   *R v Medley* (1834) 172 ER 1246.

203   *Smith v Warringah Shire* (1961) 79 WN (NSW) 436; *Walsh v Ervin* [1952] VLR 361.

204   *York Brothers (Trading) Pty Ltd v Commissioner of Main Roads* (1983) 1 NSWLR 391.

205   *R v Madden* [1975] 3 All ER 155.

9.9.1   Unreasonable and substantial interference

First, as with private nuisance, a public nuisance will only be made out where it can be said that the interference it creates is substantial and unreasonable. This is determined by applying the same principles and undertaking the same balancing task as in private nuisance. However, unlike private nuisance, such an interference will only be substantial if it affects the reasonable comfort and convenience of the life of a class of the public who come within the scope of its operation.[207] In *Attorney-General v PYA Quarries Ltd*, the Attorney-General sued the defendant owner of a quarry, due to the fact that its operations sent stones falling over the neighbourhood, caused loud noise throughout the day and night, and generated serious levels of dust that affected the health of members of the local town. The defendant argued that as the interference only affected a few local residents, if it was a nuisance at all, it was only a private one. The English Queen's Bench held that the interference was certainly a public nuisance, but declined to create a rule outlining how many people must be affected in order for the nuisance to be substantial. Rather, it stated that the question of whether the number of persons affected is sufficient to constitute a class is one of fact in every case.[208]

The House of Lords later attempted to clarify this point in *R v Rimmington*.[209] In that case, the defendant had sent 538 separate postal packages containing racially offensive material to different recipients. The House held that in order to be a substantial interference, the act or omission must be likely to inflict significant injury on a substantial section of the public exercising their ordinary rights.[210] It reasoned that because the packages caused injury to separate individuals rather than the community or a significant section of it as a whole, a substantial interference *with the public* could not be made out, and the plaintiff's claim failed.[211] This reasoning demonstrates that it is crucial to establish that a representative cross-section of a class of people has been *contemporaneously* interfered with in order for a public nuisance to be made out.

9.9.2   Special or particular damage

The second element of public nuisance, which is crucial to establishing civil liability, is that the plaintiff must have suffered special damage *different or greater than* that suffered by the public at large.[212] For example, if a defendant spilled a pollutant into drinking water, a plaintiff would not be able to sue for the mere fact that he or she could no longer drink the water just like the rest of the public. If, however, the plaintiff drank the water presuming it to be safe and later suffered an illness, this special damage would entitle the plaintiff to a civil claim in public nuisance to be compensated for that special loss.

If the plaintiff's injury is simply identical to that of the public, no civil action can be brought for public nuisance. Thus, in *Winterbottom v Lord Derby* it was held that in a case where a public highway is obstructed, a plaintiff cannot sue in public nuisance if the only

---

206   *Kent v Johnson* (1972) 21 FLR 177.
207   *A-G v PYA Quarries Ltd* [1957] 2 QB 169, 184.
208   Ibid.
209   [2006] 1 AC 459.
210   Ibid [36] (Lord Bingham).
211   Ibid [37]–[39].
212   *Walsh v Ervin* [1952] VLR 361, 368.

damage she suffered was being delayed on a few occasions, like the rest of the public.[213] The rationale for this rule is that it prevents indeterminate liability; if anyone was allowed to sue, 500 might do so and this would lead to a severe penalty being placed on the defendant. Thus, for the most part, an action in public nuisance is brought on behalf of the public by the Attorney-General.

The particular damage that must be suffered by a plaintiff need not be physical damage; it includes interference with the enjoyment of land, such as interference due to noxious fumes or even general damage due to inconvenience and delay.[214] There is authority in Queensland, however, which suggests that pure economic loss, in certain circumstances, may not be sufficient to constitute 'special' damage.[215] Furthermore, a plaintiff need not have any property interest in order to sue. Thus, in *Castle v St Augustine's Links Ltd*, the plaintiff was able to recover damages in public nuisance when he was hit by a golf ball on a public road.[216] While the general public's enjoyment of the use of the road was interfered with, the plaintiff could sue because he had suffered particular personal injury.

A final point to note about public nuisance is that the High Court of Australia has recognised that a plaintiff's personal injury will suffice as 'special' damage. In *Cartwright v McLaine & Long Pty Ltd*, the plaintiff suffered personal injury as a result of slipping on oil which had spilt onto a footpath which was opposite a derelict service station.[217] The High Court held that a public nuisance had been committed, but the defendant was not liable for other reasons.[218] It can therefore be suggested that the restrictions of the civil liability legislation on establishing liability in negligence for personal injury could be avoided by framing an action in public nuisance, rather than negligence.[219]

Case: *Ball v Consolidated Rutile Ltd* [1991] 1 Qd R 524

Facts

The plaintiffs were licensed professional fishermen who fished in Moreton Bay in Queensland. They were permitted to use nets to take prawns for commercial fishing. The defendant conducted sand mining operations on North Stradbroke Island, situated in Moreton Bay.

In the course of its operations, the defendant formed a sand dune on the Island. However, on 22 March 1982, a part of this artificial sand dune crumbled and slipped into the waters of Moreton Bay, dispersing 114000 cubic metres of sand and other types of sand dune vegetation. After the slippage, tidal currents carried the sand mass into the waters of Moreton Bay. As a result, when the plaintiffs attempted to fish in the water, their fishing gear was damaged.

---

213 (1867) LR 2 Ex 316.
214 *Walsh v Ervin* [1952] VLR 361, 371 (Sholl J).
215 See *Ball v Consolidated Rutile Ltd* [1991] 1 Qd R 524.
216 (1922) 38 TLR 615.
217 (1979) 143 CLR 549.
218 Ibid 557 (Gibbs ACJ). See also *New South Wales v Tyszyk* [2008] NSWCA 107.
219 Note, however, that the High Court has subsumed the tort of public nuisance in relation to highway maintenance by a local council with the tort of negligence: *Brodie v Singleton Shire Council* (2001) 206 CLR 512; [2001] HCA 29.

The plaintiffs sued the defendant in negligence and public nuisance. They sought compensation not only for the damage done to their fishing gear, but also for the pure economic loss they suffered due to the lost catches of prawns because they were unable to fish in Moreton Bay.

Issue

One of the primary issues in the case was whether the pure economic loss suffered by the plaintiffs constituted 'special' damage and therefore found an action in public nuisance.

Decision

Ambrose J in the Queensland Supreme Court held that pure economic loss did not constitute special damage, and thus the plaintiffs could not found an action in public nuisance to be compensated for this loss.

Ambrose J held (at [547]) that the consequential damage to the plaintiffs' commercial fishing gear was enough to establish particular damage:

> The damage to the plaintiffs' fishing gear amounting to nearly $40 000 would be sufficiently particular to enable them to recover that damage if the deposition of the material in Moreton Bay as a result of the slippage of the dune constituted a public nuisance.

His Honour then went on to find, however, that the pure economic loss suffered by the plaintiffs did not constitute particular damage so as to make it recoverable in damages for public nuisance. His reason for this conclusion was that because all commercial fishermen would not be able to fish in parts of Moreton Bay, all of them would also suffer pure economic loss. Thus, the specific economic loss suffered by the plaintiffs was not necessarily particular to them.[220]

Significance

Pure economic loss will not amount to 'special or particular damage' to found an action in public nuisance where such economic loss is also suffered by another class of the public.

Notes

This case is the only Australian authority to consider pure economic loss in the context of public nuisance. Its authoritative influence, however, is limited given that it was decided by only one Justice of the Supreme Court of Queensland.

Question

Is this case authority for the proposition that, generally, pure economic loss will not amount to 'special' or 'particular' damage?

    Guided response in the eBook

---

220 *Ball v Consolidated Rutile Ltd* [1991] 1 Qd R 524, 547.

9.10   Conclusion

Some commentators have argued that certain aspects of nuisance, particularly public nuisance, should be replaced by the tort of negligence. In some respects, Australian courts have reflected this viewpoint.[221] However, such a hasty and, arguably, irrational conclusion should be cautioned against. The tort of nuisance is exclusively underpinned by social and historical concerns for absolute rights in real property. It is the only tort which adequately protects against *consequential* harm done to land, enabling it to intelligibly hold that an individual's enjoyment of their land should not be interfered with. In contrast, the tort of negligence does not respect the legitimacy and value of the enjoyment of private rights in land, and it would be futile to allow the tort, with all its restrictions, to become all-encompassing. Nuisance, despite its ambiguities and obscurities, is a nuanced tort that still occupies an important place in the modern law of torts. Given the ever-increasing housing prices in the modern property market, combined with concerns of overpopulation and overuse, it is likely that nuisance and its robust ability to protect the use and enjoyment of land in a variety of circumstances, will only maintain its relevance and usefulness in years to come.

REVIEW QUESTIONS

(1) Is public nuisance a crime, a tort or both?

(2) What type of damage will qualify as 'special'?

(3) Does a plaintiff need to have a proprietary interest in order to sue in public nuisance?

 Guided responses in the eBook

KEY CONCEPTS

- **private nuisance:** occurs when the use and enjoyment of a plaintiff's land is unreasonably interfered with by an act or omission of the defendant. It can be made out if the plaintiff has suffered material damage (eg, property damage) or non-physical damage (eg, offensive smells, excessive noise).

- **public nuisance:** a common law crime as well as a common law tort. The tort will arise where a defendant interferes with a plaintiff's public right, which causes the plaintiff to suffer special or particular damage.

- **unreasonable interference with land:** various (and sometimes conflicting) factors determine whether a plaintiff's use and enjoyment of their land has been *unreasonably* interfered with.

---

221 See *Burnie Port Authority v General Jones Pty Ltd* (1994) 179 CLR 520; *Brodie v Singleton Shire Council* (2001) 206 CLR 512; [2001] HCA 29.

Complete the multiple-choice questions in the eBook to test your knowledge

PROBLEM-SOLVING EXERCISES

Exercise 1

In January, Tropical Camps Ltd was given planning permission to open a holiday camp on the edge of a quiet residential neighbourhood. The camp opened for business in July. In December, Andrew, an academic, moved into a house near the perimeter of the camp. He has always done much of his writing in the evening, but now he cannot work because of the loud music emanating from the camp.

Does Andrew have an action in private nuisance?

 Guided response in the eBook

Exercise 2

In January, Smart Sun Pty Ltd constructed a solar panel array in a rural area called Towral. This was a part of a government program to promote sustainable electricity generation. In the past, Towral had mainly consisted of dairy farms. However, over the past two years, Towral's population shifted and became predominantly white-collar workers who work remotely and live on hobby farms. Nadine is a banker who moved to a small farm in Towral before Smart Sun. Her farm is next to Smart Sun's solar panel array, and since the array was installed, Nadine's home office has been penetrated by extremely bright reflections from the solar panels, causing the room to heat up. This has significantly impeded her ability to work, and has caused her extreme stress. Does Nadine have an action in private nuisance?

 Guided response in the eBook

CHALLENGE YOURSELF

Exercise 1

Consider Andrew's scenario in problem-solving exercise 1. Suppose that Andrew becomes so distressed by the noise one night that he decides to go and speak to the management of the camp. Rather than entering the Tropical Camps' office via its public entrance, he decides to jump over his back fence where the camp adjoins his property. It is pitch black and on the walkway to the office, he trips on a hose leading to a tank storing machinery oil. The hose is pulled out of the tank and oil floods the public footpath outside the camp. Stephanie, on her evening jog, fails to see the oil and slips on it, falling into the gutter and breaking her leg.

Discuss all of the possible actions in tort.

 Guided response in the eBook

Exercise 2

Consider Nadine's scenario in problem-solving exercise 2. Suppose that Nadine decides to take action herself to fix the situation. Nadine plants a row of shrubs along the edge of her land between her house and Smart Sun's solar panel array, which blocks the reflections. However, in the middle of summer on a hot day, the concentrated light causes the shrubs to heat up and catch fire. This fire spreads to Nadine's property, burning her house to the ground. It also spreads to Gordon's property (her neighbour), whose house also burns down. Discuss who may be liable in private nuisance.

 Guided response in the eBook

10

VICARIOUS LIABILITY AND NON-DELEGABLE DUTY

10.1   Introduction

In this chapter we discuss two doctrines that are interrelated in that they impose liability either because of the relationship between the defendant and the tortfeasor (D2–D1) (*vicarious liability*), or the relationship between the defendant and the plaintiff (D2–P) (*non-delegable duty of care*).

We will start by examining vicarious liability, which is a form of *strict liability*. We will learn that the employer–employee relationship is the most common instance of vicarious liability. At common law, the employee who commits the tort is always liable, and so vicarious liability of the employer is in addition to the direct liability of the employee (tortfeasor). We will distinguish the employer–employee relationship from the relationship of *principal–independent contractor*, as the employer is not vicariously liable for the acts of independent contractors. Then, we will establish when the employee acts *in the course of employment*. We will also note the employer's *right of indemnity* from an employee.

HINTS AND TIPS

The concept of strict liability exists not only in tort but also in criminal law,[1] where it operates in a similar way in that some criminal offences do not require proof of fault. The application of this doctrine in criminal law, as in the law of torts, is very narrow.

You will learn that a principal is not vicariously liable for the torts of an independent contractor; nor is an employer liable for the acts of employees outside their scope of employment. You will see also that in situations generating a *non-delegable duty of care*, a principal will be *directly or personally liable* for the *negligence* of their independent contractor. It continues to be debated by judges and legal scholars whether the doctrine

---

1 See *Criminal Code Act 1995* (Cth) div 6.1.

of non-delegable duty of care is part of the tort of negligence, strict liability or a separate tort. Irrespective of which doctrine applies, it is the ultimate defendant (D2) who is liable to compensate the plaintiff for harm or loss suffered. Figure 10.1 provides an overview of the two doctrines.

10.2   Vicarious liability

Vicarious liability means that someone is liable for the wrongdoing of another person. An example is strict liability (ie, liability regardless of personal fault). Vicarious type of liability is to be distinguished from personal liability, where someone breaches a duty of care by failing to control others who cause damage to a third party (see Chapter 2).

HINTS AND TIPS

At common law, there is no general duty to control others to prevent them from doing damage to someone else, as per the statement that it is 'exceptional to find in the law a duty to control another's actions to prevent harm to strangers'.[2]

It is very important to understand, and to remember, that the tortfeasor is *always* liable to the plaintiff. The question asked in relation to vicarious liability is: *Will someone else be liable in addition to the tortfeasor?* Therefore, in actions involving vicarious liability, there will be two defendants, the tortfeasor and the person vicariously liable, making them concurrently liable (see Section 12.6). Vicarious liability is, thus, a form of *secondary liability* (in addition to *primary liability* of the tortfeasor) along with, but distinguished from, contributory negligence (see Section 5.2).

HINTS AND TIPS

Vicarious liability and contributory negligence (discussed in Section 5.2) are both examples of secondary liability. They are not the same, however, and can be distinguished because the former is based on the common law doctrine of agency, while the latter is based on the tort theory of enterprise liability.

In the context of employment relations, in New South Wales,[3] South Australia[4] and the Northern Territory,[5] the position has been altered and the employer bears liability alone unless the employee's tortious act constitutes 'serious and wilful misconduct' (see also Section 10.2.5).

---

2 *Smith v Leurs* (1945) 70 CLR 256, 262 (Dixon J), cited in *Modbury Triangle Shopping Centre Pty Ltd v Anzil* (2000) 205 CLR 254; [2000] HCA 61, [20] (Gleeson CJ).
3 *Employees Liability Act 1991* (NSW) s 3.
4 *Civil Liability Act 1936* (SA) s 59.
5 *Law Reform (Miscellaneous Provisions) Act 1956* (NT) s 22A.

Figure 10.1   Vicarious liability and non-delegable duty of care

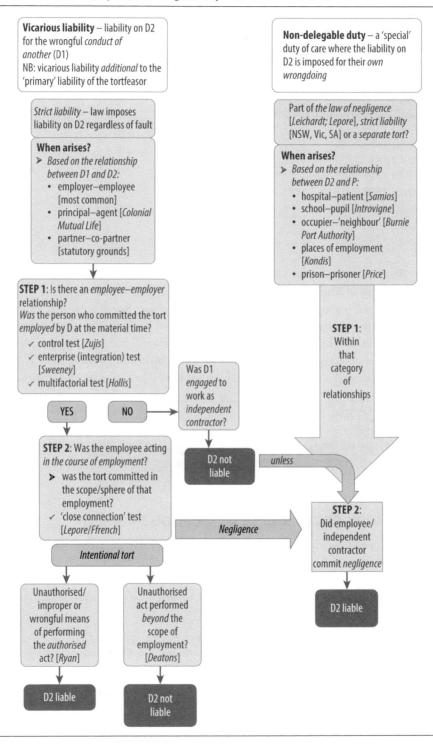

The most common type of relationship where the principle of vicarious liability may arise is that of employer–employee. It may also emerge in the relationship of principal–agent and between fellow partners (which now has a statutory basis: see Table 10.1) and in some exceptional situations (as discussed in Section 10.2.1).

Table 10.1   Statutory grounds for the vicarious liability of partners

Legislation	Section(s)
Partnership Act 1963 (ACT)	14, 16
Partnership Act 1892 (NSW)	10, 12
Partnership Act 1997 (NT)	14, 16
Partnership Act 1891 (Qld)	13, 15
Partnership Act 1891 (SA)	10, 12
Partnership Act 1891 (Tas)	15, 17
Partnership Act 1958 (Vic)	14, 16
Partnership Act 1895 (WA)	17, 19

Historically, vicarious liability did not arise between members of an unincorporated association.[6] Nor does the relationship between parent and child give rise to vicarious liability,[7] unless the parent and child are also in one of the special relationships (eg, employer–employee). In the Northern Territory, however, the parent and child will be joint tortfeasors (see Section 12.6.1) if the child commits intentional damage and is under the age of 18, ordinarily resident with that parent and not in full-time employment.[8] The liability will extend to a maximum of $5000 to be received from the parent in respect of that damage.

HINTS AND TIPS

Note that the rule on the parent–child relationship (as it relates to an analogous special parental liability) differs under the civil law system in continental Europe.[9]

10.2.1   The 'agency' theory of vicarious liability

The concept of vicarious liability has a long tradition, and its development has been inconsistent; you should keep this in mind when reading cases and applying them to current scenarios. As vicarious liability is a form of strict liability, it is closely related to the common law doctrine of agency *respondeat superior* ('let the master answer') under

---

6   See *Trustees of the Roman Catholic Church v Ellis* (2007) 70 NSWLR 565, concerning sexual abuse of a child by a priest, where it was found that because of the unincorporated nature of the Roman Catholic Church no appropriate defendant could be identified, resulting in the plaintiff's claim to fail, which has been referred to as the 'Ellis Defence'. Following the Royal Commission into Institutional Responses to Child Sexual Abuse, some jurisdictions across Australia have introduced relevant legislation to close the legal loophole (see Section 10.4.1).

7   *Moon v Towers* (1860) 8 CB NS 611.

8   *Law Reform (Miscellaneous Provisions) Act 1956* (NT) pt VIIIA.

9   See P Giliker, *Vicarious Liability in Tort: A Comparative Perspective* (Cambridge University Press, 2010) ch 7.

which the superior is responsible for the acts of their subordinate. Jurists and legal scholars still debate the extent to which the grounds for vicarious liability can be explained by the application of the notion of agency;[10] nevertheless, the term 'agency' is often employed by judges in this context.

It does not help either that the concept of 'agent' is not overly precise. Put simply, a person who does something at the request and for the benefit of another does so as an 'agent' for that person. In such a situation, the liability of the principal is based on the common law maxim *qui facit per alium, facit per se* ('one who acts through another, acts personally') which is commonly accepted to be the traditional basis of vicarious liability. In that sense, the agent (who is not necessarily a servant or a partner) acts as a *representative* for the principal (who is not necessarily a master).

Despite the various and often inconsistent applications of the term 'agency',[11] in the context of vicarious liability it is often used simply as a label to signify that vicarious liability is established. As Gleeson CJ noted in *Scott v Davis*:

> Lord Wilberforce made the point that to describe a person as the agent of another, in this context, is to express a conclusion that vicarious liability exists, rather than to state a reason for such a conclusion. Nevertheless, some judges refer to agency as a criterion of liability, similar to employment. If that is to be done, it is necessary to be more particular as to what is meant.[12]

In addition to the established master–servant relationship where the principle of vicarious liability arises (see Section 10.2.2.1), it purportedly may also arise in other instances:

(1) even though there is a lack of any contractual or fiduciary relationship between the parties (ie, between the tortfeasor and the party vicariously liable) or

(2) where the tortfeasor is found to be an 'agent' representing a principal leading to a transaction with the third party.

In *Soblusky v Egan* it was found that a motor vehicle owner might be vicariously liable for the acts of those who drive the owner's car with the owner's permission, and thus such liability would arise under instance (1) above.[13] Since *Soblusky*, the application of the doctrine has been discussed on a number of occasions by courts, including in relation to flying a plane[14] and driving a motorboat,[15] and its application rejected; courts remain reluctant to extend the application of the doctrine beyond the context of motor vehicles.

If there is property damage, under the common law there is a rebuttable presumption that the motor vehicle was driven by the owner or the 'agent' for the benefit of the owner.[16] In some jurisdictions in Australia, statutory agency has been introduced, rendering the motor vehicle owner the statutory principal of the driver for the purpose of recovery of

10 See, eg, WS Holdsworth, *History of English Law* (Sweet & Maxwell, 1925) vol 8, 477.
11 See also GE Dal Pont, *Law of Agency* (Butterworths, 2001); PG Watts, *Bowstead and Reynolds on Agency* (Thomson Reuters, 21st ed, 2017).
12 (2000) 204 CLR 333, 339; [2000] HCA 52, [4].
13 (1960) 103 CLR 215.
14 See *Scott v Davis* (2000) 204 CLR 333; [2000] HCA 52.
15 See *Gutman v McFall* (2004) 61 NSWLR 599.
16 See *Pratt v Connolly* (1994) Aust Torts Reports 81-283.

damages and compulsory third-party insurance. For example, under the *Motor Accidents Compensation Act 1999* (NSW), the presumption of agency is set out in s 112(1), which provides:

> (1) For the purposes of:
>
>   (a) any proceedings against the owner of a motor vehicle, whether severally or jointly with the driver of the vehicle, for the recovery of damages for liability in respect of the death of or injury to a person caused by the fault of the driver of the vehicle in the use or operation of the vehicle, and
>
>   (b) the third-party policy, if the vehicle concerned is an insured motor vehicle,
>
> any person (other than the owner) who was, at the time of the occurrence out of which the proceedings arose, the driver of the vehicle (whether with or without the authority of the owner) is taken to be the agent of the owner acting within the scope of the agent's authority in relation to the vehicle.

As to instance (2) above, the High Court in *Colonial Mutual Life Assurance Society Ltd v Producers and Citizens Co-operative Insurance Co of Australia Ltd* found an insurance company vicariously liable for slanderous comments by one of its 'representatives' (an insurance salesperson).[17] The principal was found liable on the grounds of 'representative agency'. Following this case, even though the general rule is that a party will not generally be found vicariously liable for an act of another person unless the other person is their servant, the principal will be vicariously liable for the actions of their representative agent in circumstances where:

- the tortfeasor represents the party that requested representation (ie, of a very narrow application)[18] and
- this representation is for the purpose of the third party to enter into legal relations with the principal.[19]

This is because the agent, as the person performing the function, 'does not act independently, but as a representative of the Company, which accordingly must be considered as itself conducting the negotiation in his person'.[20]

The use of the terms 'agent' and 'representative' can be, and often is, confusing as their meanings depend on the context. Dixon J pointed out in *Colonial Mutual Life*:

> The rule which imposes liability upon a master for the wrongs of his servant committed in the course of his employment is commonly regarded as part of the law of agency: indeed, in our case law the terms principal and agent are employed more often than not although the matter in hand arises upon the relation of master and servant.[21]

---

17 (1931) 46 CLR 41.

18 Note that Kirby J in his dissenting judgment in *Sweeney v Boylan Nominees Pty Ltd* (2006) 226 CLR 161; [2006] HCA 19 argued against such a narrow application as it would lead to 'a very confined and peculiar rule' (at [89]).

19 See *Sweeney v Boylan Nominees Pty Ltd* (2006) 226 CLR 161; [2006] HCA 19, [22].

20 *Colonial Mutual Life Assurance Society Ltd v Producers & Citizens Co-operative Insurance Co of Australia Ltd* (1931) 46 CLR 41, 49.

21 Ibid.

The majority in *Sweeney v Boylan Nominees Pty Ltd* clarified: 'as was said in [*Scott v Davis* (2000) 204 CLR 333; [2000] HCA 52] of the word 'agent', to use the word 'representative' is to begin but not to end the inquiry'.[22] Thus, in the employment context, asserting whether the contractor or worker was an employee or an independent contractor remains critical to the ambit of vicarious liability.[23]

10.2.2   Vicarious liability in the employment context

The employer–employee relationship is one of the instances where vicarious liability is most common. There are two steps that need to be fulfilled to establish vicarious liability in the context of employer–employee relationship, as shown in Figure 10.2. Both requirements need to be satisfied, since an employer is not liable for either:

- a tortious act of an independent contractor nor
- an act of an employee that was not within the course of their employment.

Figure 10.2   Vicarious liability and employment

| Step 1 | Was the person who committed the torts employed by D? |
| Step 2 | Was the tort committed in the course of that employment? |

HINTS AND TIPS

For an exception to the general rule that the employer is vicariously liable for the act committed by their employee in their course of employment, see Section 10.2.4.

The liability of the employer is based on policy.[24] As aptly expressed by the High Court in *Hollis v Vabu Pty Ltd*, 'the modern doctrine respecting the liability of an employer for the torts of an employee was adopted not by way of an exercise in analytical jurisprudence but as a matter of policy'.[25]

There have been various policy rationales provided for the vicarious liability of an employer. One is that it is often of little value to sue an employee as they are not likely to have the necessary funds to meet the costs of liability, whereas the employer is much more likely to have such a capacity, either as part of the costs of running a business or

---

22 (2006) 226 CLR 161; [2006] HCA 19, [29] (Gleeson CJ, Gummow, Hayne, Heydon and Crennan JJ).
23 *Sweeney v Boylan Nominees Pty Ltd* (2006) 226 CLR 161; [2006] HCA 19.
24 See, eg, Queensland Law Reform Commission, *Vicarious Liability* (Report No 56, December 2001) 9–13 in which the Commission identified a number of policy factors imposing vicarious liability in the context of the employer–employee relationship.
25 (2001) 207 CLR 21; [2001] HCA 44, [34] (Gleeson CJ, Gaudron, Gummow, Kirby and Hayne JJ) following Fullagar J in *Darling Island Stevedoring and Lighterage Co Ltd v Long* (1957) 97 CLR 36.

through insurance (the so-called 'deep-pocket' liability). Vicarious liability is also perceived to encourage employers to minimise risks by introducing an 'adequate' risk management system, supervising and controlling their employees with due care, providing training to their employees and insuring against third-party liability. Also, it is believed that as businesses benefit from the activities of their employees, it is only fair that the business should be prepared to compensate an injured party when it can be shown that the tortious act arose out of the course of employment.

To help understand this complex area of law, it is important to be aware of (and use) the correct terminology: employees are *employed* to work; independent contractors are *engaged* to work. Unfortunately, judges and legal text writers do not always observe this distinction, which causes unnecessary confusion. You should avoid speaking of independent contractors as being 'employed to work', as this is a contradiction.

HINTS AND TIPS

Employees are *employed* to work while independent contractors are *engaged* to work. Using the correct language will demonstrate your understanding of the type of relationship you mean.

10.2.2.1   The master–servant theory

The origin of the general rule imposing vicarious liability is the relationship between master and servant, in that if the master controls what is done and how it is done, the worker will usually be considered to be the employee.

There are two main (conflicting) approaches to the master–servant relationship:

- *The master's tort theory:*[26] The servant's 'tort' (or wrong) is attributed to the master. It is a separate and independent liability from that of the servant, as the master 'is to answer for the act as if it were his own'.[27]

- *The servant's tort theory:*[28] The master is answerable for a tort committed by the servant, and so the tort of the servant is treated as an indirect act of the master who holds liability even though they have not broken a duty of their own.

The principle of vicarious liability as it has developed in Australia seems to be based more on the servant's tort approach,[29] given that the employer can be liable for the tortious act of an employee, but not of an independent contractor.

The master's tort theory is similar to a non-delegable duty. Arguably, s 8 of the *Law Reform (Vicarious Liability) Act 1983* (NSW) follows this theory as it makes the Crown vicariously liable 'in respect of the tort committed by a person in the service of the Crown

---

26 As expressed in the majority judgment (Kitto, Taylor and Webb JJ) in *Darling Island Stevedoring and Lighterage Co Ltd v Long* (1957) 97 CLR 36.

27 *Dansey v Richardson* (1854) 3 EL & B 144, 162.

28 In line with the minority judgment by Fullagar J in *Darling Island Stevedoring and Lighterage Co Ltd v Long* (1957) 97 CLR 36.

29 See, eg, *Darling Island Stevedoring and Lighterage Co Ltd v Long* (1957) 97 CLR 36, 56–7 (Fullager J); *Commonwealth v Griffiths* (2007) 70 NSWLR 268, [100] (Beazley JA).

in the performance or purported performance by the person of a function (including an independent function)': that is, irrespective of whether or not the master had control over the servant (performing an 'independent function') (see Section 10.2.4).

Another factor suggesting that the master's tort theory operates in New South Wales as well is that s 3C of the *Civil Liability Act 2002* (NSW) clarifies that the operation of the Act allows the party vicariously liable to take advantage of the immunity attached to the primary tortfeasor. (Under s 3B this is 'in respect of an intentional act that is done by the person with intent to cause injury or death'.[30])

HINTS AND TIPS

Immunities or exclusions that are not provided for under the *Civil Liability Act 2002* (NSW) will not be extended to the employer for the purpose of establishing vicarious liability.

10.2.2.2   Establishing an employer–employee relationship

Over the years, courts have devised various tests to determine the existence of an employer–employee relationship. The most significant of those tests are the 'control' test, the 'enterprise' (integration) test and the 'multifactorial' test.

Case: *ZG Operations Australia Pty Ltd v Jamsek* (2022) 398 ALR 603

Facts

Martin Jamsek and Robert Whitby (and the other drivers) were employed as truck drivers by the predecessor of ZG Operations Australia Pty Ltd and ZG Lighting Pty Ltd (collectively referred to as 'ZG').

In 1985 or 1986, ZG informed the respondents (and the other drivers) that it would no longer employ them but offered them to enter into independent contractor arrangements. The respondents agreed and set up partnerships with their respective wives. According to the terms of the new contracts that each partnership entered into with the company, Mr Jamsek and Mr Whitby purchased their own trucks and invoiced ZG for their delivery services and the operational and maintenance costs of those trucks. The resulting income was declared as partnership income for tax purposes and split between each respondent and his wife.

Those contracts were terminated in 2017, following which Mr Jamsek and Mr Whitby filed proceedings again ZG for their statutory entitlements under the *Fair Work Act 2009* (Cth), the *Superannuation Guarantee (Administration) Act 1992* (Cth) and the *Long Service Leave Act 1955* (NSW) as employees of ZG.

---

30 See *Zorom Enterprises Pty Ltd v Zabow* (2007) 71 NSWLR 354.

Issue

The Court had to determine the nature of the employment relationship and whether the two truck drivers who provided the company with over 30 years of service were employees of the company or independent contractors.

Decision

At first instance, the Court found Mr Jamsek and Mr Whitby to be independent contractors, a decision which was subsequently overturned by the Federal Court of Appeal, which was subsequently appealed to the High Court.

The High Court unanimously held that the truck drivers were not employees of the company but independent contractors under independent contract agreements between the company and their respective partnerships.

Significance

The case highlights that courts are less likely to undermine the terms of contractual agreements when they are robust, an outcome of a thorough contract management process of engaging legitimate independent contractors and the parties have acted in accordance with those terms.

Notes

When stating its position as to why the Federal Court erred in its judgment, the High Court (Kiefel CJ, Keane and Edelman JJ) concluded that (at [63]):

> The partnerships contracted with the company and invoiced the company for delivery services provided by the operation of the trucks. The partnerships earned income from the company, incurred expenses associated with the ownership and operation of the trucks, and took advantage of tax benefits of the structure. It is not possible to square the contention that the respondents were not conducting a business of their own as partners with the circumstance that, for many years, they enjoyed the advantages of splitting the income generated by the business conducted by the partnerships with their fellow partners.

Question

Does an employer simply need to label a relationship as one of contractual delivery of services for the court to find against it being one of employment?

 Guided response in the eBook

HINTS AND TIPS

In this area of law, 'substance' is given priority over 'form'. The label used (eg, a contract stating that a person is an 'independent contractor') is not determinative of the worker's status, which will be assessed by the court as a matter of fact.[31]

THE CONTROL TEST

The control test is the traditional test which looks into the degree of control that the employer has over the employee (based on the master–servant relationship). It examines what is required to be done, but also how it was required to be done (ie, the type of task and the manner in which it was performed).

Zuijs v Wirth Brothers Pty Ltd concerned a trapeze artist who was injured while performing an act during which his partner dropped him.[32] The Court considered whether the circus (the ultimate defendant) could be liable. To do so, it needed to assess whether the contract with the defendant was one of service, thus bringing the injured party within the *Workers Compensation (Amendment) Act 1948* (NSW).

The trial judge found both trapeze artists to be independent contractors. The High Court disagreed on the ground that what needed to be assessed was the existence of the right to exercise control, rather than whether that control was in fact exercised. The Court held that both men were under the control of the defendant (Wirth Brothers); thus, they were both employees and the defendant was held liable for the negligent act.

The control test, though still applicable, is not as helpful today for dealing with highly skilled workers with high degrees of autonomy. It continues to be applied, but mainly in the context of low-skilled jobs where it might still be possible to establish the existence of 'effective control'.

THE ENTERPRISE (INTEGRATION) TEST

This test classifies workers according to the extent to which they are 'integrated' into the business. For example, the fact that they wear a uniform might be indicative (even if not determinative) of them being an employee. In *Stevenson, Jordan & Harrison Ltd v MacDonald & Evans*, Denning LJ stated:

> Under a contract of service, a man is employed as part of the business, and his work is done as an *integral part of the business*; whereas under a contract for service his work, although done for the business is not integrated into it, but is only accessory to it.[33]

The meaning of 'control' within the context of working for or within the 'organisation of the defendant's business'[34] was considered by the Court in *Sweeney v Boylan Nominees Pty Ltd*.[35]

---

31   *Zuijs v Wirth Brothers Pty Ltd* (1955) 93 CLR 561.
33   [1952] 1 TLR 101, 110 (emphasis added).
32   Ibid.
34   See ibid 111 (Lord Denning).
35   (2006) 226 CLR 161; [2006] HCA 19.

Boylan Nominees owned a commercial refrigerator that was placed in a convenience store. Boylan Nominees was under an obligation to service and maintain the refrigerator. Maria Sweeney suffered personal injury when the refrigerator door fell on her when she opened it to buy a carton of milk. Earlier that day, a mechanic, Mr Comninos, had been called in by Boylan Nominees to check and repair what was claimed to be a faulty refrigerator door. As was later established, Mr Comninos was negligent in repairing the door.

In the District Court of New South Wales, Boylan Nominees was found to be vicariously liable for the negligence of Mr Comninos. The New South Wales Court of Appeal set aside the judgment on the ground that an employer is not vicariously liable for the negligence of an independent contractor, which is what Mr Comninos was. He was found to carry on his own business as his van had his company name on it. In addition, he provided his own uniform and equipment. He was only paid by the defendant after submitting an invoice for completed work and spare parts that he supplied.

The High Court confirmed that an employer will generally be vicariously liable for the conduct of an employee, but not for the actions of an independent contractor, even if it is claimed that the independent contractor was a 'representative' of the employer. Kirby J, in his dissenting judgment, suggested that it might be possible for the Court to reconsider the application of the 'integration' test. Even though the person who caused the damage was not an employee of Boylan Nominees, 'that person was the representative agent of the party sued, performing that party's functions and advancing its economic interests, effectively as part of its enterprise'.[36] But the majority of the High Court was of the view that even if the tortfeasor was found to be 'part and parcel' of the defendant's organisation, this is not enough to render the defendant liable for the wrongs.

HINTS AND TIPS

The case law suggests that neither the control test nor the enterprise (integration) test is to be used as the sole or stand-alone test.

THE MULTIFACTORIAL TEST

It is debatable whether this is a separate test or whether the courts simply integrate the different approaches. But it is now established that, in Australia, courts look for multiple or multifaceted factors to assess the nature of the relationship.[37] This test was first applied in *Stevens v Brodribb Sawmilling Co Pty Ltd*.[38]

The facts of the case were that Roy Stevens, a trucker, was injured when a log fell while being moved into his truck by Stanley Gray, a 'snigger'. Mr Stevens sued the defendant (Brodribb) for the injury caused by Mr Gray's negligence, claiming that Mr Gray was an employee of the defendant, and that the defendant was vicariously liable for his negligent act.

---

36 Ibid [38].
37 See *Construction, Forestry, Maritime, Mining and Energy Union v Personnel Contracting Pty Ltd* (2022) 398 ALR 404; *ZG Operations Australia Pty Ltd v Jamsek* (2022) 398 ALR 603.
38 (1986) 160 CLR 161.

The High Court employed the 'multiple indicia test' to establish whether Mr Gray was an employee or an independent contractor while working for Brodribb. The factors considered included that sniggers used their own vehicles, set their own hours of work, were paid by the amount of timber they delivered, and could work for more than one mill. All these factors were found to be indicative of the contract between Brodribb and Mr Gray being a contract *for* service rather than *of* service. Therefore, the defendant was not found to be vicariously liable for the tortious act of Mr Gray. In its analysis, the High Court looked at the matter of 'control' and concluded that 'control is not now regarded as the only relevant factor. Rather it is the totality of the relationship between the parties which must be considered'.[39]

This means that no one factor is determinative; rather, the totality of the circumstances surrounding the employment relationship needs to be considered, as 'any attempt to list the relevant matters, however incompletely, may mislead because they can be no more than a guide to the existence of the relationship of master and servant'.[40]

The multifactorial test was further confirmed in *Hollis v Vabu Pty Ltd*.[41]

Case: *Hollis v Vabu Pty Ltd* (2001) 207 CLR 21

Facts

The plaintiff, Gary Hollis, was injured by a bicycle courier who was never identified. The plaintiff could remember only that the cyclist was wearing a green jacket with a label in gold lettering saying 'Crisis Couriers' on the back and front of it. The defendant, Vabu Pty Ltd, operated a business of delivering parcels and documents under the business name 'Crisis Couriers'.

Issue

Was the unidentified courier an employee (in which case Vabu was vicariously liable) or an independent contractor (in which case the company was not liable)?

Decision

The New South Wales Court of Appeal found in favour of the defendant. The plaintiff appealed. The High Court looked at the particulars of the relationship between Vabu and its couriers, including that the company offered training and provided uniforms, and that insurance and other deductions from pay were imposed on couriers without negotiations.

Although the couriers provided their own bikes, bore the costs of maintaining them and supplied many of their own accessories (other than a radio and uniforms), these were found not to be of a 'very considerable' expense (contrary to what was found by the Court of Appeal).

The High Court found that the unidentified courier was in fact an employee of Vabu, making the company vicariously liable for the tort of one of its employees.

---

39 *Stevens v Brodribb Sawmilling Co Pty Ltd* (1986) 160 CLR 16, [20] (Mason J).
40 Ibid [12] (Wilson and Dawson JJ).
41 (2001) 207 CLR 21; [2001] HCA 44.

Significance

Courts conduct a multifactorial assessment by looking into a number of factors, including whether wages are paid in a lump sum or regularly, by whom the superannuation is paid, whether any uniforms are provided, and if annual leave is provided.

Notes

The High Court found that the Court of Appeal erred in making the assessment that it was a 'considerable expense' for the couriers to provide their own bikes, bear the costs of their maintenance and supply their own accessories. The High Court distinguished this case from *Vabu Pty Ltd v Federal Commissioner of Taxation* (1966) 33 ATR 537 which found the Vabu couriers to be independent contractors. The distinguishing factor was that the taxation decision was in relation to motor vehicle and motorbike couriers. It was therefore not analogous to the case of bicycle couriers in terms of the scale of 'expense'. This led the High Court to conclude that 'the relationship between Vabu and its bicycle couriers in the present case is properly to be characterised as one of employment' (at [20]).

Question

Are courts more likely to find in favour of the defendant if workers have to provide their own vehicles and bear the costs of maintaining and running them?

    Guided response in the eBook

10.2.3   Acting in the course (scope) of employment

Even if the relationship will be found to be one of employer–employee (step 1), the employee must have been acting *in the course of employment* (step 2) when the tort was committed in order for the employer to be vicariously liable. Other phrases you might come across in relation to establishing this element are acting 'within the scope of employment' or 'within the sphere of employment', which are used interchangeably.

The principle of scope or course of employment is a limiting or controlling element in finding the employer vicariously liable for the conduct of its employee. Already in the 19th century certain limits were placed on the master's liability for an act of a servant, in that if the servant:

> was going out of his way, against his master's implied commands, when driving on his master's business, he will make his master liable; but if he was going on a *frolic of his own*, without being at all on his master's business, the master will not be liable.[42]

This limiting element was necessary to address the apparent tendency of 19th-century coachmen to drive off with their masters' coaches.[43] The test of making the master liable for

---

42   *Joel v Morison* (1834) 6 Car & P 501, 503 (Parker B) (emphasis added).
43   As noted by Diplock LJ in *Morris v CW Martin & Sons Ltd* [1966] 1 QB 716.

the acts of the servant was applied in *Sadler v Henlock* by Crompton J who confirmed that it is necessary to assess whether the party sought to be made responsible retained the power of controlling the act.[44]

As discussed later in this chapter (at Section 10.4), Gleeson CJ in *New South Wales v Lepore* noted:

> Not everything that an employee does at work, or during working hours, is sufficiently connected with the duties and responsibilities of the employee to be regarded as within the scope of the employment. And the fact that wrongdoing occurs away from the workplace, or outside normal working hours, is not conclusive against liability.[45]

It is required that the servant/employee was acting in their scope of employment for the master/employer to be liable. What constitutes a deviation or a mere detour of the servant (leaving the employer liable) and what is a 'frolic' (not giving rise to the employer's vicarious liability) has been, nevertheless, the subject of ample debate in courts and by legal scholars. This area has been subject to extensive judicial revision, and different approaches (and tests) have been devised to deal with the different types of wrongdoing (whether negligent or intentional torts) and consequently when such acts can be found to be within the scope of employment.

10.2.3.1 Establishing the scope of employment

The second step is established when the act or conduct by the employee is authorised by the employer or is sufficiently closely connected to the authorised act or is incidental to it. Over the years, courts have interpreted the requirement of acting within the scope of employment rather widely, and policy considerations have played an important role in defining the scope of this principle. Thus, even acts that might be expressly prohibited by an employee might still be found to be sufficiently closely connected to an authorised act to find the employer vicariously liable.

In *Phoenix Society Inc v Cavenagh* a drunk bus driver was found to be acting within the sphere of her employment when she collided with a car driven by the plaintiff (Ms Cavenagh) who was injured as a consequence.[46] The Supreme Court of South Australia found the employer (Phoenix Society) liable for the driver's negligent act, even though the driver had been expressly instructed not to drive the employer's bus while under the influence of alcohol. The Court found that the act was undertaken as part of her employment (ie, to drive the bus on this occasion) and stated, 'the fact that an act is illegal or committed in disobedience of an instruction does not necessarily take the act outside the course of employment'.[47]

It is a long-established principle that performing an authorised task in an unauthorised or prohibited manner falls within the scope of employment. In the early 20th-century case of *Bugge v Brown*, the employer was found to be vicariously liable for a farm worker

---

44 (1855) 119 ER 209.
45 (2003) 212 CLR 511; [2003] HCA 4, [40].
46 (1996) 25 MVR 143.
47 *Phoenix Society Inc v Cavenagh* (1996) 25 MVR 143, 145 (Debelle J).

burning down a neighbouring station as a result of making a fire outside the hut while cooking, notwithstanding that the worker had been given direct instructions to cook only inside the hut.[48]

The same principle might apply if an employee's act is intentional or criminal in nature, as that will not necessarily take it out of the scope of employment since it might still be for the employer's benefit, even if not directly approved or directed. Such cases occasionally arise in circumstances where security guards in nightclubs and pubs assault or injure patrons.

In *Starks v RSM Security Pty Ltd* Byron Starks, a patron at the Bondi Hotel, was asked to leave the premises by the security officer, Eugene Wilson.[49] When Mr Starks questioned the request, Mr Wilson headbutted him causing him personal injury. The New South Wales District Court found the security officer (the first defendant) liable for Mr Starks' injuries, but rejected the plaintiff's claims against the second defendant, the security officer's employer (RSM Security) for vicarious liability. The Court of Appeal allowed Mr Starks' appeal in regard to RMS Security. The Court confirmed that if in the execution of a security guard's duties, while maintaining order on the premises, an excessive or unnecessary force was used, the employer would be vicariously liable. Beazley JA stated:

> Although Mr Wilson's action in headbutting Mr Starks was unreasonable, uncalled for, and not a usual mode for a security officer to use to persuade a customer to leave hotel premises, the fact is, Mr Wilson acted in that way in the course of seeking to have Mr Starks leave the premises.[50]

In a similar case, *Ryan v Ann St Holdings*, the Queensland Court of Appeal considered the current case law concerning what constituted 'acting in the course of employment'.[51] In that case, a security guard assaulted a patron after closing time for no apparent or justifiable reason, causing him to lose consciousness for a time. The Court held that the club was liable as the act was committed in the course of employment. Williams JA (referring to *New South Wales v Lepore*[52]) held:

> Where, as here, the employee is authorised to use force there must ... be an increased risk that any violent propensities ... could result in harm to nightclub patrons.
>
>   ... the critical test, in broad terms, involves a comparison between the intentional wrongful conduct and the type of conduct the employee was engaged to perform. If there is a 'sufficient connection' (Gleeson J) ... or a 'sufficiently close connection' (Kirby J) ... or a 'close connection' (Gaudron, Gummow and Hayne J) ... it will be open ... to conclude that the wrongful act was done in the course of employment, albeit in an improper mode.[53]

A similar approach was adopted by the Supreme Court of South Australia but in a different context in *Ffrench v Sestili*.[54] The plaintiff (Ms Ffrench) was disabled and cared for by Ms

---

48 (1919) 26 CLR 110.
49 (2004) Aust Torts Reports 81-763.
50 Ibid [24].
51 [2006] 2 Qd R 486.
52 *New South Wales v Lepore* (2003) 212 CLR 511; [2003] HCA 4.
53 *Ryan v Ann St Holdings* [2006] 2 Qd R 486, [17]–[18].
54 (2007) 98 SASR 28.

Brown (employed by Ada Sestili who traded as Direct Personal Care Services). Ms Brown withdrew $33 350 from Ms Ffrench's account without her authorisation. The question before the Court was whether the employer of Ms Brown should be vicariously liable for her dishonest conduct. At the first instance, the Court found against the plaintiff on the basis that Ms Brown was 'on a frolic of her own' when committing the fraudulent act. On appeal, Gray J found Ms Sestili vicariously liable for the full amount misappropriated by her employee as her conduct was 'sufficiently connected with Ms Sestili's business'.

On appeal to the Full Court of the Supreme Court, Debelle J clarified the two main points:

(1) 'the fact that an employee had intentionally engaged in criminal conduct or other breach of the law may not suffice to deny vicarious liability'

(2) 'the fact that the conduct in which the employee has engaged was contrary to instructions given by the employer may not be sufficient to deny vicarious liability'.[55]

As Ms Brown was the carer of Ms Ffrench, it fell within her sphere of employment to do all sorts of domestic duties, including withdrawing money to do shopping for her. Even if Ms Brown had been instructed by Ms Sestili not to use the client's credit card, 'it was an instruction which did not limit the sphere of employment but only as to how her employment as a carer was to be performed'.[56] Thus, even if the instruction had been given, it 'did not limit the extent of the authority reposed in Ms Brown as a carer'.[57]

What would constitute an applicable test in assessing an employer's vicarious liability for an employee's intentional criminal conduct was considered at a significant length by the High Court in *New South Wales v Lepore*.[58] The case concerned sexual abuse committed by an employee (see Section 10.4.1 where this issue is discussed in more detail). The High Court Justices proposed various tests, leading to a high degree of confusion, but the tests have been subsequently applied in cases in this area. A case in point is *Blake v JR Perry Nominees Pty Ltd*.

Case: *Blake v JR Perry Nominees Pty Ltd* (2012) 38 VR 123

Facts

The case concerned fuel tanker drivers (Trevor Blake and Lindsey Jones), employed by JR Perry Nominees Pty Ltd ('JR Perry'), who were waiting to refuel a ship which had been significantly delayed.

It is believed that as Mr Blake and Mr Jones were waiting, they started playing pranks on each other. At some point, Mr Jones without warning struck Mr Blake hard on the back of the knees, causing him to fall and injure his back from which he never fully recovered.

---

55 Ibid [37]–[38] (Debelle J).
56 Ibid [39] (Debelle J).
57 Ibid.
58 (2003) 212 CLR 511; [2003] HCA 4.

Mr Blake sued JR Perry as his employer for the injury he had suffered at the hands of Mr Jones, arguing that Mr Jones acted out of boredom while waiting on the wharf.

Issue

The question before the Court was whether the employer was vicariously liable for the injuries sustained by the plaintiff.

Decision

The trial judge found that JR Perry was not vicariously liable, which decision was confirmed on appeal.

Significance

This case clearly highlights that what is within the scope of employment depends on the facts of each case, and the level of generality within which the scope of employment is assessed will affect the determination of that scope.

Notes

At first instance, the Court concluded that the question was to be determined on the basis of whether the employee's conduct (striking the applicant) constituted a deliberate action (which would result in vicarious liability) rather than an act 'solely personal to the alleged perpetrator of the tort or wrong' (at [47]), and thus concluded that was 'not able to accept that an unlawful assault by Mr Jones on a fellow employee [was] so closely connected with the employment tasks of a driver awaiting the arrival of a vessel as to be regarded as within the scope of his employment' (at [94]). Accordingly, JR Perry was not found to be directly liable to Mr Blake.

On appeal, the Court considered a number of tests to determine the employer's liability and found against it (Neave JA dissenting). The rationale was that it would be neither fair nor just to make the employer liable for the damage caused by the employee as there was no 'sufficient' or 'close' enough connection between the wrongdoing and the scope of the employee's employment. The Court of Appeal also highlighted that such cases need to be considered within the context in which the wrongdoing occurred.

Question

Is the question of 'intention' (or the lack of) on the part of the wrongdoer an important consideration for the courts in similar cases?

 Guided response in the eBook

Despite some degree of confusion or inconsistency in how the different tests have been applied to the different circumstances, in its simplest form, the 'close (or sufficient) connection' test[59] is based on two seemingly straightforward elements. That is, when assessing whether particular conduct was performed within the scope of the employee's employment, one must establish:

(1)   what constitutes an 'authorised' act in the circumstances

(2)   whether the tortious act of the employee is so connected to the authorised act that it can be seen as a mode of carrying out the task, albeit improperly or wrongfully.

Even though the test does not offer much guidance on the type or degree of such 'connection', courts will examine what was expected of the employee against the conduct in question. In *Ffrench v Sestili*, the relationship between the employee and the plaintiff was one of trust and confidence; the employee had access to confidential information (the plaintiff's credit card details and PIN); and the plaintiff was in a position of vulnerability.[60] All these factors were taken into account when assessing the degree of connection between the authorised act and the fraudulent conduct of the employee.

If the act or conduct of the employee is found to be an 'unauthorised' act (by virtue of being so unconnected with authorised acts) or if the employee acted on a 'frolic of their own', the employee will most likely be found to have acted *beyond* their scope of employment.

A good illustration of when conduct by an employee might be unconnected with authorised acts is *Deatons Pty Ltd v Flew*.[61] In this case, a barmaid (Mrs Barlow) first threw a glass of beer and then the glass in the face of the plaintiff (Mr Flew) after he had allegedly insulted her. As a result, he became blind in one eye. The question for the Court was whether throwing a beer glass was incidental to the barmaid's employment and could be said to be furthering the employer's interest. The High Court found that the barmaid had not acted in the course of her employment such that the defendant (Deatons) would be vicariously liable (see further, Table 10.2). Dixon J explained:

> For upon the plaintiff's case the assault was as unexplained as it was unprovoked and might have proceeded from private spite on the part of the barmaid or from some other cause quite unconnected with her occupation or employment … it was an act of passion and resentment done neither in furtherance of the master's interests nor under his express or implied authority nor as an incident to or in consequence of anything the barmaid was employed to do.[62]

---

59 This test is sometimes referred to as 'Salmond's test' as it was formulated by Sir John William Salmond, a prominent legal scholar and judge in New Zealand in the early 20th century. See JW Salmond, *The Law of Torts: A Treatise on the English Law of Liability for Civil Injuries* (Stevens & Haynes, 1907) 83–4.

60 (2007) 98 SASR 28.

61 (1949) 79 CLR 370.

62 Ibid 381 (Dixon J).

Table 10.2   Comparison of cases as to performing an 'unauthorised act' versus performing an 'authorised act in an unauthorised manner'

Case	*Deatons Pty Ltd v Flew* (1949) 79 CLR 370	*Ryan v Ann St Holdings* [2006] 2 Qd R 486
Facts	Barmaid employed by Deatons (hotel operator) threw a glass of beer at a patron (Flew) who had insulted her.	Security guard headbutted a patron at a nightclub after closing time.
Claims	The plaintiff brought an action for damages against the employer (Deatons).	The plaintiff brought an action for damages against the employer (Ann St Holdings).
Decision	The High Court found that the act of the barmaid was outside the scope of her employment as she was authorised to serve beer, not to control order or restore discipline at the bar.	The Queensland Court of Appeal held that the club was liable as the act was in the security guard's course of employment, which included ensuring that patrons left the nightclub in an orderly manner by closing time.
Application	The act or conduct is outside the scope of employment if the employee was not authorised to perform that particular act (as here, keep order), and the act was done in the employee's own personal interest (as here, for personal retribution).	The act or conduct is within the scope of employment if the employee was authorised to perform that particular act (as here, use physical force) but performed it in an unauthorised, prohibited or improper manner, and it would be still in pursuit of the employer's interest as incidental to the performance of the employee's work.
Outcome	Employer was not liable to the customer for damages.	Employer was found to be vicariously liable to the customer.

10.2.4   Exception to employer's vicarious liability

There is one important exception to finding an employer vicariously liable for an act committed by an employee in the course of employment. The principle of independent discretionary power or duty has been developed in public law in response to the principle of vicarious liability in tort law. This rule applies in situations when powers are conferred by common law or a statute directly upon an employee, making the employer not vicariously liable at common law for a tortious act of that employee.

The leading case is *Enever v The King* which concerned a wrongful arrest by a police constable and for which the Crown was found not to be liable.[63] The basis of the exemption rests on the principle that the employee is exercising an 'independent discretion' or 'original authority', which makes such an employee not a servant or agent of the employer (ie, not subject to the control of the employer)[64] in relation to the exercise of this independent power.

---

63   (1906) 3 CLR 969.
64   *Enever v The King* (1906) 3 CLR 969, 982–3 (Barton J).

This rule was widely criticised[65] and has now been abrogated in relation to the police and some other categories of public employees by legislation in all Australian jurisdictions. Today, the Crown can be vicariously liable for torts committed by police officers shown to have acted within their scope of employment and in good faith (see Table 10.3)

Table 10.3   Statutory grounds for vicarious liability of the Crown for acts committed by police officers

Legislation	Provision(s)
Australian Federal Police Act 1979 (Cth)	s 64B
Law Reform (Vicarious Liability) Act 1983 (NSW)	ss 7, 8, pt 4
Police Administration Act 1978 (NT)	pt VIIA
Police Service Administration Act 1990 (Qld)	s 10.5
Police Act 1998 (SA)	s 65
Police Service Act 2003 (Tas)	s 84
Victoria Police Act 2013 (Vic) (previously *Police Regulation Act 1958*)	s 74 (s 123)
Police Act 1892 (WA)	s 137

Some of the statutes have also introduced exemptions for the Crown from exemplary or punitive damages, but these are still available against the Crown for tortious acts of police officers in some jurisdictions.[66] This is despite the general tendency to exclude or limit access to exemplary and punitive damages at common law,[67] and by statute in defamation actions[68] (see Chapter 11) and negligence for personal injury[69] (see Section 12.3).

10.2.5   Employer's right of indemnity

It is not always possible to establish who the negligent employee was, as in *Hollis v Vabu Pty Ltd* (see Section 10.2.2.2).[70] In situations where the employer is found to be vicariously liable and the employee can be identified, the employer can seek indemnity from the employee. The employer can claim that the employee breached a term of their employment contract (usually an implied term) by failing to act competently. This entitlement to recover contribution or indemnity from an employee is called the employer's right of indemnity.

In New South Wales the employer's right of indemnity from the employee has been abolished in respect of a tort for which the employer is vicariously liable by s 3(1)(a) of the *Employees Liability Act 1991* (NSW) (see Table 10.4). However, s 5(a) provides that the employee will lose that protection if 'the conduct constituting the [employee's] tort … was serious and wilful conduct'. Similarly, in South Australia and the Northern Territory, an employer is bound to indemnify an employee except where the employee's liability was due to serious and wilful (or gross) misconduct. Also, s 66 of the *Insurance Contracts Act 1984*

---

65 See, eg, J Carabetta, 'Employment Statutes of the Police in Australia' (2003) 27(1) *Melbourne University Law Review* 1.

66 In New South Wales, see *New South Wales v Ibbett* (2006) 229 CLR 638; [2006] HCA 57.

67 See, eg, the High Court's call to 'moderate' the award of exemplary damages in *XL Petroleum (NSW) Pty Ltd v Caltex Oil (Australia) Pty Ltd* (1985) 155 CLR 448.

68 See, eg, *Defamation Act 2005* (NSW) s 37.

69 See, eg, *Civil Liability Act 2002* (NSW) s 21.

70 (2001) 207 CLR 21; [2001] HCA 44.

(Cth) has abolished the insurer's right to enforce the employer's right of indemnity, except where the employee's conduct was 'serious or wilful misconduct'.

Table 10.4   Overview of statutory provisions on the employer's right of indemnity

Legislation	Section(s)
Employees Liability Act 1991 (NSW)	3, 5
Law Reform (Miscellaneous Provisions) Act 1956 (NT)	22A
Civil Liability Act 1936 (SA)	59

It is also possible for the employer to claim an indemnity from the employee as a 'joint tortfeasor' under the law of contribution,[71] but only where it can be established that the employer was not at fault.[72]

Since the introduction of the civil liability legislation, a number of jurisdictions have introduced proportionate liability in relation to negligently caused property damage and economic loss (see Table 10.5). This means that the defendants will be liable only for the proportion of the damage they caused based on what is 'just and reasonable'.

Table 10.5   Overview of statutory provisions on apportionable claims

Legislation	Provision(s)
Civil Law (Wrongs) Act 2002 (ACT)	ss 107D(2), 107F
Civil Liability Act 2002 (NSW)	s 35(1)(a)(b)
Proportionate Liability Act 2005 (NT)	s 4
Civil Liability Act 2003 (Qld)	pt 2
Civil Liability Act 2002 (Tas)	pt 9A
Wrongs Act 1958 (Vic)	s 24AI
Civil Liability Act 2002 (WA)	s 5AK

REVIEW QUESTIONS

(1)   What are the types of relationships that can and cannot give rise to vicarious liability?

(2)   In the context of the employer–employee relationship, what are the requirements that need to be satisfied for the employer to be vicariously liable for the tortious conduct of its employee?

 Guided responses in the eBook

---

71   Note, however, that under *Police Act 1998* (SA) s 65 and *Police Regulation Act 1898* (Tas) s 52, in certain types of cases only the employer (not the employee) may be held liable (see Section 10.2.2.2).
72   See *Thompson v Australian Capital Television Pty Ltd* (1996) 186 CLR 574.

10.3   Non-delegable duty

At common law, a principal (delegator) is not vicariously liable for the torts of an independent contractor (delegatee). This was perceived as often leading to an unjust outcome for a plaintiff. As a result, the courts over the years have developed a doctrine that will, in certain situations or certain types of relationships, impose upon a principal a 'non-delegable' duty of care.

This doctrine sits somewhere between the doctrine of vicarious liability and negligence. That is, it was developed in response to what was perceived as a gap in placing liability on the one who is in charge or has the control. On the other hand, it is perceived as a *form* of a duty of care where a finding of 'fault' by not taking reasonable care on the part of the delegator is not necessary. The High Court in *Leichardt Municipal Council v Montgomery* held that a non-delegable duty is part of the law of negligence that involves the imposition of strict liability.[73] This might be seen as contradictory, as a negligence action usually requires finding a fault, whereas strict liability imposes liability regardless of fault (ie, negligence or tortious intent). Consequently, the doctrine of non-delegable duty is controversial and uncertain across the different jurisdictions in Australia.

HINTS AND TIPS

Not all jurisdictions have approached the issue of a non-delegable duty similarly. In Victoria,[74] New South Wales[75] and presumably South Australia (see Section 10.3.1), a non-delegable duty of care is treated as one of vicarious liability as it imposes strict liability.

This non-delegable duty of care is not an absolute duty to prevent harm, nor is the ordinary duty of care; rather, it is a duty to ensure that all reasonable care and skill is taken, which cannot be discharged by using someone else. In other words, it is not the task that cannot be delegated; it is the liability that cannot be delegated to a third party. Consequently, the duty holder, when delegating the task, will be legally responsible for any failure in the performance of the task. This means that a non-delegable duty does not disappear because of delegation; rather, it is duplicated, creating two concurrent duties. This gives the plaintiff two choices of remedy:

(1)   to sue the original tortfeasor (D1) in a regular negligence action or

(2)   to sue the delegator (D2), arguing a breach of D2's personal non-delegable duty owed directly to the plaintiff as they are in a special relationship.

The non-delegable duty arises in situations where the defendant has control over the person or property of another, or in situations when the person owed a non-delegable duty remains in a relationship of special dependency on or vulnerability to the defendant.[76] The High

---

73   (2007) 230 CLR 22; [2007] HCA 6.
74   *Wrongs Act 1958* (Vic) s 61.
75   *Civil Liability Act 2002* (NSW) s 5Q.
76   See *Northern Sandblasting Pty Ltd v Harris* (1997) 188 CLR 313.

Court has recognised that a non-delegable duty of care arises in a range of limited types of relationships (see Section 10.3.1). These categories are not closed, and so there is scope for future recognition of new non-delegable duties, although courts are generally reluctant to find non-delegable duties.[77] This is because this duty, in comparison to an 'ordinary' duty of care, does not depend on the defendant taking any reasonable steps to mitigate the risk of harm to the plaintiff, and thus puts a significant burden on the potential defendants.

10.3.1   Special relationships

A non-delegable duty of care is based on the notions of *control* (by the defendant) and *vulnerability* (of the plaintiff), which explains its development in relation to specific special relationships. The duty arises because of an antecedent relationship between the plaintiff and the defendant, and to protect a special class of persons against particular types of risk.

Thus, this duty remains personal to the defendant even if the task itself is delegated. It is a 'higher' or 'more stringent' duty than the ordinary duty of care,[78] as it is not simply a duty to *take reasonable care*[79] but to ensure that *reasonable care is taken* by the person carrying out the work, or task delegated or entrusted to them, by the defendant. In such situations, if damage is caused by negligence of an independent contractor, the principal will be directly liable because of a breach by the principal of a non-delegable duty to *see* that reasonable care is taken by the independent contractor. The origins of the doctrine lie in the law of nuisance (see Chapter 9) and a number of influential judgments of Lord Blackburn in the late 19th century – in particular *Rylands v Fletcher*.[80] As discussed in Section 10.3.1.3, it was found that the defendant's duty to prevent water escaping from his reservoir was non-delegable. Liability was not affected by the fact that the breach was caused by an independent contractor. It must be noted, though, that the application of this doctrine is very narrow.[81]

This duty cannot be discharged (by delegating the task to another) and thus it is not an issue of negligence, even though a breach of duty occurs by negligence. The scope of the doctrine includes negligence on the part of the initial wrongdoer, but does not extend to cover any intentional act of wrongdoing.

In South Australia, there are no specific provisions relating to a non-delegable duty. In practice, current legislation already applies to breaches of non-delegable duty through the application of strict liability, and thus the doctrine operates in the same way as vicarious liability. In some of the jurisdictions which introduced legislation following the 2002 *Review of the Law of Negligence* (see Chapter 1), a similar path has been followed. In Victoria[82] and

---

77 See, eg, *Davie v New Merton Board Mills Ltd* [1959] AC 604 (employer's liability and the defective tools used by employees); *D & F Estates Ltd v Church Commissioners for England* [1989] AC 177 (duty of a contractor to supervise a subcontractor when it would be unreasonable to expect such a supervision); *Rowe v Herman* [1997] 1 WLR 1390 (contractor not held liable for injury to a road user).

78 *Burnie Port Authority v General Jones Pty Ltd* (1994) 179 CLR 520, 550 (Mason CJ, Deane, Dawson, Toohey and Gaudron JJ).

79 *Kondis v State Transport Authority* (1984) 154 CLR 672, 687 (Mason J).

80 (1866) LR 1 Ex 265, affirmed by the House of Lords in *Rylands v Fletcher* (1868) LR 3 HL 330.

81 See *New South Wales v Lepore* (2003) 212 CLR 511; [2003] HCA 4; *Leichardt Municipal Council v Montgomery* (2007) 230 CLR 22; [2007] HCA 6; *Leighton Contractors Pty Ltd v Fox* (2009) 240 CLR 1.

82 *Wrongs Act 1958* (Vic) s 61.

New South Wales[83] the issue of a breach of a non-delegable duty is one of vicarious liability which implies strict liability.

Section 5Q of the *Civil Liability Act 2002* (NSW) provides:

(1) The extent of liability in tort of a person ('the defendant') for breach of a non-delegable duty to ensure that reasonable care is taken by a person in the carrying out of any work or task delegated or otherwise entrusted to the person by the defendant is to be determined as if the liability were the vicarious liability of the defendant for the negligence of the person in connection with the performance of the work or task.

(2) This section applies to an action in tort whether or not it is an action in negligence, despite anything to the contrary in section 5A.

Section 5Q does not apply to all tort actions and, as s 3B provides, actions to which the Act does not apply include intentional torts (including sexual assault or other sexual misconduct), dust diseases, actions relating to smoking or other use of tobacco products, motor accident cases and actions by an employee against an employer for a workplace injury. Section 5Q(2) clarifies that, although s 5A provides that pt 1A of the Act only applies to negligence, s 5Q also applies to other tort actions (eg, breach of statutory duty).

Over the years the High Court has held that certain relationships generate a non-delegable duty of care and that such a duty is owed by:

* a hospital to its patients
* a school to its pupils
* an occupier of premises (as to dangerous substances and activities on the premises) to their 'neighbour' (persons or property outside the premises)
* an employer to their employee
* by analogy, a duty is also owed by a prison or detention facility to its prisoners or detainees.

Let us have a closer look now at how the non-delegable duty might apply in the context of these 'special' relationships.

10.3.1.1 Hospitals

In the past, hospitals were considered to be charitable institutions that had immunity from tortious liability to relieve them of the burden of having to pay damages that they could not afford. In modern times, the charitable immunity doctrine has been largely abandoned throughout the common law world, thus allowing for the tort liability of charitable institutions. Professionally qualified staff, including consultants and anaesthetists, are held to be employees of a hospital for the purpose of vicarious liability. But, even if (or irrespective of whether) they are deemed to be non-employees, a hospital has a non-delegable duty of care towards its patients.

Denning LJ in *Cassidy v Ministry of Health* formulated the non-delegable duty of a hospital towards its patients on the basis that the hospital authorities (whether local authorities, government boards or other corporations) cannot:

---

83 *Civil Liability Act 2002* (NSW) s 5Q.

> get rid of [their] responsibility by delegating the performance of it to someone else, no matter whether the delegation be to a servant under a contract of service or to an independent contractor under a contract of services.[84]

As to the scope of that duty, Denning LJ in *Roe v Ministry of Health* clarified his view that:

> the hospital authorities are responsible for the whole of their staff, not only for the nurses and doctors, but also for the anaesthetists and the surgeons. It does not matter whether they are permanent or temporary, resident or visiting, whole time or part time. The hospital authorities are responsible for all of them.[85]

The extent of the non-delegable duty of hospitals was examined in Australia in *Samios v Repatriation Commission*.[86] In this case the Supreme Court of Western Australia had to consider whether the hospital should be held liable for the conduct of a radiologist practising in a private radiological clinic. The hospital would use the services of a private clinic whenever its resident radiologist was on leave. On this occasion, the plaintiff (Mr Samios) had injured his shoulder. It was x-rayed and in the opinion of the radiologist from the private clinic there was no evidence of dislocation or bone injury; hence, the patient was discharged. As Mr Samios continued to feel pain, he had his shoulder x-rayed again elsewhere and it was found that, in fact, it had been dislocated. Due to the lapse in time between x-rays (eight weeks), repair surgery could not be performed successfully. As a result, his shoulder became partially disabled. The hospital was found to be liable to Mr Samios, including for the negligence of the radiologist from the private clinic who Mr Samios never met in person and had no contact with. Jackson SPJ stated that 'the hospital was under a positive duty to take some steps in the matter and not to allow the plaintiff to remain uncertain until two months had elapsed by which time … it was too late to operate'.[87]

The *direct* liability is based on a breach by the principal (the hospital) of the non-delegable duty it owes to its patients to ensure that reasonable care is taken by the independent contractor (the medical staff). The hospital's non-delegable duty of care, however, does not extend to situations where the patient selects a consultant or anaesthetist, as it only applies to services provided 'directly' to the patients of the hospital. In situations where the hospital facilities are simply used by the specialist for private patients, this duty may not extend to 'catch' the hospital because the patient is not being provided with a service by the hospital.

The case of *Ellis v Wallsend District Hospital* concerned an honorary surgeon (Dr Chambers), and the question the New South Wales Court of Appeal had to consider was whether the hospital was vicariously liable for the negligence of Dr Chambers.[88] The Court discussed in length the details of the work arrangements including whether the honorary medical officer was in fact an employee of the hospital, and whether the patient (Mrs Ellis) was a public patient admitted by the hospital for treatment or advice, or a private patient admitted from Dr Chambers' practice. The Court found that Dr Chambers was not an employee and thus the hospital could not be held vicariously liable to the patient.

---

84   [1951] 2 KB 343, 360.
85   [1954] 2 QB 66, 82.
86   [1960] WAR 219.
87   *Samios v Repatriation Commission* [1960] WAR 219, 229 (Jackson SPJ).
88   *Ellis v Wallsend District Hospital* (1989) 17 NSWLR 553.

In his dissenting judgment, Kirby J held that in not finding the hospital vicariously liable to the patient (Mrs Ellis) the hospital should be found directly liable for breach of its non-delegable duty of care to her, since Dr Chambers had failed to inform her of the risk inherent in the operation. The majority held that in cases of liability arising from a non-delegable duty, 'the question of what medical services the hospital has undertaken to supply' shapes the nature and scope of that duty.[89]

On this occasion, no negligence was found on the part of the hospital in relation to the aspects of the treatment it provided (ie, the operating venue and auxiliary staff) and which Dr Chambers (like other senior physicians and surgeons) used to treat his private patients, who would pay him his fee and the hospital for nursing care and accommodation. The appellant (Mrs Ellis) failed to prove any act of negligence on Dr Chambers' part, hence her claim against the hospital also failed. Even if Dr Chambers had been found negligent, the hospital would not have been responsible for any negligence on his part, as the Court of Appeal ruled that the hospital, given the nature of the relationship with the doctor, did not hold a non-delegable duty to the doctor's patient to ensure that the procedure was carried out with due caution.[90]

EMERGING ISSUE

Following *Ellis v Wallsend District Hospital* (1989) 17 NSWLR 553, it is more likely that hospitals will not be liable where medical officers merely 'use' their facilities for private patients. The principle of non-delegable duty of care is evolving (across Commonwealth jurisdictions) and thus healthcare providers need to consider the various delegated functions and the types of relationships that their service providers, or those who 'use' their facilities, have with the relevant patient, requiring regular reviewing of the contracts in place as well as the indemnity clauses that the principals seek to rely on.

10.3.1.2 Schools

As held in *Commonwealth v Introvigne*, a school authority owes its pupils a non-delegable duty of care in relation to negligent acts.[91] In this case, a pupil was injured in school grounds which were set up by the Commonwealth and operated by the State of New South Wales. The Court established that the school owed its pupil a non-delegable duty of care because of the special relationship between the school authority and pupils. As stated by Mason J, with whom Gibbs CJ agreed: 'The duty thereby imposed on a school authority is akin to that owed by a hospital to its patient.'[92] The non-delegable duty of school authorities does not, however, extend to intentional torts of teachers against pupils (including sexual abuse) as discussed in *New South Wales v Lepore* (see Section 10.4.1.1).

---

89 Ibid 604 (Samuel JA, Meagher JA agreeing).
90 Ibid 606 (Samuel JA).
91 (1982) 150 CLR 258.
92 *Commonwealth v Introvigne* (1982) 150 CLR 258, 270 (Mason J). See also Section 2.5.6.4.

10.3.1.3 Occupiers of premises

If a person who has control of premises brings a dangerous substance onto the premises, or carries on a dangerous activity there, or allows someone else to do these, and that substance escapes causing damage to another's property, they would have been liable under the rule in *Rylands v Fletcher*.[93] That case attached strict liability to anyone carrying out dangerous activities or bringing dangerous materials onto land.[94] Today in Australia, such a person will be liable in negligence, as clarified in the next case.

In *Burnie Port Authority v General Jones Pty Ltd*, the appellant owned a warehouse, part of which was used by the respondent to store frozen vegetables.[95] In the process of developing the warehouse, the appellants engaged an independent contractor to carry out lagging for insulation purposes, which required a certain degree of welding. Due to the contractor's negligence when welding, which set alight cartons containing a highly flammable substance stored close to the welding activity, a significant part of the warehouse was destroyed, causing loss to the respondent. The respondent brought a claim against the appellant on three grounds: (1) strict liability (for the spread of the fire from its premises); (2) the *Rylands v Fletcher* rule; and (3) breach of a non-delegable duty of care. By a 5:2 majority (Brennan and McHugh JJ dissenting), the appeal was dismissed. The Court held that the respondent could not succeed on the second claim as:

> the rule in *Rylands v Fletcher*, with all its difficulties, uncertainties, qualifications and exceptions, should now be seen for the purposes of the common law of this country, as absorbed by the principles of ordinary negligence.[96]

The Court thus absorbed the rule in *Rylands v Fletcher* into the law of negligence.[97] Burnie Port Authority, which occupied and had control of the premises, was found to owe General Jones a duty of care that was non-delegable as it extended to ensuring that its independent contractor took reasonable care to prevent the cartons being set alight as a result of the welding activity, because an uncontrollable fire would most likely result.

Consequently, a person in control of land owes a non-delegable duty of care in relation to the negligent conduct of another person in carrying out dangerous operations on the land, irrespective of whether or not the occupier is vicariously liable for the person conducting the operations:

---

93 (1868) LR 3 HL 330.
94 The rule was explained thus: '[T]he person who for his own purposes brings on his lands and collects and keeps there anything likely to do mischief if it escapes, must keep it in at his peril, and, if he does not do so, is prima facie answerable for all the damage which is the natural consequence of its escape. He can excuse himself by showing that the escape was owing to the plaintiff's default; or perhaps that the escape was the consequence of *vis major*, or the act of God': *Fletcher v Rylands* (1866) LR 1 Ex 265, 279 (Blackburn J), affd in *Rylands v Fletcher* (1868) LR 3 HL 330.
95 (1994) 179 CLR 520.
96 *Burnie Port Authority v General Jones Pty Ltd* (1994) 179 CLR 520, 556 (Mason CJ, Deane, Dawson, Toohey and Gaudron JJ). Under English law this rule continues to apply in England and Wales: see *Transco plc v Stockport Metropolitan Borough Council* [2004] 2 AC 1 (HL).
97 The dissenting Justices did not agree that the rule in *Rylands* could be subsumed within the tort of negligence on the basis that *Rylands v Fletcher* liability can exist *without* any fault on the part of the independent contractor, whereas under the law of negligence the occupier can be liable only for a *negligent* act of the independent contractor. Thus, the minority believed that the claim under the rule in *Rylands v Fletcher* required separate consideration.

> [A] person who takes advantage of his or her control of premises to introduce a dangerous substance, to carry on a dangerous activity, or to allow another to do one of those things, owes a duty of reasonable care to avoid a reasonably foreseeable risk of injury or damage to the person or property of another … [T]hat duty of care … extends to ensuring that such care is taken.[98]

A 'dangerous' use of land (or a 'non-natural' use as termed in *Rylands v Fletcher*) is use that is beyond what would be considered ordinary or of no general benefit to the community. There seem to be two broad categories:

- use that has a significant magnitude of danger irrespective of the circumstances (ie, it is 'inherently' dangerous)
- use that is not always dangerous but was on this occasion.

Nonetheless, some uncertainty continues as to what would constitute 'non-natural' or 'non-ordinary' use of land. In some instances, it includes structural damage to land (caused by the negligence of contractors).[99] Courts have held that erecting scaffolding[100] and crowd surfing[101] are not 'dangerous' uses of land for the purpose of this principle.

HINTS AND TIPS

Landlords do not owe their tenants a non-delegable duty of care.[102]

10.3.1.4   Places of employment

The non-delegable duty can arise in relation to the provision of a safe system of work, as was found in *Kondis v State Transport Authority*.[103] Mason J provided the dicta for when, and in what circumstances, a non-delegable duty of care might emerge in that context, stating that the common:

> element in the relationship between the parties which generates [the] special responsibility or duty to see that care is taken … [is that] the person on whom [the duty] is imposed has undertaken the care, supervision or control of the person or property of another or is so placed in relation to that person or his property as to assume a particular responsibility for his or its safety, in circumstances where the person affected might reasonably expect that due care will be exercised.[104]

The non-delegable duty of the employer to its employees might also extend to taking reasonable care to avoid exposing them to unnecessary risk of injury. If there is a reasonably foreseeable risk to the employee of performing a particular task in the workplace, the

---

98 *Burnie Port Authority v General Jones Pty Ltd* [1994] HCA 13, [43].
99 *Dalton v Angus & Co* (1881) 6 App Cas 740.
100 *Complete Scaffold Services Pty Ltd v Adelaide Brighton Cement Ltd* [2001] SASC 199.
101 *Newcastle Entertainment Security Pty Ltd v Simpson* [1999] NSWCA 351.
102 See *Northern Sandblasting Pty Ltd v Harris* (1997) 188 CLR 313; *Jones v Bartlett* (2000) 205 CLR 166; [2000] HCA 56.
103 (1984) 154 CLR 672.
104 *Kondis v State Transport Authority* (1984) 154 CLR 672, 235 (Mason J).

employer is required to mitigate the risk by devising 'a method of operation for the performance of the task that eliminates the risk, or by the provision of adequate safeguards', as was found in *Czatyrko v Edith Cowan University*.[105] When the task in question is repetitive in nature, as it was in *Czatyrko*, the High Court instructed that the employer 'must take into account the possibility of thoughtlessness, or inadvertence or carelessness'.[106] Moreover, despite the injury in this case being caused by the employee's omission to take precautions when performing the relevant task, he had not been directed or warned by the employer to take such precautions, and thus the Court considered there should be no finding of contributory negligence (see Section 5.2).

10.3.1.5   Prisons and detention facilities

In recent times courts have found that the duty of prison authorities/detention facilities to their prisoners/detainees can be regarded as non-delegable in nature due to the level of control exercised by the authorities and the little autonomy inmates have while incarcerated. Allsop P of the New South Wales Court of Appeal described the relationship as one characterised by 'control by the [authority] of the [prisoner] and its assumption of responsibility over the [prisoner]'.[107]

In the context of immigration detention under the *Migration Act 1958* (Cth), the Full Federal Court held:

> It is well-established that a gaoler owes a duty of care under the common law to exercise reasonable care for the safety of a person held in custody …
>
> But that obligation is not a guarantee of the safety of the detainee; it is an obligation of reasonable care to avoid harm to the detainee whether that harm be inflicted by a third person or by the detainee himself or herself.[108]

The Federal Court in *S v Department of Immigration and Multicultural and Indigenous Affairs*[109] considered the Commonwealth's detention services contract with GSL Australia Pty Ltd for the management of and service provision at Baxter Detention Centre.[110] Finn J noted that:

> I consider that the Commonwealth has correctly conceded in this matter that it owes a nondelegable duty of care to the applicants because of its particular 'relationship' with detainees.[111]

Finn J drew a parallel between the relationship of hospital and patient, where the element of 'control' is present, but stated that in the context of a detention facility:

105 (2005) 214 ALR 349.
106 *Czatyrko v Edith Cowan University* (2005) 214 ALR 349, [12].
107 *Price v New South Wales* [2011] NSWCA 341, [35].
108 *SBEG v Commonwealth* (2012) 208 FCR 235, [19].
109 (2005) 143 FCR 217.
110 Baxter Immigration Reception and Processing Centre (commonly known as Baxter Detention Centre) was a purpose-built immigration detention facility near the city of Port Augusta in South Australia. Controversial in the context of the mandatory detention of asylum seekers in Australia, it was closed in August 2007.
111 *S v Department of Immigration and Multicultural and Indigenous Affairs* (2005) 143 FCR 217; [2005] FCA 549, [199].

there is … the exaggerated vulnerability of the class of detainees at significant risk of mental illnesses [in that] indefinite detainees in Baxter were known to the Commonwealth to be susceptible to serious mental illness.[112]

Two years later, in *AS v Minister for Immigration and Border Protection*, the Commonwealth further conceded that it owed 'AS and people … held [in] immigration detention [on Christmas Island] a non-delegable duty of care to ensure that reasonable care is taken of them'.[113]

REVIEW QUESTIONS

(1) Can all types of relationships generate a non-delegable duty of care?

(2) What are the potential disadvantages of extending hospitals' non-delegable duty of care to any harm suffered by a plaintiff, including where that patient was not a 'direct' patient of the hospital?

  Guided responses in the eBook

10.4   Cases on the non-delegable duty of care and vicarious liability

As you will have gathered from the discussion in this chapter, vicarious liability and the non-delegable duty of care are closely related. In many of the cases, the claims by plaintiffs have been on the basis of one or the other or, often, both doctrines. Depending on the circumstances, it might be possible to clearly determine whether the matter is of vicarious liability or non-delegable duty of care when dealing with a non-employee (an independent contractor); in other cases, the plaintiff might have more than one option.

As illustrated by Figure 10.3, within the employment context, an employer (D2) may be vicariously liable for an employee (D1) who acted within their scope of employment while committing the tortious act (whether negligent or intentional). The employer may also be liable for their own personal breach of a non-delegable duty of care to the plaintiff, if the relationship between D2 and P fits one of the recognised categories (see Section 10.3.1), but only in relation to the negligence of D1.

If D1 is an independent contractor, the principal (D2) will not normally be vicariously liable for any tort committed by D1, unless D1 acted as an 'agent' for D2 (see Section 10.2.1). D2 can be liable for a negligent tort committed by D1 under the doctrine of non-delegable duty, but not in relation to an intentional tort of D1.

---

112 Ibid [209].
113 [2017] VSC 137, [21] (Forrest J).

Figure 10.3   Comparison of employer's liability for (a) negligent torts and (b) intentional torts

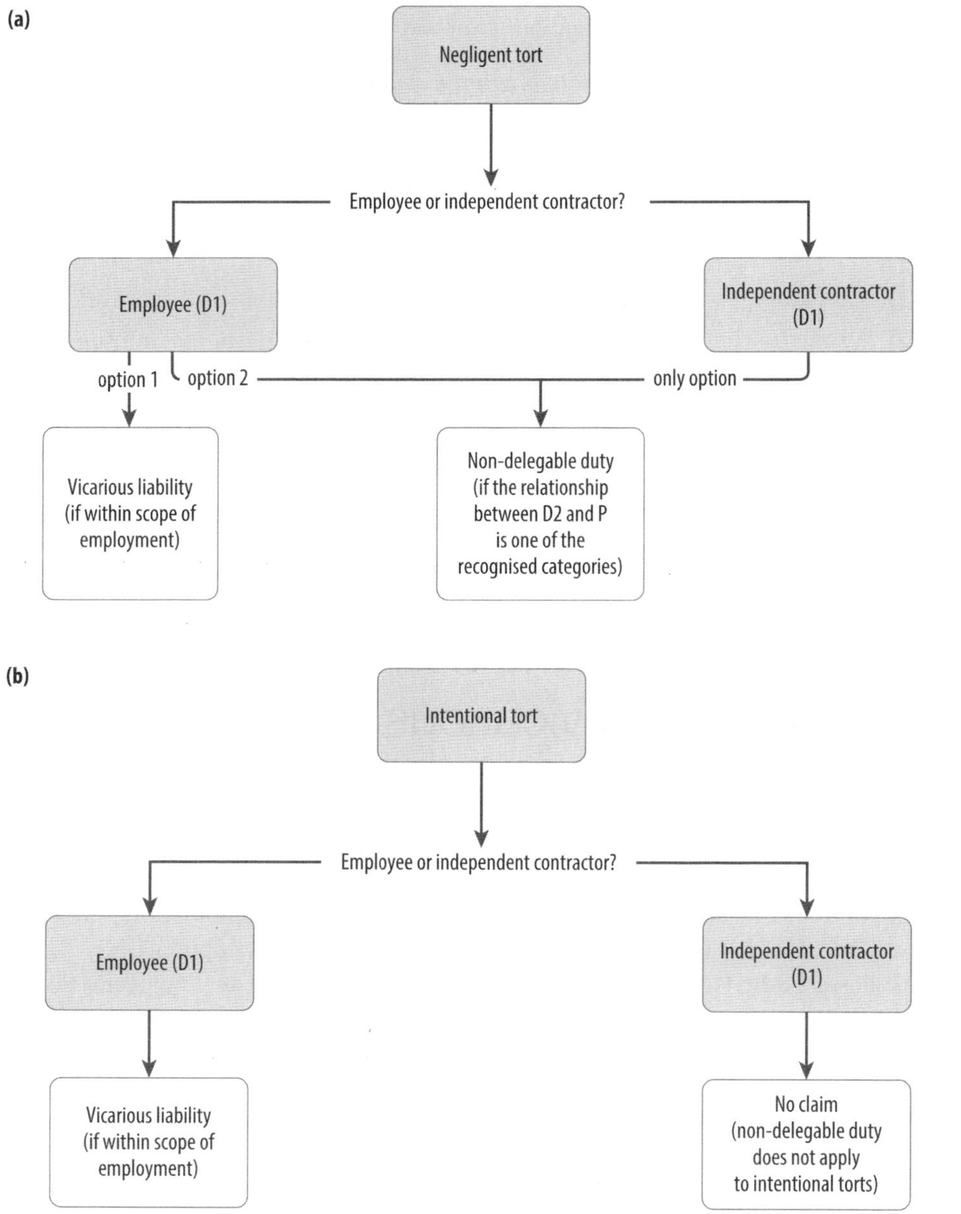

When it comes to liability for the negligent act of an employee (in relation to vicarious liability) or of an independent contractor (in relation to non-delegable duty), the law is relatively uncontroversial. It is more complicated when it comes to liability for an intentional tortious act, particularly in relation to sexual abuse, as it must be shown that the employee acted within the scope of their employment *while* committing the wrongful (including criminal) act. As the cases discussed in this section show, in Australia, as in other

Commonwealth jurisdictions, the matter of liability of employers for sexual abuse committed by employees has caused a great deal of difficulty, often bordering on confusion.

10.4.1   Legal liability of an employer for acts of sexual abuse committed by an employee

The question of whether an employer should be liable for sexual abuse committed by its employee has been the subject of intense debate across Commonwealth countries. This area relates to both vicarious liability and the non-delegable duty of care.

In relation to vicarious liability, the possibility of the employer being liable for an intentional tortious (even criminal) act is a complex matter, as it requires finding that such an act would fall within the scope of employment – in particular, satisfying the requirement that such an act was for the 'benefit' of the employer. But, as discussed in Section 10.2.3, this is not impossible since the employment created the opportunity for the wrongdoing (ie, the employee was placed in the position to do 'that class of acts'). This can be the case even when the employee acted in flagrant breach of employment obligations and instructions.

The matter of sexual abuse of children in the context of residential, educational or care institutions was first addressed in Canada in the case of *Bazley v Curry*.[114] The Supreme Court of Canada had to consider whether the defendant employer was vicariously liable for the sexual assault of some of the children residing in a residential care facility by an employee who was employed to care for them. The basis of finding liability was:

> whether the wrongful act is sufficiently related to conduct authorised by the employer
> to justify the imposition of vicarious liability. Vicarious liability is generally appropriate
> where there is a significant connection between the creation or enhancement of a risk
> and the wrong that accrues therefrom, even if unrelated to the employer's desire.[115]

In another Canadian case, *Jacobi v Griffiths*, the Supreme Court did not find a not-for-profit organisation that ran a recreational club for children liable for an assault by its program director of two children at his home.[116] The Court distinguished *Bazley v Curry* on the grounds that the club offered recreational after-school activities, run by volunteers and other members, and it did not create the same kind of relationship of power and intimacy as in *Bazley v Curry*. It was reasoned that the offender was merely provided with an opportunity to meet children.[117]

In the United Kingdom, following *Bazley v Curry*, the House of Lords found a boarding school vicariously liable for the sexual abuse of boys in its care by one of its employees in *Lister v Hesley Hall Ltd*.[118] Lord Millett stated:

> In the present case the warden's duties provided him with the opportunity to commit
> indecent assaults on the boys for his own sexual gratification, but that in itself is not

---

114   [1999] 2 SCR 534.
115   *Bazley v Curry* [1999] 2 SCR 534, [41] (McLachlin J).
116   [1999] 2 SCR 570.
117   This approach was confirmed in the later Canadian cases *Doe v Bennett* [2004] 1 SCR 436 and *EB v Order of the Oblates of Mary Immaculate in the Province of British Columbia* [2005] 3 SCR 45.
118   [2001] 1 AC 215.

enough to make the school liable … But there was far more to it than that. The school was responsible for the care and welfare of the boys. It entrusted that responsibility to the warden. He was employed to discharge the school's responsibility to the boys. For this purpose the school entrusted them to his care. He did not merely take advantage of the opportunity which employment at a residential school gave him. He abused the special position in which the school had placed him to enable it to discharge its own responsibilities, with the result that the assaults were committed by the very employee to whom the school had entrusted the care of the boys.[119]

More recently, in *Armes v Nottinghamshire County Council*, the UK Supreme Court confirmed its position that a local authority might be found vicariously liable for abuse perpetrated by foster parents, even if that local authority is not found to be negligent in relation to the foster placement.[120] The Court, however, rejected the argument that the local authority was liable on the basis of breach of a non-delegable duty of care, as this would be too wide-reaching and place too great a burden on authorities.[121]

The matter of the alleged sexual abuse of children by a public school teacher came before the High Court of Australia in *New South Wales v Lepore*,[122] which was tried at the same time as two other cases of sexual assault in Queensland: *Samin v State of Queensland*[123] and *Rich v Queensland*.[124] In all three cases, the plaintiffs based their claims solely on the basis of non-delegable duty of care, but an alternative approach based on vicarious liability of school authorities was entertained by the High Court, in line with the findings by the highest courts in Canada and the United Kingdom. These two approaches will be discussed in turn.

10.4.1.1 Non-delegable duty

In *Lepore* the question was whether the school authority should be liable in damages to the pupil for sexual abuse committed by one of its employees (a school teacher).[125] The High Court looked at earlier cases involving school authorities where the non-delegable or personal duty of the school to its pupils was found.

In *Commonwealth v Introvigne* (discussed in Section 10.3.1.2) the High Court attributed responsibility to the Commonwealth for the negligence of the teachers, in particular of the acting principal, for failing to arrange for adequate supervision, resulting in the plaintiff suffering head injuries while playing in the school grounds.[126] The plaintiff made a claim – discussed at the first instance and later at the appellate court – of vicarious liability. Nonetheless, Mason J (with whom Gibbs CJ agreed) based his decision on a non-delegable duty of care, as '[t]he duty … imposed on a school authority is akin to that owed by a

---

119 *Lister v Hesley Hall Ltd* [2001] 1 AC 215, 250 (Lord Millett). Similar reasoning was applied by the Supreme Court of the United Kingdom in *Various Claimants v Catholic Welfare Office* [2013] 2 AC 1, where Lord Philips laid down five criteria that can give rise to vicarious liability in such circumstances.
120 [2017] 3 WLR 1000.
121 Ibid [49] (Lord Reed, Hale, Kerr and Clarke LJJ agreeing), following the argument raised in *Cox v Ministry of Justice* [2016] 2 WLR 806, in relation to finding the Ministry of Justice vicariously liable for the negligence of a prisoner causing injury to the applicant employee.
122 (2003) 212 CLR 511; [2003] HCA 4.
123 [2001] QCA 295.
124 (2001) Aust Torts Reports 81-626.
125 *New South Wales v Lepore* (2003) 212 CLR 511; [2003] HCA 4.
126 (1982) 150 CLR 258.

hospital to its patient'.[127] The Commonwealth's 'personal' liability resulted from it failing to ensure that reasonable supervision was provided and thus failing to fulfil its own duty of care. That being said, even if intentional infliction of injury on another can involve a failure to take reasonable care, it can be much more: 'Intentional wrongdoing, especially intentional criminality, introduces a factor of legal relevance beyond a mere failure to take care'.[128] The majority in *Lepore* found that the school authorities did indeed owe their pupils a non-delegable duty of care, but that duty would not be breached by an intentional act of sexual assault on a pupil. Hence, the school was not liable, and could only be liable if the teacher's act was one of negligence and the school failed to ensure that reasonable care was taken. Gleeson CJ (with whom Callinan J agreed) asserted:

> At all events, to describe a duty of care as 'personal' or 'non-delegable', in the sense that the person subject to the duty has a responsibility either to perform the duty, or to see it performed, and cannot discharge that responsibility by entrusting its performance to another, conveys a reasonably clear idea; but it addresses the nature of the duty, rather than its content.[129]

As to the scope of that duty, his Honour clearly limited it to wrongful acts that are negligent in nature:

> The proposition that, because a school authority's duty of care to a pupil is non-delegable, the authority is liable for any injury, accidental or intentional, inflicted at school upon a pupil by a teacher, is too broad and the responsibility with which it fixes school authorities is too demanding.[130]

Thus, as the law currently stands, where a teacher employed by a school authority commits intentional and criminal wrongdoing (such as a sexual assault) during school hours, the school authorities will not be 'personally' liable to the pupil for breach of a non-delegable duty of care unless the school authorities were negligent in, for example, employing a particular person, supervising the employee, failing to respond to previous complaints or in some other way that facilitated or permitted the cause of the harm to the pupil.

10.4.1.2   Vicarious liability

Neither at first instance nor in the Court of Appeal was the case against the State of New South Wales based on vicarious liability[131] (likewise, *Samin* and *Rich* were argued solely on the basis of a non-delegable duty of care[132]). The potential scope of such a possibility was nevertheless discussed by the High Court.[133]

Their Honours provided an extensive analysis of the jurisprudence regarding when an employer might be held vicariously liable for the conduct of an employee. They focused in particular on the requirement that the wrongful act or omission needs to take part within the

---

127 *Commonwealth v Introvigne* (1982) 150 CLR 258, 270.
128 *New South Wales v Lepore* (2003) 212 CLR 511; [2003] HCA 4, [31].
129 Ibid [20].
130 Ibid [34].
131 *Lepore v New South Wales* (2001) 52 NSWLR 420.
132 *Rich v Queensland* (2001) Aust Torts Reports 81-626.
133 *New South Wales v Lepore* (2003) 212 CLR 511; [2003] HCA 4.

scope of employment. As we saw in Section 10.2.3, not everything that an employee does, even during work hours, will be deemed to fall within the course of employment. Similarly, the fact that wrongdoing occurred outside work hours or the place of employment will not be determinative against finding the employer liable. When an act or conduct is not directly authorised by the employer, the court needs to assess the extent to which it can be said to be incidental or 'closely connected' to the authorised acts.

In the ordinary meaning of the words, a sexual abuse of a child can never be said to be 'closely connected' to a teacher or carer's responsibility. Yet, as cases in Canada and the United Kingdom show, it might be justifiable to construe such a finding depending on the circumstances of the case. The nature of such responsibilities, and whether there is a sufficient connection between the wrongful act and what the particular teacher was employed to do, must be assessed, 'for [the sexual] misconduct fairly to be regarded as in the course of the teacher's employment [based on the type of] the relationship with pupils created by those responsibilities'.[134]

Thus, unless the circumstances are such that a teacher's responsibilities place the teacher in a position of power and intimacy in relation to a pupil, a sexual assault by the teacher committed during school hours falls outside the scope of employment and, therefore, is not the type of conduct for which the school authorities are vicariously liable.

Unsurprisingly, the decision in *Lepore* has been criticised for failing to clearly state the position in Australia as to vicarious liability for a (sexual) abuse by an employee committed in the course of employment;[135] or rather, for offering *multiple* positions. As aptly summarised by Kirby J:

> Gummow and Hayne JJ do not favour the analysis of risk adopted by the Supreme Court of Canada in *Bazley* ... Callinan J rejects the application of vicarious liability to situations of intentional wrongdoing by employees ... For McHugh J the issue does not arise for decision [as he saw the issue as one of non-delegable duty of care]. Gaudron J introduces an analysis based on the law of estoppel ... On the other hand, the reasons of Gleeson CJ are influenced by the analysis of vicarious liability in the English and Canadian decisions.[136]

As to Kirby J's opinion in relation to vicarious liability, he reiterated that as a legal principle it has emerged from 'judicial perceptions of justice and social requirements that vary over time', so it should be of no surprise that it is 'a subject fashioned by judges at different times, holding different ideas about its justification and social purpose, or "no idea at all"'.[137] As to the issue of whether non-delegable duty was applicable, he refused to provide a ruling in this case: the teacher was the employee of the school and so the claim should have been brought under vicarious liability; thus, a non-delegable duty of care would not be an issue.

---

134 Ibid [74] (Gleeson CJ).
135 See, eg, S White and G Orr, 'Precarious Liability: The High Court in *Lepore, Samin* and *Rich* on School Responsibility for Assaults by Teachers (Case Notes)' (2003) 11(2) *Torts Law Journal* 101; J Wangman, 'Liability for Institutional Child Sexual Assault' (2004) 28(1) *Melbourne University Law Review* 169.
136 *New South Wales v Lepore* (2003) 212 CLR 511; [2003] HCA 4, [298] (Kirby J).
137 Ibid [301].

The matter was discussed again in 2016 in *Prince Alfred College Inc v ADC*.[138] The High Court held that the 'relevant approach' to be taken in such situations is to examine the position of 'power' and 'intimacy' that the employee was assigned to by the employer and was thereby placed in relation to the respondent. The Court did not ultimately rule in relation to the liability of Prince Alfred College towards ADC, as it found the time extension sought by the College should not be granted (but note the passing of the *Limitation of Actions (Child Abuse) Amendment Act 2018* (SA) since, as discussed below). Nevertheless, the case continues to provide important guidance as to the liability of employers for criminal acts committed by their employees in Australia, in particular in relation to sexual abuse of children in educational institutions.

Case: *Prince Alfred College Inc v ADC* (2016) 258 CLR 134

Facts

In 1962, as a 12-year-old boarder at Prince Alfred College, ADC was sexually abused by Dean Bain on multiple occasions. Mr Bain was employed by the College as a housemaster. Shortly after Prince Alfred College was made aware of the allegations, Mr Bain was dismissed from his employment there. In his adult life, ADC was diagnosed with post-traumatic stress disorder, suffered alcoholism, would self-harm and was admitted to a psychiatric clinic on a number of occasions.

In 1997, ADC commenced civil proceedings against Mr Bain, but did not pursue a legal action against the College. In 1999, ADC and Mr Bain reached a settlement under which Mr Bain paid ADC $15 000. In 2008, ADC brought proceedings in the Supreme Court of South Australia against Prince Alfred College for:

(1) breach of a non-delegable duty of care
(2) negligence in employing Mr Bain who had prior convictions of gross indecency (in 1954) and indecent behaviour with students (in 1960), and a breach of duty in supervising Mr Bain
(3) vicarious liability for the wrongful act of its employee.

As the statutory time limitation had expired, ADC needed to apply for an extension of time to bring the proceedings.

Issue

Can an employer be vicariously liable for its employee's intentional act (such as sexual abuse)?

Decision

The Full Court of the Supreme Court of South Australia in *A, DC v Prince Alfred College Inc* [2015] SASCFC 161 allowed the claim to be brought despite the passing of the time limitation period, and found Prince Alfred College vicariously liable. Gray J also found the College had breached its duty of care. The College appealed that decision.

138 (2016) 258 CLR 134; [2016] HCA 37.

The High Court allowed the appeal, stating that ADC should not have been granted an extension of time under s 48(3) of the *Limitation of Actions Act 1936* (SA). Thus, it agreed with the primary judge that the passing of such a significant period (11 years) from 'an apparent resolution of any claim against the [College] and the commencement of proceedings was not justified by the circumstances of this case and meant that a fair trial on the merits was no longer possible' (at [8]).

Significance

In determining vicarious liability of the employer for a sexual assault by an employee, the court will look into a number of features that might give occasion for the wrongful act, which the High Court referred to as 'the relevant approach', to assess whether that employee acted in the scope of their employment. These factors include 'authority', 'control', 'power', 'trust', 'access' to the person or premises and the ability to achieve 'intimacy' with the victim.

Notes

Before the passing of the *Limitation of Actions (Child Abuse) Amendment Act 2018* (SA), which commenced on 1 February 2019 (and excluded the application of limitation periods for child abuse actions in pt 1A), one of the major hurdles experienced by the plaintiff was the application of the *Limitation of Actions Act 1936* (SA), which prescribes that claims need to be brought within three years from when the injury incurred and, as that period is usually suspended until the person turned 18, it meant the plaintiff's 21st birthday. The plaintiff was diagnosed with post-traumatic stress disorder in 1996, and it was not until December 2008 that he brought the present proceedings.

Under s 48 of the *Limitation of Actions Act 1936*, with similar provisions across most other jurisdictions in Australia, courts are allowed to extend the limitation periods for personal injury actions (which child sexual abuses would fall into) by exercising their discretion. Nevertheless, the High Court agreed with the primary judge that the longer the passage of time, the greater the risk of failing to achieve a just outcome for the defendant, which cannot be addressed merely by reducing the damages to take into account the delay during which evidence has been lost: 'To say that is simply to acknowledge that a fair trial on the merits of the case in order to do justice according to law is no longer possible' (at [8]).

Question

What would be your arguments in favour of removing limitation periods for child abuse claims in similar cases?

 Guided response in the eBook

The more recent developments in assessing vicarious liability in historical cases of sexual abuse include *PCB v Geelong College*, decided by the Supreme Court of Victoria in 2021, where also landmark damages of $2 632 319.25 were awarded to the plaintiff.

Case: *PCB v Geelong College* [2021] VSC 633

Facts

PCB was a student at Geelong College. In 1988, the plaintiff attended the House of Guilds (a complex of spaces for woodwork, ceramics and other crafts) after school, which was located on the grounds of the school which, in addition to the Geelong students, was open to students from other schools and members of the community who had to pay a membership fee.

Bert Palframan, who passed away in about 1999, was an honorary member of the House of Guilds. It was not disputed that in the period between late 1988 and mid-1990 the plaintiff was sexually abused by him at the House of Guilds, in his car and (on one occasion) in the plaintiff's home. The plaintiff had been diagnosed as having suffered psychiatric injury as a consequence of the sexual abuse.

The plaintiff argued that Palframan was, in effect, an employee of the school and the defendant was negligent and/or vicariously liable for abuse perpetrated by Palframan. PCB claimed damages on the grounds of (at [25]):

> that the 'trajectory' of his life was altered for the worse by the abuse. Among other things, he claim[ed] that he would have been either more 'successful' or 'successful' earlier and in a more sustained way but for the abuse.

Issue

The Court had to consider the school's liability for sexual abuse of a student by a non-employee on and off school premises.

Decision

O'Meare J, reviewing the evidence provided (including that the school did not assign Palframan a professional title, he was not paid by the school and the school never held any personal file about him, as one would expect from an employer), did not find the relationship to be 'akin' to an employee of the school.

His Honour also rejected the argument of the plaintiff that the case of *Prince Alfred College Inc v ADC*[139] provided a 'framework' for finding the school vicariously liable as 'the presence of a relationship of employer and employee is a necessary intermediate step or foundation in the reasoning of the High Court in Prince Alfred College' (at [303]).

As to the claim of negligence on the part of the school, his Honour did not accept that the general system of supervision was a reasonable response, including some evidence that the school had received warnings about the activities of Palframan, which should have met with a more decisive action to supervise or exclude him. Consequently, the Court found that Geelong College should bear responsibility for the consequences of the abuse suffered within and outside the school premises (as the latter was facilitated by the former) and assessed damages:

- for pain and suffering at $300 000
- for past loss of earnings at $676 583.05

---

139 (2016) 258 CLR 134; [2016] HCA 37.

- for future loss of earning capacity at $1 634 995.20
- other/medical and like expenses at $20 741.

Significance

This case shows that courts are adamant that the duty of care owed to children by schools and institutions establishes high standards to ensure the safety of those children.

Question

Should the 'standard of the day' apply when dealing with historical sexual abuse cases?

 Guided response in the eBook

As persuasively noted by Lord Philips, 'the law of vicarious liability is on the move'.[140] The matter of finding employers liable for an intentional criminal conduct committed by their employees – in particular, sexual abuse of children in educational, residential or care facilities – will continue to attract considerable judicial and scholarly attention. It is a difficult balancing act to ensure 'justice' to the applicants, on the one hand, and 'fairness' to the defendants, on the other. The general principles for vicarious liability, therefore, will most likely continue to be reformulated in light of the facts of new cases as they arise. It is also more likely than not that the 'relevant approach' will continue to differ between jurisdictions as the outcomes in this area are determined by policy choices and judges' assessments of what is 'fair and just' (the UK approach).[141] This may very well lead to a lowering of the level of legal certainty in this area, as noted by a Canadian judge: 'Overly frequent resort to general principles opens the door to subjective judicial evaluations that may promote uncertainty and litigation at the expense of predictability and settlement.'[142]

This is an area that has experienced relative developments in Australia in recent years as well, in response to the five-year enquiry by the Royal Commission into Institutional Responses to Child Sexual Abuse.[143] The Royal Commission held hearings between 2013 and 2017, including with survivors of child sexual abuse, and made 189 recommendations aiming to make institutions safer for children.[144] Since the Royal Commission's Final Report was released in 2017, states and territories have been implementing the recommendations. As

---

140 *Various Claimants v Catholic Welfare Office* [2013] 2 AC 1, [19].
141 Note also that in 2022, after seven years of public hearings and evidence from 725 victims, the Independent Inquiry into Child Sexual Abuse (IICSA) in England and Wales (UK) published its Report, making 20 recommendations, including calling for a statutory requirement for people working with children or in a position of trust to report allegations of child sexual abuse, see <www.iicsa.org.uk>.
142 *EB v Order of the Oblates of Mary Immaculate in the Province of British Columbia* [2005] 3 SCR 45, [41] (Binnie J).
143 See the Royal Commission website, <www.childabuseroyalcommission.gov.au>.
144 *Royal Commission into Institutional Responses to Child Sexual Abuse: Final Report Recommendations* (Report, December 2017), <www.childabuseroyalcommission.gov.au/sites/default/files/final%5Freport%5F-%5Frecommendations.pdf>.

a consequence, the limitation period for claims resulting from the sexual abuse of a person in an institutional context has now been removed across jurisdictions in Australia (summarised in Table 10.6), in line with the Royal Commission's recommendations.[145] There are still some differences across the jurisdictions in approaches to claims that had commenced before the limitation periods were removed, as well as some jurisdictions passing laws permitting courts to set aside previous settlements allowing plaintiffs to make new claims that would be more just.

Table 10.6   Overview of statutory provisions removing limitation periods in child sexual (and in some instances some other types of) abuses

Legislation	Provision(s)
Limitation Act 1985 (ACT)	s 21C
Limitation Act 1969 (NSW)	s 6A
Limitation Act 1981 (NT)	ss 5A, 53–5
Limitations of Actions Act 1974 (Qld)	ss 11A, 48
Limitations of Actions Act 1936 (SA)	s 3A
Limitation Act 1974 (Tas)	ss 5B, 5C, 38
Limitations of Actions Act 1958 (Vic)	pt IIA div 5
Limitation Act 2005 (WA)	s 6A, pt 7 div 1

For example, in South Australia, in addition to the passing of the *Limitation of Actions (Child Abuse) Amendment Act 2018* (SA) that amended the *Limitation of Actions Act 1936* by removing the limitation period for child abuses (covering sexual abuse, serious physical abuse and psychological abuse related to sexual abuse or serious physical abuse, pts 1A, 3A(5)), the *Civil Liability (Institutional Child Abuse Liability) Amendment Act 2021* took effect on 1 August 2022. The Amendment Act makes four key changes to the *Civil Liability Act 1936* (SA), including allowing action for previously settled claims if the courts find it just and reasonable to do so (pt 7B), as well as allowing historical abuse claims to be made against an unincorporated association, such as an associated trust, and against institutions that might have changed structure over time – for example, following a merger (pt 7A div 4).

HINTS AND TIPS

You can follow the progress of the implementation of the Royal Commission's recommendations by checking state and territory websites.[146] At the end of 2022, the Commonwealth, states and territories as well as certain institutions were required to provide their final progress reports on the implementation of the recommendations.

145   *Limitation of Actions Amendment (Child Abuse) Act 2015* (Vic); *Limitation of Actions Amendment (Child Abuse) Act 2016* (NSW); *Justice and Community Safety Legislation Amendment Act 2016 (No 2)* (ACT); *Limitation of Actions (Child Sexual Abuse) and Other Legislation Amendment Act 2016* (Qld); *Limitation Amendment (Child Abuse) Act 2017* (NT); *Civil Liability Legislation Amendment (Child Sexual Abuse Actions) Act 2018* (WA); *Limitation of Actions (Child Abuse) Amendment Act 2018* (SA); *Justice Legislation Amendment (Organisational Liability for Child Abuse) Act 2019* (Tas).

146   ACT (<www.act.gov.au/childabuseroyalcommission/documents>); NSW (<www.nsw.gov.au/projects/response-to-royal-commission>); NT (<https://rmo.nt.gov.au/updates/2020-generational-change-

The relationship between the personal, non-delegable duty of an employer and the employer's vicarious liability for the wrongdoing of its employees is a complex area, including due to the statutory differences across the jurisdictions in Australia. It can be simplified to a few key aspects which are summarised in Table 10.7.

Table 10.7   Comparison of the key principles of the doctrines of vicarious liability and non-delegable duty of care

	Vicarious liability	Non-delegable duty
When does it arise?	Is based on the relationship between the tortfeasor (D1) and the ultimate defendant (D2). Relationships giving rise to vicarious liability include: • employer (D2)–employee (D1) (most common) • partner (D2)–co-partner (D1) • principal (D2)–agent (D1) • car owner (D2)–driver (D1) (when driven with the permission of the owner).	Arises only in the context of special relationships between the defendant (D2) and the plaintiff (P): • employer (D2) to employee (P) • hospital (D2) to patient (P) • school (D2) to pupil (P) • occupier (D2) to 'neighbour' (P) (as to dangerous forces escaping) • prison or detention centre (D2) to prisoner or detainee (P).
Fault element	It is a form of strict liability, thus D2 does not need to be at fault personally but is held strictly liable for the wrongdoing of D1.	It is part of the law of negligence.[a] But in Victoria,[b] New South Wales[c] and South Australia, a breach of non-delegable duty is treated as if the delegator were vicariously liable to P (thus, it is strict liability) – though only if the tort committed by the delegate was negligent and not intentional. Also, it has been argued by Hayne J that the non-delegable duty of care is a form of vicarious liability.[d]
Conditions of application	D1 (employee, servant or agent) committed a tort (any type) against P, satisfying the conditions that: (1) D1 was an employee, servant or agent of D2, *and* (2) the tort was committed within the course of employment.	P and D2 are in one of the recognised types of special relationships that can give rise to a non-delegable duty of care. D2 (employee or independent contractor) commits negligence, as this doctrine does not apply to intentional torts.

impact-report>); Qld (<www.cyjma.qld.gov.au/about-us/reviews-inquiries/queensland-government-response-royal-commission-institutional-responses-child-sexual-abuse>); SA (<www.childprotection .sa.gov.au/child-protection-initiatives/system-reform/safe-and-well>); Tas (<www.justice.tas.gov.au/ carcru/tasmanian-response-to-the-royal-commission>); Vic (<www.vic.gov.au/victorian-government-response-royal-commission-institutional-responses-child-sexual-abuse>); WA (<www.wa.gov.au/ government/publications/2021-progress-report-safer-wa-children-and-young-people>).

Table 10.7   *(cont.)*

	Vicarious liability	Non-delegable duty
Consequences	Imposes liability on D2 for the *wrongdoing of another* (D1), even if D2 is not at fault personally.	Imposes liability on D2 for its *own wrongdoing* by failing to comply with a personal duty owed directly to P (ie, to see or ensure that reasonable care and skill is taken by another).
Choices of remedy available to P	Choice of either: (1) sue the original tortfeasor (D1) in a regular tort action, or (2) sue the employer, master or principal (D2) because (although not at fault itself) it is liable for the wrongdoing of its employees, servants or agents.	Choice of either: (1) sue the original tortfeasor (D1) in a regular negligence action, or (2) sue the delegator (D2) because it breached its personal, non-delegable duty owed directly to P with whom it is in one of the special relationships.

  ᵃ *Leichardt Municipal Council v Montgomery* (2007) 230 CLR 22; [2007] HCA 6; *New South Wales v Lepore* (2003) 212 CLR 511; [2003] HCA 4.
  ᵇ *Wrongs Act 1958* (Vic) s 61.
  ᶜ *Civil Liability Act 2002* (NSW) s 5Q.
  ᵈ *Burnie Port Authority v General Jones Pty Ltd* (1994) 179 CLR 520.

HINTS AND TIPS

In Australia only one employer can be vicariously liable as there is no recognition of the principle of 'dual vicarious liability'.[147] In other Commonwealth jurisdictions, including the United Kingdom[148] and Canada,[149] multiple unconnected employers can be found vicariously liable.

REVIEW QUESTIONS

(1) Based on the cases discussed in this section, what would be the key considerations in assessing vicarious liability of educational, residential or care institutions for the intentional and criminal wrongdoings (such as sexual abuse) of their employees (eg, teachers or carers)?

(2) Based on the judgment in *Prince Alfred College Inc v ADC*, would it be advisable to pursue a claim for breach of a personal duty of the employer to the plaintiff in relation to intentional (including criminal) wrongdoings of an employee?

 Guided responses in the eBook

147 See, eg, *Villanti v Coles Group Supply Chain Pty Ltd* (2017) 81 MVR 445.
148 See, eg, *Viasystems (Tyneside) Ltd v Thermal Transfer (Northern) Ltd* [2006] QB 510.
149 See, eg, *Blackwater v Plint* [2005] 3 SCR 3.

KEY CONCEPTS

- **contract for service:** independent contractors are engaged by an employer to work under a contract for service (in which the independent contractor directs their services as specified in their contract and are legally responsible for their own work).

- **contract of service:** employees are employed by an employer to work under a contract of service (in which the employer has the right to direct the way in which the employee does the work and so the employer is legally responsible for the employee's work).

- **master–servant:** an old-fashioned way of describing the employer–employee relationship.

- **non-delegable duty of care:** a form of liability imposed on the defendant to ensure that reasonable care and skill is taken by the defendant's delegate. The duty may arise in a small number of special relationships between the defendant and the plaintiff.

- **strict liability:** means 'liability regardless of fault'. It imposes liability on a party without a finding of fault (ie, negligence or tortious intent). An example is vicarious liability.

- **vicarious liability:** means 'liability through another person'. At common law, a person who is liable for the tort of another person is said to be vicariously liable.

 Complete the multiple-choice questions in the eBook to test your knowledge

PROBLEM-SOLVING EXERCISES

Exercise 1

Fintech is a tech start-up that specialises in providing live internet streaming to businesses that trade in bitcoin (cryptocurrency). It has been very successful in attracting new clients and its employee numbers have grown from the initial five to 25 within six months of its operation. To celebrate its first anniversary, the management of Fintech organised a party for employees in one of the trendiest bars in Melbourne. All staff were invited, with an expectation that they would all attend unless they had a valid excuse. Following the party, some of the employees moved to the bar at the hotel where some of them were staying.

Drinks continued to be served at the hotel bar, for which the company was partially paying. While at the hotel bar and having enjoyed quite a few drinks at that point, Mr Bolt (a marketing assistant) and Ms Bearing (the technology manager) started discussing work-related matters. This included chatting about which new database management system should be adopted by the company to maintain and control access to the ever-increasing size of the Fintech database and improving the speed of retrieval, which was critical for maintaining the company's initial success on the market. An argument between Mr Bolt and Ms Bearing developed, with Ms Bearing saying that she 'knew better' as she was the technology manager and warned Mr Bolt against undermining her authority in front of other employees. Mr Bolt was then assaulted by Ms Bearing, resulting in him sustaining a severe brain injury.

Mr Bolt wishes to bring a claim against Fintech alleging it is vicariously liable for Ms Bearing's action and asks for your advice.

 Guided response in the eBook

Exercise 2

Johnny, a lively and energetic 11-year-old, is a pupil at Rocky High School. He takes part in many of the activities offered during the course of a normal school day. One such activity is swimming lessons provided at the local swimming pool. Swimming lessons are provided by a swimming teacher (Mr Jones) and supervised by a lifeguard (Ms Thomas).

Mr Jones doubles as a maths teacher at Rocky High where he is employed full-time on a permanent contract. His salary is paid fortnightly with the appropriate tax deductions being made by the school. When conducting the swimming lessons, Mr Jones is required to wear a jersey with the school's logo on it.

Ms Thomas is employed by Mrs Bell (trading as Swimming Fun Services) with whom Rocky High has a contract. Swimming Fun Services is in charge of who is delegated to act as lifeguard at the swimming pool during the school's swimming lessons. On occasions when Ms Thomas is away or unwell, a substitute lifeguard is provided by Swimming Fun Services.

During one of the lessons, Johnny got into trouble while swimming. As witnessed by other pupils, as Johnny was practising his backstroke he started choking and went under the water. At the time, Ms Thomas was engaged in a phone conversation and Mr Jones was updating his Facebook page (an activity the school headmistress has reprimanded him for on previous occasions and subsequently instructed him not to do while children are in the water). Neither Mr Jones nor Ms Thomas noticed Johnny in trouble and it was only after other children raised the alarm that Ms Thomas jumped into the pool and pulled Johnny out. He was successfully resuscitated but suffered a serious hypoxic brain injury.

Advise the plaintiffs (Johnny's parents) on the possible course of action.

 Guided response in the eBook

CHALLENGE YOURSELF

Exercise 1

Consider again the scenario in problem-solving exercise 2. Now assume that Mr Jones (an employee) sexually abused Johnny in the changing room after one of the swimming lessons. Mr Jones had a previous history of indecent exposure and suspension for sexually motivated assault. Do these facts change anything in the reasoning you provided for the initial scenario? If so, how?

Guided response in the eBook

Exercise 2

Among the legal profession and legal scholars, it has been debated whether maintaining a non-delegable duty of care serves its purpose. Do you agree that non-delegable duty of care should be abandoned and replaced with vicarious liability (ie, strict liability for the wrongful act of another) in line with s 5Q of the *Civil Liability Act 2002* (NSW)? What would be your arguments *for* such a position?

 Guided response in the eBook

11

DEFAMATION

11.1   Introduction and purpose of defamation laws

The tort of defamation protects the reputation of individuals in society.[1] A cause of action arises where one individual publishes a false matter about another that lowers the reputation of the latter in the eyes of ordinary and reasonable members of the society.[2] While many of the torts covered in this book seek to protect the bodily integrity of individuals, the tort of defamation seeks to protect their reputation. Defamation laws are concerned with balancing freedom of speech with the protection of individuals' reputation, character and standing in the community.[3] The increased use of social media has a significant role to play in defamation, with the speed and ease of publication on the internet creating new sites for defamation action.[4] Additionally, the emergence of novel technologies and methods of sharing defamatory posts online – such as hashtags,[5] emojis[6] and memes[7] – have raised novel questions about application of traditional defamation principles to the modern technological landscape. This makes defamation a highly relevant tort in contemporary society.

11.1.1   What is defamation?

Defamation arises when the defendant publishes or communicates a false statement about the plaintiff to a third party and the statement adversely affects the reputation of the plaintiff in the eyes of ordinary and reasonable people.[8] Defamation is not concerned with the plaintiff's safety or mental wellbeing, but instead focuses on offering redress in circumstances where the plaintiff's good character or standing has been harmed.[9]

Defamation is a tort of strict liability.[10] The defendant does not need to be at fault but they do need to intend the act of publishing the communication.[11] Hence, a defendant may be liable even if they did not intend to harm the defendant's reputation and took reasonable care.[12]

---

1   *Radio 2UE Sydney Pty Ltd v Chesterton* (2009) 238 CLR 460; [2009] HCA 16, [1]–[3] (French CJ, Gummow, Kiefel and Bell JJ).
2   Ibid [1]–[8].
3   See, eg, *Defamation Act 2005* (Vic) s 3, which stipulates that the objects of defamation legislation are, inter alia, to provide fair remedies for reputational harm but to also ensure the law of defamation does not place unreasonable limits on freedom of expression.
4   For example, *in Mickle v Farley* [2013] NSWDC 295, defamatory posts on Facebook and Twitter by a former student about a high school teacher resulted in an award of damages for $105 000. More recently, Mildura politician and social worker Dr Anne Webster succeeded in her defamation claim for defamatory posts on a Facebook page: *Webster v Brewer (No 3)* [2020] FCA 1343.
5   *B1 v B2* [2017] NSWDC 252.
6   *McAlpine v Bercow* [2013] EWHC 1342 (QB).
7   *Mosslmani v DailyMailcom Australia Pty Ltd* [2016] NSWDC 264.
8   *Radio 2UE Sydney Pty Ltd v Chesterton* (2009) 238 CLR 460; [2009] HCA 16, [5] (French CJ, Gummow, Kiefel and Bell JJ).
9   Damages for defamation may also compensate for injury to feelings: *Carson v John Fairfax & Sons Ltd* (1993) 178 CLR 44, 71 (Brennan J), 105 (McHugh J).
10   This was recently confirmed by the High Court in *Fairfax Media Publications Pty Ltd v Voller* (2021) 273 CLR 346; [2021] HCA 27, [111] ('*Voller*').
11   Ibid [111].
12   *Google Inc v Duffy* (2017) 129 SASR 304, [25].

Historically, in some circumstances it was relatively straightforward for the defendant to establish a claim in defamation; therefore, defences played a crucial role in determining the success of such claims. However, with the introduction of the new serious harm test in 2021, the plaintiff now has the onus of convincing a judge that they have sustained serious harm, thereby reducing the likelihood that trivial claims will be brought.[13] Further, the plaintiff does not bear the onus of proof to establish that the defamatory matter is false, so the defendant's ability to establish the truth of the matter in a defence is critical.

11.1.2 Purpose of defamation law

Defamation law is found in statute and in common law. Its purpose is to attempt to balance the competing demands of freedom of speech in the public sphere with the private right of individuals to protect their reputation.[14] We should be permitted to freely express our opinion about people but not present those opinions as false statements of fact that damage others' reputations.[15] The manner in which the balance between these competing rights is struck can vary considerably among international jurisdictions. Situated at one end of a spectrum, in the United States, the right to freedom of speech is constitutionally entrenched, making defamation actions more difficult to maintain. At the opposite end, in the United Kingdom, no such constitutional protections exist and action for damaging statements was, before 2013, more easily maintained. The position in the United Kingdom changed considerably with the introduction of the *Defamation Act 2013* (UK) which requires plaintiffs to show actual or probable serious harm. Previously, Australia had adopted a middle-ground position between the two countries, but the passing of the United Kingdom's statute has shifted that positioning.[16] Further, the introduction of the new serious harm requirement in Australia – modelled on the United Kingdom's provisions – arguably align Australia more closely with the British jurisdiction.

Defamation laws can also be crucial in offering remedies in the absence of a tort of privacy in Australia.[17] In the United States, a tort of privacy is recognised in statute and common law;[18] despite the country's strong recognition of freedom of speech, it has been used by celebrities

---

13   See s 10A of the uniform defamation provisions. See also: *Lachaux v Independent Print Ltd* [2020] AC 612; *Newman v Whittington* [2022] NSWSC 249; *Wilks v Qu* [2022] VCC 620.

14   This was recognised by the High Court in *Lange v Australian Broadcasting Corporation* (1997) 189 CLR 520.

15   Unlike the United States, where the First Amendment to the American Constitution protects freedom of speech from government interference, Australia does not have a bill of rights that articulates or protects freedom of speech.

16   See D Rolph, 'A Critique of the Defamation Act 2013: Lessons For and From Australian Defamation Law Reform' (2016) 21(4) *Communications Law* 116.

17   The decision of the High Court in *Victoria Park Racing & Recreation Grounds Co Ltd v Taylor* (1937) 58 CLR 479 is thought to have precluded the development of the tort of privacy for many decades. The decision in *Australian Broadcasting Corporation v Lenah Game Meats Pty Ltd* (2001) 208 CLR 199; [2001] HCA 63 appears to have opened the door to potential development of such a tort: 'the time is ripe for consideration whether a tort of invasion of privacy should be recognised' at [335] (Callinan J); 'the law should be more astute than in the past to identify and protect interests that fall within the concept of privacy' at [40] (Gleeson J).

18   American Law Institute, *Restatement (Second) of Torts* (1977) § 652A; *Pavesich v New England Life Insurance Co*, 122 Ga 190 (1905). See also EA Meltz, 'No Harm, No Foul? "Attempted" Invasion of Privacy and the Tort of Intrusion Upon Seclusion' (2015) 83(6) *Fordham Law Review* 3431, 3434–6 for an overview of the development of the tort of privacy in the United States.

as a weapon against media intrusion.[19] In the United Kingdom, prominent celebrities have pursued action pertaining to their reputation through an action for breach of confidence.[20] In Australia, public figures may rely on the tort of defamation as a means of protection in the absence of a tort of privacy.[21] For example, Australian rugby player Andrew Ettingshausen commenced defamation proceedings for the publication of nude photographs of him in a national magazine. Interestingly, Kirby P referred to Ettingshausen's case seemingly as centred on the invasion of his privacy rather than damage to reputation, given the photographs of the plaintiff were taken without his consent.[22] Given that the tort of defamation protects *reputation* rather than *privacy*, the scope of the protection in this regard is limited.

11.1.3   Background to the 2005 and 2021 reforms to the uniform defamation legislation

11.1.3.1   Overview of the 2005 legislative reforms

For many years the legal framework pertaining to defamation in Australia was inconsistent, operating via a combination of common law and legislation. Queensland and Tasmania implemented defamation codes,[23] Western Australia relied largely on common law, while the remaining states used a mixture of common law and statute.[24] The fragmented network of defamation principles across Australian states proved problematic. For example, multiple instances of publication of a defamatory matter throughout Australian states, and even internationally, could result in a plaintiff pursuing defamation lawsuits across numerous jurisdictions.[25] The lack of consistency in the law meant that defamatory material actionable in one state was potentially not actionable in another. Following various attempts at reform, on 1 January 2006 a new uniform defamation regime came into effect and these statutes remain applicable to this day (see Table 11.1).[26] Each state and territory implemented legislation based on recommendations and a model uniform law developed by the Standing Committee of Attorneys-General.[27]

---

19   SJ Katze, 'Hunting the Hunters: AB 381 and California's Attempt to Restrain the Paparazzi' (2006) 16(4) *Fordham Intellectual Property, Media and Entertainment Law Journal* 1349.

20   See, eg, *Campbell v MGN Ltd* [2004] 2 AC 457 (model Naomi Campbell successfully sued media outlet MGN for publishing photographs of her leaving a rehabilitation clinic).

21   D Rolph, *Reputation, Celebrity and Defamation Law* (Ashgate Publishing, 2008).

22   *Australian Consolidated Press v Ettingshausen* (New South Wales Court of Appeal, Gleeson CJ, Kirby P and Clarke JA, 13 October 1993) 26–7.

23   *Defamation Act 1889* (Qld); *Defamation Act 1957* (Tas). New South Wales originally used a code but subsequently replaced it with legislation: *Defamation Act 1974* (NSW).

24   *Defamation Act 1901* (ACT); *Defamation Act 1974* (NSW); *Defamation Act 1938* (NT); *Civil Liability Act 1936* (SA); *Wrongs Act 1958* (Vic).

25   D Rolph, 'A Critique of the National, Uniform Defamation Laws' (2008) 16(3) *Torts Law Journal* 207, 209–10.

26   The law came into effect on 1 January 2006 in New South Wales, Victoria, South Australia, Western Australia, Queensland and Tasmania. On 23 February 2006 it came into effect in the Australian Capital Territory, and on 26 April 2006 in the Northern Territory.

27   Recommendations for reform are contained in Standing Committee of Attorneys-General, Working Group of State and Territory Officers, *Proposal for Uniform Defamation Laws* (July 2004). The model laws are outlined in Standing Committee of Attorneys-General, *Model Defamation Provisions* (March 2005).

Table 11.1   Key features of the uniform defamation Acts introduced in 2005

Key features	Legislative reference/further explanation
Repeal of previous defamation legislation and retention of the common law (with modifications) to assist with the determination of defamation	*Civil Law (Wrongs) Act 2002* (ACT) s 118; *Defamation Act 2005* (NSW) s 6; *Defamation Act 2005* (Qld) s 6; *Defamation Act 2005* (SA) s 6; *Defamation Act 2005* (Tas) s 6; *Defamation Act 2005* (Vic) s 6; *Defamation Act 2005* (WA) s 6; *Defamation Act 2006* (NT) s 5
Abolition of the common law distinction between *slander* (non-permanent forms of defamatory matter) and *libel* (permanent forms of defamatory matter)	Historically, an action in libel could be instigated without proof of pecuniary loss whereas an action in slander required proof of financial loss. This distinction is no longer relevant as under the uniform defamation laws action in defamation may be brought without proof of pecuniary loss
Introduction of statutory caps for non-economic loss	At the time of introduction, the cap was set at $250 000, but has increased with indexation yearly
Introduction of provisions promoting non-litigious means of resolving defamation disputes through alternative dispute resolution	For instance, through the use of an offer to amend or an apology
Confinement of the role of juries in civil trials to determination of whether the plaintiff has been defamed, and deferring determination of the award of damages to the judge	*Defamation Act 2005* (NSW) s 22; *Defamation Act 2005* (Qld) s 22; *Defamation Act 2005* (Tas) s 22; *Defamation Act 2005* (Vic) s 22; *Defamation Act 2005* (WA) s 22. No equivalent provisions exist in the ACT, NT and SA legislation
Abolition of exemplary or punitive damages in defamation	Two justifications for this are: (1) that punishment should be left to the criminal law rather than civil law; and (2) a plaintiff should not be permitted to profit from damages awarded for defamation
Introduction of justification (truth) as a defence to defamation, without a public interest requirement	*Civil Law (Wrongs) Act 2002* (ACT) s 135; *Defamation Act 2005* (NSW) s 25; *Defamation Act 2006* (NT) s 22; *Defamation Act 2005* (Qld) s 25; *Defamation Act 2005* (SA) s 23; *Defamation Act 2005* (Tas) s 25; *Defamation Act 2005* (Vic) s 25; *Defamation Act 2005* (WA) s 25
Imposition of a one-year time period for instigating a defamation action following publication	*Defamation Act 2005* (Tas) s 20A; *Limitation Act 1985* (ACT) s 21B; *Limitation Act 1969* (NSW) s 14B; *Limitation Act 1981* (NT) s 12(2)(b); *Limitation of Actions Act 1974* (Qld) s 10AA; *Limitation of Actions Act 1936* (SA) s 37; *Limitation of Actions Act 1958* (Vic) s 5(AAA); *Limitation Act 2005* (WA) s 15

The purpose of the uniform legislation was to achieve consistency and uniformity of defamation law across all Australian states and territories, to ensure that freedom of expression was not unreasonably curtailed, to promote effective and fair remedies, and to encourage speedy and non-litigious forms of dispute resolution.[28]

11.1.3.2   Overview of the 2021 legislative reforms

While the 2005 reforms were effective and worked well for many years, technology made significant advances in the decade and a half that followed, meaning that many existing defamation principles required substantial overhaul. In June 2018, the New South Wales Government published a report following a statutory review of the law of defamation, particularly relating to defamation in the digital environment.[29] In February 2019 the Council of Attorneys-General released a Discussion Paper,[30] and subsequently sought public consultation on proposals to amend the existing defamation provisions. The Discussion Paper (referring to the NSW Review of defamation provisions) highlighted that the objective of existing legislation remained valid but ought to be amended and modernised.[31] Draft amendments to existing provisions were released for public comment and consultation between November 2019 and January 2020.

On 27 July 2020, the Council of Attorneys-General approved the Model Defamation Amendment Provisions (MDAPs).[32] The proposed reforms were divided into two stages. The first tranche of reforms (Stage 1 Reforms) intended to implement reforms such as:

- the introduction of a serious harm threshold
- amendment to existing defences and introduction of new defences
- creation of the single publication rule
- clarification to non-economic loss damages.

Legislative amendments stemming from the Stage 1 Reforms came into force on or after 1 July 2021 in Victoria, New South Wales, South Australia, Queensland, Tasmania and the Australian Capital Territory. It is important to note that new provisions only apply to publication of defamation matter *after* the provisions have commenced.

Stage 2 Reforms are underway and intend to address contemporary issues in defamation pertaining to technology and the internet. Stage 2 reforms are divided into two parts. *Part A* of the reforms addresses defamation and the internet, along with questions pertaining to liability of internet intermediaries for content published by third-party users. *Part B*

---

28   Standing Committee of Attorneys-General, Working Group of State and Territory Officers, *Proposal for Uniform Defamation Laws* (July 2004) 9. See also *Civil Law (Wrongs) Act 2002* (ACT) s 115; *Defamation Act 2005* (NSW) s 3; *Defamation Act 2006* (NT) s 2; *Defamation Act 2005* (Qld) s 3; *Defamation Act 2005* (SA) s 3; *Defamation Act 2005* (Tas) s 3; *Defamation Act 2005* (Vic) s 3; *Defamation Act 2005* (WA) s 3.

29   New South Wales, Department of Justice, *Statutory Review: Defamation Act 2005* (Report, June 2018).

30   Council of Attorneys-General, *Review of Model Defamation Provisions* (2019) <www.justice.nsw.gov .au/justicepolicy/Documents/review-model-defamation-provisions/Final-CAG-Defamation-Discussion-Paper-Feb-2019.pdf>.

31   Ibid 10.

32   Parliamentary Council's Committee, *Model Defamation Amendment Provisions 2020* (27 July 2020) <https://pcc.gov.au/uniform/2020/Model_Defamation_Amendment_Provisions_2020.pdf>.

addresses the issue of whether defamation laws are having undesirable consequences on reporting of alleged criminal conduct to police and statutory investigative bodies.[33]

The following section summarises the key changes stemming from Stage 1 of the Reforms. At this stage of your study of defamation, these are only intended to be an overview of recent changes. Each of these principles will be explored in more depth throughout the chapter. (A summary of the key amendments and provisions is listed in Table 11.2.)

- **Standing to sue regarding certain corporations (s 9):** Generally, to have standing to sue, a plaintiff must be a person or confined to a certain group of individuals. Under the previous provisions, a company could bring an action in defamation if they were an 'excluded corporation' which operated not-for-profit or held less than 10 full-time employees. If plaintiffs structured their companies to use contractors rather than employees, they would bypass the restriction and would be entitled to sue in defamation. The aim of the reforms is to amend the definition of 'employee' to include contractors.[34]

- **'Serious harm' test (s 10A):** The reforms introduced a new element requiring a plaintiff to show – on the balance of probabilities – that a publication has caused, or is likely to cause, serious harm to the plaintiff's reputation. This test must be determined by a judicial officer prior to the trial commencing. This provision was modelled on s 1 of the *Defamation Act 2013* (UK).[35] The introduction of the new 'serious harm' test supersedes the previous defence of triviality which was subsequently abolished.

- **Concerns notices (ss 12A and 12B):** The reforms now require plaintiffs to serve a concerns notice on a defendant as a mandatory requirement before defamation proceedings can be issued.[36]

- **Contextual truth defence amendment (s 26):** Prior to the 2021 amendments, the wording of the provision only allowed a defendant to plead and prove an imputation that arose 'in addition to' an imputation pleaded by the plaintiff. The removal of the words 'in addition to' will streamline the operation of the defence and allow the practice of 'pleading back' which allows a defendant to plead back substantially true imputations which the plaintiff originally pleaded.[37]

- **Adoption of a new public interest defence (s 29A):** The new defence will protect a defendant if the publication concerns a matter of *public interest* and the defendant *reasonably believed* the matter was in the public interest. While the reforms do not provide a definition of 'public interest', one can envisage this defence may protect media organisations and individuals/entities discussing matters that may interest the public generally.[38]

---

33 Attorneys-General, *Review of Model Defamation Provisions – Stage 2 Discussion Paper* (31 March 2021) <www.justice.nsw.gov.au/justicepolicy/Documents/review-model-defamation-provisions/discussion-paper-stage-2.pdf>.

34 Parliamentary Council's Committee, *Model Defamation Amendment Provisions 2020* (27 July 2020) <https://pcc.gov.au/uniform/2020/Model_Defamation_Amendment_Provisions_2020.pdf> 2–3.

35 Ibid 3–4.

36 Ibid 3–5.

37 Ibid 8.

38 Ibid 7–8.

- **Qualified privilege defence amendment (s 30(3)):** The reforms modify the list of factors used in s 30(3) when determining whether conduct of a publisher is reasonable and to minimise overlap with the new public interest defence.[39]
- **Adoption of a new scientific or academic peer review defence (s 30A):** The new defence protects individuals/entities engaging in academic or scientific debate, to ensure that publications in peer-reviewed journals are protected from defamation action to allow scientists and academics to debate freely.[40]
- **Honest opinion defence amendment (s 31(5)):** The sub-provision clarifies the honest opinion defence by outlining factors that can assist the court to determine if an opinion is based on proper material (such as whether the material is notorious or accessible from a reference link).[41]
- **Amendments and clarification of caps on damages (s 35):** The reforms were in response to inconsistent decisions regarding the awarding of damages in defamation cases. The new provision stresses that the maximum damages amount is to be awarded only in a most serious case. A court is still permitted to make a separate award of aggravated damages; however, the two awards must be made separately.[42]
- **Adoption of a new single publication rule:** This reform means that the start date of a limitation period will begin to run when the publication is *first uploaded* or *sent to a recipient*, changing the previous position which allowed the date to start *each time* a publication was downloaded.[43]

Table 11.2   Summary of key amendments and provisions

Amendment	*Defamation Act* provision(s)
Standing to sue regarding certain corporations	s 9
Introduction of new 'serious harm' elements	s 10A
Concerns notices	ss 12A–12B
Contextual truth defence amended – replaces previous provision	s 26
New public interest defence	s 29A
Qualified privilege defence amended	s 30
New scientific/academic peer review defence	s 30A
Honest opinion defence amended	s 31
Changes to caps on damages	s 35
Changes to the single publication rule	See, eg, *Limitations of Actions Act 1958* (Vic) s 5A

39   Ibid 8–9.
40   Ibid 9–10.
41   Ibid 10.
42   Ibid 11.
43   Ibid 11–13.

11.1.4   Existing defamation legislative frameworks

Each Australian state and territory, with the exception of the Australian Capital Territory, contains defamation Acts. In the Australian Capital Territory, provisions relating to defamation were inserted into the existing civil liability legislation (see Table 11.3). The uniform legislation is generally structured with the following headings:

- preliminary matters (such as the object of the Act)
- general principles (retention of common law, causes of action and choice of law)
- avenues of resolving disputes without recourse to litigation
- litigation of claims (roles of the judge and jury, defences, remedies and costs)
- miscellaneous matters.

Table 11.3   Australian defamation legislation

Jurisdiction	Legislation
Australian Capital Territory	Civil Law (Wrongs) Act 2002
New South Wales	Defamation Act 2005
Northern Territory	Defamation Act 2006
Queensland	Defamation Act 2005
South Australia	Defamation Act 2005
Tasmania	Defamation Act 2005
Victoria	Defamation Act 2005
Western Australia	Defamation Act 2005

11.1.5   Common law and legislative frameworks

The introduction of the uniform defamation legislation means that many, though not all, aspects of defamation law are now contained in statute. The inclusion of a provision stipulating that the legislation does not affect the operation of the general law means that common law principles continue to apply, except where they are otherwise altered by legislation. For instance, the legislation does not define 'defamation'; nor does it outline the elements necessary to establish a cause of action save for the recently introduced 'serious harm' element; therefore, one must turn to the common law for guidance. The legislation also contains defences that either extend common law defences or introduce defences previously not available at common law. For instance, contextual truth, public interest, academic/ scientific peer review and statutory qualified privilege are new defences, while justification (substantial truth), honest opinion, absolute privilege and innocent dissemination are now enacted in statutory form. The uniform legislation maintains the common law position that only a single cause of action arises out of the publication of a matter, regardless of how many imputations can be derived.[44]

----

44   *Civil Law (Wrongs) Act 2002* (ACT) s 120; *Defamation Act 2005* (NSW) s 8; *Defamation Act 2006* (NT) s 7; *Defamation Act 2005* (Qld) s 8; *Defamation Act 2005* (SA) s 8; *Defamation Act 2005* (Tas) s 8; *Defamation Act 2005* (Vic) s 8; *Defamation Act 2005* (WA) s 8.

HINTS AND TIPS

Suppose that a magazine article contains three imputations against Celebrity A, imputing that she is a liar, a thief and unfaithful in her marriage. The uniform defamation legislation provides that Celebrity A can only take one cause of action against the magazine publisher in defamation and not three separate actions. This is because, as you have just learned, a single cause of action arises out of the publication of a matter regardless of how many imputations the matter (the article) contains.

REVIEW QUESTIONS

(1) List two benefits of the Australian uniform defamation legislation.

(2) If D writes a diary note containing a defamatory statement about P, which is inadvertently shared on the internet and read by 100 individuals, can D be held liable in defamation regardless of his or her lack of intention?

 Guided responses in the eBook

11.2   Elements of defamation

To commence defamation action, the plaintiff must establish four elements:

(1) The matter contains a defamatory imputation.

(2) The matter identifies the plaintiff.

(3) The matter was published or communicated to a third party.

(4) The plaintiff has sustained serious harm.

Even if the plaintiff satisfies these elements, the defendant may nevertheless escape liability or reduce the award of damages payable if he or she can successfully establish a defence. The plaintiff must initiate proceedings within one year of publication, or seek leave from the court of up to three years by showing that it was not reasonable to bring the proceedings earlier.[45] The steps required to establish defamation are set out in Figure 11.1 and discussed in detail in the sections following.

11.2.1   Does the matter contain a defamatory imputation?

The starting point for a plaintiff is to identify the *matter* that has been published by the defendant, then identify the *imputations* contained within the matter, then prove that the

---

45 *Defamation Act 2005* (Tas) s 20A; *Limitation Act 1985* (ACT) s 21B; *Limitation Act 1969* (NSW) s 14B; *Limitation Act 1981* (NT) s 12(2)(b); *Limitation of Actions Act 1974* (Qld) s 10AA; *Limitation of Actions Act 1936* (SA) s 37; *Limitation of Actions Act 1958* (Vic) s 5(AAA); *Limitation Act 2005* (WA) s 15.

Figure 11.1   Elements of defamation

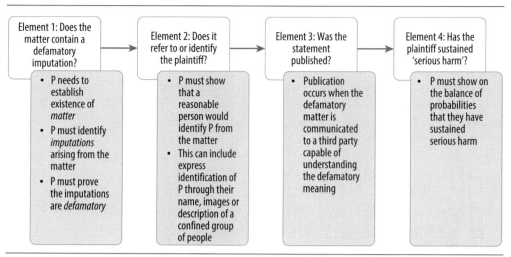

imputations are *defamatory* as interpreted by an ordinary and reasonable person, and finally that the plaintiff has sustained *serious harm*.

11.2.1.1   Definition of 'matter'

In the context of defamation, matter refers to a 'thing' that is published by the defendant. The term 'matter' is defined by the uniform legislation to include:

(a)   an article, report, advertisement or other thing communicated by means of a newspaper, magazine or other periodical; and

(b)   a program, report, advertisement or other thing communicated by means of television, radio, the Internet or any other form of electronic communication; and

(c)   a letter, note or other writing; and

(d)   a picture, gesture or oral utterance; and

(e)   any other thing by means of which something may be communicated to a person.[46]

HINTS AND TIPS

Think of 'matter' as a delivery vehicle that transports the defamatory message from the defendant to a third party. For example, in *Cornes v The Ten Group Pty Ltd* (2012) 114 SASR 46 a program communicated by means of television could be considered as the 'vehicle' which transported the defamatory message to the viewers of the television program.

---

46   *Civil Law (Wrongs) Act 2002* (ACT) s 118; *Defamation Act 2005* (NSW) s 4; *Defamation Act 2006* (NT) s 5; *Defamation Act 2005* (Qld) s 4; *Defamation Act 2005* (SA) s 4; *Defamation Act 2005* (Tas) s 6; *Defamation Act 2005* (Vic) s 6; *Defamation Act 2005* (WA) s 6.

11.2.1.2   Defamatory imputations

Defamatory imputations are central to a defamation action. The plaintiff must demonstrate that the matter contains a defamatory imputation that conveys a certain meaning and lowers the plaintiff's reputation in the eyes of the 'ordinary reasonable reader' or 'hypothetical referee'.[47] An imputation is akin to a suggestion, as it requires one to look to the meaning behind the word, phrase or image to identify the message suggested to a third party. Take the example of a statement made about a prominent athlete: 'It's not possible X has tested negative to illicit substances. He won 11 out of 12 matches following a year-long break due to injury. That is impossible! It tells you everything.'[48] The statement could be interpreted by a reasonable person as suggesting that X uses performance-enhancing substances to win matches.

Where a defamation claim is being heard before a judge and jury, the judge decides the imputations that can reasonably be drawn from the matter and put to the jury.[49] The jury must then determine whether the imputations are defamatory. For example, in *Boyd v Mirror Newspapers Ltd* the Court was required to determine whether words in a newspaper headline could give to rise to three imputations.[50] If the imputations were capable of being defamatory, they would be sent to the jury to determine whether they were, in fact, defamatory. The case is discussed in more detail in Section 11.2.1.4.

A defamatory imputation may be conveyed directly through the natural and ordinary meaning of the words used (eg, 'Y is a thief' or 'Z is a murderer'). In instances where the natural or ordinary meaning of words is used, the imputation is clear from the literal interpretation of the words; hence, it is unnecessary to 'read into' the words used. In contrast, defamatory imputations may also be communicated indirectly through innuendo. Innuendo looks at the insinuation that can be drawn or interpreted by a third party, where direct words are not used to convey the message. The difference between a true and false innuendo is significant.

11.2.1.3   True and false innuendo

Defamatory imputations can be conveyed indirectly through two types of innuendo. The first type of innuendo is known as a *false* (or sometimes *popular*) innuendo and is based on the meaning that an ordinary person would understand from their general understanding of popular culture and the contemporary meaning of words or phrases. For example, the comment by D that P 'had their hands in the till' can be understood to infer that P dishonestly misappropriated funds.[51]

The second type of innuendo is known as a *true* (or *legal*) innuendo which is conveyed to a limited group of people who assign a particular meaning to the words due to extrinsic knowledge. Essentially these individuals are privy to knowledge or an understanding of

---

47   *Haddon v Forsyth* [2011] NSWSC 123, [17]–[18] (Simpson J).
48   The example is based on Rafael Nadal's defamation action in a French court: 'Rafael Nadal Awarded Damages over French Former Minister's Doping Claim', *The Guardian* (16 November 2017).
49   *Favell v Queensland Newspapers Pty Ltd* (2005) 221 ALR 186, [9] (Gleeson CJ, McHugh, Gummow and Heydon JJ).
50   [1980] 2 NSWLR 449.
51   *Bjelke-Petersen v Warburton* [1987] 2 Qd R 465.

facts (eg, legal, medical or sports knowledge) not contained in the defamatory matter. For example, in *Brisciani v Piscioneri (No 4)* the term 'ex-lawyer' could be interpreted by individuals with knowledge of the requirement to be admitted to legal practice to infer that the plaintiff had been struck off the Supreme Court roll.[52] Without this extrinsic knowledge, one might simply believe the plaintiff had elected to change careers.

Where there are multiple meanings that can be attributed to an imputation (eg, one defamatory and one innocent) the courts have applied the single meaning rule. In *Cornes v The Ten Group Pty Ltd* prominent comedian Mick Molloy stated 'And apparently you slept with her too' on a football panel show.[53] While some audience viewers may have been familiar with the comedic nature of the show, the show also purported to provide factual information. The Court of Appeal concluded that Molloy's statement could be interpreted as defamatory by an ordinary reasonable viewer of the program. Once a court has deemed a matter as capable of being defamatory, the plaintiff is entitled to plead multiple defamatory imputations as arising from the matter.

11.2.1.4   Definition of 'defamatory'

Once the plaintiff has established the existence of matter containing imputations, the plaintiff is also required to demonstrate that the imputations are *defamatory* and carry a 'sting' that lowers the plaintiff's reputation. In *Radio 2UE Sydney Pty Ltd v Chesterton* the High Court confirmed that the tests for assessing whether statements are defamatory include determining whether the statements lower the plaintiff's reputation in the estimation of others, expose the plaintiff to ridicule or contempt or induce society to shun or exclude the plaintiff.[54] The Court also endorsed the principle that imputations will be defamatory if understood by an ordinary reasonable person who is of 'ordinary intelligence, experience and education' and 'not avid for scandal'.[55] More recently, in *Trkulja v Google LLC* the High Court considered whether a Google search of the plaintiff's name, which elicited search results of criminal underworld figures, could be defamatory.[56] The Court held that 'the test of capacity of a published matter to defame is, in this case, whether any of the search results complained of are capable of conveying any of the defamatory imputations alleged.'[57] In finding Google liable, the Court held there was 'no evidence … that it would have been apparent to an ordinary reasonable person using the Google search engine that Google made no contribution to the elements or combination of elements of those of the search results that convey a connection between Mr Trkulja and criminality'.[58]

---

52   [2016] ACTCA 32.
53   (2012) 114 SASR 46.
54   (2009) 238 CLR 460.
55   Ibid 466–7 (French CJ, Gummow, Kiefel and Bell JJ).
56   (2018) 356 ALR 178.
57   *Trkulja v Google LLC* (2018) 356 ALR 178, [52].
58   Ibid [59].

Case: *Radio 2UE Sydney Pty Ltd v Chesterton* (2009) 238 CLR 460

Facts

Ray Chesterton was a journalist on Radio 2UE Sydney. On 8 August 2005 John Laws, the presenter of a morning radio show, used numerous statements in reference to Mr Chesterton including referring to him as a 'bombastic, beer-bellied buffoon' and a 'creep'. Mr Laws alleged that Mr Chesterton was 'fired by 2UE and blames me for it'. Mr Laws also used a rather rude nickname, 'Ankles' ('I doubt you'd have any [friends], and those that you do have call you 'Ankles' and for a very good reason'). Mr Chesterton sued the radio station alleging that the broadcast contained numerous defamatory imputations. At trial, the jury found in favour of the plaintiff. The radio station appealed and the New South Wales Court of Appeal dismissed the appeal.

Issue

In issue before the High Court was the question of the legal tests to be applied to determine whether statements were defamatory.

Decision

The Court dismissed the appeal. It upheld the finding of the New South Wales Supreme Court that the statements were defamatory and carried imputations that the plaintiff was a creep, an unpleasant and repellent person, a bombastic, beer-bellied buffoon, that the plaintiff was not to be taken seriously as a journalist, that the plaintiff was fired and blamed Mr Laws for the dismissal and, finally, that the plaintiff was an ungrateful person who accepted hospitality then attacked the giver.

Significance

French CJ, Gummow, Kiefel and Bell JJ held that the test of defamation is whether the statements lower the reputation of the plaintiff in the estimation of others, expose the plaintiff to hatred, contempt or ridicule or cause the plaintiff to be shunned or avoided by society. Whether the matter is deemed defamatory is to be assessed from the perspective of a hypothetical reasonable person.

Notes

At [36] the High Court held:

> The concept of 'reputation' in the law of defamation comprehends all aspects of a person's standing in the community. It has been observed that phrases such as 'business reputation' or 'reputation for honesty' may sometimes obscure this fact. In principle therefore the general test for defamation should apply to an imputation concerning any aspect of a person's reputation. A conclusion as to whether injury to reputation has occurred is the answer to the question posed by the general test, whether it be stated as whether a person's standing in the community, or the estimation in which people hold that person, has been lowered or simply whether the imputation is likely to cause people

to think the less of a plaintiff. An imputation which defames a person in their professional or business reputation does not have a different effect. It will cause people to think the less of that person in that aspect of their reputation. For any imputation to be actionable, whether it reflects upon a person's character or their business or professional reputation, the test must be satisfied.

Question

Does the same legal test used to determine business reputation also apply to personal reputation?

 Guided response in the eBook

The defamatory matter can disparage the plaintiff by imputing, for instance, that they are dishonest, disloyal or a criminal, but the imputations must attract a level of blame or responsibility on the plaintiff's part. It is not defamatory to make comments relating to aspects of a plaintiff that he or she has no control over, such as their ethnicity or physical appearance. As the *Boyd* case demonstrates, the statement that the plaintiff was overweight did not attach any blameworthiness on his part. However, such a statement may be defamatory where it portrays the plaintiff in a ridiculous light.

Case: *Boyd v Mirror Newspapers Ltd* [1980] 2 NSWLR 449

Facts

Leslie Boyd was a well-known and successful Australian Rugby League player. In 1980 the *Daily Mirror* published an article headed 'Boyd is Fat, Slow and Predictable'. In the article the author also described Mr Boyd as having 'waddled' onto the field. Mr Boyd sued the newspaper in defamation claiming the following imputations arose from the article: (a) that he was so fat and slow that he could not properly play football; (b) that he was so fat so as to appear ridiculous when he came onto the field; and (c) that he had permitted his physical condition to degenerate so as to be hopeless in first-grade Rugby League.

Issue

The legal issue in the case: whether, construed on their natural and ordinary meaning, the words in the headline could convey the imputations alleged by the plaintiff and whether these imputations were defamatory.

Decision

The second and third imputations (that Mr Boyd was so fat and slow that he could not properly play football and that he was somehow to blame for his physical degeneration) were capable of being conveyed by the matter and capable of being defamatory of the plaintiff. Hunt J held that the first imputation was not capable of being defamatory.

Significance

The first imputation was held as not capable of being defamatory, as it would not cause the public to shun or avoid Mr Boyd or think of him in a ridiculous light.

Notes

At [32]–[35] Hunt J held:

> I turn, finally, to the first imputation, which is in these terms: 'that the plaintiff was so fat and slow that he could not properly play in his position as a second row forward in first-grade Rugby League football.'
>
> The plaintiff says that the matter complained of ascribes to him characteristics which are not expected of a first-grade Rugby League footballer – that he is fat and slow – as well as an incapacity to play properly in his position by reason of that condition. He takes the stand that, without more, the imputation is thus defamatory of him. His argument proceeds upon the basis that the ordinary reasonable reader has not construed the matter complained of as asserting that he is himself in part to blame for his condition. He says that that reader would, nevertheless, think the less of him, because as a first-grade Rugby League footballer he is in that condition.
>
> On his behalf, the analogy is drawn of a ballerina who is described as being fat and cumbersome. Although perhaps incongruous, the analogy is apt. But I do not see how, in either case, the description is defamatory unless that condition is shown or suggested to have resulted from some cause for which the plaintiff is blameworthy: *Henderson v Thompson*. There is nothing in the description of being fat and slow, even where the object being described is a first-grade Rugby League footballer, which would tend to make people shun or avoid him; nor is it, alone, capable of displaying him in a ridiculous light. To amount to defamation at common law, therefore, the imputation must be disparaging of the plaintiff personally, and without some suggestion of blameworthiness on his part I am unable to see how this imputation can be said to be so disparaging.
>
> I, therefore, hold that the first imputation is incapable of defaming the plaintiff. It cannot go to the jury. [Citations omitted.]

Question

Why did Hunt J find the first imputation was not capable of defaming the plaintiff?

 Guided response in the eBook

Case: *Random House Australia Pty Ltd v Abbott* (1999) 94 FCR 296

Facts

Random House published a book written by Bob Ellis titled *Goodbye Jerusalem: Night Thoughts of a Labor Outsider*. A paragraph in the book pertained to politicians Tony Abbott and Peter Costello:

> Abbott and Costello … they're both in the Right Wing of the Labor Party till the one woman [had sexual relations with] both of them and married one of them and inducted them into the Young Liberals.

The politicians alleged the passage was defamatory as it imputed they lacked personal integrity, their political commitment was shallow and they were weak and unreliable so as to allow political decisions to be dictated by their wives. The imprecise reference to a 'woman' in the passage allowed both Margaret Abbott and Tanya Costello to sue, alleging the passage contained imputations they were sexually promiscuous, engaged in sexual misconduct, were political manipulators, were of low morality and lacked respect for their husbands.

Issue

Did the book passage contain defamatory imputations about the politicians and their wives?

Decision

The politicians were successful in establishing the defamatory imputations against them, namely that they were prepared to abandon political allegiance in exchange for sexual favours. Mrs Abbott and Mrs Costello were successful in establishing imputations that they had engaged in sexual misconduct, were political manipulators and of low morality, but not that that this amounted to sexually promiscuous behaviour. The imputation that they lacked respect for their husbands, and that their husbands' change of political beliefs was caused by marriage, was not supported as it could only be derived through speculation rather than inference.

Significance

It was decided that a passage could be capable of being defamatory due to innuendo.

Notes

Beaumont J held at [24]:

> A defamatory imputation may be made by reliance upon the natural and ordinary meaning of the words published, or by innuendo (per Brennan J, Gibbs CJ, Stephen, Murphy and Wilson JJ agreeing) in *Reader's Digest Services Pty Ltd v Lamb*. Where no (true) innuendo is pleaded, and the published words clearly relate to the plaintiff, the issue of libel or no libel, can be determined by asking whether hypothetical referees (described in the authorities as 'reasonable' persons or 'right-thinking members of society generally' or 'ordinary (persons) not avid for scandal') would understand the words in a defamatory sense. [Citations omitted.]

Question

Were the defamatory imputations in this case derived from the natural and ordinary meaning of the words in the passage, or through true or false innuendo?

 Guided response in the eBook

Case: *Ettingshausen v Australian Consolidated Press Ltd* (1991) 23 NSWLR 443

Facts

A journalist and photographer were granted exclusive, behind-the-scenes access to the Rugby League football players for the Australian team the Kangaroos, including at training, post-match locker rooms and hotels, for the purpose of capturing images for a photo book to be auctioned for charity. As part of publicity for the book, *HQ* magazine ran an article showing images of three players (including the plaintiff, Andrew Ettingshausen) nude in the showers following a rugby match. The plaintiff alleged that the grainy black-and-white image of him showed his genitals.

Issue

Did the image contain the defamatory imputations that: (a) the plaintiff is the type of person who would deliberately allow a photo of his genitals to appear in a national magazine; or (b) the plaintiff is a person whose genitals have been exposed to readers of a national magazine?

Decision

Both imputations could be conveyed to an ordinary and reasonable reader and could be defamatory insofar as they subjected the plaintiff to more than trivial ridicule in the eyes of the public. The plaintiff was originally awarded $350 000 by a jury. On appeal the New South Wales Court of Appeal agreed as to liability but found the award of damages excessive. The matter was remitted for retrial with the jury awarding Mr Ettingshausen $100 000.

Significance

This case shows that defamatory innuendo is not simply limited to words but can also include photographs or images. Here, Mr Ettingshausen vigorously disputed the publishing of the image which suggested that he was the type of person who was comfortable with being photographed in the nude for a magazine.

Notes

Hunt J stated (in reference to the plaintiff's plea of true innuendo) at 445:

> Paragraph 4 pleaded true innuendoes … based upon the extrinsic fact that the plaintiff
> is employed as a schools and junior development promotions officer by the New South
> Wales Rugby League – which assert that he is unfit to hold such a position because
> of having posed for or allowed a photograph to be taken exposing his genitals for
> publication in the defendant's magazine.

Question

Given the protracted litigation and the relatively conservative award of $100 000, do you think the plaintiff's case ought to have been framed as an invasion of privacy action, or was an action in defamation appropriate for damage to his reputation?

 Guided response in the eBook

Case: *Hockey v Fairfax Media Publications Pty Ltd* (2015) 237 FCR 33

Facts

Three Australian newspapers published articles regarding federal Treasurer, Joe Hockey, with the headlines 'Treasurer for Sale' or 'Treasurer Hockey for Sale'. Each of the newspapers also published the headlines on their online platforms, with links to the full articles. Some of the newspapers published tweets with the same headline but without a link to the full article. Finally, one newspaper promoted the article through a poster with large and bold font 'Treasurer for Sale'.

Issue

Did the articles and the poster contain defamatory imputations, including that Mr Hockey was corrupt and that he accepted bribes to influence decisions he made as Treasurer?

Decision

Mr Hockey's action with respect to the poster and the tweets was successful. The Federal Court was satisfied there existed readers who would not take the positive step of locating the full article to read it and understand its context. However, the Court did not find the online newspaper articles and hard copies of the newspaper were open to the interpretation that Mr Hockey was corrupt and open to bribery, as the headline was capable of being placed in its true context by readers.

Significance

The case demonstrates the importance of a statement being placed in its full context by the reader. Where the majority of readers are likely to accept defamatory imputations without regard to the full context, the matter may be deemed defamatory.

Notes

At [207]–[209] White J held:

> In my opinion, it is not necessary to resort to analogies with newspaper posters in order to conclude that it may [be defamatory]. The greater ease by which the reader may obtain access to the article in question is not a reason for concluding that all readers of the tweet will exercise that access. Some may read the tweet without going further.
>
> There is some force in the submission of counsel for the respondents to the effect that the ease with which followers of tweets may obtain access to the article suggests that, if the tweet had any impact on those reading it, they are likely to have used the hyperlink to read more. However, this is a matter going to damages rather than to liability.
>
> On this basis, I consider that the first bare tweet by *The Age* does convey the same defamatory meaning as did the [*Sydney Morning Herald*] poster, namely, imputation (c) that 'the applicant corruptly solicited payments to influence his decisions as Treasurer of the Commonwealth of Australia'.

Question

The success of Mr Hockey's case with respect to the online tweets rested on the finding that ordinary and reasonable readers were unlikely to take the positive step of using the hyperlink to access and read the full articles. Does the ruling have a potentially chilling effect for social media users publishing brief posts but relying on hyperlinks to explain or add to the tweet or post?

 Guided response in the eBook

11.2.2 Does the matter identify the plaintiff?

The plaintiff must demonstrate that the matter is capable of identifying the plaintiff to an ordinary and reasonable person. Where matter expressly identifies an individual, the element of identity will be easily met. However, where the plaintiff is not expressly named, it may still be possible to determine their identity if they are described with sufficient detail or if they are a member of a small group of individuals about whom defamatory statements are made.

11.2.2.1 Express identification of plaintiff

Establishing identity is relatively uncontentious where defamatory matter expressly identifies the plaintiff. For instance, in *Wilson v Bauer Media Pty Ltd* the publishers of a women's magazine expressly named Hollywood actress Rebel Wilson in an article alleging she was a serial liar who had lied about her real name, age and upbringing.[59] However, use of the plaintiff's name is not necessary if the defendant provides sufficient information that allows people to identify him or her. In *Bateman v Shepherd* an article published by the president of a medical association contained sufficient information to identify the plaintiff, a medical practitioner, even without using the plaintiff's name.[60] As indicated earlier in this chapter, the defendant's intention to defame is irrelevant in a cause of action for defamation. Hence, where a defendant makes a defamatory statement about a plaintiff, the defendant may also risk defaming other individuals with the same name. In *Lee v Wilson* a publication by a newspaper alleging bribery against a 'Detective Lee' in the context of a police inquiry allowed two detectives with the same surname to sue.[61]

11.2.2.2   Reasonable to identify plaintiff

Where defamatory matter refers to a large group of people, the plaintiff is unlikely to be able to show that he or she was personally affected.[62] For example, if D states 'All Victorian surgeons are negligent', the statement encompasses such a large number of surgeons that it is unlikely that the statement reasonably identifies one particular surgeon as negligent. However, identification may be possible where the defamatory matter refers to a small group of people. For instance, in *Bjelke-Petersen v Warburton* the statement to media that Queensland Ministers had 'their hands in the till' was held to be defamatory because it identified a sufficiently limited class of individuals.[63] As the next two cases demonstrate, defamatory matter can be sufficient to identify the plaintiff even when depicted in a fictional context or through use of images.

Case: *E Hulton & Co v Jones* [1910] AC 20

Facts

The defendant published an article about a fictional character named Artemus Jones, an adulterous churchwarden from Peckham. Thomas Artemus Jones, a lawyer from North Wales, alleged the article was defamatory of him and produced witnesses to support his assertion that the article identified him to ordinary and reasonable readers.

Issue

Would people reasonably believe that the article, though fictitious, was based on the plaintiff?

Decision

The reference to 'Artemus Jones' was held to be defamatory of the plaintiff. The Court held that sensible and ordinary people were capable of perceiving that the article referred to the real Thomas Artemus Jones.

---

59   [2017] VSC 521.
60   (1997) Aust Torts Reports 81-417.
61   (1934) 51 CLR 276.
62   *Knupffer v London Express Newspaper Ltd* [1944] AC 116.
63   [1987] 2 Qd R 465.

Significance

Lack of intention to defame, in this case through the use of a fictitious character, is no defence to a claim for defamation.

Notes

Lord Chancellor Loreburn (stating that the trial judge correctly found for the plaintiff) said at 592:

> 'The real point upon which your verdict must turn is – Ought or ought not sensible and reasonable people reading this article to think that it was a mere imaginary person such as I have said – Tom Jones, Mr Pecksniff as a humbug, Mr Stiggins, or any name of that sort which one reads of in literature, used as a type? If you think that any reasonable person would think that, it is not actionable at all. If, on the other hand, you do not think that, but think that people would suppose it to mean some real person, those who did not know the plaintiff of course would not know who the real person was, but those who did know of the existence of the plaintiff would think that it was the plaintiff, then the action is maintainable, subject to such damages as you think under all the circumstances are fair and right to give to the plaintiff.' I see no objection in law to that passage.

Question

Does the fictitious context of the article, combined with the lack of intention to defame, have any relevance to or impact on the ultimate damage to the plaintiff's reputation?

 Guided response in the eBook

Case: *Nixon v Slater & Gordon* [2000] Aust Torts Reports 81-565

Facts

Slater & Gordon, an Australian law firm, published and distributed a booklet to medical practitioners, intending to alleviate fears of a medical negligence litigation explosion. The cover of the booklet featured a photograph of two surgeons performing a cardiothoracic surgery on a patient while a robed barrister stood at the head of the bed. The photograph was accompanied by the captions 'Medical malpractice claims … ' and ' … A litigation explosion?'. The photograph was obtained from a picture library but was of two practising surgeons, Ian Nixon and Gregory Ellis, with the image of the barrister superimposed. Mr Nixon and Mr Ellis claimed that they were identifiable through the image and alleged that the image on the booklet imputed that they were the subject of medical negligence proceedings. The applicants also claimed that the conduct of Slater & Gordon contravened the misleading and deceptive conduct provision in s 52 of the *Trade Practices Act 1974* (Cth) (now s 18 of the *Australian Consumer Law*).

Issue

Could a reasonable member of the medical profession or the general public identify Mr Nixon and Mr Ellis from the image and therefore think they were negligent?

Decision

Merkel J held that a reasonable imputation that could be conveyed from the image, to both members of the medical profession and the general public, was that Slater & Gordon was involved in a medical negligence claim against Mr Nixon and Mr Ellis, the surgeons depicted in the brochure. The imputation was manifested by the words in the photograph, combined with the presence of the barrister scrutinising the surgery.

Significance

Mr Nixon and Mr Ellis were awarded $200 000 and $100 000 in damages, respectively, for defamation and a contravention of the *Trade Practices Act 1974* (Cth). An injunction prohibiting further publication of the booklet and a letter of retraction were also granted.

Notes

Merkel J stated at [42]:

> I propose to approach the question of whether any defamatory imputation is to be derived from the medical malpractice booklet objectively, in disregard of the evidence given by various witnesses, including the applicants, as to what they took the booklet to mean to them. For that purpose the hypothetical referees in the present case are not the public at large but, rather, are members of the medical profession in the State of Victoria, the membership of which is significantly constituted by the 8531 members to whom the publication was addressed. While there is some evidence that the medical malpractice booklet was seen around hospital or medical practitioner waiting rooms and other analogous locations, it was specifically published and addressed to, and intended and expected to only be of interest to and read by, members of the medical profession. Thus, it is appropriate to treat the hypothetical referee for the purposes of the present case as the hypothetical member of the medical profession.

Question

Does a successful defamation case rest upon the plaintiff's ability to prove that all members of the community are capable of identifying the plaintiff and finding the matter defamatory?

    Guided response in the eBook

HINTS AND TIPS

Proof of identity is not limited to circumstances where a defendant expressly names a plaintiff. You ought to ask: Is it reasonable to identify the plaintiff in the description of the matter?

11.2.3   Has the statement been published?

The defamatory matter must be published to a third party. This means that an individual other than the plaintiff must see or hear the material and understand its defamatory meaning.

11.2.3.1   Definition and interpretation of 'publication'

The term 'publication' is not defined in the uniform defamation legislation and therefore we must turn to case law to interpret instances where matter will be deemed to be published. Publication is not limited to traditional forms of published items such as books or articles, but includes oral utterances, written communications and images. Various parties involved in the publication process may be deemed liable. For example, where defamatory matter is contained in a book, the author, editor, publisher and printer may all be held liable. In *Cornes v The Ten Group Pty Ltd* a defamatory statement spoken on a television program by comedian Mick Molloy meant that both he and the broadcaster had committed defamation.[64]

HINTS AND TIPS

In *Gunston v Davies Brothers Ltd* (2012) 21 Tas R 256, former Tasmanian Police sergeant Andrew Gunston sued *The Mercury* newspaper for the phrase 'Sergeant Sleaze' which he alleged was defamatory as it cast him in a low, contemptible and disreputable light. Ultimately the newspaper, the editor and four of its journalists were held liable and ordered to pay Mr Gunston damages. The case illustrates how various parties involved in a publication process may be liable.

The defendant may also be liable for an unintentional publication, provided the publication is a natural or probable consequence of his or her action. In *Theaker v Richardson* the defendant wrote and delivered a defamatory letter to the plaintiff's residence in the midst of a local council election.[65] The letter was opened and read by the plaintiff's husband. The Court held the defendant had published the defamatory matter even though he had intended that it only be read by the plaintiff, as it was a natural and probable

---

64   (2011) 114 SASR 1.
65   [1962] 1 WLR 151.

consequence that another individual in the household might open mail. A communication between the defendant and their spouse is not deemed to be a publication, in order to allow free discussion in a marital relationship. However, a communication to the plaintiff's spouse is deemed to be a publication for the purpose of defamation.[66]

The test of reasonable foreseeability also has a role in determining whether publication has occurred. A defendant may be held liable where he or she utters defamatory statements in a place where it is reasonably foreseeable others may overhear.[67] Failure to remove a defamatory matter may also constitute defamation. For instance, in *Byrne v Deane* the owners of a golf club were held liable when they became aware of a defamatory poem posted in the club and failed to remove it.[68] Finally, the location of publication may be of critical significance as it will determine where the plaintiff can institute proceedings. The uniform defamation legislation provides that if a plaintiff elects to sue in one Australian jurisdiction, they cannot subsequently initiate proceedings in other Australian states without the leave of the court.[69]

Publication on the internet has recently undergone significant reform. Historically, a significant decision of the High Court in *Dow Jones & Co Inc v Gutnick* concluded that publication occurs at the place where web pages are downloaded.[70] In that case Dow Jones, a company based in the United States, published an article in the online magazine *Barron's Online* titled 'Unholy Gains' about prominent Australian businessman Joseph Gutnick. While Gutnick held some operations in the United States, he resided in Victoria and most of his business and social activities were conducted there. The Court had to determine where the material was published. In a unanimous decision, the High Court held that Mr Gutnick could sue in Victoria as that was the jurisdiction where damage to his reputation predominantly occurred. 'Publication' occurred at the time readers interpreted the communication, rather than at the time the article was posted on the internet.

This multiple publication rule resulted in a new cause of action being created each time that online material was downloaded (ie, published to a third party). In effect, this resulted in serious unintended consequences because it could allow plaintiffs to circumvent the one-year limitation period by asserting that material was 'published' each time it was downloaded. This rule was modified in the 2021 reforms with the adoption of the single publication rule which now determines that publication occurs when material is initially uploaded on the internet.[71]

Further issues of publication have concerned online internet intermediaries. In *Duffy v Google Inc* the South Australian Supreme Court considered the liability of Google for publication of online content in search results and auto-complete suggestions.[72] The plaintiff, Dr Janice Duffy, consulted several psychics and when their predictions did not eventuate,

---

66   *Wenhak v Morgan* (1880) 20 QBD 637.
67   *White v JF Stone (Lighting & Radio) Ltd* [1939] 2 KB 827.
68   [1937] 1 KB 818.
69   *Civil Law (Wrongs) Act 2002* (ACT) s 133; *Defamation Act 2005* (NSW) s 23; *Defamation Act 2006* (NT) s 20; *Defamation Act 2005* (Qld) s 23; *Defamation Act 2005* (SA) s 21; *Defamation Act 2005* (Tas) s 23; *Defamation Act 2005* (Vic) s 23; *Defamation Act 2005* (WA) s 23.
70   (2002) 210 CLR 575.
71   *Limitation of Actions Act 1958* (Vic) s 5A.
72   (2015) 125 SASR 437.

made complaints online. Dr Duffy subsequently discovered that upon entering her name in a Google search, the auto-complete result of 'Janice Duffy Psychic Stalker' appeared. After complaining to Google, and receiving no response, Dr Duffy initiated defamation proceedings against the search provider. In the Supreme Court, Blue J found that the automatic search results did not mean Google could not be deemed to be a publisher of the search results, especially after it had notice of the defamatory content and failed to remove it.[73] On appeal in *Google Inc v Duffy*, the Full Court affirmed the decision of the trial judge, finding Google to be a secondary or subordinate publisher of the defamatory material.[74] A subsequent decision of the High Court in *Trkulja v Google LLC*[75] has confirmed the liability of internet search engines as publishers. More recently, in *Fairfax Media Publications Pty Ltd v Voller*[76] the High Court held that individuals or entities who have control over online pages may be liable for defamatory comments posted on those pages by third-party users.

Case: *Fairfax Media Publications Pty Ltd v Voller* (2021) 273 CLR 346

Facts

The plaintiff, Dylan Voller, had garnered public attention due to his mistreatment in a Northern Territory detention centre, with his story publicised by mainstream media. Mr Voller sued three media organisations (Fairfax Media, Nationwide News and Sky News) for defamatory comments made by social media users on Facebook pages created by the media companies. The Facebook pages contained links to the media stories, and online users could engage with the material by commenting, 'liking' the post or sharing it with other users.

Issue

Were the appellants (the three media companies) 'publishers' of the defamatory comments posted by third parties on Facebook pages?

Decision

The High Court held that the media companies were publishers of the comments made by third parties (ie, online users) as the media companies were hosting the Facebook pages. Essentially, by creating the pages and facilitating public discussion, the media companies were held to be 'publishers'.

Significance

The case is significant because it confirms that individuals or entities who control social media platforms can be held to be 'publishers' if they facilitate or encourage discussion on internet web

---

73   *Duffy v Google Inc* (2015) 125 SASR 437, [206].
74   (2017) 129 SASR 304.
75   (2018) 356 ALR 178.
76   (2021) 273 CLR 346; [2021] HCA 27.

pages. Further, the case is significant because the High Court confirmed that defamation is a tort of strict liability and that proof of fault is not required.

Notes

The Court held at [105] (Kiefel CJ, Keane and Gleeson JJ):

> In sum, each appellant intentionally took a platform provided by another entity, Facebook, created and administered a public Facebook page, and posted content on that page. The creation of the public Facebook page, and the posting of content on that page, encouraged and facilitated publication of comments from third parties. The appellants were thereby publishers of the third-party comments.

Question

On what basis did the High Court find that the three publishers were liable in defamation given they were not the direct publishers of the third-party comments?

 Guided response in the eBook

Case: *Google LLC v Defteros* (2022) 403 ALR 434

Facts

In this case, the plaintiff was a Melbourne solicitor whose firm had represented numerous notorious 'gangland' clients. In 2004 and 2005 the plaintiff was charged for a conspiracy to murder but the charges were subsequently dropped. The plaintiff ceased legal practice but returned years later in 2007, and by 2014 had a successful practice. In 2016 the plaintiff discovered an internet search of his name returned results from a 2004 *The Age* article, including a hyperlink to a full article. In 2017, the plaintiff subsequently became aware of further material that defamed him including a composite image of four photographs – one of the plaintiff and three Melbourne gangland figures. The plaintiff took action against Google as publisher of the material held on the internet. The trial judge found in favour of the plaintiff, and this decision was upheld by the Court of Appeal. Google subsequently appealed to the High Court.

Issue

Was the appellant liable as a 'publisher' for providing hyperlinks to potentially defamatory content?

Decision

In contrast to the *Voller* decision, in this instance a 5:2 High Court majority held that Google should not be liable because the inclusion of hyperlinks to articles in its search results did not make it a 'publisher'.

Significance

The case is significant because it clarifies that merely providing a hyperlink to a publication made by a third party (with potentially defamatory content) may not incur liability. Per Gageler J's comments below, that may require directing, enticing or encouraging the searcher to click on the hyperlink (ie, adopting a more *active* role) rather than *passively* providing search results with hyperlinks.

Notes

The Court held at [49] (Kiefel CJ and Gleeson JJ):

> It cannot be said that the appellant was involved in the communication of the defamatory material by reference to the circumstances in *Webb v Bloch* and *Voller*. It did not approve the writing of defamatory matter for the purpose of publication. It did not contribute to any extent to the publication of the Underworld article on *The Age's* webpage. It did not provide a forum or place where it could be communicated, nor did it encourage the writing of comment in response to the article which was likely to contain defamatory matter. Contrary to the finding of the trial judge, the appellant was not instrumental in communicating the Underworld article. It assisted persons searching the Web to find certain information and to access it.

Further, Gageler J clarified at [74]:

> Google does not, merely by providing the search result in a form which includes the hyperlink, direct, entice or encourage the searcher to click on the hyperlink.

Question

On what basis did the High Court differentiate the *Defteros* case from the *Voller* case?

 Guided response in the eBook

11.2.4 'Serious harm' test

Prior to the 2021 reforms, defamation law required the plaintiff to prove, on the balance of probabilities, three elements: (1) that matter was published to a third party; (2) that the matter contained defamatory imputations, meaning that they lowered the plaintiff's reputation in the eyes of ordinary and reasonable members of the community; and (3) that the publication identified the plaintiff. In short, the plaintiff was not required to establish that they had sustained harm, though this was, and continues to be, a factor relevant to an award of damages. For instance, in *Newman v Whittington* the Court confirmed that the 'seriousness or gravity of any defamation has historically been a relevant factor in relation to the award of damages.'[77]

---

77 *Newman v Whittington* [2022] NSWSC 249, [44].

The 2021 reforms introduced a fourth element, which now requires a plaintiff to show that publication of the defamatory matter would cause, or likely cause, serious harm to their reputation. This is an entirely new element in Australian defamation law, though it was modelled on s 1 of the *Defamation Act 2013* (UK).[78] Like the Australian provisions, the UK provisions do not include a definition of 'serious harm'. The UK courts considered this in *Lachaux v Independent Print Ltd*.[79] In that case, Mr Lachaux sued British newspapers regarding defamatory allegations concerning his alleged behaviour towards his wife during divorce proceedings while residing in the United Arab Emirates (UAE). The UK Supreme Court interpreted the provision to require proof of *actual facts* about the impact of the defamatory matter. Such actual facts may require the plaintiff to show how their reputation and standing has been lowered by reference to the number of recipients of the defamatory matter, the type of publication or the plaintiff's initial reputation and how that has been affected by the allegedly defamatory publication.

In Australia, s 10A(1) of the uniform defamation provisions[80] is as follows:

(1)   It is an element (the serious harm element) of a cause of action for defamation that the publication of defamatory matter about a person has caused, or is likely to cause, serious harm to the reputation of the person.

Section 10A(2) also applies to corporations by stipulating that 'harm to the reputation of an excluded corporation is not serious harm unless it has caused, or is likely to cause, the corporation serious financial loss.' Section 10A(3) states that a judicial officer (and not a jury) is to determine whether the 'serious harm' test has been satisfied. Section 10A(5) stipulates that the 'serious harm' test must be determined before trial commences. The provisions state the 'judicial officer is to determine the issue as soon as practicable before the trial commences unless satisfied that there are special circumstances justifying the postponement of the determination to a later stage of the proceeding'.

Given the recency of these provisions, judicial interpretation in Australian jurisdictions is somewhat limited. However, several decisions have provided some initial guidance. In *Newman v Whittington*,[81] Sackar J confirmed that while *Lachaux* was not binding in Australian jurisdictions, it was 'powerful and persuasive analysis' given the similarities between the Australian and UK provisions.[82] The Court confirmed that the issue of serious harm 'would normally be determined before trial unless special circumstances suggest otherwise'.[83] His Honour further confirmed that seriousness and gravity of defamation is a factor to be taken

78   *Defamation Act 2013* (UK), s 1 provides: '(1) A statement is not defamatory unless its publication has caused or is likely to cause serious harm to the reputation of the claimant. (2) For the purposes of this section, harm to the reputation of a body that trades for profit is not "serious harm" unless it has caused or is likely to cause the body serious financial loss.'
79   [2020] AC 612.
80   *Civil Law (Wrongs) Act 2002* (ACT) s 122A; *Defamation Act 2005* (NSW) s 10A; *Defamation Act 2005* (Qld) s 10A; *Defamation Act 2005* (SA) s 10A; *Defamation Act 2005* (Tas) s 10A; *Defamation Act 2005* (Vic) s 10A. (The Northern Territory and Western Australia have not enacted the 'serious harm' provisions at the time of writing.)
81   [2022] NSWSC 249.
82   At [51].
83   *Newman v Whittington* [2022] NSWSC 249, [35] (Sackar J).

into account.[84] His Honour confirmed that s 10A places an onus on the plaintiff to prove serious harm as an element of the cause of action in defamation.[85] His Honour adopted the reasoning of Lord Sumption in *Lachaux* confirming that the provision 'required its application to be determined by reference to the actual facts about its impact and not just to the meaning of the words'.[86]

Further, in *Wilks v Qu*, Clayton J confirmed that 'the legislation imposes a presumption that the special harm element *will* be heard prior to trial and the considerations ordinarily pertinent to the trial of a separate question are not applicable.'[87]

11.2.5   Standing to sue

The tort of defamation is confined to protecting the personal and professional reputation of individuals, rather than corporations. Under the uniform defamation legislation a company is excluded from taking action, unless:

- it is a non-profit organisation or
- it has fewer than 10 employees and is not related to another corporation.[88]

Government authorities and local government bodies are also excluded. In 2018, the New South Wales Government in its review of the model defamation provisions invited submissions on the section pertaining to liability of corporation.[89] Concerns were expressed that as the term 'employee' was not defined, it would adopt its ordinary meaning under the general law. This would mean that independent contractors would not be considered 'employees', and could result in undesirable consequences where a corporation could bypass the prohibition because of the way it elected to structure its business.[90]

In Australia, s 9 of the uniform defamation provisions[91] is as follows:

Section 9

(1)   A corporation has no cause of action for defamation in relation to the publication of defamatory matter about the corporation unless it was an excluded corporation at the time of the publication.

---

84   Ibid [44] (Sackar J).
85   Ibid [47] (Sackar J).
86   Ibid [64] (Sackar J).
87   *Wilks v Qu* [2022] VCC 620, [39] (Clayton J).
88   *Civil Law (Wrongs) Act 2002* (ACT) s 121; *Defamation Act 2005* (NSW) s 9; *Defamation Act 2006* (NT) s 8; *Defamation Act 2005* (Qld) s 9; *Defamation Act 2005* (SA) s 9; *Defamation Act 2005* (Tas) s 9; *Defamation Act 2005* (Vic) s 9; *Defamation Act 2005* (WA) s 9.
89   See New South Wales, Department of Justice, *Statutory Review: Defamation Act 2005* (June 2018) Recommendation 2: 'Recommend that the Council of Attorneys-General ask the Defamation Working Party to review the Model Defamation Provisions equivalent to section 9 (certain corporations do not have cause of action for defamation) to determine whether the capacity of corporations to sue for defamation should be amended.'
90   Parliamentary Council's Committee, *Model Defamation Amendment Provisions 2020* (27 July 2020) <https://pcc.gov.au/uniform/2020/Model_Defamation_Amendment_Provisions_2020.pdf> 3.
91   *Civil Law (Wrongs) Act 2002* (ACT) s 121; *Defamation Act 2005* (NSW) s 9; *Defamation Act 2005* (Qld) s 9; *Defamation Act 2005* (SA) s 9; *Defamation Act 2005* (Tas) s 9; *Defamation Act 2005* (Vic) s 9. (The Northern Territory and Western Australia have not enacted the serious harm provisions at the time of writing.)

(2)   A corporation is an excluded corporation if –

    (a)   the objects for which it is formed do not include obtaining financial gain for its members or corporators; or

    (b)   it has fewer than 10 employees and is not an associated entity of another corporation,

and the corporation is not a public body.

(3)   In counting employees for the purposes of subsection (2)(b), part-time employees are to be taken into account as an appropriate fraction of a full-time equivalent.

...

(6)   In this section –

    ...

    employee, in relation to a corporation, includes any individual (whether or not an independent contractor) who is –

    (a)   engaged in the day to day operations of the corporation other than as a volunteer; and

    (b)   subject to the control and direction of the corporation;

    ...

An individual is not prevented from taking action if matter defames both the individual and the company.[92] However, in *Triguboff v Fairfax Media Publications Pty Ltd* the Federal Court found against Michael Triguboff, founder and managing director of Meriton Property Services, finding a newspaper article about the company did not personally defame him.[93] In other words, an article about a company is not automatically an article about the owner unless a link exists within the publication. Neither deceased individuals nor their estates are permitted to take action, regardless of whether the matter was published before or after their death.[94] Tasmania is the only state that did not adopt the provision, so the common law position appears to have been retained in that state.[95]

HINTS AND TIPS

Excluded corporations, government bodies and estates of deceased individuals do not have standing to sue under the uniform defamation laws.

11.2.6   Defamation and injurious falsehood

The tort of injurious falsehood may be relied on where the defendant has made a malicious publication of a false statement regarding the plaintiff's goods or business that causes damage to the plaintiff.[96]

---

92   *Civil Law (Wrongs) Act 2002* (ACT) s 121(5); *Defamation Act 2005* (NSW) s 9(5); *Defamation Act 2006* (NT) s 8(5); *Defamation Act 2005* (Qld) s 9(5); *Defamation Act 2005* (SA) s 9(5); *Defamation Act 2005* (Tas) s 9(5); *Defamation Act 2005* (Vic) s 9(5); *Defamation Act 2005* (WA) s 9(5).

93   [2018] FCA 845.

94   *Civil Law (Wrongs) Act 2002* (ACT) s 122; *Defamation Act 2005* (NSW) s 10; *Defamation Act 2006* (NT) s 9; *Defamation Act 2005* (Qld) s 10; *Defamation Act 2005* (SA) s 10; *Defamation Act 2005* (Vic) s 10; *Defamation Act 2005* (WA) s 10.

95   Interestingly, *Defamation Act 2005* (Tas) s 10 is titled 'Section left blank' to preserve the consistency in numbering with the remaining states.

96   *Tavakoli v Imisides (No 4)* [2019] NSWSC 717, [43]–[45].

Recently, a trend has emerged of doctors suing their former patients for damage to their reputation and in some instances, loss to business income.[97] For instance, in *Tavakoli v Imisides (No 4)*,[98] the defendant posted a Google review claiming that Dr Tavakoli (a plastic surgeon) charged her for a procedure she never received. The defendant also depicted the plaintiff as having acted improperly and incompetently. The imputations in the case alleged the plaintiff was an incompetent surgeon, cruel in his dealings as a doctor, and was a bully in intimidating the patient. Ultimately the Court found that a cause of action in both defamation and injurious falsehood was established. An injunction and an award of damages were granted in this instance.

The *tort of injurious falsehood* involves malicious publication of a false statement that damages the plaintiff's business. The elements of this tort are different to the tort of defamation and require the court to find:

(a)   a false statement of or concerning the plaintiff's goods or business

(b)   publication of that statement by the defendant to a third person

(c)   malice on the part of the defendant and

(d)   proof by the plaintiff of actual damage (which may include a general loss of business) suffered as a result of the statement.

As highlighted above, these elements were satisfied in *Tavakoli* where the Court found the defendant liable for both defamation and injurious falsehood. This case provides a good example of how a cause of action in both defamation and injurious falsehood can arise simultaneously from the same factual circumstances.

REVIEW QUESTIONS

(1)   Explain the difference between defamatory imputations derived through (a) natural and ordinary meaning, (b) true innuendo, and (c) false innuendo. Provide an example of each.

(2)   Is it always necessary to identify an individual by name in order to be found liable in defamation?

(3)   If matter is posted on the internet (eg, on social media websites), in what location will it be deemed to have been published?

(4)   Critically evaluate whether the lack of standing by corporations under the uniform defamation laws is just and helpful.

(5)   Summarise the decision in *Voller* and outline why the case is significant for online publication.

 Guided responses in the eBook

---

97   See, eg, *Al Muderis v Duncan (No 3)* [2017] NSWSC 726. See also I Freckelton and T Popa, 'Doctors, Defamation and Damages: Medical Practitioners Fighting Back' (2019) 27(1) *Journal of Law and Medicine* 20.

98   [2019] NSWSC 717.

11.3   Defences

Once the plaintiff has established a prima facie case in defamation, the onus shifts to the defendant to prove a defence to avoid liability. Prior to the enactment of the uniform legislation, the defences at common law varied significantly among the states. The uniform legislation created nine statutory defences that operate alongside the common law defences.[99] Following the 2021 reforms, additional statutory defences were introduced and the defence of triviality was removed. In many instances the statutory defences have altered the nature of the common law defences substantially and this will be discussed. Figures 11.2 and 11.3 outline the defences available in statute and at common law respectively.

Figure 11.2   Statutory defences to defamation

Figure 11.3   Common law defences to defamation

HINTS AND TIPS

Defendants facing defamation action should rely on the statutory defences as a starting point to assist them to avoid liability, but common law defences continue to exist and are also available to the defendant.

11.3.1   Justification

The defence of justification allows the plaintiff to escape liability for publication of defamatory matter if the 'defendant proves that the defamatory imputations carried by

---

99   The legislation provides: 'A defence under this Division is additional to any other defence or exclusion of liability available to the defendant apart from this Act (including under the general law) and does not of itself vitiate, limit or abrogate any other defence or exclusion of liability.' See *Civil Law (Wrongs) Act 2002* (ACT) s 134; *Defamation Act 2005* (NSW) s 24; *Defamation Act 2006* (NT) s 21; *Defamation Act 2005* (Qld) s 24; *Defamation Act 2005* (SA) s 24; *Defamation Act 2005* (Tas) s 24; *Defamation Act 2005* (Vic) s 24; *Defamation Act 2005* (WA) s 24.

the matter of which the plaintiff complains are substantially true'. The uniform legislation defines 'substantially true' as 'true in substance or not materially different from the truth'.[100] The emphasis on the 'substantial truth' of imputations means that a defendant can escape liability if the defamatory matter contains minor inaccuracies.[101]

Prior to the enactment of the uniform defamation legislation, the defence of truth existed at common law. In the Northern Territory, South Australia, Victoria and Western Australia truth alone was a complete defence. However, in the Australian Capital Territory, New South Wales, Queensland and Tasmania the defendant also needed to show that disclosure of the matter was in the public interest. The statutory test omits the public interest requirement, meaning publication of private or embarrassing information is not actionable in defamation if accurately portrayed.

In order to succeed in the defence of justification, the defendant must justify the 'sting' of the defamatory matter. For example, the defendant may be able to prove the truth of some, but not all, of the alleged extramarital affairs of a plaintiff.[102] This would justify the 'common sting' that the plaintiff was unfaithful or disloyal. However, it would exclude other 'stings' that could not be justified, such as a statement alleging the plaintiff is a thief or alcoholic.

For example, *Phillips v Robab Pty Ltd* involved a dispute between Sydney osteopaths in which an allegation was made on a website that an osteopath 'stole' patient records.[103] The defence of justification was unsuccessful as Rothman J recognised that the plaintiff was entitled to gain access to patient information, hence access to the information was technically gained with authority and did not amount to 'stealing'. Therefore, if the defendant can justify only *some* and not *all* of the imputations, the defence will fail. Similarly, the defendant will not be able to rely on the defence of justification where the matter is literally, but not substantively, true, as illustrated in *Howden v Truth & Sportsman Ltd*.[104]

Case: *Howden v Truth & Sportsman Ltd* (1937) 68 CLR 416

Facts

The defendant published matter about the plaintiff, alleging he had been sentenced to a term of 15 months' imprisonment for conspiracy to commit fraud. Although this was true, the plaintiff's conviction was subsequently quashed and a new trial ordered.

---

100 *Civil Law (Wrongs) Act 2002* (ACT) s 116; *Defamation Act 2005* (NSW) s 4; *Defamation Act 2006* (NT) s 3; *Defamation Act 2005* (Qld) s 4; *Defamation Act 2005* (SA) s 4; *Defamation Act 2005* (Tas) s 4; *Defamation Act 2005* (Vic) s 4; *Defamation Act 2005* (WA) s 4.

101 In *Alexander v North Eastern Railway Co* (1865) 6 B & S 340 the defendant escaped liability in defamation despite alleging the plaintiff had been sentenced to three weeks' imprisonment, when in actual fact he had been sentenced to two weeks.

102 *Khashoggi v IPC Magazines Ltd* [1986] 1 WLR 1412.

103 (2014) 110 IPR 184.

104 (1937) 68 CLR 416.

Issue

Could the defendant rely on the defence of truth in circumstances where the defamatory matter was literally but not substantively true?

Decision

The defendant could not rely on the truth defence, as the subsequent quashing of the conviction meant that the imputation that the plaintiff was a criminal was no longer substantively true.

Significance

The defendant cannot rely on the literal meaning of words to argue their truth, but must instead justify the substantive truth or 'sting' behind the imputations.

Notes

Dixon J held at 420–1: 'The defence depends upon the substantial truth of the defamatory meaning conveyed by a libel. Every material part of the imputations upon the plaintiff contained in the words complained of must be true; otherwise the justification fails as an answer to the action.'

Question

Consider the following situation: A newspaper publishes photographs of P in handcuffs being arrested. The police subsequently released P after discovering he was mistakenly apprehended for a crime he was not involved in. Can the newspaper be held liable in defamation?

    Guided response in the eBook

The defendant must justify each of the imputations from the matter or, alternatively, that the imputations carried a 'common sting'. For instance, an imputation alleging that P, an elite athlete, is a cheater can be justified through proof that P took prohibited substances while competing in a competition. However, if the matter carried imputations that P was also a thief or promiscuous, then these imputations would need to be separately justified. In *Mutch v Sleeman*, an article contained imputations against the plaintiff including that he was not a fit and proper person to retain a position in public office, that he was addicted to vile language, that he was a wife-beater, that he was a man of 'unclean, abominable and unmanly' habits and that he was guilty of improper and corrupt conduct.[105] The Court held that to satisfy a defence of justification, the defendant must prove each statement to be true.

The common law position was outlined in *Polly Peck plc v Trelford* where the Court held that a defendant would succeed if the imputations pleaded by the plaintiff did no further harm to the plaintiff's reputation because of the truth of the broader imputations (provided these had a 'common sting').[106] This was termed the '*Polly Peck* defence'. In *David Syme &*

---

105 (1928) 29 SR (NSW) 125.
106 [1986] QB 1000.

Co Ltd v Hore-Lacey the Victorian Court of Appeal held that a jury could not find for the plaintiff 'unless the meaning they would give the publication was only a nuance or variant, not substantially different or more serious from that proposed by the plaintiff'.[107]

The defence of justification has been considered in a number of recent cases including *Cripps v Vakras* where Kyrou J considered both the common law and statutory defence in the context of proceedings brought by a gallery owner against two artists for defamatory online posts.[108] The case involved a number of defamatory imputations, including that the gallery owner was racist and a bully, with only one imputation (regarding economic duress) found to be justified.

The precision with which the truth defence must be pleaded was recently discussed in defamation proceedings instituted by actor Geoffrey Rush against Nationwide News, who alleged that he behaved inappropriately towards a female cast member in a play.[109] At trial, the defendants pleaded the defence of justification under s 25 of the NSW uniform defamation laws.[110] The defendants relied on conduct, behaviour and text messages to assert their publication was justified.[111] Ultimately, Wigney J found that the defendants 'failed to discharge their burden of proving the substantial truth of the imputations that have been found to have been conveyed by the matters complained of. Their defence of justification accordingly fails.'[112] On appeal, the Full Court of the Federal Court of Australia left the findings pertaining to the defence of justification undisturbed.[113]

Case: *Nationwide News Pty Ltd v Rush* (2020) 380 ALR 432

Facts

Actor Geoffrey Rush worked as part of a theatre production of *King Lear*. Approximately two years later, Nationwide News published three items about Mr Rush's alleged conduct during the theatre production, which the actor alleged defamed him: (1) a poster asserting inappropriate behaviour; (2) a large photograph of the actor with the line 'KING LEER'; (3) a publication in the *Daily Telegraph* purporting to support actresses who made the allegations of inappropriate behaviour. At trial, Mr Rush was awarded $2 872 753.10 in damages for economic and non-economic loss. The newspaper appealed.

Issue

The case concerned several legal issues including alleged apprehension of bias against the trial judge; whether there was an error in finding that the publication conveyed the defamatory imputation that Mr Rush was a 'pervert', and errors relating to an award of damages. Most

---

107   (2000) 1 VR 667, [21] (Ormiston JA).
108   [2014] VSC 279.
109   *Rush v Nationwide News Pty Ltd* (2018) 359 ALR 473.
110   *Rush v Nationwide News Pty Limited (No 7)* [2019] FCA 496, [220]–[229]. Particulars of pleadings by Nationwide were at [230]–[241] (Wigney J).
111   Ibid [230] (Wigney J).
112   Ibid [662] (Wigney J).
113   *Nationwide News Pty Ltd v Rush* (2020) 380 ALR 432, [316]–[344] (White, Gleeson and Wheelahan JJ).

significantly for your study of defences, the appellant newspaper alleged the trial judge had erred in rejecting the justification defence.

Decision

The Full Court of the Federal Court affirmed the trial judge's findings that the newspaper had not made out the substantial truth of the material they relied on. In other words, Mr Rush's conduct, behaviour and text messages did not amount to the inappropriate behaviour imputed by the defamatory matter.

Significance

The decision is significant not only for media companies but also for the wider community, as it emphasises the need to have a substantially true basis prior to publishing content that is potentially defamatory.

Notes

Their Honours highlighted the role of context and community values at [331]–[333], especially regarding the alleged inappropriate conduct that stemmed from text messages exchanged between Mr Rush and Ms Norvill (an actress who made allegations against Mr Rush): 'The characterisation of a comment made by one person to another as "inappropriate" involves an application of community values and mores and consideration of the context and circumstances in which the comment is made'.

Question

Consider the following situation: A newspaper publishes photographs of P with a derogatory headline based on copies of text exchanges between P and a third party. Is P entitled to sue in defamation? How does this case affect the balance between individual rights and journalism for the benefit of the public?

 Guided response in the eBook

11.3.2   Contextual truth

The contextual truth defence allows the defendant to escape liability where:

- the matter carries one or more imputations (the 'contextual imputations')
- the contextual imputations are substantially true and
- the defamatory imputations (that are not contextual imputations) that the plaintiff complains of do not further harm the plaintiff's reputation because of the substantial truth of the contextual imputations.[114]

---

114 See *Civil Law (Wrongs) Act 2002* (ACT) s 136; *Defamation Act 2005* (NSW) s 26; *Defamation Act 2005* (Qld) s 26; *Defamation Act 2005* (SA) s 24; *Defamation Act 2005* (Tas) s 26; *Defamation Act 2005* (Vic) s 26.

Since the introduction of the 2021 uniform defamation law amendments, the contextual imputations on which the defendant relies on can include the imputations of which the plaintiff is complaining about.[115]

Put simply, the defence protects the defendant in circumstances where the most damaging imputations are substantially true yet the plaintiff elects to claim on the basis of the less damaging, untrue imputations. The statutory defence of contextual truth applies to the publication of defamatory 'matter' rather than defamatory 'imputations', so that the defence of contextual truth must defeat the whole cause of action of which the plaintiff complains.[116]

Imagine that D publishes a newspaper article about P claiming that P is a murderer and thief and failed to pay a parking ticket. If D can prove P was convicted for murder and theft, but has no evidence that P failed to pay a parking ticket, the law does not permit P to claim for the defamatory imputations of the parking ticket because the untrue imputations do not do any further harm to the plaintiff's reputation. Essentially, the law does not permit P to cherrypick the defamatory imputations. A case that provides a good example is *Mizikovsky v Queensland Television Ltd*.[117] Here, the chief executive of a building company initiated proceedings against the defendant for broadcasting matter containing defamatory imputations that the plaintiff was not a competent builder and had caused financial loss and hardship to his customers. The jury ultimately found no further harm was caused to the plaintiff, due to the truth of the contextual imputations that he routinely failed to deliver promises to customers and respond to their complaints.

In 2021, the statutory defence of contextual truth received minor, but significant, changes. Prior to 2021, the provision was worded as follows:

> It is a defence to the publication of defamatory matter if the defendant proves that (a) the matter carried, in addition to the defamatory imputations of which the plaintiff complains, one or more other imputations (contextual imputations) that are substantially true.[118]

Defamation lawyer Matthew Collins succinctly puts it: 'As enacted, the defence was infected with a serious drafting error.'[119] The words 'in addition to' presented practical problems, as it meant that the defendant was required to show that imputations could be derived from the matter (ie, the contextual imputations) that have not been pleaded by the plaintiff, and that these were true. Strict interpretations of this legislative provision meant that a defendant could not plead an imputation if it was already pleaded by the plaintiff.[120] The 2021 reforms removed the words 'in addition to' and now permit a defendant to 'plead back' substantially true imputations pleaded by the plaintiff. The developments of these historical 'mischiefs'[121] are presented below.

---

115 See *Civil Law (Wrongs) Act 2002* (ACT) s 136(2); *Defamation Act 2005* (NSW) s 26(2); *Defamation Act 2005* (Qld) s 26(2); *Defamation Act 2005* (SA) s 24(2); *Defamation Act 2005* (Tas) s 26(2); *Defamation Act 2005* (Vic) s 26(2). Western Australia and the Northern Territory have not implemented the amendments to s 26.

116 *Fairfax Media Publications Pty Ltd v Kermode* (2011) 81 NSWLR 157.

117 [2014] 1 Qd R 197.

118 See, eg, *Defamation Act 2005* (Vic) s 26(a) effective October 2014.

119 M Collins, 'The Reformulated Contextual Truth Defence: More Radical Than First Appears' (2022) 50(2) *Federal Law Review* 206.

120 *Fairfax Media Publications Pty Ltd v Kermode* (2011) 81 NSWLR 157.

121 J Harrison, 'Guess Who's Back: The Reform of the Statutory Defence of Contextual Truth', *BarNews* (2021) <https://barnews.nswbar.asn.au/autumn-2021/28-guess-whos-back-the-reform-of-the-statutory-defence-of-contextual-truth>.

The case of *Irving v Penguin Books Ltd*, though decided on common law principles, provides a good example of the operation of the defence.[122]

Case: *Irving v Penguin Books Ltd* [2000] EWHC QB 115

Facts

The defendant published a book titled *Denying the Holocaust: The Growing Assault on Truth and Memory* about the plaintiff, a controversial historian, alleging he was a prominent Holocaust denier. The book contained numerous imputations about the plaintiff including that he deliberately misrepresented the treatment of Jewish people, that he painted Hitler favourably and, further, that he was anti-Semitic, racist and associated with Nazi extremists. These imputations were accepted by the Court as substantially true. The book also contained the assertion that the plaintiff had hung a picture of Hitler above his desk.

Issue

If the majority of the defamatory imputations were substantially true, could the plaintiff succeed on the basis of an imputation that added no further damage to his reputation?

Decision

The defamatory imputation that the plaintiff had hung a picture of Hitler above his desk did not have any material effect on the plaintiff's reputation when compared with the gravity of the substantially true imputations.

Significance

The plaintiff is unlikely to succeed where the defendant can prove that the defamatory imputations do not further harm the reputation of the plaintiff due to the substantial truth of the contextual imputations.

Notes

Gray J stated at [13.165]–[13.167]:

> My overall finding in relation to the plea of justification is that the Defendants have proved the substantial truth of the imputations, most of which relate to Irving's conduct as an historian ... My finding is that the defamatory meanings ... are substantially justified.
>
> But there are certain defamatory imputations which I have found to be defamatory of Irving but which have not been proved to be true. The Defendants made no attempt to prove the truth of Lipstadt's claim that Irving was scheduled to speak at an anti-Zionist conference in Sweden in 1992, which was also to be attended by various representatives of terrorist organisations such as Hezbollah and Hammas. Nor did they seek to justify Lipstadt's claim that Irving has a self-portrait by Hitler hanging over his desk. Furthermore the Defendants have, as I have held, failed in their attempt to justify

the defamatory imputations made against Irving in relation to the Goebbels diaries in the Moscow archive. The question which I have to ask myself is whether the consequence of the Defendants' failure to prove the truth of these matters is that the defence of justification fails in its entirety.

The answer to that question requires me to decide whether (I am paraphrasing section 5 of the *Defamation Act 1952*) the failure on the part of the Defendants to prove the truth of those charges materially injures the reputation of Irving, in view of the fact that the other defamatory charges made against him have been proved to be justified. The charges which I have found to be substantially true include the charges that Irving has for his own ideological reasons persistently and deliberately misrepresented and manipulated historical evidence; that for the same reasons he has portrayed Hitler in an unwarrantedly favourable light, principally in relation to his attitude towards and responsibility for the treatment of the Jews; that he is an active Holocaust denier; that he is antisemitic and racist and that he associates with right wing extremists who promote neo-Nazism. In my judgment the charges against Irving which have been proved to be true are of sufficient gravity for it be clear that the failure to prove the truth of the matters set out in paragraph 13.165 [ie, whether the plaintiff had hung a picture of Hitler above his desk] does not have any material effect on Irving's reputation.

Question

In [13.165]–[13.167] of his judgment Gray J appears to focus closely on the defence of justification. How are the defences of justification and contextual truth linked?

 Guided response in the eBook

The statutory defence of contextual truth was considered in the case of *Fairfax Media Productions Pty Ltd v Kermode*.[123] The plaintiff, Reginald Kermode, initiated proceedings against the defendant publishers for an article published in *The Sydney Morning Herald*. The plaintiff alleged that the article contained a number of defamatory imputations asserting that he had inappropriately influenced politicians to accept donations to benefit companies controlled by him. The plaintiff pleaded a number of imputations; in response, the defendant pleaded the defences of substantial truth and contextual truth. The issue was whether the wording of the statutory defence under the uniform defamation laws permitted the defendant to 'plead back' some of the plaintiff's imputations as contextual imputations. In the practice of 'pleading back', defendants would attempt to prove the truth of the imputations raised by the plaintiff, so that if some imputations were proven to be true, the true imputations would outweigh the untrue ones. Thus, no further harm would be done to the plaintiff's reputation because of the truth of some of the imputations, and the defendant would succeed.

Under the previous *Defamation Act 1974* (NSW), the wording of s 16 provided a defence of contextual truth where 'an imputation is made by a publication … and another imputation is made by the same publication'. This essentially allowed a defendant to use the imputations raised by the plaintiff as part of the defendant's case. Yet s 26 of the uniform defamation laws (prior to the 2021 reforms) was worded differently and permitted a defence of contextual truth where the imputations pleaded by the defendant were '*in addition to the defamatory imputations of which the plaintiff complains*' (emphasis added). Put simply, the defendant was required to show that imputations can be derived from the matter (contextual imputations) that have not been pleaded by the plaintiff. The New South Wales Court of Appeal upheld the trial judge's decision that the wording of the uniform defamation laws (as it was then worded) did not allow the practice of pleading back. McColl JA held: 'the words "in addition to … ", as the primary judge pointed out … correctly in my view, cannot be "contorted to include imputations pleaded by the plaintiff".'[124]

The New South Wales Court of Appeal in *Fairfax Digital Australia & New Zealand Pty Ltd v Kazal* considered whether imputations could be 'pleaded back' for a contextual truth defence.[125] As already discussed, a defendant could 'plead back' the plaintiff's imputations and argue that, because of the substantial truth of the imputations, the imputation complained of did no further harm to the plaintiff's reputation. The key issue in *Kazal* was whether 'a plea of contextual truth under *Defamation Act 2005* (NSW), s 26 may adopt, as contextual imputations, those of the imputations pleaded by a plaintiff that are subsequently found to be carried, defamatory and "substantially true".'[126] The Court of Appeal held that 'a defamatory imputation does not cease to be one "of which the plaintiff complains" (s 26(a)) if it is found by the tribunal of fact to be substantially true in the context of a different defence (s 25) which, by hypothesis, has failed'.[127] As outlined, the removal of the words 'in addition to' has reformulated the defence to create a smoother operation.

11.3.3   Absolute privilege

The defence of absolute privilege recognises the importance of free speech in certain contexts and protects communications in such circumstances by ensuring that defamation proceedings cannot be brought for potentially defamatory matter. Defamation proceedings cannot be maintained where matter was published on an occasion of privilege (eg, evidence given in judicial proceedings, debate during parliamentary proceedings or material in ministerial communications).[128] Statements made outside court or Parliament will not be protected. For example, in *O'Shane v Harbour Radio Pty Ltd*, a former magistrate successfully sued the broadcaster of a radio show where the presenter described the magistrate's decisions as 'diabolical and wrong'.[129] The action was permitted, given that the defamatory statements were made outside of court and not in the course of judicial proceedings. In *Mann v O'Neill* the

---

124 *Fairfax Media Publications Pty Ltd v Kermode* (2011) 81 NSWLR 157, [81] (McColl JA).
125 (2018) 97 NSWLR 547.
126 *Fairfax Digital Australia & New Zealand Pty Ltd v Kazal* (2018) 97 NSWLR 547, [36] (Meagher JA).
127 Ibid [149] (Gleeson JA).
128 See *Civil Law (Wrongs) Act 2002* (ACT) s 137; *Defamation Act 2005* (NSW) s 27; *Defamation Act 2006* (NT) s 24; *Defamation Act 2005* (Qld) s 27; *Defamation Act 2005* (SA) s 25; *Defamation Act 2005* (Tas) s 27; *Defamation Act 2005* (Vic) s 27; *Defamation Act 2005* (WA) s 27.
129 (2013) 85 NSWLR 698.

plaintiff questioned the mental capacity of a magistrate in letters sent to the Chief Magistrate and Minister for Justice.[130] The plaintiff argued that the letters of complaint were initiating documents for a quasi-judicial tribunal 'recognised by law' and thus attracted absolute privilege. The High Court held that the communications were not protected by absolute privilege as they were made outside court with no connection to the court proceedings.

HINTS AND TIPS

The defence of absolute privilege helps to protect freedom of speech in circumstances where it is vital to speak freely. For example, imagine if A was asked to give evidence in court proceedings and felt the need to conceal evidence out of fear of being sued in defamation.

Likewise, absolute privilege can protect politicians who may be debating issues in Parliament. However, it is important to note that defendants are *not* protected if they make defamatory comments outside of parliamentary proceedings, such as defaming politicians online. For instance:

- Politician Dr Anne Webster was successful in her defamation action against a defendant who posted defamatory posts about her online: *Webster v Brewer (No 3)* [2020] FCA 1343.
- Former deputy NSW premier John Barilaro was also successful in his defamation action against Google for defamatory videos made by a commentator which Google hosted via the YouTube channel: *Barilaro v Google LLC* [2022] FCA 650.

11.3.4   Publication of public documents

The uniform legislation provides that it is a defence to the publication of defamatory matter if the defendant proves that the matter was contained in a public document or a copy or fair summary of the document.[131] The term 'public document' is defined within the provision and includes:

- parliamentary reports or papers
- a judgment or court order
- a record of a court or tribunal relating to the judgment or determination
- a report under the law of any country that is required to be tabled in Parliament
- any documents issued by the government or document open to inspection by the public in an Australian jurisdiction
- any other document treated as a public document by a body of an Australian jurisdiction.

---

130 (1997) 191 CLR 204.
131 See *Civil Law (Wrongs) Act 2002* (ACT) s 138; *Defamation Act 2005* (NSW) s 28; *Defamation Act 2006* (NT) s 25; *Defamation Act 2005* (Qld) s 28; *Defamation Act 2005* (SA) s 26; *Defamation Act 2005* (Tas) s 28; *Defamation Act 2005* (Vic) s 28; *Defamation Act 2005* (WA) s 28.

The defence will be defeated if the plaintiff proves that the defamatory matter was not published honestly for the information of the public or the advancement of education.

Case: *Belbin v Lower Murray Urban and Rural Water Corporation* [2012] VSC 535

Facts

A Minister of the Victorian Government wrote a letter to the former customers of a water trust and the letter was posted on the internet. The letter contained imputations that the plaintiffs had broken the law, acted irresponsibly and approved last-minute secret contracts.

Issue

Did the letter constitute a 'public document' given it was written by a Government Minister?

Decision

The letter did not constitute a 'public document' as it was not issued by the Government, was informal in nature and was not created for the purpose of informing the general public.

Significance

In order to constitute a 'public document' it is imperative the document be issued in a formal public capacity and published for the information of the public.

Notes

At [89], Kaye J focused on the difference between the terms 'published' and 'issued' in determining whether the document was issued by the Government:

> Clearly, a document may be kept without being published; conversely, a document may be published without being kept. Similarly, the verb 'issue' and the verb 'publish' are not synonymous. Not every document published by a government, or by an officer, employee or agency of the government, would, per se, be issued by the government (or by the officer, employee or agency of the government). Conversely, while a document issued by the government may thereby be published by the government, it does not follow that each document, issued by a government (or an officer, employee or agency of the government), is thereby 'published' as that word is understood in defamation law.

Question

What do you think would have made the letter in this case a 'public document' so as to fall within the defence of publication of public documents?

 Guided response in the eBook

HINTS AND TIPS

The term 'public document' is defined in s 28(4) of the uniform defamation legislation so it has a specific meaning. It does not intend to cover all 'publicly available' documents, so do not be misled by the title of this defence!

11.3.5 Fair report of proceedings of public concern

The uniform defamation legislation provides that it is a defence to the publication of defamatory matter if the defendant proves that the matter was, or was contained in, a fair report of any proceedings of public concern.[132] The defendant will succeed if he or she can prove that: (1) the matter was contained in an earlier published report of proceedings of a public concern; (2) the matter was a fair copy, fair summary or fair extract of the earlier published report; and (3) the defendant had no knowledge that would make the defendant reasonably aware that the earlier published report was not fair.[133] Like the defence of publication of public documents, the defence will be defeated if the plaintiff proves the defamatory matter was not published honestly for the information of the public or the advancement of education. The provision defines 'proceedings of public concern' to include proceedings of:

- a parliamentary body
- an international organisation
- an international government conference
- a court or tribunal
- a public inquiry
- a local government body
- a learned society (including a sport or recreational association)
- a trade association
- a public meeting
- an ombudsman
- a law reform body.

The defence of fair report of proceedings of a public concern was raised in *Defteros v Google LLC*. Mr Defteros, a Melbourne solicitor, sued Google for hyperlinks to articles published by a third party, which he alleged defamed him. In the trial decision, Richards J explored whether an article by *The Age* which reported on a bail application heard in the Magistrates' Court was a fair report. Ultimately, Richards J found that the article 'published by Google was a fair copy of the whole of the earlier published report in *The Age*.'[134] While the matter

---

132 See *Civil Law (Wrongs) Act 2002* (ACT) s 139; *Defamation Act 2005* (NSW) s 29; *Defamation Act 2006* (NT) s 26; *Defamation Act 2005* (Qld) s 29; *Defamation Act 2005* (SA) s 27; *Defamation Act 2005* (Tas) s 29; *Defamation Act 2005* (Vic) s 29; *Defamation Act 2005* (WA) s 29.

133 Ibid.

134 *Defteros v Google LLC* [2020] VSC 219.

was subsequently appealed to the High Court on legal issues pertaining to hyperlinks, the trial decision nevertheless provides a good example of the circumstances in which the defence may be raised.

HINTS AND TIPS

Think of a reporter on your favourite evening news program and try to recall an occasion where the reporter reported on a prominent trial in court. The defence of fair report permits the journalist to provide a fair summary of the court proceedings without being sued for defamation.

11.3.6   Publication of matter concerning an issue of public interest

The 2021 reforms introduced a new defence of publication of matter concerning an issue of public interest. In essence, a defendant can rely on the defence if:

- the matter concerns an issue of public interest and
- the defendant reasonably believed that publication of the matter was in the public interest.[135]

Pursuant to s 29A(2), the court is required to take into account all of the 'circumstances of the case'. Section 29A(3) provides some guidance by outlining nine factors that a court may take into account and they include the seriousness of the defamatory imputation, the extent to which the matter published relates to the performance of a person's public functions or activities and sources of the information. Section 29A(4) stipulates that not all of the factors must be taken into account, which means the provision is not to be used as a 'checklist'. Further, the list of factors is not exhaustive so it does not limit the matters a court can take into account when deciding whether the defence has been established. Finally, the legislative provisions make it clear that the jury, if there is one, is to determine whether the defence is established, rather than a judge.

HINTS AND TIPS

The Explanatory Memorandum to the statutory amendments outline that the purpose of the provision is to ensure that freedom of expression is not limited. It may aid journalists and media organisations in more freely reporting on matters that are in the public interest.

---

135 *Civil Law (Wrongs) Act 2002* (ACT) s 139AA; *Defamation Act 2005* (NSW) s 29A; *Defamation Act 2005* (Qld) s 29A; *Defamation Act 2005* (SA) s 27A; *Defamation Act 2005* (Tas) s 29A; *Defamation Act 2005* (Vic) s 29A. The Northern Territory and Western Australian statutes do not contain this provision.

In *Barilaro v Google LLC*,[136] Google pleaded the new statutory defence under s 29A of the NSW *Uniform Defamation Act*. It claimed that hosting the videos containing defamatory matter pertaining to former deputy premier John Barilaro were in the public interest. Given the videos were uploaded prior to the commencement of the new provisions on 1 July 2022, Rares J stated: 'I am of opinion that s 29A provides a defence only to the publication of defamatory matter in electronic form that is first uploaded on or after 1 July 2021.'[137] However, his Honour went on to say that even if the material had been published after the commencement of the new provisions, Google would need to satisfy the Court that publication was in the public interest. His Honour was not convinced that was satisfied given Google 'did not particularise any enquiry or research that it had made about the content of [the video]'.[138]

11.3.7 Qualified privilege

At common law the defence of qualified privilege protects the publication of material that might otherwise be considered defamatory provided it is communicated on an occasion of partial (or qualified) privilege. An instance of qualified privilege arises where person A has a legal, moral or social duty to communicate the matter to person B who has a reciprocal interest in receiving the material.[139] Where an individual is giving a reference regarding a job applicant or responding to questions from police he or she will be protected by qualified privilege. For instance, in *Stuart v Bell* the defendant was protected by qualified privilege when he informed the plaintiff's potential employer that the plaintiff was suspected of theft.[140] The defence will not stand where the defendant is motivated by malice.[141]

An extended form of the common law defence of qualified privilege applies to the publication of political discussion or commentary.[142] In *Lange v Australian Broadcasting Commission* the plaintiff, a former New Zealand Prime Minister, sued the Australian Broadcasting Commission for publication of alleged defamatory material while he was a member of the New Zealand Parliament.[143] The High Court upheld the existence of an implied right to freedom of political comment under the Constitution but required the publisher to show that its conduct was reasonable in all the circumstances. The reasonableness requirement means the publisher must show it:

- had reasonable grounds for believing the statement was true
- took proper steps to verify the accuracy of the material and
- sought a response from the plaintiff and published the response.

Two High Court decisions have considered the application of the common law defence of qualified privilege.

---

136 [2022] FCA 650.
137 Ibid [381] (Rares J).
138 Ibid [382] (Rares J).
139 *Adam v Ward* [1917] AC 309, 344.
140 [1891] 2 QB 341.
141 *Robert v Bass* (2002) 212 CLR 1; [2002] HCA 57. Honesty is presumed and the plaintiff has the onus of proof of negating it.
142 See *Lange v Australian Broadcasting Corporation* (1997) 189 CLR 520; *Marshall v Megna* [2013] NSWCA 30.
143 (1997) 189 CLR 520.

Case: *Aktas v Westpac Banking Corporation Ltd* (2010) 241 CLR 570

Facts

The plaintiff operated a real estate business that held a trust account (a highly regulated account containing funds belonging to clients). A garnishee order was issued against the plaintiff to deduct funds to pay for an outstanding debt. To comply with the order, the defendant bank changed the status of the plaintiff's account to post credit only, meaning that funds could not be withdrawn from the account. In error, the bank also changed the status of the trust account. Subsequently, cheques issued from the account were dishonoured and an automated message 'Refer to Drawer' was sent by the bank to the intended payees, despite there being sufficient funds in the trust account.

Issue

Was the act of dishonouring the cheque and issuing an automatic message defamatory of the plaintiff? Was the bank protected by qualified privilege?

Decision

The act of dishonouring the cheque was not defamatory, but issuing the message 'Refer to Drawer' was defamatory. The defendant bank was not protected by the defence of qualified privilege because it had provided clients with additional information about the reason for the dishonoured cheque beyond the mere notice of dishonour.

Significance

No reciprocity of interest will exist for the purpose of qualified privilege at common law where the defendant's actions create an error with no genuine need for the communication.

Notes

Heydon and Kiefel JJ wrote separate dissenting judgments in this case. At [116], Kiefel J held:

> The only feature which assumes relevance with respect to the communications in question in this case is that they resulted from a mistake as to the application of a garnishee order to the type of account in question. Here the law recognises the imperfection of human reasoning and understanding and the possibility of carelessness. Mistake does not deny the operation of the defence. The question is whether, given the honest belief of its employee that the account could not be utilised to pay cheques, the bank could fairly be said to consider itself obliged to communicate its decision, a decision in which others were necessarily interested. In my view the answer must be 'yes'.

Question

Do you think Westpac's mistake should have denied it the defence of qualified privilege?

 Guided response in the eBook

Case: *Cush v Dillon* (2011) 243 CLR 298

Facts

James Croft was the chairperson and Amanda Cush the general manager of the Border Rivers-Gwydir Catchment Management Authority (CMA), and Meryl Dillon and Leslie Boland were board members. At a meeting on 8 April 2005, Mrs Dillon stated to Mr Croft, 'It is common knowledge among people in the CMA that Ms Cush and Mr Boland are having an affair'. Ms Cush and Mr Boland alleged that defamatory imputations arose from the comment that both were acting unprofessionally in their roles at CMA, that Mr Boland was being unfaithful to his wife and that Ms Cush was undermining his marriage.

Issue

Could Mrs Dillon rely on the statutory defence of qualified privilege?

Decision

The High Court held that the defence of qualified privilege applied to Mrs Dillon's communications. While the affair was not true, the communication about the *rumours* of an affair was accurate. Mrs Dillon had a duty to disclose, and Mr Croft had an interest in receiving, information concerning the nature of the relationship between members of the board and members of staff.

Significance

The judgment reaffirms that the defence of qualified privilege is likely to succeed even where communications are inaccurate, provided statements are made on an occasion of privilege and without malice.

Notes

French CJ, Crennan and Kiefel JJ held at [23]:

> In this case it cannot be said that the necessary connection was absent. As Bergin CJ in Eq held, the duty Mrs Dillon had in disclosing and the interest Mr Croft had in receiving the information concerning CMA staff-related matters, including the nature of the relationship between members of the Board and members of staff, gave rise to an occasion of privilege. The concession, properly made, was that the occasion of the privilege extended to the communication of the existence of the rumour. It could not, in our view, then be suggested that the communication of the fact of an affair was less relevant to the matters discussed than a rumour. The error inherent in the statement does not deny the privilege.

Question

Did the Justices of the High Court give a broad or narrow construction of the defence of qualified privilege in this judgment?

 Guided response in the eBook

The statutory defence of qualified privilege requires the defendant to satisfy three elements:

(1) The recipient has an interest or apparent interest in having information on some subject.

(2) The matter is published to the recipient in the course of giving to the recipient information on that subject.

(3) The conduct of the defendant in publishing that matter is reasonable in the circumstances.[144]

The requirements that need to be satisfied for the statutory defence of qualified privilege are outlined in Figure 11.4.

Figure 11.4   Requirements for the statutory defence of qualified privilege

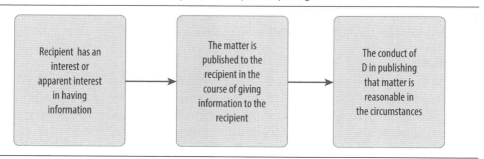

The focus on an *apparent* interest invokes a 'reasonableness' test, with the defendant needing to show that at the time of the publication the defendant believed on reasonable grounds that the recipient had an interest in receiving the information.[145] A court may take into consideration a number of factors in determining whether the defendant's conduct was reasonable. Prior to the 2021 reforms, this list was extensive, but has since been reduced to five factors:

(a) the seriousness of the defamatory imputations

(b) the extent to which the matter published distinguishes between suspicions, allegations and proven facts

(c) the nature of the defendant's business environment

(d) whether it was appropriate for the matter to be published expeditiously and

(e) steps taken to verify the information in the published matter.[146]

---

144 The wording used here derives from the statutory provisions contained in the following legislation: *Civil Law (Wrongs) Act 2002* (ACT) s 139A; *Defamation Act 2005* (NSW) s 30; *Defamation Act 2006* (NT) s 27; *Defamation Act 2005* (Qld) s 30; *Defamation Act 2005* (SA) s 28; *Defamation Act 2005* (Tas) s 30; *Defamation Act 2005* (Vic) s 30; *Defamation Act 2005* (WA) s 30.

145 *Civil Law (Wrongs) Act 2002* (ACT) s 139A(2); *Defamation Act 2005* (NSW) s 30(2); *Defamation Act 2006* (NT) s 27(2); *Defamation Act 2005* (Qld) s 30(2); *Defamation Act 2005* (SA) s 28(2); *Defamation Act 2005* (Tas) s 30(2); *Defamation Act 2005* (Vic) s 30(2); *Defamation Act 2005* (WA) s 30(2).

146 *Civil Law (Wrongs) Act 2002* (ACT) s 139A(3); *Defamation Act 2005* (NSW) s 30(3); *Defamation Act 2006* (NT) s 27(3); *Defamation Act 2005* (Qld) s 30(3); *Defamation Act 2005* (SA) s 28(3); *Defamation Act 2005* (Tas) s 30(3); *Defamation Act 2005* (Vic) s 30(3); *Defamation Act 2005* (WA) s 30(3). The Northern Territory and Western Australian provisions remain unaltered.

The new provisions stipulate that there is no requirement to satisfy all of the factors listed in sub-s 3, and further clarifies that the sub-section does not purport to limit the factors a court can consider when assessing whether the defence has been made out.[147] This means the list is not exhaustive and other factors may be taken into consideration. Further, the new provisions clarify that there is no need for a public interest requirement to be met for the defence to be satisfied.[148] The statutory defence will be defeated if the defendant's actions were perpetuated by malice.[149] Finally, the new provisions also clarify that the jury (and not a judicial officer) determines whether the defence has been made out.[150]

11.3.8   Scientific or academic peer review

The defence of scientific or academic peer review has recognised the need to protect scientists and academics' freedom of expression when publishing research, and when debating or critiquing research for the purpose of peer review. This is a new defence stemming from the 2021 reforms which provides that a defendant will have a defence provided:

- the matter was published in a scientific or academic journal
- the matter relates to a scientific or academic issue
- an independent review of the matter's scientific or academic merit was undertaken by the editor of the journal or a person with the relevant scientific/academic expertise.[151]

The provisions also protect individuals who undertake an assessment of the same matter for the purposes of peer review, as well as for the creation of a fair summary or fair extract of the relevant matter. To illustrate the operation of the defence: suppose that Professor X is a law academic who writes an article on a contentious law reform topic. Provided that Professor X's article is published in an academic journal, relates to an academic issue – in this case, law reform – and is subjected to peer review, Professor X can rely on this defence for any allegedly defamatory content that is raised in their article. However, the defence will be defeated if the plaintiff can establish that the matter was not published honestly for the purpose of information for the public or advancing education.

---

147   *Civil Law (Wrongs) Act 2002* (ACT) s 139A(3A); *Defamation Act 2005* (NSW) s 30(3A); *Defamation Act 2005* (Qld) s 30(3A); *Defamation Act 2005* (SA) s 28(3A); *Defamation Act 2005* (Tas) s 30(3A); *Defamation Act 2005* (Vic) s 30(3A).

148   *Civil Law (Wrongs) Act 2002* (ACT) s 139A(3B); *Defamation Act 2005* (NSW) s 30(3B); *Defamation Act 2005* (Qld) s 30(3B); *Defamation Act 2005* (SA) s 28(3B); *Defamation Act 2005* (Tas) s 30(3B); *Defamation Act 2005* (Vic) s 30(3B).

149   *Civil Law (Wrongs) Act 2002* (ACT) s 139A(4); *Defamation Act 2005* (NSW) s 30(4); *Defamation Act 2006* (NT) s 27(4); *Defamation Act 2005* (Qld) s 30(4); *Defamation Act 2005* (SA) s 28(4); *Defamation Act 2005* (Tas) s 30(4); *Defamation Act 2005* (Vic) s 30(4); *Defamation Act 2005* (WA) s 30(4).

150   *Civil Law (Wrongs) Act 2002* (ACT) s 139A(6); *Defamation Act 2005* (NSW) s 30(6); *Defamation Act 2005* (Qld) s 30(6); *Defamation Act 2005* (SA) s 28(6); *Defamation Act 2005* (Tas) s 30(6); *Defamation Act 2005* (Vic) s 30(6).

151   *Civil Law (Wrongs) Act 2002* (ACT) s 139AB(1); *Defamation Act 2005* (NSW) s 30A(1); *Defamation Act 2005* (Qld) s 30A(1); *Defamation Act 2005* (SA) s 28A(1); *Defamation Act 2005* (Tas) s 30A(1); *Defamation Act 2005* (Vic) s 30A(1).

While the defence was modelled on s 6 of the UK *Defamation Act*, the Australian provisions contain several notable differences:

- The independent review may be conducted by *either* the journal's editor or an independent peer reviewer (rather than both, a requirement in the UK *Defamation Act*).
- The defence is not a defence of qualified privilege (as is the case with the UK *Defamation Act*).
- The defence can be defeated if not published honestly.
- Publication with malice does not necessarily defeat the defence.[152]

11.3.9   Honest opinion

The defence of honest opinion (or 'fair comment' at common law) protects our freedom to express opinions. Under both the common law and statutory defences, a statement is protected if it was an honestly held opinion on a matter of public interest. The purpose of the defence is to allow commentary, opinion pieces, critical reviews or editorial pieces to be published provided these are of legitimate interest to the public. If A has an unpleasant dining experience at a restaurant or B dislikes the acting of a famous Hollywood actor in a movie, both A and B should be permitted to share their opinion without fear of defamation lawsuits.

The common law defence of fair comment requires that:

- the matter is a statement of opinion rather than fact
- the matter is of public interest
- the facts on which the opinion is based are true or arise out of an occasion of privilege
- the opinion is honestly held.

The statement must be objectively perceived to be one of opinion rather than fact, and there must be sufficient material on which to base the opinion. For instance, in *Herald & Weekly Times Ltd v Popovic* a prominent journalist attempted to rely on the defence of fair comment for an opinion piece he wrote about the presiding magistrate's comments to the police prosecutor during a criminal trial.[153] The defence failed as the defendant could not establish that the opinion was based on facts truly stated or arising out of an occasion of privilege. The next case demonstrates the operation of the fair comment defence, particularly the need for information to be presented as *opinion* rather than *fact*.

---

152 Parliamentary Council's Committee, *Model Defamation Amendment Provisions 2020* (27 July 2020) <https://pcc.gov.au/uniform/2020/Model_Defamation_Amendment_Provisions_2020.pdf> 10.
153 (2003) 9 VR 1.

Case: *Channel Seven Adelaide Pty Ltd v Manock* (2007) 232 CLR 245

Facts

Forensic pathologist Dr Colin Manock gave evidence at the murder trial of Henry Keogh. Dr Manock initiated defamation proceedings against Channel Seven, the broadcaster of television program *Today Tonight* for airing a segment advertised with new facts and an image of Dr Manock. The plaintiff claimed that the program defamed him by imputing he deliberately concealed evidence at the trial.

Issue

Did the program represent the information as commentary or fact?

Decision

The High Court held that the program was defamatory of Dr Manock as the statements were presented as fact, not comment.

Significance

The judgment reinforces the need for statements to objectively be recognised as opinion rather than fact, regardless of the defendant's intention.

Notes

Gleeson CJ stated at [9]:

> To be protected by the defence of fair comment, the defamatory matter had to be recognisable as comment and not as a statement of fact. The facts on which the matter was based were neither stated nor indicated with sufficient clarity to make it clear that it was comment on those facts.

Question

Review Gleeson CJ's judgment at [9]–[11]. What factors persuaded his Honour that the advertisement was portrayed as fact rather than opinion?

 Guided response in the eBook

Under the *statutory* defence of honest opinion, the defendant must demonstrate three factors:

(1)   The matter was a statement of opinion rather than fact.

(2)   The opinion related to a matter of public interest.

(3)   The opinion was based on proper material.[154]

The 2021 reforms inserted a new provision (replacing the previous position) to clarify the phrase 'based on proper material'. Under the new sub-section, the opinion is *based on proper material* provided it is:

• set out in specific or general terms in the published matter or

• notorious or

• accessible from a reference, link or other reference point (such as a hyperlink or web page) or

• otherwise apparent from the context in which the matter is published.

Further, the material must be:

• substantially true or

• published on an occasion of absolute or qualified privilege or

• published on an occasion that attracted the defence of publication of public documents or fair report of public proceedings.[155]

HINTS AND TIPS

Both the statutory defence of honest opinion (under s 31 of the uniform defamation legislation) and the common law defence of fair comment can be raised simultaneously by a defendant. For instance, in *Dutton v Bazzi* [2021] FCA 1474 the plaintiff, politician Peter Dutton, took defamation action against refugee advocate Shane Bazzi who tweeted the phrase 'Peter Dutton is a rape apologist' in response to an article in *The Guardian* newspaper. Bazzi raised both defences of honest opinion and fair comment at trial, but neither defence was successful. While the matter was subsequently appealed on the issue of whether the tweet conveyed the alleged imputation (see *Bazzi v Dutton* (2022) 289 FCR 1), the findings relating to defences were not challenged.

---

154   See *Civil Law (Wrongs) Act 2002* (ACT) s 139B(1); *Defamation Act 2005* (NSW) s 31(1); *Defamation Act 2006* (NT) s 28(1); *Defamation Act 2005* (Qld) s 31(1); *Defamation Act 2005* (SA) s 29(1); *Defamation Act 2005* (Tas) s 31(1); *Defamation Act 2005* (Vic) s 31(1); *Defamation Act 2005* (WA) s 31(1).

155   See *Civil Law (Wrongs) Act 2002* (ACT) s 139B(5); *Defamation Act 2005* (NSW) s 31(5); *Defamation Act 2006* (NT) s 28(5); *Defamation Act 2005* (Qld) s 31(5); *Defamation Act 2005* (SA) s 29(5); *Defamation Act 2005* (Tas) s 31(5); *Defamation Act 2005* (Vic) s 31(5); *Defamation Act 2005* (WA) s 31(5). Note that the Western Australian and Northern Territory legislation does not contain the sub-section requiring the matter to be set out in specific terms, be notorious, accessible and otherwise apparent.

11.3.10   Innocent dissemination

All individuals involved in the publication process – including authors, editors, printers, publishers and broadcasters – are technically liable for defamation. If this principle were upheld strictly, the practical consequence would be that distributors such as newspaper vendors and libraries could be held responsible even though they have no direct involvement or control of the defamatory matter. To set some limits, the defence of innocent dissemination protects defendants if they published the matter in their capacity as employee or agent of a subordinate distributor, and neither knew or ought to have known that the matter was defamatory and their lack of knowledge was not due to negligence on their part.[156] An individual is a 'subordinate distributor' if they:

- were not the first or primary distributor of the matter
- were not the author or originator of the matter and
- were not able to exercise editorial control over the matter prior to publication.

Some examples of a 'subordinate distributor' include a bookseller, newsagent, wholesaler, provider of postal services or broadcaster of a live program.

The advent of social media, together with the ability to easily re-tweet or share content on platforms such as Twitter and Facebook, raises interesting questions about how the defence of innocent dissemination operates in the online environment. The recent High Court decision in *Trkulja v Google LLC* demonstrates that search results are capable of conveying defamatory imputations and that search engine providers will not necessarily be deemed to be passive internet intermediaries.[157] International decisions have shown that liability can also be imposed for posting a tweet on a website[158] and tagging another individual in defamatory posts.[159]

11.3.11   Triviality defence abolished

With the introduction of the serious harm threshold most jurisdictions (with the exception of Western Australia and the Northern Territory) have abolished the defence of triviality. The defence of triviality could be used where the defendant can prove that the circumstances of publication were such that the plaintiff was unlikely to sustain any harm.[160] In *Smith v Lucht* the Court considered the meaning of 'harm' for the purposes of the triviality defences in circumstances where the former son-in-law of a solicitor referred to the solicitor as a 'Dennis Denuto', a fictional incompetent lawyer in the movie *The Castle*.[161] The comment was made to the plaintiff and the plaintiff's son and daughter-in-law. The Court upheld the defence of

---

156 See *Civil Law (Wrongs) Act 2002* (ACT) s 139C; *Defamation Act 2005* (NSW) s 32; *Defamation Act 2006* (NT) s 29; *Defamation Act 2005* (Qld) s 32; *Defamation Act 2005* (SA) s 30; *Defamation Act 2005* (Tas) s 32; *Defamation Act 2005* (Vic) s 32; *Defamation Act 2005* (WA) s 32.
157 (2018) 356 ALR 178.
158 *Cairns v Modi* [2013] 1 WLR 1015.
159 *Isparta v Richter* [2013] 6 SA 529 (High Court).
160 See *Civil Law (Wrongs) Act 2002* (ACT) s 139D; *Defamation Act 2005* (NSW) s 33; *Defamation Act 2006* (NT) s 30; *Defamation Act 2005* (Qld) s 33; *Defamation Act 2005* (SA) s 31; *Defamation Act 2005* (Tas) s 33; *Defamation Act 2005* (Vic) s 33; *Defamation Act 2005* (WA) s 33.
161 [2017] 2 Qd R 489.

triviality, stressing the need for reputational harm rather than merely emotional harm for the purpose of defamation.

Yet in *Kostov v Nationwide News Pty Ltd*, the New South Wales Supreme Court considered whether the plaintiff's claim surmounted a 'threshold of seriousness'.[162] The plaintiff instigated proceedings against the publisher of an article, imputing that Adriana Kostov, by providing a character reference for her former boyfriend in criminal proceedings, was inter alia condoning criminal activity or failing to appreciate its seriousness. In finding that the article was not capable of being defamatory, McCallum J also addressed the threshold of seriousness. Referring to the decision in *Thornton v Telegraph Media Group Ltd*[163] McCallum J held: 'Justice Tugendhat's carefully reasoned judgment has persuaded me that the definition of "defamatory" adopted in Australia must equally comprehend a qualification or threshold of seriousness so as to exclude trivial claims'.[164] This issue has now been legislatively stated with the introduction of the serious harm threshold, requiring the plaintiff to establish they have, in fact, sustained serious harm. This threshold makes the operation of this defence (largely) redundant in the majority of Australian jurisdictions.

Review questions

(1) How do the statutory defences affect previous common law defences?

(2) In what contexts does the defence of absolute privilege apply? Why is the defence necessary in judicial proceedings?

(3) What is the difference between the defences of fair comment and honest opinion?

 Guided responses in the eBook

11.4   Remedies and dispute resolution

Where a plaintiff is able to establish a cause of action in defamation by satisfying the four elements (see Section 11.2), and the defendant is unable to establish a defence, the plaintiff will be entitled to a remedy. Remedies for defamation are outlined in the uniform defamation legislation.

11.4.1   Damages

'Damages' refers to compensation paid by a defendant to a plaintiff. The purpose of compensation is to restore the plaintiff as far as possible to the position he or she would

---

162 (2018) 97 NSWLR 1073.
163 [2011] 1 WLR 1985.
164 *Kostov v Nationwide News Pty Ltd* (2018) 97 NSWLR 1073, [37].

have been in had the wrong not occurred.[165] In *Carson v John Fairfax & Sons Ltd*, the Court held that an award of damages serves three purposes: (1) consolation to the plaintiff for personal distress and hurt; (2) reparation for the harm to the plaintiff's reputation; and (3) vindication of the plaintiff's reputation.[166] A successful plaintiff may be awarded economic loss, non-economic loss and/or aggravated damages, but is no longer entitled to claim exemplary damages as these have been abolished in defamation.

11.4.1.1 Economic loss

Economic loss damages (also termed 'special damages') compensate the plaintiff for the pecuniary loss sustained as a result of defamatory imputations.[167] The plaintiff can claim for loss of earnings, lost income, loss of employment, loss of contracts or lost opportunities to earn income.[168] There is no limit on the amount of economic loss that a court can award a plaintiff. The highly publicised trial initiated by actress Rebel Wilson highlighted the extent of damages that could potentially be awarded for economic loss. In *Wilson v Bauer Media Pty Ltd* economic loss damages for loss of opportunity to earn income (future movie contracts) were awarded in the sum of $3 917 472.[169] However, on appeal to the Victorian Court of Appeal the economic loss damages were set aside.

In *Rayney v Western Australia (No 9)* the Western Australian Supreme Court considered the plaintiff's claim for economic loss as a result of damage to his professional reputation as a barrister following a police conference, where the words spoken by police could give rise to the imputation that the plaintiff had murdered his wife.[170] The Court held that economic loss could be claimed between the making of the defamatory statement until the plaintiff's arrest and charge with murder.

11.4.1.2 Non-economic loss

Damages for non-economic loss (also termed 'general damages') are awarded for harm to a plaintiff's reputation and are difficult to quantify with precision. An example of an award of non-economic loss damages can be seen in *Hockey v Fairfax Media Publications Pty Ltd* where Joe Hockey was awarded $120 000 in general damages for the defamatory advertising posters and $80 000 for each of the two defamatory tweets.[171] In *Carolan v Fairfax Media Publications Pty Ltd (No 6)* a personal trainer defamed by four articles was awarded $300 000 as the articles contained serious imputations alleging that he had conducted tests on Rugby League players and passed on the test results to organised crime figures.[172]

Non-economic loss damages are subject to a maximum cap, with that figure increasing yearly through indexation. Rebel Wilson's proceedings against Bauer Media demonstrate the ability of courts to somewhat 'exceed' the cap by awarding aggravated damages. At trial, Ms

---

165 *Todorovic v Waller* (1981) 150 CLR 402.
166 (1993) 178 CLR 44, 60–1.
167 *Wilson v Bauer Media Pty Ltd* [2017] VSC 521, [137] (Dixon J).
168 The ability to claim for lost opportunities to earn income is potentially contentious following *Bauer Media Pty Ltd v Wilson (No 2)* (2018) 56 VR 674.
169 [2017] VSC 521.
170 [2017] WASC 367.
171 (2015) 237 FCR 33.
172 [2016] NSWSC 1091.

Wilson was awarded \$650 000 in non-economic loss damages, with the award exceeding the cap because it included aggravated damages.[173] On appeal the non-economic loss damages were reduced to \$600 000 (including aggravated damages).[174]

This decision resulted in some uncertainty which has since been clarified via statutory reform. In *Bauer Media Pty Ltd v Wilson (No 2)*,[175] the Victorian Court of Appeal stated that the cap on damages (in s 35 of the *Defamation Act*) did not represent a scale of damages to be awarded depending on the gravity or seriousness of a case. Further, the Court stated that the legislation did not require separate awards of general and aggravated damages to be made. The current provisions preserve the 'cap' on damages. However, they contain two points of clarification:

- the maximum damages amount is to be awarded only in a most serious case
- an award of aggravated damages is to be made separately to any award of non-economic loss damages.[176]

11.4.1.3   Aggravated damages

Aggravated damages may be awarded when a court considers that the defendant's conduct has aggravated or increased the hurt suffered by the plaintiff.[177] For instance, in *Mickle v Farley* the judge awarded a school teacher \$85 000 in compensatory damages with an added \$20 000 in aggravated damages for the defendant's conduct in publishing defamatory material on social media platforms.[178] In *Wilson v Bauer Media Pty Ltd*, Dixon J awarded the plaintiff \$650 000 (including aggravated damages) for publication of defamatory magazine articles; however, as noted earlier, this award of damages was reduced on appeal.[179] The award of aggravated damages in that case allowed the plaintiff to receive compensation that exceeded the statutory cap for non-economic loss.

11.4.1.4   Exemplary damages prohibited

The purpose of exemplary damages was to include punishment for the defendant for blatant disregard of the plaintiff's rights and to deter future wrongdoing. Exemplary damages can be distinguished from aggravated damages, the latter being compensatory in nature. Exemplary damages were abolished by the uniform defamation laws.[180]

---

173   *Wilson v Bauer Media Pty Ltd* [2017] VSC 521.
174   *Bauer Media Pty Ltd v Wilson (No 2)* (2018) 56 VR 674.
175   (2018) 56 VR 674.
176   *Civil Law (Wrongs) Act 2002* (ACT) s 139F; *Defamation Act 2005* (NSW) s 35; *Defamation Act 2005* (Qld) s 35; *Defamation Act 2005* (SA) s 33; *Defamation Act 2005* (Tas) s 35; *Defamation Act 2005* (Vic) s 35. Western Australian and the Northern Territory legislation do not contain the amended provisions.
177   *Uren v John Fairfax & Sons Pty Ltd* (1966) 117 CLR 118, 149 (Windeyer J).
178   [2013] NSWDC 295.
179   [2017] VSC 521.
180   See *Civil Law (Wrongs) Act 2002* (ACT) s 139H; *Defamation Act 2005* (NSW) s 37; *Defamation Act 2006* (NT) s 34; *Defamation Act 2005* (Qld) s 37; *Defamation Act 2005* (SA) s 35; *Defamation Act 2005* (Tas) s 37; *Defamation Act 2005* (Vic) s 37; *Defamation Act 2005* (WA) s 37.

11.4.2   Injunction

An injunction is a court order compelling a party to engage in or refrain from certain conduct. In the defamation context, an injunction may be awarded preventing publication or republication of defamatory matter. An injunction is an equitable remedy which is awarded at the court's discretion and requires the plaintiff to persuade the court that an injunction is an appropriate remedy in the circumstances. In *Nixon v Slater & Gordon*, apart from an award of damages, an injunction prohibiting further publication of the booklet and a letter of retraction were also granted.[181]

Injunctions will only be awarded in exceptional circumstances, with the courts acknowledging the potential adverse impact on freedom of expression. In *Australian Broadcasting Corporation v O'Neill* the High Court acknowledged the impact on freedom of speech and the need to take caution when exercising discretion to award an injunction in defamation proceedings.[182] Further, the difficulty of using an injunction to restrain internet publication was addressed in *Macquarie Bank Ltd v Berg*:

> The consequence is that, if I were to make the order sought (and the defendant were to obey it) he would be restrained from publishing anywhere in the world via the medium of the Internet.
>
> The difficulties are obvious. An injunction to restrain defamation in NSW is designed to ensure compliance with the laws of NSW, and to protect the rights of plaintiffs, as those rights are defined by the law of NSW. Such an injunction is not designed to superimpose the law of NSW relating to defamation on every other state, territory and country of the world. Yet that would be the effect of an order restraining publication on the Internet.[183]

11.4.3   Role of apology

Apologies can be a powerful tool in resolving disputes without the need for court proceedings or other forms of dispute resolution.[184] The uniform defamation laws encourage resolution of disputes without recourse to litigation. The publisher may make an offer to make amends and the offer may include an apology.[185] The uniform defamation laws provide that an apology does not constitute an express or implied admission of fault or liability in connection with the matter and is not relevant to determination of fault or liability. Evidence of the apology is not admissible in subsequent court proceedings as proof of fault or liability.[186]

---

181 [2000] Aust Torts Reports 81-565.
182 (2006) 227 CLR 57; [2006] HCA 46, [16]–[19] (Gleeson CJ and Crennan J), [73]–[83] (Gummow and Hayne JJ).
183 [1999] NSWSC 526, [13]–[14] (Simpson J).
184 R Carroll, 'Apologies as a Legal Remedy' (2013) 35(2) *Sydney Law Review* 317.
185 See *Civil Law (Wrongs) Act 2002* (ACT) ss 125–7; *Defamation Act 2005* (NSW) ss 13–15; *Defamation Act 2006* (NT) ss 12–14; *Defamation Act 2005* (Qld) ss 13–15; *Defamation Act 2005* (SA) ss 13–15; *Defamation Act 2005* (Tas) ss 13–15; *Defamation Act 2005* (Vic) ss 13–15; *Defamation Act 2005* (WA) ss 13–15.
186 See *Civil Law (Wrongs) Act 2002* (ACT) s 132; *Defamation Act 2005* (NSW) s 20; *Defamation Act 2006* (NT) s 19; *Defamation Act 2005* (Qld) s 20; *Defamation Act 2005* (SA) s 20; *Defamation Act 2005* (Tas) s 20; *Defamation Act 2005* (Vic) s 20; *Defamation Act 2005* (WA) s 20.

11.4.4 Dispute resolution

Plaintiffs are now required to issue a concerns notice prior to issuing legal proceedings for defamation.[187] This is a departure from the previous legislative provision which did not impose mandatory requirements for plaintiffs to issue such a notice. A *concerns notice* is a notice sent by the potential plaintiff to the publisher of the allegedly defamatory material. The concerns notice sets out the publication that the plaintiff is complaining of.

Section 12A of the uniform defamation provisions requires a concerns notice to:

- be in writing
- specify the location of the material (eg, in a magazine, book or web page)
- outline the allegedly defamatory imputations
- inform the publisher of the harm that constitutes 'serious harm'.
- If an aggrieved person is an excluded corporation, then the plaintiff must outline the financial loss that has been sustained.[188]

Plaintiffs are required to wait 28 days after issuing the concerns notice before they can instigate legal proceedings. The practical effect of the provisions relating to the concerns notice will mean that plaintiffs will be required to articulate imputations carefully and ensure they wait until the statutory period has passed before issuing proceedings. In essence, this creates a hurdle for the plaintiff to overcome, along with matters already outlined pertaining to the need to establish serious harm. This may potentially create a more onerous process for plaintiffs when instigating proceedings.

REVIEW QUESTIONS

(1) What is the difference between economic loss damages and non-economic loss damages in defamation?

(2) Does a defendant admit liability if he or she chooses to apologise to a plaintiff?

 Guided responses in the eBook

---

187 *Civil Law (Wrongs) Act 2002* (ACT) s 124B; *Defamation Act 2005* (NSW) s 12B; *Defamation Act 2005* (Qld) s 12B; *Defamation Act 2005* (SA) s 12B; *Defamation Act 2005* (Tas) s 12B; *Defamation Act 2005* (Vic) s 12B.

188 *Civil Law (Wrongs) Act 2002* (ACT) s 124A; *Defamation Act 2005* (NSW) s 12A; *Defamation Act 2005* (Qld) s 12A; *Defamation Act 2005* (SA) s 12A; *Defamation Act 2005* (Tas) s 12A; *Defamation Act 2005* (Vic) s 12A.

11.5   Defamation and social media

The rise of social media has made publication on the internet quicker and easier than ever before. The speed with which comments can be published or shared on online platforms and viewed by millions around the globe within minutes has undoubtedly reinvigorated defamation as a cause of action in the online environment. In fact, many of the cases that are now brought before the courts were instigated because of online publication. To a large degree, online defamation has become part of defamation law and the statutory reforms recognise this development. However, online communications nevertheless contain intricacies not usually available in mainstream media, such as hashtags, hyperlinks, emojis, liking and sharing of content. This section will canvass the ability to take defamation action for matter published in the online environment and highlights key developments in the online space.

11.5.1   Introduction to defamation and the internet

The principles of defamation remain the same regardless of whether defamatory material is published in a traditional medium such as a book or newspaper, or whether publication occurs on an internet web page, blog site or social media platform. However, the increase in internet publications has challenged the legislature and the courts to develop new principles to meet technological developments in society. Publication of defamatory matter over the internet raises novel questions for the courts. For instance, can a plaintiff sue if publication is made by an anonymous user? Can a search engine be liable for images produced in search results? Can an individual be liable for 'sharing' defamatory content created by another? These are all pertinent questions that courts have had to consider.

11.5.2   Liability of anonymous users

Individuals attempting to use anonymity as a cover to make defamatory remarks on internet web pages may face liability if the plaintiff is able to produce sufficient evidence of the defendant's identity before a court, as the case of *Applause Store Productions Ltd v Raphael* demonstrates.[189] In this case, the granting of a *Norwich Pharmacal* order ensured the disclosure of the identity of a Facebook user who posted defamatory content online.[190] In *Applause*, the defendant created a fake account on Facebook in the name of the claimant, Matthew Firsht. The defamatory material was posted to a Facebook group with a hyperlink titled 'Has Mathew Firsht lied to you?' The plaintiff initiated proceedings in defamation on his own behalf and on behalf of his company, Applause. A court granted an order compelling Facebook to release information about the identity of the user, which showed that the creation of the fake profile originated from the defendant's address. The defendant alleged that 'strangers' attending a party at his residence had broken into his computer and created the fake profile. The Deputy Judge of the English High Court rejected the defendant's version of events as 'utterly implausible' and found in favour of the plaintiff. The case shows that an action in defamation may be possible against 'anonymous' users who post defamatory material via the internet.

---

189 [2008] All ER (D) 321.
190 See *Norwich Pharmacal Co v Customs and Excise Commissioners* [1974] AC 133.

11.5.3 Liability of intermediaries

A plaintiff who is unable to determine the identity of the publisher of defamatory material, or who does not have the resources to investigate the true identity of an anonymous website user, may still instigate proceedings against an internet intermediary responsible for hosting the defamatory matter. The intermediary could include a social media company such as Facebook or Twitter or a search engine such as Google. Previous cases have suggested that intermediaries may be able to avoid defamation liability if their role was passive in hosting the material rather than actively publishing it.[191] However, more recent judgments have indicated that intermediaries may be liable if defamatory matter is brought to their attention and they actively refuse to remove it. The litigation involving Trkulja and Google is an example of this.

In *Trkulja v Google Inc LLC (No 5)*,[192] Mr Trkulja (the plaintiff) sued Google, alleging an internet search of his name using a search engine controlled by Google produced results affiliating him with high-profile Melbourne criminal figures. The plaintiff's lawyers had written to the defendant requesting the material be removed, but the defendant failed to do so. The defendant was found to be liable for publishing the defamatory material, as it had failed to stop the defamation from occurring once it had notice of the existence of defamatory matter. Subsequently in *Google Inc v Trkulja*,[193] Mr Trkulja alleged that an internet search of phrases such as 'Melbourne criminal underworld photos' and 'Melbourne underworld criminals' using the defendant's search engine produced results that were defamatory of him. The Victorian Court of Appeal found that Google could not be held liable as the primary publisher of the allegedly defamatory material, in the manner framed by the plaintiff. As a secondary publisher, it could rely on the defence of innocent dissemination. Further, the material was held not to convey the defamatory imputations raised by the plaintiff, as a reasonable internet user would be capable of understanding that the search result may result in a random compilation of images. Finally, the High Court determined Mr Trkulja's appeal pertaining to Google's liability as publisher of the defamatory material.

Case: *Trkulja v Google LLC* (2018) 356 ALR 178

Facts

The High Court granted special leave to Mr Trkulja to determine legal issues pertaining to the liability of search engines for defamation, for publishing photos in search results capable of conveying that he was a criminal.

Issue

Were the Google image search results, which displayed Mr Trkulja's images in conjunction with images of convicted Melbourne criminals, capable of being defamatory?

---

191 *Bunt v Tilley* [2007] 1 WLR 1243; *Metropolitan International Schools Ltd v Designtechnica Corporation* [2011] 1 WLR 1743.
192 [2012] VSC 533.
193 (2016) 342 ALR 504.

Decision

The High Court allowed Mr Trkulja's appeal, finding that the images in the search engine results were *capable* of being defamatory. The issue of defamatory *capacity* was addressed by the High Court at [52]:

> As has been observed, the test of capacity of a published matter to defame is, in this case, whether any of the search results complained of are capable of conveying any of the defamatory imputations alleged.

The High Court further elaborated on the ordinary and reasonable search engine user at [53]:

> [A]lthough it might be correct to say that the capacity of the search results to convey the alleged defamatory imputations is to be judged by reference to the 'ordinary reasonable user of a search engine such as the Google search engine', by analogy, say, to the way it is said that the capacity of a newspaper article to defame is to be judged by reference to the standards of an ordinary reasonable reader, to do so would be correct only so long as the expression were understood to mean an ordinary reasonable person who has made the Google search in issue.

Significance

The decision that search term auto-completions are capable of being defamatory means that internet search providers are no longer viewed as passive agents and thus not immune from defamation proceedings. The decision also calls into question how search engine providers will continue to rely on the defence of innocent dissemination in the online environment.

Notes

Kiefel CJ, Bell, Keane, Nettle and Gordon JJ stated at [62]:

> So to conclude, as the Court of Appeal observed, might result in the list of persons potentially defamed being large and diverse. But contrary to the Court of Appeal's apparent reasoning, that does not mean that the conclusion is unsound. It means no more than that, in such cases, the liability of a search engine proprietor, like Google, may well turn more on whether the search engine proprietor is able to bring itself within the defence of innocent dissemination than on whether the content of what has been published has the capacity to defame.

Question

What repercussions does the *Trkulja* decision have for the defence of innocent dissemination?

 Guided response in the eBook

In recent times, courts have considered numerous legal issues pertaining to liability over internet postings. For instance, the Court in *Cairns v Modi* held that one can be liable for re-tweeting content.[194] In *Mosslmani v DailyMail.com Australia Pty Ltd* a judge of the New South Wales District Court considered whether a photo of a mullet haircut turned into a meme (a typically humorous image) was defamatory.[195] Gibson DCJ held the meme was not defamatory given that people 'liked' the image online. In *Al Muderis v Duncan (No 3)* a respected Sydney surgeon was awarded $480000 in damages after the plaintiff created a website in the surgeon's name and posted content and videos imputing that the surgeon was a 'butcher' and 'medically negligent'.[196] The following two cases illustrate how Australian judges are likely to find that content posted on social media can be defamatory.

Case: *Mickle v Farley* [2013] NSWDC 295

Facts

The defendant, a young man, posted derogatory untruthful remarks regarding a music teacher at his former school on Facebook and Twitter.

Issue

Was the defendant liable for the publication of the defamatory matter online?

Decision

Elkaim DCJ found the posts defamatory and awarded $85000 in compensatory damages and $20000 in aggravated damages.

Significance

The judgment reinforces the ability to sue for posting defamatory remarks on social media.

Notes

Elkaim DCJ stated at [13]:

> The plaintiff is obviously entitled to an award of compensatory damages flowing from the established defamatory publications. I have had the benefit of concise submissions on damages from learned counsel for the plaintiff who has set out a number of the principles that I will apply. As he has submitted to me, the general damage to reputation is presumed to be the natural and probable consequence of a defamatory publication. The compensation is intended to vindicate the person's reputation in the eyes of the general community and compensate the person for the distress and insult felt. There must be a consolation for the personal distress and hurt caused to the plaintiff by the publication as well as an attempt through an award of monetary compensation to achieve as far as possible a reparation and vindication of the plaintiff's reputation.

194 [2013] 1 WLR 1015.
195 [2016] NSWDC 264.
196 [2017] NSWSC 726.

Question

Do you think an award of damages is sufficient to restore reputational harm or does the act of bringing a successful lawsuit achieve more in repairing the plaintiff's reputation in some circumstances?

 Guided response in the eBook

Case: *Hockey v Fairfax Media Publications Pty Ltd* (2015) 237 FCR 33

Facts

The facts of this case are set out in Section 11.2.1.4.

Issue

Were the tweets and hyperlinked articles capable of being defamatory?

Decision

The online headlines with hyperlinks to the full article *were not* held to be defamatory as the reader was capable of placing the headline into context. However, the tweets containing only the headline *were* held to be defamatory as a reasonable reader was unlikely to take the initiative to locate the full article.

Significance

The case raises questions regarding the extent to which hyperlinked material is relevant in determining whether internet posts are defamatory. The case also raises broader concerns about using social media, particularly short snippets, to promote material.

Question

How do the principles outlined in the *Hockey* judgment align with more recent decisions in *Voller* and *Defteros* concerning liability of online publishers for hyperlinks?

 Guided response in the eBook

EMERGING ISSUE

Can you be liable for an online defamatory post in which you permit yourself to be tagged? In *Isparta v Richter* a South African court awarded damages to the plaintiff in circumstances where the first defendant tagged the second defendant on defamatory Facebook posts, suggesting that courts may be open to imposing liability in such circumstances.[197] Can you also be liable for creating a defamatory meme? What about for using hashtags to further promote your defamatory posts? These are all intricacies of social media that courts must continue to grapple with as communication online evolves. Table 11.4 highlights some of these online issues that continue to evolve.

Table 11.4   Overview of defamation in the online social environment

Issue	Case examples
Liability of search engines	• *Google Inc v Duffy* (2017) 129 SASR 304 • *Trkulja v Google LLC* (2018) 356 ALR 178
Hyperlinks	*Google LLC v Defteros* (2022) 403 ALR 434
Comments made by third parties on pages	*Fairfax Media Publications Pty Ltd v Voller* (2021) 273 CLR 346; [2021] HCA 27
Sharing material online	Prior to the statutory reforms this issue was akin to republication as outlined in *Dow Jones & Company Inc v Gutnick* (2002) 210 CLR 575; [2002] HCA 56
Facebook/Twitter	• *Webster v Brewer (No 3)* [2020] FCA 1343 • *Mickle v Farley* [2013] NSWDC 295 • *Hockey v Fairfax Media Publications Pty Ltd* (2015) 237 FCR 33
Hashtags	*B1 v B2* [2017] NSWDC 252 (the use of a popular white ribbon day hashtag increased exposure to the defamatory content)
Emojis	*McAlpine v Bercow* [2013] EWHC 1342 (QB)
Memes	*Mosslmani v DailyMail.com Australia Pty Ltd* [2016] NSWDC 264
Anonymous users	*Kabbabe v Google LLC* [2020] FCA 126

REVIEW QUESTIONS

(1)   Is defamation actionable regardless of the medium in which the defamatory matter is contained?

(2)   Are there circumstances where an individual who is not the original creator of a defamatory post can be liable for defamation?

 Guided responses in the eBook

11.6   Privacy and breach of confidentiality

Historically, the Australian legislature and courts have been reluctant to recognise a tort of privacy in Australia.[198] Australian privacy legislation assists with the regulation of data maintenance but offers no real protection against invasion of privacy.[199] The High Court has also been reluctant to recognise a common law right to privacy,[200] but recently it has left the door slightly ajar and appeared more receptive to the development of a tort of privacy.[201] As indicated at the beginning of this chapter, in the absence of a tort of privacy, individuals may turn to defamation laws or an equitable action for breach of confidence to attain relief. For instance, in *Wilson v Ferguson* the Court granted an injunction and equitable compensation for the defendant's breach of confidence for publishing online intimate images of the plaintiff (obtained while they were in a relationship).[202] The following three cases evidence judicial movement towards the development of a tort of privacy in Australian states; however, in the absence of a decision from the High Court, they should be treated with caution.

Case: *Grosse v Purvis* [2003] QDC 151

Facts

Following a brief intimate relationship, the defendant developed an obsessive infatuation with the plaintiff and became hostile and abusive when she became intimate with other men. The plaintiff took action against the defendant for behaviour which resembled stalking, including causes of action for harassment, nuisance, negligence, trespass to person and the intentional infliction of physical harm.

Issue

Was evidence of the defendant's stalking behaviour sufficient to amount to an action for invasion of privacy?

Decision

Skoien DCJ held in favour of the plaintiff, finding that the defendant's behaviour amounted to stalking in breach of the state's criminal code and had also caused the plaintiff embarrassment, hurt and distress.

Significance

The case recognises the right to damages for invasion of an individual's privacy which causes emotional harm. However, as a decision of a single judge, the case is merely persuasive in Australian states.

---

198 N Witzleb, 'A Statutory Cause of Action for Privacy? A Critical Appraisal of Three Recent Australian Law Reform Proposals' (2011) 19(2) *Torts Law Journal* 104.

199 See, eg, the *Privacy Act 1988* (Cth).

200 *Victoria Park Racing & Recreation Grounds Co Ltd v Taylor* (1937) 58 CLR 479.

201 *Australian Broadcasting Corporation v Lenah Game Meats Pty Ltd* (2001) 208 CLR 199; [2001] HCA 63.

202 [2015] WASC 15.

Notes

Skoien DCJ stated at [444]–[445]:

> It is not my task nor my intent to state the limits of the cause of action nor any special defences other than is necessary for the purposes of this case. In my view the essential elements would be:
> (a) a willed act by the defendant,
> (b) which intrudes upon the privacy or seclusion of the plaintiff,
> (c) in a manner which would be considered highly offensive to a reasonable person of ordinary sensibilities,
> (d) and which causes the plaintiff detriment in the form of mental psychological or emotional harm or distress or which prevents or hinders the plaintiff from doing an act which she is lawfully entitled to do … I have found the defendant to have committed many of such acts, beginning in 1994. The suffering of embarrassment, hurt, distress and, a fortiori, PTSD would be actionable detriment as would enforced changes of lifestyle caused by the intrusion. I have found that the plaintiff has suffered such detriment.

Question

Prior to this case, had Australian judges attempted to develop the elements of a potential cause of action for the tort of privacy?

 Guided response in the eBook

Case: *Jane Doe v Australian Broadcasting Corporation* [2007] VCC 281

Facts

The plaintiff was attacked and raped by her estranged husband. A news bulletin published by the defendant broadcast details of the offence, including that the offence had occurred in Jane Doe's home. It identified the suburb the home was located in and also identified Jane Doe by name as the victim. The publication was also a breach of the *Judicial Proceedings Reports Act 1958* (Vic). The plaintiff claimed she suffered psychiatric harm as a result of the publication and sued for breach of statutory duty, negligence, breach of privacy and breach of confidence.

Issue

Did the defendant's action in broadcasting the details of the offence constitute an invasion of privacy?

Decision

The plaintiff succeeded on all four grounds and was awarded $234190 in damages. Hampel J considered previous High Court authorities and *Grosse v Purvis* in finding that the publication of personal information contravened existing legislation (where there was no public interest in the information being disclosed) and had infringed the plaintiff's right to privacy.

Significance

A civil action may arise for invasion of privacy where personal information is disclosed without any public interest requirement, showing that a tort of privacy and breach of confidence are closely linked.

Notes

Hampel J stated at [163]:

> The wrong that was done here was the publication of personal information, in circumstances where there was no public interest in publishing it, and where there was a prohibition on its publication. In publishing the information, the defendants failed to exercise the care which could be reasonably required of them to protect the plaintiff's privacy and comply with the prohibition on publication imposed by [the Act]. This, coupled with the absence of public interest, the clearly private nature of the information, and the prohibition on publication, all point to the publication being unjustified.

Question

Do you consider that the outcome of the case might have been different had the plaintiff been a celebrity rather than a victim of crime?

 Guided response in the eBook

Case: *Giller v Procopets* (2008) 24 VR 1

Facts

The defendant filmed himself and the plaintiff during sexual encounters, first secretly and then with the plaintiff's consent. After their relationship ended, the defendant shared the videotapes with the plaintiff's family, friends and employer. The plaintiff sought damages for breach of privacy, breach of confidence and intentional infliction of mental harm.

Issue

Could the non-consensual disclosure of private material constitute a breach of privacy?

Decision

While the Victorian Court of Appeal declined to directly confirm the existence of a common law tort of privacy, it permitted damages for emotional distress arising from the equitable claim for breach of confidence.

Significance

Breach of confidence can be used as a cause of action to respond to breaches of privacy arising from non-consensual disclosure of private information.

Notes

Neave J stated at [423]:

> By parity of reasoning there should be no barrier to the making of an order for equitable compensation to compensate a claimant for the embarrassment or distress she has suffered as the result of a breach of an equitable duty of confidence which has already occurred.

Question

Do you consider that an award of damages for breach of confidence in this case adequately responded to the invasion of the plaintiff's privacy, or is a separate tort of privacy required?

    Guided response in the eBook

EMERGING ISSUE

In New Zealand, a general tort of invasion of privacy exists at common law: *P v D* [2000] 2 NZLR 591 (HC); *Peters v Attorney-General on behalf of Ministry of Social Development* [2021] NZCA 355. Is it time for the Australian Parliament to introduce a tort of privacy, or do existing common law principles provide sufficient protection?

REVIEW QUESTIONS

(1) Outline the arguments in favour of and against the development of a tort of privacy.

(2) What impact did the High Court judgments in *Victoria Park Racing and Recreation Grounds Co Ltd v Taylor* (1937) 58 CLR 479 and *Australian Broadcasting Corporation v Lenah Game Meats Pty Ltd* (2001) 208 CLR 199 have on the right to privacy?

 Guided responses in the eBook

KEY CONCEPTS

- **action for defamation:** must commence within 12 months.

- **defamation:** protects the personal and professional reputation of individuals. Australian defamation law derives from uniform legislation and the common law.

- **defences for defamation:** the defendant may rely on statutory or common law defences.

- **elements of defamation:** comprise: (1) the existence of defamatory matter; (2) which identifies the plaintiff; (3) which has been published; and (4) serious harm threshold.

- **interpretation and innuendo:** the matter must contain imputations capable of being derived through the natural and ordinary interpretation of the words, or through true or false innuendo.

- **remedies for defamation:** can consist of the publication of an apology, retraction, injunction and damages for economic and non-economic loss.

- **reputation:** the plaintiff must establish that the imputations are defamatory as interpreted by an ordinary and reasonable person, insofar as they ridicule or lower the reputation of the plaintiff.

 Complete the multiple-choice questions in the eBook to test your knowledge

PROBLEM-SOLVING EXERCISES

Exercise 1

Gina is a client of Ronald, the head personal trainer at a prominent Melbourne gym, Sweat Town. Gina has been training with Ronald for six months but, despite effort on her part, has failed to see physical results of regular training. After a particularly disastrous training session with Ronald, when Gina tripped on the treadmill and injured her knee, she decides she's had enough. On her way to work, she logs into *Social Friends*, a social media website, and posts the following:

> The Head Trainer at Sweat Town is an incompetent monkey. I don't know why I'm paying him so much money when he doesn't know how to use equipment and prescribes me programs that are utterly useless! I'd get fitter sooner by eating fried chicken than training with that goose #SweatTownMonkey #RubbishRonald.

Unfortunately, through Gina's use of hashtags, one of Ronald's colleagues sees the post and immediately notifies him. The hashtag attracts much publicity, and many of Ronald's clients see the post. As a result, he has seen a significant decline in clients. Ronald is furious and wishes to sue Gina for defamation.

Assume that publication occurred in the preceding 12 months. Advise Gina as to her liability in defamation.

 Guided response in the eBook

Exercise 2

Mini Max is a prominent Australian chef and celebrity. Foxy News recently ran a story about Mini's controversial views on using herbal treatments to cure ailments, rather than relying on medicinal treatments that are backed by scientific research. The story was posted on Foxy News' page on social media website *Social Friends*. The posts referred to Mini by name and contained her image. Foxy News has control over the stories that are posted on its *Social Friends* page, and with 10 000 subscribers and counting, it wants to garner as much publicity as possible. The post concerning Mini Max gained substantial public attention, with many *Social Friends* users taking an immediate dislike to Mini's views on herbal treatment. Hundreds of users posted false, derogatory and nasty comments in response to the post, including allegations that Mini allowed her child's health to drastically deteriorate because she would not accept Western medical treatment.

The posts caused Mini's personal and professional reputation to deteriorate; in the space of a month, she lost a publishing contract worth $10 000 and a stint on a television program worth $20 000. She has also lost several sponsorship deals with various companies, worth $50 000, because these companies no longer wish to be affiliated with her.

Mini Max has sought your advice regarding her potential to take action in the tort of defamation against Foxy News for the damage to her reputation.

 Guided response in the eBook

CHALLENGE YOURSELF

Exercise 1

How might the outcome in the Gina and Ronald scenario in problem-solving exercise I differ if:

(1) Gina had taken an unflattering photo of Ronald and turned it into a meme, mocking Ronald's fitness? Assume the meme was 'liked' by 50 online users.

(2) Gina and Ronald were in an intimate relationship and Gina released intimate photographs taken of Ronald without his consent?

  Guided responses in the eBook

Exercise 2

Dr Fifi Eves is a prominent Australian dentist at Paris Street Dental who specialises in cosmetic dentistry and helping her patients attain a Hollywood smile. She is highly regarded in the Australian dental community, not only for her great dentistry skill but also for her philanthropic work in underprivileged communities. She is highly respected by her patients, dental peers and colleagues.

In February this year, Dr Eves met with a new patient, Carolina Campbell. Carolina came to Dr Eves seeking a smile makeover and with a desire to look 'exactly' like her favourite movie star. Dr Eves explained that she could use various techniques such as veneers and implants to help Carolina achieve a dazzling smile. However, she cautioned that Carolina's facial features were naturally different to her favourite movie star, so she couldn't guarantee that results would precisely match her Hollywood idol.

Dr Eves explained all risks affiliated with the procedure and Carolina signed all necessary consent forms. The cosmetic makeover was conducted in April, and by all independent medical accounts it was conducted competently. However, Carolina was not happy and decided to take out her dissatisfaction publicly. She jumped online and posted the following:

> Avoid Dr Fifi Eves – she ain't no teeth transformer – teeth destroyer is more like it! She does not care and does not help patients. She charged me a fortune for cosmetic work that was utterly terrible – a monkey could have done a better job. #DrEForEvil *devil emoji*

Unfortunately, the hashtag propelled the post on social media and within a week it was seen by thousands of members of the Australian community. Within weeks, Dr Eves observed a significant drop in her income, due to patient cancellations. Dr Eves' secretary has told her that patients are calling the practice and stating they do not wish to see Dr Eves because of the post alleging she is 'evil' and 'incompetent'. Further, an invitation Dr Eves had to speak at an international dental conference has been revoked. Finally, Dr Eves' contract for a new book has been revoked.

Dr Eves has come to your office seeking legal advice. Draft a piece of advice for Dr Eves regarding the harm to her reputation and addressing: (1) the tort of defamation; and (2) injurious falsehood.

 Guided response in the eBook

12

REMEDIES

12.1   Introduction

In a tort action, if the plaintiff's claims are successful and no relevant defences are available to the defendant, the plaintiff will be entitled to an order or award by the court for an appropriate remedy. Such judicial remedies include:

* damages
* injunctions
* declarations.

If the plaintiff seeks one of these remedies, they must plead the details of the loss sustained (or that will be sustained), produce evidence to support them, and prove them on the balance of probabilities. Generally, the plaintiff bears the onus of proving such matters.

In addition, self-help remedies are available and include:

* eviction of trespassers and re-entry of land
* self-defence
* abatement
* apology.

The focus of this chapter will be on judicial remedies, especially damages.

These judicial and self-help remedies, together with statutory compensation schemes and compensation, comprise the remedies available in torts (as shown in Figure 12.1).

Figure 12.1 Remedies in torts

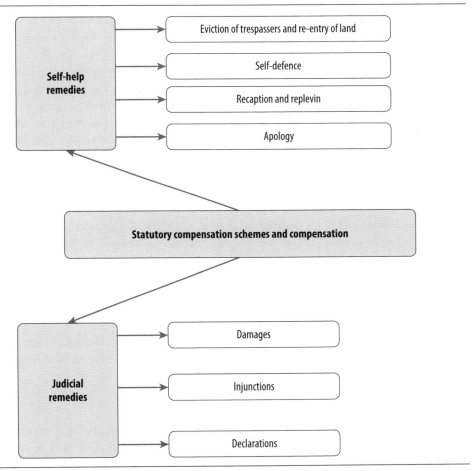

12.2   Self-help remedies

Self-help remedies involve the plaintiff making good his or her own right without the intervention of the judiciary (ie, the court).[1]

In a strict sense, self-help remedies are not remedies since they do not involve a court order; instead, the court gives permission to a plaintiff to act in a particular way. But in a more general sense, the plaintiff is given a means to redress his or her grievance by vindicating his or her own rights. Some commentators reason that an important function of

---

1   For what follows, see K Barnett and S Harder, *Remedies in Australian Private Law* (Cambridge University Press, 2nd ed, 2018) 370–1.

tort law is to prevent persons engaging in violent recourse against one another when they have been wronged; rather, the courts vindicate the rights of the victim in a public forum. Consistent with the views of these 'civil recourse theorists', self-help remedies in tort are exceptional and there is a strong requirement that they be reasonable.[2]

12.2.1   Eviction of trespassers and re-entry of land

A person entitled to possession of land may evict a trespasser, but only so long as no more than reasonable force is used.[3] As noted in Section 8.2.5.2, this notion comprises a defence known as re-entry of land, which overlaps with the defence of property and necessity. It is available by the actual or rightful possessor against any action by the trespasser against the possessor arising from the use of reasonable force by the possessor (eg, battery or assault).

In assessing whether the use and degree of force were reasonable, it is relevant to consider whether a reasonable opportunity was given to the trespasser to terminate the trespass (eg, by leaving the premises),[4] and whether legal proceedings against a trespasser would have been more appropriate than self-help because of its likely risk of a breach of the peace.[5]

The degree of force that might reasonably be used against a trespasser, such as a thief or burglar, presents a difficult question of degree, since the law does not value interests in property as highly as those in the person. For this reason the use of force in defence of property is harder to justify than in the case of self-defence of the person. This is illustrated by the case of *Hackshaw v Shaw*.[6]

12.2.2   Self-defence of the person

Self-defence is usually dealt with by the courts as a defence, but it is equally fitting to regard it as a remedy. (See, as defences to trespass, Section 8.2.1 on self-defence and Section 8.2.2 on defence of another.)

12.2.2.1   Elements of self-defence

Self-defence has two elements. The first element is that the defendant believed on reasonable grounds that he or she needed to protect himself or herself. As stated by the High Court the question to be asked is 'whether the accused [defendant] believed on reasonable grounds that it was necessary in self-defence to do what he did'.[7] The second element is that the force used in doing so was reasonable.[8] The same issues arise regarding self-defence in both tort and criminal actions.

These principles also apply to cases in which a defendant acts in defence of another.[9]

---

2 Eg, using reasonable force to expel a trespasser or taking necessary steps to abate a nuisance: see below.
3 *Cowell v Rosehill Racecourse Co Ltd* (1937) 56 CLR 605, 631 (Dixon J).
4 Ibid.
5 See, eg, *Horkin v North Melbourne Football Club Social Club* [1983] 1 VR 153, 157 (Brooking J) (ejecting a drunken interloper from a social function).
6 (1984) 155 CLR 614.
7 *Zecevic v DPP (Vic)* (1987) 162 CLR 645, 661 (Wilson, Dawson and Toohey JJ, Mason CJ agreeing).
8 *Fontin v Katapodis* (1962) 108 CLR 177, 182.
9 *R v Portelli* (2004) 10 VR 259.

12.2.2.2   Reasonable need to protect oneself

There are two sub-elements in this first element of reasonable need, namely: (1) the defendant must have believed at the time of committing the relevant act that what he or she was doing was necessary; and (2) that belief must be based on reasonable grounds.[10] The second sub-element of reasonable grounds takes into account:

(a)   the defendant's subjective understanding of the circumstances (rather than the reasonable person's perception of the circumstances; ie, an objective test)

(b)   whether such an action was by way of an instant reaction, in which case its proportionality should be given less weight

(c)   the proportionality of the defendant's response as just one factor.[11]

12.2.2.3   Force used was reasonable

On the second test of reasonable force, this is a question of fact in each case. The question to be determined is whether the force used was reasonable and proportionate to the perceived threat.

In *Fontin v Katapodis* the High Court discussed the issue in terms of whether, in all the circumstances, it was reasonably necessary for the defendant to act in the way he did.[12] Katapodis had repeatedly but lightly struck Fontin with a T-square. In response and to avoid further blows, Fontin threw a jagged piece of glass that struck Katapodis and severely injured his hand. The Court held that the response was not reasonable, taking into account the nature of response, the nature of the perceived threat, and the availability of other more reasonable means to avert the perceived threat (eg, escape).

12.2.3   Abatement

As noted in Section 8.2.5, abatement is where a person takes reasonable steps to mitigate or end a tortious interference with their goods or land and is regarded as both a remedy and a defence to trespass. There are a variety of actions by way of abatement; eviction of trespassers and re-entry of land has been dealt with above. This section deals with recaption and replevin of goods and abatement of nuisance.

12.2.3.1   Recaption

The common law right of recaption allows a person who has been deprived of the possession of goods to recover those goods immediately and without recourse to legal action.[13]

The common law has, however, been the subject of considerable statutory modification and the scope of the common law remedy is much reduced as a consequence.[14]

Longstanding English authority established the right of recaption as a defence to an action in trespass provided that reasonable force was used to retake goods wrongfully withheld.[15] But

---

10   *Watkins v Victoria* (2010) 27 VR 543, [71]–[75] (Ashley JA and Beach AJA, Mandie JA agreeing).
11   Ibid [71]–[73] (Ashley JA and Beach AJA, Mandie JA agreeing).
12   (1962) 108 CLR 177.
13   See Section 8.2.5.1.
14   See, eg, *National Credit Code* pt 5 div 2 (enforcement of mortgages of goods), pt 11 div 3 (consumer leases) (contained in the *National Consumer Credit Protection Act 2009* (Cth) sch 1).

while such authority suggests that recaption is available when the original taking was lawful but later possession became unlawful, a majority of the New South Wales Court of Appeal indicated that recaption is only available if the taking was unlawful from the beginning.[16] The Court of Appeal criticised the right of recaption as unnecessarily encouraging 'forcible, perhaps violent, redress'; it determined that the earlier English decision of *Blades v Higgs* was not based in precedent and so refused the remedy of recaption on the facts before it.[17]

The right of recaption is a defence to trespass to land in circumstances where the defendant enters the plaintiff's land to retake goods.[18] But the exact circumstances of this right of recaption remain unclear because, while a right of peaceable entry exists, the use of reasonable force to do so may not.[19]

12.2.3.2   Replevin

Replevin is another action in which a person can recover goods that have been wrongfully detained by another.

In cases in which a plaintiff is deprived of the possession of goods by the defendant, the action of replevin allows the defendant to obtain delivery-up of the goods as interim relief until the question of who is entitled to the goods is determined at the trial of the action. The circumstances of the deprivation of the goods need to be wrongful, such as a landlord taking (or 'distraining') a tenant's property for non-payment of rent. The plaintiff, then, must apply for a warrant or for restitution of the goods and provide security (by way of a bond or deposit) and pledge that he or she will prosecute the action of replevin and, if unsuccessful, allow the defendant to retain the goods. If successful, the replevin action will require the sheriff to restore the goods to the plaintiff.[20]

There have been few reported cases on replevin in recent decades and so, arguably, it has little modern relevance.

12.2.3.3   Abatement of nuisance

A person who has an action in nuisance may remove the source of the interference through abatement, as noted in Section 8.2.5.3. For example, a person may remove overhanging tree branches or tree roots growing into their land.[21] This self-help remedy has origins dating back to the 13th century.

Abatement refers to the *act of removal* of the source of the nuisance, but it does not extend to acts undertaken to *alleviate* the effects of the interference. For example, in one case the plaintiff was unable to recover the costs of installing PVC pipes that were resistant to cypress roots; yet the removal of the roots would have constituted abatement.[22]

It is unclear whether the costs of abatement are recoverable. Although it has been held that the plaintiff is entitled to recover the cost of erecting a wall to prevent water from the

15 *Blades v Higgs* (1861) 10 CB (NS) 713, 720.
16 *Toyota Finance Australia Ltd v Dennis* (2002) 58 NSWLR 101.
17 Ibid.
18 *Cox v Bath* (1893) 14 LR (NSW) 263, 266.
19 *Beneficial Finance Corporation Ltd v Alzden Pty Ltd* (Supreme Court of New South Wales, Equity Division, 10 May 1993) 2.
20 R Sutton, *Personal Actions at Common Law* (Butterworths, 1929) 66–71.
21 *Lemmon v Webb* [1895] AC 1.
22 *Young v Wheeler* [1987] Aust Torts Reports 80-126.

defendant's pool flooding his property,[23] a series of cases has suggested that the cost of abatement is not recoverable where the abatement destroys the nuisance.[24] But an exception is made for acts of abatement occurring only on the plaintiff's land and representing a reasonable attempt to mitigate the damages.[25]

A person may only do what is necessary or reasonable to avert the harm; if there are two ways of abating a nuisance, the less harmful must be adopted unless it would injure a third party or the public.[26] For example, it was considered unreasonable for a defendant to enter a plaintiff's land without notice to cut a bank that was impeding a natural water flow from the defendant's land onto the plaintiff's land; nor was the defendant entitled to an injunction preventing the plaintiff repairing the bank because the defendant had elected to abate by cutting the bank.[27]

12.2.4   Apology

As noted in Section 11.4.3 dealing with defamation, apologies can be a powerful tool in resolving all kinds of disputes without the need for court proceedings. Consistently with the defamation laws, the civil liability legislation provides that an apology does not constitute an admission of fault or liability and is not admissible.[28]

REVIEW QUESTIONS

(1) Why has the common law traditionally been loath to recognise self-help remedies?

(2) What self-help remedies are most commonly encountered in modern legal contexts?

(3) In what circumstances are these self-help remedies usually used?

 Guided responses in the eBook

12.3   Damages

12.3.1   Introduction

The most common remedy in tort law is damages: the provision of monetary satisfaction for the wrong suffered by the plaintiff.

---

23 *Corbett v Pallas* (1995) 86 LGERA 312.
24 *Young v Wheeler* [1987] Aust Torts Reports 80-126; *City of Richmond v Scantelbury* [1991] 2 VR 38, 48.
25 *Proprietors of Strata Plan No 14198 v Cowell* (1989) 24 NSWLR 478, 487.
26 *Lagan Navigation Co v Lambeg Bleaching Co* [1927] AC 226, 245.
27 *Lagan Navigation Co v Lambeg Bleaching Co* [1927] AC 226.
28 See, eg, *Wrongs Act 1958* (Vic) s 14J.

12.3.1.1 'Damage' and 'damages'

There is a distinction between the terms 'damage' and 'damages'. 'Damage' generally refers to the legally recognised loss, harm or injury – the detrimental difference in the plaintiff's position – suffered as a consequence of the defendant's tort. For example, damage is the 'gist' of an action in negligence;[29] in contrast, such damage is not required to establish an action in trespass, which is actionable 'per se'.[30] 'Damages' is the word used to describe the sum of money that a court may award to a successful plaintiff in an action in tort (and other types of action) for the damage suffered. As discussed below, awards of damages compensate for this damage suffered, but also serve other purposes.

12.3.1.2 'Special' and 'general' damages

Also note the distinction between the terms 'special damages' and 'general damages'.[31] Special damages refers to those awards of damages that usually can be quantified with a degree of precision. The prime example of a head of special damages is past economic loss, which is the amount of financial or pecuniary loss that the plaintiff has sustained between the date of the injury and the date of the trial verdict. On the other hand, general damages cannot be quantified with the same degree of precision and are more open-ended. The prime examples of general damages are future economic loss and non-economic loss measurable from the date of the verdict up until retirement age or the death of the plaintiff.

Arguably, the distinction between the two has been blurred[32] (discussed in Section 12.3.5.6). It is common today for the term 'general damages' to be used interchangeably with the term 'non-pecuniary loss damages', while the term 'special damages' often refers to all damages measurable in money, even those relating to the future.

12.3.1.3 Damages awarded for torts actionable 'per se' versus torts in which damage is the 'gist' of the action

As noted above, causes of action where damage is the 'gist' of the action include negligence and nuisance. In such actions, emotional or transient conditions, such as humiliation, embarrassment, distress, indignity, grief or general anxiety suffered by the plaintiff as a result of the wrongdoing are normally not considered sufficient to constitute legally recognised 'damage'; as a consequence, they do not give rise to an award of damages.[33]

Trespass torts, on the other hand, are actionable 'per se', that is, without proof of damage, since damage is not the 'gist' of the action. But where the plaintiff suffers humiliation, embarrassment, distress or indignity as a result of such trespass torts, even in the absence of other legally recognised damage, this may lead to an award of either compensatory, aggravated or exemplary damages.[34]

---

29 See Section 4.1.1.
30 See Section 6.3.3 and Chapter 7.
31 *Paff v Speed* (1961) 105 CLR 549, 558–9 (Fullagar J).
32 See, eg, *Griffiths v Kerkemeyer* (1977) 139 CLR 161.
33 See Section 4.1.1; see also *Mount Isa Mines Ltd v Pusey* (1970) 125 CLR 383, 394 (Windeyer J); *Jaensch v Coffey* (1984) 155 CLR 549, 587 (Deane J).
34 See Sections 6.5, 8.3.1 and 12.3.2.

12.3.2   Types of damages

Consistent with the distinction between damage and damages noted in Section 12.3.1.1, the various types of harm or loss are known as 'heads of *damage*', while the corresponding amounts of money awarded are known as 'heads of *damages*'.[35] The High Court has recently referred to the latter as '*categories* of damages', so we will use this term to avoid confusion between the two.[36] The different categories of damages have been dealt with elsewhere in this book in respect of remedies for trespass[37] and defamation,[38] and include:

- compensatory damages, including:
  - aggravated damages
  - statutory damages and compensation
  - exemplary or punitive damages
- nominal damages
- contemptuous damages
- 'vindicatory damages'
- other damages, including:
  - Lord Cairns' Act damages (also referred to mistakenly as 'restitutionary damages')
  - gain-based awards.

These categories or types of damages are outlined in Figure 12.2 and discussed in the following sections.

Figure 12.2   Types or categories of damages

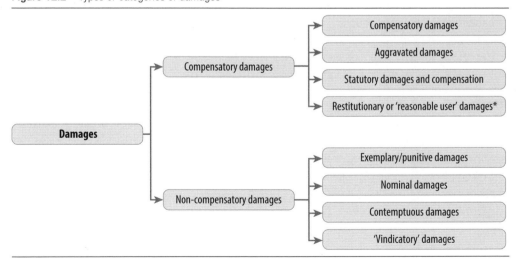

* Damages awarded instead of/in addition to injunction ('equitable' or Lord Cairns' Act damages)

---

35 H Luntz and S Harder, *Assessment of Damages for Personal Injury and Death* (LexisNexis, 5th ed, 2021) [1.7.1], p. 143.
36 *Lewis v Australian Capital Territory* (2020) 271 CLR 192; [2020] HCA 26, [117] (Gordon J).
37 See Section 8.3.
38 See Section 11.4.1.

12.3.2.1   Compensatory damages

Compensatory damages are governed by the 'compensatory principle', as articulated by the High Court in *Haines v Bendall*[39] and reaffirmed in *Lewis v Australian Capital Territory*,[40] 'that the injured party should receive compensation in a sum which, so far as money can do, will put that party in the same position as he or she would have been in if the contract had been performed or the tort had not been committed'.

The classic formulation of this principle was by Lord Blackburn in the House of Lords: 'damages should as nearly as possible get at that sum of money which will put the party who has been injured, or who has suffered, in the same position as he would have been in if he had not sustained the wrong for which he is now getting his compensation'.[41]

This compensatory principle is also known as the principle of *restitutio in integrum* ('restoration to wholeness').[42]

The High Court in *Lewis* has reasoned, from this compensatory principle, that an award of compensatory damages is assessed on the basis of any 'loss' to the plaintiff caused by the wrongdoing, and this loss is to be assessed by a 'but for' test or 'counter-factual' analysis of the position the plaintiff would have been in had the wrongdoing not occurred.[43]

Case: *Lewis v Australian Capital Territory* (2020) 271 CLR 192

Facts

The plaintiff, Lewis, was serving a 12-month periodic detention order that required him to be detained on weekends but not otherwise. He failed to attend this periodic detention on four occasions and, as a consequence, his periodic detention was cancelled by the sentencing board and he was detained full-time. After 82 days of full-time detention it was realised that the decision to cancel his periodic detention was wrongful as he had been denied procedural fairness. It was not in dispute before the High Court that this constituted 82 days, false imprisonment.

Issue

The issue in dispute was whether the plaintiff was entitled to a 'substantial' award of damages for having been falsely imprisoned when he would have been detained lawfully anyway by operation of the sentencing legislation and a warrant for his arrest even if the false imprisonment not taken place. The plaintiff suffered no physical or mental injury as a consequence of the false imprisonment.

---

39 (1991) 172 CLR 60, 63 (Mason CJ, Dawson, Toohey and Gaudron JJ).
40 (2020) 271 CLR 192; [2020] HCA 26, [2] (Kiefel CJ and Keane J); [30]–[31] (Gageler J); [50], [63], [65] (Gordon J); [139], [150] (Edelman J).
41 *Livingstone v Rawyards Coal Co* (1880) 5 App Cas 25, 39, cited in *Lewis v Australian Capital Territory* (2020) 271 CLR 192; [2020] HCA 26, [139] (Edelman J).
42 *Owners of Dredger Liesbosch and Owners of Steamship Edison* [1933] AC 449, 463 (Lord Wright).
43 *Lewis v Australian Capital Territory* (2020) 271 CLR 192; [2020] HCA 26, [2] (Kiefel CJ and Keane J), [30]–[31] (Gageler J), [50], [65], [69] (Gordon J), [151] (Edelman J).

Decision

The High Court unanimously ruled that the plaintiff was not entitled to a substantial award of so-called vindicatory damages for the false imprisonment. He was entitled to a sum of $1 only by way of nominal damages since he had not established that he had suffered any harm, loss or damage as a result of the false imprisonment.

Significance

The High Court used a 'but for' test, or 'counter-factual' test, for assessing damages: would the plaintiff have suffered loss if the wrongdoing had not occurred? This notion of 'loss' appears to encompass both the legally recognised 'damage' that is required for an action in negligence as well as loss to those interests whose interference constitutes torts actionable 'per se'. On the facts of the case in *Lewis*, the High Court referred to the plaintiff's failure to prove any *loss* of liberty resulting from his false imprisonment, since the plaintiff would have been detained anyway by operation of the relevant legislation, as fatal to any award of substantial damages.

Notes

In its determinations, the High Court divided into four separate judgments. Nevertheless, the Court agreed on several matters, namely that:

- There was no category of damages at common law called 'vindicatory damages', in the sense of an award of damages that was substantial and awarded in recognition or vindication of wrongdoing itself even if no loss to the plaintiff had been suffered, such as in the case of torts actionable per se like false imprisonment.[44]
- According to the 'compensation principle' of *Haines v Bendall*,[45] the purpose of damages was to put the plaintiff back in the position he was in as if the wrongdoing had not occurred. This required determining the *loss* suffered by the plaintiff as a result of the wrongdoing by using a 'but for', or 'counter-factual', analysis.[46]
- The 'counter-factual' test to be applied was: 'but for the decision of the Board made in denial of procedural fairness' whether the plaintiff 'would *lawfully* have been subject to the same imprisonment'.[47] Kiefel CJ and Keane J agreed with Edelman J, while Gordon and Gageler JJ expressed themselves in substantially the same terms.[48]
- On the application of this test to facts, the plaintiff had suffered no loss since he would have been detained anyway even if the false imprisonment had not occurred.[49] Kiefel CJ and Keane J distinguished their application of the 'but for' test from Edelman J by saying that the test was not engaged in the first place since the plaintiff had not suffered any 'real loss'; his right of liberty was 'so qualified and attenuated … that he suffered no real loss.'[50]

44 Ibid [2] (Kiefel CJ and Keane J), [22] (Gageler J agreeing with Gordon J), [51] (Gordon J), [173] (Edelman J).
45 (1991) 172 CLR 60.
46 Ibid [2] (Kiefel CJ and Keane J, agreeing with Edelman J), [30]–[31] (Gageler J), [50], [65], [69], (Gordon J), [151] (Edelman J).
47 Ibid [179] (Edelman J, emphasis added).
48 Ibid [2] (Kiefel CJ and Keane J agreeing with Edelman J), [91] (Gordon J), [36]–[40] (Gageler J).
49 Ibid [41], [42] (Gageler J), [74] (Gordon J), [179] (Edelman J).
50 Ibid [3], [4], [6] (Kiefel CJ and Keane J).

- Accordingly, the plaintiff was not entitled to substantial damages; the plaintiff was entitled to nominal damages in the sum of $1 only because he had not suffered any loss.[51]

Question
What was the notion of 'vindicatory' damages that the High Court rejected?

 Guided response in the eBook

12.3.2.2 Statutory damages and compensation

As outlined in Section 1.3, Australian statutory compensations schemes, such as transport accident compensation, workers' compensation, the National Disability Insurance Scheme (NDIS), and victims of crime compensation schemes, provide remedies to claimants.

Such claimants are able to seek either no-fault compensation (eg, periodic payments in lieu of wages, medical expenses, lump sum payments, or other supports) by following the claims procedure in the statute or by making a claim for damages at common law after satisfying certain thresholds that are stipulated in the statute. In this way, statutory compensation schemes enable both self-help and judicial remedies.

Note also that the *Australian Consumer Law*, comprising sch 2 of the *Competition and Consumer Act 2010* (Cth), provides for the award of damages for breaches of its provisions.

12.3.2.3 Nominal damages

Nominal damages are awarded where a plaintiff has proven a violation of legal rights but without suffering any harm or damage as a consequence.[52]

Nominal damages are available for torts that are actionable per se (eg, trespass to land, trespass to person and trespass to goods), where there is no need to prove loss or damage.[53] But nominal damages cannot be awarded where damage is the gist of the plaintiff's cause of action, as in an action for the tort of negligence.

The High Court in *Lewis* determined that the plaintiff was not entitled to 'substantive' damages since he had not suffered any harm, loss or damage, and so did not disturb the nominal damages award of $1 made by the ACT Court of Appeal.[54]

The amount of nominal damages awarded must be no more than a 'token sum', although it need not be extremely small.[55] A 'token' amount in a case involving a breach of contract

---

51 Ibid [2], (Kiefel CJ and Keane J), [21] (Gageler J), [50] (Gordon J), [125], [179], [184] (Edelman J).
52 *The Mediana* [1900] AC 113, 116 (Lord Halsbury LC), whose obiter dicta was cited with approval in *Baume v Commonwealth* (1906) 4 CLR 97, 116 and *Lewis v Australian Capital Territory* (2020) 271 CLR 192; [2020] HCA 26, [4] (Kiefel CJ and Keane J), [21], [47], [86], [114]–[115] (Gordon J), [125], [156] (Edelman J).
53 See Sections 8.3.1.1 (trespass to person), 8.3.2.1 (trespass to land) and 8.3.3.1 (trespass to goods).
54 *Lewis v Australian Capital Territory* (2020) 271 CLR 192; [2020] HCA 26, [2] (Kiefel CJ and Keane J), [21] (Gageler J), [50] (Gordon J), [125], [179], [184] (Edelman J).
55 *New South Wales v Stevens* (2012) 82 NSWLR 106 (Sackville AJA and McColl JA in separate judgments, Ward JA agreeing with both Justices).

with no actual loss or damage to the plaintiff gave rise to an award of nominal damages of $100 in *New South Wales v Stevens*;[56] this sum was considerably more than the award to the plaintiff in *Lewis* for his false imprisonment of $1.[57]

Previously an award of nominal damages carried with it the entitlement to the costs of the action, and so was important for a plaintiff from this perspective. But under modern procedural reforms, the court's discretion in relation to costs means that the difference is less significant than it once was.[58]

12.3.2.4   Contemptuous damages

Contemptuous damages, rarely awarded other than by a jury in defamation cases, are of a very small amount and their purpose is to indicate the court's view that, although the plaintiff has technically established the right, the action should never have been brought. They differ from nominal damages in that they can be awarded for any tort – whether actionable per se or not – and indicate the court's contempt for the character and conduct of the plaintiff.[59] The amount awarded is usually described as 'the lowest coin of the realm' or derisory.[60] In the past, it was important to distinguish nominal from contemptuous damages because the former (but not the latter) carried with it the entitlement to the costs of the action; a court could use its discretion to deprive the plaintiff of the costs of the action despite the technical victory on the merits of the case.[61] The significance of this has diminished, however, in light of the court's broad discretion to award costs, as noted above.

12.3.2.5   Vindicatory damages

Where a tort actionable per se occurred but the plaintiff suffered no actual loss as a result, the question arises as to whether the defendant is liable to pay more than mere nominal damages. Some commentators assert that the answer to this question is 'yes'; the defendant ought to pay substantial damages, known as 'vindicatory' damages, on the basis that the damages vindicate the plaintiff's right or interest that has been interfered with.[62] These have also been called 'normative' damages since they recognise the 'normative' loss sustained by the plaintiff, as distinguished from the lack of 'consequential' or 'factual' loss suffered by the

---

56 *New South Wales v Stevens* (2012) 82 NSWLR 106.

57 See *Lewis v Australian Capital Territory* (2020) 271 CLR 192; [2020] HCA 26, [131].

58 *Motium Pty Ltd v Arrow Electronics Australia Pty Ltd* [2011] WASCA 65 (plaintiff entitled to nominal damages for breach of contract, but that did not carry with it an entitlement to full costs because the plaintiff failed in an attempt to recover substantial damages); *Actrol Parts Pty Ltd v Coppi (No 3)* (2015) 49 VR 573 (award of nominal damages refused and proceedings dismissed with indemnity costs to defendant).

59 For example, *Connolly v Sunday Times Publishing Co Ltd* (1908) 7 CLR 263, 268 (Griffith CJ), 272 (Barton J), 276 (O'Connor J) (jury verdict awarding plaintiff one shilling in damages for defamation considered contemptuous damages); *Bailey v Truth & Sportsman Ltd* (1938) 60 CLR 700, 709 (Latham CJ), 725 (Dixon J in dissent), 727–8, 731 (McTiernan J) (jury verdict awarding plaintiff one farthing in damages for defamation described as contemptuous damages); *Earnshaw v Loy (No 2)* [1959] VR 252, 253–4 (jury verdict awarding plaintiff a small amount of damages for assault and malicious prosecution, which Sholl J said was 'contemptuous' in the sense of recognising infringement of the plaintiff's legal rights but that his conduct and general character 'deserved the contempt of decent people').

60 See *Allen v Lloyd-Jones (No 6)* [2014] NSWDC 40, [139]–[140] (Gibson DCJ).

61 See, eg, *Connolly v Sunday Times Publishing Co Ltd* (1908) 7 CLR 263.

62 JNE Varuhas, *Damages and Human Rights* (Hart Publishing, 2016) 46; JNE Varuhas, 'Before the High Court v Lewis v Australian Capital Territory: Valuing Freedom' (2020) 42(1) *Sydney Law Review* 123.

plaintiff.[63] Robert Stevens has called these 'substitutive' damages since they are damages that substitute for the value of the right infringed.[64]

The High Court in *Lewis* explicitly confirmed that there was no category of damages called 'vindicatory damages', in the sense of an award of damages that was substantial in nature awarded as recognition or vindication of the wrongdoing itself even if no loss to the plaintiff has been suffered.[65] In that decision Edelman J also observed that the decision of *Plenty v Dillon* – often cited as a paradigmatic authority for the notion of vindicatory damages – did not provide support for the proposition that vindicatory damages were a part of the common law.[66]

Note that vindicatory damages also refer to the conceptually distinct category of damages recognised in a series of Privy Council appeals from the Caribbean, which recognise 'the sense of public outrage … the importance of constitutional right and the gravity of the breach, and deter further breaches', thus performing a role akin to exemplary damages although with the aim of vindication rather than punishment.[67]

12.3.2.6 Restitutionary damages or 'reasonable user fee' damages

A defendant who uses or interferes with the defendant's land or personal property without permission is liable to pay damages to the owner even if the owner fails to establish any loss caused by that wrongful use (ie, cost of replacement or the consequences of its depletion). The basis of this award of damages is for a 'reasonable user fee', that is, it is a 'gain-based' award reflecting the value for the defendant wrongfully having the benefit of the use of the property.[68] Note that the terminology here is confusing since 'reasonable user fee' awards are also called 'restitutionary damages' or 'user' awards, among other terms.

'Reasonable user fee' awards are made in two kinds of case: trespass to land (eg, *LJP Investments Pty Ltd v Howard Chia Investments (No 2)*)[69] and trespass to goods (*Strand Electric & Engineering Co Ltd v Brisford Entertainments Ltd*) ('*Strand*').[70] The decision in *Strand* was considered by the New South Wales Court of Appeal in *Bunnings Group Ltd v CHEP Australia Ltd*, which ultimately determined that the plaintiff's loss of use of its pallets due to their detention by the defendants could be adequately conceptualised in terms of compensatory principles in respect of the 'use' of the pallets, and so there was no need to resort to restitutionary principles.[71]

12.3.2.7 Aggravated damages

Aggravated damages may be awarded, in addition to compensatory damages for actual harm suffered, to compensate the plaintiff for injury (frequently intangible) resulting from

---

63 JNE Varuhas, *Damages and Human Rights* (Hart Publishing, 2016) 46; JNE Varuhas, 'Before the High Court v Lewis v Australian Capital Territory: Valuing Freedom" (2020) 42(1) *Sydney Law Review* 123.

64 R Stevens, *Torts and Rights* (Oxford University Press, 2007) 59–91, 137–44.

65 *Lewis v Australian Capital Territory* (2020) 271 CLR 192; [2020] HCA 26, [2] (Kiefel CJ and Keane J), [22] (Gageler J) (agreeing with Gordon J), [51] (Gordon J), [173] (Edelman J).

66 Ibid [161].

67 See, eg, *Attorney-General of Trinidad and Tobago v Ramanoop* [2006] 1 AC 328.

68 K Barnett and S Harder, *Remedies in Australian Private Law* (Cambridge University Press, 2nd ed, 2018) 445–6.

69 (1989) 24 NSWLR 499.

70 [1952] 2 QB 246, see Section 8.3.

71 (2011) 82 NSWLR 420, [170]–[179] (Allsop P), [193]–[201] (Giles P).

the 'circumstances and manner of the wrongdoing' by the defendant.[72] Aggravated damages are awarded to compensate the plaintiff for the *manner* in which the defendant behaved in committing the wrong or thereafter.[73] While the same factors may be relevant to both aggravated and exemplary damages, the difference is that aggravated damages are assessed from the plaintiff's point of view while exemplary damages focus on the defendant's conduct.[74] Such damages are awarded where the circumstances 'increase the hurt to the plaintiff'.[75]

The intangible' injuries for which aggravated damages may be awarded are 'for injury to the plaintiff's feelings caused by insult, humiliation and the like'.[76] The injury suffered need not be a recognised psychiatric illness; in fact, such damages are in effect 'compensation for mental suffering falling short of a recognised psychiatric illness'.[77] Note that in causes of action where damage is the 'gist' of the action (eg, negligence, nuisance and deceit), intangible responses of this sort to the wrong (such as grief, general anxiety or emotional disturbance) will normally not constitute legally recognised damage and so not give rise to an award of damages.[78]

An award of aggravated damages for the intangible injury to the plaintiff's hurt feelings is distinct from an ordinary award of compensatory damages for injury to the plaintiff's feelings. According to the New South Wales Court of Appeal in *New South Wales v Riley*, the latter is caused by ordinary wrongdoing of a kind consistent with 'human fallibility' and therefore to be quantified towards the 'centre of the wide range of damages' whereas the former is caused by wrongdoing 'that goes beyond ordinary human fallibility … [or] serious misconduct' and therefore to be awarded 'towards the upper limit of the range'.[79]

AGGRAVATED DAMAGES AWARDED FOR CERTAIN TORTS

Aggravated damages are most frequently awarded for the trespass torts (also known as torts actionable per se), which protect a plaintiff's feelings or liberty, such as false imprisonment[80] or assault.[81] They are also available for torts that protect reputation, namely defamation.[82] Similarly, they are available for torts protecting proprietary interests, such as trespass to land.[83]

---

72 *New South Wales v Ibbett* (2006) 229 CLR 638; [2006] HCA 57, [31] (coram), citing *Uren v John Fairfax & Sons Pty Ltd* (1966) 117 CLR 118, 129–30 (Taylor J).

73 *Uren v John Fairfax & Sons Pty Ltd* (1966) 117 CLR 118, 149 (Windeyer J).

74 *New South Wales v Ibbett* [2005] NSWCA 445, [83] (Spigelman CJ), quoted with approval in *New South Wales v Ibbett* (2006) 229 CLR 638; [2006] HCA 57, [34] and in *Lewis v Australian Capital Territory* (2020) 271 CLR 192; [2020] HCA 26, [112] (Gordon J).

75 *New South Wales v Ibbett* (2006) 229 CLR 638; [2006] HCA 57, [35].

76 *Lamb v Cotogno* (1987) 164 CLR 1, 8 (coram).

77 *New South Wales v Riley* (2003) 57 NSWLR 496, [129] (Hodgson JA); *New South Wales v Corby* (2010) 76 NSWLR 439, [48] (Basten JA).

78 See Section 4.1.1, citing *Leonard v Pollock* [2012] WASCA 108. See also *Public Trustee v Zoanetti* (1945) 70 CLR 266, 279 (Dixon J); *Jaensch v Coffey* (1984) 155 CLR 549, 587 (Deane J), citing *Mount Isa Mines Ltd v Pusey* (1970) 125 CLR 383, 394 (Windeyer J).

79 (2003) 57 NSWLR 496, [131], [133] (Hodgson JA) (Nicholas J and Sheller JA agreeing).

80 *Myer Stores Ltd v Soo* [1991] 2 VR 597; *McFadzean v Construction, Forestry, Mining and Energy Union* (2007) 20 VR 250.

81 *New South Wales v Ibbett* (2006) 229 CLR 638; [2006] HCA 57.

82 See, eg, *Uren v John Fairfax & Sons Pty Ltd* (1966) 117 CLR 118; *Bauer Media Pty Ltd v Wilson (No 2)* (2018) 56 VR 674; *Defamation Act 2005* (Vic) s 35(2).

83 *TCN Channel Nine Pty Ltd v Anning* (2002) 54 NSWLR 333, [179].

AGGRAVATED DAMAGES AWARDED FOR NEGLIGENCE?

In addition to the issue of establishing legally recognised damage for the tort of negligence mentioned above, it is controversial as to whether aggravated damages are available in actions in negligence at all, particularly in personal injury cases.[84] The Victorian Court of Appeal has presumed that aggravated damages are available for such personal injury cases.[85] But the New South Wales Court of Appeal stated that there is 'no clear guidance in Australian case law on the broad question whether aggravated damages are capable of being awarded in a negligence action.'[86] Despite obiter statements confirming this position of uncertainty in other appellate courts,[87] the Court of Appeal of the Australian Capital Territory decided to award aggravated damages in a case of sexual abuse, finding support in the case law for this position.[88]

AGGRAVATED DAMAGES LIMITED BY CIVIL LIABILITY LEGISLATION

Only a few jurisdictions have abolished aggravated damages. Civil liability legislation in New South Wales and Queensland prohibits an award of aggravated damages in actions for personal injury caused by the defendant's negligence.[89]

In Australian jurisdictions where they have not otherwise been abolished, aggravated damages are available at common law.

Likewise, ss 87E and 87ZB of the *Competition and Consumer Act 2010* (Cth) preclude an award of aggravated damages for negligent personal injury arising from product liability.

12.3.2.8   Exemplary damages

Exemplary damages are damages over and above those necessary to compensate the plaintiff. Exemplary damages are awarded to punish the defendant; to act as a deterrent to the defendant and their conduct and 'other like-minded persons' engaging in conduct 'of the same reprehensible kind'; 'to mark the court's condemnation' of such conduct; and to provide retribution by assuaging 'any urge for revenge … and … any temptation to engage in self-help likely to endanger the peace'.[90]

Note that exemplary damages are 'parasitic' on compensatory damages, and so the plaintiff is unable to recover the former unless entitled to an award of the latter.[91]

Exemplary damages are also known as 'punitive' damages (particularly in the United States), and in the past have been referred to as 'penal', 'retributory' or 'vindictive' damages.[92]

---

84   *Willoughby Municipal Council v Halstead* (1916) 22 CLR 352 (court divided 2:2 on the issue); *Oldham v Lawson (No 1)* [1976] VR 654, 658–9 (Harris J doubted their availability).

85   *Backwell v AAA* [1997] 1 VR 182, 214 (Ormiston JA).

86   *Hunter Area Health Service v Marchlewski* (2000) 51 NSWLR 268, [110] (Mason P).

87   *Delta Corporation v Davies* [2002] WASCA 125, [155].

88   *John XXIII College v SMA* [2022] ACTCA 32, [202], [228] (coram).

89   *Civil Liability Act 2002* (NSW) s 21; *Civil Liability Act 2003* (Qld) s 52. Some exceptions remain for tobacco and smoking claims, and the New South Wales legislation also makes an exception for intentional acts in s 3B(1)(a). See Section 8.3.1.3.

90   *Lamb v Cotogno* (1987) 164 CLR 1, 9–10 (coram); *Uren v John Fairfax & Sons Pty Ltd* (1966) 117 CLR 118, 138 (Taylor J), 149 (Windeyer J).

91   *XL Petroleum (NSW) Pty Ltd v Caltex Oil (Australia) Pty Ltd* (1985) 155 CLR 448, 468–9 (Brennan J).

92   *Whitfield v De Lauret & Co Ltd* (1920) 29 CLR 71, 81.

The House of Lords has confined English law to three particular circumstances in which exemplary damages may be awarded: (1) for 'oppressive, arbitrary or unconstitutional action by the servants of the government'; (2) where the defendant's conduct 'has been calculated by him to make a profit for himself which may well exceed the compensation payable to the plaintiff'; and (3) where 'expressly authorised by statute'.[93] No such restrictions apply in Australia.[94]

In Australia, by contrast, exemplary damages are available at common law whenever the conduct of the defendant is 'high-handed, insolent, vindictive or malicious or … in some other way exhibit[s] a contumelious disregard of the plaintiff's rights'.[95]

Although the High Court in *Lamb v Cotogno* observed that 'in some cases it may be difficult to differentiate between aggravated damages and exemplary damages', the crucial difference is that exemplary damages are awarded with the intent of punishing, deterring or marking the 'detestation' of the conduct whereas aggravated damages are intended to compensate the plaintiff for these intangible injuries.[96] In practice, some cases have awarded both types of damages for the same wrongdoing.[97]

Case: *Lamb v Cotogno* (1987) 164 CLR 1

Facts

Lamb, a process server, attempted to serve a summons on Cotogno. In a rage, Cotogno threw himself on the bonnet of Lamb's car. Lamb drove off quickly and attempted to dislodge Cotogno by weaving back and forth. Lamb braked suddenly and Cotogno was seriously injured when he fell off. Lamb drove off, leaving Cotogno lying on the side of the road screaming in pain. Cotogno sued Lamb for trespass to the person and received both compensatory and exemplary damages.

In the Supreme Court of New South Wales, Cotogno was awarded compensatory damages of $198 570 and exemplary damages of $5000, the latter on the basis that, although there was 'nothing malicious' in Lamb's actions, he nevertheless 'did callously abandon the plaintiff on the road and sped off in the night leaving him lying on a darkened road' (at 6). Further, the injury to Cotogno arose from the use of the vehicle, which was covered by a policy of compulsory insurance.

Issue

First, could exemplary damages be awarded for the 'callous' manner in which Lamb committed the tort, even though this did not amount to malice or reckless indifference and was provoked?

Second, could exemplary damages be awarded even if the defendant, Lamb, was covered by insurance and so the punitive element of awarding exemplary damages was arguably defeated?

---

93 *Rookes v Barnard* [1964] AC 1129, 1226–7 (Lord Devlin).
94 *Uren v John Fairfax & Sons Pty Ltd* (1966) 117 CLR 118; *Australian Consolidated Press Ltd v Uren* (1966) 117 CLR 185, affd in [1969] 1 AC 590 (PC).
95 *Uren v John Fairfax & Sons Pty Ltd* (1966) 117 CLR 118, 129 (Taylor J).
96 (1987) 164 CLR 1, 8.
97 For example, *New South Wales v Ibbett* (2006) 229 CLR 638 and *Canterbury Bankstown Rugby League Football Club Ltd v Rogers* [1993] Aust Torts Reports 81-246, both discussed in the section below.

Decision

On the first issue, the High Court held that the conduct in abandoning Cotogno in the manner Lamb did displayed 'a cruel or reckless disregard for the welfare of the plaintiff and indifference to his plight' and so amounted to an 'insult' to Cotogno, which justified an award of exemplary damages (at 12–13). Further, although his actions were without malice, Lamb's act in abandoning Cotogno was callous and sufficient to indicate that he acted 'in a humiliating manner and in wanton disregard of the plaintiff's welfare' (at 13). The Court said that, while there can be no malice without intent, 'the intent or recklessness necessary to justify an award of exemplary damages may be found in contumelious behaviour which falls short of being malicious or is not aptly described by the use of that word' (at 13).

On the second issue, although it was argued that the aims of deterrence and punishment were defeated because the defendant Lamb was insured in this case, the Court reasoned that nevertheless the social aim of exemplary damages extended to general deterrence and to preventing plaintiffs from taking revenge, and so exemplary damages should nevertheless be awarded (at 9–12).

Significance

The High Court clarified the meaning of contumelious behaviour as not necessarily requiring malice. It also clarified that insurance would not prevent an award of exemplary damages.

Note

The judgment of the High Court (at 9) analyses the aim of exemplary damages as being to punish the defendant, but as not necessarily the only aim of such damages.

Question

What did the High Court set out as the aims of exemplary damages, in addition to punishment and deterrence?

 Guided response in the eBook

EXEMPLARY DAMAGES AWARDED FOR INTENTIONAL TORTS

It follows from this notion of contumelious disregard, or contempt, shown to the plaintiff that exemplary damages are generally awarded in respect of those torts in which intention is normally an element. Accordingly, exemplary damages may be awarded in cases involving intentional torts, such as trespass to the person,[98] trespass to goods, trespass to land,[99]

---

98   See, eg, *Canterbury Bankstown Rugby League Football Club Ltd v Rogers* [1993] Aust Torts Reports 81-246.

99   See, eg, *New South Wales v Ibbett* (2006) 229 CLR 638; [2006] HCA 57.

intentional torts affecting the plaintiff's business interests,[100] actions in deceit, and actions in nuisance causing property damage.

EXEMPLARY DAMAGES AWARDED FOR NEGLIGENCE

Exemplary damages are available in negligence actions.[101]

The High Court in *Gray v Motor Accident Commission* indicated that exemplary damages could not be awarded in cases of alleged negligence where there was 'no conscious wrongdoing' by the defendant, but they could be awarded where the defendant was shown to have acted 'consciously in contumelious disregard of the rights of the plaintiff or persons in the position of the plaintiff'.[102] The Court gave an example of such cases, namely those involving a defendant employer's failure to provide a safe system of work where the employer knew of an extreme danger created by this failure but persisted in using the unsafe system.[103]

Other examples include claims against an asbestos supplier for mesothelioma,[104] claims against a doctor by a patient[105] and a breach by a public trustee of a common law duty to the beneficiary of an estate.[106]

Where the defendant has deliberately or recklessly invaded the plaintiff's right in order to make a profit or save an expense, exemplary damages may be awarded, which may include a restitutionary element so as to exceed the gain that the defendant hoped to make.[107]

EXEMPLARY DAMAGES LIMITED BY CIVIL LIABILITY LEGISLATION AND OTHER STATUTORY LIMITATIONS

As noted in Sections 8.3.1.4 and 12.3.2.7 regarding aggravated damages, the same provisions abolishing aggravated damages have abolished exemplary damages in New South Wales and Queensland.[108]

The prohibitions in the civil liability legislation against awards of exemplary damages do not apply to liability that arises from an 'intentional act' that is done by a person 'with intent to cause injury or death' or that is sexual assault or other sexual misconduct committed by the person. The uniform defamation statutes, which came into effect in all jurisdictions in 2006, prohibit exemplary damages.[109] Under Commonwealth consumer protection laws, exemplary damages are prohibited.[110] The award of exemplary damages, but not aggravated damages, is prohibited in motor and workplace accident cases in New South Wales and Victoria.[111]

---

100 See, eg, *Whitfield v De Lauret & Co Ltd* (1920) 29 CLR 71.
101 *Gray v Motor Accident Commission* (1998) 196 CLR 1, 22.
102 Ibid.
103 Ibid.
104 *Amaca Pty Ltd v Banton* (2007) 5 DDCR 314.
105 *Backwell v AAA* [1997] 1 VR 182.
106 *McDonald v Public Trustee* [2010] NSWSC 684.
107 *Dean v Phung* [2012] NSWCA 223, [80]–[82] (taking into account in the award of exemplary damages the extent to which a dentist who fraudulently over-serviced a plaintiff remained unjustly enriched).
108 *Civil Liability Act 2002* (NSW) s 21; *Civil Liability Act 2003* (Qld) s 52.
109 See, eg, *Defamation Act 2005* (NSW).
110 *Competition and Consumer Act 2010* (Cth) s 87ZB (subject to s 87E).
111 *Motor Accidents Compensation Act 1999* (NSW) s 144; *Workers Compensation Act 1987* (NSW) s 151R; *Transport Accident Act 1986* (Vic); *Workplace Injury Rehabilitation and Compensation Act 2013* (Vic) s 340(c).

EXEMPLARY DAMAGES AWARDED IF CRIMINAL PUNISHMENT HAS ALREADY BEEN IMPOSED ON THE DEFENDANT

The availability of exemplary damages in the law of torts, which relates to rights and liabilities between individuals and other individuals, overlaps with criminal law, which relates to rights and liabilities between individuals and the State. Punishment is not commonly recognised as a central aim of civil law, and some commentators argue that it should therefore have no role, or at most a limited role, in tort law.

Case: *Gray v Motor Accident Commission* (1998) 196 CLR 1

Facts

The defendant, while driving, deliberately ran down the plaintiff as he crossed the road. The defendant was convicted of intentionally causing grievous bodily harm and sentenced to seven years' imprisonment. The plaintiff then sued the defendant in negligence, but the case was conducted as if it were a claim for trespass to the person.

Issue

Can exemplary damages be awarded if a defendant has already been convicted of a criminal offence, and therefore arguably already 'punished'?

Decision

The fact that the defendant had already been punished was a reason to decline an award of punitive damages since: (a) the purposes of punishment and deterrence had been achieved if 'substantial punishment' was exacted; and (b) awarding exemplary damages would amount to 'double punishment'.

Significance

Prior criminal conviction is grounds for disallowing a subsequent award of exemplary damages in civil proceedings.

Notes

The High Court also made another significant comment on exemplary damages. It explained that the presence of compulsory insurance in this case (which covered the costs of the personal injuries inflicted on the plaintiff) was not a bar to an award of exemplary damages.

Question

How does the criminal law and tort law deal with the issue of damages in respect of a verdict of wrongdoing on the same set of facts?

    Guided response in the eBook

EXAMPLES OF EXEMPLARY DAMAGES AWARDS

The case of *Canterbury Bankstown Rugby League Football Club Ltd v Rogers*, heard in the New South Wales Court of Appeal, illustrates the application of several aspects just discussed in the awarding of aggravated and exemplary damages.[112] Another example arises from the case of *New South Wales v Ibbett*.[113]

Case: *New South Wales v Ibbett* (2006) 229 CLR 638

Facts

Police officers unlawfully entered Mrs Ibbett's property when attempting to arrest her son, and one of them pointed a gun at her when she asked them to leave. Mrs Ibbett was successful in suing the officer and the police force for both assault and trespass to land, and recovered compensatory, aggravated and exemplary damages. The State of New South Wales appealed the amounts of the awards.

Issue

Was it appropriate to award exemplary damages in this case? What amount was appropriate?

Decision

The High Court held that the following amounts were appropriate:

- Assault
    - Compensatory damages $15000
    - Aggravated damages $10000
    - Exemplary damages $25000
- Trespass to land
    - Compensatory damages $10000
    - Aggravated damages $20000
    - Exemplary damages $20000
- Total $100000.

Significance

This case is a further illustration of the application and interaction of compensatory, aggravated and exemplary damages.

Notes

In this case, there may well have been issues as to whether the aggravated or exemplary damages were to be awarded against the police force as a corporate entity or against the individual officers personally, but the issue of vicarious liability was conceded by NSW Police.

---

112 [1993] Aust Torts Reports 81-246.
113 (2006) 229 CLR 638; [2006] HCA 57.

Question

What was the difference between the award of exemplary damages in this case and the award in *Canterbury Bankstown Rugby League Football Club Ltd v Rogers* [1993] Aust Torts Reports 81-246?

    Guided response in the eBook

12.3.3   Compensatory damages for property damage

Compensating a plaintiff for damage or loss to his or her property is a relatively straightforward matter when compared to compensation for personal injury, since the estimation of the loss is usually more certain in the former case than the latter. Restitution for the loss of value of property usually represents the difference in the value of the property before and after the loss or damage.

The main issue in property damage is how that amount will be calculated. Compensation for property damage will be different according to the manner in which that loss is reckoned, namely whether that loss comprises:

- the cost of repair, in the case of property that is partially destroyed[114]
- the diminution in the value of property that is partially destroyed[115]
- the total replacement cost in the case of *total* deprivation or destruction of the property.[116]

Any loss that the plaintiff suffers as a consequence of the damage to or loss of the property may also be compensable ('consequential loss').

12.3.3.1   Cost of repair or diminished value

Depending on the circumstances, a court may award compensatory damages for a tort causing loss to property by an amount representing either: (a) the reduced or diminished value of that property; or (b) the cost of reinstating or repairing it. The amounts recoverable for the costs of repair or reinstatement will be the reasonable commercial cost of repair or reinstatement.[117]

In cases where the plaintiff seeks the higher of these two amounts as compensation, the plaintiff must convince the court of the appropriate measure, and that it is reasonable in the circumstances.[118] The Victorian Supreme Court set out the following approach (as applied to real property, or land):

114 *Murphy v Brown* (1985) 1 NSWLR 131; *Pargiter v Alexander* (1995) 5 Tas R 158.
115 *Davidson v JS Gilbert Fabrications Pty Ltd* [1986] 1 Qd R 1.
116 *Wheeler v Riverside Coal Transport Co Pty Ltd* [1964] Qd R 113.
117 *Powercor Australia Ltd v Thomas* (2012) 43 VR 220, [25] (Osborn JA, Warren CJ and Bongiorno JA agreeing).
118 *Hansen v Gloucester Developments Pty Ltd* [1992] 1 Qd R 14; *Evans v Balog* [1976] 1 NSWLR 36, 39; *Jones v Shire of Perth* [1970] WAR 56; *Pargiter v Alexander* (1995) 5 Tas R 158.

Courts will start with what the plaintiff has asked for, and then consider whether that measure of damages is fair and reasonable in light of the injury suffered, the difference between the diminution in value on the one hand and the reinstatement costs on the other, and any special value in the land.[119]

Where the plaintiff has received some sort of benefit from the damage to his or her property, the court may take that into account by reducing the damages payable. An example of this is the case of *Gagner Pty Ltd v Canturi Corporation Pty Ltd*.[120]

Case: *Gagner Pty Ltd v Canturi Corporation Pty Ltd* (2009) 262 ALR 691

Facts

The respondent's business premises were damaged by flooding caused by the appellant's negligence. The flooding affected approximately 10 per cent of the respondent's floor area, but the respondent took the opportunity to completely refurbish the premises and to close the business for 29 days while doing so, both at a substantial cost. The trial judge awarded damages to reflect the costs of rectifying the premises to the condition as close as possible before the flood and the loss of profits for only 10 days. On appeal, the appellant argued that the respondent had not suffered any loss because of the complete refurbishment, and that the award of damages was, in the circumstances, a claim for betterment.

Issue

The Court upheld the principle that the plaintiff should ordinarily be entitled to damages for the cost of repairs; only in the most exceptional case would the plaintiff be denied damages for the cost of repairs on the ground that it was unreasonable when compared to the diminution in value of the property.

Decision

The New South Wales Court of Appeal upheld the decision at first instance that the respondent was entitled to the reasonable costs of rectification of damage resulting from the flooding of the shop caused by the appellant's negligence. The fact that the respondent chose to go beyond such rectification to effect a total refurbishment did not preclude recovery of an amount that a precise rectification of water damage would have cost. As Campbell JA put it at [111]: 'it was the judge's task to assess the compensation that would make good those consequences properly attributable to the flooding. This she did by allowing the amount that a precise rectification of the water damage alone would have cost, and leaving the respondent to bear any amount it had spent in excess of that.'

---

119 *Winky Pop Pty Ltd v Mobil Refining Australia Pty Ltd* [2015] VSC 348, [182].
120 (2009) 262 ALR 691.

Significance

The appropriate measure of the respondent's claim for damages was not a claim for betterment, but reasonable compensation in the circumstances.

Notes

Campbell JA discussed cases that measured damage for tortious damage to property and concluded that the appropriate principle was 'making good the damage' in assessing damages for torts, at [105]–[106]:

> What counts as making good the damage, for the purpose of assessing damages for torts, needs to be understood bearing in mind what the purpose is for which one is asking what counts as 'making good'. That purpose is ascertaining what the work is that is necessary to undo the consequences of the tort having been committed. The only interest of the defendant that bears upon the question of whether rectification work is reasonable is a financial one, sometimes expressed in the principle that a plaintiff must mitigate his damage …
>
> The cost of making good is merely one way of putting a dollar figure on the damage that the plaintiff has suffered, for the purposes of carrying through the compensatory principle. There are circumstances, of which the present is one, when the fact that money has not been spent on the precise items that would need to be acquired to restore property to its pre-damage condition does not prevent the cost of acquiring those items being the appropriate way of giving effect to the compensatory principle …

Campbell JA also referred to an exceptional circumstance when a plaintiff was entitled to the costs of reinstating or repairing property, even where those costs appeared unreasonable when compared to the diminution in the value of the property. This was the case of *Evans v Balog*, in which the land that was damaged was the plaintiffs' family home. That was a reasonable factor in establishing the reasonableness of reinstating it, even though the costs of restoration exceeded the diminution in value of the land that had arisen from the damage (at [103]).

Question

On what basis will the court differentiate between a claim for betterment and one for mere rectification of damage? What happens if a plaintiff goes beyond mere rectification of damage? Will this necessarily mean that it will be denied an award of damages by a court?

 Guided response in the eBook

COST OF REPAIRS NOT PAID FOR BY THE PLAINTIFF

It is noteworthy that, although the general principle supports the notion that it is the actual cost of repair that is the relevant measure of damages, if the plaintiff is able to have the repairs done without cost, this will not result in a reduction to that amount.[121]

REPLACEMENT COSTS

In cases where the property has been destroyed or the plaintiff has been permanently deprived of possession, damages will be assessed as the cost of replacement (ie, the market value of the property destroyed).[122]

Further, if a reasonable substitute is available for a price significantly less than the cost of repair, that replacement cost is the measure of the damages.[123]

BETTERMENT

In the event that the plaintiff is awarded damages measured by the cost of replacement or repairs, an allowance is to be made for any improvement or betterment that the superior replacement brings. The plaintiff can recover the cost of such repair or replacement if it is not unreasonable or extravagant.

So, in the New South Wales Court of Appeal decision of *Hyder Consulting (Australia) Pty Ltd v Wilh Wilhelmsen Agency Pty Ltd*,[124] the respondent owner was awarded damages against the appellant engineer for the costs of replacing a negligently constructed pavement that collapsed within four years of being built despite having an expected lifespan of 20 years. The Court differed on whether this 'new for old' damages amount represented a windfall to the appellant. Meagher JA held that it did and ordered a 20 per cent discount on the damages payable.[125] But the majority of the New South Wales Court of Appeal disagreed with this 'crude' method of discount.[126]

In the Victorian Court of Appeal decision of *Powercor Australia Ltd v Thomas*,[127] the respondent's business premises were damaged by flooding caused by the appellant's negligence. Although the respondent took the opportunity to completely refurbish those premises, the Court limited the damages payable to the reasonable reinstatement of the premises and 10 days of lost business, rather than the full cost of the refurbishment and the entire period of the closure. A similar finding was made by the New South Wales Court of Appeal in *Gagner Pty Ltd v Canturi Corporation Pty Ltd* as discussed above.[128]

CONSEQUENTIAL LOSS

As discussed in Section 8.3.3.1, consequential loss flowing from a tort in trespass to personal property is recoverable. Similar principles apply to other torts, such as negligence. If the

---

121 *The Endeavour* (1890) 6 Asp 511, 512; *Jones v Stroud District Council* [1988] 1 All ER 5, 13–14; *Powercor Australia Ltd v Thomas* (2012) 43 VR 220.
122 *Powercor Australia Ltd v Thomas* (2012) 43 VR 220.
123 Ibid.
124 [2001] NSWCA 313.
125 Ibid [22] (Meagher JA).
126 Ibid [55] (Sheller JA), [107] (Giles JA).
127 (2012) 43 VR 220.
128 (2009) 262 ALR 691.

property is profit-making, the plaintiff is entitled to the consequential loss of profits or the costs of hiring a substitute.[129]

MITIGATION OF LOSS

Where the plaintiff's conduct involves a failure to take reasonable action to lessen the damage of the wrongdoing, it may be considered unjust that the defendant compensate the whole of the loss that occurred as a consequence.

In the case of *Powercor Australia Ltd v Thomas* the principles of consequential loss and mitigation were interrelated.[130]

Case: *Powercor Australia Ltd v Thomas* (2012) 43 VR 220

Facts

The case concerned representative proceedings which arose out of a bushfire near Horsham in regional Victoria on 7 February 2009 ('Black Saturday') and which were settled. Certain questions relating to damages were reserved for the decision of the Court, including the assessment of the damages payable to the lead plaintiff for damage to fixtures on his farm. In particular, the lead plaintiff sustained the destruction of fences that he subsequently repaired after the fire; he was assisted in this by volunteers, who reinstated some of the fences and fixtures without charging the plaintiff.

Issue

Mitigation of loss and consequential loss.

Decision

The Court of Appeal held (per Osborn JA's leading judgment) that the loss occurred at the time of the destruction of the fences and other fixtures by the fire (ie, at the time of the wrongdoing by the defendant) and therefore the duty to mitigate had no relevant application: at [56]. Further, any obligation to mitigate if it existed did not bear on the relevant measure of direct loss; that is, Osborn JA rejected the notion that 'the fact a plaintiff undertakes or proposes to undertake repairs himself or herself displaces the ordinary measure of loss resulting from direct damage': at [59].

Osborn JA went on to explain how the consequential losses claimed by the plaintiff differed from the direct losses claimed by him, albeit both were in respect of repairing fencing:

> [67] Moreover, in cases such as the present, the undertaking of fence repairs may itself be reasonably necessary to mitigate consequential losses which would otherwise be suffered by way of agistment costs or loss of profit. Counsel for Powercor acknowledged in the course of argument that professional fencers were in short supply after the

---

129 *The Liesbosch v The SS Edison* [1933] AC 449, 446 (Lord Wright); *Glenmont Investments Pty Ltd v O'Loughlin* (2000) 79 SASR 185; *Powercor Australia Ltd v Thomas* (2012) 43 VR 220; *Winky Pop Pty Ltd v Mobil Refining Australia Pty Ltd* [2015] VSC 348, [145].
130 (2012) 43 VR 220.

Horsham fire. There was no suggestion that it was unreasonable for Thomas to himself repair his fences.

[68] In such circumstances, there is no necessary inconsistency between a claim for loss measured by reference to the reasonable cost of fencing and a claim for loss of profits in part resulting from the time spent effecting repairs.

Significance

Although a plaintiff normally has a duty to mitigate his or her loss, this principle does not apply in circumstances when the loss or damage occurs at the very moment of the defendant's wrongdoing (eg, the destruction of fences by bushfire), when it would be impossible or very difficult for the plaintiff to mitigate his or her loss.

In circumstances where the plaintiff has mitigated his or her loss, including by undertaking such repairs or reinstatement himself or herself, the 'ordinary measure' of the 'direct loss' or damage is not lessened or otherwise affected.

Where the mitigation of the loss by the plaintiff involves repairs or reinstatement by the plaintiff himself or herself, the amount of damages may be quantified by reference either to the loss of profits resulting from the plaintiff's time spent in effecting repairs or to the reasonable cost of fencing.

Question

How does the decision in *Powercor* impact on the common law principles relating to mitigation of loss and consequential loss?

    Guided response in the eBook

In a case where the plaintiff's large mechanical dinosaur, intended for profit-making activities, was damaged by the defendant, the Full Court of the South Australian Supreme Court allowed a claim for loss of profits as a consequential loss, although it lowered the amount payable.[131] The Court rejected the argument by the defendant that, because it was more probable than not that profits from the lost opportunity to display the dinosaur in America, to use it in a film, sequels, etc., would *not* have been made, no award at all should be made for loss of profits. Instead the Court considered that the approach of the trial judge was correct in principle, namely 'to assess the profits that might have been made, to assess the degree of likelihood that those profits would in fact have been realised, and then to adjust the award of damages accordingly'.[132]

Even if a plaintiff is deprived of non-profit-earning property, damages will be recoverable in principle. For example, plaintiffs deprived of their spare lightship for a period of repair

---

131 *Glenmont Investments Pty Ltd v O'Loughlin* (2000) 79 SASR 185.
132 Ibid [429] (Doyle CJ, Nyland and Martin JJ).

were entitled to substantial damages.[133] The explanation for this is on the basis of the 'need' principle (ie, the need to keep or replace that item of property).[134] This 'need' principle has been recognised by the High Court.[135]

12.3.4 Compensatory damages for personal injury

As observed in Section 12.3.2.1, compensatory damages compensate a plaintiff for the loss, harm or damage (what we have termed 'damage' in this chapter) suffered at the hands of the defendant, and aim to restore the plaintiff to the position they would have been in had the wrongdoing not occurred, which is known as the compensatory principle.

The High Court in *Lewis v Australian Capital Territory* reasoned that, consistent with the compensatory principle in *Haines v Bendall*, a 'counter-factual' or 'but for' test of causation was to be used for determining the 'loss' (what we have termed 'damage' in this chapter) suffered by the plaintiff by comparing the position of the plaintiff following the wrongdoing and their hypothetical position had the wrongdoing not occurred.[136]

12.3.4.1 Four basic principles

The High Court has stated four basic principles that apply to an award of compensatory damages for personal injury:

> Certain fundamental principles are so well established that it is unnecessary to cite authorities in support of them. In the first place, a plaintiff who has been injured by the negligence of the defendant should be awarded such a sum of money as will, as nearly as possible, put him in the same position as if he had not sustained the injuries. Secondly, damages for one cause of action must be recovered once and forever, and (in the absence of any statutory exception) must be awarded as a lump sum; the court cannot order a defendant to make periodic payments to the plaintiff. Thirdly, the court has no concern with the manner in which the plaintiff uses the sum awarded to him; the plaintiff is free to do what he likes with it. Fourthly, the burden lies on the plaintiff to prove the injury or loss for which he seeks damages.[137]

We will deal with each of these four principles in turn.

The first principle is the compensatory principle referred to in Section 12.3.2.1; namely, the aim to put the plaintiff in the monetary position he or she would have been in if the injury had not been sustained. Since it is impossible to restore to a condition of physical wholeness a person who has suffered serious physical injury, the *restitutio* or compensatory

---

133 *The Mediana* [1900] AC 113.

134 *Anthanasopoulos v Moseley* (2001) 52 NSWLR 262, [80] (Ipp AJA explaining such cases as *The Mediana* [1900] AC 113).

135 *Griffiths v Kerkemeyer* (1977) 139 CLR 161. See also *Yates v Mobile Marine Repairs Pty Ltd* [2007] NSWSC 1463 (loss of use of a pleasure yacht).

136 *Lewis v Australian Capital Territory* (2020) 271 CLR 192; [2020] HCA 26, [2] (Kiefel CJ and Keane J), [30]–[31] (Gageler J), [50], [63], [65] (Gordon J), [151] (Edelman J). Note the objection to this approach articulated in H Luntz and S Harder, *Assessment of Damages for Personal Injury and Death* (LexisNexis, 5th ed, 2021) [1.10.2], 202.

137 *Todorovic v Waller* (1981) 150 CLR 402, 412 (Gibbs CJ and Wilson J).

principle, therefore, must be qualified by the phrase 'so far as money can do so'.[138] The second principle is the once-and-for-all rule. This is the notion that damages are awarded on one occasion and cannot be varied later. Two consequences follow from this.

The first consequence is that damages, usually awarded as a lump sum, cannot later be varied if it becomes apparent that the award was not sufficient. This 'once for all' rule was established in the case of *Fetter v Beal*.[139] In that case, the plaintiff sued in battery claiming that the defendant broke his skull. The defendant was found liable and ordered to pay £11 in damages. Eight years later, the plaintiff, having recovered damages, brought a second action, because a portion of his skull had to be removed by trepanning (a surgical operation removing part of the bone of the skull with a cylindrical saw known as a trepan). The defendant successfully defended the action. Holt CJ stated that the 'once for all' rule was a matter of settled law and would not be overturned (it went back to the *wergeld* tariffs), and that if 'this matter' (presumably the additional damage) had been raised in earlier evidence, as a probable consequence of the battery, the plaintiff would have recovered damages for it.[140] Conversely, once fixed, the sum of damages is not decreased on the basis that subsequently the claimant might miraculously recover or die soon after the verdict.

The second consequence of the once-and-for-all rule is that it is necessary for courts to make predictions about the plaintiff's future circumstances in the making of damages awards. It is necessary for the court to estimate two matters: (1) what would have happened if not for the injury; and (2) what will now happen in the future to the plaintiff. The impossibility of these tasks has been recognised by the courts. In respect of restoring plaintiffs to the position they would have been in if they had not been injured, difficulties stem from the absence of a yardstick for non-economic loss, the inherent uncertainty about predicting the future, and not knowing what would have happened without the injury.[141] In respect of predicting what will now happen, the House of Lords commented:

> Knowledge of the future being denied to mankind, so much of the award as is to be attributed to future loss and suffering – in many cases the major part of the award – will almost surely be wrong. There really is only one certainty: the future will prove the award to be either too high or too low.[142]

It is arguable that the best that can be done is to base such awards on empirical research on probabilities of events rather than merely judicial hunch.

But note that the civil liability legislation has provided modifications to the once-and-for-all rule by way of various means: periodic payments, interim payments pending a final once-and-for-all payment, provisional payments with a specified event permitting further assessment and payment, and so-called structured settlements that provide for court-approved periodic payments of all or part of the damages.

Structured settlements are permitted under the civil liability legislation as set out in Table 12.1, although in reality many actions are settled and both parties generally prefer to settle for a lump sum.

---

138 *Harriton v Stephens* (2004) 59 NSWLR 694, [226]–[230] (Ipp JA).
139 (1701) 91 ER 1122, 1123.
140 Ibid 1123.
141 *Todorovic v Waller* (1981) 150 CLR 402, 413 (Gibbs CJ and Wilson J).
142 *Lim v Canada & Islington Area Health Authority* [1980] AC 174, 183.

Table 12.1   Provisions on structured settlements

Legislation	Section(s)
Similar legislation repealed by *Justice and Community Safety Legislation Amendment Act 2006* (ACT)	2.62
Civil Liability Act 2002 (NSW)	22–6
Personal Injuries (Civil Claims) Act 2003 (NT)	12
Personal Injuries (Liabilities and Damages) Act 2003 (NT)	31–2
Civil Liability Act 2003 (Qld)	63–7
Supreme Court Act 1935 (SA)	30BA
Civil Liability Act 2002 (Tas)	8
Wrongs Act 1958 (Vic)	28M, 28N
Civil Liability Act 2002 (WA)	14, 15

The advantages of these structured settlements are that they have no tax consequences and allow the plaintiff to manage his or her future finances with the prospect of future reassessment. Yet such arrangements do not apply to court awards, but only to settlements between the parties that are submitted to the court for approval.

The third principle is that the court does not care *how* the plaintiff spends the money. In addition, the court is not concerned *if* the plaintiff spends the award of damages, since damages may be awarded to a plaintiff who is permanently unconscious and thus incapable of making use of the money.[143]

The fourth principle is that the plaintiff bears the burden of proof on the issue of damages. In *Watts v Rake*[144] the High Court held that the plaintiff may rely on the difference between the pre- and post-accident condition; it is not for the plaintiff to disprove that the pre-accident condition would have eventually led to a similar incapacity. A change in the plaintiff's condition, once causally proven, is enough to raise a presumption of fact in the plaintiff's favour for the defendant to overcome.[145]

12.3.4.2   The impact of the civil liability legislation on compensatory damages

The principles governing the assessment of common law damages generally apply to personal injury cases. However, since 2001 there have been significant statutory modification of these principles in respect of personal injuries damages by the civil liability legislation in the Australian states and territories.

As discussed in Section 12.3.2.8, the introduction of the civil liability legislation led to greater uniformity across the states and territories in terms of exemplary damages; this has also been the case for compensatory damages. We will look at these provisions more closely in the following sections.

---

143   *Skelton v Collins* (1966) 115 CLR 94.
144   *Watts v Rake* (1960) 108 CLR 158.
145   Ibid 160 (Dixon CJ).

Several matters are worthy of note in respect of these pieces of legislation. First, the changes to personal injuries damages apply only to 'an award of personal injury damages'.[146] This specifically excludes 'an award where the fault concerned is an intentional act that is done with intent to cause death or injury or that is sexual assault or other sexual misconduct'[147] (see Table 12.1). Such 'intentional acts' may well include trespass torts (ie, the so-called intentional torts) but *only* where such torts *additionally* are 'done with intent to cause death or injury'. So, for instance, a battery caused by the negligence of the plaintiff may well satisfy the first intention requirement but not the second.[148] On the other hand, assault or intentional infliction of harm will likely satisfy both intention requirements.[149] Second, it must be remembered that the source of the damages award is the common law, not the legislation – the latter merely modifies the common law principles. Third, the provisions of the civil liability legislation have continued to be amended since their original implementation in 2003.

We now turn to the various 'heads of damage' that we referred to earlier to consider the types of loss that are claimed and awarded.

12.3.4.3 Heads of damage

How do the courts go about assessing damages? In the past the courts would simply award a 'global' sum of damages,[150] but today an itemisation of the award is made due to the application of civil liability statutes governing caps on all or part of the award and the application of different interest rates to different parts of the award.

The High Court has identified three types of loss that a plaintiff could recover if he or she suffers personal injury:

> A plaintiff who has suffered negligently caused personal injury is traditionally seen as able to recover three types of loss.
>
> The first covers non-pecuniary losses such as pain and suffering, disfigurement, loss of limbs or organs, loss of the senses – sight, taste, hearing, smell and touch; and loss of the capacity to engage in hobbies, sport, work, marriage and child-bearing. Damages can be recovered in relation to these losses even if no actual financial loss is caused and even if the damage caused by them cannot be measured in money.
>
> The second type of loss is loss of earning capacity both before the trial and after it. Although the damages recoverable in relation to reduced future income are damages for loss of earning capacity, not damages for loss of earnings simpliciter, those damages are awardable only to the extent that the loss has been or may be productive of financial loss. Hence 'the valuation of the loss of earning capacity involves the consideration of what moneys could have been produced by the exercise of the [plaintiff's] former earning capacity'.

---

146 See, eg, *Wrongs Act 1958* (Vic) s 28C(1).
147 See, eg, ibid s 28C(2).
148 See Section 8.3.1.2. See also *Fede v Gray by his tutor New South Wales Trustee and Guardian* (2018) 98 NSWLR 1149, [206] (Basten JA, Meagher JA agreeing, McColl JA dissenting) held that the defendant satisfied the first intention requirement in biting the plaintiff but not the second since he did not understand the nature of his actions and so did not 'intentionally cause injury to the plaintiff'.
149 See, eg, *Balven v Thurston* [2013] NSWSC 210, [41] (Latham J in obiter stated that the *Civil Liability Act 2002* (NSW) would not apply to assault on the basis of s 3B(1)).
150 *Arthur Robinson (Grafton) Pty Ltd v Carter* (1968) 122 CLR 649, 660 (Barwick CJ).

The third type of recoverable loss is actual financial loss, for example, ambulance charges; charges for medical, hospital and professional nursing services; travel and accommodation expenses incurred in obtaining those services; the costs of rehabilitation needs, special clothing and special equipment; the costs of modifying houses; the costs of funds management; and the costs of professionally supplied home maintenance services. It is not necessary for the costs actually to have been incurred by the time of the trial, but it is necessary that they will be incurred.[151]

The three 'heads of damage' referred to are organised slightly differently in what follows; that organisational structure is set out in Figure 12.3.

Figure 12.3 Three heads of damage in compensatory damages for personal injury

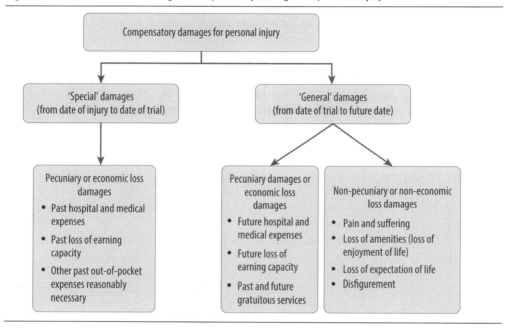

HINTS AND TIPS

The terms 'special damages' and 'general damages' are often used to divide awards of compensatory damages, although the terms can cause confusion. Special damages are awarded in respect of actual losses incurred and which are capable of precise calculation or estimation, such as from the date of the injury up to the date of verdict.[152] Such losses are also 'pecuniary' or economic or monetary, as they may be translated into monetary terms.[153]

---

151 *CSR Ltd v Eddy* (2005) 226 CLR 1; [2005] HCA 64, [28]–[31] (Gleeson CJ, Gummow and Heydon JJ).
152 *Paff v Speed* (1961) 105 CLR 549, 558–9 (Fullagar J, as discussed in Section 12.3.1.2).
153 *McRae v Commonwealth Disposals Commission* (1951) 84 CLR 377.

Special damages may be claimed for the following pecuniary or monetary or economic losses:

- past hospital and medical expenses
- past loss of earning capacity
- other monetary claims arising from the injury up until judgment or settlement.

General damages, on the other hand, are not capable of precise arithmetical calculation or estimation, and so are regarded as 'at large'; they rely for their estimation on tests developed in the common law and in statute to place a monetary value on such damages and which are therefore less certain than the tests used in calculating special damages.[154]

Pecuniary general damages compensate a plaintiff for:

- future hospital and medical expenses
- past and future gratuitous services
- any future loss of earning capacity.

Non-pecuniary general damages or non-economic loss damages compensate the plaintiff for:

- pain and suffering (past, present and future)
- loss of amenities/loss of enjoyment of life (past, present and future)
- loss of expectation of life
- disfigurement.

As can be observed in Figure 12.3, general and special damages can overlap; for instance, many of the types of damages referred to relate to both past and future harm or loss and so should be classified as both general and special damages, yet they are also incapable of precise calculation (eg, pain and suffering damages) and so are classified in the figure as 'general' damages. There has been some judicial comment on the blurring of this distinction between general and special damages.[155] In some High Court decisions, the term 'general damages' is usually a substitute for damages for non-pecuniary loss, while the term 'special damages' often includes all damages measurable in money, even those relating to the future (eg, future loss of earning capacity).[156] In the interests of clarity, it is perhaps better to avoid the terms 'general' and 'special' damages and instead refer to them as 'pecuniary' or 'economic loss', on the one hand, or 'non-pecuniary' or 'non-economic loss' damages, on the other, together with specific mention of the nature of the loss they are compensating (ie, medical expenses or loss of earning capacity).

---

154 *Paff v Speed* (1961) 105 CLR 549, 558–9 (Fullagar J).
155 *CSR Ltd v Eddy* (2005) 226 CLR 1; [2005] HCA 64, [90] (McHugh J) (referring to the introduction of *Griffiths v Kerkemeyer* damages).
156 See, eg, *Sharman v Evans* (1977) 138 CLR 563.

12.3.5 Pecuniary damages

Pecuniary damages or economic loss damages compensate the plaintiff for monetary loss caused by the injury. Following the High Court, the two principal heads of pecuniary loss are: (1) 'loss of earning capacity both before trial and after it'; and (2) actual financial loss because of 'needs' created by the injury.[157] These correspond to, respectively: (1) loss of earnings and loss of earning capacity; and (2) the costs of medical and other associated expenses due to the injury.

12.3.5.1 Loss of earning capacity and loss of earnings

The head of damage is 'loss of earning *capacity*' rather than 'loss of earnings'; but the loss is for the periods both 'before trial and after it'[158] and so, in practice, both the loss from the injury to the date of verdict and future loss of earning capacity from the date of verdict to retirement age are recoverable as damages.

The High Court has explained the difference between earning capacity and loss of earnings in this way:

> In Australia, a plaintiff is compensated for loss of earning capacity, not loss of earnings. In practice, there is usually little difference in result irrespective of whether the damages are assessed by reference to loss of earning capacity or by reference to loss of earnings. That is because 'an injured plaintiff recovers not merely because his earning capacity has been diminished but because the diminution of his earning capacity is or may be productive of financial loss'. Nevertheless, there is a difference between the two approaches, and the loss of earning capacity principle more accurately compensates a plaintiff for the effect of an accident on the plaintiff's ability to earn income. Earning capacity is an intangible asset. Its value depends on what it is capable of producing. Earnings are evidence of the value of earning capacity, but they are not synonymous with its value. When loss of earnings rather than loss of capacity to earn is the criterion, the natural tendency is to compare the plaintiff's pre-accident and post-accident earnings. This sometimes means that no attention is paid to that part of the plaintiff's capacity to earn that was not exploited before the accident. Further, there is a tendency to assume that if pre-accident and post-accident incomes are comparable, no loss has occurred.[159]

Further, loss of earning capacity means that 'damages are awardable only to the extent that the loss has been or may be productive of financial loss'.[160] So, 'on general principle, if a salaried ambulance worker and a volunteer ambulance worker are injured by the same tort which impairs their capacity to perform ambulance work, the former can recover damages calculated by reference to the probable earnings of ambulance workers, but not the latter.'[161]

---

157 *CSR Ltd v Eddy* (2005) 226 CLR 1; [2005] HCA 64, [28]–[31] (Gleeson CJ, Gummow and Heydon JJ).

158 Ibid.

159 *Medlin v State Government Insurance Commission* (1995) 182 CLR 1, 16 (McHugh J) (citations omitted).

160 *Graham v Baker* (1961) 106 CLR 340, 347, quoted in *CSR Ltd v Eddy* (2005) 226 CLR 1; [2005] HCA 64, [28]–[31] (Gleeson CJ, Gummow and Heydon JJ).

161 *CSR Ltd v Eddy* (2005) 226 CLR 1; [2005] HCA 64, [41].

When assessing a plaintiff's loss of earning capacity, the court compares 'the economic benefit' or earning capacity before injury and 'the economic benefit from exercising capacity after injury'.[162] This is a comparison of 'before' or 'without injury' earnings and 'after' or 'with injury' earnings.[163] The latter comparator will be the residual earning capacity and the possibility of the plaintiff being able to exploit that capacity for financial gain. Evidence of past earnings (eg, through income tax records) is the 'best evidential basis to assess the earning capacity of the claimant, but for the injury, subject to adjustment for the passage of time since that income was last earned'.[164] Further, although the plaintiff must show a diminution in earning capacity resulting from the injury to obtain an award of damages under this head, he or she is not required to identify the precise value of the loss.[165]

Sometimes 'loss of earning capacity' will include income earned by a partnership and so be different from that income earned by the plaintiff in his or her individual capacity.[166]

If a plaintiff provides evidence that his or her earnings in the future would have increased (eg, by promotion) had he or she not been injured, this may be taken into account by a court.[167]

As indicated, the loss of earning capacity for which the plaintiff is to be compensated must take into account anything that the plaintiff does earn or is capable of earning after the injury (ie, their 'residual' earning capacity). In the case of *McCracken v Melbourne Storm Rugby League Football Club Ltd*, a well-known footballer increased his property development activities after his injury, thus resulting in greater financial gains than his loss of earning capacity as a footballer.[168] The New South Wales Court of Appeal held that there were no damages to be awarded for his loss of earning capacity because he failed to show that he would have made similar gains if he had continued as a footballer.

12.3.5.2 Net earnings

The earnings taken into account in Australia are the net earnings that the plaintiff would have derived from the exercise of his or her earning capacity if not injured. That is, the plaintiff's loss of earning capacity is based on the weekly gross income of the plaintiff:

- Less tax. The amount awarded for loss of earning capacity is calculated at a net amount (ie, less income tax that would have been paid on the gross amount).[169] This includes deduction of the Medicare levy, as it is regarded as a tax.[170]

---

162 *Penrith City Council v Parks* [2004] NSWCA 201, [3] (Giles JA).

163 *Kallouf v Middis* [2008] NSWCA 61.

164 *Allianz Australia Insurance Ltd v Kerr* (2012) 83 NSWLR 302, [24]–[25] (Basten JA).

165 Ibid.

166 *Husher v Husher* (1999) 197 CLR 138; [1999] HCA 47, [21].

167 *Malec v JC Hutton Pty Ltd* (1990) 169 CLR 638. See also *Norris v Blake (No 2)* (1997) 41 NSWLR 49 (promising actor showed that his future earnings likely to be significant despite his earnings to the date of the trial being relatively modest).

168 [2007] NSWCA 353.

169 *British Transport Commission v Gourley* [1956] AC 185; *Cullen v Trappell* (1980) 146 CLR 1.

170 Queensland and Victoria have confirmed this common law rule, legislating that notional income tax is taken into account: *Civil Proceedings Act 2011* (Qld) s 60; *Wrongs Act 1958* (Vic) s 28A. In the other jurisdictions, the High Court decision in *Cullen v Trappell* (1980) 146 CLR 1 is followed so as to require the deduction of income tax, including the Medicare levy.

- Less deductible expenses. The plaintiff's gross earnings must be reduced by expenses that the plaintiff would have incurred in producing those earnings.[171] Thus, transport expenses, union dues, uniform expenses and the like may be deducted. Childcare expenses, however, and other expenses not 'necessary' for earning are not to be deducted.[172]

- Plus lost superannuation contributions compulsorily paid by employers in some states. This amount is capped to the minimum level of compulsory employers' contribution required under the relevant Commonwealth legislation as a percentage of the lost earning capacity by the civil liability legislation in some states.[173] The NSW Court of Appeal has considered some of the issues concerning the inclusion of superannuation contributions in a damages award for loss of earning capacity; in particular, (1) how to take into account its 'present value' and (2) whether that contribution needed to be calculated by actuarial means.[174]

- Less the 'discount rate' (discussed in Section 12.3.5.8).

12.3.5.3 Assessment period

For *past* loss of earning capacity, the relevant period of assessment is the period from the date of injury to the date of verdict or judgment.

For *future* loss of earning capacity, the period of assessment is from the date of judgment to the pre-accident expected date of retirement, if there is permanent impairment, or up until the date when the plaintiff will be able to resume their full capacity to work again. Accordingly, the court must take into account the likely duration of the plaintiff's incapacity for work and the probable duration of the plaintiff's remaining working life, comparing what this was before the accident to what it is post the accident.[175] The calculation of the plaintiff's loss of earning capacity is made over the period during which the plaintiff might have been expected to earn if the injury had not occurred, as illustrated in *Skelton v Collins*.[176]

In *Skelton v Collins* a 17-year-old plaintiff suffered severe brain injury that rendered him permanently unconscious. At issue before the High Court was whether damages for loss of future earning capacity should be assessed by reference to the reduced period of the plaintiff's life expectancy due to his injuries (it was agreed that the plaintiff would live only another six months beyond the trial) or by reference to the whole period during which he would have been capable of earning had he not been injured. The Court determined that it was the latter; the amount should be calculated by reference to the plaintiff's pre-accident lifespan.[177]

But this assessment period may be reduced or extended on evidence presented about the particular plaintiff: for example, evidence demonstrating that the plaintiff had a pre-existing

171 *Sharman v Evans* (1977) 138 CLR 563.
172 *Wynn v NSW Insurance Ministerial Corporation* (1995) 184 CLR 485.
173 *Civil Liability Act 2002* (NSW) s 15C; *Civil Liability Act 2003* (Qld) s 56; *Civil Liability Act 1936* (SA) s 56A (motor vehicle accidents); *Civil Liability Act 2002* (Tas) s 25.
174 *Zorom Enterprises Pty Ltd v Zabow* (2007) 71 NSWLR 354.
175 A Stickley, *Australian Torts Law* (LexisNexis Butterworths, 4th ed, 2016) [15.78], 401.
176 *Skelton v Collins* (1966) 115 CLR 94.
177 Ibid 121 (Taylor J, Kitto, Menzies, Windeyer and Owen JJ agreeing).

medical condition that meant he would not have worked all the way up to normal retirement age; or, the corollary, that he would have worked beyond the normal retirement age.[178]

The period of time by which the plaintiff's working life is shortened due to the defendant's negligence is taken into account by the court. Damages are still awarded for this period, referred to as the 'lost years' component (ie, the calculation of the number of years between the post-accident age of death to the pre-accident date of retirement). But the loss of earning capacity for these 'lost years' is reduced by deducting the likely living expenses of the plaintiff (since the plaintiff will no longer incur such living expenses when they are dead).[179] This deduction for expenses saved during the 'lost years' would be 'at a standard which the plaintiff's job and career prospects at time of death would suggest he was reasonably likely to achieve'.[180]

12.3.5.4 Earnings cap

All Australian jurisdictions have placed limits on the amount of an award for loss of earning capacity. Except for South Australia, all jurisdictions have capped such damages at three times the average weekly earnings. In South Australia, damages for loss of earning capacity must not exceed the prescribed maximum amount for total damages.

The earnings caps in the relevant civil liability statutes in each state are set out in Table 12.2.

Table 12.2   Caps on awards of loss of earning capacity damages

Legislation	Section
Civil Law (Wrongs) Act 2002 (ACT)	98
Civil Liability Act 2002 (NSW)	12
Personal Injuries (Liabilities and Damages) Act 2003 (NT)	20
Civil Liability Act 2003 (Qld)	54
Civil Liability Act 1936 (SA)	54
Civil Liability Act 2002 (Tas)	26
Wrongs Act 1958 (Vic)	28F
Civil Liability Act 2002 (WA)	11

In all jurisdictions, except Queensland and Victoria, the relevant provisions require that the court disregard the amount (if any) by which the plaintiff's average weekly earnings would (but for the death or injury) have exceeded the three times average weekly earnings cap.

This has been interpreted as meaning that the cap must be applied to the first component in the calculation of lost earnings (earnings 'but for' the injury) *before* deducting actual earnings after the injury and before making a deduction for vicissitudes.[181] The anomalous consequence of this approach is that, of two persons with differing amounts of actual loss, the person with the higher loss may obtain a lower amount of damages (or no damages at all, as in the case of *Tuohey v Freemasons Hospital*). The relevant provisions in Queensland

---

178 *Ascic v Westel Co-operative Ltd* [1992] Aust Torts Reports 81-159.
179 *Skelton v Collins* (1966) 115 CLR 94; *Sharman v Evans* (1977) 138 CLR 563.
180 *Gammell v Wilson* [1982] AC 27, 78 (Lord Scarman), approved in *Fitch v Cates* (1982) 150 CLR 482.
181 *Tuohey v Freemasons Hospital* (2012) 37 VR 180.

and Victoria initially adopted wording to this effect, but recent amendments to them mean that the cap now applies to the 'amount of damages' and thus to the end result of calculating lost earnings. Therefore, although it remains possible in Queensland and Victoria for two persons with differing amounts of actual loss to obtain the same amount of damages, it is no longer possible that the person with the higher loss obtains a lower amount of damages (or no damages).

12.3.5.5   Hospital and medical expenses

A plaintiff may claim the reasonable and necessary expenses arising from hospital and medical treatments due to their injuries.[182]

The general rule is that a plaintiff can recover damages where the disabilities caused by the tortious act of the defendant had caused or might cause financial loss.[183] This head of damages might include such items as pharmaceutical expenses, costs of future medical aids and equipment, and future hospital costs (eg, future operations or therapies).

In respect of past hospital and medical expenses arising between the date of injury and the date of judgment, and so classified as 'special' damages, a plaintiff need not have actually disbursed the fees, provided they are due and payable.[184] Nor is it necessary that the plaintiff be under any legal liability to reimburse some other party who has paid such expenses.[185]

Future hospital and medical expenses include those costs payable for the period from the date of judgment until the expected date of recovery or, if the plaintiff is permanently injured, until the expected date of death.[186]

The requirement, for both past and future hospital and medical expenses, is that they are (1) reasonable and (2) necessary to the plaintiff's injuries.[187] This was expressed by the High Court in the following terms in *Sharman v Evans*:

> The touchstone of reasonableness in the case of the cost of providing nursing and medical care for the plaintiff in the future is, no doubt, cost matched against health benefits to the plaintiff. If the cost is very great and benefits to health slight or speculative the cost-involving treatment will clearly be unreasonable, the more so if there is available an alternative and relatively inexpensive mode of treatment, affording equal or only slightly lesser benefits.[188]

On the facts of *Sharman v Evans*, the plaintiff was rendered a quadriplegic as a result of her injuries; the issue before the High Court was whether it was reasonable for the defendant to pay the expenses for the costs of caring for her at home, since they were approximately four

---

182   *Sharman v Evans* (1977) 138 CLR 563.
183   *Graham v Baker* (1961) 106 CLR 340.
184   *Blundell v Musgrave* (1956) 96 CLR 73.
185   *Donnelly v Joyce* [1974] QB 454; *Renner v Orchard* [1967] QWN 3.
186   *Sharman v Evans* (1977) 138 CLR 563.
187   Ibid.
188   Ibid 573 (Gibbs and Stephen JJ, Jacobs J agreeing on this point).

times the cost of caring for her in hospital. The Court held that the benefit to the plaintiff being cared for at home was not reasonable because it did not result in:

> any benefit to her health but rather to her future enjoyment of life which would be enhanced by the home atmosphere; her life would not thereby be prolonged nor would her physical condition be at all improved; indeed she would be somewhat more at risk physically than in hospital. There is no evidence suggesting any likely psychiatric benefits, probable though these might appear to the layman.[189]

The cost of home care in the case of a serious injury is considerably more expensive than the cost of institutional care. But in all cases the court must consider the reasonableness of the cost.

Although the High Court found the costs of home care versus institutional care unreasonable on the basis of the evidence in the case of *Sharman v Evans*, it appears that community attitudes and institutional healthcare costs have changed since then. A series of cases have awarded the costs of stay-at-home care because the significant health benefits made such expenses reasonable.[190]

The costs of the treatment itself must be reasonable. The cost of a surgical operation, required only because medical advice had not been followed in the first instance, was not allowed by way of damages by the Supreme Court of Western Australia.[191] The costs of physiotherapy expenses that were $2000 more than the fees recommended by the Australian Physiotherapists Association were reduced by the South Australian Supreme Court by that amount representing the difference between the two.[192] The cost of a visit to Lourdes was held not to be reasonably necessary for the plaintiff's condition by the Supreme Court of the Australian Capital Territory.[193]

In a similar vein, the cost of home renovations or vehicle modifications must be judged as reasonable by the court in terms of conferring a health benefit sufficient to justify the cost of those changes. In *Diamond v Simpson (No 1)*, the plaintiff suffered cerebral palsy as a result of a negligent forceps delivery by the defendant medical practitioner.[194] The plaintiff succeeded in recovering damages for the costs of having a home purpose built for her or modified for her disabilities. However, the New South Wales Court of Appeal rejected the plaintiff's claim for the costs of modifying her parents' home, as she would no longer be living there. It also rejected her claim for the costs of modifying a holiday house owned by her parents, as this house was only used a few times per year.

---

189 Ibid 573–4 (Gibbs and Stephen JJ).
190 See, eg, *Government Insurance Office (NSW) v Mackie* [1990] Aust Torts Reports 81-053; *Burford v Allen* (1993) 60 SASR 428; *Rosecrance v Rosecrance* (1995) 105 NTR 1, 25 (Mildren J) (SC), upheld in (1998) 8 NTLR 1, 27–8 (CA).
191 *Laut & Loughlin v White Feather Main Reefs* (1905) 7 WALR 203.
192 *Kostik v Giannakopoulos* (1989) Aust Torts Reports 80-274.
193 *Lipovac v Hamilton Holdings Pty Ltd* (1997) 136 FLR 400. See also *Neal v CSR Ltd* (1990) Aust Torts Reports 81-052; *Perry v Australian Rail Track Corporation Ltd* (2013) 64 MVR 121.
194 *Diamond v Simpson (No 1)* (2003) Aust Torts Reports 81-695.

Case: *Sharman v Evans* (1977) 138 CLR 563

Facts

The plaintiff was injured in a road accident at the age of 20. She suffered quadriplegia, epilepsy, severe respiratory impairment and ongoing pain in her right shoulder, and had lost her power of speech and some intellectual capacity; however, she remained aware of her predicament. The plaintiff was awarded $150 000 to $175 000 to provide for future costs of nursing and medical care, which involved an assumption that the plaintiff would not spend all of the rest of her life in hospital but would instead spend periods being cared for at home.

Issue

The issue before the High Court was whether it was reasonable for the defendant to pay for the costs of caring for the plaintiff at home, since they were approximately four times the cost of caring for her in hospital. Gibbs and Stephens JJ (the leading majority of the High Court) explained at 573 [14] what 'reasonable' meant:

> The appropriate criterion must be that such expenses as the plaintiff may reasonably incur should be recoverable from the defendant; as Barwick CJ put it in *Arthur Robinson (Grafton) Pty Ltd v Carter*: 'The question here is not what are the ideal requirements but what are the reasonable requirements of the respondent'. The touchstone of reasonableness in the case of the cost of providing nursing and medical care for the plaintiff in the future is, no doubt, cost matched against health benefits to the plaintiff. If cost is very great and benefits to health slight or speculative the cost-involving treatment will clearly be unreasonable, the more so if there is available an alternative and relatively inexpensive mode of treatment, affording equal or only slightly lesser benefits [citations omitted].

Decision

It was held, by a majority of 3:2 (Barwick CJ at 567, Gibbs and Stephen JJ at 573–4) that it was not reasonable to make an award for the costs of care for the plaintiff for those periods in which the plaintiff would be cared for by nurses at home (in addition to the expenses for her care in hospital).

Significance

The High Court clarified that the notion of 'reasonableness' as a criterion for the award of damages in nursing and medical care is to be determined on the basis of cost versus health benefits to the plaintiff.

Question

How do you think the High Court would decide the issue in *Sharman v Evans* (1977) 138 CLR 563 if it came before the Court today, particularly in light of subsequent decisions?

 Guided response in the eBook

12.3.5.6   Gratuitous services provided to the plaintiff

While the ordinary rule for the recovery of damages was that a plaintiff could recover damages only where the disabilities had caused or might cause *financial loss*,[195] the High Court has introduced the principle that a plaintiff could recover damages in respect of the (hypothetical) costs to a family member of fulfilling the natural obligations to attend to the injuries and disabilities caused to the plaintiff by the tort.[196] These damages are provided on the basis of the *need* of the plaintiff for the care, not the cost to the plaintiff of obtaining that care.

Damages that are awarded for home care, despite the fact that the care is provided gratuitously, are called at common law '*Griffiths v Kerkemeyer* damages' after this seminal case.

Case: *Griffiths v Kerkemeyer* (1977) 139 CLR 161

Facts

The plaintiff was rendered a quadriplegic as the result of the defendant's negligent act in a motor vehicle accident. He was awarded damages, which included a sum representing the value of services rendered and to be provided to him by his fiancée and members of his family. The services had been provided to him gratuitously.

Issue

The High Court held that damages for economic loss were payable to the plaintiff based on the need of the plaintiff for care, but not the actual costs of obtaining that care.

Decision

The High Court held that the gratuitous services were recoverable as damages. Further:

- The sum in question was recoverable as damages even though the plaintiff was under no legal liability to pay for the services.
- The value of such services in general should be calculated by reference to their standard or market cost, and not by the loss suffered by the person who provides them.

Significance

The High Court departed from its previous decision in *Blundell v Musgrave* (1956) 96 CLR 73, 79 and 92, in which it had held that expenses in an action for damages for personal injuries could only be recovered where there was, or would be, a legal obligation to pay them.

---

195 *Blundell v Musgrave* (1956) 96 CLR 73.
196 *Griffiths v Kerkemeyer* (1977) 139 CLR 161.

Question

On what basis did the High Court explain its rationale to award damages in this case?

 Guided response in the eBook

The High Court has confirmed that the true basis of a claim for gratuitous care damages is the *need* of the plaintiff for those services, and that the plaintiff does not have to show that the need is or may be productive of financial loss.[197]

The High Court has awarded damages for gratuitous attendant care services, even in circumstances where it was the tortfeasor defendant who was providing the services gratuitously to the plaintiff.[198] The Court rejected as artificial the defendant's argument that this would result in 'double' compensation to the plaintiff. The Court pointed out that the plaintiff's needs remained the same, regardless of who provided the services.[199] The Court also recognised that the 'vicissitudes of life … could throw the plaintiff back on others, including commercial caregivers, for services no longer provided by the tortfeasor'; in such a case, the compensation was necessary.[200]

The manner in which such damages are valuated and the limitations on them are covered next.

VALUATION OF GRATUITOUS SERVICES

In *Van Gervan v Fenton*, the High Court considered the principles governing the valuation of gratuitous care services.[201] The Court confirmed that, given that the true basis of a claim for gratuitous care damages was the *need* of the plaintiff for those services, the plaintiff's damages 'are not determined by reference to the actual cost to the plaintiff of having [the care or services] provided or by reference to the income foregone by the provider of the services', but generally by reference to 'the market cost of [providing the] services'.[202] In that case, the High Court awarded damages for gratuitous attendant care services at the market rate, not on the basis of the service provider's (the plaintiff's wife) 'lost' income as a nurse's aide.

Statutory provisions provide caps on the amount of damages payable for gratuitous services and on how those services are valued.

STATUTORY LIMITATIONS ON GRATUITOUS SERVICES

Provisions in the states' civil liability legislation provide some limitations to these *Griffiths v Kerkemeyer* damages, namely by:

- defining the *types* of services recoverable as damages under this head

---

197 *Kars v Kars* (1996) 187 CLR 345, 379–82 (Toohey, McHugh, Gummow and Kirby JJ).
198 Ibid (in this case, the plaintiff's husband was the tortfeasor defendant).
199 Ibid 382 (Toohey, McHugh, Gummow and Kirby JJ).
200 Ibid.
201 (1992) 175 CLR 327, 333 (Mason CJ, Toohey and McHugh JJ).
202 Ibid.

- setting out thresholds for the duration and frequency of such services to be recoverable under this head
- providing a cap on the quantum of damages under this head.

The limitations on damages for gratuitous services provisions in the relevant civil liability statutes in each state are set out in Table 12.3. In South Australia, s 58(4) of the *Civil Liability Act 1936* (SA) is confined to persons suffering personal injuries in a motor vehicle accident.

Table 12.3 Limitations on damages for gratuitous services

Legislation	Terminology	Thresholds	Caps
No legislation in ACT restricting awards			
Civil Liability Act 2002 (NSW)	s 15(1) defines concepts of 'attendant care services' and 'gratuitous attendant care services'	s 15(2)–(3)	s 15(4)–(5)
Personal Injuries (Liabilities and Damages) Act 2003 (NT)	s 18(1) defines 'gratuitous services'	s 23(1)	s 23(3), (4)
Civil Liability Act 2003 (Qld)	Concept of 'gratuitous services provided to an injured person' (s 59) not defined	s 59(1)	none
Civil Liability Act 1936 (SA)	No definition of 'gratuitous services' (s 58)	s 58(1) s 58(4)	s 58(2)–(3) s 58(4)
Civil Liability Act 2002 (Tas)	s 3 defines 'gratuitous services' (s 28B)	s 28B(1)–(2)	s 28B(3)
Wrongs Act 1958 (Vic)	s 28B defines concepts of 'attendant care services' and 'gratuitous attendant care services'	s 28IA(1)–(2)	s 28IB
Civil Liability Act 2002 (WA)	No definitions but s 12(1) refers to 'the awarding of damages for gratuitous services of a domestic nature or gratuitous services relating to nursing and attendance that have been or are to be provided to the person in whose favour the award is sought by a member of the same household or family as the person'	s 12(2)–(5)	s 12(5)–(7)

As can be seen in Table 12.3, the terminology used in the civil liability legislation to refer to these *Griffiths v Kerkemeyer* damages is not uniform. However, generally, the relevant services are those provided by way of home care that are akin to nursing services. For instance, the term 'attendant care services' is defined in s 28B of the *Wrongs Act 1958* (Vic) as 'any of the following':

- services of a domestic nature
- services relating to nursing or
- services that aim to alleviate the consequences of an injury.

Of course, it is essential that these services are provided at no cost to the plaintiff (ie, for free). The term 'gratuitous attendant care services' is defined in s 28B of the *Wrongs Act 1958* (Vic) as 'attendant care services' that have to be provided or are provided by another person to the plaintiff for which the plaintiff 'has not paid or is not liable to pay'. Significantly, the definition requires that the services are provided *to the plaintiff*; services that are provided to someone other than the plaintiff (eg, the plaintiff's children or dependants) are dealt with under a separate head of damages, namely damages for the loss of ability to provide gratuitous care for *others*.[203]

The thresholds in the legislation require the plaintiff to show that the services have been provided based on the need of that plaintiff, namely a substantial need for the services caused by the effects of the personal injury suffered due to the wrongdoer's negligence. Illustrative of this is s 28IA(1) of the *Wrongs Act 1958* (Vic), which provides that damages for gratuitous attendant care services are not to be awarded unless three conditions are satisfied, namely:

    (a)   there is (or was) a reasonable need for the services to be provided; and

    (b)   the need has arisen (or arose) *solely* because of the injury to which the damages relate; and

    (c)   the services would not be (or would not have been) provided ... but for the injury.[204]

Section 28IA(1) reflects the common law requirement of reasonableness and the need for a causal link between the wrong and the injury that is claimed. But s 28IA alters the common law by precluding a plaintiff from claiming for gratuitous care where that care is minor (ie, the costs do not exceed the monetary threshold) and is of the kind that would normally be provided by family members or others (ie, not for injuries).

The court needs to make a comparison between provision of gratuitous services before and after the accident. This was illustrated in the case of *Woolworths Ltd v Lawlor*, in which the plaintiff's husband provided services of a domestic nature to the plaintiff following her injury.[205] The defendant argued that part of these services should not be compensable as damages because they were provided for the benefit of the household and not just in respect of the plaintiff's post-injury condition. The New South Wales Court of Appeal rejected this argument and held that the services were 'solely' due to the accident. In obiter, however, Beazley JA (Hodgson and Tobias JJA agreeing) considered a hypothetical example of a plaintiff with a pre-existing condition who required assistance of 5 hours per week before the accident, and 15 hours per week of post-accident gratuitous care. Beazley JA interpreted s 15(2)(b) of the *Civil Liability Act 2002* (NSW) as allowing for an award of 10 hours for gratuitous attendant care services because the need for those additional 10 hours had arisen 'solely because of the injury to which the damages relate'.[206]

In addition to this requirement for a causal nexus between the injury and the gratuitous services, those services must be of a certain minimum level in terms of their intensity/ frequency and duration, before damages will be awarded. The basis for these requirements was a recommendation of the *Review of the Law of Negligence* ('Ipp Report') that two preconditions should apply to such awards, namely: (1) the intensity of such services should be for at least six hours per week; and (2) their duration should be for at least six months.[207]

---

203 See Section 12.3.5.7.
204 Emphasis added.
205 [2004] NSWCA 209.
206 Ibid [28].
207 *Review of the Law of Negligence* (Final Report, September 2002) 203–5.

It has become apparent that this recommendation was not implemented by the wording of the relevant civil liability provisions, as illustrated by the divergence that exists between Victoria, on the one hand, and New South Wales and Queensland, on the other.

In Victoria s 28IA(2) of the *Wrongs Act 1958* (Vic) states:

> [N]o damages may be awarded to a claimant for gratuitous attendant care services if the services are provided, or are to be provided –
>
> (a)   for less than 6 hours per week; and
>
> (b)   for less than 6 months.

In New South Wales s 15(3) of the *Civil Liability Act 2002* (NSW) states:[208]

> [N]o damages may be awarded to a claimant for gratuitous attendant care services unless the services are provided (or to be provided):
>
> (a)   for at least 6 hours per week, and
>
> (b)   for a period of at least 6 consecutive months.

The critical difference in wording is the use of 'if' in the Victorian provision in contrast to 'unless' in the New South Wales and Queensland equivalents. The Victorian Supreme Court of Appeal interpreted s 28IA(2) of the *Wrongs Act 1958* (Vic) as *precluding* a common law right (to gratuitous damages); as such this prohibition *did not* operate unless those services were of a kind that fell within *both* paragraphs (a) and (b).[209] In contrast, the New South Wales Court of Appeal interpreted s 51(3) as prohibiting the common law right to gratuitous damages unless both paragraphs (a) and (b) were satisfied; both needed to be met before an entitlement arose.[210] In a similar manner to this, the Queensland Court of Appeal characterised s 59(1)(c) of the *Civil Liability Act 2003* (Qld) as restricting a plaintiff's previously unfettered common law right, and interpreted the provision, on its 'ordinary meaning', to require that both conditions in paragraphs (a) and (b) be met for the entitlement to arise.[211]

As indicated in *Van Gervan v Fenton*, the High Court calculated gratuitous services based on their ordinary market value.[212] This market value links the amount recoverable by way of damages to 'average weekly earnings'. For instance, s 28IB of the *Wrongs Act 1958* (Vic) refers to 'average weekly total earnings of all employees in Victoria'. Where the services are for more than 40 hours per week, gratuitous damages cannot exceed the 'average weekly total earnings of all employees in Victoria', as published by the Australian Bureau of Statistics; and where the services are for less than 40 hours per week, the damages will be pro-rated to an hourly rate, being one-fortieth of the 'average weekly total earnings of all employees in Victoria'.

---

208   The *Civil Liability Act 2003* (Qld) s 59(1)(c) is in substantially the same form.

209   *Alcoa Portland Aluminium Pty Ltd v Victorian WorkCover Authority* (2007) 18 VR 146, [40] (Chernov JA, Maxwell ACJ and Neave JA agreeing).

210   *Hill v Forrester* (2010) 79 NSWLR 470, [2] (Tobias JA), [105] (Sackville AJA).

211   *Kriz v King* [2007] 1 Qd R 327, [18] (McMurdo P, Jerrard and Helman JJ agreeing). In *Grice v Queensland* [2006] 1 Qd R 222, [24] (McMurdo P, McPherson and Williams JJA agreeing) the Court of Appeal considered the precursor civil liability legislation, which contained virtually identical wording, and held that both conditions needed to be met.

212   *Van Gervan v Fenton* (1992) 175 CLR 327.

12.3.5.7 Loss of ability of plaintiff to provide gratuitous services to others

If the plaintiff, after suffering injury, is no longer able to care for others, is this recoverable as a head of damages? For instance, if the plaintiff was a caregiver to an ill wife or husband, and those services were replaced after the plaintiff's injury by another family member who provided them gratuitously, would the cost of those services be recoverable as damages by the plaintiff?

PREVIOUS POSITION AT COMMON LAW

The previous position at common law was that the recovery of such damages by the plaintiff (known as 'Sullivan v Gordon damages') was controversial. In *Sullivan v Gordon*, it was held by the New South Wales Court of Appeal that a plaintiff could claim damages for their lost capacity to provide gratuitous services to others because of their injury.[213] The damages were payable at the ordinary market or commercial rate for such services.

This decision was followed by some, but not all, states and territories. It was followed in the Australian Capital Territory[214] and Western Australia[215] and such damages were recoverable in Queensland.[216]

PRESENT POSITION AT COMMON LAW

At common law, this head of damages is no longer available as a separate head of damages following the High Court decision in *CSR Ltd v Eddy*.[217] In that case the plaintiff, prior to trial, died of mesothelioma. He had also been the carer for his disabled wife. It was held that the plaintiff's estate was entitled to the costs of caring for the plaintiff's wife after his death. The High Court concluded:

- There was a distinction between loss of services rendered *by* the plaintiff prior to the accident and services rendered *to* the plaintiff afterwards. *Griffiths v Kerkemeyer* applied to the latter, but the former loss (dealt with by *Sullivan v Gordon*) was not one suffered by the plaintiff, but one suffered by the persons to whom the services were formerly rendered.

- There were sound policy reasons for allowing the plaintiff to recover *Sullivan v Gordon* damages for loss of services rendered *by* the plaintiff prior to the accident, but this must be a matter of legislative intervention.[218]

- If a plaintiff were no longer able to provide services to another, such a loss may be compensated as a loss of amenity.[219]

CIVIL LIABILITY LEGISLATION

In response to the decision in *CSR Ltd v Eddy*, some jurisdictions have amended the civil liability legislation to allow compensation in limited circumstances. For example, New

---

213 *Sullivan v Gordon* (1999) 47 NSWLR 319, 322 [2] (Mason P); 332 [59] (Beazley JA, with whom the rest of the Court agreed).
214 *Brown v Willington* [2001] ACTSC 100.
215 *Easther v Amaca Pty Ltd* [2001] WASC 328; *Thomas v Kula* [2001] WASCA 362.
216 *Sturch v Wilmott* [1997] 2 Qd R 310; *Waters v Mussig* [1986] 1 Qd R 224.
217 (2005) 226 CLR 1; [2005] HCA 64.
218 Ibid [66]–[67].
219 Ibid [76].

South Wales passed legislation effectively restoring the position in *Sullivan v Gordon*, as did Queensland and the Australian Capital Territory; but the Northern Territory, South Australia and Western Australia have not (see Table 12.4). The relevant civil liability legislation providing for damages for the plaintiff's loss of ability to provide gratuitous services to others in each state is set out in Table 12.4.

Table 12.4   Provisions providing for damages for the plaintiff's loss of ability to provide gratuitous services to others

Legislation	Section(s)
Civil Law (Wrongs) Act 2002 (ACT)	100
Civil Liability Act 2002 (NSW)	15B
Civil Liability Act 2003 (Qld)	59A–59B
Civil Liability Act 2002 (Tas)	28BA
Wrongs Act 1958 (Vic)	28ID, 28IE

Victoria had already passed legislation before *CSR Ltd v Eddy* was decided, a case that stated limited damages were recoverable but did not confer a positive statutory right to damages. In 2015, however, s 28ID of the *Wrongs Act 1958* (Vic) was amended to provide a positive statutory right of damages for the plaintiff's loss of ability to provide gratuitous services to family members only if the care:

- was provided to the plaintiff's 'dependants' (defined in s 28B as 'any persons who are wholly, mainly or in part dependent on the claimant at the time of the injury')[220] and

- was being provided for at least six hours per week and

- had been provided for at least six consecutive months before the injury (or there was a reasonable expectation that they would have been).

It seems clear from the wording of the provision that these are *cumulative* provisions; in other words, all must be satisfied before the plaintiff will be entitled to the damages. In addition, the Victorian legislation imposes the same monetary caps as for the loss of gratuitous services provided *to* the plaintiff under s 28IA.[221]

In respect of the New South Wales provisions, an issue has arisen regarding the phrase 'gratuitous domestic services' in s 15B(1) of the *Civil Liability Act 2002* (NSW). In a case in which the injured plaintiff had cared for his 14-year-old daughter who had spina bifida, by providing daily basic physiotherapy and massage, the defendant argued that such services were not 'domestic' in nature but rather palliative or nursing care, and so were not compensable. The Court of Appeal held that 'the phrase "domestic services" in s 15B should be given its ordinary meaning and not given a restricted meaning', since the outer limits of the meaning of that term were not clear and it could well go beyond the provision of housework and the like.[222]

---

220 Not limited to persons whom the plaintiff had a legal obligation to maintain: *Amaca Pty Ltd v Novek* [2009] NSWCA 50.

221 *Wrongs Act 1958* (Vic) s 28IE.

222 *Liverpool City Council v Laskar* (2010) 77 NSWLR 666, [61]–[62] (Whealy J, Beazley and Macfarlane JJA agreeing with this construction).

12.3.5.8   Deductions or allowances

Where awards of damages are for injuries that are serious and extend into the future, it is necessary that such awards take into account circumstances after the judgment. These include adjustments for the following:

- 'discount rate'
- contingencies or 'vicissitudes'
- 'saved' items of expenditure
- tax
- income from 'lost years'
- overlap between heads of damage
- collateral benefits.

Other matters to be taken into account, and which must usually be added to any calculation of an award of damages, include:

- interest on damages
- superannuation entitlements.

'DISCOUNT RATE'

The sum awarded for future economic losses, such as future medical expenses and loss of earning capacity, is discounted to bring it back to its present value. This discount is applied to take into account the fact that the plaintiff receives the money in the 'present', not at some future time, and so can theoretically invest the money immediately and earn interest on it, thus potentially obtaining a windfall.

The policy behind the idea of discounting to present value and its application was discussed in the case of *Todorovic v Waller*.[223]

Case: *Todorovic v Waller* (1981) 150 CLR 402

Facts

The case involved two appeals to the High Court. The first (*Todorovic v Waller*) involved a man aged 35 at the date of the trial, who had suffered brain damage that rendered him virtually unemployable. The second (*Jetson v Hankin*) concerned a man, aged 34 at the date of the trial, who also suffered brain damage and was unlikely to obtain further gainful employment.

---

223 (1981) 150 CLR 402.

Issue

What 'discount rate', if any, was appropriate to apply to the assessment of damages for loss of future earning capacity and for the cost of goods and services which the plaintiff would need in the future because of his injury?

Decision

The appropriate discount rate to be applied was 3 per cent. Five members of the Court were of the opinion, for different reasons, that a discount rate was necessary: Gibbs CJ and Wilson, Mason, Aickin and Brennan JJ. Individually, they would have applied different discount rates, but in order to settle the differences that had emerged among the state courts, they reached a compromise among themselves of a 3 per cent discount rate. Stephen and Murphy JJ dissented, on the basis that there was no justification for a discount rate at all. Thus, the High Court issued the following statement, which appears before its judgment at 409:

> In an action for damages for personal injuries, evidence as to the likely course of inflation, or of possible future changes in rates of wages or of prices, is inadmissible. Where there has been a loss of earning capacity which is likely to lead to financial loss in the future, or where the plaintiff's injuries will make it necessary to expend in the future money to provide medical or other services, or goods necessary for the plaintiff's health or comfort, the present value of the future loss ought to be quantified by adopting a discount rate of 3 per cent in all cases, subject, of course, to any relevant statutory provisions. This rate is intended to make the appropriate allowance for inflation, for future changes in rates of wages generally or of prices, and for tax (either actual or notional) upon income from investment of the sum awarded. No further allowance should be made for these matters.

Significance

This decision established that the applicable rate for the discount rate is 3 per cent at common law, which varies from the statutory discount rate of 5 per cent.

Question

Why was this issue of the appropriate rate to apply for the discount rate so controversial among members of the High Court?

 Guided response in the eBook

The 5 per cent discount rate is provided for in the civil liability legislation in each state except Western Australia (6 per cent), as set out in Table 12.5.

Table 12.5 Discount rates

Legislation	Section (s)
No legislation in ACT; therefore, 3% at common law	
Civil Liability Act 2002 (NSW)	14
Personal Injuries (Liabilities and Damages) Act 2003 (NT)	22
Civil Liability Act 2003 (Qld)	57
Civil Liability Act 1936 (SA)	3, 55
Civil Liability Act 2002 (Tas)	28A
Wrongs Act 1958 (Vic)	28I
Civil Liability Act 2002 (WA)	5 (6%)

Thus, if the civil liability legislation applies to the award of damages, namely if it is 'an award of personal injury damages' (eg, s 28C(1) of the *Wrongs Act 1958* (Vic)), the 5 per cent discount rate will apply. If, on the other hand, that legislation does not apply (eg, if the 'award where the fault concerned is an intentional act that is done with intent to cause death or injury or that is sexual assault or other sexual misconduct'[224]), then the common law 3 per cent rate will apply by default.[225]

CONTINGENCIES OR 'VICISSITUDES'

Consistent with the aim of putting the plaintiff back in the same position as if the accident had not occurred, the award of a lump sum to the plaintiff for the loss now is perceived to be of greater value than the loss in the future. This is because receipt of a lump sum in the present is certain, but the loss is contingent on events in the future such as the plaintiff living up until the time when the loss would have been incurred.

This means that a damages award is adjusted to take into account the normal vicissitudes of life that may affect future earning capacity and future needs for medical and other services.

With regard to loss of earning capacity, the court must always take into account the chances that the plaintiff might in any event have been affected by:

> Ill health, unemployment, road or rail accidents, wars, changes in industrial emphasis, so
> that industries move their location, or are superseded by new and different techniques,
> the onset and effect of automation and the mere daily vicissitudes of life.[226]

These contingencies need not be negative; all contingencies are not adverse: 'A particular plaintiff might have had prospects or chances of advancement and increasingly remunerative employment. Why count the buffets and ignore the rewards of fortune? Each case depends on its facts.'[227] In practice, however, lower courts almost always reduce the damages for future loss of earning capacity by a substantial amount.

---

224 *Wrongs Act 1958* (Vic) s 28C(2).
225 *Raper v Bowden* (2016) 76 MVR 369, [103]–[106].
226 *Arthur Robinson (Grafton) Pty Ltd v Carter* (1968) 122 CLR 649, 659 (Barwick CJ), cited favourably in *Wynn v NSW Insurance Ministerial Corporation* (1995) 184 CLR 485, 497 (Dawson, Toohey, Gaudron and Gummow JJ).
227 *Bresatz v Przibilla* (1962) 108 CLR 541, 544 (Windeyer J).

In terms of future needs for medical and other services in the future, the court must take into account whether the plaintiff will require institutional support or home support (see the discussion of *Wynn* in the case box), or particular surgical operations or devices, and so on.

What is the appropriate rate for contingencies in respect of loss of earning capacity? The discount is rarely more than 15 per cent, with a range usually between 10 and 15 per cent, according to the Western Australian Court of Appeal.[228] Professor Luntz claims that the 'conventional' rate in New South Wales is 15 per cent.[229] The High Court has expressed the view that prospective life expectancy tables issued by the Australian Bureau of Statistics (rather than 'historical' tables) should be used, as they make allowance for future improvement in life expectancy and so are more accurate than the alternative.[230]

An example of the application of these principles is illustrated in the decision in *Wynn v NSW Insurance Ministerial Corporation*.[231]

Case: *Wynn v NSW Insurance Ministerial Corporation* (1995) 184 CLR 485

Facts

The plaintiff aggravated a pre-existing spinal injury when she was 30 years old. At the time of this aggravation, she was working in a management role with American Express; she was ambitious with prospects of promotion. Prior to the accident she had needed to pay for child care in order to carry out her work. After the accident, she no longer needed that child care because she was working in a family business and could look after the children herself.

Issue

The issues before the High Court were as to the correct percentage rate to be applied to make allowance for the vicissitudes of life or contingencies and what particular factors should be taken into account in doing so in respect of the plaintiff's future loss of earning capacity.

Decision

The High Court held that the correct contingency rate to be applied on the facts was 12.5 per cent (Dawson, Toohey, Gaudron and Gummow JJ at 500, Brennan CJ agreeing); this was in contrast to the trial judge, who held that 5 per cent was appropriate and the Court of Appeal who held that 28 per cent was appropriate. The High Court came to this finding after taking into account the four usual contingencies of sickness, accident, unemployment, and industrial disputes (Dawson, Toohey, Gaudron and Gummow JJ at 498).

---

228 *Villasevil v Pickering* (2001) 24 WAR 167, [38].
229 H Luntz, *Torts: Cases and Commentary* (LexisNexis Butterworths, 9th ed, 2021) [9.2.40].
230 *Golden Eagle International Trading Pty Ltd v Zhang* (2007) 229 CLR 498; [2007] HCA 15, [68]–[70] (Kirby and Hayne JJ, Gummow, Callinan and Crennan JJ agreeing).
231 *Wynn v NSW Insurance Ministerial Corporation* (1995) 184 CLR 485.

Significance

The High Court confirmed the four matters that should be applied for the vicissitudes of life. These were mostly matters to do with the plaintiff's earning capacity and prospects for advancement and promotion or otherwise, rather than having regard to traditional and perhaps outmoded gender stereotypes, such as leaving the workforce because of the demands of parenting. The High Court rejected the Court of Appeal's finding that a 28 per cent deduction for contingencies was required based on a presumption that the plaintiff would 'at some stage [choose] or [be] forced to accept a less demanding job' (Dawson, Toohey, Gaudron and Gummow JJ at 494).

Question

How did the High Court apply the four matters relevant to contingencies on the facts to come to a finding that a 12.5 per cent adjustment was appropriate?

 Guided response in the eBook

When allowing for contingencies, the courts will distinguish between facts that are theoretically capable of being established with certainty and facts that can never be known for certain. This issue was discussed in *Malec v JC Hutton Pty Ltd*.[232]

Case: *Malec v JC Hutton Pty Ltd* (1990) 169 CLR 638

Facts

Joze Malec, a labourer in a meatworks between 1972 and 1980, developed brucellosis, an animal-borne disease, as a result of the negligence of his employer. This resulted in Mr Malec suffering a neurotic condition (ie, depression) that rendered him incapacitated for employment. From 1982 Mr Malec also suffered from a degenerative spinal condition, which was not caused by the brucellosis and which alone would have rendered him incapacitated for employment.

Issue

What method was to be used for allowing for future contingencies in the award of damages? The appeal was from a decision of the Full Court of the Supreme Court of Queensland, which refused to award Malec any damages for future loss of earnings or for future expenses for his neurotic condition on the basis that it was 'likely' (ie, more probable than not) that the deteriorating back condition would have led to a similar neurotic condition, even if he had not contracted the brucellosis.

---

232 (1990) 169 CLR 638.

Decision

The High Court held that the Full Court was wrong to deny all damages. For past losses, such as loss of income between the accident and the trial, the normal civil standard applies (ie, on the balance of probabilities); satisfaction of that standard means that the past loss is 'certain'. But the assessment of future or 'hypothetical' loss is not on the basis of the balance of probabilities standard. Rather, future losses will be given a value according to an estimate of their probability, unless the chance of the hypothetical event occurring was so small as to be disregarded or so likely as to be certain. Accordingly, the percentage probability of that contingency occurring will be applied to the future damages to either decrease or increase that amount.

As Deane, Gaudron and McHugh JJ said in respect of assessing future damages, at 642–3 [7]:

> If the law is to take account of future or hypothetical events in assessing damages, it can only do so in terms of the degree of probability of those events occurring. The probability may be very high – 99.9 per cent – or very low – 0.1 per cent. But unless the chance is so low as to be regarded as speculative – say less than 1 per cent – or so high as to be practically certain – say over 99 per cent – the court will take that chance into account in assessing the damages. Where proof is necessarily unattainable, it would be unfair to treat as certain a prediction which has a 51 per cent probability of occurring, but to ignore altogether a prediction which has a 49 per cent probability of occurring. Thus, the court assesses the degree of probability that an event would have occurred, or might occur, and adjusts its award of damages to reflect the degree of probability. The adjustment may increase or decrease the amount of damages otherwise to be awarded.

Their Honours went on to point out the erroneous reasoning of the Full Court. First, as explained, it was mistaken in treating a future contingency as 'certain' on the basis merely that a future event was more probable than not on the balance of probabilities. Second, the future scenario that the Full Court relied on was based on a contingency dependent on a further contingency, at 645 [9]:

> If, for example, and only by way of illustration, there was a 75 per cent probability of his becoming unemployable by reason of his back condition even if he had not contracted brucellosis and a 75 per cent chance that that unemployability would have caused a similar neurotic condition, there was only a 56.25 per cent chance (75% × 75%) that, if he had not contracted brucellosis, he would have developed a similar neurotic condition.

The High Court set aside the Full Court's award of damages and substituted an order that damages be assessed and reductions made for Malec in accordance with its own judgment.

Significance

The High Court determined that it was appropriate to take into account future hypothetical events by scaling damages as a percentage of the degree of probability of those events occurring rather than on an 'all-or-nothing' basis on the balance of probabilities. Rather, the relevant degree of probability that an event would have occurred or might occur, expressed as a percentage, was used to scale the award of damages upwards or downwards.

Notes

The High Court referred the matter to the Master to assess damages in accordance with his or her own judgment and the evidence on damages put before the Court of Appeal.

Questions

(1) How did the High Court's method of taking into account future hypothetical events (ie, the degree of probability that the plaintiff would have been incapacitated for employment due to the non-work-related degenerative spinal condition) differ from the approach taken by the Full Court of the Supreme Court of Queensland?

(2) Is the approach by the High Court in *Lewis v Australian Capital Territory* (discussed in Section 12.3.2.1) in treating as 'certain' the likelihood that Lewis would be detained even if he had not been falsely imprisoned, consistent with its approach in *Malec v JC Hutton Pty Ltd* [1990] HCA 20; (1990) 169 CLR 638 in treating future events as not legally certain and losses given a value dependant on an estimate of their probability?

 Guided responses in the eBook

SAVED EXPENDITURE

Where the plaintiff's working life is shortened by the injury, any items of expenditure that the plaintiff would usually expend for work-related purposes that have been saved because he or she can no longer work, or can no longer work full time, must be deducted from the award of damages for loss of earning capacity.

Such saved expenditure has been referred to as 'outgoings … necessarily incurred in or in connection with the employment or undertaking by which earning capacity is realised' and includes such items as the cost of clothing suitable to the particular employment, public transport costs, tools and equipment.[233] Trade magazines would also fall into this category.

The plaintiff's costs of maintaining herself or her dependants is not something for which a deduction is to be made when awarding damages for loss of earning capacity. For example, the plaintiff's living expenses, comprising board and lodging in the case of *Sharman v Evans*, was such a cost for which no deduction would ordinarily be made.[234] But the High Court added that if such costs gave rise to 'an element of double compensation', then they would be deducted; in that case, the plaintiff's board and lodging would doubly compensate because they would be part of any damages awarded for future hospital expenses.

In *Wynn v NSW Insurance Ministerial Corporation* the majority of the High Court determined that the plaintiff's childcare expenses could not be regarded as costs 'necessarily

---

233 *Wynn v NSW Insurance Ministerial Corporation* (1995) 184 CLR 485, 495 (Dawson, Toohey, Gaudron and Gummow JJ), citing *Sharman v Evans* (1977) 138 CLR 563, 577 (Gibbs and Stephen JJ).

incurred in or in connection with the employment or undertaking by which earning capacity is realised' since they merely provided 'an opportunity to realise that capacity' and were one of a number of discretionary costs associated with having children that parents could choose or not choose to pay and so were 'essentially private or domestic in nature'.[235]

TAX TO BE DEDUCTED

Tax is to be deducted from the amount of damages payable by way of lost earning capacity. The High Court in *Cullen v Trappell*[236] determined that an amount awarded for lost earning capacity must take into account (ie, deduct) income tax that would have been payable.

The Medicare levy is an amount paid in addition to the tax paid on taxable income under s 251S of the *Income Tax Assessment Act 1936* (Cth). Like income tax, the Medicare levy is a tax and so deducted in the same way.[237]

Queensland and Victoria have legislated that notional income tax is taken into account.[238] As for the other states and territories, a deduction representing income tax must be made in accordance with the position at common law.[239]

COLLATERAL SOURCE RULE

A plaintiff will often receive payments in respect of his or her injuries from third-party sources other than the defendant. This is inevitable given the usual delay between the plaintiff suffering the personal injury and receiving damages as compensation; this period is likely to be a minimum of three years and possibly extend to more than 10 years. These 'collateral benefits' might include sick pay, pensions, unemployment benefits, disability benefits, insurance policy payments, charitable assistance from friends or relatives, etc.

In each case, a court has to decide whether or not to take these collateral benefits into account in reduction of the loss for which the injured plaintiff is to receive compensation; or to ignore them, allowing the injured plaintiff to retain both. On the one hand, the plaintiff may be required to repay the collateral benefit so it is appropriate for the court to ignore them. On the other hand, in other instances, the effect of the court ignoring the collateral benefits is that the plaintiff is in theory over-compensated, since they receive more than their true loss from the combination of sources. The counter-argument to this position is that the tortfeasor will pay less than the true loss they have caused.

The High Court has established a set of general principles in assessing damages for personal injury in respect of benefits that a plaintiff has received or is to receive from any source other than the defendant.[240] These principles are that the court is required to consider the nature of the benefit that is considered to be 'collateral' by inquiring whether the person

---

234 *Sharman v Evans* (1977) 138 CLR 563.
235 *Wynn v NSW Insurance Ministerial Corporation* (1995) 184 CLR 485, 495–6 (Dawson, Toohey, Gaudron and Gummow JJ).
236 (1980) 146 CLR 1.
237 *Port Sorell Bowls Club Inc v Dann* [2022] TASFC 2, [92] (Blow CJ and Pearce J).
238 *Civil Proceedings Act 2011* (Qld) s 60; *Wrongs Act 1958* (Vic) s 28A.
239 *Cullen v Trappell* (1980) 146 CLR 1.
240 *National Insurance Co of New Zealand Ltd v Espagne* (1961) 105 CLR 569, 573 (Dixon CJ, Fullagar and Windeyer JJ agreeing), 599 (Windeyer J, Dixon CJ and Fullagar J agreeing), accepted subsequently in *Radding v Lee* (1983) 151 CLR 117; *Manser v Spry* (1994) 181 CLR 428; *Harris v Commercial Minerals Ltd* (1986) CLR 1. See also *Zheng v Cai* (2009) 239 CLR 446; [2009] HCA 52, [28]–[29].

or body supplying that benefit intended that the plaintiff should enjoy it *in addition to* the plaintiff's right to damages and to full compensation by way of damages from the defendant.

The following provides an overview of how the courts have attempted to apply these principles to specific types of collateral benefits:

- *Gifts by third parties:* The High Court has unanimously held that payments made to the plaintiff by her church were not to be deducted from her damages for loss of earning capacity, since the intention of the donor was benevolence to the plaintiff as victim of the tort.[241]

- *Gifts by the defendant:* These will be taken into account in reduction of the damages, since they lack the quality of benevolence (or the intention that they should be additional to the damages payable).[242]

- *Sick pay:* If a plaintiff receives sick pay in lieu of wages, any such amount will be set off against the award for loss of earning capacity, since the plaintiff will have suffered no loss of earning capacity productive of financial loss.[243]

- *Redundancy payments:* A plaintiff's receipt from their employer of a redundancy package (ie, a payment that arises on termination of employment based on the number of years of service) will not ordinarily be set off unless the defendant can prove that the redundancy was for the purpose of replacing lost income independent of an action against the defendant.[244]

- *Voluntary payments by an employer:* The Queensland Supreme Court has held that if an employer makes a gift of money to an employee injured by the negligence of another party, usually this payment is not taken into account when assessing damages unless the payment was intended to replace wages.[245] Accordingly, when an employer paid wages to an injured employee beyond his entitlement to sick pay, there was no loss of income suffered.[246] But where the employee entered into an agreement to repay to the employer a sum equal to lost wages advanced as a loan when his claim was finalised, this amount was not set off.[247]

- *Medicare benefits:* Medicare benefits paid under the *Health Insurance Act 1973* (Cth) are not available to a person who has received a damages award; they should, therefore, be ignored for the purpose of damages assessment. If a plaintiff has already been paid Medicare benefits, that plaintiff must repay them.[248] The Health Insurance Commission is a body established by the *Health and Other Services (Compensation) Act 1995* (Cth) for recouping expenditure on medical insurance costs made to accident victims.

---

241 *Zheng v Cai* (2009) 239 CLR 446; [2009] HCA 52, [20].
242 *Silverbrook Research Pty Ltd v Lindley* [2010] NSWCA 357, [12]–[14].
243 *Graham v Baker* (1961) 106 CLR 340.
244 *Hall v Cramer* (2003) 40 MVR 477.
245 *Hobbelen v Nunn* [1965] Qd R 105.
246 *Koremans v Sweeney* [1966] QWN 46.
247 *Treloar v Wickham* (1961) 105 CLR 102.
248 *Health Insurance Act 1973* (Cth) s 18.

- *Social security benefits:* The effect of High Court decisions is that social security payments should be set off.[249] But the *Social Security Act 1991* (Cth) imposes a regime similar in nature to that used in respect of Medicare benefits, in that:
  - compensation payments made to a plaintiff (including workers' compensation, motor vehicle accident and common law damages for personal injury) are taken into account for the purposes of determining the plaintiff's eligibility for certain pensions, benefits or allowances, and[250]
  - past payments of social security made to the plaintiff may be recovered from the plaintiff following the plaintiff's receipt of a lump sum damages award.[251] This is done by means of a notice being served on the plaintiff requiring repayment.[252] These past payments are recoverable as debts owed to the Commonwealth.
- *No-fault workers' compensation, motor accident legislation and criminal injuries compensation schemes:* These schemes attempt to ensure that the plaintiff does not obtain a double benefit in respect of a particular loss.

12.3.6   Non-pecuniary damages

Assessment of non-pecuniary damages, for non-economic loss, requires the court to consider losses that are subjective to the plaintiff.

12.3.6.1   Heads of damage

Prior to the civil liability legislation, non-pecuniary damages were assessed according to the following heads of damage:

- pain and suffering
- loss of amenities/loss of enjoyment of life
- loss of expectation of life.

Each of these non-pecuniary heads of damage was considered separately and itemised.

Under the civil liability legislation there is no uniform definition of 'non-economic loss'. While some jurisdictions use the term 'non-economic loss', others use 'general damages' or 'non-pecuniary loss' (see Table 12.6). Nevertheless, there is consistency in including within it the following heads of damage:

- pain and suffering
- loss of amenities/loss of enjoyment of life
- loss of expectation of life (but not included in s 28B of the *Wrongs Act 1958* (Vic))
- disfigurement or bodily harm (but not included in s 28B of the *Wrongs Act 1958* (Vic)).

---

249 See, eg, *National Insurance Co of New Zealand Ltd v Espagne* (1961) 105 CLR 569.
250 *Social Security Act 1991* (Cth) s 17(1).
251 Ibid s 1178.
252 Ibid s 1184.

Table 12.6   Non-pecuniary damages definitions, caps, thresholds and methods of assessment

Legislation	Non-pecuniary damages definition	Cap	Threshold	Method of assessment
Civil Law (Wrongs) Act 2002 (ACT)	Non-economic loss: s 99(4)	No cap	No threshold	s 99(1) court to have regard to earlier decisions ('tariffs')
Civil Liability Act 2002 (NSW)	Non-economic loss: s 3	s 16(2)	s 16(1) at least 15% of most extreme case	s 16 as a percentage figure – proportion of 'a most extreme case' but also court to have regard to earlier decisions ('tariffs') (s 17A)
Personal Injuries (Liabilities and Damages) Act 2003 (NT)	'Permanent impairment suffered as a consequence of a personal injury': s 18	s 27(1)	s 27(2)	s 27(3) as a percentage figure on the basis of the 'degree of impairment' as a percentage of specified maximum amount
Civil Liability Act 2003 (Qld)	General damages: s 51	s 62 *Civil Liability Regulation 2014* (Qld) sch 7	s 62 *Civil Liability Regulation 2014* (Qld) sch 7 minimum award	s 61 as a percentage figure based on 'injury scale value' provided for in *Civil Liability Regulation 2014* (Qld) sch 7
Civil Liability Act 1936 (SA)	Non-economic loss: s 3	s 52(2)	s 52(1) significant impairment for at least 7 days or medical expenses of the minimum prescribed amount	s 52(2) as a figure on a 'scale value' from 0 to 60
Civil Liability Act 2002 (Tas)	Non-economic loss: s 3	None: s 27(3)	s 27(1) financial threshold	s 28 court to have regard to earlier decisions ('tariffs')
Wrongs Act 1958 (Vic)	Non-economic loss: s 28B	s 28G	s 28LE 'significant injury', being at least 5% for physical injury and 10% for psychiatric injury	s 28HA court to have regard to earlier decisions ('tariffs')
Civil Liability Act 2002 (WA)	Non-pecuniary loss: s 9(4)	s 10	s 9(1) financial threshold	s 10A court to have regard to earlier decisions ('tariffs')

12.3.6.2 Thresholds and caps

The legislation imposes legislative caps and contains thresholds for the recovery of non-pecuniary loss damages.

All the jurisdictions, except Tasmania, have imposed set maximum amounts (caps) that can be recovered by way of non-pecuniary loss damages, which amounts are indexed annually. The purpose is to contain awards even in the most extreme cases.

All jurisdictions, except Queensland, have established thresholds for the recovery of non-pecuniary loss damages. The threshold is a level below which no claim can be made. The purpose is to exclude the high volume of minor injuries that are costly to administer. For instance, s 16(1) of the *Civil Liability Act 2002* (NSW) states that no damages may be recovered 'for non-economic loss unless the severity of the non-economic loss is at least 15 per cent of a most extreme case'. Victoria's *Wrongs Act 1958* (Vic) requires 'significant injury',[253] with a minimum 'threshold level'[254] defined as an impairment of 5 per cent for physical injury and 10 per cent for psychiatric injury.[255] Tasmania and Western Australia set a minimum financial threshold. In South Australia, the threshold impairment must last at least seven days and significant medical expenses must be incurred. There are no thresholds on the recovery of non-economic losses in Queensland, although the legislation does set a minimum award amount.

The relevant civil liability statutes in each state deal with non-pecuniary damages as set out in Table 12.6.

12.3.6.3 Method for assessment of damages

The civil liability legislation in different jurisdictions uses different methods to assess damages for non-economic loss.

As shown in Table 12.6, New South Wales, Queensland, South Australia and the Northern Territory use a percentage figure method of assessment. For example, under s 16 of the *Civil Liability Act 2002* (NSW), the severity of the non-economic loss is determined as a percentage proportion of 'a most extreme case' (this must be 15 per cent or more) and then applied to the corresponding percentage of the maximum amount in the table, which represents the amount of damages payable.[256]

Other jurisdictions, such as the ACT, Victoria, Tasmania and Western Australia, permit the 'tariff' method of assessment, which permits the parties to refer the court to previous awards of such damages for the purposes of calculating the amount. The reference to 'tariffs' is a practice employed by English courts to assess an award of non-economic loss damages depending on the severity of the injury, not as a 'fixed' point on a scale, but as varying within a range or 'bracket', depending on factors peculiar to the plaintiff (eg, age and the pursuits of which he or she has been deprived).[257] Although the High Court discouraged the use of such a scale on the basis that cases are not truly comparable with one another,[258] this has now been changed by the civil liability legislation just discussed, which permits courts to refer to earlier awards.

The methods of assessment for non-pecuniary damages are set out in Table 12.6.

We will now consider the following three heads of damage for non-pecuniary loss:

* pain and suffering
* loss of amenities/loss of enjoyment of life
* loss of expectation of life.

---

253 *Wrongs Act 1958* (Vic) s 28LE.
254 Ibid s 28LF.
255 Ibid s 28LB.
256 See also *Southgate v Waterford* (1990) 21 NSWLR 427.
257 *Heil v Rankin* [2001] QB 272; *Simmons v Castle* [2013] 1 WLR 1239.
258 *Planet Fisheries Pty Ltd v La Rosa* (1968) 119 CLR 118, 124–5 (coram).

12.3.6.4   Pain and suffering

This category of damages is designed to provide pleasure or comfort, 'in so far as [money] can', for the 'actual physical pain' suffered in the accident and its aftermath.[259] The assessment of damages here depends on the consequences to the individual plaintiff of the accident.[260] Given that such physical pain can only be subjectively felt by the plaintiff himself or herself, the High Court in principle held that there can never be a 'tariff' with which a particular plaintiff's damages can be compared; rather, as already discussed, legislatures have authorised courts to refer to earlier decisions in order to establish an appropriate award.

Relevant factors in assessing the extent of the pain and suffering include:

- the extent and duration of the pain and suffering[261]
- the circumstances giving rise to the injury, such as the plaintiff being caught underneath the defendant's vehicle and dragged[262]
- the distress, worry or anxiety caused by medication made necessary by the pain and suffering[263]
- mental illness arising from the physical injuries.[264]

The nature of the award of damages for pain and suffering was made apparent by the High Court in *Skelton v Collins*, where the plaintiff was rendered permanently unconscious.[265] The Court held that, given such damages are assessed on a subjective basis in order to provide solace for the physical hurt felt by the plaintiff, no award can be made for a plaintiff who is 'insensible to physical pain and suffering' and so 'does not experience pain and, consequently, does not suffer on that account'.[266]

12.3.6.5   Loss of amenities of life/loss of enjoyment of life

Loss of amenities of life (or 'enjoyment of life') is used to describe compensation for 'the deprivation of the ability to participate in normal activities and thus to enjoy life to the full'.[267] Under this head of loss are included such matters as the inability to engage in recreational pastimes and sport,[268] the deprivation of sexual pleasure[269] and the loss of opportunity for cultural fulfilment.[270]

Damages for pain and suffering, on the one hand, and for loss of amenities of life, on the other, are 'usually' assessed together as one lump sum.[271] But they are intended to relate

---

259 *Teubner v Humble* (1963) 108 CLR 491, 507 (Windeyer J).
260 *Bresatz v Przibilla* (1962) 108 CLR 541, 548 (Windeyer J).
261 *O'Shea v Sullivan* (1994) Aust Torts Reports 81-273; *Casey v Zurgalo* [1968] ALR 134.
262 *Freudhofer v Poledano* [1972] VR 287.
263 *O'Shea v Sullivan* [1994] Aust Torts Reports 81-273 (plaintiff required to take morphine).
264 *Admiralski v Stehbens* [1960] Qd R 510.
265 (1966) 115 CLR 94.
266 Ibid 108 (Taylor J).
267 *Teubner v Humble* (1963) 108 CLR 491, 507–8 (Windeyer J).
268 See, eg, *Motor Accidents Insurance Board v Pulford* (1993) Aust Torts Reports 81-235, 62421 (Cox J).
269 See, eg, *Vassilef v BCG Marine Services (NSW) Pty Ltd* [1980] Qd R 21.
270 See, eg, *Namala v Northern Territory* (1996) 131 FLR 468, 474 (Kearney J).
271 D Rolph et al, *Balkin & Davis Law of Torts* (LexisNexis, 6th ed, 2021) [11.27].

to different aspects of the plaintiff's loss. Compensation for pain and suffering is meant to provide 'pleasure or ... comfort' in so far as money can for 'actual physical pain', past and future, whereas compensation for loss of amenities compensates for 'the distress of mind and the feeling of frustration that come from an incapacity to take part in activities'.[272]

This head of damage is related to loss of earning capacity, but in an inverse manner: to the extent that damages for loss of earning capacity replace funds that the victim would have spent on pleasurable pursuits, the award for loss of amenities should be proportionately reduced.[273]

Like pain and suffering, loss of amenities is largely subjective but 'the primary purpose of compensation under this head is the plaintiff's realisation that the accident has deprived him or her of the opportunity to enjoy life as fully as was the case prior to the injury'.[274] Accordingly, 'if the plaintiff is rendered permanently unconscious by the accident, only a modest and conventional sum is to be awarded'.[275]

12.3.6.6   Loss of expectation of life

This category of non-pecuniary damages is awarded when the plaintiff's life expectancy has been shortened as a result of the accident. Its purpose is to seek to provide the plaintiff with 'consolation or solace', rather than 'recompense', 'caused by a knowledge of the curtailment of life'.[276] This is 'the loss of a measure of prospective happiness'.[277]

The High Court has accepted the approach of the House of Lords[278] that, because of the extraordinary difficulty in putting a monetary value on such an item as the balance of joy over sorrow, the courts should award no more than a modest and conventional sum. This sum should not vary depending on the age of the plaintiff or on the years by which his or her life had been cut short. Modest awards of between $10 000 and $20 000 have been considered appropriate.[279]

Since the amount for loss of expectation of life is no more than a conventional award, and so does not place a money value on such an item as the balance of joy over sorrow, or the age of the victim, or the number of years by which his or her life has been shortened, that conventional sum will be awarded even if the plaintiff is rendered permanently unconscious by the accident.[280]

---

272   *Teubner v Humble* (1963) 108 CLR 491, 507–8 (Windeyer J).
273   *Sharman v Evans* (1977) 138 CLR 563, 583 (Gibbs and Stephen JJ); *Campbell v Nangle* (1985) 40 SASR 161, 200 (Jacobs J).
274   D Rolph et al, *Balkin & Davis Law of Torts* (LexisNexis, 6th ed, 2021) [11.29]; *Sharman v Evans* (1977) 138 CLR 563, 584 (Gibbs and Stephen JJ).
275   Ibid. The sum of $1500 was awarded for both loss of amenities and loss of expectation of life in *Skelton v Collins* (1966) 115 CLR 94.
276   *Skelton v Collins* (1966) 115 CLR 94, 131–2 (Windeyer J).
277   Ibid 117, 120 (Taylor J).
278   Ibid 98 (Kitto J); *Benham v Gambling* [1941] AC 157.
279   *Sullivan v Micallef* (1994) Aust Torts Reports 81-308, 61790 (Mahoney AP) (appropriate figure accepted as being between $5000 and $20 000); *McGilvray v Amaca Pty Ltd* [2001] WASC 345 ($15 000 awarded).
280   *Skelton v Collins* (1966) 115 CLR 94.

HINTS AND TIPS

Sections 12.3.1–12.3.6 analyse types of damages that are available in cases of personal injury. Table 12.7 provides an overview of the similarities and differences between them by having regard to two criteria: first, whether harm, loss or damage (referred to as 'damage' in this chapter) needs to be proven before this kind of damages can be awarded to a plaintiff and, second, the purpose behind an award of this kind of damages.

Table 12.7   Categories of damages compared by requirement for 'damage' and purpose

	Compensatory	Aggravated	Exemplary/ punitive	Nominal	Contemptuous
Requirement for 'damage'?	Yes	Yes	Yes	No	No
Purpose	To compensate plaintiff for damage	To compensate plaintiff for the manner of the defendant's conduct	To punish, deter or show disapproval of the defendant's conduct	To acknowledge the wrongdoing	To acknowledge the wrongdoing but show the court's disapproval of the plaintiff's conduct

12.3.7   Claims upon the death of a person

In circumstances where a person who is the victim of the tortious act of another dies, two types of action are available:

(1)   claim by the *estate* of the deceased victim (survival of causes of action claim)

(2)   claim by the *dependants* of the deceased victim for loss of financial support (dependants' claim).

The two types of claim may be available in conjunction, since it is common for the beneficiaries of the deceased's estate to also be dependants of the deceased.

The existence of these two types of claims represents a departure from the previous common law position that a plaintiff's cause of action in tort died with the death of that plaintiff (*actio personalis moritur cum persona*) and did not survive for the benefit of the deceased's estate.[281]

Legislation now provides for compensation in both of these situations as separate causes of action that are available in conjunction with each other.

---

281   *Baker v Bolton* (1808) 170 ER 1033, confirmed in *Barclay v Penberthy* (2012) 246 CLR 258; [2012] HCA 40.

12.3.7.1   Claims by the estate of the deceased (survival of causes of action claim)

The estate of a person killed, whether wrongfully or not, retains any cause of action the deceased would have had if alive.

The 'survival' of causes of action' provisions are found in the pieces of legislation across Australian jurisdictions outlined in Table 12.8.

Table 12.8   Claims by the estate of the deceased

Legislation	Section
Civil Law (Wrongs) Act 2002 (ACT)	16
Law Reform (Miscellaneous Provisions) Act 1944 (NSW)	2
Law Reform (Miscellaneous Provisions) Act 1956 (NT)	6
Succession Act 1981 (Qld)	66
Survival of Causes of Action Act 1940 (SA)	2
Administration and Probate Act 1935 (Tas)	27
Administration and Probate Act 1958 (Vic)	29
Law Reform (Miscellaneous Provisions) Act 1941 (WA)	4

By way of example of the operation of these provisions, s 29(1) of the *Administration and Probate Act 1958* (Vic) provides for the survival of the cause of action as follows:

> Subject to the provisions of this section, on the death of any person, all causes of action subsisting against or vested in him shall survive against or (as the case may be) for the benefit of his estate.

DAMAGES

The estate cannot claim for any loss that the deceased could not have recovered.

The nature of the legislative provisions is to limit the damages payable in a survival of causes of action case. For example, s 29(2) of the *Administration and Probate Act 1958* (Vic) relevantly provides:

> Where a cause of action survives as aforesaid for the benefit of the estate of a deceased person the damages recoverable for the benefit of the estate of that person –
>
> (a)   shall not include any exemplary damages;
>
> ...
>
> (c)   where the death of that person has been caused by the act or omission which gives rise to the cause of action –
>
> (i)   shall be calculated without reference to any loss or gain to his estate consequent on his death, except that a sum in respect of funeral expenses may be included;
>
> (ii)   shall not, except as provided in subsection (2A), include any damages for his pain or suffering or for any bodily or mental harm suffered by him or for the curtailment of his expectation of life;
>
> (iii)   shall be calculated without reference to the future probable earnings of the deceased had he survived and without any allowance for the loss of his earning capacity that relates to any period after his death.

The damages recoverable under this cause of action are therefore limited to:

- funeral expenses (sub-para (i))
- pecuniary damages, such as loss of earning capacity and medical, hospital and other expenses, such as gratuitous services – *but only for the period between the accident and the death* (sub-para (iii)).

Specifically excluded by the legislation are damages for:

- non-pecuniary losses, such as pain and suffering, loss of amenities and loss of expectation of life (sub-para (ii))
- future pecuniary loss, such as loss of earning capacity (sub-para (iii))
- exemplary damages (para (a))
- defamation (sub-s (1)).[282]

The rationale for these limitations and exclusions is that the estate itself could not recover these heads of loss as it had not, nor would, suffer them and so it was contrary to the basic principle of compensatory damages to receive them.[283]

If the deceased's action was in respect of a dust disease – for example, exposure to asbestos – the legislation provides that non-pecuniary damages may be claimed if the proceedings were commenced before the deceased died.[284]

The legislation requires that the damages be calculated without reference to any loss or gain to the estate.[285] This means no set-off is made for any insurance payments or any other collateral benefits payable on the death.

The survival of action claim survives no matter the order of death of the deceased of the estate making the claim and the deceased of the estate defending the claim.[286]

12.3.7.2   Claims by the dependants of the deceased (dependants' action)

We now turn to causes of action by the deceased's dependants that exist in cases where the defendant's wrongful conduct resulted in the death of the deceased person. Such an action contrasts with the 'survival' of causes of action discussed in Section 12.3.7.1, which ensure that any cause of action that the plaintiff had before his or her death will survive beyond that plaintiff's death, whether or not that wrongful act caused the plaintiff's death or just his or her injury.

The origin of this cause of action existing in the deceased's dependants to recover in circumstances where the deceased died because of the defendant's wrongful conduct was

---

282 Tasmania is the only Australian jurisdiction that allows claims in defamation by deceased estates; the remaining jurisdictions provide that a person cannot assert, continue or enforce a cause of action for defamation if either party is dead: *Uniform Defamation Acts* s 10; *Civil Law (Wrongs) Act 2002* (ACT) s 122; *Defamation Act 2006* (NT) s 9; cf *Administration and Probate Act 1935* (Tas) s 27(1).

283 *Workcover Queensland v Amaca Pty Ltd* (2010) 241 CLR 420; [2010] HCA 34, [50].

284 *Dust Diseases Tribunal Act 1989* (NSW) s 12B; *Succession Act 1981* (Qld) s 66(2A), (2B); *Survival of Causes of Actions Act 1940* (SA) s 3(2), (3); *Administration and Probate Act 1935* (Tas) s 27(3A), (3B); *Administration and Probate Act 1958* (Vic) s 29(2A).

285 See, eg, *Administration and Probate Act 1958* (Vic) s 29(2)(c)(i).

286 *Administration and Probate Act 1958* (Vic), considered in *Partridge v Chick* (1951) 84 CLR 611.

enshrined in the United Kingdom's *Fatal Accidents Act 1846* (also known as *Lord Campbell's Act*).[287] As noted earlier, prior to this legislation, at common law at that time, the cause of action of a deceased plaintiff died with the plaintiff, and so the plaintiff's dependants could not recover. The legislation created a statutory cause of action for the benefit of the immediate dependants or family members of a person wrongfully killed, in cases where the deceased would have had a cause of action in respect of the wrongful conduct.

Successors to *Lord Campbell's Act*, which give rise to dependants' actions, exist in the Australian jurisdictions, as per Table 12.9.

Table 12.9   Dependants' action

Legislation	Section
Civil Law (Wrongs) Act 2002 (ACT)	24
Compensation to Relatives Act 1897 (NSW)	3(1)
Compensation (Fatal Injuries) Act 1974 (NT)	7
Civil Proceedings Act 2011 (Qld)	64
Civil Liability Act 1936 (SA)	23
Fatal Accidents Act 1934 (Tas)	4
Wrongs Act 1958 (Vic)	16
Fatal Accidents Act 1959 (WA)	4

By way of illustration, s 16 of the *Wrongs Act 1958* (Vic) provides:

> Whensoever the death of a person is caused by a wrongful act neglect or default and the act neglect or default is such as would (if death had not ensued) have entitled the party injured to maintain an action and recover damages in respect thereof, then and in every such case the person who would have been liable if death had not ensued shall be liable to an action for damages notwithstanding the death of the person injured.

Accordingly, in order to bring a dependant's claim, it must be proven that:

- if the deceased had not died, he or she would have brought an action in relation to the injury and would have recovered damages
- there is a causal link between the defendant's wrongful conduct and the death and
- the claimants are dependants of the deceased, as defined by the legislation.

We will discuss each of these factors in turn.

RIGHT OF ACTION

An action cannot be brought unless the deceased could have brought an action at the time of death.[288] The deceased will not have had a right of action, for instance, if:

- a complete defence would have been available to the defendant (eg, voluntary assumption of risk)[289]
- the relevant time limitation period had expired

---

287   9 & 10 Vict, c 93.
288   See, eg, *Wrongs Act 1958* (Vic) s 16.
289   *Williams v Birmingham Battery & Metal Co* [1899] 2 QB 338; *Murphy v Culhane* [1977] QB 94.

- the deceased contracted out of the benefit[290]
- the deceased had satisfied the cause of action prior to death (eg, by accepting an award of compensation)[291]
- the deceased had recovered damages for personal injuries prior to death.[292]

CAUSATION

Both the injury and the death must have been caused by the defendant. According to the Full Court of the Victorian Supreme Court in *Haber v Walker*, the legal principle of remoteness need not be satisfied when 'simple causation' was established on the basis of the 'but for' test and the lack of any intervening acts.[293]

The eggshell skull rule applies to such dependency claims; the fact that the deceased plaintiff may have been vulnerable to suffering depression is irrelevant when assessing damages.[294]

DEPENDANTS

To be entitled to compensation, the claimant must prove that he or she is a dependant, as defined by the relevant Act. The legislation specifies who may seek damages, although the language referable to who is a dependant varies (see Table 12.10).

Table 12.10   Definitions of dependants

Legislation	Language used for dependants	Provision(s)
Civil Law (Wrongs) Act 2002 (ACT)	'people for whose benefit the action is brought (the beneficiaries)'	s 25
Compensation to Relatives Act 1897 (NSW)	members of the deceased's family	s 4
Compensation (Fatal Injuries) Act 1974 (NT)	members of the deceased's family	s 8
Civil Proceedings Act 2011 (Qld)	members of the deceased's family	s 62
Civil Liability Act 1936 (SA)	members of the deceased's family	s 24(1)
Fatal Accidents Act 1934 (Tas)	members of the deceased's family	s 5
Wrongs Act 1958 (Vic)	dependants	s 17(2)
Fatal Accidents Act 1959 (WA)	relatives	s 3, sch 2

In all jurisdictions, a dependant includes the spouse, including a same-sex spouse, of the deceased.[295] Victoria does not do so explicitly: s 17(2) of the *Wrongs Act 1958* (Vic) defines 'dependants' as 'such persons as were wholly mainly or in part dependent on the person deceased', which would arguably include same-sex spouses.

290 *Central Queensland Speleological Society Inc v Central Queensland Cement (No 1)* [1989] 2 Qd R 512.
291 *Read v Great Eastern Railway Co* (1868) LR 3 QB 555.
292 *Brunsden v Humphrey* (1884) 14 QBD 141.
293 [1963] VR 339, 358 (Smith J, with whom Lowe J agreed).
294 *Lisle v Bruce* [2002] 2 Qd R 168.
295 *Compensation to Relatives Act 1897* (NSW) ss 4(2), 7(4); *Interpretation Act 1987* (NSW) s 21C; *Civil Proceedings Act 2011* (Qld) ss 63, 67(7); *Acts Interpretation Act 1974* (Qld) ss 32DA(5), 36; *Civil Liability Act 1936* (SA) s 3; *Family Relationships Act 1975* (SA) ss 11, 11A; *Fatal Accidents Act 1934* (Tas) s 3; *Relationships Act 2003* (Tas) ss 4–6; *Fatal Accidents Act 1959* (WA) s 6(1), sch 2 cl (h); *Interpretation Act 1984* (WA) s 13A(3).

Whichever term is used, damages are only awarded if the dependant has suffered pecuniary loss, or has lost the reasonable expectation of a pecuniary advantage, due to the wrongful death of the deceased. As explained by the High Court in *De Sales v Ingrilli*, damages are awarded 'for the chance that the deceased would have provided the relative with financial support or its equivalent in the future'.[296] Accordingly, there must be evidence of pecuniary dependency on the deceased, not merely a personal relationship. For example, in a case where the claimant sought damages for the death of her de facto husband, the evidence indicated that it was the deceased who was dependent on the claimant as the deceased was setting up a new business at the time of his death and so there was no net pecuniary benefit in the claimant's favour.[297] The Court held that, on the balance of probabilities, there was no evidence to indicate that, had the deceased not died, the claimant would have received a net pecuniary benefit from the relationship.

Further, the dependency must have arisen from a familial rather than some other relationship.[298] So, if the deceased and the dependant were also in a commercial relationship, a distinction would need to be made between the benefits arising from the familial relationship and those from the commercial relationship.[299] Further, the High Court has held that an employer could not recover damages for the death of its employees,[300] due to the rule at common law that a person cannot recover damages for the death of another.[301] In addition, the legislation succeeding *Lord Campbell's Act* confined the right of recovery in certain limited circumstances to dependants.

The statutory right of action lies against the party who would have been liable at the suit of the deceased had he or she lived.[302] This right of action on behalf of the dependants against the defendant is a single cause of action, and is generally brought in the name of the executor or administrator of the deceased's estate.[303] Where the deceased has no executor or administrator, or no action is brought within six months of the death, the dependants may themselves be given the right to commence the action.[304]

---

296 (2002) 212 CLR 338; [2002] HCA 52, [91] (McHugh J).
297 *Campbell v Li-Pina* (2007) 47 MVR 279.
298 *Burgess v Florence Nightingale Hospital for Gentlewomen* [1955] 1 QB 349; *Chief Commissioner of Railways and Tramways (NSW) v Boylson* (1915) 19 CLR 505. However, note that *Civil Liability Act 1936* (SA) s 66 allows compensation for loss if the deceased and his or her spouse or domestic partner were jointly engaged in business and the business is impaired or ceases.
299 See *Schimke v Clement* (2011) 58 MVR 390. See also *Di Battista v Molton* [1971] VR 656, in which the Full Court held that there was substantial income that was derived from a shareholding in a company that was derived from the relationship of husband and wife, rather than the employment of the wife by the husband's company.
300 *Barclay v Penberthy* (2012) 246 CLR 258; [2012] HCA 40.
301 *Baker v Bolton* (1808) 170 ER 1033.
302 *Nominal Defendant v Taylor* (1982) 154 CLR 106.
303 *Compensation to Relatives Act 1897* (NSW) ss 4(1), 5; *Civil Proceedings Act 2011* (Qld) s 65(1), (2); *Civil Liability Act 1936* (SA) ss 24, 25(1); *Fatal Accidents Act 1934* (Tas) ss 5, 6; *Wrongs Act 1958* (Vic) s 18; *Fatal Accidents Act 1959* (WA) ss 6(1B), 7.
304 *Compensation to Relatives Act 1897* (NSW) s 6B(1); *Civil Liability Act 1936* (SA) s 27(1); *Fatal Accidents Act 1934* (Tas) s 8(1); *Wrongs Act 1958* (Vic) s 18; *Fatal Accidents Act 1959* (WA) s 9(1). In the *Civil Proceedings Act 2011* (Qld) s 65(2), the personal representative or one or more members of the deceased's family may bring the proceeding.

12.3.7.3   Damages

The dependants' action aims to compensate the dependants for the loss of the contribution by the deceased for their support or the loss of expectation of financial support. Accordingly, the common law in Australia awards damages for pecuniary loss rather than non-pecuniary loss (ie, consolation for grief or suffering).[305] Statutory exceptions do permit compensation for consolation for grief or suffering, discussed below.

PECUNIARY LOSS

Compensation for the pecuniary loss is damages representing the financial contribution to the household by the deceased. The pecuniary loss may be actual or prospective.[306] In this way, any loss of income that contributed to the support of the dependants and other pecuniary losses stemming from the death are recoverable.[307] The court requires only that the beneficiary of the dependants' claim to prove evidence of a reasonable expectation of benefit had the deceased lived. It is not necessary to prove that deriving such a benefit was probable; but a mere speculative chance is not enough.[308]

One such pecuniary loss is the loss of services. Thus, the High Court in *Nguyen v Nguyen* held that loss of domestic services previously provided by the deceased had a pecuniary value capable of assessment and should be included in a dependant's claim.[309] In that case, a father and his two young children were the plaintiffs claiming damages under the Queensland legislation for the death of their wife and mother, who had provided childcare and household services. The plaintiff father had not engaged anyone to perform the household services for him and the two children, and had no intention of doing so; he looked after the children himself. The Full Court of the Queensland Supreme Court held that the plaintiffs could not recover since the husband was performing the services at no cost. This was overruled by the High Court, which indicated that the damages here were not to be assessed according to the principles of need as in *Griffiths v Kerkemeyer*.[310] Rather, Dawson, Toohey and McHugh JJ pointed out that the claim here was for compensation for some 'tangible advantage' lost by reason of the death of the deceased – it was based on the plaintiffs' loss of the financial contribution made by the deceased to the household and the entitlement to recover that loss, regardless of whether the plaintiffs intended to use the damages to replace the services or not.[311]

Some jurisdictions have placed thresholds on claims for gratuitous services that were previously provided by the deceased, such as those in *Nguyen v Nguyen*. For example, s 19A of the *Wrongs Act 1958* (Vic) requires that such damages will only be awarded where those services were provided to the dependants for more than six hours per week and for more than six consecutive months prior to the accident, or were expected to be provided for more

---

305   *Victorian Railways Commissioners v Speed* (1928) 40 CLR 43, 444 (Higgins J); *Public Trustee v Zoanetti* (1945) 70 CLR 266, 276 (Dixon J).
306   *Berry v Humm & Co* [1915] 1 KB 627.
307   *Robertson v Robin* [1967] SASR 151.
308   *Davies v Taylor* [1974] AC 207.
309   *Nguyen v Nguyen* (1990) 169 CLR 245.
310   (1977) 139 CLR 161.
311   *Nguyen v Nguyen* (1990) 169 CLR 245, 264.

than six hours per week for more than six consecutive months. The damages are capped or pro-rated at the average weekly earnings rate under s 19B of the Act.

NON-PECUNIARY LOSS

A non-pecuniary loss claim may be for payment of a monetary solace ('solatium') for the grief and suffering of the dependants for the death, but this is available only under the South Australian legislation.[312]

A further non-pecuniary loss is the loss of consortium, namely the sharing of companionship and lives, including sexual intercourse.[313] This is available under the Queensland and South Australian legislation.[314] But in Victoria and Western Australia the loss of consortium is not recoverable, and this common law position has not been changed by legislation in those states. Claims for loss of consortium have been abolished in New South Wales and Tasmania.[315]

ASSESSING DAMAGES

A court must determine the amount of damages that represents the value of the loss to each dependant from the date of the death until the date of trial or settlement as well as anticipated future loss. Accordingly, events between the death and trial must be taken into account, as well as future probable events, in order to assess this amount.

Relevant factors in determining the pecuniary support provided by the deceased to the dependant are:

- the deceased's life expectancy and actual prospective net earning capacity[316]
- the likely period and extent of the dependant's dependency.[317] The court looks beyond just the age of dependants; the High Court has provided two examples: a surviving spouse could reasonably expect to receive a benefit measured as a share of the deceased's income until the deceased's expected retirement age, while a child of the deceased could reasonably expect such a benefit until that child reached the age of expected financial independence.[318]

To ensure that a dependant is not over-compensated, certain gains received by that claimant on the death of the deceased must be taken into account and set off against the damages awarded according to principles established by the High Court:[319]

- The general principle is that damages should be calculated by reference to the reasonable expectation of benefit or support had the deceased lived, with a balancing of any gains and losses of the dependant.[320]
- Benefits received by the claimant from the deceased's estate will be set off against any damages awarded, but not where those benefits involved property enjoyed

312   *Civil Liability Act 1936* (SA) ss 28, 29.
313   *Toohey v Hollier* (1955) 92 CLR 618.
314   *Civil Liability Act 2003* (Qld) s 58(1)(a); *Civil Liability Act 1936* (SA) s 65.
315   *Law Reform (Marital Consortium) Act 1984* (NSW) s 3; *Civil Liability Act 2002* (Tas) s 28D.
316   *Lincoln v Gravil* (1954) 94 CLR 430; *Parker v Commonwealth* (1965) 112 CLR 295.
317   *Scholefield v Bates* [1958] SASR 317.
318   *De Sales v Ingrilli* (2002) 212 CLR 338; [2002] HCA 52, [14].
319   *Nguyen v Nguyen* (1990) 169 CLR 245.
320   *Public Trustee v Zoanetti* (1945) 70 CLR 266, 276–7 (Dixon J).

during the deceased's lifetime and that continued to be enjoyed by the deceased's relatives after the death.[321]

• As a general rule, benefits accruing to the dependants as a result of the death ('collateral benefits') must be deducted from the loss suffered. In some jurisdictions, legislation has abrogated this rule or limited its application.[322]

• The court must take into account the vicissitudes of life or future contingencies to safeguard against over-compensation. The prospect that the dependant may suffer an existing illness that leads to a premature death is a matter that may require discounting the damages payable.[323]

• One such contingency, the prospect that the surviving spouse may remarry or re-partner, was previously considered to represent a financial benefit and would be taken into account by a court and discount the award of damages.[324] But the High Court in *De Sales v Ingrilli* considered that this was an archaic principle and by a majority of 4:3 held that there should be no separate deduction for vicissitudes of life for the prospects of remarriage or re-partnering.[325] This was merely one of the usual vicissitudes. Some of the legislation codifies this principle.[326]

12.3.8 Other factors affecting the assessment of damages

Evidence of contributory negligence on the part of the deceased may reduce the amount of damages recoverable by the relatives under the statutes.[327]

Some statutory restrictions are placed on loss of earnings. Given that dependants' claims must consider the earnings of the deceased, statutory caps placed on damages for loss of earning capacity may be relevant. The issue here is that in some jurisdictions, it is clear that the restrictions apply to dependants' claims, but in others it is not. The Queensland, South

---

321 *Darroch v Dennis* [1952] VLR 282; *Peipman v Turner* [1961] NSWR 252; *McCullagh v Lawrence* [1989] 1 Qd R 163.

322 For example, *Civil Proceedings Act 2011* (Qld) s 70 lists certain benefits resulting from death that are not to be set off (eg, insurance, superannuation or pension payouts) and *Fatal Accidents Act 1934* (Tas) s 10(1)(b) excludes the 'accelerated' benefit to the dependants, where they are heirs of the deceased, of the value of the deceased's estate.

323 *De Sales v Ingrilli* (2002) 212 CLR 338; [2002] HCA 52, [15] (Gleeson CJ).

324 The High Court in *Nguyen v Nguyen* (1990) 169 CLR 245, 264 treated this as a well-established principle, citing *Carroll v Purcell* (1961) 107 CLR 73.

325 (2002) 212 CLR 338; [2002] HCA 52.

326 For example, *Civil Proceedings Act 2011* (Qld) s 67 provides that the *possibility* that a surviving spouse may enter a new relationship should have no effect on the assessment of damages; but if the surviving spouse has entered into a new relationship, this should be taken into account: s 67(6). The *Wrongs Act 1958* (Vic) s 19(2)–(5) provides that there is no reduction for the prospect of or a new relationship.

327 *Law Reform Act 1995* (Qld) s 10(5); *Wrongs Act 1954* (Tas) s 4(4); *Law Reform (Contributory Negligence and Tortfeasors' Contribution) Act 1947* (WA) s 4(2)(a). In New South Wales the court may reduce damages but is not compelled to do so: *Civil Liability Act 2002* (NSW) s 5T; *Law Reform (Miscellaneous Provisions) Act 1965* (NSW) s 13. In South Australia the court is to 'have regard to' any contributory negligence by the deceased: *Civil Liability Act 1936* (SA) s 45. In Victoria, the legislation does not allow the damages to be reduced for the contributory negligence of the deceased: *Wrongs Act 1958* (Vic) s 18.

Australian, Victorian and Western Australian legislation make clear reference to dependency claims, and require the court to disregard the deceased's earnings above three times the average weekly earnings or cap damages at that or another amount.[328] In New South Wales and Tasmania, it is not so clear whether the restrictions will apply; this will depend on the ambiguous interpretation of the relevant provisions[329] (considered in Sections 2.1 and 12.3.5.4).

REVIEW QUESTIONS

(1) In the case of *New South Wales v Ibbett* the Court made substantial awards of exemplary damages for the assault of Mrs Ibbett ($25 000) and the trespass on her land ($20 000). This was far greater than the exemplary damages awarded to Rogers against Bugden of $7500 in *Canterbury Bankstown Rugby League Football Club Ltd v Rogers*. How do you account for this difference?

(2) Will a court award damages for (a) the reduced value of a property, or (b) the costs of repairing or reinstating it?

(3) What are 'heads of damage'?

(4) What is the difference between a 'discount' rate and a discount or reduction for the vicissitudes of life?

(5) What are the two kinds of claims that can be brought for wrongful death? Do these two kinds of claims operate independently of one another, or do they complement one another?

 Guided responses in the eBook

12.4 Injunctions

An injunction is a coercive remedy originating in equity. It takes the form of a court order compelling a party to do or not to do something.

The jurisdiction of courts to order injunctions has a number of sources. First, many statutes confer on common law courts a power to grant remedies, reflecting Judicature Acts reforms.[330] Such injunctions are 'legal' because they are equitable remedies given in relation to a common law cause of action (called the 'auxiliary' jurisdiction of equity). Second, courts have an inherent jurisdiction to grant injunctions to preserve the status quo and to prevent

---

328 *Civil Liability Act 2003* (Qld) s 54; *Civil Liability Act 1936* (SA) s 54(3); as does *Wrongs Act 1958* (Vic) s 28F; *Civil Liability Act 2002* (WA) s 11(1).

329 *Civil Liability Act 2002* (NSW) s 12 refers to 'the claimant's gross weekly earnings'; *Civil Liability Act 2002* (Tas) s 26 refers to 'a person' entitled under the *Fatal Accidents Act 1934* (Tas) and that a court is to disregard the person's earnings above the limit. The New South Wales provision was considered by the High Court in *Taylor v Owners Strata Plan No 11564* (2014) 253 CLR 531.

330 See, eg, *Supreme Court Act 1986* (Vic) s 37.

proceedings being frustrated.[331] Third, legislation may explicitly provide a court with the power to grant an injunction.[332]

12.4.1 Types of injunctions

An injunction may take a number of forms. It may either prohibit a party from doing something ('prohibitory' injunction) or require a party to do a specific act ('mandatory' injunction). It may be final (or 'perpetual') if it confers an ongoing right, usually at the conclusion of the trial; or it may be temporary (known as an 'interlocutory' injunction), if it merely seeks to maintain the status quo before the trial has occurred. One particular type of interlocutory injunction is the 'quia timet' interlocutory injunction, granted to prevent a prospective infringement of the plaintiff's rights.

12.4.2 In what circumstances is an injunction ordered?

In order to obtain an injunction, a plaintiff must establish three preliminary matters:

(1) that the defendant has committed (or, in the case of a quia timet injunction, is about to commit) a tort

(2) that damages are not an adequate remedy

(3) that there is no discretionary bar to relief.

12.4.2.1 Is a proprietary interest required?

It is sometime suggested that a plaintiff must have a proprietary right before he or she can be awarded an injunction, but this view has been rejected by the High Court.[333] The better view is that proprietary rights are often the kind of rights where damages are likely to be *inadequate* to compensate the plaintiff for injury to the right and so an injunction is often necessary, although other rights might also be protected by injunction.

12.4.2.2 Adequacy of damages as a remedy

When an injunction is granted in aid of a common law cause of action such as tort, in equity's 'auxiliary' jurisdiction, as explained earlier, it must be shown that damages are an inadequate remedy before an injunction will be granted.

The historical basis for this requirement stems from the 18th-century Court of Chancery's concern to avoid interfering in common law proceedings.

An intermediate appellate court has accepted that, instead of the adequacy of damages, the requirement should be reformulated as to whether it is just in all the circumstances that a plaintiff shall be confined to his or her remedy in damages.[334]

---

331 *Simsek v Macphee* (1982) 148 CLR 636.
332 See, eg, *Australian Consumer Law* s 232 (contained in *Competition and Consumer Act 2010* (Cth) sch 2).
333 *Cardile v LED Builders Pty Ltd* (1999) 198 CLR 380; [1999] HCA 18, [30] (Gaudron, McHugh, Gummow and Callinan JJ); *Australian Broadcasting Corporation v Lenah Game Meats Pty Ltd* (2001) 208 CLR 199; [2001] HCA 63, [90].
334 *Belgrave Nominees Pty Ltd v Barlin-Scott Airconditioning (Australia) Pty Ltd* [1984] VR 947, 955.

It is significant that the *Australian Consumer Law*, comprising sch 2 of the *Competition and Consumer Act 2010* (Cth), does not require the plaintiff to establish that damages are inadequate before granting an injunction. Section 232 provides that a court has the power to award an injunction to prevent a contravention of the provisions of the *Australian Consumer Law* and is interpreted broadly because it is a public interest provision.[335]

12.4.2.3 Rights protected by injunction

A large range of injuries to a variety of rights in tort may give rise to an injunction. These may be categorised as:

- proprietary rights in land
- property rights in goods and funds of money
- economic rights
- right to bodily integrity
- right to protect one's reputation.[336]

PROPRIETARY RIGHTS IN LAND

The proprietary torts that protect plaintiffs from infringement of their rights in land are trespass, private nuisance and public nuisance. If the plaintiff has committed a proprietary tort in relation to land and will not desist from doing so in the future, courts will grant an injunction.[337] Damages may be awarded in place of or in addition to an injunction and are known as 'equitable damages';[338] but such damages will rarely be an adequate remedy for injury to property rights in land.[339] Injunctions may be given for relatively minor trespasses, such as encroachment of scaffolding into the plaintiff's airspace[340] or the passage of a crane jib over the plaintiff's land.[341]

PROPERTY RIGHTS IN GOODS

The proprietary rights that protect plaintiffs from injury to their rights in goods are trespass to goods, conversion and detinue. Courts are less likely to award an injunction restraining the defendant from committing a proprietary tort in relation to goods than they are in relation to land.[342] But where the goods are unique, scarce or irreplaceable, an injunction is more likely to be awarded, reflecting the necessity of establishing that damages are inadequate.[343]

---

335 See, eg, *ICI Ltd v Trade Practices Commission* (1992) 38 FCR 248, 256 (Lockhart J commenting on the predecessor provision).
336 K Barnett and S Harder, *Remedies in Australian Private Law* (Cambridge University Press, 2nd ed, 2018) 330.
337 *LJP Investments Pty Ltd v Howard Chia Investments Pty Ltd (No 2)* (1989) 24 NSWLR 499. See Section 8.3.2.5.
338 See Section 8.3.2.5 and *Shelfer v City of London Electric Lighting Co* [1895] 1 Ch 287.
339 *Beswicke v Alner* [1926] VLR 72, 76–7.
340 *Break Fast Investments Pty Ltd v PCH Melbourne Pty Ltd* (2007) 20 VR 311. Compare *LJP Investments v Howard Chia Investments Pty Ltd (No 2)* (1989) 24 NSWLR 499.
341 *Woollerton & Wilson Ltd v Richard Costain Ltd* [1970] 1 WLR 411; *Graham v KD Morris & Sons Pty Ltd* [1974] Qd R 1.
342 *Cook v Rodgers* (1946) 46 SR (NSW) 229.
343 *Collier-Garland (Properties) Pty Ltd v O'Hair* (1963) 63 SR (NSW) 500.

ECONOMIC RIGHTS

A variety of intentional torts seek to prevent interference with a plaintiff's economic rights. These torts include injurious falsehood, passing off, inducing breach of contract, interfering with contractual relations and conspiracy. Injunctions are available for many of these torts (eg, passing off)[344] as damages are rarely adequate to compensate the plaintiff for the loss, particularly because the loss is difficult to measure.

BODILY INTEGRITY

The intentional torts that seek to protect trespass to the person are assault, battery and false imprisonment. Injunctions to prevent battery or false imprisonment are rarely sought, since a tortfeasor will not announce such a tort in advance and an injunction serves no purpose once the tort is committed. As noted, equitable injunctions in the auxiliary jurisdiction were said to extend to the protection of property, not the person.[345] In exceptional circumstances only will a threat of assault be dealt with by means of an injunction.[346]

REPUTATION

Defamation occurs where a defendant publishes to third parties imputations that tend to harm the reputation of the plaintiff in the eyes of the public. A plaintiff seeking a final injunction restraining a threatened publication by a defendant needs to show that the publication would be defamatory of the plaintiff and that the defendant would have no defence.[347] Many cases in defamation involve applications for interlocutory injunctions, as plaintiffs typically seek to restrain imminent publication prior to trial. The test for interlocutory injunction will only be granted in 'exceptional' or 'very' clear cases.[348]

12.4.2.4 Quia timet injunctions

An important function of the injunction is to prevent prospective damage from occurring. Quia timet literally means 'because he or she is afraid' in Latin. A quia timet injunction is awarded where no damage has yet been sustained by the plaintiff, but the defendant has threatened both 'imminent and substantial' damage to the plaintiff's property or interests.[349] In this way it is necessary to prove that the common law cause of action has crystallised.[350]

12.4.2.5 Discretionary factors and bars to relief

Legal injunctions (ie, in the auxiliary jurisdiction of equity) are always subject to the discretion of the court as well as a number of general bars to relief that apply to all equitable relief. These include factors such as hardship and public interest;[351] lack of 'clean hands'; and 'laches' or delay.[352]

---

344 *Erven Warnink Bv v J Townsend & Sons (Hull) Ltd* [1979] AC 731, 742 (Lord Diplock).
345 *Palmer Bruyn & Parker Pty Ltd v Parsons* (2001) 208 CLR 388; [2001] HCA 69, [58].
346 *Parry v Crooks* (1981) 27 SASR 1, 9 (King CJ); *Corvisy v Corvisy* [1982] 2 NSWLR 557; *Nguyen v Scheiff* (2002) 29 Fam LR 177.
347 *Naoum v Dannawi* (2009) 75 NSWLR 216, [32].
348 *Australian Broadcasting Corporation v O'Neill* (2006) 227 CLR 57; [2006] HCA 46.
349 *Proctor v Bayley* (1889) 42 Ch D 390, 398; *Bendigo & Country Districts Trustees & Executors Co Ltd v Sandhurst & Northern District Trustees, Executors & Agency Co Ltd* (1909) 9 CLR 474, 478.
350 *Associated Newspapers Group plc v Insert Media Ltd* (1989) IPR 345, 358 (Mummery J).
351 *Miller v Jackson* [1977] QB 966; *Wrotham Park Estate Co Ltd v Parkside Homes Ltd* [1974] 1 WLR 798, 811 (Brightman J).
352 *Wroth v Tyler* [1974] Ch 30, 53.

12.4.2.6   Interlocutory injunctions: requirements

Interlocutory injunctions are injunctions granted prior to final judgment. They are generally sought to preserve the status quo until the trial takes place.

In order to obtain an interlocutory injunction,[353] a plaintiff must first identify a legal, equitable or statutory right that the injunction supports.[354] Then, the court must be satisfied of two matters. The first is that there is a 'serious question to be tried'[355] or that there is a 'prima facie' case.[356] Although the High Court has expressed its preference for the latter test, it has noted the similarity of the two tests.[357] The second matter the court must be satisfied of is that the balance of convenience supports the order of an injunction, taking into account the impact of the order for injunction on both the plaintiff and the defendant and the nature of the rights affected.[358] An example of this process of balancing is afforded by a decision of the Federal Court.[359]

12.4.2.7   Damages awarded instead of or in addition to injunction

As noted in Section 8.3.5, a court may award damages instead of or in addition to an injunction in certain circumstances as set out in *Shelfer v City of London Electric Lighting Co*,[360] which we labelled 'equitable damages'. They are also called 'Lord Cairns' Act damages' since they have their origin in English legislation known as the *Lord Cairns' Act* that awarded damages only in limited circumstances for equitable causes of action.[361]

Such damages have been awarded in cases of proprietary torts such as trespass to land and goods and nuisance. In *Isenberg v East India House Estate Co Ltd*,[362] in a case of nuisance where the defendant's houses blocked out the plaintiff's light, the Court ordered an inquiry into the measure of damage rather than an injunction to pull down the offending buildings.

REVIEW QUESTIONS

(1)   What types of injunction can apply (if at all) to torts?

(2)   In what circumstances will an injunction be ordered?

 Guided responses in the eBook

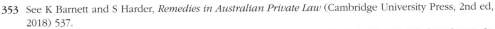

353   See K Barnett and S Harder, *Remedies in Australian Private Law* (Cambridge University Press, 2nd ed, 2018) 537.

354   *Australian Broadcasting Corporation v Lenah Game Meats Pty Ltd* (2001) 208 CLR 199; [2001] HCA 63, [15]–[16] (Gleeson CJ), [61] (Gaudron J), [86]–[105] (Gummow and Hayne JJ).

355   *American Cynamid Co v Ethicon Ltd* [1975] AC 396, 407 (Lord Diplock).

356   *Beecham Group Ltd v Bristol Laboratories Pty Ltd* (1968) 118 CLR 618, 622 (Kitto, Taylor, Menzies and Owen JJ).

357   *Australian Broadcasting Corporation v O'Neill* (2006) 227 CLR 57; [2006] HCA 46, [65]–[72].

358   *Beecham Group Ltd v Bristol Laboratories Pty Ltd* (1968) 118 CLR 618, 622–3 (Kitto, Taylor, Menzies and Owen JJ).

359   *Textile Clothing and Footwear Union of Australia v Huyck Wangner Australia Pty Ltd* [2008] FCA 1504.

360   [1895] 1 Ch 287.

361   *Chancery Amendment Act 1858* (21 & 22 Vict c 27) s 2.

362   (1863) 3 De GJ & S 263.

12.5 Declarations

A declaration judgment is an order made by the court that conclusively pronounces the existence or non-existence of rights or obligations concerning the parties before it.[363] It is not an enforceable order of the court and so stands in contrast to judgments for damages, which can be enforced against a defendant. The power of the court to award declarations exists by statute.[364]

In the context of torts, because common law courts could not award declarations before the UK *Judicature Acts* of 1873 and 1875, they developed nominal damages as an analogue to a declaratory judgment. That is, when the court awarded nominal damages, it was making a declaration that the defendant had committed a wrong but caused no damage and so awarded only a 'token' amount of nominal damages.[365]

Some scholars have described declarations as 'vindicatory' in that they 'vindicate the plaintiff's rights by a public statement of those rights'.[366] Justice Gordon of the High Court confirmed this understanding in *Lewis v Australian Capital Territory* when her Honour stated that 'an award of substantial compensatory damages is not required in order to vindicate Mr Lewis' rights. That is achieved by the finding of unlawful detention made in this case, akin to a declaration, together with an award of nominal damages.'[367]

REVIEW QUESTION

Is the category of nominal damages still needed in the law of torts, given the existence of the court's power to make declarations and so vindicate the plaintiff's rights by this means?

 Guided response in the eBook

12.6 Multiple tortfeasors

12.6.1 Liability

On occasion the loss or damage that the plaintiff has suffered is attributable to more than one tortfeasor. In such cases, the plaintiff may sue as many defendants as are legally responsible

---

363 K Barnett and S Harder, *Remedies in Australian Private Law* (Cambridge University Press, 2nd ed, 2018) 420.

364 *Court Procedures Rules 2006* (ACT) r 2900(2); *Supreme Court Act 1970* (NSW) s 75; *Supreme Court Act 1979* (NT) s 18(1); *Civil Proceedings Act 2011* (Qld) s 102(2); *Supreme Court Act 1935* (SA) s 31; *Supreme Court Rules 2000* (Tas) r 103(2); *Supreme Court Act 1986* (Vic) s 36; *Supreme Court Act 1935* (WA) s 25(6).

365 *New South Wales v Stevens* (2012) 82 NSWLR 106.

366 K Barnett and S Harder, *Remedies in Australian Private Law* (Cambridge University Press, 2nd ed, 2018) 416.

367 *Lewis v Australian Capital Territory* (2020) 271 CLR 192; [2020] HCA 26, [98] (Gordon J).

for the loss, provided that the plaintiff may never recover more than the total loss suffered.[368]

It is important to review some basic concepts in order to understand how the law allocates responsibility in such cases.[369] These concepts are:

- joint tortfeasors versus several tortfeasors
- concurrent liability
- solidary liability
- proportionate liability.

12.6.1.1   Joint tortfeasors versus several tortfeasors

Where two or more defendants are held liable to the plaintiff for the *same wrong*, they are described as 'joint tortfeasors'. This may occur in a variety of circumstances, including where:[370]

- One defendant is vicariously liable for the tort of the other (see Section 10.2).
- One defendant committed the tort as an agent for the other.
- Both defendants shared (and breached) the very same duty of care towards the plaintiff (eg, joint occupiers of land breached the duty of care each owed to a visitor).
- Both defendants were acting 'in concert' towards a common end.

By contrast, 'several tortfeasors' are liable for *different wrongs* and are unconnected to one another save in the respect that their wrongs all caused the plaintiff harm.[371]

12.6.1.2   Concurrent liability

Where multiple tortfeasors, joint or several, are liable for the *same damage*, their liability is said to be 'concurrent'.[372] As stated by the High Court: 'Concurrent tortfeasors are persons whose acts concur to produce the same damage'.[373] Following from this proposition:[374]

- All joint tortfeasors are necessarily liable concurrently because, if the first defendant (D1) and the second defendant (D2) are liable for the same wrong, they are inevitably liable for the same damage flowing from that wrong.
- But several tortfeasors can either be liable concurrently for causing the plaintiff the *same* injury (eg, two negligent drivers cause an accident causing a leg injury to the plaintiff), or their liability can be non-concurrent where their separate wrongs may cause the plaintiff *distinct* injuries (eg, driver 1 negligently causes the plaintiff a broken leg and driver 2 independently causes the plaintiff a broken arm).

---

368 *D'Angola v Rio Pioneer Gravel Co Pty Ltd* [1979] 1 NSWLR 495.
369 See generally K Barker et al, *The Law of Torts in Australia* (Oxford University Press, 5th ed, 2012) ch 18.
370 *Baxter v Obacelo Pty Ltd* (2001) 205 CLR 635; [2001] HCA 66, [24] (Gleeson CJ and Callinan J).
371 Ibid.
372 Ibid.
373 Ibid.
374 K Barker et al, *The Law of Torts in Australia* (Oxford University Press, 5th ed, 2012) [18.11].

The distinction between concurrent and non-concurrent tortfeasors is important:

(1)   In cases where tortfeasors are non-concurrently liable for causing the plaintiff distinct items of damage, each tortfeasor is only liable for the separate damage he or she caused (and so 'severally' liable).

(2)   In cases where tortfeasors (whether joint or several) are concurrently liable for the same damage, liability for the plaintiff's damage is usually 'solidary'.

12.6.1.3   Solidary liability

Solidary liability means that each and every tortfeasor is liable to the plaintiff for the *whole* of the plaintiff's loss, not just the portion he or she caused. This principle applies whether the defendant's concurrent liability is joint or several.[375] Solidary liability is commonly referred to as 'joint and several' liability; but the phrase 'joint and several' liability fails to distinguish between joint tortfeasors, who are necessarily concurrently liable, and several tortfeasors, who may be liable concurrently or non-concurrently – and in the latter case, not liable for the whole of the damage but only that portion he or she caused.

HINTS AND TIPS

Note the distinction between the term 'solidary' liability, which means that each tortfeasor is liable for the whole of the loss, and the concept of 'joint and several' liability, which means that each tortfeasor is liable for the whole of the loss but does not specify whether that tortfeasor is a joint concurrent tortfeasor or a several concurrent tortfeasor.

Solidary liability was once the governing principle for all cases of concurrent wrongdoing and remains the rule at common law. But legislation has led to its replacement in a significant number of situations by the concept of 'proportionate liability'.

12.6.1.4   Proportionate liability

Under the principles of proportionate liability, concurrent wrongdoers (whether joint or several) are liable to the plaintiff only for such proportion of the damage as represents the measure of their own responsibility for it. We examine some of the details of the legislative proportionate liability system in Section 12.6.1.6. Significantly, these proportionate liability provisions apply only to economic loss and property damage and so *do not apply to personal injuries claims.*

12.6.1.5   Joint tortfeasors: what is the effect of judgment and a release?

What is the effect of a judgment? Previously at common law, a rule known as the rule in *Brinsmead v Harrison*[376] provided that a judgment against one joint tortfeasor barred an action against any of the others, even if the judgment remained unsatisfied (unpaid). This

375   *Bell v Thompson* (1934) SR (NSW) 431, 435 (Jordan CJ on joint liability); *Barisic v Devenport* [1978] 2 NSWLR 111, 116–17 (Moffitt P on several liability).
376   (1871) LR 6 CP 584.

rule was designed to avoid a multiplicity of actions,[377] but operated harshly against plaintiffs if they happened to sue an impecunious defendant. The rule has now been abolished by legislation (see Section 12.6.1.6). Accordingly:

- The fact that a plaintiff has obtained a judgment against one joint tortfeasor no longer prevents the plaintiff subsequently bringing actions against others in respect of the same damage.

- The same is true where a plaintiff joins a number of joint tortfeasors in the *same* action and obtains judgment against one of them: despite having obtained a judgment against one defendant, the plaintiff may therefore go on to obtain judgment against other defendants in the same proceedings.

The legislation abolishing the rule in *Brinsmead v Harrison* achieves the policy aim of protecting plaintiffs who obtain judgment against impecunious tortfeasors, but opens the door to the other policy concern, namely the possibility of a multiplicity of unnecessary actions. Such legislation contains two types of provisions to offset this risk:

(1) If the plaintiff brings more than one action in respect of the same damage, the judgment obtained in the first action sets an upper limit on the total amount that the plaintiff can recover under all of them.[378]

(2) A plaintiff bringing more than one action may also have to pay the costs of later actions (a 'sanction in costs') unless he or she had reasonable grounds for bringing the latter action or actions. The impecuniosity of the first defendant may be just such a reasonable ground. In Victoria, this second rule applies.[379]

What is the effect of a release by which a plaintiff releases a joint tortfeasor from liability? Does this prevent the plaintiff suing other joint tortfeasors? It was once thought that a release by the plaintiff of one joint tortfeasor automatically operated to release them all, in the same way that a judgment did.[380] But the various statutory provisions have been held to have impliedly abolished this rule also.[381] So a release of one defendant does not release a second defendant. However, if the plaintiff accepts a sum from the first defendant in satisfaction of *all* of its claims (against both defendants), it has been suggested that the plaintiff may not then bring an action against the second defendant (or the first defendant).[382]

12.6.1.6   Proportionate liability under legislation

The insurance crisis of the early 2000s, and the legislative reform that followed, resulted in the introduction of proportionate liability and the abolition of solidary liability in all Australian jurisdictions. Significantly, these reforms do not apply to cases of death and personal injury.

Solidary liability remains in cases of death and personal injury because the policy argument prevailed that solidary liability was justified in those cases despite its unfair operation in cases of property damage and economic loss. Hence, proportionate liability

---

377 *Nau v Kemp & Associates Pty Ltd* (2010) 77 NSWLR 687, [139] (Campbell JA).
378 *Baxter v Obacelo Pty Ltd* (2001) 205 CLR 635; [2001] HCA 66.
379 *Wrongs Act 1958* (Vic) ss 24AA, 24AB.
380 *Cutter v McPhail* [1962] 2 QB 292.
381 *Thompson v Australian Capital Television Pty Ltd* (1996) 186 CLR 574.
382 *Baxter v Obacelo Pty Ltd* (2001) 205 CLR 635; [2001] HCA 66, [48] (Gleeson CJ and Callinan J).

and the abolition of solidary liability in the legislation only operates in situations of property damage and economic loss.

The proportionate liability framework is set out in Table 12.11.

Table 12.11   Proportionate liability

Legislation	Provision(s)
Civil Law (Wrongs) Act 2002 (ACT)	ch 7A
Civil Liability Act 2002 (NSW)	pt 4
Personal Injuries (Liabilities and Damages) Act 2003 (NT)	pt 2
Civil Liability Act 2003 (Qld)	ch 2 pt 2
Law Reform (Contributory Negligence and Apportionment of Liability) Act 2001 (SA)	ss 8, 9
Civil Liability Act 2002 (Tas)	pt 9A
Wrongs Act 1958 (Vic)	pt IVAA
Civil Liability Act 2002 (WA)	pt 1F

The significant aspects of the proportionate liability legislation are:

- Proportionate liability applies to all 'apportionable' claims, defined as claims for economic loss or damage to property arising from breach of duty of care, as well as claims arising from the breach of statutory prohibitions on misleading and deceptive conduct. Accordingly, the proportionate liability provisions *do not apply to personal injuries claims*.

- The legislation applies to the liability of 'concurrent wrongdoers', defined as one of two or more persons whose act or omission caused, independently of each other or jointly, the *same* damage for which the plaintiff makes his or her claim. This meaning of 'concurrent' wrongdoers is consistent with the common law definition.[383] The provision includes both joint tortfeasors and several tortfeasors. But the Queensland and South Australian legislation refer only to several tortfeasors, thus excluding joint tortfeasors from the proportionate liability regime; their liability remains solidary.

- In the situation of claims that are not 'apportionable' or claims that are specifically excluded, namely in those cases where the wrongdoer's liability rests on intention to cause damage or fraud, liability rests on prior common law principles (ie, solidary liability).

- Where the regime of proportionate liability applies, a defendant's liability is limited to an amount reflecting that proportion of the damage that the court considers just having regard to the extent of that defendant's responsibility for the loss. This gives the court a wide discretion akin to that provided for in legislation allowing apportionment for a plaintiff's contributory negligence and for contribution between defendants.

- Except in Victoria, the legislation also provides that the court may (or, in some jurisdictions, must) consider the comparative responsibility of any concurrent wrongdoer who is not a party to the proceedings.

- A defendant against whom a proportionate liability judgment has been made cannot be required to pay contribution to, or indemnify, another concurrent wrongdoer.

383 *St George Bank Ltd v Quinerts Pty Ltd* (2009) 25 VR 666, [63]–[67].

These situations just discussed apply to concurrent tortfeasors (ie, multiple tortfeasors responsible for the same harm).

12.6.1.7   Liability of several tortfeasors for distinct damage

What is the situation regarding several tortfeasors for distinct damage? These tortfeasors are not covered by the legislation. The situation for several tortfeasors who cause the plaintiff *distinct* harm is that each is responsible only for the separate loss he or she has caused.

Thus, by way of example, if D1 negligently injures P's arm and D2 independently injures P's leg (whether at the same time or later), D1 is liable only for damages to the arm and D2 only for damage to the leg. But, while their liability may be so limited in respect of damages for non-economic loss, both will be liable on a solidary basis for any loss of earnings or psychiatric harm.[384]

12.6.2   Contribution

In cases in which a defendant is liable on a solidary basis for the whole of a plaintiff's damage, he or she has the right to claim a monetary contribution from any other person liable in respect of the same damage, whether this is a joint or several tortfeasor. Rights to contribution arise only where a defendant's liability is solidary, not where he or she is merely liable for a defined proportion of the plaintiff's loss.

At common law the rule in *Merryweather v Nixan* provided that there could be no contribution between tortfeasors.[385] But all Australian jurisdictions now have legislation abolishing this rule. The legislation, however, does vary considerably in detail from one jurisdiction to the next, which gives rise to some complexity.

The contribution provisions are set out in Table 12.12.

Table 12.12   Contribution provisions

Legislation	Provision
Civil Law (Wrongs) Act 2002 (ACT)	pt 2.5
Law Reform (Miscellaneous Provisions) Act 1946 (NSW)	s 5
Law Reform (Miscellaneous Provisions) Act 1956 (NT)	pt IV
Law Reform Act 1995 (Qld)	pt 3 div 2
Law Reform (Contributory Negligence and Apportionment of Liability) Act 2001 (SA)	s 6
Wrongs Act 1954 (Tas)	s 3
Wrongs Act 1958 (Vic)	pt IV
Law Reform (Contributory Negligence and Tortfeasors' Contribution) Act 1947 (WA)	s 7

The contribution provisions take two different forms:

(1)   In New South Wales, Queensland, Western Australia and Tasmania, the provision reads, with minor differences, that 'any tortfeasor liable' can recover contribution from 'any other tortfeasor' who is also liable for the same harm or damage.

(2)   In the Australian Capital Territory, Northern Territory, South Australia and Victoria, the legislation refers generally to 'a person' who is liable for harm or damage suffered by another being able to recover contribution from another 'person' who is also liable for the same harm or damage.

384   *Dingle v Associated Newspapers* [1961] 2 QB 162, 188–9 (Devlin LJ).
385   (1799) 101 ER 1337.

The different wording gives rise to issues of who is liable and who's contribution can be claimed against.

12.6.2.1   Who, as a liable tortfeasor, may claim contribution?

The wording in the first-mentioned provision of 'any tortfeasor liable', or its equivalents, means any person whose liability has been ascertained by judgment of a court, including a consent judgment,[386] or by an out-of-court settlement reached without the court's sanction.[387] In the case of settlements, the party seeking contribution (A) must show that, had the claim gone to judgment, A would have been liable to pay in whole or in part. Therefore, whether or not an admission of liability was made at settlement, the party seeking contribution must ultimately admit liability.[388]

12.6.2.2   Against whom may contribution be claimed?

The first-mentioned legislation variously states that the contribution proceedings may be brought against 'any other tortfeasor who is ... liable', 'someone else liable for the same damage or harm' and 'third person[s] liable for the same damage or harm'. They clearly include concurrent tortfeasors against whom a judgment has actually been entered by a court; and they exclude persons against whom the injured plaintiff has not and could not have recovered.[389]

12.6.2.3   Assessment of contribution

Courts in all jurisdictions have a wide discretion to award such contribution as they consider to be 'just and equitable'. This ranges from nothing[390] to complete indemnity.[391]

In typical cases of two or more negligent defendants, the apportionment exercise requires a court to examine both the relative blameworthiness of each defendant (the extent to which he or she departed from the standards of a reasonable person)[392] and the relative causal significance of their acts.

REVIEW QUESTIONS

(1)   What is the difference between joint and several tortfeasors?

(2)   What is the difference between concurrent liability, solidary liability and proportionate liability?

(3)   What is contribution?

   Guided responses in the eBook

---

386   *Bitumen & Oil Refineries (Australia) Ltd v Commissioner for Government Transport* (1955) 92 CLR 220, 211–12.

387   *Stott v West Yorkshire Road Car Co Ltd* [1971] 2 QB 651; *Bakker v Joppich & Bitumax Pty Ltd* (1980) 25 SASR 468; *Ahrens Engineering Pty Ltd v Leroy Palmer & Associates* (2010) 106 SASR 160.

388   *Stott v West Yorkshire Road Car Co Ltd* [1971] 2 QB 651, 565–657 (Lord Denning MR); *Thompson v Australian Capital Television Pty Ltd* (1996) 186 CLR 574.

389   *Amaca Pty Ltd v New South Wales* (2003) 199 ALR 596.

390   *Rolls Royce Industrial Power (Pacific) Ltd v James Hardie & Co Pty Ltd* (2001) 53 NSWLR 626.

391   *Pantalone v Alaouie* (1989) 18 NSWLR 119.

392   See, eg, *Amaca Pty Ltd v New South Wales* (2003) 199 ALR 596.

KEY CONCEPTS

- **death following personal injury:** in the case of death following personal injury, the deceased person's estate or dependants may be entitled to take action for the tort.

- **multiple defendants:** in the case of multiple defendants, issues of liability and contribution arise between the defendants depending on whether the liability is joint or several, concurrent or non-concurrent.

- **remedies:** usually provided by a court, and in tort cases generally take the form of awards of damages or injunctions. The plaintiff is entitled to a remedy once they have established the requirements of a case in negligence or another tort, and the defendant has been unable to prove the existence of a relevant defence.

- **self-help measures:** remedies also exist in the form of self-help measures, in which the parties take remedial action without a court award or order.

 Complete the multiple-choice questions in the eBook to test your knowledge

PROBLEM-SOLVING EXERCISES

Exercise 1

Penny, 26, was a successful jazz dancer earning a gross income of about $4300 per week. Two years ago she suffered a spinal cord injury in a skiing accident, which was caused by the negligence of the instructor, Roy. Penny is paralysed from the waist down as a result of the accident. She is confined to a wheelchair. A medical report indicates that she has an impairment of her spine of 55 per cent, based on the AMA Guides.

Penny has incurred $278 000 in hospital and medical expenses in the two years to date, and will require ongoing medical treatment and rehabilitation. She and her husband (a highly paid financial adviser) have also incurred expenses of $250 000 in making changes to their home to make it wheelchair-accessible, and a further $28 000 to modify their vehicle.

Penny can generally manage to look after herself, but sometimes needs help with dressing and grooming (approximately five hours per week). Her mother and sister have been providing this care in the two years since the accident, and will continue to provide this care on an ongoing basis. Since the accident, her mother and sister have also been assisting with caring for Penny's four-year-old son for approximately three hours per week, performing tasks that Penny herself is no longer able to do because of the accident. Again, this care will be ongoing. Penny looked after her son prior to the accident.

Following the accident, Penny has been working as an administrative assistant to a children's dance company, earning about $1400 gross per week.

Six months ago Penny suffered a mild stroke (this was nothing to do with the skiing accident). The medical specialist treating Penny for her stroke estimates that (even had she not been paralysed in the skiing accident) there was a 65 per cent chance that in five years she would have been unable to work as a dancer because of the risk of suffering a stroke, and that it is almost definite that she would have been completely incapacitated for work of any kind in 10 years.

Advise Penny of her entitlement to compensation for damages. Use the *Wrongs Act 1958* (Vic) as appropriate.

   Guided response in the eBook

Exercise 2

Taking the facts of Penny in problem-solving exercise 1, provide your advice to Penny's estate on the assumption that two years after the accident she dies as a result of a spinal cord abscess (caused by the trauma of the accident). You should act on the assumption that she did not commence proceedings to recover damages before she died.

Advise Penny's estate on what actions it may bring in tort to seek damages following the death of Penny.

   Guided response in the eBook

CHALLENGE YOURSELF

Exercise 1

If the *Malec v Hutton* approach to contingencies had been applied by the High Court to the facts in *Lewis v Australian Capital Territory*, would there have been a different outcome?

   Guided response in the eBook

Exercise 2

The High Court in *Lewis v Australian Capital Territory* definitively rejected the concept of 'vindicatory damages' forming a part of the Australian law of torts. In doing so, it arguably failed to properly distinguish between torts that are actionable per se and those in which damage is the gist of the action. This is yet another example of the monopolisation of the law of torts by negligence. Discuss.

   Guided response in the eBook

13

TORTS ARISING FROM STATUTORY DUTIES AND POWERS

13.1   Introduction

The common law principles of duty of care and negligence potentially apply to all actors, public and private, and earlier chapters have discussed their application to government actors (see Section 2.5.4). This chapter analyses two distinct forms of tortious action which are connected to the performance or non-performance of statutory duties and powers. The first, the action for breach of a statutory duty of care, exists where Parliament intends a legislative duty to be enforced by a private cause of action. This action in essence facilitates the enforcement of specific types of legislative duties which are aimed at the protection of certain interests. The second cause of the action, misfeasance in public office, exists as an action to prevent the bad-faith use of statutory power by public officers performing public functions.

13.2   Action for breach of statutory duty

13.2.1   When will this action be available?

As stated by Crennan and Kiefel JJ in *Stuart v Kirkland-Veenstra*, 'the action for breach of statutory duty, although itself a tort, is regarded as distinct from the tort of negligence'.[1] The action is commonly pleaded concurrently with an action for negligence. It is important to be clear that not all breaches of statutory duty give rise to this action – a duty must be accompanied by an express or implied parliamentary intention for the cause of action to attach to a particular duty. Action for breach of statutory duty has its historical roots in a common law presumption, expressed by Gaudron J in *Slivak v Lurgi*, that 'as a general rule, legislation which imposes duties with respect to the safety of others is construed as conferring a right of civil action unless a contrary intention appears'.[2]

---

1 (2009) 237 CLR 215; [2009] HCA 15, [130]. As discussed in Chapter 2, the existence of legal powers (including statutory powers) is necessary but not sufficient to establish a common law duty of care.
2 (2001) 205 CLR 304; [2001] HCA 6, [49].

As Justice Mark Leeming has noted, the historical roots of this presumption are contested, and its use has waxed and waned.[3] Successful actions for breach of statutory duty have often clustered around the area of industrial and workplace safety. The clearest statement of principle as to when the action will exist was provided by the joint judgment of Brennan CJ, Dawson and Toohey JJ in the High Court case of *Byrne v Australian Airlines Ltd* ('*Byrne*'):

> A cause of action for damages for breach of statutory duty arises where a statute which imposes an obligation for the protection or benefit of a particular class of persons is, upon its proper construction, intended to provide a ground of civil liability when the breach of the obligation causes injury or damage of a kind against which the statute was designed to afford protection.[4]

Where the criteria regulating its recognition are met, the action for breach of statutory duty thus grants a private individual the right to enforce a statutory duty against another person, and recover damages for harm suffered.

13.2.2   Elements of the action

The elements of the action for breach of statutory duty are summarised in Figure 13.1.

13.2.2.1   Did Parliament intend to allow an action under the particular statute?

There are examples where Parliament has expressly chosen to provide individuals with the right to take a private tort action to enforce the requirements of a statute.[5] Granting such a right to take private action can replace or supplement the enforcement activities of agencies or regulators. Far more difficult, however, are instances where a statute prescribes some methods of enforcement and it falls to the court to decide whether there was an intent for the alternative remedy of action to recover damages to be available. In *O'Connor v SP Bray Ltd*, Dixon J observed the potential excesses involved in applying a presumption to the 'silences' of a statute:

> The difficulty is that in such a case the legislature has in fact expressed no intention upon the subject, and an interpretation of the statute, according to ordinary canons of construction, will rarely yield a necessary implication positively giving a civil remedy. As an examination of the decided cases will show, an intention to give, or not to give, a private right has more often than not been ascribed to the legislature as a result of presumptions or by reference to matters governing the policy of the provision rather

---

3 Justice M Leeming, 'Theories and Principles Underlying the Development of the Common Law: The Statutory Elephant in the Room' (2013) 36(3) *University of New South Wales Law Journal* 1002, 1017. The fact that early precedents were almost entirely centred on industrial and workplace safety led the famous jurist Glanville Williams to remark that 'when [penal legislation] concerns industrial welfare, such legislation results in absolute liability in tort. In all other cases it is ignored': G Williams, 'The Effect of Penal Legislation in the Law of Tort' (1960) 23(3) *Modern Law Review* 233, 233.

4 (1995) 185 CLR 410, 424 (citations omitted).

5 The most prominent example is s 236 of the *Australian Consumer Law* (contained in *Competition and Consumer Act 2010* (Cth) sch 2) which makes breaches of consumer law such as misleading or deceptive conduct or unfair contract terms actionable in private law.

Figure 13.1   Elements of breach of statutory duty

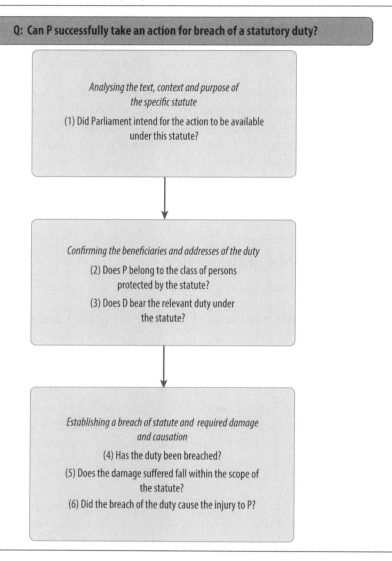

Q: Can P successfully take an action for breach of a statutory duty?

Analysing the text, context and purpose of the specific statute

(1) Did Parliament intend for the action to be available under this statute?

Confirming the beneficiaries and addresses of the duty

(2) Does P belong to the class of persons protected by the statute?

(3) Does D bear the relevant duty under the statute?

Establishing a breach of statute and required damage and causation

(4) Has the duty been breached?

(5) Does the damage suffered fall within the scope of the statute?

(6) Did the breach of the duty cause the injury to P?

than the meaning of the instrument. Sometimes it almost appears that a complexion is given to the statute upon very general considerations without either the authority of any general rule of law or the application of any definite rule of construction.[6]

Thus, as Professor Neil Foster has written, complex and interacting principles of interpretation will arise when a court is asked to identify whether the cause of action exists:

Does the statute itself prescribe a penalty, or not? Is the statutory provision designed for the benefit of a limited class of persons, or is it meant for the benefit of the public at large? Is the obligation concerned a specific and confined obligation, or is it more

6 (1937) 56 CLR 464, 477–8.

general and ill-defined? Does the provision occur in a statutory context where other obligations are likely to be actionable, or not? Has this obligation, or an obligation analogous to this in previous legislation, been already held by the courts to give rise to a civil action?[7]

This quote by Foster should be read closely, as it condenses much complexity. First, the reader should acknowledge that an actionable duty will be found in balancing competing factors. This is an area shaped by a finding about a specific statute of a particular character. The answer is not driven by absolute principles, but by what Parliament is found to have intended. Second, Foster highlights three factors which, as we will see, nearly always fall to be negotiated in determining if an actionable duty exists:

- Does the statute prescribe *alternative remedies* of such a nature that it is unlikely that Parliament intended to allow for the imposition of a supplementary actionable statutory duty by the plaintiff inappropriate?

- What is the *character of the duty* defined by the statute? If the duty is expressed solely in terms of ends, the general avoidance of an absolute outcome or prohibition, it is less likely to ground an actionable duty. If it is rather expressed in terms of both means *and* ends, the situation may differ. A statutory duty which addresses the steps a specific entity is meant to take to avoid a result is more likely to ground an actionable duty.

- Does the statute involve the protection of the safety or interests of a specific class of people, or is it directed towards a broad public interest?

There is a general principle that the likelihood of a private action being available will increase if the duty involves or regulates private interests and concerns, not merely the public as a whole. In a recent piece of scholarship, Professor Neil Foster argues that the 'limited class' principle does not operate as a bright line rule. It is likely better thought of as a factor to be taken into account in discerning Parliament's intention to allow civil action for breach of a statutory duty. Take, for instance, the statement of the High Court of Australia in *Brodie v Singleton Shire Council*:[8]

> Ordinarily, the more general the statutory duty and the wider the class of persons in the community who it may be expected will derive benefit from its performance, the less likely is it that the statute can be construed as conferring an individual right of action for damages for its non-performance.[9]

This statement is compatible with an understanding that a duty targeted at a limited class is more likely to be recognised, not a blanket exclusion of duties owed to the public at large.

Nevertheless, while not a separate condition existing outside the interpretation process, duties which are directed towards the common good or broad public interest are less likely to be actionable. This was seen in the Victorian bushfires case of *Matthews v SPI Electricity Pty Ltd (Ruling No 2)* ('*Matthews*') where the Court stressed that an obligation to prepare a

---

7   N Foster, 'The Merits of the Civil Action for Breach of Statutory Duty' (2011) 33(1) *Sydney Law Review* 67, 74.
8   (2001) 206 CLR 512; [2001] HCA 29, [326].
9   *Brodie v Singleton Shire Council* (2001) 206 CLR 512; [2001] HCA 29, [326].

bushfire emergency response was directed at protecting the public as a whole, rather than at a specific class to whom a private right of action would then attach.[10]

Case: *Matthews v SPI Electricity Pty Ltd (Ruling No 2)* (2011) 34 VR 584

Facts

The plaintiffs were a group of residents who had suffered the loss of loved ones and physical and psychological harm as a result of the Black Saturday fires of 7 February 2009. The plaintiffs alleged that Victoria Police breached their duty of care under relevant legislation in failing to warn residents of the Kilmore East fire.

The plaintiffs argued that the lack of warning on the day contravened the relevant disaster plan (DISPLAN), which bodies were required to create under the *Emergency Management Act 1986* (Vic). They argued that they, as private individuals, could take an action for breach of statutory duty where the plan provisions were not complied with.

Issue

Were the plaintiffs permitted to take an action for breach of statutory duty if there was a failure to follow the procedures included in the disaster plan?

Decision

The action was dismissed, with the Supreme Court of Victoria ruling that Parliament did not intend for any right of private action to be permitted under the relevant statute.

(Read paras [70]–[87] of the ruling for the Court's analysis of the specific statutory provisions.) The Court first stressed that the primary purpose of the *Emergency Management Act 1986* (Vic) was to demand coordination between emergency bodies by requiring the creation of an emergency plan. The Court found that the purpose of the statute was thus 'to provide those bodies with the knowledge and understanding as to who is responsible for what particular activity in the event of an emergency' (at [76]).

The statute also did not address the form and nature that the DISPLAN should take. Section 10(1) of the Act merely required that a plan be put into place and be reviewed periodically. This was a powerful consideration against the argument of the plaintiffs. The Court found that if Parliament had intended to allow individuals to take action for breach of a statutory duty in the event of non-compliance with the plan's contents, the statute would have specified the nature and form of the issues to be included in a DISPLAN.

The DISPLAN applicable to the Black Saturday bushfires contained a requirement that coordinators (police officers) consider the giving of warnings and, by cl 3.4, stated that there was an obligation, in certain circumstances, to give warnings. The primary Act did not, however, create any obligation regarding the giving of warnings, a pattern of emphasis which rendered it unlikely that Parliament intended the obligations within the DISPLAN to be actionable by tort.

---

10 (2011) 34 VR 584.

The DISPLAN was ultimately a creature of that broader statute in its text, purpose and context, and the statute did not disclose sufficient intention for the action to be ruled available (see [80]).

The Court found that the goal of the legislation was the protection of the public as a whole, rather than any specific class of private individuals. The Act could not be construed as being directed at protecting a certain class of persons, but was directed at the community at large.

Significance

The ruling underlines that the specificity of the duties contained in the statute is a key variable in determining whether action for breach of a statutory duty is available.

Where an Act is directed at the interests of the community as a whole, rather than benefiting certain classes of individuals, the duties contained within it are less likely to be found actionable by private individuals.

Question

Why is the nature of the duty included in the legislation such an important factor in determining if imposition of liability is appropriate?

    Guided response in the eBook

Having read through *Matthews*, the reader can see that the relevant statutory provision must be clearly framed to impose a legal obligation. In *AS v Minister for Immigration and Border Protection*,[11] the Victorian Court of Appeal held that s 4AA(1) of the *Migration Act 1958* (Cth) did not create an actionable duty. This provision read: 'the Parliament affirms as a principle that a minor shall only be detained as a measure of last resort.'

The Court held that the subsection was not framed as a prohibition of an imperative character, but as an abstract or indirect affirmation of a principle to be valued in decision-making. In *Waugh v Kippen*, it was similarly underlined that the more specific the statute is about the actions required to comply with a duty, the more likely a private cause of action will be found to exist.[12]

Many statutes will expressly specify remedies such as criminal sanctions or injunctive relief, to ensure relevant duties are complied with. Where such remedies are provided for, the interpretive principle of *expressio unius est exclusion alterius* ('the expression of one is the exclusion of others') counts against the recognition of additional remedies such as a private action for breach of statutory duties. This is, however, only a general principle, which must be balanced against other specific elements of the particular statute.

A recent case which explored the likelihood of a duty arising in the context of criminal sanctions is *Jane Doe v Fairfax Media Publications Pty Ltd*.[13] This case concerned the alleged

11 *AS v Minister for Immigration and Border Protection* (2016) 312 FLR 67.
12 *Waugh v Kippen* (1986) 160 CLR 156.
13 [2018] NSWSC 1996.

disclosure of identifying information of a sexual assault complainant by a newspaper group. The section in question was s 578A of the *Crimes Act 1900* (NSW), which bars the publication of material identifying or likely to identify a complainant in prescribed sexual assault proceedings. The defendants had not actually been criminally prosecuted for the alleged publication upon which the plaintiff had sued. New South Wales Police had not spoken to the defendant and no complaint had been lodged. The defendants maintained they had complied with the duty of non-publication, but the availability of the action still fell before the Court for determination.

Justice Fullerton ultimately found that the statutory duty did not confer a private right of action for a number of reasons. The most compelling of these were the express provision of a mechanism for enforcing breaches of the duty through criminal law sanctions. While the existence of a criminal law sanction had been present in older cases involving workplace health and safety, the Court ultimately found that 'more recent cases paint a different picture'. It cited, in particular, the judgment of Wood CJ in *Preston v Star City Pty Ltd*.[14] There the plaintiff argued that a casino had induced him to incur substantial gaming losses in breach of relevant legislation. Despite its awareness of his existing losses, it had induced him to continue gambling through complimentary services and privileges as a 'high roller' gambler. Ultimately, his Honour found that s 70 of the *Casino Control Act 1992* (NSW) did not evince sufficient intention, citing:

> [T]he comprehensive regulatory scheme set up under the Act and Regulations, which includes the establishment of a body charged with monitoring legal casino gaming in the State and supervising compliance by casino operators and staff, and which provides for criminal and civil sanctions, as well as for disciplinary action in the event of any contravention of the Act, Regulations or licence conditions …[15]

In the current matter, Justice Fullerton emphasised that the Court's 'overwhelming impression' was that the only remedy the legislature intended to provide was the imposition of a criminal sanction. The section also permitted a judge to exercise a discretion, permitting publication of the identify of a complainant where the public interest required it, also militated against an actionable duty being established. The legislation also did not prescribe steps by which publication might be avoided and was of a blanket nature. As a result, it was held that there was no obligation to take 'a specific precaution' or 'measures for the safety of others' in the language of the section. It merely prescribed an end rather than a means, a factor which militates against the recognition of an actionable duty.

HINTS AND TIPS

You should avoid absolute statements such as, 'if the statute already expressly provides for a remedy, then action for breach of a statutory duty will never be available.'

Ultimately, there are multiple interacting factors involved in considering whether the action exists under the statute. This dynamic of duelling interpretive principles was

---

14 [1999] NSWSC 1273.
15 *Jane Doe v Fairfax Media Publications Pty Limited* [2018] NSWSC 1996, [87].

present in the early case of *Groves v Lord Wimborne* [1898] 2 QB 402 where, based upon the general scope of the Act, the nature of the duty and the seriousness of the consequence, the Court ultimately decided that the express penalty in the Act was intended to add to, not exclude, a private individual's right to action for damages. The presumption that the existence of alternative remedies excludes the private cause of action can thus be rebutted by the inadequacy of the penalty or where the specified remedy addresses damage of only a certain nature: *Dairy Farmers Co-operative Ltd v Azar* (1990) 170 CLR 293.

Construing parliamentary intention will also require an examination of the legislative history of the statute. In *Byrne*, the High Court found that there is a strong inference that a private cause of action exists where the current statute has replaced one that previously allowed for the action.[16]

In its ruling in *Seiko Epson Corporation v Calidad Pty Ltd*, the Federal Court quoted Brennan CJ, Dawson and Toohey JJ in *Byrne*:

> One generalisation that can be made is that where the persons upon whom the statutory obligation is imposed are under an existing common law duty of care towards the persons whom the statute is intended to benefit or protect, the statutory prescription of a higher or more specific standard of care may, in the absence of any indication of a contrary intention, properly be construed as creating a private right.[17]

As Forrest J stated in the Victorian case of *Acir v Frosster Pty Ltd*, decisions conferring a private right of action in workplace safety statutes usually rely on the combination of a clear parliamentary intention to promote health and safety and the existing legal relationship between employer and employee.[18]

The need to evaluate each particular statutory duty to discover whether it creates an implied right to take the action makes generalisation inevitably difficult. Ultimately, it is the interaction and balancing of various principles of interpretation that shape the court's response to a claim. Thus the question of whether a right to take a private action subsists within the statutory framework is best explored through a worked case example.

Case: *Seiko Epson Corporation v Calidad Pty Ltd* (2017) 133 IPR 1

Facts

This case concerned an unsuccessful allegation of trademark tampering. A third party outside Australia legitimately obtained used Epson printer cartridges. They refilled and modified these so that they would work again, and then sold them in Australia as cartridges suitable for Epson printers. Seiko argued that Calidad had contravened s 148 of the *Trade Marks Act 1995* (Cth).

16　*Byrne v Australian Airlines Ltd* (1995) 185 CLR 410, 424 ('*Byrne*').
17　(2017) 133 IPR 1, [341], quoting *Byrne* (1995) 185 CLR 410, 424.
18　[2009] VSC 454, [225].

Issue

Section 148 of the Act makes it an offence to deal with products on which a registered trademark has been tampered with (in the absence of the trademark holder's consent).

Decision

The Federal Court determined that s 148 did not, on balance, bestow a right to take private action for damages.

Significance

This case establishes that s 148 cannot be used to take private action for damages.

Questions

(1)   What purpose did the Court attach to s 148 of the *Trade Marks Act 1995* (Cth)? How did the Explanatory Memorandum to the Intellectual Property Laws Amendment (Raising the Bar) Bill 2012 (Cth) support this interpretation?

(2)   How did the existence of a criminal penalty and a specific mechanism for recovering damages incurred due to trademark infringements affect the Court's reasoning?

(3)   What role did the previous case of *British American Tobacco Exports BV v Trojan Trading Co Pty Ltd* [2010] VSC 572 play in the Court's reasoning?

 Guided responses in the eBook

13.2.2.2   Does the plaintiff belong to the class of persons protected by the statute?

If the action is to be made out, the plaintiff must fall within the class of persons who are protected by the statute. The plaintiff must show that he or she enjoys a 'personal right to due observance' of a statutory provision which has been denied.[19]

It is important to underline, however, that legislation might not directly identify the class on its face, but rather identify a harm which only a certain group of people can suffer. Those who suffer the harm contemplated by the legislation can thus form a class to whom an action is available. This was seen in *Pask v Owen*, where the relevant legislation prohibited a person from knowingly supplying a firearm for the use of a 'prevented person'.[20] The defendants provided their 15-year-old son with an air gun and ammunition. When their son permitted the plaintiff (a 13-year-old child) to handle the weapon, the plaintiff accidentally shot himself in the eye. The Court held that action for breach of statutory duty was available as the plaintiff was 'within the class sought to be protected' – individuals who came into contact with prevented persons who had been given arms. In such cases, the class is defined

19   *Sovar v Henry Lane Pty Ltd* (1967) 116 CLR 397, 404 (Kitto J).
20   [1987] Qd R 421.

by the circumstance affecting the relevant members of the public. A further illustrative example is the United Kingdom case of *Knapp v Railway Executive*, where a majority of the Court held that a defendant's duty to ensure that gates at level crossings were down was fundamentally aimed at ensuring benefits for road users rather than train drivers.[21]

13.2.2.3 Does the defendant bear the relevant duty under the statute?

The third element of the tort requires the litigant to establish that the defendant falls within the class of persons upon whom the duty is imposed. This can be complicated by the issue of whether or not the ordinary principles of vicarious liability can be applied to statutory terms. Ultimately, the question of whom Parliament intended to make liable is based on an interpretation of the legislation. When confronting the legislation, the court is asking whether there is sufficient evidence from the text, purpose and context of the provision setting out the duty that Parliament intended for the individual or class specified to be 'singled out' as the sole subject of the obligation, and thus as the liable party. Where this is not present, there is likely to be scope to 'read in' the ordinary principles of vicarious liability (discussed in Chapter 10).

Darling Island Stevedoring and Lighterage Co Ltd v Long is regarded as the classic case exploring these interpretive tensions.[22] There, an accident had occurred in breach of statutory duty, with the relevant regulations providing for a £100 fine for breach by the 'person in charge'. The High Court found that the relevant 'person in charge' was the foreman of the stevedoring gang involved in the unloading operation, not the employer, and that the principles of vicarious liability did not therefore apply.

The decision to impose liability on the fellow employee has been criticised, and could be viewed as being out of step with the principles of vicarious liability discussed in Chapter 10. In the United Kingdom case of *Majrowski v Guy's and St Thomas' NHS Trust*, the House of Lords unanimously found that there should be a presumption that the principle of vicarious liability applies where an employee breaches a statutory duty in the course of his or her employment.[23] This presumption could be rebutted by a contrary intention in the particular piece of legislation. Australian cases such as *Hollis v Vabu Pty Ltd* (discussed in Section 10.2.2.2) show that it may be equally appropriate in Australia for the wrong and the concomitant liability to be transferred to the employer.[24]

13.2.2.4 Was the duty breached?

The question of whether a statutory duty may have been breached is ultimately a question of interpretation and does not necessarily (or even commonly) embrace the common law's 'reasonable care' standard. While there are standard phrases for setting the scope of statutory duties (eg, 'so far as is reasonably practicable'), such phrases ultimately fall to be determined in the light of the text, context and purpose of the legislation in which they feature. The question of what is 'reasonably practicable' often depends upon, for example, a contextual consideration of whether the time, trouble and expense of the precautions suggested are

---

21 [1949] 2 All ER 508.
22 (1957) 97 CLR 36.
23 [2006] 3 WLR 125.
24 (2001) 207 CLR 21; [2001] HCA 44.

disproportionate to the risk protected by the statute.[25] The need to interpret the specific language of the statute, and to avoid falling back on common law concepts or policy values, was underlined in *Deal v Father Pius Kodakkathanath*.[26]

Case: *Deal v Father Pius Kodakkathanath* (2016) 258 CLR 281

Facts

The appellant was a teacher who had fallen from a stepladder when taking down artwork from the classroom wall. She was stepping back off the ladder, attempting not to damage multiple papier-mâché displays, when she missed a step and fell, injuring her knee.

Issue

This concerned a private action for breach of reg 3.1.2 of the *Occupational Health and Safety Regulations 2007* (Vic) which provided that an employer was to ensure the elimination of the risk of a musculoskeletal disorder 'associated with' a 'hazardous manual handling task' *as far as practicable*.

Decision

In the Victorian Court of Appeal, the majority had found that in order for a harm to be 'associated with' a task, there must be a 'close connection' between the activity and the risk. It found that the task of taking down the displays did not have a sufficient connection with what is usually defined as 'hazardous manual handling' and was a generic task. As injuries covered by falls did not have a close connection to the activity of manual handling, the Court held that the claim for statutory breach should not be permitted to be put to the jury at trial.

The High Court overturned this approach, finding that 'associated with' should not be given such a narrow interpretation. It emphasised that the definition of a 'hazardous manual handling task' under the relevant regulations included the manual handling of unstable loads, or loads that are difficult to hold. In this case, the papier-mâché displays had to be held in a certain manner to prevent them bending, which meant it was open to the jury to conclude that falling off the ladder was a 'risk' associated with a hazardous manual handling task.

Significance

This case broadened the definition of 'associated with' and 'hazardous manual handling task'.

Question

How did the High Court criticise the Victorian Court of Appeal's approach to the statute? (See paras [36]–[55] of the case.)

   Guided response in the eBook

---

25 See, generally, *Marshall v Gotham Co Ltd* [1954] AC 300.

26 (2016) 258 CLR 281; [2016] HCA 31.

The question of whether the statute imposes an absolute obligation is one of interpretation. In the occupational health and safety context, an obligation to 'ensure' has often been taken to impose absolute liability.

EMERGING ISSUE

Recent law reforms increase the burden on those taking action against *public authorities* for breach of a statutory duty. All states except South Australia and the Northern Territory now require that an act or omission must have been so unreasonable that no reasonable public decision-maker in the defendant's position would have made or omitted to perform it. These laws were passed in response to the Ipp Report recommendation which called for a policy defence to tort actions reflecting the then-prevailing *Wednesbury* 'unreasonableness' standard in public law.[27] For instance, s 84 of the *Wrongs Act 1958* (Vic) provides:

(1) This section applies to a proceeding for damages for an alleged breach of statutory duty by a public authority in connection with the exercise of or a failure to exercise a function of the authority.

(2) For the purpose of the proceeding, an act or omission of the public authority relating to a function conferred on the public authority specifically in its capacity as a public authority does not constitute a breach of statutory duty unless the act or omission was in the circumstances so unreasonable that no public authority having the functions of the authority in question could properly consider the act or omission to be a reasonable exercise of its functions.

The practical result of such provisions is that they substantially increase the barriers to establishing a breach of statutory duty. Public authorities are the most common addressees of any legislative duty, and their actions will be evaluated according to this high standard of inaction or action. A useful overview of the distinct impacts of the 'so unreasonable' standard was provided in *Queensland Bulk Water Supply Authority v Rodriguez & Sons Pty Ltd* (2021) 393 ALR 162. The Court emphasised that the ordinary test – that a person or entity failed to take precautions against a risk of harm which a reasonable person in its position would have taken – did not apply to public authorities. Instead, it will need to be established that *no* proper authority would have considered the action or inaction grossly unreasonable.[28]

This is aggravated by the fact that the statutory language arguably expresses a conservative version of the *Wednesbury* test – which was recently restated by the High Court as requiring 'evident and intelligible justification' for decisions.[29] The Court in *Rodriguez* expressly noted that 'it would invite error to reformulate the statute by

---

27 *Review of the Law of Negligence* (Final Report, September 2002) 153–8 Recommendation 39. The label derives from *Associated Provincial Picture Houses Ltd v Wednesbury Corporation* [1948] 1 KB 223, which established that in order to be quashed for unreasonableness in public law, a decision by a public authority must be so unreasonable that no reasonable authority would have made it.

28 *Queensland Bulk Water Supply Authority v Rodriguez & Sons Pty Ltd* (2021) 393 ALR 162, [278].

29 *Minister for Immigration and Citizenship v Li* (2013) 249 CLR 332; [2013] HCA 18.

reference to subsequent explanations by the High Court of the unreasonableness standard in administrative law cases'. As a result, it is arguable that Australian tort law is now shaped by statutory provisions reflecting language which is generally reserved for more extreme forms of unreasonableness findings in administrative law. The ruling of the plurality in *Minister for Immigration and Citizenship v Li* states:[30]

> *Wednesbury* is not the starting point for the standard of reasonableness, nor should it be considered the end point. The legal standard of unreasonableness should not be considered as limited to what is in effect an irrational, if not bizarre, decision – which is to say one that is so unreasonable that no reasonable person could have arrived at it …[31]

Leave to appeal the New South Wales Court of Appeal ruling on questions including the standard of care applying to public authorities was refused by the High Court in 2022. The *Rodriguez* decision confirming the relevant section applies to both breach of a statutory duty and common law negligence.[32] The application of the 'so unreasonable' standard will therefore grow in coming years and it may be that legislatures will need to consider whether it involves adequate norms for judging the conduct of modern governmental entities.

13.2.2.5   Does the damage suffered fall within the scope of the statute?

The New South Wales case of *Kebewar Pty Ltd v Harkin* provides an example of the requirement that, in order to be compensable, the harm caused by a breach of statutory duty must be of a kind that the duty was intended to prevent.[33] The case concerned a local government ordinance. The plaintiff argued that the ordinance imposed a duty on those excavating land to prevent harm arising from soil moving from the land on which the excavation was being carried. The Court, however, held that the duty to prevent damage had been limited by Parliament to situations where an excavation extended below the level of the base of the relevant building. Given that there was no right to excavate below a house of an adjoining property, the legislation was not intended to cover risks of damage to buildings belonging to a neighbour. As a result, no claim for breach of statutory duty could be advanced by the owner of a neighbouring house.

Similar reasoning was employed in *Quality Roads Pty Ltd v Baw Baw Shire Council (Ruling No 1)*,[34] a Victorian case which involved s 40 of the *Roads Management Act 2004* (Vic). This provision imposed a statutory duty on road authorities to inspect, maintain and repair public roads to the standard specified in the management plan for that road, or to a reasonable standard having regard to the principles set out in the Act. In this case, a contractor who was providing maintenance services under a road maintenance contract

---

30 Ibid.
31 Ibid (Hayne, Kiefel and Bell JJ).
32 *Queensland Bulk Water Supply Authority v Rodriguez & Sons Pty Ltd* (2021) 393 ALR 162
33 (1987) 9 NSWLR 738.
34 (2016) 223 LGERA 1.

argued that the defendant Council had breached its statutory duty by failing to maintain the road network within its municipal area to the required standard. The contractors argued that this failure had caused it an economic loss (the loss of variation payments for additional potholing and grading works), for which they were entitled to recover. This argument was rejected by the Victorian Supreme Court, which held that the duty was directed solely at harm caused to public users of the road arising from hazards and poor maintenance by the authority.

13.2.2.6   Did the breach cause the injury suffered by the plaintiff?

As with other causes of action, the defendant must prove that the breach of statutory duty caused or materially contributed to the plaintiff's injury. A specific point of emphasis in the action for statutory breach is that the issue of causation cannot be divorced from the legal framework that gives rise to the cause of action. As noted by the High Court in *Henville v Walker*:

> In some situations, the legal framework may require a finding that, despite a causal connection in a physical sense between the breach and damage, no causal connection exists for legal purposes. In other situations, the legal framework may require a finding that a causal connection exists even though no more appears than that the damage followed after breach of a legal norm.[35]

In the Victorian case of *Duma v Mader International Pty Ltd*, the Court attempted this summary of the current trends in causation in breach of statutory actions:

> It is true that courts have readily upheld causal inferences drawn from a breach of statutory duty where it is clear that the injury suffered was of a kind that would obviously result from a breach, especially where an injury of the type suffered was a foreseeable risk ... Yet it cannot be correct at law that a breach of a regulation, no matter how remote from the injury, can be taken in all instances as automatically establishing a causal presumption that must be rebutted by a defendant.[36]

This passage underlines that, in practice, where legislation drafted with the purpose of ensuring that a form of harm is prevented is breached, showing that the conduct amounting to breach made some material contribution to an injury or harm contemplated by the legislation will usually suffice to establish causation.

13.2.2.7   Defences

There are few defences available to the action for breach of a statutory duty, with contributory negligence (discussed in Section 5.2) being the most common way of reducing liability.[37] After a period of initial resistance,[38] the High Court endorsed the availability of contributory negligence in actions for breach of statutory duty in the 1943 case of *Piro v W Foster & Co*

---

35 (2001) 206 CLR 459; [2001] HCA 52, [100].
36 (2013) 42 VR 351, [63].
37 *Booksan Pty Ltd v Wehbe* (2006) Aust Torts Reports 81-830.
38 *Burke v Butterfield & Lewis Ltd* (1926) 38 CLR 354.

Ltd.[39] This common law position has only been varied by the Australian Capital Territory, where the relevant apportionment legislation exempts breach of statutory duty.[40]

It should also be noted that voluntary assumption of risk (discussed in Section 5.3) is not a defence to this action. Liability can, however, be denied on the basis that the plaintiff was solely responsible for the harm.

REVIEW QUESTIONS

The *Educational Inclusion Act* (Cth) (fictional) contains the following provisions:

Section 11 – Duty to create a plan

(a) A school must create an educational inclusion plan (hereinafter 'Plan'). This Plan should contain procedures and policies for dealing with diversity and inclusion issues defined by the Act.

(b) Following the creation of its Plan, a school must, to the extent practicable in the circumstances, endeavour to disseminate the Plan in the manner accessible to its staff, students and parents.

(c) Following the creation of its Plan, a school must promote its use by individual staff members.

Section 12 – Financial penalty

A school which fails to create a Plan within the requisite time period shall be liable for payment of a fine not greater than $2000.

Parents of a child have approached you complaining that their child was excluded from a sports activity due to her visual impairment. While the relevant public high school has created an inclusion Plan, the angry parents argue that it was never communicated to them properly and the staff member was obviously unaware of the requirement that parents be consulted before a child is excluded from an activity. The school's Plan is available on its staff intranet and public website, and discussion of its contents is part of new staff orientation. At the start of each school term, staff are invited to study its contents.

(1) Identify the arguments for and against whether there was sufficient intention on the part of Parliament to create a right of action for breach of a statutory duty for s 11(b) and (c)?

(2) If the action exists, are the parents likely to succeed in establishing a breach of the statutory duty in this case?

 Guided responses in the eBook

---

39 (1943) 68 CLR 313.
40 *Civil Law (Wrongs) Act 2002* (ACT) s 102(2).

13.3   Misfeasance in public office

13.3.1   A public law tort

The tort of misfeasance in public office allows an individual to seek restitution for loss and damage suffered due to certain bad faith actions of the holder of a public office. In the High Court case of *Sanders v Snell*, Gleeson CJ, Gaudron, Kirby and Hayne JJ underlined that the tort 'is concerned with misuse of public power', with the policy rationale being to ensure that a person injured by the intentional or knowing misuse of public power will have an effective means of redress.[41] The tort also protects the community interest by, in the words of Lord Steyn in *Three Rivers District Council v Bank of England (No 3)*, ensuring 'that in a legal system based on the rule of law, executive or administrative law may be exercised only for the public good and not for ulterior or improper purposes'.[42] As Professor Jim Davis commented, the tort 'has had only a relatively brief exposure to judicial consideration, and that … exposure is relatively recent'.[43] Misfeasance in public office was first considered by the High Court in *Northern Territory v Mengel* in 1995.[44] The recent case of *Nyoni v Shire of Kellerberrin* also represents a leading analysis of the tort at the federal level.[45] In that case, the joint judgment of North and Rares JJ provided this fundamental statement of the elements of the tort:

> The tort requires, *first*, a misuse of an office or power, *secondly*, the intentional element that the officer did so either with the intention of harming a person or class of persons or knowing that he, she or it was acting in excess of his, her or its power, and, *thirdly*, that the plaintiff (or applicant) suffered special damage or, to use Lord Bingham's more modern characterisation, 'material damage' such as financial loss, physical or mental injury, including recognised psychiatric injury (but not merely distress, injured feelings, indignation or annoyance).[46]

The Victorian case of *De Reus v Gray* provides an illustrative example of the tort being successfully pled.[47]

This case concerned a single mother of four who, upon non-payment of $400 in parking fines, had a warrant issued for her arrest. Upon her arrest she was taken to a Melbourne police station, where the officer in charge of the cells asked for her to be strip searched. Despite no justification for this request being provided, the search was carried out by a male constable and a female constable at the end of a corridor at the entrance to a cell. Following the search of the clothes, during which Ms Gray was not provided with alternative clothing,

---

41   (1998) 196 CLR 329, 344.
42   [2003] 2 AC 1, 190 (approving what Nourse LJ had held in *Jones v Swansea City Council* [1990] 1 WLR 54, 85). Lord Steyn's view reflects what Gummow, Hayne, Heydon and Crennan JJ had held in *Commissioner of Taxation v Futuris Corporation Ltd* (2008) 237 CLR 146, 153–4.
43   J Davis, 'Misfeasance in Public Office, Exemplary Damages and Vicarious Liability' (2010) 64 *Australian Institute of Administrative Law Forum* 59, 59.
44   (1995) 185 CLR 307.
45   (2017) 248 FCR 311; [2017] FCAFC 59.
46   *Nyoni v Shire of Kellerberrin* (2017) 248 FCR 311; [2017] FCAFC 59, citing *Watkins v Home Department* [2006] 2 AC 395, 403, 410.
47   (2003) 9 VR 432.

she was detained for four hours. The following day, she completed two hours of community service at the police station to discharge the fines.

The jury at trial, and the Victorian Court of Appeal on appeal, held that the relevant charging officer was a holder of public office and that he knew that he was not authorised to conduct a strip search or had recklessly disregarded whether he had that power. The Court of Appeal ordered an award of $60 000 in compensatory (including aggravated) damages, and exemplary damages of $50 000 and $25 000 in relation to the conduct of two police officers.

13.3.2   Elements of the tort

Figure 13.2 summarises the elements of misfeasance in public office.

Figure 13.2   Elements of misfeasance in public office

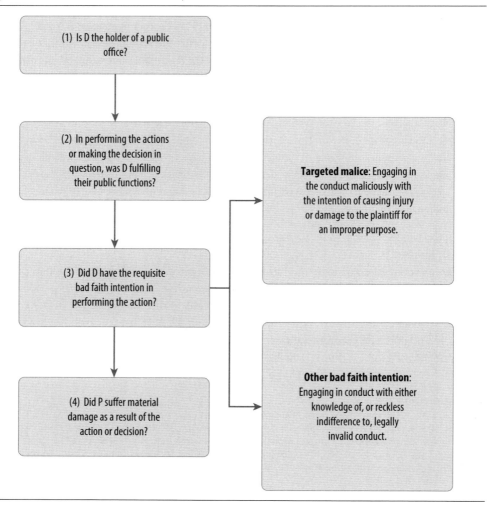

13.3.2.1   Is the defendant the 'holder of a public office'?

The action of misfeasance in public office is available only against individuals or bodies who are the holders of a public office. As Professor Mark Aronson has noted: 'A person might be a public employee but not a public officer. There is in fact no single definition of "public officer" across all contexts.'[48] Given the growth in the outsourcing of public service delivery to private entities, there are challenges to defining the term 'holder of a public office' and the degree to which the tort should reflect changes in the nature of government activity.

Positions which have been recognised as falling within the ambit of this tort include: prison, parole and police officers;[49] a Minister making a funding or statutory decision; and departmental officers engaged in the vaccination of animals.[50] Corporate entities (ie, statutory corporations or councils) can also be liable. The key outstanding question is whether the term 'public officer' is to be judged by reference to the *formal position* held or whether the term is used to underline that the person must enjoy *independent* statutory decision-making powers or functions which they can exercise personally without direction from others.

The term 'holder of public office', in the Commonwealth context, has potential links to the constitutional jurisprudence regarding the 'Officer of the Commonwealth'.[51] In *Leerdam v Noori*, Spigelman CJ held that a firm of solicitors engaged by the federal Minister for Immigration and Multicultural and Indigenous Affairs to represent the Department at the Administrative Appeals Tribunal did not qualify. His Honour stated:

> In the present case there is no 'office' or governmental power of any character. The concept of an 'office', in the context of liability for abuse of power, connotes an official position to which continuing functions or duties are assigned. Those duties or functions must be of a 'public' nature. It is not sufficient merely to be employed by a public authority for public purposes.[52]

In *Obeid v Lockley*, the New South Wales Court of Appeal stated that the term 'public office' must be given an interpretation which furthers the purpose of the tort – namely, the prevention of abuse of public power:

> The concept clearly would not include all public employees, particularly those with minimal responsibilities. However, it does not seem to me that the tort of misfeasance in public office is confined only to a person appointed to a particular statutory office which expressly confers statutory powers and responsibilities ... Such a narrow definition of 'public officer' would defeat the rationale of the tort as expressed by Lord Steyn in *Three Rivers* at 190, that 'executive and administrative power "may be exercised only for the public good" and not for ulterior or improper purposes'.[53]

---

48 M Aronson, 'Misfeasance in Public Office: A Very Peculiar Tort' (2011) 35(1) *Melbourne University Law Review* 1, 43.

49 *De Reus v Gray* (2003) 9 VR 432.

50 *Northern Territory v Mengel* (1995) 185 CLR 307.

51 For a discussion of the continuing gap in Australian constitutional jurisprudence, see N Boughey and G Week, '"Officers of the Commonwealth" in the Private Sector: Should the High Court Review Outsourced Exercises of Power?' (2013) 36(1) *University of New South Wales Law Journal* 31.

52 *Leerdam v Noori* (2009) 255 ALR 553, 554.

53 (2018) 98 NSWLR 258, [113] (citations omitted). See discussion in T Cockburn and M Thomas, 'Personal Liability of Public Officers in the Tort of Misfeasance in Public Office: Part 1' (2001) 9(1) *Torts Law Journal* 1, 7–8.

Invoking this principle, the Court of Appeal proceeded to overturn the trial finding that senior investigators at the Independent Commission Against Corruption were not themselves individually the holders of public office. The Court underlined that the *Independent Commission Against Corruption Act 1988* (NSW) bestowed powers of search and seizure upon them and, in their position descriptions, they were said to be responsible for the management of investigations.

13.3.2.2   Is the defendant fulfilling a public function?

The boundaries of the concept of 'public function' were the subject of judicial analysis in *Emanuele v Hedley*.[54] This case concerned a senior public official who allegedly falsely reported to his superiors the substance of a conversation that suggested the commission of a crime. Their Honours observed that whether the official's report were true or false, his compilation and delivery of it 'were not actions done in the exercise of powers attaching to a public office. They were simply the actions of an employee reporting an alleged event to superior officers.'[55] Similarly, in *Calveley v Chief Constable of Merseyside Police* ('*Calveley*'), it was held that internal investigations within police departments did not fall within the scope of the duty.[56] Lord Bridge found that if, for instance, a police officer made a false report to a disciplinary investigation team, an action in defamation could be pursued. His Lordship cautioned that 'the report is defamation not misfeasance in public office, since the mere making of a report is not a relevant exercise of power or authority by the investigating officer'.[57] This finding was discussed in *Nyoni v Shire of Kellerberrin* where (as outlined in Section 13.3.2.3) Darren Friend, the chief executive officer of a local council, had made a complaint about the local pharmacist to two regulators.[58] At first instance, the Federal Court found that Mr Friend's actions in sending the email of complaint to regulators, and in assisting another individual to prepare a letter that would support later regulatory action, was similar in character to that in *Calveley*.[59]

The Full Court of the Federal Court rejected this, however, ultimately finding that the complaint to regulators was not of the same character as an internal communication from an employee passing on concerns about a colleague to their superiors:

> Mr Friend was using the authority of the Shire and his own office to seek to cause two governmental institutions to send officers to Kellerberrin the next day with a view to them taking action adverse to Mr Nyoni because of the disconnection of the electricity supply to the pharmacy. Hence, Mr Friend's question at the conclusion of the 14 October 2010 email, 'I assume I will see you both tomorrow?' In effect, Mr Friend was making a complaint, using his office, to two regulatory bodies that a pharmacy in the Shire, that was an important, if not essential, service in Kellerberrin, could not operate properly without electricity … Mr Friend also procured the production and despatch

---

54 (1998) 179 FCR 290.
55 Ibid 300.
56 [1989] AC 1228.
57 Ibid 1240–1.
58 (2017) 248 FCR 311; [2017] FCAFC 59.
59 *Calveley v Chief Constable of Merseyside Police* [1989] AC 1228.

to the two regulators of Mr Mitchell's letter of 14 October 2010, that confirmed that the power supply had been disconnected, with the intention of harming Mr Nyoni.[60]

The Full Court thus held that the email was effectively an official complaint on behalf of the Shire, designed to initiate investigative and disciplinary actions by regulators against the pharmacist, rather than a commercial or private act. Interestingly, Dowsett J dissented, finding that it had not been demonstrated that safeguarding the availability of pharmaceutical services in the town was part of the Shire's functions. His Honour reasoned that the situation was thus similar to the reporting of a conversation to a superior,[61] as in *Emanuele v Hedley*.[62]

13.3.2.3   Did the defendant have the requisite 'bad faith' intention?

The tort of misfeasance is a 'deliberate tort'.[63] We will commence with the most extreme intention: the intention to harm. The presence of 'targeted malice' as the driving force of a decision will generally result in an unlawful decision. Public power is held on trust to the Australian public to exercise for public, not private or vengeful, ends. Second, the presence of malice will necessarily display the required intention to impose harmful consequences on the person.

MALICIOUS INTENTION

The case of *Nyoni v Shire of Kellerberrin* ('*Nyoni*') has confirmed that, in Australia, a misfeasance claim may succeed where the malicious intention accompanies the use of what would have been otherwise *lawful* action.[64] The question of whether illegality was a requirement was previously the subject of academic discussion, centring in particular on the example provided by Harper J in *Grimwade v Victoria*:

> Malice of itself is insufficient unless the exercise of the power is only valid if done without malice: a parking officer may be as malicious as he likes in giving a parking ticket to his worst enemy whose vehicle is illegally parked. And the fact that the officer intends to cause harm (by fixing the enemy with an obligation to pay the fine) is wholly beside the point.[65]

The Full Federal Court in *Nyoni* rejected this parking ticket example. The Court found it 'overlooked that the causative role of the officer's intention' in giving the parking ticket 'would be to injure the "enemy", as opposed to carrying out his lawful duties'.[66] It noted the Canadian case of *Odhavji Estate v Woodhouse*, where the Court held that malicious action, combined with knowledge of likely injury, establishes the action:

> the fact that the public officer has acted for the express purpose of harming the plaintiff is sufficient to satisfy each ingredient of the tort, owing to the fact that a public officer

---

60 *Nyoni v Shire of Kellerberin* (2017) 248 FCR 311; [2017] FCAFC 59, [107].
61 Ibid [152]–[154]. Leave to appeal the Full Federal Court ruling to the High Court was sought by the appellants but was refused.
62 (1998) 179 FCR 290.
63 *Northern Territory v Mengel* (1995) 185 CLR 307, 345.
64 (2017) 248 FCR 311; [2017] FCAFC 59 ('*Nyoni*').
65 (1997) 90 A Crim R 526, 556.
66 (2017) 248 FCR 311; [2017] FCAFC 59, [88].

does not have the authority to exercise his or her powers for an improper purpose, such as deliberately harming a member of the public. In each instance, the tort involves deliberate disregard of official duty coupled with knowledge that the misconduct is likely to injure the plaintiff.[67]

The majority of the Full Federal Court was thus satisfied that the position at law was that 'if the officer used his power for the dominant purpose of injuring the "enemy", then that would be an improper use of the power'.[68] Targeted malice is a misuse of power grounding action in tort, provided the intention to inflict harm was the 'actuating motive'.[69] The facts of *Nyoni* were held to involve such a scenario.

Case: *Nyoni v Shire of Kellerberrin* (2017) 248 FCR 311

Facts

Emson Nyoni was the operator of the only pharmacy in Kellerberrin, Western Australia. He argued that the chief executive officer of the Kellerberrin Shire Council, Darren Friend, had maliciously provided false information about his business to the Pharmaceutical Council of Western Australia and the State Department of Health. The regulatory investigations resulted in Mr Nyoni's business closing and being replaced.

Issue

The misfeasance action had failed at trial when the primary judge held that Mr Friend had not been exercising the powers attached to his public office as chief executive officer when he sent the relevant communications to the regulatory bodies.

Decision

This was overturned by the joint judgment of the Full Federal Court, which ruled that the making of complaints about local service providers fell within the purview of the Shire's responsibilities. The Court found that Mr Friend had acted as part of a continuing campaign by the Shire to persuade the regulators that Mr Nyoni was not a suitable pharmacist for the town. Mr Friend had alerted the regulators to the fact that power at the pharmacy had been disconnected, and had also ensured that the contractor who had disconnected it immediately sent a letter outlining this fact. When it later emerged that the disconnection was made in error and not due to any default by Mr Nyoni, the former chief executive officer failed to notify the regulators of this fact.

Significance

This case is a useful example of how the presence of malice – a private desire to punish an individual – can discharge the elements of this tort. Where malice is the motive, this can result in an otherwise lawful action being carried out for an improper purpose. It is not sufficient that a later

---

67 [2003] 3 SCR 263, 280–2, quoted in *Nyoni* ibid [90].
68 *Nyoni* (2017) 248 FCR 311; [2017] FCAFC 59, [91].
69 Ibid [94], citing the Full Federal Court in *Sanders v Snell* (2003) 130 FCR 149, 178.

justification centring on the public interest has been advanced, if malice towards the individual is proven as the moving force for the decision.

Question

Do you think that targeted malice is easy to establish in cases involving the use of punitive powers?

 Guided response in the eBook

HINTS AND TIPS

Despite the *Nyoni* case, courts have regularly underlined that malice will not be lightly inferred and is a question to be determined on the facts of the particular matter. In line with the *Briginshaw v Briginshaw* principle, the plaintiff bears the onus of properly satisfying the court before the court will proceed to make any finding of wrongdoing against an individual.[70]

In *Commonwealth v Fernando*, the Acting Minister for Immigration, Multicultural and Indigenous Affairs had cancelled the applicant's visa four days before the Department received Mr Fernando's submissions arguing that he should be allowed to remain in the country.[71] Despite the fact that the action represented a clear breach of procedural fairness, the Court refused to infer malice and award compensation. The Court underlined that it was possible to infer that the Acting Minister had made his decision on the basis that Mr Fernando, like previous applicants in his position, had chosen not to meet the 14-day deadline. The Court observed:

> A finding that a Commonwealth Government Minister has deliberately exercised an important statutory power knowing that, in doing so, he was acting unlawfully is properly to be characterised as grave. The legal consequences are potentially serious as too is the effect on the Minister's reputation. In circumstances in which, on the facts found, conflicting inferences are open and one of those inferences is favourable to the respondent, the Court will not be satisfied that the applicant's case has been proved to the necessary standard.[72]

---

70 (1938) 60 CLR 336.
71 (2012) 200 FCR 1; [2012] FCAFC 18.
72 Ibid [130].

OTHER BAD FAITH INTENTION

The fact that a governmental officer has engaged in actions beyond his or her power is not sufficient to establish the tort unless those actions are accompanied by the requisite state of mind. This requires that:

- the person either had direct knowledge that the act was in excess of his or her lawful powers or was recklessly indifferent to the possibility of a lack of power
- the person also needs to have knowledge of, or be recklessly indifference to, the harm their action or inaction will cause to affected people.

The key point of emphasis is a 'bad faith' element. Liability will not flow from good faith misinterpretations or misapplications of the law; the individual must also have knowledge of the likely harm which would flow from their action.[73] Liability for misfeasance needs to be sufficiently distinct from a finding of gross negligence. It is shaped by a dishonest exercise of public powers – the deliberate ignoring of a risk.

The assessment of a person's state of mind – whether it is actual knowledge or reckless indifference – is also *subjective*. That is, simply imputing knowledge – saying the person 'should' have known of the harm or the lack of legal basis for actions – is not enough. Instead, it must be shown that the specific individual actually held the required state of mind. This, again, ensures that negligence (failure to exercise due care in relation to a risk) is kept distinct from the bad faith that underpins misfeasance. Misfeasance involves a 'wilful blindness' – an active disregarding of a risk, rather than a failure to appreciate it.

Due to this high threshold of knowledge and intention required to establish misfeasance, the action has long been viewed as one that is necessarily rare in practice. Notwithstanding this, the recent case of *Brett Cattle Company Pty Ltd v Minister for Agriculture* saw a high-profile successful invocation of the tort.

Case: *Brett Cattle Co Pty Ltd v Minister for Agriculture* (2020) 274 FCR 337

Facts

This action was taken by farmers and other businesses who were affected by a government decision to suspend live export of Australian cattle to Indonesia in 2011. In May 2011, the Australian Broadcasting Corporation broadcast a program detailing inhumane practices in an Indonesian abattoir. Acting swiftly in response to public outcry, the Minister for Agriculture, Fisheries and Forestry issued an order which banned exports to the facilities featured in the original report, at least until exemptions were considered. When, five days later, the political outcry had not abated, the Minister issued a revised order which effectively amounted to an absolute ban on live cattle exports to Indonesia for a period of six months. This case assessed whether the approval of that second order constituted misfeasance in public office. The plaintiffs

---

73 *Northern Territory v Mengel* (1995) 185 CLR 307, 345 ('*Mengel* ').

argued that the order was unlawful, as it was unreasonable due to its lack of proportionality. It was submitted that in creating it, the Minister had been recklessly indifferent to its legality and to the harm it would cause.

Issue

How was the Minister's state of knowledge around the making of the order approached by Justice Rares in the Federal Court?

Decision

The Court was satisfied that the order was unlawful – that those aspects of the case are best dealt with an administrative law context. It is worth noting that the Court's imposition of a requirement of proportionality on the making of delegated legislation has been queried by academic commentators. Regardless of this public law issue, however, the case provides a useful canvas of the principles that apply to establishing misfeasance in public office.

In determining the mental state that accompanied the decision, Justice Rares relied on the information that was before the Minister, drawing inferences as to his state of mind. The Court did not have access to cabinet documents which might have revealed more. The Court found that the Minister had not received any departmental or Solicitor-General advice as to the legality of his second absolute ban order. The advice available was either marked draft or overly general. It was found that the Minister knew that some exporters had the ability to track their animals to slaughter and to ensure compliance with international standards. Despite this, the Minister pressed on with an order which did not allow for any exceptions. This supported a finding, in the Court's view, that the Minister had 'closed his mind' and 'shut his eyes' to the reasonableness of the order. The refusal to take legal advice on the scope of the order, the Court inferred, represented the deliberate taking of a risk that it might turn out invalid. The Court stated it was comfortable that the Minister 'did not care whether it turned out to be so'.

The Court also confirmed the existence of the second 'bad faith' requirement – that there be knowledge or reckless indifference as to the harm that flows from the unlawful act. The Court stressed that subjective knowledge of or indifference to the harm must be shown; it cannot merely be said that the harm was a foreseeable consequence. Nevertheless, the Court was satisfied that even this higher standard was made out. Justice Rares was satisfied that the Minister 'knew that the order itself would cause immediate economic loss to many persons', but had proceeded. This element of 'not caring' was enough to show that the Minister had acted with reckless indifference as to the impact on the farmers.

Significance

The case confirms the current approach of Australian courts to misfeasance actions. Reckless indifference represents the key 'limit' concept for analysing the state of mind accompanying any ultra vires act. It must be distinguished from gross negligence, which involves serious carelessness in failing to understand the existence of risk.[74]

---

74 T Howe QC and A Berger, 'Misfeasance' (2012) 98 *Legal Briefing* 1.

The leading discussion of 'reckless indifference' is that of the United Kingdom House of Lords in *Three Rivers District Council v Bank of England (No 3)*.[75] The subjective nature of the recklessness analysis is best described by Lord Hobhouse:

> The official does the act intentionally being aware that it risks directly causing loss to the plaintiff or an identifiable class to which the plaintiff belongs and the official wilfully disregards that risk.
>
> ... His recklessness arises because he chooses wilfully to disregard that risk ... Subjective recklessness comes into the formulation at the first and last stage because it is, in law, tantamount to knowledge and therefore gives rise to the same liability.[76]

It is important to note that the preferred understanding of the current law is that the official must be recklessly indifferent to both their lack of power *and* the harm which may result to the plaintiff. This requires that the defendant knew they were running the risk that their actions were illegal and harmful but recklessly went ahead anyway. The defendant must be either aware of or recklessly indifferent to any risk of harm caused by their unlawful actions. In *Obeid v Lockley*, the New South Wales Court of Appeal favoured the view that the tort cannot be made out where a person recklessly exceeds their powers in circumstances where they *ought* to have foreseen the possibility of harm arising.[77] The plaintiff will need to prove subjective awareness of harm on the facts.

Questions

(1) Why did the Court condemn the order as capricious and unreasonable? (See [358]–[361].)

(2) Why was the fact that the Minister specifically asked for more information about the estimated costs of ex gratia payments under the Commonwealth's Scheme for Compensation for Detriment Caused by Defective Administration? (See [380].)

  Guided responses in the eBook

13.3.2.4   Did the plaintiff suffer material damage?

Proving the tort of misfeasance in public office also requires showing that the plaintiff or applicant has suffered actual or special or material damage.[78] This requirement was not made out in the United Kingdom case of *Watkins v Home Office*.[79] This case concerned the allegedly malicious opening by three prison officers of letters to a prisoner. The House of Lords found that the prisoner had not established 'material damage' despite the unlawful character of the officers' actions.

The majority ruling in *Nyoni* found that material damage was made out by the damage which flowed from the baseless complaints being sent to the regulators, alleging Mr Nyoni's unfitness to hold a licence. The Court held that:

75 [2003] 2 AC 1.
76 Ibid 192.
77 (2018) 98 NSWLR 258, [153]–[172] (Bathurst CJ), [242] (Leeming JA).
78 *Nyoni* (2017) 248 FCR 311; [2017] FCAFC 59, [98].
79 [2006] 2 AC 395.

> The making of such an allegation by a public officer or body, such as Mr Friend or the Shire, to another government agency or authority with regulatory powers over a person in Mr Nyoni's position should be presumed (as it would in cases of slander) to cause sufficient material or actual damage to support the action of misfeasance in public office.[80]

The Court held that damages for both economic and reputational harm were recoverable, as there was 'no reason why the law should ignore the reality that a professional person must suffer some real, material harm' when a wrongful complaint is made to a professional regulator.

The assessment of liability in *Brett Cattle Co Pty Ltd v Minister for Agriculture* was complex, and the Federal Court was effectively drawn into considering what a fair order would have looked like.[81] It refused to assess damages on the basis that no export ban of any kind should have been made. Instead, the Court turned to its reasoning about the lack of exceptions as the key thing that drove a loss. Justice Rates ultimately decided that it was likely that the Minister would have adopted the 'obvious and compelling' option of imposing an order allowing the exemption of exporters who did meet international standards. Ultimately, the award of damages was calculated on the 'lost export period' for compliant slaughtering and costs related to retaining the cattle.

HINTS AND TIPS

Reflecting the policy behind the tort, courts also retain a discretion to award exemplary damages. The United Kingdom case of *Kuddus v Chief Constable of Leicestershire* [2002] 2 AC 122, 149 saw Lord Hutton underline the appropriateness of exemplary damages as it 'serves to uphold and vindicate the rule of law because it makes clear that the courts will not tolerate such conduct'.

It is important to note that the availability of financial compensation is central to the practical utility of misfeasance as a 'public law' tort. While judicial review of government power exists, there is no right of action for damages for loss caused by invalid administrative action. Neither s 16(1) of the *Administrative Decisions (Judicial Review) Act 1977* (Cth) nor the Australian Constitution include the award of damages within their available remedies. There is, however, an ex gratia Commonwealth scheme which operates as an informal recovery mechanism for damage caused by errors in government decision-making.[82] This scheme can be useful for practitioners seeking an informal method of redress for their clients in circumstances where more formal legal avenues are unavailable.

---

80   (2017) 248 FCR 311; [2017] FCAFC 59, [101].
81   (2020) 274 FCR 337.
82   The Scheme for Compensation for Detriment Caused by Defective Administration is an important form of alternative remediation for clients who may have suffered damage as a result of government error. Its limitations must be highlighted, however, as it is ex gratia and requires the exhaustion of alternative legal remedies.

13.3.3   Liability of government entities for misfeasance of individuals

The question of when the actions of a tortfeasor, and in particular his or her malicious intention, should be imputed to the tortfeasor's employer can be of great practical significance to the recovery of compensation. It is, first, possible that a government entity can become directly liable for any misfeasance in public office. In *Nyoni*, the joint judgment found that the chief executive officer's actions were consistent with an established campaign by the Shire and that 'in pursuing a complaint against Mr Nyoni he was acting as the Shire, not merely as its representative'.[83] Given these circumstances, where the individual was acting on the instructions of and with the authority of the Shire, the Court held that the Shire was directly liable for 'exercising the Shire's power to make a complaint' with the intention of causing economic and reputational harm. The case therefore fell into the category of cases identified by Professor Aronson:

> In the right circumstances, the mental state of their staff can be imputed to the organisations themselves. For example, if all the members of a local government council voted unanimously to cancel a land use development consent, and if they did that entirely out of a sense of revenge and self-interest, and in the knowledge that they were acting illegally, then they will have been guilty of bad faith sufficient for the purposes of misfeasance.[84]

Indeed, in some cases, despite each participating individual bearing the requisite mental state towards the affected individual, *only* the public entity as a whole, as the holder of the relevant power, could fulfil the requirement of having *caused* the underlying loss.

Given the traditional view of ministerial responsibility for the actions of a department, and their leadership role in guiding actions through policy, it is unsurprising that departments may be held vicariously liable for the actions of their Ministers, despite their not being employees. In *Commonwealth v Fernando*, the Department of Immigration and Multicultural and Indigenous Affairs conceded that it would be vicariously liable for any tortious conduct of the Minister were it established in the proceedings.[85] Vicarious liability for the actions of police officers has also received specific statutory treatment in each Australian jurisdiction, with the Crown being held to be vicariously liable for torts committed in the exercise or purported exercise of duties. In the Commonwealth and Queensland, the Crown is joint tortfeasor. As Professor Davis has noted, in all jurisdictions outside of New South Wales, a police officer does not incur any personal civil liability where there is a 'good faith' use of his or her powers, but liability rather transfers to the state.[86] Generally, in order to establish vicarious liability it must be shown that the individual is an employee of the defendant and committed the tort in the course of that employment. A finding that a malicious exercise of public power falls within the course of employment obviously presents difficulties. This was recognised in *Northern Territory v Mengel* when the High Court commented that 'although

---

83 *Nyoni v Shire of Kellerberin* (2017) 248 FCR 311; [2017] FCAFC 59, [85].
84 M Aronson, 'Misfeasance in Public Office: A Very Peculiar Tort' (2011) 35(1) *Melbourne University Law Review* 1, 44.
85 (2012) 200 FCR 1; [2012] FCAFC 18.
86 On this point, see the leading piece on vicarious liability for misfeasance: J Davis, 'Misfeasance in Public Office, Exemplary Damages and Vicarious Liability' (2010) 64 *Australian Institute of Administrative Law Forum* 59.

the tort is the tort of a public officer, he or she is liable personally and, unless there is a de facto authority, there will ordinarily only be personal liability'.[87] Outside of instances of malicious intention, where there has been reckless disregard, but no active impropriety, vicarious liability may be easier to establish as the tasks are connected to employment.[88]

Vicarious liability can also be opposed in instances where the tortfeasor was exercising an independent (if public) function. Many administrative officers will enjoy a variety of discretionary powers which are centred on their personal judgment and subject to varying degrees of line management control. Where an individual officeholder is directly vested with a personal power under statute, it is not legally valid for him or her to act under the dictation of another. This would seem to underline an absence of employer control or direction.

In practice, however, it must be stressed that the defence of misfeasance claims is commonly undertaken at the taxpayer's expense. Appendix E of the *Legal Services Directions 2017* (Cth) states that assistance will be provided where a public employee has 'acted reasonably and responsibly'. However, assistance will only be ruled out where there is 'serious or wilful misconduct or culpable negligence'.[89]

HINTS AND TIPS

The case of *Plaintiff M83A/2019 v Morrison (No 2)*[90] provides useful insight into the factual challenges of pleading a misfeasance action in practice. As discussed previously, misfeasance is an inquiry into the state of mind held by particular individuals exercising powers. Plaintiff M83A saw a misfeasance claim against multiple Ministers for Immigration and two departmental secretaries were summarily dismissed due to an insufficient factual basis being advanced for the pleadings. The Court warned plaintiffs against merely speculating about the requisite mental state and hoping the necessary evidence would emerge in the course of discovery or cross-examination. Justice Mortimer underlined the importance of a factual basis for a claim, even in a context where the applicants inevitably face an 'information asymmetry'. There is no doubt that plaintiffs face significant hurdles in assessing whether to embark on a claim given the confidentiality that necessarily surrounds the legal advice available to decision-makers and sensitive government decision-making. Nevertheless, Justice Mortimer remarked:

> In the context of any proceeding, let alone one making the grave allegation of misfeasance in public office against Commonwealth Ministers and Departmental Secretaries, the hope that a basis for a cause of action might emerge in the witness box will be unlikely ever to justify permitting applicants to re-plead their case, and proceed to trial so as to keep the possibility of that moment in the witness box alive.[91]

---

87 (1995) 185 CLR 307, 344–5.
88 See M Aronson, 'Misfeasance in Public Office: A Very Peculiar Tort' (2011) 35(1) *Melbourne University Law Review* 1, 45.
89 *Legal Services Directions 2017* (Cth) app E cl 6. The Directions are a set of binding rules issued by the Attorney-General about the performance of Commonwealth legal work.
90 [2020] FCA 1198.
91 Ibid [122].

REVIEW QUESTIONS

IT Solutions Australia is the (fictional) contracted provider of phone services for the (fictional) Department of Social Protection. The (fictional) *Social Security Act* requires that the individual have a 'reasonable opportunity' to submit their income report via their chosen communication method. Susan, a student, calls the reporting line operated by IT Solutions on behalf of the Department. Before reporting her income, Susan indicates to the staff member that she has a question about a separate matter that she wants to ask. The operator responds by saying, 'I don't have time for a chat, watch your tone. Actually, you know what? Goodbye' and hangs up. The contract with IT Solutions Australia requires that 'the contractor's staff must provide an efficient and professional phone service to commercial standards'. As the 5 pm deadline has elapsed by the time her next call is put through to another operator, Susan's study payment is delayed, causing serious financial consequences for her.

(1) Is the staff member 'the holder of a public officer fulfilling a public function' for the purposes of a misfeasance in public office claim?

(2) Regardless of whether they satisfy this first requirement, has the phone operator formed the necessary intention for a misfeasance claim to be made out?

   Guided responses in the eBook

KEY CONCEPTS

• **action for breach of statutory duty:** available where the relevant legislation created by Parliament expressly or impliedly contemplates the enforcement of the statutory duty it contains by private individuals through an action in tort.

• **bad faith intention:** in order to be proven, a claim for misfeasance in public office must establish one of the requisite forms of intention: (1) malicious intent, where the public officer uses a legal power in bad faith with the intention of causing damage to the individual; or (2) subjective (not imputed) knowledge of or reckless indifference to *both* the lawfulness of an action and to the harm which follows for the people affected by it.

• **intention of Parliament:** to permit a private action is identified through analysis of the text, context and purpose of the relevant duty. Key factors which go against the creation of such a duty are the existence of a specific remedy, or where the duty protects the interests of the public as a whole, rather than that of private individuals.

• **misfeasance in public office:** an action that is available where the holder of a public office uses their public powers in bad faith and in a manner which causes material damage to the affected individual.

Complete the multiple-choice questions in the eBook to test your knowledge

PROBLEM-SOLVING EXERCISES

Exercise 1

The (fictional) *Legal Workplace Health and Safety Act 2017* (Cth) imposes the following duty on the management of legal firms and workplaces:

Section 12 – Duty to ensure a safe working environment

(1)   The managers and supervising lawyers of law firms and workplaces under this Act must, so far as is reasonably practicable, ensure a healthy workplace, free from intimidation and harassment.

(2)   For the purposes of section 12(1):

'Intimidation' includes the making of threats by any manager about future employment status or progression within the firm, outside the context of formal review.

'Harassment' consists of any course of conduct by a manager which is inappropriately personal or unwelcome, resulting in offence to the individual. The conduct in question must not be an ordinary act of workplace supervision or professional development activities undertaken by management.

Section 13 – Penalty for breach of section 12

(1)   Where section 12 has been breached, the Department shall secure an enforceable undertaking as to future conduct within the firm. This undertaking may include a direction to remove management responsibilities from an individual.

(2)   Where an enforceable undertaking issued under subsection (1) is not complied with, the Department may impose a civil penalty of up to 2% of the annual turnover of the firm or workplace in question.

The objects clause states the following:

Section 3 – Objects of Act

(1)   The objects of this Act are to:

(a)   ensure that practices in the legal profession reflect community values, particularly in relation to non-discrimination and the promotion of diversity in the profession;

(b)   promote a safe and healthy working environment for individuals; and

(c)   avoid unnecessary workplace litigation and reduce the existing regulatory burden on law firms.

In the second reading speech (fictional), the Minister stated that the creation of the new statutory duty was reflected in the following policy:

Recent media reports regarding the treatment of young lawyers have raised widespread public concern. The Australian community, through the provision of student loans and supports, has invested their taxpayer dollars into training these students. This Act expresses the public interest in ensuring that these students, a resource for our future, are not, through mistreatment, excluded from future participation in the workplace. A key aspect is the fact that the Act does not depend on a complaint from an individual but can be triggered by a whistleblower's report about conduct.

Young & Sons is a law firm for the purposes of the legislation. Gary Young is a lead partner concerning whom a s 12 matter is currently being determined by the (fictional) Department of Professional Affairs. Following a court proceeding one day, Mr Young told a young lawyer he was supervising, John Sullivan, that his voice when making submissions 'sounds like you are 12; not something you can change, I suppose, but annoying and unprofessional'. Upon being criticised for the tone of this comment by another lawyer who was present, Mr Young responded: 'Performance reviews are coming up. He'd better be listening to and accepting anything I say. He can't run crying to you about it, either.' The young lawyer was extremely upset and felt humiliated and insecure about his position in the workplace. He later received a negative annual performance review which stated: 'Feedback from your supervising lawyer indicates you are not a cultural fit for our firm and have reacted badly to the feedback provided to you.' He has since left the firm early and will have to locate a new position.

Under s 14 of the Act, the Department of Professional Affairs is responsible for investigating any potential breaches of the statutory duty. Section 15 requires that prior to the making of any enforcement order:

An investigator must ensure that any firm or individual investigated under section 14 has a reasonable opportunity to respond to the grounds for the allegation of breach and the scope and nature of any proposed penalty prior to the issuing of a penalty.

The investigator in this case, Mr Holland, has informed Mr Young that he and his firm have been found in breach of s 12 due to his conduct towards Mr Sullivan. The Department has decided that it will issue the enforceable undertaking within 48 hours and that it will be taking submissions on its terms because 'Mr Young has already had an opportunity to make submissions on the events'.

Mr Young is frustrated by his inability to make additional submissions regarding penalty. He would like to receive the reasons for the breach and the findings about why his conduct was unacceptable. While he had the chance to make submissions on the penalties before breach was found, he was addressing a hypothetical: the investigator had not made any findings concerning what it was about his conduct that was unacceptable. Mr Young believes a failure to allow him to make submissions is an obvious breach of s 14.

Nevertheless, Mr Holland proceeds to impose a penalty without any further interaction. He demands an enforceable undertaking to remove Mr Young from any day-to-day supervision of new clerks in the firm. Mr Young is furious, as he had input into the design of this undertaking. He believes Mr Holland has a personal grudge against him, and begins proceedings for misfeasance in public office. The Department provides an initial response, stating that Mr Young had the opportunity to make a submission prior to the decision.

A process of discovery reveals the following email correspondence between Mr Holland and his fellow departmental group members, including his group leader. It was sent the same day as the letter informing Mr Young that there would be no further consultation:

I am making the call now. Mr Young has been continually lodging freedom of information requests and made a load of procedural claims, disrupting the progress of this matter. He has that 'lawyer's attitude' to everything. I've had confrontation after confrontation with him and I'm done. I'm going to block this one immediately, let Appeal spend some time sorting it out. The only thing I care about is getting some time to progress this file, free from having to document everything as I go. Clearly, the decision to move this to an enforcement action was made to remove this guy from any position of responsibility as a matter of priority.

(1)   Was there sufficient intention on the part of Parliament to allow actions for breach of a statutory duty where conduct breaching s 12 occurs?

(2)   Can Mr Young take an action of misfeasance in public office against Mr Holland?

    Guided responses in the eBook

Exercise 2

The *Responsible Protests Act 2021* (Vic) is a fictional piece of state legislation which regulates the holding of protests by organisations. Under the legislation, State Protest Commission officers can ban individuals from being involved in organising future protests for a period of up to a year and restrain individuals' use of social media to promote protest actions or movements.

This order to restrain communications can be triggered under s 5 of the Act, where:

(a)   the Commission believes on reasonable grounds that the individual engaged in conduct in all circumstances, to have substantially impeded the effective policing of a protest.

(b)   For the avoidance of the doubt, the conduct or impediment referred to in subsection (a) does not refer solely to physical actions such as obstruction but can cover any act or communication which consists of persuading, encouraging, instigating or pressuring others to substantially impede effective policing.

Cassandra Page has recently been made subject to restrictions under the Act, and is barred from being involved in the organisation of protests for the next six months. She currently works as Advocacy Coordinator at Defend the Planet, an environmental non-governmental organisation. She is also restrained from social media posting on certain organisational pages, including the one she operates for Defend the Planet. As a result of the order it has been suggested she take unpaid leave from her job, as there are no other duties she can perform in the interim.

The basis for the order is a social media post that Cassandra sent out before a recent protest. It stated that protestors should 'use noise as a tactic on the day to attract attention and make sure any members of the public or the media observe any unfair police interventions in our protest action'.

She received a decision identifying a breach of the 2021 Act from a Commission officer, Conor Rorke, the following day. It stated that her communication 'clearly encouraged others to substantially impede the effective policing of protests'. Cassandra is outraged, as in her view, noise is just an ordinary part of a protest. Her post was simply aimed at making people feel comfortable about attending a protest and ensuring that any heavy-handed police interventions did not go unremarked by the media.

The Commission officer is well known to her from online interactions. Rorke has joined social media groups she is involved in. He has regularly posted provocative views under an initially anonymous account on the page. These posts often occurred outside of work hours, and were often targeted at 'hippies who don't have real jobs'. The day after the order was received by Cassandra, she noticed the following message from the account operated by Rorke:

> We won't be seeing any more pile-ons and snark from Cassandra on here. Delighted a clear message was sent about that. Shame your job will be impacted, but rules are rules!

Cassandra put in a freedom of information request to gain insight into how Rorke had constructed his decision. This revealed that he had spent a total of 13 minutes generating the decision. Its issuance involved the use of a pre-populated decision letter template, which assists decision-makers' reasoning. As part of this, Rorke received the following warning:

> Are you satisfied that conduct was such that it would substantially impede effective policing? There is a threshold of seriousness which applies to your decision-making. You should consider, even if the conduct might impede policing, why the matter is grave enough to warrant penalty under the Act.

Rorke responded: 'Not needed, self-evident from the post and her past actions.' The system then warned him that 'insufficient justification recorded [word length]. Please add further details', but he overrode this and issued the pro forma decision.

Cassandra would like to evaluate whether there are grounds for a misfeasance in public office action against Conor Rorke.

 Guided response in the eBook

CHALLENGE YOURSELF

Exercise 1

Returning to the scenario in the first problem-solving exercise, was Mr Young's comment the 'making of a threat' under s 12?

 Guided response in the eBook

Exercise 2

Consider if we expand the *Responsible Protest Act 2021* in problem-solving exercise 2 to include the following provision:

> Protest organisers must take all reasonably practicable actions to ensure that protests organised by them are conducted in an orderly manner that minimises disruption to the operation of private business premises.

The Act then prescribes penalties for a failure to take reasonably practicable actions, including:

- A fine payable to the Commission.
- A ban from organising future protests which require licensing from the Commission.

The non-governmental organisation Defend our Planet has encountered some difficulties after a recent protest action it organised. The protest was held in Melbourne's Central Business District, outside the State Parliament. Unfortunately, attendance was larger than expected, and the crowds gathered across the entrance to a well-known restaurant. Protestors effectively blocked the entrance to this restaurant for a period of two hours. They also leant against the windows, damaging a distinctive piece of etched artwork which was a well-known feature of the premises. Having been unable to identify the individuals involved from CCTV footage, the restaurant is now exploring an action for breach of statutory duty against Defend our Planet as the organisers of the protest. They argue that the organisers failed to direct crowds adequately, allowing the group to congregate where they did.

Defend our Planet argue that their standard 'if attending' social media post uploaded ahead of the event warned protestors against interfering with local businesses. They also encouraged people to move closer to the stage where possible. They argue that the expectations of the restaurant are way beyond those contemplated by the legislation, and that responsibility ultimately lies with the individuals involved.

 Guided response in the eBook

INDEX

does the matter contain a defamatory
imputation, 515–16
defamatory imputations, 517
definition of 'defamatory', 518–25
definition of 'matter', 516–17
true and false innuendo, 517–18
does the matter identify the plaintiff, 525
express identification of plaintiff, 525–6
reasonable to identify plaintiff, 526–9
has the statement been published, 529
definition and interpretation of 'publication',
529–33
'serious harm' test, 533–5
standing to sue, 535–6
employees
contributory negligence and, 239–40
non-delegable duties, 113
standard of care for, 239–40
employer–employee relationship, 467–9
control test, 469
enterprise (integration) test, 469–70
multifactorial test, 470–2
employers
duty of care, 68–72, 113
legal liability of employer for acts of sexual
abuse committed by employee, 491–2
vicarious liability
employers' right of indemnity, 479–80
exception to employers' vicarious liability,
478–9
exemplary damages, 369, 594–6
awarded for intentional torts, 596
awarded for negligence, 597
awarded if criminal punishment already
imposed on defendant, 598–9
examples of exemplary damages awards,
599–600
limited by civil liability legislation and other
statutory limitations, 597
prohibited for defamation, 562
trespass to land, 404
trespass to the person, 399–400

factual causation, 26, 188
civil liability legislation, 192–5
'necessary condition' test, 195–200
common law, 200–1
'but for' test, 201–5
'common sense' test, 205–6
'material contribution' test, 206–8
onus and standard of proof, 188–9
res ipsa loquitur, 189–91
false imprisonment, 292–3
defendant at fault, 305–7
direct interference, 293–6

restraint in all directions, 296–300
knowledge of the restraint, 304–5
no reasonable means to escape, 300–2
physical restraint not necessary, 302–4
foreseeability, 81, 83
reasonable foreseeability, *see* reasonable
foreseeability

Gillick competence, 389
goods
property rights in goods, 651
recaption of goods, 379–82
trespass to goods, *see* trespass to goods
Griffiths v Kerkemeyer damages, 619, 620, 621

hospitals, non-delegable duty and, 483–5
human rights
constraints on Australian protection and
enforcement measures
absence of a Bill of Rights, 16–17
lack of regional human rights system, 17–18
tort law and, 13–18

illegality, 27
as a defence, 256
common law position, 256–7
state legislative variations, 257
incapacity, 396–7
independent contractors, 112–13
injunctions, 649–50
circumstances in which injunction ordered
adequacy of damages as remedy, 650–1
damages awarded instead of or in addition
to injunction, 653
discretionary factors and bars to relief, 652
is proprietary interest required, 650
quia timet injunctions, 652
requirements of interlocutory injunctions,
653
rights protected by injunction, *see* rights
protected by injunction
defamation, 563
trespass to land, 400
trespass to the person, 400
types of, 650
injurious falsehood, 537
innuendo, 517–18
institutional child abuse
civil liability reforms, 44–5
National Redress Scheme, 49
'reasonable person' standard and, 144–5
intentional torts, 4
exemplary damages awarded for, 596
overview, 18–21
interlocutory injunctions, requirements of, 653